WÖRTERBUCH DER KABELTECHNIK
DEUTSCH · ENGLISCH · FRANZÖSISCH

DICTIONARY OF CABLE ENGINEERING
ENGLISH · GERMAN · FRENCH

DICTIONNAIRE DE LA TECHNIQUE DES CÂBLES
FRANÇAIS · ALLEMAND · ANGLAIS

von
CHRISTEL RICHLING und INGEBURG DREWITZ
SIEMENS AG

herausgegeben von
K.-H. BRINKMANN und E. TANKE

1976

OSCAR BRANDSTETTER VERLAG KG · WIESBADEN

CIP-Kurztitelaufnahme der Deutschen Bibliothek

Richling, Christel
Wörterbuch der Kabeltechnik: dt., engl., franz./
von Christel Richling u. Ingeburg Drewitz. Hrsg.
von K.-H. Brinkmann u. E. Tanke. – 1. Aufl. –
Wiesbaden: Brandstetter, 1976. – 610 S.
ISBN 3-87097-072-3 Lin.

NE: Drewitz, Ingeburg:

In diesem Wörterbuch werden, wie in Nachschlagewerken allgemein üblich, etwa bestehende Patente, Gebrauchsmuster oder Warenzeichen nicht erwähnt. Wenn ein solcher Hinweis fehlt, heißt das also nicht, daß eine Ware oder ein Warenname frei ist.

In this dictionary, as in reference works in general, no mention is made of patents, trademark rights, or other proprietary rights which may attach to certain words or entries. The absence of such mention, however, in no way implies that the words or entries in question are exempt from such rights.

Conformément à l'usage général pour les ouvrages de référence, nous avons renoncé à toute mention des brevets, modèles déposés et marques de fabrique. L'absence d'une telle indication ne signifie donc pas que le produit ou terme mentionné ne soit pas protégé.

Copyright © 1976 by

OSCAR BRANDSTETTER VERLAG KG, WIESBADEN

Textverarbeitung und Lichtsatzsteuerung: Siemens
Programmsystem TEAM

Satz: Digiset-Lichtsetzanlage der Satz AG, Zürich
Druck: Oscar Brandstetter Druckerei KG, Wiesbaden

ISBN 3870970723
Printed in Germany

GELEITWORT

Die in allen Industrie-Ländern fortschreitende Entwicklung der modernen Technik und die damit in vielen Sprachen anfallende Flut von Fachliteratur, sowie die immer stärkere weltweite wirtschaftliche Verflechtung erfordern mehr denn je mehrsprachige Fachwörterbücher, in denen die sprachlichen Besonderheiten des einzelnen Wirtschaftszweiges erfaßt werden.

Angesichts der internationalen Harmonisierung der Kabelkonstruktionen und Prüfvorschriften und ihrer Auswirkungen auf die nationalen Bestimmungen und den Welthandel ist es nicht mehr ausreichend, wenn nur eine kleine Gruppe von Spezialisten mit der fachbezogenen technischen Terminologie vertraut ist.

Das vorliegende Wörterbuch soll dem großen Kreis der interessierten Fachleute, seien es Ingenieure, Kaufleute oder Studenten, die Möglichkeit zur besseren Verständigung mit ausländischen Kollegen vermitteln und das Studium der Fachliteratur erleichtern.

Wir wünschen dem dreisprachigen Kabel-Wörterbuch, daß es dazu beitragen möge, weltweit sprachliche Grenzen zu überwinden.

SIEMENS AKTIENGESELLSCHAFT

FOREWORD

The continuing advance of technology throughout the industrialized world has been attended by a flood of polyglot, technical literature, and this, together with an increasing interdependence of national economies, makes more urgent than ever before the need for specialized multilingual dictionaries in every sector of science and industry.

In view of the international harmonization of cable design and test specifications and its effect on national regulations and world trade, it is no longer sufficient for the terminology of cable engineering to be accessible solely to a small group of specialists.

This trilingual cable dictionary is intended to serve a large, international community of engineers, businessmen, and students as a means of achieving better understanding, and as an aid to more effective professional reading.

It is our hope that it will contribute worldwide to the overcoming of language barriers.

SIEMENS AKTIENGESELLSCHAFT

AVANT-PROPOS

Pour répondre au défi de notre société moderne, faire face à l'accélération croissante de l'évolution technologique, mieux comprendre le flot de littérature spécialisée qui nous submerge, et nous intégrer dans un monde marqué par l'interpénétration des économies nationales, nous devons de plus en plus nous armer de dictionnaires techniques multilingues faisant la part des particularités de l'usage linguistique dans les divers secteurs de l'économie.

Vu l'harmonisation internationale des normes de construction et de sécurité applicables aux câbles et son incidence sur les législations nationales et le commerce mondial, la terminologie propre à cette technique doit quitter le «ghetto» réservé aux rares initiés, afin d'être mise à la portée du non-spécialiste.

Avec ce dictionnaire, les auteurs se sont donné pour but de fournir leur modeste contribution à cette libération «terminologique», en donnant à un vaste cercle d'intéressés, ingénieurs, agents commerciaux, étudiants, un instrument qui devrait leur faciliter l'étude de la littérature spécialisée et améliorer la qualité des contacts avec leurs collègues étrangers.

Nous espérons que ce dictionnaire trilingue sur les câbles contribuera à une meilleure compréhension par-delà les frontières linguistiques.

SIEMENS AKTIENGESELLSCHAFT

VORWORT

Das vorliegende dreisprachige Wörterbuch der Kabeltechnik soll eine Lücke in der Reihe der technischen Fachwörterbücher schließen. Obwohl die Kabeltechnik ein bedeutender Wirtschaftszweig ist, wurde, bedingt durch die starke Spezialisierung dieses Bereichs der Technik, das Fachvokabular bisher noch in keinem Wörterbuch ausreichend erfaßt. Um diesem Mangel abzuhelfen, entstand dieses Wörterbuch aus der unmittelbaren Praxis eines Industrie-Übersetzungsbüros, in dem Texte sämtlicher Zweige der Kabeltechnik und der Randgebiete im weitesten Sinne als Übersetzungs- und Dolmetscher-Aufgaben zu bearbeiten sind. Das Fachglossarium der Energie- und Nachrichtenkabeltechnik soll Ingenieuren, Übersetzern und allen, die in irgendeiner Form mit dem Kabelgebiet zu tun haben, möglichst viele Verständigungshilfen geben, sei es beim Lesen, Übersetzen oder Verhandeln.

Infolge unterschiedlicher technischer Entwicklung und sprachlicher Gewohnheiten sowie wegen Fehlens klarer Definitionen und Abgrenzungen war es – selbst nach Diskussionen mit französischen und englischen Fachkollegen – nicht immer möglich, präzise gleichwertige Ausdrücke zuzuordnen. Ein Teil der französischen und englischen Begriffe mußte umschrieben werden, um eine Übersetzungsmöglichkeit zu schaffen. Für Änderungs- und Ergänzungsvorschläge aus dem Benutzerkreis unseres Wörterbuchs, die in einer späteren Neu-Auflage erfaßt werden sollen, wären die Autoren daher sehr dankbar.

Unser Dank für tatkräftige Mithilfe bei den Vorarbeiten gilt unseren Mitarbeiterinnen Frau Jutta Hinz und Frau Erika Cherrier.

Wir danken ferner der Firma Kabel- und Metallwerke Gutehoffnungshütte, Hannover, die uns freundlicherweise eine eigene Wortsammlung zur Auswertung überlassen hat.

Berlin im Frühjahr 1976   Die Verfasser

PREFACE

This trilingual dictionary of cable engineering is intended to fill a longstanding need. Although the cable industry is of major economic importance, its highly specialized nature has until now discouraged dictionary makers from attempting a full-scale compilation of its terminology. The present dictionary was conceived to compensate for this deficiency. It is based on the day-to-day work of an industrial translating and interpreting service, and incorporates the terminology employed in actual texts drawn from all sectors of cable engineering and allied fields. Its aim is to assist engineers, translators and other practitioners in the field of power and communication cables to improve their proficiency in the use of its specialized vocabulary – whether for reading, translating, or engaging in business negotiations.

Due to differences in technical development and language usage, as well as to imprecision or overlapping of definitions, it has not always been possible, even after consultation with French and English speaking experts, to provide exact equivalents for all terms. For some French and English terms a descriptive expression is given instead, in view of which the authors would welcome any suggestions from users for changes or additions that might be incorporated in later editions of the dictionary.

We wish to thank Mrs. Jutta Hinz and Mrs. Erika Cherrier for their invaluable assistance in preparing this work for publication.

We are also indebted to Kabel- und Metallwerke Gutehoffnungshütte, Hanover, for allowing us to evaluate a glossary of terms which they had compiled themselves.

Berlin, spring 1976   The authors

PRÉFACE

Alors que le secteur des câbles occupe une place nullement négligeable dans notre économie, nous ne disposions, à ce jour, d'aucun dictionnaire spécialisé contenant un nombre suffisant de termes relatifs à cette technique. Désireux de remédier à cette situation vraisemblablement imputable au caractère particulier de ce sujet, nous avons donc décidé de tirer profit de l'expérience acquise par les traducteurs et interprètes d'une grande entreprise ayant à traiter toute la technique des câbles et ses domaines annexes. Le dictionnaire trilingue que nous vous présentons est le fruit de cette somme de travail et est destiné à faciliter la tâche des ingénieurs, traducteurs et autres personnes amenées à lire, traduire ou interpréter des textes relatifs aux câbles d'énergie et de télécommunications.

En dépit de la consultation de spécialistes français et anglais, nos efforts dans la recherche d'équivalents ont parfois échoué sur certaines divergences dans l'évolution technologique et dans l'usage linguistique, ainsi que sur l'absence occasionnelle de définitions précises ou de séparations bien nettes entre les domaines. C'est pourquoi certains termes français et anglais ont dû être rendus par une approximation. Aussi les auteurs sauraient-ils gré aux utilisateurs de cet ouvrage de bien vouloir leur signaler les erreurs et omissions qu'ils ne manqueront pas de relever. Il en sera tenu compte dans une prochaine édition revue et complétée.

Pour clôturer, nous tenons à remercier vivement nos collègues, Mmes Jutta Hinz et Erika Cherrier, du précieux concours qu'elles ont apporté à l'exécution de tous les travaux préparatoires ayant permis la publication de ce dictionnaire.

Nous nous devons, par ailleurs, d'exprimer notre sincère gratitude envers la société Kabel- und Metallwerke Gutehoffnungshütte, Hanovre, qui a eu l'extrême amabilité de contribuer à l'enrichissement de ce dictionnaire en nous donnant toute liberté d'exploiter ses fichiers terminologiques.

Berlin, printemps 1976   Les Auteurs

In diesem Wörterbuch verwendete und weitere im Rahmen der Kabeltechnik gebräuchliche Abkürzungen.

Abbreviations used in this dictionary and others connected with cable engineering.

Abréviations utilisées dans ce dictionnaire et autres relatives à la technique des câbles.

acc.	*D* Akkusativ *m* *E* accusative *F* accusatif *m*	c. access.	*E* cable accessories
acess. c.	*F* accessoires de câble	caout.	*F* caoutchouc
adh.	*E* adhesive	c. com.	*F* câbles de communication
adj	*D* Adjektiv *n* *E* adjective *F* adjectif *m*	c.c.r.	*E* continuous casting and rolling
air cond.	*E* air conditioning	CEGB	Central Electricity Generating Board (GB)
ASTM	American Society for Testing and Materials	c. én.	*F* câble d'énergie
A.W.G. awg	*E* American Wire Gage = Brown & Sharpe (B&S) gauge *F* jauge *f* américaine pour fils métalliques *D* amerikanische Drahtlehre	CERL	Central Electricity Research Laboratory (GB)
		chem.	*D* Chemie *E* chemistry
		chim	*F* chimie
		CIGRE	*F* Conférence Internationale des Grands Réseaux Electriques *E* International Conference on Large High Voltage Electric Systems *D* Internationale Konferenz über Hochspannungsanlagen
Bdspinn.	*D* Bandspinnen		
BS	*E* British Standard *F* norme anglaise *D* britische Norm		
B & S gauge (Brown & Sharpe)	*E* A.W.G.		
		c. install.	*E* cable installation
BTU	*E* British Thermal Unit *F* unité anglaise de chaleur *D* britische Wärmeeinheit	CIRED	*F* Congrès International des Réseaux Electriques de Distribution *E* International Congress on Electricity Distribution *D* Internationale Tagung über elektrische Verteilersysteme
cab.	*E* cable *F* câble		
câblage	*F* câblage/assemblage et câbleuses/assembleuses		

CM	*E*	circular mil (US) (cross section unit)		
	F	unité américaine pour sections droites		
	D	amerikanische Querschnitts-Einheit		
c.n.e.	*E*	combined neutral and earth		
	F	neutre *m* mis à la terre		
	D	geerdeter Nulleiter		
col.	*F*	colle		
com.	*E*	communications engineering		
	F	communications		
com. c.	*E*	communications cables		
cond. d'air	*F*	conditionnement d'air		
contr.	*E*	control		
coul. cont. lam.	*F*	coulée continue laminage		
c. tel.	*F*	câbles téléphoniques		
dB	*D*	Dezibel *n*		
	E	decibel		
	F	décibel *m*		
deg.	*E*	degrees		
	F	degrés *m pl*		
	D	Grad *m (pl)*		
dia.	*E*	diameter		
	F	diamètre *m*		
	D	Durchmesser *m*		
DIN	*D*	Deutsche Industrie-Norm Deutsches Institut für Normung e. V.		
	E	German standard		
	F	norme allemande		
Drahth.	*D*	Drahtherstellung		
DV	*D*	Datenverarbeitung		
	E	data processing		
	F	traitement *m* des informations		
EDF		Electricité de France		
EDP	*E*	electronic data processing		
	F	traitement *m* électronique des données		
	D	elektronische Datenverarbeitung		
EDV	*D*	elektronische Datenverarbeitung		
	E	electronic data processing		
	F	traitement *m* électronique des données		
el.	*E*	electrical		
	F	électrique		
	D	elektrisch		
En. K.	*D*	Energiekabel		
ess.	*F*	essai		
extr.	*E*	extruder		
	F	extrudeuse		
	D	Extruder		
f	*D*	feminin		
	E	feminine		
	F	féminin		
fabr. fils mét.	*F*	fabrication de fils métalliques		
FEX	*E*	Far-End Cross-Talk		
	F	télédiaphonie *f*		
	D	Fernnebensprechen *n*		
GB		Great Britain		
Gi.	*D*	Gummi/Kautschuk		
Gießw.	*D*	Gießwalzen		
Hütt.	*D*	Hüttenwesen		
I.D.	*E*	inner diameter		
	F	diamètre *m* intérieur		
	D	Innendurchmesser *m*		
I.E.C.	*E*	International Electrotechnical Commission		
	F	Commission Electrotechnique Internationale (CEI)		
	D	Internationale Elektrotechnische Kommission		
IEE		Institution of Electrical Engineers (GB)		
IEEE		Institute of Electrical and Electronic Engineers (US)		
IPCEA		Insulated Power		

		Cable Engineers Association (US)
Kab.	D	Kabel
K. Garn	D	Kabelgarnituren
Klebst.	D	Klebstoff
Klimat.	D	Klimatechnik
kV	D	Kilovolt n
	E	kilovolt
	F	kilovolt m
kVA	D	Kilovoltampere n
	E	kilovolt-ampere
	F	kilovoltampère m
K. Verl.	D	Kabelverlegung
lam.	F	laminoir
lapp.	E	lapping
m	D	maskulin
	E	masculine
	F	masculin
mach.	E	machines
	F	machines
Masch.	D	Maschinen
math.	D	Mathematik
	E	mathematics
	F	mathématiques
MCM	E	1000 circular mils (US) (cross-section unit)
	F	unité américaine pour sections droites
	D	amerikanische Querschnitts-Einheit (das 1000fache der Kreisfläche mit dem Durchmesser 1 mil) (1 MCM = 0,5067 mm²)
meas.	E	measure
méc.	F	mécanique
mech.	D	mechanisch
	E	mecanical
mes.	F	mesures
Mess.	D	Meßtechnik
met.	D	Metall
	E	metal
	F	métal
métallurg.	F	métallurgie
met. extr. pr.	E	metal extrusion press
Met.-Strangpr.	D	Metall-Strangpresse
n	D	Neutrum n
	E	neuter
	F	neutre
n	E	noun
	F	substantif m
	D	Substantiv n
Nachr.	D	Nachrichtentechnik
Nachr. K.	D	Nachrichtenkabel
N.E.M.A.		National Electric Manufacturers Association (US)
NEX	E	Near-End-Cross-Talk
	F	paradiaphonie f
	D	Nahnebensprechen n
NF	F	Norme Française
	E	French standard
	D	französische Norm
O.D.	E	outer diameter
	F	diamètre m extérieur
	D	Außendurchmesser m
opt.	D	optisch
pl	D	Plural m
	E	plural
	F	pluriel m
plast.	D	Kunststoffe, Plaste
	E	plastics
	F	plastiques
plt		Pluraletantum
pose c.	F	pose des câbles
pow. c.	E	power cable
pr. à filer	F	presse à filer
prod.	D	Produktion
	E	production
	F	production
Prüf.	D	Prüfung
re	D	rund eindrähtig (Leiter)
	E	round solid
	F	rond massif
Regl.	D	Regeltechnik
régl.	F	réglage

rm	*D*	rund mehrdrähtig (Leiter)	Tel. K.	*D* Telefonkabel
	E	round stranded	test	test
	F	rond câblé	UL	Underwriters' Laboratory (US)
r.m.s.	*E*	root mean square (value)	U.R.D.	*E* underground residential distribution, underground rural distribution
	F	moyenne *f* quadratique, valeur *f* effective		*F* distribution *f* souterraine dans les quartiers résidentiels, distribution *f* souterraine rurale
	D	quadratischer Mittelwert, Effektivwert *m*		*D* erdverlegte Verteilernetze in Wohnbezirken, erdverlegte Verteilernetze auf dem Lande
rm/v	*D*	rund mehrdrähtig, verdichtet (Leiter)		
	E	round stranded, compacted		
	F	rond câblé, rétreint		
roll. m	*E*	rolling mill	US	USA
rub.	*E*	rubber	UTE	Union Technique de l'Electricité
	F	rubanage		
se	*D*	sektorförmig eindrähtig (Leiter)	v	*D* Verb *n*
				E verb
	E	sector-shaped solid		*F* verbe *m*
	F	sectoral massif	Vers.	*D* Verseilung und Verseilmaschinen
sg	*D*	Singular *m*		
	E	singular	vi	*D* Verb *n*, intransitiv
	F	singulier *m*		*E* verb, intransitive
sm	*D*	sektorförmig mehrdrähtig (Leiter)		*F* verbe *m* intransitif
			VIR	*E* vulcanized India rubber (GB)
	E	sector-shaped stranded		*F* caoutchouc *m* naturel vulcanisé
	F	sectoral câblé		
smelt.	*E*	smelting		*D* vulkanisierter Naturkautschuk
SRX	*E*	Self-Return Cross-Talk		
	F	diaphonie *f* par réaction automatique	vis.	*E* visual
				D visuel
	D	rückgekoppeltes Nebensprechen *n*		*F* visuel
strand.	*E*	stranding and stranding machines	vt	*D* Verb *n*, transitiv
				E verb, transitive
S.W.G.	*E*	Standard Wire Gauge (GB)		*F* verbe *m* transitif
	F	jauge *f* anglaise pour fils métalliques	vulc.	*E* vulcanization
				F vulcanisation
	D	englische Drahtlehre	Vulk.	*D* Vulkanisation
tel.	*D*	Telefonie *f*	Walzw.	*D* Walzwerk
	E	telephony	wire manuf.	*E* wire manufacture
	F	téléphonie *f*		
tel. c.	*E*	telephone cables		

WÖRTERBUCH
DER KABELTECHNIK

TEIL I

DEUTSCH-ENGLISCH-FRANZÖSISCH

A

abändern v
  E: modify v, alter v, change v, revise v
  F: modifier v, changer v, réviser v
Abbau m (Werkstoffe)
  E: degradation n, decomposition n
  F: dégradation f
Abbau m (Kautschuk)
  E: thermal degradation
  F: dégradation f thermique
abbauen v (Masch.)
  E: dismantle v, disassemble v
  F: désassembler v
abbinden v [Kab.]
  E: bind v, lace v, tie v
  F: lier v
abbinden v [Klebst.]
  E: harden v, set v
  F: durcir v
abblättern v
  E: flake v (off), scale v (off), peel v (off)
  F: écailler v (s'), décoller v (se)
Abbrand m [Hütt.]
  E: scale loss, melting loss
  F: perte f au feu, déchet m
abbremsen v
  E: brake v, slow down v
  F: freiner v
Abbrühmasse f
  E: scalding compound
  F: matière f d'échaudage
Abdeckblech n
  E: covering sheet, cover plate
  F: tôle f de recouvrement, tôle f de protection
Abdeckhaube f
  E: cover n, hood n
  F: capot m
Abdeckplatte f
  E: covering plate, guard plate
  F: plaque f protectrice, plaque f de recouvrement
Abdeckung f
  E: cover n, covering n
  F: recouvrement m, couverture f
abdichten v
  E: seal v
  F: rendre v étanche, boucher v, étancher v
Abdichtmasse f
  E: sealing compound
  F: matière f d'étanchéité
Abdichtung f
  E: sealing n, tightness n
  F: étanchéité f
Abfall der Temperatur
  E: temperature drop, temperature decrease
  F: chute f de température, baisse f de la température
Abfall des Öldrucks
  E: drop of the oil pressure
  F: baisse f de la pression d'huile, chute f de la pression d'huile
Abfall einer Kurve
  E: decline of a curve, slope of a curve
  F: inclinaison f d'une courbe, pente f d'une courbe
Abfälle m pl
  E: scrap n
  F: déchets m pl
Abfallschere f
  E: cobble shears pl, scrap cutter
  F: cisailles f pl à déchets
abfließen v
  E: drain v
  F: écouler v (s')
Abflußleitung f
  E: discharge line, drain pipe
  F: conduit m de décharge, conduite f d'écoulement
Abgangskasten m
  E: tapping-off unit
  F: coffret m de branchement
abgeflacht adj
  E: flattened adj
  F: méplat adj
abgepaßt, in ~en Längen
  E: cut to length
  F: coupé adj à longueur
abgerundete Kante
  E: rounded edge
  F: côté m arrondi, tranche f arrondie
abgeschirmt, einzeln ~e Kabeladern
  E: individually screened cable cores
  F: conducteurs m pl de câble avec écran individuel
abgeschirmtes Kabel
  E: screened cable, shielded cable
  F: câble m sous écran, câble m blindé
abgeschrägte Kante
  E: beveled edge
  F: tranche f biseautée

abgestopftes

abgestopftes Kabel [Tel.]
  E: filled cable
  F: câble *m* rempli

abgestopftes Kabel, diskontinuierlich
  ~ [Tel. K.]
  E: cable with water blocks
  F: câble *m* rempli de façon discontinue

abgestopftes Kabel, über die ganze Länge ~ [Tel. K.]
  E: fully filled cable, continuously filled cable
  F: câble *m* rempli de façon continue, câble *m* à remplissage total, câble *m* à remplissage continu

abgestuft *adj*
  E: staggered *adj*, graded *adj*
  F: en quinconce, échelonné *adj*, décalé *adj*, gradué *adj*, étagé *adj*

abgetuftes Kabel
  E: drained cable, non-bleeding cable
  F: câble *m* à matière écoulée

abgleichen *v*
  E: adjust *v*, compensate *v*, trim *v*, balance *v*, tune *v*
  F: ajuster *v*, compenser *v*, accorder *v*

abgleichen *v* [Masch.]
  E: align *v*
  F: équilibrer *v*

Abgleichung *f*
  E: adjustment *n*, compensation *n*, trimming *n*, alignment *n*, tuning *n*
  F: ajustement *n*, compensation *f*, équilibrage *m*, accord *m*

Abhängigkeit, in ~ von [Math.]
  E: as a function of, versus
  F: en fonction de

abisolieren *v*
  E: to remove the insulation, to strip the insulation
  F: dénuder *v*, désisoler *v*

Abisoliermaschine *f*
  E: cable stripper
  F: machine *f* à dénuder

abklingeln *v* [Tel. K.]
  E: buzz out *v*, ring out *v*
  F: sonner *v*

Abklingeln *n* [Tel. K.]
  E: ringing test, ring-out procedure, buzz-out operation
  F: contrôle *m* de continuité, sonnage *m*

abkühlen *v*
  E: cool *v*
  F: refroidir *v* (se)

Abkühlkurve *f*
  E: cooling curve, heat dissipation diagram
  F: courbe *f* de refroidissement

Ablaßventil *n*
  E: outlet valve, drain valve, discharge valve, exhaust valve
  F: soupape *f* de décharge, soupape *f* de vidange, soupape *f* d'émission, soupape *f* de sortie

Ablauf *m* [Drahth., Kab.]
  E: pay-off *n*
  F: déroulement *m*

Ablaufbock *m* [Drahth., Kab.]
  E: pay-off stand, supply stand, feed stand, take-off stand
  F: bâti *m* départ, dévidoir *m*, dérouleur *m*

Ablaufdiagramm *n*
  E: flow chart, flow diagram, process (flow) chart
  F: organigramme *m* (prod.), ordinogramme *m*, graphique *m* de processus, diagramme *m* de déroulement

Ablaufgestell *n* [Drahth., Kab.]
  E: pay-off stand, supply stand, feed stand, take-off stand
  F: bâti *m* départ, dévidoir *m*, dérouleur *m*

Ablaufplan *m*
  E: flow chart, flow diagram, process (flow) chart
  F: organigramme *m* (prod.), ordinogramme *m*, graphique *m* de processus, diagramme *m* de déroulement

Ablaufspule *f*
  E: pay-off reel, supply reel
  F: bobine *f* débitrice, bobine *f* d'alimentation, bobine *f* de dévidage

Ablauftrommel *f*
  E: pay-off reel, supply reel
  F: bobine *f* débitrice, bobine *f* d'alimentation, bobine *f* de dévidage

Ableiter *m*
  E: arrester *n*
  F: conducteur *m* de dérivation, déchargeur *m*

Ableitung f
  E: leakage n, leakance n
  F: dérivation f
Ableitung f [Nachr. K.]
  E: conductance n
  F: perditance f
Ableitungsdämpfung f [Nachr. K.]
  E: leakage attenuation, leakage loss, leakage current loss
  F: affaiblissement m dû à la perditance
Ableit(ungs)strom m
  E: leakage current, fault current, stray current
  F: courant m de fuite, courant m de défaut, courant m vagabond
Ableitungsverlust m
  E: leakage current loss, leakage loss
  F: perte f par dérivation
Ableitungsverlust m [Nachr. K.]
  E: conductance n
  F: perditance f
Ablesung, eine ~ vornehmen
  E: to take a reading
  F: faire v une lecture
ablösen v (Folie, Schicht)
  E: peel v, separate v, detach v
  F: peler v, séparer v, décoller v
Ablösen n (Trennen)
  E: peeling n, detachment n, detaching n
  F: pelage m, décollement m
abmanteln v
  E: to strip the cable sheath
  F: enlever v la gaine du câble, dépouiller v la gaine du câble
Abmessung f
  E: dimension n
  F: dimension f
abmontieren v
  E: remove v, dismount v
  F: démonter v, enlever v
Abnahme im Werk
  E: factory acceptance
  F: réception f en usine
Abnahmebeamter m
  E: inspection officer
  F: réceptionnaire m
Abnahmeprotokoll n
  E: acceptance certificate
  F: procès-verbal m de réception, certificat m de réception
Abnahmeprüfung f
  E: acceptance test, approval inspection
  F: essai m de réception
abnehmbar adj
  E: detachable adj, removable adj, dismountable adj
  F: amovible adj, démontable adj
Abreißen von Papierband oder Draht
  E: break of paper tape or wire
  F: rupture f du ruban de papier ou du fil métallique
Abrieb m
  E: abrasion n, wear n
  F: abrasion f
Abriebfestigkeit f
  E: abrasion resistance
  F: résistance f à l'abrasion
abrunden v (Kante)
  E: round v, round off v
  F: arrondir v
Absauganlage f
  E: suction system, exhaust system
  F: installation f d'aspiration
absaugen v
  E: suck v
  F: aspirer v
Absaughaube f
  E: suction hood, ventilation hood
  F: collecteur m de fumées
Absaugrohr n
  E: suction pipe
  F: tube m d'aspiration
Absaugung f
  E: exhaust n, suction n
  F: exhaustion f, aspiration f
Absaugung von Dämpfen
  E: drawing off of fumes
  F: captage m de fumées
abschalten v [el.]
  E: switch off v, interrupt v, disconnect v, turn off (US) v, de-energize v, cut out v
  F: couper v, interrompre v, déconnecter v
abschalten v [Masch.]
  E: shut down v
  F: arrêter v
Abschalter m
  E: circuit breaker, cut-out switch, disconnecting switch
  F: discontacteur m, disjoncteur m, interrupteur m
Abschaltleistung f

Abschaltleistung
- E: breaking capacity (GB), interrupting capacity (US)
- F: puissance *f* de rupture, pouvoir *m* de coupure

Abschaltstrom *m*
- E: breaking current
- F: courant *m* de coupure

Abschaltstromkreis *m*
- E: breaking circuit
- F: circuit *m* de courant de rupture

Abschaltzeit *f* [el.]
- E: cut-out time
- F: temps *m* de coupure

abscheren *v*
- E: shear off *v*
- F: cisailler *v*

abschirmen *v* [el.]
- E: shield *v*, screen *v*
- F: blinder *v*

Abschirmfaktor gegen elektrische Störungen
- E: electrical interference screening factor
- F: facteur *m* de blindage contre les perturbations électriques

Abschirmgeflecht *n*
- E: screening braid, woven shield, shielding braid
- F: écran *m* guipé

Abschirmung *f* [el.]
- E: shield *n*, shielding *n*, screen *n*, screening *n*
- F: écran *m*, blindage *m*

Abschleiffestigkeit *f*
- E: abrasion resistance
- F: résistance *f* à l'abrasion

Abschlußhülse, Kabel-~ *f*
- E: cable lug, terminal lug, cable eye
- F: cosse *f* de câble, attache *f* de conducteur, cosse *f* terminale

abschneiden *v*
- E: crop *v*, trim *v*, cut *v*
- F: couper *v*, rogner *v*, cisailler *v*

Abschnitt *m*
- E: section *n*
- F: section *f*

Abschnitt einer Strecke [K. Verl.]
- E: route section
- F: tronçon *m* de ligne, tronçon *m* de liaison

abschnittweise *adj*
- E: in sections
- F: en sections

abschrägen *v*
- E: bevel *v*, chamfer *v*
- F: chanfreiner *v*, biseauter *v*

abschrauben *v*
- E: unscrew *v*, screw off *v*
- F: dévisser *v*

abschrecken *v*
- E: chill *v*, quench *v*
- F: tremper *v*

absetzen *v* (Isolierung, Mantel)
- E: cut back *v*, remove *v*
- F: enlever *v*, découper *v*

Absicherung *f* [el.]
- E: fusing *n*, protection by fuses
- F: protection *f* par fusibles

Absinken der Temperatur
- E: temperature drop, temperature decrease
- F: chute *f* de température, baisse *f* de la température

absolute Dielektrizitätskonstante
- E: absolute permittivity
- F: permittivité *f* absolue

absolute Fehlergrenze
- E: absolute limit of error
- F: limite *f* absolue d'erreur

Absonderung *f*
- E: segregation *n*, separation *n*, exudation *n*
- F: ségrégation *f*, séparation *f*

abspalten *v*
- E: split off *v*, set free *v*
- F: fendre *v*, libérer *v*

Abspaltung *f* [Chem.]
- E: liberation *n*, cleavage *n*
- F: libération *f*, dégagement *m*

Abspanndraht *m*
- E: anchoring wire
- F: fil *m* d'ancrage

abspannen *v* [el.]
- E: to step down the voltage
- F: abaisser *v* la tension

Absperrhahn *m*
- E: stop cock
- F: robinet *m* d'arrêt

Absperrventil *n*
- E: stop valve, shut-off valve
- F: soupape *f* d'arrêt

Abspritzen (von Isolatoren) im Betrieb
- E: live-washing *n* (of insulators)
- F: rinçage *m* sous tension (des isolateurs)

Abspritzvorrichtung *f*

abspulen v
  E: spray equipment
  F: dispositif *m* de pulvérisation, pulvérisateur *m*

abspulen v
  E: unwind v, pay off v, uncoil v
  F: dérouler v, dévider v

Abstand *m*
  E: distance *n*, clearance *n*, interval *n*, space *n*
  F: distance *f*, écart *m*, intervalle *m*

Abstände, in gleichen ~n
  E: equispaced *adj*
  F: à distances égales

Abstandhalter *m*
  E: spacer *n*
  F: séparateur *m*

Abstandscheibe *f*
  E: disc spacer, disc insulator
  F: disque *m* séparateur, disque *m* d'écartement

Abstichöffnung *f* [Met.]
  E: tap hole
  F: trou *m* de percée, trou *m* de coulée

abstimmen v
  E: tune v, adjust v, match v
  F: accorder v, régler v

Abstimmung *f* [Regl.]
  E: tuning *n*, adjustment *n*
  F: accord *m*, réglage *m*

Abstopfen *n* [Tel. K.]
  E: filling *n*, blocking *n*
  F: remplissage *m*

Abstopfen mit Petrol-jelly [Tel. K.]
  E: petroleum jelly filling
  F: remplissage *m* en gelée de pétrole

Abstopfmasse *f* [Tel. K.]
  E: filling compound
  F: matière *f* de remplissage

Abstreifer *m* (an der Armiermaschine)
  E: stripping device, wiper *n*
  F: râcloir *m*

Abstreifmesser *n*
  E: doctor blade
  F: râcloir *m*

abtasten v
  E: scan v, sense v
  F: palper v, sonder v, balayer v

Abtast-Führungsrollen *f pl* [Vulk.]
  E: sensing guide rollers
  F: chandelles *f pl* de palpage

Abtastvorrichtung *f*
  E: scanning device, scanner *n*, sensing device, sensor *n*, detecting element
  F: palpeur *m*, scanner *m*, sonde *f*

Abtrommeln *n* [Kab.]
  E: unreeling *n*, unwinding *n*
  F: déroulement *m*

Abtropfprüfung *f* [Kab.]
  E: drainage test
  F: essai *m* d'écoulement

abwandern v (Masse, Weichmacher)
  E: migrate v
  F: migrer v

abwandernde Masse [Kab.]
  E: migrating compound, draining compound
  F: matière *f* migrante

Abwanderung des Weichmachers
  E: migration of plasticizer
  F: migration *f* du plastifiant

Abwanderung von Masse [Kab.]
  E: migration of compound, draining of compound
  F: migration *f* de matière, écoulement *m* de matière

Abwickelei *f* [Drahth., Kab.]
  E: pay-off stand, supply stand, feed stand, take-off stand
  F: bâti *m* départ, dévidoir *m*, dérouleur *m*

abwickeln v
  E: unwind v, pay off v, uncoil v
  F: dérouler v, dévider v

Abwickeltrommel *f*
  E: pay-off reel, supply reel
  F: bobine *f* débitrice, bobine *f* d'alimentation, bobine *f* de dévidage

abziehen v (Folie, Schicht)
  E: peel v, separate v, detach v
  F: peler v, séparer v, décoller v

abziehen, Schlacke ~
  E: to skim off the dross
  F: soutirer v la scorie, écraser v

Abzug *m* (Lüftung)
  E: exhaust *n*, exhaust hood, fume hood
  F: hotte *f*, chapelle *f*, collecteur *m* de fumées, capteur *m* de fumées

Abzugscheibe *f*
  E: pull-off capstan, haul-off capstan
  F: cabestan *m* de tirage, roue *f* de tirage, cabestan *m* tireur

Abzugsgeschwindigkeit *f*
  E: pull-off speed
  F: vitesse *f* de tirage

Abzugsvorrichtung f
  E: pull-off device, haul-off device
  F: dispositif m de tirage

Abzweigdose f
  E: branch box, distributing box, branch joint, distributor box (US), distribution cabinet, connecting box
  F: boîte f de dérivation, boîte f de branchement, boîte f de distribution

abzweigen v
  E: branch v, tap v
  F: brancher v, dériver v

Abzweigkabel n
  E: branch cable, stub cable
  F: câble m de branchement, câble m de dérivation

Abzweigkasten m
  E: branch box, distributing box, branch joint, distributor box (US), distribution cabinet, connecting box
  F: boîte f de dérivation, boîte f de branchement, boîte f de distribution

Abzweigklemme f
  E: tee connector, T-connector n, branch connector, branch terminal
  F: borne f en forme de T, borne f de dérivation, té m de dérivation

Abzweigleitung f
  E: branch circuit, tap line
  F: ligne f de branchement, ligne f de dérivation, dérivation f

Abzweigmuffe f (T-Muffe; spitzwinklige Muffe)
  E: branch joint
  F: boîte f de dérivation

Abzweigstecker m
  E: socket-outlet adapter, distribution plug
  F: fiche f de dérivation

Abzweigstromkreis m
  E: branch circuit, shunt n
  F: circuit m dérivé, shunt m

Abzweigung f
  E: branch n, tap n, junction n
  F: dérivation f, raccordement m, branchement m

Acetylenruß m
  E: acetylene black
  F: noir m d'acétylène

Achsabstand m
  E: centre-to-centre distance, centre spacing
  F: distance f d'axe en axe, distance f des centres

Achsbohrung f (Kabeltrommel)
  E: spindle hole
  F: trou m central

Achsenspiel n
  E: play of axis, backlash of axis
  F: jeu m sur axe, jeu m à l'entraînement

ACSR-Leiterseil n (Al-Leiter um einen Stahlkerndraht verseilt)
  E: aluminium conductor steel reinforced (ACSR)
  F: âme f ACSR (fils d'aluminium câblés autour d'un fil central en acier)

Ader f [Kab.]
  E: core n, conductor n, insulated wire, insulated conductor
  F: conducteur m isolé, fil m isolé

Aderabschirmung f
  E: insulation screen, core screen (GB), insulation shield (US)
  F: écran m sur l'isolant

Aderisolierung f
  E: core insulation
  F: isolation f du conducteur

Aderkennzeichnung f
  E: core identification, tracer n (US)
  F: repérage m des conducteurs

Aderleitung f
  E: general purpose single-core non-sheathed cable, insulated wire
  F: conducteur m (à âme rigide ou souple)

Adermischung f
  E: insulating compound
  F: mélange m isolant

Aderpaar n
  E: pair of cores
  F: paire f de conducteurs

Aderumhüllung, gemeinsame gepreßte ~
  E: extruded inner covering, inner filling sheath
  F: gaine f de bourrage, gaine f formant bourrage

Aderumhüllung, gemeinsame gewickelte ~
  E: taped inner covering, lapped inner

Aderverseilmaschine f
- E: core-stranding machine, laying-up machine, core-strander n, cabler n
- F: assembleuse f

Aderverseilung f
- E: core stranding, laying up n, cabling n
- F: assemblage m (des conducteurs)

Aderzahl f
- E: number of cores
- F: nombre m des conducteurs

Aderzählfolge f
- E: numbering of cable cores
- F: ordre m de numération des conducteurs

Adhäsion f
- E: adhesion n, adherence n, bonding n, sticking n
- F: adhésion f, adhérance f, collage m

Agglomerat n
- E: agglomeration n, agglomerate n
- F: aggloméré m

Aggregat n
- E: aggregate n, set n, unit n
- F: agrégat m, groupe m

aggressive Lösung
- E: corrosive solution
- F: solution f corrosive

Akkordarbeit f
- E: piecework n, incentive scheme
- F: travail m à la pièce, travail m à forfait

akkumulierter Fehler
- E: accumulated error
- F: erreur f cumulée

akustisches Warnsignal
- E: audible warning
- F: signal m avertisseur acoustique

Al-PE-Schichtenmantel m
- E: Alpeth-sheath n (US)
- F: gaine f d'aluminium polyéthylène contrecollé

altern v
- E: age v
- F: vieillir v

Alterung f
- E: ag(e)ing n
- F: vieillissement m

Alterung durch Lagerung
- E: shelf ag(e)ing
- F: vieillissement m au stockage

covering
F: revêtement m interne rubané

Alterung im Umluftofen
- E: ventilated air oven ag(e)ing, circulating air ag(e)ing
- F: vieillissement m en étuve à circulation d'air, vieillissement m par circulation d'air

Alterung unter Öl
- E: oil immersion ag(e)ing
- F: vieillissement m dans l'huile

Alterung, durch Wärme beschleunigte ~
- E: thermo-accelerated ag(e)ing
- F: vieillissement m thermo-accéléré

alterungsbeständig adj
- E: resistant to ag(e)ing
- F: non-vieillissant adj

Alterungsbeständigkeit f
- E: ag(e)ing resistance
- F: résistance f au vieillissement

Alterungsprüfung f
- E: ag(e)ing test
- F: essai m de vieillissement

Alterungsschutzmittel n
- E: antioxidant, oxidation inhibitor
- F: inhibiteur m d'oxydation, antioxidant m, antioxygène m

Altkupfer n
- E: scrap copper, copper scrap
- F: déchets m pl de cuivre

Aluminiumbarren m
- E: aluminium ingot
- F: lingot m d'aluminium

Aluminiumbolzen m
- E: aluminium billet
- F: billette f d'aluminium

Aluminiumdraht m
- E: aluminium wire
- F: fil m d'aluminium

Aluminiumdraht mit Kupfermantel
- E: copper-clad aluminium wire
- F: fil m d'aluminium plaqué de cuivre

Aluminiumkerbblock m
- E: aluminium ingot
- F: lingot m d'aluminium

Aluminiumlegierung f
- E: aluminium alloy
- F: alliage m d'aluminium

Aluminiumleiter m (ACSR)
- E: aluminium conductor steel reinforced (ACSR)
- F: âme f ACSR (fils d'aluminium câblés autour d'un fil central en acier)

Aluminiumleiterkabel n
  E: aluminium conductor cable
  F: câble m à âme en aluminium, câble m à conducteur en aluminium

Aluminiummantel m
  E: aluminium sheath
  F: gaine f d'aluminium

Aluminiummantelkabel n
  E: aluminium-sheathed cable
  F: câble m sous gaine d'aluminium

Aluminium-(Mantel)-Presse f
  E: aluminium press, aluminium sheathing press
  F: presse f à aluminium

Aluminiummassel f
  E: aluminium ingot
  F: lingot m d'aluminium

Aluminiumpreßbolzen m
  E: aluminium billet
  F: billette f d'aluminium

Aluminiumrundbarren m
  E: aluminium billet
  F: billette f d'aluminium

Aluminium-Wellmantel m
  E: corrugated aluminium sheath
  F: gaine f ondulée en aluminium

Amt n [Tel.]
  E: exchange n (GB), central n (US), central office
  F: central m

Amtskabel n [Tel.]
  E: exchange cable
  F: câble m principal

Amtsverbindungskabel n [Tel.]
  E: inter-exchange trunk cable
  F: câble m de jonction entre centraux téléphoniques

Anbrennen n (im Extruder)
  E: scorching n (in extruder cylinder)
  F: grillage m (dans l'extrudeuse)

Anbrennen der Isolierung
  E: charring of the insulation
  F: carbonisation f de l'isolant

ändern v
  E: modify v, alter v, change v, revise v
  F: modifier v, changer v, réviser v

Andruckrolle f
  E: press roll
  F: rouleau m de pression, rouleau m de serrage

anfahren v [Masch.]
  E: start v, start up v
  F: démarrer v, mettre v en marche

Anfahrstellung f
  E: starting position
  F: position f de mise en marche

Anfangsdruck m
  E: initial pressure
  F: pression f initiale

Anfangskurzschluß-Wechselstrom m
  E: initial symmetric short-circuit current
  F: courant m initial symétrique de court-circuit

anfeuchten v
  E: wet v, moisten v
  F: mouiller v, tremper v, humecter v

Anforderung f
  E: requirement n, demand n
  F: exigence f, impératif m

Angaben f pl
  E: data pl and sg, details pl, particulars pl
  F: données f pl, renseignements m pl

angespitzte Isolierung
  E: pencilled insulation
  F: isolation f appointée

angetrieben von
  E: powered by, driven by
  F: entraîné adj par

Anhalten n [Masch.]
  E: stoppage n
  F: arrêt m

Anhaltevorrichtung f
  E: stopping device
  F: dispositif m d'arrêt

Anhäufung von Kabeln [K. Verl.]
  E: grouping of cables, accumulation of cables
  F: accumulation f de câbles, groupement m de câbles

Anlage f [Masch.]
  E: plant n, unit n, installation n, equipment n, line n
  F: installation f

Anlage f (Auslegung)
  E: layout n, arrangement n
  F: disposition f, groupement m

Anlage einer Werkstatt
  E: shop lay-out
  F: disposition f dans un atelier

Anlage im Betriebsmaßstab
  E: commercial size plant
  F: installation f à l'échelle industrielle

anlappende Bandumspinnung
  E: butted taping

Anlaufzeit f[Masch.]
  E: starting time, acceleration time, running-in period
  F: temps m de démarrage, temps m d'accélération

anlegen, eine Spannung ~
  E: to apply a voltage
  F: mettre v sous tension, appliquer v une tension

anlegen, einen Strom ~
  E: to inject a current, to apply a current
  F: faire v passer un courant

Anlehnung, in ~ an
  E: similar to, taking pattern from
  F: suivant l'exemple de

Anlieferungszustand, im ~
  E: in as-received condition, at the received stage, as delivered
  F: à l'état vierge, à la livraison

anmelden, ein Patent ~
  E: to apply for a patent, to file a patent application
  F: déposer v une demande de brevet, demander v un brevet

Annäherungswert m
  E: approximate value
  F: valeur f approchée, valeur f approximative

Anodenschlamm m
  E: anode mud
  F: boue f anodique

Anordnung f
  E: layout n, arrangement n
  F: disposition f, groupement m

anorganisch adj
  E: inorganic adj
  F: inorganique adj

Anpassung f[Nachr.]
  E: matching n
  F: adaptation f

Anpassungsdämpfung f
  E: matching attenuation, matching loss, return loss
  F: affaiblissement m d'adaptation

Anpassungsübertrager m[Nachr.]
  E: matching relay repeater, matching transformer
  F: transformateur m d'adaptation

Ansatz einer Mischung
  E: compound formulation
  F: formulation f d'un mélange

ansaugen v
  E: suck v
  F: aspirer v

anschalten v[Masch.]
  E: start v, start up v
  F: démarrer v, mettre v en marche

anschalten v[el.]
  E: switch on v, turn on (US) v
  F: enclencher v (él.), mettre v sous tension, fermer v (circuit), mettre v en circuit

Anschlag m (Arretierung)
  E: stop n, lock n, limit stop
  F: butée f, arrêt m

Anschlußdose f
  E: connection box, junction box
  F: boîte f de jonction, boîte f de raccordement

Anschlußdrähte, einseitig herausgeführte ~
  E: single-ended terminal wires
  F: fils m pl de jonction unidirectionnels

Anschlüsse, elektrische ~
  E: electrical connections
  F: liaisons f pl électriques, raccords m pl électriques

Anschlußkabel n
  E: connection cable, service cable
  F: câble m de raccordement

Anschlußkasten m[el.]
  E: distribution panel, terminal box, junction box, connection box
  F: coffret m de distribution, boîte f de distribution, boîte f de dérivation, boîte f de connexion, coffret m de raccordement, boîte f de jonction, boîte f à bornes

Anschlußklemme f[el.]
  E: terminal n, connector n, connecting terminal
  F: borne f, connecteur m, borne f de raccordement

Anschlußklemme f[Nachr. K.]
  E: binding post
  F: borne f

Anschlußlasche f
  E: cable lug, terminal lug, cable eye
  F: cosse f de câble, attache f de conducteur, cosse f terminale

Anschlußleiste f[el.]
  E: terminal block, terminal strip, terminal board, connecting block,

Anschlußleiste
   connection strip
   F: bloc *m* de connexion, réglette *f* de raccordement, réglette *f* à bornes, barrette *f* à bornes

Anschlußleistung *f*
   E: power rating, connected load
   F: puissance *f* connectée, puissance *f* absorbée

Anschlußleitung *f* [Tel.]
   E: direct line, subscriber's line
   F: ligne *f* d'abonné

Anschlußmuffe *f*
   E: junction box
   F: manchon *m* de raccordement

Anschlußöse *f*
   E: cable lug, terminal lug, cable eye
   F: cosse *f* de câble, attache *f* de conducteur, cosse *f* terminale

Anschlußschnur *f*
   E: flexible cord, flexible *n*, connecting cord
   F: câble *m* souple, cordon *m* de raccordement

Anschlußschnur, Geräte-~ *f*
   E: appliance cord
   F: cordon *m* de raccordement d'appareil, cordon *m* d'alimentation d'appareil, cordon *m* souple, câble *m* souple de raccordement

Anschlußstecker *m*
   E: connector *n*, connecting plug
   F: fiche *f* de raccordement

Anschlußstück *n*
   E: intermediate piece, connecting piece, adapter *n*, connector *n*, fitting *n*
   F: pièce *f* intermédiaire, pièce *f* de raccordement, raccord *m*, pièce *f* de jonction, adaptateur *m*

Anschlußwert *m*
   E: power rating, connected load
   F: puissance *f* connectée, puissance *f* absorbée

Ansetzen einer Mischung
   E: preparation of a compound, compound preparation
   F: préparation *f* d'un mélange

anspitzen *v* (Isolierung)
   E: pencil *v*
   F: appointer *v*

anspitzen *v* (Draht)
   E: point *v*
   F: appointer *v*

Anspitzmaschine und Einziehmaschine (Draht)
   E: wire sharpening and threading machine
   F: machine *f* à appointer et enfiler le fil métallique

Ansprechgeschwindigkeit *f*
   E: rapidity of response, responding speed
   F: rapidité *f* de réponse

Ansprechzeit *f*
   E: response time, reaction time
   F: temps *m* de réponse

Anstieg der Spannung
   E: voltage rise
   F: montée *f* de tension

Anstieg der Temperatur
   E: temperature rise, temperature increase
   F: élévation *f* de température, montée *f* de température

Anstieg einer Kurve
   E: slope of a curve
   F: pente *f* d'une courbe, montée *f* d'une courbe

Anstrich *m*
   E: paint *n*, finish *n*
   F: peinture *f*, enduit *m*

Antenne *f*
   E: aerial *n*, antenna *n*
   F: antenne *f*

Antennendurchführung *f*
   E: antenna duct, antenna lead-in (tube)
   F: traversée *f* d'antenne, passage *m* d'antenne

Antennenherabführung *f*
   E: antenna down-lead, aerial lead-in
   F: descente *f* d'antenne

Antennenkabel *n*
   E: antenna cable, aerial cable
   F: câble *m* d'antenne

Antennenleitung *f*
   E: antenna wire
   F: conducteur *m* d'antenne

Antennenniederführung *f*
   E: antenna down-lead, aerial lead-in
   F: descente *f* d'antenne

Antennenspeiseleitung *f*
   E: antenna feeder, aerial feeder, antenna lead
   F: feeder *m* d'antenne, ligne *f* d'alimentation d'antenne, descente

Arbeitsbühne

    f d'antenne, câble m d'antenne
Antennenzuleitung f
    E: antenna feeder, aerial feeder, antenna lead
    F: feeder m d'antenne, ligne f d'alimentation d'antenne, descente f d'antenne, câble m d'antenne
Antimon n
    E: antimony n
    F: antimoine m
Antimon-Blei n
    E: antimonial lead
    F: plomb m antimonié
Antioxidans n
    E: antioxidant n, oxidation inhibitor
    F: inhibiteur m d'oxydation, antioxidant m, antioxygène m
Antrieb, doppelseitiger ~
    E: bilateral drive
    F: commande f bilatérale
Antrieb, einseitiger ~
    E: unilateral drive
    F: commande f unilatérale
Antriebsaggregat, hydraulisches ~
    E: hydraulic power pack
    F: unité f d'entraînement hydraulique
Antriebsmotor m
    E: driving motor
    F: moteur m d'entraînement
Antriebsrad n
    E: drive gear, driving gear
    F: pignon m de commande
Antriebswelle f
    E: transmission shaft, driving shaft
    F: arbre m de commande
Anvulkanisation f (Elastomere)
    E: scorching n
    F: carbonisation f
Anvulkanisieren n (Vorvulkanisieren)
    E: pre-vulcanisation n
    F: prévulcanisation f
Anwalzgrad m (Leiter)
    E: compression degree, shaping degree
    F: coefficient m de rétreint
Anwendeldraht m (Luftkabel)
    E: lashing wire
    F: fil m hélice de support
Anwendelmaschine f (Luftkabel)
    E: lashing machine
    F: machine f à poser l'hélice de support
Anwendungsbereich m
    E: range of application
    F: sphère f d'application
Anwendungsgebiet n
    E: field of application
    F: champ m d'application, domaine m d'application, domaine m d'utilisation
Anzapfung f
    E: tap n, tapping n
    F: prise f
Anzeige f
    E: indication n, display n, reading n
    F: indication f, signalisation f, lecture f, affichage m
Anzeigelampe f
    E: pilot lamp, signal lamp, indicating lamp, pilot light
    F: voyant m lumineux, signal m lumineux, lampe-témoin f
Anzeigestromkreis m
    E: indicator circuit
    F: circuit m indicateur
Anzeigetafel f
    E: indicator panel, signal board, display panel
    F: panneau m indicateur de fonctionnement, tableau m indicateur
Anzeigevorrichtung f
    E: indicator n, display unit
    F: indicateur m
Arbeitsablauf m
    E: flow of operation, operating sequence, flow process, operating cycle
    F: phases f pl de travail, suite f des opérations, cycle m de travail, déroulement m des opérations
Arbeitsablaufdiagramm n
    E: flow chart, flow diagram, process (flow) chart
    F: organigramme m (prod.), ordinogramme m, graphique m de processus, diagramme m de déroulement
Arbeitsanweisung f
    E: working instructions pl
    F: instructions f pl de travail
Arbeitsbühne f
    E: operator's control platform, operating platform
    F: plate-forme f de commande, plate-forme f de service

Arbeitsbühne

Arbeitsbühne, höhenverstellbare ~
 E: elevator n (working platform)
 F: élévateur m (plateforme de travail)

Arbeitsgang, in einem einzigen ~
 E: in a single operation
 F: en une seule passe, en une même operation

Arbeitsgeschwindigkeit f [Masch.]
 E: line speed, production speed, running speed, production rate, operating speed, processing speed
 F: vitesse de marche f, vitesse f de fabrication, vitesse f de production, vitesse f de travail

Arbeitsplatzgestaltung f
 E: workplace layout
 F: implantation f du poste de travail

Arbeitsprogramm n (Prod.)
 E: production programme, manufacturing programme, production scheme, manufacturing schedule
 F: programme m de fabrication

Arbeitsstudie f
 E: time and motion study
 F: étude f du travail

Arbeitsvorbereitung f
 E: manufacturing planning, work planning, production planning
 F: préparation f du travail

Arbeitswalze f
 E: work(ing) roll
 F: cylindre m de travail

Arbeitsweise f
 E: mode of operation, functioning n, operation n
 F: fonctionnement m, mode m de fonctionnement, opération f

Arbeitszyklus einer Maschine
 E: machine cycle
 F: cycle m de marche d'une machine

Arbeitszylinder m [Met.-Strangpr.]
 E: main cylinder
 F: cylindre m de pression

Armiermaschine f
 E: armo(u)ring machine
 F: armeuse f

armiert adj
 E: armo(u)red adj
 F: armé adj

armiertes Kabel für flache Küstengewässer
 E: shore-end cable, shallow-water cable, shelf cable
 F: câble m d'atterrissement, câble m côtier, câble m de bas fond

Armierung f
 E: armo(u)ring n, armo(u)r n
 F: armure f

Armierung, doppellagige ~
 E: double armo(u)ring
 F: armure f double

Armierungsdraht m
 E: armo(u)ring wire
 F: fil m d'armure

Asbest m
 E: asbestos n
 F: amiante m

Asbestzementrohr n
 E: asbestos cement pipe
 F: tube m en amiante-ciment

Aschegehalt m
 E: ash content
 F: teneur f en cendres, taux m de cendre

Äthylen-Propylen-Kautschuk m (EPR)
 E: ethylene-propylene rubber (EPR) n
 F: caoutchouc m d'éthylène propylène (EPR)

Äthylen-Vinyl-Azetat (EVA) n
 E: ethylene vinyl acetate (EVA)
 F: acétate m d'éthylène vinyle (EVA)

atmen v [mech.]
 E: breathe v
 F: respirer v

atmender Speicher (SZ-Verseilung)
 E: breathing accumulator
 F: moufle m respirant

Aufbau m
 E: installation n, erection n, set-up n, assembly n
 F: implantation f, montage m, assemblage m

Aufbau eines Kabels
 E: cable design, cable make-up, construction of a cable, cable build-up, design of a cable
 F: construction f d'un câble, constitution f d'un câble

Aufbau-Daten pl
 E: design data
 F: données f pl de construction, caractéristiques f pl dimensionelles, données f pl constructives

Aufbocken einer Kabeltrommel

aufschließen

aufbringen v
  E: apply v
  F: appliquer v, mettre v en place
Aufbringen n (Masse, Kleber, Korrosionsschutz)
  E: flooding n, coating n
  F: enduction f
Aufbringung f
  E: application n
  F: pose f, mise f en place
aufdrehen v (sich)
  E: unwind v, open v, birdcage v, basket v, untwist v
  F: détordre v (se)
Auffangbehälter m
  E: sump n
  F: bâche f
Auffindung einer Störstelle
  E: fault location, fault finding, trouble finding, fault detection, trouble shooting (US), locating the trouble (GB)
  F: localisation f d'un défaut
auffüllen v
  E: replenish v, resupply v, refill v
  F: remplir v, refaire v le plein
Auffüllen n (Kabelgraben)
  E: backfilling n
  F: remplissage m (caniveau de câble)
Auffüllmaterial n [K. Verl.]
  E: backfill n
  F: matériel m de remplissage
aufgepreßter Aluminiummantel
  E: extruded aluminium sheath
  F: gaine f d'aluminium filée sur câble
aufgepreßter Deflektor
  E: mo(u)lded deflector
  F: déflecteur m surmoulé
aufgeschrumpfter Endverschluß
  E: shrunk-on termination
  F: extrémité f emmanchée à chaud
Aufhängung f
  E: suspension n
  F: suspension f
Aufheizzeit f
  E: warm-up time, heating-up time
  F: temps m de chauffage
aufklappbar adj
  E: hinged adj, swivelling adj, pivoted adj
  F: pivotant adj, articulé adj

aufkorben v (Armierungsdrähte)
  E: unwind v, open v, birdcage v, basket v, untwist v
  F: détordre v (se)
Aufkorben n (Armierungsdrähte)
  E: birdcaging n, basketing n
  F: détorsion f (formation de paniers/corbeilles des fils d'armure)
Auflagedruck m
  E: contact pressure
  F: pression f de serrage
Aufnehmer m [Met.-Strangpr.]
  E: billet container
  F: conteneur m de billettes, pot m de presse
Aufnehmerhalter m [Met.-Strangpr.]
  E: container holder
  F: support m du conteneur, porte-conteneur m
Aufnehmerheizung f [Met.-Strangpr.]
  E: container heating system
  F: chauffage m du conteneur
Aufnehmer-Verschiebevorrichtung f [Met.-Strangpr.]
  E: container shifting device
  F: dispositif m de déplacement du conteneur
aufpressen, Bleimantel ~
  E: lead-sheath v, to apply the lead sheath
  F: mettre v sous gaine de plomb
Aufpressen des Mantels auf das Kabel
  E: extrusion of the sheath on to the cable
  F: filage m de la gaine sur le câble, extrusion f de la gaine sur le câble
Aufputz-Installation f
  E: surface mounting, installation on the surface
  F: pose f sur crépi, pose f apparente
Aufputz-Schalter m
  E: surface-mounted switch
  F: interrupteur m monté sur crépi
aufschieben v
  E: slip on v
  F: enfiler v
Aufschieb-Endverschluß m
  E: slip-on termination
  F: extrémité f emmanchable
aufschließen v [Chem.]
  E: decompose v
  F: attaquer v, dissoudre v, désagréger v

Aufschluß m (in der Wurzschmitt-Bombe)
  E: decomposition n (in the Wurzschmitt-bomb)
  F: dissolution f (dans la bombe Wurzschmitt)

Aufschluß geben über (z.B. Betriebsverhalten)
  E: to be indicative of, to permit conclusions as to
  F: fournir v des renseignements sur

aufschrumpfbarer Endverschluß
  E: shrink-on termination, heat-shrinkable termination
  F: extrémité f emmanchable à chaud

aufschrumpfen v
  E: heat-shrink v, shrink on v
  F: emmancher v à chaud

Aufschrumpfmuffe f
  E: heat-shrinkage insulating sleeve, shrink-on sleeve, heat-shrinkable sleeve
  F: manchon m emmanché à chaud

Aufschrumpftechnik f
  E: shrink-on technique, heat-shrinkage technique
  F: technique f d'emmanchement à chaud

Aufsetzen n (Prüflast)
  E: application n (test load)
  F: application f (charge d'essai)

aufspulen v
  E: wind v, wind up v, take up v, spool v, reel v, coil v
  F: enrouler v, bobiner v

Aufsteck-Endverschluß m
  E: plug-in termination, plug-on termination
  F: extrémité f embrochable

Aufstellungszeichnung f
  E: assembly drawing, erection drawing, installation drawing
  F: plan m d'assemblage, plan m de montage

Aufteilungskabel n [Nachr.]
  E: distribution cable
  F: câble m de distribution

Aufteilungskappe f
  E: spreader head, spreader cap
  F: cornet m de division

Aufteilungsmuffe f
  E: spreading box, spreader box, multiple joint box, distribution sleeve
  F: boîte f de distribution, boîte f de division, boîte f de trifurcation

Aufteilungsmuffe für drei Adern
  E: trifurcating joint, trifurcating box
  F: boîte f tri-mono, boîte f de trifurcation

Aufteilungs-Ortskabel n
  E: local distribution cable
  F: câble m urbain de distribution

Auftragsschweißung f
  E: welded hard surfacing, build-up welding, surface layer welding
  F: soudure f à superposition

auftrommeln v
  E: wind v, wind up v, take up v, spool v, reel v, coil v
  F: enrouler v, bobiner v

aufvulkanisierter Endenabschluß
  E: sealing end vulcanized to the cable
  F: extrémité f vulcanisée sur le câble

aufvulkanisierter Stecker
  E: plug vulcanized to the cable
  F: fiche f vulcanisée sur le câble

aufweiten v
  E: expand v, bulge v, bell out v, flare v
  F: élargir v, évaser v, mandriner v

aufwendiges Verfahren
  E: elaborate process
  F: méthode f élaborée, technique f recherchée

Aufwickelei f
  E: take-up unit, take-up n, take-up stand
  F: enrouleur m, bobinoir m

aufwickeln v
  E: wind v, wind up v, take up v, spool v, reel v, coil v
  F: enrouler v, bobiner v

Aufwickeln von Draht (Faßwickler)
  E: wire packaging (barrel take-up)
  F: enroulement m du fil (tonneau d'enroulement)

Aufwickelspule f
  E: take-up reel
  F: bobine f réceptrice

Aufwickeltrommel f
  E: take-up reel, reeling drum
  F: bobine f réceptrice

Aufzugsleitung f
  E: lift cable
  F: câble m d'ascenseur

Auge, mit bloßem ~ sichtbar

E: visible to the naked eye
F: visible adj à l'œil nu

ausbauen v
E: remove v, dismount v
F: démonter v, enlever v

Ausbauleistung f
E: installed capacity, total rated power
F: puissance f installée

Ausbiegen von Kabeladern
E: fanning out of the cable cores, bending out of the cable cores
F: épanouissement m des conducteurs de câble

Ausblühung f
E: bloom n, blooming n
F: efflorescence f

Ausbluten n (Farbe)
E: bleeding n
F: migration f

ausbreiten v (sich)
E: spread v, propagate v
F: étendre v (s'), propager v (se)

Ausbreitung f
E: propagation n, spreading n
F: propagation f, diffusion f

ausdehnen v (sich)
E: expand vi, dilate vi
F: dilater v (se)

Ausdehnung f
E: expansion n, extension n, dilatation n
F: dilatation f, expansion f, extension f

Ausdehnungskoeffizient m
E: coefficient of expansion, expansion coefficient
F: coefficient m de dilatation

auseinandernehmen v
E: dismantle v, disassemble v
F: désassembler v

Auseinanderspreizen der Kabeladern
E: fanning out of the cable cores, bending out of the cable cores
F: épanouissement m des conducteurs de câble

Ausfall m (Anlage, Kabel)
E: failure n, breakdown n, outage n
F: défaut m, panne f, défaillance f, incident m de fonctionnement

Ausfallmuster n
E: reference sample, quality sample
F: échantillon m de qualité, échantillon m type

Ausfallrate f
E: failure rate
F: taux m de défaillances

Ausfallwahrscheinlichkeit f
E: failure probability
F: probabilité f de claquage

Ausfallzeit f [Masch.]
E: down-time n, outage time
F: temps m d'arrêt, temps m de panne, temps m d'immobilisation

Ausgangsmaterial n
E: original material, basic material, raw material, feed stock
F: matière f de base, produit m de base, matière f première, matériel m rudimentaire

Ausgangswert m
E: initial value
F: valeur f initiale

ausgeglichene Übertragungsleitung [Tel.]
E: balanced transmission line
F: ligne f de transmission équilibrée

ausgelastet, voll ~
E: loaded to capacity, operating at full capacity
F: utilisé adj à pleine capacité, utilisé adj à plein

ausgezogene Platte
E: rolled sheet
F: plaque f laminée

Ausgleich m
E: compensation n, balance n, balancing n, counterbalancing n, equalization n
F: compensation f, équilibrage m, équilibre m, balance f, égalisation f

Ausgleichen durch Dralländerung [Nachr. K.]
E: compensation by alteration of twist
F: compensation f par changement du pas de câblage

Ausgleichen durch Gruppieren nach elektrischen Werten [Nachr. K.]
E: compensation by grouping according to electrical values
F: compensation f par groupement suivant les valeurs électriques

Ausgleichen durch Kreuzen [Nachr. K.]
E: compensation by crossing
F: compensation f par croisement

Ausgleichsgefäß n (Ölkabel)
E: oil expansion tank, variable oil

Ausgleichsgefäß

pressure tank, oil pressure tank, oil reservoir
F: réservoir m à pression d'huile variable

Ausgleichsleitung f
E: equalizer n, equipotential connection, balancing circuit, equalizing circuit
F: fil m de compensation, circuit m d'équilibrage

Ausgleichsnetzwerk n
E: balancing network
F: réseau m de compensation

Ausgleichsstrom m
E: equalizing current, transient current, balancing current
F: courant m compensateur, courant m transitoire

Ausgußmasse f [K. Garn.]
E: filling compound, sealing compound, flooding compound
F: matière f de remplissage

aushalten v
E: withstand v, resist v to ...
F: supporter v, résister v à ..., tenir v, soutenir v

Aushärten n [Plast.]
E: curing n
F: cuisson f, durcissement m

ausklappbar adj
E: hinged adj, swivelling adj, pivoted adj
F: pivotant adj, articulé adj

Auskleidung f
E: lining n
F: doublure f, revêtement m, fourrure f

Ausklingeln n [Tel. K.]
E: ringing test, ring-out procedure, buzz-out operation
F: contrôle m de continuité, sonnage m

Auskreuzen von Kabelmänteln
E: cross-bonding of cable sheaths
F: transposition f des gaines de câbles

Auskreuzungskasten m [Kab.]
E: link box, cross-bonding box
F: boîte f de raccordement à la terre, boîte f de transposition

Auslaßventil n
E: outlet valve, drain valve, discharge valve, exhaust valve
F: soupape f de décharge, soupape f de vidange, soupape f d'émission, soupape f de sortie

Auslauf-Ende n (Draht)
E: back-end n (wire)
F: fin f (fil métallique)

Auslaufzeit f (Viskositätsmessung)
E: time of efflux, flow time
F: temps m d'écoulement

Auslegemaschine für Kabel
E: cable laying machine
F: machine f à poser les câbles

auslegen v [Kab.]
E: lay v, install v
F: poser v

auslegen v (Werk, Anlage)
E: lay out v, set out v
F: disposer v, arranger v

Auslegeschrift f
E: published patent application, examined patent application
F: demande f de brevet examinée

Auslegung f (Planung)
E: layout n, arrangement n
F: disposition f, groupement m

Auslösestrom m
E: release current, tripping current
F: courant m de déclenchement

Ausnutzungsgrad m [Masch.]
E: utilisation factor, unit capacity factor
F: coefficient m d'utilisation

Ausrüstung f [Masch.]
E: equipment n, facilities pl
F: équipement m, matériel m

aussagekräftig adj (Werte)
E: meaningful adj, significant adj
F: significatif adj

ausschalten v [el.]
E: switch off v, interrupt v, disconnect v, turn off (US) v, de-energize v, cut out v
F: couper v, interrompre v, déconnecter v

ausschalten v [Masch.]
E: shut down v
F: arrêter v

Ausschalter m
E: circuit breaker, cut-out switch, disconnecting switch
F: discontacteur m, disjoncteur m, interrupteur m

Ausschaltleistung f
E: breaking capacity (GB),

interrupting capacity (US)
F: puissance f de rupture, pouvoir m de coupure

Ausscheidung f
E: segregation n, separation n, exudation n
F: ségrégation f, séparation f

Ausscheidung f [Chem.]
E: precipitate n
F: précipité m, dépôt m

ausschwenkbar adj
E: hinged adj, swivelling adj, pivoted adj
F: pivotant adj, articulé adj

Ausschwenken n
E: swinging-out n, swivelling-out n
F: pivotement m

ausschwitzen v
E: exude v
F: exsuder v

Ausschwitzen n (auf der Oberfläche von Kunststoffen)
E: exudation n
F: exsudation f

Aussehen n (Oberfläche)
E: appearance n
F: aspect m

Außenabmessungen f pl
E: overall dimensions
F: dimensions f pl extérieures

Außendruckkabel n
E: compression cable
F: câble m à compression

Außendurchmesser m
E: overall diameter, outer diameter (OD)
F: diamètre m extérieur

Außenleiter m
E: outer conductor
F: âme f extérieure, conducteur m extérieur

Außenmantel m
E: outer sheath
F: gaine f extérieure, gaine d'étanchéité f

Außenschutz m [Kab.]
E: serving n, oversheath n
F: revêtement m extérieur

außer Betrieb
E: out of operation, out of order, out of service
F: hors service

äußere Leitschicht [Kab.]
E: outer semi-conducting layer
F: couche f semi-conductrice externe

äußere Schutzhülle [Kab.]
E: serving n, oversheath n
F: revêtement m extérieur

aussetzen v (einwirken lassen)
E: expose v
F: exposer v

Aussetzen n (dem Licht, der Wärme)
E: exposure n (to)
F: exposition f (à la lumière; à la chaleur)

Aussetzen des Bleiflusses
E: lead starvation
F: raté m du flux de plomb

aussetzender Betrieb [el.]
E: intermittent operation
F: service m intermittent, service m avec charge intermittente, régime m temporaire

Aussparung f
E: recess n, clearance n, slot n
F: découpe f, évidement m

Ausstanzen n (Prüfkörper)
E: punching with a die, cutting with a die, die-cutting n
F: découpage m, poinçonnage m

Ausstoß m [Masch.]
E: performance n, output n, efficiency n, capacity n
F: performance f, débit m, efficacité f, rendement m, capacité f

Ausstoßen des Preßrestes [Met.-Strangpr.]
E: ejection of the discard
F: expulsion f du culot de filage

Ausstoßvorrichtung f
E: ejector n
F: éjecteur m

austauschbar adj
E: interchangeable adj, replaceable adj
F: interchangeable adj

Austritt m
E: outlet n, exit n, orifice n
F: sortie f

Austrittstemperatur f
E: outlet temperature
F: température f de sortie

austrocknen v
E: dry out v, desiccate vt, dehydrate vt
F: sécher v, dessécher v

Austrocknung 18

Austrocknung des Erdbodens
 E: drying (out)
   of the soil
 F: séchage *m* du sol, dessèchement *m*
   du sol
Auswahlprüfung *f*
 E: sample test, screening *n*
 F: essai *m* de prélèvement
auswechselbar *adj*
 E: interchangeable *adj*, replaceable
   adj
 F: interchangeable *adj*
Auswerfer *m*
 E: ejector *n*
 F: éjecteur *m*
Auswertung *f*
 E: evaluation *n*
 F: évaluation *f*
auswickeln *v* (Isolierung)
 E: build up *v*
 F: reconstituer *v*
Auswickeln einer Verbindungsstelle
 E: lapping of a joint, build-up of a
   joint
 F: reconstitution *f* d'une jonction
ausziehbar *adj*
 E: extensible *adj*, telescopic *adj*
 F: extensible *adj*, télescopique *adj*
automatische Doppelaufwickelei
 E: automatic double spooler
 F: enrouleur *m* automatique à double
   bobine
automatische Drahtführung (Wickler)
 E: automatic wire guide
 F: trancanage *m* automatique du fil
   métallique
automatische Leckstellenanzeige
 E: automatic leakage detection
 F: détection *f* automatique de fuites
automatische Nulleinstellung
 E: automatic reset
 F: remise *f* à zéro automatique
automatischer Spulapparat
 E: automatic spooler
 F: bobinoir *m* automatique

B

Babbeln *n* [Tel.]
 E: babbling *n*

 F: murmure *m* confus
Baggerkabel *n*
 E: trailing cable, dredge cable
 F: câble *m* de drague
Baggerleitung *f*
 E: trailing cable, dredge cable
 F: câble *m* de drague
Bahn *f* (Papier, Stoff)
 E: web *n*, sheeting *n*, sheet *n*
 F: bande *f*
Bahnhofsfernmeldekabel *n*
 E: railway station telecommunication
   cable
 F: câble *m* de télécommunication
   pour gares ferroviaires
Bahnkabel *n*
 E: railway cable
 F: câble *m* de chemin de fer
Bajonett-Schnellverschluß mit Schnecke und Schneckenrad für Tränkgefäße
 E: quick-acting lock with worm gear
   for impregnating tanks
 F: fermeture *f* rapide à baïonnette avec
   roue hélicoïdale pour cuves
   d'imprégnation
Bajonettverschluß *m*
 E: bayonet joint
 F: verrouillage *m* à baïonnette
„Ballon"-Isolierung *f*
 E: balloon insulation
 F: isolation *f* ballon
Ballung von Kabeln [K. Verl.]
 E: grouping of cables, accumulation
   of cables
 F: accumulation *f* de câbles,
   groupement *m* de câbles
Ballungsfaktor *m*
 E: grouping factor
 F: coefficient *m* d'accumulation
Ballungszentrum *n* [K. Verl.]
 E: heavily loaded locality, congested
   area
 F: grande agglomération urbaine,
   zone *f* de forte agglomération
Bambusringe *m pl* (durch Rastzeiten
   beim Aufbringen von Kabelmänteln
   aus Blei oder Aluminium)
 E: bamboo rings, stop marks
 F: nœuds *m pl* de bambou
Banbury-Kneter *m*
 E: rubber kneader, Banbury-mixer *n*,
   Banbury-kneader *n*

Band n
  E: tape n, strip n, band n
  F: ruban m, bande f
Bandagen f pl (für Ziehscheiben an der Drahtziehmaschine)
  E: pullblock tyres
  F: bandages m pl (pour les cônes de tréfilage)
Bandarmierung f
  E: steel tape armo(u)ring, steel tape armo(u)r
  F: armure f en feuillard d'acier
Bandbewehrung f
  E: steel tape armo(u)ring, steel tape armo(u)r
  F: armure f en feuillard d'acier
Bandbreite f [Nachr.]
  E: band width
  F: largeur f de bande
Bandeisen n
  E: steel tape, steel strip
  F: feuillard m d'acier
Bandeisen-Armierung f
  E: steel tape armo(u)ring, steel tape armo(u)r
  F: armure f en feuillard d'acier
bandeisenbewehrtes Kabel
  E: steel-tape-armo(u)red cable
  F: câble m armé en feuillard d'acier
Bandeisenbewehrung f
  E: steel tape armo(u)ring, steel tape armo(u)r
  F: armure f en feuillard d'acier
Bandeisen-Spinner m
  E: steel tape spinner, steel taping head
  F: enrouleur m à feuillard d'acier, tête f à feuillard
Bandeisen-Wickler m
  E: steel tape spooler
  F: bobinoir m à feuillard d'acier
Bandisolierung f
  E: tape insulation, taped insulation, lapped insulation
  F: isolation f rubanée
Bandkupfer n
  E: copper tape, copper strip, copper strap
  F: bande f de cuivre, ruban m de cuivre
Bandriß m (Papier)

F: mélangeur m à caoutchouc, mélangeur m Banbury, malaxeur m Banbury

  E: tape break
  F: déchirure f du ruban, rupture f du ruban
Bandrißwächter m (Papier)
  E: tape break monitor
  F: détecteur m de rupture du ruban
Bandscheibe f
  E: pad n (paper), coil n (metal tape)
  F: galette f
Bandschreiber m
  E: chart recorder, strip chart recorder
  F: enregistreur m à papier déroulant
Bandumspinnung f
  E: lapping n, taping n, tape(d) wrapping
  F: rubanage m
Bandwickelmaschine f
  E: taping machine, lapping machine
  F: rubaneuse f
Bandwickler m
  E: spinner n, lapping head, tape lapping head
  F: tête f de rubanage, tête f rubaneuse
Basisschaltung f [el.]
  E: grounded-base circuit
  F: circuit m de base, montage m de base
Bauart f [Kab.]
  E: design n, type n, construction n
  F: construction f, type m
Bauelement n [Kab.]
  E: constructional element, component n
  F: élément m constitutif, élément m de construction
Bäumchenbildung f (in Isolierstoffen unter el. Beanspruchung)
  E: treeing n
  F: treeing m, arborescence f
Baumwollband, gummibeschichtetes ~
  E: proofed cotton tape
  F: ruban m de coton caoutchouté
Baumwollbindeband n
  E: cotton binder tape
  F: ruban m de coton de ligature
Baumwollgeflecht n
  E: cotton braiding, braided cotton covering
  F: tresse f de coton
Baumwollumklöppelung f
  E: cotton braiding, braided cotton covering
  F: tresse f de coton

Bausatz

Bausatz m
  E: kit n
  F: trousse f
Baustelle, auf der ~ [K. Verl.]
  E: at site
  F: sur chantier
Baustellen-Bedingungen f pl [K. Verl.]
  E: field conditions
  F: conditions f pl sur chantier
Baustellen-Verhältnisse n pl [K. Verl.]
  E: field conditions
  F: conditions f pl sur chantier
beanspruchen v [el., mech.]
  E: stress v, strain v, load v
  F: contraindre v, solliciter v, charger v
Beanspruchung f [el., mech.]
  E: stress n, strain n, load n
  F: contrainte f, sollicitation f, charge f
Beanspruchungshäufung f
  E: stress concentration
  F: concentration f de contraintes
Bearbeitungszugabe f
  E: oversize n, overdimension n
  F: surépaisseur f
bedienbar, leicht ~
  E: easy to operate
  F: facilement manœuvrable
bedienen, eine Maschine ~
  E: to run a machine, to operate a machine
  F: faire v marcher une machine, opérer v une machine
Bedienung f
  E: operation n, handling n, actuation n, control n
  F: commande f, manœuvre f, manipulation f
Bedienung, leichte ~
  E: ease of manipulation, ease of operation, working ease
  F: aisance f de manipulation, aisance f de manœuvre
Bedienungsanleitung f
  E: operating instruction, instructions pl for use, operating manual
  F: mode m opératoire, mode m d'emploi, notice f d'utilisation, manuel m d'instruction
Bedienungsfehler m
  E: faulty operation, operating error, operator's error
  F: fausse manœuvre f, erreur f de conduite, erreur f de manœuvre, erreur f de l'opérateur, erreur f de manipulation
Bedienungsfeld n
  E: control panel, operator panel
  F: panneau m de commande
Bedienungshebel m
  E: hand lever, actuating lever, operating lever
  F: levier m de commande
Bedienungsperson f
  E: operator n, attendant n
  F: opérateur m, machiniste m
Bedienungspult n
  E: control desk, operator's desk, control console
  F: pupitre m de commande, poste m de commande
Bedienungsseite f [Masch.]
  E: side of attendance, service side, operating side, working side
  F: côté commande m, côté m manœuvre, côté m service
Bedingung, eine ~ erfüllen
  E: to meet a requirement
  F: satisfaire v à une demande, satisfaire v à une exigence
Bedingungen auf der Baustelle [K. Verl.]
  E: field conditions
  F: conditions f pl sur chantier
bedrucken v
  E: print v
  F: imprimer v
Bedruckung f
  E: printing n
  F: marquage m par impression
Bedruckungsvorrichtung f
  E: printer n, printing device
  F: dispositif m d'impression
Beeinflussung f
  E: interference n (effect)
  F: effet m de perturbation, perturbation f, interférence f
Beeinflussung von Nachrichtenleitungen durch Energieanlagen
  E: interference of power cables with communication cables
  F: perturbation f des lignes de télécommunication par des lignes de transport d'énergie
Beeinflussung, induktive ~ benachbarter Kabel

E: inductive influence on neighbouring cables, inductive interference with neighbouring cables
F: effet m inductif sur des câbles voisins

Beeinflussungsspannung f
E: interference voltage, disturbing voltage
F: tension f perturbatrice, tension f parasite

Befeilen des Aluminiummantels (zum Verbinden)
E: filing of the aluminium sheath (for jointing)
F: limure f de la gaine d'aluminium (pour la jonction)

befestigen v
E: fasten v, fix v, attach v
F: attacher v, fixer v

befestigen, Kabel mit Schellen ~
E: to clamp a cable
F: brider v le câble

Befestigungsklemme f
E: mounting clip, mounting bracket
F: pince f d'ancrage, collier de fixation m

Befestigungsschelle f
E: clamp n, bracket n, clip n, cleat n
F: collier m, bride f

befeuchten v
E: wet v, moisten v
F: mouiller v, tremper v, humecter v

Beflechtung f
E: braid n, braiding n
F: tresse f

Befräsen n (Kupfer-Drahtbarren)
E: scalping n, chipping n
F: scalpage m, décortiquage m

begehbarer Tunnel
E: man-sized tunnel
F: tunnel m à dimension d'homme

Behandlung f
E: treatment n
F: traitement n

Beharrungszustand m
E: steady state condition
F: état m stationnaire, régime m établi, régime m permanent

Beheizung f
E: heating n
F: chauffage m

Beilauf m [Kab.]
E: filler n, valley sealer
F: bourrage m

Beilaufschnüre f pl
E: filler strings
F: cordelettes f pl

Beimengung f
E: addition n, admixture n
F: addition f, adjonction f

Beiwert m
E: coefficient n, factor n
F: coefficient m

Beizanlage f
E: pickling plant
F: installation f de décapage

Beizbad n
E: pickling bath
F: bain m de décapage

beizen v
E: pickle v
F: décaper v

Beizlösung f
E: pickling solution
F: solution f de décapage

Belastbarkeit f [el.]
E: current-carrying capacity, current rating, ampacity n, power rating
F: capacité f de charge, charge f limite, puissance f limite

belasten v
E: charge v, load v
F: charger v

belasten v [el., mech.]
E: stress v, strain v, load v
F: contraindre v, solliciter v, charger v

belastete Leitung
E: loaded line, line under load
F: ligne f chargée, ligne f en charge

belastetes dünndrähtiges Kabel [Tel. K.]
E: loaded thin-wire cable
F: câble m chargé avec âme en fils fins

Belastung f [el., mech.]
E: stress n, strain n, load n
F: contrainte f, sollicitation f, charge f

Belastungsdiagramm n
E: loading diagram
F: diagramme m de charge

Belastungsgrenze f
E: ultimate load, load limit
F: charge f limite

Belastungspause f
E: load pause

Belastungspause
F: intervalle *m* de charge

Belastungsspule f
E: Pupin coil, loading coil
F: bobine f Pupin, bobine f de charge

Belastungsstrom *m*
E: load current
F: courant *m* de charge

Belastungszyklen *m pl* [el.]
E: load cycles, current loading cycles
F: cycles *m pl* de charge

belegte Räume, stark ~ [Kab.]
E: congested areas
F: zones f pl à forte accumulation

Belegung f [Tel.]
E: engagement *n*, holding *n*
F: occupation f, prise f

Belegung mit Kabeln [K. Verl.]
E: grouping of cables, accumulation of cables
F: accumulation f de câbles, groupement *m* de câbles

Beleuchtungskabel *n*
E: lighting cable
F: câble *m* pour éclairage luminescent

belüften v
E: ventilate v, aerate v
F: aérer v, ventiler v

belüfteter Kabelkanal
E: forced ventilated cable tunnel
F: caniveau *m* de câble à ventilation forcée

Belüftung f
E: ventilation *n*, aeration *n*
F: ventilation f, aération f

Bemessungsspannung f
E: specified voltage
F: tension f spécifiée

benetzen v
E: wet v, moisten v
F: mouiller v, tremper v, humecter v

Benetzungsmittel *n*
E: wetting agent
F: agent *m* mouillant, agent *m* humidificateur

Beobachtungsfenster *n* [Masch.]
E: peephole *n*, sight glass, observation window, inspection glass
F: hublot *m* de regard, voyant *m*

Bereich *m*
E: range *n*, field *n*, scope *n*, area *n*
F: gamme f, domaine *m*, plage f

Bergwerkskabel *n*
E: mining cable, mine cable
F: câble *m* de mines

Berstdruck *m*
E: bursting pressure
F: pression f d'éclatement

Berstdruckfestigkeit f
E: bursting strength
F: résistance f à la pression d'éclatement

Berstdruckprüfung f
E: bursting test
F: essai *m* d'éclatement

Berührungsschutz *m* [el.]
E: protection from contact, shock protection
F: protection f contre des contacts accidentels

Berührungsspannung f
E: contact voltage, touch voltage, touch potential
F: tension f de contact

Beschädigung des Kabelmantels
E: damage to the cable sheath
F: endommagement *m* de la gaine de câble

beschichten v
E: coat v
F: revêtir v, enduire v

Beschichtung f
E: coating *n*
F: revêtement *m*, enrobage *m*

beschicken v
E: feed v, charge v, load v, supply v
F: alimenter v, charger v

Beschickungsmaterial *n*
E: feed material
F: matière f d'alimentation

Beschleuniger *m* [Vulk.]
E: accelerator *n*
F: accélérateur *m*

beschleunigte Alterung
E: accelerated ag(e)ing
F: vieillissement *m* accéléré

beschleunigte Lebensdauerprüfung
E: accelerated life test
F: essai *m* accéléré de durée de vie

beschneiden v
E: crop v, trim v, cut v
F: couper v, rogner v, cisailler v

besichtigen v
E: inspect v, survey v
F: examiner v, inspecter v

Bespinnung f(mit Kordel, Garn)
  E: spinning n
  F: guipage m
bespulte Leitung
  E: coil-loaded line
  F: ligne f pupinisée
bespultes dünndrähtiges Kabel
  E: loaded thin-wire cable
  F: câble m pupinisé avec âme en fils fins
bespultes Kabel
  E: loaded cable
  F: câble m chargé
Bespulung f
  E: coil-loading n, Pupin loading
  F: pupinisation f, charge f au moyen de bobines en série
Beständigkeit f
  E: stability n, durability n, resistance n, strength n
  F: résistance f, stabilité f, tenue f
bestehen, eine Prüfung ~
  E: to pass a test, to withstand a test
  F: passer v un essai, tenir v un essai, résister v à un essai
Bestimmung f[Prüf.]
  E: determination n, analysis n
  F: détermination f, analyse f
Bestimmungen f pl (Vorschriften)
  E: specifications pl, rules pl, regulations pl, standards pl
  F: prescriptions f pl, règles f pl
Bestimmungsgröße f
  E: parameter n, characteristic value
  F: paramètre m, valeur f caractéristique
bestrahltes PE
  E: irradiated PE
  F: polyéthylène m irradié
Betätigung f
  E: operation n, handling n, actuation n, control n
  F: commande f, manœuvre f, manipulation f
Betrieb m [Kab., Masch.]
  E: operation n, service n, duty n
  F: fonctionnement m, service m, exploitation f, régime m
Betrieb m (Werk, Anlage)
  E: factory n, plant n, workshop n
  F: usine f, atelier m
Betrieb mit aussetzender Belastung [el.]
  E: intermittent operation
  F: service m intermittent, service m avec charge intermittente, régime m temporaire
Betrieb mit zyklischer Belastung
  E: operation with cyclic loading
  F: régime m cyclique
Betrieb, außer ~
  E: out of operation, out of order, out of service
  F: hors service
Betrieb, in ~ nehmen
  E: to put to service, to set working, to take into commission, to bring into commercial operation
  F: mettre v en service, mettre v en œuvre
Betriebsablauf m
  E: flow of operation, operating sequence, flow process, operating cycle
  F: phases f pl de travail, suite f des opérations, cycle m de travail, déroulement m des opérations
Betriebsableitung f[Nachr.]
  E: operational leakage
  F: perditance f de transmission
Betriebsanleitung f
  E: operating instruction, instructions pl for use, operating manual
  F: mode m opératoire, mode m d'emploi, notice f d'utilisation, manuel m d'instruction
Betriebsart f
  E: method of operation, mode of operation, type of service
  F: mode m d'exploitation, régime m de marche
Betriebsbeanspruchung f
  E: operating stress
  F: contrainte f de service
Betriebsbedingungen f pl
  E: operational conditions, operating conditions, service conditions
  F: conditions f pl de travail, conditions f pl de fonctionnement, conditions f pl d'exploitation
betriebsbereit adj
  E: operational adj, ready for operation, in working order
  F: prêt adj à fonctionner, prêt adj à la mise en marche, , en ordre de marche
Betriebsdämpfung f[Tel.]

Betriebsdämpfung

  E: effective attenuation, overall loss, operative attenuation
  F: affaiblissement *m* composite
Betriebsdämpfungsmaß *n*[Tel.]
  E: operative attenuation unit
  F: unité *f* d'affaiblissement composite
Betriebsdruck *m*
  E: operating pressure, working pressure
  F: pression *f* de service
Betriebseigenschaften *f pl*
  E: operational characteristics
  F: caractéristiques *f pl* de service, caractéristiques *f pl* de fonctionnement
Betriebsfeldstärke *f*
  E: operating stress, operating field strength
  F: intensité *f* de service, gradient *m* de service
Betriebsflüssigkeit *f*
  E: working fluid
  F: liquide *m* de service
Betriebsfrequenz *f*[el.]
  E: power frequency
  F: fréquence *f* de régime
Betriebsingenieur *m*
  E: manufacturing engineer, production engineer
  F: ingénieur *m* de fabrication
Betriebskapazität *f*[Tel.]
  E: mutual capacitance
  F: capacité *f* mutuelle
Betriebskapazität *f*(Anlage)
  E: operating capacity
  F: capacité *f* de service
Betriebskosten *pl t*
  E: operating cost, operating expenses *pl*, running cost
  F: coût *m* d'exploitation
Betriebsmaßstab, Versuch im ~
  E: commercial scale trial
  F: essai *m* à l'échelle industrielle
betriebssichere Kabel
  E: operationally reliable cables, fail-safe cables
  F: câbles *m pl* de bonne sécurité de fonctionnement, câbles *m pl* de fonctionnement sûr
Betriebssicherheit *f*
  E: operating reliability, operating safety, service reliability, functional reliability, reliability of operation, operational reliability
  F: sécurité *f* de fonctionnement, fiabilité *f* de service
Betriebsspannung *f*
  E: operating voltage, service voltage
  F: tension *f* de service, tension *f* de régime
Betriebsstörung *f*
  E: failure *n*, breakdown *n*, outage *n*
  F: défaut *m*, panne *f*, défaillance *f*, incident *m* de fonctionnement
Betriebstemperatur *f*
  E: operating temperature
  F: température *f* de service, température *f* de fonctionnement
betriebsuntauglich *adj*
  E: unserviceable *adj*
  F: inutilisable *adj*
Betriebsverhalten *n*
  E: operating performance, service performance
  F: performance *f*(en service), tenue *f* (en service)
Betriebsversuch *m*
  E: field test, field trial, factory trial
  F: essai *m* sur chantier, essai *m* en service, essai *m* en usine
Betriebszustand *m*
  E: working order, operating condition
  F: état *m* de service
Betriebszuverlässigkeit *f*
  E: operating reliability, operating safety, service reliability, functional reliability, reliability of operation, operational reliability
  F: sécurité *f* de fonctionnement, fiabilité *f* de service
Bettungsmaterial *n*[K. Verl.]
  E: bedding material
  F: remblai *m*
Bettungstiefe *f*[K. Verl.]
  E: laying depth, depth of laying, depth below ground, depth under surface, installation depth
  F: profondeur *f* de pose
bewährt *adj*
  E: proved *adj*, proven *adj*, time-tested *adj*
  F: éprouvé *adj*
bewährt, im Betrieb ~
  E: field-proved *adj*
  F: qui a fait ses épreuves en service
bewährtes Verfahren

E: established practice
F: méthode f éprouvée
beweglich (fliegend) angeordnet
E: flying adj
F: volant adj, mobile adj
bewegliche Leitung
E: flexible cable, flexible cord, flexible n
F: câble m souple, cordon m souple
bewegliche Starkstromleitung
E: flexible portable power cord
F: câble m souple mobile d'énergie
Beweglichkeit f
E: flexibility n, mobility n
F: souplesse f, flexibilité f, mobilité f
bewehrt adj
E: armo(u)red adj
F: armé adj
Bewehrung f
E: armo(u)ring n, armo(u)r n
F: armure f
Bewehrungsdraht m
E: armo(u)ring wire
F: fil m d'armure
Bewehrungsmaschine f
E: armo(u)ring machine
F: armeuse f
bewickeln v [Kab.]
E: wrap v, wind v, cover v
F: recouvrir v, enrouler v
bewickeln v (mit Band)
E: lap v, tape v, wrap v
F: enrubanner v, rubaner v
Bewicklung f (mit Band)
E: lapping n, taping n, tape(d) wrapping
F: rubanage m
bewittern v
E: weather v
F: exposer v aux intempéries
Bewitterungsversuch m
E: weathering test
F: essai m atmosphérique, essai m de résistance aux intempéries
Bezirkskabel n
E: exchange cable, trunk cable, intercity cable
F: câble m régional, câble m suburbain
Bezugsdämpfung f
E: reference equivalent
F: équivalent m de référence
Bezugsgröße f

E: reference quantity
F: grandeur f de référence
Bezugskreis m
E: reference circuit
F: circuit m de référence
Bezugsspannung f
E: reference voltage
F: tension f de référence
Biegbarkeit f
E: flexibility n
F: souplesse f, flexibilité f
Biegefähigkeit f
E: bending capacity
F: aptitude f au pliage
Biegefestigkeit f
E: bending strength, flexural strength
F: résistance f au pliage
Biegen n
E: bending n
F: pliage m, flexion f
Biegeprüfung f
E: bending test, flexural test
F: essai m de pliage
Biegeradius m
E: bending radius
F: rayon m de courbure
Biegewechselfestigkeit f
E: reversed bending strength
F: résistance f aux pliages alternés
Biegezahl f
E: bending limit, bending value
F: nombre m de pliages alternés
Biegezyklen m pl
E: bending cycles
F: flexions f pl répétées
biegsam adj
E: flexible adj
F: flexible adj, souple adj
biegsame Schnur
E: flexible cord
F: cordon m souple
Biegsamkeit f
E: flexibility n
F: souplesse f, flexibilité f
Biegung f
E: curvature n, bend n, deflection n
F: courbure f, incurvation f, courbe f
Bildschirm m
E: screen n, image screen, viewing screen
F: écran m, écran m de vision
Bildtelegraphie-Übertragungsleitung f

Bindedraht m
 E: binding wire
 F: fil m de ligature, fil m d'attache

Bindefestigkeit f
 E: bond strength, bonding strength, adhesiveness n
 F: résistance f d'adhésion, pouvoir m adhésif, propriété f adhésive, adhésion f

Bindemittel n
 E: binder n, bonding agent
 F: liant m

Bindung f [Chem.]
 E: bond n
 F: liaison f

Birkenstämme m pl (zum Polen beim Kupferschmelzen)
 E: birch trunks, birch poles
 F: troncs m pl de bouleaux

Bitumen n
 E: bitumen n
 F: bitume m

Bitumenkasten m
 E: bitumen vat
 F: bac m à bitume

Bitumenkreppapier n
 E: bituminized crepe paper
 F: papier m crêpé bituminé

Bitumenmasse f
 E: bitumen compound
 F: matière f de bitume

bituminiert adj
 E: bituminized adj
 F: bituminé adj

Blähmittel n
 E: blowing agent
 F: agent m soufflant, agent m de gonflement

blank adj
 E: plain adj, bright adj, bare adj
 F: nu adj, brillant adj

Blankdraht m
 E: bare wire
 F: fil m nu

blanker Leiter
 E: bare conductor, plain conductor
 F: âme f nue

blankes Bleimantelkabel
 E: cable with bare lead sheath, plain lead-covered cable
 F: câble m sous gaine de plomb nu

Blankglühen n
 E: bright annealing
 F: recuit m brillant

Blankglühofen m
 E: bell type (annealing) furnace, hood type (annealing) furnace, top hat (annealing) furnace
 F: four m à tremper, four m pour recuit brillant

Blase f
 E: bubble n, blister n
 F: vessie f, bulle f

Blasenbildung f
 E: blistering n
 F: formation f de bulles

bleibende Dehnung
 E: permanent set, residual set, retained elongation
 F: allongement m permanent, allongement m rémanent

bleibende Verformung
 E: permanent deformation, plastic deformation
 F: déformation f permanente

Bleihülse f
 E: lead sleeve
 F: manchon m de plomb

Bleikappe f
 E: lead cap
 F: capot m de plomb

Bleikugelbad n
 E: lead ball bath, lead-shot bath
 F: bain m de grenaille de plomb

Bleilegierung f
 E: lead alloy
 F: alliage m de plomb

Bleimantel m
 E: lead sheath
 F: gaine f de plomb

Bleimantel aufpressen
 E: lead-sheath v, to apply the lead sheath
 F: mettre v sous gaine de plomb

Bleimantel mit Drahtarmierung
 E: wire-reinforced lead sheath
 F: gaine f de plomb avec armure en fils

Bleimantelkabel n
 E: lead-sheathed cable, lead-covered cable
 F: câble m sous gaine de plomb

Bleimantelkabel mit Außenschutz
 E: served lead-covered cable
 F: câble m sous gaine de plomb avec revêtement extérieur

Bleimantelleitung f
 E: lead-sheathed cable
 F: conducteur m sous gaine de plomb

Blei-(Mantel)-Presse f
 E: lead-sheathing press, lead press
 F: presse f de gainage à plomb, presse f à plomb

Bleimennige f
 E: red lead
 F: minium m de plomb

Bleimuffe f
 E: lead sleeve
 F: manchon m de plomb

Bleioxid n
 E: lead oxide
 F: oxyde m de plomb

Bleischmelzwanne f
 E: lead melting kettle
 F: creuset m à plomb

Bleistearat n
 E: lead stearate
 F: stéarate m de plomb

Blindelement n[Tel. K.]
 E: dummy n
 F: faux-élément m

Blindleistung f
 E: reactive power
 F: puissance f réactive

Blindleitwert m
 E: susceptance n
 F: susceptance f

Blindmuffe f
 E: dummy joint, dummy joint box
 F: fausse boîte de jonction

Blindstrom m
 E: reactive current, idle current
 F: courant m réactif

Blindversuch m
 E: blank trial, blank experiment, blank test
 F: essai m à blanc

Blindwiderstand m
 E: reactive impedance, reactance n
 F: réactance f

Blisterkupfer n
 E: blister copper
 F: cuivre m blister

Blitzableiter m
 E: lightning conductor, lightning arrester
 F: parafoudre m

Blitzbeeinflussung f
 E: effects pl of lightning
 F: effets m pl de foudre

Blitzschutz m
 E: lightning protection
 F: protection f contre la foudre

Blockaufnehmer m[Met.-Strangpr.]
 E: billet container
 F: conteneur m de billettes, pot m de presse

Blockblei n
 E: pig lead
 F: saumon m de plomb

blockieren v
 E: block v, interlock v
 F: bloquer v

Blockkondensator m
 E: blocking capacitor
 F: condensateur m de blocage

Blocklader m[Met.-Strangpr.]
 E: billet loader
 F: chargeur m de billettes

Blockstraße f(Walzw.)
 E: roughing train, blooming train
 F: train m dégrossiseur, train m ébaucheur

Blocktransportvorrichtung f[Met.-Strangpr.]
 E: billet handling device
 F: dispositif m de transport des billettes

bloß, mit ~em Auge sichtbar
 E: visible to the naked eye
 F: visible adj à l'œil nu

blutender Endverschluß
 E: bleeding sealing end
 F: extrémité f non étanche

Bodenaustrocknung f
 E: drying (out) of the soil
 F: séchage m du sol, dessèchement m du sol

Bodenleitfähigkeit f
 E: soil conductance
 F: conductivité f du sol

Bodensatz m
 E: bottom settling, deposit n, sediment n
 F: dépôt m, sédiment m

Bodensenkung f
 E: subsidence of ground

Bodensenkung

F: tassement *m* de terre

Bohrung *f*
E: bore *n*, hole *n*
F: trou *m*, alésage *m*

Bohrung *f*(für den Kabeldurchlauf)
E: cable passage, clear bore (for cable)
F: passage *m* pour cable

Bolzen *m*[Met.-Strangpr.]
E: billet *n*
F: billette *f*

Bolzenaufnehmer *m*[Met.-Strangpr.]
E: billet container
F: conteneur *m* de billettes, pot *m* de presse

Bolzenbeschickung *f*[Met.-Strangpr.]
E: billet loading
F: alimentation *f* en billettes

Bolzenende *n*[Met.-Strangpr.]
E: billet butt
F: bout *m* de la billette

Bolzenspitze *f*[Met.-Strangpr.]
E: billet nose
F: tête *f* de la billette

Bolzenvorwärmofen *m*[Met.-Strangpr.]
E: billet preheater
F: four *m* de réchauffage des billettes

bördeln *v*
E: fold back *v*, flange *v*
F: rabattre *v*, border *v*, bordeler *v*

Brachzeit einer Maschine
E: machine downtime
F: temps *m* d'attente d'une machine

Brand, einen ~ weiterleitend
E: flame-resistant *adj*, non fire propagating
F: non propagateur de la flamme *adj*, non propagateur de l'incendie *adj*, non transmettant la flamme

Brasilien-Kanarische Inseln-Kabel *n*
E: Brazil-Canary Islands telephone cable (BRACAN cable)
F: câble *m* téléphonique du Brésil aux Iles Canaries

Brechpunkt *m*
E: breaking point
F: point *m* de fragilité

Brechungsindex *m*
E: refraction index
F: indice *m* de réfraction

Breitbahnwicklung *f*(Papier)
E: broad-web paper wrapping
F: enroulement *m* papier à large bande

Breitbandkabel *n*
E: wide-band cable, broad-band cable
F: câble *m* à large bande

Breitbandkommunikationsnetz *n*
E: broad-band communications network, broad-band system
F: réseau *m* de communication à large bande, système *m* à large bande

Breitbandsystem *n*
E: broad-band communications network, broad-band system
F: réseau *m* de communication à large bande, système *m* à large bande

Breitband-Trägerfrequenz-Sprechkreis *m*
E: broad-band carrier telephony speech circuit
F: circuit *m* téléphonique à fréquence porteuse à large bande

Breitband-Trägerfrequenzsystem *n*
E: broad-band carrier system
F: système *m* à large bande à fréquence porteuse

Breitband-Übertragung *f*
E: wide-band transmission, broad-band transmission
F: transmission *f* à large bande

Breite *f*
E: width *n*, breadth *n*
F: largeur *f*

Bremskraft *f*
E: braking effort
F: effort *m* de freinage

Bremszug *m*
E: back pull, back tension
F: traction *f* de retenue

brennbar *adj*
E: flammable *adj*(US), inflammable *adj*(GB), , combustible *adj*
F: combustible *adj*, inflammable *adj*

Brennpunkt *m*(chem.)
E: fire point, ignition point, flash point
F: point *m* d'inflammation

Bruch *m*
E: fracture *n*, break *n*, rupture *n*
F: rupture *f*, brisure *f*, cassure *f*

Bruchdehnung *f*
E: elongation at break, ultimate elongation, elongation at rupture
F: allongement *m* à la rupture

Brüchigkeit *f*

Bruchdehnung f
E: brittleness n
F: fragilité f

Bruchlast f
E: breaking load, ultimate load
F: charge f de rupture

Bruchstelle f
E: fracture n, break n, rupture n
F: rupture f, brisure f, cassure f

Brückenkran m
E: bridge crane, overhead travelling crane
F: pont-grue m

Brückenmatrize f
E: spider type die
F: filière f type croisillon

Brückenschaltung f
E: bridge circuit
F: circuit m en pont

Brumm-Modulation f
E: hum-modulation n
F: ronflement m de modulation

Buchse f
E: bushing n, bush n, sleeve n
F: manchon m, douille f

Bügel-Doppelschlag-Schnellverseilmaschine f
E: double-twist flyer-type high-speed stranding machine
F: câbleuse f inversée (à flyer) double torsion à grande vitesse

Bügelverseilmaschine f
E: flyer-type stranding machine
F: câbleuse f inversée (à flyer)

Bühne f (Arbeitsplattform)
E: platform n
F: plate-forme f

Bull-Block m (Einscheiben-Vorsatzblock für große Profil-Abmessungen) [Drahth.]
E: bull-block n
F: bull-block m

Buna S (Butadien-Styrol-Kautschuk) m
E: Buna S (butadiene-styrene rubber), GRS (butadiene-styrene rubber) (US)
F: Buna m S (caoutchouc butadiène styrène)

Bündel n [Nachr. K.]
E: unit n, bunch n
F: faisceau m

Bündel unregelmäßig zusammenschlagen [Vers.]
E: to oscillate cable units

F: osciller v les faisceaux de câbles

Bündel-Haltewendel f
E: unit binder
F: frettage m sur faisceaux

Bündelkabel n
E: unit cable, unit-stranded cable, bunched cable, unit-type stranded cable
F: câble m en faisceaux, câble m à conducteurs en faisceaux

Bündel-Spinner m
E: unit binder
F: tête f à lier les faisceaux

Bündelungsvorrichtung für Draht
E: pack-former for wire
F: dispositif m à empaqueter les fils métalliques

Bündelverseilmaschine f
E: bunching machine, unit stranding machine
F: tordeuse f

bündelverseilter Leiter
E: rope lay strand
F: âme f câblée par faisceaux

bündelverseiltes Kabel
E: unit cable, unit-stranded cable, bunched cable, unit-type stranded cable
F: câble m en faisceaux, câble m à conducteurs en faisceaux

Bündelverseilung f
E: unit stranding, unit lay-up
F: assemblage m par faisceaux, câblage m par faisceaux

Bundwickler m
E: coiling basket
F: corbeille f d'enroulement, panier m d'enroulement

Butylkautschuk m
E: butyl rubber
F: caoutchouc m (de) butyle

C

CATV
(Ortsgemeinschaftsantennenfernsehen, Gemeinschaftsantennenfernsehen)
E: Community Antenna Television (CATV)
F: réception f collective d'antenne de

CATV

télévision (CATV)
Ceander-Kabel n
 E: Waveconal-cable n (GB)
 F: câble m à neutre concentrique en fils métalliques disposés en méandres
Ceander-Leiter m
 E: wave-form concentric neutral conductor
 F: neutre m concentrique en fils métalliques disposés en méandres
Chargenbetrieb m
 E: intermittent process, discontinuous operation, batch type process, batch operation
 F: procédé m discontinu, service m en discontinu
Chargenmischer m
 E: batch mixer
 F: mélangeur m à charges, mélangeur m discontinu
chargenweise adj
 E: in batch quantities
 F: en charges
chargenweise Fertigung
 E: batch type manufacturing process
 F: fabrication f discontinue
chargenweises Beizen [Drahth.]
 E: batch type pickling
 F: décapage m discontinu
chemisch vernetztes Polyäthylen (VPE)
 E: chemically cross-linked polyethylene (XLPE)
 F: polyéthylène m réticulé chimiquement (PRC)
chemische Vernetzung
 E: chemical cross-linking
 F: réticulation f chimique
chlorsulfoniertes PE (CSPE)
 E: chlorosulphonated PE (CSPE)
 F: polyéthylène m chlorosulfoné (CSPE)
Commonwealth-Pazifik-Kabel n
 E: Commonwealth-Pacific telephone cable (COMPAC cable)
 F: câble m téléphonique Commonwealth-Pacifique
compoundierte Jute
 E: compounded jute
 F: jute f compoundée
Copolymer n
 E: copolymer n

 F: copolymère m
CSPE (s. chlorsulfoniertes PE)
CV (s. kontinuierliche Vulkanisation)
CV-Anlage f
 E: CV-line n, continuous vulcanization line
 F: chaîne f CV, chaîne f de vulcanisation en continu

D

DAB (s. Dauerbetrieb mit aussetzender Belastung)
dachziegelartig aufgebrachte Bänder
 E: intercalated tapes, interlocked tapes
 F: rubans m pl imbriqués
dachziegelartig aufgebrachtes Rußpapier und metallisiertes Papier
 E: carbon-loaded paper interlocked with metallized paper
 F: papier m carbone et papier métallisé imbriqués
Dampf m [Vulk.]
 E: steam n, vapour n
 F: vapeur f
Dampfabsperrventil n [Vulk.]
 E: steam stop valve
 F: vanne f à vapeur
Dampfatmosphäre f
 E: steam atmosphere
 F: atmosphère f de vapeur
Dampfdruck m [Vulk.]
 E: steam pressure
 F: pression f de vapeur
Dampfhochdruckrohr zur kontinuierlichen Vulkanisation
 E: continuous vulcanization high-pressure steam pipe
 F: tube m de vulcanisation continue à vapeur à haute pression
Dämpfung f
 E: damping n, attenuation n
 F: atténuation f, affaiblissement m
Dämpfungsausgleich m
 E: attenuation equalization, attenuation compensation
 F: équilibrage m d'affaiblissement
Dämpfungsentzerrung f
 E: attenuation equalization,

attenuation compensation
F: équilibrage *m* d'affaiblissement
Dämpfungsfaktor *m*
E: attenuation factor, damping coefficient
F: coefficient *m* d'affaiblissement
Dämpfungskonstante *f*
E: attenuation constant
F: constante *f* d'affaiblissement
Dämpfungsmaß *n*
E: attenuation unit, attenuation equivalent, total transmission equivalent, total attenuation
F: unité *f* d'affaiblissement, équivalent *m* d'affaiblissement
Dämpfungsverzerrung *f*
E: attenuation distortion, frequency distortion
F: distorsion *f* d'affaiblissement
Dampfvulkanisation *f*
E: steam vulcanization, steam cure, vapour cure
F: vulcanisation *f* à vapeur
Darstellung, schematische ~
E: schematic representation, diagrammatic representation
F: représentation *f* schématique, schéma *m* de principe
Daten *pl*
E: data *pl and sg*, details *pl*, particulars *pl*
F: données *f pl*, renseignements *m pl*
Datenerfassung *f*
E: data collection, data acquisition
F: acquisition *f* des données
Datenerfassungsanlage *f*
E: data logging system
F: poste *m* d'acquisition des données
Datenfernübertragungsleitung *f*
E: long distance data transmission line
F: ligne *f* de transmission d'informations à longue distance
Daten-Fernverarbeitung, direkte ~
E: on-line remote data processing, direct remote data processing
F: télétraitement *m* d'informations direct, télétraitement *m* d'informations on-line
Datenübertragung *f*
E: data transmission
F: transmission *f* d'informations, transmission *f* de données

Datenübertragung, Kabel für ~
E: data transmission cable
F: câble *m* pour transmissions numériques
Datex-Netz *n*
E: datex network
F: réseau *m* datex
Daube *f* (Kabeltrommeln)
E: plank *n*, batten *n*
F: douve *f*
Dauer der Trocknung und Tränkung
E: duration of the drying and impregnating process
F: durée *f* du séchage et de l'imprégnation
Dauerabriebprüfung *f*
E: repeated abrasion test
F: essai *m* d'abrasion répétée
Daueralterungsprüfung *f*
E: long-time ag(e)ing test
F: essai *m* de vieillissement de longue durée
Dauerbeanspruchung *f*
E: continuous stress
F: sollicitation *f* permanente, contrainte *f* continue
Dauerbelastung *f*
E: continuous load, sustained load
F: charge *f* continue, charge *f* permanente
Dauerbetrieb *m* (ununterbrochener Betrieb von mindestens 2,5 Std.) [el.]
E: long-time operation
F: service *m* de longue durée
Dauerbetrieb mit aussetzender Belastung (DAB) [el.]
E: continuous duty with intermittent loading
F: service *m* ininterrompu à charge intermittente
Dauerbetrieb mit gleichbleibender Belastung [el.]
E: continuous duty, continuous operation
F: régime *m* permanent, service *m* continu
Dauerbetrieb mit kurzzeitiger Belastung [el.]
E: continuous duty with short-time loading
F: régime *m* permanent à charge temporaire
Dauerbetrieb mit periodisch

Dauerbetrieb

veränderlicher Belastung [el.]
  E: periodic load duty
  F: service m permanent à charge variant périodiquement, régime m permanent à charge variant périodiquement

Dauerbetrieb mit veränderlicher Belastung [el.]
  E: continuous duty with variable load
  F: service m ininterrompu à charge variable

Dauerbiegefestigkeit f
  E: resistance to bending fatigue, bending endurance, bending fatigue strength, flexural fatigue strength
  F: résistance f de fatigue à la flexion, endurance f à la flexion

Dauerfestigkeit f [el.]
  E: long-time strength
  F: tenue f en longue durée, longévité f

Dauerfestigkeit f [Met.]
  E: fatigue strength, fatigue resistance
  F: résistance f à la fatigue

Dauerfestigkeitsgrenze f
  E: fatigue limit, endurance limit
  F: résistance f limite de fatigue, limite f d'endurance

Dauerkurzschlußstrom m
  E: sustained short-circuit current
  F: courant m de court-circuit permanent

Dauerlast f
  E: continuous load, sustained load
  F: charge f continue, charge f permanente

Dauer-Spannungsfestigkeit eines Kabels
  E: voltage life of a cable, long-time dielectric strength of a cable
  F: durée f de vie d'un câble, tenue f en longue durée d'un câble

Dauerspannungsprüfung f
  E: voltage life test
  F: essai m de durée de vie

Dauerstandfestigkeit f [Met.]
  E: creep resistance, fatigue strength, creep strength, long-time rupture strength
  F: résistance f au fluage, résistance f à la rupture sous charge permanente

Dauerstrombelastungsprüfung f
  E: continuous current carrying test
  F: essai m de capacité de charge en courant permanent

Dauerversuch m
  E: long-time test, continuous test
  F: essai m de (longue) durée, essai m continu

Dauerversuch m [mech.]
  E: endurance test, fatigue test
  F: essai m d'endurance, essai m de fatigue

Dauerwechselfestigkeit f
  E: endurance strength
  F: résistance f aux efforts répétés, résistance f aux efforts alternatifs

Dauerzustand m
  E: steady state condition
  F: état m stationnaire, régime m établi, régime m permanent

Deflektor m [K. Garn.]
  E: deflector n
  F: déflecteur m

Deflektor, aufgepreßter ~
  E: mo(u)lded deflector
  F: déflecteur m surmoulé

Deflektor, einteiliger ~
  E: one-piece deflector
  F: déflecteur m en une seule pièce

Deflektorhalter m
  E: deflector support
  F: support m de déflecteur

Deformation in der Wärme
  E: heat deformation, heat distortion
  F: déformation f à chaud

Dehnbarkeit f
  E: elasticity n, extensibility n, ductility n
  F: élasticité f, extensibilité f, ductilité f

dehnen v
  E: elongate v, extend v, expand vt
  F: allonger v, étendre v, étirer v

Dehn(ungs)grenze f
  E: yield point, yield strength, elastic limit
  F: limite f d'élasticité, limite f d'allongement

Dehnung f
  E: elongation n, extension n, stretch n
  F: allongement m, extension f, étirage m

Dehnung, Prüfung auf bleibende ~
  E: hot-set-test n
  F: essai m d'allongement permanent

dehnungsarm adj

E: with limited extensibility
F: à extensibilité réduite
Dehnungsbeanspruchung f
E: tensile stress
F: contrainte f de traction, effort m de traction
Dehnungsmuffe f [Kab.]
E: expansion box
F: manchon m de dilatation
Dehnungsrest m
E: residual elongation
F: allongement m résiduel
Dehnungs-Spannungs-Kurve f
E: stress-strain curve
F: courbe f de tension-allongement
demineralisieren v
E: desalt v, desalinate v, demineralize v, deionize v
F: déminéraliser v, dessaler v
Depolymerisation f
E: depolymerisation n
F: dépolymérisation f
Destillationsrückstand m
E: distillation residue
F: résidu m de distillation
Dezentrierung f
E: decentering n
F: décentrage m
Diagramm n
E: diagram n, graph n, graphic representation, chart n
F: diagramme m, représentation f graphique, graphique m
Diamantziehsteine m pl [Drahth.]
E: diamond dies
F: filières f pl en diamant
dicht besiedeltes Gebiet [K. Verl.]
E: heavily loaded locality, congested area
F: grande agglomération urbaine, zone f de forte agglomération
Dichte f
E: density n
F: densité f
Dichtigkeit f
E: sealing n, tightness n
F: étanchéité f
Dichtigkeitsprüfung f
E: tightness control, leakage test
F: contrôle m d'étanchéité
Dichtung f
E: seal n, packing n
F: joint m, joint m d'étanchéité

Dichtungsring m
E: sealing ring, joint ring
F: anneau m d'étanchéité, bague f d'étanchéité, joint m annulaire
Dichtungsscheibe f
E: packing ring, sealing washer, gasket n, sealing disc
F: rondelle f d'étanchéité
Dichtungswickel m [Kab.]
E: sealing wrap
F: rubanage m d'étanchéité
Dicke f
E: thickness n
F: épaisseur f
Dickenausgleich m
E: thickness compensation
F: compensation f de l'épaisseur
Dickenmessung f
E: thickness measurement
F: mesure f d'épaisseur
Dickflüssigkeit f
E: ropiness n, high viscosity
F: haute viscosité f
Dielektrikum n
E: insulation n, dielectric n
F: isolation f, isolant m, enveloppe f isolante, diélectrique m, isolement m
dielektrische Festigkeit
E: dielectric strength, breakdown strength, puncture resistance, electric strength
F: rigidité f diélectrique
dielektrische Verluste
E: dielectric losses
F: pertes f pl diélectriques
Dielektrizitätskonstante (DK) f
E: dielectric constant, permittivity n
F: constante f diélectrique, permittivité f
Dielektrizitätskonstante, absolute ~
E: absolute permittivity
F: permittivité f absolue
Dielektrizitätskonstante, relative ~
E: relative permittivity
F: permittivité f relative
Dieselhorst-Martin-Verseilung f
E: multiple-twin quad formation
F: câblage m à quartes à paires
Dieselhorst-Martin-Vierer m
E: multiple-twin quad, DM-quad n
F: quarte f Dieselhorst-Martin, quarte f DM

Dieselhorst-Martin-Vierer-verseiltes Kabel
  E: cable with multiple-twin quad formation, multiple-twin quad cable
  F: câble *m* à quartes Dieselhorst-Martin, câble *m* à quartes DM

direkte Daten-Fernverarbeitung
  E: on-line remote data processing, direct remote data processing
  F: télétraitement *m* d'informations direct, télétraitement *m* d'informations on-line

direkte Kühlung von Kabeln
  E: integral cooling of cables, direct cooling of cables
  F: refroidissement *m* intégral des câbles, refroidissement *m* direct des câbles

diskontinuierlich abgestopftes Kabel [Tel. K.]
  E: cable with water blocks
  F: câble *m* rempli de façon discontinue

diskontinuierliches Verfahren
  E: intermittent process, discontinuous operation, batch type process, batch operation
  F: procédé *m* discontinu, service *m* en discontinu

DK (s. Dielektrizitätskonstante)

DM-Verseilung *f*
  E: multiple-twin quad formation
  F: câblage *m* à quartes à paires

DM-Vierer *m*
  E: multiple-twin quad, DM-quad *n*
  F: quarte *f* Dieselhorst-Martin, quarte *f* DM

DM-Viererkabel *n*
  E: cable with multiple-twin quad formation, multiple-twin quad cable
  F: câble *m* à quartes Dieselhorst-Martin, câble *m* à quartes DM

DM-Vierer-verseiltes Kabel
  E: cable with multiple-twin quad formation, multiple-twin quad cable
  F: câble *m* à quartes Dieselhorst-Martin, câble *m* à quartes DM

Doppelader *f* [Nachr. K.]
  E: pair *n*, twin-wire *n*, dual wire
  F: paire *f*, fil *m* double, conducteur *m* jumelé

doppeladrig *adj*
  E: bifilar *adj*, twin *adj*
  F: bifilaire *adj*

doppeladriges Kabel
  E: double-core cable (GB), two-conductor cable (US), twin cable
  F: câble *m* biphasé, câble *m* à deux conducteurs

Doppelaufwickelei, automatische ~
  E: automatic double spooler
  F: enrouleur *m* automatique à double bobine

Doppelbindung *f* [Chem.]
  E: double bond
  F: liaison *f* double

Doppelerdschluß *m*
  E: double earth fault (GB), double ground fault (US)
  F: défaut *m* à la terre double

Doppelglockenisolator *m*
  E: double shed insulator
  F: isolateur *m* à double cloche

Doppelkopf *m* [Extr.]
  E: twin (extruder) head, double (extruder) head, dual (extruder) head
  F: tête *f* double de boudineuse, tête *f* double extrusion

Doppelkopf-Extrusion *f*
  E: twin-head extrusion
  F: extrusion *f* tête double

doppellagig *adj*
  E: double-layer *adj*, twin-layer *adj*, duplex *adj*
  F: en double couche, en deux couches

doppellagige Armierung
  E: double armo(u)ring
  F: armure *f* double

Doppellangsieb-Papiermaschine *f*
  E: twin-wire paper-making machine
  F: machine *f* à papier à toile double sans fin

Doppelschlag *m*
  E: double twist
  F: double torsion *f*

Doppelschlag-Bündel-Schnellverseilmaschine *f*
  E: double-twist high-speed bunching machine
  F: tordeuse *f* double-torsion à grande vitesse

Doppelschlag-Verseilmaschine *f*

E: double-twist strander
F: câbleuse *f* double torsion
doppelseitiger Antrieb
E: bilateral drive
F: commande *f* bilatérale
Doppelspeicher *m* [Vers.]
E: double accumulator
F: accumulateur *m* double
Doppelspinnkopf *m*
E: duplicate lapping head, dual lapping head
F: tête *f* double de rubanage
Doppelsprechen *n*
E: two-way telephone conversation, phantom telephony
F: téléphonie *f* fantôme, téléphonie *f* duplex
Doppelsprechschaltung *f*
E: phantom phone connection
F: montage *m* en fantôme
Doppelspulapparat *m*
E: double-reel spooler, dual-reel take-up
F: enrouleur *m* à double bobine, bobinoir *m* double
Doppelspuler *m*
E: double-reel spooler, dual-reel take-up
F: enrouleur *m* à double bobine, bobinoir *m* double
Doppelstempel-Kabelmantelpresse *f*
E: twin-ram cable sheathing press, double-acting cable sheathing press, double-ram cable sheathing press
F: presse *f* de gainage à fouloir double
Doppelstempel-Presse *f*
E: double-ram press, twin-ram press, double-acting press
F: presse *f* à fouloir double
Doppelsternvierer *m*
E: pair stranded in quad pair formation
F: paire *f* câblée en étoile
doppelt-ummanteltes Kabel
E: double-sheathed cable
F: câble *m* sous gaine double
doppeltwirkender Plunger
E: double-acting plunger
F: piston *m* à double effet, piston *m* à action double
Dorn *m*
E: mandrel *n*
F: mandrin *m*, broche *f*, poinçon *m*
Dornstapler *m*
E: ram truck
F: empileuse *f* à mandrins
Dornwickelprüfung *f*
E: mandrel test, wrapping test
F: essai *m* d'enroulement
Dosierung *f*
E: dosage *n*, proportioning *n*, metering *n*
F: dosage *m*
Draht *m*
E: wire *n*
F: fil *m* métallique
Draht, dicker ~
E: large-diameter wire, large-size wire
F: gros fil *m*, fil *m* de gros diamètre
Draht, dünner ~
E: small-diameter wire
F: fil *m* de petit diamètre, fil *m* mince
Draht, harter ~
E: hard-drawn wire
F: fil *m* dur, fil *m* écroui
drahtarmiertes Kabel
E: wire-armo(u)red cable
F: câble *m* armé en fils métalliques
Drahtarmierung *f*
E: wire armo(u)ring, wire armo(u)r
F: armure *f* en fils métalliques
Drahtbarren *m*
E: wire bar, ingot *n*
F: lingot *m*
drahtbewehrtes Kabel
E: wire-armo(u)red cable
F: câble *m* armé en fils métalliques
Drahtbewehrung *f*
E: wire armo(u)ring, wire armo(u)r
F: armure *f* en fils métalliques
Drahtbewicklung *f*
E: wire wrapping
F: enroulement *m* de fil
Drahtbruch *m*
E: wire break, wire breakage
F: casse-fil *m*, rupture *f* du fil
Drahtbruchschalter *m*
E: wire break switch
F: casse-fil *m* électrique
Drahtbund *m*
E: coil of wire, wire coil
F: couronne *f* de fil métallique
Drahtbund *m* [K. Garn.]
E: field-controlling wire binding

Drahtbund

 F: frettage *m* en fil métallique pour l'orientation du champ électrique, frette *f* en fil métallique

Drahtbürste, Behandlung mit der ~
 E: scratch brushing
 F: traitement *m* à la brosse métallique

Drahtdicke *f*
 E: wire gauge, wire size
 F: grosseur *f* du fil métallique, jauge *f* des fils

Drahtdurchmesser *m*
 E: wire diameter
 F: diamètre *m* du fil métallique

Drähte ziehen auf dicke, mittlere, kleine Durchmesser
 E: to draw wires down to large, medium, small diameters
 F: tréfiler *v* des fils de gros, moyens, petits diamètres

Drahtführung *f*
 E: wire guide
 F: guide-fil *m*

Drahtführung, automatische ~ (Wickler)
 E: automatic wire guide
 F: trancanage *m* automatique du fil métallique

Drahtgeflecht *n*
 E: wire braid
 F: tresse *f* de fil métallique

Drahtklasse *f*
 E: wire gauge, wire size
 F: grosseur *f* du fil métallique, jauge *f* des fils

Drahtklemme *f*
 E: wire grip, wire clamp
 F: serre-fil *m*

Drahtlack *m*
 E: wire enamel
 F: vernis *m* pour fils

Drahtlage *f*
 E: layer of wires
 F: couche *f* de fils

Drahtlehre *f*
 E: wire gauge, wire size
 F: grosseur *f* du fil métallique, jauge *f* des fils

Drahtrichtvorrichtung *f*
 E: wire straightening device
 F: redresseur *m* de fil

Drahtring *m*
 E: coil of wire, wire coil
 F: couronne *f* de fil métallique

Drahtriß *m*
 E: wire break, wire breakage
 F: casse-fil *m*, rupture *f* du fil

Drahtrißwächter *m*
 E: wire break monitor
 F: détecteur *m* de casses-fil, détecteur *m* de ruptures du fil métallique

Drahtumflechtmaschine *f*
 E: wire braiding machine
 F: machine *f* à tresser en fils métalliques

Drahtumspinnmaschine *f*
 E: wire covering machine
 F: machine *f* à recouvrir le fil métallique

Drahtumspinnung *f*
 E: wire covering
 F: recouvrement *m* du fil métallique

Drahtumwickelei *f*
 E: wire rewinding stand
 F: bobineuse *f* de fil métallique (pour rebobinage)

Drahtvormaterial *n* [Drahth.]
 E: wire rod, redraw rod
 F: fil *m* machine, fil *m* ébauche, fil *m* pour retréfilage

Drahtvorwärmer *m*
 E: wire preheater
 F: réchauffeur *m* de fil métallique

Drahtwalzwerk *n*
 E: wire rolling mill, rod rolling mill
 F: laminoir *m* à fils métalliques

Drahtwickelmaschine *f*
 E: wire winding machine, wire spooler
 F: bobineuse de fil métallique *f*

Drahtwickler *m* (stationär)
 E: dead block
 F: enrouleur *m* de fil métallique

Drahtziehen *n*
 E: wire drawing
 F: tréfilage *m*

Drahtzieherei *f*
 E: wire drawing department
 F: tréfilerie *f*

Drahtziehgeschwindigkeit *f*
 E: wire drawing speed
 F: vitesse *f* de tréfilage

Drahtziehmaschine *f*
 E: wire drawing machine
 F: tréfileuse *f*, machine *f* à tréfiler

Drainage, elektrische ~

Drall m [Vers.]
  E: lay n, twist n
  F: pas m, torsion f

Drallänge f [Vers.]
  E: length of lay, pitch n, length of twist
  F: longueur f du pas

Drall-Ausgleichsvorrichtung f
  E: twist compensator
  F: compensateur m de torsion

Drallrichtung f [Vers.]
  E: direction of lay, direction of twist
  F: sens m du pas de câblage, sens m de câblage, sens m de torsion, sens m du pas de torsion, direction f du pas, direction f de la torsion

Drallrichtung, periodisch wechselnde ~
  E: periodically changing lay
  F: pas m de câblage changeant périodiquement

Drallwechsel m
  E: reversal of lay, change of lay
  F: inversion f de la torsion, changement m de la torsion, changement m du pas de câblage

Drallwechselgetriebe n
  E: lay changing gear, twist changing gear
  F: variateur m de torsion

Drallwechselstelle f
  E: lay reversal point, twist changing point
  F: point m d'inversion de la torsion, point m de changement de la torsion

Drallzuschlag m [Vers.]
  E: stranding allowance, laying-up allowance
  F: supplément m de torsion

drehbar gelagert
  E: hinged adj, swivelling adj, pivoted adj
  F: pivotant adj, articulé adj

drehbarer Werkzeugkopf
  E: rotary die head
  F: tête f d'outils rotative

Drehgeschwindigkeit f
  E: speed of rotation
  F: vitesse f de rotation

Drehrichtung f [Masch.]
  E: direction of rotation
  F: sens m de rotation

Drehsicherungsscheibe f
  E: lock washer
  F: bague f de frein

Drehstrom m
  E: three-phase current
  F: courant m triphasé

Drehstromkabel n
  E: three-phase (current) cable
  F: câble m à courant triphasé

Drehstromnetz mit Nulleiter
  E: three-phase system with neutral
  F: secteur m triphasé avec conducteur neutre

Drehtrommelofen m
  E: rotary furnace
  F: four m tubulaire tournant

Drehzahl f (Umdrehungen pro Minute = U/Min)
  E: number of revolutions per minute (r.p.m.), rotational speed, speed n
  F: nombre m de tours par minute (t.p.m.), vitesse f de rotation, vitesse f

Drehzahländerung f
  E: speed variation
  F: changement m de vitesse

Drehzahlbereich m
  E: speed range
  F: gamme f de vitesses

dreiadriges Kabel
  E: three-core cable, three-conductor cable, triple-core cable
  F: câble m triphasé, câble m à trois conducteurs

Dreibleimantelkabel n
  E: three-core single lead sheath cable, SL-cable n
  F: câble m triplomb, câble m triplomb trigaine

Dreiecksanordnung f [K.Verl.]
  E: trefoil arrangement, triangular arrangement
  F: disposition f en triangle, disposition f en trèfle

Dreieckschaltung, in ~
  E: delta-connected adj
  F: monté adj en triangle, monté adj en delta

Dreieck-verseiltes Kabel
  E: triangular-shape cable
  F: câble m assemblé en forme triangulaire

Dreieinhalbleiterkabel n
  E: three-and-a-half core cable
  F: câble m à trois conducteurs et demi
Dreier m [Tel. K.]
  E: triple n
  F: câble m téléphonique à trois conducteurs
Dreifach-Extrusion f
  E: triple extrusion
  F: extrusion f triple
Dreifachkabel n
  E: three-core cable, three-conductor cable, triple-core cable
  F: câble m triphasé, câble m à trois conducteurs
Dreifach-Kopf m [Extr.]
  E: triple extruder head
  F: tête f triple de boudineuse, tête f triple extrusion
Dreifach-Spritzkopf m [Extr.]
  E: triple extruder head
  F: tête f triple de boudineuse, tête f triple extrusion
Dreileiter-Endverschluß m
  E: three-core termination
  F: boîte f d'extrémité tripolaire
Dreileiterkabel n
  E: three-core cable, three-conductor cable, triple-core cable
  F: câble m triphasé, câble m à trois conducteurs
Dreileiterölkabel n
  E: three-core oil-filled cable
  F: câble m tripolaire à huile fluide
Dreimantelkabel n
  E: three-core single lead sheath cable, SL-cable n
  F: câble m triplomb, câble m triplomb trigaine
Dreiphasengleichrichter m
  E: three-phase rectifier
  F: redresseur m triphasé
dreipolig adj
  E: three-pole adj, three-phase adj
  F: tripolaire adj
dreipoliger Kurzschluß m
  E: three-phase fault
  F: court-circuit m tripolaire
Dreiwalzenkalander m
  E: three-roll calender, three-bowl calender
  F: calandre f à trois cylindres, calandre f à trois rouleaux

Drillingsleitung f
  E: three-core cord
  F: conducteur m trifil
Dritte-Kreise-Kopplung f
  E: third-circuits coupling
  F: couplage m de tiers circuits
Druck, ohne ~
  E: depressurized adj
  F: en dépression
Druck, unter ~ setzen
  E: pressurize v
  F: mettre v sous pression
Druckabfall m
  E: pressure drop, pressure loss, head loss
  F: chute f de pression, dépression f, perte f de pression
Druckanlage f
  E: pressurizing plant
  F: installation f de mise sous pression
Druck-Ausgleichsgefäß n (Ölkabel)
  E: oil expansion tank, variable oil pressure tank, oil pressure tank, oil reservoir
  F: réservoir m à pression d'huile variable
Druckbeanspruchung f
  E: compressive stress
  F: contrainte f de compression, effort m de compression
Druckbeständigkeit f
  E: pressure resistance, compressive strength, crushing strength
  F: résistance f à l'écrasement, résistance f à la pression
druckdicht adj
  E: pressure-tight adj
  F: étanche adj à la pression
Druckdichtigkeit f
  E: pressure tightness
  F: étanchéité f à la pression
druckfester Mantel
  E: pressure-retaining sheath
  F: gaine f d'étanchéité à la pression
Druckfestigkeit f
  E: pressure resistance, compressive strength, crushing strength
  F: résistance f à l'écrasement, résistance f à la pression
Druckgas n
  E: compressed gas, pressure gas
  F: gaz m comprimé
druckgasdichte Muffe

E: gas pressure-tight joint
F: manchon *m* de jonction étanche au gaz comprimé

Druckgasschutz und -überwachung von Telefonkabeln
E: telephone cable pressurization, gas pressure supervision of telephone cables, gas pressure control of telephone cables
F: contrôle *m* des câbles téléphoniques à gaz comprimé

druckgasüberwacht *adj*
E: gas pressure controlled
F: contrôlé *adj* à gaz comprimé

Druckgas-Überwachungssystem *n*
E: gas pressure alarm system
F: système *m* de contrôle à gaz comprimé

Druckgeber *m* [Nachr.]
E: pressure transducer
F: transmetteur *m* de pression

Druckhaltestation *f*
E: pressure maintaining unit
F: poste *m* de tenue de la pression

Druckkabel *n*
E: pressure cable
F: câble *m* sous pression

Druckknopfsteuerung *f*
E: push-button control
F: commande *f* par bouton-poussoir

Druckluft *f*
E: compressed air
F: air *m* comprimé

Druckluftbetätigung *f*
E: pneumatic operation, compressed-air control
F: commande *f* à air comprimé, commande *f* pneumatique

Druckluftkühlung *f*
E: cooling by compressed air
F: refroidissement *m* à air comprimé

Druckmeßgerät *n*
E: pressure gauge, pressure control device, manometer *n*
F: dispositif *m* de contrôle de la pression, manomètre *m*

Druckminderungsventil *n*
E: pressure reducing valve
F: manodétendeur *m*

Druckpumpe *f*
E: pressure pump, forcing pump
F: pompe *f* foulante, pompe *f* refoulante, refouleur *m*

Druckregler *m*
E: pressure regulator, pressure control(ler)
F: régulateur *m* de pression

Druckschutzspinner *m* [Kab.]
E: reinforcement tape spinner
F: enrouleur *m* du frettage

Druckschutzwendel *f* [Kab.]
E: circumferential reinforcement tape, holding tape, reinforcement helix
F: frettage *m*

Druckschwankungen *f pl*
E: pressure variations
F: alternance *f* des pressions et des dépressions

Druckspritzverfahren *n* [Extr.]
E: controlled pressure extrusion
F: extrusion *f* en bourrage, extrusion *f* «pression bourrage»

Drucküberträger *m* [Nachr.]
E: pressure transducer
F: transmetteur *m* de pression

Druckverlust *m*
E: pressure drop, pressure loss, head loss
F: chute *f* de pression, dépression *f*, perte *f* de pression

Druckversuch *m*
E: pressure test, compression test
F: essai *m* de pression, essai *m* de compression

Druckversuch *m* (Rohre, Schaumkunststoffe)
E: crush(ing) test
F: essai *m* d'écrasement

Druckwächter *m*
E: pressure contactor, pressure monitor, pressure control device
F: dispositif *m* de contrôle de pression, avertisseur *m* de pression

Druckwasser *n*
E: pressurized water
F: eau *f* sous pression, eau *f* pressurisée

dunkelgefärbt *adj*
E: dark-coloured *adj*
F: de couleur foncée

dünndrähtiges Kabel, bespultes ~
E: loaded thin-wire cable
F: câble *m* pupinisé avec âme en fils fins

Dünnflüssigkeit *f*

Dünnflüssigkeit
  E: low viscosity
  F: faible viscosité f
Dünnschicht-Lackdraht m
  E: thin-film insulated magnet wire
  F: fil m verni en couche mince
dünnwandiger Überzug
  E: thin-wall coating
  F: revêtement m mince
Duplex-Papier n (Doppellagenpapier)
  E: duplex paper, double-ply paper
  F: papier m duplex, papier m en deux couches
durchbrennen v[el.]
  E: blow v, fuse v
  F: fuser v, fondre v
Durchdringung f[Nachr.]
  E: telephone density, line density
  F: densité f téléphonique, densité f de lignes principales
Durchdrückfestigkeit f
  E: cut-through resistance
  F: résistance f à l'enfoncement
Durchdrückprüfung f
  E: cut-through test
  F: essai m d'enfoncement
Durchdrücktemperatur f
  E: cut-through temperature
  F: température f d'enfoncement
Durchflußmenge f
  E: flow rate, flow volume
  F: débit m
Durchflußmischer m (Mischungsherstellung)
  E: flow mixer, pipeline mixer
  F: mélangeur m en continu à courant
durchführbar adj
  E: practicable adj, realizable adj
  F: réalisable adj, faisable adj, praticable adj
durchführen, eine Prüfung ~
  E: to perform a test, to carry out a test, to conduct a test
  F: faire v un essai, effectuer v un essai
Durchführung f[K. Garn.]
  E: bushing n
  F: traversée f, douille f
Durchführungs-Isolator m
  E: bushing insulator
  F: isolateur m de traversée
Durchführungsrohr n
  E: wall tube, wall duct
  F: douille f de traversée
Durchgang m[Walzw.]
  E: pass n
  F: passe f
Durchgang, elektrischer ~
  E: electrical continuity
  F: continuité f électrique
Durchgang, in einem ~
  E: in a single operation
  F: en une seule passe, en une même opération
Durchgangsleitung f[Tel.]
  E: through circuit, through line
  F: ligne f de transit
Durchgangsmuffe f
  E: straight joint, straight-through joint
  F: jonction f droite
Durchgangsprüfgerät n[el.]
  E: continuity tester
  F: dispositif m d'essai de la continuité électrique
Durchgangsprüfung f[el.]
  E: continuity check, continuity test
  F: contrôle m de continuité, essai m de continuité
Durchgangsverkehr m[Nachr.]
  E: through-traffic n
  F: trafic m de transit
Durchgangswiderstand m (ohne Oberflächenwiderstand)
  E: volume resistance (exclusive of surface resistance)
  F: résistance f intérieure
durchgefärbte Mischung
  E: colo(u)red compound
  F: mélange m coloré dans la masse
durchgehende Linie
  E: full line
  F: trait m plein
Durchhang m
  E: sag n
  F: flèche f, mou m
Durchhang-Abtastgerät n[Vulk.]
  E: sag sensing unit, catenary sensing unit (on catenary vulcanization line)
  F: détecteur m de flèche
Durchhängen n
  E: sagging n, slackening n
  F: fléchissement m
durchhängender Draht
  E: slack wire
  F: fil m lâche, fil m faisant flèche
Durchhanghöhe f

Durchhangregelung f [Vulk.]
- E: catenary control, sag control
- F: contrôle m de la flèche

E: sag clearance
F: écart m de flèche, hauteur f de flèche

Durchhärtung f
- E: through-hardening n
- F: durcissement m à cœur

Durchklingeln n [Tel. K.]
- E: ringing test, ring-out procedure, buzz-out operation
- F: contrôle m de continuité, sonnage m

durchlässig adj
- E: permeable adj, pervious adj
- F: perméable adj

Durchlässigkeit für Gas
- E: permeability to gas
- F: perméabilité f au gaz

Durchlaufgeschwindigkeit f [Prod.]
- E: feed rate, line speed, running speed
- F: vitesse f de passage

Durchlaufglühanlage f
- E: continuous annealing plant, continuous annealer
- F: installation f de recuit en continu, recuiseur m en continu

Durchlaufglühanlage f (gekoppelt mit Feindraht-Ziehmaschine)
- E: tandem annealer, continuous wire drawing and annealing machine
- F: installation f de recuit en tandem, tréfileuse f et recuiseur m en continu

Durchlaufprüfgerät n [Kab.]
- E: on-line spark tester, continuous discharge detection apparatus, sparker n, spark tester
- F: appareil m de contrôle d'ionisation par défilement continu, détecteur m de défauts à sec

Durchlauf-Prüfung f
- E: scanning test
- F: essai m d'ionisation par défilement, essai m de «scanning»

Durchlaufverfahren, im ~
- E: in continuous operation
- F: en continu

Durchlaufvulkanisation f
- E: continuous vulcanization (CV)
- F: vulcanisation f continue (CV)

Durchlaufzeit f [Prod.]
- E: production flow time
- F: temps m de passage

Durchmesser, großer, mittlerer, kleiner ~
- E: large, medium, small diameter
- F: gros, moyen, petit diamètre

Durchmessermeßgerät n
- E: diameter gauge, diameter measuring device
- F: appareil m de mesure du diamètre, mesureur m du diamètre

Durchmesser-Überwachungsgerät n
- E: diameter control device
- F: dispositif m de contrôle du diamètre

Durchmesserverringerung f
- E: diameter reduction, thinning n
- F: réduction f du diamètre, rétreint m

Durchsatz m
- E: throughput n
- F: débit m

durchschalten v [Tel.]
- E: to connect through, put through v, switch through v
- F: relier v, mettre v en communication

Durchschlag m [el.]
- E: breakdown n, dielectric breakdown, puncture n
- F: claquage m, amorçage m, décharge f disruptive

durchschlagen v [el.]
- E: break down v
- F: claquer v

Durchschlagfeldstärke f
- E: breakdown stress, breakdown gradient, breakdown field strength
- F: intensité f de claquage

Durchschlagfestigkeit f
- E: dielectric strength, breakdown strength, puncture resistance, electric strength
- F: rigidité f diélectrique

Durchschlagspannung f
- E: breakdown voltage, disruptive voltage
- F: tension f de claquage, tension f de perforation, tension f disruptive

Durchschnittsprobe f
- E: representative sample, average sample
- F: échantillon m de la qualité moyenne

durchsickern v

durchsickern
   E: ooze *v*, filter through *v*, leak *v*
   F: suinter *v*, filtrer *v*(se)

durchtränkt *adj*
   E: impregnated *adj*
   F: imprégné *adj*

durchverbundenes Kabelsystem
   E: system with the cable sheaths connected across the joints
   F: réseau *m* de câbles dont les gaines sont reliées entre elles à travers les jonctions

Durometer *n*
   E: hardness tester, durometer *n*
   F: appareil *m* de contrôle de la dureté, duromètre *m*

Düse *f*
   E: nozzle *n*, jet *n*, orifice *n*
   F: buse *f*, injecteur *m*, tuyère *f*

Dusche *f*(zum Kühlen)
   E: spray *n*
   F: pulvérisateur *m*

Düse *f*[Extr.]
   E: die *n*
   F: filière *f*

Dynamodraht *m*
   E: magnet wire
   F: fil *m* de bobinage, fil *m* de dynamo

E

Ebene, in einer ~ liegende Kabel
   E: cables in flat formation, cables laid in parallel, cables laid side by side
   F: câbles *m pl* disposés en nappe

EC-Aluminium (s. Leitaluminium)

Echodämpfung *f*
   E: echo attenuation, active return loss
   F: affaiblissement *m* d'écho

Echosperre *f*
   E: echo suppressor
   F: suppresseur *m* d'écho

Echostörungen *f pl*
   E: disturbances due to echo, echo troubles
   F: dérangement *m* par les effets d'écho

Eckrollen *f pl* [K. Verl.]
   E: corner rollers
   F: rouleaux *m pl* d'angle

EC-Kupfer (s. Leitkupfer)

effektiv übertragenes Frequenzband
   E: effectively transmitted frequency band
   F: bande *f* de fréquences transmise de façon effective

effektive Dielektrizitätskonstante
   E: effective dielectric constant
   F: constante *f* diélectrique effective

Effektivleistung *f*
   E: active power
   F: puissance *f* effective

Effektivspannung *f*
   E: active voltage, in-phase voltage, effective voltage, r.m.s.-voltage *n*
   F: tension *f* efficace, tension *f* active

Effektivwert *m*
   E: effective value, root mean square (r.m.s.) value
   F: valeur *f* efficace

Eichkreis *m*
   E: calibration circuit
   F: circuit *m* d'étalonnage

Eichkurve *f*
   E: calibration curve
   F: courbe *f* d'étalonnage

Eichmaß *n*
   E: gauge *n*, standard *n*
   F: jauge *f*, étalon *m*

Eichung *f*
   E: calibration *n*, adjusting *n*, gauging *n*
   F: étalonnage *m*, calibrage *m*, jaugeage *m*

Eichwiderstand *m*
   E: standard resistance, calibrating resistance
   F: résistance *f* étalon

Eigenimpedanz *f*
   E: self-impedance *n*
   F: auto-impédance *f*

Eigenschaft, elektrische ~
   E: electrical characteristic, electrical property
   F: caractéristique *f* électrique, propriété *f* électrique

Eigenschaft, mechanische ~
   E: mechanical characteristic, mechanical property
   F: charactéristique *f* mécanique, propriété *f* mécanique

eigensichere Anlage
   E: intrinsically safe installation
   F: installation *f* à sécurité intrinsèque

Eigenspannung f[mech.]
  E: internal stress
  F: contrainte f interne, tension f interne
Eigenviskosität f
  E: intrinsic viscosity
  F: viscosité f intrinsèque
Eignung f
  E: suitability n
  F: aptitude f, qualification f
einadrige Leitung
  E: single-core cable (with or without sheath)
  F: monoconducteur m (avec ou sans gaine)
einadrige Leitung mit Mantel
  E: single-core sheathed conductor
  F: monoconducteur m sous gaine
einadriges Kabel
  E: single-core cable, single-conductor cable
  F: câble m monophasé, câble m unipolaire, câble m monoconducteur, câble m monopolaire
einbauen v
  E: insert v, mount v, fit v
  F: mettre v, placer v, insérer v
einbetten v
  E: embed v
  F: encastrer v, enrober v, noyer v
Einbrennlack m
  E: baking enamel, baking varnish
  F: vernis-émail m
eindrähtiger Leiter
  E: solid conductor
  F: âme f massive, âme f à un seul brin
Eindringen von Feuchtigkeit
  E: ingress of moisture, penetration of moisture, moisture permeation
  F: pénétration f d'humidité
Eindringen von Wasser (in Kabel)
  E: water seeping, water seepage, water penetration
  F: infiltration f d'eau, pénétration f d'eau
Eindringprüfung f
  E: penetration test
  F: essai m de pénétration
Eindringtiefe f
  E: depth of penetration
  F: profondeur f de pénétration
Eindringung f
  E: penetration n
  F: pénétration f
Eindrücklast f
  E: indentation load
  F: charge f d'empreinte
Eindrucktiefe f
  E: indentation depth
  F: profondeur f de l'empreinte
Eindrückzeit f
  E: indentation time
  F: temps m d'empreinte
Einfach-Erdschluß m
  E: single fault to earth (GB), single fault to ground (US)
  F: défaut m à la terre simple
Einfädeln n (Drahtziehmaschine)
  E: stringing-up n, threading-up n
  F: enfilage m
Einfrierpunkt m
  E: solidification point, freezing point
  F: point m de solidification, point m de congélation
einführen v
  E: insert v, introduce v, lead in v
  F: insérer v, introduire v
einführen, Kabel in elektrische Anlagen ~
  E: to terminate cables on to electrical plant
  F: introduire v les câbles dans des installations électriques
Einführen in einen Kanalzug [K. Verl.]
  E: duct rodding
  F: introduction f dans un conduit
Einführung f (Kabel)
  E: inlet n, entrance n
  F: entrée f
Einführungsdraht m
  E: drop wire (telephone cable to connect open wire lines on poles to subscribers' premises) (US), subscriber('s) drop wire, telephone drop, lead(ing)-in wire
  F: ligne f d'abonné téléphonique (raccord à la ligne aérienne), ligne f de desserte d'abonné, fil m d'entrée d'abonné
Einführungsisolator m
  E: inlet insulator, lead-in insulator
  F: isolateur m d'entrée
Einführungskabel n
  E: lead(ing)-in cable, stub cable
  F: câble m d'entrée

Einführungskanal für Kabel
  E: conduit for leading in cables
  F: conduite f pour l'introduction des câbles

Einführungsleitung f
  E: drop wire (telephone cable to connect open wire lines on poles to subscribers' premises) (US), subscriber('s) drop wire, telephone drop, lead(ing)-in wire
  F: ligne f d'abonné téléphonique (raccord à la ligne aérienne), ligne f de desserte d'abonné, fil m d'entrée d'abonné

Einführungtrichter m [K. Garn.]
  E: terminal bell, entrance bell
  F: cornet m d'entrée

Einfüllöffnung f
  E: filling hole
  F: trou m de remplissage

Einfülltemperatur f
  E: pouring temperature, filling temperature
  F: température f de remplissage

Einfülltrichter m [Extr.]
  E: feeding hopper
  F: trémie f d'alimentation, entonnoir m de chargement

eingängige Schnecke [Extr.]
  E: single-flighted screw
  F: vis f à un seul filet

Eingangsimpedanz f
  E: input impedance
  F: impédance f d'entrée

Eingangskreis m
  E: input circuit
  F: circuit m d'entrée

Eingangswiderstand m
  E: input resistance
  F: résistance f d'entrée

eingebaut adj
  E: built-in adj, enclosed adj
  F: incorporé adj

eingehende Prüfung
  E: exhaustive test, close examination, thorough examination
  F: essai m détaillé, examen m détaillé, contrôle m minutieux

eingekerbt adj
  E: notched adj
  F: entaillé adj

eingelagert adj
  E: intercalated adj, sandwiched adj between,
  F: interposé adj, entreposé adj

eingeschlossene Luft
  E: entrapped air
  F: air m enfermé

einhalten v (Werte, Bedingungen)
  E: meet v, observe v, comply with v
  F: respecter v, observer v

einheitlich adj
  E: uniform adj, consistent adj, homogeneous adj
  F: homogène adj, uniforme adj

Einlagerung f
  E: incorporation n, insertion n, intercalation n
  F: interposition f, entreposage m

Einlaßventil n
  E: inlet valve
  F: soupape f d'admission

Einlauf m (in eine Maschine)
  E: inlet n, entrance n
  F: entrée f

einlaufen, in die Maschine ~
  E: to enter the machine, to run into the machine
  F: entrer v dans la machine

Einlaufzeit f [Masch.]
  E: starting time, acceleration time, running-in period
  F: temps m de démarrage, temps m d'accélération

Einleiter-Endverschluß m
  E: single-core termination
  F: boîte f d'extrémité unipolaire

Einleiterkabel n
  E: single-core cable, single-conductor cable
  F: câble m monophasé, câble m unipolaire, câble m monoconducteur, câble m monopolaire

Einleiterölkabel n
  E: single-core oil-filled cable
  F: câble m unipolaire à huile fluide

Einmannbedienung f
  E: one-man operation
  F: commande f par une personne

Einmoden-Lichtleiter m [Nachr.]
  E: single-mode optical fibre
  F: fibre f optique monomode

Einphasenstrom m
  E: single-phase current
  F: courant m monophasé

einpoliger Erdschluß
 E: single-line-to-earth fault
 F: défaut *m* à la terre unipolaire
Einreißfestigkeit *f*
 E: resistance to tearing, tear resistance, tearing strength
 F: résistance *f* au déchirement
einrichten *v*[Masch.]
 E: set up *v*
 F: régler *v*
Einrichtezeit *f*[Masch.]
 E: set-up time
 F: temps *m* de préparation, temps *m* de réglage
Einsatz von Materialien
 E: use of materials, employment of materials, application of materials
 F: mise *f* au point de matériaux, utilisation *f* de matériaux
einsatzbereit *adj*
 E: ready for use, ready for service
 F: prêt *adj* au service, prêt *adj* à l'usage, prêt *adj* à la mise en œuvre
Einsatzspule *f*
 E: input bobbin, input reel, processing reel, processing drum
 F: bobine *f* d'alimentation
Einsatztrommel *f*
 E: input bobbin, input reel, processing reel, processing drum
 F: bobine *f* d'alimentation
Einschaltdauer *f*
 E: duty factor, switch-on time
 F: facteur *m* de marche, durée *f* de mise en circuit
einschalten *v*[Masch.]
 E: start *v*, start up *v*
 F: démarrer *v*, mettre *v* en marche
einschalten *v*[el.]
 E: switch on *v*, turn on (US) *v*
 F: enclencher *v*(él.), mettre *v* sous tension, fermer *v*(circuit), mettre *v* en circuit
Einschaltstrom *m*
 E: starting current
 F: courant *m* de démarrage
Einschichtbetrieb, im ~
 E: on a single shift basis
 F: en une seule équipe
einschießen, Kabel in den Schiffsladeraum ~
 E: to coil the cable into the ship's hold
 F: enrouler *v* le câble dans la cale d'un navire, stocker *v* le cable dans la cale d'un navire, lover *v* le câble dans la cale d'un navire
Einschlüsse *m pl*
 E: inclusions *pl*
 F: inclusions *f pl*, occlusions *f pl*
Einschnürungen *f pl*(Met.-Strangpr.)
 E: bamboo rings, stop marks
 F: nœuds *m pl* de bambou
einseitig geerdetes System
 E: system earthed at one end only
 F: réseau *m* mis à la terre d'un côté seulement
einseitig herausgeführte Anschlußdrähte
 E: single-ended terminal wires
 F: fils *m pl* de jonction unidirectionnels
einseitiger Antrieb
 E: unilateral drive
 F: commande *f* unilatérale
einsetzen *v*
 E: insert *v*, mount *v*, fit *v*
 F: mettre *v*, placer *v*, insérer *v*
Einsetzen von Spulen
 E: positioning of reels, loading of reels
 F: montage *m* des bobines
Einsetzen von Trommeln
 E: positioning of reels, loading of reels
 F: montage *m* des bobines
Einspannklaue *f*
 E: jaw *n*, fixing clamp, clamping jaw
 F: mâchoire *f* de serrage, mordache *f*
Einspannklemme *f*
 E: jaw *n*, fixing clamp, clamping jaw
 F: mâchoire *f* de serrage, mordache *f*
Einspannlänge *f*[Prüf.]
 E: free length (of specimen) between clamps, clamping length
 F: longueur *f* libre entre mâchoires
einspeisen *v*[mech., el.]
 E: feed *v*, charge *v*, load *v*, supply *v*
 F: alimenter *v*, charger *v*
Einspeisung *f*[el.]
 E: power supply, feed-in *n*
 F: alimentation *f*, arrivée *f*
Einspeisungskabel *n*
 E: feeder *n*, feeder cable
 F: câble *m* d'alimentation, feeder *m*
Einspruchsverfahren *n*
 E: public inquiry
 F: enquête *f* publique

einstellbar

einstellbar *adj*
 E: adjustable *adj*, variable *adj*
 F: ajustable *adj*, réglable *adj*, orientable *adj*

Einstellgenauigkeit *f*
 E: accuracy of adjustment, precision of adjustment
 F: exactitude *f* de réglage, précision *f* de réglage

Einstellknopf *m*
 E: control knob
 F: bouton *m* de réglage

Einstellschraube *f*
 E: set screw, adjusting screw
 F: vis *f* d'ajustage, vis *f* de réglage

Einstellung *f*
 E: adjustment *n*, regulation *n*, setting *n*
 F: réglage *m*

Einstempel-Presse *f*
 E: single-ram press
 F: presse *f* à un (seul) fouloir

Einstiegöffnung *f* [K. Verl.]
 E: entrance *n*, manhole *n*
 F: entrée *f*, accès *m*, trou *m* d'homme, regard *m* de visite

eintauchen *v*
 E: immerse *v*, dip *v*
 F: immerger *v*, tremper *v*, plonger *v*

Eintauchen in Wasser
 E: immersion in water, water immersion
 F: immersion *f* dans l'eau

einteilig *adj*
 E: single-piece... *adj*, one-piece... *adj*, monobloc *adj*
 F: monobloc *adj*, indivisé *adj*, en une seule pièce

Eintritt *m*
 E: inlet *n*, entrance *n*
 F: entrée *f*

Eintrittstemperatur *f*
 E: inlet temperature, initial temperature
 F: température *f* d'entrée

Einwegtrommel *f* [Kab.]
 E: non-returnable reel
 F: touret *m* perdu

Einzelader *f*
 E: single conductor
 F: brin *m*, élément *m*, monoconducteur *m*

Einzelantrieb *m*
 E: single drive, direct drive
 F: commande *f* individuelle, commande *f* directe

Einzelblock mit Doppelscheibe [Drahth.]
 E: double-deck drawing block
 F: banc *m* à deux cônes de tréfilage

Einzeldraht *m*
 E: single wire
 F: brin *m*

Einzelleiter *m*
 E: single conductor
 F: brin *m*, élément *m*, monoconducteur *m*

einzeln abgeschirmte Kabeladern
 E: individually screened cable cores
 F: conducteurs *m pl* de câble avec écran individuel

Einzelpaar *n*
 E: single pair
 F: mono-paire *f*

Einzelzeichnung *f*
 E: detail drawing, component drawing
 F: plan *m* de détail

einziehen *v* (in Rohre) [K. Verl.]
 E: pull *v*
 F: tirer *v*

einziehen, ein Kabel von Hand ~
 E: to manhandle a cable
 F: tirer *v* un câble à la main

Einziehen *n* (von Kabeln in Rohre)
 E: pulling in, pull-in *n*, drawing in
 F: tirage *m*

Einziehmaschine, Anspitzmaschine und ~ (Draht)
 E: wire sharpening and threading machine
 F: machine *f* à appointer et enfiler le fil métallique

einzügiger Rohrstrang
 E: single duct conduit
 F: caniveau *m* à passage simple

Einzugszone *f* [Extr.]
 E: feeding zone
 F: zone *f* d'alimentation

Eisenbahnerde *f* [Nachr. K.]
 E: railway earth
 F: terre *f* de voie ferrée

Eisenband-Wickler *m*
 E: steel tape spinner, steel taping head
 F: enrouleur *m* à feuillard d'acier, tête *f* à feuillard

E-Kupfer n (Kupfer für die Elektrotechnik)
  E: high-conductivity copper, electrical grade copper, ETP-Copper (electrolytic tough pitch copper) n
  F: cuivre m à haute conductivité, cuivre m raffiné électrolytique
elastische Dehnung
  E: stretch n
  F: allongement m élastique
elastische Erholung
  E: elastic recovery, recovery from stretching
  F: reprise f élastique
elastische Verformung
  E: elastic deformation
  F: déformation f élastique
Elastizitätsgrenze f
  E: yield point, yield strength, elastic limit
  F: limite f d'élasticité, limite f d'allongement
Elastizitätsmodul m
  E: modulus of elasticity
  F: module m d'élasticité
Elastomer n
  E: elastomer n
  F: élastomère m
elektrisch leitend
  E: electrically conductive
  F: conducteur adj du courant électrique
elektrische Anschlüsse
  E: electrical connections
  F: liaisons f pl électriques, raccords m pl électriques
elektrische Drainage
  E: electrical drainage
  F: drainage m électrique
elektrische Eigenschaft
  E: electrical characteristic, electrical property
  F: caractéristique f électrique, propriété f électrique
elektrische Entkopplung
  E: electrical decoupling
  F: découplage m électrique
elektrische Festigkeit
  E: dielectric strength, breakdown strength, puncture resistance, electric strength
  F: rigidité f diélectrique

elektrischer Durchgang
  E: electrical continuity
  F: continuité f électrique
elektrischer Übertragungsweg
  E: electrical transmission route
  F: voie f de transmission électrique
Elektrizitäts-Versorgungsunternehmen (EVU) n
  E: electricity supply undertaking, electricity undertaking, utility (US) n
  F: société f de distribution d'électricité, entreprise f d'électricité, centrale f électrique
Elektrodenabstand m
  E: electrode spacing, distance between electrodes, spark gap
  F: écartement m des électrodes, distance f entre électrodes
elektrolytisch verzinnter Draht
  E: electro-tinned wire
  F: fil m métallique étamé électrolytiquement
elektrolytische Korrosion
  E: electrolytic corrosion
  F: corrosion f électrolytique
Elektrolytkupfer n
  E: electrolytic copper
  F: cuivre m électrolytique
elektro-motorische Kabellegerolle
  E: motor-driven roller for cable laying
  F: rouleau m entraîné par moteur pour la pose du câble
elektrostatischer Schirm
  E: electrostatic screen, electrostatic shield
  F: écran m électrostatique
Elektrotechnik f
  E: electrical engineering
  F: électrotechnique f
Empfindlichkeit f
  E: sensibility n, sensitivity n
  F: sensibilité f
empirische Versuche
  E: trial-and-error experiments
  F: essais m pl empiriques
Endbearbeitung f
  E: finishing n, completion n
  F: finissage m, finition f
Endenabschluß m
  E: sealing end, termination n, terminal n, pothead n

Endenabschluß
F: extrémité f, accessoire m d'extrémité

Endenanschlußklemme f[el.]
E: terminal n, connector n, connecting terminal
F: borne f, connecteur m, borne f de raccordement

Endfertigung f
E: finishing n, completion n
F: finissage m, finition f

Endgestell für Kabel
E: cable supporting rack, cable terminating rack, terminal rack
F: bâti m pour têtes de câbles, bâti m terminal

Endschalter m
E: limit switch
F: interrupteur m de fin de course, interrupteur m terminal

Endverschluß m
E: sealing end, termination n, terminal n, pothead n
F: extrémité f, accessoire m d'extrémité

Endverschluß, Aufsteck-~ m
E: plug-in termination, plug-on termination
F: extrémité f embrochable

Endverschluß, leicht aufsteckbarer ~
E: easy-on termination
F: extrémité f facilement embrochable

Energie f
E: power n, energy n
F: énergie f, puissance f

Energiebedarf m
E: power requirement, power demand
F: demande f d'énergie, puissance f nécessaire

Energiekabel n
E: power cable
F: câble m d'énergie

Energiequelle f
E: source of energy, source of power, power source
F: source f d'énergie

Energieübertragung f
E: power transmission
F: transport m d'énergie

Energieverbrauch m
E: current consumption, power consumption
F: consommation f de courant, consommation f électrique, consommation f d'énergie

Energieversorgung f
E: power supply, power distribution
F: alimentation f en énergie électrique, distribution f d'énergie électrique, alimentation f en courant électrique

Energieverteilung f
E: power supply, power distribution
F: alimentation f en énergie électrique, distribution f d'énergie électrique, alimentation f en courant électrique

enge Toleranz
E: close tolerance
F: tolérance f étroite

Englergrad m (Öl-Viskosität)
E: Engler degree
F: degré m Engler

Entdämpfung f[Tel. K.]
E: damping reduction, transmission gain
F: compensation f de l'affaiblissement, compensation f de l'amortissement

enteiweißter Kautschuk
E: deproteinised rubber
F: caoutchouc m sans protéine

entflammbar adj
E: flammable adj (US), inflammable adj (GB), , combustible adj
F: combustible adj, inflammable adj

Entgasung f
E: degassing n, degasification n
F: dégazage m

entgegengesetzt der Fertigungsrichtung
E: upstream adv
F: en amont

Entgraten n
E: deburring n, trimming n
F: ébarbage m, ébavurage m

Enthärtungsanlage f
E: softening plant
F: installation f d'adoucissement, décarbonateur m

entkoppeln v
E: balance out v, decouple v, uncouple v
F: neutraliser v, désaccoupler v

Entkopplung, elektrische ~
E: electrical decoupling
F: découplage m électrique

Entladestrom m
 E: discharge current
 F: courant m de décharge
Entladungsdurchschlag m
 E: ionizing discharge
 F: décharge f ionisante
Entladungsfigur f
 E: discharge pattern
 F: figure f de décharges
Entladungsintensität f
 E: discharge intensity
 F: intensité f de décharge
Entladungskanal m
 E: streamer n, discharge channel
 F: voie f de décharge
Entladungsspannung f
 E: discharge voltage
 F: tension f de décharge
Entlasten n [Prüf.]
 E: removal of load
 F: déchargement m
Entleeren n
 E: unloading n, emptying n
 F: vidage m, vidange f, évacuation f
Entlüfter m
 E: exhaust fan
 F: désaérateur m
Entlüftung f
 E: exhaust n, deaeration n
 F: désaération f, ventilation f
Entlüftungsloch n
 E: vent hole, vent n
 F: évent m
Entlüftungsrohr n
 E: exhaust pipe, exhaust flue, ventilation pipe
 F: cheminée f d'aération, tube m d'évacuation, tube m de ventilation
Entmischung f
 E: segregation n, decomposition n, separation n
 F: ségrégation f, décomposition f, déshomogénéisation f
entsalzen v
 E: desalt v, desalinate v, demineralize v, deionize v
 F: déminéraliser v, dessaler v
Entschäumer m
 E: anti-foaming agent
 F: agent m anti-mousse
Entspannungsglühen n
 E: stress-relieving annealing
 F: recuit m de détente

Entstörung f
 E: interference elimination, interference suppression, noise suppression
 F: suppression f des parasites, déparasitage m
entwickelt, bis zur Fertigungsreife ~
 E: developed to the production stage
 F: étudié jusqu'au stade de fabrication
Entwicklungsarbeiten f pl
 E: development work
 F: études f pl
entziehen v
 E: extract v, remove v
 F: retirer v, enlever v, ôter v
Entzündbarkeit f
 E: inflammability n
 F: inflammabilité f
entzundern v
 E: descale v
 F: décalaminer v
Entzündungspunkt m (Öle)
 E: fire point, ignition point, flash point
 F: point m d'inflammation
Epoxidharz n
 E: epoxy resin, epoxide resin
 F: résine f époxy, résine f époxyde, résine f époxydique
EPR-Kautschuk m
 E: ethylene-propylene rubber (EPR) n
 F: caoutchouc m d'éthylène propylène (EPR)
Erdanschluß m
 E: earth connection (GB), ground connection (US)
 F: prise f de terre, connexion f de terre
Erdarbeiten f pl [K.Verl.]
 E: earth work, excavation work
 F: travaux m pl de terrassement
Erdboden m
 E: soil n, ground n, earth n
 F: terre f
Erdboden, Austrocknung des ~s
 E: drying (out) of the soil
 F: séchage m du sol, dessèchement m du sol
Erddraht m
 E: earth lead (GB), ground lead (US)
 F: fil m de terre
Erde f [el.]

Erde
- E: earth n (GB), ground n (US)
- F: terre f

Erde, gegen ~
- E: to ground, to earth
- F: par rapport à la terre

erden v
- E: earth v (GB), to connect to earth, ground (US) v
- F: mettre v à la terre, relier v à la terre

Erdkabel n
- E: buried cable, underground cable
- F: câble m souterrain

Erdklemme f
- E: ground clamp (US), ground terminal (US), earth terminal (GB), earth clamp (GB)
- F: borne f de terre, prise f de terre

Erdkopplung f
- E: unbalance to ground, earth coupling (GB)
- F: déséquilibre m par rapport à la terre

Erdleiter m
- E: earthing conductor (GB), grounding conductor (US), earth wire (GB), ground wire (US), guard wire
- F: conducteur m de terre, fil de garde m

Erdleitung f
- E: earthing conductor (GB), grounding conductor (US), earth wire (GB), ground wire (US), guard wire
- F: conducteur m de terre, fil de garde m

Erdpotential n
- E: earth potential (GB), ground potential (US)
- F: potentiel m de terre

Erdrückleitung f
- E: earth return circuit (GB), ground return circuit (US)
- F: circuit m de retour par la terre

Erdschelle f
- E: earth(ing) clip (GB), ground(ing) clip (US)
- F: collier m de mise à la terre

Erdschluß m
- E: earth fault (GB), ground fault (US)
- F: contact m à la terre, défaut m à la terre

Erdschlußkompensation f
- E: earth fault compensation (GB), ground fault compensation (US)
- F: compensation f des défauts à la terre

Erdschlußschutz m
- E: earth fault protection (GB), ground fault protection (US)
- F: protection f contre les défauts à la terre

Erdschlußstrom m
- E: earth leakage current (GB), earth fault current (GB), ground fault current (US)
- F: courant m de court-circuit à la terre, courant m à la terre

Erdseil n
- E: earthing conductor (GB), grounding conductor (US), earth wire (GB), ground wire (US), guard wire
- F: conducteur m de terre, fil de garde m

Erdung f
- E: earthing n (GB), grounding n (US), connection to earth (GB), connection to ground (US)
- F: mise f à la terre

Erdungsanlage f
- E: earth(ing) system (GB), ground(ing) system (US)
- F: système m de mise à la terre

Erdungsanschluß m
- E: earth connection (GB), ground connection (US)
- F: prise f de terre, connexion f de terre

Erdungsklemme f
- E: ground clamp (US), ground terminal (US), earth terminal (GB), earth clamp (GB)
- F: borne f de terre, prise f de terre

Erdungsleitung f
- E: earthing circuit (GB), grounding circuit (US)
- F: circuit m de mise à la terre

Erdungspunkt m
- E: earth point
- F: point m de (mise à la) terre

Erdungsschelle f
- E: earth(ing) clip (GB), ground(ing) clip (US)
- F: collier m de mise à la terre

Erdungsschirm m

Erdungswiderstand m
E: earth resistance (GB), ground resistance (US)
F: résistance f de terre

Erdverbindung f
E: earth connection (GB), ground connection (US)
F: prise f de terre, connexion f de terre

erdverlegt adj [K. Verl.]
E: laid in earth, buried adj, laid underground
F: posé adj en terre, enterré adj

Erdverlegung f
E: direct burial (in earth), burying n (in ground), underground laying, laying in earth
F: pose f en pleine terre, pose f souterraine

Erfahrung mit einer Fertigungsmethode
E: process experience
F: expérience f faite avec une méthode de fabrication

erfassen, die Messungen ~ kleine Entladungen nicht mehr
E: the measurements are insensitive to small discharges
F: les mesures sont insensibles aux décharges de faible importance

erfüllen, eine Bedingung ~
E: to meet a requirement
F: satisfaire v à une demande, satisfaire v à une exigence

erfüllen, eine Forderung ~
E: to meet a requirement
F: satisfaire v à une demande, satisfaire v à une exigence

Erhöhung f
E: increase n, raise n, rise n
F: augmentation f, élévation f

Erholung, elastische ~
E: elastic recovery, recovery from stretching
F: reprise f élastique

Ermüdung f
E: fatigue n
F: fatigue f

Ermüdungsbruch m
E: fatigue crack, fatigue failure, fatigue fracture, stress cracking
F: cassure f de fatigue, rupture f de fatigue

Ermüdungsfestigkeit f [Met.]
E: fatigue strength, fatigue resistance
F: résistance f à la fatigue

Ermüdungsversuch m [mech.]
E: endurance test, fatigue test
F: essai m d'endurance, essai m de fatigue

Erprobung f (s. Prüfung)

errichten v
E: set up v, install v, mount v, erect v, assemble v
F: monter v, ériger v, installer v, assembler v

Errichtung f
E: installation n, erection n, set-up n, assembly n
F: implantation f, montage m, assemblage m

Errichtungsvorschrift f
E: installation rule, installation standard
F: prescription f d'installation, règle f d'installation

Ersatzaderpaar n [Nachr. K.]
E: reserve pair, spare pair, extra pair
F: paire f de réserve

Ersatzmaterial n
E: substitute n
F: matériau m de remplacement

Ersatzteil n
E: spare part, spare n
F: pièce f de rechange

ersetzen v
E: replace v, substitute v
F: remplacer v, substituer v

erstarren v
E: solidify v, freeze v, set v, harden v
F: solidifier v (se), congéler v, durcir v

Erstarrung f
E: solidification n, setting n, hardening n, freezing v
F: solidification f, congélation f

Erstarrungspunkt m
E: solidification point, freezing point
F: point m de solidification, point m de congélation

Erstarrungspunkt m (Öle)
E: pour point, cloud point
F: point m de figeage

Erstarrungsschrumpfung f
  E: solidification shrinkage
  F: retrait m par solidification
erteilen, ein Patent ~
  E: to grant a patent
  F: accorder v un brevet, délivrer v un brevet
Erwärmung f
  E: heating n, temperature rise
  F: chauffage m, échauffement m
Erwärmungs- und Abkühlungszyklen
  E: heating and cooling cycles
  F: cycles m pl d'échauffement et de refroidissement
Erweicher m
  E: softener n
  F: émollient m
Erweichung f
  E: softening n
  F: ramollissement m
Erweichungspunkt m (Massen)
  E: softening point
  F: point m de ramollissement
Erweichungstemperatur f
  E: heat distortion temperature
  F: température f de ramollissement, température f de déformation à chaud
Erweiterung f
  E: extension n, enlargement n, widening n, expansion n
  F: extension f, élargissement m
EVA (s. Äthylen-Vinyl-Azetat)
evakuieren v
  E: evacuate v
  F: évacuer v, mettre v sous vide
EVU (s. Elektrizitäts-Versorgungsunternehmen)
EVU-Last f
  E: public utilities load
  F: charge f des centrales électriques
EVU-Netz n
  E: public distribution network
  F: réseau m de distribution public
Extrudat n
  E: extruded material, extrudate n
  F: produit m d'extrusion
Extruder m
  E: extruder n
  F: boudineuse f, extrudeuse f
Extruder mit Entgasungssystem
  E: vent extruder
  F: boudineuse f à aération

Extruderkopf m
  E: extrusion head, extruder head
  F: tête f de boudineuse, tête f d'extrusion
Extruderschnecke f
  E: extrusion screw
  F: vis f de boudineuse
Extruderwerkzeuge n pl
  E: extruder dies pl, extrusion dies pl
  F: outillage m de boudineuse
Extrudierbarkeit f
  E: extrudability n
  F: extrudabilité f
extrudieren v
  E: extrude v
  F: extruder v, boudiner v
Extrudieren n
  E: extrusion n
  F: extrusion f, boudinage m
Extrudieren, hydrostatisches ~ [Met.]
  E: hydrostatic extrusion
  F: extrusion f hydrostatique
Extrusion f
  E: extrusion n
  F: extrusion f, boudinage m
Extrusion mit engen Toleranzen
  E: close tolerance extrusion
  F: extrusion f avec tolérances étroites
Extrusionsverfahren n
  E: extrusion process
  F: méthode f d'extrusion
Exzentrizitäts-Meßvorrichtung f
  E: eccentricity gauge
  F: jauge f d'excentricité, appareil m de mesure de l'excentricité

F

Fabrikatespektrum, breites ~
  E: highly diversified range of products, broad spectrum of manufacturing activities
  F: gamme f de produits largement diversifiée
Facharbeiter m
  E: skilled worker
  F: ouvrier m qualifié
Fachung f (Garn)
  E: folding number
  F: nombre m des fils

fadenziehend adj (Viskosität)
  E: ropy adj
  F: filant adj
fahrbares Gerät
  E: mobile unit, mobile equipment
  F: équipement m mobile
Fahrdraht m
  E: trolley wire, overhead contact wire, slide wire
  F: fil m (de) trolley, fil m de contact
fahren, eine Maschine ~
  E: to run a machine, to operate a machine
  F: faire v marcher une machine, opérer v une machine
Fahrgeschwindigkeit f [Masch.]
  E: line speed, production speed, running speed, production rate, operating speed, processing speed
  F: vitesse f de marche f, vitesse f de fabrication, vitesse f de production, vitesse f de travail
Fahrstuhlkabel n
  E: lift cable
  F: câble m d'ascenseur
fällen v [Chem.]
  E: precipitate v
  F: précipiter v
fallender Guß
  E: top-pouring n
  F: coulée f en chute, coulée f en plan incliné
Fallprüfung f
  E: drop test
  F: essai m de résistance aux secousses
Falte f
  E: crease n, wrinkle n
  F: pli m
Faltenbildung f
  E: creasing n, wrinkling n
  F: plissement m, formation f de plis
faltenfrei adj
  E: wrinkle-free adj, crease-free adj
  F: exempt de plis, sans plis
falzen v
  E: fold v
  F: plier v, replier v
Falzfestigkeit f
  E: folding endurance
  F: résistance f aux pliages répétés
Falzzahl f
  E: number of double folds
  F: nombre m de pliages répétés

Farbbatch n
  E: master batch, colo(u)r batch, colo(u)r concentrate
  F: mélange m coloré maître
Farbbeständigkeit f
  E: colo(u)r-fastness, colo(u)r retention
  F: permanence f de la teinte, stabilité f de la couleur
Farbe f
  E: colo(u)r n
  F: couleur f
farbecht adj
  E: colo(u)r-fast adj
  F: de couleur résistante
färben v
  E: colo(u)r v, dye v, stain v, pigment v
  F: colorer v, teindre v
farbige Kennzeichnung
  E: colo(u)r code, colo(u)r coding
  F: repérage m coloré, code m de couleur
farbige Spirale
  E: colo(u)red spiral, colo(u)red helix
  F: spirale f colorée, hélice f colorée
farbige Wendel
  E: colo(u)red spiral, colo(u)red helix
  F: spirale f colorée, hélice f colorée
Farbkonzentrat n
  E: master batch, colo(u)r batch, colo(u)r concentrate
  F: mélange m coloré maître
farbloser Kunststoff
  E: uncoloured plastic, natural-coloured plastic, unpigmented plastic, natural plastic (US)
  F: matière f plastique de couleur naturelle, matière f plastique non colorée, matière f plastique incolore
Farbmarkierung f
  E: ink-marking n, colo(u)r marking
  F: marquage m à l'encre, marquage m coloré
Farbstoff m
  E: pigment n, colo(u)rant n
  F: pigment m, matière colorante f
Farbtönung f
  E: colo(u)r shade
  F: nuance f de couleur, teinte f
Färbung f
  E: colo(u)ring n
  F: coloration f

Fassung *f*
  E: plug socket, connector socket, receptacle *n*, female contact, socket *n*
  F: prise *f* femelle, fiche *f* femelle, douille *f*

Fassungsader *f*
  E: flexible wire for fittings (sockets)
  F: fil *m* de douille

Faßwickler *m*
  E: pail-pack *n*, drum-pack *n*, pay-off-pak *n*, draw-pak *n*, D-pak *n*
  F: enrouleur *m* en forme de tonneau, fût *m* de bobinage pour fils métalliques

Fehlanpassung *f*
  E: mismatching *n*
  F: désadaptation *f*

Fehlausrichtung *f*
  E: misalignment *n*
  F: désalignement *m*

Fehlbedienung *f*
  E: faulty operation, operating error, operator's error
  F: fausse manœuvre *f*, erreur *f* de conduite, erreur *f* de manœuvre, erreur *f* de l'opérateur, erreur *f* de manipulation

Fehler *m*
  E: defect *n*, error *n*, failure *n*, fault *n*
  F: défaut *m*, erreur *f*, défaillance *f*

Fehleranzeige *f*
  E: error display, fault indication
  F: affichage *m* d'erreur, signalisation *f* de défauts

Fehleranzeige-Einrichtung *f*
  E: error indicator, fault indicator
  F: indicateur *m* d'erreur, indicateur *m* de défauts

Fehleranzeiger *m*
  E: error indicator, fault indicator
  F: indicateur *m* d'erreur, indicateur *m* de défauts

Fehlerdämpfung *f*
  E: reflection attenuation, balance return loss, return loss between line and network (US), reflection loss, balance attenuation
  F: atténuation *f* de réflexion, affaiblissement *m* d'équilibrage, affaiblissement *m* des courants réfléchis

Fehlerdämpfungsmaß *n* [Nachr. K.]
  E: return loss unit
  F: équivalent *m* d'affaiblissement d'équilibrage

fehlerfrei *adj*
  E: correct *adj*, faultless *adj*, free from defects
  F: sans défauts, exempt *adj* de défauts,

Fehlergrenze, absolute ~
  E: absolute limit of error
  F: limite *f* absolue d'erreur

fehlerhaft *adj*
  E: defective *adj*, faulty *adj*
  F: défectueux *adj*

Fehlerhäufigkeit *f*
  E: error rate
  F: taux *m* d'erreur, fréquence *f* d'erreurs

Fehlerort *m*
  E: position of a fault
  F: position *f* d'un défaut

Fehlerort-Meßbrücke *f*
  E: fault location measuring bridge
  F: pont *m* de localisation de défauts

Fehlerortsbestimmung *f*
  E: fault location, fault finding, trouble finding, fault detection, trouble shooting (US), locating the trouble (GB)
  F: localisation *f* d'un défaut

Fehlerortung *f*
  E: fault location, fault finding, trouble finding, fault detection, trouble shooting (US), locating the trouble (GB)
  F: localisation *f* d'un défaut

Fehlerortungsgerät *n*
  E: fault detector, fault location unit
  F: localisateur *m* de défauts, détecteur *m* de défauts

Fehlerstelle *f*
  E: position of a fault
  F: position *f* d'un défaut

Fehlerstrom *m*
  E: leakage current, fault current, stray current
  F: courant *m* de fuite, courant *m* de défaut, courant *m* vagabond

Fehlersuche *f*
  E: fault location, fault finding, trouble finding, fault detection, trouble shooting (US), locating the trouble (GB)
  F: localisation *f* d'un défaut

Fehlersuchgerät n
 E: fault detector, fault location unit
 F: localisateur m de défauts, détecteur m de défauts

Fehlerwahrscheinlichkeit f
 E: failure probability
 F: probabilité f de claquage

Fehlmessung f
 E: faulty measurement, measuring error
 F: raté m de mesure, erreur f de mesure

Feindraht m
 E: fine wire, fine drawn wire
 F: fil m fin

feindrähtiger Leiter
 E: fine wire conductor, flexible stranded conductor
 F: âme f en fils fins

Feineinstellung f
 E: fine adjustment, precision adjustment
 F: réglage m minutieux, réglage m précis

feinkörnige Struktur
 E: fine-grain structure
 F: structure f à grains fins

feinpulverig adj
 E: powdery adj, pulverulent adj
 F: en poudre, pulvérulent adj

Feinstdraht m
 E: super-fine wire, extra-fine wire
 F: fil m super-fin, fil m extra-fin

feinstdrähtiger Leiter
 E: extra-fine wire conductor, super-fine wire conductor, extra-flexible stranded conductor
 F: âme f en fils extra-fins, âme f en fils super-fins

Feinvakuum n
 E: vacuum 1 to 10^{-3} torr
 F: vide m de 1 à 10^{-3} torr

Feinzug m [Drahth.]
 E: finishing pass
 F: tréfilage m à dimensions fines

Feldbegrenzung f [el.]
 E: limitation of the electrical field, field limitation
 F: limitation du champ électrique f

Feldkonzentrationen f pl [el.]
 E: stress concentrations
 F: concentrations f pl du champ électrique

Feldregulierung f [el.]
 E: stress control, stress relief, field control
 F: orientation f du champ électrique, régularisation f du champ électrique, régulation f du champ électrique

Feldstärke f [el.]
 E: field strength
 F: intensité f du champ

feldsteuernd adj [el.]
 E: field-controlling adj, stress-controlling adj
 F: orientant adj le champ électrique

feldsteuerndes Element [K. Garn.]
 E: stress cone
 F: cône m de contrainte

Feldsteuerung f [el.]
 E: stress control, stress relief, field control
 F: orientation f du champ électrique, régularisation f du champ électrique, régulation f du champ électrique

Feldverteilung f [el.]
 E: stress grading, stress distribution
 F: répartition f du champ électrique, distribution f du champ électrique

Fell n [Gi.]
 E: sheet of masticated rubber, milled crepe (rubber)
 F: nappe f de caoutchouc malaxé

Fell von der Mischwalze abschneiden [Gi.]
 E: to break the batch loose from the rolls
 F: briser v la nappe de caoutchouc malaxé sur les cylindres

Fernamt n
 E: trunk exchange (GB), toll exchange (US), long distance exchange
 F: central m interurbain

Fernbedienung f
 E: remote control, telecontrol n
 F: télécommande f, commande f à distance

Ferngespräch n
 E: trunk call (GB), toll call (US), long distance call (US)
 F: conversation f interurbaine

Fernmeldeanlage
 E: telecommunications system
 F: installation f de télécommunication

Fernmeldekabel
  E: telecommunications cable, communications cable
  F: câble m de télécommunication, câble m de communication

Fernmeldenetz n
  E: telecommunications network, telecommunications system
  F: réseau m de télécommunication

Fernmeldetechnik f
  E: telecommunications engineering
  F: technique f de télécommunication

Fernmeldeverkehr m
  E: telecommunication n
  F: télécommunication f

Fernmeßkabel n
  E: telemetering cable
  F: câble m de télémesure

Fernnebensprechdämpfung f
  E: far-end crosstalk attenuation
  F: affaiblissement m télédiaphonique

Fernnebensprechen n
  E: far-end cross talk (FEX)
  F: télédiaphonie f

Fernschreibnetz n
  E: telex network
  F: réseau m télex

Fernsehfrequenz f
  E: video frequency
  F: vidéo-fréquence f

Fernsehgegensprechen n
  E: combined television telephone service
  F: service m téléphonique et télévision combiné

Fernsehkanal m
  E: television channel
  F: voie de télévision f

Fernsehpaar n
  E: video pair
  F: paire f de télévision

Fernsehübertragung f
  E: television transmission
  F: transmission f de télévision

Fernsprechamt n
  E: telephone exchange, telephone central office
  F: bureau m téléphonique, central m téléphonique

Fernsprechanschluß m
  E: telephone connection
  F: abonnement m téléphonique, abonné m téléphonique

Fernsprechdoppelleitung f
  E: two-wire telephone circuit, telephone loop
  F: circuit m téléphonique bifilaire

Fernsprechfrequenz f
  E: voice frequency, telephone frequency, speech frequency
  F: fréquence f vocale, fréquence f téléphonique

Fernsprechkabel n
  E: telephone cable
  F: câble m téléphonique

Fernsprechkanal m
  E: telephone channel, voice channel, speech channel
  F: canal m téléphonique, voie f téléphonique

Fernsprechleitung f
  E: telephone circuit, voice circuit, speech circuit
  F: circuit m téléphonique

Fernsprechnetz n
  E: telephone system, telephone network
  F: réseau m téléphonique

Fernsprechschnellverkehr m
  E: no-delay telephone system
  F: service m téléphonique instantané

Fernsprech-Selbstanschluß m
  E: automatic telephone
  F: téléphone m automatique

Fernsprechteilnehmerleitung f
  E: drop wire (telephone cable to connect open wire lines on poles to subscribers' premises) (US), subscriber('s) drop wire, telephone drop, lead(ing)-in wire
  F: ligne f d'abonné téléphonique (raccord à la ligne aérienne), ligne f de desserte d'abonné, fil m d'entrée d'abonné

Fernsprechverkehr m
  E: telephone traffic, line telephony, intercommunication n
  F: trafic m téléphonique

Fernsteuerung f
  E: remote control, telecontrol n
  F: télécommande f, commande f à distance

Fernübertragung f
  E: long distance transmission, teletransmission n
  F: transmission f à grande distance

Fernüberwachung f
  E: remote supervision, remote monitoring
  F: télésurveillance f, surveillance f à distance
Fernvermittlungsstelle f
  E: trunk exchange (GB), toll exchange (US), long distance exchange
  F: central m interurbain
Fertigdraht m
  E: final wire size
  F: fil m de diamètre final
fertiges Kabel
  E: finished cable
  F: câble m fini, câble m terminé
Fertigmaß n
  E: finishing dimension, finished size
  F: dimension f finale
Fertigungsablauf m
  E: production sequence
  F: cycle m de fabrication
Fertigungsabteilung f
  E: production department, manufacturing department
  F: service m de production, atelier m de fabrication
Fertigungsbereich m
  E: range of production
  F: gamme f de fabrication
Fertigungsfehler m
  E: manufacturing defect, manufacturing flaw
  F: vice m de fabrication, défaut m de fabrication
Fertigungsflußschema n
  E: flow chart, flow diagram, process (flow) chart
  F: organigramme m (prod.), ordinogramme m, graphique m de processus, diagramme m de déroulement
Fertigungsgeschwindigkeit f [Masch.]
  E: line speed, production speed, running speed, production rate, operating speed, processing speed
  F: vitesse f de marche f, vitesse f de fabrication, vitesse f de production, vitesse f de travail
Fertigungskontrolle f
  E: process control, manufacturing control, production control
  F: contrôle m en cours de fabrication
Fertigungslänge f
  E: manufacturing length, production length, factory length
  F: longueur f de fabrication
Fertigungsmaßstab, hergestellt im ~
  E: produced on an industrial scale, commercially produced
  F: réalisé adj à l'échelle industrielle
Fertigungsprogramm n
  E: production programme, manufacturing programme, production scheme, manufacturing schedule
  F: programme m de fabrication
Fertigungsreife, bis zur ~ entwickelt
  E: developed to the production stage
  F: étudié jusqu'au stade de fabrication
Fertigungsrichtung, entgegengesetzt der ~
  E: upstream adv
  F: en amont
Fertigungsrichtung, in ~
  E: downstream adv
  F: en aval
Fertigungsspektrum n
  E: range of production
  F: gamme f de fabrication
Fertigungsspektrum, breites ~
  E: highly diversified range of products, broad spectrum of manufacturing activities
  F: gamme f de produits largement diversifiée
Fertigungsstraße f
  E: manufacturing line, production line
  F: chaîne f de fabrication
Fertigungstechnik f
  E: production engineering
  F: technique f de fabrication, technique f de production
fertigungstechnische Entwicklung
  E: production engineering development
  F: étude f de la technique de fabrication
Fertigungstrommel f
  E: machine drum
  F: touret m d'atelier
Fertigungsvorbereitung f
  E: manufacturing planning, work planning, production planning
  F: préparation f du travail
Fertigungsvorschrift f
  E: manufacturing specification

Fertigungsvorschrift
  F: mode m opératoire
Fertigwalzstraße f
  E: finishing train
  F: train m finisseur
Fertigzug m [Drahth.]
  E: finishing pass
  F: tréfilage m à dimensions fines
fest anliegend
  E: giving a tight fit, close-fitting adj, tight-fitting adj, making a tight fit
  F: étant bien serré
Festader f [Nachr. K.]
  E: air-space(d) paper-insulated core (tightly wrapped)
  F: conducteur m à isolement air/papier (rubanage serré)
feste Verdrahtung
  E: permanent wiring, fixed wiring
  F: filerie f fixe
feste Verlegung [Kab.]
  E: fixed installation, permanent installation
  F: installation f fixe
Festigkeit f
  E: stability n, durability n, resistance n, strength n
  F: résistance f, stabilité f, tenue f
festklemmen v
  E: cleat v, clamp v, cramp v
  F: brider v, attacher v, serrer v, agrafer v
Festlegung von Kabeln
  E: cable anchorage
  F: fixation f du câble
Festpunkt für Spulenabstände [Nachr. K.]
  E: section point for loading coil spacing
  F: point m de section pour l'écartement entre bobines de charge
festsitzend adj
  E: giving a tight fit, close-fitting adj, tight-fitting adj, making a tight fit
  F: étant bien serré
feststehend adj
  E: stationary adj, fixed adj
  F: stationnaire adj, fixe adj
Feststellschraube f
  E: locking screw, locking bolt
  F: vis f de blocage
Fettsäure-Weichmacher m
  E: fatty acid plasticizer
  F: plastifiant m derivé d'acide gras
Feuchtegehalt m
  E: moisture content
  F: degré m d'humidité, teneur f en humidité
Feuchtigkeit f
  E: humidity n, moisture n
  F: humidité f
Feuchtigkeit entziehen
  E: dehumidify v, to extract humidity
  F: déshydrater v, déshumidifier v, enlever v l'humidité
Feuchtigkeitsaufnahme f
  E: moisture absorption
  F: reprise f d'humidité, absorption f d'humidité
feuchtigkeitsbeständig adj
  E: moisture-resistant adj
  F: résistant adj à l'humidité
Feuchtigkeitsgehalt m
  E: moisture content
  F: degré m d'humidité, teneur f en humidité
Feuchtigkeitssperre f
  E: moisture barrier
  F: barrière f d'humidité
Feuchtkugel-Temperatur f [Klimat.]
  E: wet bulb temperature
  F: température f au thermomètre humide
Feuchtraumleitung f
  E: damp-proof wiring cable
  F: câble m hydrofuge, câble m pour locaux humides
Feuchtthermometer-Temperatur f [Klimat.]
  E: wet bulb temperature
  F: température f au thermomètre humide
feuerbeständig adj
  E: fire-resistant adj, fire-proof adj, flame-proof adj
  F: résistant adj au feu, résistant adj à la flamme
Feuerbeständigkeit f
  E: fire-resistance n
  F: résistance f au feu
Feuerfestigkeit f
  E: fire-resistance n
  F: résistance f au feu
Feuerraffination f
  E: fire refining
  F: raffinage m au feu

feuerraffiniertes Kupfer
E: fire-refined copper
F: cuivre m raffiné au feu

Filzabstreifer m
E: felt stripper
F: râcloir m en feutre

Firmenkennfaden m
E: manufacturers' identification thread
F: fil m distinctif du fournisseur

Firmenkennzeichen n
E: trademark n, brand mark
F: marque f de fabrique, marque f du fabricant

Flachdraht m
E: flat wire
F: fil m plat, fil m méplat

Flachdrahtarmierung f
E: flat wire armo(u)ring
F: armure f en fils méplats

Flachdrahtbewehrung f
E: flat wire armo(u)ring
F: armure f en fils méplats

Flächenbelegung f
E: space requirement, occupancy n
F: encombrement m

Flächengewicht n
E: weight per square meter
F: poids m au mètre carré

Flächengewicht n (Papier)
E: substance n (paper weight in g/m²)
F: grammage m

Flachkabel n
E: flat type cable
F: câble m méplat

Flachleitung f
E: flat flexible cable, flat twin cable
F: câble m souple méplat

Flachstecker m
E: flat plug
F: fiche f plate, fiche f méplate

Flachwähl-Anlage f
E: panel switching equipment
F: installation f de sélecteurs à panneau

flammenbeständig adj
E: fire-resistant adj, fire-proof adj, flame-proof adj
F: résistant adj au feu, résistant adj à la flamme,

flammenhemmend adj
E: flame-retardant adj
F: retardant adj la flamme

flammenverzögernd adj
E: flame-retardant adj
F: retardant adj la flamme

Flammofen m
E: reverberatory furnace
F: four m à réverbère, fourneau m à réverbère

Flammpunkt m
E: fire point, ignition point, flash point
F: point m d'inflammation

Flammpunkt im geschlossenen Tiegel
E: flash point in a closed cup
F: point m d'éclair en vase fermé, point m d'éclair en coupe fermé

Flammpunkt im offenen Tiegel
E: flash point in an open cup
F: point m d'éclair en vase ouvert, point m d'éclair en coupe ouverte

flammwidrig adj
E: flame-resistant adj, non fire propagating
F: non propagateur de la flamme adj, non propagateur de l'incendie adj, non transmettant la flamme

Flammwidrigkeit f
E: flame resistance
F: non-propagation f de la flamme, non-propagation f de l'incendie, résistance f à la propagation de la flamme

Flammwidrigkeitsprüfung f
E: flame resisting test, flame resistance test
F: essai m de résistance à la propagation de la flamme, essai m de non-propagation de la flamme

Flanschdurchmesser m (Kabeltrommel)
E: flange diameter
F: diamètre m de la joue

Flechtmaschine f
E: braiding machine, braider n
F: machine f à tresser

flexible Leitung
E: flexible cable, flexible cord, flexible n
F: câble m souple, cordon m souple

flexible Verdrahtung
E: flexible wiring
F: filerie f souple

fliegende Säge
E: flying saw
F: scie f volante

fliegende 60

fliegende Schere
  E: flying shear(s)
  F: cisailles *f pl* à porte-à-faux
Fließbeständigkeit *f* [Plast.]
  E: flow resistance
  F: résistance *f* au fluage
Fließen eines Stroms
  E: flow of a current
  F: écoulement *m* d'un courant
Fließen mit Gefälle
  E: gravity flow
  F: écoulement *m* par gravité
Fließgeschwindigkeit *f*
  E: flow rate, flow velocity, rate of flow
  F: vitesse *f* d'écoulement
Fließgrenze *f*
  E: flow limit
  F: limite *f* d'écoulement, limite *f* de fluage, seuil *m* de fluage
Fließkanal *m* [Extr.]
  E: flow channel
  F: profil *m* d'écoulement plastique
Fließpunkt *m*
  E: flow point
  F: point *m* d'écoulement
Fließverhalten *n*
  E: flow behaviour
  F: tenue *f* au fluage
Fließvermögen *n*
  E: fluidity *n*, flow *n*
  F: fluidité *f*
Flitter *m* (Draht)
  E: sliver *n*, spill *n*
  F: paillette *f*
fluchten *v*
  E: to be flush, to be in alignment, to be in line with
  F: affleurer *v*, aligner *v* (s')
Fluchten, zum ~ bringen
  E: align *v*
  F: aligner *v*
flüchtige Bestandteile *m pl*
  E: volatile components
  F: constituants *m pl* volatils, composants *m pl* volatils
Flugplatzbeleuchtungskabel *n*
  E: airport lighting cable
  F: câble *m* pour l'éclairage d'aéroports
Flugzeug-Bordleitung *f*
  E: aircraft wire
  F: câble *m* d'avion
Fluidmischer *m*

  E: fluid mixer
  F: mélangeur *m* du type à fluidification
Flurförderfahrzeug *n*
  E: shop floor transport vehicle
  F: chariot *m* de manutention
Flurförderwesen *n*
  E: floor handling
  F: manutention *f*
Flußdiagramm *n*
  E: flow chart, flow diagram, process (flow) chart
  F: organigramme *m* (prod.), ordinogramme *m*, graphique *m* de processus, diagramme *m* de déroulement
Flüssigkeitstemperierung *f* [Extr.]
  E: thermal liquid control, temperature control by a liquid medium
  F: réglage *m* de la température par un liquide thermique
Flußkabel *n*
  E: river cable
  F: câble *m* sous-fluvial
Flußmittel *n*
  E: flux *n*, soldering flux
  F: flux *m*, fondant *m*
Folie *f* [Plast.]
  E: film *n*
  F: feuille *f*
Folie *f* [Met.]
  E: foil *n*
  F: feuille *f*
Folienband *n*
  E: film tape
  F: ruban *m* de feuille
Förderanlage *f*
  E: conveying system, conveyor *n*, feed system
  F: installation *f* de transport, convoyeur *m*
Förderanlage, pneumatische ~
  E: pneumatic conveying system
  F: installation *f* de transport pneumatique
Förderleistung einer Pumpe
  E: pump output, delivery of a pump
  F: capacité *f* de pompage, débit *m* d'une pompe
Förderschnecke *f* [Extr.]
  E: stockscrew *n*
  F: vis d'extrusion *f*
Forderung, eine ~ erfüllen

Fremdkühlung

- *E:* to meet a requirement
- *F:* satisfaire v à une demande, satisfaire v à une exigence

Form f (Gießen, Pressen)
- *E:* mo(u)ld n
- *F:* moule m

Formänderung f
- *E:* deformation n, distortion n
- *F:* déformation f

Formänderungsbeständigkeit f
- *E:* form-stability n, dimensional stability, resistance to deformation, deformation resistance
- *F:* stabilité f de forme, résistance f à la déformation

Formate n pl [Met.]
- *E:* ingots pl
- *F:* lingots m pl

Formbarkeit f
- *E:* plasticity n, workability n
- *F:* plasticité f, aptitude au façonnage f, aptitude f au moulage, malléabilité f

formbeständig adj
- *E:* form-stable adj, resistant to deformation
- *F:* stable adj de forme

Formbeständigkeit f
- *E:* form-stability n, dimensional stability, resistance to deformation, deformation resistance
- *F:* stabilité f de forme, résistance f à la déformation

Formbrett für Kabel
- *E:* cable forming board, cable lacing board
- *F:* gabarit m pour câbles, planche f de préparation pour câbles

Formenschwindmaß n
- *E:* mo(u)ld shrinkage
- *F:* retrait m au moulage

Formstein m [Kab.]
- *E:* duct block
- *F:* bloc-tube m

Formsteinzug m [K. Verl.]
- *E:* duct-bank n
- *F:* fourreau m porte-cables

Formteil n
- *E:* mo(u)lding n, mo(u)lded part
- *F:* pièce f moulée

fortlaufende Untersuchungen
- *E:* continuing studies
- *F:* études f pl continues

Fourdrinier-Papiermaschine f
- *E:* continuous traveling wire cloth paper machine, Fourdrinier paper machine
- *F:* machine f à papier à toile sans fin, machine f à papier Fourdrinier

fräsen v (Drahtbarren)
- *E:* scalp v
- *F:* scalper v

frei von Hohlräumen
- *E:* void-free adj
- *F:* exempt adj de bulles d'air, exempt adj de poches d'air,

frei von Luftblasen
- *E:* void-free adj
- *F:* exempt adj de bulles d'air, exempt adj de poches d'air,

frei von Lufteinschlüssen
- *E:* void-free adj
- *F:* exempt adj de bulles d'air, exempt adj de poches d'air,

freigeben, für die Fertigung ~
- *E:* to release for factory production
- *F:* relâcher v pour la fabrication, passer v à la fabrication

Freigelände-Prüfung f
- *E:* field test
- *F:* essai m sur chantier

Freilegen des Leiters
- *E:* baring of the conductor, stripping of the conductor
- *F:* dénudage m du conducteur

Freileitung f
- *E:* overhead line
- *F:* ligne f aérienne

Freileitung f [Nachr. K.]
- *E:* open wire line
- *F:* fil m aérien

Freiluft-Anlage f
- *E:* outdoor plant
- *F:* installation f extérieure

Freiluft-Endverschluß m
- *E:* outdoor termination
- *F:* extrémité f extérieure

freitragend adj
- *E:* cantilevered adj
- *F:* non soutenu adj

Fremdkörper m
- *E:* impurity n, foreign matter
- *F:* impureté f, corps m étranger

Fremdkühlung f [Kab.]
- *E:* forced cooling, artificial cooling
- *F:* refroidissement m forcé

Fremdspannung f
  E: external voltage, unweighted noise voltage
  F: tension f non pondérée
Fremdstoff m
  E: impurity n, foreign matter
  F: impureté f, corps m étranger
Fremdstrom m
  E: parasitic current
  F: courant m parasitique
frequenzabhängig adj
  E: dependent on frequency, frequency-dependent adj
  F: dépendant adj de la fréquence
Frequenzband n
  E: frequency band, frequency range
  F: bande f de fréquences, plage f de fréquences, gamme f de fréquences
Frequenzband, effektiv übertragenes ~
  E: effectively transmitted frequency band
  F: bande f de fréquences transmise de façon effective
Frequenzbereich m
  E: frequency band, frequency range
  F: bande f de fréquences, plage f de fréquences, gamme f de fréquences
Frequenzschwankung f
  E: frequency variation, frequency fluctuation
  F: variation f de fréquence
frisches Material [Prüf.]
  E: virgin material
  F: matière f neuve
Fuge f [Papierspinn.]
  E: butt space, butt gap, gap n
  F: déjoint m, joint m
Fühler m
  E: scanning device, scanner n, sensing device, sensor n, detecting element
  F: palpeur m, scanner m, sonde f
Führungsnippel m [Extr.]
  E: guider tip
  F: poinçon m guide
Führungsrolle f
  E: guide roller, guide pulley
  F: rouleau-guide m, poulie f de guidage
Führungsschiene f
  E: guide rail
  F: rail m de guidage, rail m de roulement
Füllen n
  E: filling n
  F: remplissage m
Füllfaktor m
  E: space factor, bulk factor
  F: coefficient m de remplissage, coefficient m de volume
Füllmasse f [K. Garn.]
  E: filling compound, sealing compound, flooding compound
  F: matière f de remplissage
Füllstandsanzeiger m
  E: level indicator
  F: indicateur m du niveau
Füllstandswächter m
  E: level control(ler)
  F: contrôleur m du niveau
Füllstoff m
  E: filler n, loading material
  F: matière f de charge, charge f
füllstoffreich adj
  E: heavily loaded
  F: fortement chargé, à haute teneur en charge
Fülltrichter m [Extr.]
  E: feeding hopper
  F: trémie f d'alimentation, entonnoir m de chargement
Füllung f
  E: filling n
  F: remplissage m
Fundamentrahmen m
  E: base frame
  F: cadre m de base, bâti m d'ensemble
Fundamentschraube f
  E: foundation bolt
  F: boulon m de fondation
Fundamentzeichnung f
  E: foundation drawing
  F: plan m de fondation, dessin m de fondation
Funken m
  E: spark n
  F: étincelle f
Funkenentladung f
  E: spark discharge
  F: décharge f par étincelles
Funkenhorn n
  E: arcing horn
  F: corne f d'arc, corne f de protection
Funkenstrecke f
  E: spark gap
  F: éclateur m
Funkenüberschlag m

Funkenüberschlag (continued)
- E: flash-over *n*, arc-over *n*, spark-over *n*
- F: contournement *m*, amorçage *m*

Funktionsprüfung *f*
- E: functional test
- F: essai *m* de fonctionnement

Funktionsreichweite *f*
- E: operational range
- F: portée *f* de fonctionnement

Funktionsschema *n*
- E: functional diagram, block diagram
- F: schéma *m* fonctionnel

Futter
- E: lining *n*
- F: doublure *f*, revêtement *m*, fourrure *f*

G

Gabelmuffe für drei Adern
- E: trifurcating joint, trifurcating box
- F: boîte *f* tri-mono, boîte *f* de trifurcation

Gabelmuffe für zwei Adern
- E: bifurcating joint
- F: boîte *f* de bifurcation

Gabelstapler *m*
- E: forklift truck
- F: chariot *m* élévateur à fourche

galvanische Kopplung
- E: galvanic coupling
- F: couplage *m* galvanique, couplage *m* par dérivation

galvanische Verzinnung
- E: electro-tinning *n*
- F: étamage *m* galvanique, étamage *m* électrolytique

Ganghöhe einer Schnecke/Schraube
- E: lead of a screw
- F: pas *m* d'une vis

Gangversatz *m* [Bdspinn.]
- E: registration *n*, staggering *n*
- F: chevauchement *m*

Garnituren *f pl*
- E: accessories *pl*
- F: accessoires *m pl*, appareillage *m*

Garn-Nummer *f*
- E: count *n* (of yarn)
- F: numéro *m* de fil

Garnspinnkopf *m*
- E: yarn spinning head
- F: tête *f* à filin

Gasaufnahme *f*
- E: gas absorption
- F: absorption *f* de gaz

Gasaußendruck-Kabel *n*
- E: compression cable, impregnated gas-pressure cable, external gas pressure cable
- F: câble *m* à compression externe de gaz

Gasaußendruck-Kabel im Stahlrohr
- E: pipeline compression cable
- F: câble *m* en tube sous compression externe de gaz

Gasblase *f*
- E: gas bubble
- F: bulle *f* de gaz, bulle *f* gazeuse

Gaschromatographie *f*
- E: gas chromatographic analysis, gas chromatography
- F: chromatographie *f* en phase gazeuse

Gasdichtigkeit *f*
- E: impermeability to gas, gas-tightness *n*, gas impermeability
- F: étanchéité *f* au gaz, imperméabilité *f* au gaz

Gasdruck-Kabel *n*
- E: gas pressure cable, gas-filled cable
- F: câble *m* sous pression de gaz

Gasdruck-Rohrkabel *n*
- E: gas pressure pipe type cable
- F: câble *m* en tube sous pression de gaz

Gasdurchlässigkeit *f*
- E: permeability to gas
- F: perméabilité *f* au gaz

Gasen *n*
- E: gassing *n*
- F: gazage *m*

gasförmiger Isolierstoff
- E: gaseous insulating material
- F: isolant *m* gazeux

Gasinnendruck-Kabel *n*
- E: gas-filled internal pressure cable, internal gas pressure cable
- F: câble *m* à pression interne de gaz

Gasruß *m*
- E: gas black
- F: noir *m* de gaz

Gasspürgerät *n* [Nachr. K.]
- E: cable sniffer

Gasspürgerät
- F: appareil *m* détecteur de gaz

gasundurchlässig *adj*
- E: gas-tight *adj*, impermeable to gas
- F: étanche *adj* au gaz, imperméable *adj* au gaz,

Gasundurchlässigkeit *f*
- E: impermeability to gas, gas-tightness *n*, gas impermeability
- F: étanchéité *f* au gaz, imperméabilité *f* au gaz

Gaußsche Verteilung
- E: Gaussian (distribution) law
- F: loi *f* gaussienne, répartition *f* gaussienne

Gebläse *n*
- E: fan *n*, blower *n*, ventilator *n*
- F: ventilateur *m*

geblasenes Bitumen
- E: blown bitumen, oxidized bitumen
- F: bitume *m* soufflé

gedämpft schwingende Wellen
- E: damped oscillation waves
- F: ondes *f pl* d'oscillation amortie

Geer-Alterungsofen *m*
- E: Geer ag(e)ing oven
- F: étuve *f* de vieillissement Geer

geerdet *adj*
- E: earthed *adj* (GB), grounded *adj* (US),
- F: mis *adj* à la terre

geerdeter Sternpunkt (Nullpunkt)
- E: earthed neutral (GB), grounded neutral (US)
- F: neutre *m* à la terre, neutre *m* mis à la terre

Gefällezuführung *f*
- E: gravity feed
- F: alimentation *f* par gravité

gefalzter Aluminiummantel
- E: folded aluminium sheath
- F: gaine *f* repliée en aluminium

Geflecht *n*
- E: braid *n*, braiding *n*
- F: tresse *f*

gefüllt, kontinuierlich ~es Kabel [Tel. K.]
- E: fully filled cable, continuously filled cable
- F: câble *m* rempli de façon continue, câble *m* à remplissage total, câble *m* à remplissage continu

Gegenholm *m* [Met.-Strangpr.]
- E: counterplaten *n*
- F: contre-traverse *f*

Gegeninduktivität *f*
- E: mutual inductance
- F: induction *f* mutuelle

Gegenkopplung *f*
- E: negative feed-back
- F: contre-réaction *f*

Gegenmitsprechen *n*
- E: side-to-phantom far-end crosstalk
- F: télédiaphonie *f* entre réel et fantôme

Gegennebensprechdämpfung *f*
- E: far-end crosstalk attenuation
- F: affaiblissement *m* télédiaphonique

Gegennebensprechen *n*
- E: far-end cross talk (FEX)
- F: télédiaphonie *f*

Gegenschlagverseilung *f*
- E: reverse(d) lay stranding
- F: câblage *m* en couches croisées, câblage *m* en sens alterné

gegenseitige Erwärmung
- E: mutual heating
- F: échauffement *m* mutuel

gegenseitige Störungen
- E: mutual interference
- F: interférence *f* mutuelle

Gegenübersprechen *n*
- E: side-to-side far-end crosstalk
- F: télédiaphonie *f* entre réel et réel

Gegenwendel *f*
- E: anti-twist tape, counter helix
- F: hélice *f* anti-torsion

Gehäuse *n*
- E: housing *n*, casing *n*, cabinet *n*
- F: boîte *f*, caisse *f*

gekapselte Schaltanlagen
- E: metal-clad switch-gear, cubicle type switch-gear
- F: disjoncteurs *m pl* enfermés, disjoncteurs *m pl* blindés

gekoppelt mit
- E: tied in with, interlocked with
- F: lié *adj* à, couplé *adj* avec,

gekreuzte Adern
- E: transposed conductors, transposed cores
- F: conducteurs *m pl* transposés

Geltungsbereich *m*
- E: scope *n* (of application)
- F: domaine *m* d'emploi

gemeinsame gepreßte Aderumhüllung

gemeinsame gewickelte Aderumhüllung
- E: taped inner covering, lapped inner covering
- F: revêtement *m* interne rubané

Gemeinschaftsantenne *f*
- E: community antenna
- F: antenne *f* collective

Gemeinschaftsantennenfernsehen *n*
- E: Community Antenna Television (CATV)
- F: réception *f* collective d'antenne de télévision

Gemeinschaftsleitung *f*
- E: party line
- F: ligne *f* partagée

Gemisch *n*
- E: mixture *n*, blend *n*, compound *n*, composition *n*
- F: mélange *m*, composition *f*

Genauigkeit, mit einer ~ von ... mm
- E: to nearest ... mm, accurate within ... mm
- F: à ... mm près, avec une précision de ... mm

genügen, einer Anforderung ~
- E: to meet a requirement
- F: satisfaire *v* à une demande, satisfaire *v* à une exigence

gepreßt, gemeinsame ~e Aderumhüllung
- E: extruded inner covering, inner filling sheath
- F: gaine *f* de bourrage, gaine *f* formant bourrage

Geradeausstecker *m*
- E: straight plug
- F: fiche *f* droite

geradkettiges PE
- E: straight-chain PE, linear PE
- F: polyéthylène *m* à chaîne droite, polyéthylène *m* linéaire

Gerät *n*
- E: apparatus *n*, instrument *n*, device *n*, equipment *n*
- F: appareil *m*, instrument *m*

Geräte-Anschlußschnur *f*
- E: appliance cord
- F: cordon *m* de raccordement d'appareil, cordon *m* d'alimentation d'appareil, cordon *m* souple, câble *m* souple de raccordement

Geräteschnur *f* (für vielbewegte Verbindungen)
- E: retractile cord
- F: cordon *m* souple rétractile

Gerätesteckdose *f*
- E: appliance connector
- F: connecteur *m* (d'appareil)

Geräuschfilter *m*
- E: noise suppressor
- F: filtre *m* de bruit

Geräuschpegel *m* [Nachr. K.]
- E: noise level, interference level
- F: niveau *m* de bruit, niveau *m* des perturbations

Geräuschspannung *f*
- E: noise voltage
- F: tension *f* de bruit, tension *f* psophométrique

geriffelt *adj*
- E: grooved *adj*, ribbed *adj*
- F: cannelé *adj*, strié *adj*, rainé *adj*

Gesamtdämpfung *f*
- E: total cable equivalent, total loss, total attenuation
- F: atténuation *f* totale

Gesamtkopplung *f*
- E: total coupling
- F: couplage *m* total

geschichtete Papierisolierung
- E: graded paper insulation
- F: isolant *m* papier échelonné

geschirmtes Kabel
- E: screened cable, shielded cable
- F: câble *m* sous écran, câble *m* blindé

geschirmtes Paar
- E: screened pair, shielded pair
- F: paire *f* sous écran

geschlossene Ringwellung
- E: closed corrugation
- F: ondulation *f* à anneaux fermés

geschlossene Wendel
- E: closed helix
- F: hélice *f* fermée

geschlossener Kreis
- E: closed circuit
- F: circuit *m* fermé

geschützt *adj*
- E: protected *adj*
- F: protégé *adj*

Geschwindigkeit *f*

Geschwindigkeit

    E: number of revolutions per minute (r.p.m.), rotational speed, speed *n*
    F: nombre *m* de tours par minute (t.p.m.), vitesse *f* de rotation, vitesse *f*

Geschwindigkeitsbereich *m*
    E: speed range
    F: gamme *f* de vitesses

gestaffelt *adj*
    E: staggered *adj*, graded *adj*
    F: en quinconce, échelonné *adj*, décalé *adj*, gradué *adj*, étagé *adj*

Gestell *n*
    E: rack *n*, frame *n*
    F: bâti *m*

gesteuert, Kabel mit ~em Dielektrikum (Ölkabel, Gasdruckkabel)
    E: cable with controlled dielectric, controlled dielectric cable
    F: câble *m* à diélectrique contrôlé

gestreckte Verseilung
    E: stranding without pretwist
    F: câblage *m* sans prétorsion

gestrecktes Kabelmuster
    E: straightened cable sample
    F: échantillon *m* de câble étiré

gestrichelte Linie
    E: dashed line
    F: ligne *f* brisée, tireté *m*

Gestrickband, Kupfer-~ (verzinnt) *n* [Kab.]
    E: tinned copper braid, tinned copper mesh
    F: tresse *f* en cuivre étamé

geteilt *adj*
    E: split *adj*, two-piece *adj*
    F: en deux pièces, divisé *adj*

getränktes Papier
    E: impregnated paper
    F: papier *m* imprégné

Getriebe *n*
    E: gear(ing) *n*
    F: engrenage *m*, agencement *m*

Gewebe *n*
    E: fabric *n*
    F: toile *f*, tissu *m*

Gewebeband *n*
    E: fabric tape, textile tape
    F: ruban *m* textile

gewellter Mantel
    E: corrugated sheath
    F: gaine *f* ondulée

Gewichtsprozent *n*
    E: percentage by weight, percent in weight
    F: pourcent(age) *m* en poids

Gewichtsteil *n*
    E: part by weight
    F: partie *f* en poids

Gewichtsverlust *m*
    E: weight loss
    F: perte *f* de masse, perte *f* de poids

gewickelt, gemeinsame ~e Aderumhüllung
    E: taped inner covering, lapped inner covering
    F: revêtement *m* interne rubané

gewickelte Isolierung
    E: tape insulation, taped insulation, lapped insulation
    F: isolation *f* rubanée

gewickelte Muffe
    E: lapped joint
    F: jonction *f* reconstituée

gewickelte Umhüllung
    E: taped covering, lapped covering
    F: revêtement *m* rubané

gewickelter Endverschluß
    E: lapped termination
    F: extrémité *f* reconstituée

Gewinde, linksgängiges ~
    E: left-hand(ed) thread
    F: filet *m* à gauche

Gewinde, rechtsgängiges ~
    E: right-hand(ed) thread
    F: filet *m* à droite

Gewindegang der Schnecke [Extr.]
    E: flight of the screw, thread of the screw
    F: filet *m* de la vis, pas *m* de la vis, spire *f* de la vis

GGA (s. Großgemeinschaftsantennen-Anlage)

Gießen *n* (in Formen)
    E: casting *n*
    F: coulage *m*, coulée *f*

Gießgeschwindigkeit *f*
    E: casting speed, pouring speed, casting rate
    F: vitesse *f* de coulée

Gießharz *n*
    E: casting resin, cast resin
    F: résine *f* moulée

Gießharz-Isolator *m*
    E: casting resin insulator
    F: isolateur *m* en résine moulée

Gießharz-Muffe f
 E: casting resin joint
 F: jonction f en résine moulée
Gießling m
 E: casting n
 F: pièce f coulée
Gießpfanne f [Gießw.]
 E: tundish n, pouring ladle
 F: poche f de coulée
Gießrad n [Gießw.]
 E: casting wheel
 F: roue f de coulée
Gießrinne f [Gießw.]
 E: launder n, transfer launder, transfer trough
 F: rigole f de transfert, rigole f de coulée
Gießstrang m [Gießw.]
 E: cast bar
 F: barre f coulée
Gießtemperatur f
 E: pouring temperature, casting temperature
 F: température f de coulée
Gießtopf m [Gießw.]
 E: tundish n, pouring ladle
 F: poche f de coulée
Gießtülle f
 E: pouring spout
 F: bec m de coulée
Gießwalzanlage f
 E: continuous casting and rolling plant
 F: installation f de coulée continue laminage
Gießwalzdraht m
 E: continuously cast and rolled rod
 F: fil m fabriqué en coulée continue laminage
Gießwalzen n
 E: continuous casting and rolling (CCR)
 F: coulée f continue laminage
Glasfaser f
 E: glass fibre (GB), glass fiber (US)
 F: fibre f de verre
Glasfasergewebe n
 E: glass fibre fabric
 F: tissu m de verre
Glasfaser-Wellenleiter m
 E: glass fibre waveguide
 F: guide m d'ondes en fibres de verre
Glasisolator m
 E: glass insulator
 F: isolateur m en verre
Glasseide f
 E: glass fibre yarn
 F: soie f de verre
Glasseidenband n
 E: glass fibre tape
 F: ruban m en soie de verre
glatte Oberfläche
 E: smooth surface, plain surface
 F: surface f lisse
glatter Mantel
 E: plain sheath
 F: gaine f lisse
gleichbleibende Belastung
 E: constant load
 F: charge f constante
Gleichgewichtstemperatur f
 E: equilibrium temperature
 F: température f d'équilibre
Gleichgewichtszustand m
 E: state of equilibrium
 F: état m d'équilibre
Gleichlaufregler m
 E: synchronous speed regulating device
 F: régulateur m de synchronisation de vitesses
gleichmäßige Verteilung
 E: even distribution, uniform distribution
 F: répartition f uniforme
Gleichspannung f
 E: direct voltage, d.c. voltage, continuous voltage
 F: tension f continue
Gleichspannungsfestigkeit f
 E: d.c. voltage strength
 F: tenue f sous tension continue
Gleichstrom m
 E: direct current (d.c.), continuous current
 F: courant m continu
Gleichstrom-Datenübertragung mit niedriger Sendespannung
 E: low transmission voltage d.c. data transmission
 F: transmission f d'informations en courant continu à basse tension d'émission
Gleichstromübertrager m [Nachr.]
 E: d.c. relay repeater
 F: répéteur m à relais en courant

Gleichstromübertrager

continu

Gleitdraht m
 E: skid wire
 F: fil m de glissement

Gleitentladung f
 E: surface discharge
 F: décharge f superficielle

Gleitmittel n
 E: grease n, lubricant n
 F: matière f lubrifiante, lubrifiant m

Gleitmodul n
 E: shear modulus
 F: module m d'élasticité au cisaillement

Gleitschiene f
 E: slide bar, slide rail
 F: glissière f, chemin m de glissement, patin m

Glimmbeständigkeit f
 E: corona resistance, glow stability
 F: résistance f à l'effet de couronne, résistance f à l'effet de corona

Glimmen n [el.]
 E: corona
 F: couronne f, effet m de couronne

Glimmentladung f
 E: corona discharge, ionization discharge
 F: effluve f, décharge f par ionisation, décharge f en couronne

Glimmergewebeband n
 E: mica tape
 F: ruban m mica

glimmfrei adj [el.]
 E: corona-free adj
 F: exempt adj d'effet de couronne

Glimmschutz m
 E: corona protection
 F: protection f contre l'effet de couronne

Glockenisolator m
 E: shed insulator, cup insulator, bell-shaped insulator, dome-shaped insulator, petticoat insulator, insulating bell
 F: isolateur m à cloche, cloche f isolante

Glockenisolator mit doppelter Bundrille
 E: double groove insulator
 F: isolateur m à double rainure

Glockenisolator mit zwei Halsrillen
 E: double groove insulator
 F: isolateur m à double rainure

Glühanlage f
 E: annealer n, annealing plant
 F: recuiseur m

glühen v
 E: anneal v
 F: recuire v

glühen, spannungsfrei ~
 E: normalize v
 F: normaliser v

Glühen n
 E: annealing n
 F: recuit m

Glührückstand m
 E: ash n, ignition residue
 F: résidu m de calcination, résidu m de recuit

Glühverlust m
 E: annealing loss
 F: perte f au recuit

Graben m (s. Kabelgraben)

Gradient m
 E: gradient n
 F: gradient m

Grädigkeit f (Temp.Unterschr.zw. Kühlmedien)
 E: temperature difference
 F: différence f de température

Granulat n
 E: granules pl, pellets pl, granulate n
 F: granulés m pl

Granulator m
 E: granulator n, granulating machine, dicer n, pelletizer n
 F: granulateur m

Granulatsilo m
 E: granules storage bin
 F: silo m à granulés

granulieren v
 E: pelletize v, granulate v
 F: granuler v

graphisch darstellen
 E: to plot a graph, to plot graphically
 F: représenter v graphiquement

graphische Darstellung
 E: diagram n, graph n, graphic representation, chart n
 F: diagramme m, représentation f graphique, graphique m

Grat m
 E: fin n, burr n, flash n
 F: bavure f, arête f

Greifer m (Raupenabzug)

Grenzbedingungen f pl
  E: boundary conditions
  F: conditions f pl aux limites

Grenz-Dauerfestigkeit f
  E: maximum long-time strength
  F: tenue f maximale en longue durée

Grenzfall m
  E: border-line case
  F: cas m limite

Grenzfläche f
  E: interface n
  F: surface f de séparation, interface f

Grenzflächendruck m
  E: interface pressure
  F: pression f à la surface de séparation

Grenzleistung f
  E: ultimate load, load limit
  F: charge f limite

Grenzschicht-Effekt m
  E: interfacial effect
  F: effet m interfacial

Grenztemperatur f
  E: limit temperature, temperature limit
  F: température f limite

Grenzwert m
  E: limiting value, limit n
  F: valeur f limite, limite f

Grobdraht m [Drahtl.]
  E: wire rod, redraw rod
  F: fil m machine, fil m ébauche, fil m pour retréfilage

Grobdrahtring m
  E: rod coil, coil of rod
  F: couronne f de fil machine

Grobdrahtziehmaschine f
  E: rod breakdown machine
  F: tréfileuse f pour fil machine

Grobdrahtzug m
  E: rod breakdown
  F: tréfilage m du fil machine

Grobeinstellung f
  E: coarse adjustment
  F: réglage m approximatif, réglage m grossier

grobkörnige Struktur
  E: coarse-grain structure
  F: structure f à gros grains

Grobvakuum n
  E: vacuum 760 to 100 torr
  F: vide m de 760 à 100 torr

Großgemeinschaftsantennen-Anlage (GGA) f
  E: Community Antenna Television System (CATV)
  F: installation f de réception collective d'antenne de télévision

Großversuch m
  E: large-scale trial
  F: essai m à grande échelle

Grubenkabel n
  E: mining cable, mine cable
  F: câble m de mines

Grubenschachtkabel n
  E: mine shaft cable, shaft cable
  F: câble m pour puits de mines

Grubenstreckenkabel n
  E: gallery cable, mine gallery cable
  F: câble m pour galeries de mines

Grundbündel n [Nachr. K.]
  E: primary unit, primary core unit, basic unit, sub-unit n
  F: faisceau m élémentaire, faisceau m de base

Grundgesamtheit f [Math.]
  E: population n
  F: population f

Grundlagenforschung f
  E: fundamental research, basic research
  F: recherche f fondamentale

Grundmischung f
  E: master batch, pre-mix n
  F: mélange m mère, mélange m maître

Grundplatte f
  E: base plate, mounting base
  F: plaque f de base, socle m

Grundrahmen m
  E: base frame
  F: cadre m de base, bâti m d'ensemble

Grundring m [Met.-Strangpr.]
  E: base ring
  F: anneau m de fond, bague f de fond

Grundrißzeichnung f
  E: layout drawing
  F: plan m d'ensemble

Grundviskosität f
  E: intrinsic viscosity
  F: viscosité f intrinsèque

Grundwasser n [K. Verl.]
  E: ground water, subsoil water
  F: eau f souterraine, nappe f d'eau

grüngelbe Ader
 E: green-yellow core
 F: conducteur *m* vert-jaune

Gruppenlaufzeit *f* [Nachr.]
 E: group propagation time, group delay time
 F: temps *m* de propagation de groupe

Gruppenumsetzer *m* [Nachr.]
 E: group modulator
 F: équipement *m* de modulation de groupe

Gruppieren von Fertigungslängen
 E: grouping of factory lengths
 F: groupement *m* de longueurs de fabrication

Gruppieren, Ausgleichen durch ~ nach elektrischen Werten [Nachr. K.]
 E: compensation by grouping according to electrical values
 F: compensation *f* par groupement suivant les valeurs électriques

Gummi *m* (vulkanisierter Kautschuk)
 E: rubber *n*
 F: caoutchouc *m* (vulcanisé)

Gummiaderleitung mit erhöhter Wärmebeständigkeit
 E: rubber-insulated wire with increased heat resistance
 F: conducteur *m* isolé au caoutchouc avec résistance accrue aux températures élevées

Gummiaderleitung, wärmebeständige ~
 E: heat-resistant rubber-insulated cable
 F: conducteur *m* (à âme souple) isolé au caoutchouc résistant à la chaleur

Gummiaderschnur *f*
 E: braided flexible cord
 F: cordon *m* souple sous tresse

gummibeschichtetes Baumwollband
 E: proofed cotton tape
 F: ruban *m* de coton caoutchouté

Gummi-Einführungstülle *f* (gegen Ausfransen von Kabelenden)
 E: wire binding sleeve
 F: passe-fil *m* en caoutchouc

gummiertes Textilband
 E: proofed textile tape, rubber-coated textile tape
 F: ruban *m* textile caoutchouté

Gummiisolierung *f*
 E: rubber insulation
 F: isolation *f* caoutchouc

Gummikneter *m*
 E: rubber kneader, Banbury-mixer *n*, Banbury-kneader *n*
 F: mélangeur *m* à caoutchouc, mélangeur *m* Banbury, malaxeur *m* Banbury

Gummi-Mantel *m*
 E: rubber sheath
 F: gaine *f* de caoutchouc

Gummimantelmischung für starke Beanspruchung
 E: tough-rubber sheathing compound
 F: mélange *m* gaine de caoutchouc pour contraintes fortes

Gummimischerei *f*
 E: rubber mixing plant
 F: installation *f* de préparation des mélanges de caoutchouc

Gummimischung *f*
 E: rubber compound
 F: mélange *m* de caoutchouc

Gummischlauchleitung *f*
 E: tough-rubber sheathed cable, rubber jacket core
 F: câble *m* souple sous gaine de caoutchouc

Gummischlauchleitung, leichte ~
 E: ordinary tough-rubber sheathed flexible cord
 F: câble *m* souple sous gaine ordinaire de caoutchouc

Gummischlauchleitung, schwere ~
 E: heavy tough-rubber sheathed flexible cable
 F: câble *m* souple sous gaine épaisse de caoutchouc

Gummitülle *f* (für Kabelenden)
 E: wire binding sleeve
 F: passe-fil *m* en caoutchouc

Gürtelkabel
 E: belted cable
 F: câble *m* à ceinture

Gußblock *m*
 E: wire bar, ingot *n*
 F: lingot *m*

gußeisernes Muffengehäuse
 E: cast iron joint box
 F: boîte *f* de jonction en fonte

Gußgrat *m*
 E: fin *n*, burr *n*, flash *n*

Gußhaut f
- E: skin n (casting)
- F: croûte f de la fonte, peau f de la fonte, pellicule f de coulée

Güteklasse f
- E: quality grade, quality n
- F: classe f de qualité, qualité f

Güteprüfung f
- E: quality inspection, quality test, quality control
- F: contrôle m de qualité, surveillance f de la qualité

Gütevorschrift f
- E: quality specification
- F: spécification f de qualité

Guttapercha f
- E: gutta percha
- F: gutta-percha f

H

haften v
- E: adhere v, bond v, stick v
- F: adhérer v, coller v

Haftgrundierung f
- E: primer n, wash primer
- F: couche f de fond

Haftmasse f
- E: non-draining compound, nd-compound n
- F: matière f non migrante, matière f nd

Haftmassekabel n
- E: non-draining cable, nd-cable n
- F: câble m à matière non migrante, câble m nd

Haftung f
- E: adhesion n, adherence n, bonding n, sticking n
- F: adhésion f, adhérance f, collage m

Haftvermittler m
- E: adhesive n, bonding agent
- F: adhésif m, colle f

Haftvermögen n
- E: tackiness n, adhesive power, peel strength
- F: adhérence f, adhésivité f

halber Leiter
- E: conductor with reduced cross-sectional area
- F: âme f à section réduite

Halbfertigfabrikat n
- E: semi-finished product
- F: semi-produit m, demi-produit m, produit m semi-fini

Halbleiter-Verstärkung f
- E: solid-state amplification
- F: amplification f par semi-conducteurs, amplification f à transistors

Halbschale f
- E: half shell
- F: demi-coquille f

Haltbarkeit f (Werkstoffe)
- E: shelf life, storage stability
- F: limite f de stockage, stabilité f au stockage

Halterung f
- E: holder n, support n
- F: support m

Haltestellenmarkierungen f pl (Met.-Strangpr.)
- E: bamboo rings, stop marks
- F: nœuds m pl de bambou

Haltewendel f [Kab.]
- E: binder n, holding tape, reinforcement helix
- F: frettage m, spirale f de fixation

Haltezeiten f pl [Met.-Strangpr.]
- E: stoppage periods
- F: temps m pl d'arrêt

Hand, von ~ aufgebracht
- E: hand-applied adj
- F: posé adj à la main

Handapparateschnur f (kleingewendelt, dehnbar)
- E: retractile cord
- F: cordon m souple rétractile

handbetätigt adj
- E: hand-operated adj, manually operated
- F: commandé adj manuellement, à commande manuelle

Handbetrieb m
- E: manual operation, hand operation, manual control
- F: opération f manuelle, commande f manuelle, opération f à main

handelsüblich adj
- E: commercial adj
- F: commercial adj, du type commercial

Handhabung

Handhabung, leichte ~
 E: ease of manipulation, ease of operation, working ease
 F: aisance f de manipulation, aisance f de manœuvre

Handloch n [Nachr.]
 E: handhole n
 F: trou m de poing

Handsteuerung f
 E: manual operation, hand operation, manual control
 F: opération f manuelle, commande f manuelle, opération f à main

Hängeisolator m
 E: suspension insulator, chain insulator
 F: isolateur m suspendu, isolateur m de suspension

hantelförmig adj
 E: dumb-bell shaped
 F: en forme d'haltère

hantelförmiges Prüfstück
 E: dumb-bell shaped test piece
 F: éprouvette f en forme d'haltère

härtbar adj
 E: hardenable adj
 F: durcissable adj

Härtbarkeit f
 E: hardenability n
 F: aptitude au durcissement f

harte Kunststoffe
 E: rigid plastics
 F: matières f pl plastiques rigides

Härte f
 E: hardness n
 F: dureté f

Härtegrad m [Met.]
 E: degree of hardness, temper n
 F: degré m de dureté

härten v [Plast.]
 E: cure v
 F: durcir v

Härteprüfer m
 E: hardness tester, durometer n
 F: appareil m de contrôle de la dureté, duromètre m

harter Draht
 E: hard-drawn wire
 F: fil m dur, fil m écroui

Härter m
 E: hardener n, curing agent
 F: durcisseur m, agent de durcissement m

Hartgewebe n
 E: synthetic resin-bonded fabric, laminated fabric
 F: stratifié m, tissu m revêtu de résin synthétique

hartgezogener Draht
 E: hard-drawn wire
 F: fil m dur, fil m écroui

Hartlot n
 E: brass solder, brazing solder, hard solder, brazing alloy
 F: brasure f

hartlöten v
 E: braze v
 F: braser v

Hartmetall-Ziehstein m
 E: hard metal (drawing) die, tungsten carbide (drawing) die
 F: filière f (de tréfilage) en métal dur, filière f (de tréfilage) en carbure de tungstène

Hartpapier n
 E: synthetic resin-bonded paper, laminated paper
 F: papier m dur, papier m imprégné de résine synthétique

Hart-PVC n
 E: rigid PVC
 F: PVC m rigide

Härtung f
 E: hardening n
 F: durcissement m

hartwerden v
 E: solidify v, freeze v, set v, harden v
 F: solidifier v (se), congéler v, durcir

Harz n (Kunstharz)
 E: resin n
 F: résine f

Harz n (Naturharz)
 E: rosin n, gum rosin
 F: colophane f

Haubenglühofen m
 E: bell type (annealing) furnace, hood type (annealing) furnace, top hat (annealing) furnace
 F: four m à tremper, four m pour recuit brillant

Häufung von Kabeln [K. Verl.]
 E: grouping of cables, accumulation of cables
 F: accumulation f de câbles, groupement m de câbles

Hauptbündel n [Nachr. K.]

auptkabel n
- E: main unit, main core unit
- F: faisceau *m* principal

auptkabel n
- E: main cable, mains cable
- F: câble *m* principal

auptspeisekabel n
- E: main cable, mains cable
- F: câble *m* principal

auptverstärkerstelle f
- E: main repeater station
- F: station *f* principale de répéteurs

ausanschlußkabel n [En. K.]
- E: service cable, branch cable, service drop cable
- F: câble *m* de raccordement domestique, câble *m* de branchement domestique

ausanschlußleitung f [Tel.]
- E: direct line, subscriber's line
- F: ligne *f* d'abonné

ausanschlußmuffe f
- E: house service box
- F: boîte *f* de raccordement domestique

ausgeräteleitung f
- E: appliance wire
- F: câble *m* pour appareils électrodomestiques, câble *m* pour appareils électroménagers

ausinstallation f
- E: house wiring
- F: installation *f* intérieure

ausinstallationsleitung f [En. K.]
- E: house wiring cable
- F: câble *m* domestique

auszuführungsleitung f
- E: drop wire (telephone cable to connect open wire lines on poles to subscribers' premises) (US), subscriber(s) drop wire, telephone drop, lead(ing)-in wire
- F: ligne *f* d'abonné téléphonique (raccord à la ligne aérienne), ligne *f* de desserte d'abonné, fil *m* d'entrée d'abonné

auteffekt m [el.]
- E: skin effect
- F: effet *m* de peau

ißluftschweißen mit Kunststoff-Drahtzufuhr
- E: hot-air welding with plastic welding rod
- F: soudage *m* à air chaud avec fil de soudage plastique

Heißstelle f
- E: hot spot
- F: point *m* chaud, pointe *f* locale de température

Heizband n
- E: heating collar
- F: ruban *m* de chauffage, collier chauffant *m*

Heizbandage f
- E: heating tapes *pl*
- F: frette *f* de chauffage

Heizkabel n
- E: heating cable
- F: câble *m* de chauffage, câble *m* chauffant

Heizkessel m [Vulk.]
- E: vulcanizing pan, autoclave *n*
- F: autoclave *m* de vulcanisation

Heizleistung f
- E: heating power
- F: puissance *f* de chauffage

Heizleitung f
- E: heating wire
- F: câble *m* de chauffage, conducteur *m* chauffant

Heizschlange f
- E: heating coil
- F: serpentin *m* de chauffage

Heizung f
- E: heating *n*
- F: chauffage *m*

Heizwiderstand m
- E: heating resistor
- F: résistance *f* de chauffage

Heizzone f [Extr.]
- E: heating zone
- F: zone *f* de chauffage

Hertz (Hz)
- E: cycles per second (cps), hertz
- F: cycles *m pl* par seconde, hertz, périodes *f pl* par seconde

herunterziehen v (auf) [Drahth.]
- E: draw down v (to)
- F: réduire *v* le diamètre (à)

herunterziehen v (Metallmantel)
- E: die down *v*
- F: rétrécir *v*, rétreindre *v*

Hessianband n (Jute)
- E: hessian tape
- F: ruban *m* Hessian

HF (s. Hochfrequenz)

HF-Antennenkabel n

HF-Antennenkabel

    E: high-frequency antenna cable
    F: câble *m* d'antenne à haute fréquence

HGÜ (s. Hochspannungs-Gleichstrom-Übertragung)

Hilfsabzugsscheibe *f*
    E: auxiliary pull-off capstan
    F: cabestan *m* de tirage auxiliaire

Hilfsader *f*
    E: test(ing) wire, pilot wire, test(ing) conductor, pilot core, pilot conductor
    F: fil *m* d'essai, fil *m* pilote

Hilfsarbeiter *m*
    E: helper *n*, unskilled worker
    F: aide *m*, auxiliaire *m*

Hilfsspannung *f*
    E: auxiliary voltage
    F: tension *f* auxiliaire

Hilfsvorrichtung *f*
    E: auxiliary device
    F: dispositif *m* auxiliaire

Hintereinanderschaltung *f*
    E: series circuit, series connection
    F: montage *m* en série, connexion *f* en série, couplage *m* en série

Hintereinander-Schaltung *f* [mech.]
    E: tandem arrangement, tandem connection
    F: disposition *f* en tandem

Hin- und Herbewegung *f*
    E: reciprocation *n*, reciprocating motion, to-and-fro movement
    F: mouvement *m* de va-et-vient, mouvement *m* alternatif

hitzebeständige Aderleitung
    E: heat-resistant insulated wire
    F: conducteur *m* résistant aux températures élevées

hitzebeständige Schlauchleitung
    E: heat-resistant sheathed flexible cable
    F: câble *m* souple sous gaine résistant aux températures élevées

Hitzebeständigkeit *f*
    E: heat resistance, thermal resistance, thermal stability
    F: résistance *f* à la chaleur, résistance *f* thermique, stabilité *f* thermique

H-Kabel (s. Höchstädter-Kabel)

hochbeansprucht *adj*
    E: heavily loaded, heavily stressed, highly stressed
    F: fortement chargé

hochbelastet *adj*
    E: heavily loaded, heavily stressed, highly stressed
    F: fortement chargé

hochbewegliche Verbindungsschnur
    E: retractile cord
    F: cordon *m* souple rétractile

Hochdruck-Ölkabel im Stahlrohr
    E: high-pressure oil-filled pipe type cable, Oilostatic-cable *n*
    F: câble *m* en tube d'acier sous haute pression d'huile, câble *m* Oléostatique

Hochdruck-PE *n*
    E: low-density PE (LD-PE), high-pressure PE (HP-PE)
    F: polyéthylène *m* basse densité, polyéthylène *m* haute pression

Hochfrequenz (HF) *f*
    E: high frequency (HF), radio frequency
    F: haute fréquence *f* (HF), fréquence *f* radioélectrique

Hochfrequenz-Antennenkabel *n*
    E: high-frequency antenna cable
    F: câble *m* d'antenne à haute fréquence

Hochfrequenzkabel *n*
    E: radio frequency cable, high-frequency cable
    F: câble *m* à haute fréquence, câble *m* à fréquence radioélectrique

Hochfrequenz-Koaxialkabel *n*
    E: high-frequency coaxial cable, radio frequency coaxial cable, coaxial cable for high-frequency transmission
    F: câble *m* coaxial à haute fréquence, câble *m* coaxial à fréquence radioélectrique

Hochführung *f* [Kab.]
    E: vertical installation
    F: installation *f* verticale

Hochführungsschacht *m* [Kab.]
    E: cable shaft, vertical wall duct
    F: puits *m* de montée

Hochleistungs-Doppelschlag-Bündelverseilmaschine *f*
    E: double-twist high-speed bunching machine
    F: tordeuse *f* double-torsion à grande vitesse

Hochleistungskabel n
  E: high power cable, heavy duty cable
  F: câble m à grande puissance
Hochleistungsmaschine f
  E: high-capacity machine, high-speed machine, heavy-duty machine
  F: machine f à grand rendement, machine f à grand débit, machine f à grande puissance, machine f à grande vitesse
Hochleistungsübertragung f
  E: bulk power transmission
  F: transport m de grandes (fortes) puissances
hochleitfähig adj
  E: highly conductive, high-conductivity...
  F: à haute conductibilité
hochmolekular adj
  E: of high molecular weight, high-molecular... adj
  F: à haut poids moléculaire
hochohmig adj
  E: high-ohmic adj, of high resistance, highly resistive
  F: de haute valeur ohmique, de grande résistance
hochpaariges Kabel [Tel.]
  E: multiple pair cable, multipair cable, multipaired cable, large-capacity cable
  F: câble m multipaire, câble m multitoron, câble m à grande capacité
Hochpolymerisat n
  E: high-polymer n
  F: haut polymère m
hochsiedend adj
  E: with a high boiling point
  F: à point d'ébullition élevé
Hochspannung f
  E: high voltage (HV), high tension
  F: haute tension f (HT)
Hochspannungs-Gleichstrom-Übertragung (HGÜ) f
  E: high-voltage d.c. transmission
  F: transport m de courant continu à haute tension
Hochspannungskabel n
  E: high-voltage cable, H.V. cable, high-tension cable
  F: câble m à haute tension, câble m
HT
Hochspannungsschaltanlage f
  E: high-voltage switchgear
  F: installation f de disjoncteurs haute tension
Hochspannungstransformator m
  E: high-voltage transformer, high-tension transformer
  F: transformateur m (de) haute tension
Höchstädter-Kabel (H-Kabel) n
  E: Hochstadter cable, 'H'-type cable, metallized paper screened cable, shielded conductor cable
  F: câble m du type Hochstadter, câble m à écran en papier métallisé
Höchstspannung f
  E: extra-high voltage (EHV), supertension n
  F: très haute tension f (THT)
Höchstspannungskabel n
  E: extra-high voltage cable, supertension cable, EHV-cable n
  F: câble m à très haute tension (THT)
Hochvakuum n
  E: high vacuum (10^{-3} to 10^{-6} torr)
  F: vide m poussé (10^{-3} à 10^{-6} torr)
hochviskoses Öl
  E: high-viscosity oil
  F: huile f à viscosité élevée
Höhe, in der ~ verstellbar
  E: vertically adjustable
  F: réglable adj en hauteur
Höhenunterschied m
  E: difference of level
  F: dénivellation f, différence f de niveau
höhenverstellbare Arbeitsbühne
  E: elevator n (working platform)
  F: élévateur m (plateforme de travail)
Hohlader f [Nachr. K.]
  E: air-space(d) paper-insulated core (loosely wrapped)
  F: conducteur m à isolement air/papier (rubanage lâche)
Hohldorn m [Met.-Strangpr.]
  E: hollow mandrel
  F: mandrin m creux
Hohlleiter m [En. K.]
  E: hollow conductor
  F: âme f creuse
Hohlleiter m [Nachr.]
  E: waveguide n

Hohlleiter
   F: guide *m* d'ondes
Hohlraum *m*
   E: void *n*, cavity *n*
   F: vide *m*, cavité *f*
Hohlraumbildung *f*
   E: void formation
   F: formation *f* de vides
Hohlstempel *m* [Met.-Strangpr.]
   E: hollow ram
   F: fouloir *m* creux
Hohlwelle eines Verseilkorbes
   E: cage barrel, barrel of a stranding cage
   F: arbre *m* creux d'une cage de câblage
Holztrommel *f*
   E: wooden reel, wooden drum
   F: touret *m* en bois
Homogenisierzone einer Schnecke [Extr.]
   E: metering section of a screw
   F: zone *f* d'homogénéisation d'une vis
Hubwagen *m*
   E: lifting carriage
   F: chariot *m* élévateur
Hülle *f*
   E: sheath *n*, covering *n*, jacket *n*
   F: enveloppe *f*, revêtement *m*
Hülse *f* [K. Garn.]
   E: sleeve *n*
   F: manchon *m*
hydraulisches Antriebsaggregat
   E: hydraulic power pack
   F: unité *f* d'entraînement hydraulique
hydrostatisches Extrudieren [Met.]
   E: hydrostatic extrusion
   F: extrusion *f* hydrostatique
Hz (s. Hertz)

I

IACS (Standardwert des spezifischen Widerstandes von weichgeglühtem Kupfer) (nach IEC)
   E: IACS (International Annealed Copper Standard) (according to IEC)
   F: IACS (valeur standard de la résistivité du cuivre recuit) (selon la CEI)

I.A.C.S.-Leitfähigkeit *f* (Kupfer)
   E: I.A.C.S. conductivity (International Annealed Copper Standard/IEC)
   F: conductivité *f* I.A.C.S. (cuivre), conductibilité *f* I.A.C.S. (cuivre)
Impedanz-Prüfung *f*
   E: impedance test
   F: contrôle *m* d'impédance
Imprägniermasse *f*
   E: impregnating compound
   F: matière *f* d'imprégnation
Imprägnierung *f*
   E: impregnation *n*
   F: imprégnation *f*
Impulsfrequenz *f*
   E: pulse frequency, impulse frequency
   F: fréquence *f* d'impulsion
Imvierer-Kopplung *f*
   E: inherent quad coupling, internal quad coupling
   F: couplage *m* inhérent à la quarte, couplage *m* à l'intérieur de la quarte
Inbetriebnahme *f*
   E: commissioning *n*, putting to service, taking into commission
   F: mise *f* en oeuvre, mise *f* en service
indirekte Kühlung von Kabeln
   E: lateral cooling of cables
   F: refroidissement *m* latéral des câbles, refroidissement *m* indirect des câbles
induktionsfreies Kabel
   E: screened conductor cable, non-inductive cable
   F: câble *m* non-inductif
induktionsgeschützt *adj*
   E: protected against interference
   F: protégé *adj* contre les interférences
Induktionsheizung *f*
   E: induction heating
   F: chauffage *m* à induction
Induktionsofen *m*
   E: induction furnace
   F: four *m* à induction
Induktionsspannung *f*
   E: induced voltage
   F: tension *f* induite
Induktionsstrom *m*
   E: induction current, induced current, inductive current
   F: courant *m* induit, courant *m*

induktive Beeinflussung benachbarter Kabel
 E: inductive influence on neighbouring cables, inductive interference with neighbouring cables
 F: effet m inductif sur des câbles voisins

induktive Kopplung
 E: inductive coupling
 F: couplage m inductif

induktive Leiterheizung
 E: inductive conductor heating
 F: chauffage m de l'âme par induction

induktiver Widerstand
 E: inductive resistance
 F: résistance f inductive

Induktivität f
 E: inductance n
 F: inductance f

Industriefernsehen n
 E: closed-circuit television (factory), industrial television
 F: télévision f industrielle

induzierte Spannung
 E: induced voltage
 F: tension f induite

Inertgas n
 E: inert gas, protective gas, reducing gas
 F: gaz m inerte, gaz m de protection, gaz m réducteur

Informationsschritt m [Nachr.]
 E: signal element
 F: élément m de signal

Infrarot-Spektroskopie f
 E: infra-red spectroscopy, IR-spectroscopy n
 F: spectroscopie f infrarouge, spectroscopie f IR

Inhibitor m
 E: inhibitor n
 F: inhibiteur m

Innenbüchse f
 E: liner n
 F: fourrure f

Innendurchmesser m
 E: inner diameter (ID), inside diameter, internal diameter
 F: diamètre m intérieur

Innenleiter m
 E: inner conductor
 F: conducteur m intérieur

Innenmischer m
 E: internal mixer, kneader n, masticator n
 F: mélangeur m interne, malaxeur m

Innenraum-Anlage f
 E: indoor plant
 F: installation f intérieure

Innenraum-Endverschluß m
 E: indoor termination
 F: extrémité f intérieure

Innenraumleitung f
 E: indoor wiring cable
 F: câble m pour installation intérieure

Innenraum-Verlegung f
 E: indoor installation
 F: pose f à l'intérieur

innere Leitschicht
 E: strand shield, inner semi-conducting layer
 F: écran m sur l'âme, écran m interne, couche f semi-conductrice interne

innere Verdrahtung
 E: inside wiring, internal wiring
 F: filerie f interne

innige Verbindung
 E: intimate bond, close bond
 F: liaison f intime

Installationsdrähte $m\,pl$ (für Fernsprech- und Signalanlagen)
 E: installation wires
 F: fils $m\,pl$ d'installation

Installationsleitung f [En. K.]
 E: house wiring cable
 F: câble m domestique

Installationszeichnung f
 E: assembly drawing, erection drawing, installation drawing
 F: plan m d'assemblage, plan m de montage

installierte Leistung
 E: installed capacity, total rated power
 F: puissance f installée

Instandhaltung f
 E: maintenance n, service n, servicing n
 F: entretien m, service m, maintenance f

Instandsetzung f
 E: overhauling n, repair n
 F: remise f en état, réparation f, dépannage m

integrierter Schaltkreis
  E: integrated circuit (IC)
  F: circuit *m* intégré
interkristalline Brüchigkeit [Met.]
  E: intercrystalline brittleness, cleavage brittleness
  F: fragilité *f* intercristalline
interkristalliner Bruch [Met.]
  E: intercrystalline crack
  F: cassure *f* intercristalline, cassure *f* intergranulaire
Ionenaustauscher *m*
  E: ion exchanger
  F: échangeur *m* d'ions
Ionisation *f*
  E: ionization *n*
  F: ionisation *f*
Ionisations-Aussetzspannung *f*
  E: ionization extinction voltage
  F: tension *f* d'extinction d'ionisation
Ionisations-Einsetzspannung *f*
  E: ionization inception voltage
  F: seuil *m* d'ionisation
Ionisationspegel *m*
  E: ionization level
  F: seuil *m* d'ionisation
Ionisationsprüfung *f*
  E: scanning test
  F: essai *m* d'ionisation par défilement, essai *m* de «scanning»
IR-Spektroskopie *f*
  E: infra-red spectroscopy, IR-spectroscopy *n*
  F: spectroscopie *f* infrarouge, spectroscopie *f* IR
Island-Kanada-Kabel *n*
  E: Iceland-Canada telephone cable (ICECAN cable)
  F: câble *m* téléphonique d'Islande au Canada
Isolation *f*
  E: isolation *n*
  F: isolation *f*, isolement *m*
Isolation gegen Erde
  E: insulation against ground
  F: isolement *m* par rapport à la terre
Isolationsfehler *m*
  E: insulation fault, insulation defect
  F: défaut *m* d'isolement
Isolationsmesser *m*
  E: insulation tester
  F: appareil *m* de mesure d'isolement
Isolationspegel *m*
  E: insulation level
  F: niveau *m* d'isolement
Isolationsprüfung *f*
  E: insulation test
  F: essai *m* d'isolement
Isolationsstörung *f*
  E: insulation fault, insulation defect
  F: défaut *m* d'isolement
Isolationswiderstand *m*
  E: insulation resistance
  F: résistance *f* d'isolement, résistance *f* diélectrique
Isolator *m*
  E: insulator *n*
  F: isolateur *m*
Isolatorenkette *f*
  E: insulator string
  F: chaîne *f* d'isolateurs
Isolator-Rippen *f pl*
  E: insulator corrugation
  F: ondulation *f* d'isolateur
Isolierband *n*
  E: insulating tape, friction tape (US)
  F: ruban *m* isolant
Isolierbuchse *f*
  E: insulating bush(ing), insulating sleeve
  F: manchon *m* isolant, douille *f* isolante
Isolierdicke *f*
  E: insulation thickness
  F: épaisseur *f* d'isolant
isolieren *v*
  E: insulate *v*, isolate *v*
  F: isoler *v*
Isolierflüssigkeit *f*
  E: insulating fluid, insulating liquid
  F: liquide *m* isolant
Isolierglocke *f*
  E: shed insulator, cup insulator, bell-shaped insulator, dome-shaped insulator, petticoat insulator, insulating bell
  F: isolateur *m* à cloche, cloche *f* isolante
Isolierhülse *f*
  E: insulating bush(ing), insulating sleeve
  F: manchon *m* isolant, douille *f* isolante
Isolierlack *m*
  E: insulating varnish
  F: vernis *m* isolant, vernis *m*

d'émaillage
Isoliermaterial n
  E: insulating material, insulant n
  F: isolant m
Isoliermischung f
  E: insulating compound
  F: mélange m isolant
Isolieröl n
  E: insulating oil
  F: huile f isolante
Isolierpapier n
  E: insulating paper
  F: papier m isolant
Isolierschicht f
  E: insulating layer
  F: couche f isolante, paroi f isolante
Isolierstoff m
  E: insulating material, insulant n
  F: isolant m
isolierter Sternpunkt
  E: insulated neutral, isolated neutral
  F: neutre m isolé
Isolierung f
  E: insulation n, dielectric n
  F: isolation f, isolant m, enveloppe f isolante, diélectrique m, isolement m
Isolierung f (Trennung)
  E: isolation n
  F: isolation f, isolement m
Isolierung aus extrudiertem homogenem Material
  E: solid insulation, solid dielectric
  F: isolant m solide, isolant m sec
Isolierung aus Papierbandumspinnung
  E: paper tape insulation, lapped paper insulation, spiral strip paper insulation (US), paper ribbon insulation (US)
  F: isolation f rubanée en papier, rubanage m en papier
Isolierung, massearme ~
  E: mass-impregnated and drained insulation
  F: isolant m égoutté après imprégnation
Isolierung, vollimprägnierte ~
  E: fully impregnated insulation
  F: isolation f à imprégnation totale
Isolierung, vorimprägnierte ~
  E: pre-impregnated insulation
  F: isolation f préimprégnée
Isoliervermögen n
  E: insulating properties pl
  F: pouvoir m isolant
Isolierwickel m
  E: insulation build-up
  F: reconstitution f d'isolant
Istwert m
  E: actual value, real value
  F: valeur f réelle

J

Joch n [Vers.]
  E: cradle n
  F: porte-bobine m, berceau m
Jochbügel m
  E: stranding flyer, twisting flyer
  F: archet m de câblage, flyer m de câblage
Jute-Beilauf m
  E: jute filler
  F: bourrage m jute
Jute-Garn n
  E: jute yarn
  F: filin m de jute
Jute-Polster n
  E: jute bedding
  F: matelas m de jute
Jute-Umspinnung f
  E: jute wrapping
  F: revêtement m en jute
Jute-Wickler m
  E: jute serving head, jute spinner
  F: tête f à jute

K

Kabel n
  E: cable n
  F: câble m
Kabel für Datenübertragung
  E: data transmission cable
  F: câble m pour transmissions numériques
Kabel für Gegensprechanlagen
  E: intercom cable, intercommunication cable
  F: câble m d'intercommunication

Kabel

Kabel für leichte Beanspruchungen
  E: light-duty cable
  F: câble *m* pour contraintes faibles
Kabel für (Orts-)Gemeinschafts-Fernsehantennen
  E: CATV cable (Community Antenna Television cable)
  F: câble *m* CATV (câble de réception collective d'antenne de télévision)
Kabel für schwere Beanspruchungen
  E: heavy-duty cable
  F: câble *m* pour contraintes sévères
Kabel für Tauchpumpen in Bohrlöchern
  E: borehole cable
  F: câble *m* pour trou de forage
Kabel in den Schiffsladeraum einschießen
  E: to coil the cable into the ship's hold
  F: enrouler *v* le câble dans la cale d'un navire, stocker *v* le cable dans la cale d'un navire, lover *v* le câble dans la cale d'un navire
Kabel in elektrische Anlagen einführen
  E: to terminate cables on to electrical plant
  F: introduire *v* les câbles dans des installations électriques
Kabel in unbelastetem Zustand [En. K.]
  E: cable at no-load
  F: câble *m* non chargé, câble *m* en exploitation sans charge
Kabel mit abgeschirmten Leitern
  E: screened conductor cable
  F: câble *m* à conducteurs sous écran
Kabel mit geringer Aderzahl [Tel.]
  E: small capacity cable, small make-up cable, small-sized cable
  F: câble *m* à faible capacité, câble *m* à petit nombre de paires
Kabel mit geringer Paarzahl [Tel.]
  E: small capacity cable, small make-up cable, small-sized cable
  F: câble *m* à faible capacité, câble *m* à petit nombre de paires
Kabel mit gesteuertem Dielektrikum (Ölkabel, Gasdruckkabel)
  E: cable with controlled dielectric, controlled dielectric cable
  F: câble *m* à diélectrique contrôlé
Kabel mit getränkter Papierisolierung
  E: impregnated paper insulated cable
  F: câble *m* isolé au papier imprégné
Kabel mit großen Querschnitten
  E: cables with big cross-sectional areas, large-size cables
  F: câbles *m pl* de grosses sections, gros câbles *m pl*
Kabel mit kleinen Querschnitten
  E: cables with small cross-sectional areas, small-size cables
  F: câbles *m pl* de petites sections
Kabel mit kunststoffisolierten Leitern
  E: plastic-insulated conductor cable, PIC-cable *n* (US)
  F: câble *m* à conducteurs isolés au plastique
Kabel mit Kunststoff-Isolierung
  E: plastics cable, plastic-insulated cable
  F: câble *m* (isolé) à matière plastique
Kabel mit metallener Leiterglättung
  E: smooth-conductor cable
  F: câble *m* à écran métallique sur l'âme
Kabel mit nicht abwandernder Tränkmasse
  E: non-draining cable, nd-cable *n*
  F: câble *m* à matière non migrante, câble *m* nd
Kabel mit nicht radialem Feld
  E: non-radial field cable
  F: câble *m* à champ non radial
Kabel mit Schellen befestigen
  E: to clamp a cable
  F: brider *v* le câble
Kabel mit skineffektarmen Leitern
  E: Milliken conductor cable
  F: câble *m* à conducteurs Milliken
Kabel mit vorimprägnierter Papierisolierung
  E: pre-impregnated cable
  F: câble *m* isolé au papier préimprégné, câble *m* préimprégné
Kabel zum Auftrommeln
  E: trailing cable
  F: câble *m* de remorque, câble *m* d'enrouleur, câble *m* pour engin mobile
Kabel, abgetropftes ~
  E: drained cable, non-bleeding cable
  F: câble *m* à matière écoulée
Kabel, armiertes ~ für flache Küstengewässer
  E: shore-end cable, shallow-water

cable, shelf cable
F: câble m d'atterrissement, câble m côtier, câble m de bas fond
Kabel, bandeisenbewehrtes ~
E: steel-tape-armo(u)red cable
F: câble m armé en feuillard d'acier
Kabel, bespultes ~
E: loaded cable
F: câble m chargé
Kabel, drahtarmiertes ~
E: wire-armo(u)red cable
F: câble m armé en fils métalliques
Kabel, drahtbewehrtes ~
E: wire-armo(u)red cable
F: câble m armé en fils métalliques
Kabel, ein ~ an Land ziehen
E: to float a cable ashore
F: atterrir v un câble
Kabel, in einer Ebene liegende ~
E: cables in flat formation, cables laid in parallel, cables laid side by side
F: câbles m pl disposés en nappe
Kabel, kombiniertes ~
E: composite cable
F: câble m composite
Kabel, nebeneinander liegende ~
E: cables in flat formation, cables laid in parallel, cables laid side by side
F: câbles m pl disposés en nappe
Kabel, paarverseiltes ~
E: cable with pair formation, twin cable, paired cable
F: câble m à paires, câble m jumelé, câble m pairé
Kabel, stahlbandarmiertes ~
E: steel-tape-armo(u)red cable
F: câble m armé en feuillard d'acier
Kabel-Abschlußhülse f
E: cable lug, terminal lug, cable eye
F: cosse f de câble, attache f de conducteur, cosse f terminale
Kabelabschnitt m
E: cable section
F: tronçon m de câble
Kabelader, numerierte ~
E: numbered cable core
F: conducteur m de câble numéroté
Kabelanlage f
E: cable installation
F: liaison f de câbles, canalisation f (câb.)
Kabelanordnung f
E: cable arrangement

F: disposition f des câbles
Kabelanschluß m
E: cable connection
F: raccord m de câble
Kabelaufbau m
E: cable design, cable make-up, construction of a cable, cable build-up, design of a cable
F: construction f d'un câble, constitution f d'un câble
Kabelaufführungspunkt m
E: cable distribution point, cable lifting point
F: point m de montée de cable
Kabelaufteilungskeller m (Fernsprechamt)
E: cable vault (tel. exchange)
F: sous-sol m de distribution des câbles, cave f des câbles
Kabelbaum m
E: cable harness, wiring harness, cable assembly
F: harnais m de câbles, faisceau m de câbles, forme f de câbles
Kabelblei n
E: cable lead
F: plomb m de câble
Kabeleinführung f
E: cable entrance, cable inlet
F: entrée f de câble
Kabel-Einziehvorrichtung f
E: cable puller
F: dispositif m de tirage des câbles
Kabelendgestell n
E: cable supporting rack, cable terminating rack, terminal rack
F: bâti m pour têtes de câbles, bâti m terminal
Kabelendverschluß m
E: cable termination
F: boîte f d'extrémité de câble
Kabelendverschluß, umgekehrter ~
E: inverted type cable termination
F: extrémité f de câble du type inverti
Kabelfehler m
E: cable defect, cable failure, cable fault
F: défaut m de câble
Kabelfernsehen n
E: closed-circuit television
F: télévision f par câble
Kabelfestlegung f
E: cable anchorage

Kabelfestlegung
 F: fixation f du câble
Kabelformbrett n
 E: cable forming board, cable lacing board
 F: gabarit m pour câbles, planche f de préparation pour câbles
Kabelgarnituren f pl
 E: cable accessories
 F: accessoires m pl de câble
Kabelgraben m
 E: cable trench
 F: tranchée f de câble
Kabelgruppe f
 E: cable group
 F: famille f de câbles
Kabelhersteller m
 E: cable maker, cable manufacturer
 F: fabricant m de câbles, câbleur m
Kabelherstellung f
 E: cable making, cable manufacture
 F: fabrication f des câbles
Kabelkanal m
 E: cable duct
 F: conduite f de câble, caniveau m de câble
Kabelklemme f
 E: cable clamp, cable cleat, cable clip, cable grip
 F: collier m de câble, attache f de câble, serre-câble m
Kabelklemme f [el.]
 E: cable terminal
 F: borne f de câble
Kabelklemme, pneumatische ~ [Vulk.]
 E: air clamp
 F: serre-câble m pneumatique
Kabelkonstrukteur m
 E: cable design engineer
 F: ingénieur m de construction des câbles
Kabelkonstruktion f
 E: cable design, cable make-up, construction of a cable, cable build-up, design of a cable
 F: construction f d'un câble, constitution f d'un câble
Kabellänge f
 E: cable length
 F: longueur f du câble
Kabellegerolle, elektro-motorische ~
 E: motor-driven roller for cable laying
 F: rouleau m entraîné par moteur pour la pose du câble
Kabellegeschiff n
 E: cable ship
 F: navire m câblier, câblier m
Kabellitze f
 E: cable strand
 F: toron m de câble
Kabelmantel m
 E: cable sheath, cable jacket
 F: gaine f de câble
Kabelmantelpresse, kontinuierliche ~
 E: continuous cable sheathing press
 F: presse f de gainage en continu
Kabelmesser n
 E: cable stripping knife
 F: couteau m pour câbles
Kabelmeßkoffer m
 E: portable cable measuring set
 F: valise f de mesure pour câbles
Kabelmeßwagen m
 E: cable testing truck
 F: voiture-laboratoire f pour l'essai des câbles
Kabelpflug m
 E: cable laying plough (GB), cable laying plow (US)
 F: charrue f de pose pour câbles
Kabelpritsche f [K. Verl.]
 E: cable tray, cable rack
 F: tablette f à câbles, charpente pour câbles f
Kabelprüfautomat m
 E: automatic cable tester
 F: appareil m automatique d'essai de câbles
Kabelrolle f [K. Verl.]
 E: cable roller
 F: rouleau m de câble
Kabelrost m [K. Verl.]
 E: cable grate
 F: grille f à câbles, râtelier m à câbles
Kabelsatz m
 E: cable harness, wiring harness, cable assembly
 F: harnais m de câbles, faisceau m de câbles, forme f de câbles
Kabelschacht m
 E: cable pit, cable jointing chamber, cable jointing manhole, cable vault
 F: trou m d'homme, puits m de visite, puits m de jonction, chambre f de répartition, puits m à câbles
Kabelschelle f

E: cable clamp, cable cleat, cable clip, cable grip
F: collier *m* de câble, attache *f* de câble, serre-câble *m*

Kabelschrank *m* [Nachr.]
E: cable cabinet
F: armoire *f* à câbles

Kabelschuh *m*
E: cable lug, terminal lug, cable eye
F: cosse *f* de câble, attache *f* de conducteur, cosse *f* terminale

Kabelseele *f*
E: cable core (assembly)
F: assemblage *m* des conducteurs du câble

Kabelstrecke *f*
E: cable route
F: liaison *f* de câble

Kabelstumpf *m*
E: stub cable, sealed cable end
F: bout *m* de câble

Kabeltechnik *f*
E: cable engineering
F: technique *f* des câbles

Kabeltragdraht *m*
E: cable suspension wire
F: fil *m* porte-câble

Kabeltraggerüst *n* [K. Verl.]
E: cable tray, cable rack
F: tablette *f* à câbles, charpente pour câbles *f*

Kabeltrommel *f*
E: cable drum, cable reel
F: touret *m* de câble, bobine *f* de câble

Kabeltrommel-Anhänger *m*
E: cable trailer, cable trolley
F: chariot *m* à câbles, chariot *m* à touret de câble

Kabeltunnel *m*
E: cable subway, cable tunnel, cable gallery
F: tunnel *m* des câbles, galérie *f* des câbles

Kabelverbindungen herstellen
E: to joint cables
F: faire *v* des jonctions sur câble

Kabelverlegung *f* (s. Verlegung von Kabeln)

Kabelverteilerschrank *m*
E: cable distribution cabinet
F: armoire *f* de distribution de câbles

Kabelverzweiger *m*
E: branch box, distributing box, branch joint, distributor box (US), distribution cabinet, connecting box
F: boîte *f* de dérivation, boîte *f* de branchement, boîte *f* de distribution

Kabelwagen *m*
E: cable trailer, cable trolley
F: chariot *m* à câbles, chariot *m* à touret de câble

Kabelwanne *f* [K. Verl.]
E: cable trough
F: goulotte *f* à câbles

Kabelwerk *n*
E: cable works, cable factory
F: câblerie *f*, usine *f* de câbles

Kabelwiderstand *m*
E: characteristic cable impedance
F: impédance *f* caractéristique de câble

Kabelwinde *f*
E: cable winch
F: treuil *m* de câble

Kabelziehstrumpf *m* (s. Ziehstrumpf)

Kalander *m*
E: calender *n*
F: calandre *f*

Kalkmilch *f*
E: lime milk
F: lait *m* de chaux

Kalkschicht *f*
E: chalk layer
F: couche de chaux *f*

Kalküberzug *m*
E: chalk layer
F: couche de chaux *f*

Kaltbiegeprüfung *f*
E: cold bending test, bending test at low temperature
F: essai *m* de pliage à froid, essai *m* de pliage à basse température, essai *m* d'enroulement à basse température

kältebeständig *adj*
E: resistant to cold, cold-resistant *adj*, resistant to low temperatures
F: résistant *adj* au froid, résistant *adj* aux basses températures,

Kältebeständigkeit *f*
E: low temperature resistance, resistance to low temperatures
F: résistance *f* aux basses températures

Kältebiegeprüfung *f*

Kältebiegeprüfung

Kältebiegeprüfung
- *E:* cold bending test, bending test at low temperature
- *F:* essai *m* de pliage à froid, essai *m* de pliage à basse température, essai *m* d'enroulement à basse température

Kältedehnungsprüfung *f*
- *E:* elongation test at low temperature
- *F:* essai *m* d'allongement à froid

Kälteeigenschaften unter 0 °C
- *E:* sub-zero properties
- *F:* caractéristiques *f pl* aux températures en dessous de zéro

Kälteraum *m*
- *E:* cold-chamber *n*
- *F:* frigorifère *m*

Kälteschlagprüfung *f*
- *E:* impact resistance test at low temperature
- *F:* essai *m* de choc à basse température

Kältesprödigkeit *f*
- *E:* low temperature brittleness
- *F:* fragilité *f* à basse température

Kälteverhalten *n*
- *E:* behaviour at low temperatures
- *F:* comportement *m* à basse température

Kältewickelprüfung *f*
- *E:* cold bending test, bending test at low temperature
- *F:* essai *m* de pliage à froid, essai *m* de pliage à basse température, essai *m* d'enroulement à basse température

Kaltfließbeständigkeit *f*
- *E:* cold flow resistance
- *F:* résistance *f* au fluage à froid

Kaltformung *f*
- *E:* cold-working *n*
- *F:* façonnage *m* à froid, formage *m* à froid

Kaltfüllmasse *f*
- *E:* cold filling compound, cold pouring compound
- *F:* matière *f* de remplissage à froid

Kalthärten *n* (Gießharze)
- *E:* cold-setting *n*
- *F:* durcissage *m* à froid

kalthärtende Masse
- *E:* cold-setting compound
- *F:* matière *f* durcissable à froid

Kaltlötstelle *f*
- *E:* cold solder joint
- *F:* soudure *f* froide

Kaltpreßschweißen *n*
- *E:* cold welding, cold pressure welding
- *F:* soudage *m* à froid

Kaltschweißen *n*
- *E:* cold welding, cold pressure welding
- *F:* soudage *m* à froid

Kaltschweißstelle *f*
- *E:* cold shut, cold lap
- *F:* rebut *m*

Kaltumformung *f*
- *E:* cold-working *n*
- *F:* façonnage *m* à froid, formage *m* à froid

Kaltverfestigung *f*
- *E:* strain hardening
- *F:* écrouissage *m*

Kaltvergußmasse *f*
- *E:* cold filling compound, cold pouring compound
- *F:* matière *f* de remplissage à froid

Kaltvulkanisation *f*
- *E:* cold cure, cold vulcanization
- *F:* vulcanisation *f* à froid

kaltwalzen *v*
- *E:* cold-roll *v*
- *F:* laminer *v* à froid

Kaltwalzwerk *n*
- *E:* cold rolling mill
- *F:* laminoir *m* à froid

Kammer *f*
- *E:* chamber *n*, cabinet *n*, compartment *n*
- *F:* chambre *f*, compartiment *m*

Kanada-Schottland-Kabel *n*
- *E:* Canada-Scotland transatlantic telephone cable (CANTAT cable)
- *F:* câble *m* téléphonique du Canada à l'Ecosse

Kanalruß *m*
- *E:* channel black
- *F:* noir *m* au tunnel

Kanalzug *m* [K. Verl.]
- *E:* duct *n*
- *F:* conduit *m*, caniveau *m*

Kanalzugöffnung *f* [K. Verl.]
- *E:* duct entrance
- *F:* entrée *f* de conduit

Kante *f*
- *E:* edge *n*
- *F:* bord *m*, arête *f*, tranche *f*

Kante, abgerundete ~

Kennzeichnung

    E: rounded edge
    F: côté *m* arrondi, tranche *f* arrondie
Kante, abgeschrägte ~
    E: beveled edge
    F: tranche *f* biseautée
Kantenfestigkeit *f*
    E: edge tear resistance
    F: résistance *f* des bords au déchirement
Kantenradius *m* (Sektorleiter)
    E: corner radius, edge radius
    F: rayon *m* de coude
Kaolin
    E: china clay, kaolin *n*
    F: caolin *m*, kaolin *m*
Kapazität *f* [el.]
    E: capacitance *n*
    F: capacité *f*
Kapazität gegen Erde
    E: capacitance to earth
    F: capacité *f* par rapport à la terre
Kapazitätsmessung *f*
    E: capacitance measurement
    F: mesure *f* de capacité
Kapazitätssymmetrie *f*
    E: capacitance balance
    F: équilibre *m* de capacité
Kapazitätsunsymmetrie *f*
    E: capacitance unbalance, capacitance imbalance (US)
    F: déséquilibre *m* de capacité
kapazitive Kopplung
    E: capacitance unbalance, capacitance imbalance (US)
    F: déséquilibre *m* de capacité
kapazitiver Widerstand
    E: capacitive resistance, capacitive reactance
    F: résistance *f* capacitive
Kapelle *f* (Abzug)
    E: hood *n*
    F: hotte *f*
Kappe *f* [K.Garn.]
    E: cap *n*
    F: capot *m*, capuchon *m*
kaschiert mit ...
    E: coated with ..., laminated with ..., backed with ...
    F: contrecouché *adj* de ..., contrecollé *adj* de ..., revêtu *adj* de ..., doublé *adj* de ...,
Kaskadenkühler *m* (Granulat)
    E: cascades cooler
    F: installation *f* de refroidissement en cascades
Kaskadenschaltung *f*
    E: cascade connection
    F: montage *m* en cascade
Kathodenkupfer *n*
    E: cathode copper
    F: cuivre *m* cathodique
kathodischer Korrosionsschutz
    E: cathodic protection
    F: protection *f* cathodique
Kautschuk *m* (unvulkanisiert)
    E: rubber *n*
    F: caoutchouc *m*
Kautschukregenerat *n*
    E: reclaimed rubber
    F: caoutchouc *m* régénéré
Kavernenkraftwerk *n*
    E: underground power station
    F: centrale *f* hydroélectrique souterraine
Keilriemen *m*
    E: V-belt *n*
    F: courroie *f* trapézoïdale
Keilring *m*
    E: wedge ring
    F: bague *f* conique
KE-Kupfer *n* (Kathoden-Elektrolyt-Kupfer)
    E: CATH-copper *n* (electrolytic cathode copper)
    F: cuivre *m* cathodique électrolytique
Kennfaden *m*
    E: identification thread, marker thread, tracer thread
    F: fil *m* d'identification, fil *m* distinctif, filin *m* de reconnaissance
Kennlinie *f*
    E: characteristic curve
    F: caractéristique *f*, courbe *f* caractéristique
Kennwert *m*
    E: parameter *n*, characteristic value
    F: paramètre *m*, valeur *f* caractéristique
Kennzeichen *n* [Kab.]
    E: mark *n*, code *n*
    F: marque *f*, code *m*
Kennzeichnung *f* [Kab.]
    E: identification *n*, marking *n*, coding *n*
    F: désignation *f*, identification *f*, marquage *m*, repérage *m*

Kennzeichnung, farbige ~
 E: colo(u)r code, colo(u)r coding
 F: repérage *m* coloré, code *m* de couleur

Kennziffer *f* [Kab.]
 E: code number
 F: chiffre *m* distinctif, numéro-repère *m*, repère *m* numérique

Kerbempfindlichkeit *f*
 E: notch sensitivity
 F: sensibilité *f* à l'entaille

Kerbkabelschuh *m*
 E: notch type cable lug
 F: cosse *f* de câble à sertir

Kerbschlagprobe *f*
 E: notched bar impact test
 F: essai *m* de choc sur éprouvette entaillée

Kerbverbinder *m*
 E: notched type sleeve
 F: manchon *m* à sertir

Kerbverbindung *f*
 E: notch type joint
 F: raccord *m* à sertir

Kerbzähigkeit *f*
 E: tear resistance (from a nick), notch toughness
 F: résistance *f* au déchirement (à partir de l'entaille), dureté *f* à l'entaille

Kern einer Papierscheibe [Bdspinn.]
 E: centre of a paper pad
 F: centre *m* d'une galette à papier, bague *f* d'une galette à papier

Kerndurchmesser *m* (Kabeltrommel)
 E: barrel diameter
 F: diamètre *m* du tambour

Kernkraftwerk *n*
 E: nuclear power station
 F: centrale *f* nucléaire, centrale *f* atomique

Kettenantrieb *m*
 E: chain drive
 F: transmission *f* par chaîne, commande *f* par chaîne

Kettenisolator *m*
 E: suspension insulator, chain insulator
 F: isolateur *m* suspendu, isolateur *m* de suspension

Kettenleiter *m* [el.]
 E: recurrent network, lattice network
 F: réseau *m* récurrent, système *m* itératif

Kettenlinie *f*
 E: catenary *n*
 F: chaînette *f*

Kettenlinien-Vulkanisation *f*
 E: catenary vulcanization
 F: vulcanisation *f* en chaînette

Kinke *f*
 E: kink *n*
 F: coque *f*

Kinkenbildung *f*
 E: kinking *n*
 F: formation *f* de coques

kippbar *adj*
 E: inclinable *adj*, tiltable *adj*
 F: inclinable *adj*, basculant *adj*, renversable *adj*

kippbarer Drehtrommelofen
 E: tiltable rotary furnace
 F: four *m* tubulaire tournant basculant

Kippmischer *m*
 E: tilting mixer
 F: mélangeur *m* basculant, mélangeur *m* renversable

Klebeband *n*
 E: adhesive tape
 F: ruban *m* adhésif

kleben *vi*
 E: adhere *v*, bond *v*, stick *v*
 F: adhérer *v*, coller *v*

kleben *vt*
 E: cement *vt*, glue *vt*, paste *vt*, bond *vt*
 F: coller *vt*, attacher *vt*

Kleber *m*
 E: adhesive *n*, bonding agent
 F: adhésif *m*, colle *f*

Klebrigkeit *f*
 E: stickiness *n*, tackiness *n*
 F: glutinosité *f*, état *m* collant

Klebstoff *m*
 E: adhesive *n*, bonding agent
 F: adhésif *m*, colle *f*

Kleinkoaxialpaar *n*
 E: small-diameter coaxial pair
 F: paire *f* coaxiale de petit diamètre

Klemmbacke *f*
 E: jaw *n*, fixing clamp, clamping jaw
 F: mâchoire *f* de serrage, mordache *f*

Klemme *f*
 E: clamp *n*, clip *n*
 F: pince *f*, attache *f*

Klemme *f* [el.]
 E: terminal *n*, connector *n*,

Klemmenkasten *m* [el.]
- E: distribution panel, terminal box, junction box, connection box
- F: coffret *m* de distribution, boîte *f* de distribution, boîte *f* de dérivation, boîte *f* de connexion, coffret *m* de raccordement, boîte *f* de jonction, boîte *f* à bornes

Klemmleiste *f* [el.]
- E: terminal block, terminal strip, terminal board, connecting block, connection strip
- F: bloc *m* de connexion, réglette *f* de raccordement, réglette *f* à bornes, barrette *f* à bornes

Klemmplatte *f*
- E: terminal plate
- F: plaque *f* à bornes

Klemmring *m*
- E: clamp ring, clamping ring, locking ring
- F: bague *f* de serrage

Klemmschraube *f* [el.]
- E: terminal screw, binding screw, screw terminal
- F: vis *f* de borne, borne *f* à vis

Klemmverbindung *f*
- E: clamped joint
- F: raccord *m* boulonné

Klimaanlage *f*
- E: air-conditioner *n*
- F: conditionneur *m* d'air

klimatisierte Atmosphäre
- E: conditioned atmosphere, conditioned air
- F: atmosphère *f* conditionnée

klimatisierter Raum
- E: air-conditioned room
- F: enceinte *f* climatisée

Klimatisierung *f*
- E: air-conditioning *n*
- F: climatisation *f*, conditionnement *m* d'air

Klinge *f*
- E: blade *n*
- F: lame *f*

Klingeldraht *m*
- E: bell wire
- F: fil *m* de sonnerie

Klingelprüfung *f* [Tel. K.]
- E: ringing test, ring-out procedure, buzz-out operation
- F: contrôle *m* de continuité, sonnage *m*

Klirrfaktor *m*
- E: distortion factor
- F: facteur *m* de distorsion

Klöppelmaschine *f*
- E: braiding machine, braider *n*
- F: machine *f* à tresser

Knetarm *m*
- E: blade *n* (of kneader)
- F: pale *f*, palette *f*, bras *m* (de malaxeur)

kneten *v*
- E: masticate *v*, knead *v*
- F: malaxer *v*

Kneter *m*
- E: internal mixer, kneader *n*, masticator *n*
- F: mélangeur *m* interne, malaxeur *m*

Knetlegierung *f*
- E: wrought alloy
- F: alliage *m* de pétrissage

Knick *m* (in Leitung oder Kabel)
- E: kink *n*
- F: coque *f*

Knicken *n* [Bdspinn.]
- E: creasing *n*
- F: pliage *n*

Knickfestigkeit *f*
- E: buckling resistance, buckling strength
- F: résistance *f* au flambage

Knickschutz *m* [Kab.]
- E: protection against kinking
- F: protection *f* contre la formation de coques

Knierohr *n*
- E: pipe bend, conduit bend, elbow *n*, knee *n*
- F: coude *m*, raccord *m* coudé

Knotenpunkt *m*
- E: intersection *n*, junction point
- F: intersection *f*, point *m* nodal, nœud *m*, point *m* de jonction

Knüppel *m* [Met.-Strangpr.]
- E: billet *n*
- F: billette *f*

koaxiales Fernkabel
- E: long distance coaxial cable
- F: câble *m* coaxial à longue distance

koaxiales Hochfrequenzkabel

koaxiales

Koaxialkabel
- E: high-frequency coaxial cable, radio frequency coaxial cable, coaxial cable for high-frequency transmission
- F: câble *m* coaxial à haute fréquence, câble *m* coaxial à fréquence radioélectrique

Koaxialkabel *n*
- E: coaxial cable, concentric cable
- F: câble *m* coaxial, câble *m* concentrique

Koaxialleitung *f*
- E: coaxial line, concentric-conductor line
- F: ligne *f* coaxiale, liaison *f* coaxiale, ligne *f* à conducteur concentrique

Koaxialleitung für den Fernverkehr
- E: coaxial line for long distance traffic
- F: ligne *f* coaxiale pour trafic à longue distance

Koaxialpaar *n*
- E: coaxial pair
- F: paire *f* coaxiale

Koax-Tube *f*
- E: coaxial tube
- F: tube *m* coaxial

Kohlenwasserstoffpolymere *n pl*
- E: hydrocarbon polymers
- F: polymères *m pl* d'hydrocarbure

Kokille *f*
- E: mo(u)ld *n*
- F: coquille *f*

Kokillenguß *m*
- E: ingot mo(u)ld casting, gravity die-casting
- F: coulée *f* en coquille

Kolben *m* [Masch.]
- E: piston *n*, ram *n*, plunger *n*
- F: piston *m*, fouloir *m*

Kolbenhub *m*
- E: piston stroke
- F: course *f* de piston

Kolbenpresse *f*
- E: ram press, plunger press
- F: presse *f* à piston

Kollergang *m*
- E: muller mixer, edge runner mixer
- F: mélangeur *m* à meules

Kolophonium *n*
- E: rosin *n*, gum rosin
- F: colophane *f*

kombiniertes Kabel
- E: composite cable
- F: câble *m* composite

Kombizange *f*
- E: combination pliers *pl*
- F: pince *f* universelle

Komponente *f*
- E: component *n*, constituent *n*
- F: composante *f*

Kondensator *m*
- E: capacitor *n*
- F: condensateur *m*

Kondensatorkeule *f*
- E: capacitor cone, condenser cone
- F: cône *m* de condensateur

Kondensatoröl *n*
- E: capacitor oil, condenser oil
- F: huile *f* de condensateur

Kondensatorwickel *m*
- E: capacitor roll, capacitor coil
- F: bobinage *m* de condensateur

konditionierte Luft
- E: conditioned atmosphere, conditioned air
- F: atmosphère *f* conditionnée

konditionierter Raum
- E: air-conditioned room
- F: enceinte *f* climatisée

konfektionierte Leitungen
- E: pre-assembled flexible cables and cords, cord sets
- F: cordons *m pl* et conducteurs façonnés, conducteurs *m pl* préassemblés

Kongo-Rot-Prüfung *f*
- E: Congo Red test
- F: essai *m* au rouge de Congo

konisch *adj*
- E: tapered *adj*, conic(al) *adj*
- F: effilé *adj*, à section décroissante, conique *adj*

Konstruktionsblatt *n*
- E: design sheet
- F: feuille *f* de construction

Konstruktionsbüro *n*
- E: drawing office, engineering department, designing office
- F: bureau *m* d'études, bureau *m* de dessins

Konstruktionsdaten *pl*
- E: design data
- F: données *f pl* de construction, caractéristiques *f pl* dimensionelles, données *f pl* constructives

Konstruktionsstahl *m*

Konstruktionsstahl *m*
- *E:* structural steel
- *F:* acier *m* de construction

Konstruktionszeichnung *f*
- *E:* construction drawing, design drawing
- *F:* plan *m* de construction, dessin *m* d'atelier

Kontaktkorrosion *f*
- *E:* galvanic corrosion, bimetallic corrosion
- *F:* corrosion *f* par contact

Kontaktmanometer *n*
- *E:* contact manometer, contact-making pressure gauge
- *F:* manomètre *m* à contact, manostat *m*

Kontaktrolle *f*
- *E:* contact sheave
- *F:* galet *m* de contact

kontinuierlich *adj*
- *E:* continuous *adj*, non-intermittent *adj*
- *F:* continu *adj*, en continu

kontinuierlich gefülltes Kabel [Tel. K.]
- *E:* fully filled cable, continuously filled cable
- *F:* câble *m* rempli de façon continue, câble *m* à remplissage total, câble *m* à remplissage continu

kontinuierliche Drahtzieh- und Glühanlage
- *E:* tandem annealer, continuous wire drawing and annealing machine
- *F:* installation *f* de recuit en tandem, tréfileuse *f* et recuiseur en continu

kontinuierliche Drahtzieh-, Glüh- und Isolier-Anlage
- *E:* tandem wire drawing, annealing and insulating line
- *F:* installation *f* continue de tréfilage, recuit et isolement

kontinuierliche Fertigung
- *E:* continuous manufacture
- *F:* fabrication *f* en continu

kontinuierliche Kabelmantelpresse
- *E:* continuous cable sheathing press
- *F:* presse *f* de gainage en continu

kontinuierliche Vulkanisation (CV)
- *E:* continuous vulcanization (CV)
- *F:* vulcanisation *f* continue (CV)

kontinuierliche Vulkanisationsanlage
- *E:* CV-line *n*, continuous vulcanization line
- *F:* chaîne *f* CV, chaîne *f* de vulcanisation en continu

kontinuierliche Widerstandsglühanlage
- *E:* continuous resistance annealer
- *F:* recuiseur *m* continu par résistance, installation *f* continue de recuit par résistance

kontinuierlicher Betrieb
- *E:* continuous operation
- *F:* marche *f* continue, opération *f* continue, service *m* continu

Kontroll-/Schreibgerät *n*
- *E:* controller/recorder *n*
- *F:* contrôleur/enregistreur *m*

Konturenstecker *m*
- *E:* shaped plug
- *F:* fiche *f* profilée

Konusschneider *m*
- *E:* pencilling tool
- *F:* dispositif *m* d'appointage

konzentrische Leitung
- *E:* coaxial line, concentric-conductor line
- *F:* ligne *f* coaxiale, liaison *f* coaxiale, ligne *f* à conducteur concentrique

konzentrischer Leiter
- *E:* concentric conductor
- *F:* âme *f* concentrique

konzentrischer Nulleiter
- *E:* concentric neutral conductor
- *F:* neutre *m* concentrique, neutre *m* périphérique

konzentrischer Prüfschirm
- *E:* concentric test-shield
- *F:* écran *m* d'essai concentrique

konzentrisches Dreileiterkabel
- *E:* triple concentric cable
- *F:* câble *m* triphasé concentrique

konzentrisches Kabel
- *E:* coaxial cable, concentric cable
- *F:* câble *m* coaxial, câble *m* concentrique

konzentrisches Zweileiterkabel
- *E:* coaxial cable, concentric cable
- *F:* câble *m* coaxial, câble *m* concentrique

köpfen *v* (Drahtenden)
- *E:* crop *v*, trim *v*, cut *v*
- *F:* couper *v*, rogner *v*, cisailler *v*

Koppelkondensator *m*
- *E:* coupling capacitor
- *F:* condensateur *m* de couplage

Kopplung *f*
  E: coupling *n*
  F: couplage *m*

Kopplung zwischen nicht-benachbarten Verseilelementen
  E: coupling between non-adjacent strands
  F: couplage *m* entre éléments câblés non voisins

Kopplung, kapazitive ~
  E: capacitance unbalance, capacitance imbalance (US)
  F: déséquilibre *m* de capacité

Kopplungsfaktor *m* [Tel.]
  E: coupling coefficient
  F: coefficient *m* de couplage

Kopplungsmeßplatz *m*
  E: capacity unbalance testing equipment
  F: poste *m* de mesure des déséquilibres de capacité

Kopplungsniveau *n*
  E: unbalance level, coupling level
  F: niveau *m* de couplage

Kopplungswiderstand *m*
  E: coupling resistance, surface transfer impedance
  F: résistance *f* de couplage

Korb *m* [Vers.]
  E: cage *n*
  F: cage *f*

Korbspinner, horizontaler ~
  E: horizontal cage lapper, horizontal cage type lapping machine
  F: rubaneuse *f* horizontale à cage

Korbspinner, vertikaler ~
  E: vertical cage lapper, vertical cage type lapping machine
  F: rubaneuse *f* verticale à cage

Korbverseilmaschine *f*
  E: planetary strander, planet-type stranding machine, cage strander, slow-speed strander
  F: câbleuse *f* à cage, assembleuse *f* à cage

Kordel *f*
  E: string *n*
  F: ficelle *f*, cordelette *f*

Kordelbespinnung *f*
  E: string spinning
  F: guipage *m*

Kordelspinnmaschine *f*
  E: string spinning machine
  F: guipeuse *f*

Korngrenzen *f pl*
  E: grain boundaries
  F: limites *f pl* des grains, joints *m pl* des grains

Korngröße *f*
  E: grain size
  F: grosseur *f* du grain

Korngrößenverteilung *f*
  E: particle size distribution
  F: répartition *f* granulométrique

körnig *adj*
  E: grained *adj*, granular *adj*
  F: granuleux *adj*, granulaire *adj*, grenu *adj*

körnige Einschlüsse
  E: grained inclusions
  F: inclusions *f pl* granuleuses

körnige Oberfläche
  E: surface of granular structure
  F: surface *f* de structure granulaire

Kornwachstum *n*
  E: grain growth
  F: croissance *f* des grains, grossissement *m* des grains

Korona *f* [el.]
  E: corona *n*
  F: couronne *f*, effet *m* de couronne

Koronabeständigkeit *f*
  E: corona resistance, glow stability
  F: résistance *f* à l'effet de couronne, résistance *f* à l'effet de corona

Korona-Entladung *f*
  E: corona discharge, ionization discharge
  F: effluve *f* en couronne, décharge *f* par ionisation, décharge *f* en couronne

korrodieren *v*
  E: corrode *v*, attack *v*
  F: corroder *v*, attaquer *v*

Korrosion, elektrolytische ~
  E: electrolytic corrosion
  F: corrosion *f* électrolytique

korrosionsfest *adj*
  E: corrosion-resistant *adj*, corrosion-proof *adj*, anti-corrosive *adj*
  F: résistant *adj* à la corrosion

Korrosionsschutz *m*
  E: anti-corrosion protection
  F: protection *f* anti-corrosive, protection *f* anticorrosion

Korrosionsschutz, kathodischer ~

E: cathodic protection
F: protection f cathodique

Kraftfahrzeugleitung f
E: vehicle cable
F: câble m pour automobile

kräftig adj
E: sturdy adj, robust adj, rigid adj, solid adj
F: robuste adj

Kraft-Isolierpapier n
E: Kraft insulating paper
F: papier m isolant Kraft

kraftschlüssig verbunden
E: positively connected
F: rendu adj solidaire, relié adj de façon positive

Kraftwerk n
E: power station, generating station
F: centrale f électrique

Kranbahn f
E: crane rail
F: chemin m de roulement de la grue

Krarupisieren n
E: continuous loading
F: charge f continue, krarupisation f

Krarup-Kabel n
E: Krarup cable, continuously loaded cable
F: câble m Krarup, câble m krarupisé, câble m à charge continue, câble m ferromagnétique

Krätze f [Met.]
E: dross n
F: crasse f

Kratzgeräusch n [Nachr.]
E: scratchy noise
F: bruit m de friture

Kreide f
E: calcium carbonate, chalk n
F: carbonate m de calcium, craie f

Kreidekasten m (Kabelfertigung)
E: lime box, chalk box
F: bac m à craie

Kreideüberzug m
E: coating of whiting
F: enduction f en craie

Kreisdiagrammschreiber m
E: circular chart recorder
F: enregistreur m à diagramme circulaire

Kreislauf, geschlossener ~
E: closed circuit
F: circuit m fermé

Kreisvierer m
E: phantom circuit, superposed circuit
F: circuit m fantôme, circuit m superposé, circuit m combiné

Krepp-Papier n
E: crepe paper
F: papier m plissé, papier m crêpé

kreuzen v (Leitungen)
E: cross-connect v, cross-splice v
F: transposer v

kreuzen v (Drähte zum Induktionsschutz)
E: transpose v
F: transposer v

Kreuzen n [Nachr. K.]
E: crossing n, cross-connection n, cross-splicing n
F: croisement m, transposition f

Kreuzen von Straßen [K. Verl.]
E: crossing of roadways
F: croisement m de routes

Kreuzschlagverseilung f
E: reverse(d) lay stranding
F: câblage m en couches croisées, câblage m en sens alterné

Kriechen n
E: creep n
F: fluage m

Kriechstrom m
E: surface leakage current
F: courant m de fuite superficiel

Kriechstromfestigkeit f
E: track(ing) resistance
F: résistance f au cheminement

Kriechweg m
E: leakage path
F: ligne f de fuite

Kriechwegbildung f
E: tracking n
F: cheminement m

kristallines Gefüge
E: crystalline structure
F: structure f cristalline

Kristallinität f
E: crystallinity n
F: cristallinité f

Kristallit m (PE)
E: crystal n, crystallite n
F: cristal m, cristallite m

Krümmer m (Rohr)
E: pipe bend, conduit bend, elbow n, knee n

Krümmer
  F: coude m, raccord m coudé
Krümmung f
  E: curvature n, bend n, deflection n
  F: courbure f, incurvation f, courbe f
Krümmungsradius m (Sektorleiter)
  E: corner radius, edge radius
  F: rayon m de coude
Kryo-Kabel n
  E: cryogenic cable
  F: câble m cryogénique, cryocâble m
kugelförmig adj
  E: spherical-shaped adj
  F: sphérique adj
Kugelfunkenstrecke f
  E: sphere gap
  F: éclateur m à sphères
Kugellager n
  E: ball-bearing n
  F: palier m à billes, roulement m à billes
Kühlaggregat n
  E: cooling set, refrigeration unit
  F: agrégat m réfrigérant, groupe m réfrigérant
Kühlbad n
  E: cooling bath
  F: bain m de refroidissement
Kühlflüssigkeit f
  E: cooling liquid
  F: liquide m de refroidissement
Kühlkreis m
  E: cooling circuit
  F: circuit m de refroidissement
Kühlmischer m
  E: cooling mixer
  F: mélangeur m réfrigérant
Kühlmittel n
  E: coolant n, cooling medium, cooling agent
  F: réfrigérant m
Kühlrinne f
  E: cooling trough
  F: goulotte f de refroidissement, gouttière f de refroidissement, bac m de refroidissement
Kühlrohr n
  E: cooling tube
  F: tube m de refroidissement
Kühlstrecke f
  E: cooling section
  F: section f de refroidissement
Kühlturm m
  E: cooling tower
  F: tour f de réfrigération
Kühlung, direkte ~ von Kabeln
  E: integral cooling of cables, direct cooling of cables
  F: refroidissement m intégral des câbles, refroidissement m direct des câbles
Kühlung, indirekte ~ von Kabeln
  E: lateral cooling of cables
  F: refroidissement m latéral des câbles, refroidissement m indirect des câbles
Kühlwanne f
  E: cooling trough
  F: goulotte f de refroidissement, gouttière f de refroidissement, bac m de refroidissement
Kühlwasser n
  E: cooling water
  F: eau f de refroidissement, eau f réfrigérante
Kühlwasserrohr n
  E: cooling water pipe
  F: tube m à eau de refroidissement
Kühlwasserrücklauf m
  E: recirculation of cooling water
  F: retour m d'eau de refroidissement
Kühlwasserumlauf m
  E: cooling water circulation
  F: circulation f d'eau de refroidissement
Kumaronharz n
  E: Coumarone resin
  F: résine f de coumarone
Kunstharz n
  E: synthetic resin
  F: résine f synthétique, résine f de synthèse, résine f artificielle
Kunstharzkitt m
  E: synthetic resin cement
  F: ciment m de résine synthétique
künstliche Belüftung
  E: forced ventilation
  F: ventilation f forcée
künstliche Kühlung [Kab.]
  E: forced cooling, artificial cooling
  F: refroidissement m forcé
Kunststoff m
  E: plastic material, synthetic material, synthetic resin
  F: matière f plastique, matière f synthétique, plastique m
Kunststoff-Aderleitung f

kunststoffisolierte Aderleitung
 E: thermoplastic-insulated building wire
 F: conducteur *m* isolé à matière plastique

kunststoffbeschichtetes Papierband
 E: polymer/paper laminated tape
 F: ruban *m* papier contrecouché d'un polymère

Kunststoff-Energiekabel *n*
 E: plastics power cable, plastic-insulated power cable
 F: câble *m* d'énergie (isolé) à matière plastique

kunststoffisolierte Ader
 E: plastic-insulated core
 F: conducteur *m* isolé au plastique

kunststoffisolierte Ader [Nachr. K.]
 E: PIC (plastic insulated conductor) (US)
 F: conducteur *m* isolé au plastique

Kunststoff-Isolierung *f*
 E: plastic insulation, synthetic insulation
 F: isolant *m* plastique, isolant *m* synthétique

Kunststoffkabel *n*
 E: plastics cable, plastic-insulated cable
 F: câble *m* (isolé) à matière plastique

kunststoffkaschierte Metallfolie
 E: plastics-coated metal foil
 F: feuille *f* métallique doublée de matière plastique

Kunststoffmantel *m*
 E: plastic sheath
 F: gaine *f* plastique

Kunststoffmantelkabel *n*
 E: plastic-sheathed cable, non-metallic-sheathed cable
 F: câble *m* sous gaine plastique, câble *m* sous gaine non-métallique

Kunststoff-Mischerei *f*
 E: plastics mixing plant
 F: installation *f* de préparation des mélanges plastiques

Kunststoff-Mischung *f*
 E: plastics compound, synthetic resin compound
 F: mélange *m* plastique

Kunststoffschlauchleitung *f*
 E: plastic-sheathed flexible cord
 F: câble *m* souple sous gaine en plastique

Kunststoffschlauchleitung, leichte ~
 E: light plastic-sheathed flexible cord
 F: câble *m* souple sous gaine légère en plastique

Kunststoffschlauchleitung, mittlere ~
 E: ordinary plastic-sheathed flexible cord
 F: câble *m* souple sous gaine ordinaire en plastique

Kupfer für die Elektrotechnik (s. E-Kupfer)

Kupfer, feuerraffiniertes ~
 E: fire-refined copper
 F: cuivre *m* raffiné au feu

Kupferabfälle *m pl*
 E: scrap copper, copper scrap
 F: déchets *m pl* de cuivre

Kupferband *n*
 E: copper tape, copper strip, copper strap
 F: bande *f* de cuivre, ruban *m* de cuivre

Kupferdraht, weichgeglüht
 E: copper wire, soft-annealed
 F: fil *m* de cuivre recuit

Kupferdrahtbarren *m pl*
 E: copper wirebars
 F: lingots *m pl* de cuivre

Kupferdrahtgeflecht *n*
 E: copper wire braiding, copper braiding
 F: tresse *f* en fils de cuivre

Kupfer-Gestrickband *n* (verzinnt) [Kab.]
 E: tinned copper braid, tinned copper mesh
 F: tresse *f* en cuivre étamé

Kupferleiter *m*
 E: copper conductor
 F: âme *f* en cuivre

Kupferleiterkabel *n*
 E: copper conductor cable
 F: câble *m* à âme en cuivre, câble *m* à conducteur en cuivre

kupferplattierter Aluminiumdraht
 E: copper-clad aluminium wire
 F: fil *m* d'aluminium plaqué de cuivre

kupferplattierter Aluminiumleiter
 E: copper-clad aluminium conductor
 F: âme *f* en aluminium plaqué de cuivre

Kupferraffination *f*
 E: copper refining
 F: raffinage *m* du cuivre

Kupferschirm m
 E: copper screen
 F: écran m en cuivre

Kupferschirmgeflecht n
 E: copper-mesh shield, copper braid shielding, copper-mesh screen, braided copper screen
 F: écran m en tresse de cuivre

Kupferschmelze f
 E: molten copper
 F: cuivre m fondu

kupferumhüllter Aluminiumdraht
 E: copper-clad aluminium wire
 F: fil m d'aluminium plaqué de cuivre

Kupferverluste m pl [el.]
 E: ohmic losses
 F: pertes f pl dans le cuivre

Kupferwellmantel m
 E: corrugated copper sheath
 F: gaine f ondulée en cuivre

Kupferwellrohr n
 E: corrugated copper tube
 F: tube m ondulée en cuivre

Kurve, Abfall einer ~
 E: decline of a curve, slope of a curve
 F: inclinaison f d'une courbe, pente f d'une courbe

Kurve, Anstieg einer ~
 E: slope of a curve
 F: pente f d'une courbe, montée f d'une courbe

Kurvenbild n
 E: diagram n, graph n, graphic representation, chart n
 F: diagramme m, représentation f graphique, graphique m

Kurvenverlauf m
 E: characteristic of a curve
 F: allure f d'une courbe

kurzschließen v
 E: short-circuit v
 F: mettre v en court-circuit, court-circuiter v

Kurzschlußdauer f
 E: short-circuit time, short-circuit duration
 F: temps m de court-circuit, durée f de court-circuit

Kurzschlußfall, im ~
 E: under short-circuit conditions
 F: en cas de court-circuit

Kurzschlußfestigkeit f
 E: short-circuit strength
 F: résistance f aux courts-circuits

Kurzschlußleistung f
 E: short-circuit rating
 F: puissance f de court-circuit

kurzschlußsicher adj
 E: short-circuit proof
 F: résistant adj au court-circuit

Kurzschlußstrom m
 E: short-circuit current
 F: courant m de court-circuit

Kurzschlußverhalten n
 E: short-circuit behaviour
 F: tenue f en court-circuit

Kurzschlußwindung f
 E: short-circuited turn, short-circuit winding
 F: spire f de court-circuit

Kurzschlußzeit f
 E: short-circuit time, short-circuit duration
 F: temps m de court-circuit, durée f de court-circuit

Kurzzeitbetrieb m (mit gleichbleibender Last) [el.]
 E: short-time service, short-time duty, short-time operation
 F: service m temporaire, régime m temporaire, service m de courte durée

Kurzzeitbetrieb m (mit veränderlicher Last) [el.]
 E: variable temporary duty
 F: service m temporaire variable, régime m temporaire variable

Kurzzeit-Durchschlagfestigkeit f
 E: short-time dielectric strength
 F: tenue f au claquage de courte durée

Kurzzeitfestigkeit f
 E: short-time strength
 F: tenue f en courte durée

Kurzzeitprüfung f
 E: short-time test
 F: essai m de courte durée

Kurzzeitverhalten n
 E: short-time performance
 F: comportement m en courte durée

Kurzzeitversuch m
 E: short-time test
 F: essai m de courte durée

Küstenkabel n
 E: shore-end cable, shallow-water cable, shelf cable
 F: câble m d'atterrissement, câble m

côtier, câble *m* de bas fond

L

Labormaßstab, Versuch im ~
E: laboratory-scale trial
F: essai *m* à l'échelle de laboratoire

Laboruntersuchung *f*
E: laboratory test, laboratory investigation
F: essai *m* de laboratoire

Laborwalze *f*
E: laboratory roller mill
F: malaxeur *m* de laboratoire à cylindres

Lack *m*
E: varnish *n*, enamel *n*
F: vernis *m*

Lackband *n*
E: varnished tape
F: ruban *m* verni, ruban *m* laqué

Lackbandkabel *n*
E: varnished cambric (insulated) cable
F: câble *m* isolé à la toile vernie

Lackbaumwolldraht *m*
E: cotton-covered enamelled wire
F: fil *m* émail-coton, fil *m* émaillé guipé de coton

Lackdraht *m*
E: enamel(l)ed wire, magnet wire
F: fil *m* émaillé, fil *m* verni

Lackgewebe-Band *n*
E: varnished cambric tape
F: ruban *m* en toile vernie

Lackgewebe-Isolierung *f*
E: varnished cambric insulation
F: isolation *f* en toile vernie

Lackierturm *m*
E: enamelling tower
F: tour *f* de vernissage

Lackimprägnierung *f*
E: varnish impregnation
F: imprégnation *f* en vernis

Lackpapierkabel *n*
E: varnished paper cable
F: câble *m* isolé au papier verni

Lacküberzug *m*
E: varnish coating
F: couche *f* de vernis, couche *f* de laque

laden *v*
E: charge *v*, load *v*
F: charger *v*

Ladestrom *m*
E: capacitance current, charging current
F: courant *m* de charge

Ladung *f* [el.]
E: charge *n*
F: charge *f*

Ladungsträger *m*
E: charge carrier
F: porteur *m* de charge

Lage *f*
E: layer *n*
F: couche *f*

Lage-Lage Kopplung
E: inter-layer coupling
F: couplage *m* entre couches

Lagenkabel *n*
E: layer-stranded cable, concentric layer cable, layered cable, layer type cable
F: câble *m* à couches concentriques, câble *m* en couches

Lagenversatz *m* [Bdspinn.]
E: registration *n*, staggering *n*
F: chevauchement *m*

lagenverseiltes Kabel
E: layer-stranded cable, concentric layer cable, layered cable, layer type cable
F: câble *m* à couches concentriques, câble *m* en couches

Lagenverseilung *f*
E: layer-stranding *n*, stranding in layers
F: assemblage *m* par (en) couches, câblage *m* par (en) couches

lagenweise *adj*
E: in consecutive layers
F: en couches consécutives

Lagerfähigkeit *f* (Werkstoffe)
E: shelf life, storage stability
F: limite *f* de stockage, stabilité *f* au stockage

Lagerlänge *f*
E: stock length
F: longueur *f* standard

Lagerung in Wasser
E: immersion in water, water immersion
F: immersion *f* dans l'eau

Lagerungsbeständigkeit

Lagerungsbeständigkeit f
- E: shelf life, storage stability
- F: limite f de stockage, stabilité f au stockage

Lahnlitzenleiter m
- E: tinsel conductor
- F: fil m rosette

Lampenschnur f
- E: lamp cord
- F: cordon m de lampe

Land, ein Kabel an ~ ziehen
- E: to float a cable ashore
- F: atterrir v un câble

Landleitung f [Tel.]
- E: rural line
- F: ligne f rurale

Länge, auf die gewünschte ~ schneiden
- E: to cut to the required length
- F: couper v à la longueur voulue

Länge/Durchmesser-Verhältnis (L/D) (Extruder-Schnecke) n
- E: L/D ratio
- F: rapport m L/D

Längenmarkierung f
- E: meter marking, length marking
- F: marquage m métré

Längenmeßband n [Kab.]
- E: measuring tape
- F: bande f métreuse

Längenmeßvorrichtung f
- E: meter counter
- F: compteur m métreur

Längenspeicher m [Drahth., Vers.]
- E: accumulator n
- F: accumulateur m, moufle f de régulation

Längenzählgerät n
- E: meter counter
- F: compteur m métreur

langkettige Polymere
- E: long-chain polymers
- F: polymères m pl à longues chaînes

Längsaufbringung f (Bänder)
- E: longitudinal application
- F: pose f longitudinale, disposition f longitudinale

längsaufgebracht adj
- E: longitudinally applied
- F: posé adj longitudinalement, disposé adj en long,

Längsausgleich m [Tel. K.]
- E: balancing of the mutual capacities
- F: égalisation f des capacités mutuelles

Längsbedecken n
- E: longitudinal covering
- F: recouvrement m longitudinal

Längsbedeckungsmaschine f
- E: longitudinal covering machine
- F: machine f à revêtir en sens longitudinal

Langsieb-Papier n
- E: Fourdrinier-machine paper
- F: papier m fabriqué sur machine Fourdrinier

Langsieb-Papiermaschine f
- E: continuous traveling wire cloth paper machine, Fourdrinier paper machine
- F: machine f à papier à toile sans fin, machine f à papier Fourdrinier

Längsmarkierung f
- E: longitudinal marking
- F: marquage m longitudinal, repérage m longitudinal

Längsrichtung f
- E: longitudinal direction, axial direction
- F: sens m longitudinal, sens m de l'axe

Längsriß m (Draht)
- E: split n
- F: crique f

längswasserdicht adj
- E: longitudinally water-proof
- F: étanche adj à l'eau en sens longitudinal

längswasserdichtes Kabel
- E: water-proof cable, water-tight cable
- F: câble m étanche à l'eau, câble m imperméable à l'eau

Längswasserdichtigkeit f
- E: longitudinal water tightness
- F: étanchéité f longitudinale

Längswiderstand m
- E: series resistance, ohmic resistance, positive-sequence resistance
- F: résistance f longitudinale, résistance f en série

Langzeit-Alterungs-Eigenschaften f pl
- E: long-time age(i)ng properties
- F: propriétés f pl de vieillissement de longue durée

Langzeitfestigkeit f [el.]

Langzeitprüfung f
  E: long-time test, continuous test
  F: essai m de (longue) durée, essai m continu

Langzeitverhalten n
  E: long-time behaviour
  F: comportement m en (longue) durée

Langzeitversuch m
  E: long-time test, continuous test
  F: essai m de (longue) durée, essai m continu

Last f [el., mech.]
  E: stress n, strain n, load n
  F: contrainte f, sollicitation f, charge f

Last, mit ~ [el.]
  E: under load
  F: en charge

Last, ohne ~ [el.]
  E: at no-load
  F: sans charge

Lastdichte f
  E: load density
  F: densité f de charge

Lastfaktor m
  E: load factor
  F: facteur m de charge

Lastschwankung f
  E: load fluctuation, load variation
  F: fluctuation f de charge, variation f de charge

Lastschwerpunkt m [el.]
  E: load centre
  F: centre m de grande consommation

Lastspiel n
  E: alternation of load
  F: alternance f

Lastspitze f [el.]
  E: peak load, load peak
  F: pointe f de charge, charge f de pointe

Lastverteilung f
  E: load distribution, dispatching n
  F: répartition f de la charge, dispatching m

Lastwechsel m
  E: reversal of load, change of load
  F: alternance f de l'effort, cycle m de l'effort, cycle m de charge

Lastzyklen m pl [el.]
  E: load cycles, current loading cycles
  F: cycles m pl de charge

Laufboden m
  E: catwalk n
  F: passerelle f

Laufbühne f
  E: catwalk n
  F: passerelle f

laufen, Kabel durch eine Maschine ~ lassen
  E: to feed a cable through a machine
  F: faire v passer un câble par une machine

Laufholm m [Met.-Strangpr.]
  E: moving crosshead
  F: traverse f mobile

Laufkran m
  E: overhead crane, travelling crane
  F: pont m roulant

Laufkranz m
  E: stranding cage disc, carriage n (carrying stranding cradles)
  F: couronne f d'assemblage

Laufrichtung f [Masch.]
  E: direction of running, sense of running
  F: sens m de marche, sens m de défilement

Laufrichtung des Kabels durch eine Maschine
  E: direction of cable travel
  F: sens m de passage du câble

Laufschiene f
  E: guide rail
  F: rail m de guidage, rail m de roulement

Laufzeit einer Maschine
  E: running time of a machine
  F: durée f de fonctionnement d'une machine

L/D (s. Länge/Durchmesser-Verhältnis)

Lebensdauer f
  E: life n, service life
  F: durée f de vie, vie f, durée f d'exploitation

Lebensdauerprüfung f
  E: life test
  F: essai m de (durée) de vie

Lebensdauerprüfung, beschleunigte ~
  E: accelerated life test
  F: essai m accéléré de durée de vie

Leckbildung f
  E: leakage formation
  F: formation f de fuites

Leckortung f

Leckortung
- E: leakage detection
- F: localisation f de fuites

Leckstelle f
- E: leakage n
- F: fuite f, non-étanchéité f

Leckstellenanzeige, automatische ~
- E: automatic leakage detection
- F: détection f automatique de fuites

Leerlaufrolle f
- E: idler pulley
- F: poulie f de marche à vide

Leerlaufspannung f
- E: open-circuit voltage, no-load voltage
- F: tension f à vide, tension f à circuit ouvert

Leerlaufstrom m
- E: no-load current
- F: courant m à vide

Legeverhältnisse n pl
- E: laying conditions, installation conditions
- F: conditions f pl de pose

Legierung f
- E: alloy n
- F: alliage m

Legungstiefe f [K. Verl.]
- E: laying depth, depth of laying, depth below ground, depth under surface, installation depth
- F: profondeur f de pose

leicht zugänglich
- E: easily accessible
- F: facilement accessible

Leichtbau-Koaxialkabel n
- E: lightweight coaxial cable
- F: câble m coaxial léger

Leichtbau-Luftkabel n
- E: figure-eight cable, lightweight aerial cable
- F: câble m aérien léger

leichte Bedienung
- E: ease of manipulation, ease of operation, working ease
- F: aisance f de manipulation, aisance f de manœuvre

leichte Gummischlauchleitung
- E: ordinary tough-rubber sheathed flexible cord
- F: câble m souple sous gaine ordinaire de caoutchouc

leichte Handhabung
- E: ease of manipulation, ease of operation, working ease
- F: aisance f de manipulation, aisance f de manœuvre

leichte Kunststoffschlauchleitung
- E: light plastic-sheathed flexible cord
- F: câble m souple sous gaine légère en plastique

leichte (PVC-)Schlauchleitung
- E: light (PVC-)sheathed flexible cord
- F: câble m souple sous gaine légère (en PVC)

leichte Zwillingsleitung
- E: flat twin tinsel cord
- F: câble m souple méplat à fil rosette

Leihtrommel f [Kab.]
- E: returnable reel
- F: touret m non perdu

Leistung f [Masch.]
- E: performance n, output n, efficiency n, capacity n
- F: performance f, débit m, efficacité f, rendement m, capacité f

Leistung f [el.]
- E: power n
- F: puissance f

Leistungsabgabe f
- E: power output
- F: puissance f disponible

Leistungsaufnahme f
- E: power consumption, power input
- F: puissance f absorbée

Leistungsbedarf m
- E: power requirement, power demand
- F: demande f d'énergie, puissance f nécessaire

Leistungsfaktor m
- E: power factor
- F: facteur m de puissance

Leistungspegel m
- E: power level
- F: niveau m de puissance

Leistungsverlust m [el.]
- E: power loss
- F: perte f de puissance

Leitaluminium (EC-Aluminium) n
- E: electrical conductor grade aluminium (EC-aluminium), high-conductivity aluminium
- F: aluminium m à haute conductibilité

leitend adj
- E: conductive adj
- F: conducteur adj (-trice), conductible adj

Leiter *m*
  E: conductor *n*
  F: âme *f* conductrice, conducteur *m*
Leiter aus konzentrisch verseilten Drahtlagen
  E: concentric lay conductor, concentric strand
  F: âme *f* câblée en couches concentriques
Leiter mit kleinem Querschnitt
  E: small-size conductor, small-gauge conductor
  F: âme *f* de petite section
Leiteraufbau *m*
  E: conductor design
  F: constitution *f* de l'âme conductrice
Leiterbruch *m*
  E: conductor break
  F: rupture *f* de l'âme
Leiterbündel *n*
  E: conductor unit
  F: faisceau *m* d'âmes
Leiterdeckschicht *f* (schwachleitend)
  E: strand shield, inner semi-conducting layer
  F: écran *m* sur l'âme, écran *m* interne, couche *f* semi-conductrice interne
Leiter-Erdspannung *f*
  E: phase-to-earth voltage, line-to-earth voltage
  F: tension *f* étoilée
Leiterfeldstärke *f*
  E: conductor field strength, conductor gradient
  F: intensité *m* de champ au conducteur, gradient *m* au conducteur
Leiterglättung *f*
  E: strand shield, inner semi-conducting layer
  F: écran *m* sur l'âme, écran *m* interne, couche *f* semi-conductrice interne
Leiterglättung, Kabel mit metallener ~
  E: smooth-conductor cable
  F: câble *m* à écran métallique sur l'âme
Leiterheizung, induktive ~
  E: inductive conductor heating
  F: chauffage *m* de l'âme par induction
Leiterseil *n*
  E: conductor strand
  F: toron *m*
Leitertemperatur *f*
  E: conductor temperature
  F: température *f* à l'âme
Leiterverdichtung *f* (s. Verdichtung des Leiters)
Leiterverluste *m pl*
  E: conductor losses
  F: pertes *f pl* sur l'âme
Leiterverseilung *f*
  E: conductor stranding, bunching *n*, stranding *n*, twisting *n*
  F: câblage *m* (âme)
Leiterwiderstand *m*
  E: electrical resistance of conductor, conductor resistance
  F: résistance *f* électrique de l'âme
leitfähig *adj*
  E: conductive *adj*
  F: conducteur *adj* (-trice), conductible *adj*
Leitfähigkeit *f*
  E: conductivity *n*
  F: conductibilité *f*, conductivité *f*
Leitfähigkeit, elektrische ~
  E: electrical conductivity
  F: conductibilité *f* électrique
Leitfähigkeit, magnetische ~
  E: permeability *n*
  F: perméabilité *f*
Leitgummi *m*
  E: semi-conducting rubber
  F: caoutchouc *m* semi-conducteur
Leitkupfer (EC-Kupfer) *n*
  E: electrical conductor grade copper (EC-copper), high-conductivity copper
  F: cuivre *m* à haute conductibilité
Leitlack *m*
  E: semi-conducting varnish, conducting varnish
  F: vernis *m* semi-conducteur
Leitrolle *f*
  E: guide roller, guide pulley
  F: rouleau-guide *m*, poulie *f* de guidage
Leitschicht *f*
  E: semi-conducting layer, semi-conductive layer
  F: couche *f* semi-conductrice
Leitung *f*
  E: insulated wire
  F: fil *m* isolé
Leitung *f* [Nachr.]
  E: line *n*

Leitung
  F: ligne f
Leitung für feste Verlegung
  E: cable for fixed installation
  F: câble m pour installation fixe
Leitung für Tauchpumpen in Bohrlöchern
  E: borehole cable
  F: câble m pour trou de forage
Leitung mit Kreuzungsausgleich [Nachr. K.]
  E: transposed transmission line
  F: ligne f de transmission avec transpositions
Leitung mit punktförmiger Ladung
  E: lump loaded circuit
  F: circuit m à charge concentrée
Leitung, belastete ~
  E: loaded line, line under load
  F: ligne f chargée, ligne f en charge
Leitungsabschnitt m [Nachr. K.]
  E: line section
  F: tronçon m de ligne
Leitungsberührung f
  E: line to line fault
  F: contact m entre fils
Leitungsdämpfung f [Tel. K.]
  E: line attenuation, transmission loss, line loss
  F: affaiblissement m de la ligne
Leitungsdraht m
  E: line wire
  F: fil m de ligne
Leitungseinführung f
  E: cable entrance, cable inlet
  F: entrée f de câble
Leitungsgeräusch n
  E: line noise
  F: bruit m de circuit, bruit m de ligne
Leitungsinduktivität f
  E: line inductance
  F: inductance f de ligne
Leitungskonstante f
  E: line constant
  F: constante f de ligne
Leitungsnachbildung f
  E: artificial balancing line, artificial line, balancing network
  F: équilibreur m, ligne f artificielle
Leitungstrosse f
  E: trailing cable
  F: câble m de remorque, câble m d'enrouleur, câble m pour engin mobile

Leitungswiderstand m
  E: line resistance
  F: résistance f de ligne
Leitvermögen n
  E: conductivity n
  F: conductibilité f, conductivité f
Leitwert m
  E: conductance n
  F: conductance f
Leuchtanzeige f
  E: visual indication
  F: voyant m lumineux
Leuchtbildwarte f
  E: luminous control panel
  F: tableau m de commande lumineux
Leuchtröhrenleitung f
  E: fluorescent tube cable
  F: câble m pour tubes fluorescentes
lichtbeständig adj
  E: light-fast adj, light-stable adj
  F: stable adj à la lumière, résistant adj à la lumière,
Lichtbeständigkeit f (Mischungen)
  E: light-stability n
  F: stabilité f à la lumière
Lichtbeständigkeit f (Farben)
  E: fastness to light
  F: résistance f à la lumière
Lichtbogenbeständigkeit f
  E: arc resistance
  F: résistance f à l'arc électrique
Lichtbogenschweißen n
  E: arc welding
  F: soudage m à l'arc
lichte Weite
  E: inside diameter, inside width
  F: diamètre m intérieur, largeur f intérieure, ouverture f
lichtecht adj
  E: light-fast adj, light-stable adj
  F: stable adj à la lumière, résistant adj à la lumière,
Lichtempfindlichkeit f
  E: light-sensitivity n, luminous sensitivity
  F: sensibilité f à la lumière, sensibilité f lumineuse
Lichtfestigkeit f (Mischungen)
  E: light-stability n
  F: stabilité f à la lumière
Lichtleiter m
  E: optical fibre
  F: fibre f optique

Lichtleiterkabel n
  E: optical fibre cable
  F: câble m à fibres optiques
Lichtleiter-Nachrichtenübertragung f
  E: optical fibre transmission
  F: transmission f par fibre optique
Lichtleiter-Nachrichten-Übertragungsanlage f
  E: optical fibre transmission line
  F: ligne f de transmission par fibre optique
Lichtriß m
  E: sun-crack n, light-crack n
  F: craquelure f due à l'effet de la lumière
Lichtrißbildung f
  E: sun-cracking n, light-cracking n
  F: fissuration f sous l'effet de la lumière solaire
Lichtschutzmittel n
  E: light-stabilizer n, sun-cracking inhibitor
  F: stabilisant m contre l'effet de la lumière
Lieferlänge f
  E: supply length, delivery length
  F: longueur f de livraison, longueur f de bobine
Liefertrommel f
  E: despatch reel, shipping reel, delivery reel
  F: bobine f d'expédition
Liefervorschrift f
  E: purchase specification
  F: spécification f d'achat
lineare Verzerrung
  E: linear distortion
  F: distorsion f linéaire
linearer Ausdehnungskoeffizient
  E: longitudinal expansion coefficient, coefficient of linear expansion
  F: coefficient m de dilatation linéaire
linearer Widerstand
  E: linear resistance
  F: résistance f linéique
Linksdrall m [Vers.]
  E: left-hand lay, left-hand twist
  F: pas m à gauche
Linksdrehung f [Masch.]
  E: counter-clockwise rotation
  F: rotation f en sens inverse des aiguilles d'une montre
linksgängiges Gewinde
  E: left-hand(ed) thread
  F: filet m à gauche
Linksschlag m [Vers.]
  E: left-hand lay, left-hand twist
  F: pas m à gauche
Linksschlag-Verseilung f
  E: left-hand stranding
  F: assemblage m à pas gauche, câblage m à pas gauche
Litze f
  E: strand n, bunch strand, stranded wire
  F: toron m, cordon m
Litzendraht m
  E: tinsel wire
  F: fil m torsadé
Litzenleiter m
  E: bunched conductor
  F: torsade f
Litzenleitung f
  E: tinsel cord
  F: cordon m, toron m
Lizenzgebühr f
  E: royalty n
  F: taxe f et annuités sur brevet
Lochfraß m
  E: local(ized) corrosion, pitting n
  F: corrosion f localisée, corrosion f locale, corrosion f ponctuelle, pitting m
Lochplatte f [Vers.]
  E: assembling plate, lay plate
  F: plaque f de répartition, plaque f de guidage
Lochscheibe f [Extr.]
  E: breaker plate
  F: répartiteur m de flux
Lockerung f [Bdspinn.]
  E: loosening n
  F: ramollissement m
Lockerwerden n [Bdspinn.]
  E: loosening n
  F: ramollissement m
Lokalelement n
  E: local cell
  F: pile f locale, élément m galvanique localisé
Lokalkorrosion f
  E: local(ized) corrosion, pitting n
  F: corrosion f localisée, corrosion f locale, corrosion f ponctuelle, pitting m
Los n [Kab.]

Los

- *E:* lot *n*
- *F:* lot *m*

Lösung *f*
- *E:* solution *n*
- *F:* solution *f*

Lösungsmittelbeständigkeit *f*
- *E:* solvent resistance
- *F:* résistance *f* aux solvants

Lot *n*
- *E:* solder *n*
- *F:* métal *m* d'apport, soudure *f*, brasure *f*

Lötbarkeit *f*
- *E:* solderability *n*
- *F:* soudabilité *f*

Lötdraht *m*
- *E:* cored solder, soldering wire, wire solder
- *F:* fil *m* de soudure, soudure *f* en fil

Löten *n*
- *E:* soldering *n*
- *F:* soudage *m*

lötfreie gewickelte Verbindung
- *E:* wire-wrap connection
- *F:* connexion *f* enroulée, raccord *m* sans soudure

Lötkabelschuh *m*
- *E:* soldered terminal lug
- *F:* cosse *f* de câble soudée

Lotstab *m*
- *E:* solder stick
- *F:* barre *f* de soudure

Lötstelle *f*
- *E:* soldered joint, soldering joint
- *F:* jonction *f* par soudure, soudure *f*, joint *m* soudé

Lötverbindung *f* (hart)
- *E:* brazed joint, brazing joint
- *F:* brasure *f*

Lötverbindung *f* (weich)
- *E:* soldered joint, soldering joint
- *F:* jonction *f* par soudure, soudure *f*, joint *m* soudé

Lötzinn *n*
- *E:* tinning solder, soldering tin
- *F:* étain *m* à souder, étain *m* de soudage

Lückenfüllung *f* [Kab.]
- *E:* filler *n*, valley sealer
- *F:* bourrage *m*

Luft, eingeschlossene ~
- *E:* entrapped air
- *F:* air *m* enfermé

Luftabschluß *m*
- *E:* exclusion of air, hermetic seal
- *F:* étanchéité *f* à l'air

Luftbombe *f*
- *E:* air bomb
- *F:* bombe *f* à air

luftdicht *adj*
- *E:* air-tight *adj*, hermetically sealed
- *F:* étanche *adj* à l'air

Luftdurchlässigkeit *f*
- *E:* permeability to air
- *F:* perméabilité *f* à l'air

Luftdurchlässigkeit *f* (Papier)
- *E:* porosity *n*
- *F:* porosité *f*

Luftdurchsatz *m* (im Wärmeschrank)
- *E:* air flow
- *F:* débit *m* d'air

Lufteinschlüsse *m pl*
- *E:* air inclusions, air pockets, voids *pl*
- *F:* occlusions *f pl* d'air, poches *f pl* d'air, bulles *f pl* d'air

Luftfeuchtigkeit *f*
- *E:* atmospheric humidity, humidity of the air
- *F:* humidité *f* de l'air

Luftfeuchtigkeit, relative ~
- *E:* relative humidity
- *F:* degré *m* hygrométrique, humidité *f* relative

luftgekühlt *adj*
- *E:* air-cooled *adj*
- *F:* refroidi *adj* à l'air

Luftkabel *n*
- *E:* aerial cable, overhead cable
- *F:* câble *m* aérien, fil *m* aérien

Luftkabel, selbsttragendes ~
- *E:* self-supporting aerial cable, self-supporting overhead cable
- *F:* câble *m* aérien autoporteur

Luftkabeltragseil *n* [Tel. K.]
- *E:* supporting strand, suspension strand, aerial messenger, messenger wire
- *F:* câble *m* porteur, corde *f* de suspension

Luftkühlstrecke *f*
- *E:* air cooling section
- *F:* section *f* de refroidissement par air

Luftumwälzung, Ofen mit ~
- *E:* forced-air oven, air oven
- *F:* étuve *f* à circulation d'air, étuve *f* ventilé

Lüftung f
 E: ventilation n, aeration n
 F: ventilation f, aération f
Lunker m
 E: shrinkhole n
 F: retassure f

M

magnetische Kopplung
 E: magnetic coupling
 F: couplage m magnétique
magnetische Leitfähigkeit
 E: permeability n
 F: perméabilité f
magnetischer Schirm
 E: magnetic shield
 F: écran m magnétique
Magnetventil n
 E: solenoid valve
 F: électrovanne f
Mannloch n [K. Verl.]
 E: entrance n, manhole n
 F: entrée f, accès m, trou m d'homme, regard m de visite
Mannlochdeckel m
 E: manhole cover
 F: couvercle m de trou d'homme
Manometer n
 E: pressure gauge, pressure control device, manometer n
 F: dispositif m de contrôle de la pression, manomètre m
Mantel m [Kab.]
 E: sheath n, jacket n
 F: gaine f
Mantelabstreifmaschine f
 E: sheath stripping machine
 F: dépouilleuse f de gaine
Manteldicke f [Kab.]
 E: sheath thickness
 F: épaisseur f de la gaine
Mantelleitung f
 E: light PVC-sheathed cable
 F: câble m rigide sous gaine légère en PVC
Mantelmischung f
 E: sheathing compound
 F: mélange m gaine
Mantelverluste m pl

 E: sheath losses
 F: pertes f pl sur la gaine
Markierung durch Prägen
 E: marking by embossing
 F: marquage m en relief
Markierung für fehlerhaftes Paar
 E: marker n (com. c.), defective pair marker
 F: marqueur m de paires défectueuses
Markierungselement n [Nachr. K.]
 E: marker n
 F: élément m de marquage
Markierungsfarbe f
 (Aderkennzeichnung)
 E: tracer colo(u)r
 F: couleur f de repérage
Markierungsstrich m
 E: marker line
 F: trait m de repère
Maschine, bei laufender ~
 E: under running conditions of a machine
 F: la machine étant en marche
maschinell adj
 E: mechanical adj
 F: mécanique adj
Maschinenführer m
 E: operator n, attendant n
 F: opérateur m, machiniste m
Maschinenspule f
 E: input bobbin, input reel, processing reel, processing drum
 F: bobine f d'alimentation
Maschinentrommel f
 E: input bobbin, input reel, processing reel, processing drum
 F: bobine f d'alimentation
Masse, abwandernde ~ [Kab.]
 E: migrating compound, draining compound
 F: matière f migrante
Masseabwanderung f [Kab.]
 E: migration of compound, draining of compound
 F: migration f de matière, écoulement m de matière
massearme Isolierung
 E: mass-impregnated and drained insulation
 F: isolant m égoutté après imprégnation
Masseaustritt m
 E: bleeding of compound

Masseaustritt
F: fuite f de matière

Masse-Druck m [Extr.]
E: melt pressure
F: pression f de la matière en fusion

massegetränkt adj
E: mass-impregnated adj, compound-impregnated adj
F: imprégné adj de matière

massegetränktes Papierkabel
E: paper-insulated mass-impregnated cable
F: câble m isolé à papier imprégné à matière visqueuse

Massekabel n
E: paper-insulated mass-impregnated cable
F: câble m isolé à papier imprégné à matière visqueuse

Massel f (Blei)
E: pig n, cake n
F: saumon m

Masse-Temperatur f [Extr.]
E: melt temperature
F: température f de la matière en fusion

Masseverarmung f [Kab.]
E: migration of compound, draining of compound
F: migration f de matière, écoulement m de matière

maßgerecht adj
E: true to size, accurate to size
F: à dimensions exactes, conforme adj à l'échelle,

maßhaltig adj
E: true to size, accurate to size
F: à dimensions exactes, conforme adj à l'échelle,

Maßhaltigkeit f
E: accuracy to size, dimensional accuracy, dimensional stability, dimensional precision
F: exactitude f des dimensions prescrites

Massivleiter m
E: solid conductor
F: âme f massive, âme f à un seul brin

Maßstab, Versuch im praktischen ~
E: full-scale trial
F: essai m à l'échelle naturelle

maßstäbliche Zeichnung
E: scale drawing, dimensional drawing, drawing to scale
F: dessin m à l'échelle

Mast-Endverschluß m
E: pole-mounted termination
F: isolateur m de poteau

Materialfehler m
E: material defect
F: défaut m du matériel

Materialfluß m (innerbetrieblich)
E: materials handling
F: transport m des matériaux

Materialprüfung f
E: material testing
F: essai m des matériaux

Matrize f
E: ring die, female die
F: filière f

Matrizenhalter m
E: die holder
F: fourreau m

Matrizenkühlung f
E: die cooling
F: refroidissement m de la filière

Matrizenring m
E: die ring
F: anneau m de filière

Matrizenversteller m
E: die adjuster
F: dispositif m de réglage de filière

maximal zulässige Betriebstemperatur
E: maximum admissible operating temperature
F: température f de service maximale admissible

mechanisch betätigt
E: mechanically operated
F: à commande mécanique

mechanische Eigenschaft
E: mechanical characteristic, mechanical property
F: charactéristique f mécanique, propriété f mécanique

mechanische Festigkeit
E: mechanical strength
F: résistance mécanique f

Medianwert m
E: median value
F: valeur f médiane

mehradriges Kabel
E: multicore cable, multiconductor cable, multiple core cable
F: câble m multipolaire, câble m multiconducteur

mehrdrähtiger Leiter

Mehrfachextrusion f
- E: multiple extrusion
- F: extrusion f multiple

Mehrfachschutzerdung f
- E: protective multiple earthing (p.m.e.)
- F: protection f par mise à la terre multiple, mise f à la terre de protection multiple, mise f au neutre

Mehrfachstecker m
- E: multicontact plug, multiple plug
- F: fiche f multiple

Mehrfachverseilung f
- E: multiple stranding
- F: câblage m multiple

mehrgängige Trommelverseilmaschine
- E: multi-pass drum twisting machine
- F: câbleuse f à tambour à plusieures passes

Mehrleiterkabel n
- E: multicore cable, multiconductor cable, multiple core cable
- F: câble m multipolaire, câble m multiconducteur

Mehrlochkanal m
- E: line of ducts, multiple duct conduit, multiple way duct
- F: conduit m à plusieurs passages, caniveau m à passage multiple

Mehrmoden-Lichtleiter m
- E: multimode optical fibre
- F: fibre f optique multimode

mehrpaariges Kabel [Tel.]
- E: multiple pair cable, multipair cable, multipaired cable, large-capacity cable
- F: câble m multipaire, câble m multitoron, câble m à grande capacité

mehrpoliger Stecker
- E: multiple pin plug
- F: fiche f multipolaire

Mehrschichtbetrieb m
- E: multiple shift operation
- F: travail m en plusieurs équipes

Mehrschicht-Isolierung f
- E: laminated insulation, laminar insulation, composite bonded laminar insulation
- F: isolation f stratifiée, isolation f laminée

mehrzügiger Rohrstrang
- E: line of ducts, multiple duct conduit, multiple way duct
- F: conduit m à plusieurs passages, caniveau m à passage multiple

Membranen f pl (im Öldruckausgleichsgefäß)
- E: cells pl, membrane cells
- F: cellules f pl

Meßader f [Nachr. K.]
- E: second wire, test wire
- F: fil m de test

Meßanordnung f
- E: measuring arrangement, connections pl for measurement
- F: disposition f de mesure, montage m de mesure, couplage m de mesure

Meßband n [Kab.]
- E: measuring tape
- F: bande f métreuse

Meßbrücke f
- E: measuring bridge
- F: pont m de mesure

Meßelektrode f
- E: measuring electrode
- F: électrode f de mesure, sonde f

Meßergebnis n
- E: measuring result
- F: résultat m de mesure

Meßfehler m
- E: faulty measurement, measuring error
- F: raté m de mesure, erreur f de mesure

Meßgenauigkeit f
- E: accuracy of measurement, measuring precision
- F: précision f de mesure

Meßgerät n
- E: measuring device, measuring instrument, measuring equipment
- F: appareil m de mesure

Meßgröße f
- E: quantity to be measured, measured quantity
- F: grandeur f mesurée

Meßkabel n
- E: measuring cable
- F: câble m de mesure

Meßkoffer m (s. Kabelmeßkoffer)

Meßkreis m

Meßkreis
 E: measuring circuit
 F: circuit *m* de mesure
Meßmethode f
 E: method of measurement
 F: méthode f de mesure
Meßplatz m
 E: measuring setup, bench-mounted testing equipment
 F: table f d'essai, poste *m* de mesure
Meßpunkt m
 E: measuring point, check point
 F: point *m* de mesure
Meßraum m
 E: measuring room, test room
 F: salle f de mesure
Meßschaltung f
 E: measuring arrangement, connections pl for measurement
 F: disposition f de mesure, montage *m* de mesure, couplage *m* de mesure
Meßschleife f
 E: measuring loop
 F: boucle f de mesure
Meßspannung f
 E: measuring voltage
 F: tension f de mesure
Meßuhr f
 E: indicating dial
 F: compteur *m*, indicateur *m* à cadran
Meßwagen für Kabel
 E: cable testing truck
 F: voiture-laboratoire f pour l'essai des câbles
Meßwert m
 E: measured value
 F: valeur f mesurée
Meßwertschreiber m
 E: recording instrument, recorder *n*
 F: enregistreur *m*
Meßwiderstand m
 E: measuring resistance
 F: résistance f de mesure
Metallband n
 E: metal strip, metal tape
 F: feuillard *m*, bande f métallique
Metallfolie f
 E: metal foil
 F: feuille f métallique
metallisiertes Papier (Höchstädter Folie)
 E: metallized paper
 F: papier *m* métallisé
Metallmantel m
 E: metal sheath
 F: gaine f métallique
metallographische Prüfung
 E: metallographic examination, metallographic test
 F: examen *m* métallographique, analyse f métallographique
metallumhüllter Leiter
 E: metal clad conductor
 F: âme f plaquée de métal
Meterzähler m
 E: meter counter
 F: compteur *m* métreur
Methode f
 E: process *n*, method *n*, technique *n*, procedure *n*
 F: procédé *m*, méthode f, technique f
mikrokristallines Wachs
 E: microcrystalline wax
 F: cire f microcristalline
Mikrometerschraube f
 E: micrometer screw
 F: vis f micrométrique, palmer *m*
Mikrophonleitung f
 E: microphone cable
 F: câble *m* de microphone
mikroskopische Untersuchung
 E: microscopic inspection
 F: inspection f microscopique
Mikrowelle f
 E: microwave *n*
 F: micro-onde f
Milliken-Leiter *m* (s. skineffektarmer Leiter)
Millikenleiter-Kabel n
 E: Milliken conductor cable
 F: câble *m* à conducteurs Milliken
mineralisoliertes Kabel
 E: mineral-insulated cable
 F: câble *m* à isolation minérale
Mineralöl n
 E: mineral oil
 F: huile f minérale
Miniatur-Kabel n
 E: miniature cable
 F: câble *m* miniature
Minusleiter m
 E: negative lead, negative conductor
 F: conducteur *m* négatif
Mischanlage f
 E: mixing plant
 F: installation f de préparation des mélanges

mischen v [Gi., Plast.]
 E: mix v, blend v, compound v
 F: mélanger v

mischen v
 E: blend v, mix v, intermingle v
 F: mélanger v, mêler v

Mischer m
 E: mixer n
 F: mélangeur m

Mischerei f
 E: mixing shop
 F: atelier m de préparation des mélanges

Mischfolge f
 E: order-of-addition schedule (mixing)
 F: ordre m d'addition des ingrédients

Mischkneter m
 E: kneader mixer
 F: malaxeur-mélangeur m

Mischpolymerisat n
 E: copolymer n
 F: copolymère m

Mischschnecke f [Extr.]
 E: mixing screw
 F: vis f de mélangeage

Mischung f
 E: compound n
 F: mélange m

Mischungsansatz m
 E: compound formulation
 F: formulation f d'un mélange

Mischungsaufbereitung f
 E: preparation of a compound, compound preparation
 F: préparation f d'un mélange

Mischungsbestandteile m pl
 E: ingredients of a compound
 F: ingrédients m pl d'un mélange, composants m pl d'un mélange

Mischwalzwerk n
 E: mixing mill, mixing rolls pl
 F: mélangeur m à cylindres, mélangeur m à rouleaux, cylindre m malaxeur

Mitsprechen n
 E: side-to-phantom crosstalk
 F: diaphonie f entre réel et fantôme

Mitsprechkopplung f
 E: phantom-to-side unbalance
 F: couplage m de diaphonie

Mittelblindader f
 E: centre blind core, centre filler
 F: bourrage m central

Mitteldraht m [Drahth.]
 E: intermediate wire
 F: fil m intermédiaire

Mitteldraht m (Leiter)
 E: core wire
 F: fil m central

Mittelleiter m
 E: middle conductor, centre conductor
 F: conducteur m médian

Mittellinie einer Maschine
 E: centre line of a machine
 F: ligne f centrale d'une machine, axe m médian d'une machine

Mittelpunktsleiter m
 E: neutral conductor, neutral wire, zero conductor
 F: conducteur m neutre, fil m neutre, neutre m

Mittelspannungskabel n
 E: medium voltage cable
 F: câble m à moyenne tension

Mittelwert m
 E: mean value, average value
 F: valeur f moyenne

Mittenabstand m
 E: centre-to-centre distance, centre spacing
 F: distance f d'axe en axe, distance f des centres

mittlere Kunststoffschlauchleitung
 E: ordinary plastic-sheathed flexible cord
 F: câble m souple sous gaine ordinaire en plastique

mittlere (PVC-)Schlauchleitung
 E: ordinary (PVC-)sheathed flexible cord
 F: câble m souple sous gaine ordinaire (en PVC)

Modellanfertigung f
 E: pattern-making n
 F: fabrication f de maquettes

Modellkabel n
 E: model cable
 F: maquette f de câble, modèle m de câble

Molch m (Rohrreiniger)
 E: go-devil n
 F: écouvillon m

Molekulargefüge n
 E: molecular structure

Molekulargefüge
 F: structure f moléculaire
Molekulargewicht, mit hohem ~
 E: of high molecular weight, high-molecular... adj
 F: à haut poids moléculaire
Montage f
 E: installation n, erection n, set-up n, assembly n
 F: implantation f, montage m, assemblage m
Montageanleitung f
 E: fitting instructions pl, installation instructions pl
 F: instructions f pl de montage, notice f de montage
Montageort, am ~ [K. Verl.]
 E: at site
 F: sur chantier
Montagesatz m
 E: installation kit
 F: ensemble m de montage
Montagezeichnung f
 E: assembly drawing, erection drawing, installation drawing
 F: plan m d'assemblage, plan m de montage
Monteur m
 E: jointer n, fitter n, erector n
 F: monteur m
Motor mit regulierbarer Geschwindigkeit
 E: adjustable speed motor, variable speed motor
 F: moteur m à vitesse réglable, moteur m à vitesse variable
motorangetrieben adj
 E: motor-driven adj, motorized adj
 F: commandé adj par moteur, motorisé adj, entraîné adj par moteur,
motorisch adj
 E: motor-driven adj, motorized adj
 F: commandé adj par moteur, motorisé adj, entraîné adj par moteur,
Muffe f [Kab.]
 E: joint n
 F: jonction f
Muffenbauwerk n
 E: cable pit, cable jointing chamber, cable jointing manhole, cable vault
 F: trou m d'homme, puits m de visite, puits m de jonction, chambre f de répartition, puits m à câbles
Muffenbauwerks-Sohle f
 E: floor of vault, floor of manhole
 F: fond m du trou d'homme
Muffenbunker m
 E: cable pit, cable jointing chamber, cable jointing manhole, cable vault
 F: trou m d'homme, puits m de visite, puits m de jonction, chambre f de répartition, puits m à câbles
Muffenbunker-Sohle f
 E: floor of vault, floor of manhole
 F: fond m du trou d'homme
Muffengehäuse n
 E: joint box, casing of a joint
 F: boîte f de jonction
Mundstück n [Extr.]
 E: die n
 F: filière f
Muster n
 E: specimen n, sample n
 F: éprouvette f, échantillon m

N

Nachbarvierer-Nebensprech-Kopplung f
 E: side-to-side crosstalk coupling
 F: couplage m diaphonique entre réel et réel, couplage m diaphonique entre quartes voisines
nachbilden v
 E: simulate v
 F: simuler v
nachdunkeln v
 E: darken v
 F: foncer v (se)
nacheilende Phase
 E: lagging phase
 F: phase f en retard
nachfüllen v
 E: replenish v, resupply v, refill v
 F: remplir v, refaire v le plein
Nachrichten-Außenkabel n
 E: outdoor communications cable
 F: câble m de communication extérieur
Nachrichtenkabel n
 E: telecommunications cable, communications cable

Nachrichtennetz n
 E: communications network
 F: réseau m de communications

Nachrichtentechnik f
 E: communications engineering
 F: technique f de communication

Nachrichtenübermittlung f
 E: telecommunication n
 F: télécommunication f

nachstellen v
 E: reset v
 F: rajuster v, réajuster v

Nagetier-Schäden m pl
 E: rodent attack
 F: détériorations f pl causées par des rongeurs

Näheeffekt m
 E: proximity effect
 F: effet m de proximité

Näherungswert m
 E: approximate value
 F: valeur f approchée, valeur f approximative

Nahnebensprechdämpfung f
 E: near-end crosstalk attenuation
 F: affaiblissement m paradiaphonique

Nahnebensprechen n
 E: near-end cross talk (NEX)
 F: paradiaphonie f

nahtloses Pressen von Metallmänteln
 E: seamless extrusion of metal sheaths
 F: filage m sans soudure des gaines métalliques

nahtloses Rohr
 E: seamless tube
 F: tube m sans soudure

Nahtschweißen n
 E: seam welding
 F: soudage m en ligne continue

naphtenbasisches Rohöl
 E: naphthene base crude oil
 F: huile f brute naphténique

Naßanalyse f
 E: wet analysis
 F: analyse f humide

Naturkautschuk m
 E: natural rubber
 F: caoutchouc m naturel

nd-Kabel n
 E: non-draining cable, nd-cable n
 F: câble m à matière non migrante, câble m nd

nd-Masse f
 E: non-draining compound, nd-compound n
 F: matière f non migrante, matière f nd

nebeneinander liegende Kabel
 E: cables in flat formation, cables laid in parallel, cables laid side by side
 F: câbles m pl disposés en nappe

nebeneinander, Verlegung ~
 E: laying side by side, laying in parallel, parallel arrangement
 F: disposition f côte à côte, disposition f en nappe horizontale, disposition f en parallèle

Nebenschluß m
 E: branch circuit, shunt n
 F: circuit m dérivé, shunt m

Nebensprechausgleich m
 E: crosstalk balancing
 F: équilibrage m de diaphonies

Nebensprechdämpfung f
 E: crosstalk attenuation, crosstalk transmission equivalent
 F: affaiblissement m diaphonique

Nebensprechdämpfungsmaß n
 E: crosstalk attenuation unit
 F: unité f d'affaiblissement diaphonique, équivalent m d'affaiblissement diaphonique

Nebensprechdämpfungsmesser m
 E: crosstalk meter
 F: diaphonomètre m

Nebensprechen n
 E: crosstalk
 F: diaphonie f

Nebensprechen, unverständliches ~ [Tel.]
 E: babbling n
 F: murmure m confus

nebensprechfrei adj
 E: crosstalk-proof adj
 F: exempt adj de diaphonie

Nebensprechkopplung f
 E: crosstalk circuit, crosstalk coupling
 F: couplage m diaphonique

Nebensprechmesser m
 E: crosstalk meter
 F: diaphonomètre m

Nebensprechstrom m
 E: crosstalk current, unbalance(d) current

Nebensprechstrom
  F: courant *m* diaphonique
Nebenzeit *f* [Masch.]
  E: ancillary time, non-productive time, handling time, down time
  F: temps *m* auxiliaire, temps *m* mort
Neigung *f*
  E: inclination *n*, tilting *n*, tilt *n*
  F: inclinaison *f*, basculement *m*
Neigung einer Kurve
  E: decline of a curve, slope of a curve
  F: inclinaison *f* d'une courbe, pente *f* d'une courbe
Neigungswinkel *m*
  E: angle of inclination, tilt angle
  F: angle *m* d'inclinaison
Nennbelastung *f*
  E: rated load, nominal load
  F: charge *f* nominale
Nennleistung *f* [Masch.]
  E: rated output, nominal output
  F: debit *m* nominal
Nennleistung *f* [el.]
  E: rated power, nominal power
  F: puissance *f* nominale
Nennquerschnitt *m*
  E: nominal cross-section
  F: section *f* nominale
Nennspannung *f*
  E: nominal voltage, rated voltage
  F: tension *f* nominale
Nennwert *m*
  E: nominal value, rated value
  F: valeur *f* nominale
Neoprene *n* (Polychloropren-Kautschuk der Du Pont)
  E: Neoprene *n*
  F: Neoprene *n*
Netz *n* [el.]
  E: network *n*, system *n*, mains *n*
  F: réseau *m*, secteur *m*
Netz mit isoliertem Sternpunkt
  E: system with insulated neutral
  F: réseau *m* avec neutre isolé
Netz mit starr geerdetem Sternpunkt
  E: solidly earthed system (GB), solidly grounded system (US)
  F: réseau *m* avec mise à la terre rigide du neutre, réseau *m* rigidement relié à la terre
Netzanschluß *m*
  E: line connection, mains supply, power supply
  F: branchement *m* au réseau, connexion *f* au réseau, alimentation *f* (sur) secteur
Netzanschlußkabel *n*
  E: line cable
  F: câble *m* d'alimentation réseau
Netzausfall *m*
  E: power failure
  F: manque *m* de tension secteur, défaillance *f* du secteur
Netzkabel *n*
  E: mains cable, distribution cable
  F: câble *m* de réseau, câble *m* de distribution
Netzmittel *n*
  E: wetting agent
  F: agent *m* mouillant, agent *m* humidificateur
Netzschalter *m*
  E: power switch
  F: interrupteur *m* de réseau
Netzspannung *f*
  E: mains voltage, line voltage, system voltage
  F: tension *f* de réseau, tension *f* du secteur
Netzstecker *m*
  E: power plug
  F: fiche *f* de prise de courant
Netzstörung *f*
  E: system fault
  F: dérangement *m* sur réseau
Netzstrom *m*
  E: line current, mains current
  F: courant *m* secteur, courant *m* de réseau
Netztransformator *m*
  E: power transformer
  F: transformateur *m* d'alimentation
netzunabhängig *adj*
  E: non-system-dependent *adj*, non-system-connected *adj*
  F: indépendant *adj* du réseau
Netzwiderstand *m*
  E: network impedance
  F: impédance *f* du réseau
Netzzuleitung *f*
  E: mains supply lead
  F: conduite *f* d'amenée de secteur
neues Material [Prüf.]
  E: virgin material
  F: matière *f* neuve
Neutralisationszahl (NZ) *f*
  E: neutralisation number

F: indice *m* de neutralisation

nicht abwandernde Tränkmasse
- *E:* non-draining compound, nd-compound *n*
- *F:* matière *f* non migrante, matière *f* nd

nicht geerdeter Sternpunkt (Nullpunkt)
- *E:* unearthed neutral (GB), ungrounded neutral (US)
- *F:* neutre *m* non mis à la terre

nicht kompensierte Länge (beim Platzwechsel einer Blankdrahtleitung)
- *E:* non-compensated length
- *F:* longueur *f* non compensée

nicht verdichteter Leiter
- *E:* non-compacted conductor
- *F:* âme *f* non rétreinte

nichtrostend *adj*
- *E:* stainless *adj*, rust-resisting *adj*
- *F:* inoxydable *adj*

Niederdruckölkabel *n*
- *E:* low pressure oil-filled cable
- *F:* câble *m* sous basse pression d'huile

Niederdruckölkabel *n* (mit aufgepreßtem Metallmantel)
- *E:* self-contained oil-filled cable
- *F:* câble *m* sous basse pression d'huile (sous gaine métallique)

Niederdruck-PE *n*
- *E:* high-density PE (HD-PE), low pressure PE (LP-PE)
- *F:* polyéthylène *m* haute densité, polyéthylène *m* basse pression

Niederfrequenz *f*
- *E:* audio frequency, voice frequency, low frequency
- *F:* audio-fréquence *f*, fréquence *f* vocale, basse fréquence *f*

Niederfrequenzfernsprechen *n*
- *E:* audio frequency telephony
- *F:* téléphonie *f* à audio-fréquence

Niederfrequenz-Schaltkabel *n*
- *E:* voice frequency switchboard cable
- *F:* câble *m* de connexion basse fréquence

Niederfrequenz-Übertragungssystem *n*
- *E:* audio frequency transmission system
- *F:* système *m* de transmission basse fréquence

niedermolekular *adj*
- *E:* of low molecular weight
- *F:* à faible poids moléculaire

niederohmig *adj*
- *E:* low-ohmic *adj*, of low resistance
- *F:* de faible valeur ohmique, de faible résistance

Niederschlag *m* [Chem.]
- *E:* precipitate *n*
- *F:* précipité *m*, dépôt *m*

Niederspannung *f*
- *E:* low voltage (LV)
- *F:* basse tension *f* (BT)

Niederspannungskabel *n*
- *E:* low voltage cable
- *F:* câble *m* à basse tension

Niederspannungsschaltanlage *f*
- *E:* low voltage switchgear
- *F:* installation *f* de disjoncteurs basse tension

niedrigpaariges Kabel [Tel.]
- *E:* small capacity cable, small make-up cable, small-sized cable
- *F:* câble *m* à faible capacité, câble *m* à petit nombre de paires

niedrigsiedend *adj*
- *E:* with a low boiling point
- *F:* à bas point d'ébullition

niedrigviskoses Öl
- *E:* low-viscosity oil
- *F:* huile *f* à faible viscosité

Nippel *m* [Extr.]
- *E:* tip *n*
- *F:* poinçon *m*

Nippelbock *m* [Vers.]
- *E:* nipple stand
- *F:* bâti *m* de filière

Nitrilkautschuk *m*
- *E:* nitrile butadiene rubber
- *F:* caoutchouc *m* nitrile

Niveauwächter *m*
- *E:* level control(ler)
- *F:* contrôleur *m* du niveau

Nominalwert *m*
- *E:* nominal value, rated value
- *F:* valeur *f* nominale

Norm *f*
- *E:* standard specification
- *F:* norme *f*, spécification *f*

Normalbeanspruchung *f*
- *E:* standard stress
- *F:* charge *f* normale

Normalkoaxialpaar *n*
- *E:* standard coaxial pair
- *F:* paire *f* coaxiale standard

Normenausschuß *m*
  E: standardization committee
  F: comité *m* de normalisation
Normteil *n*
  E: standard part
  F: pièce *f* standard, pièce *f* normalisée
Normung *f*
  E: standardisation *n*, normalization *n*, unification *n*
  F: standardisation *f*, normalisation *f*, unification *f*
Notabschaltung *f*
  E: emergency shut-down
  F: arrêt *m* d'urgence
Notbetrieb *m*
  E: emergency operation, emergency service
  F: régime *m* de secours
Notstrom-Aggregat *n*
  E: stand-by power unit, emergency generator set
  F: groupe *m* électrogène de secours
Notstromversorgung *f*
  E: emergency power supply
  F: alimentation *f* en énergie de secours
Nulleinstellung, automatische ~
  E: automatic reset
  F: remise *f* à zéro automatique
Nulleiter *m*
  E: neutral conductor, neutral wire, zero conductor
  F: conducteur *m* neutre, fil *m* neutre, neutre *m*
Nulleiter, konzentrischer ~
  E: concentric neutral conductor
  F: neutre *m* concentrique, neutre *m* périphérique
Nullpunkt *m*
  E: neutral point, zero point
  F: neutre *m*, point *m* neutre, zéro *m*
Nullsystem *n*
  E: zero phase-sequence system
  F: système *m* homopolaire
Nullung *f*
  E: protective multiple earthing (p.m.e.)
  F: protection *f* par mise à la terre multiple, mise *f* à la terre de protection multiple, mise *f* au neutre
numerierte Kabelader
  E: numbered cable core
  F: conducteur *m* de câble numéroté
Numerierung *f*
  E: numbering *n*
  F: numérotage *m*
Nut *f*
  E: groove *n*, slot *n*, recess *n*, notch *n*, nick *n*
  F: rainure *f*, encoche *f*, découpe *f*, évidement *m*, entaille *f*
Nut und Feder
  E: slot and tongue
  F: rainure *f* et languette
Nutzdämpfung *f*
  E: effective transmission, effective transmission equivalent, overall transmission loss
  F: équivalent *m* de transmission effective
Nutzleistung *f* [el.]
  E: useful power
  F: puissance *f* utile
Nutzungsdauer *f*
  E: life *n*, service life
  F: durée *f* de vie, vie *f*, durée *f* d'exploitation
NZ (s. Neutralisationszahl)

O

Oberflächenbehandlung *f*
  E: surface treatment
  F: traitement *m* de surface
Oberflächenbeschaffenheit *f*
  E: surface finish, surface quality
  F: qualité *f* de surface
Oberflächenfehler *m*
  E: surface defect, surface imperfection, surface irregularity
  F: défaut *m* superficiel, défaut *m* de surface, imperfection *f* superficielle
Oberflächengüte *f*
  E: surface finish, surface quality
  F: qualité *f* de surface
Oberflächenrauhigkeit *f*
  E: surface roughness
  F: rugosité *f* de la surface
Oberflächenrisse *m pl*
  E: surface cracks
  F: craquelures *f pl* en surface
Oberflächenschutz *m*

E: surface protection
F: protection f superficielle

Oberflächenverluste m pl
E: surface losses
F: pertes f pl superficielles

Oberflächenwiderstand m
E: surface resistance
F: résistance f superficielle

Oberflächenwiderstand, spezifischer ~
E: surface resistivity
F: résistivité f de surface

Ofen mit Luftumwälzung
E: forced-air oven, air oven
F: étuve f à circulation d'air, étuve f ventilé

Ofenauskleidung f
E: furnace lining
F: revêtement m de four

Ofenruß m
E: furnace black
F: suie f

offene Wendel
E: open helix
F: hélice f de vide

Offenlegungsschrift f
E: unexamined patent application
F: demande f de brevet non examinée

Öffnung f
E: opening n, orifice n, aperture n, bore n
F: orifice m, ouverture f

OFHC-Kupfer n (sauerstoffreies hochleitfähiges Kupfer)
E: OFHC-copper n (oxygen free high conductivity copper)
F: cuivre m OFHC (cuivre exempt d'oxygène, à haute conductivité)

Ohmsche Kopplung
E: ohmic coupling
F: couplage m ohmique

ohmscher Widerstand
E: ohmic resistance
F: résistance f ohmique

ohne Last [el.]
E: at no-load
F: sans charge

Ohrkurve f [Nachr. K.]
E: psophonetic curve
F: courbe f psophonétique

Oilostatic-Kabel n
E: high-pressure oil-filled pipe type cable, Oilostatic-cable n
F: câble m en tube d'acier sous haute pression d'huile, câble m Oléostatique

Ölausgleichsgefäß n
E: oil expansion tank, variable oil pressure tank, oil pressure tank, oil reservoir
F: réservoir m à pression d'huile variable

Ölbeständigkeit f
E: oil resistance
F: résistance f à l'huile

Ölbewegung f (im Kabel)
E: oil oscillation
F: oscillation f d'huile

Öldruck m
E: oil pressure
F: pression f d'huile

Öldruck-Ausgleichsgefäß n
E: oil expansion tank, variable oil pressure tank, oil pressure tank, oil reservoir
F: réservoir m à pression d'huile variable

Öldruckkabel n
E: oil pressure cable, pressure-assisted oil-filled cable
F: câble m à pression d'huile

Öldruck-Rohrkabel n
E: oil pressure pipe type cable
F: câble m en tube à pression d'huile

Öleinspeisungsvorrichtung f
E: oil feeding equipment
F: dispositif m d'alimentation en huile

Ölfestigkeit f
E: oil resistance
F: résistance f à l'huile

Ölharzgemisch n
E: oil-rosin compound
F: mélange m oléo-résineux, mélange m huile-résine

Ölharzlack m
E: oleoresinous enamel
F: vernis m oléo-résineux

Öl-Hochdruck-Kabel n
E: high-pressure oil-filled cable
F: câble m à huile fluide à haute pression, câble m sous haute pression d'huile

Ölkabel n
E: oil-filled cable
F: câble m à huile fluide

Ölkanal m [Kab.]
E: oil duct

Ölkanal
  F: canal *m* de circulation d'huile
Ölkreislauf *m*
  E: oil circulation
  F: circulation *f* d'huile
Ölleckstelle *f*
  E: oil leakage
  F: fuite *f* d'huile
öllösliches Harz
  E: oil soluble resin
  F: résine *f* oléosoluble
Öl/Papier-Dielektrikum *n*
  E: oil/paper dielectric
  F: diélectrique *m* papier/huile
Ölstandsanzeiger *m*
  E: oil level indicator
  F: indicateur *m* du niveau d'huile
Ölumlaufkühlung *f*
  E: oil circulation cooling
  F: refroidissement *m* par circulation d'huile
optimale Gestaltung
  E: optimization *n*
  F: optimisation *f*, optimalisation *f*
Optimierung *f*
  E: optimization *n*
  F: optimisation *f*, optimalisation *f*
Organisationsplan *m*
  E: organization chart
  F: organigramme *m*
örtlich begrenzt
  E: locally confined, locally limited
  F: limité *adj* localement, localisé *adj*
Ortsanschlußkabel *n*
  E: local exchange connection cable, telephone distribution cable, local junction cable
  F: câble *m* téléphonique de réseau local
Ortsantennen-Fernsehen *n*
  E: Community Antenna Television (CATV)
  F: réception *f* collective d'antenne de télévision
Ortsgemeinschaftsantennen-Fernsehkabel *n*
  E: community antenna television (CATV) cable
  F: câble *m* de réception collective d'antenne de télévision
Ortsgespräch *n*
  E: local call
  F: conversation *f* urbaine
Ortskabel *n*
  E: local subscriber('s) connection cable, telephone distribution cable, subscriber('s) cable, local cable
  F: câble *m* urbain, câble *m* d'abonné
Ortsnetz *n* [Tel.]
  E: local exchange network, municipal network
  F: réseau *m* urbain, réseau *m* local, réseau *m* municipal
ortsveränderliches Gerät
  E: portable appliance, mobile equipment, portable equipment
  F: appareil *m* portatif, appareil *m* mobile
Ortsverbindungskabel *n*
  E: local exchange connection cable, telephone distribution cable, local junction cable
  F: câble *m* téléphonique de réseau local
Ortsvermittlungsstelle *f*
  E: local exchange
  F: central *m* urbain
oszillierende Verseilscheibe
  E: oscillating face plate
  F: plaque *f* de répartition oscillante
Oxideinschlüsse *m pl*
  E: oxide inclusions
  F: inclusions *f pl* d'oxyde
Oxidhaut *f*
  E: oxide film, oxide skin
  F: peau *f* oxydée, couche *f* d'oxyde
Oxydationsinhibitor *m*
  E: antioxidant *n*, oxidation inhibitor
  F: inhibiteur *m* d'oxydation, antioxidant *m*, antioxygène *m*
Oxydationsverzögerer *m*
  E: antioxidant *n*, oxidation inhibitor
  F: inhibiteur *m* d'oxydation, antioxidant *m*, antioxygène *m*
oxydativer Abbau
  E: oxidative decomposition, oxidative degradation
  F: décomposition *f* par oxydation
oxydieren *v*
  E: oxidize *v*
  F: oxyder *v*
Ozonbeständigkeit *f*
  E: ozone resistance, resistance to ozone
  F: résistance *f* à l'ozone

P

PA (s. Polyamid)
Paar *n* [Nachr. K.]
  E: pair *n*, twin-wire *n*, dual wire
  F: paire *f*, fil *m* double, conducteur *m* jumelé
paarig verseiltes Kabel
  E: cable with pair formation, twin cable, paired cable
  F: câble *m* à paires, câble *m* jumelé, câble *m* pairé
Paarverseilmaschine *f*
  E: twinning machine, pair stranding machine, pair twisting machine
  F: paireuse *f*
paarverseilte Leitung [Nachr. K.]
  E: pair *n*, twin-wire *n*, dual wire
  F: paire *f*, fil *m* double, conducteur *m* jumelé
paarverseiltes Kabel
  E: cable with pair formation, twin cable, paired cable
  F: câble *m* à paires, câble *m* jumelé, câble *m* pairé
Paarverseilung *f*
  E: pairing *n*, twinning *n*, pair twisting
  F: pairage *m*, assemblage *m* par paires
Palette, auf ~n packen
  E: palletize *v*
  F: palettiser *v*
Panzerkabel *n*
  E: armo(u)red cable, shielded cable
  F: câble *m* armé, câble *m* blindé
Papierbänder schneiden
  E: to slit paper tapes
  F: découper *v* des rubans de papier
Papierbandisolierung *f*
  E: paper tape insulation, lapped paper insulation, spiral strip paper insulation (US), paper ribbon insulation (US)
  F: isolation *f* rubanée en papier, rubanage *m* en papier
Papierbandriß *m*
  E: paper tape break
  F: déchirure *f* du ruban de papier, rupture *f* du ruban de papier
Papierbandscheibe *f* [Bdspinn.]
  E: paper pad
  F: galette *f* de papier
Papierbandschneidemaschine *f*
  E: paper tape cutting machine, paper-slitting machine
  F: machine *f* à couper les rubans de papier, machine *f* à découper le papier, découpeuse *f* à papier
Papier-Bleikabel *n*
  E: paper-insulated lead-sheathed cable, paper-insulated lead-covered cable, PILC cable (US)
  F: câble *m* isolé à papier sous gaine de plomb
Papier-Hohlraumisolierung *f*
  E: air-space(d) paper insulation
  F: isolant *m* air/papier
papierisolierte Ader
  E: paper-insulated wire, paper-insulated core
  F: conducteur *m* isolé au papier
papierisoliertes Bleimantelkabel
  E: paper-insulated lead-sheathed cable, paper-insulated lead-covered cable, PILC cable (US)
  F: câble *m* isolé à papier sous gaine de plomb
papierisoliertes Kabel
  E: paper-insulated cable
  F: câble *m* isolé au papier
Papierisolierung *f*
  E: paper insulation
  F: isolant *m* papier
Papierkabel *n*
  E: paper-insulated cable
  F: câble *m* isolé au papier
Papierkordel *f*
  E: paper string
  F: ficelle *f* de papier
Papierkordelader *f*
  E: paper string wire (core)
  F: conducteur *m* à ficelle de papier
Papier/Kunststoff-Schichtenisolierung *f*
  E: paper/plastic laminate insulation
  F: isolant *m* stratifié en papier/matière plastique
Papier/Kunststoff-Schichtenmaterial *n* (Bänder)
  E: bonded laminar material (paper/plastic tapes), bonded laminate (paper/plastic tapes)
  F: rubanage *m* stratifié (rubans papier/synthétiques)
Papier-Luftraumisolierung *f*

Papier-Luftraumisolierung
  E: air-space(d) paper insulation
  F: isolant *m* air/papier
Papier-Masse-Kabel *n*
  E: paper-insulated mass-impregnated cable
  F: câble *m* isolé à papier imprégné à matière visqueuse
Papierpulpisolierung *f*
  E: paper pulp insulation
  F: isolant *m* pâte à papier
Papierrolle *f*
  E: paper roll
  F: rouleau *m* de papier
Papierscheibe *f* [Bdspinn.]
  E: paper pad
  F: galette *f* de papier
Papierscheibenhalter *m* [Bdspinn.]
  E: pad holder
  F: porte-galette *m*
Papierschneidemaschine *f*
  E: paper tape cutting machine, paper-slitting machine
  F: machine *f* à couper les rubans de papier, machine *f* à découper le papier, découpeuse *f* à papier
Papierspinnen *n*
  E: paper lapping
  F: rubanage *m* de papier
Papierspinnkopf *m*
  E: paper lapping head
  F: tête *f* de rubaneuse à papier, tête *f* à papier
Papierspinnmaschine *f*
  E: paper lapping machine
  F: rubaneuse *f* à papier
Papierstreifen *m*
  E: paper strip
  F: bande *f* de papier
Papiervorschub *m*
  E: paper feed
  F: défilement *m* du papier
Papierwickel *m* (vorgefertigt) [K. Garn.]
  E: paper tube
  F: fuseau *m* long de papier
paraffinbasisches Rohöl
  E: paraffin base crude oil
  F: huile *f* brute à la base de paraffine
parallel zum Kabel verlegte Wasserrohre
  E: separate lateral water pipes
  F: tubes *m pl* à eau latéraux disposés séparément du câble
Parallelanordnung *f*
  E: laying side by side, laying in parallel, parallel arrangement
  F: disposition *f* côte à côte, disposition *f* en nappe horizontale, disposition *f* en parallèle
Parallelschaltung *f*
  E: parallel circuit, parallel connection
  F: montage *m* en parallèle, couplage *m* en parallèle
Paßsitz *m*
  E: snug fit, tight fit
  F: ajustement *m*
Patent, ein ~ anmelden
  E: to apply for a patent, to file a patent application
  F: déposer *v* une demande de brevet, demander *v* un brevet
Patent, ein ~ erteilen
  E: to grant a patent
  F: accorder *v* un brevet, délivrer *v* un brevet
Patentanspruch *m*
  E: patent claim
  F: revendication *f* d'un brevet, spécification *f* d'un brevet
Patentmeldung *f*
  E: patent application
  F: demande *f* de brevet
Patentverletzung *f*
  E: patent infringement, infringement of a patent
  F: violation *f* d'un brevet, contrefaçon *f* d'un brevet
Patrize *f*
  E: core die, male die
  F: poinçon *m*
PCM-Kabel *n*
  E: pulse-code modulation cable, PCM cable
  F: câble *m* de modulation par impulsion et codage, câble *m* MIC
PCP (s. Polychloropren)
PE (s. Polyäthylen)
PE-Mantel *m*
  E: PE-sheath *n*
  F: gaine *f* de PE
PE-Mischung *f*
  E: PE-compound *n*
  F: mélange *m* de PE
Penetration *f*
  E: penetration *n*
  F: pénétration *f*
periodisch wechselnde Drallrichtung

periodically changing lay
E: periodically changing lay
F: pas m de câblage changeant périodiquement

periodischer Betrieb
E: periodic operation, intermittent operation, intermittent service
F: régime m périodique

Peroxid n
E: peroxide n
F: peroxyde m

Peschelrohr n
E: Peschel conduit (for house wiring)
F: tube m en tôle plombée

Petrol-jelly n
E: petroleum jelly, petrol jelly
F: vaseline f, gelée f de pétrole

Pfeiffrequenz f
E: singing frequency
F: fréquence f de sifflement

Pflichtenheft n
E: specification n
F: cahier m des charges

Pfropfpolymerisat n
E: graft-polymer n
F: polymère m greffé

Phantomausnutzung f
E: use of phantom circuits
F: utilisation f de circuits fantôme

Phantomkreis m
E: phantom circuit, superposed circuit
F: circuit m fantôme, circuit m superposé, circuit m combiné

Phantomkreis mit Erdrückleitung
E: ground phantom circuit
F: circuit m fantôme avec retour par la terre

Phantomleitung f
E: phantom circuit, superposed circuit
F: circuit m fantôme, circuit m superposé, circuit m combiné

Phantompupinspule f
E: phantom circuit loading coil
F: bobine f de charge pour circuit fantôme

Phantomschaltung f
E: phantom circuit, superposed circuit
F: circuit m fantôme, circuit m superposé, circuit m combiné

Phase gegen Erde
E: phase to earth, phase to ground
F: phase f par rapport à la terre

Phase gegen Phase
E: phase to phase
F: phase f à phase

Phasenausfall-Überwachungsgerät n
E: phase monitor
F: dispositif m de contrôle des phases

Phasenausgleich m
E: phase compensation
F: compensation f des phases

Phasengeschwindigkeit f
E: phase velocity
F: vitesse f de phase

phasengleich adj
E: in phase
F: en phase

Phasengleichheit f
E: phase balance, phase coincidence
F: équilibre m des phases, concordance f des phases

Phasenlaufzeit f
E: phase delay
F: temps m de propagation de phase

Phasenleiter m
E: phase conductor, line conductor
F: conducteur m de phase

Phasenmaß n
E: phase constant
F: constante f de phase

Phasennacheilung f
E: phase lag
F: retard m de phase

Phasenspannung f
E: phase voltage
F: tension f de phase

Phasenstrom m
E: phase current
F: courant m de phase

Phasenverkettung f
E: interlinking of phases
F: interconnexion f des phases

Phasenverschiebung f
E: phase displacement, phase shift
F: déphasage m

Phasenverzerrung f
E: phase distortion
F: distorsion f de phase

Phasenvoreilung f
E: phase lead
F: avance f de phase

Phasenwinkel m
E: phase angle
F: angle m de phase

Pilzisolator
  E: mushroom insulator
  F: isolateur m en forme de champignon

Pinole, in ~n gelagert
  E: pintle-mounted adj
  F: monté adj entre pointes

Pinolen-Wickler m
  E: pintle-type spooler
  F: bobinoir m à pointes, enrouleur m à pointes

Planetenrührwerk n
  E: planetary mixer
  F: agitateur m planétaire

Planung und Betrieb von Stromnetzen
  E: system planning and operation
  F: conception f et exploitation de réseaux électriques

Planung von Kabelanlagen
  E: planning of cable installations
  F: planification f d'installations de câbles

Plast m
  E: plastic material, synthetic material, synthetic resin
  F: matière f plastique, matière f synthétique, plastique m

Plastifikator m
  E: plastifier n, plastificator n
  F: plastificateur m

Plastifizierung f
  E: plastification n
  F: plastification f

plastisches Fließen
  E: plastic flow
  F: écoulement m plastique

plastizieren v (mech.)
  E: masticate v, knead v
  F: malaxer v

Plastizität f
  E: plasticity n
  F: plasticité f

Plastometer n
  E: plastometer n
  F: plastomètre m

Platte f
  E: sheet n, plate n, slab n
  F: plaque f, plateau m

Plattenziehen n [Gi., Plast.]
  E: sheeting-out n
  F: tirage m en nappes

Plattiermaschine f
  E: paper lapping machine
  F: rubaneuse f à papier

Platzbedarf m
  E: space requirement, occupancy n
  F: encombrement m

Platzwechsel m (bei einer Fernsprechfreileitung)
  E: transposition n
  F: transposition f

Plunger m [Masch.]
  E: piston n, ram n, plunger n
  F: piston m, fouloir m

Plunger, doppeltwirkender ~
  E: double-acting plunger
  F: piston m à double effet, piston m à action double

pneumatische Förderanlage
  E: pneumatic conveying system
  F: installation f de transport pneumatique

pneumatische Kabelklemme [Vulk.]
  E: air clamp
  F: serre-câble m pneumatique

Poise n (Viskosität)
  E: poise n
  F: poise f

Pole, gleichnamige ~
  E: like poles, similar poles
  F: pôles m pl homologues, pôles m pl similaires

Polen n [Hütt.]
  E: poling n
  F: travail m avec la perche

Polster n (unter der Bewehrung)
  E: bedding n
  F: matelas m

Polwechsel m
  E: change of polarity, pole reversal, pole changing
  F: inversion f de polarité

Polyamid (PA) n
  E: polyamide n
  F: polyamide m

Polyäthylen (PE) n
  E: polyethylene (PE) n
  F: polyéthylène m (PE)

Polychloropren (PCP) n
  E: polychloroprene (PCP) n
  F: polychloroprène m (PCP)

Polyesterharz n
  E: polyester resin
  F: résine f polyester

Polyisobutylen n
  E: polyisobutylene n

F: polyisobutylène *m*

Polymerisat *n*
 E: polymer *n*
 F: polymère *m*

Polymerisation *f*
 E: polymerisation *n*
 F: polymérisation *f*

Polyolefin, verzweigtes ~
 E: branched polyolefin
 F: polyoléfine *m* ramifié

Polypropylen *n*
 E: polypropylene *n*
 F: polypropylène *m*

Polystyrol *n*
 E: polystyrene *n*
 F: polystyrène *m*

Polytetrafluoräthylen (PTFE) *n*
 E: polytetrafluorethylene (PTFE) *n*
 F: polytétrafluoréthylène *m* (PTFE)

Polyvinylchlorid (PVC) *n*
 E: polyvinyl chloride (PVC)
 F: chlorure *m* de polyvinyle (PVC), polychlorure *m* de vinyle (PCV)

Pore *f*
 E: pore *n*, pinhole *n*
 F: pore *m*

porenfrei *adj*
 E: pore-free *adj*, free of pinholes
 F: exempt *adj* de pores

Porenfreiheit, einen Überzug auf ~ prüfen
 E: to test the continuity of a coating
 F: essayer *v* la continuité d'un revêtement

Porenprüfgerät *n* (Papier)
 E: porosimeter *n*
 F: porosimètre *m*

Portalkran *m*
 E: gantry crane
 F: grue *f* (à) portique

Portalwickler *m* (abwickelnd)
 E: portal type pay-off
 F: dérouleur *m* à portique

Portalwickler *m* (aufwickelnd)
 E: portal type take-up
 F: enrouleur *m* à portique

Porzellanisolator *m*
 E: porcelain insulator
 F: isolateur *m* en porcelaine, porcelaine *f*

Positionsregelung *f*
 E: position control
 F: réglage *m* de position

Potentiometer *n*
 E: voltage divider, potentiometer *n*
 F: réducteur *m* de tension, potentiomètre *m*

prägen *v*
 E: emboss *v*
 F: estamper *v*, imprimer *v*

Prägerad *n*
 E: embossing wheel
 F: galet *m* d'estampage

Prägung *f*
 E: embossing *n*
 F: estampage *m*, impression *f*

Preßbarkeit *f*
 E: extrudability *n*
 F: extrudabilité *f*

Preßdraht *m*
 E: extruded rod
 F: fil *m* machine filé

Preßdruck *m* [Extr., Met.-Strangpr.]
 E: extrusion pressure
 F: pression *f* d'extrusion, pression *f* de filage

Pressen mit Schale [Met.-Strangpr.]
 E: extrusion with shell
 F: filage *m* avec croûte

Pressen ohne Schale [Met.-Strangpr.]
 E: extrusion without shell
 F: filage *m* sans croûte

Pressen, nahtloses ~ von Metallmänteln
 E: seamless extrusion of metal sheaths
 F: filage *m* sans soudure des gaines métalliques

Preßgeschwindigkeit *f*
 E: extrusion rate
 F: vitesse *f* d'extrusion

Preßkabelschuh *m*
 E: crimped type cable termination, compression type cable lug
 F: cosse *f* de câble à poinçonner, cosse *f* de câble à sertir

Preßkopf *m* [Met.-Strangpr.]
 E: die block, press block
 F: bloc *m* de presse, tête *f* d'outillage

Preßling *m*
 E: mo(u)lding *n*, mo(u)lded part
 F: pièce *f* moulée

Preßrest *m* [Met.-Strangpr.]
 E: discard *n*, butt-end *n*
 F: culot *m* de filage

Preßrest, Ausstoßen des ~es [Met.-Strangpr.]

Preßrest

- E: ejection of the discard
- F: expulsion f du culot de filage

Preßschale f [Met.-Strangpr.]
- E: shell n, skin n
- F: croûte f, chemise f

Preßscheibe f [Met.-Strangpr.]
- E: dummy block
- F: grain m de poussée

Preßscheibentrenner m [Met.-Strangpr.]
- E: dummy block separator
- F: séparateur m du grain de poussée

Preßstempel m
- E: pressure ram
- F: fouloir m de la presse

Preßteil n
- E: mo(u)lding n, mo(u)lded part
- F: pièce f moulée

Preßtemperatur f
- E: extrusion temperature
- F: température f d'extrusion, température f de filage

Preßtopf m [Met.-Strangpr.]
- E: billet container
- F: conteneur m de billettes, pot m de presse

Preßverbinder m
- E: compression type sleeve, crimped sleeve
- F: manchon m à poinçonner

Preßverbindung f
- E: compressed joint, crimped joint
- F: raccord m poinçonné

Preßwerkzeug n [K. Garn.]
- E: compression tool, crimping tool
- F: outil m de poinçonnage

Primärkreislauf m
- E: primary circuit
- F: circuit m primaire

Primärleiter m
- E: prime conductor
- F: conducteur m primaire

Primärspannung f
- E: primary voltage, input voltage
- F: tension f primaire

Primärwicklung f
- E: primary winding
- F: enroulement m primaire

Prinzipschaltbild n
- E: schematic wiring diagram, elementary circuit diagram
- F: schéma m de principe

Pritsche f [K. Verl.]
- E: cable tray, cable rack
- F: tablette f à câbles, charpente pour câbles f

Probe f
- E: specimen n, sample n
- F: éprouvette f, échantillon m

Probefertigung f
- E: trial production, production trial, manufacturing trial
- F: essai m de fabrication, production f à l'échelle expérimentale

Probelänge f
- E: trial length, experimental length, test length
- F: longueur f d'essai

Probelauf m
- E: trial run, test run
- F: marche f d'essai

Probenahme f
- E: sampling n, taking of samples
- F: prélèvement m d'échantillons, échantillonnage m

Produktionsablauf m
- E: production sequence
- F: cycle m de fabrication

Profil n
- E: section n
- F: profilé m

Profildraht m
- E: profile wire, shaped wire, strip n
- F: brin m profilé, fil m profilé

Profilleiter m
- E: shaped conductor
- F: âme f profilée

Profilwalze f
- E: sizing roll, section roll
- F: cylindre m à profilés

Programmsteuerung f
- E: program(me) control
- F: commande f par programme

Projektierung f
- E: planning n
- F: étude f, élaboration f d'un projet

Protodur-Kabel n
- E: Protodur-cable n
- F: câble m au Protodur

Protothen-Kabel n
- E: Protothen-cable n
- F: câble m au Protothen

Prozeßrechner m
- E: process-control computer
- F: calculateur m pour la conduite des processus industriels

Prüfader f

Prüfanforderungen *f pl*
  E: test requirements
  F: exigences *f pl* d'essai

Prüfanordnung *f*
  E: experimental arrangement, test(ing) arrangement, test setup
  F: montage *m* d'essai, montage *m* expérimental, disposition *f* d'essai

Prüfbedingungen *f pl*
  E: test conditions
  F: conditions *f pl* d'expérience, conditions *f pl* d'essai

Prüfbefund *m*
  E: test result
  F: résultat *m* d'essai

Prüfbericht *m*
  E: test report
  F: procès-verbal *m* d'essai

Prüfbescheinigung *f*
  E: test certificate
  F: certificat *m* d'essai

Prüfdauer *f*
  E: test duration, testing time, testing period
  F: durée *f* d'expérience, durée *f* d'essai

Prüfdraht *m*
  E: test(ing) wire, pilot wire, test(ing) conductor, pilot core, pilot conductor
  F: fil *m* d'essai, fil *m* pilote

Prüfeinrichtung *f*
  E: testing equipment, test set, testing device
  F: équipement *m* d'essai, dispositif *m* d'essai

prüfen *v*
  E: check *v*, test *v*, verify *v*, control *v*
  F: essayer *v*, vérifier *v*, contrôler *v*

Prüfergebnis *n*
  E: test result
  F: résultat *m* d'essai

Prüffeld *n*
  E: test field
  F: champ *m* d'essai

Prüfgerät *n*
  E: testing equipment, test set, testing device
  F: équipement *m* d'essai, dispositif *m* d'essai

Prüfhantel *f*
  E: dumb-bell shaped test piece
  F: éprouvette *f* en forme d'haltère

Prüfkennzeichen *n*
  E: test mark, inspection mark
  F: marque *f* de contrôle

Prüfkörper *m*
  E: test sample, test piece, test specimen
  F: échantillon *m*, éprouvette *f*

Prüflänge *f*
  E: test length
  F: longueur *f* d'essai

Prüfleiter *m*
  E: test(ing) wire, pilot wire, test(ing) conductor, pilot core, pilot conductor
  F: fil *m* d'essai, fil *m* pilote

Prüfleitung *f*
  E: test line
  F: ligne *f* d'essai

Prüfmethode *f*
  E: test method
  F: méthode *f* d'essai

Prüfprotokoll *n*
  E: test report
  F: procès-verbal *m* d'essai

Prüfschirm, konzentrischer ~
  E: concentric test-shield
  F: écran *m* d'essai concentrique

Prüfspannung *f*
  E: test voltage
  F: tension *f* d'essai

Prüfstand *m*
  E: test stand, test floor, test bench
  F: plate-forme *f* d'essai, poste *m* d'essai

Prüfstelle *f*
  E: approval organization, testing station
  F: institut *m* de certification, station *f* d'essai, organisme *m* d'approbation

Prüfstrom *m*
  E: test current
  F: courant *m* d'essai

Prüfstromkreis *m*
  E: temporary circuit, test circuit, experimental circuit
  F: montage *m* expérimental (él.), couplage *m* expérimental, circuit *m*

Prüfstück *n*
  E: test sample, test piece, test

Prüfstück
   specimen
   F: échantillon m, éprouvette f
Prüfung f (Kontrolle)
   E: inspection n, check n, examination n, investigation n, analysis n
   F: examen m, analyse f, contrôle m
Prüfung f (Erprobung)
   E: test n, trial n, experiment n
   F: essai m, épreuve f, expérience f
Prüfung an verlegten Kabeln
   E: site test on cables
   F: essai m de câbles sur chantier
Prüfung auf bleibende Dehnung
   E: hot-set-test n
   F: essai m d'allongement permanent
Prüfung auf Durchgang [el.]
   E: continuity check, continuity test
   F: contrôle m de continuité, essai m de continuité
Prüfung der Zerreißfestigkeit
   E: tensile test, tensile strength test
   F: essai m de traction
Prüfung mit Belastungszyklen
   E: loading cycle test, cyclic loading test
   F: essai m aux cycles de charge
Prüfung mit wechselnder Polarität
   E: polarity inversion test
   F: essai m à inversion de la polarité
Prüfung während der Fertigung
   E: production test, in-process testing
   F: essai m en cours de fabrication
Prüfung, eine ~ durchführen
   E: to perform a test, to carry out a test, to conduct a test
   F: faire v un essai, effectuer v un essai
Prüfung, nicht zerstörungsfreie ~
   E: destructive test
   F: essai m destructif
Prüfung, zerstörungsfreie ~
   E: non-destructive test
   F: essai m non-destructif
Prüfverfahren n
   E: test procedure
   F: mode m d'essai
Prüfvorrichtung f
   E: testing equipment, test set, testing device
   F: équipement m d'essai, dispositif m d'essai
Prüfvorschrift f
   E: test specification
   F: règle f d'essai

Prüfzelle f
   E: test cell
   F: logette f d'essai
PTFE (s. Polytetrafluoräthylen)
Pulp-Ader f
   E: pulped wire, pulp-insulated wire
   F: conducteur m isolé à la pâte de papier
pulpisolierte Ader
   E: pulped wire, pulp-insulated wire
   F: conducteur m isolé à la pâte de papier
Pulscode-Modulationskabel n
   E: pulse-code modulation cable, PCM cable
   F: câble m de modulation par impulsion et codage, câble m MIC
pulverförmig adj
   E: powdery adj, pulverulent adj
   F: en poudre, pulvérulent adj
Pumpenleistung f
   E: pump output, delivery of a pump
   F: capacité f de pompage, débit m d'une pompe
Pumpspeicher(kraft)werk n
   E: pumped storage (hydroelectric) power station
   F: centrale f électrique à accumulation par pompage
Pumpstation f
   E: pumping station
   F: station f de pompage
punktierte Linie
   E: dotted line
   F: ligne f brisée
punktweises Messen
   E: pointwise measurement
   F: mesure f par points
pupinisiert adj
   E: coil-loaded adj
   F: pupinisé adj
Pupinisierung f
   E: coil-loading n, Pupin loading
   F: pupinisation f, charge f au moyen de bobines en série
Pupinkabel n
   E: loaded audio cable, coil-loaded cable
   F: câble m pupinisé
Pupinleitung f
   E: coil-loaded circuit
   F: circuit m pupinisé
Pupin-Spule f

Pupinspule
- E: Pupin coil, loading coil
- F: bobine f Pupin, bobine f de charge

Pupinspulenkasten m [Nachr.]
- E: loading (coil) pot, loading coil case
- F: boîte f de charge, pot m de charge

Pupinspulensatz m
- E: loading coil unit, loading unit (tel. c.)
- F: jeu m de bobines de charge, unité f de charge (c. tél.)

Puppe f (Rolle aus Walzfell)
- E: billet n, puppet n
- F: billette f, poupée f

Putz, auf ~ [K. Verl.]
- E: on the surface, open adj
- F: à la surface, apparent adj, sur crépi

Putz, unter ~ [K. Verl.]
- E: under plaster, concealed adj
- F: encastré adj, sous enduit, sous crépi

PVC (s. Polyvinylchlorid)

PVC-Isolierung f
- E: PVC insulation
- F: isolation f PVC

PVC-Mantel m
- E: PVC sheath
- F: gaine f de PVC

PVC-Mantelleitung f
- E: light PVC-sheathed cable
- F: câble m rigide sous gaine légère en PVC

PVC-Mischung f
- E: PVC compound
- F: mélange m de PVC

Q

Qualitätskontrolle f
- E: quality inspection, quality test, quality control
- F: contrôle m de qualité, surveillance f de la qualité

Quecksilbersäule f
- E: mercury column
- F: colonne f de mercure

Quellbeständigkeit f
- E: resistance to swelling
- F: résistance f au gonflement

quellen v
- E: swell v
- F: enfler v(s'), gonfler v(se)

Querbewegung f
- E: crosswise movement, transverse motion
- F: mouvement m transversal

Querkopf m [Extr.]
- E: cross-head n
- F: tête f équerre, tête f transversale

Querschnitt m
- E: cross-section n, cross-sectional area
- F: section f (droite)

Querschnitt, berechneter wirksamer ~
- E: calculated effective area
- F: section f efficace calculée

Querschnitt, elektrisch wirksamer ~
- E: electrically effective cross-section
- F: section f électriquement efficace

Querschnitt, geometrischer ~
- E: geometrical cross-section
- F: section f géométrique

querschnittsgleich adj
- E: of equal cross-sectional area
- F: de section égale

Querschnittsverringerung f
- E: area reduction
- F: réduction f de la section

Querspannung f [el.]
- E: transverse voltage, quadrature-axis component of the voltage
- F: tension f transversale, composante f transversale d'une tension

Quervebindungskabel n [Tel.]
- E: tie line cable
- F: câble m de jonction transversal

R

Radialfeldkabel n
- E: radial field cable, screened cable, shielded conductor cable
- F: câble m à champ radial

Radischneider m
- E: pencilling tool
- F: dispositif m d'appointage

Raffinade-Kupfer n
- E: fire-refined copper
- F: cuivre m raffiné au feu

Raffination f
- E: refining n

Raffination
    F: raffinage m
Rahmen m
    E: rack n, frame n
    F: bâti m
Randbedingungen f pl
    E: boundary conditions
    F: conditions f pl aux limites
Raumbedarf m
    E: space requirement, occupancy n
    F: encombrement m
Raumgewicht n
    E: volumetric weight, density n, weight per unit of volume
    F: poids m par (unité de) volume, densité f
Raumladung f
    E: space charge
    F: charge f d'espace, charge f spatiale
Raumtemperatur f
    E: room temperature, ambient temperature
    F: température f ambiante
Raupenabzug m
    E: caterpillar pull-off, caterpuller n
    F: chenille f de tirage
Raupenglied n
    E: caterpillar pad
    F: patin m de chenille
Rauschpegel m [Nachr. K.]
    E: noise level, interference level
    F: niveau m de bruit, niveau m des perturbations
reaktionsträge adj
    E: inert adj
    F: inerte adj
rechnergesteuert adj
    E: computer-controlled adj
    F: commandé adj par ordinateur
rechnerischer Wert
    E: calculated value, theoretical value
    F: valeur f théorique
Rechteckdraht m
    E: rectangular wire, rectangular section wire
    F: fil m rectangulaire, fil m de section rectangulaire
Rechteck-Hohlleiter m
    E: rectangular waveguide
    F: guide m d'ondes rectangulaire
rechteckiger Querschnitt
    E: rectangular cross-section
    F: section f rectangulaire
Rechtsdrall m [Vers.]
    E: right-hand lay, right-hand twist
    F: pas m à droite
Rechtsdrehung f [Masch.]
    E: clockwise rotation
    F: rotation f en sens des aiguilles d'une montre
rechtsgängiges Gewinde
    E: right-hand(ed) thread
    F: filet m à droite
Rechtsschlag m [Vers.]
    E: right-hand lay, right-hand twist
    F: pas m à droite
Rechtsschlag-Verseilung f
    E: right-hand stranding
    F: assemblage m à pas droit, câblage m à pas droit
recken v
    E: straighten v, stretch v
    F: allonger v, étendre v, tendre v
Reckung des Leiters
    E: stretching of the conductor
    F: étirage m du conducteur
Reduktionsfaktor m
    E: reduction factor
    F: facteur m réducteur, coefficient m de réduction
Reduktionsgetriebe n
    E: reduction gear
    F: réducteur m, engrenage m réducteur, démultiplicateur m
reduzierendes Gas
    E: inert gas, protective gas, reducing gas
    F: gaz m inerte, gaz m de protection, gaz m réducteur
Reflexionsdämpfung f
    E: reflection attenuation, balance return loss, return loss between line and network (US), reflection loss, balance attenuation
    F: atténuation f de réflexion, affaiblissement m d'équilibrage, affaiblissement m des courants réfléchis
reflexionsfrei adj [Nachr. K.]
    E: flat adj, free of reflection
    F: non réfléchissant adj
regelbar adj
    E: adjustable adj, variable adj
    F: ajustable adj, réglable adj, orientable adj
Regelbereich m
    E: control range, regulating range

F: plage f de régulation, gamme f de réglage
Regelkreis m
E: control circuit
F: circuit m de réglage, circuit m de commande
Regelmotor m
E: adjustable speed motor, variable speed motor
F: moteur m à vitesse réglable, moteur m à vitesse variable
Regelspannung f
E: control voltage, control tension
F: tension f de réglage, tension f de commande
Regeltransformator m
E: regulating transformer, variable ratio transformer
F: transformateur m de réglage
Regelung f
E: adjustment n, regulation n, setting n
F: réglage m
Regenerat n
E: reclaim n
F: régénéré m
Registriergerät n
E: recording instrument, recorder n
F: enregistreur m
Regler m
E: regulator n, control n, controller n
F: régulateur m, appareil m de réglage
regulierbar adj
E: adjustable adj, variable adj
F: ajustable adj, réglable adj, orientable adj
Regulierventil n
E: control valve
F: soupape f de réglage
Reibelot n
E: tinning solder, soldering tin
F: étain m à souder, étain m de soudage
Reibkorrosion f
E: fretting corrosion
F: fretting m
Reibschweißen n
E: friction welding
F: soudage m à friction
Reibung f
E: friction n
F: friction f, frottement m

reibungsarm adj
E: low friction ...
F: à faible friction
Reibungskoeffizient m
E: friction coefficient
F: coefficient m de frottement
Reihenschaltung f
E: series circuit, series connection
F: montage m en série, connexion f en série, couplage m en série
Reihenspannung f
E: insulation (class) rating
F: tension f nominale d'isolement
Reinheitsgrad m
E: degree of purity
F: degré m de pureté
reinigen v [Extr.]
E: purge v
F: purger v
Reinigungsmischung f [Extr.]
E: purging compound
F: mélange m de purification
Reinigungsmolch m (für Rohrleitungen)
E: go-devil n
F: écouvillon m
Reißdehnung f
E: elongation at break, ultimate elongation, elongation at rupture
F: allongement m à la rupture
Reißen n
E: tearing n, breaking n, tear n, break n
F: rupture f, déchirure f, déchirement m
Reißfaden m
E: slitting cord
F: fil m de déchirement
Reißfestigkeit f
E: tensile strength (at break), ultimate tensile strength
F: résistance f à la rupture
Reißlänge f (Papier)
E: breaking length
F: longueur f de rupture
Rekristallisation f
E: recrystallization n
F: récristallisation f
Rekristallisationsglühung f
E: process annealing, subcritical annealing
F: recuit m de récristallisation
relative Dielektrizitätskonstante
E: relative permittivity

relative
- F: permittivité f relative

relative Luftfeuchtigkeit
- E: relative humidity
- F: degré m hygrométrique, humidité f relative

Reparatur f
- E: overhauling n, repair n
- F: remise f en état, réparation f, dépannage m

Reproduzierbarkeit f
- E: reproducibility n
- F: reproductibilité f

Reserveaggregat n
- E: stand-by unit, stand-by aggregate
- F: agrégat m de réserve, agrégat m de secours, poste m de secours

Reservepaar n [Nachr. K.]
- E: reserve pair, spare pair, extra pair
- F: paire f de réserve

Reservevierer m
- E: reserve quad
- F: quarte f de réserve

Restdämpfung f
- E: net attenuation, net loss, overall attenuation, overall transmission loss
- F: équivalent m net de transmission, affaiblissement m résiduel, affaiblissement m effectif

Restdämpfungsmessung zwischen den Leitungsenden
- E: overall attenuation measurement
- F: mesure f d'équivalents de transmission

Restladung f
- E: residual charge
- F: charge f résiduelle

Rezept einer Mischung
- E: compound formula
- F: formule f d'un mélange

Rezipient m [Met.-Strangpr.]
- E: billet container
- F: conteneur m de billettes, pot m de presse

richten v (Draht)
- E: straighten v
- F: redresser v

Richtrolle f
- E: dressing roll
- F: rouleau m dresseur

Richtung, in wechselnder ~
- E: in alternating direction
- F: en sens alterné

Richtungsader f
- E: direction core
- F: conducteur m de direction

Richtungselement n
- E: direction element
- F: élément m de direction

Richtungspaar n
- E: direction pair
- F: paire f de direction

Richtwert m
- E: reference value, standard value, approximate value
- F: valeur f indicative, valeur f de référence, valeur f standard, valeur f approximée

Riemenantrieb m
- E: belt drive
- F: commande f à courroie

Rillkopf m (Wellmaschine)
- E: corrugating head
- F: porte-outils m (machine à onduler), tête f à onduler

Ring m (Draht/Kabel)
- E: coil n
- F: couronne f (fil métallique/câble)

Ring- und Kugelmethode (zur Bestimmung des Erweichungspunktes von Massen)
- E: ring and ball method
- F: méthode f bille et anneau

Ringkabel n
- E: link cable, junction cable
- F: câble m de liaison circulaire

Ringmarkierung von Kabeladern
- E: ring marking of cable cores, ring code of cable cores
- F: repérage m annulaire des conducteurs de câble

Ringspalt m
- E: annular gap, annular passage
- F: espace m annulaire

Ringwellung, geschlossene ~
- E: closed corrugation
- F: ondulation f à anneaux fermés

Rippenisolator m
- E: ribbed insulator
- F: isolateur m à nervures

Rippenrohr n
- E: fin tube
- F: tuyau m à ailettes

Riß m
- E: crack n, fissure n
- F: craquelure f, fissure f

Rißbeständigkeit f
 E: cracking resistance
 F: tenue f aux craquelures

rissig adj
 E: cracked adj, fissured adj
 F: fissuré adj, craquelé adj

Rißwächter m (s. Bandrißwächter, Drahtrißwächter)

robust adj
 E: sturdy adj, robust adj, rigid adj, solid adj
 F: robuste adj

Rohdichte f
 E: apparent density (paper)
 F: masse f volumique apparente

Rohöl, naphtenbasisches ~
 E: naphthene base crude oil
 F: huile f brute naphténique

Rohr n
 E: tube n, pipe n
 F: tube n, tuyau m

Rohraufhängung f [Vulk.]
 E: pipe suspension, pipe hangers pl
 F: berceau m

Rohrbogen m
 E: pipe bend, conduit bend, elbow n, knee n
 F: coude m, raccord m coudé

Rohrdraht m
 E: metal-clad wiring cable
 F: câble m cuirassé

Rohrdraht, umhüllter ~
 E: sheathed metal-clad wiring cable
 F: câble m cuirassé sous gaine

Rohrdüker m [K. Verl.]
 E: sink-pipe n, underwater pipe
 F: tuyau m placé en lit de canal

Röhrenkabel n
 E: conduit cable
 F: câble m posé en conduites

Rohrformwerkzeug n
 E: tube forming tool
 F: outil m pour le formage de tuyaux

Rohrkabel n
 E: pipe type cable
 F: câble m en tube

Rohrknie n
 E: pipe bend, conduit bend, elbow n, knee n
 F: coude m, raccord m coudé

Rohrkrümmung f
 E: pipe bend, conduit bend, elbow n, knee n
 F: coude m, raccord m coudé

Rohrleitung f
 E: pipeline n
 F: tubulure f, conduite f

Rohrleitungssystem n
 E: pipe system, piping n
 F: tuyauterie f

Rohrmast, nach oben verjüngter ~
 E: tapered tube pole, tapered tubular mast
 F: poteau m tubulaire à section décroissante

Rohrschelle f
 E: collar band, wall clamp, pipe clip
 F: bride f d'attache, collier m pour tubes

Rohrschlange f
 E: coiled pipe
 F: serpentin m, tuyau m serpentin

Rohrstrang m
 E: pipeline conduit
 F: conduit m, caniveau m

Rohrstrang, einzügiger ~
 E: single duct conduit
 F: caniveau m à passage simple

Rohrstrang, mehrzügiger ~
 E: line of ducts, multiple duct conduit, multiple way duct
 F: conduit m à plusieurs passages, caniveau m à passage multiple

Rohrverbindung f
 E: pipe connection, pipe joint
 F: joint m de tuyeaux

Rohrverseilmaschine f
 E: tubular stranding machine, tube strander
 F: toronneuse f tubulaire

Rohrzug m [K. Verl.]
 E: duct n
 F: conduit m, caniveau m

Rohstoff m
 E: material n, raw material
 F: matière f, matière f première

Rolle f
 E: sheave n, roller n, pulley n
 F: rouleau m, galet m

Rollenförderer m
 E: roller (type) conveyor
 F: installation f de transport par rouleaux

Rollenspeicher m [Vers.]
 E: roller-type accumulator
 F: accumulateur m du type rouleau

Rost *m* [K. Verl.]
  E: cable grate
  F: grille *f* à câbles, râtelier *m* à câbles
rostbeständig *adj*
  E: stainless *adj*, rust-resisting *adj*
  F: inoxydable *adj*
rostfreier Stahl
  E: stainless steel
  F: acier *m* inoxydable
Rostschutz *m*
  E: rust prevention, rust protection
  F: protection *f* contre la rouille
Rostschutzanstrich *m*
  E: anti-corrosion coating
  F: enduit *m* anti-corrosif
rotierender Speicher [Vers.]
  E: rotating accumulator
  F: moufle *f* rotative
Rückdrehung, mit ~ [Vers.]
  E: with backtwist
  F: à détorsion
Rückdrehung, ohne ~ [Vers.]
  E: without backtwist
  F: à torsion, sans détorsion
Rückdruck *m* [Extr.]
  E: back pressure
  F: contre-pression *f*, pression *f* de refoulement
Rückflußdämpfung *f*
  E: structural return loss
  F: affaiblissement *m* de régularité
Rückfüllung *f* [K. Verl.]
  E: backfill *n*
  F: matériel *m* de remplissage
Rückgewinnung *f*
  E: recovery *n*
  F: récupération *f*
Rückgewinnungsanlage für Draht aus Kabelabfällen
  E: wire reclaiming system
  F: installation *f* de récupération du fil métallique à partir des déchets de câble
Rückkopplung *f*
  E: feedback *n*
  F: réaction *f*
Rückkopplungsspule *f*
  E: reaction coil, feedback coil
  F: bobine *f* de réaction
Rückkühlung von Kühlwasser
  E: re-cooling of cooling water
  F: refroidissement *m* d'eau de retour
Rücklaufrohr *n*
  E: return pipe
  F: tube *m* de retour
Rückleiter *m*
  E: return conductor, return wire
  F: conducteur *m* de retour, fil *m* de retour
Rückschlagventil *n*
  E: return valve, check valve, back-pressure valve, non-return valve
  F: soupape *f* de retenue
Rückzugbewegung des Preßstempels
  E: return stroke of the ram
  F: retour *m* du fouloir, recul *m* du fouloir
Rückzugskolben *m*
  E: pull-back ram
  F: piston *m* de remontée, piston *m* de rappel
Rückzugzylinder *m*
  E: pull-back cylinder
  F: cylindre *m* de retour
Rufreichweite *f* [Nachr. K.]
  E: calling range
  F: portée *f* d'appel
Rührwerk *n*
  E: agitator *n*, mixer *n*
  F: agitateur *m*, mélangeur *m*
Rundbolzen *m*
  E: round billet
  F: billette *f* cylindrique
Runddraht *m*
  E: round wire
  F: fil *m* rond
Runddraht-Armierung *f*
  E: round wire armo(u)ring
  F: armure *f* en fils ronds
Runddraht-Bewehrung *f*
  E: round wire armo(u)ring
  F: armure *f* en fils ronds
Rundfunkpaar *n*
  E: broadcast pair
  F: paire *f* radio
Rundknüppel *m*
  E: round billet
  F: billette *f* cylindrique
Rundleiter *m*
  E: round conductor, circular conductor
  F: âme *f* ronde, âme *f* circulaire
Rundschälwerkzeug *n* (zum schichtweisen Abtragen von extrudierten Kabel-Isolierungen und schwachleitenden Schichten) [Kab.]

Schachtofen

- E: jacket removal tool
- F: dispositif *m* de décortiquage (des couches isolantes et semiconductrices d'un câble), outil *m* de pelage, dispositif *m* de coupes minces

Rundsieb(papier-)maschine *f*
- E: cylinder paper machine
- F: machine *f* à papier à tamis cylindrique

Rundsieb-Papier *n*
- E: cylinder machine paper
- F: papier *m* (fabriqué sur) machine à tamis cylindrique

Rundversuch *m*
- E: round-robin test
- F: essai *m* interlaboratoire

Ruß *m*
- E: carbon black
- F: noir *m* de fumée, noir *m* de carbone

rußgefüllt *adj*
- E: carbon black loaded
- F: chargé *adj* en noir

Rußpapier *n*
- E: carbon black paper
- F: papier *m* carbone

Rüstzeit *f* [Masch.]
- E: set-up time
- F: temps *m* de préparation, temps *m* de réglage

Rüttelsieb *n*
- E: vibratory screen
- F: tamis *m* à secousses

S

Salzbad *n*
- E: salt bath
- F: bain *m* de sel

Sammelbehälter *m*
- E: sump *n*
- F: bâche *f*

Sammelschiene *f*
- E: bus-bar *n*, bus-duct *n*
- F: barre *f* omnibus, barre *f* collectrice

satiniertes Papier
- E: satin paper, satiny paper, satined paper
- F: papier *m* satiné

sattgetränkt *adj*
- E: fully impregnated
- F: imprégné *adj* jusqu'à saturation

Sättigungsdruck *m*
- E: saturation pressure
- F: pression *f* de saturation

Sättigungsgrad *m*
- E: degree of saturation
- F: degré *m* de saturation

Sauerstoffanteil *m*
- E: oxygen content
- F: degré *m* d'oxygène

Sauerstoffbombe *f*
- E: oxygen bomb
- F: bombe *f* à oxygène

Sauerstoffentzug *m*
- E: removal of oxygen, deoxidation *n*
- F: réduction *f* d'oxygène

Saugfähigkeit *f*
- E: absorption capacity
- F: capacité *f* d'absorption

Saugleitung *f*
- E: suction line
- F: tubulure *f* d'aspiration, conduite *f* d'aspiration

säurebeständig *adj*
- E: acid-resistant *adj*, acid-proof *adj*
- F: résistant *adj* aux acides

Säurebeständigkeit *f*
- E: acid resistance
- F: résistance *f* aux acides

Säurerückgewinnungsanlage *f*
- E: acid recovery plant
- F: installation *f* de récupération d'acide

Säurezahl *f*
- E: acid number
- F: indice *m* d'acide

SB (s. Siedebeginn)

„Scanning"-Prüfung *f*
- E: scanning test
- F: essai *m* d'ionisation par défilement, essai *m* de «scanning»

Schaben *n* [Drahth.]
- E: shaving *n*
- F: rasage *n*

Schachtdeckel *m*
- E: manhole cover
- F: couvercle *m* de trou d'homme

Schachtkabel *n*
- E: mine shaft cable, shaft cable
- F: câble *m* pour puits de mines

Schachtofen *m*
- E: shaft furnace, stack furnace

Schachtofen

F: four *m* à cuve

Schachtsohle *f*
E: floor of vault, floor of manhole
F: fond *m* du trou d'homme

schädlich *adj*
E: harmful *adj*, detrimental *adj*
F: néfaste *adj*, nocif *adj*, nuisible *adj*

schälen *v*(Draht, Isolierung)
E: shave *v*
F: raser *v*

schälen *v*(eine Schicht)
E: peel *v*
F: peler *v*

Schaltader *f*
E: jumper wire, cross-connecting wire, hook-up wire
F: fil *m* de connexion, jarretière *f*

Schaltanlage *f*
E: switching station, switch gear
F: installation *f* de distribution, disjoncteur *m*, installation *f* de commutation

Schaltanlageneinführungs-Endverschluß *m*[Kab.]
E: cable termination for metal-clad substations
F: extrémité *f* de câble pour les coffrets de disjoncteurs-interrupteurs

Schaltdraht *m*
E: jumper wire, cross-connecting wire, hook-up wire
F: fil *m* de connexion, jarretière *f*

schalten *v*[el.]
E: switch *v*, connect *v*
F: connecter *v*, brancher *v*, monter *v*, relier *v*

schalten *v*[mech.]
E: change *v*(gear)
F: changer *v* de vitesse (engrenage)

Schalter *m*
E: switch *n*
F: interrupteur *m*, disjoncteur *m*

Schaltkabel *n*
E: switchboard cable
F: câble *m* de connexion

Schaltkasten *m*[Kab.]
E: link box, cross-bonding box
F: boîte *f* de raccordement à la terre, boîte *f* de transposition

Schaltkreis, integrierter ~
E: integrated circuit (IC)
F: circuit *m* intégré

Schaltlitze *f*
E: stranded hook-up wire
F: fil *m* à brins multiples

Schaltplan *m*
E: wiring diagram, wiring scheme, circuit diagram
F: schéma *m* électrique, plan *m* de câblage, plan *m* des circuits, schéma *m* des connexions

Schaltpult *n*
E: control desk, operator's desk, control console
F: pupitre *m* de commande, poste *m* de commande

Schaltschema *n*
E: wiring diagram, wiring scheme, circuit diagram
F: schéma *m* électrique, plan *m* de câblage, plan *m* des circuits, schéma *m* des connexions

Schaltschrank *m*
E: control cabinet
F: armoire *f* de commande, armoire *f* d'appareillage, armoire *f* de régulation

Schaltschütz *n*
E: contactor *n*, relay switch
F: contacteur-disjoncteur *m*, contacteur-interrupteur *m*

Schalttafel *f*
E: control panel, switchboard *n*
F: tableau *m* de distribution, tableau *m* de commande

Schaltüberspannung *f*
E: switching surge, maneuver overvoltage, transient caused by switching
F: surtension *f* de commutation, surtension *f* de manœuvre

Schaltung *f*
E: circuitry *n*, circuit arrangement, wiring *n*, cabling *n*, interconnection *n*
F: circuit *m*, montage *m*, schéma *m* de connexions, filerie *f*

Schaltwarte *f*
E: control station
F: station *f* de commande, poste *m* de commande

Schälwerkzeug *n*[Kab.]
E: jacket removal tool
F: dispositif *m* de décortiquage (des couches isolantes et

semiconductrices d'un câble), outil *m* de pelage, dispositif *m* de coupes minces

Schaufelmischer *m*
  E: paddle mixer
  F: mélangeur *m* à palettes

Schauglas *n* [Masch.]
  E: peephole *n*, sight glass, observation window, inspection glass
  F: hublot *m* de regard, voyant *m*

Schauloch *n* [Masch.]
  E: peephole *n*, sight glass, observation window, inspection glass
  F: hublot *m* de regard, voyant *m*

Schaum-Kunststoff *m*
  E: foamed plastic, expanded plastic, cellular plastic
  F: mousse *f* (synthétique), plastique *m* cellulaire

Schauzeichen *n*
  E: lamp indicator, visual signal
  F: signalisation *f* visible

Scheibe *f*
  E: sheave *n*, disc *n*, pulley *n*
  F: roue *f*, galet *m*, poulie *f*, disque *m*

Scheibenabzug *m*
  E: pull-off capstan, haul-off capstan
  F: cabestan *m* de tirage, roue *f* de tirage, cabestan *m* tireur

Scheibenhalter *m* [Bdspinn.]
  E: pad holder
  F: porte-galette *m*

Scheibenisolierung *f* [Nachr. K.]
  E: disc insulation
  F: isolation *f* par disques

Scheindämpfung *f*
  E: apparent attenuation
  F: affaiblissement *m* apparent

Scheinleistung *f*
  E: apparent power
  F: puissance *f* apparente

Scheinwiderstand *m*
  E: impedance *n*
  F: impédance *f*

Scheitelspannung *f*
  E: peak voltage, crest voltage
  F: tension *f* de crête, tension *f* de pointe

Scheitelwert *m*
  E: peak value, crest value, amplitude *n*
  F: valeur *f* de crête

Schelle *f*
  E: clamp *n*, bracket *n*, clip *n*, cleat *n*
  F: collier *m*, bride *f*

schematische Darstellung
  E: schematic representation, diagrammatic representation
  F: représentation *f* schématique, schéma *m* de principe

Scherbeanspruchung *f*
  E: shear stress
  F: effort *m* de cisaillement, contrainte *f* de cisaillement

Schere, fliegende ~
  E: flying shear(s)
  F: cisailles *f pl* à porte-à-faux

Scherfestigkeit *f*
  E: shear strength
  F: résistance *f* au cisaillement

Schering-Brücke *f*
  E: Schering bridge
  F: pont *m* Schering

Schicht *f*
  E: layer *n*
  F: couche *f*

Schichtbetrieb *m*
  E: shift operation
  F: travail *m* en équipes

Schichtdicke *f*
  E: layer thickness
  F: épaisseur *f* de couche

Schichtenmantel *m*
  E: composite layer sheath, laminated sheath, multiple sheath
  F: gaine *f* composite, gaine *f* complexe

Schichtisolierung *f*
  E: laminated insulation, laminar insulation, composite bonded laminar insulation
  F: isolation *f* stratifiée, isolation *f* laminée

Schichtleistung *f*
  E: output per shift
  F: production *f* par équipe

Schichtstoff *m*
  E: laminate *n*, laminated plastic, laminated material
  F: laminé *m*, stratifié *m*, plastique *m* laminé, produit *m* laminé

Schichtung der Papier-Isolierung
  E: gradation of the paper insulation
  F: échelonnement *m* de l'isolant papier, étagement *m* de l'isolant

Schichtung

papier

schichtweise Bedeckung
 E: sandwich covering
 F: revêtement *m* en sandwich

Schiffskabel *n*
 E: ship wiring cable
 F: câble *m* de navire, câble *m* de bord

Schirm *m* [el.]
 E: shield *n*, shielding *n*, screen *n*, screening *n*
 F: écran *m*, blindage *m*

Schirm (schwachleitend) über dem Leiter
 E: strand shield, inner semi-conducting layer
 F: écran *m* sur l'âme, écran *m* interne, couche *f* semi-conductrice interne

Schirm aus Kupfer-Drahtgeflecht
 E: copper-mesh shield, copper braid shielding, copper-mesh screen, braided copper screen
 F: écran *m* en tresse de cuivre

Schirm aus metallisiertem Papier [Kab.]
 E: metallized paper screen
 F: écran *m* en papier métallisé

Schirm über der Isolierung
 E: insulation screen, core screen (GB), insulation shield (US)
 F: écran *m* sur l'isolant

Schirmfaktor *m*
 E: screening factor (GB), shield factor (US)
 F: facteur *m* d'écran

Schirmisolator *m*
 E: umbrella type insulator
 F: isolateur *m* type parapluie

Schirmquerschnitt *m* [Kab.]
 E: screen cross-section
 F: section *f* de l'écran

Schlacke *f*
 E: slag *n*, dross *n*
 F: scorie *f*

Schlacke abziehen
 E: to skim off the dross
 F: soutirer *v* la scorie, écraser *v*

Schlag *m* [Vers.]
 E: lay *n*, twist *n*
 F: pas *m*, torsion *f*

Schlagfestigkeit *f*
 E: impact strength, impact resistance
 F: résistance *f* au choc mécanique, résilience *f*

Schlaglänge *f* [Vers.]
 E: length of lay, pitch *n*, length of twist
 F: longueur *f* du pas

Schlaglängen-Faktor *m*
 E: lay ratio
 F: taux *m* du pas

Schlagprobe *f*
 E: impact test
 F: essai *m* au choc

Schlagrichtung *f* [Vers.]
 E: direction of lay, direction of twist
 F: sens *m* du pas de câblage, sens *m* de câblage, sens *m* de torsion, sens *m* du pas de torsion, direction *f* du pas, direction *f* de la torsion

Schlagweite *f* [el.]
 E: flash-over distance
 F: distance *f* de contournement

Schlagzähigkeit *f*
 E: impact strength, impact resistance
 F: résistance *f* au choc mécanique, résilience *f*

Schlämmanalyse *f*
 E: analysis by elutriation, analysis by decantation
 F: analyse *f* à décantation, analyse *f* par élutriation

Schlangenverlegung von Kabeln
 E: snaking of cables, laying cables in a wave formation
 F: pose *f* des câbles en serpentins

Schlauch *m*
 E: tube *n*, hose *n*
 F: tuyau *m*

schlauchförmiges Prüfstück
 E: tubular test piece
 F: éprouvette *f* de forme tubulaire

Schlauchreckverfahren *n* [Extr.]
 E: tube-on method, tubing extrusion, vacuum smearing
 F: extrusion *f* cône avec vide sur le poinçon, boudinage *m* sous vide

Schleifdraht *m*
 E: trolley wire, overhead contact wire, slide wire
 F: fil *m* (de) trolley, fil *m* de contact

Schleife *f* (Leitungszusammenführung)
 E: loop *n*, closed circuit
 F: boucle *f*, circuit *m* fermé

Schleifenkapazität *f*
 E: loop capacity, wire-to-wire capacity
 F: capacité *f* de boucle

Schleifenmessung *f*

Schleifenwiderstand m
   E: loop test
   F: mesure *f* en boucle

Schleifenwiderstand m
   E: loop resistance
   F: résistance *f* de boucle

Schleppleitung f
   E: trailing cable
   F: câble *m* de remorque, câble *m* d'enrouleur, câble *m* pour engin mobile

schlüsselfertige Anlage
   E: turnkey installation
   F: installation *f* (achevée) clé en main

Schmalbandwicklung f
   E: lapping *n*, taping *n*, tape(d) wrapping
   F: rubanage *m*

Schmelzdraht m
   E: fuse wire, fusing conductor
   F: fil *m* fusible, fil *m* de fusion

Schmelze f
   E: melt *n*, molten material
   F: matière *f* en fusion, fonte *f* (mét.)

Schmelzen n
   E: melting *n*, fusion *n*
   F: fonte *f*, fusion *f*

Schmelzen-Temperatur f [Extr.]
   E: melt temperature
   F: température *f* de la matière en fusion

Schmelzindex m
   E: melt (flow) index
   F: indice *m* de fluidité, indice *m* de fluage, indice *m* de fusion

Schmelzkessel m (Bleipresse)
   E: melting pot
   F: pot *m* de presse

Schmelzleiter m
   E: fuse wire, fusing conductor
   F: fil *m* fusible, fil *m* de fusion

Schmelzofen m
   E: melting furnace
   F: four(neau) *m* de fusion

Schmelzpunkt m
   E: melting point
   F: point *m* de fusion

Schmelztemperatur f
   E: melting temperature
   F: température *f* de fusion

Schmelztopf m (Bleipresse)
   E: melting pot
   F: pot *m* de presse

Schmierlot n
   E: wiping solder
   F: soudure *f* liquide

Schmiermittel n
   E: grease *n*, lubricant *n*
   F: matière *f* lubrifiante, lubrifiant *m*

Schmierplombe f
   E: wiped solder joint, wiping nipple, wiping gland, wiping solder seal
   F: soudure *f* à la louche

Schmierung f
   E: lubrication *n*, greasing *n*
   F: lubrification *f*, graissage *m*

Schmirgelleinen n
   E: emery cloth, abrasive cloth
   F: toile *f* (d')émeri

schmirgeln v
   E: sand *v*, emery *v*
   F: émeriller *v*

Schmirgelpapier n
   E: abrasive paper
   F: papier *m* abrasif, papier *m* émerisé

Schnecke f [Extr.]
   E: screw
   F: vis *f*

Schnecke f (bei einer Kabeltrommel)
   E: ramp
   F: escargot *m*

Schneckenausstoßvorrichtung f [Extr.]
   E: screw pushout device
   F: extracteur *m* de vis

Schneckendrehzahl f [Extr.]
   E: screw speed
   F: tours *m pl* de vis par minute, vitesse *f* de la vis

Schneckengang m [Extr.]
   E: flight of the screw, thread of the screw
   F: filet *m* de la vis, pas *m* de la vis, spire *f* de la vis

Schneckengehäuse n [Extr.]
   E: barrel *n*, cylinder *n*
   F: cylindre *m*

Schneckengewinde n [Extr.]
   E: flight of the screw, thread of the screw
   F: filet *m* de la vis, pas *m* de la vis, spire *f* de la vis

Schneckenlänge nD (D = Durchmesser) [Extr.]
   E: screw length nD (D = diameter)
   F: longueur *f* de la vis nD (D = diamètre)

Schneckenpresse f

Schneckenpresse
- E: extruder n
- F: boudineuse f, extrudeuse f

Schneckenspitze f [Extr.]
- E: tip of a screw
- F: pointe f de la vis

Schneckensteg m [Extr.]
- E: land of the screw
- F: crête f de la vis

schneiden, auf die gewünschte Länge ~
- E: to cut to the required length
- F: couper v à la longueur voulue

schneiden, Papierbänder ~
- E: to slit paper tapes
- F: découper v des rubans de papier

Schneidvorrichtung f
- E: cutting device
- F: dispositif m de coupe

Schnellaufwickelei für Draht
- E: high-speed continuous wire take-up
- F: enrouleur m de fil métallique à grande vitesse

Schnelltrennstecker m
- E: quick disconnect plug
- F: fiche f de coupure rapide

Schnellverschluß m
- E: quick-action locking device, rapid-action locking device
- F: fermeture f rapide

Schnellverseilmaschine f
- E: high-speed strander
- F: câbleuse f à grande vitesse

Schnellverseilmaschine, vertikale ~ [Nachr. K.]
- E: high speed vertical twister
- F: câbleuse f verticale à grande vitesse

Schnittstellenkabel n
- E: interface cable
- F: câble m d'interface

Schnur f [el.]
- E: cord n
- F: cordon m

Schnur, biegsame ~
- E: flexible cord
- F: cordon m souple

Schopfschere f
- E: crop shear
- F: cisaille f à ébouter

Schottland-Island-Kabel n
- E: Scotland-Iceland telephone cable (SCOTICE cable)
- F: câble m téléphonique de l'Ecosse à l'Islande

schräg adj
- E: inclined adj, oblique adj
- F: incliné adj, oblique adj

schräg geschnitten
- E: bias-cut adj
- F: coupé adj en biais

Schrägkopf m [Extr.]
- E: oblique head
- F: tête f oblique

Schrämleitung f
- E: coal cutter cable
- F: câble m de haveuse

Schraubklemme f [el.]
- E: terminal screw, binding screw, screw terminal
- F: vis f de borne, borne f à vis

Schraublehre f
- E: screw callipers pl
- F: calibre m à vis

Schraubverbinder m
- E: bolt-on connector
- F: connecteur m à vis

Schraubverbindung f
- E: screw connection, bolted connection, bolted joint, screw(ed) joint
- F: vissage m, boulonnage m, raccord m à vis, raccord m fileté

Schrotkugelbad n
- E: lead ball bath, lead-shot bath
- F: bain m de grenaille de plomb

Schrott m
- E: scrap n
- F: déchets m pl

schrumpfen v
- E: shrink v, contract v
- F: rétrécir v(se), contracter v(se)

Schrumpfmaß n
- E: shrinkage allowance
- F: grandeur f de retrait

Schrumpfmuffe f
- E: heat-shrinkage insulating sleeve, shrink-on sleeve, heat-shrinkable sleeve
- F: manchon m emmanché à chaud

Schrumpfschlauch m
- E: heat-shrinkable tubing, shrink-on tube
- F: tuyau m emmanchable à chaud, gaine f thermorétractable, manchon m thermorétractable

Schrumpfung f
  E: shrinkage n, contraction n
  F: retrait m, contraction f
Schrumpfung beim Erwärmen
  E: heat-shrinkage n
  F: retrait m au chauffage
Schulfernsehen n
  E: Educational Television (ETV)
  F: Télévision Scolaire
Schuppen f pl
  E: flakes pl, scales pl
  F: écailles f pl, paillettes f pl
Schuppenbildung f
  E: flaking n, scaling n
  F: écaillement m
Schürze f (Mischwalzwerk)
  E: tray n
  F: plateau m
Schüttelrutsche f
  E: vibratory feeder
  F: goulotte f oscillante, goulotte f à secousses
Schüttgewicht n
  E: bulk density, apparent density
  F: densité f apparente
Schutzabdeckung f
  E: guard n, protective covering, safety guard
  F: carter m de sécurité, carter m enveloppe, carter m de protection
Schutzanstrich m
  E: protective varnish coating
  F: couche f de peinture protectrice, enduit m protecteur
Schutzerdung f
  E: protective earth (GB), protective ground (US)
  F: protection f par mise à la terre, mise f à la terre de protection
Schutzfunkenstrecke f
  E: protective spark gap
  F: éclateur m de protection
Schutzgas n
  E: inert gas, protective gas, reducing gas
  F: gaz m inerte, gaz m de protection, gaz m réducteur
Schutzgasatmosphäre f
  E: controlled atmosphere, protective atmosphere
  F: atmosphère f contrôlée, atmosphère f protectrice
Schutzgasschweißen n

  E: inert gas arc welding
  F: soudage m à arc en atmosphère protectrice
Schutzgitter n
  E: wire mesh guard
  F: grille f protectrice
Schutzhülle f
  E: protective coating, protective cover(ing)
  F: revêtement m protecteur, revêtement m de protection, enveloppe f protectrice
Schutzhülle, äußere ~ [Kab.]
  E: serving n, oversheath n
  F: revêtement m extérieur
Schutzkontakt m
  E: protective contact, earthing contact (GB)
  F: contact m de mise à la terre
Schutzleiter m
  E: protective conductor
  F: conducteur m de protection
Schutzmantel m
  E: protective jacket, protective sheath
  F: gaine f de protection
Schutzmuffe f
  E: joint protection box
  F: manchon m protecteur
Schutzrechte n pl
  E: patent rights, trademark rights
  F: droits m pl de protection
Schutzschalter m
  E: line protection switch, overcurrent cut-out switch, protective switch
  F: disjoncteur m de protection, interrupteur m de sécurité
Schutzüberzug m
  E: protective coating, protective cover(ing)
  F: revêtement m protecteur, revêtement m de protection, enveloppe f protectrice
Schutzvorrichtung f
  E: safety device, protective device
  F: dispositif m de sécurité, dispositif m de protection
schwachleitende Mischung
  E: semi-conducting compound, semi-conductive compound
  F: mélange m semi-conducteur
schwachleitende Schicht
  E: semi-conducting layer, semi-

schwachleitende
conductive layer
F: couche f semi-conductrice

Schwachstelle f [Kab.]
E: weak point
F: point m faible

Schwefelhexafluorid (SF₆) n
E: sulphur hexafluoride (SF₆)
F: hexafluorure f de soufre (SF₆)

Schwefelvernetzung f
E: sulphur cross-linking
F: réticulation f au soufre

Schweißdraht m
E: welding wire
F: fil m de soudage

Schweißen n
E: welding n
F: soudage m

Schweißleitung f
E: welding cable
F: câble m de soudure

Schweißnaht f
E: welding seam
F: ligne f de soudure

Schweißraupe f
E: welding bead
F: cordon m de soudure

Schweißstab m
E: welding rod, filler rod
F: baguette f de soudage

Schweißstelle f
E: welded joint
F: soudure f, joint m soudé

Schweißverbindung f
E: welded joint
F: soudure f, joint m soudé

Schwenkarm m
E: swivel arm, swing-out arm
F: bras m pivotant, bras m amovible

schwenkbar adj
E: hinged adj, swivelling adj, pivoted adj
F: pivotant adj, articulé adj

schwere Gummischlauchleitung
E: heavy tough-rubber sheathed flexible cable
F: câble m souple sous gaine épaisse de caoutchouc

Schwimmerschalter m [el.]
E: float (type) switch
F: interrupteur m à flotteur

schwimmfähiges Kabel
E: buoyant cable
F: câble m flottable

Schwingung f [el.]
E: oscillation n
F: oscillation f

Schwingung f [mech.]
E: vibration n
F: vibration f

Schwingungsfestigkeit f
E: resistance to vibrations
F: résistance f aux vibrations

schwingungsfrei adj
E: vibration-free adj, non-vibrating adj, anti-vibration ...
F: anti-vibratoire adj

Sechskantpressung f [K.Garn.]
E: hexagonal compression
F: sertissage m hexagonal

Seekabel n
E: submarine cable
F: câble m sous-marin

Seekabelverstärker m
E: submerged repeater, underwater amplifier
F: répéteur m immergé

Seekoaxialkabel n
E: submarine coaxial cable
F: câble m coaxial sousmarin

Seele f [Kab.]
E: core n (assembly)
F: assemblage m des conducteurs

Seelenbedeckung f
E: core covering, core wrap(ping)
F: revêtement m sur l'assemblage

Seelenbewicklung f
E: core covering, core wrap(ping)
F: revêtement m sur l'assemblage

Seelen-Haltewendel f
E: core binder
F: frettage m sur l'assemblage

Seelenspinnkopf m [Kab.]
E: core binder head
F: tête f de revêtement d'assemblage

Seelenverseilmaschine f
E: core-stranding machine, laying-up machine, core-strander n, cabler n
F: assembleuse f

Seelenverseilung f
E: core stranding, laying up n, cabling n
F: assemblage m (des conducteurs)

Segmentleiter m
E: segmental conductor, split conductor
F: âme f segmentée

Seidenbaumwolldraht m
  E: silk and cotton covered wire
  F: fil m revêtu de soie et de coton
Seil n
  E: rope n, strand n
  F: câble m, corde f
Sektorbreite f (des Leiters)
  E: sector width
  F: largeur f du secteur
Sektorhöhe f (des Leiters)
  E: sector height
  F: hauteur f du secteur
Sektorkante f
  E: sector edge
  F: arête f de secteur
Sektorleiter m
  E: sector-shaped conductor
  F: âme f sectorale
Sektorspitze f
  E: sector peak, sector crest
  F: sommet m d'un secteur
Sektorverdichtungswalzen f pl
  E: sector rollers
  F: rouleaux m pl (de rétreint) de secteur
Sekundärkreislauf m
  E: secondary circuit
  F: circuit m secondaire
Sekundärkühlung f
  E: secondary cooling
  F: refroidissement m secondaire
Sekundärspannung f
  E: secondary voltage, output voltage
  F: tension f secondaire
selbstausschaltend adj [Masch.]
  E: self-disengaging adj
  F: à débrayage automatique
Selbstausschalter m
  E: automatic cut-out
  F: interrupteur m automatique
selbsterlöschend adj
  E: self-extinguishing adj
  F: auto-extinguible adj
selbstklebend adj
  E: self-bonding adj, self-adhering adj, self-adhesive adj
  F: auto-collant adj, auto-adhésif adj
selbstklebendes Band
  E: self-adhesive tape, pressure-sensitive tape
  F: ruban m auto-adhésif, ruban m auto-collant
selbsttragendes Kabel
  E: self-supporting cable
  F: câble m autoporteur
selbsttragendes Luftkabel
  E: self-supporting aerial cable, self-supporting overhead cable
  F: câble m aérien autoporteur
selbstverschweißendes Band
  E: self-amalgamating tape, self-fusing tape
  F: ruban m autosoudable, ruban m autosoudant, ruban m autoamalgamant
selbstvulkanisierend adj
  E: self-curing adj, self-vulcanizing adj
  F: auto-vulcanisant adj
Selbstwählbetrieb m
  E: automatic telephone service, automatic dialling, automatic dial service
  F: exploitation f (téléphonique) automatique, sélection f automatique, service m téléphonique automatique
Selbstwählsystem n
  E: automatic telephone service, automatic dialling, automatic dial service
  F: exploitation f (téléphonique) automatique, sélection f automatique, service m téléphonique automatique
selbstzentrierend adj
  E: self-ali(g)ning adj, self-centering adj, autocentering adj
  F: à centrage automatique
senkrechte Anordnung
  E: vertical arrangement
  F: disposition f verticale
Senkung des Erdbodens
  E: subsidence of ground
  F: tassement m de terre
Serienstörspannung f
  E: series interference voltage
  F: tension f perturbatrice série
SF$_6$ (s. Schwefelhexafluorid)
SF$_6$-isoliertes Leitersystem
  E: gas(SF$_6$)-insulated conductor system, compressed gas(SF$_6$)-insulated transmission line, SF$_6$-insulated metal clad tubular bus, SF$_6$-insulated bus duct
  F: liaison f blindée isolée au SF$_6$,

SF-isoliertes

canalisation *f* blindée isolée au SF₆

SF₆-Rohrleiter *m*
- *E:* gas(SF₆)-insulated conductor system, compressed gas(SF₆)-insulated transmission line, SF₆-insulated metal clad tubular bus, SF₆-insulated bus duct
- *F:* liaison *f* blindée isolée au SF₆, canalisation *f* blindée isolée au SF₆

SF₆-Rohrschiene *f*
- *E:* gas(SF₆)-insulated conductor system, compressed gas(SF₆)-insulated transmission line, SF₆-insulated metal clad tubular bus, SF₆-insulated bus duct
- *F:* liaison *f* blindée isolée au SF₆, canalisation *f* blindée isolée au SF₆

Sicherheitsabdeckung *f*
- *E:* guard *n*, protective covering, safety guard
- *F:* carter *m* de sécurité, carter *m* enveloppe, carter *m* de protection

Sicherheitsvorrichtung *f*
- *E:* safety device, protective device
- *F:* dispositif *m* de sécurité, dispositif *m* de protection

Sicherung *f* [el.]
- *E:* fuse *n*
- *F:* fusible *m*, coupe-circuit *m*

Siebanalyse *f*
- *E:* sieve analysis, screen analysis
- *F:* analyse *f* au tamis

Siebeinsatz *m* [Extr.]
- *E:* strainer *n*
- *F:* plaque-filtre *f*

Siebpackung *f* [Extr.]
- *E:* screen pack
- *F:* paquet *m* de filtres

Siebrückstand *m*
- *E:* screen residue
- *F:* refus *m* de criblage, refus *m* du tamis

Siebung *f*
- *E:* sieving *n*, screening *n*
- *F:* criblage *m*, tamisage *m*

Siedebeginn (SB) *m*
- *E:* initial boiling point (I.B.P.)
- *F:* début *m* d'ébullition

Siedebereich *m*
- *E:* boiling range
- *F:* zone *f* d'ébullition, domaine *m* d'ébullition

Siedekurve *f*
- *E:* boiling curve
- *F:* courbe *f* des points d'ébullition

Siedepunkt *m*
- *E:* boiling point
- *F:* point *m* d'ébullition

Signalader *f*
- *E:* signalling core
- *F:* fil *m* de signalisation

Signalkabel *n*
- *E:* signalling cable
- *F:* câble *m* de signalisation

Signallampe *f*
- *E:* pilot lamp, signal lamp, indicating lamp, pilot light
- *F:* voyant *m* lumineux, signal *m* lumineux, lampe-témoin *f*

Signal-Schaltkabel *n*
- *E:* signal switchboard cable
- *F:* câble *m* de connexion pour installations de signalisation

Silikonkautschuk *m*
- *E:* silicone rubber
- *F:* caoutchouc *m* silicone

Simplex-Papier *n* (Einfachlagenpapier)
- *E:* simplex paper, single-ply paper, single-wire paper
- *F:* papier *m* simplex, papier *m* en une couche

Skalenteilung *f*
- *E:* scale division
- *F:* graduation *f* d'échelle

Skineffekt *m* [el.]
- *E:* skin effect
- *F:* effet *m* de peau

skineffektarmer Leiter (Milliken-Leiter)
- *E:* Milliken conductor
- *F:* conducteur *m* Milliken

Sofortdurchschlagfestigkeit *f*
- *E:* instantaneous breakdown strength
- *F:* tenue *f* au claquage instantané

Sollwert *m*
- *E:* specified value, desired value
- *F:* valeur *f* spécifiée

Sonder-Gummiaderleitung *f*
- *E:* special rubber insulated cable
- *F:* câble *m* spécial isolé au caoutchouc

Spaltbreite *f* [Walzw.]
- *E:* gap width
- *F:* écartement *m*

spanabhebende Bearbeitung

E: cutting *n*, machining *n*
F: usinage *m* (à l'outil de coupe)
spanlose Bearbeitung
E: non-cutting shaping
F: mise *f* en forme plastique
Spanndraht *m*
E: guy wire, span wire
F: fil *m* tendeur, fil *m* d'arrêt
spannen *v*
E: straighten *v*, stretch *v*
F: allonger *v*, étendre *v*, tendre *v*
Spannrad *n* (Properzi-Gießmaschine)
E: tension wheel
F: roue *f* de serrage
Spannung *f*
E: voltage *n*, tension *n*
F: tension *f*
Spannung gegen Erde
E: voltage to earth
F: tension *f* par rapport à la terre, tension *f* simple
Spannung im Material [mech.]
E: strain in the material
F: tension *f* dans le matériau
Spannung, die ~ abschalten
E: to cut off the voltage, to cut out the voltage
F: mettre *v* hors tension
Spannung, eine ~ anlegen
E: to apply a voltage
F: mettre *v* sous tension, appliquer *v* une tension
spannungführend *adj*
E: live *adj*, current-carrying *adj*
F: sous tension, parcouru *adj* de courant,
Spannungsabfall *m*
E: voltage drop
F: chute *f* de tension
Spannungs-Abgriff *m*
E: voltage tap
F: prise *f* de tension
Spannungsanstieg *m*
E: voltage rise
F: montée *f* de tension
Spannungsausgleich *m*
E: compensation of voltage
F: équilibrage *m* de la tension
Spannungsbeanspruchung *f*
E: voltage stress, electric stress
F: contrainte *f* de tension, contrainte *f* électrique
Spannungsfestigkeit *f*
E: dielectric strength, breakdown strength, puncture resistance, electric strength
F: rigidité *f* diélectrique
spannungsfrei glühen
E: normalize *v*
F: normaliser *v*
Spannungsgradient *m*
E: voltage gradient
F: gradient *m* de potentiel
spannungslose Periode [el.]
E: dead time interval, off-load period
F: repos *m*
spannungslose Verseilung (Rundleiter)
E: stranding with backtwist
F: câblage *m* à détorsion
spannungslose Verseilung (Sektorleiter)
E: stranding with pretwist
F: câblage *m* à préformage, câblage *m* à prétorsion
Spannungspegel *m*
E: voltage level
F: niveau *m* de tension
Spannungsprüfgerät *n*
E: voltage detector, spark tester
F: détecteur *m* de tension
Spannungsprüfung *f*
E: dielectric test, voltage test, spark test
F: essai *m* diélectrique, essai *m* de tension
Spannungsquelle *f*
E: voltage source
F: source *f* de tension
Spannungsregelung *f*
E: voltage control
F: réglage *m* de tension
Spannungsrißbeständigkeit *f*
E: stress cracking resistance
F: résistance *f* à la fissuration sous contrainte, résistance *f* à la fissuration de contact
Spannungsrißbildung *f* [Plast.]
E: environmental stress cracking
F: fissuration *f* de contact, fissuration *f* sous contrainte
Spannungsschwankung *f*
E: voltage fluctuation, voltage variation
F: fluctuation *f* de tension, variation *f* de tension
Spannungsstabilisator *m* (Zusatz in

Spannungsstabilisator Isoliermischungen)
 E: voltage stabilizer (additive in insulating compounds)
 F: stabilisant m de tension
spannungsstabilisierend adj (Mischungsadditiv)
 E: voltage-stabilizing adj
 F: stabilisant adj électriquement
Spannungssteigerung, stufenweise ~
 E: voltage increase in steps
 F: élévation f de tension par paliers
Spannungsstoß m [el.]
 E: impulse n (el.), voltage surge
 F: onde f de choc
Spannungsstufe f
 E: voltage step
 F: gradin m de tension, palier m de tension
Spannungsteiler m
 E: voltage divider, potentiometer n
 F: réducteur m de tension, potentiomètre m
Spannungsunterschied m
 E: potential difference
 F: différence f de potentiel
Spannungsverlust m
 E: voltage loss, potential loss
 F: perte f de tension, perte f de potentiel
Speicher m [Drahtk., Vers.]
 E: accumulator n
 F: accumulateur m, moufle f de régulation
Speicher, atmender ~ (SZ-Verseilung)
 E: breathing accumulator
 F: moufle m respirant
Speicher, rotierender ~ [Vers.]
 E: rotating accumulator
 F: moufle f rotative
Speicherinhalt m [Drahtk., Vers.]
 E: accumulator capacity
 F: capacité f d'accumulateur, capacité f de moufle
Speisekabel n
 E: feeder n, feeder cable
 F: câble m d'alimentation, feeder m
Speiseleitung f
 E: feeding line, feeder n
 F: circuit m d'alimentation, feeder m
speisen v [mech., el.]
 E: feed v, charge v, load v, supply v
 F: alimenter v, charger v
Speisepunkt m
 E: feeding point
 F: point m d'alimentation
Speisespannung f
 E: supply voltage
 F: tension f d'alimentation
Speisestrom m
 E: feed current
 F: courant m d'alimentation
Speisung f
 E: feed n
 F: alimentation f
Spektralanalyse f
 E: spectral analysis
 F: analyse f spectrale
spektrographische Analyse
 E: spectrographic(al) analysis
 F: analyse f spectrographique
Spektrum n [Prod.]
 E: range n, spectrum n
 F: gamme f, éventail m
Sperrbereich m [Nachr.]
 E: cut-off range suppression band
 F: bande f éliminée, intervalle m imperméable
Sperre f
 E: barrier n
 F: barrière f, arrêt m
Sperrkreis m
 E: block circuit, trap circuit
 F: circuit-bouchon m
Sperrmuffe f
 E: stop joint
 F: joint m d'arrêt
Sperrspannung f
 E: inverse voltage, reverse voltage
 F: tension f inverse, tension f d'arrêt
spezifischer Durchgangswiderstand
 E: volume resistivity
 F: résistivité f de volume
spezifischer Isolationswiderstand
 E: specific insulation resistance
 F: résistance f spécifique d'isolement
spezifischer Oberflächenwiderstand
 E: surface resistivity
 F: résistivité f de surface
spezifischer Wärmewiderstand des Bodens
 E: thermal resistivity of the soil
 F: résistivité f thermique du sol
spezifischer Widerstand
 E: volume resistivity, resistivity n, specific resistance
 F: résistivité f

spezifisches Gewicht
  E: specific gravity, volume weight
  F: poids *m* spécifique, masse *f* volumique

Spinner *m* (Band)
  E: spinner *n*, lapping head, tape lapping head
  F: tête *f* de rubanage, tête *f* rubaneuse

Spinnerdrehzahl *f* [Bdspinn.]
  E: lapping head speed
  F: vitesse *f* de tête rubaneuse

Spinnfuge *f* [Papierspinn.]
  E: butt space, butt gap, gap *n*
  F: déjoint *m*, joint *m*

Spinnkopf *m* (Band)
  E: spinner *n*, lapping head, tape lapping head
  F: tête *f* de rubanage, tête *f* rubaneuse

Spinnkopf *m* (Garn, Kordel)
  E: spinning head
  F: tête *f* guipeuse

Spinnmaschine *f* (Band)
  E: taping machine, lapping machine
  F: rubaneuse *f*

Spinnrichtung *f* [Bdspinn.]
  E: lapping direction
  F: sens *m* de rubanage, sens *m* d'enroulement

Spinnspannung *f* [Bdspinn.]
  E: lapping tension
  F: tension *f* de rubanage

Spinnwinkel *m* [Bdspinn.]
  E: lapping angle
  F: angle *m* de rubanage

Spinnzug *m* [Bdspinn.]
  E: lapping tension
  F: tension *f* de rubanage

Spirale, farbige ~
  E: colo(u)red spiral, colo(u)red helix
  F: spirale *f* colorée, hélice *f* colorée

Spitze *f* (Spannung, Leistung)
  E: peak *n*, crest *n*
  F: pointe *f*, crête *f*

Spitzenbelastung *f* [el.]
  E: peak load, load peak
  F: pointe *f* de charge, charge *f* de pointe

Spitzenbelastungszeit *f*
  E: peak hours *pl*
  F: heures *f pl* de pointe

Spitzenspannung *f*
  E: peak voltage, crest voltage
  F: tension *f* de crête, tension *f* de pointe

Spitzenwert *m*
  E: peak value, crest value, amplitude *n*
  F: valeur *f* de crête

Spitzenwinkel *m* (Sektorleiter)
  E: sector angle
  F: angle *m* au sommet

spitzwinklige Abzweigmuffe
  E: tangential joint
  F: boîte *f* tangentielle

Spleiß *m*
  E: splice *n*, spliced joint
  F: épissure *f*, joint *m*, jonction épissée *f*

spleißen *v*
  E: splice *v*
  F: épisser *v*

Spleißgerät *n*
  E: splicing tool
  F: outil *m* à épisser

Spleißmuffengehäuse *n* [Nachr. K.]
  E: splice case, splice closure
  F: manchon *m* sur jonction épissée

Spleißstelle *f*
  E: splice *n*, spliced joint
  F: épissure *f*, joint *m*, jonction épissée *f*

Spleißverbindung *f*
  E: splice *n*, spliced joint
  F: épissure *f*, joint *m*, jonction épissée *f*

Sprachreichweite *f* [Nachr. K.]
  E: audio range
  F: portée *f* téléphonique

Sprachsperre *f*
  E: audio-suppression device, guard circuit
  F: dispositif *m* d'audio-supression

Sprechader *f*
  E: speaking wire, speech wire
  F: fil *m* téléphonique

Sprechfrequenz *f*
  E: voice frequency, telephone frequency, speech frequency
  F: fréquence *f* vocale, fréquence *f* téléphonique

Sprechfrequenzübertragung *f*
  E: voice frequency transmission
  F: transmission *f* de fréquences vocales

Sprechkanal *m*
  E: telephone channel, voice channel, speech channel

Sprechkanal

- F: canal *m* téléphonique, voie *f* téléphonique

Sprechkreis *m*
- E: speaking circuit, voice circuit, speech circuit
- F: circuit *m* téléphonique

Sprechleistung *f*
- E: speech power
- F: puissance *f* vocale

Sprechstelle *f*
- E: telephone set, telephone instrument (US), telephone station
- F: appareil *m* téléphonique, poste *m* téléphonique

Sprechstrom *m*
- E: telephone current, speaking current
- F: courant *m* téléphonique

Sprechverkehr *m*
- E: telephone traffic, line telephony, intercommunication *n*
- F: trafic *m* téléphonique

Sprechzeichen *n*
- E: voice signal
- F: signal *m* vocal

Spreizen der Kabeladern
- E: fanning out of the cable cores, bending out of the cable cores
- F: épanouissement *m* des conducteurs de câble

Spritzguß *m*
- E: injection mo(u)lding
- F: moulage *m* par injection, fonte *f* injectée

Spritzkopf *m* (Extruder)
- E: extrusion head, extruder head
- F: tête *f* de boudineuse, tête *f* d'extrusion

Spritzverfahren *n*
- E: extrusion process
- F: méthode *f* d'extrusion

Spritzwerkzeuge *n pl*
- E: extruder dies *pl*, extrusion dies *pl*
- F: outillage *m* de boudineuse

Sprödbruch *m*
- E: brittle fracture
- F: rupture *f* fragile

spröde *adj*
- E: brittle *adj*
- F: cassant *adj*, fragile *adj*

Sprödigkeit *f*
- E: brittleness *n*
- F: fragilité *f*

Sprödigkeitstemperatur *f*
- E: brittleness temperature
- F: température *f* de fragilité

Sprühdüse *f*
- E: spray nozzle, jet nozzle
- F: pulvérisateur *m*, atomiseur *m*

Sprüheinrichtung *f*
- E: spray equipment
- F: dispositif *m* de pulvérisation, pulvérisateur *m*

Sprühentladung *f*
- E: corona discharge, ionization discharge
- F: effluve *f* en couronne, décharge *f* par ionisation, décharge *f* en couronne

Sprühschirm *m* (gegen el. Entladungen)
- E: corona shield
- F: écran *m* contre les effluves

Spulapparat, automatischer ~
- E: automatic spooler
- F: bobinoir *m* automatique

Spule *f*
- E: coil *n*, reel *n*, bobbin *n*, spool *n*
- F: bobine *f*

spulen *v*
- E: wind *v*, wind up *v*, take up *v*, spool *v*, reel *v*, coil *v*
- F: enrouler *v*, bobiner *v*

spülen *v*
- E: rinse *v*, flush *v*
- F: rincer *v*

Spulendrehzahl *f*
- E: bobbin speed
- F: vitesse *f* de la bobine

Spulenfeld *n*
- E: loading (coil) section
- F: section *f* de charge, section *f* de bobines Pupin

Spulenfeldlänge *f*
- E: loading (coil) section
- F: section *f* de charge, section *f* de bobines Pupin

Spulenflansch *m*
- E: reel flange, spool flange
- F: joue *f* de bobine

Spulenhalter *m* [Vers.]
- E: cradle *n*
- F: porte-bobine *m*, berceau *m*

Spulenkasten *m* [Nachr.]
- E: loading (coil) pot, loading coil case
- F: boîte *f* de charge, pot *m* de charge

Spulenpunkt *m* (Pupinisierung)
- E: pupinization point

F: point m de charge
Spulensatz m
  E: loading coil unit, loading unit (tel. c.)
  F: jeu m de bobines de charge, unité f de charge (c. tél.)
Spulenträger m [Vers.]
  E: cradle n
  F: porte-bobine m, berceau m
Spulenwechsel m
  E: reel change
  F: changement m de bobine
Spürgas n
  E: tracer gas
  F: gaz m détecteur
Stabilisator m
  E: stabilizing agent, stabilizer n
  F: agent m stabilisant, stabilisant m
stabilisierender Zusatz
  E: stabilizing agent, stabilizer n
  F: agent m stabilisant, stabilisant m
Stadium der Fertigung
  E: stage of production, manufacturing stage
  F: étape f de fabrication, phase f de fabrication
Stadtgemeinschaftsantennen-Fernsehen n
  E: Community Antenna Television (CATV)
  F: réception f collective d'antenne de télévision
Stadtnetz n [el.]
  E: urban network, urban supply system
  F: réseau m urbain
Stahlband n
  E: steel tape, steel strip
  F: feuillard m d'acier
stahlbandarmiertes Kabel
  E: steel-tape-armo(u)red cable
  F: câble m armé en feuillard d'acier
Stahlbandarmierung f
  E: steel tape armo(u)ring, steel tape armo(u)r
  F: armure f en feuillard d'acier
Stahlbandbewehrung f
  E: steel tape armo(u)ring, steel tape armo(u)r
  F: armure f en feuillard d'acier
Stahlbandwendel f
  E: steel tape helix
  F: hélice f de feuillard d'acier

Stahldraht m
  E: steel wire
  F: fil m d'acier
Stahldrahtarmierung f
  E: steel wire armouring
  F: armure f en fils d'acier
Stahldrahtbewehrung f
  E: steel wire armouring
  F: armure f en fils d'acier
Stahlflachdraht-Armierung f
  E: flat steel wire armouring
  F: armure f en fils d'acier méplats
Stahlflachdraht-Bewehrung f
  E: flat steel wire armouring
  F: armure f en fils d'acier méplats
Stahlrohr n
  E: steel pipe
  F: tuyau m en acier, tube m d'acier
Stahlwellmantel m
  E: corrugated steel sheath
  F: gaine f d'acier ondulée
Stalpeth-Mantel m (Stahl-Al-PE-Schichtenmantel)
  E: Stalpeth-sheath n
  F: gaine f Stalpeth
Stammkreis m
  E: side circuit, physical circuit, combining circuit
  F: circuit m combinant, circuit m réel
Stammkreisspule f
  E: side circuit loading coil
  F: bobine f de charge du circuit combinant
Stammleitung f
  E: side circuit, physical circuit, combining circuit
  F: circuit m combinant, circuit m réel
Stammleitungsspule f
  E: side circuit loading coil
  F: bobine f de charge du circuit combinant
Stammpupinspule f
  E: side circuit loading coil
  F: bobine f de charge du circuit combinant
Stampfdichte f
  E: apparent density after vibration
  F: densité f apparente après vibration
Stampffutter bei Schmelzöfen
  E: rammed refractory lining
  F: revêtement m de fourneau réfractaire damé
Standard-Leitfähigkeit nach IEC

Standard-Leitfähigkeit (Kupfer)
  E: I.A.C.S. conductivity (International Annealed Copper Standard/IEC)
  F: conductivité f I.A.C.S. (cuivre), conductibilité f I.A.C.S. (cuivre)

Standard-Schnittstellenkabel n
  E: standard interface cable
  F: câble m d'interface standard

Standard-Widerstand nach IEC (Kupfer)
  E: I.A.C.S. resistance (International Annealed Copper Standard/IEC)
  F: résistance f I.A.C.S. (cuivre)

Stand der Technik, nach dem neuesten ~
  E: according to the latest state of the art
  F: selon les dernières règles de l'art

Standort eines Werkes
  E: location of a factory
  F: implantation f d'une usine

Standzeit f [Masch.]
  E: life n, service life
  F: vie f

Standzeit f (von Mischungen)
  E: time until thermal-oxidative decomposition
  F: temps m jusqu'à la décomposition thermo-oxydative

Stanzwerkzeug n
  E: blanking die, punching tool
  F: outil m de découpage

Stapelbühne f
  E: collection platform
  F: plate-forme f d'empilage

Stärke f [mech.]
  E: strength n, power n, force n
  F: puissance f, force f

Stärke f [el.]
  E: intensity n
  F: intensité f, puissance f

Starkstrom m
  E: power current
  F: courant m fort

Starkstromfrequenz f
  E: power frequency
  F: fréquence f industrielle

Starkstromgeräusch n [Nachr. K.]
  E: power induced noise, power supply noise
  F: bruit m induit

Starkstromkabel n
  E: power cable
  F: câble m d'énergie

Starkstromleitung f
  E: power cable, flexible power cord
  F: câble m (souple) d'énergie

Starkstromleitung f (System)
  E: power line, power circuit
  F: ligne f à courant fort

Starkstromnetz n
  E: mains n, power system, power transmission network, power distribution network
  F: réseau m de distribution d'énergie, réseau m de transport d'énergie

Starkstromtechnik f
  E: power engineering
  F: technique f des courants forts

starr geerdeter Sternpunkt
  E: solidly earthed neutral (GB), solidly grounded neutral (US)
  F: neutre m rigidement relié à la terre

starr geerdetes Netz
  E: solidly earthed system (GB), solidly grounded system (US)
  F: réseau m avec mise à la terre rigide du neutre, réseau m rigidement relié à la terre

starre Sternpunkterdung
  E: solid earthing of neutral (GB), solid grounding of neutral (US)
  F: mise f à la terre rigide du neutre

stationär adj
  E: stationary adj, fixed adj
  F: stationnaire adj, fixe adj

statischer Schirm
  E: electrostatic screen, electrostatic shield
  F: écran m électrostatique

Stauring m [Extr.]
  E: retaining ring
  F: bague f de laminage

Stearinsäure f
  E: stearic acid
  F: acide m stéarique

Steckanschluß m
  E: plug and socket connection
  F: jonction f débrochable, prise f complète mâle et femelle, prise f débrochable

Steckbuchse f
  E: plug socket, connector socket, receptacle n, female contact, socket n
  F: prise f femelle, fiche f femelle,

Steckdose f
  E: socket n, socket outlet
  F: prise f de courant

Stecker m
  E: plug n, plug connector
  F: fiche f, prise f mâle

Stecker, mehrpoliger ~
  E: multiple pin plug
  F: fiche f multipolaire

Steckerbuchse f
  E: plug socket, connector socket, receptacle n, female contact, socket n
  F: prise f femelle, fiche f femelle, douille f

Steckverbindung f
  E: plug and socket connection
  F: jonction f débrochable, prise f complète mâle et femelle, prise f débrochable

Stegleitung f
  E: flat webbed building wire
  F: conducteur m à gaine séparable

stehende Welle [el.]
  E: standing wave
  F: onde f stationnaire

stehender Guß
  E: vertical cast
  F: coulée f verticale

Stehspannung f
  E: withstand voltage
  F: tension f de tenue

Stehstoßspannung f
  E: impulse withstand voltage
  F: tension f de tenue au choc, tension f de tenue aux ondes de choc

Stehwechselspannung f
  E: a.c. withstand voltage
  F: tension f de tenue au courant alternatif

Steigerung f
  E: increase n, raise n, rise n
  F: augmentation f, élévation f

Steigleitung f
  E: rising main, vertical riser cable
  F: colonne f montante

Steigung f (Gewinde, Schnecke, Bandspinnen)
  E: pitch n
  F: pas m

Steigungswinkel m
  E: angle of pitch
  F: angle m d'inclinaison, angle m de pas

Steilhangkabel n
  E: cable for installation on steep slopes
  F: câble m pour installation sur pentes raides

Steinkohlenteer m
  E: coal tar
  F: goudron m minéral, goudron m de houille

Stellfläche f [Masch.]
  E: floor space, floor area
  F: surface f

Stellschraube f
  E: set screw, adjusting screw
  F: vis f d'ajustage, vis f de réglage

Stelltransformator m
  E: regulating transformer, variable ratio transformer
  F: transformateur m de réglage

Stempel m [Masch.]
  E: piston n, ram n, plunger n
  F: piston m, fouloir m

Stempelpresse f
  E: ram press, plunger press
  F: presse f à piston

Sternpunkt m
  E: neutral point, zero point
  F: neutre m, point m neutre, zéro m

Sternpunkt, geerdeter ~ (Nullpunkt)
  E: earthed neutral (GB), grounded neutral (US)
  F: neutre m à la terre, neutre m mis à la terre

Sternpunkt, isolierter ~
  E: insulated neutral, isolated neutral
  F: neutre m isolé

Sternpunkt, Netz mit starr geerdetem ~
  E: solidly earthed system (GB), solidly grounded system (US)
  F: réseau m avec mise à la terre rigide du neutre, réseau m rigidement relié à la terre

Sternpunkt, nicht geerdeter ~ (Nullpunkt)
  E: unearthed neutral (GB), ungrounded neutral (US)
  F: neutre m non mis à la terre

Sternpunkt, starr geerdeter ~
  E: solidly earthed neutral (GB), solidly grounded neutral (US)
  F: neutre m rigidement relié à la terre

Sternpunkterdung f
- E: earthing of neutral (GB), grounding of neutral (US)
- F: mise f à la terre du neutre

Sternpunkterdung, starre ~
- E: solid earthing of neutral (GB), solid grounding of neutral (US)
- F: mise f à la terre rigide du neutre

Sternvierer m
- E: star-quad n, spiral quad (US), spiral four quad (US)
- F: quarte f étoile

sternviererverseiltes Kabel
- E: cable with star quad combination, star quad cable
- F: câble m à quartes en étoile

Sternviererverseilung f
- E: star quad formation, star quad twisting, star quadding
- F: câblage m par quartes en étoile, fabrication f de quartes étoile

Steuerader f
- E: control core
- F: conducteur m de commande

Steuerelement n [K. Garn.]
- E: stress cone
- F: cône m de contrainte

Steuerimpuls m
- E: control signal pulse
- F: impulsion f de contrôle

Steuerkabel n
- E: control cable
- F: câble m de commande

Steuerkreis m
- E: control circuit
- F: circuit m de réglage, circuit m de commande

steuern v
- E: control v
- F: régler v, commander v

Steuerpult n
- E: control desk, operator's desk, control console
- F: pupitre m de commande, poste m de commande

Steuerspannung f
- E: control voltage, control tension
- F: tension f de réglage, tension f de commande

Steuerstrom m
- E: control current
- F: courant m de commande

Steuerung f [el., mech.]
- E: control n
- F: commande f, réglage m

Stich m [Walzw.]
- E: pass n
- F: passe f

Stichkabel n [En. K.]
- E: service cable, branch cable, service drop cable
- F: câble m de raccordement domestique, câble m de branchement domestique

Stichprobe f
- E: random sample
- F: échantillon m pris au hasard, éprouvette f prise au hasard

Stichprobenmessung f
- E: random measurement
- F: mesure f sur prélèvement

Stichprobenprüfung f
- E: sampling test, random test, spot check
- F: essai m sur prélèvement

Stiftschelle f [K. Verl.]
- E: clip n
- F: attache f

Stillstandszeit f [Masch.]
- E: down-time n, idle time, dead time
- F: temps m d'arrêt, temps m mort

Stockpunkt m
- E: solidification point, freezing point
- F: point m de solidification, point m de congélation

Stockpunkt m (Öle)
- E: pour point, cloud point
- F: point m de figeage

Stokes n (St) (Viskosität)
- E: stokes n
- F: stokes n

Stopfbüchse f
- E: stuffing box, gland n
- F: presse-étoupe f

Stöpselschnur f
- E: plug-ended cord
- F: cordon m avec fiche, cordon m de liaison

Störanfälligkeit f [Nachr.]
- E: sensibility to disturbances
- F: sensibilité f aux parasites, sensibilité f aux perturbations

Störbeeinflussung f
- E: interference n (effect)
- F: effet m de perturbation, perturbation f, interférence f

Störbeseitigung f
  E: interference elimination, interference suppression, noise suppression
  F: suppression f des parasites, déparasitage m

Störfeld n [Nachr.]
  E: noise field, interference field
  F: champ m perturbateur, champ m parasite

Störgeräusch n
  E: interfering noise, parasitic noise
  F: bruit m parasite, bruit m perturbateur

Störpegel m [Nachr. K.]
  E: noise level, interference level
  F: niveau m de bruit, niveau m des perturbations

Störquelle f
  E: interference source, source of disturbance
  F: source f de perturbation

Störschutz m
  E: interference protection
  F: antiparasitage m

Störschutzeinrichtung f
  E: interference eliminator, interference suppression device
  F: dispositif m antiparasites

Störschutzkondensator m
  E: anti-interference capacitor, anti-noise capacitor
  F: condensateur m antiparasites

Störschwingung f
  E: parasitic oscillation
  F: onde f perturbatrice, oscillation f parasite

Störspannung f
  E: interference voltage, disturbing voltage
  F: tension f perturbatrice, tension f parasite

Störsperre f [Nachr.]
  E: interference suppressor
  F: suppresseur m d'interférences

Störung, eine ~ beseitigen
  E: to clear a fault
  F: éliminer v un défaut, supprimer v un défaut, dépanner v

Störung, eine ~ eingrenzen
  E: to locate a fault
  F: localiser v un défaut

Störung, eine ~ suchen
  E: to trace a fault
  F: détecter v un défaut

Stoß, auf ~ [Bdspinn.]
  E: without butt gaps, in a closed helix
  F: en hélice fermée, en spires jointives

Stoßdurchschlagfestigkeit f
  E: impulse breakdown strength
  F: résistance f au claquage sous tension de choc

Stoßfuge f [Papierspinn.]
  E: butt space, butt gap, gap n
  F: déjoint m, joint m

Stoßionisation f
  E: ionization by collision, impact ionization
  F: ionisation f par choc

Stoßkantenzwischenraum m [Papierspinn.]
  E: butt space, butt gap, gap n
  F: déjoint m, joint m

Stoßkurzschlußstrom m
  E: maximum asymmetric short-circuit current
  F: courant m maximum asymétrique de court circuit

Stoßpegel m
  E: impulse level
  F: seuil m de choc

Stoßprüfung f (el.)
  E: impulse voltage test, impulse test, surge test
  F: essai m aux ondes de choc, essai m au choc

Stoßspannung f
  E: impulse voltage, surge voltage
  F: tension f de choc

Stoßspannungsanlage f
  E: impulse generator
  F: génératrice f de choc

Stoßspannungsfestigkeit f
  E: impulse (voltage) strength, surge voltage strength, surge resistance
  F: résistance f aux ondes de choc, tenue f aux ondes de choc

Stoßspannungs-Prüfung f
  E: impulse voltage test, impulse test, surge test
  F: essai m aux ondes de choc, essai m au choc

Stoßspannungsverhalten n
  E: impulse voltage behaviour
  F: comportement m aux ondes de choc

Stoßstellen, die ~ überdeckend [Bdspinn.]
 E: covering the butt joints
 F: faisant couvre-joint

Stoßstrom m
 E: surge current, impulse current
 F: courant m de choc

Stoßwelle f [el.]
 E: impulse n (el.), voltage surge
 F: onde f de choc

strahlenvernetzbare Mischung
 E: irradiation cross-linkable compound
 F: mélange m réticulable par irradiation

strahlenvernetzt adj
 E: cross-linked by irradiation
 F: réticulé adj par irradiation

Strahlenvernetzung f
 E: cross-linking by irradiation
 F: réticulation f par irradiation

Strahlung f
 E: radiation n
 F: radiation f

Strahlungsbund m [K. Garn.]
 E: field-controlling wire binding
 F: frettage m en fil métallique pour l'orientation du champ électrique, frette f en fil métallique

Strahlungsring m [K. Garn.]
 E: stress relief ring
 F: anneau m de répartition du champ électrique

Strammheit f (Gummimischungen)
 E: stiffness n
 F: raideur f

Strangguß m
 E: continuous casting
 F: coulée f continue, coulage m continu

Strangpresse f
 E: ram press, plunger press
 F: presse f à piston

Strangpresse für Kabelmäntel [Met.]
 E: cable sheathing press
 F: presse f à filer pour gaines de câbles

Strangpresse in Viersäulenbauart [Met.]
 E: four-column type metal extrusion press
 F: presse f à filer type à quatre colonnes

Strangpresse in Zweisäulenbauart [Met.]
 E: two-column type metal extrusion press
 F: presse f à filer type à deux colonnes

strecken v
 E: straighten v, stretch v
 F: allonger v, étendre v, tendre v

Streckenabschnitt m [K. Verl.]
 E: route section
 F: tronçon m de ligne, tronçon m de liaison

Streckenfernmeldekabel n
 E: railway telecommunication cable
 F: câble m de télécommunication de parcours ferroviaire

Streckenfernsprecher m
 E: portable telephone set
 F: poste m téléphonique mobile

Streckgrenze f
 E: yield point, yield strength, elastic limit
 F: limite f d'élasticité, limite f d'allongement

Streckmittel n (Gummimischungen)
 E: extender n
 F: extendeur m

Streichharz n
 E: wiping resin
 F: résine f à enduire

strenge Prüfung
 E: severe test, rigorous test, rigid test, stringent test, severe control, strict control, exacting control
 F: essai m rigoureux, contrôle m serré, contrôle m rigoureux, contrôle m sévère

Streubereich m
 E: range of scattering, range of dispersion
 F: plage f de dispersion

Streufeld n
 E: leakage field
 F: champ m de fuite

Streustrom m
 E: leakage current, fault current, stray current
 F: courant m de fuite, courant m de défaut, courant m vagabond

Streuung f [Prüf.]
 E: scattering n, dispersion n
 F: dispersion f

strichpunktiert adj
 E: dash-dotted adj

F: ponctué *adj* et rayé
Strohverseilung f
 E: straw-rope stranding
 F: câblage *m* en tortillon de paille
Strom m
 E: current *n*
 F: courant *m*
Stromabfall m
 E: current drop, current decrease
 F: chute *f* de courant
stromabhängige Verluste
 E: current-dependent losses, current-controlled losses
 F: pertes *f pl* dépendant du courant
Stromanzeiger m
 E: current indicator
 F: indicateur *m* de courant
Stromausfall m
 E: power failure, current breakdown
 F: panne *f* de courant, manque *m* de courant
Strombegrenzer m
 E: current limiter
 F: limiteur *m* de courant
Strombelastbarkeit f [el.]
 E: current-carrying capacity, current rating, ampacity *n*, power rating
 F: capacité *f* de charge, charge *f* limite, puissance *f* limite
Strombelastung f
 E: current load, power load
 F: charge *f* électrique
Stromdichte f
 E: current density
 F: densité *f* de courant
stromführend *adj*
 E: live *adj*, current-carrying *adj*
 F: sous tension, parcouru *adj* de courant,
Stromgegenkopplung f
 E: current feedback
 F: réaction *f* négative d'intensité
stromgespeist *adj*
 E: current-fed *adj*
 F: alimenté *adj* en courant
Stromkreis m
 E: circuit *n*, electric circuit
 F: circuit *m* électrique
Stromkreis für Zweidraht-Getrenntlage-Verfahren [Nachr.]
 E: four-wire type circuit
 F: circuit *m* assimilé à un circuit à quatre fils

Stromkreis mit Verstärkung
 E: repeater circuit
 F: circuit *m* à répéteur
stromlos *adj*
 E: currentless *adj*
 F: sans courant
Stromquelle f
 E: current source
 F: source *f* de courant
Stromschiene f
 E: conductor rail, contact rail
 F: rail *m* de contact
Stromschwankung f
 E: current variation, fluctuation of current
 F: variation *f* de courant, fluctuation *f* de courant
Stromstärke f
 E: current intensity, amperage *n*
 F: intensité *f* de courant, ampérage *m*
Strömungseinsatz m [Extr.]
 E: flow fixture
 F: mandrin *m* de répartition de matière
Strömungsgeschwindigkeit f
 E: flow rate, flow velocity, rate of flow
 F: vitesse *f* d'écoulement
Strömungsmesser m
 E: flow meter
 F: rhéomètre *m*
Strömungsverlust m
 E: flow loss
 F: perte *f* d'écoulement
Strömungswächter m
 E: flow monitor
 F: contrôleur *m* d'écoulement
Strömungswiderstand m
 E: flow resistance, hydrodynamic resistance
 F: résistance *f* hydraulique
Stromverbrauch m
 E: current consumption, power consumption
 F: consommation *f* de courant, consommation *f* électrique, consommation *f* d'énergie
Stromverdrängung f [el.]
 E: skin effect
 F: effet *m* de peau
Stromversorgung f
 E: power supply, power distribution
 F: alimentation *f* en énergie électrique, distribution *f* d'énergie

Stromversorgung

électrique, alimentation f en courant électrique

Stromversorgungsgeräusch n [Nachr. K.]
- E: power induced noise, power supply noise
- F: bruit m induit

Stromwandler m
- E: current transformer
- F: transformateur m du courant

Stromwärmeverlust m
- E: resistance loss
- F: perte f par effet Joule

Strossenleitung f
- E: stope cable
- F: câble m de stross

Stückprüfung f
- E: routine test, sample test
- F: essai m de routine

Stufe, in ~n von ...
- E: in steps of ..., in increments of ...
- F: par paliers de ..., par échelons de ...

Stufenheizung f [Vulk.]
- E: vulcanization in stages, "step-up" cure
- F: vulcanisation f échelonnée, vulcanisation f par paliers

stufenlos regelbar
- E: stepless adj, continuously adjustable, infinitely variable
- F: réglable sans à-coups, sans intervalles

stufenlos regelbares Getriebe
- E: infinitely variable gear
- F: engrenage m réglable sans à-coups

Stufenmuster n [Kab.]
- E: stepped sample, telescoped sample
- F: échantillon m étagé

stufenweise Spannungssteigerung
- E: voltage increase in steps
- F: élévation f de tension par paliers

Stumpfschweißen n
- E: butt welding
- F: soudage m par rapprochement, soudure f bout à bout

Stumpfschweißmaschine f
- E: butt welding machine
- F: soudeuse f par rapprochement

Stutzen m
- E: connecting piece, connection n
- F: manchon m, raccord m, tubulure f

Stützisolator m
- E: post insulator, pin insulator, pole-mounted insulator
- F: isolateur m support, isolateur m rigide

Stützrolle f
- E: supporting roller
- F: galet m support, rouleau m d'appui

Stützwendel f (im Hohlleiter)
- E: central spiral, support helix
- F: hélice f de support

Styroflex-isolierte Ader
- E: Styroflex-insulated wire
- F: conducteur m isolé au Styroflex

Styroflex-Wendel f [Kab.]
- E: Styroflex-helix n
- F: spirale f de Styroflex

Styrol-Butadien-Kautschuk m
- E: styrene butadiene rubber (SBR)
- F: caoutchouc m styrène butadiène

Südatlantisches Telefonkabel
- E: Southatlantic telephone cable (SAT cable)
- F: câble m téléphonique de l'Atlantique du Sud

Summenhäufigkeit f [Math.]
- E: cumulative frequency
- F: probabilité f cumulée, fréquence f cumulée

supraleitend adj
- E: superconducting adj, superconductive adj
- F: supraconducteur adj (-trice)

Supraleiter m
- E: superconductor n
- F: supraconducteur m

Supraleiterkabel n
- E: superconducting cable
- F: câble m supraconducteur

Supraleitung f
- E: superconductivity n
- F: supraconductibilité f

Suspension-PVC
- E: suspension PVC
- F: PVC m de suspension

Suspensionspolymerisation f
- E: suspension polymerisation
- F: polymérisation f en suspension

symmetrisches Kabel [Tel.]
- E: balanced pair cable
- F: câble m symétrique

symmetrisches Paar
- E: symmetric pair
- F: paire f symétrique

SZ-Verseilung f

T-Abzweigmuffe f
  E: T-joint n, tee-joint n, tee-off fitting
  F: jonction f en forme de T
Tageslastdiagramm n
  E: daily load curve
  F: courbe f journalière de charge
Talkum n
  E: talc n, talc powder
  F: talc m
Tandemanordnung f [mech.]
  E: tandem arrangement, tandem connection
  F: disposition f en tandem
Tandembetrieb m
  E: tandemized operation
  F: fonctionnement m en tandem, opération f en tandem
Tangentialmuffe f
  E: tangential joint
  F: boîte f tangentielle
Tangentialspinner m [Bdspinn.]
  E: tangential lapper, tangential type lapping machine
  F: rubaneuse f tangentielle
Tänzerrolle f
  E: float roll, floating roller, dancer n
  F: poulie f mobile, poulie f flottante, moufle f
TAT-Kabel (s. Transatlantik-Telefonkabel)
Tatzenklemme f
  E: claw-type clamp
  F: borne f en forme de griffe
Tauchplunger m [Met.-Strangpr.]
  E: plunger piston
  F: fouloir m plongeur
Tauchpumpenleitung f
  E: submersible-pump cable, submerged-pump cable
  F: câble m pour pompe immergée
Tauchziehen n [Drahtz.]
  E: dip forming (General Electric process for production of copper wire)

E: SZ-stranding n
F: câblage m SZ

F: formage m par immersion, dipforming m
Teer m
  E: tar n, pitch n
  F: goudron m
Teilchengrößenanalyse f
  E: particle size analysis
  F: analyse f granulométrique
Teilchengrößenverteilung f
  E: particle size distribution
  F: répartition f granulométrique
Teilentladung f [el.]
  E: partial discharge
  F: décharge f partielle
Teilentladungs-Beständigkeit f
  E: partial discharge resistance
  F: résistance f aux décharges partielles
teilentladungsfrei adj
  E: free from partial discharges, partial discharge-free
  F: exempt adj de décharges partielles
Teilentladungsmessung f
  E: partial discharge measurement
  F: mesure f des décharges partielles
Teilentladungsprüfung f
  E: partial discharge level test, corona level test
  F: essai m de décharges partielles
Teilnehmer m [Tel.]
  E: subscriber n
  F: abonné m
Teilnehmeranschluß m
  E: subscriber's station
  F: poste m d'abonné
Teilnehmer-Anschlußkabel n
  E: local subscriber('s) connection cable, telephone distribution cable, subscriber('s) cable, local cable
  F: câble m urbain, câble m d'abonné
Teilnehmer-Anschlußleitung f
  E: drop wire (telephone cable to connect open wire lines on poles to subscribers' premises) (US), subscriber('s) drop wire, telephone drop, lead(ing)-in wire
  F: ligne f d'abonné téléphonique (raccord à la ligne aérienne), ligne f de desserte d'abonné, fil m d'entrée d'abonné
Teilnehmereinführungsleitung f
  E: drop wire (telephone cable to connect open wire lines on poles to

Teilnehmereinführungsleitung

subscribers' premises) (US), subscriber('s) drop wire, telephone drop, lead(ing)-in wire
F: ligne *f* d'abonné téléphonique (raccord à la ligne aérienne), ligne *f* de desserte d'abonné, fil *m* d'entrée d'abonné

Teilnehmer-Kabel *n*
E: local subscriber('s) connection cable, telephone distribution cable, subscriber('s) cable, local cable
F: câble *m* urbain, câble *m* d'abonné

Teilnehmer-Ortskabel *n*
E: local subscriber('s) connection cable, telephone distribution cable, subscriber('s) cable, local cable
F: câble *m* urbain, câble *m* d'abonné

Teilzeichnung *f*
E: detail drawing, component drawing
F: plan *m* de détail

Telefonapparat *m*
E: telephone set, telephone instrument (US), telephone station
F: appareil *m* téléphonique, poste *m* téléphonique

Telefon-Fernkabel *n*
E: long distance telephone cable, trunk cable (GB), toll cable (US)
F: câble *m* téléphonique à grande distance, câble *m* interurbain

Telefongespräch *n*
E: telephone call, telephone conversation
F: conversation *f* téléphonique

Telefonkabel *n*
E: telephone cable
F: câble *m* téléphonique

Telefonleitung *f*
E: telephone line
F: ligne *f* téléphonique

Telefonnetz *n*
E: telephone system, telephone network
F: réseau *m* téléphonique

Telefonzentrale *f*
E: telephone exchange, telephone central office
F: bureau *m* téléphonique, central *m* téléphonique

Telegrafiegeräusch *n*
E: telegraphic noise
F: bruit *m* télégraphique

Teleskop-Rohr *n* [Vulk.]
E: telescoping tube, splice box
F: tube *m* télescopique

Telex-Netz *n*
E: telex network
F: réseau *m* télex

Tellur *n*
E: tellurium *n*
F: tellure *m*

Temperaturabfall *m*
E: temperature drop, temperature decrease
F: chute *f* de température, baisse *f* de la température

temperaturabhängig *adj*
E: temperature-dependent *adj*
F: dépendant *adj* de la température, influencé *adj* par la température,

Temperaturabhängigkeit *f*
E: temperature dependence
F: dépendance *f* de la température

Temperaturanzeiger *m*
E: temperature indicator
F: indicateur *m* de température

Temperaturausgleich *m*
E: equalization of temperature, compensation of temperature
F: égalisation *f* de la température, compensation *f* de la température

Temperaturbeiwert *m*
E: temperature coefficient
F: coefficient *m* de température

Temperaturerhöhung *f*
E: temperature rise, temperature increase
F: élévation *f* de température, montée *f* de température

Temperaturfühler *m*
E: temperature pick-up, temperature sensor
F: palpeur *m* de température, sonde *f* pyrométrique

Temperaturgefälle *n*
E: temperature gradient, thermal gradient
F: gradient *m* de température, gradient *m* thermique

Temperaturkoeffizient *m*
E: temperature coefficient
F: coefficient *m* de température

Temperaturmessung *f*
E: temperature measurement
F: mesure *f* de température

Temperaturprofil n
  E: temperature profile
  F: profil m de température
Temperaturregelung f
  E: temperature control
  F: réglage m de la température
Temperaturregler m
  E: temperature controller, thermostat n, temperature regulator
  F: thermostat m, régulateur m de température
Temperaturschreiber m
  E: temperature recorder
  F: enregistreur m de température
Temperaturspiel n
  E: temperature difference
  F: différence f de température
temperaturunabhängig adj
  E: temperature-independent adj
  F: indépendant adj de la température
Temperaturzonen f pl
  E: temperature zones
  F: zones f pl de température
tempern v [Plast.]
  E: anneal v
  F: recuire v
tempern v [Met.]
  E: malleableise v (GB), malleableize v (US)
  F: malléabiliser v
Termitenschäden m pl
  E: termite attack
  F: détériorations f pl causées par les termites
Test m
  E: test n, trial n, experiment n
  F: essai m, épreuve f, expérience f
Testanordnung f
  E: experimental arrangement, test(ing) arrangement, test setup
  F: montage m d'essai, montage m expérimental, disposition f d'essai
Textilband n
  E: fabric tape, textile tape
  F: ruban m textile
Textilband mit eingewebten Kupferdrähten
  E: fabric tape with interwoven copper wires, copper threaded textile tape
  F: ruban m textile tissu de fils de cuivre
Textilband mit eingewebten Metalldrähten
  E: textile tape with interwoven metal wires
  F: toile f métallisée
TFH-Telephonie f (Trägerfrequenzübertragung auf Hochspannungs-Leitungen)
  E: power line carrier telephony
  F: téléphonie f à fréquence porteuse sur ligne à haute tension
TF-System n (Trägerfrequenzsystem)
  E: carrier system
  F: système m à courant porteur
thermische Leitfähigkeit
  E: thermal conductivity
  F: conductivité f calorifique, conductibilité f thermique
thermischer Abbau (Kautschuk)
  E: thermal degradation
  F: dégradation f thermique
Thermoelement n
  E: thermocouple n
  F: thermocouple m, thermoélément m
thermooxidativer Abbau
  E: thermooxidative degradation
  F: dégradation f thermo-oxydative
Thermoplaste m pl
  E: thermoplastics pl, thermoplastic materials
  F: matières f pl thermoplastiques
Thermostat m
  E: temperature controller, thermostat n, temperature regulator
  F: thermostat m, régulateur m de température
Thomson-(Doppel)brücke f
  E: Thomson bridge, double bridge
  F: pont m (double) de Thomson
tiefgekühltes Kabel
  E: cryogenic cable
  F: câble m cryogénique, cryocâble m
Tiefseekabel n
  E: deep sea submarine cable, deep sea cable
  F: câble m de haute mer, câble m de grand fond
Tiegel, Flammpunkt im geschlossenen ~
  E: flash point in a closed cup
  F: point m d'éclair en vase fermé, point m d'éclair en coupe fermé
Tiegel, Flammpunkt im offenen ~
  E: flash point in an open cup

Tiegel

F: point *m* d'éclair en vase ouvert, point *m* d'éclair en coupe ouvert

Titanweiß *n*
E: titanium white
F: blanc *m* de titane

Titer *m* (Feinheitsmaß für Fasern/Garn; Einheit: Denier (den))
E: titer *n* (yarn count; unit: denier)
F: titre *m* de fil (numéro de fil; unité: denier)

Toleranz *f*
E: tolerance *n*, permissible variation, allowance *n*
F: tolérance *f*

Toleranzbereich *m*
E: tolerance bandwith, tolerance range
F: gamme *f* de tolérances

Tonfrequenz *f*
E: audio frequency, voice frequency, low frequency
F: audio-fréquence *f*, fréquence *f* vocale, basse fréquence *f*

Tordierstrecke *f* [Vers.]
E: twisting section
F: distance *f* de torsion

Torsionsbeanspruchung *f*
E: torsional stress
F: contrainte *f* de torsion

Torsionsprüfung *f*
E: twisting test, torsion test
F: essai *m* de torsion

Torsionssteifheit *f*
E: torsional rigidity
F: rigidité *f* de torsion

Totwalzen *n* (Kautschuk)
E: over-milling *n*, over-mastication *n*, "killing" of rubber
F: mastication *f* à mort, malaxage *m* à mort

Totzeit *f* [Masch.]
E: down-time *n*, idle time, dead time
F: temps *m* d'arrêt, temps *m* mort

Tragband *n* (Luftkabel)
E: cable suspender
F: bride *f* de suspension

tragbar *adj*
E: portable *adj*
F: portatif *adj*

Tragdraht *m*
E: supporting wire
F: fil *m* porteur, câble *m* de support

Tragdraht *m* (für Fahrdraht)

E: catenary wire, suspension wire
F: fil *m* de suspension (pour fil de contact)

Trägerfrequenz *f* (TF)
E: carrier frequency
F: fréquence *f* porteuse

Trägerfrequenz-Fernkabel *n*
E: long distance carrier frequency cable
F: câble *m* à courant porteur à grande distance

Trägerfrequenzkabel *n*
E: carrier frequency cable, carrier cable
F: câble *m* à courant porteur

Trägerfrequenz-Kanalwahl *f*
E: carrier frequency channel selection
F: sélection *f* de la voie à fréquence porteuse

Trägerfrequenz-Sternvierer *m*
E: carrier frequency star quad
F: quarte *f* en étoile à courant porteur

Trägerfrequenz-Übertragungssystem *n*
E: carrier frequency transmission system
F: système *m* de transmission à courants porteurs

Trägerstrom *m*
E: carrier current
F: courant *m* porteur

Trägerstromfernsprechen *n*
E: carrier current telephony
F: téléphonie *f* à courants porteurs

Tragorgan *n* [En. K.]
E: suspension strand, suspension unit
F: élément *m* porteur, porteur *m*

Tragorgan *n* [Nachr. K.]
E: strength member
F: élément *m* de support

Tragseil *n* [Tel. K.]
E: supporting strand, suspension strand, aerial messenger, messenger wire
F: câble *m* porteur, corde *f* de suspension

tränken *v*
E: impregnate *v*
F: imprégner *v*

Tränkgefäß *n*
E: impregnating tank
F: cuve *f* d'imprégnation

Tränkharz *n*

Tränkharz *(continued)*
- E: impregnating resin
- F: résine f imprégnatrice

Tränkkorb m
- E: impregnating tray
- F: panier m d'imprégnation

Tränklack m
- E: impregnating varnish
- F: vernis m d'imprégnation

Tränkmasse f
- E: impregnating compound
- F: matière f d'imprégnation

Tränkmittel n
- E: impregnating medium, impregnant n
- F: imprégnant m

Tränkung f
- E: impregnation n
- F: imprégnation f

Transatlantik-Telefonkabel (TAT-Kabel) n
- E: Transatlantic telephone cable (TAT cable)
- F: câble m téléphonique transatlantique

Transformator-Anzapfung f
- E: transformer tap
- F: prise f de transformateur

Transformator-Einführung f
- E: transformer termination, transformer connection, transformer entry
- F: prise f de transformateur, raccord m de transformateur, entrée f de transformateur

Transformatoreinführungs-Endverschluß m [Kab.]
- E: transformer type cable termination
- F: extrémité f de câble pour transformateur

Transistor-Verstärkung f
- E: solid-state amplification
- F: amplification f par semi-conducteurs, amplification f à transistors

Transpazifik-Kabel n
- E: Transpacific telephone cable (TRANSPAC cable)
- F: câble m téléphonique transpacifique

Transport m (innerbetrieblich)
- E: handling n
- F: manutention f

Trasse f [Kab.]
- E: route n, run n
- F: parcours m, tracé m

Treibmittel n (Schaumstoffe)
- E: blowing agent
- F: agent m soufflant, agent m de gonflement

Trennelement n [Nachr. K.]
- E: separating element
- F: élément m de séparation

Trennfolie f
- E: separator n (film)
- F: séparateur m

Trennmittel n
- E: release agent
- F: agent m séparateur

Trennschalter m
- E: isolating switch, disconnecting switch
- F: sectionneur m, disjoncteur m

Trennschicht f
- E: separator n (film)
- F: séparateur m

Treppenspannung f
- E: staircase-type voltage
- F: tension f échelonnée

Trichter m
- E: hopper n, funnel n
- F: trémie f, entonnoir m

Trichtermündung f [Extr.]
- E: hopper throat, feed throat
- F: embouchure f de trémie

Trockenkugel-Temperatur f [Klimat.]
- E: dry bulb temperature
- F: température f au thermomètre sec

Trockenprüfgerät n [Kab.]
- E: on-line spark tester, continuous discharge detection apparatus, sparker n, spark tester
- F: appareil m de contrôle d'ionisation par défilement continu, détecteur m de défauts à sec

Trockenthermometer-Temperatur f [Klimat.]
- E: dry bulb temperature
- F: température f au thermomètre sec

Trocknung f
- E: drying n
- F: séchage m

Trocknungsgefäß n
- E: drying tank
- F: cuve f de séchage

Trocknungsmittel n
- E: desiccant n

Trocknungsmittel
F: desséchant m, déshydratant m

Trocknungs- und Tränkvorgang, Überwachung des ~s
E: monitoring of the drying and impregnating process
F: contrôle m du séchage et de l'imprégnation

Trog m
E: trough n
F: bac m, cuve f, goulotte f

Trogmischer m
E: trough mixer
F: mélangeur m à cuve

Trommel f[Kab.]
E: reel n, drum n
F: touret m, bobine f

Trommelflansch m[Kab.]
E: reel flange, drum flange
F: joue f de touret

Trommelkern m[Kab.]
E: barrel of a reel
F: tambour m de touret, traverse f de touret, fût m de touret

Trommelleitung f
E: trailing cable
F: câble m de remorque, câble m d'enrouleur, câble m pour engin mobile

Trommelmischer m
E: barrel mixer, drum mixer
F: mélangeur m à tambour, mélangeur m à tonneau

Trommelscheibe f[Kab.]
E: reel flange, drum flange
F: joue f de touret

Trommelverseilmaschine, mehrgängige ~
E: multi-pass drum twisting machine
F: câbleuse f à tambour à plusieurs passes

tropenfest adj
E: tropicalized adj, resistant to tropical conditions, tropic-proof adj
F: tropicalisé adj, résistant adj aux conditions tropicales,

Tropfprüfung f (an Tränkmassen)
E: dripping test
F: essai m d'égouttement

Tropfpunkt m
E: drop point
F: point m de goutte

Tropfschirm m (Isolator)
E: drop shield
F: cloche f d'égouttement

Tropf- und Ablaufprüfung f[Kab.]
E: drainage test
F: essai m d'écoulement

Tube f[Nachr. K.]
E: tube n
F: tube m

Typ m[Kab.]
E: design n, type n, construction n
F: construction f, type m

Typenbezeichnung f
E: code designation, type designation
F: code m de désignation

Typenkurzzeichen n
E: code designation, type designation
F: code m de désignation

Typenspektrum n
E: pattern of types, range of types, type spectrum
F: gamme f de types, éventail m de types

Typprüfung f
E: type test
F: essai m de type

U

überdeckend, die Stoßstellen ~ [Bdspinn.]
E: covering the butt joints
F: faisant couvre-joint

Überdicke f
E: oversize n, overdimension n
F: surépaisseur f

Überdruck m
E: overpressure n, excess pressure
F: surpression f

Überdruckventil n
E: pressure relief valve
F: soupape f de sûreté, soupape f de surpression

Überführungsrinne f[Gießw.]
E: launder n, transfer launder, transfer trough
F: rigole f de transfert, rigole f de coulée

Übergangsbetrieb m
E: transient operation, transient conditions pl

Übergangsmuffe f
  E: transition joint, transition sleeve
  F: joint *m* de transition

Übergangsstrom *m*
  E: equalizing current, transient current, balancing current
  F: courant *m* compensateur, courant *m* transitoire

Übergangswiderstand *m*
  E: contact resistance, transition resistance
  F: résistance *f* de contact, résistance *f* de passage

Überkopfablauf *m*
  E: overhead pay-off
  F: dévidoir *m* au-dessus de la hauteur de la tête, dérouleur *m* au-dessus de la hauteur de la tête

Überkopfabzug *m*
  E: overhead pull-off
  F: cabestan *m* de tirage au-dessus de la hauteur de la tête

Überkopf-Aufwickelei f [Gießw.]
  E: orbital laying head coiler
  F: enrouloir *m* au-dessus de la hauteur de la tête

überlagern v
  E: superpose v, superimpose v
  F: superposer v

überlagerter Stromkreis
  E: superposed circuit
  F: circuit *m* superposé

Überlagerung f
  E: superposition *n*, superimposition *n*
  F: superposition *f*

Überlandleitung f
  E: long distance transmission line
  F: ligne *f* à grand transport d'énergie

überlappen v
  E: overlap v
  F: chevaucher v, recouvrir v (se)

überlappend adj
  E: overlapping adj
  F: à recouvrement, chevauchant adj

Überlappung f
  E: overlap(ping) *n*
  F: recouvrement *m*, chevauchement *m*

Überlappung, mit 50% ~
  E: half-lapped adj, with 50% overlap, with 50% registration
  F: à 50% de recouvrement

Überlast f
  E: overload *n*
  F: surcharge *f*

Überlastbetrieb, bei ~
  E: under overload conditions
  F: en surcharge

Überlastschalter *m*
  E: overload circuit breaker
  F: interrupteur *m* de surcharge

Überlasttemperatur f
  E: emergency temperature, overload temperature
  F: température *f* en surcharge

Überlauf *m* [Extr.]
  E: scrap *n*, purging *n*
  F: purges *f pl*

Überlaufrohr *n*
  E: overflow pipe
  F: tuyau *m* de trop-plein, trop-plein

Überlaufventil *n*
  E: overflow valve, by-pass valve
  F: soupape *f* de trop-plein

Übermaß *n*
  E: oversize *n*, overdimension *n*
  F: surépaisseur *f*

übermäßige Erwärmung
  E: overheating *n*
  F: surchauffe *f*, surchauffage *m*

Überschlag *m* [el.]
  E: flash-over *n*, spark-over *n*, arc-over *n*
  F: contournement *m*, amorçage *m*

Überschlagspannung f
  E: flash-over voltage, spark-over voltage, arc-over voltage
  F: tension *f* de contournement, tension *f* d'éclatement, tension *f* d'amorçage

Überschlag-Stoßspannung f
  E: impulse flashover voltage, impulse spark-over voltage
  F: tension *f* de contournement au choc

überschreiten v
  E: exceed v
  F: dépasser v, excéder v

Übersetzungsverhältnis *n* [mech.]
  E: gear-ratio *n*, transmission ratio
  F: rapport *m* d'engrenage, rapport *m* de transmission

Überspannung f
  E: overvoltage *n*, surge voltage

Überspannung
  F: surtension f
Überspannungsableiter m
  E: surge diverter, surge voltage arrester, overvoltage arrester
  F: parasurtension m
Überspannungsschalter m
  E: overvoltage circuit-breaker, maximum voltage circuit-breaker
  F: interrupteur m à maximum de tension, disjoncteur m de surtension
Überspannungsschutz m
  E: overvoltage protection, surge protection
  F: protection f contre les surtensions
Übersprechdämpfung f
  E: crosstalk attenuation, crosstalk transmission equivalent
  F: affaiblissement m diaphonique
Übersprechen n
  E: side-to-side crosstalk
  F: diaphonie f entre réel et réel
Übersprechkopplung f
  E: side-to-side crosstalk coupling
  F: couplage m diaphonique entre réel et réel, couplage m diaphonique entre quartes voisines
Überstromschutz m
  E: overcurrent protection, overload protection, excess current protection
  F: protection f contre les surintensités
übertragbare Leistung
  E: transmission power
  F: puissance f à transporter
übertragen v
  E: carry v, transmit v
  F: transporter v, transmettre v
Übertrager m [Nachr.]
  E: transformer n, translator n
  F: transformateur m, translateur m
Übertragung f
  E: transmission n
  F: transmission f
Übertragung hoher Leistungen
  E: bulk power transmission
  F: transport m de grandes puissances
Übertragungsbandbreite f
  E: transmission band-width
  F: largeur f de bande de transmission
Übertragungs-Eigenschaften f pl
  E: transmission characteristics
  F: caractéristiques f pl de transmission
Übertragungs-Gleichungen f pl [Nachr.]
  E: transmission equations
  F: équations f pl de transmission
Übertragungsgüte f
  E: transmission quality
  F: qualité f de transmission
Übertragungskanal m
  E: transmission path, transmission channel, channel n
  F: voie f de transmission, voie f de transport
Übertragungskapazität f
  E: transmission capacity
  F: capacité f de transport, capacité f de transmission
Übertragungskonstante f
  E: propagation coefficient
  F: exposant m linéique de propagation
Übertragungsleistung f
  E: transmission power
  F: puissance f à transporter
Übertragungsleitung, ausgeglichene ~ [Tel.]
  E: balanced transmission line
  F: ligne f de transmission équilibrée
Übertragungsmaß n
  E: propagation unit
  F: équivalent m de transmission, exposant m de transfert, unité f de propagation
Übertragungsnetz n
  E: transmission system
  F: système m de transmission, réseau m de transmission, réseau m de transport
Übertragungsqualität f
  E: transmission quality
  F: qualité f de transmission
Übertragungsspannung f
  E: transmission voltage
  F: tension f de transmission, tension f de transport
Übertragungssystem n
  E: transmission system
  F: système m de transmission, réseau m de transmission, réseau m de transport
Übertragungsverlust m
  E: transmission loss
  F: perte f de transmission, perte f de

Übertragungsweg m
　E: transmission path, transmission channel, channel n
　F: voie f de transmission, voie f de transport

Übertragungsweg, elektrischer ~
　E: electrical transmission route
　F: voie f de transmission électrique

Überwachung f
　E: monitoring n, supervision n
　F: surveillance f

Überwachungspaar n
　E: alarm pair
　F: paire f de surveillance

Überwalzen n (Kautschuk)
　E: over-milling n, over-mastication n, "killing" of rubber
　F: mastication f à mort, malaxage m à mort

Überwalzung f (bei gewalztem Draht)
　E: spill n
　F: repliure f de laminage

Überziehen n (Masse, Kleber, Korrosionsschutz)
　E: flooding n, coating n
　F: enduction f

Überzug m
　E: coating n
　F: revêtement m, enrobage m

Uhrzeigersinn, gegen den ~
　E: counterclockwise adj, anti-clockwise adj
　F: dans le sens inverse des aiguilles d'une montre

Uhrzeigersinn, im ~
　E: clockwise adj
　F: dans le sens des aiguilles d'une montre

Ultra-Hochspannung f
　E: ultra-high voltage (UHV)
　F: ultra-haute tension f (UHT)

umbördeln v
　E: fold back v, flange v
　F: rabattre v, border v, bordeler v

Umbördelung f
　E: flanging n
　F: bord m rabattu

Umbruchfestigkeit f (Isolator)
　E: cantilever strength
　F: résistance f à la rupture en flexion

Umdrehung f (Achse)
　E: rotation n
　F: rotation f

Umdrehungen pro Minute (U/min, Upm)
　E: revolutions per minute (r.p.m.)
　F: tours m pl par minute (t/min)

Umdrehungsgeschwindigkeit f
　E: speed of rotation
　F: vitesse f de rotation

Umfangsgeschwindigkeit f
　E: peripheral speed, circumferential speed
　F: vitesse f périphérique, vitesse f circonférentielle

Umflechtung f
　E: braid n, braiding n
　F: tresse f

Umflechtungsmaschine f
　E: braiding machine, braider n
　F: machine f à tresser

Umgebungstemperatur f
　E: ambient temperature
　F: température f ambiante

umgekehrter Kabelendverschluß
　E: inverted type cable termination
　F: extrémité f de câble du type inverti

umhüllter Rohrdraht
　E: sheathed metal-clad wiring cable
　F: câble m cuirassé sous gaine

Umhüllung f
　E: sheath n, covering n, jacket n
　F: enveloppe f, revêtement m

Umhüllungslinie f (z.B. bei Leitern)
　E: contour line
　F: enveloppante f

U/min, Upm (s. Umdrehungen pro Minute)

Umkehr der Polarität
　E: change of polarity, pole reversal, pole changing
　F: inversion f de polarité

Umlauf m
　E: circulation n, recirculation n, recycling n
　F: circulation f

Umlaufbügel m
　E: flier n, flyer n
　F: flyer m

Umlenkkopf m
　E: transfer head
　F: tête f de renvoi

Umlenkrolle f
　E: deflector roll, reversing sheave
　F: roue f de renvoi, galet m de renvoi,

Umlenkrolle
   poulie *f* de renvoi

Umlenkvorrichtung *f*
   E: transfer device
   F: dispositif *m* de renvoi

Umluftalterung *f*
   E: ventilated air oven ag(e)ing, circulating air ag(e)ing
   F: vieillissement *m* en étuve à circulation d'air, vieillissement *m* par circulation d'air

Umluftofen *m*
   E: forced-air oven, air oven
   F: étuve *f* à circulation d'air, étuve *f* ventilé

Umluftofen, Alterung im ~
   E: ventilated air oven ag(e)ing, circulating air ag(e)ing
   F: vieillissement *m* en étuve à circulation d'air, vieillissement *m* par circulation d'air

Ummanteln mit Blei
   E: lead-sheathing *n*
   F: mise *f* sous plomb

Ummantelung *f*
   E: sheathing *n*
   F: gainage *m*

Umpolung *f*
   E: change of polarity, pole reversal, pole changing
   F: inversion *f* de polarité

Umpumpen *n*
   E: recycling *n*, recirculation *n*
   F: circulation *f* par pompage, recyclage *m*

Umrechnungsfaktor *m*
   E: conversion factor
   F: coefficient *m* de transformation

Umschalter *m*
   E: change-over switch
   F: commutateur *m*

Umschaltung *f*
   E: change-over *n*, switch-over *n*
   F: commutation *f*

umschlagen *v*
   E: fold back *v*, flange *v*
   F: rabattre *v*, border *v*, bordeler *v*

Umschlingungswinkel *m*
   E: contact angle, angle of wrap
   F: angle *m* de contact, arc *m* d'enroulement

Umspannwerk *n*
   E: substation *n*, transforming station, transformer station
   F: sous-station *f*, poste *m* de transformation

umspinnen *v* [Kab.]
   E: wrap *v*, wind *v*, cover *v*
   F: recouvrir *v*, enrouler *v*

umspinnen *v* (mit Band)
   E: lap *v*, tape *v*, wrap *v*
   F: enrubanner *v*, rubaner *v*

umspinnen, mit Papierkordel ~
   E: to apply the paper string, to spin the paper string
   F: guiper *v*

Umspinnung *f* (mit Band)
   E: lapping *n*, taping *n*, tape(d) wrapping
   F: rubanage *m*

Umspinnung *f* (mit Kordel, Garn)
   E: spinning *n*
   F: guipage *m*

umspritzen *v*
   E: extrude *v*
   F: extruder *v*, boudiner *v*

Umtrommeln *n*
   E: rewinding *n*
   F: rebobinage *m*, réenroulement *m*

Umwälzpumpe *f*
   E: circulating pump
   F: pompe *f* de (à) circulation

Umwandlungstemperatur *f* [Plast.]
   E: transition temperature
   F: température *f* de transformation

Umwickelei *f*
   E: rewinding stand
   F: bobineuse *f*

umwickeln *v* [Kab.]
   E: wrap *v*, wind *v*, cover *v*
   F: recouvrir *v*, enrouler *v*

umwickeln *v* (mit Band)
   E: lap *v*, tape *v*, wrap *v*
   F: enrubanner *v*, rubaner *v*

Umwickeln *n* (Umspulen)
   E: rewinding *n*
   F: rebobinage *m*, réenroulement *m*

Umwicklung *f* (mit Band)
   E: wrapping *n*, winding *n*
   F: enrubannage *m*, recouvrement *m*

Umwicklungsmaschine *f*
   E: wrapping machine
   F: machine *f* à revêtir, machine *f* à enrouler

unauslöschlich *adj* (Farbe)
   E: indelible *adj*, fast *adj*
   F: indélébile *adj*

unbearbeitet adj
  E: untreated adj, unmachined adj, unfinished adj
  F: non travaillé adj, non usiné adj

unbelastet adj [Tel. K.]
  E: unloaded adj, non-loaded adj
  F: non chargé adj, non pupinisé adj

unbelastet, Kabel in ~em Zustand [En. K.]
  E: cable at no-load
  F: câble m non chargé, câble m en exploitation sans charge

unbelastetes dünndrähtiges Kabel [Tel. K.]
  E: unloaded thin wire cable
  F: câble m non chargé avec âme en fils fins

unbelastetes Kabel [En. K.]
  E: cable at no-load
  F: câble m non chargé, câble m en exploitation sans charge

unbeschädigt adj
  E: intact adj, undamaged adj
  F: intact adj

unbespult adj [Tel. K.]
  E: unloaded adj, non-loaded adj
  F: non chargé adj, non pupinisé adj

unbespulte symmetrische Leitung
  E: unloaded balanced line, non-loaded balanced line
  F: ligne f symétrique non pupinisée, ligne f symétrique non chargée

unbrennbar adj
  E: non-inflammable adj, flame-proof adj, non-combustible adj, incombustible adj
  F: non-inflammable adj, incombustible adj

Unbrennbarkeit f
  E: incombustibility n
  F: non-inflammabilité f, incombustibilité f

undicht adj
  E: leaky adj, untight adj
  F: non étanche adj

Undichtigkeit f
  E: leakage n
  F: fuite f, non-étanchéité f

undurchlässig für ...
  E: impermeable to ..., impervious to ..., impenetrable to ...
  F: imperméable adj à, impénétrable adj pour,

Undurchlässigkeit f
  E: impermeability n
  F: imperméabilité f

uneben adj
  E: uneven adj
  F: inégal adj, non plan adj

unempfindlich adj
  E: sturdy adj, robust adj, rigid adj, solid adj
  F: robuste adj

unempfindlich gegen ...
  E: insensitive to ...
  F: insensible adj à ...

ungefärbter Kunststoff
  E: uncoloured plastic, natural-coloured plastic, unpigmented plastic, natural plastic (US)
  F: matière f plastique de couleur naturelle, matière f plastique non colorée, matière f plastique incolore

ungelernter Arbeiter
  E: unskilled worker
  F: ouvrier m non qualifié, manœuvre m

ungenau adj
  E: inexact adj, inaccurate adj
  F: inexact adj, imprécis adj

Ungenauigkeit f (Anzeige, Messung)
  E: inaccuracy n, inexactitude n
  F: imprécision f, inexactitude f

ungeschirmtes Kabel
  E: unscreened cable
  F: câble m sans écran

unmagnetische Bewehrung
  E: non-magnetic armo(u)ring
  F: armure f amagnétique

unregelmäßig, Bündel ~ zusammenschlagen [Vers.]
  E: to oscillate cable units
  F: osciller v les faisceaux de câbles

Unsymmetrie f
  E: unbalance n, unsymmetry n, asymmetry n
  F: déséquilibre m, asymétrie f, dissymétrie f

unsystematische Kopplung
  E: unsystematic coupling
  F: couplage m non systématique

Unterflur-Installation f
  E: subsurface installation, installation below floor level
  F: installation f en sous-sol,

Unterflur-Installation
  installation *f* souterraine
unterirdisches Kabelnetz
  E: underground cable system
  F: réseau *m* de câbles souterrain
Unterlagen *f pl* (beschreibende oder zeichnerische Angaben)
  E: information material, data *pl*, documents *pl*
  F: documents *m pl*, données *f pl*, documentation *f*
Unterputz-Installation *f*
  E: buried wiring, concealed wiring, installation under plaster
  F: installation *f* sous crépi, pose *f* sous crépi, pose *f* encastrée
unterschreiten *v*
  E: to fall short of
  F: être *v* inférieur à
Unterseeverstärker *m*
  E: submerged repeater, underwater amplifier
  F: répéteur *m* immergé
Untersetzungsgetriebe *n*
  E: reduction gear
  F: réducteur *m*, engrenage *m* réducteur, démultiplicateur *m*
Untersuchung *f*
  E: inspection *n*, check *n*, examination *n*, investigation *n*, analysis *n*
  F: examen *m*, analyse *f*, contrôle *m*
unterteilen *v*
  E: sectionalize *v*, subdivide *v*
  F: subdiviser *v*, sectionner *v*
Unterwasserkabel *n*
  E: submarine cable
  F: câble *m* sous-marin
Unterwasserlänge *f*
  E: immersed length
  F: longueur *f* immergée, longueur *f* plongée
Unterwasserverlegung *f*
  E: submarine laying
  F: pose *f* sous-marine
Unterwasserverstärker *m*
  E: submerged repeater, underwater amplifier
  F: répéteur *m* immergé
unverständliches (nicht lineares) Nebensprechen
  E: unintelligible (non linear) crosstalk
  F: diaphonie *f* inintelligible (non linéaire)

unwirksam *adj*
  E: ineffective *adj*, inoperative *adj*
  F: inefficace *adj*
unzugänglich *adj*
  E: inaccessible *adj*
  F: inaccessible *adj*
unzulässig *adj*
  E: inadmissible *adj*
  F: inadmissible *adj*

V

vagabundierender Strom
  E: leakage current, fault current, stray current
  F: courant *m* de fuite, courant *m* de défaut, courant *m* vagabond
Vakuum, unter ~
  E: under vacuum
  F: sous vide
vakuumdicht *adj*
  E: vacuum-tight *adj*, vacuum-sealed *adj*
  F: étanche *adj* au vide, hermétique *adj*
Vakuumglühanlage *f*
  E: vacuum annealing plant
  F: installation *f* de recuit sous vide
Vakuumpumpe *f*
  E: vacuum pump
  F: pompe *f* à vide
Vakuumröhren-Verstärker *m*
  E: vacuum tube amplifier
  F: amplificateur *m* à tube à vide
Vakuumtrocknung *f*
  E: vacuum drying
  F: séchage *m* sous vide
Vaseline *f*
  E: petroleum jelly, petrol jelly
  F: vaseline *f*, gelée *f* de pétrole
VDE (s. Verband Deutscher Elektrotechniker e.V.)
VDE-Bestimmungen *f pl*
  E: VDE Regulations, VDE Rules, VDE Standards
  F: normes *f pl* VDE, règles *f pl* VDE, spécifications *f pl* VDE, pl
VDE-Kennfaden *m*
  E: VDE tracer thread, VDE identification thread
  F: fil *m* distinctif VDE, fil *m*

d'identification VDE
VDE-Kennzeichen n
  E: VDE approval mark
  F: marque f d'approbation VDE
VDE-Regeln f pl
  E: VDE Regulations, VDE Rules, VDE Standards
  F: normes f pl VDE, règles f pl VDE, spécifications f pl VDE, pl
VDE-Vorschriften f pl
  E: VDE Regulations, VDE Rules, VDE Standards
  F: normes f pl VDE, règles f pl VDE, spécifications f pl VDE, pl
VDI (s. Verein Deutscher Ingenieure)
Ventil n
  E: valve n
  F: valve f, soupape f
Verarbeitbarkeit f
  E: processability n
  F: aptitude f à la mise en œuvre
verarbeiten v
  E: process v, convert v
  F: mettre v en œuvre, travailler v, convertir v
Verarbeitung f
  E: processing n
  F: mise f en œuvre
Verarbeitungstemperatur f
  E: processing temperature
  F: température f de mise en œuvre
Veraschung f
  E: incineration n
  F: incinération f
Verband Deutscher Elektrotechniker e.V. (VDE)
  E: Association of German Electrical Engineers
  F: Association f des Electrotechniciens Allemands
Verbesserung f
  E: improvement n
  F: amélioration f
verbinden v
  E: join v, joint v, connect v, link v
  F: raccorder v, lier v, joindre v, réunir v
Verbinden n [Kab.]
  E: jointing n, splicing n, connecting n
  F: raccordement m
Verbindung f
  E: joint n, connection n
  F: jonction f

Verbindungsdraht m
  E: bond wire
  F: fil m de connexion
Verbindungshülse f
  E: joint sleeve, connecting sleeve
  F: manchon m de jonction, manchon m de raccordement
Verbindungskabel n
  E: junction cable, connecting cable, interconnecting cable, switchboard cable
  F: câble m de jonction, câble m de connexion
Verbindungsklemme f [el.]
  E: terminal n, connector n, connecting terminal
  F: borne f, connecteur m, borne f de raccordement
Verbindungsmuffe f
  E: connecting box, joint box, straight joint
  F: boîte f de jonction, jonction f
Verbindungsstelle f
  E: joint n, connection n
  F: jonction f
Verbindungsstück n
  E: intermediate piece, connecting piece, adapter n, connector n, fitting n
  F: pièce f intermédiaire, pièce f de raccordement, raccord m, pièce f de jonction, adaptateur m
verblassen v
  E: fade v
  F: perdre v sa couleur, décolorer v
verbrennen vi
  E: burn v, scorch v, combust v
  F: brûler v, carboniser v
Verbundnetz n
  E: interconnected system, interconnection system, grid (system) n
  F: réseau m d'interconnexion, réseau m de liaison
Verbundwerkstoff m
  E: composite material, multilayer material, composite n
  F: complexe m, matériau m composite
Verdampfung f
  E: evaporation n
  F: évaporation f
verdichten v

verdichten

- E: compact v, compress v
- F: rétreindre v, compacter v, comprimer v

Verdichter m [Vers.]
- E: compacting head
- F: tête f de compression

verdichteter Leiter
- E: compact(ed) conductor, compacted strand, compressed strand
- F: âme f rétreinte, âme f compactée

verdichteter Sand
- E: compacted sand
- F: sable m compacté

Verdichtung des Erdbodens [K. Verl.]
- E: compression of the soil, compaction of the soil
- F: compression f du sol

Verdichtung des Leiters
- E: compression of the conductor, compaction of the conductor
- F: compactage m de l'âme, rétreint m de l'âme

Verdichtungsgrad m (Leiter)
- E: compression degree, shaping degree
- F: coefficient m de rétreint

Verdichtungswerkzeug n
- E: compacting tool
- F: filière f de rétreint

Verdrahtung f
- E: wiring n
- F: filerie f

Verdrahtung, feste ~
- E: permanent wiring, fixed wiring
- F: filerie f fixe

Verdrahtung, flexible ~
- E: flexible wiring
- F: filerie f souple

Verdrahtung, innere ~
- E: inside wiring, internal wiring
- F: filerie f interne

Verdrahtungsleitung f
- E: single-core non-sheathed cable for internal wiring, wiring cable
- F: conducteur m pour filerie interne, fil m de câblage

Verdrahtungsplan m
- E: wiring diagram, wiring scheme, circuit diagram
- F: schéma m électrique, plan m de câblage, plan m des circuits, schéma m des connexions

Verdrehung f
- E: torsion n, twist n
- F: torsion f, giration f

verdrehungsfreies Kabel
- E: anti-twist cable
- F: câble m anti-giratoire

verdrillen v
- E: twist v
- F: torsader v

Verdünnungsmittel n
- E: diluent n, thinner n
- F: agent m de dilution, diluant m

Verein Deutscher Ingenieure (VDI)
- E: Association of German Engineers
- F: Association f des Ingénieurs Allemands

Vereinheitlichung f
- E: standardisation n, normalization n, unification n
- F: standardisation f, normalisation f, unification f

Verfahren n
- E: process n, method n, technique n, procedure n
- F: procédé m, méthode f, technique f

Verfärbung f
- E: discoloration n, staining n
- F: décoloration f, changement m de couleur

verflüchtigen v
- E: volatilize v
- F: volatiliser v

Verformung f
- E: deformation n, distortion n
- F: déformation f

Verformung, bleibende ~
- E: permanent deformation, plastic deformation
- F: déformation f permanente

Verformung, elastische ~
- E: elastic deformation
- F: déformation f élastique

vergießen v [K. Garn.]
- E: encapsulate v, fill v, seal v
- F: surmouler v, sceller v

Vergleichsmessung f
- E: comparative measurement
- F: mesure f comparative

Vergleichsmuster n
- E: reference sample, control sample
- F: échantillon m témoin, échantillon m de comparaison, échantillon m de contrôle

Vergleichsprüfung f
  E: comparative test
  F: essai m comparatif
Vergleichswert m
  E: reference value, comparative value
  F: valeur f de référence, valeur f comparative
Vergleichswiderstand m
  E: reference resistance, comparative resistance
  F: résistance f de comparaison
vergrößern v
  E: increase v, extend v, enlarge v, magnify v
  F: augmenter v, élargir v, grossir v, agrandir v
Vergrößerung f
  E: enlargement n, magnification n increase n
  F: agrandissement m, augmentation f, élargissement m
Vergußmasse f [K. Garn.]
  E: filling compound, sealing compound, flooding compound
  F: matière f de remplissage
Vergüten n [Met.]
  E: hardening and tempering operation, heat treatment
  F: traitement m thermique, trempe f
Verhalten n
  E: behaviour n, performance n
  F: tenue f, allure f, comportement m, performance f
verjüngt adj
  E: tapered adj, conic(al) adj
  F: effilé adj, à section décroissante, conique adj
Verjüngung f
  E: tapering n, taper n
  F: conicité f, cône m
verkabeln v
  E: cable v, wire v
  F: câbler v
verkappen v
  E: cap-seal v
  F: fermer v par un capuchon, terminer v par un capuchon
Verkaufstrommel f [Kab.]
  E: non-returnable reel
  F: touret m perdu
verkettete Spannung
  E: phase-to-phase voltage, line-to-line voltage, voltage between phases
  F: tension f composée, tension f entre phases
Verkohlen der Isolierung
  E: charring of the insulation
  F: carbonisation f de l'isolant
verkohlt adj
  E: charred adj, carbonized adj
  F: carbonisé adj
Verlagerung f
  E: movement n, shifting n, displacement n
  F: déplacement m, décalage m
Verlängerungsschnur f
  E: extension cord
  F: cordon m prolongateur, corde f d'allongement
Verlauf einer Kurve
  E: characteristic of a curve
  F: allure f d'une courbe
Verlegearm m (Aufwickelei)
  E: distributor n, traverser n, traversing unit
  F: dispositif de trancanage m, palpeur-guide m
Verlegeart f [Kab.]
  E: method of laying, method of installation
  F: mode m de pose
Verlegebedingungen f pl
  E: laying conditions, installation conditions
  F: conditions f pl de pose
Verlegegeschwindigkeit f (beim Aufspulen)
  E: distribution speed, traversing speed
  F: vitesse f de trancanage
Verlegemaschine für Kabel
  E: cable laying machine
  F: machine f à poser les câbles
verlegen v [Kab.]
  E: lay v, install v
  F: poser v
Verlegerollen f pl [Kab.]
  E: laying rollers
  F: galets m pl de pose
Verlegetiefe f [K. Verl.]
  E: laying depth, depth of laying, depth below ground, depth under surface, installation depth
  F: profondeur f de pose
Verlegevorrichtung f (Aufwickelei)

E: distributor *n*, traverser *n*, traversing unit
F: dispositif de trancanage *m*, palpeur-guide *m*

Verlegung von Kabeln
E: cable installation, cable laying
F: pose *f* de câbles

Verlegung auf Pritschen
E: laying on racks
F: pose *f* sur tablettes

Verlegung auf Putz
E: surface mounting, installation on the surface
F: pose *f* sur crépi, pose *f* apparente

Verlegung im Freien
E: outdoor installation
F: pose *f* à l'extérieur

Verlegung in Erde
E: direct burial (in earth), burying *n* (in ground), underground laying, laying in earth
F: pose *f* en pleine terre, pose *f* souterraine

Verlegung in Formsteinen [Nachr. K.]
E: laying in ducts
F: pose *f* en blocs-tube

Verlegung in Kanälen
E: laying in conduits, laying in ducts
F: pose *f* en caniveaux

Verlegung in Luft
E: installation in free air
F: pose *f* à l'air libre

Verlegung in Röhren
E: laying in conduits, laying in ducts
F: pose *f* en caniveaux

Verlegung nebeneinander
E: laying side by side, laying in parallel, parallel arrangement
F: disposition *f* côte à côte, disposition *f* en nappe horizontale, disposition *f* en parallèle

Verlegung unter Putz
E: buried wiring, concealed wiring, installation under plaster
F: installation *f* sous crépi, pose *f* sous crépi, pose *f* encastrée

Verlegung von Kabeln in Schlangenlinien
E: snaking of cables, laying cables in a wave formation
F: pose *f* des câbles en serpentins

verlitzen *v*
E: bunch-strand *v*, bunch *v*
F: torsader *v*, toronner *v*

Verlust *m*
E: loss *n*
F: perte *f*

verlustarm *adj*
E: low-loss... *adj*
F: à faibles pertes

verlustarmes Kabel [Nachr.]
E: low capacitance cable, LoCap cable
F: câble *m* à faible capacitance

Verluste im Dielektrikum
E: dielectric losses
F: pertes *f pl* diélectriques

Verlustfaktor *m*
E: loss factor tg δ, dissipation factor, dielectric power factor cos φ
F: facteur *m* de perte tg δ, facteur de puissance cos φ, tangente de l'angle de perte tg δ

Verlustleistung *f*
E: power loss, power dissipation
F: puissance *f* de perte, dissipation *f* de puissance, puissance *f* dissipée

Verluststrom *m*
E: leakage current, fault current, stray current
F: courant *m* de fuite, courant *m* de défaut, courant *m* vagabond

Verlustwärme *f*
E: heat due to losses
F: chaleur *f* due aux pertes

Verlustwinkel *m* (tan δ)
E: loss angle (tan δ)
F: angle *m* de perte (tan δ)

vermaschtes Netz
E: meshed network
F: réseau *m* maillé

vermindern *v*
E: reduce *v*, decrease *v*
F: réduire *v*, diminuer *v*

vermischen *v*
E: blend *v*, mix *v*, intermingle *v*
F: mélanger *v*, mêler *v*

Vermittlungseinrichtung *f* [Nachr.]
E: switching equipment
F: équipement *m* de commutation

vernachlässigbar *adj*
E: negligible *adj*
F: négligeable *adj*

vernetzbar *adj*
E: cross-linkable *adj*
F: réticulable *adj*

Vernetzer m
  E: cross-linking agent
  F: agent m de réticulation
vernetztes Polyäthylen (VPE)
  E: cross-linked polyethylene (XLPE)
  F: polyéthylène m réticulé
Vernetzung f
  E: cross-linking n
  F: réticulation f
Vernetzung, chemische ~
  E: chemical cross-linking
  F: réticulation f chimique
Vernetzungsmittel n
  E: cross-linking agent
  F: agent m de réticulation
Verriegelung f
  E: blocking n, interlocking n, locking n
  F: blocage m, verrouillage m
verringern v
  E: reduce v, decrease v
  F: réduire v, diminuer v
Versandspule f
  E: despatch reel, shipping reel, delivery reel
  F: bobine f d'expédition
Versandtrommel f
  E: shipping drum, shipping reel
  F: touret m d'expédition
Verschalbrett n
  E: plank n, batten n
  F: douve f
Verschalung f (Kabeltrommeln)
  E: lagging n
  F: douvage m
verschäumtes PE
  E: foamed PE, cellular PE, expanded PE
  F: polyéthylène m mousse, polyéthylène m cellulaire
verschiebbar adj
  E: displaceable adj, shiftable adj, movable adj
  F: déplaçable adj
Verschiebung f
  E: movement n, shifting n, displacement n
  F: déplacement m, décalage m
Verschlechterung f
  E: deterioration n
  F: détérioration f
Verschleiß m
  E: wear n

  F: usure f
Verschleißteil n
  E: wearing part, part subject to wear
  F: pièce f d'usure
Verschlußkappe f [Kab.]
  E: sealing cap
  F: capot m d'étanchéité
Verschraubung f
  E: screw connection, bolted connection, bolted joint, screw(ed) joint
  F: vissage m, boulonnage m, raccord m à vis, raccord m fileté
verschweißen v
  E: weld v, fuse v
  F: souder v
Verseifungszahl f
  E: saponification value, saponification number
  F: coefficient m de saponification, indice m de saponification
Verseilachse f
  E: stranding axis
  F: axe m de câblage
Verseilbügel m
  E: stranding flyer, twisting flyer
  F: archet m de câblage, flyer m de câblage
Verseilelement n
  E: stranding element, stranded element
  F: élément m de câblage, élément m câblé, élément m d'assemblage
verseilen v (Leiter)
  E: strand v
  F: câbler v
verseilen v (Kabelseele)
  E: lay up v, strand v
  F: assembler v
Verseilkopf m
  E: stranding head, stranding support
  F: tête f de câblage, tête f d'assemblage
Verseilkorb m
  E: stranding cage
  F: cage f d'assemblage
Verseilmaschine f
  E: stranding machine, strander n, cabler n, twister n, stranding cabler (US)
  F: câbleuse f, assembleuse f
Verseilnippel m
  E: stranding nipple, stranding closer,

Verseilnippel

    twisting closer, closing die
    F: filière *f* d'assemblage, filière *f* de câblage

Verseilpunkt *m*
    E: stranding point, die point
    F: point *m* de câblage

Verseilscheibe *f*
    E: assembling plate, lay plate, face plate
    F: plaque *f* de répartition, plaque *f* de guidage

Verseilung *f* (Leiter)
    E: conductor stranding, bunching *n*, stranding *n*, twisting *n*
    F: câblage *m* (âme)

Verseilung *f* (Seele)
    E: core stranding, laying up *n*, cabling *n*
    F: assemblage *m* (des conducteurs)

Verseilung im Gegenschlag
    E: reverse(d) lay stranding
    F: câblage *m* en couches croisées, câblage *m* en sens alterné

Verseilung im Gleichschlag
    E: same lay stranding
    F: câblage *m* en même sens

Verseilung im Längsschlag
    E: long lay stranding, Lang's lay stranding
    F: câblage *m* long, câblage *m* Lang

Verseilung im Wechselschlag
    E: reverse(d) lay stranding
    F: câblage *m* en couches croisées, câblage *m* en sens alterné

Verseilung mit Rückdrehung (Rundleiter)
    E: stranding with backtwist
    F: câblage *m* à détorsion

Verseilung mit Vordrall (Sektorleiter)
    E: stranding with pretwist
    F: câblage *m* à préformage, câblage *m* à prétorsion

Verseilung ohne Rückdrehung
    E: stranding without backtwist
    F: câblage *m* sans détorsion

Verseilung, gestreckte ~
    E: stranding without pretwist
    F: câblage *m* sans prétorsion

Verseilwinkel *m*
    E: stranding angle
    F: angle *m* de câblage

versetzt *adj* (stufenweise)
    E: staggered *adj*, graded *adj*
    F: en quinconce, échelonné *adj*, décalé *adj*, gradué *adj*, étagé *adj*

versetzt um ... % [Bdspinn.]
    E: with ... % registration
    F: décalé *adj* de ... %

Versorgung aus dem Netz
    E: mains supply, power supply
    F: alimentation *f* par le réseau, alimentation *f* (sur) secteur

Versorgungsleitung *f*
    E: feeding line, feeder *n*
    F: circuit *m* d'alimentation, feeder *m*

Versorgungsnetz *n*
    E: supply network, supply system, mains *n*
    F: réseau *m* d'alimentation

Versorgungsspannung *f*
    E: distribution voltage
    F: tension *f* d'alimentation, tension *f* de distribution

verständliches (lineares) Nebensprechen
    E: intelligible (linear) cross-talk
    F: diaphonie *f* intelligible (linéaire)

Verstärker *m*
    E: amplifier *n*, repeater *n*
    F: amplificateur *m*, répéteur *m*

Verstärkerfeld *n*
    E: repeater section
    F: section *f* (élémentaire) d'amplification

Verstärkergeräusch *n*
    E: amplifier noise
    F: bruit *m* d'amplificateur

Verstärkerspule *f*
    E: Pupin coil, loading coil
    F: bobine *f* Pupin, bobine *f* de charge

verstärkter Kunststoff
    E: reinforced plastic
    F: plastique *m* renforcé

Verstärkung *f* [mech.]
    E: reinforcement *n*, strengthening *n*
    F: renforcement *m*

Verstärkung *f* [Nachr.]
    E: amplification *n*
    F: amplification *n*

verstellbar *adj*
    E: adjustable *adj*, variable *adj*
    F: ajustable *adj*, réglable *adj*, orientable *adj*

verstellbar, in der Höhe ~
    E: vertically adjustable
    F: réglable *adj* en hauteur

Verstellschraube f
 E: set screw, adjusting screw
 F: vis f d'ajustage, vis f de réglage

Versuch m
 E: test n, trial n, experiment n
 F: essai m, épreuve f, expérience f

Versuch im Betriebsmaßstab
 E: commercial scale trial
 F: essai m à l'échelle industrielle

Versuch im Labormaßstab
 E: laboratory-scale trial
 F: essai m à l'échelle de laboratoire

Versuch im praktischen Maßstab
 E: full-scale trial
 F: essai m à l'échelle naturelle

Versuchsanlage f
 E: test(ing) installation, trial installation, pilot installation
 F: installation f d'essai, installation f expérimentale

Versuchsanordnung f
 E: test(ing) arrangement, test(ing) arrangement, test setup
 F: montage m d'essai, montage m expérimental, disposition f d'essai

Versuchsbedingungen f pl
 E: test conditions
 F: conditions f pl d'expérience, conditions f pl d'essai

Versuchsdauer f
 E: test duration, testing time, testing period
 F: durée f d'expérience, durée f d'essai

Versuchsergebnis n
 E: test result
 F: résultat m d'essai

Versuchsfertigung f
 E: trial production, production trial, manufacturing trial
 F: essai m de fabrication, production f à l'échelle expérimentale

Versuchskabel n
 E: test cable, experimental cable, trial cable
 F: câble m expérimental, câble m d'essai

Versuchslänge f
 E: trial length, experimental length, test length
 F: longueur f d'essai

Versuchsschaltung f
 E: temporary circuit, test circuit, experimental circuit
 F: montage m expérimental (él.), couplage m expérimental, circuit m d'essai

Versuchsstadium n
 E: trial stage, experimental stage, laboratory stage
 F: stade m expérimental

Versuchsstraße f [Prod.]
 E: pilot line
 F: ligne f expérimentale, ligne f d'essai

versuchsweise adv
 E: tentatively adv
 F: à titre d'essai

verteilen v
 E: distribute v, disperse v
 F: distribuer v

Verteiler m (Aufwickelei)
 E: distributor n, traverser n, traversing unit
 F: dispositif de trancanage m, palpeur-guide m

Verteilergestell für Nachrichtenanlagen
 E: distribution frame for telecommunications systems
 F: répartiteur m d'installations de télécommunication

Verteilerkabel n
 E: distribution cable
 F: câble m de distribution

Verteilerkasten m
 E: branch box, distributing box, branch joint, distributor box (US), distribution cabinet, connecting box
 F: boîte f de dérivation, boîte f de branchement, boîte f de distribution

Verteilung f
 E: dispersion n, distribution n
 F: distribution f, répartition f

vertikale Schnellverseilmaschine [Nachr. K.]
 E: high speed vertical twister
 F: câbleuse f verticale à grande vitesse

vertikaler Korbspinner
 E: vertical cage lapper, vertical cage type lapping machine
 F: rubaneuse f verticale à cage

Vertikal-Extrusion f
 E: vertical extrusion
 F: extrusion f verticale

Vertikal-Spinnmaschine f
  E: vertical lapping machine
  F: rubaneuse f verticale
Verträglichkeit f
  E: compatibility
  F: compatibilité f
Verträglichkeitsprüfung f
  E: compatibility test
  F: essai m de compatibilité, essai m de non-contamination
Verunreinigung f
  E: contamination n, impurity n
  F: contamination f, impureté f
Verweilzeit f [Extr.]
  E: residence time
  F: temps m de séjour, durée f de traitement
verwürgen v
  E: bunch-strand v, bunch v
  F: torsader v, toronner v
verzelltes PE
  E: foamed PE, cellular PE, expanded PE
  F: polyéthylène m mousse, polyéthylène m cellulaire
Verzerrung f
  E: distortion n
  F: distorsion f
verzinkter Stahldraht
  E: galvanized steel wire, zinc-coated steel wire
  F: fil m d'acier galvanisé
verzinnter Draht
  E: tinned wire
  F: fil m étamé
Verzinnung f
  E: tinning n, tin-coating n
  F: étamage m
Verzögerer m
  E: retarder n
  F: retardateur m
Verzögerungsrelais n
  E: time-lag relay, slow-acting relay
  F: relais m temporisé
Verzweiger m [Nachr.]
  E: cross-connection point (C.C.P.), branching point
  F: point m de sous-répartition, point m de branchement
Verzweigergehäuse für Kabel [Nachr.]
  E: cable distribution cabinet
  F: coffret m de dérivation pour câbles
verzweigtes Polyolefin
  E: branched polyolefin
  F: polyoléfine m ramifié
Verzweigung der Molekülketten
  E: branching of the molecular chains, ramification of the molecular chains
  F: ramification f des chaînes moléculaires
Verzweigungsmuffe für drei Adern
  E: trifurcating joint, trifurcating box
  F: boîte f tri-mono, boîte f de trifurcation
Verzweigungsmuffe für zwei Adern
  E: bifurcating joint
  F: boîte f de bifurcation
Verzweigungspunkt m [Nachr.]
  E: cross-connection point (C.C.P.), branching point
  F: point m de sous-répartition, point m de branchement
Vibrations-Prüfmaschine f
  E: vibration test machine
  F: machine f à contrôler la tenue aux vibrations
Vielbandkabel n
  E: multi-channel cable
  F: câble m à bandes multiples
Vierdraht-Abschluß m [Nachr.]
  E: four-wire termination
  F: terminaison f à 4 fils
Vierer m
  E: quad n
  F: quarte f
Viererkreis m
  E: phantom circuit, superposed circuit
  F: circuit m fantôme, circuit m superposé, circuit m combiné
Viererverseilmaschine f
  E: quad twisting machine, quadding machine
  F: quarteuse f
vierer-verseiltes Kabel
  E: cable with quad formation
  F: câble m à quartes
Viererverseilung f
  E: quadding n, quad twisting
  F: quartage m
Vierpoldämpfung f
  E: image attenuation constant
  F: affaiblissement m sur images
Vierwalzenkalander m
  E: four roll calender

F: calandre *f* à quatre cylindres, calandre *f* à quatre rouleaux

Viskosität *f*
 E: viscosity *n*
 F: viscosité *f*

visuelle Prüfung
 E: visual examination, visual control, inspection *n*
 F: examen *m* visuel, inspection *f*

voll ausgelastet
 E: loaded to capacity, operating at full capacity
 F: utilisé *adj* à pleine capacité, utilisé *adj* à plein,

Vollast *f*
 E: full load
 F: pleine charge *f*

Vollastprüfung *f*
 E: full-load test
 F: essai *m* à pleine charge

Vollaststrom *m*
 E: full-load current
 F: courant *m* de pleine charge

vollautomatisch *adj*
 E: fully automatic, fully automated
 F: entièrement automatique, complètement automatisé

vollautomatisiert *adj*
 E: fully automatic, fully automated
 F: entièrement automatique, complètement automatisé

vollimprägnierte Isolierung
 E: fully impregnated insulation
 F: isolation *f* à imprégnation totale

voll-isoliert und gekapselt (Schaltelemente)
 E: fully insulated and enclosed
 F: isolé *adj* et blindé entièrement

Voll-PE *n*
 E: solid PE
 F: polyéthylène *m*

Volumenänderung *f*
 E: volume variation
 F: changement *m* du volume

Vorbehandlung *f*
 E: preparation *n*, preliminary treatment, pretreatment *n*
 F: préparation *f*, traitement *m* préalable

Vorbereitung *f*
 E: preparation *n*, preliminary treatment, pretreatment *n*
 F: préparation *f*, traitement *m* préalable

vordralliert *adj*
 E: pretwisted *adj*, prespiralled *adj*
 F: préformé *adj*, prétordu *adj*

Vordrallierung *f*
 E: pretwisting *n*, prespiralling *n*
 F: préformage *m*, prétorsion *f*

voreilende Phase
 E: leading phase
 F: phase *f* en avance

Voreinstellung *f*
 E: presetting *n*, preselection *n*, preadjustment *n*
 F: préréglage *m*

Vorentladung *f*
 E: predischarge *n*
 F: prédécharge *f*

Vorgabezeit *f*
 E: allowed time
 F: temps *m* alloué

vorgefertigter Endverschluß
 E: pre-mo(u)lded termination
 F: extrémité *f* prémoulée

vorgeformt *adj*
 E: pre-formed *adj*
 F: préformé *adj*

vorgetränktes Kabel
 E: pre-impregnated cable
 F: câble *m* isolé au papier préimprégné, câble *m* préimprégné

vorgewölbter Draht
 E: curved wire
 F: fil *m* métallique courbé

Vorheizzone *f*
 E: preheat zone
 F: zone *f* de préchauffage

vorimprägnierte Isolierung
 E: pre-impregnated insulation
 F: isolation *f* préimprégnée

Vormischung *f*
 E: master batch, pre-mix *n*
 F: mélange *m* mère, mélange *m* maître

Vornorm *f*
 E: tentative standard
 F: norme *f* provisoire

Vorratsader *f* [Nachr. K.]
 E: spare wire
 F: fil *m* de réserve

Vorratsbehälter *m*
 E: storage tank, supply tank, reservoir *n*
 F: réservoir *m*

Vorratstrommel f
  E: pay-off reel, supply reel
  F: bobine f débitrice, bobine f d'alimentation, bobine f de dévidage

Vorrichtung f
  E: device n, equipment n, facility n, appliance n
  F: dispositif m

Vorschub m
  E: feed n, advance n
  F: avance f

Vorspannung f[el.]
  E: bias n
  F: tension f de polarisation, polarisation f

Vorverseilkopf m
  E: prespiralling head
  F: tête f de prétorsion

vorwalzen v
  E: rough v, bloom v
  F: cingler v, dégrossir v, ébaucher v

Vorwalzstraße f
  E: roughing train, blooming train
  F: train m dégrossiseur, train m ébaucheur

Vorwalzwerk n
  E: blooming mill, roughing mill
  F: laminoir m ébaucheur

vorwärmen v
  E: preheat v
  F: préchauffer v

Vorwärmofen m
  E: preheater n, preheating furnace
  F: four m de (pré-)chauffage

Vorwärtsbewegung f
  E: forward motion
  F: marche f en avant

Vorziehdraht m[Drahth.]
  E: wire rod, redraw rod
  F: fil m machine, fil m ébauche, fil m pour retréfilage

VPE (s. vernetztes Polyäthylen)

Vulkanisat n
  E: vulcanized material, vulcanizate n
  F: produit m de vulcanisation

Vulkanisation f
  E: vulcanization n, curing n
  F: vulcanisation f

Vulkanisationsbereich m
  E: curing range, vulcanization range
  F: intervalle m de vulcanisation

Vulkanisationsdauer f
  E: time of cure, vulcanization time
  F: durée f de vulcanisation

Vulkanisationsgeschwindigkeit f
  E: rate of cure, vulcanization rate
  F: vitesse f de vulcanisation

Vulkanisationsgrad m
  E: state of cure, degree of cure
  F: degré m de vulcanisation, stade m de vulcanisation

Vulkanisationsmittel n
  E: vulcanizing agent
  F: agent m de vulcanisation

Vulkanisationsrohr n
  E: vulcanizing tube
  F: tube m de vulcanisation

vulkanisieren v
  E: vulcanize v, cure v
  F: vulcaniser v

Vulkanisierkessel m
  E: vulcanizing pan, autoclave n
  F: autoclave m de vulcanisation

vulkanisiertes Bitumen
  E: vulcanized bitumen
  F: bitume m vulcanisé

W

Wachs, mikrokristallines ~
  E: microcrystalline wax
  F: cire f microcristalline

Wählschalter m
  E: selector n (switch)
  F: commutateur-sélecteur m

Wahrscheinlichkeitskurve f
  E: probability curve
  F: courbe f de probabilité

Wahrscheinlichkeitsrechnung f
  E: probability theory, probability calculus
  F: calcul m des probabilités

Walzdraht m
  E: wire rod
  F: fil m machine laminé

Walzdrahtring m
  E: rod coil, coil of rod
  F: couronne f de fil machine

Walze f
  E: roll n, bowl n (calender)
  F: rouleau m, cylindre m

walzen v[Met.]

E: roll *v*
F: laminer *v*

walzen *v* [Gi., Plast.]
E: mill *v*
F: malaxer *v*, mélanger *v*

Walzenkaliber *n*
E: roll groove
F: calibre *m* des cylindres, cannelure *f* des cylindres

Walzenspalt *m* (Mischungsherstellung)
E: gap between rolls, nip between rolls
F: écartement *m* entre cylindres, jeu *m* entre cylindres

Walzenstellung *f* (Mischungsherstellung)
E: gap between rolls, nip between rolls
F: écartement *m* entre cylindres, jeu *m* entre cylindres

Walzfell *n* (Mischungsherstellung)
E: band *n* (as taken from a mill), sheet *n* (as taken from a mill)
F: nappe *f*

Walzgang *m* [Met.]
E: rolling cycle, rolling pass
F: passe *f* de laminage, cycle *m* de laminage

Walzgerüst *n* [Met.]
E: roll stand
F: cage *f* de laminoir

Walzhaut *f*
E: rolling skin, scale *n*
F: pellicule *f* de laminage, croûte *f* de laminage

Walzplatte *f* (Mischungsherstellung)
E: slab *n*
F: mélange *m* en plaque

Walzsplitter *m*
E: sliver *n*
F: paille *f* de laminage

Walzstraße *f* [Met.]
E: rolling train
F: train *m* de laminoirs

Walzwerk *n* [Met.]
E: rolling mill
F: laminoir *m*

Wanddicke *f*
E: wall thickness
F: épaisseur *f* de la paroi

Wanderwelle *f*
E: travelling wave, transient wave
F: onde *f* progressive, onde *f* mobile

Wanne *f*
E: trough *n*
F: bac *m*, cuve *f*, goulotte *f*

Wareneingangskontrolle *f*
E: incoming inspection, testing of incoming materials, quality control of raw material consignments
F: contrôle *m* à la livraison, contrôle *m* à la réception du matériel

Warmbiegeprüfung *f*
E: hot bending test
F: essai *m* de pliage à chaud

warmbrüchig *adj*
E: hot-short *adj*
F: cassant *adj* à chaud

Wärme, die ~ ableiten
E: to conduct away the heat, to carry away the heat, to dissipate the heat
F: dissiper *v* la chaleur

Wärmeableitung *f*
E: heat dissipation, heat removal
F: dissipation *f* de la chaleur, évacuation *f* des calories

Wärmealterung *f*
E: thermal ag(e)ing
F: vieillissement *m* thermique

Wärmeaufnahme *f*
E: heat absorption
F: absorption *f* de chaleur

Wärmeausdehnungskoeffizient *m*
E: thermal expansion coefficient
F: coefficient *m* de dilatation thermique

Wärmeaustausch *m*
E: heat exchange
F: échange *m* de chaleur, échange *m* thermique

Wärmeaustauscher *m*
E: heat exchanger
F: échangeur *m* de chaleur, échangeur *m* thermique

Wärmebehandlung *f*
E: heat treatment
F: traitement *m* thermique

wärmebeständig *adj*
E: heat-proof *adj*, heat-resistant *adj*
F: résistant *adj* à la chaleur

Wärmebeständigkeit *f*
E: heat resistance, thermal resistance, thermal stability
F: résistance *f* à la chaleur, résistance *f* thermique, stabilité *f* thermique

Wärmedruckbeständigkeit *f*

Wärmedruckbeständigkeit
  E: resistance to pressure at high temperatures, hot deformation resistance, hot deformation strength
  F: résistance *f* à la pression aux températures élevées

Wärmedruckprüfung *f*
  E: hot pressure test
  F: essai *m* de pression à température élevée, essai *m* de compression à chaud, essai *m* d'écrasement à chaud

Wärmedurchgangswiderstand *m*
  E: thermal resistance
  F: résistance *f* thermique

wärmeempfindlich *adj*
  E: heat-sensitive *adj*
  F: sensible *adj* à la chaleur

wärmehärtbare Kunststoffe
  E: thermosetting synthetic materials, thermosetting plastics, thermosetting resins
  F: matières *f pl* plastiques thermodurcissables

Wärmeklasse *f*
  E: insulation class, thermal classification
  F: classe *f* d'isolement

Wärmekraftwerk *n*
  E: thermal power station
  F: centrale *f* thermique

Wärmeleitfähigkeit *f*
  E: thermal conductivity
  F: conductivité *f* calorifique, conductibilité *f* thermique

Wärmequelle *f*
  E: heat source
  F: source *f* de chaleur

Wärmeschock *m*
  E: thermal shock, heat shock
  F: choc *m* thermique

Wärmeschockbeständigkeit *f*
  E: heat shock resistance
  F: résistance *f* aux craquelures

Wärmeschockprüfung *f*
  E: heat shock test
  F: essai *m* de choc thermique

Wärmeschrank *m*
  E: oven *n*, heating cabinet, heated cabinet
  F: étuve *f*

wärmeschrumpfende Kabelgarnituren
  E: shrink-on cable accessories, heat-shrinkable cable accessories
  F: accessoires *m pl* de câbles emmanchables à chaud

wärmeschrumpfender Endverschluß
  E: shrink-on termination, heat-shrinkable termination
  F: extrémité *f* emmanchable à chaud

Wärmeschrumpftechnik *f*
  E: shrink-on technique, heat-shrinkage technique
  F: technique *f* d'emmanchement à chaud

Wärmeschrumpfung *f*
  E: heat-shrinkage *n*
  F: retrait *m* au chauffage

Wärmeschutz *m* (über Kabelisolierung)
  E: heat barrier, thermal barrier
  F: isolation *f* thermique

Wärmestandfestigkeit *f*
  E: heat resistance, thermal resistance, thermal stability
  F: résistance *f* à la chaleur, résistance *f* thermique, stabilité *f* thermique

Wärmeübergang *m*
  E: heat transfer, heat transmission, transfer of heat
  F: transmission *f* calorifique, transmission *f* de chaleur

Wärmeübergangswiderstand *m*
  E: heat transfer resistance, heat transmission resistance
  F: résistance *f* de transmission de chaleur

Wärmeübertragung *f*
  E: heat transfer, heat transmission, transfer of heat
  F: transmission *f* calorifique, transmission *f* de chaleur

Wärmeübertragungskoeffizient *m*
  E: coefficient of heat transfer
  F: coefficient *m* de transmission calorifique

Wärmeverhalten *n*
  E: thermal behaviour
  F: comportement *m* à la chaleur

Wärmewiderstand *m*
  E: thermal resistance
  F: résistance *f* thermique

Wärmezyklen *m pl*
  E: heat cycles
  F: cycles *m pl* de chauffage, cycles *m pl* thermiques

Warmformbarkeit *f*

E: hot-workability n
F: malléabilité f à chaud

Warmformung f
E: hot forming, hot-working n
F: mise f en forme à chaud, façonnage m à chaud

Warmhalteofen m [Gießw.]
E: holding furnace
F: four m de maintien à température, four m d'attente

warmhärtend adj
E: thermosetting adj, heat-curing adj, thermal-curing adj
F: thermodurcissable adj

warmhärtender Klebstoff
E: thermosetting adhesive
F: colle f thermodurcissable

Warmverarbeitung f
E: hot forming, hot-working n
F: mise f en forme à chaud, façonnage m à chaud

Warmverformbarkeit f
E: hot-workability n
F: malléabilité f à chaud

Warmverformung f
E: hot forming, hot-working n
F: mise f en forme à chaud, façonnage m à chaud

Warmvergußmasse f
E: hot filling compound, hot pouring compound
F: matière f de remplissage à chaud

warmverschweißen v
E: heat-seal v
F: thermosouder v

warmverschweißendes Band
E: heat fusing tape
F: ruban m thermosoudant

warmwalzen v
E: hot-roll v
F: laminer v à chaud

Warmwalzwerk n
E: hot-rolling mill
F: laminoir m à chaud

Warnsignal, akustisches ~
E: audible warning
F: signal m avertisseur acoustique

wartungsfreie Anlage
E: self-contained system
F: installation f indépendante ne nécessitant pas d'entretien

Wartungsvorschrift f
E: maintenance instructions pl
F: instructions f pl d'entretien, manuel m d'entretien

wasserabstoßend adj
E: water repellent, hydrophobic adj
F: hydrofuge adj, hydrophobe adj

Wasseraufnahme f
E: water absorption
F: absorption f d'eau

Wasseraufnahmefähigkeit f
E: water absorption capacity
F: faculté f hygroscopique

wasserbeständig adj
E: water resistant
F: résistant adj à l'eau

Wasserdampf m
E: water vapour, steam n
F: vapeur f d'eau

Wasserdampfdurchlässigkeit f
E: water vapour permeability
F: perméabilité f à la vapeur d'eau

Wasserdichtigkeit f
E: water tightness
F: étanchéité f à l'eau

Wasserdichtung f [Vulk.]
E: water seal
F: joint m d'eau

Wasserdruck m
E: hydraulic pressure, water pressure
F: pression f hydraulique, pression f d'eau

wassergekühlt adj
E: water-cooled adj
F: refroidi adj à l'eau

Wasserkraftwerk n
E: hydro-electric power station
F: centrale f hydroélectrique

Wasserkühlstrecke f
E: water cooling section
F: section f de refroidissement par eau

Wasserkühlung f
E: water cooling
F: refroidissement m à l'eau

Wasserlagerung f
E: immersion in water, water immersion
F: immersion f dans l'eau

Wasserstandsanzeiger m
E: water level indicator
F: indicateur m de niveau d'eau

wäßriger Auszug
E: aqueous extract
F: extrait m aqueux

Webkante

Webkante f
  E: selvage n, selvedge n
  F: lisière f

Wechselbiegefestigkeit f
  E: reversed bending strength
  F: résistance f aux pliages alternés

Wechselbiegeprüfung f
  E: reversed bending test
  F: essai m de pliages alternés

Wechselgetriebe n
  E: change gear
  F: variateur m de vitesse, engrenage m de changement de vitesse

wechselnd, in ~er Richtung
  E: in alternating direction
  F: en sens alterné

wechselnd, Prüfung mit ~er Polarität
  E: polarity inversion test
  F: essai m à inversion de la polarité

wechselnde Belastung
  E: variable load, alternating load
  F: charge f variable

Wechselschlag, Verseilung im ~
  E: reverse(d) lay stranding
  F: câblage m en couches croisées, câblage m en sens alterné

Wechselspannung f
  E: a.c. voltage, alternating voltage
  F: tension f alternative

Wechselspannungsfestigkeit f
  E: a.c. voltage strength
  F: tenue f sous tension alternative

Wechselspannungsnetz n
  E: a.c. voltage system
  F: réseau m à courant alternatif

Wechselspannungsprüfung f
  E: a.c. voltage test
  F: essai m de tension alternative

Wechselspannungssystem n
  E: a.c. voltage system
  F: réseau m à courant alternatif

Wechselstrom m
  E: alternating current (a.c.)
  F: courant m alternatif

Wechselstromgenerator m
  E: a.c. generator
  F: génératrice f à courant alternatif

Wechselstrommotor m
  E: a.c. motor
  F: moteur m à courant alternatif

Wechselwirkung f
  E: interplay n, interaction n
  F: interaction f, action f réciproque

Wegerecht n [K. Verl.]
  E: right of way
  F: droit m de passage

Weibull-Kurve f
  E: Weibull-curve n
  F: courbe f de Weibull

Weibull-Regel f (Weibull-Verteilung)
  E: Weibull's (distribution) law
  F: loi f de Weibull

weichgeglühter Draht
  E: soft annealed wire
  F: fil m recuit

Weichglühen n
  E: soft annealing
  F: recuit m d'adoucissement

Weichlot n
  E: wiping solder
  F: soudure f liquide

weichlöten v
  E: soft-solder v
  F: souder v

Weichlöten n
  E: soft soldering
  F: soudage m tendre

Weichmacher m
  E: plasticizer
  F: plastifiant m

weichmacherfreies PVC
  E: rigid PVC
  F: PVC m rigide

Weichmacherwanderung f
  E: migration of plasticizer
  F: migration f du plastifiant

Weich-PVC n
  E: plasticized PVC
  F: PVC m plastifié

weiterleitend, einen Brand nicht ~
  E: flame-resistant adj, non fire propagating
  F: non propagateur de la flamme adj, non propagateur de l'incendie adj, non transmettant la flamme

Weiterreißfestigkeit f
  E: resistance to tearing, tear resistance, tearing strength
  F: résistance f au déchirement

Weitverkehrs-Fernsprechtechnik f
  E: long distance telephony
  F: téléphonie f à longue distance

Weitverkehrskabel n
  E: long distance telephone cable, trunk cable (GB), toll cable (US)
  F: câble m téléphonique à grande

distance, câble *m* interurbain
Weitverkehrsnetz *n*
  E: long distance network, trunk network (GB), toll network (US)
  F: réseau *m* de câbles à grande distance
Weitverkehrs-Telefonkabel *n*
  E: long distance telephone cable, trunk cable (GB), toll cable (US)
  F: câble *m* téléphonique à grande distance, câble *m* interurbain
Welle *f*
  E: wave *n*
  F: onde *f*
Welle *f* [Masch.]
  E: shaft *n*
  F: arbre *m*
Wellenbereich *m* (Schwingung)
  E: wave range, wave band
  F: gamme *f* d'ondes
Wellendämpfung *f*
  E: image attenuation constant
  F: affaiblissement *m* sur images
Wellenkamm *m* [Kab.]
  E: crest of a wave
  F: crête *f* d'une onde
Wellenlänge *f*
  E: wavelength *n*
  F: longueur *f* d'onde
Wellenlänge *f* (Wellmantel)
  E: pitch of corrugation
  F: pas *m* d'ondulation
Wellenleiter *m* [Nachr.]
  E: waveguide *n*
  F: guide *m* d'ondes
Wellenleiterbündel *n*
  E: waveguide bundle
  F: faisceau *m* de guide d'ondes
Wellenspitze *f* (beim Wellmantel)
  E: peak of corrugation
  F: crête *f* d'ondulation
Wellental *n* (beim Wellmantel)
  E: valley of corrugation
  F: fond *m* d'ondulation, gorge *f* d'ondulation
Wellentiefe *f* (beim Wellmantel)
  E: depth of corrugation
  F: profondeur *f* d'ondulation
Wellenwiderstand *m*
  E: characteristic impedance
  F: impédance *f* caractéristique
Welligkeit *f*
  E: waviness *n*

F: ondulation *f*
Wellkopf *m*
  E: corrugating head
  F: porte-outils *m* (machine à onduler), tête *f* à onduler
Wellmantel *m*
  E: corrugated sheath
  F: gaine *f* ondulée
Wellmantelkabel *n*
  E: cable with corrugated sheath
  F: câble *m* à gaine ondulée
Wellvorrichtung *f*
  E: corrugating device
  F: dispositif *m* à onduler
Wendel, farbige ~
  E: colo(u)red spiral, colo(u)red helix
  F: spirale *f* colorée, hélice *f* colorée
Wendel, geschlossene ~
  E: closed helix
  F: hélice *f* fermée
Wendel, offene ~
  E: open helix
  F: hélice *f* de vide
wendelförmig aufbringen
  E: to apply helically, to apply spirally
  F: poser *v* en hélice, enrouler *v* en hélice
wendelförmige Aufbringung
  E: helical application
  F: enroulement *m* hélicoïdal
Wendelmarkierung *f*
  E: helical marking
  F: marquage *m* hélicoïdal, repérage *m* hélicoïdal
Wendelspinner *m* (für Haltewendel)
  E: binder head
  F: tête *f* de frettage
Werksbesichtigung *f*
  E: tour through the factory (GB), plant visitation (US)
  F: tour *m* de l'usine
Werkstatt *f*
  E: factory *n*, plant *n*, workshop *n*
  F: usine *f*, atelier *m*
Werkstatttrommel *f*
  E: input bobbin, input reel, processing reel, processing drum
  F: bobine *f* d'alimentation
Werkstoff *m*
  E: material *n*, raw material
  F: matière *f*, matière *f* première
Werkstoff-Technologie *f*
  E: materials technology

Werkstoff-Technologie

F: technologie f des matières

Werkzeugbestückung f
E: tooling n
F: outillage m

Werkzeuge n pl [Extr., Met.-Strangpr., Drahth.]
E: dies pl, tools pl
F: outils m pl

Werkzeugkopf, drehbarer ~
E: rotary die head
F: tête f d'outils rotative

Werkzeugmaschinenleitung f
E: machine tool wire
F: conducteur m pour machines-outils

Werkzeugschlitten m
E: die slide
F: chariot m porte-outils

Werkzeugtasche f
E: kit n
F: trousse f

Wetterbeständigkeit f
E: weatherability n, weather resistance
F: résistance f aux intempéries

Wetterfestigkeit f
E: weatherability n, weather resistance
F: résistance f aux intempéries

Wickeldorn m (s. Dorn)

Wickeldraht m
E: winding wire
F: fil m de bobinage

Wickelgeschwindigkeit f
E: winding speed
F: vitesse f de bobinage

Wickelkeule f [K. Garn.]
E: stress cone
F: cône m de contrainte

Wickelkorb m
E: coiling basket
F: corbeille f d'enroulement, panier m d'enroulement

Wickellocke f
E: helical coil
F: hélice f d'essai

Wickelmaschine f
E: winding machine (for rewinding)
F: bobinoir m

Wickelmuffe f
E: lapped joint
F: jonction f reconstituée

wickeln v

E: wind v, wind up v, take up v, spool v, reel v, coil v
F: enrouler v, bobiner v

wickeln v (Band)
E: lap v, tape v, wrap v
F: enrubanner v, rubaner v

Wickelrichtung f
E: winding direction
F: sens m d'enroulement

Wickelverbindung f (lötfrei)
E: wire-wrap connection
F: connexion f enroulée, raccord m sans soudure

Wickler m
E: coiler n, spooler n, take-up n, rewinding stand
F: enrouleuse f, enrouleur m, bobineuse f

Wicklung f
E: winding n, wrapping n, coil n
F: enroulement m, bobinage m

Widerstand m (als el. Wert)
E: resistance n
F: résistance f

Widerstand m (Gerät)
E: resistor n
F: rhéostat m

Widerstandsbrücke f
E: resistance bridge, Wheatstone bridge
F: pont m de résistances

Widerstandsfähigkeit f
E: stability n, durability n, resistance n, strength n
F: résistance f, stabilité f, tenue f

Widerstandsglühanlage, kontinuierliche ~
E: continuous resistance annealer
F: recuiseur m continu par résistance, installation f continue de recuit par résistance

Widerstandsheizung f
E: resistance heating
F: chauffage m par résistance

Widerstandsschweißen n
E: resistance welding
F: soudage m par résistance

wiederaufbereiten v
E: regenerate v
F: régénérer v

wieder einschalten, den Strom ~
E: to restore power
F: réenclencher v la puissance

Wiederholbarkeit f
  E: repeatability n
  F: reproductibilité f
Wiegenanordnung, in ~ [K. Verl.]
  E: in cradled arrangement
  F: disposé adj en berceau
Windsichten n
  E: air classification
  F: triage m pneumatique
Windsichter m
  E: air classification plant, air-classifier, air-sifter n
  F: cribleur m à air, séparateur m pneumatique
Windung f
  E: winding n (of coil, reel), turn n, loop n
  F: spire f
Windungen eines aufgetrommelten Kabels
  E: convolutions of a cable on a reel
  F: spires f pl d'un câble sur un touret
Winkelstecker m
  E: angular plug, right-angle plug, right-angle connector
  F: fiche f angulaire, fiche f rectangulaire
Wirbelstrom m [el.]
  E: eddy current
  F: courant m parasite, courant m de Foucault
Wirbelstromverluste m pl [el.]
  E: eddy current losses
  F: pertes f pl de Foucault, pertes f pl par courants parasites
Wirkleistung f
  E: active power
  F: puissance f effective
Wirkspannung f
  E: active voltage, in-phase voltage, effective voltage, r.m.s.-voltage n
  F: tension f efficace, tension f active
Wirkstrom m
  E: active current, wattful current
  F: courant m actif, courant m watté
Wirkungsgrad m
  E: efficiency n
  F: efficacité f, rendement m
Wirkwiderstand m
  E: active resistance, effective resistance
  F: résistance f effective
Wischlot n
  E: wiping solder
  F: soudure f liquide
Witterungsbeständigkeit f
  E: weatherability n, weather resistance
  F: résistance f aux intempéries
Witterungseinfluß m
  E: atmospheric influence
  F: influence f atmosphérique, intempéries f pl
Wulst m (am Gummi-Mischwalzwerk)
  E: bank of rubber on a mill
  F: bourrelet m (sur mélangeur à caoutchouc)
Würgelitze f
  E: bunched conductor
  F: torsade f
Würgelitze, Seil aus ~n
  E: compound bunch
  F: corde f de torsades

Z

zähflüssig adj
  E: viscous adj
  F: visqueux adj
Zähflüssigkeit f
  E: ropiness n, high viscosity
  F: haute viscosité f
zähgepoltes Kupfer
  E: tough-pitch copper (t.p.c.)
  F: cuivre m raffiné, cuivre m tenace
Zähigkeit f
  E: toughness n
  F: ténacité f
Zählader f
  E: pilot wire, marked wire, tracer wire
  F: fil m pilote, fil m compteur
Zählelement n
  E: marking element
  F: élément m de comptage
Zählpaar n [Nachr. K.]
  E: tracer pair
  F: paire f de comptage
Zahnradgetriebe n
  E: gear(ing) n
  F: engrenage m, agencement m
Zeichengeschwindigkeit f [Nachr. K.]
  E: symbol rate
  F: vitesse f des symboles

Zeichenmarkierung f
  E: sign marking
  F: marquage m par symboles

Zeichnung, maßstäbliche ~
  E: scale drawing, dimensional drawing, drawing to scale
  F: dessin m à l'échelle

Zeitkonstante f
  E: time constant, time factor
  F: constante f de temps

Zeitschalter m
  E: time switch, timer n
  F: automate m temporisé

Zeit-Spannungsfestigkeit eines Kabels
  E: voltage life of a cable, long-time dielectric strength of a cable
  F: durée f de vie d'un câble, tenue f en longue durée d'un câble

Zeit-Spannungsfestigkeits-Kurve f [Kab.]
  E: voltage life characteristic curve
  F: courbe f de vie

Zeitstudie f
  E: work measurement, time study
  F: mesure f du travail

Zellen f pl (im Öldruckausgleichsgefäß)
  E: cells pl, membrane cells
  F: cellules f pl

Zell-PE n
  E: foamed PE, cellular PE, expanded PE
  F: polyéthylène m mousse, polyéthylène m cellulaire

Zell-PE-isolierte Ader
  E: cellular PE-insulated wire (core)
  F: conducteur m isolé au PE cellulaire

Zentralspinner m
  E: central spinner, concentric lapping machine, concentric lapper
  F: rubaneuse f centrale

Zentralspinnkopf m
  E: concentric lapping head
  F: tête f rubaneuse centrale, tête f de rubanage centrale

Zentralwickler m
  E: central spinner, concentric lapping machine, concentric lapper
  F: rubaneuse f centrale

Zentrierring m
  E: eccentric ring
  F: bague f de centrage, anneau m de centrage

Zentrierung f
  E: centering n
  F: centrage m

Zentrierung am Führungsnippel [Extr.]
  E: pilot on guider tip
  F: dispositif m de centrage sur le poinçon guide

Zentrierung von Mundstück und Nippel [Extr.]
  E: adjustment of the gum space
  F: centrage m de l'écart entre la filière et le poinçon

Zentrizität f
  E: centricity n
  F: centricité f

zerhackte Gleichspannung
  E: chopped d.c. voltage
  F: tension f continue vibrée

Zerkleinerungsanlage für Kabelabfälle
  E: cable scrap granulators pl
  F: installation f de broyage des déchets de câbles

zerlegbare Kabeltrommel
  E: knock-down returnable shipping reel
  F: touret m de câble démontable non perdu

zerlegen
  E: dismantle v, disassemble v
  F: désassembler v

zerreißen v
  E: break v, tear v, rupture v
  F: déchirer v

Zerreißfestigkeit f
  E: tensile strength (at break), ultimate tensile strength
  F: résistance f à la rupture

Zerreißfestigkeit, Prüfung der ~
  E: tensile test, tensile strength test
  F: essai m de traction

Zerreißfestigkeits-Prüfmaschine f
  E: tensile strength testing machine
  F: machine f à essayer la résistance à la traction, machine f de traction

Zerreißprüfung f
  E: tensile test, tensile strength test
  F: essai m de traction

Zersetzung f
  E: degradation n, decomposition n
  F: dégradation f

zerstörungsfreie Prüfung
  E: non-destructive test
  F: essai m non-destructif

zerstörungsfreie Prüfung, nicht ~
  E: destructive test
  F: essai *m* destructif
Ziehbad *n* [Drahth.]
  E: drawing bath
  F: bain *m* de tréfilage
Ziehdiamanten *m pl* [Drahth.]
  E: diamond dies
  F: filières *f pl* en diamant
ziehen, Drähte ~ auf dicke, mittlere, kleine Durchmesser
  E: to draw wires down to large, medium, small diameters
  F: tréfiler *v* des fils de gros, moyens, petits diamètres
Ziehen *n* (von Stangen, Profilen oder Draht)
  E: drawing *n*
  F: étirage *m*
Ziehflüssigkeit *f*
  E: drawing fluid
  F: liquide *m* de tréfilage
Ziehfolgen *f pl* [Drahth.]
  E: reduction steps
  F: étapes *f pl* de tréfilage
Ziehkonus *m* [Drahth.]
  E: drawing cone
  F: cône *m* de tréfilage
Ziehkopf *m* [Kab.]
  E: pulling eye, pulling head, pulling grip
  F: œillet *m* de tirage, tête *f* de tirage, agrafe *f* de tirage, clou *m* de tirage
Ziehlösung *f*
  E: drawing solution
  F: solution *f* de tréfilage
Ziehöl *n* [Drahth.]
  E: drawing oil
  F: huile *f* de tréfilage
Ziehöse *f* [Kab.]
  E: pulling eye, pulling head, pulling grip
  F: œillet *m* de tirage, tête *f* de tirage, agrafe *f* de tirage, clou *m* de tirage
Ziehscheibe *f* [Drahth.]
  E: drawing cone
  F: cône *m* de tréfilage
Ziehstein *m*
  E: drawing die
  F: filière *f* de tréfilage
Ziehsteinauslauf *m* [Drahth.]
  E: die back relief
  F: sortie *f* de filière

Ziehsteineinlauf *m* [Drahth.]
  E: die approach
  F: entrée *f* de filière
Ziehstein-Einlaufwinkel *m* [Drahth.]
  E: die approach angle
  F: angle *m* d'entrée à la filière
Ziehsteinhalter *m* [Drahth.]
  E: die holder
  F: dispositif *m* de serrage pour filière
Ziehstrumpf *m* (für Kabel)
  E: cable stocking, cable grip
  F: grip *m* de câble
Ziehstrumpf mit zwei Schlaufen
  E: double-eye cable grip
  F: grip *m* de câble à double agrafe
Ziehstufen *f pl* [Drahth.]
  E: reduction steps
  F: étapes *f pl* de tréfilage
Ziehwerkzeug *n*
  E: drawing die
  F: filière *f* de tréfilage
Ziffernbedruckung *f*
  E: number-printing *n*
  F: repérage *m* par chiffres imprimés
Zinkbad *n*
  E: galvanizing bath
  F: bain *m* de zinc
Zinkoxid *n*
  E: zinc oxide
  F: oxyde *m* de zinc
Zinn *n*
  E: tin *n*
  F: étain *m*
Zuführung *f*
  E: feed *n*
  F: alimentation *f*
Zuführungskabel *n*
  E: feeder *n*, feeder cable
  F: câble *m* d'alimentation, feeder *m*
zugänglich, leicht ~
  E: easily accessible
  F: facilement accessible
Zugbeanspruchung *f*
  E: tensile stress
  F: contrainte *f* de traction, effort *m* de traction
Zug-Dehnungskurve *f*
  E: stress-strain curve
  F: courbe *f* de tension-allongement
Zugdruckversuch *m*
  E: tension and compression test
  F: essai *m* de traction/compression
Zugentlastung *f* [Kab.]

Zugentlastung
- E: strain-bearing element, strain relief, strain-bearing member
- F: allégement *m* de contrainte, élément *m* compensateur de traction

zugfestes Kabel
- E: cable for high tensile stresses
- F: câble *m* pour grands efforts de traction

Zugfestigkeit *f*
- E: tensile strength
- F: résistance *f* à la traction

Zugfestigkeitsprüfer *m*
- E: tensile strength testing machine
- F: machine *f* à essayer la résistance à la traction, machine *f* de traction

Zugfestigkeitsprüfung *f*
- E: tensile test, tensile strength test
- F: essai *m* de traction

Zugkraft *f*
- E: pull *n*, tractive force
- F: effort *m* de traction, force *f* de traction

Zugöse *f* [Kab.]
- E: pulling eye, pulling head, pulling grip
- F: œillet *m* de tirage, tête *f* de tirage, agrafe *f* de tirage, clou *m* de tirage

Zugseil *n*
- E: pulling rope
- F: corde *f* de tirage

Zugspannung *f*
- E: tension *n*
- F: tension *f* de traction

zugspannungsloser Draht
- E: slack wire
- F: fil *m* lâche, fil *m* faisant flèche

Zugspannungsmeßvorrichtung *f*
- E: tension meter
- F: dispositif *m* de mesure de la tension de traction

Zugspannungs-Regelvorrichtung *f*
- E: tension control device, tension compensating device, tension compensator
- F: dispositif *m* de régulation de la traction, dispositif *m* de compensation de la tension

zulässig *adj*
- E: admissible *adj*, permissible *adj*
- F: admissible *adj*

Zulassung *f*
- E: approval *n*, certification *n*
- F: homologation *f*

Zulassungsprüfung *f*
- E: approval test
- F: essai *m* d'homologation

Zulassungszeichen *n*
- E: approbation mark, certification mark
- F: marque *f* d'homologation

Zuleitung *f*
- E: lead *n*, feeder *n*, lead-in *n*, supply line
- F: conducteur *m* d'amenée, conducteur *m* d'alimentation

Zuleitungsdraht *m*
- E: lead-in wire
- F: fil *m* d'amenée

Zuleitungskabel *n*
- E: feeder *n*, feeder cable
- F: câble *m* d'alimentation, feeder *m*

Zunder *m*
- E: scale *n*, scab *n*
- F: calamine *f*

Zündkabel *n*
- E: ignition cable
- F: câble *m* d'allumage

Zündpunkt *m*
- E: ignition point
- F: point *m* d'allumage

zurückschneiden, die Isolierung ~ (an der Verbindungs- oder Reparaturstelle)
- E: to taper down the original dielectric (for jointing or repairing)
- F: couper *v* l'isolant coniquement

zusammenbacken *v*
- E: agglomerate *v*, conglomerate *v*, cake *v*
- F: agglomérer *v*, agglutiner *v*, coller *v*

Zusammenballung *f*
- E: agglomeration *n*, conglomeration *n*
- F: agglomération *f*, agglutination *f*

Zusammendrückung *f*
- E: compression *n*
- F: compression *f*

zusammenfallen *v*
- E: collapse *v*
- F: effondrer *v* (s'), écrouler *v* (s')

Zusammenstellungszeichnung *f*
- E: assembly drawing
- F: plan *m* d'ensemble

Zusatzeinrichtung *f*
- E: additional equipment, auxiliary

equipment, ancillary equipment
F: dispositif *m* additionnel,
appareillage *m* complémentaire,
appareillage *m* accessoire,
équipement *m* supplémentaire

Zusatzstoff *m*
E: additive *n*
F: additif *m*, adjuvant *m*

Zusatzverluste *m pl*
E: extra losses
F: pertes *f pl* supplémentaires

Zuteilvorrichtung *f*
E: metering device
F: doseur *m*

Zuverlässigkeit *f*
E: reliability *n*
F: fiabilité *f*

Zuverlässigkeit im Betrieb
E: operating reliability, operating safety, service reliability, functional reliability, reliability of operation, operational reliability
F: sécurité *f* de fonctionnement, fiabilité *f* de service

Zwangskühlung *f* [Kab.]
E: forced cooling, artificial cooling
F: refroidissement *m* forcé

Zwangsumlauf *m* (Flüssigkeiten)
E: forced circulation
F: circulation *f* forcée

zweifacher Eisenband-Wickler
E: dual steel taping head
F: tête *f* à deux feuillards

Zweifach-Extrusion *f*
E: twin-head extrusion
F: extrusion *f* tête double

Zweifach-Spritzkopf *m* [Extr.]
E: twin (extruder) head, double (extruder) head, dual (extruder) head
F: tête *f* double de boudineuse, tête *f* double extrusion

zweigeteilt *adj*
E: split *adj*, two-piece *adj*
F: en deux pièces, divisé *adj*

zweipoliger Kurzschluß
E: two-phase fault, phase-to-phase fault
F: court-circuit *m* bipolaire

zweiteilig *adj*
E: split *adj*, two-piece *adj*
F: en deux pièces, divisé *adj*

Zweiwalzenmischwerk *n*
E: two-roller mill
F: malaxeur *m* à deux cylindres

Zwickelfüllung *f* [Kab.]
E: filler *n*, valley sealer
F: bourrage *m*

Zwickelmantel *m*
E: extruded inner covering, inner filling sheath
F: gaine *f* de bourrage, gaine *f* formant bourrage

Zwickelmantelmischung *f*
E: inner filling compound
F: mélange *m* de bourrage

Zwickelölkabel *n*
E: three-core oil-filled cable
F: câble *m* triphasé à huile fluide

Zwickelräume *m pl* (zwischen den Kabeladern)
E: interstices *pl*
F: interstices *m pl*

Zwillingsleitung *f*
E: flat twin flexible cord
F: câble *m* souple méplat sans gaine

Zwillingsleitung, leichte ~
E: flat twin tinsel cord
F: câble *m* souple méplat à fil rosette

Zwischendraht *m*
E: intermediate wire gauge size
F: fil *m* de diamètre intermédiaire

zwischengelagert *adj*
E: intercalated *adj*, sandwiched *adj* between,
F: interposé *adj*, entreposé *adj*

Zwischenglühen *n* [Met.]
E: intermediate annealing, process annealing
F: recuit *m* intermédiaire

Zwischenlagerung *f*
E: incorporation *n*, insertion *n*, intercalation *n*
F: interposition *f*, entreposage *m*

Zwischenprüfung *f*
E: intermediate test
F: essai *m* intermédiaire

Zwischenraum *m*
E: clearance *n*, gap *n*, interstice *n*, interspace *n*, interval *n*, spacing *n*
F: espace *m*, intervalle *m*, jeu *m*

zwischenschalten *v*
E: interpose *v*, insert *v*
F: interposer *v*

Zwischenstück *n*
E: intermediate piece, connecting

Zwischenstück
  piece, adapter *n*, connector *n*,
  fitting *n*
F: pièce *f* intermédiaire, pièce *f* de
  raccordement, raccord *m*, pièce *f*
  de jonction, adaptateur *m*

Zwischenvakuum *n*
  E: vacuum 100 to 1 torr
  F: vide *m* de 100 à 1 torr

zyklische Belastung
  E: cyclic loading
  F: charge *f* cyclique

Zylinder *m* [Extr.]
  E: barrel *n*, cylinder *n*
  F: cylindre *m*

Zylinder-Endverschluß *m*
  E: cylinder pot-head
  F: extrémité *f* cylindrique

DICTIONARY
OF CABLE ENGINEERING

PART II

ENGLISH-GERMAN-FRENCH

A

abrasion n
  D: Abrieb m
  F: abrasion f
abrasion resistance
  D: Abriebfestigkeit f, Abschleiffestigkeit f
  F: résistance f à l'abrasion
abrasive cloth
  D: Schmirgelleinen n
  F: toile f (d')émeri
abrasive paper
  D: Schmirgelpapier n
  F: papier m abrasif, papier m émerisé
absolute limit of error
  D: absolute Fehlergrenze
  F: limite f absolue d'erreur
absolute permittivity
  D: absolute Dielektrizitätskonstante
  F: permittivité f absolue
absorption, moisture ~
  D: Feuchtigkeitsaufnahme f
  F: reprise f d'humidité, absorption f d'humidité
absorption capacity
  D: Saugfähigkeit f
  F: capacité f d'absorption
accelerated ag(e)ing
  D: beschleunigte Alterung
  F: vieillissement m accéléré
accelerated life test
  D: beschleunigte Lebensdauerprüfung
  F: essai m accéléré de durée de vie
acceleration time [mach.]
  D: Anlaufzeit f, Einlaufzeit f
  F: temps m de démarrage, temps m d'accélération
accelerator n [vulc.]
  D: Beschleuniger m
  F: accélérateur m
acceptance, factory ~
  D: Abnahme im Werk
  F: réception f en usine
acceptance certificate
  D: Abnahmeprotokoll n
  F: procès-verbal m de réception, certificat m de réception
acceptance test
  D: Abnahmeprüfung f
  F: essai m de réception
accessible, easily ~
  D: leicht zugänglich
  F: facilement accessible
accessories pl
  D: Garnituren f pl
  F: accessoires m pl, appareillage m
accumulated error
  D: akkumulierter Fehler
  F: erreur f cumulée
accumulation of cables [c. install.]
  D: Häufung von Kabeln, Anhäufung von Kabeln, Ballung von Kabeln, Belegung mit Kabeln
  F: accumulation f de câbles, groupement m de câbles
accumulator n [wire manuf., strand.]
  D: Speicher m, Längenspeicher m
  F: accumulateur m, moufle f de régulation
accumulator, breathing ~ [strand.]
  D: atmender Speicher (SZ-Verseilung)
  F: moufle m respirant
accumulator capacity [wire manuf., strand.]
  D: Speicherinhalt m
  F: capacité f d'accumulateur, capacité f de moufle
accuracy of adjustment
  D: Einstellgenauigkeit f
  F: exactitude f de réglage, précision f de réglage
accuracy of measurement
  D: Meßgenauigkeit f
  F: précision f de mesure
accuracy to size
  D: Maßhaltigkeit f
  F: exactitude f des dimensions prescrites
accurate to size
  D: maßhaltig adj, maßgerecht adj
  F: à dimensions exactes, conforme adj à l'échelle,
accurate within ... mm
  D: mit einer Genauigkeit von ... mm
  F: à ... mm près, avec une précision de ... mm
acetylene black
  D: Acetylenruß m
  F: noir m d'acétylène

a.c. generator
 D: Wechselstromgenerator m
 F: génératrice f à courant alternatif

acid number
 D: Säurezahl f
 F: indice m d'acide

acid-proof adj
 D: säurebeständig adj
 F: résistant adj aux acides

acid recovery plant
 D: Säurerückgewinnungsanlage f
 F: installation f de récupération d'acide

acid resistance
 D: Säurebeständigkeit f
 F: résistance f aux acides

acid-resistant adj
 D: säurebeständig adj
 F: résistant adj aux acides

a.c. motor
 D: Wechselstrommotor m
 F: moteur m à courant alternatif

ACSR (s. aluminium conductor steel reinforced)

active current
 D: Wirkstrom m
 F: courant m actif, courant m watté

active power
 D: Wirkleistung f, Effektivleistung f
 F: puissance f effective

active resistance
 D: Wirkwiderstand m
 F: résistance f effective

active return loss
 D: Echodämpfung f
 F: affaiblissement m d'écho

active voltage
 D: Effektivspannung f, Wirkspannung f
 F: tension f efficace, tension f active

actual value
 D: Istwert m
 F: valeur f réelle

actuating lever
 D: Bedienungshebel m
 F: levier m de commande

actuation n
 D: Betätigung f, Bedienung f
 F: commande f, manœuvre f, manipulation f

a.c. voltage
 D: Wechselspannung f
 F: tension f alternative

a.c. voltage strength
 D: Wechselspannungsfestigkeit f
 F: tenue f sous tension alternative

a.c. voltage system
 D: Wechselspannungssystem n, Wechselspannungsnetz n
 F: réseau m à courant alternatif

a.c. voltage test
 D: Wechselspannungsprüfung f
 F: essai m de tension alternative

a.c. withstand voltage
 D: Stehwechselspannung f
 F: tension f de tenue au courant alternatif

adapter n
 D: Zwischenstück n, Verbindungsstück n, Anschlußstück n
 F: pièce f intermédiaire, pièce f de raccordement, raccord m, pièce f de jonction, adaptateur m

addition n
 D: Beimengung f
 F: addition f, adjonction f

additional equipment
 D: Zusatzeinrichtung f
 F: dispositif m additionnel, appareillage m complémentaire, appareillage m accessoire, équipement m supplémentaire

additive n
 D: Zusatzstoff m
 F: additif m, adjuvant m

adhere v
 D: haften v, kleben vi
 F: adhérer v, coller v

adherence n
 D: Haftung f, Adhäsion f
 F: adhésion f, adhérance f, collage m

adhesion n
 D: Haftung f, Adhäsion f
 F: adhésion f, adhérance f, collage m

adhesive n
 D: Kleber m, Haftvermittler m, Klebstoff m
 F: adhésif m, colle f

adhesiveness n
 D: Bindefestigkeit f
 F: résistance f d'adhésion, pouvoir m adhésif, propriété f adhésive, adhésion f

adhesive power
 D: Haftvermögen n

adhesive tape
 D: Klebeband n
 F: ruban m adhésif
adjust v
 D: abgleichen v
 F: ajuster v, compenser v, accorder v
adjust v [contr.]
 D: abstimmen v
 F: accorder v, régler v
adjustable adj
 D: verstellbar adj, einstellbar adj, regelbar adj, regulierbar adj
 F: ajustable adj, réglable adj, orientable adj
adjustable, vertically ~
 D: in der Höhe verstellbar
 F: réglable adj en hauteur
adjustable speed motor
 D: Motor mit regulierbarer Geschwindigkeit, Regelmotor m
 F: moteur m à vitesse réglable, moteur m à vitesse variable
adjusting n
 D: Eichung f
 F: étalonnage m, calibrage m, jaugeage m
adjusting screw
 D: Verstellschraube f, Einstellschraube f, Stellschraube f
 F: vis f d'ajustage, vis f de réglage
adjustment n
 D: Abgleichung f
 F: ajustement m, compensation f, équilibrage m, accord m
adjustment n
 D: Regelung f, Einstellung f
 F: réglage m
adjustment n [contr.]
 D: Abstimmung f
 F: accord m, réglage m
adjustment of the gum space [extr.]
 D: Zentrierung von Mundstück und Nippel
 F: centrage m de l'écart entre la filière et le poinçon
admissible adj
 D: zulässig adj
 F: admissible adj
admixture n
 D: Beimengung f
 F: addition f, adjonction f
advance n
 D: Vorschub m
 F: avance f
aerate v
 D: belüften v
 F: aérer v, ventiler v
aeration n
 D: Belüftung f, Lüftung f
 F: ventilation f, aération f
aerial n
 D: Antenne f
 F: antenne f
aerial cable
 D: Antennenkabel n
 F: câble m d'antenne
aerial cable
 D: Luftkabel n
 F: câble m aérien, fil m aérien
aerial feeder
 D: Antennenspeiseleitung f, Antennenzuleitung f, Antennenkabel n
 F: feeder m d'antenne, ligne f d'alimentation d'antenne, descente f d'antenne, câble m d'antenne
aerial lead-in
 D: Antennenherabführung f, Antennenniederführung f
 F: descente f d'antenne
aerial messenger [tel. c.]
 D: Tragseil n, Luftkabeltragseil n
 F: câble m porteur, corde f de suspension
age v
 D: altern v
 F: vieillir v
ag(e)ing n
 D: Alterung f
 F: vieillissement m
ag(e)ing, circulating air ~
 D: Alterung im Umluftofen, Umluftalterung f
 F: vieillissement m en étuve à circulation d'air, vieillissement m par circulation d'air
ag(e)ing, ventilated air oven ~
 D: Alterung im Umluftofen, Umluftalterung f
 F: vieillissement m en étuve à circulation d'air, vieillissement m par circulation d'air
ag(e)ing resistance
 D: Alterungsbeständigkeit f
 F: résistance f au vieillissement

ag(e)ing

ag(e)ing test
- D: Alterungsprüfung f
- F: essai m de vieillissement

agglomerate v
- D: zusammenbacken v
- F: agglomérer v, agglutiner v, coller v

agglomerate n
- D: Agglomerat n
- F: aggloméré m

agglomeration n
- D: Agglomerat n
- F: aggloméré m

agglomeration n
- D: Zusammenballung f
- F: agglomération f, agglutination f

aggregate n
- D: Aggregat n
- F: agrégat m, groupe m

agitator n
- D: Rührwerk n
- F: agitateur m, mélangeur m

air, entrapped ~
- D: eingeschlossene Luft
- F: air m enfermé

air bomb
- D: Luftbombe f
- F: bombe f à air

air clamp [vulc.]
- D: pneumatische Kabelklemme
- F: serre-câble m pneumatique

air classification
- D: Windsichten n
- F: triage m pneumatique

air classification plant
- D: Windsichter m
- F: cribleur m à air, séparateur m pneumatique

air-classifier n
- D: Windsichter m
- F: cribleur m à air, séparateur m pneumatique

air-conditioned room
- D: klimatisierter Raum, konditionierter Raum
- F: enceinte f climatisée

air-conditioner n
- D: Klimaanlage f
- F: conditionneur m d'air

air-conditioning n
- D: Klimatisierung f
- F: climatisation f, conditionnement m d'air

air-cooled adj
- D: luftgekühlt adj
- F: refroidi adj à l'air

air cooling section
- D: Luftkühlstrecke f
- F: section f de refroidissement par air

aircraft wire
- D: Flugzeug-Bordleitung f
- F: câble m d'avion

air flow
- D: Luftdurchsatz m (im Wärmeschrank)
- F: débit m d'air

air inclusions
- D: Lufteinschlüsse m pl
- F: occlusions f pl d'air, poches f pl d'air, bulles f pl d'air

air oven
- D: Ofen mit Luftumwälzung, Umluftofen m
- F: étuve f à circulation d'air, étuve f ventilé

air pockets
- D: Lufteinschlüsse m pl
- F: occlusions f pl d'air, poches f pl d'air, bulles f pl d'air

airport lighting cable
- D: Flugplatzbeleuchtungskabel n
- F: câble m pour l'éclairage d'aéroports

air-sifter n
- D: Windsichter m
- F: cribleur m à air, séparateur m pneumatique

air-space(d) paper-insulated core (tightly wrapped) [com. c.]
- D: Festader f
- F: conducteur m à isolement air/papier (rubanage serré)

air-space(d) paper-insulated core (loosely wrapped) [com. c.]
- D: Hohlader f
- F: conducteur m à isolement air/papier (rubanage lâche)

air-space(d) paper insulation
- D: Papier-Luftraumisolierung f, Papier-Hohlraumisolierung f
- F: isolant m air/papier

air-tight adj
- D: luftdicht adj
- F: étanche adj à l'air

air wiper
- D: Gebläse n
- F: ventilateur m

alarm pair
  D: Überwachungspaar *n*
  F: paire *f* de surveillance
align *v* [mach.]
  D: abgleichen *v*
  F: équilibrer *v*
align *v*
  D: zum Fluchten bringen
  F: aligner *v*
alignment *n*
  D: Abgleichung *f*
  F: ajustement *m*, compensation *f*, équilibrage *m*, accord *m*
alignment, to be in ~
  D: fluchten *v*
  F: affleurer *v*, aligner *v* (s')
allowance *n*
  D: Toleranz *f*
  F: tolérance *f*
allowed time
  D: Vorgabezeit *f*
  F: temps *m* alloué
alloy *n*
  D: Legierung *f*
  F: alliage *m*
Alpeth-sheath *n* (US)
  D: Al-PE-Schichtenmantel *m*
  F: gaine *f* d'aluminium polyéthylène contrecollé
alter *v*
  D: abändern *v*, ändern *v*
  F: modifier *v*, changer *v*, réviser *v*
alternating current (a.c.)
  D: Wechselstrom *m*
  F: courant *m* alternatif
alternating direction, in ~
  D: in wechselnder Richtung
  F: en sens alterné
alternating load
  D: wechselnde Belastung
  F: charge *f* variable
alternating voltage
  D: Wechselspannung *f*
  F: tension *f* alternative
alternation of load
  D: Lastspiel *n*
  F: alternance *f*
aluminium alloy
  D: Aluminiumlegierung *f*
  F: alliage *m* d'aluminium
aluminium billet
  D: Aluminiumbolzen *m*, Aluminiumpreßbolzen *m*, Aluminiumrundbarren *m*
  F: billette *f* d'aluminium
aluminium conductor cable
  D: Aluminiumleiterkabel *n*
  F: câble *m* à âme en aluminium, câble *m* à conducteur en aluminium
aluminium conductor steel reinforced (ACSR)
  D: ACSR-Leiterseil *n* (Al-Leiter um einen Stahlkerndraht verseilt), Aluminiumleiter *m* (ACSR)
  F: âme *f* ACSR (fils d'aluminium câblés autour d'un fil central en acier)
aluminium ingot
  D: Aluminiumbarren *m*, Aluminiummassel *f*, Aluminiumkerbblock *m*
  F: lingot *m* d'aluminium
aluminium press
  D: Aluminium-(Mantel)-Presse *f*
  F: presse *f* à aluminium
aluminium sheath
  D: Aluminiummantel *m*
  F: gaine *f* d'aluminium
aluminium-sheathed cable
  D: Aluminiummantelkabel *n*
  F: câble *m* sous gaine d'aluminium
aluminium sheathing press
  D: Aluminium-(Mantel)-Presse *f*
  F: presse *f* à aluminium
aluminium wire
  D: Aluminiumdraht *m*
  F: fil *m* d'aluminium
ambient temperature
  D: Raumtemperatur *f*
  F: température *f* ambiante
ambient temperature
  D: Umgebungstemperatur *f*
  F: température *f* ambiante
ampacity *n*
  D: Belastbarkeit *f*, Strombelastbarkeit *f*
  F: capacité *f* de charge, charge *f* limite, puissance *f* limite
amperage *n*
  D: Stromstärke *f*
  F: intensité *f* de courant, ampérage *m*
amplification *n* [com.]
  D: Verstärkung *f*
  F: amplification *f*
amplifier *n*
  D: Verstärker *m*

amplifier
   F: amplificateur m, répéteur m

amplifier noise
   D: Verstärkergeräusch n
   F: bruit m d'amplificateur

amplitude n
   D: Scheitelwert m, Spitzenwert m
   F: valeur f de crête

analysis n
   D: Untersuchung f, Prüfung f (Kontrolle)
   F: examen m, analyse f, contrôle m

analysis n [test]
   D: Bestimmung f
   F: détermination f, analyse f

analysis by decantation
   D: Schlämmanalyse f
   F: analyse f à décantation, analyse f par élutriation

analysis by elutriation
   D: Schlämmanalyse f
   F: analyse f à décantation, analyse f par élutriation

anchorage, cable ~
   D: Kabelfestlegung f, Festlegung von Kabeln
   F: fixation f du câble

anchoring wire
   D: Abspanndraht m
   F: fil m d'ancrage

ancillary equipment
   D: Zusatzeinrichtung f
   F: dispositif m additionnel, appareillage m complémentaire, appareillage m accessoire, équipement m supplémentaire

ancillary time [mach.]
   D: Nebenzeit f
   F: temps m auxiliaire, temps m mort

angle of inclination
   D: Neigungswinkel m
   F: angle m d'inclinaison

angle of pitch
   D: Steigungswinkel m
   F: angle m d'inclinaison, angle m de pas

angle of wrap
   D: Umschlingungswinkel m
   F: angle m de contact, arc m d'enroulement

angular plug
   D: Winkelstecker m
   F: fiche f angulaire, fiche f rectangulaire

anneal v
   D: glühen v
   F: recuire v

anneal v [plast.]
   D: tempern v
   F: recuire v

annealer n
   D: Glühanlage f
   F: recuiseur m

annealing n
   D: Glühen n
   F: recuit m

annealing loss
   D: Glühverlust m
   F: perte f au recuit

annealing plant
   D: Glühanlage f
   F: recuiseur m

annular gap
   D: Ringspalt m
   F: espace m annulaire

annular passage
   D: Ringspalt m
   F: espace m annulaire

anode mud
   D: Anodenschlamm m
   F: boue f anodique

antenna n
   D: Antenne f
   F: antenne f

antenna cable
   D: Antennenkabel n
   F: câble m d'antenne

antenna down-lead
   D: Antennenherabführung f, Antennenniederführung f
   F: descente f d'antenne

antenna duct
   D: Antennendurchführung f
   F: traversée f d'antenne, passage m d'antenne

antenna feeder
   D: Antennenspeiseleitung f, Antennenzuleitung f, Antennenkabel n
   F: feeder m d'antenne, ligne f d'alimentation d'antenne, descente f d'antenne, câble m d'antenne

antenna lead
   D: Antennenspeiseleitung f, Antennenzuleitung f, Antennenkabel n
   F: feeder m d'antenne, ligne f

antenna lead-in (tube)
  D: Antennendurchführung f
  F: traversée f d'antenne, passage m d'antenne

antenna wire
  D: Antennenleitung f
  F: conducteur m d'antenne

anti-clockwise *adj*
  D: gegen den Uhrzeigersinn
  F: dans le sens inverse des aiguilles d'une montre

anti-corrosion coating
  D: Rostschutzanstrich m
  F: enduit m anti-corrosif

anti-corrosion protection
  D: Korrosionsschutz m
  F: protection f anti-corrosive, protection f anticorrosion

anti-corrosive *adj*
  D: korrosionsfest *adj*
  F: résistant *adj* à la corrosion

anti-foaming agent
  D: Entschäumer m
  F: agent m anti-mousse

anti-interference capacitor
  D: Störschutzkondensator m
  F: condensateur m antiparasites

antimonial lead
  D: Antimon-Blei n
  F: plomb m antimonié

antimony n
  D: Antimon n
  F: antimoine m

anti-noise capacitor
  D: Störschutzkondensator m
  F: condensateur m antiparasites

antioxidant n
  D: Oxydationsinhibitor m, Oxydationsverzögerer m, Alterungsschutzmittel n, Antioxidans n
  F: inhibiteur m d'oxydation, antioxidant m, antioxygène m

anti-twist cable
  D: verdrehungsfreies Kabel
  F: câble m anti-giratoire

anti-twist tape
  D: Gegenwendel f
  F: hélice f anti-torsion

anti-vibration ...
  D: schwingungsfrei *adj*

  F: anti-vibratoire *adj*

aperture n
  D: Öffnung f
  F: orifice m, ouverture f

apparatus n
  D: Gerät n
  F: appareil m, instrument m

apparent attenuation
  D: Scheindämpfung f
  F: affaiblissement m apparent

apparent density
  D: Schüttgewicht n
  F: densité f apparente

apparent density (paper)
  D: Rohdichte f
  F: masse f volumique apparente

apparent density after vibration
  D: Stampfdichte f
  F: densité f apparente après vibration

apparent power
  D: Scheinleistung f
  F: puissance f apparente

appearance n
  D: Aussehen n (Oberfläche)
  F: aspect m

appliance n
  D: Vorrichtung f
  F: dispositif m

appliance connector
  D: Gerätesteckdose f
  F: connecteur m (d'appareil)

appliance cord
  D: Geräte-Anschlußschnur f
  F: cordon m de raccordement d'appareil, cordon m d'alimentation d'appareil, cordon m souple, câble m souple de raccordement

appliance wire
  D: Hausgeräteleitung f
  F: câble m pour appareils électrodomestiques, câble m pour appareils électroménagers

application
  D: Aufbringung f
  F: pose f, mise f en place

application n (test load)
  D: Aufsetzen n (Prüflast)
  F: application f (charge d'essai)

application of materials
  D: Einsatz von Materialien
  F: mise f au point de matériaux, utilisation f de matériaux

apply v

apply

apply
- D: aufbringen v
- F: appliquer v, mettre v en place

apply, to ~ a current
- D: einen Strom anlegen
- F: faire v passer un courant

apply, to ~ a voltage
- D: eine Spannung anlegen
- F: mettre v sous tension, appliquer v une tension

apply, to ~ for a patent
- D: ein Patent anmelden
- F: déposer v une demande de brevet, demander v un brevet

apply, to ~ helically
- D: wendelförmig aufbringen
- F: poser v en hélice, enrouler v en hélice

apply, to ~ spirally
- D: wendelförmig aufbringen
- F: poser v en hélice, enrouler v en hélice

apply, to ~ the lead sheath
- D: Bleimantel aufpressen
- F: mettre v sous gaine de plomb

apply, to ~ the paper string
- D: mit Papierkordel umspinnen
- F: guiper v

approbation mark
- D: Zulassungszeichen n
- F: marque f d'homologation

approval n
- D: Zulassung f
- F: homologation f

approval inspection
- D: Abnahmeprüfung f
- F: essai m de réception

approval organization
- D: Prüfstelle f
- F: institut m de certification, station f d'essai, organisme m d'approbation

approval test
- D: Zulassungsprüfung f
- F: essai m d'homologation

approximate value
- D: Annäherungswert m, Näherungswert m
- F: valeur f approchée, valeur f approximative

aqueous extract
- D: wäßriger Auszug
- F: extrait m aqueux

arcing horn
- D: Funkenhorn n
- F: corne f d'arc, corne f de protection

arc-over n
- D: Funkenüberschlag m, Überschlag m
- F: contournement m, amorçage m

arc-over voltage
- D: Überschlagspannung f
- F: tension f de contournement, tension f d'éclatement, tension f d'amorçage

arc resistance
- D: Lichtbogenbeständigkeit f
- F: résistance f à l'arc électrique

arc welding
- D: Lichtbogenschweißen n
- F: soudage m à l'arc

area n
- D: Bereich m
- F: gamme f, domaine m, plage f

area reduction
- D: Querschnittsverringerung f
- F: réduction f de la section

armo(u)r n
- D: Bewehrung f, Armierung f
- F: armure f

armo(u)red adj
- D: bewehrt adj, armiert adj
- F: armé adj

armo(u)red cable
- D: Panzerkabel n
- F: câble m armé, câble m blindé

armo(u)ring n
- D: Bewehrung f, Armierung f
- F: armure f

armo(u)ring, double ~
- D: doppellagige Armierung
- F: armure f double

armo(u)ring machine
- D: Armiermaschine f, Bewehrungsmaschine f
- F: armeuse f

armo(u)ring wire
- D: Bewehrungsdraht m, Armierungsdraht m
- F: fil m d'armure

arrangement n
- D: Auslegung f (Planung), Anordnung f, Anlage f (Auslegung)
- F: disposition f, groupement m

arrester n
- D: Ableiter m
- F: conducteur m de dérivation, déchargeur m

artificial balancing line
  D: Leitungsnachbildung f
  F: équilibreur m, ligne f artificielle
artificial cooling [cab.]
  D: Fremdkühlung f, Zwangskühlung f, künstliche Kühlung
  F: refroidissement m forcé
artificial line
  D: Leitungsnachbildung f
  F: équilibreur m, ligne f artificielle
asbestos n
  D: Asbest m
  F: amiante m
asbestos cement pipe
  D: Asbestzementrohr n
  F: tube m en amiante-ciment
ash n
  D: Glührückstand m
  F: résidu m de calcination, résidu m de recuit
ash content
  D: Aschegehalt m
  F: teneur f en cendres, taux m de cendre
as-received, in ~ condition
  D: im Anlieferungszustand
  F: à l'état vierge, à la livraison
assemble v
  D: errichten v
  F: monter v, ériger v, installer v, assembler v
assembling plate [strand.]
  D: Verseilscheibe f, Lochplatte f
  F: plaque f de répartition, plaque f de guidage
assembly n
  D: Errichtung f, Montage f, Aufbau m
  F: implantation f, montage m, assemblage m
assembly drawing
  D: Montagezeichnung f, Installationszeichnung f, Aufstellungszeichnung f
  F: plan m d'assemblage, plan m de montage
Association of German Electrical Engineers
  D: Verband Deutscher Elektrotechniker e.V. (VDE)
  F: Association f des Electrotechniciens Allemands
Association of German Engineers
  D: Verein Deutscher Ingenieure (VDI)
  F: Association f des Ingénieurs Allemands
asymmetry n
  D: Unsymmetrie f
  F: déséquilibre m, asymétrie f, dissymétrie f
atmospheric humidity
  D: Luftfeuchtigkeit f
  F: humidité f de l'air
atmospheric influence
  D: Witterungseinfluß m
  F: influence f atmosphérique, intempéries f pl
attach v
  D: befestigen v
  F: attacher v, fixer v
attack v
  D: korrodieren v
  F: corroder v, attaquer v
attendant n
  D: Maschinenführer m, Bedienungsperson f
  F: opérateur m, machiniste m
attenuation n
  D: Dämpfung f
  F: atténuation f, affaiblissement m
attenuation compensation
  D: Dämpfungsausgleich m, Dämpfungsentzerrung f
  F: équilibrage m d'affaiblissement
attenuation constant
  D: Dämpfungskonstante f
  F: constante f d'affaiblissement
attenuation distortion
  D: Dämpfungsverzerrung f
  F: distorsion f d'affaiblissement
attenuation equalization
  D: Dämpfungsausgleich m, Dämpfungsentzerrung f
  F: équilibrage m d'affaiblissement
attenuation equivalent
  D: Dämpfungsmaß n
  F: unité f d'affaiblissement, équivalent m d'affaiblissement
attenuation factor
  D: Dämpfungsfaktor m
  F: coefficient m d'affaiblissement
attenuation unit
  D: Dämpfungsmaß n
  F: unité f d'affaiblissement, équivalent m d'affaiblissement
audible warning

audible
D: akustisches Warnsignal
F: signal *m* avertisseur acoustique

audio frequency
D: Tonfrequenz *f*, Niederfrequenz *f*
F: audio-fréquence *f*, fréquence *f* vocale, basse fréquence *f*

audio frequency telephony
D: Niederfrequenzfernsprechen *n*
F: téléphonie *f* à audio-fréquence

audio frequency transmission system
D: Niederfrequenz-Übertragungssystem *n*
F: système *m* de transmission basse fréquence

audio range [com. c.]
D: Sprachreichweite *f*
F: portée *f* téléphonique

audio-suppression device
D: Sprachsperre *f*
F: dispositif *m* d'audio-supression

autocentering *adj*
D: selbstzentrierend *adj*
F: à centrage automatique

autoclave
D: Heizkessel *m*, Vulkanisierkessel *m*
F: autoclave *m* de vulcanisation

automatic cable tester
D: Kabelprüfautomat *m*
F: appareil *m* automatique d'essai de câbles

automatic cut-out
D: Selbstausschalter *m*
F: interrupteur *m* automatique

automatic dialling
D: Selbstwählbetrieb *m*, Selbstwählsystem *n*
F: exploitation *f* (téléphonique) automatique, sélection *f* automatique, service *m* téléphonique automatique

automatic dial service
D: Selbstwählbetrieb *m*, Selbstwählsystem *n*
F: exploitation *f* (téléphonique) automatique, sélection *f* automatique, service *m* téléphonique automatique

automatic double spooler
D: automatische Doppelaufwickelei
F: enrouleur *m* automatique à double bobine

automatic leakage detection
D: automatische Leckstellenanzeige
F: détection *f* automatique de fuites

automatic reset
D: automatische Nulleinstellung
F: remise *f* à zéro automatique

automatic spooler
D: automatischer Spulapparat
F: bobinoir *m* automatique

automatic telephone
D: Fernsprech-Selbstanschluß *m*
F: téléphone *m* automatique

automatic telephone service
D: Selbstwählbetrieb *m*, Selbstwählsystem *n*
F: exploitation *f* (téléphonique) automatique, sélection *f* automatique, service *m* téléphonique automatique

automatic wire guide
D: automatische Drahtführung (Wickler)
F: trancanage *m* automatique du fil métallique

auxiliary device
D: Hilfsvorrichtung *f*
F: dispositif *m* auxiliaire

auxiliary equipment
D: Zusatzeinrichtung *f*
F: dispositif *m* additionnel, appareillage *m* complémentaire, appareillage *m* accessoire, équipement *m* supplémentaire

auxiliary pull-off capstan
D: Hilfsabzugsscheibe *f*
F: cabestan *m* de tirage auxiliaire

auxiliary voltage
D: Hilfsspannung *f*
F: tension *f* auxiliaire

average sample
D: Durchschnittsprobe *f*
F: échantillon *m* de la qualité moyenne

average value
D: Mittelwert *m*
F: valeur *f* moyenne

axial direction
D: Längsrichtung *f*
F: sens *m* longitudinal, sens *m* de l'axe

B

babbling n [tel.]
  D: Babbeln n, unverständliches Nebensprechen
  F: murmure m confus
backed with ...
  D: kaschiert mit ...
  F: contrecouché adj de ..., contrecollé adj de ..., revêtu adj de ..., doublé adj de ...,
back-end n (wire)
  D: Auslauf-Ende n (Draht)
  F: fin f (fil métallique)
backfill n [c. install.]
  D: Rückfüllung f, Auffüllmaterial n
  F: matériel m de remplissage
backfilling n
  D: Auffüllen n (Kabelgraben)
  F: remplissage m (caniveau de câble)
backlash of axis
  D: Achsenspiel n
  F: jeu m sur axe, jeu m à l'entraînement
back pressure [extr.]
  D: Rückdruck m
  F: contre-pression f, pression f de refoulement
back-pressure valve
  D: Rückschlagventil n
  F: soupape f de retenue
back pull
  D: Bremszug m
  F: traction f de retenue
back tension
  D: Bremszug m
  F: traction f de retenue
backtwist, with ~ [strand.]
  D: mit Rückdrehung
  F: à détorsion
backtwist, without ~ [strand.]
  D: ohne Rückdrehung
  F: à torsion, sans détorsion
baking enamel
  D: Einbrennlack m
  F: vernis-émail m
baking varnish
  D: Einbrennlack m
  F: vernis-émail m
balance n
  D: Ausgleich m
  F: compensation f, équilibrage m, équilibre m, balance f, égalisation f
balance attenuation
  D: Reflexionsdämpfung f, Fehlerdämpfung f
  F: atténuation f de réflexion, affaiblissement m d'équilibrage, affaiblissement m des courants réfléchis
balanced pair cable [tel.]
  D: symmetrisches Kabel
  F: câble m symétrique
balanced transmission line [tel.]
  D: ausgeglichene Übertragungsleitung
  F: ligne f de transmission équilibrée
balance out v
  D: entkoppeln v
  F: neutraliser v, désaccoupler v
balance return loss
  D: Reflexionsdämpfung f, Fehlerdämpfung f
  F: atténuation f de réflexion, affaiblissement m d'équilibrage, affaiblissement m des courants réfléchis
balancing n
  D: Ausgleich m
  F: compensation f, équilibrage m, équilibre m, balance f, égalisation f
balancing circuit
  D: Ausgleichsleitung f
  F: fil m de compensation, circuit m d'équilibrage
balancing current
  D: Ausgleichsstrom m, Übergangsstrom m
  F: courant m compensateur, courant m transitoire
balancing network
  D: Ausgleichsnetzwerk n
  F: réseau m de compensation
balancing network
  D: Leitungsnachbildung f
  F: équilibreur m, ligne f artificielle
balancing of the mutual capacities [tel. c.]
  D: Längsausgleich m
  F: égalisation f des capacités mutuelles
ball-bearing n
  D: Kugellager n
  F: palier m à billes, roulement m à billes

balloon 196

balloon insulation
D: „Ballon"-Isolierung f
F: isolation f ballon

bamboo rings
D: Bambusringe m pl (durch Rastzeiten beim Aufbringen von Kabelmänteln aus Blei oder Aluminium), Einschnürungen f pl (Met.-Strangpr.), Haltestellenmarkierungen f pl (Met.-Strangpr.)
F: nœuds m pl de bambou

Banbury-kneader n
D: Gummikneter m, Banbury-Kneter m
F: mélangeur m à caoutchouc, mélangeur m Banbury, malaxeur m Banbury

Banbury-mixer n
D: Gummikneter m, Banbury-Kneter m
F: mélangeur m à caoutchouc, mélangeur m Banbury, malaxeur m Banbury

band n
D: Band n
F: ruban m, bande f

band n (as taken from a mill)
D: Walzfell n (Mischungsherstellung)
F: nappe f

band width [com.]
D: Bandbreite f
F: largeur f de bande

bank of rubber on a mill
D: Wulst m (am Gummi-Mischwalzwerk)
F: bourrelet m (sur mélangeur à caoutchouc)

bare adj
D: blank adj
F: nu adj, brillant adj

bare conductor
D: blanker Leiter
F: âme f nue

bare wire
D: Blankdraht m
F: fil m nu

baring of the conductor
D: Freilegen des Leiters
F: dénudage m du conducteur

barrel n [extr.]
D: Zylinder m, Schneckengehäuse n
F: cylindre m

barrel diameter
D: Kerndurchmesser m (Kabeltrommel)
F: diamètre m du tambour

barrel mixer
D: Trommelmischer m
F: mélangeur m à tambour, mélangeur m à tonneau

barrel of a reel [cab.]
D: Trommelkern m
F: tambour m de touret, traverse f de touret, fût m de touret

barrel of a stranding cage
D: Hohlwelle eines Verseilkorbes
F: arbre m creux d'une cage de câblage

barrier n
D: Sperre f
F: barrière f, arrêt m

base frame
D: Grundrahmen m, Fundamentrahmen m
F: cadre m de base, bâti m d'ensemble

base plate
D: Grundplatte f
F: plaque f de base, socle m

base ring [met. extr. pr.]
D: Grundring m
F: anneau m de fond, bague f de fond

basic material
D: Ausgangsmaterial n
F: matière f de base, produit m de base, matière f première, matériel m rudimentaire

basic research
D: Grundlagenforschung f
F: recherche f fondamentale

basic unit [com. c.]
D: Grundbündel n
F: faisceau m élémentaire, faisceau m de base

basket v
D: aufkorben v (Armierungsdrähte), aufdrehen v (sich)
F: détordre v (se)

basketing n
D: Aufkorben n (Armierungsdrähte)
F: détorsion f (formation de paniers/corbeilles des fils d'armure)

batch, to break the ~ loose from the rolls [rub.]
D: Fell von der Mischwalze abschneiden

bending

batch mixer (continued)
- F: briser v la nappe de caoutchouc malaxé sur les cylindres

batch mixer
- D: Chargenmischer m
- F: mélangeur m à charges, mélangeur m discontinu

batch operation
- D: diskontinuierliches Verfahren, Chargenbetrieb m
- F: procédé m discontinu, service m en discontinu

batch quantities, in ~
- D: chargenweise adj
- F: en charges

batch type manufacturing process
- D: chargenweise Fertigung
- F: fabrication f discontinue

batch type pickling [wire manuf.]
- D: chargenweises Beizen
- F: décapage m discontinu

batch type process
- D: diskontinuierliches Verfahren, Chargenbetrieb m
- F: procédé m discontinu, service m en discontinu

batten n
- D: Daube f (Kabeltrommeln), Verschalbrett n
- F: douve f

bayonet joint
- D: Bajonettverschluß m
- F: verrouillage m à baïonnette

bedding n
- D: Polster n (unter der Bewehrung)
- F: matelas m

bedding material [c. install.]
- D: Bettungsmaterial n
- F: remblai m

behaviour n
- D: Verhalten n
- F: tenue f, allure f, comportement m, performance f

behaviour at low temperatures
- D: Kälteverhalten n
- F: comportement m à basse température

bell out v
- D: aufweiten v
- F: élargir v, évaser v, mandriner v

bell-shaped insulator
- D: Glockenisolator m, Isolierglocke f
- F: isolateur m à cloche, cloche f isolante

bell type (annealing) furnace
- D: Haubenglühofen m, Blankglühofen m
- F: four m à tremper, four m pour recuit brillant

bell wire
- D: Klingeldraht m
- F: fil m de sonnerie

belt drive
- D: Riemenantrieb m
- F: commande f à courroie

belted cable
- D: Gürtelkabel n
- F: câble m à ceinture

bench-mounted testing equipment
- D: Meßplatz m
- F: table f d'essai, poste m de mesure

bend n
- D: Krümmung f, Biegung f
- F: courbure f, incurvation f, courbe f

bending n
- D: Biegen n
- F: pliage m, flexion f

bending capacity
- D: Biegefähigkeit f
- F: aptitude f au pliage

bending cycles
- D: Biegezyklen m pl
- F: flexions f pl répétées

bending endurance
- D: Dauerbiegefestigkeit f
- F: résistance f de fatigue à la flexion, endurance f à la flexion

bending fatigue strength
- D: Dauerbiegefestigkeit f
- F: résistance f de fatigue à la flexion, endurance f à la flexion

bending limit
- D: Biegezahl f
- F: nombre m de pliages alternés

bending out of the cable cores
- D: Spreizen der Kabeladern, Auseinanderspreizen der Kabeladern, Ausbiegen von Kabeladern
- F: épanouissement m des conducteurs de câble

bending radius
- D: Biegeradius m
- F: rayon m de courbure

bending strength
- D: Biegefestigkeit f
- F: résistance f au pliage

bending test
  D: Biegeprüfung f
  F: essai m de pliage
bending test at low temperature
  D: Kältebiegeprüfung f,
    Kaltbiegeprüfung f,
    Kältewickelprüfung f
  F: essai m de pliage à froid, essai m de pliage à basse température, essai m d'enroulement à basse température
bending value
  D: Biegezahl f
  F: nombre m de pliages alternés
bevel v
  D: abschrägen v
  F: chanfreiner v, biseauter v
beveled edge
  D: abgeschrägte Kante
  F: tranche f biseautée
bias n [el.]
  D: Vorspannung f
  F: tension f de polarisation, polarisation f
bias-cut adj
  D: schräg geschnitten
  F: coupé adj en biais
bifilar adj
  D: doppeladrig adj
  F: bifilaire adj
bifurcating joint
  D: Gabelmuffe für zwei Adern, Verzweigungsmuffe für zwei Adern
  F: boîte f de bifurcation
bilateral drive
  D: doppelseitiger Antrieb
  F: commande f bilatérale
billet n [met. extr. pr.]
  D: Bolzen m, Knüppel m
  F: billette f
billet n
  D: Puppe f (Rolle aus Walzfell)
  F: billette f, poupée f
billet butt [met. extr. pr.]
  D: Bolzenende n
  F: bout m de la billette
billet container [met. extr. pr.]
  D: Blockaufnehmer m, Bolzenaufnehmer m, Aufnehmer m, Preßtopf m, Rezipient m
  F: conteneur m de billettes, pot m de presse
billet handling device [met. extr. pr.]
  D: Blocktransportvorrichtung f
  F: dispositif m de transport des billettes
billet loader [met. extr. pr.]
  D: Blocklader m
  F: chargeur m de billettes
billet loading [met. extr. pr.]
  D: Bolzenbeschickung f
  F: alimentation f en billettes
billet nose [met. extr. pr.]
  D: Bolzenspitze f
  F: tête f de la billette
billet preheater [met. extr. pr.]
  D: Bolzenvorwärmofen m
  F: four m de réchauffage des billettes
bimetallic corrosion
  D: Kontaktkorrosion f
  F: corrosion f par contact
bind v [cab.]
  D: abbinden v
  F: lier v
binder n
  D: Bindemittel n
  F: liant m
binder n [cab.]
  D: Haltewendel f
  F: frettage m, spirale f de fixation
binder head
  D: Wendelspinner m (für Haltewendel)
  F: tête f de frettage
binding post [com. c.]
  D: Anschlußklemme f
  F: borne f
binding screw [el.]
  D: Klemmschraube f, Schraubklemme f
  F: vis f de borne, borne f à vis
binding wire
  D: Bindedraht m
  F: fil m de ligature, fil m d'attache
birch poles
  D: Birkenstämme m pl (zum Polen beim Kupferschmelzen)
  F: troncs m pl de bouleaux
birch trunks
  D: Birkenstämme m pl (zum Polen beim Kupferschmelzen)
  F: troncs m pl de bouleaux
birdcage v
  D: aufkorben v (Armierungsdrähte), aufdrehen v (sich)
  F: détordre v (se)

birdcaging n
  D: Aufkorben n (Armierungsdrähte)
  F: détorsion f (formation de paniers/corbeilles des fils d'armure)

bitumen n
  D: Bitumen n
  F: bitume m

bitumen compound
  D: Bitumenmasse f
  F: matière f de bitume

bitumen vat
  D: Bitumenkasten m
  F: bac m à bitume

bituminized adj
  D: bituminiert adj
  F: bituminé adj

bituminized crepe paper
  D: Bitumenkreppapier n
  F: papier m crêpé bituminé

blade n
  D: Klinge f
  F: lame f

blade n (of kneader)
  D: Knetarm m
  F: pale f, palette f, bras m (de malaxeur)

blank experiment
  D: Blindversuch m
  F: essai m à blanc

blanking die
  D: Stanzwerkzeug n
  F: outil m de découpage

blank test
  D: Blindversuch m
  F: essai m à blanc

blank trial
  D: Blindversuch m
  F: essai m à blanc

blast n
  D: Gebläse n
  F: ventilateur m

bleeding n
  D: Ausbluten n (Farbe)
  F: migration f

bleeding of compound
  D: Masseaustritt m
  F: fuite f de matière

bleeding sealing end
  D: blutender Endverschluß
  F: extrémité f non étanche

blend v
  D: vermischen v, mischen v
  F: mélanger v, mêler v

blend v [rub., plast.]
  D: mischen v
  F: mélanger v

blend n
  D: Gemisch n
  F: mélange m, composition f

blister n
  D: Blase f
  F: vessie f, bulle f

blister copper
  D: Blisterkupfer n
  F: cuivre m blister

blistering n
  D: Blasenbildung f
  F: formation f de bulles

block v
  D: blockieren v
  F: bloquer v

block circuit
  D: Sperrkreis m
  F: circuit-bouchon m

block diagram
  D: Funktionsschema n
  F: schéma m fonctionnel

blocking n [tel. c.]
  D: Abstopfen n
  F: remplissage m

blocking n
  D: Verriegelung f
  F: blocage m, verrouillage m

blocking capacitor
  D: Blockkondensator m
  F: condensateur m de blocage

bloom v
  D: vorwalzen v
  F: cingler v, dégrossir v, ébaucher v

bloom n
  D: Ausblühung f
  F: efflorescence f

blooming n
  D: Ausblühung f
  F: efflorescence f

blooming mill
  D: Vorwalzwerk n
  F: laminoir m ébaucheur

blooming train
  D: Vorwalzstraße f, Blockstraße f (Walzw.)
  F: train m dégrossiseur, train m ébaucheur

blow v [el.]
  D: durchbrennen v
  F: fuser v, fondre v

blower

blower n
  D: Gebläse n
  F: ventilateur m

blowing agent
  D: Treibmittel n (Schaumstoffe), Blähmittel n
  F: agent m soufflant, agent m de gonflement

blown bitumen
  D: geblasenes Bitumen
  F: bitume m soufflé

bobbin n
  D: Spule f
  F: bobine f

bobbin speed
  D: Spulendrehzahl f
  F: vitesse f de la bobine

boiling curve
  D: Siedekurve f
  F: courbe f des points d'ébullition

boiling point
  D: Siedepunkt m
  F: point m d'ébullition

boiling point, with a high ~
  D: hochsiedend adj
  F: à point d'ébullition élevé

boiling point, with a low ~
  D: niedrigsiedend adj
  F: à bas point d'ébullition

boiling range
  D: Siedebereich m
  F: zone f d'ébullition, domaine m d'ébullition

bolted connection
  D: Verschraubung f, Schraubverbindung f
  F: vissage m, boulonnage m, raccord m à vis, raccord m fileté

bolted joint
  D: Verschraubung f, Schraubverbindung f
  F: vissage m, boulonnage m, raccord m à vis, raccord m fileté

bolt-on connector
  D: Schraubverbinder m
  F: connecteur m à vis

bond v
  D: haften v, kleben vi
  F: adhérer v, coller v

bond vt
  D: kleben vt
  F: coller vt, attacher vt

bond n [chem.]
  D: Bindung f
  F: liaison f

bonded laminar material (paper/plastic tapes)
  D: Papier/Kunststoff-Schichtenmaterial n (Bänder)
  F: rubanage m stratifié (rubans papier/synthétiques)

bonded laminate (paper/plastic tapes)
  D: Papier/Kunststoff-Schichtenmaterial n (Bänder)
  F: rubanage m stratifié (rubans papier/synthétiques)

bonding n
  D: Haftung f, Adhäsion f
  F: adhésion f, adhérance f, collage m

bonding agent
  D: Kleber m, Haftvermittler m, Klebstoff m
  F: adhésif m, colle f

bonding agent
  D: Bindemittel n
  F: liant m

bonding strength
  D: Bindefestigkeit f
  F: résistance f d'adhésion, pouvoir m adhésif, propriété f adhésive, adhésion f

bond strength
  D: Bindefestigkeit f
  F: résistance f d'adhésion, pouvoir m adhésif, propriété f adhésive, adhésion f

bond wire
  D: Verbindungsdraht m
  F: fil m de connexion

border-line case
  D: Grenzfall m
  F: cas m limite

bore n
  D: Öffnung f
  F: orifice m, ouverture f

bore n
  D: Bohrung f
  F: trou m, alésage m

borehole cable
  D: Kabel für Tauchpumpen in Bohrlöchern, Leitung für Tauchpumpen in Bohrlöchern
  F: câble m pour trou de forage

bottom settling
  D: Bodensatz m
  F: dépôt m, sédiment m

boundary conditions
 D: Grenzbedingungen f pl, Randbedingungen f pl
 F: conditions f pl aux limites

bowl n (calender)
 D: Walze f
 F: rouleau m, cylindre m

BRACAN cable (s. Brazil-Canary Islands telephone cable)

bracket n
 D: Schelle f, Befestigungsschelle f
 F: collier m, bride f

braid n
 D: Beflechtung f, Geflecht n, Umflechtung f
 F: tresse f

braided copper screen
 D: Schirm aus Kupfer-Drahtgeflecht, Kupferschirmgeflecht n
 F: écran m en tresse de cuivre

braided cotton covering
 D: Baumwollumklöppelung f, Baumwollgeflecht n
 F: tresse f de coton

braided flexible cord
 D: Gummiaderschnur f
 F: cordon m souple sous tresse

braider n
 D: Flechtmaschine f, Umflechtungsmaschine f, Klöppelmaschine f
 F: machine f à tresser

braiding n
 D: Beflechtung f, Geflecht n, Umflechtung f
 F: tresse f

braiding machine
 D: Flechtmaschine f, Umflechtungsmaschine f, Klöppelmaschine f
 F: machine f à tresser

brake v
 D: abbremsen v
 F: freiner v

braking effort
 D: Bremskraft f
 F: effort m de freinage

branch v
 D: abzweigen v
 F: brancher v, dériver v

branch n
 D: Abzweigung f
 F: dérivation f, raccordement m, branchement m

branch box
 D: Abzweigkasten m, Abzweigdose f, Kabelverzweiger m, Abzweigmuffe f, Verteilerkasten m
 F: boîte f de dérivation, boîte f de branchement, boîte f de distribution

branch cable
 D: Abzweigkabel n
 F: câble m de branchement, câble m de dérivation

branch cable [pow. c.]
 D: Stichkabel n, Hausanschlußkabel n
 F: câble m de raccordement domestique, câble m de branchement domestique

branch circuit
 D: Abzweigstromkreis m, Nebenschluß m
 F: circuit m dérivé, shunt m

branch circuit
 D: Abzweigleitung f
 F: ligne f de branchement, ligne f de dérivation, dérivation f

branch connector
 D: Abzweigklemme f
 F: borne f en forme de T, borne f de dérivation, té m de dérivation

branched polyolefin
 D: verzweigtes Polyolefin
 F: polyoléfine m ramifié

branching of the molecular chains
 D: Verzweigung der Molekülketten
 F: ramification f des chaînes moléculaires

branching point [com.]
 D: Verzweiger m, Verzweigungspunkt m
 F: point m de sous-répartition, point m de branchement

branch joint
 D: Abzweigmuffe f
 F: boîte f de dérivation

branch terminal
 D: Abzweigklemme f
 F: borne f en forme de T, borne f de dérivation, té m de dérivation

brand mark
 D: Firmenkennzeichen n
 F: marque f de fabrique, marque f du fabricant

brass solder

brass

braze v
  D: hartlöten v
  F: braser v
brazed joint
  D: Lötverbindung f (hart)
  F: brasure f
Brazil-Canary Islands telephone cable (BRACAN cable)
  D: Brasilien-Kanarische Inseln-Kabel n
  F: câble m téléphonique du Brésil aux Iles Canaries
brazing alloy
  D: Hartlot n
  F: brasure f
brazing joint
  D: Lötverbindung f (hart)
  F: brasure f
brazing solder
  D: Hartlot n
  F: brasure f
breadth n
  D: Breite f
  F: largeur f
break v
  D: zerreißen v
  F: déchirer v
break n
  D: Reißen n
  F: rupture f, déchirure f, déchirement m
break n
  D: Bruch m, Bruchstelle f
  F: rupture f, brisure f, cassure f
break, to ~ the batch loose from the rolls [rub.]
  D: Fell von der Mischwalze abschneiden
  F: briser v la nappe de caoutchouc malaxé sur les cylindres
break down v [el.]
  D: durchschlagen v
  F: claquer v
breakdown n
  D: Ausfall m (Anlage, Kabel), Betriebsstörung f
  F: défaut m, panne f, défaillance f, incident m de fonctionnement
breakdown n [el.]
  D: Durchschlag m
  F: claquage m, amorçage m, décharge f disruptive
breakdown field strength
  D: Durchschlagfeldstärke f
  F: intensité f de claquage
breakdown gradient
  D: Durchschlagfeldstärke f
  F: intensité f de claquage
breakdown strength
  D: Durchschlagfestigkeit f, Spannungsfestigkeit f, elektrische Festigkeit, dielektrische Festigkeit
  F: rigidité f diélectrique
breakdown stress
  D: Durchschlagfeldstärke f
  F: intensité f de claquage
breakdown voltage
  D: Durchschlagspannung f
  F: tension f de claquage, tension f de perforation, tension f disruptive
breaker plate [extr.]
  D: Lochscheibe f
  F: répartiteur m de flux
breaking n
  D: Reißen n
  F: rupture f, déchirure f, déchirement m
breaking capacity (GB)
  D: Ausschaltleistung f, Abschaltleistung f
  F: puissance f de rupture, pouvoir m de coupure
breaking circuit
  D: Abschaltstromkreis m
  F: circuit m de courant de rupture
breaking current
  D: Abschaltstrom m
  F: courant m de coupure
breaking length
  D: Reißlänge f (Papier)
  F: longueur f de rupture
breaking load
  D: Bruchlast f
  F: charge f de rupture
breaking point
  D: Brechpunkt m
  F: point m de fragilité
break of paper tape or wire
  D: Abreißen von Papierband oder Draht
  F: rupture f du ruban de papier ou du fil métallique
breathe v [mech.]
  D: atmen v

F: respirer *v*

breathing accumulator [strand.]
D: atmender Speicher (SZ-Verseilung)
F: moufle *m* respirant

bridge circuit
D: Brückenschaltung *f*
F: circuit *m* en pont

bridge crane
D: Brückenkran *m*
F: pont-grue *m*

bright *adj*
D: blank *adj*
F: nu *adj*, brillant *adj*

bright annealing
D: Blankglühen *n*
F: recuit *m* brillant

brittle *adj*
D: spröde *adj*
F: cassant *adj*, fragile *adj*

brittle fracture
D: Sprödbruch *m*
F: rupture *f* fragile

brittleness
D: Brüchigkeit *f*, Sprödigkeit *f*
F: fragilité *f*

brittleness, low temperature ~
D: Kältesprödigkeit *f*
F: fragilité *f* à basse température

brittleness temperature
D: Sprödigkeitstemperatur *f*
F: température *f* de fragilité

broad-band cable
D: Breitbandkabel *n*
F: câble *m* à large bande

broad-band carrier system
D: Breitband-Trägerfrequenzsystem *n*
F: système *m* à large bande à fréquence porteuse

broad-band carrier telephony speech circuit
D: Breitband-Trägerfrequenz-Sprechkreis *m*
F: circuit *m* téléphonique à fréquence porteuse à large bande

broad-band communications network
D: Breitbandkommunikationsnetz *n*, Breitbandsystem *n*
F: réseau *m* de communication à large bande, système *m* à large bande

broad-band system
D: Breitbandkommunikationsnetz *n*, Breitbandsystem *n*
F: réseau *m* de communication à large bande, système *m* à large bande

broad-band transmission
D: Breitband-Übertragung *f*
F: transmission *f* à large bande

broadcast pair
D: Rundfunkpaar *n*
F: paire *f* radio

broad-web paper wrapping
D: Breitbahnwicklung *f* (Papier)
F: enroulement *m* papier à large bande

bubble *n*
D: Blase *f*
F: vessie *f*, bulle *f*

buckling resistance
D: Knickfestigkeit *f*
F: résistance *f* au flambage

buckling strength
D: Knickfestigkeit *f*
F: résistance *f* au flambage

building, flat webbed ~ wire
D: Stegleitung *f*
F: conducteur *m* à gaine séparable

build up *v*
D: auswickeln *v* (Isolierung)
F: reconstituer *v*

build-up of a joint
D: Auswickeln einer Verbindungsstelle
F: reconstitution *f* d'une jonction

build-up welding
D: Auftragsschweißung *f*
F: soudure *f* à superposition

built-in *adj*
D: eingebaut *adj*
F: incorporé *adj*

bulge *v*
D: aufweiten *v*
F: élargir *v*, évaser *v*, mandriner *v*

bulk density
D: Schüttgewicht *n*
F: densité *f* apparente

bulk factor
D: Füllfaktor *m*
F: coefficient *m* de remplissage, coefficient *m* de volume

bulk power transmission
D: Hochleistungsübertragung *f*
F: transport *m* de grandes (fortes) puissances

bull-block *n* [wire manuf.]

bull-block

    D: Bull-Block *m* (Einscheiben-Vorsatzblock für große Profil-Abmessungen)
    F: bull-block *m*

Buna S (butadiene-styrene rubber)
    D: Buna S *m* (Butadien-Styrol-Kautschuk)
    F: Buna *m* S (caoutchouc butadiène styrène)

bunch *v*
    D: verwürgen *v*, verlitzen *v*
    F: torsader *v*, toronner *v*

bunch *n* [com. c.]
    D: Bündel *n*
    F: faisceau *m*

bunched cable
    D: Bündelkabel *n*, bündelverseiltes Kabel
    F: câble *m* en faisceaux, câble *m* à conducteurs en faisceaux

bunched conductor
    D: Würgelitze *f*, Litzenleiter *m*
    F: torsade *f*

bunching *n*
    D: Leiterverseilung *f*, Verseilung *f*
    F: câblage *m* (âme)

bunching machine
    D: Bündelverseilmaschine *f*
    F: tordeuse *f*

bunch-strand *v*
    D: verwürgen *v*, verlitzen *v*
    F: torsader *v*, toronner *v*

bunch strand
    D: Litze *f*
    F: toron *m*, cordon *m*

buoyant cable
    D: schwimmfähiges Kabel
    F: câble *m* flottable

buried *adj* [c. install.]
    D: erdverlegt *adj*
    F: posé *adj* en terre, enterré *adj*

buried cable
    D: Erdkabel *n*
    F: câble *m* souterrain

buried wiring
    D: Unterputz-Installation *f*, Verlegung unter Putz
    F: installation *f* sous crépi, pose *f* sous crépi, pose *f* encastrée

burn *v*
    D: verbrennen *vi*
    F: brûler *v*, carboniser *v*

burr *n*
    D: Grat *m*, Gußgrat *m*
    F: bavure *f*, arête *f*

bursting pressure
    D: Berstdruck *m*
    F: pression *f* d'éclatement

bursting strength
    D: Berstdruckfestigkeit *f*
    F: résistance *f* à la pression d'éclatement

bursting test
    D: Berstdruckprüfung *f*
    F: essai *m* d'éclatement

burying *n* (in ground)
    D: Verlegung in Erde, Erdverlegung *f*
    F: pose *f* en pleine terre, pose *f* souterraine

bus-bar *n*
    D: Sammelschiene *f*
    F: barre *f* omnibus, barre *f* collectrice

bus-duct *n*
    D: Sammelschiene *f*
    F: barre *f* omnibus, barre *f* collectrice

bush *n*
    D: Buchse *f*
    F: manchon *m*, douille *f*

bushing *n*
    D: Buchse *f*
    F: manchon *m*, douille *f*

bushing *n* [c. access.]
    D: Durchführung *f*
    F: traversée *f*, douille *f*

bushing insulator
    D: Durchführungs-Isolator *m*
    F: isolateur *m* de traversée

butted taping
    D: anlappende Bandumspinnung
    F: rubanage *m* jointif

butt-end *n* [met. extr. pr.]
    D: Preßrest *m*
    F: culot *m* de filage

butt gap [paper lapp.]
    D: Spinnfuge *f*, Fuge *f*, Stoßfuge *f*, Stoßkantenzwischenraum *m*
    F: déjoint *m*, joint *m*

butt gaps, without ~ [lapp.]
    D: auf Stoß
    F: en hélice fermée, en spires jointives

butt space [paper lapp.]
    D: Spinnfuge *f*, Fuge *f*, Stoßfuge *f*, Stoßkantenzwischenraum *m*
    F: déjoint *m*, joint *m*

butt welding

- D: Stumpfschweißen n
- F: soudage m par rapprochement, soudure f bout à bout

butt welding machine
- D: Stumpfschweißmaschine f
- F: soudeuse f par rapprochement

butyl rubber
- D: Butylkautschuk m
- F: caoutchouc m (de) butyle

buzz out v [tel. c.]
- D: abklingeln v
- F: sonner v

buzz-out operation [tel. c.]
- D: Abklingeln n, Durchklingeln n, Ausklingeln n, Klingelprüfung f
- F: contrôle m de continuité, sonnage m

by-pass valve
- D: Überlaufventil n
- F: soupape f de trop-plein

C

cabinet n
- D: Gehäuse n
- F: boîte f, caisse f

cabinet n
- D: Kammer f
- F: chambre f, compartiment m

cable v
- D: verkabeln v
- F: câbler v

cable n
- D: Kabel n, Leitung f
- F: câble m

cable accessories
- D: Kabelgarnituren f pl
- F: accessoires m pl de câble

cable anchorage
- D: Kabelfestlegung f, Festlegung von Kabeln
- F: fixation f du câble

cable arrangement
- D: Kabelanordnung f
- F: disposition f des câbles

cable assembly
- D: Kabelbaum m, Kabelsatz m
- F: harnais m de câbles, faisceau m de câbles, forme f de câbles

cable at no-load [pow. c.]
- D: unbelastetes Kabel, Kabel in unbelastetem Zustand
- F: câble m non chargé, câble m en exploitation sans charge

cable build-up
- D: Kabelaufbau m, Aufbau eines Kabels, Kabelkonstruktion f
- F: construction f d'un câble, constitution f d'un câble

cable cabinet [com.]
- D: Kabelschrank m
- F: armoire f à câbles

cable clamp
- D: Kabelschelle f, Kabelklemme f
- F: collier m de câble, attache f de câble, serre-câble m

cable cleat
- D: Kabelschelle f, Kabelklemme f
- F: collier m de câble, attache f de câble, serre-câble m

cable clip
- D: Kabelschelle f, Kabelklemme f
- F: collier m de câble, attache f de câble, serre-câble m

cable connection
- D: Kabelanschluß m
- F: raccord m de câble

cable core (assembly)
- D: Kabelseele f
- F: assemblage m des conducteurs du câble

cable defect
- D: Kabelfehler m
- F: défaut m de câble

cable design
- D: Kabelaufbau m, Aufbau eines Kabels, Kabelkonstruktion f
- F: construction f d'un câble, constitution f d'un câble

cable design engineer
- D: Kabelkonstrukteur m
- F: ingénieur m de construction des câbles

cable distribution cabinet
- D: Kabelverteilerschrank m
- F: armoire f de distribution de câbles

cable distribution cabinet [com.]
- D: Verzweigergehäuse für Kabel
- F: coffret m de dérivation pour câbles

cable distribution point
- D: Kabelaufführungspunkt m
- F: point m de montée de cable

cable drum

cable

cable
- D: Kabeltrommel f
- F: touret m de câble, bobine f de câble

cable duct
- D: Kabelkanal m
- F: conduite f de câble, caniveau m de câble

cable engineering
- D: Kabeltechnik f
- F: technique f des câbles

cable entrance
- D: Kabeleinführung f, Leitungseinführung f
- F: entrée f de câble

cable eye
- D: Kabelschuh m, Kabel-Abschlußhülse f, Anschlußöse f, Anschlußlasche f
- F: cosse f de câble, attache f de conducteur, cosse f terminale

cable factory
- D: Kabelwerk n
- F: câblerie f, usine f de câbles

cable failure
- D: Kabelfehler m
- F: défaut m de câble

cable fault
- D: Kabelfehler m
- F: défaut m de câble

cable for fixed installation
- D: Leitung für feste Verlegung
- F: câble m pour installation fixe

cable for high tensile stresses
- D: zugfestes Kabel
- F: câble m pour grands efforts de traction

cable for installation on steep slopes
- D: Steilhangkabel n
- F: câble m pour installation sur pentes raides

cable forming board
- D: Kabelformbrett n, Formbrett für Kabel
- F: gabarit m pour câbles, planche f de préparation pour câbles

cable gallery
- D: Kabeltunnel m
- F: tunnel m des câbles, galérie f des câbles

cable grate [c. install.]
- D: Kabelrost m, Rost m
- F: grille f à câbles, râtelier m à câbles

cable grip
- D: Kabelschelle f, Kabelklemme f
- F: collier m de câble, attache f de câble, serre-câble m

cable grip
- D: Ziehstrumpf m (für Kabel)
- F: grip m de câble

cable group
- D: Kabelgruppe f
- F: famille f de câbles

cable harness
- D: Kabelbaum m, Kabelsatz m
- F: harnais m de câbles, faisceau m de câbles, forme f de câbles

cable inlet
- D: Kabeleinführung f, Leitungseinführung f
- F: entrée f de câble

cable installation
- D: Kabelanlage f
- F: liaison f de câbles, canalisation f (câb.)

cable installation
- D: Verlegung von Kabeln
- F: pose f de câbles

cable jacket
- D: Kabelmantel m
- F: gaine f de câble

cable jointing chamber
- D: Muffenbunker m, Muffenbauwerk n, Kabelschacht m
- F: trou m d'homme, puits m de visite, puits m de jonction, chambre f de répartition, puits m à câbles

cable jointing manhole
- D: Muffenbunker m, Muffenbauwerk n, Kabelschacht m
- F: trou m d'homme, puits m de visite, puits m de jonction, chambre f de répartition, puits m à câbles

cable lacing board
- D: Kabelformbrett n, Formbrett für Kabel
- F: gabarit m pour câbles, planche f de préparation pour câbles

cable laying
- D: Verlegung von Kabeln
- F: pose f de câbles

cable laying machine
- D: Auslegemaschine für Kabel, Verlegemaschine für Kabel
- F: machine f à poser les câbles

cable laying plough (GB)
- D: Kabelpflug m
- F: charrue f de pose pour câbles

cable laying plow (US)
 D: Kabelpflug m
 F: charrue f de pose pour câbles

cable lead
 D: Kabelblei n
 F: plomb m de câble

cable length
 D: Kabellänge f
 F: longueur f du câble

cable lifting point
 D: Kabelaufführungspunkt m
 F: point m de montée de cable

cable lug
 D: Kabelschuh m, Kabel-Abschlußhülse f, Anschlußöse f, Anschlußlasche f
 F: cosse f de câble, attache f de conducteur, cosse f terminale

cable maker
 D: Kabelhersteller m
 F: fabricant m de câbles, câbleur m

cable make-up
 D: Kabelaufbau m, Aufbau eines Kabels, Kabelkonstruktion f
 F: construction f d'un câble, constitution f d'un câble

cable making
 D: Kabelherstellung f
 F: fabrication f des câbles

cable manufacture
 D: Kabelherstellung f
 F: fabrication f des câbles

cable manufacturer
 D: Kabelhersteller m
 F: fabricant m de câbles, câbleur m

cable passage
 D: Bohrung f (für den Kabeldurchlauf)
 F: passage m pour cable

cable pit
 D: Muffenbunker m, Muffenbauwerk n, Kabelschacht m
 F: trou m d'homme, puits m de visite, puits m de jonction, chambre f de répartition, puits m à câbles

cable puller
 D: Kabel-Einziehvorrichtung f
 F: dispositif m de tirage des câbles

cabler n
 D: Verseilmaschine f
 F: câbleuse f, assembleuse f

cable rack [c. install.]
 D: Kabelpritsche f, Kabeltraggerüst n, Pritsche f
 F: tablette f à câbles, charpente pour câbles f

cable reel
 D: Kabeltrommel f
 F: touret m de câble, bobine f de câble

cable roller [c. install.]
 D: Kabelrolle f
 F: rouleau m de câble

cable route
 D: Kabelstrecke f
 F: liaison f de câble

cable scrap granulators pl
 D: Zerkleinerungsanlage für Kabelabfälle
 F: installation f de broyage des déchets de câbles

cable section
 D: Kabelabschnitt m
 F: tronçon m de câble

cable shaft [cab.]
 D: Hochführungsschacht m
 F: puits m de montée

cable sheath
 D: Kabelmantel m
 F: gaine f de câble

cable sheathing press [met.]
 D: Strangpresse für Kabelmäntel
 F: presse f à filer pour gaines de câbles

cable ship
 D: Kabellegeschiff n
 F: navire m câblier, câblier m

cables in flat formation
 D: nebeneinander liegende Kabel, in einer Ebene liegende Kabel
 F: câbles m pl disposés en nappe

cables laid in parallel
 D: nebeneinander liegende Kabel, in einer Ebene liegende Kabel
 F: câbles m pl disposés en nappe

cables laid side by side
 D: nebeneinander liegende Kabel, in einer Ebene liegende Kabel
 F: câbles m pl disposés en nappe

cable sniffer [com. c.]
 D: Gasspürgerät n
 F: appareil m détecteur de gaz

cable stocking
 D: Ziehstrumpf m (für Kabel)
 F: grip m de câble

cable strand
 D: Kabellitze f
 F: toron m de câble

cable stripper
D: Abisoliermaschine f
F: machine f à dénuder

cable stripping knife
D: Kabelmesser n
F: couteau m pour câbles

cable subway
D: Kabeltunnel m
F: tunnel m des câbles, galérie f des câbles

cable suspender
D: Tragband n (Luftkabel)
F: bride f de suspension

cable suspension wire
D: Kabeltragdraht m
F: fil m porte-câble

cables with big cross-sectional areas
D: Kabel mit großen Querschnitten
F: câbles m pl de grosses sections, gros câbles m pl

cables with small cross-sectional areas
D: Kabel mit kleinen Querschnitten
F: câbles m pl de petites sections

cable terminal
D: Kabelklemme f
F: borne f de câble

cable termination
D: Kabelendverschluß m
F: boîte f d'extrémité de câble

cable termination for metal-clad substations
D: Schaltanlageneinführungs-Endverschluß m
F: extrémité f de câble pour les coffrets de disjoncteurs-interrupteurs

cable tester, automatic ~
D: Kabelprüfautomat m
F: appareil m automatique d'essai de câbles

cable testing truck
D: Kabelmeßwagen m, Meßwagen für Kabel
F: voiture-laboratoire f pour l'essai des câbles

cable trailer
D: Kabelwagen m, Kabeltrommel-Anhänger m
F: chariot m à câbles, chariot m à touret de câble

cable tray [c. install.]
D: Kabelpritsche f, Kabeltraggerüst n, Pritsche f

F: tablette f à câbles, charpente pour câbles f

cable trench
D: Kabelgraben m
F: tranchée f de câble

cable trolley
D: Kabelwagen m, Kabeltrommel-Anhänger m
F: chariot m à câbles, chariot m à touret de câble

cable trough [c. install.]
D: Kabelwanne f
F: goulotte f à câbles

cable tunnel
D: Kabeltunnel m
F: tunnel m des câbles, galérie f des câbles

cable vault
D: Muffenbunker m, Muffenbauwerk n, Kabelschacht m
F: trou m d'homme, puits m de visite, puits m de jonction, chambre f de répartition, puits m à câbles

cable vault (tel. exchange)
D: Kabelaufteilungskeller m (Fernsprechamt)
F: sous-sol m de distribution des câbles, cave f des câbles

cable winch
D: Kabelwinde f
F: treuil m de câble

cable with bare lead sheath
D: blankes Bleimantelkabel
F: câble m sous gaine de plomb nu

cable with controlled dielectric
D: Kabel mit gesteuertem Dielektrikum (Ölkabel, Gasdruckkabel)
F: câble m à diélectrique contrôlé

cable with corrugated sheath
D: Wellmantelkabel n
F: câble m à gaine ondulée

cable with multiple-twin quad formation
D: Dieselhorst-Martin-Viererverseiltes Kabel, DM-Viererverseiltes Kabel, DM-Viererkabel n
F: câble m à quartes Dieselhorst-Martin, câble m à quartes DM

cable with pair formation [com. c.]
D: paarverseiltes Kabel, paarig verseiltes Kabel

cable with quad formation
D: vierer-verseiltes Kabel
F: câble *m* à quartes

cable with star quad combination
D: sternviererverseiltes Kabel
F: câble *m* à quartes en étoile

cable with water blocks [tel. c.]
D: diskontinuierlich abgestopftes Kabel
F: câble *m* rempli de façon discontinue

cable works
D: Kabelwerk *n*
F: câblerie *f*, usine *f* de câbles

cabling *n*
D: Schaltung *f*, Verdrahtung *f*
F: circuit *m*, montage *m*, schéma *m* de connexions, filerie *f*

cabling *n* [cab.]
D: Seelenverseilung *f*, Aderverseilung *f*, Verseilung *f* (Seele)
F: assemblage *m* (des conducteurs)

cage *n* [strand.]
D: Korb *m*
F: cage *f*

cage barrel
D: Hohlwelle eines Verseilkorbes
F: arbre *m* creux d'une cage de câblage

cage lapper, horizontal ~
D: horizontaler Korbspinner
F: rubaneuse *f* horizontale à cage

cage lapper, vertical ~
D: vertikaler Korbspinner
F: rubaneuse *f* verticale à cage

cage strander
D: Korbverseilmaschine *f*
F: câbleuse *f* à cage, assembleuse *f* à cage

cage type lapping machine, horizontal ~
D: horizontaler Korbspinner
F: rubaneuse *f* horizontale à cage

cage type lapping machine, vertical ~
D: vertikaler Korbspinner
F: rubaneuse *f* verticale à cage

cake *v*
D: zusammenbacken *v*
F: agglomérer *v*, agglutiner *v*, coller *v*

cake *n*
D: Massel *f* (Blei)
F: saumon *m*

calcium carbonate
D: Kreide *f*
F: carbonate *m* de calcium, craie *f*

calculated effective area
D: berechneter wirksamer Querschnitt
F: section *f* efficace calculée

calculated value
D: rechnerischer Wert
F: valeur *f* théorique

calender *n*
D: Kalander *m*
F: calandre *f*

calibrating resistance
D: Eichwiderstand *m*
F: résistance *f* étalon

calibration *n*
D: Eichung *f*
F: étalonnage *m*, calibrage *m*, jaugeage *m*

calibration circuit
D: Eichkreis *m*
F: circuit *m* d'étalonnage

calibration curve
D: Eichkurve *f*
F: courbe *f* d'étalonnage

calling range [com. c.]
D: Rufreichweite *f*
F: portée *f* d'appel

Canada-Scotland transatlantic telephone cable (CANTAT cable)
D: Kanada-Schottland-Kabel *n*
F: câble *m* téléphonique du Canada à l'Ecosse

cantilevered *adj*
D: freitragend *adj*
F: non soutenu *adj*

cantilever strength
D: Umbruchfestigkeit *f* (Isolator)
F: résistance *f* à la rupture en flexion

cap *n* [c. access.]
D: Kappe *f*
F: capot *m*, capuchon *m*

capacitance *n* [el.]
D: Kapazität *f*
F: capacité *f*

capacitance balance
D: Kapazitätssymmetrie *f*
F: équilibre *m* de capacité

capacitance current
D: Ladestrom *m*
F: courant *m* de charge

capacitance imbalance (US)
D: kapazitive Kopplung, Kapazitätsunsymmetrie f
F: déséquilibre m de capacité

capacitance measurement
D: Kapazitätsmessung f
F: mesure f de capacité

capacitance to earth
D: Kapazität gegen Erde
F: capacité f par rapport à la terre

capacitance unbalance
D: kapazitive Kopplung, Kapazitätsunsymmetrie f
F: déséquilibre m de capacité

capacitive reactance
D: kapazitiver Widerstand
F: résistance f capacitive

capacitive resistance
D: kapazitiver Widerstand
F: résistance f capacitive

capacitor n
D: Kondensator m
F: condensateur m

capacitor coil
D: Kondensatorwickel m
F: bobinage m de condensateur

capacitor cone
D: Kondensatorkeule f
F: cône m de condensateur

capacitor oil
D: Kondensatoröl n
F: huile f de condensateur

capacitor roll
D: Kondensatorwickel m
F: bobinage m de condensateur

capacity n [mach.]
D: Leistung f, Ausstoß m
F: performance f, débit m, efficacité f, rendement m, capacité f

capacity, loaded to ~
D: voll ausgelastet
F: utilisé adj à pleine capacité, utilisé adj à plein,

capacity, operating at full ~
D: voll ausgelastet
F: utilisé adj à pleine capacité, utilisé adj à plein,

capacity unbalance testing equipment
D: Kopplungsmeßplatz m
F: poste m de mesure des déséquilibres de capacité

cap-seal v
D: verkappen v
F: fermer v par un capuchon, terminer v par un capuchon

capstan, haul-off ~
D: Scheibenabzug m, Abzugscheibe f
F: cabestan m de tirage, roue f de tirage, cabestan m tireur

capstan, pull-off ~
D: Scheibenabzug m, Abzugscheibe f
F: cabestan m de tirage, roue f de tirage, cabestan m tireur

carbon black
D: Ruß m
F: noir m de fumée, noir m de carbone

carbon black loaded
D: rußgefüllt adj
F: chargé adj en noir

carbon black paper
D: Rußpapier n
F: papier m carbone

carbonized adj
D: verkohlt adj
F: carbonisé adj

carbon-loaded paper interlocked with metallized paper
D: dachziegelartig aufgebrachtes Rußpapier und metallisiertes Papier
F: papier m carbone et papier métallisé imbriqués

carriage n (carrying stranding cradles)
D: Laufkranz m
F: couronne f d'assemblage

carrier cable
D: Trägerfrequenzkabel n
F: câble m à courant porteur

carrier current
D: Trägerstrom m
F: courant m porteur

carrier current telephony
D: Trägerstromfernsprechen n
F: téléphonie f à courants porteurs

carrier frequency
D: Trägerfrequenz f (TF)
F: fréquence f porteuse

carrier frequency cable
D: Trägerfrequenzkabel n
F: câble m à courant porteur

carrier frequency channel selection
D: Trägerfrequenz-Kanalwahl f
F: sélection f de la voie à fréquence porteuse

carrier frequency star quad
D: Trägerfrequenz-Sternvierer m

carrier frequency transmission system
F: quarte f en étoile à courant porteur
carrier frequency transmission system
D: Trägerfrequenz-Übertragungssystem n
F: système m de transmission à courants porteurs
carrier system
D: TF-System n (Trägerfrequenzsystem)
F: système m à courant porteur
carry v
D: übertragen v
F: transporter v, transmettre v
carry, to ~ away the heat
D: die Wärme ableiten
F: dissiper v la chaleur
carry, to ~ out a test
D: eine Prüfung durchführen
F: faire v un essai, effectuer v un essai
cascade connection
D: Kaskadenschaltung f
F: montage m en cascade
cascades cooler
D: Kaskadenkühler m (Granulat)
F: installation f de refroidissement en cascades
casing n
D: Gehäuse n
F: boîte f, caisse f
casing of a joint
D: Muffengehäuse n
F: boîte f de jonction
cast bar [c. c. r.]
D: Gießstrang m
F: barre f coulée
casting n
D: Gießling m
F: pièce f coulée
casting n
D: Gießen n (in Formen)
F: coulage m, coulée f
casting, continuous ~
D: Strangguß m
F: coulée f continue, coulage m continu
casting, continuous ~ and rolling plant
D: Gießwalzanlage f
F: installation f de coulée continue laminage
casting rate
D: Gießgeschwindigkeit f
F: vitesse f de coulée
casting resin
D: Gießharz n
F: résine f moulée
casting resin insulator
D: Gießharz-Isolator m
F: isolateur m en résine moulée
casting resin joint
D: Gießharz-Muffe f
F: jonction f en résine moulée
casting speed
D: Gießgeschwindigkeit f
F: vitesse f de coulée
casting temperature
D: Gießtemperatur f
F: température f de coulée
casting wheel [c. c. r.]
D: Gießrad n
F: roue f de coulée
cast iron joint box
D: gußeisernes Muffengehäuse
F: boîte f de jonction en fonte
cast resin
D: Gießharz n
F: résine f moulée
catenary n
D: Kettenlinie f
F: chaînette f
catenary control [vulc.]
D: Durchhangregelung f
F: contrôle m de la flèche
catenary sensing unit (on catenary vulcanization line) [vulc.]
D: Durchhang-Abtastgerät n
F: détecteur m de flèche
catenary vulcanization
D: Kettenlinien-Vulkanisation f
F: vulcanisation f en chaînette
catenary wire
D: Tragdraht m (für Fahrdraht)
F: fil m de suspension (pour fil de contact)
caterpillar pad
D: Raupenglied n
F: patin m de chenille
caterpillar pull-off
D: Raupenabzug m
F: chenille f de tirage
caterpuller
D: Raupenabzug m
F: chenille f de tirage
CATH-copper n (electrolytic cathode copper)
D: KE-Kupfer n (Kathoden-Elektrolyt-Kupfer)

F: cuivre *m* cathodique électrolytique

cathode copper
D: Kathodenkupfer *n*
F: cuivre *m* cathodique

cathodic protection
D: kathodischer Korrosionsschutz
F: protection *f* cathodique

CATV (s. Community Antenna Television)

CATV cable (Community Antenna Television cable)
D: Kabel für (Orts-)Gemeinschafts-Fernsehantennen
F: câble *m* CATV (câble de réception collective d'antenne de télévision)

catwalk *n*
D: Laufboden *m*, Laufbühne *f*
F: passerelle *f*

cavity *n*
D: Hohlraum *m*
F: vide *m*, cavité *f*

C.C.P. (s. cross-connection point)

cells *pl*
D: Zellen *f pl* (im Öldruckausgleichsgefäß), Membranen *f pl* (im Öldruckausgleichsgefäß), *pl*
F: cellules *f pl*

cellular PE
D: Zell-PE *n*, verschäumtes PE, verzelltes PE
F: polyéthylène *m* mousse, polyéthylène *m* cellulaire

cellular PE-insulated wire (core)
D: Zell-PE-isolierte Ader
F: conducteur *m* isolé au PE cellulaire

cellular plastic
D: Schaum-Kunststoff *m*
F: mousse *f* (synthétique), plastique *m* cellulaire

cement *vt*
D: kleben *vt*
F: coller *vt*, attacher *vt*

center (US) (s. centre (GB))

centering *n*
D: Zentrierung *f*
F: centrage *m*

central *n* (US) [tel.]
D: Amt *n*
F: central *m*

central office [tel.]
D: Amt *n*
F: central *m*

central spinner
D: Zentralspinner *m*, Zentralwickler *m*
F: rubaneuse *f* centrale

central spiral
D: Stützwendel *f* (im Hohlleiter)
F: hélice *f* de support

centre blind core
D: Mittelblindader *f*
F: bourrage *m* central

centre conductor
D: Mittelleiter *m*
F: conducteur *m* médian

centre filler
D: Mittelblindader *f*
F: bourrage *m* central

centre line of a machine
D: Mittellinie einer Maschine
F: ligne *f* centrale d'une machine, axe *m* médian d'une machine

centre of a paper pad [lapp.]
D: Kern einer Papierscheibe
F: centre *m* d'une galette à papier, bague *f* d'une galette à papier

centre spacing
D: Mittenabstand *m*, Achsabstand *m*
F: distance *f* d'axe en axe, distance *f* des centres

centre-to-centre distance
D: Mittenabstand *m*, Achsabstand *m*
F: distance *f* d'axe en axe, distance *f* des centres

centricity *n*
D: Zentrizität *f*
F: centricité *f*

certification *n*
D: Zulassung *f*
F: homologation *f*

certification mark
D: Zulassungszeichen *n*
F: marque *f* d'homologation

chain drive
D: Kettenantrieb *m*
F: transmission *f* par chaîne, commande *f* par chaîne

chain insulator
D: Kettenisolator *m*, Hängeisolator *m*
F: isolateur *m* suspendu, isolateur *m* de suspension

chalk *n*
D: Kreide *f*
F: carbonate *m* de calcium, craie *f*

chalk box

chalk layer
- D: Kreidekasten *m* (Kabelfertigung)
- F: bac *m* à craie

chalk layer
- D: Kalkschicht *f*, Kalküberzug *m*
- F: couche de chaux *f*

chamber *n*
- D: Kammer *f*
- F: chambre *f*, compartiment *m*

chamber, cable jointing ~
- D: Muffenbunker *m*, Muffenbauwerk *n*, Kabelschacht *m*
- F: trou *m* d'homme, puits *m* de visite, puits *m* de jonction, chambre *f* de répartition, puits *m* à câbles

chamfer *v*
- D: abschrägen *v*
- F: chanfreiner *v*, biseauter *v*

change *v*
- D: abändern *v*, ändern *v*
- F: modifier *v*, changer *v*, réviser *v*

change *v* (gear) [mech.]
- D: schalten *v*
- F: changer *v* de vitesse (engrenage)

change gear
- D: Wechselgetriebe *n*
- F: variateur *m* de vitesse, engrenage *m* de changement de vitesse

change of lay
- D: Drallwechsel *m*
- F: inversion *f* de la torsion, changement *m* de la torsion, changement *m* du pas de câblage

change of load
- D: Lastwechsel *m*
- F: alternance *f* de l'effort, cycle *m* de l'effort, cycle *m* de charge

change of polarity
- D: Umpolung *f*, Polwechsel *m*, Umkehr der Polarität
- F: inversion *f* de polarité

change-over *n*
- D: Umschaltung *f*
- F: commutation *f*

change-over switch
- D: Umschalter *m*
- F: commutateur *m*

channel *n*
- D: Übertragungsweg *m*, Übertragungskanal *m*
- F: voie *f* de transmission, voie *f* de transport

channel black
- D: Kanalruß *m*
- F: noir *m* au tunnel

characteristic cable impedance
- D: Kabelwiderstand *m*
- F: impédance *f* caractéristique de câble

characteristic curve
- D: Kennlinie *f*
- F: caractéristique *f*, courbe *f* caractéristique

characteristic impedance
- D: Wellenwiderstand *m*
- F: impédance *f* caractéristique

characteristic of a curve
- D: Kurvenverlauf *m*, Verlauf einer Kurve
- F: allure *f* d'une courbe

characteristic value
- D: Kennwert *m*, Bestimmungsgröße *f*
- F: paramètre *m*, valeur *f* caractéristique

charge *v*
- D: laden *v*, belasten *v*
- F: charger *v*

charge *v* [mech., el.]
- D: speisen *v*, einspeisen *v*, beschicken *v*
- F: alimenter *v*, charger *v*

charge *n* [el.]
- D: Ladung *f*
- F: charge *f*

charge carrier
- D: Ladungsträger *m*
- F: porteur *m* de charge

charging current
- D: Ladestrom *m*
- F: courant *m* de charge

charred *adj*
- D: verkohlt *adj*
- F: carbonisé *adj*

charring of the insulation
- D: Anbrennen der Isolierung, Verkohlen der Isolierung
- F: carbonisation *f* de l'isolant

chart *n*
- D: Kurvenbild *n*, Diagramm *n*, graphische Darstellung
- F: diagramme *m*, représentation *f* graphique, graphique *m*

chart recorder
- D: Bandschreiber *m*
- F: enregistreur *m* à papier déroulant

check *v*
- D: prüfen *v*

check
  F: essayer v, vérifier v, contrôler v
check n
  D: Untersuchung f, Prüfung f (Kontrolle)
  F: examen m, analyse f, contrôle m
check point
  D: Meßpunkt m
  F: point m de mesure
check valve
  D: Rückschlagventil n
  F: soupape f de retenue
chemical cross-linking
  D: chemische Vernetzung
  F: réticulation f chimique
chemically cross-linked polyethylene (XLPE)
  D: chemisch vernetztes Polyäthylen (VPE)
  F: polyéthylène m réticulé chimiquement (PRC)
chill v
  D: abschrecken v
  F: tremper v
china clay
  D: Kaolin n
  F: caolin m, kaolin m
chipping n
  D: Befräsen n (Kupfer-Drahtbarren)
  F: scalpage m, décortiquage m
chlorosulphonated PE (CSPE)
  D: chlorsulfoniertes PE (CSPE)
  F: polyéthylène m chlorosulfoné (CSPE)
chopped d.c. voltage
  D: zerhackte Gleichspannung
  F: tension f continue vibrée
circuit n
  D: Stromkreis m
  F: circuit m électrique
circuit arrangement
  D: Schaltung f, Verdrahtung f
  F: circuit m, montage m, schéma m de connexions, filerie f
circuit breaker
  D: Ausschalter m, Abschalter m
  F: discontacteur m, disjoncteur m, interrupteur m
circuit diagram
  D: Schaltplan m, Schaltschema n, Verdrahtungsplan m
  F: schéma m électrique, plan m de câblage, plan m des circuits, schéma m des connexions

circuitry n
  D: Schaltung f, Verdrahtung f
  F: circuit m, montage m, schéma m de connexions, filerie f
circular chart recorder
  D: Kreisdiagrammschreiber m
  F: enregistreur m à diagramme circulaire
circular conductor
  D: Rundleiter m
  F: âme f ronde, âme f circulaire
circulating air ag(e)ing
  D: Alterung im Umluftofen, Umluftalterung f
  F: vieillissement m en étuve à circulation d'air, vieillissement m par circulation d'air
circulating pump
  D: Umwälzpumpe f
  F: pompe f de (à) circulation
circulation n
  D: Umlauf m
  F: circulation f
circulation, cooling water ~
  D: Kühlwasserumlauf m
  F: circulation f d'eau de refroidissement
circumferential reinforcement tape [cab.]
  D: Druckschutzwendel f
  F: frettage m
circumferential speed
  D: Umfangsgeschwindigkeit f
  F: vitesse f périphérique, vitesse f circonférentielle
clamp v
  D: festklemmen v
  F: brider v, attacher v, serrer v, agrafer v
clamp n
  D: Klemme f
  F: pince f, attache f
clamp, to ~ a cable
  D: Kabel mit Schellen befestigen
  F: brider v le câble
clamped joint
  D: Klemmverbindung f
  F: raccord m boulonné
clamping jaw
  D: Einspannklaue f, Einspannklemme f, Klemmbacke f
  F: mâchoire f de serrage, mordache f
clamping length [test]

clamping ring
D: Einspannlänge f
F: longueur f libre entre mâchoires

clamping ring
D: Klemmring m
F: bague f de serrage

clamp ring
D: Klemmring m
F: bague f de serrage

claw-type clamp
D: Tatzenklemme f
F: borne f en forme de griffe

clear, to ~ a fault
D: eine Störung beseitigen
F: éliminer v un défaut, supprimer v un défaut, dépanner v

clearance n
D: Aussparung f
F: découpe f, évidement m

clearance n
D: Zwischenraum m
F: espace m, intervalle m, jeu m

clear bore (for cable)
D: Bohrung f (für den Kabeldurchlauf)
F: passage m pour cable

cleat v
D: festklemmen v
F: brider v, attacher v, serrer v, agrafer v

cleat n
D: Schelle f, Befestigungsschelle f
F: collier m, bride f

cleavage n [chem.]
D: Abspaltung f
F: libération f, dégagement m

cleavage brittleness [met.]
D: interkristalline Brüchigkeit
F: fragilité f intercristalline

clip n
D: Klemme f
F: pince f, attache f

clip n
D: Schelle f, Befestigungsschelle f
F: collier m, bride f

clip n [c. install.]
D: Stiftschelle f
F: attache f

clockwise adj
D: im Uhrzeigersinn
F: dans le sens des aiguilles d'une montre

clockwise rotation [mach.]
D: Rechtsdrehung f
F: rotation f en sens des aiguilles d'une montre

close bond
D: innige Verbindung
F: liaison f intime

closed circuit
D: geschlossener Kreis, geschlossener Kreislauf
F: circuit m fermé

closed circuit [el.]
D: Schleife f (Leitungszusammenführung)
F: boucle f, circuit m fermé

closed-circuit television
D: Kabelfernsehen n
F: télévision f par câble

closed-circuit television (factory)
D: Industriefernsehen n
F: télévision f industrielle

closed corrugation
D: geschlossene Ringwellung
F: ondulation f à anneaux fermés

closed helix
D: geschlossene Wendel
F: hélice f fermée

closed helix, in a ~ [lapp.]
D: auf Stoß
F: en hélice fermée, en spires jointives

close examination
D: eingehende Prüfung
F: essai m détaillé, examen m détaillé, contrôle m minutieux

close-fitting adj
D: fest anliegend, festsitzend adj
F: étant bien serré

close tolerance
D: enge Toleranz
F: tolérance f étroite

close tolerance extrusion
D: Extrusion mit engen Toleranzen
F: extrusion f avec tolérances étroites

closing die
D: Verseilnippel m
F: filière f d'assemblage, filière f de câblage

cloud point
D: Erstarrungspunkt m (Öle), Stockpunkt m (Öle)
F: point m de figeage

coal cutter cable
D: Schrämleitung f
F: câble m de haveuse

coal tar
D: Steinkohlenteer m

coal

F: goudron *m* minéral, goudron *m* de houille

coarse adjustment
D: Grobeinstellung *f*
F: réglage *m* approximatif, réglage *m* grossier

coarse-grain structure
D: grobkörnige Struktur
F: structure *f* à gros grains

coat *v*
D: beschichten *v*
F: revêtir *v*, enduire *v*

coated with ...
D: kaschiert mit ...
F: contrecouché *adj* de ..., contrecollé *adj* de ..., revêtu *adj* de ..., doublé *adj* de ...,

coating *n*
D: Überzug *m*, Beschichtung *f*
F: revêtement *m*, enrobage *m*

coating *n*
D: Überziehen *n* (Masse, Kleber, Korrosionsschutz), Aufbringen *n* (Masse, Kleber, Korrosionsschutz)
F: enduction *f*

coating of whiting
D: Kreideüberzug *m*
F: enduction *f* en craie

coaxial cable
D: Koaxialkabel *n*, konzentrisches Zweileiterkabel, konzentrisches Kabel
F: câble *m* coaxial, câble *m* concentrique

coaxial cable for high-frequency transmission
D: Hochfrequenz-Koaxialkabel *n*, koaxiales Hochfrequenzkabel
F: câble *m* coaxial à haute fréquence, câble *m* coaxial à fréquence radioélectrique

coaxial line
D: Koaxialleitung *f*, konzentrische Leitung
F: ligne *f* coaxiale, liaison *f* coaxiale, ligne *f* à conducteur concentrique

coaxial line for long distance traffic
D: Koaxialleitung für den Fernverkehr
F: ligne *f* coaxiale pour trafic à longue distance

coaxial pair
D: Koaxialpaar *n*
F: paire *f* coaxiale

coaxial tube
D: Koax-Tube *f*
F: tube *m* coaxial

cobble shears *pl*
D: Abfallschere *f*
F: cisailles *f pl* à déchets

code *n* [cab.]
D: Kennzeichen *n*
F: marque *f*, code *m*

code designation
D: Typenbezeichnung *f*, Typenkurzzeichen *n*
F: code *m* de désignation

code number [cab.]
D: Kennziffer *f*
F: chiffre *m* distinctif, numéro-repère *m*, repère *m* numérique

coding *n* [cab.]
D: Kennzeichnung *f*
F: désignation *f*, identification *f*, marquage *m*, repérage *m*

coefficient *n*
D: Beiwert *n*
F: coefficient *m*

coefficient of expansion
D: Ausdehnungskoeffizient *m*
F: coefficient *m* de dilatation

coefficient of heat transfer
D: Wärmeübertragungskoeffizient *m*
F: coefficient *m* de transmission calorifique

coefficient of linear expansion
D: linearer Ausdehnungskoeffizient
F: coefficient *m* de dilatation linéaire

coil *v*
D: aufwickeln *v*, aufspulen *v*, spulen *v*, wickeln *v*, auftrommeln *v*
F: enrouler *v*, bobiner *v*

coil *n*
D: Ring *m* (Draht/Kabel)
F: couronne *f* (fil métallique/câble)

coil *n*
D: Spule *f*
F: bobine *f*

coil *n*
D: Wicklung *f*
F: enroulement *m*, bobinage *m*

coil *n* (metal tape)
D: Bandscheibe *f*
F: galette *f*

coil, to ~ the cable into the ship's hold
D: Kabel in den Schiffsladeraum

einschießen
F: enrouler *v* le câble dans la cale d'un navire, stocker *v* le câble dans la cale d'un navire, lover *v* le câble dans la cale d'un navire

coiled pipe
D: Rohrschlange *f*
F: serpentin *m*, tuyau *m* serpentin

coiler *n*
D: Wickler *m*, Umwickelei *f*
F: enrouleuse *f*, enrouleur *m*, bobineuse *f*

coiling basket
D: Bundwickler *m*, Wickelkorb *m*
F: corbeille *f* d'enroulement, panier *m* d'enroulement

coil-loaded *adj*
D: pupinisiert *adj*
F: pupinisé *adj*

coil-loaded cable
D: Pupinkabel *n*
F: câble *m* pupinisé

coil-loaded circuit
D: Pupinleitung *f*
F: circuit *m* pupinisé

coil-loaded line
D: bespulte Leitung
F: ligne *f* pupinisée

coil-loading *n*
D: Bespulung *f*, Pupinisierung *f*
F: pupinisation *f*, charge *f* au moyen de bobines en série

coil of rod
D: Walzdrahtring *m*, Grobdrahtring *m*
F: couronne *f* de fil machine

coil of wire
D: Drahtring *m*, Drahtbund *m*
F: couronne *f* de fil métallique

cold bending test
D: Kältebiegeprüfung *f*, Kaltbiegeprüfung *f*, Kältewickelprüfung *f*
F: essai *m* de pliage à froid, essai *m* de pliage à basse température, essai *m* d'enroulement à basse température

cold-chamber *n*
D: Kälteraum *m*
F: frigorifère *m*

cold cure
D: Kaltvulkanisation *f*
F: vulcanisation *f* à froid

cold filling compound
D: Kaltvergußmasse *f*, Kaltfüllmasse *f*
F: matière *f* de remplissage à froid

cold flow resistance
D: Kaltfließbeständigkeit *f*
F: résistance *f* au fluage à froid

cold lap
D: Kaltschweißstelle *f*
F: rebut *m*

cold pouring compound
D: Kaltvergußmasse *f*, Kaltfüllmasse *f*
F: matière *f* de remplissage à froid

cold pressure welding
D: Kaltschweißen *n*, Kaltpreßschweißen *n*
F: soudage *m* à froid

cold-resistant *adj*
D: kältebeständig *adj*
F: résistant *adj* au froid, résistant *adj* aux basses températures,

cold-roll *v*
D: kaltwalzen *v*
F: laminer *v* à froid

cold rolling mill
D: Kaltwalzwerk *n*
F: laminoir *m* à froid

cold-setting *n*
D: Kalthärten *n* (Gießharze)
F: durcissage *m* à froid

cold-setting compound
D: kalthärtende Masse
F: matière *f* durcissable à froid

cold shut
D: Kaltschweißstelle *f*
F: rebut *m*

cold solder joint
D: Kaltlötstelle *f*
F: soudure *f* froide

cold vulcanization
D: Kaltvulkanisation *f*
F: vulcanisation *f* à froid

cold welding
D: Kaltschweißen *n*, Kaltpreßschweißen *n*
F: soudage *m* à froid

cold-working *n*
D: Kaltformung *f*, Kaltumformung *f*
F: façonnage *m* à froid, formage *m* à froid

collapse *v*
D: zusammenfallen *v*
F: effondrer *v* (s'), écrouler *v* (s')

collar band
D: Rohrschelle *f*

collar
F: bride f d'attache, collier m pour tubes

collection platform
D: Stapelbühne f
F: plate-forme f d'empilage

colo(u)r v
D: färben v
F: colorer v, teindre v

colo(u)r n
D: Farbe f
F: couleur f

colo(u)rant n
D: Farbstoff m
F: pigment m, matière colorante f

colo(u)r batch
D: Farbkonzentrat n, Farbbatch n
F: mélange m coloré maître

colo(u)r code
D: farbige Kennzeichnung
F: repérage m coloré, code m de couleur

colo(u)r coding
D: farbige Kennzeichnung
F: repérage m coloré, code m de couleur

colo(u)r concentrate
D: Farbkonzentrat n, Farbbatch n
F: mélange m coloré maître

colo(u)r compound
D: durchgefärbte Mischung
F: mélange m coloré dans la masse

colo(u)red helix
D: farbige Spirale, farbige Wendel
F: spirale f colorée, hélice f colorée

colo(u)red spiral
D: farbige Spirale, farbige Wendel
F: spirale f colorée, hélice f colorée

colo(u)r-fast adj
D: farbecht adj
F: de couleur résistante

colo(u)r-fastness
D: Farbbeständigkeit f
F: permanence f de la teinte, stabilité f de la couleur

colo(u)ring n
D: Färbung f
F: coloration f

colo(u)r marking
D: Farbmarkierung f
F: marquage m à l'encre, marquage m coloré

colo(u)r retention
D: Farbbeständigkeit f
F: permanence f de la teinte, stabilité f de la couleur

colo(u)r shade
D: Farbtönung f
F: nuance f de couleur, teinte f

combination pliers pl
D: Kombizange f
F: pince f universelle

combining circuit
D: Stammkreis m, Stammleitung f
F: circuit m combinant, circuit m réel

combust v
D: verbrennen vi
F: brûler v, carboniser v

combustible adj
D: brennbar adj, entflammbar adj
F: combustible adj, inflammable adj

commercial adj
D: handelsüblich adj
F: commercial adj, du type commercial

commercial, to bring into ~ operation
D: in Betrieb nehmen
F: mettre v en service, mettre v en œuvre

commercially produced
D: hergestellt im Fertigungsmaßstab
F: réalisé adj à l'échelle industrielle

commercial scale trial
D: Versuch im Betriebsmaßstab
F: essai m à l'échelle industrielle

commercial size plant
D: Anlage im Betriebsmaßstab
F: installation f à l'échelle industrielle

commission, to take into ~
D: in Betrieb nehmen
F: mettre v en service, mettre v en œuvre

commissioning n
D: Inbetriebnahme f
F: mise f en oeuvre, mise f en service

Commonwealth-Pacific telephone cable (COMPAC cable)
D: Commonwealth-Pazifik-Kabel n
F: câble m téléphonique Commonwealth-Pacifique

communications cable
D: Fernmeldekabel n, Nachrichtenkabel n
F: câble m de télécommunication, câble m de communication

communications engineering
D: Nachrichtentechnik f

communications network
 D: Nachrichtennetz *n*
 F: réseau *m* de communications
community antenna
 D: Gemeinschaftsantenne *f*
 F: antenne *f* collective
Community Antenna Television (CATV)
 D: Gemeinschaftsantennenfernsehen *n*, Ortsantennen-Fernsehen *n*, Stadtgemeinschaftsantennen-Fernsehen *n*
 F: réception *f* collective d'antenne de télévision
community antenna television (CATV) cable
 D: Ortsgemeinschaftsantennen-Fernsehkabel *n*
 F: câble *m* de réception collective d'antenne de télévision
Community Antenna Television System (CATV)
 D: Großgemeinschaftsantennen-Anlage (GGA) *f*
 F: installation *f* de réception collective d'antenne de télévision
COMPAC cable (s. Commonwealth-Pacific telephone cable)
compact *v*
 D: verdichten *v*
 F: rétreindre *v*, compacter *v*, comprimer *v*
compact(ed) conductor
 D: verdichteter Leiter
 F: âme *f* rétreinte, âme *f* compactée
compacted sand
 D: verdichteter Sand
 F: sable *m* compacté
compacted strand
 D: verdichteter Leiter
 F: âme *f* rétreinte, âme *f* compactée
compacting head [strand.]
 D: Verdichter *m*
 F: tête *f* de compression
compacting tool
 D: Verdichtungswerkzeug *n*
 F: filière *f* de rétreint
compaction of the conductor
 D: Verdichtung des Leiters
 F: compactage *m* de l'âme, rétreint *m* de l'âme
compaction of the soil [c. install.]
 D: Verdichtung des Erdbodens
 F: compression *f* du sol
comparative measurement
 D: Vergleichsmessung *f*
 F: mesure *f* comparative
comparative resistance
 D: Vergleichswiderstand *m*
 F: résistance *f* de comparaison
comparative test
 D: Vergleichsprüfung *f*
 F: essai *m* comparatif
comparative value
 D: Vergleichswert *m*
 F: valeur *f* de référence, valeur *f* comparative
compartment *n*
 D: Kammer *f*
 F: chambre *f*, compartiment *m*
compatibility *n*
 D: Verträglichkeit *f*
 F: compatibilité *f*
compatibility test
 D: Verträglichkeitsprüfung *f*
 F: essai *m* de compatibilité, essai *m* de non-contamination
compensation *n*
 D: Ausgleich *m*
 F: compensation *f*, équilibrage *m*, équilibre *m*, balance *f*, égalisation *f*
compensation by alteration of twist [com. c.]
 D: Ausgleichen durch Dralländerung
 F: compensation *f* par changement du pas de câblage
compensation by crossing [com. c.]
 D: Ausgleichen durch Kreuzen
 F: compensation *f* par croisement
compensation by grouping according to electrical values [com. c.]
 D: Ausgleichen durch Gruppieren nach elektrischen Werten
 F: compensation *f* par groupement suivant les valeurs électriques
compensation of temperature
 D: Temperaturausgleich *m*
 F: égalisation *f* de la température, compensation *f* de la température
compensation of voltage
 D: Spannungsausgleich *m*
 F: équilibrage *m* de la tension
completion *n*
 D: Endbearbeitung *f*, Endfertigung *f*
 F: finissage *m*, finition *f*

comply with v[test]
  D: einhalten v (Werte, Bedingungen)
  F: respecter v, observer v
component n[cab.]
  D: Bauelement n
  F: élément m constitutif, élément m de construction
component n
  D: Komponente f
  F: composante f
component drawing
  D: Einzelzeichnung f, Teilzeichnung f
  F: plan m de détail
composite n
  D: Verbundwerkstoff m
  F: complexe m, matériau m composite
composite bonded laminar insulation
  D: Mehrschicht-Isolierung f, Schichtisolierung f
  F: isolation f stratifiée, isolation f laminée
composite cable
  D: kombiniertes Kabel
  F: câble m composite
composite layer sheath
  D: Schichtenmantel m
  F: gaine f composite, gaine f complexe
composite material
  D: Verbundwerkstoff m
  F: complexe m, matériau m composite
composition n
  D: Gemisch n
  F: mélange m, composition f
compound v[rub., plast.]
  D: mischen v
  F: mélanger v
compound n
  D: Mischung f
  F: mélange m
compound, migrating ~ [cab.]
  D: abwandernde Masse
  F: matière f migrante
compound bunch
  D: Seil aus Würgelitzen
  F: corde f de torsades
compounded jute
  D: compoundierte Jute
  F: jute f compoundée
compound formula
  D: Rezept einer Mischung
  F: formule f d'un mélange
compound formulation
  D: Ansatz einer Mischung, Mischungsansatz m
  F: formulation f d'un mélange
compound-impregnated adj
  D: massegetränkt adj
  F: imprégné adj de matière
compound preparation
  D: Ansetzen einer Mischung, Mischungsaufbereitung f
  F: préparation f d'un mélange
compress v
  D: verdichten v
  F: rétreindre v, compacter v, comprimer v
compressed air
  D: Druckluft f
  F: air m comprimé
compressed-air control
  D: Druckluftbetätigung f
  F: commande f à air comprimé, commande f pneumatique
compressed gas
  D: Druckgas n
  F: gaz m comprimé
compressed gas(SF$_6$)-insulated transmission line
  D: SF$_6$-isoliertes Leitersystem, SF$_6$-Rohrleiter m, SF$_6$-Rohrschiene f
  F: liaison f blindée isolée au SF$_6$, canalisation f blindée isolée au SF$_6$
compressed joint
  D: Preßverbindung f
  F: raccord m poinçonné
compressed strand
  D: verdichteter Leiter
  F: âme f rétreinte, âme f compactée
compression n
  D: Zusammendrückung f
  F: compression f
compression cable
  D: Außendruckkabel n
  F: câble m à compression
compression degree
  D: Verdichtungsgrad m (Leiter), Anwalzgrad m (Leiter)
  F: coefficient m de rétreint
compression of the conductor
  D: Verdichtung des Leiters
  F: compactage m de l'âme, rétreint m de l'âme
compression of the soil [c. install.]

compression test
D: Druckversuch *m*
F: essai *m* de pression, essai *m* de compression

compression tool [c. access.]
D: Preßwerkzeug *n*
F: outil *m* de poinçonnage

compression type cable lug
D: Preßkabelschuh *m*
F: cosse *f* de câble à poinçonner, cosse *f* de câble à sertir

compression type sleeve
D: Preßverbinder *m*
F: manchon *m* à poinçonner

compressive strength
D: Druckbeständigkeit *f*, Druckfestigkeit *f*
F: résistance *f* à l'écrasement, résistance *f* à la pression

compressive stress
D: Druckbeanspruchung *f*
F: contrainte *f* de compression, effort *m* de compression

computer-controlled *adj*
D: rechnergesteuert *adj*
F: commandé *adj* par ordinateur

concealed *adj* [c. install.]
D: unter Putz
F: encastré *adj*, sous enduit, sous crépi

concealed wiring
D: Unterputz-Installation *f*, Verlegung unter Putz
F: installation *f* sous crépi, pose *f* sous crépi, pose *f* encastrée

concentric cable
D: Koaxialkabel *n*, konzentrisches Zweileiterkabel, konzentrisches Kabel
F: câble *m* coaxial, câble *m* concentrique

concentric conductor
D: konzentrischer Leiter
F: âme *f* concentrique

concentric-conductor line
D: Koaxialleitung *f*, konzentrische Leitung
F: ligne *f* coaxiale, liaison *f* coaxiale, ligne *f* à conducteur concentrique

concentric lapper
D: Zentralspinner *m*, Zentralwickler *m*
F: rubaneuse *f* centrale

concentric lapping head
D: Zentralspinnkopf *m*
F: tête *f* rubaneuse centrale, tête *f* de rubanage centrale

concentric lapping machine
D: Zentralspinner *m*, Zentralwickler *m*
F: rubaneuse *f* centrale

concentric lay conductor
D: Leiter aus konzentrisch verseilten Drahtlagen
F: âme *f* câblée en couches concentriques

concentric layer cable
D: lagenverseiltes Kabel, Lagenkabel *n*
F: câble *m* à couches concentriques, câble *m* en couches

concentric neutral conductor
D: konzentrischer Nulleiter
F: neutre *m* concentrique, neutre *m* périphérique

concentric strand
D: Leiter aus konzentrisch verseilten Drahtlagen
F: âme *f* câblée en couches concentriques

concentric test-shield
D: konzentrischer Prüfschirm
F: écran *m* d'essai concentrique

conclusions, to permit ~ as to
D: Aufschluß geben über (z.B. Betriebsverhalten)
F: fournir *v* des renseignements sur

condenser cone
D: Kondensatorkeule *f*
F: cône *m* de condensateur

condenser oil
D: Kondensatoröl *n*
F: huile *f* de condensateur

conditioned air
D: klimatisierte Atmosphäre, konditionierte Luft
F: atmosphère *f* conditionnée

conditioned atmosphere
D: klimatisierte Atmosphäre, konditionierte Luft
F: atmosphère *f* conditionnée

conduct, to ~ a test
D: eine Prüfung durchführen
F: faire *v* un essai, effectuer *v* un essai

conduct, to ~ away the heat
D: die Wärme ableiten
F: dissiper v la chaleur

conductance n
D: Leitwert m
F: conductance f

conductance n [com. c.]
D: Ableitung f, Ableitungsverlust m
F: perditance f

conducting varnish
D: Leitlack m
F: vernis m semi-conducteur

conductive adj
D: leitfähig adj, leitend adj
F: conducteur adj (-trice), conductible adj

conductivity n
D: Leitfähigkeit f, Leitvermögen n
F: conductibilité f, conductivité f

conductivity, I.A.C.S. ~ (International Annealed Copper Standard/IEC)
D: Standard-Leitfähigkeit nach IEC (Kupfer), I.A.C.S.-Leitfähigkeit f (Kupfer)
F: conductivité f I.A.C.S. (cuivre), conductibilité f I.A.C.S. (cuivre)

conductor n
D: Leiter m
F: âme f conductrice, conducteur m

conductor break
D: Leiterbruch m
F: rupture f de l'âme

conductor design
D: Leiteraufbau m
F: constitution f de l'âme conductrice

conductor field strength
D: Leiterfeldstärke f
F: intensité m de champ au conducteur, gradient m au conducteur

conductor gradient
D: Leiterfeldstärke f
F: intensité m de champ au conducteur, gradient m au conducteur

conductor losses
D: Leiterverluste m pl
F: pertes f pl sur l'âme

conductor rail
D: Stromschiene f
F: rail m de contact

conductor resistance
D: Leiterwiderstand m
F: résistance f électrique de l'âme

conductor strand
D: Leiterseil n
F: toron m

conductor stranding
D: Leiterverseilung f, Verseilung f
F: câblage m (âme)

conductor temperature
D: Leitertemperatur f
F: température f à l'âme

conductor unit
D: Leiterbündel n
F: faisceau m d'âmes

conductor with reduced cross-sectional area
D: halber Leiter
F: âme f à section réduite

conduit bend
D: Rohrbogen m, Rohrkrümmung f, Rohrknie n, Knierohr n, Krümmer m (Rohr)
F: coude m, raccord m coudé

conduit cable
D: Röhrenkabel n
F: câble m posé en conduites

conduit for leading in cables
D: Einführungskanal für Kabel
F: conduite f pour l'introduction des câbles

congested area [c. install.]
D: dicht besiedeltes Gebiet, Ballungszentrum n
F: grande agglomération urbaine, zone f de forte agglomération

congested areas [cab.]
D: stark belegte Räume
F: zones f pl à forte accumulation

conglomerate v
D: zusammenbacken v
F: agglomérer v, agglutiner v, coller v

conglomeration n
D: Zusammenballung f
F: agglomération f, agglutination f

Congo Red test
D: Kongo-Rot-Prüfung f
F: essai m au rouge de Congo

conic(al) adj
D: verjüngt adj, konisch adj
F: effilé adj, à section décroissante, conique adj

connect v
D: verbinden v

F: raccorder v, lier v, joindre v, réunir v

connect v [el.]
D: schalten v
F: connecter v, brancher v, monter v, relier v

connect, to ~ through [tel.]
D: durchschalten v
F: relier v, mettre v en communication

connect, to ~ to earth
D: erden v
F: mettre v à la terre, relier v à la terre

connected load
D: Anschlußleistung f, Anschlußwert m
F: puissance f connectée, puissance f absorbée

connecting n [cab.]
D: Verbinden n
F: raccordement m

connecting block [el.]
D: Anschlußleiste f, Klemmleiste f
F: bloc m de connexion, réglette f de raccordement, réglette f à bornes, barrette f à bornes

connecting box
D: Verbindungsmuffe f
F: boîte f de jonction, jonction f

connecting box
D: Abzweigkasten m, Abzweigdose f, Kabelverzweiger m, Abzweigmuffe f, Verteilerkasten m
F: boîte f de dérivation, boîte f de branchement, boîte f de distribution

connecting cable
D: Verbindungskabel n, Schaltkabel n
F: câble m de jonction, câble m de connexion

connecting cord
D: Anschlußschnur f
F: câble m souple, cordon m de raccordement

connecting piece
D: Zwischenstück n, Verbindungsstück n, Anschlußstück n
F: pièce f intermédiaire, pièce f de raccordement, raccord m, pièce f de jonction, adaptateur m

connecting piece
D: Stutzen m
F: manchon m, raccord m, tubulure f

connecting plug
D: Anschlußstecker m
F: fiche f de raccordement

connecting sleeve
D: Verbindungshülse f
F: manchon m de jonction, manchon m de raccordement

connecting terminal [el.]
D: Klemme f, Anschlußklemme f, Verbindungsklemme f, Endenanschlußklemme f
F: borne f, connecteur m, borne f de raccordement

connection n
D: Verbindung f, Verbindungsstelle f
F: jonction f

connection n
D: Stutzen m
F: manchon m, raccord m, tubulure f

connection box [el.]
D: Anschlußkasten m, Klemmenkasten m
F: coffret m de distribution, boîte f de distribution, boîte f de dérivation, boîte f de connexion, coffret m de raccordement, boîte f de jonction, boîte f à bornes

connection box
D: Anschlußdose f
F: boîte f de jonction, boîte f de raccordement

connection cable
D: Anschlußkabel n
F: câble m de raccordement

connections, electrical ~
D: elektrische Anschlüsse
F: liaisons f pl électriques, raccords m pl électriques

connections pl **for measurement**
D: Meßanordnung f, Meßschaltung f
F: disposition f de mesure, montage m de mesure, couplage m de mesure

connection strip [el.]
D: Anschlußleiste f, Klemmleiste f
F: bloc m de connexion, réglette f de raccordement, réglette f à bornes, barrette f à bornes

connection to earth (GB)
D: Erdung f
F: mise f à la terre

connection to ground (US)
D: Erdung f

connection

F: mise f à la terre

connector n
D: Zwischenstück n, Verbindungsstück n, Anschlußstück n
F: pièce f intermédiaire, pièce f de raccordement, raccord m, pièce f de jonction, adaptateur m

connector n [el.]
D: Klemme f, Anschlußklemme f, Verbindungsklemme f, Endenanschlußklemme f
F: borne f, connecteur m, borne f de raccordement

connector n
D: Anschlußstecker m
F: fiche f de raccordement

connector socket
D: Steckbuchse f, Steckerbuchse f, Fassung f
F: prise f femelle, fiche f femelle, douille f

consistent adj
D: einheitlich adj
F: homogène adj, uniforme adj

constant load
D: gleichbleibende Belastung
F: charge f constante

constituent n
D: Komponente f
F: composante f

construction n [cab.]
D: Bauart f, Typ m
F: construction f, type m

constructional element [cab.]
D: Bauelement n
F: élément m constitutif, élément m de construction

construction drawing
D: Konstruktionszeichnung f
F: plan m de construction, dessin m d'atelier

construction of a cable
D: Kabelaufbau m, Aufbau eines Kabels, Kabelkonstruktion f
F: construction f d'un câble, constitution f d'un câble

contact angle
D: Umschlingungswinkel m
F: angle m de contact, arc m d'enroulement

contact-making pressure gauge
D: Kontaktmanometer n

F: manomètre m à contact, manostat m

contact manometer
D: Kontaktmanometer n
F: manomètre m à contact, manostat m

contactor n
D: Schaltschütz n
F: contacteur-disjoncteur m, contacteur-interrupteur m

contact pressure
D: Auflagedruck m
F: pression f de serrage

contact rail
D: Stromschiene f
F: rail m de contact

contact resistance
D: Übergangswiderstand m
F: résistance f de contact, résistance f de passage

contact sheave
D: Kontaktrolle f
F: galet m de contact

contact voltage
D: Berührungsspannung f
F: tension f de contact

contact wire, overhead ~
D: Fahrdraht m, Schleifdraht m
F: fil m (de) trolley, fil m de contact

container, billet ~ [met. extr. pr.]
D: Blockaufnehmer m, Bolzenaufnehmer m, Aufnehmer m, Preßtopf m, Rezipient m
F: conteneur m de billettes, pot m de presse

container heating system [met. extr. pr.]
D: Aufnehmerheizung f
F: chauffage m du conteneur

container holder [met. extr. pr.]
D: Aufnehmerhalter m
F: support m du conteneur, porte-conteneur m

container shifting device [met. extr. pr.]
D: Aufnehmer-Verschiebevorrichtung f
F: dispositif m de déplacement du conteneur

contamination n
D: Verunreinigung f
F: contamination f, impureté f

continuing studies
D: fortlaufende Untersuchungen
F: études f pl continues

continuity, electrical ~
 D: elektrischer Durchgang
 F: continuité f électrique
continuity, to test the ~ of a coating
 D: einen Überzug auf Porenfreiheit prüfen
 F: essayer v la continuité d'un revêtement
continuity check [el.]
 D: Durchgangsprüfung f, Prüfung auf Durchgang
 F: contrôle m de continuité, essai m de continuité
continuity test [el.]
 D: Durchgangsprüfung f, Prüfung auf Durchgang
 F: contrôle m de continuité, essai m de continuité
continuity tester [el.]
 D: Durchgangsprüfgerät n
 F: dispositif m d'essai de la continuité électrique
continuous adj
 D: kontinuierlich adj
 F: continu adj, en continu
continuous annealer
 D: Durchlaufglühanlage f
 F: installation f de recuit en continu, recuiseur m en continu
continuous annealing plant
 D: Durchlaufglühanlage f
 F: installation f de recuit en continu, recuiseur m en continu
continuous cable sheathing press
 D: kontinuierliche Kabelmantelpresse
 F: presse f de gainage en continu
continuous casting
 D: Strangguß m
 F: coulée f continue, coulage m continu
continuous casting and rolling (CCR)
 D: Gießwalzen n
 F: coulée f continue laminage
continuous casting and rolling plant
 D: Gießwalzanlage f
 F: installation f de coulée continue laminage
continuous current
 D: Gleichstrom m
 F: courant m continu
continuous current carrying test
 D: Dauerstrombelastungsprüfung f
 F: essai m de capacité de charge en courant permanent
continuous discharge detection apparatus [cab.]
 D: Durchlaufprüfgerät n, Trockenprüfgerät n
 F: appareil m de contrôle d'ionisation par défilement continu, détecteur m de défauts à sec
continuous duty [el.]
 D: Dauerbetrieb mit gleichbleibender Belastung
 F: régime m permanent, service m continu
continuous duty with intermittent loading [el.]
 D: Dauerbetrieb mit aussetzender Belastung (DAB)
 F: service m ininterrompu à charge intermittente
continuous duty with short-time loading [el.]
 D: Dauerbetrieb mit kurzzeitiger Belastung
 F: régime m permanent à charge temporaire
continuous duty with variable load [el.]
 D: Dauerbetrieb mit veränderlicher Belastung
 F: service m ininterrompu à charge variable
continuous load
 D: Dauerbelastung f, Dauerlast f
 F: charge f continue, charge f permanente
continuous loading [com. c.]
 D: Krarupisieren n
 F: charge f continue, krarupisation f
continuously adjustable
 D: stufenlos regelbar
 F: réglable sans à-coups, sans intervalles
continuously cast and rolled rod
 D: Gießwalzdraht m
 F: fil m fabriqué en coulée continue laminage
continuously filled cable [tel. c.]
 D: über die ganze Länge abgestopftes Kabel, kontinuierlich gefülltes Kabel
 F: câble m rempli de façon continue, câble m à remplissage total, câble m à remplissage continu
continuously loaded cable

continuously

continuous manufacture (cont.)
- D: Krarup-Kabel n
- F: câble m Krarup, câble m krarupisé, câble m à charge continue, câble m ferromagnétique

continuous manufacture
- D: kontinuierliche Fertigung
- F: fabrication f en continu

continuous operation
- D: kontinuierlicher Betrieb
- F: marche f continue, opération f continue, service m continu

continuous operation [el.]
- D: Dauerbetrieb mit gleichbleibender Belastung
- F: régime m permanent, service m continu

continuous operation, in ~
- D: im Durchlaufverfahren
- F: en continu

continuous resistance annealer
- D: kontinuierliche Widerstandsglühanlage
- F: recuiseur m continu par résistance, installation f continue de recuit par résistance

continuous stress
- D: Dauerbeanspruchung f
- F: sollicitation f permanente, contrainte f continue

continuous test
- D: Langzeitprüfung f, Langzeitversuch m, Dauerversuch m
- F: essai m de (longue) durée, essai m continu

continuous traveling wire cloth paper machine
- D: Langsieb-Papiermaschine f, Fourdrinier-Papiermaschine f
- F: machine f à papier à toile sans fin, machine f à papier Fourdrinier

continuous voltage
- D: Gleichspannung f
- F: tension f continue

continuous vulcanization (CV)
- D: kontinuierliche Vulkanisation (CV), Durchlaufvulkanisation f
- F: vulcanisation f continue (CV)

continuous vulcanization high-pressure steam pipe
- D: Dampfhochdruckrohr zur kontinuierlichen Vulkanisation
- F: tube m de vulcanisation continue à vapeur à haute pression

continuous vulcanization line
- D: CV-Anlage f, kontinuierliche Vulkanisationsanlage
- F: chaîne f CV, chaîne f de vulcanisation en continu

continuous wire drawing and annealing machine
- D: Durchlaufglühanlage f (gekoppelt mit Feindraht-Ziehmaschine), kontinuierliche Drahtzieh- und Glühanlage
- F: installation f de recuit en tandem, tréfileuse f et recuiseur en continu

contour line
- D: Umhüllungslinie f (z.B. bei Leitern)
- F: enveloppante f

contract v
- D: schrumpfen v
- F: rétrécir v(se), contracter v(se)

contraction n
- D: Schrumpfung f
- F: retrait m, contraction f

control v
- D: steuern v
- F: régler v, commander v

control v
- D: prüfen v
- F: essayer v, vérifier v, contrôler v

control n
- D: Regler m
- F: régulateur m, appareil m de réglage

control n
- D: Betätigung f, Bedienung f
- F: commande f, manœuvre f, manipulation f

control n [el., mech.]
- D: Steuerung f
- F: commande f, réglage m

control cabinet
- D: Schaltschrank m
- F: armoire f de commande, armoire f d'appareillage, armoire f de régulation

control cable
- D: Steuerkabel n
- F: câble m de commande

control circuit
- D: Steuerkreis m, Regelkreis m
- F: circuit m de réglage, circuit m de commande

control console

control core
D: Steuerader f
F: conducteur m de commande

control current
D: Steuerstrom m
F: courant m de commande

control desk
D: Schaltpult n, Bedienungspult n, Steuerpult n
F: pupitre m de commande, poste m de commande

control knob
D: Einstellknopf m
F: bouton m de réglage

controlled atmosphere
D: Schutzgasatmosphäre f
F: atmosphère f contrôlée, atmosphère f protectrice

controlled dielectric cable
D: Kabel mit gesteuertem Dielektrikum (Ölkabel, Gasdruckkabel)
F: câble m à diélectrique contrôlé

controlled pressure extrusion [extr.]
D: Druckspritzverfahren n
F: extrusion f en bourrage, extrusion f «pression bourrage»

controller n
D: Regler m
F: régulateur m, appareil m de réglage

controller/recorder n
D: Kontroll-/Schreibgerät n
F: contrôleur/enregistreur m

control panel
D: Schalttafel f
F: tableau m de distribution, tableau m de commande

control range
D: Regelbereich m
F: plage f de régulation, gamme f de réglage

control sample
D: Vergleichsmuster n
F: échantillon m témoin, échantillon m de comparaison, échantillon m de contrôle

control signal pulse
D: Steuerimpuls m
F: impulsion f de contrôle

control station
D: Schaltwarte f
F: station f de commande, poste m de commande

control tension
D: Steuerspannung f, Regelspannung f
F: tension f de réglage, tension f de commande

control valve
D: Regulierventil n
F: soupape f de réglage

control voltage
D: Steuerspannung f, Regelspannung f
F: tension f de réglage, tension f de commande

conversion factor
D: Umrechnungsfaktor m
F: coefficient m de transformation

convert v
D: verarbeiten v
F: mettre v en œuvre, travailler v, convertir v

conveying system
D: Förderanlage f
F: installation f de transport, convoyeur m

conveyor n
D: Förderanlage f
F: installation f de transport, convoyeur m

convolutions of a cable on a reel
D: Windungen eines aufgetrommelten Kabels
F: spires f pl d'un câble sur un touret

cool v
D: abkühlen v
F: refroidir v (se)

coolant n
D: Kühlmittel n
F: réfrigérant m

cooling, direct ~ of cables
D: direkte Kühlung von Kabeln
F: refroidissement m intégral des câbles, refroidissement m direct des câbles

cooling, integral ~ of cables
D: direkte Kühlung von Kabeln
F: refroidissement m intégral des câbles, refroidissement m direct des câbles

cooling, lateral ~ of cables
  D: indirekte Kühlung von Kabeln
  F: refroidissement m latéral des câbles, refroidissement m indirect des câbles
cooling agent
  D: Kühlmittel n
  F: réfrigérant m
cooling bath
  D: Kühlbad n
  F: bain m de refroidissement
cooling by compressed air
  D: Druckluftkühlung f
  F: refroidissement m à air comprimé
cooling circuit
  D: Kühlkreis m
  F: circuit m de refroidissement
cooling curve
  D: Abkühlkurve f
  F: courbe f de refroidissement
cooling liquid
  D: Kühlflüssigkeit f
  F: liquide m de refroidissement
cooling medium
  D: Kühlmittel n
  F: réfrigérant m
cooling mixer
  D: Kühlmischer m
  F: mélangeur m réfrigérant
cooling section
  D: Kühlstrecke f
  F: section f de refroidissement
cooling set
  D: Kühlaggregat n
  F: agrégat m réfrigérant, groupe m réfrigérant
cooling tower
  D: Kühlturm m
  F: tour f de réfrigération
cooling trough
  D: Kühlrinne f, Kühlwanne f
  F: goulotte f de refroidissement, gouttière f de refroidissement, bac m de refroidissement
cooling tube
  D: Kühlrohr n
  F: tube m de refroidissement
cooling water
  D: Kühlwasser n
  F: eau f de refroidissement, eau f réfrigérante
cooling water circulation
  D: Kühlwasserumlauf m
  F: circulation f d'eau de refroidissement
cooling water pipe
  D: Kühlwasserrohr n
  F: tube m à eau de refroidissement
copolymer n
  D: Mischpolymerisat n, Copolymer n
  F: copolymère m
copper braid, tinned ~ [cab.]
  D: Kupfer-Gestrickband n (verzinnt)
  F: tresse f en cuivre étamé
copper braiding
  D: Kupferdrahtgeflecht n
  F: tresse f en fils de cuivre
copper braid shielding
  D: Schirm aus Kupfer-Drahtgeflecht, Kupferschirmgeflecht n
  F: écran m en tresse de cuivre
copper-clad aluminium conductor
  D: kupferplattierter Aluminiumleiter
  F: âme f en aluminium plaqué de cuivre
copper-clad aluminium wire
  D: kupferplattierter Aluminiumdraht, kupferumhüllter Aluminiumdraht, Aluminiumdraht mit Kupfermantel
  F: fil m d'aluminium plaqué de cuivre
copper conductor
  D: Kupferleiter m
  F: âme f en cuivre
copper conductor cable
  D: Kupferleiterkabel n
  F: câble m à âme en cuivre, câble m à conducteur en cuivre
copper mesh, tinned ~ [cab.]
  D: Kupfer-Gestrickband n (verzinnt)
  F: tresse f en cuivre étamé
copper-mesh screen
  D: Schirm aus Kupfer-Drahtgeflecht, Kupferschirmgeflecht n
  F: écran m en tresse de cuivre
copper-mesh shield
  D: Schirm aus Kupfer-Drahtgeflecht, Kupferschirmgeflecht n
  F: écran m en tresse de cuivre
copper refining
  D: Kupferraffination f
  F: raffinage m du cuivre
copper scrap
  D: Altkupfer n, Kupferabfälle m pl
  F: déchets m pl de cuivre
copper screen
  D: Kupferschirm m

copper strap
 F: écran *m* en cuivre
copper strap
 D: Kupferband *n*, Bandkupfer *n*
 F: bande *f* de cuivre, ruban *m* de cuivre
copper strip
 D: Kupferband *n*, Bandkupfer *n*
 F: bande *f* de cuivre, ruban *m* de cuivre
copper tape
 D: Kupferband *n*, Bandkupfer *n*
 F: bande *f* de cuivre, ruban *m* de cuivre
copper threaded textile tape
 D: Textilband mit eingewebten Kupferdrähten
 F: ruban *m* textile tissu de fils de cuivre
copper wire, soft-annealed
 D: Kupferdraht, weichgeglüht
 F: fil *m* de cuivre recuit
copper wirebars
 D: Kupferdrahtbarren *m pl*
 F: lingots *m pl* de cuivre
copper wire braiding
 D: Kupferdrahtgeflecht *n*
 F: tresse *f* en fils de cuivre
cord *n* [el.]
 D: Schnur *f*
 F: cordon *m*
cord sets
 D: konfektionierte Leitungen
 F: cordons *m pl* et conducteurs façonnés, conducteurs *m pl* préassemblés
core *n*
 D: Ader *f*
 F: conducteur *m* isolé, fil *m* isolé
core *n* (assembly) [cab.]
 D: Seele *f*
 F: assemblage *m* des conducteurs
core binder
 D: Seelen-Haltewendel *f*
 F: frettage *m* sur l'assemblage
core binder head [cab.]
 D: Seelenspinnkopf *m*
 F: tête *f* de revêtement d'assemblage
core covering
 D: Seelenbedeckung *f*, Seelenbewicklung *f*
 F: revêtement *m* sur l'assemblage
core die
 D: Patrize *f*
 F: poinçon *m*
cored solder
 D: Lötdraht *m*
 F: fil *m* de soudure, soudure *f* en fil
core identification
 D: Aderkennzeichnung *f*
 F: repérage *m* des conducteurs
core insulation
 D: Aderisolierung *f*
 F: isolation *f* du conducteur
core screen (GB)
 D: Aderabschirmung *f*, Schirm über der Isolierung
 F: écran *m* sur l'isolant
core-strander *n*
 D: Seelenverseilmaschine *f*, Aderverseilmaschine *f*
 F: assembleuse *f*
core stranding [cab.]
 D: Seelenverseilung *f*, Aderverseilung *f*, Verseilung *f* (Seele)
 F: assemblage *m* (des conducteurs)
core-stranding machine
 D: Seelenverseilmaschine *f*, Aderverseilmaschine *f*
 F: assembleuse *f*
core wire
 D: Mitteldraht *m* (Leiter)
 F: fil *m* central
core wrap(ping)
 D: Seelenbedeckung *f*, Seelenbewicklung *f*
 F: revêtement *m* sur l'assemblage
corner radius
 D: Kantenradius *m* (Sektorleiter), Krümmungsradius *m* (Sektorleiter)
 F: rayon *m* de coude
corner rollers [c. install.]
 D: Eckrollen *f pl*
 F: rouleaux *m pl* d'angle
corona *n* [el.]
 D: Korona *f*, Glimmen *n*
 F: couronne *f*, effet *m* de couronne
corona discharge
 D: Glimmentladung *f*, Korona-Entladung *f*, Sprühentladung *f*
 F: effluve *f* en couronne, décharge *f* par ionisation, décharge *f* en couronne
corona-free *adj* [el.]
 D: glimmfrei *adj*
 F: exempt *adj* d'effet de couronne
corona level test
 D: Teilentladungsprüfung *f*

corona
   F: essai *m* de décharges partielles
corona protection
   D: Glimmschutz *m*
   F: protection *f* contre l'effet de couronne
corona resistance
   D: Koronabeständigkeit *f*, Glimmbeständigkeit *f*
   F: résistance *f* à l'effet de couronne, résistance *f* à l'effet de corona
corona shield
   D: Sprühschirm *m* (gegen el. Entladungen)
   F: écran *m* contre les effluves
correct *adj*
   D: fehlerfrei *adj*
   F: sans défauts, exempt *adj* de défauts,
corrode v
   D: korrodieren v
   F: corroder v, attaquer v
corrosion, electrolytic ~
   D: elektrolytische Korrosion
   F: corrosion *f* électrolytique
corrosion-proof *adj*
   D: korrosionsfest *adj*
   F: résistant *adj* à la corrosion
corrosion-resistant *adj*
   D: korrosionsfest *adj*
   F: résistant *adj* à la corrosion
corrosive solution
   D: aggressive Lösung
   F: solution *f* corrosive
corrugated aluminium sheath
   D: Aluminium-Wellmantel *m*
   F: gaine *f* ondulée en aluminium
corrugated copper sheath
   D: Kupferwellmantel *m*
   F: gaine *f* ondulée en cuivre
corrugated copper tube
   D: Kupferwellrohr *n*
   F: tube *m* ondulée en cuivre
corrugated sheath
   D: Wellmantel *m*, gewellter Mantel
   F: gaine *f* ondulée
corrugated steel sheath
   D: Stahlwellmantel *m*
   F: gaine *f* d'acier ondulée
corrugating device
   D: Wellvorrichtung *f*
   F: dispositif *m* à onduler
corrugating head
   D: Rillkopf *m* (Wellmaschine), Wellkopf *m*

   F: porte-outils *m* (machine à onduler), tête *f* à onduler
corrugation, closed ~
   D: geschlossene Ringwellung
   F: ondulation *f* à anneaux fermés
cotton binder tape
   D: Baumwollbindeband *n*
   F: ruban *m* de coton de ligature
cotton braiding
   D: Baumwollumklöppelung *f*, Baumwollgeflecht *n*
   F: tresse *f* de coton
cotton-covered enamelled wire
   D: Lackbaumwolldraht *m*
   F: fil *m* émail-coton, fil *m* émaillé guipé de coton
cotton tape, proofed ~
   D: gummibeschichtetes Baumwollband
   F: ruban *m* de coton caoutchouté
Coumarone resin
   D: Kumaronharz *n*
   F: résine *f* de coumarone
count *n* (of yarn)
   D: Garn-Nummer *f*
   F: numéro *m* de fil
counterbalancing *n*
   D: Ausgleich *m*
   F: compensation *f*, équilibrage *m*, équilibre *m*, balance *f*, égalisation *f*
counterclockwise *adj*
   D: gegen den Uhrzeigersinn
   F: dans le sens inverse des aiguilles d'une montre
counter-clockwise rotation [mach.]
   D: Linksdrehung *f*
   F: rotation *f* en sens inverse des aiguilles d'une montre
counter helix
   D: Gegenwendel *f*
   F: hélice *f* anti-torsion
counterplaten *n* [met. extr. pr.]
   D: Gegenholm *m*
   F: contre-traverse *f*
coupling *n*
   D: Kopplung *f*
   F: couplage *m*
coupling between non-adjacent strands
   D: Kopplung zwischen nichtbenachbarten Verseilelementen
   F: couplage *m* entre éléments câblés non voisins

coupling capacitor
D: Koppelkondensator *m*
F: condensateur *m* de couplage

coupling coefficient [tel.]
D: Kopplungsfaktor *m*
F: coefficient *m* de couplage

coupling level
D: Kopplungsniveau *n*
F: niveau *m* de couplage

coupling resistance
D: Kopplungswiderstand *m*
F: résistance *f* de couplage

cover *v* [cab.]
D: bewickeln *v*, umwickeln *v*, umspinnen *v*
F: recouvrir *v*, enrouler *v*

cover *n*
D: Abdeckung *f*
F: recouvrement *m*, couverture *f*

cover *n*
D: Abdeckhaube *f*
F: capot *m*

covering *n*
D: Abdeckung *f*
F: recouvrement *m*, couverture *f*

covering *n*
D: Hülle *f*, Umhüllung *f*
F: enveloppe *f*, revêtement *m*

covering plate
D: Abdeckplatte *f*
F: plaque *f* protectrice, plaque *f* de recouvrement

covering sheet
D: Abdeckblech *n*
F: tôle *f* de recouvrement, tôle *f* de protection

covering the butt joints [lapp.]
D: die Stoßstellen überdeckend
F: faisant couvre-joint

cover plate
D: Abdeckblech *n*
F: tôle *f* de recouvrement, tôle *f* de protection

cps (s. cycles per second)

crack *n*
D: Riß *m*
F: craquelure *f*, fissure *f*

cracked *adj*
D: rissig *adj*
F: fissuré *adj*, craquelé *adj*

cracking resistance
D: Rißbeständigkeit *f*
F: tenue *f* aux craquelures

cradle *n* [strand.]
D: Spulenhalter *m*, Spulenträger *m*, Joch *n*
F: porte-bobine *m*, berceau *m*

cradled, in ~ arrangement [c. install.]
D: in Wiegenanordnung
F: disposé *adj* en berceau

cramp *v*
D: festklemmen *v*
F: brider *v*, attacher *v*, serrer *v*, agrafer *v*

crane rail
D: Kranbahn *f*
F: chemin *m* de roulement de la grue

crease *n*
D: Falte *f*
F: pli *m*

crease-free *adj*
D: faltenfrei *adj*
F: exempt de plis, sans plis

creasing *n*
D: Faltenbildung *f*
F: plissement *m*, formation *f* de plis

creasing *n* [lapp.]
D: Knicken *n*
F: pliage *m*

creep *n*
D: Kriechen *n*
F: fluage *m*

creep resistance [met.]
D: Dauerstandfestigkeit *f*
F: résistance *f* au fluage, résistance *f* à la rupture sous charge permanente

creep strength [met.]
D: Dauerstandfestigkeit *f*
F: résistance *f* au fluage, résistance *f* à la rupture sous charge permanente

crepe paper
D: Krepp-Papier *n*
F: papier *m* plissé, papier *m* crêpé

crest *n*
D: Spitze *f* (Spannung, Leistung)
F: pointe *f*, crête *f*

crest of a wave [cab.]
D: Wellenkamm *m*
F: crête *f* d'une onde

crest value
D: Scheitelwert *m*, Spitzenwert *m*
F: valeur *f* de crête

crest voltage
D: Spitzenspannung *f*, Scheitelspannung *f*
F: tension *f* de crête, tension *f* de

pointe
crimped joint
 D: Preßverbindung f
 F: raccord m poinçonné
crimped sleeve
 D: Preßverbinder m
 F: manchon m à poinçonner
crimped type cable termination
 D: Preßkabelschuh m
 F: cosse f de câble à poinçonner,
 cosse f de câble à sertir
crimping tool [c. access.]
 D: Preßwerkzeug n
 F: outil m de poinçonnage
crop v
 D: köpfen v (Drahtenden),
 beschneiden v, abschneiden v
 F: couper v, rogner v, cisailler v
crop shear
 D: Schopfschere f
 F: cisaille f à ébouter
cross-bonding box [cab.]
 D: Auskreuzungskasten m,
 Schaltkasten m
 F: boîte f de raccordement à la terre,
 boîte f de transposition
cross-bonding of cable sheaths
 D: Auskreuzen von Kabelmänteln
 F: transposition f des gaines de câbles
cross-connect v
 D: kreuzen v (Leitungen)
 F: transposer v
cross-connecting wire
 D: Schaltader f, Schaltdraht m
 F: fil m de connexion, jarretière f
cross-connection n [com. c.]
 D: Kreuzen n
 F: croisement m, transposition f
cross-connection point (C.C.P.) [com.]
 D: Verzweiger m,
 Verzweigungspunkt m
 F: point m de sous-répartition, point
 m de branchement
cross-head n [extr.]
 D: Querkopf m
 F: tête f équerre, tête f transversale
crossing n [com. c.]
 D: Kreuzen n
 F: croisement m, transposition f
crossing of roadways [c. install.]
 D: Kreuzen von Straßen
 F: croisement m de routes
cross-linkable adj

 D: vernetzbar adj
 F: réticulable adj
cross-linked by irradiation
 D: strahlenvernetzt adj
 F: réticulé adj par irradiation
cross-linked polyethylene (XLPE)
 D: vernetztes Polyäthylen (VPE)
 F: polyéthylène m réticulé
cross-linking n
 D: Vernetzung f
 F: réticulation f
cross-linking, chemical ~
 D: chemische Vernetzung
 F: réticulation f chimique
cross-linking agent
 D: Vernetzungsmittel n, Vernetzer m
 F: agent m de réticulation
cross-linking by irradiation
 D: Strahlenvernetzung f
 F: réticulation f par irradiation
cross-section n
 D: Querschnitt m
 F: section f (droite)
cross-section, electrically effective ~
 D: elektrisch wirksamer Querschnitt
 F: section f électriquement efficace
cross-section, geometrical ~
 D: geometrischer Querschnitt
 F: section f géométrique
cross-sectional area
 D: Querschnitt m
 F: section f (droite)
cross-sectional area, of equal ~
 D: querschnittsgleich adj
 F: de section égale
cross-splice v
 D: kreuzen v (Leitungen)
 F: transposer v
cross-splicing n [com. c.]
 D: Kreuzen n
 F: croisement m, transposition f
crosstalk n
 D: Nebensprechen n
 F: diaphonie f
crosstalk, side-to-side ~
 D: Übersprechen n
 F: diaphonie f entre réel et réel
crosstalk attenuation
 D: Nebensprechdämpfung f,
 Übersprechdämpfung f
 F: affaiblissement m diaphonique
crosstalk attenuation unit
 D: Nebensprechdämpfungsmaß n

crosstalk balancing
 F: unité f d'affaiblissement diaphonique, équivalent m d'affaiblissement diaphonique
crosstalk balancing
 D: Nebensprechausgleich m
 F: équilibrage m de diaphonies
crosstalk circuit
 D: Nebensprechkopplung f
 F: couplage m diaphonique
crosstalk coupling
 D: Nebensprechkopplung f
 F: couplage m diaphonique
crosstalk current
 D: Nebensprechstrom m
 F: courant m diaphonique
crosstalk meter
 D: Nebensprechdämpfungsmesser m, Nebensprechmesser m
 F: diaphonomètre m
crosstalk-proof adj
 D: nebensprechfrei adj
 F: exempt adj de diaphonie
crosstalk transmission equivalent
 D: Nebensprechdämpfung f, Übersprechdämpfung f
 F: affaiblissement m diaphonique
crosswise movement
 D: Querbewegung f
 F: mouvement m transversal
crude, naphthene base ~ oil
 D: naphthenbasisches Rohöl
 F: huile f brute naphténique
crushing strength
 D: Druckbeständigkeit f, Druckfestigkeit f
 F: résistance f à l'écrasement, résistance f à la pression
crush(ing) test
 D: Druckversuch m (Rohre, Schaumkunststoffe)
 F: essai m d'écrasement
cryogenic cable
 D: tiefgekühltes Kabel, Kryo-Kabel n
 F: câble m cryogénique, cryocâble m
crystal n
 D: Kristallit m (PE)
 F: cristal m, cristallite m
crystalline structure
 D: kristallines Gefüge
 F: structure f cristalline
crystallinity n
 D: Kristallinität f
 F: cristallinité f

crystallite n
 D: Kristallit m (PE)
 F: cristal m, cristallite m
CSPE (s. chlorosulphonated PE)
cubicle type switch-gear
 D: gekapselte Schaltanlagen
 F: disjoncteurs m pl enfermés, disjoncteurs m pl blindés
cumulative frequency [math.]
 D: Summenhäufigkeit f
 F: probabilité f cumulée, fréquence f cumulée
cup, flash point in a closed ~
 D: Flammpunkt im geschlossenen Tiegel
 F: point m d'éclair en vase fermé, point m d'éclair en coupe fermé
cup, flash point in an open ~
 D: Flammpunkt im offenen Tiegel
 F: point m d'éclair en vase ouvert, point m d'éclair en coupe ouverte
cup insulator
 D: Glockenisolator m, Isolierglocke f
 F: isolateur m à cloche, cloche f isolante
cure v
 D: vulkanisieren v
 F: vulcaniser v
cure v [plast.]
 D: härten v
 F: durcir v
cure, rate of ~
 D: Vulkanisationsgeschwindigkeit f
 F: vitesse f de vulcanisation
cure, state of ~
 D: Vulkanisationsgrad m
 F: degré m de vulcanisation, stade m de vulcanisation
cure, time of ~
 D: Vulkanisationsdauer f
 F: durée f de vulcanisation
curing n [plast.]
 D: Aushärten n
 F: cuisson f, durcissement m
curing n
 D: Vulkanisation f
 F: vulcanisation f
curing agent
 D: Härter m
 F: durcisseur m, agent de durcissement m
curing range
 D: Vulkanisationsbereich m

curing
   F: intervalle *m* de vulcanisation
current *n*
   D: Strom *m*
   F: courant *m*
current breakdown
   D: Stromausfall *m*
   F: panne *f* de courant, manque *m* de courant
current-carrying *adj*
   D: stromführend *adj*, spannungführend *adj*
   F: sous tension, parcouru *adj* de courant,
current-carrying capacity
   D: Belastbarkeit *f*, Strombelastbarkeit *f*
   F: capacité *f* de charge, charge *f* limite, puissance *f* limite
current consumption
   D: Stromverbrauch *m*, Energieverbrauch *m*
   F: consommation *f* de courant, consommation *f* électrique, consommation *f* d'énergie
current-controlled losses
   D: stromabhängige Verluste
   F: pertes *f pl* dépendant du courant
current decrease
   D: Stromabfall *m*
   F: chute *f* de courant
current density
   D: Stromdichte *f*
   F: densité *f* de courant
current-dependent losses
   D: stromabhängige Verluste
   F: pertes *f pl* dépendant du courant
current drop
   D: Stromabfall *m*
   F: chute *f* de courant
current-fed *adj*
   D: stromgespeist *adj*
   F: alimenté *adj* en courant
current feedback
   D: Stromgegenkopplung *f*
   F: réaction *f* négative d'intensité
current indicator
   D: Stromanzeiger *m*
   F: indicateur *m* de courant
current intensity
   D: Stromstärke *f*
   F: intensité *f* de courant, ampérage *m*
currentless *adj*
   D: stromlos *adj*
   F: sans courant
current limiter
   D: Strombegrenzer *m*
   F: limiteur *m* de courant
current load
   D: Strombelastung *f*
   F: charge *f* électrique
current loading cycles [el.]
   D: Lastzyklen *m pl*, Belastungszyklen *m pl*
   F: cycles *m pl* de charge
current rating
   D: Belastbarkeit *f*, Strombelastbarkeit *f*
   F: capacité *f* de charge, charge *f* limite, puissance *f* limite
current source
   D: Stromquelle *f*
   F: source *f* de courant
current transformer
   D: Stromwandler *m*
   F: transformateur *m* du courant
current variation
   D: Stromschwankung *f*
   F: variation *f* de courant, fluctuation *f* de courant
curvature *n*
   D: Krümmung *f*, Biegung *f*
   F: courbure *f*, incurvation *f*, courbe *f*
curve, decline of a ~
   D: Abfall einer Kurve, Neigung einer Kurve
   F: inclinaison *f* d'une courbe, pente *f* d'une courbe
curve, slope of a ~
   D: Anstieg einer Kurve
   F: pente *f* d'une courbe, montée *f* d'une courbe
curved wire
   D: vorgewölbter Draht
   F: fil *m* métallique courbé
cut *v*
   D: köpfen *v* (Drahtenden), beschneiden *v*, abschneiden *v*
   F: couper *v*, rogner *v*, cisailler *v*
cut, to ~ to the required length
   D: auf die gewünschte Länge schneiden
   F: couper *v* à la longueur voulue
cut back *v* [cab.]
   D: absetzen *v* (Isolierung, Mantel)
   F: enlever *v*, découper *v*
cut-off range suppression band [com.]

D: Sperrbereich *m*
F: bande *f* éliminée, intervalle *m* imperméable

cut out *v*[el.]
D: abschalten *v*, ausschalten *v*
F: couper *v*, interrompre *v*, déconnecter *v*

cut-out switch
D: Ausschalter *m*, Abschalter *m*
F: discontacteur *m*, disjoncteur *m*, interrupteur *m*

cut-out time [el.]
D: Abschaltzeit *f*
F: temps *m* de coupure

cut-through resistance
D: Durchdrückfestigkeit *f*
F: résistance *f* à l'enfoncement

cut-through temperature
D: Durchdrücktemperatur *f*
F: température *f* d'enfoncement

cut-through test
D: Durchdrückprüfung *f*
F: essai *m* d'enfoncement

cutting *n*
D: spanabhebende Bearbeitung
F: usinage *m* (à l'outil de coupe)

cutting device
D: Schneidvorrichtung *f*
F: dispositif *m* de coupe

cutting with a die
D: Ausstanzen *n* (Prüfkörper)
F: découpage *m*, poinçonnage *m*

cut to length
D: in abgepaßten Längen
F: coupé *adj* à longueur

CV (s. continuous vulcanization)

CV-line *n*
D: CV-Anlage *f*, kontinuierliche Vulkanisationsanlage
F: chaîne *f* CV, chaîne *f* de vulcanisation en continu

cycles per second (cps)
D: Hertz (Hz)
F: cycles *m pl* par seconde, hertz, périodes *f pl* par seconde

cyclic loading
D: zyklische Belastung
F: charge *f* cyclique

cyclic loading, operation with ~
D: Betrieb mit zyklischer Belastung
F: régime *m* cyclique

cyclic loading test
D: Prüfung mit Belastungszyklen
F: essai *m* aux cycles de charge

cylinder *n* [extr.]
D: Zylinder *m*, Schneckengehäuse *n*
F: cylindre *m*

cylinder, main ~ [met. extr. pr.]
D: Arbeitszylinder *m*
F: cylindre *m* de pression

cylinder machine paper
D: Rundsieb-Papier *n*
F: papier *m* (fabriqué sur) machine à tamis cylindrique

cylinder paper machine
D: Rundsieb(papier-)maschine *f*
F: machine *f* à papier à tamis cylindrique

cylinder pot-head
D: Zylinder-Endverschluß *m*
F: extrémité *f* cylindrique

D

damage to the cable sheath
D: Beschädigung des Kabelmantels
F: endommagement *m* de la gaine de câble

damped oscillation waves
D: gedämpft schwingende Wellen
F: ondes *f pl* d'oscillation amortie

damping *n*
D: Dämpfung *f*
F: atténuation *f*, affaiblissement *m*

damping coefficient
D: Dämpfungsfaktor *m*
F: coefficient *m* d'affaiblissement

damping reduction [tel. c.]
D: Entdämpfung *f*
F: compensation *f* de l'affaiblissement, compensation *f* de l'amortissement

damp-proof wiring cable
D: Feuchtraumleitung *f*
F: câble *m* hydrofuge, câble *m* pour locaux humides

dancer *n*
D: Tänzerrolle *f*
F: poulie *f* mobile, poulie *f* flottante, moufle *f*

dark-coloured *adj*
D: dunkelgefärbt *adj*
F: de couleur foncée

darken *v*

darken
D: nachdunkeln v
F: foncer v(se)
dash-dotted adj
D: strichpunktiert adj
F: ponctué adj et rayé
dashed line
D: gestrichelte Linie
F: ligne f brisée, tireté m
data pl
D: Unterlagen f pl (beschreibende oder zeichnerische Angaben)
F: documents m pl, données f pl, documentation f
data pl and sg
D: Daten pl, Angaben f pl
F: données f pl, renseignements m pl
data acquisition
D: Datenerfassung f
F: acquisition f des données
data collection
D: Datenerfassung f
F: acquisition f des données
data logging system
D: Datenerfassungsanlage f
F: poste m d'acquisition des données
data processing, direct remote ~
D: direkte Daten-Fernverarbeitung
F: télétraitement m d'informations direct, télétraitement m d'informations on-line
data processing, on-line remote ~
D: direkte Daten-Fernverarbeitung
F: télétraitement m d'informations direct, télétraitement m d'informations on-line
data transmission
D: Datenübertragung f
F: transmission f d'informations, transmission f de données
data transmission, low transmission voltage d.c. ~
D: Gleichstrom-Datenübertragung mit niedriger Sendespannung
F: transmission f d'informations en courant continu à basse tension d'émission
data transmission cable
D: Kabel für Datenübertragung
F: câble m pour transmissions numériques
datex network
D: Datex-Netz n
F: réseau m datex

d.c. relay repeater [com.]
D: Gleichstromübertrager m
F: répéteur m à relais en courant continu
d.c. voltage
D: Gleichspannung f
F: tension f continue
d.c. voltage strength
D: Gleichspannungsfestigkeit f
F: tenue f sous tension continue
dead block
D: Drahtwickler m (stationär)
F: enrouleur m de fil métallique
dead time [mach.]
D: Stillstandszeit f, Totzeit f
F: temps m d'arrêt, temps m mort
dead time interval [el.]
D: spannungslose Periode
F: repos m
deaeration n
D: Entlüftung f
F: désaération f, ventilation f
deburring n
D: Entgraten n
F: ébarbage m, ébavurage m
decentering n
D: Dezentrierung f
F: décentrage m
decline of a curve
D: Abfall einer Kurve, Neigung einer Kurve
F: inclinaison f d'une courbe, pente f d'une courbe
decompose v [chem.]
D: aufschließen v
F: attaquer v, dissoudre v, désagréger v
decomposition n
D: Abbau m (Werkstoffe), Zersetzung f
F: dégradation f
decomposition n
D: Entmischung f
F: ségrégation f, décomposition f, déshomogénéisation f
decomposition n (in the Wurzschmitt-bomb)
D: Aufschluß m (in der Wurzschmitt-Bombe)
F: dissolution f (dans la bombe Wurzschmitt)
decouple v
D: entkoppeln v

decoupling, electrical ~
 D: elektrische Entkopplung
 F: découplage m électrique

decrease v
 D: vermindern v, verringern v
 F: réduire v, diminuer v

de-energize v [el.]
 D: abschalten v, ausschalten v
 F: couper v, interrompre v, déconnecter v

deep sea cable
 D: Tiefseekabel n
 F: câble m de haute mer, câble m de grand fond

deep sea submarine cable
 D: Tiefseekabel n
 F: câble m de haute mer, câble m de grand fond

defect n
 D: Fehler m
 F: défaut m, erreur f, défaillance f

defective adj
 D: fehlerhaft adj
 F: défectueux adj

defective pair marker
 D: Markierung für fehlerhaftes Paar
 F: marqueur m de paires défectueuses

deflection n
 D: Krümmung f, Biegung f
 F: courbure f, incurvation f, courbe f

deflector n [c. access.]
 D: Deflektor m
 F: déflecteur m

deflector, one-piece ~
 D: einteiliger Deflektor
 F: déflecteur m en une seule pièce

deflector roll
 D: Umlenkrolle f
 F: roue f de renvoi, galet m de renvoi, poulie f de renvoi

deflector support
 D: Deflektorhalter m
 F: support m de déflecteur

deformation n
 D: Formänderung f, Verformung f
 F: déformation f

deformation, elastic ~
 D: elastische Verformung
 F: déformation f élastique

deformation, permanent ~
 D: bleibende Verformung
 F: déformation f permanente

deformation resistance
 D: Formbeständigkeit f, Formänderungsbeständigkeit f
 F: stabilité f de forme, résistance f à la déformation

degasification n
 D: Entgasung f
 F: dégazage m

degassing n
 D: Entgasung f
 F: dégazage m

degradation n
 D: Abbau m (Werkstoffe), Zersetzung f
 F: dégradation f

degradation, thermal ~
 D: Abbau m (Kautschuk), thermischer Abbau (Kautschuk)
 F: dégradation f thermique

degree of cure
 D: Vulkanisationsgrad m
 F: degré m de vulcanisation, stade m de vulcanisation

degree of hardness [met.]
 D: Härtegrad m
 F: degré m de dureté

degree of purity
 D: Reinheitsgrad m
 F: degré m de pureté

degree of saturation
 D: Sättigungsgrad m
 F: degré m de saturation

dehumidify v
 D: Feuchtigkeit entziehen
 F: déshydrater v, déshumidifier v, enlever v l'humidité

dehydrate vt
 D: austrocknen v
 F: sécher v, dessécher v

deionize v
 D: entsalzen v, demineralisieren v
 F: déminéraliser v, dessaler v

delivered, as ~
 D: im Anlieferungszustand
 F: à l'état vierge, à la livraison

delivery length
 D: Lieferlänge f
 F: longueur f de livraison, longueur f de bobine

delivery of a pump
 D: Pumpenleistung f, Förderleistung einer Pumpe
 F: capacité f de pompage, débit m

delivery   238

    d'une pompe
delivery reel
    D: Versandspule *f*, Versandtrommel *f*, Liefertrommel *f*
    F: bobine *f* d'expédition
delta-connected *adj*
    D: in Dreieckschaltung
    F: monté *adj* en triangle, monté *adj* en delta
demand *n*
    D: Anforderung *f*
    F: exigence *f*, impératif *m*
demineralize *v*
    D: entsalzen *v*, demineralisieren *v*
    F: déminéraliser *v*, dessaler *v*
density *n*
    D: Dichte *f*
    F: densité *f*
density *n*
    D: Raumgewicht *n*
    F: poids *m* par (unité de) volume, densité *f*
deoxidation *n*
    D: Sauerstoffentzug *m*
    F: réduction *f* d'oxygène
dependent on frequency
    D: frequenzabhängig *adj*
    F: dépendant *adj* de la fréquence
depolymerisation *n*
    D: Depolymerisation *f*
    F: dépolymérisation *f*
deposit *n*
    D: Bodensatz *m*
    F: dépôt *m*, sédiment *m*
depressurized *adj*
    D: ohne Druck
    F: en dépression
deproteinised rubber
    D: enteiweißter Kautschuk
    F: caoutchouc *m* sans protéine
depth below ground [c. install.]
    D: Bettungstiefe *f*, Verlegetiefe *f*, Legungstiefe *f*
    F: profondeur *f* de pose
depth of corrugation
    D: Wellentiefe *f* (beim Wellmantel)
    F: profondeur *f* d'ondulation
depth of laying [c. install.]
    D: Bettungstiefe *f*, Verlegetiefe *f*, Legungstiefe *f*
    F: profondeur *f* de pose
depth of penetration
    D: Eindringtiefe *f*
    F: profondeur *f* de pénétration
depth under surface [c. install.]
    D: Bettungstiefe *f*, Verlegetiefe *f*, Legungstiefe *f*
    F: profondeur *f* de pose
desalinate *v*
    D: entsalzen *v*, demineralisieren *v*
    F: déminéraliser *v*, dessaler *v*
desalt *v*
    D: entsalzen *v*, demineralisieren *v*
    F: déminéraliser *v*, dessaler *v*
descale *v*
    D: entzundern *v*
    F: décalaminer *v*
desiccant *n*
    D: Trocknungsmittel *n*
    F: desséchant *m*, déshydratant *m*
desiccate *vt*
    D: austrocknen *v*
    F: sécher *v*, dessécher *v*
design *n* [cab.]
    D: Bauart *f*, Typ *m*
    F: construction *f*, type *m*
design data
    D: Aufbau-Daten *pl*, Konstruktionsdaten *pl*
    F: données *f pl* de construction, caractéristiques *f pl* dimensionelles, données *f pl* constructives
design drawing
    D: Konstruktionszeichnung *f*
    F: plan *m* de construction, dessin *m* d'atelier
designing office
    D: Konstruktionsbüro *n*
    F: bureau *m* d'études, bureau *m* de dessins
design of a cable
    D: Kabelaufbau *m*, Aufbau eines Kabels, Kabelkonstruktion *f*
    F: construction *f* d'un câble, constitution *f* d'un câble
design sheet
    D: Konstruktionsblatt *n*
    F: feuille *f* de construction
desired value
    D: Sollwert *m*
    F: valeur *f* spécifiée
despatch reel
    D: Versandspule *f*, Versandtrommel *f*, Liefertrommel *f*
    F: bobine *f* d'expédition
destructive test

detach v
  D: ablösen v (Folie, Schicht), abziehen v
  F: peler v, séparer v, décoller v

detachable adj
  D: abnehmbar adj
  F: amovible adj, démontable adj

detaching n
  D: Ablösen n (Trennen)
  F: pelage m, décollement m

detachment n
  D: Ablösen n (Trennen)
  F: pelage m, décollement m

detail drawing
  D: Einzelzeichnung f, Teilzeichnung f
  F: plan m de détail

details pl
  D: Daten pl, Angaben f pl
  F: données f pl, renseignements m pl

detecting element
  D: Abtastvorrichtung f, Fühler m
  F: palpeur m, scanner m, sonde f

deterioration n
  D: Verschlechterung f
  F: détérioration f

determination n [test]
  D: Bestimmung f
  F: détermination f, analyse f

detrimental adj
  D: schädlich adj
  F: néfaste adj, nocif adj, nuisible adj

development work
  D: Entwicklungsarbeiten f pl
  F: études f pl

device n
  D: Vorrichtung f
  F: dispositif m

diagram n
  D: Kurvenbild n, Diagramm n, graphische Darstellung
  F: diagramme m, représentation f graphique, graphique m

diagrammatic representation
  D: schematische Darstellung
  F: représentation f schématique, schéma m de principe

diameter, large, medium, small ~
  D: großer, mittlerer, kleiner Durchmesser
  F: gros, moyen, petit diamètre

diameter control device
D: nicht zerstörungsfreie Prüfung
F: essai m destructif

D: Durchmesser-Überwachungsgerät n
F: dispositif m de contrôle du diamètre

diameter gauge
  D: Durchmessermeßgerät n
  F: appareil m de mesure du diamètre, mesureur m du diamètre

diameter measuring device
  D: Durchmessermeßgerät n
  F: appareil m de mesure du diamètre, mesureur m du diamètre

diameter reduction
  D: Durchmesserverringerung f
  F: réduction f du diamètre, rétreint m

diamond dies [wire manuf.]
  D: Ziehdiamanten m pl, Diamantziehsteine m pl
  F: filières f pl en diamant

dicer n
  D: Granulator m
  F: granulateur m

die n [extr.]
  D: Mundstück n, Düse f
  F: filière f

die adjuster
  D: Matrizenversteller m
  F: dispositif m de réglage de filière

die approach [wire manuf.]
  D: Ziehsteineinlauf m
  F: entrée f de filière

die approach angle [wire manuf.]
  D: Ziehstein-Einlaufwinkel m
  F: angle m d'entrée à la filière

die back relief [wire manuf.]
  D: Ziehsteinauslauf m
  F: sortie f de filière

die block [met. extr. pr.]
  D: Preßkopf m
  F: bloc m de presse, tête f d'outillage

die cooling
  D: Matrizenkühlung f
  F: refroidissement m de la filière

die-cutting n
  D: Ausstanzen n (Prüfkörper)
  F: découpage m, poinçonnage m

die down v
  D: herunterziehen v (Metallmantel)
  F: rétrécir v, rétreindre v

die head, rotary ~
  D: drehbarer Werkzeugkopf
  F: tête f d'outils rotative

die holder

die

   D: Matrizenhalter m
   F: fourreau m

die holder [wire manuf.]
   D: Ziehsteinhalter m
   F: dispositif m de serrage pour filière

dielectric n
   D: Isolierung f, Dielektrikum n
   F: isolation f, isolant m, enveloppe f isolante, diélectrique m, isolement m

dielectric breakdown [el.]
   D: Durchschlag m
   F: claquage m, amorçage m, décharge f disruptive

dielectric constant
   D: Dielektrizitätskonstante (DK) f
   F: constante f diélectrique, permittivité f

dielectric losses
   D: dielektrische Verluste, Verluste im Dielektrikum
   F: pertes f pl diélectriques

dielectric power factor cos φ
   D: Verlustfaktor m
   F: facteur m de perte tg δ, facteur de puissance cos φ, tangente de l'angle de perte tg δ

dielectric strength
   D: Durchschlagfestigkeit f, Spannungsfestigkeit f, elektrische Festigkeit, dielektrische Festigkeit
   F: rigidité f diélectrique

dielectric test
   D: Spannungsprüfung f
   F: essai m diélectrique, essai m de tension

die point
   D: Verseilpunkt m
   F: point m de câblage

die ring
   D: Matrizenring m
   F: anneau m de filière

dies pl [extr., met.extr.pr., wire manuf.]
   D: Werkzeuge n pl
   F: outils m pl

die slide
   D: Werkzeugschlitten m
   F: chariot m porte-outils

difference of level
   D: Höhenunterschied m
   F: dénivellation f, différence f de niveau

dilatation n
   D: Ausdehnung f
   F: dilatation f, expansion f, extension f

dilate vi
   D: ausdehnen v (sich)
   F: dilater v (se)

diluent n
   D: Verdünnungsmittel n
   F: agent m de dilution, diluant m

dimension n
   D: Abmessung f
   F: dimension f

dimensional accuracy
   D: Maßhaltigkeit f
   F: exactitude f des dimensions prescrites

dimensional drawing
   D: maßstäbliche Zeichnung
   F: dessin m à l'échelle

dimensional precision
   D: Maßhaltigkeit f
   F: exactitude f des dimensions prescrites

dimensional stability
   D: Maßhaltigkeit f
   F: exactitude f des dimensions prescrites

dimensional stability
   D: Formbeständigkeit f, Formänderungsbeständigkeit f
   F: stabilité f de forme, résistance f à la déformation

dip v
   D: eintauchen v
   F: immerger v, tremper v, plonger v

dip forming (General Electric process for production of copper wire)
   D: Tauchziehen n
   F: formage m par immersion, dipforming m

direct burial (in earth)
   D: Verlegung in Erde, Erdverlegung f
   F: pose f en pleine terre, pose f souterraine

direct cooling of cables
   D: direkte Kühlung von Kabeln
   F: refroidissement m intégral des câbles, refroidissement m direct des câbles

direct current (d.c.)
   D: Gleichstrom m
   F: courant m continu

direct drive
   D: Einzelantrieb m

F: commande *f* individuelle, commande *f* directe
direction, in alternating ~
D: in wechselnder Richtung
F: en sens alterné
direction core
D: Richtungsader *f*
F: conducteur *m* de direction
direction element
D: Richtungselement *n*
F: élément *m* de direction
direction of cable travel
D: Laufrichtung des Kabels durch eine Maschine
F: sens *m* de passage du câble
direction of lay [strand.]
D: Drallrichtung *f*, Schlagrichtung *f*
F: sens *m* du pas de câblage, sens *m* de câblage, sens *m* de torsion, sens *m* du pas de torsion, direction *f* du pas, direction *f* de la torsion
direction of rotation [mach.]
D: Drehrichtung *f*
F: sens *m* de rotation
direction of running [mach.]
D: Laufrichtung *f*
F: sens *m* de marche, sens *m* de défilement
direction of twist [strand.]
D: Drallrichtung *f*, Schlagrichtung *f*
F: sens *m* du pas de câblage, sens *m* de câblage, sens *m* de torsion, sens *m* du pas de torsion, direction *f* du pas, direction *f* de la torsion
direction pair
D: Richtungspaar *n*
F: paire *f* de direction
direct line [tel.]
D: Anschlußleitung *f*, Hausanschlußleitung *f*
F: ligne *f* d'abonné
direct remote data processing
D: direkte Daten-Fernverarbeitung
F: télétraitement *m* d'informations direct, télétraitement *m* d'informations on-line
direct voltage
D: Gleichspannung *f*
F: tension *f* continue
disassemble *v*
D: abbauen *v* (Masch.), auseinandernehmen *v*, zerlegen *v*
F: désassembler *v*

disc *n*
D: Scheibe *f*
F: roue *f*, galet *m*, poulie *f*, disque *m*
discard *n* [met. extr. pr.]
D: Preßrest *m*
F: culot *m* de filage
discard, ejection of the ~ [met. extr. pr.]
D: Ausstoßen des Preßrestes
F: expulsion *f* du culot de filage
discharge channel
D: Entladungskanal *m*
F: voie *f* de décharge
discharge current
D: Entladestrom *m*
F: courant *m* de décharge
discharge intensity
D: Entladungsintensität *f*
F: intensité *f* de décharge
discharge line
D: Abflußleitung *f*
F: conduit *m* de décharge, conduite *f* d'écoulement
discharge pattern
D: Entladungsfigur *f*
F: figure *f* de décharges
discharge valve
D: Ablaßventil *n*, Auslaßventil *n*
F: soupape *f* de décharge, soupape *f* de vidange, soupape *f* d'émission, soupape *f* de sortie
discharge voltage
D: Entladungsspannung *f*
F: tension *f* de décharge
disc insulation [com. c.]
D: Scheibenisolierung *f*
F: isolation *f* par disques
disc insulator
D: Abstandscheibe *f*
F: disque *m* séparateur, disque *m* d'écartement
discoloration *n*
D: Verfärbung *f*
F: décoloration *f*, changement *m* de couleur
disconnect *v* [el.]
D: abschalten *v*, ausschalten *v*
F: couper *v*, interrompre *v*, déconnecter *v*
disconnecting switch
D: Trennschalter *m*
F: sectionneur *m*, disjoncteur *m*
discontinuous operation
D: diskontinuierliches Verfahren,

discontinuous
Chargenbetrieb m
F: procédé m discontinu, service m en discontinu

disc spacer
D: Abstandscheibe f
F: disque m séparateur, disque m d'écartement

disk (s. disc)

dismantle v
D: abbauen v (Masch.), auseinandernehmen v, zerlegen v
F: désassembler v

dismount v
D: ausbauen v, abmontieren v
F: démonter v, enlever v

dismountable adj
D: abnehmbar adj
F: amovible adj, démontable adj

dispatching n
D: Lastverteilung f
F: répartition f de la charge, dispatching m

disperse v
D: verteilen v
F: distribuer v

dispersion n [test]
D: Streuung f
F: dispersion f

dispersion n
D: Verteilung f
F: distribution f, répartition f

displaceable adj
D: verschiebbar adj
F: déplaçable adj

displacement n
D: Verschiebung f, Verlagerung f
F: déplacement m, décalage m

display n [el., vis.]
D: Anzeige f
F: indication f, signalisation f, lecture f, affichage m

display panel
D: Anzeigetafel f
F: panneau m indicateur de fonctionnement, tableau m indicateur

display unit
D: Anzeigevorrichtung f
F: indicateur m

disruptive voltage
D: Durchschlagspannung f
F: tension f de claquage, tension f de perforation, tension f disruptive

dissipate, to ~ the heat
D: die Wärme ableiten
F: dissiper v la chaleur

dissipation factor
D: Verlustfaktor m
F: facteur m de perte tg δ, facteur de puissance cos φ, tangente de l'angle de perte tg δ

distance n
D: Abstand m
F: distance f, écart m, intervalle m

distance between electrodes
D: Elektrodenabstand m
F: écartement m des électrodes, distance f entre électrodes

distillation residue
D: Destillationsrückstand m
F: résidu m de distillation

distortion n
D: Formänderung f, Verformung f
F: déformation f

distortion n
D: Verzerrung f
F: distorsion f

distortion factor
D: Klirrfaktor m
F: facteur m de distorsion

distribute v
D: verteilen v
F: distribuer v

distributing box
D: Abzweigkasten m, Abzweigdose f, Kabelverzweiger m, Abzweigmuffe f, Verteilerkasten m
F: boîte f de dérivation, boîte f de branchement, boîte f de distribution

distribution n
D: Verteilung f
F: distribution f, répartition f

distribution cabinet
D: Abzweigkasten m, Abzweigdose f, Kabelverzweiger m, Abzweigmuffe f, Verteilerkasten m
F: boîte f de dérivation, boîte f de branchement, boîte f de distribution

distribution cable
D: Verteilerkabel n
F: câble m de distribution

distribution cable [com.]
D: Aufteilungskabel n
F: câble m de distribution

distribution frame for telecommunications systems
  D: Verteilergestell für Nachrichtenanlagen
  F: répartiteur *m* d'installations de télécommunication

distribution panel [el.]
  D: Anschlußkasten *m*, Klemmenkasten *m*
  F: coffret *m* de distribution, boîte *f* de distribution, boîte *f* de dérivation, boîte *f* de connexion, coffret *m* de raccordement, boîte *m* de jonction, boîte *f* à bornes

distribution plug
  D: Abzweigstecker *m*
  F: fiche *f* de dérivation

distribution sleeve
  D: Aufteilungsmuffe *f*
  F: boîte *f* de distribution, boîte *f* de division, boîte *f* de trifurcation

distribution speed
  D: Verlegegeschwindigkeit *f* (beim Aufspulen)
  F: vitesse *f* de trancanage

distribution voltage
  D: Versorgungsspannung *f*
  F: tension *f* d'alimentation, tension *f* de distribution

distributor *n*
  D: Verlegearm *m* (Aufwickelei), Verlegevorrichtung *f* (Aufwickelei), Verteiler *m* (Aufwickelei)
  F: dispositif de trancanage *m*, palpeur-guide *m*

distributor box (US)
  D: Abzweigkasten *m*, Abzweigdose *f*, Kabelverzweiger *m*, Abzweigmuffe *f*, Verteilerkasten *m*
  F: boîte *f* de dérivation, boîte *f* de branchement, boîte *f* de distribution

disturbances due to echo
  D: Echostörungen *f pl*
  F: dérangement *m* par les effets d'écho

disturbing voltage
  D: Störspannung *f*, Beeinflussungsspannung *f*
  F: tension *f* perturbatrice, tension *f* parasite

diversified, highly ~ range of products
  D: breites Fabrikatespektrum, breites Fertigungsspektrum
  F: gamme *f* de produits largement diversifiée

DM-quad *n*
  D: Dieselhorst-Martin-Vierer *m*, DM-Vierer *m*
  F: quarte *f* Dieselhorst-Martin, quarte *f* DM

doctor blade
  D: Abstreifmesser *n*
  F: râcloir *m*

documents *pl*
  D: Unterlagen *f pl* (beschreibende oder zeichnerische Angaben)
  F: documents *m pl*, données *f pl*, documentation *f*

dome-shaped insulator
  D: Glockenisolator *m*, Isolierglocke *f*
  F: isolateur *m* à cloche, cloche *f* isolante

dosage *n*
  D: Dosierung *f*
  F: dosage *m*

dotted line
  D: punktierte Linie
  F: ligne *f* brisée

double accumulator [strand.]
  D: Doppelspeicher *m*
  F: accumulateur *m* double

double-acting cable sheathing press
  D: Doppelstempel-Kabelmantelpresse *f*
  F: presse *f* de gainage à fouloir double

double-acting plunger
  D: doppeltwirkender Plunger
  F: piston *m* à double effet, piston *m* à action double

double-acting press
  D: Doppelstempel-Presse *f*
  F: presse *f* à fouloir double

double armo(u)ring
  D: doppellagige Armierung
  F: armure *f* double

double bond [chem.]
  D: Doppelbindung *f*
  F: liaison *f* double

double bridge
  D: Thomson-(Doppel)brücke *f*
  F: pont *m* (double) de Thomson

double-core cable (GB)
  D: doppeladriges Kabel
  F: câble *m* biphasé, câble *m* à deux

double-core

conducteurs

double-deck drawing block [wire manuf.]
 D: Einzelblock mit Doppelscheibe
 F: banc m à deux cônes de tréfilage

double earth fault (GB)
 D: Doppelerdschluß m
 F: défaut m à la terre double

double-eye cable grip
 D: Ziehstrumpf mit zwei Schlaufen
 F: grip m de câble à double agrafe

double groove insulator
 D: Glockenisolator mit doppelter Bundrille, Glockenisolator mit zwei Halsrillen
 F: isolateur m à double rainure

double ground fault (US)
 D: Doppelerdschluß m
 F: défaut m à la terre double

double (extruder) head
 D: Zweifach-Spritzkopf m, Doppelkopf m
 F: tête f double de boudineuse, tête f double extrusion

double-layer adj
 D: doppellagig adj
 F: en double couche, en deux couches

double-ply paper
 D: Duplex-Papier n (Doppellagenpapier)
 F: papier m duplex, papier m en deux couches

double-ram cable sheathing press
 D: Doppelstempel-Kabelmantelpresse f
 F: presse f de gainage à foulour double

double-ram press
 D: Doppelstempel-Presse f
 F: presse f à foulour double

double-reel spooler
 D: Doppelspulapparat m, Doppelspuler m
 F: enrouleur m à double bobine, bobinoir m double

double-sheathed cable
 D: doppelt-ummanteltes Kabel
 F: câble m sous gaine double

double shed insulator
 D: Doppelglockenisolator m
 F: isolateur m à double cloche

double spooler, automatic ~
 D: automatische Doppelaufwickelei
 F: enrouleur m automatique à double bobine

double twist
 D: Doppelschlag m
 F: double torsion f

double-twist flyer-type high-speed stranding machine
 D: Bügel-Doppelschlag-Schnellverseilmaschine f
 F: câbleuse f inversée (à flyer) double torsion à grande vitesse

double-twist high-speed bunching machine
 D: Hochleistungs-Doppelschlag-Bündelverseilmaschine f, Doppelschlag-Bündel-Schnellverseilmaschine f
 F: tordeuse f double-torsion à grande vitesse

double-twist strander
 D: Doppelschlag-Verseilmaschine f
 F: câbleuse f double torsion

downstream adv
 D: in Fertigungsrichtung
 F: en aval

down-time n [mach.]
 D: Ausfallzeit f
 F: temps m d'arrêt, temps m de panne, temps m d'immobilisation

D-pak
 D: Faßwickler m
 F: enrouleur m en forme de tonneau, fût m de bobinage pour fils métalliques

drain v
 D: abfließen v
 F: écouler v (s')

drainage, electrical ~
 D: elektrische Drainage
 F: drainage m électrique

drainage test [cab.]
 D: Abtropfprüfung f, Tropf- und Ablaufprüfung f
 F: essai m d'écoulement

drained, mass-impregnated and ~ insulation
 D: massearme Isolierung
 F: isolant m égoutté après imprégnation

drained cable
 D: abgetropftes Kabel
 F: câble m à matière écoulée

draining compound [cab.]
 D: abwandernde Masse
 F: matière f migrante

draining of compound [cab.]
  D: Masseverarmung f,
  Masseabwanderung f,
  Abwanderung von Masse
  F: migration f de matière, écoulement m de matière

drain pipe
  D: Abflußleitung f
  F: conduit m de décharge, conduite f d'écoulement

drain valve
  D: Ablaßventil n, Auslaßventil n
  F: soupape f de décharge, soupape f de vidange, soupape f d'émission, soupape f de sortie

draw, to ~ wires down to large, medium, small diameters
  D: Drähte ziehen auf dicke, mittlere, kleine Durchmesser
  F: tréfiler v des fils de gros, moyens, petits diamètres

draw down (to) v [wire manuf.]
  D: herunterziehen v (auf)
  F: réduire v le diamètre (à)

drawing
  D: Ziehen n (von Stangen, Profilen oder Draht)
  F: étirage n

drawing bath [wire manuf.]
  D: Ziehbad n
  F: bain m de tréfilage

drawing cone [wire manuf.]
  D: Ziehkonus m, Ziehscheibe f
  F: cône m de tréfilage

drawing die
  D: Ziehstein m, Ziehwerkzeug n
  F: filière f de tréfilage

drawing fluid
  D: Ziehflüssigkeit f
  F: liquide m de tréfilage

drawing in
  D: Einziehen n (von Kabeln in Rohre)
  F: tirage m

drawing office
  D: Konstruktionsbüro n
  F: bureau m d'études, bureau m de dessins

drawing off of fumes
  D: Absaugung von Dämpfen
  F: captage m de fumées

drawing oil [wire manuf.]
  D: Ziehöl n
  F: huile f de tréfilage

drawing solution
  D: Ziehlösung f
  F: solution f de tréfilage

drawing to scale
  D: maßstäbliche Zeichnung
  F: dessin m à l'échelle

draw-pak n
  D: Faßwickler m
  F: enrouleur m en forme de tonneau, fût m de bobinage pour fils métalliques

dredge cable
  D: Baggerkabel n, Baggerleitung f
  F: câble m de drague

dressing roll
  D: Richtrolle f
  F: rouleau m dresseur

dripping test
  D: Tropfprüfung f (an Tränkmassen)
  F: essai m d'égouttement

drive, bilateral ~
  D: doppelseitiger Antrieb
  F: commande f bilatérale

drive, unilateral ~
  D: einseitiger Antrieb
  F: commande f unilatérale

drive gear
  D: Antriebsrad n
  F: pignon m de commande

driven by
  D: angetrieben von
  F: entraîné adj par

driving gear
  D: Antriebsrad n
  F: pignon m de commande

driving motor
  D: Antriebsmotor m
  F: moteur m d'entraînement

driving shaft
  D: Antriebswelle f
  F: arbre m de commande

drop of the oil pressure
  D: Abfall des Öldrucks
  F: baisse f de la pression d'huile, chute f de la pression d'huile

drop point
  D: Tropfpunkt m
  F: point m de goutte

drop shield
  D: Tropfschirm m (Isolator)
  F: cloche f d'égouttement

drop test
  D: Fallprüfung f

drop
   F: essai *m* de résistance aux secousses

drop wire (telephone cable to connect open wire lines on poles to subscribers' premises) (US)
   D: Teilnehmer-Anschlußleitung *f*, Hauszuführungsleitung *f*, Teilnehmereinführungsleitung *f*, Einführungsleitung *f*, Einführungsdraht *m*, Fernsprechteilnehmerleitung *f*
   F: ligne *f* d'abonné téléphonique (raccord à la ligne aérienne), ligne *f* de desserte d'abonné, fil *m* d'entrée d'abonné

dross *n*
   D: Schlacke *f*
   F: scorie *f*

dross *n* [met.]
   D: Krätze *f*
   F: crasse *f*

dross, to skim off the ~
   D: Schlacke abziehen
   F: soutirer *v* la scorie, écrasser *v*

drum *n* [cab.]
   D: Trommel *f*
   F: touret *m*, bobine *f*

drum flange [cab.]
   D: Trommelscheibe *f*, Trommelflansch *m*
   F: joue *f* de touret

drum mixer
   D: Trommelmischer *m*
   F: mélangeur *m* à tambour, mélangeur *m* à tonneau

drum-pack *n*
   D: Faßwickler *m*
   F: enrouleur *m* en forme de tonneau, fût *m* de bobinage pour fils métalliques

drum twisting, multi-pass ~ machine
   D: mehrgängige Trommelverseilmaschine
   F: câbleuse *f* à tambour à plusieures passes

dry bulb temperature [air cond.]
   D: Trockenkugel-Temperatur *f*, Trockenthermometer-Temperatur *f*
   F: température *f* au thermomètre sec

drying *n*
   D: Trocknung *f*
   F: séchage *m*

drying and impregnating process, monitoring of the ~
   D: Überwachung des Trocknungs- und Tränkvorgangs
   F: contrôle *m* du séchage et de l'imprégnation

drying of the soil
   D: Austrocknung des Erdbodens, Bodenaustrocknung *f*
   F: séchage *m* du sol, dessèchement *m* du sol

drying out of the soil
   D: Austrocknung des Erdbodens, Bodenaustrocknung *f*
   F: séchage *m* du sol, dessèchement *m* du sol

drying tank
   D: Trocknungsgefäß *n*
   F: cuve *f* de séchage

dry out *v*
   D: austrocknen *v*
   F: sécher *v*, dessécher *v*

dual (extruder) head
   D: Zweifach-Spritzkopf *m*, Doppelkopf *m*
   F: tête *f* double de boudineuse, tête *f* double extrusion

dual lapping head
   D: Doppelspinnkopf *m*
   F: tête *f* double de rubanage

dual-reel take-up
   D: Doppelspulapparat *m*, Doppelspuler *m*
   F: enrouleur *m* à double bobine, bobinoir *m* double

dual steel taping head
   D: zweifacher Eisenband-Wickler
   F: tête *f* à deux feuillards

dual wire [com. c.]
   D: Doppelader *f*, paarverseilte Leitung, Paar *n*
   F: paire *f*, fil *m* double, conducteur *m* jumelé

duct *n* [c. install.]
   D: Kanalzug *m*, Rohrzug *m*
   F: conduit *m*, caniveau *m*

duct-bank *n* [c. install.]
   D: Formsteinzug *m*
   F: fourreau *m* porte-cables

duct block
   D: Formstein *m*
   F: bloc-tube *m*

duct entrance [c. install.]
   D: Kanalzugöffnung *f*

ductility n
  D: Dehnbarkeit f
  F: élasticité f, extensibilité f, ductilité f

duct rodding [c. install.]
  D: Einführen in einen Kanalzug
  F: introduction f dans un conduit

dumb-bell shaped
  D: hantelförmig adj
  F: en forme d'haltère

dumb-bell shaped test piece
  D: Prüfhantel f, hantelförmiges Prüfstück
  F: éprouvette f en forme d'haltère

dummy n [tel. c.]
  D: Blindelement n
  F: faux-élément m

dummy block [met. extr. pr.]
  D: Preßscheibe f
  F: grain m de poussée

dummy block separator [met. extr. pr.]
  D: Preßscheibentrenner m
  F: séparateur m du grain de poussée

dummy joint
  D: Blindmuffe f
  F: fausse boîte de jonction

dummy joint box
  D: Blindmuffe f
  F: fausse boîte de jonction

duplex adj
  D: doppellagig adj
  F: en double couche, en deux couches

duplex paper
  D: Duplex-Papier n (Doppellagenpapier)
  F: papier m duplex, papier m en deux couches

duplicate lapping head
  D: Doppelspinnkopf m
  F: tête f double de rubanage

durability
  D: Beständigkeit f, Festigkeit f, Widerstandsfähigkeit f
  F: résistance f, stabilité f, tenue f

duration of the drying and impregnating process
  D: Dauer der Trocknung und Tränkung
  F: durée f du séchage et de l'imprégnation

durometer n
  D: Härteprüfer m, Durometer n
  F: appareil m de contrôle de la dureté, duromètre m

duty n [cab., mach.]
  D: Betrieb m
  F: fonctionnement m, service m, exploitation f, régime m

duty factor
  D: Einschaltdauer f
  F: facteur m de marche, durée f de mise en circuit

dye v
  D: färben v
  F: colorer v, teindre v

E

earth v (GB)
  D: erden v
  F: mettre v à la terre, relier v à la terre

earth n
  D: Erdboden m
  F: terre f

earth n (GB) [el.]
  D: Erde f
  F: terre f

earth, to ~
  D: gegen Erde
  F: par rapport à la terre

earth clamp (GB)
  D: Erdungsklemme f, Erdklemme f
  F: borne f de terre, prise f de terre

earth(ing) clip (GB)
  D: Erdungsschelle f, Erdschelle f
  F: collier m de mise à la terre

earth connection (GB)
  D: Erdanschluß m, Erdungsanschluß m, Erdverbindung f
  F: prise f de terre, connexion f de terre

earth coupling (GB)
  D: Erdkopplung f
  F: déséquilibre m par rapport à la terre

earthed adj (GB)
  D: geerdet adj
  F: mis adj à la terre

earthed, system ~ at one end only
  D: einseitig geerdetes System
  F: réseau m mis à la terre d'un côté seulement

earthed neutral (GB)

earthed

    D: geerdeter Sternpunkt (Nullpunkt)
    F: neutre m à la terre, neutre m mis à la terre

earth fault (GB)
    D: Erdschluß m
    F: contact m à la terre, défaut m à la terre

earth fault compensation (GB)
    D: Erdschlußkompensation f
    F: compensation f des défauts à la terre

earth fault current (GB)
    D: Erdschlußstrom m
    F: courant m de court-circuit à la terre, courant m à la terre

earth fault protection (GB)
    D: Erdschlußschutz m
    F: protection f contre les défauts à la terre

earthing n (GB)
    D: Erdung f
    F: mise f à la terre

earthing circuit (GB)
    D: Erdungsleitung f
    F: circuit m de mise à la terre

earthing conductor (GB)
    D: Erdleiter m, Erdleitung f, Erdseil n
    F: conducteur m de terre, fil de garde m

earthing contact (GB)
    D: Schutzkontakt m
    F: contact m de mise à la terre

earthing of neutral (GB)
    D: Sternpunkterdung f
    F: mise f à la terre du neutre

earth lead (GB)
    D: Erddraht m
    F: fil m de terre

earth leakage current (GB)
    D: Erdschlußstrom m
    F: courant m de court-circuit à la terre, courant m à la terre

earth point
    D: Erdungspunkt m
    F: point m de (mise à la) terre

earth potential (GB)
    D: Erdpotential n
    F: potentiel m de terre

earth resistance (GB)
    D: Erdungswiderstand m
    F: résistance f de terre

earth return circuit (GB)
    D: Erdrückleitung f
    F: circuit m de retour par la terre

earth shield (GB)
    D: Erdungsschirm m
    F: écran m de mise à la terre, écran m de terre

earth(ing) system (GB)
    D: Erdungsanlage f
    F: système m de mise à la terre

earth terminal (GB)
    D: Erdungsklemme f, Erdklemme f
    F: borne f de terre, prise f de terre

earth wire (GB)
    D: Erdleiter m, Erdleitung f, Erdseil n
    F: conducteur m de terre, fil de garde m

earth work [c.install.]
    D: Erdarbeiten f pl
    F: travaux m pl de terrassement

ease of manipulation
    D: leichte Bedienung, leichte Handhabung
    F: aisance f de manipulation, aisance f de manœuvre

ease of operation
    D: leichte Bedienung, leichte Handhabung
    F: aisance f de manipulation, aisance f de manœuvre

easily accessible
    D: leicht zugänglich
    F: facilement accessible

easy-on termination
    D: leicht aufsteckbarer Endverschluß
    F: extrémité f facilement embrochable

easy to operate
    D: leicht bedienbar
    F: facilement manœuvrable

EC-aluminium (s. electrical conductor grade aluminium)

eccentricity gauge
    D: Exzentrizitäts-Meßvorrichtung f
    F: jauge f d'excentricité, appareil m de mesure de l'excentricité

eccentric ring
    D: Zentrierring m
    F: bague f de centrage, anneau m de centrage

EC-copper (s. electrical conductor grade copper)

echo attenuation
    D: Echodämpfung f
    F: affaiblissement m d'écho

echo suppressor
 D: Echosperre f
 F: suppresseur m d'écho

echo troubles
 D: Echostörungen f pl
 F: dérangement m par les effets d'écho

eddy current [el.]
 D: Wirbelstrom m
 F: courant m parasite, courant m de Foucault

eddy current losses [el.]
 D: Wirbelstromverluste m pl
 F: pertes f pl de Foucault, pertes f pl par courants parasites

edge n
 D: Kante f
 F: bord m, arête f, tranche f

edge, rounded ~
 D: abgerundete Kante
 F: côté m arrondi, tranche f arrondie

edge radius
 D: Kantenradius m (Sektorleiter), Krümmungsradius m (Sektorleiter)
 F: rayon m de coude

edge runner mixer
 D: Kollergang m
 F: mélangeur m à meules

edge tear resistance
 D: Kantenfestigkeit f
 F: résistance f des bords au déchirement

Educational Television (ETV)
 D: Schulfernsehen n
 F: Télévision Scolaire

effective attenuation [tel.]
 D: Betriebsdämpfung f
 F: affaiblissement m composite

effective dielectric constant
 D: effektive Dielektrizitätskonstante
 F: constante f diélectrique effective

effectively transmitted frequency band
 D: effektiv übertragenes Frequenzband
 F: bande f de fréquences transmise de façon effective

effective resistance
 D: Wirkwiderstand m
 F: résistance f effective

effective transmission [tel. c.]
 D: Nutzdämpfung f
 F: équivalent m de transmission effective

effective transmission equivalent [tel. c.]
 D: Nutzdämpfung f
 F: équivalent m de transmission effective

effective value
 D: Effektivwert m
 F: valeur f efficace

effective voltage
 D: Effektivspannung f, Wirkspannung f
 F: tension f efficace, tension f active

effects pl **of lightning**
 D: Blitzbeeinflussung f
 F: effets m pl de foudre

efficiency n [mach.]
 D: Leistung f, Ausstoß m
 F: performance f, débit m, efficacité f, rendement m, capacité f

efficiency n
 D: Wirkungsgrad m
 F: efficacité f, rendement m

efflux, time of ~
 D: Auslaufzeit f (Viskositätsmessung)
 F: temps m d'écoulement

EHV (s. extra-high voltage)

EHV-cable n
 D: Höchstspannungskabel n
 F: câble m à très haute tension (THT)

ejection of the discard [met. extr. pr.]
 D: Ausstoßen des Preßrestes
 F: expulsion f du culot de filage

ejector n
 D: Ausstoßvorrichtung f, Auswerfer m
 F: éjecteur m

elaborate process
 D: aufwendiges Verfahren
 F: méthode f élaborée, technique f recherchée

elastic deformation
 D: elastische Verformung
 F: déformation f élastique

elasticity n
 D: Dehnbarkeit f
 F: élasticité f, extensibilité f, ductilité f

elastic limit
 D: Streckgrenze f, Dehn(ungs)grenze f, Elastizitätsgrenze f
 F: limite f d'élasticité, limite f d'allongement

elastic recovery
 D: elastische Erholung
 F: reprise f élastique

elastomer

elastomer *n*
 D: Elastomer *n*
 F: élastomère *m*

elbow *n*
 D: Rohrbogen *m*, Rohrkrümmung *f*, Rohrknie *n*, Knierohr *n*, Krümmer *m* (Rohr)
 F: coude *m*, raccord *m* coudé

electrical characteristic
 D: elektrische Eigenschaft
 F: caractéristique *f* électrique, propriété *f* électrique

electrical conductivity
 D: elektrische Leitfähigkeit
 F: conductibilité *f* électrique

electrical conductor grade aluminium (EC-aluminium)
 D: Leitaluminium (EC-Aluminium) *n*
 F: aluminium *m* à haute conductibilité

electrical conductor grade copper (EC-copper)
 D: Leitkupfer (EC-Kupfer) *n*
 F: cuivre *m* à haute conductibilité

electrical connections
 D: elektrische Anschlüsse
 F: liaisons *f pl* électriques, raccords *m pl* électriques

electrical continuity
 D: elektrischer Durchgang
 F: continuité *f* électrique

electrical decoupling
 D: elektrische Entkopplung
 F: découplage *m* électrique

electrical drainage
 D: elektrische Drainage
 F: drainage *m* électrique

electrical engineering
 D: Elektrotechnik *f*
 F: électrotechnique *f*

electrical field, limitation of the ~
 D: Feldbegrenzung *f*
 F: limitation du champ électrique *f*

electrical grade copper
 D: E-Kupfer *n* (Kupfer für die Elektrotechnik)
 F: cuivre *m* à haute conductivité, cuivre *m* raffiné électrolytique

electrically conductive
 D: elektrisch leitend
 F: conducteur *adj* du courant électrique

electrically effective cross-section
 D: elektrisch wirksamer Querschnitt
 F: section *f* électriquement efficace

electrical property
 D: elektrische Eigenschaft
 F: caractéristique *f* électrique, propriété *f* électrique

electrical transmission route
 D: elektrischer Übertragungsweg
 F: voie *f* de transmission électrique

electric circuit
 D: Stromkreis *m*
 F: circuit *m* électrique

electricity supply undertaking
 D: Elektrizitäts-Versorgungsunternehmen (EVU) *n*
 F: société *f* de distribution d'électricité, entreprise *f* d'électricité, centrale *f* électrique

electricity undertaking
 D: Elektrizitäts-Versorgungsunternehmen (EVU) *n*
 F: société *f* de distribution d'électricité, entreprise *f* d'électricité, centrale *f* électrique

electric strength
 D: Durchschlagfestigkeit *f*, Spannungsfestigkeit *f*, elektrische Festigkeit, dielektrische Festigkeit
 F: rigidité *f* diélectrique

electric stress
 D: Spannungsbeanspruchung *f*
 F: contrainte *f* de tension, contrainte *f* électrique

electrode spacing
 D: Elektrodenabstand *m*
 F: écartement *m* des électrodes, distance *f* entre électrodes

electrolytic copper
 D: Elektrolytkupfer *n*
 F: cuivre *m* électrolytique

electrolytic corrosion
 D: elektrolytische Korrosion
 F: corrosion *f* électrolytique

electrostatic screen
 D: statischer Schirm, elektrostatischer Schirm
 F: écran *m* électrostatique

electrostatic shield
 D: statischer Schirm, elektrostatischer Schirm
 F: écran *m* électrostatique

electro-tinned wire

electro-tinning
   D: elektrolytisch verzinnter Draht
   F: fil m métallique étamé électrolytiquement

electro-tinning n
   D: galvanische Verzinnung
   F: étamage m galvanique, étamage m électrolytique

elementary circuit diagram
   D: Prinzipschaltbild n
   F: schéma m de principe

elevator n (working platform)
   D: höhenverstellbare Arbeitsbühne
   F: élévateur m (plateforme de travail)

elongate v
   D: dehnen v
   F: allonger v, étendre v, étirer v

elongation n
   D: Dehnung f
   F: allongement m, extension f, étirage m

elongation at break
   D: Bruchdehnung f, Reißdehnung f
   F: allongement m à la rupture

elongation at rupture
   D: Bruchdehnung f, Reißdehnung f
   F: allongement m à la rupture

elongation test at low temperature
   D: Kältedehnungsprüfung f
   F: essai m d'allongement à froid

embed v
   D: einbetten v
   F: encastrer v, enrober v, noyer v

emboss v
   D: prägen v
   F: estamper v, imprimer v

embossing n
   D: Prägung f
   F: estampage m, impression f

embossing wheel
   D: Prägerad n
   F: galet m d'estampage

emergency generator set
   D: Notstrom-Aggregat n
   F: groupe m électrogène de secours

emergency operation
   D: Notbetrieb m
   F: régime m de secours

emergency power supply
   D: Notstromversorgung f
   F: alimentation f en énergie de secours

emergency service
   D: Notbetrieb m
   F: régime m de secours

emergency shut-down
   D: Notabschaltung f
   F: arrêt m d'urgence

emergency temperature
   D: Überlasttemperatur f
   F: température f en surcharge

emery v
   D: schmirgeln v
   F: émeriller v

emery cloth
   D: Schmirgelleinen n
   F: toile f (d')émeri

employment of materials
   D: Einsatz von Materialien
   F: mise f au point de matériaux, utilisation f de matériaux

emptying n
   D: Entleeren n
   F: vidage m, vidange f, évacuation f

enamel n
   D: Lack m
   F: vernis m

enamel(l)ed wire
   D: Lackdraht m
   F: fil m émaillé, fil m verni

enamelling tower
   D: Lackierturm m
   F: tour f de vernissage

encapsulate v [c. access.]
   D: vergießen v
   F: surmouler v, sceller v

enclosed adj
   D: eingebaut adj
   F: incorporé adj

endurance limit
   D: Dauerfestigkeitsgrenze f
   F: résistance f limite de fatigue, limite f d'endurance

endurance strength
   D: Dauerwechselfestigkeit f
   F: résistance f aux efforts répétés, résistance f aux efforts alternatifs

endurance test [mech.]
   D: Dauerversuch m, Ermüdungsversuch m
   F: essai m d'endurance, essai m de fatigue

energy n
   D: Energie f
   F: énergie f, puissance f

engagement n [tel.]
   D: Belegung f

engagement
F: occupation f, prise f

engineering department
D: Konstruktionsbüro n
F: bureau m d'études, bureau m de dessins

Engler degree
D: Englergrad m (Öl-Viskosität)
F: degré m Engler

enlarge v
D: vergrößern v
F: augmenter v, élargir v, grossir v, agrandir v

enlargement n
D: Vergrößerung f
F: agrandissement m, augmentation f, élargissement m

enter, to ~ the machine
D: in die Maschine einlaufen
F: entrer v dans la machine

entrance n [c. install.]
D: Einstiegöffnung f, Mannloch n
F: entrée f, accès m, trou m d'homme, regard m de visite

entrance n
D: Einlauf m (in eine Maschine), Eintritt m, Einführung f (Kabel)
F: entrée f

entrance bell [c. access.]
D: Einführungstrichter m
F: cornet m d'entrée

entrapped air
D: eingeschlossene Luft
F: air m enfermé

environmental stress cracking [plast.]
D: Spannungsrißbildung f
F: fissuration f de contact, fissuration f sous contrainte

epoxide resin
D: Epoxidharz n
F: résine f époxy, résine f époxyde, résine f époxydique

epoxy resin
D: Epoxidharz n
F: résine f époxy, résine f époxyde, résine f époxydique

EPR (s. ethylene-propylene rubber)

equalization n
D: Ausgleich m
F: compensation f, équilibrage m, équilibre m, balance f, égalisation f

equalization of temperature
D: Temperaturausgleich m
F: égalisation f de la température, compensation f de la température

equalizer n
D: Ausgleichsleitung f
F: fil m de compensation, circuit m d'équilibrage

equalizing circuit
D: Ausgleichsleitung f
F: fil m de compensation, circuit m d'équilibrage

equalizing current
D: Ausgleichsstrom m, Übergangsstrom m
F: courant m compensateur, courant m transitoire

equilibrium, state of ~
D: Gleichgewichtszustand m
F: état m d'équilibre

equilibrium temperature
D: Gleichgewichtstemperatur f
F: température f d'équilibre

equipment n
D: Ausrüstung f
F: équipement m, matériel m

equipment n
D: Vorrichtung f
F: dispositif m

equipotential connection
D: Ausgleichsleitung f
F: fil m de compensation, circuit m d'équilibrage

equispaced adj
D: in gleichen Abständen
F: à distances égales

erect v
D: errichten v
F: monter v, ériger v, installer v, assembler v

erection n
D: Errichtung f, Montage f, Aufbau m
F: implantation f, montage m, assemblage m

erection drawing
D: Montagezeichnung f, Installationszeichnung f, Aufstellungszeichnung f
F: plan m d'assemblage, plan m de montage

erector n
D: Monteur m
F: monteur m

error n
D: Fehler m
F: défaut m, erreur f, défaillance f

error display
 D: Fehleranzeige f
 F: affichage m d'erreur, signalisation f de défauts
error indicator
 D: Fehleranzeiger m, Fehleranzeige-Einrichtung f
 F: indicateur m d'erreur, indicateur m de défauts
error rate
 D: Fehlerhäufigkeit f
 F: taux m d'erreur, fréquence f d'erreurs
established practice
 D: bewährtes Verfahren
 F: méthode f éprouvée
ethylene-propylene rubber (EPR) n
 D: EPR-Kautschuk m, Äthylen-Propylen-Kautschuk m (EPR)
 F: caoutchouc m d'éthylène propylène (EPR)
ethylene vinyl acetate (EVA)
 D: Äthylen-Vinyl-Azetat (EVA) n
 F: acétate m d'éthylène vinyle (EVA)
ETP-Copper n (electrolytic tough pitch copper)
 D: E-Kupfer n (Kupfer für die Elektrotechnik)
 F: cuivre m à haute conductivité, cuivre m raffiné électrolytique
ETV (s. Educational Television)
EVA (s. ethylene vinyl acetate)
evacuate v
 D: evakuieren v
 F: évacuer v, mettre v sous vide
evaluation n
 D: Auswertung f
 F: évaluation f
evaporation n
 D: Verdampfung f
 F: évaporation f
even distribution
 D: gleichmäßige Verteilung
 F: répartition f uniforme
exacting control
 D: strenge Prüfung
 F: essai m rigoureux, contrôle m serré, contrôle m rigoureux, contrôle m sévère
examination n
 D: Untersuchung f, Prüfung f (Kontrolle)
 F: examen m, analyse f, contrôle m

examined patent application
 D: Auslegeschrift f
 F: demande f de brevet examinée
excavation work [c.install.]
 D: Erdarbeiten f pl
 F: travaux m pl de terrassement
exceed v
 D: überschreiten v
 F: dépasser v, excéder v
excess current protection
 D: Überstromschutz m
 F: protection f contre les surintensités
excess pressure
 D: Überdruck m
 F: surpression f
exchange n (GB) [tel.]
 D: Amt n
 F: central m
exchange cable
 D: Bezirkskabel n
 F: câble m régional, câble m suburbain
exchange cable [tel.]
 D: Amtskabel n
 F: câble m principal
exclusion of air
 D: Luftabschluß m
 F: étanchéité f à l'air
exhaust n
 D: Absaugung f
 F: exhaustion f, aspiration f
exhaust fan
 D: Entlüfter m
 F: désaérateur m
exhaust flue
 D: Entlüftungsrohr n
 F: cheminée f d'aération, tube m d'évacuation, tube m de ventilation
exhaust hood
 D: Abzug m (Lüftung), Absaughaube f
 F: hotte f, chapelle f, collecteur m de fumées, capteur m de fumées
exhaustive test
 D: eingehende Prüfung
 F: essai m détaillé, examen m détaillé, contrôle m minutieux
exhaust pipe
 D: Entlüftungsrohr n
 F: cheminée f d'aération, tube m d'évacuation, tube m de ventilation
exhaust system
 D: Absauganlage f
 F: installation f d'aspiration

exhaust

exhaust valve
 D: Ablaßventil n, Auslaßventil n
 F: soupape f de décharge, soupape f de vidange, soupape f d'émission, soupape f de sortie

exit n
 D: Austritt m
 F: sortie f

expand vi
 D: ausdehnen v (sich)
 F: dilater v (se)

expand vt
 D: dehnen v
 F: allonger v, étendre v, étirer v

expanded PE
 D: Zell-PE n, verschäumtes PE, verzelltes PE
 F: polyéthylène m mousse, polyéthylène m cellulaire

expanded plastic
 D: Schaum-Kunststoff m
 F: mousse f (synthétique), plastique m cellulaire

expansion n
 D: Ausdehnung f
 F: dilatation f, expansion f, extension f

expansion n
 D: Erweiterung f
 F: extension f, élargissement m

expansion box [cab.]
 D: Dehnungsmuffe f
 F: manchon m de dilatation

expansion coefficient
 D: Ausdehnungskoeffizient m
 F: coefficient m de dilatation

experience, process ~
 D: Erfahrung mit einer Fertigungsmethode
 F: expérience f faite avec une méthode de fabrication

experiment n
 D: Versuch m, Prüfung f (Erprobung), Test m
 F: essai m, épreuve f, expérience f

experimental arrangement
 D: Testanordnung f, Prüfanordnung f, Versuchsanordnung f
 F: montage m d'essai, montage m expérimental, disposition f d'essai

experimental cable
 D: Versuchskabel n
 F: câble m expérimental, câble m d'essai

experimental circuit
 D: Versuchsschaltung f, Prüfstromkreis m
 F: montage m expérimental (él.), couplage m expérimental, circuit m d'essai

experimental length
 D: Versuchslänge f, Probelänge f, Prüflänge f
 F: longueur f d'essai

experimental stage
 D: Versuchsstadium n
 F: stade m expérimental

expose v
 D: aussetzen v (einwirken lassen)
 F: exposer v

exposure n (to)
 D: Aussetzen n (dem Licht, der Wärme)
 F: exposition f (à la lumière; à la chaleur)

extend v
 D: dehnen v
 F: allonger v, étendre v, étirer v

extender
 D: Streckmittel n (Gummimischungen)
 F: extendeur m

extensibility n
 D: Dehnbarkeit f
 F: élasticité f, extensibilité f, ductilité f

extensibility, with limited ~
 D: dehnungsarm adj
 F: à extensibilité réduite

extensible adj
 D: ausziehbar adj
 F: extensible adj, télescopique adj

extension n
 D: Ausdehnung f
 F: dilatation f, expansion f, extension f

extension n
 D: Dehnung f
 F: allongement m, extension f, étirage m

extension cord
 D: Verlängerungsschnur f
 F: cordon m prolongateur, corde f d'allongement

external gas pressure cable
 D: Gasaußendruck-Kabel n
 F: câble m à compression externe de gaz

external voltage

extract v
 D: entziehen v
 F: retirer v, enlever v, ôter v

extract, to ~ humidity
 D: Feuchtigkeit entziehen
 F: déshydrater v, déshumidifier v, enlever v l'humidité

extra-fine wire
 D: Feinstdraht m
 F: fil m super-fin, fil m extra-fin

extra-fine wire conductor
 D: feinstdrähtiger Leiter
 F: âme f en fils extra-fins, âme f en fils super-fins

extra-flexible stranded conductor
 D: feinstdrähtiger Leiter
 F: âme f en fils extra-fins, âme f en fils super-fins

extra-high voltage (EHV)
 D: Höchstspannung f
 F: très haute tension f (THT)

extra-high voltage cable
 D: Höchstspannungskabel n
 F: câble m à très haute tension (THT)

extra losses
 D: Zusatzverluste m pl
 F: pertes f pl supplémentaires

extra pair [com. c.]
 D: Reservepaar n, Ersatzaderpaar n
 F: paire f de réserve

extrudability n
 D: Extrudierbarkeit f, Preßbarkeit f
 F: extrudabilité f

extrudate n
 D: Extrudat n
 F: produit m d'extrusion

extrude v
 D: extrudieren v, umspritzen v
 F: extruder v, boudiner v

extruded aluminium sheath
 D: aufgepreßter Aluminiummantel
 F: gaine f d'aluminium filée sur câble

extruded inner covering
 D: gemeinsame gepreßte Aderumhüllung, Zwickelmantel m
 F: gaine f de bourrage, gaine f formant bourrage

extruded material
 D: Extrudat n
 F: produit m d'extrusion

extruded rod
 D: Preßdraht m
 F: fil m machine filé

extruder n
 D: Schneckenpresse f, Extruder m
 F: boudineuse f, extrudeuse f

extruder dies pl
 D: Extruderwerkzeuge n pl, Spritzwerkzeuge n pl
 F: outillage m de boudineuse

extruder head
 D: Spritzkopf m (Extruder), Extruderkopf m
 F: tête f de boudineuse, tête f d'extrusion

extrusion n
 D: Extrudieren n, Extrusion f
 F: extrusion f, boudinage m

extrusion of the sheath on to the cable
 D: Aufpressen des Mantels auf das Kabel
 F: filage m de la gaine sur le câble, extrusion f de la gaine sur le câble

extrusion dies pl
 D: Extruderwerkzeuge n pl, Spritzwerkzeuge n pl
 F: outillage m de boudineuse

extrusion head
 D: Spritzkopf m (Extruder), Extruderkopf m
 F: tête f de boudineuse, tête f d'extrusion

extrusion pressure
 D: Preßdruck m
 F: pression f d'extrusion, pression f de filage

extrusion process
 D: Spritzverfahren n, Extrusionsverfahren n
 F: méthode f d'extrusion

extrusion rate
 D: Preßgeschwindigkeit f
 F: vitesse f d'extrusion

extrusion screw
 D: Extruderschnecke f
 F: vis f de boudineuse

extrusion temperature
 D: Preßtemperatur f
 F: température f d'extrusion, température f de filage

extrusion without shell [met. extr. pr.]
 D: Pressen ohne Schale
 F: filage m sans croûte

extrusion with shell [met. extr. pr.]

extrusion
   D: Pressen mit Schale
   F: filage *m* avec croûte

exudation *n*
   D: Ausscheidung *f*, Absonderung *f*
   F: ségrégation *f*, séparation *f*

exudation *n* [plast.]
   D: Ausschwitzen *n* (auf der Oberfläche von Kunststoffen)
   F: exsudation *f*

exude *v*
   D: ausschwitzen *v*
   F: exsuder *v*

F

fabric *n*
   D: Gewebe *n*
   F: toile *f*, tissu *m*

fabric tape
   D: Gewebeband *n*, Textilband *n*
   F: ruban *m* textile

fabric tape with interwoven copper wires
   D: Textilband mit eingewebten Kupferdrähten
   F: ruban *m* textile tissu de fils de cuivre

face plate [strand.]
   D: Verseilscheibe *f*, Lochplatte *f*
   F: plaque *f* de répartition, plaque *f* de guidage

facilities *pl*
   D: Ausrüstung *f*
   F: équipement *m*, matériel *m*

facility *n*
   D: Vorrichtung *f*
   F: dispositif *m*

factor *n*
   D: Beiwert *m*
   F: coefficient *m*

factory *n*
   D: Betrieb *m* (Werk, Anlage), Werkstatt *f*
   F: usine *f*, atelier *m*

factory acceptance
   D: Abnahme im Werk
   F: réception *f* en usine

factory length
   D: Fertigungslänge *f*
   F: longueur *f* de fabrication

factory trial
   D: Betriebsversuch *m*
   F: essai *m* sur chantier, essai *m* en service, essai *m* en usine

fade *v*
   D: verblassen *v*
   F: perdre *v* sa couleur, décolorer *v*

fail-safe cables
   D: betriebssichere Kabel
   F: câbles *m pl* de bonne sécurité de fonctionnement, câbles *m pl* de fonctionnement sûr

failure *n*
   D: Ausfall *m* (Anlage, Kabel), Betriebsstörung *f*
   F: défaut *m*, panne *f*, défaillance *f*, incident *m* de fonctionnement

failure probability
   D: Ausfallwahrscheinlichkeit *f*, Fehlerwahrscheinlichkeit *f*
   F: probabilité *f* de claquage

failure rate
   D: Ausfallrate *f*
   F: taux *m* de défaillances

fall, to ~ short of
   D: unterschreiten *v*
   F: être *v* inférieur à

fan *n*
   D: Gebläse *n*
   F: ventilateur *m*

fanning out of the cable cores
   D: Spreizen der Kabeladern, Auseinanderspreizen der Kabeladern, Ausbiegen von Kabeladern
   F: épanouissement *m* des conducteurs de câble

far-end cross talk (FEX)
   D: Fernnebensprechen *n*, Gegennebensprechen *n*
   F: télédiaphonie *f*

far-end crosstalk attenuation
   D: Fernnebensprechdämpfung *f*, Gegennebensprechdämpfung *f*
   F: affaiblissement *m* télédiaphonique

fast *adj*
   D: unauslöschlich *adj* (Farbe)
   F: indélébile *adj*

fasten *v*
   D: befestigen *v*
   F: attacher *v*, fixer *v*

fastness to light
   D: Lichtbeständigkeit *f* (Farben)

fatigue n
  D: Ermüdung f
  F: fatigue f
fatigue crack
  D: Ermüdungsbruch m
  F: cassure f de fatigue, rupture f de fatigue
fatigue failure
  D: Ermüdungsbruch m
  F: cassure f de fatigue, rupture f de fatigue
fatigue fracture
  D: Ermüdungsbruch m
  F: cassure f de fatigue, rupture f de fatigue
fatigue limit
  D: Dauerfestigkeitsgrenze f
  F: résistance f limite de fatigue, limite f d'endurance
fatigue resistance [met.]
  D: Dauerfestigkeit f, Ermüdungsfestigkeit f
  F: résistance f à la fatigue
fatigue strength [met.]
  D: Dauerfestigkeit f, Ermüdungsfestigkeit f
  F: résistance f à la fatigue
fatigue test [mech.]
  D: Dauerversuch m, Ermüdungsversuch m
  F: essai m d'endurance, essai m de fatigue
fatty acid plasticizer
  D: Fettsäure-Weichmacher m
  F: plastifiant m derivé d'acide gras
fault n
  D: Fehler m
  F: défaut m, erreur f, défaillance f
fault current
  D: Ableit(ungs)strom m, Fehlerstrom m, Streustrom m, vagabundierender Strom, Verluststrom m
  F: courant m de fuite, courant m de défaut, courant m vagabond
fault detection
  D: Fehlersuche f, Fehlerortsbestimmung f, Fehlerortung f, Auffindung einer Störstelle
  F: localisation f d'un défaut
fault detector
  D: Fehlerortungsgerät n, Fehlersuchgerät n
  F: localisateur m de défauts, détecteur m de défauts
fault finding
  D: Fehlersuche f, Fehlerortsbestimmung f, Fehlerortung f, Auffindung einer Störstelle
  F: localisation f d'un défaut
fault indication
  D: Fehleranzeige f
  F: affichage m d'erreur, signalisation f de défauts
fault indicator
  D: Fehleranzeiger m, Fehleranzeige-Einrichtung f
  F: indicateur m d'erreur, indicateur m de défauts
faultless adj
  D: fehlerfrei adj
  F: sans défauts, exempt adj de défauts,
fault location
  D: Fehlersuche f, Fehlerortsbestimmung f, Fehlerortung f, Auffindung einer Störstelle
  F: localisation f d'un défaut
fault location measuring bridge
  D: Fehlerort-Meßbrücke f
  F: pont m de localisation de défauts
fault location unit
  D: Fehlerortungsgerät n, Fehlersuchgerät n
  F: localisateur m de défauts, détecteur m de défauts
faulty adj
  D: fehlerhaft adj
  F: défectueux adj
faulty measurement
  D: Fehlmessung f, Meßfehler m
  F: raté m de mesure, erreur f de mesure
faulty operation
  D: Bedienungsfehler m, Fehlbedienung f
  F: fausse manœuvre f, erreur f de conduite, erreur f de manœuvre, erreur f de l'opérateur, erreur f de manipulation
feed v [mech., el.]
  D: speisen v, einspeisen v, beschicken v

feed
   F: alimenter v, charger v
feed n
   D: Vorschub m
   F: avance f
feed n
   D: Zuführung f, Speisung f
   F: alimentation f
feed, to ~ a cable through a machine
   D: Kabel durch eine Maschine laufen lassen
   F: faire v passer un câble par une machine
feedback n
   D: Rückkopplung f
   F: réaction f
feedback coil
   D: Rückkopplungsspule f
   F: bobine f de réaction
feed current
   D: Speisestrom m
   F: courant m d'alimentation
feeder n
   D: Zuleitung f
   F: conducteur m d'amenée, conducteur m d'alimentation
feeder n
   D: Einspeisungskabel n, Speisekabel n, Zuführungskabel n, Zuleitungskabel n
   F: câble m d'alimentation, feeder m
feeder cable
   D: Einspeisungskabel n, Speisekabel n, Zuführungskabel n, Zuleitungskabel n
   F: câble m d'alimentation, feeder m
feed-in n [el.]
   D: Einspeisung f
   F: alimentation f, arrivée f
feeding hopper [extr.]
   D: Fülltrichter m, Einfülltrichter m
   F: trémie f d'alimentation, entonnoir m de chargement
feeding line
   D: Versorgungsleitung f, Speiseleitung f
   F: circuit m d'alimentation, feeder m
feeding point
   D: Speisepunkt m
   F: point m d'alimentation
feeding zone [extr.]
   D: Einzugszone f
   F: zone f d'alimentation
feed material
   D: Beschickungsmaterial n
   F: matière f d'alimentation
feed rate [prod.]
   D: Durchlaufgeschwindigkeit f
   F: vitesse f de passage
feed stand [wire manuf., cab.]
   D: Ablaufbock m, Ablaufgestell n, Abwickelei f
   F: bâti m départ, dévidoir m, dérouleur m
feed stock
   D: Ausgangsmaterial n
   F: matière f de base, produit m de base, matière f première, matériel m rudimentaire
feed system
   D: Förderanlage f
   F: installation f de transport, convoyeur m
feed throat [extr.]
   D: Trichtermündung f
   F: embouchure f de trémie
felt stripper
   D: Filzabstreifer m
   F: râcloir m en feutre
female contact
   D: Steckbuchse f, Steckerbuchse f, Fassung f
   F: prise f femelle, fiche f femelle, douille f
female die
   D: Matrize f
   F: filière f
FEX (s. far-end cross talk)
field n
   D: Bereich m
   F: gamme f, domaine m, plage f
field conditions [c. install.]
   D: Baustellen-Bedingungen f pl, Baustellen-Verhältnisse n pl, Bedingungen auf der Baustelle
   F: conditions f pl sur chantier
field control [el.]
   D: Feldsteuerung f, Feldregulierung f
   F: orientation f du champ électrique, régularisation f du champ électrique, régulation f du champ électrique
field-controlling adj [el.]
   D: feldsteuernd adj
   F: orientant adj le champ électrique
field-controlling wire binding [c. access.]
   D: Strahlungsbund m, Drahtbund m

field limitation
 D: Feldbegrenzung f
 F: limitation du champ électrique f

field of application
 D: Anwendungsgebiet n
 F: champ m d'application, domaine m d'application, domaine m d'utilisation

field-proved adj
 D: im Betrieb bewährt
 F: qui a fait ses épreuves en service

field strength [el.]
 D: Feldstärke f
 F: intensité f du champ

field test
 D: Freigelände-Prüfung f
 F: essai m sur chantier

field trial
 D: Betriebsversuch m
 F: essai m sur chantier, essai m en service, essai m en usine

figure-eight cable
 D: Leichtbau-Luftkabel n
 F: câble m aérien léger

file, to ~ a patent application
 D: ein Patent anmelden
 F: déposer v une demande de brevet, demander v un brevet

filing of the aluminium sheath (for jointing)
 D: Befeilen des Aluminiummantels (zum Verbinden)
 F: limure f de la gaine d'aluminium (pour la jonction)

fill v [c. access.]
 D: vergießen v
 F: surmouler v, sceller v

filled cable [tel.]
 D: abgestopftes Kabel
 F: câble m rempli

filled cable, continuously ~ [tel. c.]
 D: über die ganze Länge abgestopftes Kabel, kontinuierlich gefülltes Kabel
 F: câble m rempli de façon continue, câble m à remplissage total, câble m à remplissage continu

filler
 D: Füllstoff m
 F: matière f de charge, charge f

filler n [cab.]
 D: Beilauf m, Zwickelfüllung f, Lückenfüllung f
 F: bourrage m

filler rod
 D: Schweißstab m
 F: baguette f de soudage

filler strings
 D: Beilaufschnüre f pl
 F: cordelettes f pl

filling n
 D: Füllen n, Füllung f
 F: remplissage m

filling n [tel. c.]
 D: Abstopfen n
 F: remplissage m

filling compound [tel. c.]
 D: Abstopfmasse f
 F: matière f de remplissage

filling compound [c. acc.]
 D: Vergußmasse f, Ausgußmasse f, Füllmasse f
 F: matière f de remplissage

filling hole
 D: Einfüllöffnung f
 F: trou m de remplissage

filling temperature
 D: Einfülltemperatur f
 F: température f de remplissage

film n [plast.]
 D: Folie f
 F: feuille f

film tape
 D: Folienband n
 F: ruban m de feuille

filter through v
 D: durchsickern v
 F: suinter v, filtrer v(se)

fin n
 D: Grat m, Gußgrat m
 F: bavure f, arête f

final wire size
 D: Fertigdraht m
 F: fil m de diamètre final

fine adjustment
 D: Feineinstellung f
 F: réglage m minutieux, réglage m précis

fine drawn wire
 D: Feindraht m
 F: fil m fin

fine-grain structure
 D: feinkörnige Struktur

fine-grain
   F: structure f à grains fins

fine wire
   D: Feindraht m
   F: fil m fin

fine wire conductor
   D: feindrähtiger Leiter
   F: âme f en fils fins

finish n
   D: Anstrich m
   F: peinture f, enduit m

finished cable
   D: fertiges Kabel
   F: câble m fini, câble m terminé

finished size
   D: Fertigmaß n
   F: dimension f finale

finishing
   D: Endbearbeitung f, Endfertigung f
   F: finissage m, finition f

finishing dimension
   D: Fertigmaß n
   F: dimension f finale

finishing pass [wire manuf.]
   D: Feinzug m, Fertigzug m
   F: tréfilage m à dimensions fines

finishing train
   D: Fertigwalzstraße f
   F: train m finisseur

fin tube
   D: Rippenrohr n
   F: tuyau m à ailettes

fire, non ~ propagating
   D: flammwidrig adj, einen Brand nicht weiterleitend
   F: non propagateur de la flamme adj, non propagateur de l'incendie adj, non transmettant la flamme

fire point
   D: Entzündungspunkt m (Öle), Flammpunkt m, Brennpunkt m (chem.)
   F: point m d'inflammation

fire-proof adj
   D: feuerbeständig adj, flammenbeständig adj
   F: résistant adj au feu, résistant adj à la flamme,

fire-refined copper
   D: feuerraffiniertes Kupfer, Raffinade-Kupfer n
   F: cuivre m raffiné au feu

fire refining
   D: Feuerraffination f
   F: raffinage m au feu

fire-resistance n
   D: Feuerbeständigkeit f, Feuerfestigkeit f
   F: résistance f au feu

fire-resistant adj
   D: feuerbeständig adj, flammenbeständig adj
   F: résistant adj au feu, résistant adj à la flamme,

fissure n
   D: Riß m
   F: craquelure f, fissure f

fissured adj
   D: rissig adj
   F: fissuré adj, craquelé adj

fit v
   D: einsetzen v, einbauen v
   F: mettre v, placer v, insérer v

fitter n
   D: Monteur m
   F: monteur m

fitting n
   D: Zwischenstück n, Verbindungsstück n, Anschlußstück n
   F: pièce f intermédiaire, pièce f de raccordement, raccord m, pièce f de jonction, adaptateur m

fitting instructions pl
   D: Montageanleitung f
   F: instructions f pl de montage, notice f de montage

fix v
   D: befestigen v
   F: attacher v, fixer v

fixed adj
   D: stationär adj, feststehend adj
   F: stationnaire adj, fixe adj

fixed installation [cab.]
   D: feste Verlegung
   F: installation f fixe

fixed wiring
   D: feste Verdrahtung
   F: filerie f fixe

fixing clamp
   D: Einspannklaue f, Einspannklemme f, Klemmbacke f
   F: mâchoire f de serrage, mordache f

flake v (off)
   D: abblättern v
   F: écailler v (s'), décoller v (se)

flakes pl

flaking n
- D: Schuppen f pl
- F: écailles f pl, paillettes f pl

flaking n
- D: Schuppenbildung f
- F: écaillement m

flame-proof adj
- D: feuerbeständig adj, flammenbeständig adj
- F: résistant adj au feu, résistant adj à la flamme

flame resistance
- D: Flammwidrigkeit f
- F: non-propagation f de la flamme, non-propagation f de l'incendie, résistance f à la propagation de la flamme

flame resistance test
- D: Flammwidrigkeitsprüfung f
- F: essai m de résistance à la propagation de la flamme, essai m de non-propagation de la flamme

flame-resistant adj
- D: flammwidrig adj, einen Brand nicht weiterleitend
- F: non propagateur de la flamme adj, non propagateur de l'incendie adj, non transmettant la flamme

flame resisting test
- D: Flammwidrigkeitsprüfung f
- F: essai m de résistance à la propagation de la flamme, essai m de non-propagation de la flamme

flame-retardant adj
- D: flammhemmend adj, flammenverzögernd adj
- F: retardant adj la flamme

flammable adj (US)
- D: brennbar adj, entflammbar adj
- F: combustible adj, inflammable adj

flange v
- D: umschlagen v, umbördeln v, bördeln v
- F: rabattre v, border v, bordeler v

flange, reel ~ [cab.]
- D: Trommelscheibe f, Trommelflansch m
- F: joue f de touret

flange diameter
- D: Flanschdurchmesser m (Kabeltrommel)
- F: diamètre m de la joue

flanging n
- D: Umbördelung f
- F: bord m rabattu

flare v
- D: aufweiten v
- F: élargir v, évaser v, mandriner v

flash n
- D: Grat m, Gußgrat m
- F: bavure f, arête f

flash-over n
- D: Funkenüberschlag m, Überschlag m
- F: contournement m, amorçage m

flash-over distance [el.]
- D: Schlagweite f
- F: distance f de contournement

flash-over voltage
- D: Überschlagspannung f
- F: tension f de contournement, tension f d'éclatement, tension f d'amorçage

flash point
- D: Entzündungspunkt m (Öle), Flammpunkt m, Brennpunkt m (chem.)
- F: point m d'inflammation

flash point in a closed cup
- D: Flammpunkt im geschlossenen Tiegel
- F: point m d'éclair en vase fermé, point m d'éclair en coupe fermé

flash point in an open cup
- D: Flammpunkt im offenen Tiegel
- F: point m d'éclair en vase ouvert, point m d'éclair en coupe ouverte

flat adj [com. c.]
- D: reflexionsfrei adj
- F: non réfléchissant adj

flat, cables in ~ formation
- D: nebeneinander liegende Kabel, in einer Ebene liegende Kabel
- F: câbles m pl disposés en nappe

flat flexible cable
- D: Flachleitung f
- F: câble m souple méplat

flat plug
- D: Flachstecker m
- F: fiche f plate, fiche f méplate

flat steel wire armouring
- D: Stahlflachdraht-Bewehrung f, Stahlflachdraht-Armierung f
- F: armure f en fils d'acier méplats

flattened adj
- D: abgeflacht adj
- F: méplat adj

flat twin cable
D: Flachleitung f
F: câble m souple méplat

flat twin flexible cord
D: Zwillingsleitung f
F: câble m souple méplat sans gaine

flat twin tinsel cord
D: leichte Zwillingsleitung f
F: câble m souple méplat à fil rosette

flat type cable
D: Flachkabel n
F: câble m méplat

flat webbed building wire
D: Stegleitung f
F: conducteur m à gaine séparable

flat wire
D: Flachdraht m
F: fil m plat, fil m méplat

flat wire armo(u)ring
D: Flachdrahtbewehrung f, Flachdrahtarmierung f
F: armure f en fils méplats

flexibility n
D: Biegsamkeit f, Biegbarkeit f
F: souplesse f, flexibilité f

flexible n
D: Anschlußschnur f
F: câble m souple, cordon m de raccordement

flexible n
D: bewegliche Leitung, flexible Leitung
F: câble m souple, cordon m souple

flexible adj
D: biegsam adj
F: flexible adj, souple adj

flexible cable
D: bewegliche Leitung, flexible Leitung
F: câble m souple, cordon m souple

flexible cord
D: Anschlußschnur f
F: câble m souple, cordon m de raccordement

flexible cord
D: bewegliche Leitung, flexible Leitung
F: câble m souple, cordon m souple

flexible portable power cord
D: bewegliche Starkstromleitung f
F: câble m souple mobile d'énergie

flexible power cord
D: Starkstromleitung f
F: câble m (souple) d'énergie

flexible stranded conductor
D: feindrähtiger Leiter
F: âme f en fils fins

flexible wire for fittings (sockets)
D: Fassungsader f
F: fil m de douille

flexible wiring
D: flexible Verdrahtung f
F: filerie f souple

flexural fatigue strength
D: Dauerbiegefestigkeit f
F: résistance f de fatigue à la flexion, endurance f à la flexion

flexural strength
D: Biegefestigkeit f
F: résistance f au pliage

flexural test
D: Biegeprüfung f
F: essai m de pliage

flier (s. flyer)

flight of the screw [extr.]
D: Schneckengang m, Gewindegang der Schnecke, Schneckengewinde n
F: filet m de la vis, pas m de la vis, spire f de la vis

float, to ~ a cable ashore
D: ein Kabel an Land ziehen
F: atterrir v un câble

floating roller
D: Tänzerrolle f
F: poulie f mobile, poulie f flottante, moufle f

float roll
D: Tänzerrolle f
F: poulie f mobile, poulie f flottante, moufle f

float (type) switch [el.]
D: Schwimmerschalter m
F: interrupteur m à flotteur

flooding n
D: Überziehen n (Masse, Kleber, Korrosionsschutz), Aufbringen n (Masse, Kleber, Korrosionsschutz)
F: enduction f

flooding compound [c. acc.]
D: Vergußmasse f, Ausgußmasse f, Füllmasse f
F: matière f de remplissage

floor area [mach.]
D: Stellfläche f
F: surface f

floor handling
D: Flurförderwesen *n*
F: manutention *f*

floor of manhole
D: Muffenbauwerks-Sohle *f*,
Muffenbunker-Sohle *f*,
Schachtsohle *f*
F: fond *m* du trou d'homme

floor of vault
D: Muffenbauwerks-Sohle *f*,
Muffenbunker-Sohle *f*,
Schachtsohle *f*
F: fond *m* du trou d'homme

floor space [mach.]
D: Stellfläche *f*
F: surface *f*

flow
D: Fließvermögen *n*
F: fluidité *f*

flow behaviour
D: Fließverhalten *n*
F: tenue *f* au fluage

flow channel [extr.]
D: Fließkanal *m*
F: profil *m* d'écoulement plastique

flow chart
D: Ablaufplan *m*, Ablaufdiagramm *n*,
Arbeitsablaufdiagramm *n*,
Flußdiagramm *n*,
Fertigungsflußschema *n*
F: organigramme *m* (prod.),
ordinogramme *m*, graphique *m* de
processus, diagramme *m* de
déroulement

flow diagram
D: Ablaufplan *m*, Ablaufdiagramm *n*,
Arbeitsablaufdiagramm *n*,
Flußdiagramm *n*,
Fertigungsflußschema *n*
F: organigramme *m* (prod.),
ordinogramme *m*, graphique *m* de
processus, diagramme *m* de
déroulement

flow fixture [extr.]
D: Strömungseinsatz *m*
F: mandrin *m* de répartition de
matière

flow limit
D: Fließgrenze *f*
F: limite *f* d'écoulement, limite *f* de
fluage, seuil *m* de fluage

flow loss
D: Strömungsverlust *m*
F: perte *f* d'écoulement

flow meter
D: Strömungsmesser *m*
F: rhéomètre *m*

flow mixer
D: Durchflußmischer *m*
(Mischungsherstellung)
F: mélangeur *m* en continu à courant

flow monitor
D: Strömungswächter *m*
F: contrôleur *m* d'écoulement

flow of a current
D: Fließen eines Stroms
F: écoulement *m* d'un courant

flow of operation
D: Arbeitsablauf *m*, Betriebsablauf *m*
F: phases *f pl* de travail, suite *f* des
opérations, cycle *m* de travail,
déroulement *m* des opérations

flow point
D: Fließpunkt *m*
F: point *m* d'écoulement

flow process
D: Arbeitsablauf *m*, Betriebsablauf *m*
F: phases *f pl* de travail, suite *f* des
opérations, cycle *m* de travail,
déroulement *m* des opérations

flow rate
D: Strömungsgeschwindigkeit *f*,
Fließgeschwindigkeit *f*
F: vitesse *f* d'écoulement

flow rate
D: Durchflußmenge *f*
F: débit *m*

flow resistance
D: Strömungswiderstand *m*
F: résistance *f* hydraulique

flow resistance [plast.]
D: Fließbeständigkeit *f*
F: résistance *f* au fluage

flow time
D: Auslaufzeit *f* (Viskositätsmessung)
F: temps *m* d'écoulement

flow velocity
D: Strömungsgeschwindigkeit *f*,
Fließgeschwindigkeit *f*
F: vitesse *f* d'écoulement

flow volume
D: Durchflußmenge *f*
F: débit *m*

fluctuation of current
D: Stromschwankung *f*
F: variation *f* de courant, fluctuation *f*

fluidity n
  D: Fließvermögen n
  F: fluidité f

fluid mixer
  D: Fluidmischer m
  F: mélangeur m du type à fluidification

fluorescent tube cable
  D: Leuchtröhrenleitung f
  F: câble m pour tubes fluorescentes

flush v
  D: spülen v
  F: rincer v

flush, to be ~
  D: fluchten v
  F: affleurer v, aligner v (s')

flux n
  D: Flußmittel n
  F: flux m, fondant m

flyer n
  D: Umlaufbügel m
  F: flyer m

flyer-type stranding machine
  D: Bügelverseilmaschine f
  F: câbleuse f inversée (à flyer)

flying adj
  D: beweglich (fliegend) angeordnet
  F: volant adj, mobile adj

flying saw
  D: fliegende Säge
  F: scie f volante

flying shear(s)
  D: fliegende Schere
  F: cisailles f pl à porte-à-faux

foamed PE
  D: Zell-PE n, verschäumtes PE, verzelltes PE
  F: polyéthylène m mousse, polyéthylène m cellulaire

foamed plastic
  D: Schaum-Kunststoff m
  F: mousse f (synthétique), plastique m cellulaire

foil n [met.]
  D: Folie f
  F: feuille f

fold v
  D: falzen v
  F: plier v, replier v

fold back v
  D: umschlagen v, umbördeln v, bördeln v
  F: rabattre v, border v, bordeler v

folded aluminium sheath
  D: gefalzter Aluminiummantel
  F: gaine f repliée en aluminium

folding endurance
  D: Falzfestigkeit f
  F: résistance f aux pliages répétés

folding number
  D: Fachung f (Garn)
  F: nombre m des fils

force n [mech.]
  D: Stärke f
  F: puissance f, force f

forced-air oven
  D: Ofen mit Luftumwälzung, Umluftofen m
  F: étuve f à circulation d'air, étuve f ventilé

forced circulation
  D: Zwangsumlauf m (Flüssigkeiten)
  F: circulation f forcée

forced cooling [cab.]
  D: Fremdkühlung f, Zwangskühlung f, künstliche Kühlung
  F: refroidissement m forcé

forced ventilated cable tunnel
  D: belüfteter Kabelkanal
  F: caniveau m de câble à ventilation forcée

forced ventilation
  D: künstliche Belüftung
  F: ventilation f forcée

forcing pump
  D: Druckpumpe f
  F: pompe f foulante, pompe f refoulante, refouleur m

foreign matter
  D: Fremdkörper m, Fremdstoff m
  F: impureté f, corps m étranger

forklift truck
  D: Gabelstapler m
  F: chariot m élévateur à fourche

forming board, cable ~
  D: Kabelformbrett n, Formbrett für Kabel
  F: gabarit m pour câbles, planche f de préparation pour câbles

form-stability n
  D: Formbeständigkeit f, Formänderungsbeständigkeit f
  F: stabilité f de forme, résistance f à la déformation

form-stable adj

formula, compound ~
D: Rezept einer Mischung
F: formule f d'un mélange

formulation, compound ~
D: Ansatz einer Mischung, Mischungsansatz m
F: formulation f d'un mélange

forward motion
D: Vorwärtsbewegung f
F: marche f en avant

foundation bolt
D: Fundamentschraube f
F: boulon m de fondation

foundation drawing
D: Fundamentzeichnung f
F: plan m de fondation, dessin m de fondation

four-column type metal extrusion press
D: Strangpresse in Viersäulenbauart
F: presse f à filer type à quatre colonnes

Fourdrinier-machine paper
D: Langsieb-Papier n
F: papier m fabriqué sur machine Fourdrinier

Fourdrinier paper machine
D: Langsieb-Papiermaschine f, Fourdrinier-Papiermaschine f
F: machine f à papier à toile sans fin, machine f à papier Fourdrinier

four roll calender
D: Vierwalzenkalander m
F: calandre f à quatre cylindres, calandre f à quatre rouleaux

four-wire termination [com.]
D: Vierdraht-Abschluß m
F: terminaison f à 4 fils

four-wire type circuit [com.]
D: Stromkreis für Zweidraht-Getrenntlage-Verfahren
F: circuit m assimilé à un circuit à quatre fils

fracture n
D: Bruch m, Bruchstelle f
F: rupture f, brisure f, cassure f

frame n
D: Gestell n, Rahmen m
F: bâti m

free from defects
D: fehlerfrei adj
F: sans défauts, exempt adj de défauts,

free from partial discharges
D: teilentladungsfrei adj
F: exempt adj de décharges partielles

free length (of specimen) between clamps [test]
D: Einspannlänge f
F: longueur f libre entre mâchoires

free of pinholes
D: porenfrei adj
F: exempt adj de pores

freeze v
D: erstarren v, hartwerden v
F: solidifier v (se), congéler v, durcir v

freezing v
D: Erstarrung f
F: solidification f, congélation f

freezing point
D: Stockpunkt m, Einfrierpunkt m, Erstarrungspunkt m
F: point m de solidification, point m de congélation

frequency band
D: Frequenzband n, Frequenzbereich m
F: bande f de fréquences, plage f de fréquences, gamme f de fréquences

frequency band, effectively transmitted ~
D: effektiv übertragenes Frequenzband
F: bande f de fréquences transmise de façon effective

frequency-dependent adj
D: frequenzabhängig adj
F: dépendant adj de la fréquence

frequency distortion
D: Dämpfungsverzerrung f
F: distorsion f d'affaiblissement

frequency fluctuation
D: Frequenzschwankung f
F: variation f de fréquence

frequency range
D: Frequenzband n, Frequenzbereich m
F: bande f de fréquences, plage f de fréquences, gamme f de fréquences

frequency variation
D: Frequenzschwankung f
F: variation f de fréquence

fretting corrosion
D: Reibkorrosion f
F: fretting m

friction n
　D: Reibung f
　F: friction f, frottement m
friction, low ~ ...
　D: reibungsarm adj
　F: à faible friction
friction coefficient
　D: Reibungskoeffizient m
　F: coefficient m de frottement
friction tape (US)
　D: Isolierband n
　F: ruban m isolant
friction welding
　D: Reibschweißen n
　F: soudage m à friction
full line
　D: durchgehende Linie
　F: trait m plein
full load
　D: Vollast f
　F: pleine charge f
full-load current
　D: Vollaststrom m
　F: courant m de pleine charge
full-load test
　D: Vollastprüfung f
　F: essai m à pleine charge
full-scale trial
　D: Versuch im praktischen Maßstab
　F: essai m à l'échelle naturelle
fully automated
　D: vollautomatisch adj,
　　vollautomatisiert adj
　F: entièrement automatique,
　　complètement automatisé
fully automatic
　D: vollautomatisch adj,
　　vollautomatisiert adj
　F: entièrement automatique,
　　complètement automatisé
fully filled cable [tel. c.]
　D: über die ganze Länge abgestopftes
　　Kabel, kontinuierlich gefülltes
　　Kabel
　F: câble m rempli de façon continue,
　　câble m à remplissage total, câble
　　m à remplissage continu
fully impregnated insulation
　D: vollimprägnierte Isolierung
　F: isolation f à imprégnation totale
fully insulated and enclosed
　D: voll-isoliert und gekapselt
　　(Schaltelemente)

　F: isolé adj et blindé entièrement
fume hood
　D: Abzug m (Lüftung), Absaughaube f
　F: hotte f, chapelle f, collecteur m de
　　fumées, capteur m de fumées
function, as a ~ of [math.]
　D: in Abhängigkeit von
　F: en fonction de
functional diagram
　D: Funktionsschema n
　F: schéma m fonctionnel
functional reliability
　D: Betriebssicherheit f,
　　Betriebszuverlässigkeit f,
　　Zuverlässigkeit im Betrieb
　F: sécurité f de fonctionnement,
　　fiabilité f de service
functional test
　D: Funktionsprüfung f
　F: essai m de fonctionnement
functioning n
　D: Arbeitsweise f
　F: fonctionnement m, mode m de
　　fonctionnement, opération f
fundamental research
　D: Grundlagenforschung f
　F: recherche f fondamentale
funnel n
　D: Trichter m
　F: trémie f, entonnoir m
furnace black
　D: Ofenruß m
　F: suie f
furnace lining
　D: Ofenauskleidung f
　F: revêtement m de four
fuse v
　D: verschweißen v
　F: souder v
fuse v [el.]
　D: durchbrennen v
　F: fuser v, fondre v
fuse n [el.]
　D: Sicherung f
　F: fusible m, coupe-circuit m
fuse wire
　D: Schmelzdraht m, Schmelzleiter m
　F: fil m fusible, fil m de fusion
fusing n
　D: Absicherung f
　F: protection f par fusibles
fusing conductor
　D: Schmelzdraht m, Schmelzleiter m

F: fil *m* fusible, fil *m* de fusion
fusion *n*
D: Schmelzen *n*
F: fonte *f*, fusion *f*

G

gallery cable
D: Grubenstreckenkabel *n*
F: câble *m* pour galeries de mines
galvanic corrosion
D: Kontaktkorrosion *f*
F: corrosion *f* par contact
galvanic coupling
D: galvanische Kopplung
F: couplage *m* galvanique, couplage *m* par dérivation
galvanized steel wire
D: verzinkter Stahldraht
F: fil *m* d'acier galvanisé
galvanizing bath
D: Zinkbad *n*
F: bain *m* de zinc
gantry crane
D: Portalkran *m*
F: grue *f* (à) portique
gap *n*
D: Zwischenraum *m*
F: espace *m*, intervalle *m*, jeu *m*
gap *n* [paper lapp.]
D: Spinnfuge *f*, Fuge *f*, Stoßfuge *f*, Stoßkantenzwischenraum *m*
F: déjoint *m*, joint *m*
gap between rolls
D: Walzenspalt *m* (Mischungsherstellung), Walzenstellung *f* (Mischungsherstellung)
F: écartement *m* entre cylindres, jeu *m* entre cylindres
gap width [roll. m.]
D: Spaltbreite *f*
F: écartement *m*
gas absorption
D: Gasaufnahme *f*
F: absorption *f* de gaz
gas black
D: Gasruß *m*
F: noir *m* de gaz
gas bubble
D: Gasblase *f*
F: bulle *f* de gaz, bulle *f* gazeuse
gas chromatographic analysis
D: Gaschromatographie *f*
F: chromatographie *f* en phase gazeuse
gas chromatography
D: Gaschromatographie *f*
F: chromatographie *f* en phase gazeuse
gaseous insulating material
D: gasförmiger Isolierstoff
F: isolant *m* gazeux
gas-filled cable
D: Gasdruck-Kabel *n*
F: câble *m* sous pression de gaz
gas-filled internal pressure cable
D: Gasinnendruck-Kabel *n*
F: câble *m* à pression interne de gaz
gas impermeability
D: Gasdichtigkeit *f*, Gasundurchlässigkeit *f*
F: étanchéité *f* au gaz, imperméabilité *f* au gaz
gas(SF$_6$)-insulated conductor system
D: SF$_6$-isoliertes Leitersystem, SF$_6$-Rohrleiter *m*, SF$_6$-Rohrschiene *f*
F: liaison *f* blindée isolée au SF$_6$, canalisation *f* blindée isolée au SF$_6$
gasket *n*
D: Dichtungsscheibe *f*
F: rondelle *f* d'étanchéité
gas pressure alarm system
D: Druckgas-Überwachungssystem *n*
F: système *m* de contrôle à gaz comprimé
gas pressure cable
D: Gasdruck-Kabel *n*
F: câble *m* sous pression de gaz
gas pressure controlled
D: druckgasüberwacht *adj*
F: contrôlé *adj* à gaz comprimé
gas pressure control of telephone cables
D: Druckgasschutz und -überwachung von Telefonkabeln
F: contrôle *m* des câbles téléphoniques à gaz comprimé
gas pressure pipe type cable
D: Gasdruck-Rohrkabel *n*
F: câble *m* en tube sous pression de gaz
gas pressure supervision of telephone

cables
 D: Druckgasschutz und -
    überwachung von Telefonkabeln
 F: contrôle m des câbles
    téléphoniques à gaz comprimé

gas pressure-tight joint
 D: druckgasdichte Muffe
 F: manchon m de jonction étanche au
    gaz comprimé

gassing n
 D: Gasen n
 F: gazage m

gas-tight adj
 D: gasundurchlässig adj
 F: étanche adj au gaz, imperméable
    adj au gaz,

gas-tightness n
 D: Gasdichtigkeit f,
    Gasundurchlässigkeit f
 F: étanchéité f au gaz, imperméabilité
    f au gaz

gauge n
 D: Eichmaß n
 F: jauge f, étalon m

gauging n
 D: Eichung f
 F: étalonnage m, calibrage m,
    jaugeage m

Gaussian (distribution) law
 D: Gaußsche Verteilung
 F: loi f gaussienne, répartition f
    gaussienne

gear(ing) n
 D: Zahnradgetriebe n, Getriebe n
 F: engrenage m, agencement m

gear-ratio n [mech.]
 D: Übersetzungsverhältnis n
 F: rapport m d'engrenage, rapport m
    de transmission

Geer ag(e)ing oven
 D: Geer-Alterungsofen m
 F: étuve f de vieillissement Geer

**general purpose single-core non-
sheathed cable**
 D: Aderleitung f
 F: conducteur m (à âme rigide ou
    souple)

generating station
 D: Kraftwerk n
 F: centrale f électrique

gland n
 D: Stopfbüchse f
 F: presse-étoupe f

glass fiber (US)
 D: Glasfaser f
 F: fibre f de verre

glass fibre (GB)
 D: Glasfaser f
 F: fibre f de verre

glass fibre fabric
 D: Glasfasergewebe n
 F: tissu m de verre

glass fibre tape
 D: Glasseidenband n
 F: ruban m en soie de verre

glass fibre waveguide
 D: Glasfaser-Wellenleiter m
 F: guide m d'ondes en fibres de verre

glass fibre yarn
 D: Glasseide f
 F: soie f de verre

glass insulator
 D: Glasisolator m
 F: isolateur m en verre

glow stability
 D: Koronabeständigkeit f,
    Glimmbeständigkeit f
 F: résistance f à l'effet de couronne,
    résistance f à l'effet de corona

glue vt
 D: kleben vt
 F: coller vt, attacher vt

go-devil n
 D: Reinigungsmolch m (für
    Rohrleitungen), Molch m
    (Rohrreiniger)
 F: écouvillon m

gradation of the paper insulation
 D: Schichtung der Papier-Isolierung
 F: échelonnement m de l'isolant
    papier, étagement m de l'isolant
    papier

graded adj
 D: gestaffelt adj, abgestuft adj,
    versetzt adj (stufenweise),
 F: en quinconce, échelonné adj,
    décalé adj, gradué adj, étagé adj

graded paper insulation
 D: geschichtete Papierisolierung
 F: isolant m papier échelonné

gradient n
 D: Gradient m
 F: gradient m

graft-polymer n
 D: Pfropfpolymerisat n
 F: polymère m greffé

grain boundaries
 D: Korngrenzen f pl
 F: limites f pl des grains, joints m pl des grains

grained adj
 D: körnig adj
 F: granuleux adj, granulaire adj, grenu adj

grained inclusions
 D: körnige Einschlüsse
 F: inclusions f pl granuleuses

grain growth
 D: Kornwachstum n
 F: croissance f des grains, grossissement m des grains

grain size
 D: Korngröße f
 F: grosseur f du grain

grant, to ~ a patent
 D: ein Patent erteilen
 F: accorder v un brevet, délivrer v un brevet

granular adj
 D: körnig adj
 F: granuleux adj, granulaire adj, grenu adj

granulate v
 D: granulieren v
 F: granuler v

granulate n
 D: Granulat n
 F: granulés m pl

granulating machine
 D: Granulator m
 F: granulateur m

granulator n
 D: Granulator m
 F: granulateur m

granulators, cable scrap ~ pl
 D: Zerkleinerungsanlage für Kabelabfälle
 F: installation f de broyage des déchets de câbles

granules pl
 D: Granulat n
 F: granulés m pl

granules storage bin
 D: Granulatsilo m
 F: silo m à granulés

graph n
 D: Kurvenbild n, Diagramm n, graphische Darstellung
 F: diagramme m, représentation f graphique, graphique m

graphic representation
 D: Kurvenbild n, Diagramm n, graphische Darstellung
 F: diagramme m, représentation f graphique, graphique m

grate, cable ~ [c. install.]
 D: Kabelrost m, Rost m
 F: grille f à câbles, râtelier m à câbles

gravity die-casting
 D: Kokillenguß m
 F: coulée f en coquille

gravity feed
 D: Gefällezuführung f
 F: alimentation f par gravité

gravity flow
 D: Fließen mit Gefälle
 F: écoulement m par gravité

grease n
 D: Gleitmittel n, Schmiermittel n
 F: matière f lubrifiante, lubrifiant m

greasing n
 D: Schmierung f
 F: lubrification f, graissage m

green-yellow core
 D: grüngelbe Ader
 F: conducteur m vert-jaune

grid n (system)
 D: Verbundnetz n
 F: réseau m d'interconnexion, réseau m de liaison

groove n
 D: Nut f, Aussparung f
 F: rainure f, encoche f, découpe f, évidement m, entaille f

grooved adj
 D: geriffelt adj
 F: cannelé adj, strié adj, rainé adj

ground v (US)
 D: erden v
 F: mettre v à la terre, relier v à la terre

ground n
 D: Erdboden m
 F: terre f

ground n (US) [el.]
 D: Erde f
 F: terre f

ground, to ~
 D: gegen Erde
 F: par rapport à la terre

ground clamp (US)
 D: Erdungsklemme f, Erdklemme f
 F: borne f de terre, prise f de terre

ground(ing) clip (US)
- D: Erdungsschelle f, Erdschelle f
- F: collier m de mise à la terre

ground connection (US)
- D: Erdanschluß m, Erdungsanschluß m, Erdverbindung f
- F: prise f de terre, connexion f de terre

grounded adj (US)
- D: geerdet adj
- F: mis adj à la terre

grounded-base circuit [el.]
- D: Basisschaltung f
- F: circuit m de base, montage m de base

grounded neutral (US)
- D: geerdeter Sternpunkt (Nullpunkt)
- F: neutre m à la terre, neutre m mis à la terre

ground fault (US)
- D: Erdschluß m
- F: contact m à la terre, défaut m à la terre

ground fault compensation (US)
- D: Erdschlußkompensation f
- F: compensation f des défauts à la terre

ground fault current (US)
- D: Erdschlußstrom m
- F: courant m de court-circuit à la terre, courant m à la terre

ground fault protection (US)
- D: Erdschlußschutz m
- F: protection f contre les défauts à la terre

grounding n (US)
- D: Erdung f
- F: mise f à la terre

grounding circuit (US)
- D: Erdungsleitung f
- F: circuit m de mise à la terre

grounding conductor (US)
- D: Erdleiter m, Erdleitung f, Erdseil n
- F: conducteur m de terre, fil m de garde

grounding of neutral (US)
- D: Sternpunkterdung f
- F: mise f à la terre du neutre

ground lead (US)
- D: Erddraht m
- F: fil m de terre

ground phantom circuit
- D: Phantomkreis mit Erdrückleitung
- F: circuit m fantôme avec retour par la terre

ground potential (US)
- D: Erdpotential n
- F: potentiel m de terre

ground resistance (US)
- D: Erdungswiderstand m
- F: résistance f de terre

ground return circuit (US)
- D: Erdrückleitung f
- F: circuit m de retour par la terre

ground shield (US)
- D: Erdungsschirm m
- F: écran m de mise à la terre, écran m de terre

ground(ing) system (US)
- D: Erdungsanlage f
- F: système m de mise à la terre

ground terminal (US)
- D: Erdungsklemme f, Erdklemme f
- F: borne f de terre, prise f de terre

ground water [c. install.]
- D: Grundwasser n
- F: eau f souterraine, nappe f d'eau souterraine

ground wire (US)
- D: Erdleiter m, Erdleitung f, Erdseil n
- F: conducteur m de terre, fil m de garde m

group delay time [com.]
- D: Gruppenlaufzeit f
- F: temps m de propagation de groupe

grouping factor
- D: Ballungsfaktor m
- F: coefficient m d'accumulation

grouping of cables [c. install.]
- D: Häufung von Kabeln, Anhäufung von Kabeln, Ballung von Kabeln, Belegung mit Kabeln
- F: accumulation f de câbles, groupement m de câbles

grouping of factory lengths
- D: Gruppieren von Fertigungslängen
- F: groupement m de longueurs de fabrication

group modulator [com.]
- D: Gruppenumsetzer m
- F: équipement m de modulation de groupe

group propagation time [com.]
- D: Gruppenlaufzeit f
- F: temps m de propagation de groupe

GRS (butadiene-styrene rubber) (US)

guard n [mach.]
D: Schutzabdeckung f, Sicherheitsabdeckung f
F: carter m de sécurité, carter m enveloppe, carter m de protection

guard circuit
D: Sprachsperre f
F: dispositif m d'audio-supression

guard plate
D: Abdeckplatte f
F: plaque f protectrice, plaque f de recouvrement

guard wire
D: Erdleiter m, Erdleitung f, Erdseil n
F: conducteur m de terre, fil de garde m

guide pulley
D: Führungsrolle f, Leitrolle f
F: rouleau-guide m, poulie f de guidage

guide rail
D: Führungsschiene f, Laufschiene f
F: rail m de guidage, rail m de roulement

guide roller
D: Führungsrolle f, Leitrolle f
F: rouleau-guide m, poulie f de guidage

guider tip [extr.]
D: Führungsnippel m
F: poinçon m guide

gum rosin
D: Harz n (Naturharz), Kolophonium n
F: colophane f

gutta percha
D: Guttapercha f
F: gutta-percha f

guy wire
D: Spanndraht m
F: fil m tendeur, fil m d'arrêt

H

half-lapped adj
D: mit 50% Überlappung
F: à 50% de recouvrement

half shell
D: Halbschale f
F: demi-coquille f

hand-applied adj
D: von Hand aufgebracht
F: posé adj à la main

handhole n [com.]
D: Handloch n
F: trou m de poing

hand lever
D: Bedienungshebel m
F: levier m de commande

handling
D: Transport m (innerbetrieblich)
F: manutention f

handling
D: Betätigung f, Bedienung f
F: commande f, manœuvre f, manipulation f

handling time [mach.]
D: Nebenzeit f
F: temps m auxiliaire, temps m mort

hand-operated adj
D: handbetätigt adj
F: commandé adj manuellement, à commande manuelle

hand operation
D: Handbetrieb m, Handsteuerung f
F: opération f manuelle, commande f manuelle, opération f à main

hard-drawn wire
D: harter Draht, hartgezogener Draht
F: fil m dur, fil m écroui

harden v
D: erstarren v, hartwerden v
F: solidifier v (se), congéler v, durcir v

harden v [adh.]
D: abbinden v
F: durcir v

hardenability n
D: Härtbarkeit f
F: aptitude au durcissement f

hardenable adj
D: härtbar adj
F: durcissable adj

hardener n
D: Härter m
F: durcisseur m, agent de durcissement m

hardening n
D: Härtung f
F: durcissement m

hardening

hardening n
D: Erstarrung f
F: solidification f, congélation f

hardening and tempering operation [met.]
D: Vergüten n
F: traitement m thermique, trempe f

hard metal (drawing) die
D: Hartmetall-Ziehstein m
F: filière f (de tréfilage) en métal dur, filière f (de tréfilage) en carbure de tungstène

hardness n
D: Härte f
F: dureté f

hardness tester
D: Härteprüfer m, Durometer n
F: appareil m de contrôle de la dureté, duromètre m

hard solder
D: Hartlot n
F: brasure f

harmful adj
D: schädlich adj
F: néfaste adj, nocif adj, nuisible adj

haul-off capstan
D: Scheibenabzug m, Abzugscheibe f
F: cabestan m de tirage, roue f de tirage, cabestan m tireur

haul-off device
D: Abzugsvorrichtung f
F: dispositif m de tirage

HD-PE (s. high-density PE)

head loss
D: Druckabfall m, Druckverlust m
F: chute f de pression, dépression f, perte f de pression

heat, to carry away the ~
D: die Wärme ableiten
F: dissiper v la chaleur

heat, to conduct away the ~
D: die Wärme ableiten
F: dissiper v la chaleur

heat, to dissipate the ~
D: die Wärme ableiten
F: dissiper v la chaleur

heat absorption
D: Wärmeaufnahme f
F: absorption f de chaleur

heat barrier
D: Wärmeschutz m (über Kabelisolierung)
F: isolation f thermique

heat-curing adj
D: warmhärtend adj
F: thermodurcissable adj

heat cycles
D: Wärmezyklen m pl
F: cycles m pl de chauffage, cycles m pl thermiques

heat deformation
D: Deformation in der Wärme
F: déformation f à chaud

heat dissipation
D: Wärmeableitung f
F: dissipation f de la chaleur, évacuation f des calories

heat dissipation diagram
D: Abkühlkurve f
F: courbe f de refroidissement

heat distortion
D: Deformation in der Wärme
F: déformation f à chaud

heat distortion temperature
D: Erweichungstemperatur f
F: température f de ramollissement, température f de déformation à chaud

heat due to losses
D: Verlustwärme f
F: chaleur f due aux pertes

heated cabinet
D: Wärmeschrank m
F: étuve f

heat exchange
D: Wärmeaustausch m
F: échange m de chaleur, échange m thermique

heat exchanger
D: Wärmeaustauscher m
F: échangeur m de chaleur, échangeur m thermique

heat fusing tape
D: warmverschweißendes Band
F: ruban m thermosoudant

heating n
D: Beheizung f, Heizung f
F: chauffage m

heating n
D: Erwärmung f
F: chauffage m, échauffement m

heating and cooling cycles
D: Erwärmungs- und Abkühlungszyklen m
F: cycles m pl d'échauffement et de refroidissement

heating cabinet
D: Wärmeschrank m
F: étuve f

heating cable
D: Heizkabel n
F: câble m de chauffage, câble m chauffant

heating coil
D: Heizschlange f
F: serpentin m de chauffage

heating collar
D: Heizband n
F: ruban m de chauffage, collier chauffant m

heating power
D: Heizleistung f
F: puissance f de chauffage

heating resistor
D: Heizwiderstand m
F: résistance f de chauffage

heating tapes pl
D: Heizbandage f
F: frette f de chauffage

heating-up time
D: Aufheizzeit f
F: temps m de chauffage

heating wire
D: Heizleitung f
F: câble m de chauffage, conducteur m chauffant

heating zone [extr.]
D: Heizzone f
F: zone f de chauffage

heat-proof adj
D: wärmebeständig adj
F: résistant adj à la chaleur

heat removal
D: Wärmeableitung f
F: dissipation f de la chaleur, évacuation f des calories

heat resistance
D: Wärmebeständigkeit f, Hitzebeständigkeit f, Wärmestandfestigkeit f
F: résistance f à la chaleur, résistance f thermique, stabilité f thermique

heat-resistant adj
D: wärmebeständig adj
F: résistant adj à la chaleur

heat-resistant insulated wire
D: hitzebeständige Aderleitung
F: conducteur m résistant aux températures élevées

heat-resistant rubber-insulated cable
D: wärmebeständige Gummiaderleitung
F: conducteur m (à âme souple) isolé au caoutchouc résistant à la chaleur

heat-resistant sheathed flexible cable
D: hitzebeständige Schlauchleitung
F: câble m souple sous gaine résistant aux températures élevées

heat-seal v
D: warmverschweißen v
F: thermosouder v

heat-sensitive adj
D: wärmeempfindlich adj
F: sensible adj à la chaleur

heat shock
D: Wärmeschock m
F: choc m thermique

heat shock resistance
D: Wärmeschockbeständigkeit f
F: résistance f aux craquelures

heat shock test
D: Wärmeschockprüfung f
F: essai m de choc thermique

heat-shrink v
D: aufschrumpfen v
F: emmancher v à chaud

heat-shrinkable cable accessories
D: wärmeschrumpfende Kabelgarnituren
F: accessoires m pl de câbles emmanchables à chaud

heat-shrinkable sleeve
D: Schrumpfmuffe f, Aufschrumpfmuffe f
F: manchon m emmanché à chaud

heat-shrinkable termination
D: wärmeschrumpfender Endverschluß, aufschrumpfbarer Endverschluß
F: extrémité f emmanchable à chaud

heat-shrinkable tubing
D: Schrumpfschlauch m
F: tuyau m emmanchable à chaud, gaine f thermorétractable, manchon m thermorétractable

heat-shrinkage n
D: Schrumpfung beim Erwärmen, Wärmeschrumpfung f
F: retrait m au chauffage

heat-shrinkage insulating sleeve
D: Schrumpfmuffe f,

heat-shrinkage
    Aufschrumpfmuffe f
  F: manchon *m* emmanché à chaud

heat-shrinkage technique
  D: Wärmeschrumpftechnik f,
    Aufschrumpftechnik f
  F: technique f d'emmanchement à chaud

heat source
  D: Wärmequelle f
  F: source f de chaleur

heat transfer
  D: Wärmeübergang m, Wärmeübertragung f
  F: transmission f calorifique, transmission f de chaleur

heat transfer resistance
  D: Wärmeübergangswiderstand m
  F: résistance f de transmission de chaleur

heat transmission
  D: Wärmeübergang m, Wärmeübertragung f
  F: transmission f calorifique, transmission f de chaleur

heat transmission resistance
  D: Wärmeübergangswiderstand m
  F: résistance f de transmission de chaleur

heat treatment
  D: Wärmebehandlung f
  F: traitement *m* thermique

heat treatment [met.]
  D: Vergüten n
  F: traitement *m* thermique, trempe f

heavily loaded
  D: hochbeansprucht *adj*, hochbelastet *adj*
  F: fortement chargé

heavily loaded locality [c. install.]
  D: dicht besiedeltes Gebiet, Ballungszentrum n
  F: grande agglomération urbaine, zone f de forte agglomération

heavily stressed
  D: hochbeansprucht *adj*, hochbelastet *adj*
  F: fortement chargé

heavy-duty cable
  D: Kabel für schwere Beanspruchungen
  F: câble *m* pour contraintes sévères

heavy-duty machine
  D: Hochleistungsmaschine f
  F: machine f à grand rendement, machine f à grand débit, machine f à grande puissance, machine f à grande vitesse

heavy tough-rubber sheathed flexible cable
  D: schwere Gummischlauchleitung
  F: câble *m* souple sous gaine épaisse de caoutchouc

helical application
  D: wendelförmige Aufbringung
  F: enroulement *m* hélicoïdal

helical coil
  D: Wickellocke f
  F: hélice f d'essai

helically, to apply ~
  D: wendelförmig aufbringen
  F: poser *v* en hélice, enrouler *v* en hélice

helical marking
  D: Wendelmarkierung f
  F: marquage *m* hélicoïdal, repérage *m* hélicoïdal

helix, closed ~
  D: geschlossene Wendel
  F: hélice f fermée

helix, in a closed ~ [lapp.]
  D: auf Stoß
  F: en hélice fermée, en spires jointives

helix, open ~
  D: offene Wendel
  F: hélice f de vide

helper n
  D: Hilfsarbeiter m
  F: aide *m*, auxiliaire *m*

hermetically sealed
  D: luftdicht *adj*
  F: étanche *adj* à l'air

hermetic seal
  D: Luftabschluß m
  F: étanchéité f à l'air

hertz
  D: Hertz (Hz)
  F: cycles *m pl* par seconde, hertz, périodes *f pl* par seconde

hessian tape
  D: Hessianband n (Jute)
  F: ruban *m* Hessian

hexagonal compression [c. access.]
  D: Sechskantpressung f
  F: sertissage *m* hexagonal

HF (s. high frequency)

high-capacity machine

high-conductivity...
 D: hochleitfähig adj
 F: à haute conductibilité

high-conductivity aluminium
 D: Leitaluminium (EC-Aluminium) n
 F: aluminium m à haute conductibilité

high-conductivity copper
 D: Leitkupfer (EC-Kupfer) n
 F: cuivre m à haute conductibilité

high-density PE (HD-PE)
 D: Niederdruck-PE n
 F: polyéthylène m haute densité,
    polyéthylène m basse pression

high frequency (HF)
 D: Hochfrequenz (HF) f
 F: haute fréquence f (HF), fréquence f
    radioélectrique

high-frequency antenna cable
 D: Hochfrequenz-Antennenkabel n,
    HF-Antennenkabel n
 F: câble m d'antenne à haute
    fréquence

high-frequency cable
 D: Hochfrequenzkabel n
 F: câble m à haute fréquence, câble m
    à fréquence radioélectrique

high-frequency coaxial cable
 D: Hochfrequenz-Koaxialkabel n,
    koaxiales Hochfrequenzkabel n
 F: câble m coaxial à haute fréquence,
    câble m coaxial à fréquence
    radioélectrique

highly conductive
 D: hochleitfähig adj
 F: à haute conductibilité

highly resistive
 D: hochohmig adj
 F: de haute valeur ohmique, de grande
    résistance

highly stressed
 D: hochbeansprucht adj,
    hochbelastet adj
 F: fortement chargé

high-molecular...
 D: mit hohem Molekulargewicht,
    hochmolekular adj
 F: à haut poids moléculaire

high-ohmic adj

D: Hochleistungsmaschine f
F: machine f à grand rendement,
   machine f à grand débit, machine f
   à grande puissance, machine f à
   grande vitesse

 D: hochohmig adj
 F: de haute valeur ohmique, de grande
    résistance

high-polymer
 D: Hochpolymerisat n
 F: haut polymère m

high power cable
 D: Hochleistungskabel n
 F: câble m à grande puissance

high-pressure oil-filled cable
 D: Öl-Hochdruck-Kabel n
 F: câble m à huile fluide à haute
    pression, câble m sous haute
    pression d'huile

high-pressure oil-filled pipe type cable
 D: Hochdruck-Ölkabel im Stahlrohr,
    Oilostatic-Kabel n
 F: câble m en tube d'acier sous haute
    pression d'huile, câble m
    Oléostatique

high-pressure PE (HP-PE)
 D: Hochdruck-PE n
 F: polyéthylène m basse densité,
    polyéthylène m haute pression

high-speed continuous wire take-up
 D: Schnellaufwickelei für Draht
 F: enrouleur m de fil métallique à
    grande vitesse

high-speed machine
 D: Hochleistungsmaschine f
 F: machine f à grand rendement,
    machine f à grand débit, machine f
    à grande puissance, machine f à
    grande vitesse

high-speed strander
 D: Schnellverseilmaschine f
 F: câbleuse f à grande vitesse

high speed vertical twister [com. c.]
 D: vertikale Schnellverseilmaschine
 F: câbleuse f verticale à grande
    vitesse

high tension
 D: Hochspannung f
 F: haute tension f (HT)

high-tension cable
 D: Hochspannungskabel n
 F: câble m à haute tension, câble m
    HT

high-tension transformer
 D: Hochspannungstransformator m
 F: transformateur m (de) haute
    tension

high vacuum (10^{-3} to 10^{-6} torr)
  D: Hochvakuum n
  F: vide m poussé (10^{-3} à 10^{-6} torr)
high-viscosity oil
  D: hochviskoses Öl
  F: huile f à viscosité élevée
high voltage (HV)
  D: Hochspannung f
  F: haute tension f (HT)
high-voltage cable
  D: Hochspannungskabel n
  F: câble m à haute tension, câble m HT
high-voltage d.c. transmission
  D: Hochspannungs-Gleichstrom-Übertragung (HGÜ) f
  F: transport m de courant continu à haute tension
high-voltage switchgear
  D: Hochspannungsschaltanlage f
  F: installation f de disjoncteurs haute tension
high-voltage transformer
  D: Hochspannungstransformator m
  F: transformateur m (de) haute tension
hinged adj
  D: ausschwenkbar adj, ausklappbar adj, schwenkbar adj, aufklappbar adj, drehbar gelagert
  F: pivotant adj, articulé adj
Hochstadter cable
  D: Höchstädter-Kabel (H-Kabel) n
  F: câble m du type Hochstadter, câble m à écran en papier métallisé
holder n
  D: Halterung f
  F: support m
holding n [tel.]
  D: Belegung f
  F: occupation f, prise f
holding furnace [c. c. r.]
  D: Warmhalteofen m
  F: four m de maintien à température, four m d'attente
holding tape [cab.]
  D: Haltewendel f
  F: frettage m, spirale f de fixation
hole n
  D: Bohrung f
  F: trou m, alésage m
hollow conductor [pow. c.]
  D: Hohlleiter m
  F: âme f creuse
hollow mandrel [met. extr. pr.]
  D: Hohldorn m
  F: mandrin m creux
hollow ram [met. extr. pr.]
  D: Hohlstempel m
  F: fouloir m creux
homogeneous adj
  D: einheitlich adj
  F: homogène adj, uniforme adj
hood n
  D: Abdeckhaube f
  F: capot m
hood n
  D: Kapelle f (Abzug)
  F: hotte f
hood type (annealing) furnace
  D: Haubenglühofen m, Blankglühofen m
  F: four m à tremper, four m pour recuit brillant
hook-up wire
  D: Schaltader f, Schaltdraht m
  F: fil m de connexion, jarretière f
hopper n
  D: Trichter m
  F: trémie f, entonnoir m
hopper throat [extr.]
  D: Trichtermündung f
  F: embouchure f de trémie
horizontal cage type lapping machine
  D: horizontaler Korbspinner
  F: rubaneuse f horizontale à cage
hose n
  D: Schlauch m
  F: tuyau m
hot-air welding with plastic welding rod
  D: Heißluftschweißen mit Kunststoff-Drahtzufuhr
  F: soudage m à air chaud avec fil de soudage plastique
hot bending test
  D: Warmbiegeprüfung f
  F: essai m de pliage à chaud
hot deformation resistance
  D: Wärmedruckbeständigkeit f
  F: résistance f à la pression aux températures élevées
hot deformation strength
  D: Wärmedruckbeständigkeit f
  F: résistance f à la pression aux températures élevées

hot filling compound
  D: Warmvergußmasse *f*
  F: matière *f* de remplissage à chaud
hot forming
  D: Warmverformung *f,*
  Warmformung *f,*
  Warmverarbeitung *f*
  F: mise *f* en forme à chaud, façonnage *m* à chaud
hot pouring compound
  D: Warmvergußmasse *f*
  F: matière *f* de remplissage à chaud
hot pressure test
  D: Wärmedruckprüfung *f*
  F: essai *m* de pression à température élevée, essai *m* de compression à chaud, essai *m* d'écrasement à chaud
hot-roll *v*
  D: warmwalzen *v*
  F: laminer *v* à chaud
hot-rolling mill
  D: Warmwalzwerk *n*
  F: laminoir *m* à chaud
hot-set-test
  D: Prüfung auf bleibende Dehnung
  F: essai *m* d'allongement permanent
hot-short *adj*
  D: warmbrüchig *adj*
  F: cassant *adj* à chaud
hot spot
  D: Heißstelle *f*
  F: point *m* chaud, pointe *f* locale de température
hot-workability *n*
  D: Warmverformbarkeit *f,*
  Warmformbarkeit *f*
  F: malléabilité *f* à chaud
hot-working *n*
  D: Warmverformung *f,*
  Warmformung *f,*
  Warmverarbeitung *f*
  F: mise *f* en forme à chaud, façonnage *m* à chaud
house service box
  D: Hausanschlußmuffe *f*
  F: boîte *f* de raccordement domestique
house wiring
  D: Hausinstallation *f*
  F: installation *f* intérieure
house wiring cable [pow. c.]
  D: Installationsleitung *f,*
  Hausinstallationsleitung *f*
  F: câble *m* domestique
housing *n*
  D: Gehäuse *n*
  F: boîte *f,* caisse *f*
HP-PE (s. high-pressure PE)
'H'-type cable
  D: Höchstädter-Kabel (H-Kabel) *n*
  F: câble *m* du type Hochstadter, câble *m* à écran en papier métallisé
humidity *n*
  D: Feuchtigkeit *f*
  F: humidité *f*
humidity, relative ~
  D: relative Luftfeuchtigkeit
  F: degré *m* hygrométrique, humidité *f* relative
humidity of the air
  D: Luftfeuchtigkeit *f*
  F: humidité *f* de l'air
hum-modulation *n*
  D: Brumm-Modulation *f*
  F: ronflement *m* de modulation
HV (s. high voltage)
H.V. cable
  D: Hochspannungskabel *n*
  F: câble *m* à haute tension, câble *m* HT
hydraulic power pack
  D: hydraulisches Antriebsaggregat
  F: unité *f* d'entraînement hydraulique
hydraulic pressure
  D: Wasserdruck *m*
  F: pression *f* hydraulique, pression *f* d'eau
hydrocarbon polymers
  D: Kohlenwasserstoffpolymere *n pl*
  F: polymères *m pl* d'hydrocarbure
hydrodynamic resistance
  D: Strömungswiderstand *m*
  F: résistance *f* hydraulique
hydro-electric power station
  D: Wasserkraftwerk *n*
  F: centrale *f* hydroélectrique
hydrophobic *adj*
  D: wasserabstoßend *adj*
  F: hydrofuge *adj,* hydrophobe *adj*
hydrostatic extrusion [met.]
  D: hydrostatisches Extrudieren
  F: extrusion *f* hydrostatique

I

IACS (International Annealed Copper Standard) (according to IEC)
  D: IACS (Standardwert des spezifischen Widerstandes von weichgeglühtem Kupfer) (nach IEC)
  F: IACS (valeur standard de la résistivité du cuivre recuit) (selon la CEI)

I.A.C.S. conductivity (International Annealed Copper Standard/IEC)
  D: Standard-Leitfähigkeit nach IEC (Kupfer), I.A.C.S.-Leitfähigkeit f (Kupfer)
  F: conductivité f I.A.C.S. (cuivre), conductibilité f I.A.C.S. (cuivre)

I.A.C.S. resistance (International Annealed Copper Standard/IEC)
  D: Standard-Widerstand nach IEC (Kupfer)
  F: résistance f I.A.C.S. (cuivre)

I.B.P. (s. initial boiling point)

IC (s. integrated circuit)

Iceland-Canada telephone cable (ICECAN cable)
  D: Island-Kanada-Kabel n
  F: câble m téléphonique d'Islande au Canada

identification n [cab.]
  D: Kennzeichnung f
  F: désignation f, identification f, marquage m, repérage m

identification thread
  D: Kennfaden m
  F: fil m d'identification, fil m distinctif, filin m de reconnaissance

idle current
  D: Blindstrom m
  F: courant m réactif

idler pulley
  D: Leerlaufrolle f
  F: poulie f de marche à vide

idle time [mach.]
  D: Stillstandszeit f, Totzeit f
  F: temps m d'arrêt, temps m mort

ignition cable
  D: Zündkabel n
  F: câble m d'allumage

ignition point
  D: Zündpunkt m
  F: point m d'allumage

ignition point
  D: Entzündungspunkt m (Öle), Flammpunkt m, Brennpunkt m (chem.)
  F: point m d'inflammation

ignition residue
  D: Glührückstand m
  F: résidu m de calcination, résidu m de recuit

image attenuation constant
  D: Vierpoldämpfung f, Wellendämpfung f
  F: affaiblissement m sur images

image screen
  D: Bildschirm m
  F: écran m, écran m de vision

immerse v
  D: eintauchen v
  F: immerger v, tremper v, plonger v

immersed length
  D: Unterwasserlänge f
  F: longueur f immergée, longueur f plongée

immersion in water
  D: Lagerung in Wasser, Wasserlagerung f, Eintauchen in Wasser
  F: immersion f dans l'eau

impact ionization
  D: Stoßionisation f
  F: ionisation f par choc

impact resistance
  D: Schlagzähigkeit f, Schlagfestigkeit f
  F: résistance f au choc mécanique, résilience f

impact resistance test at low temperature
  D: Kälteschlagprüfung f
  F: essai m de choc à basse température

impact strength
  D: Schlagzähigkeit f, Schlagfestigkeit f
  F: résistance f au choc mécanique, résilience f

impact test
  D: Schlagprobe f
  F: essai m au choc

impedance n
  D: Scheinwiderstand m
  F: impédance f

impedance test
 D: Impedanz-Prüfung f
 F: contrôle m d'impédance
impenetrable to ...
 D: undurchlässig für ...
 F: imperméable adj à, impénétrable adj pour,
impermeability n
 D: Undurchlässigkeit f
 F: imperméabilité f
impermeability to gas
 D: Gasdichtigkeit f, Gasundurchlässigkeit f
 F: étanchéité f au gaz, imperméabilité f au gaz
impermeable to ...
 D: undurchlässig für ...
 F: imperméable adj à, impénétrable adj pour,
impermeable to gas
 D: gasundurchlässig adj
 F: étanche adj au gaz, imperméable adj au gaz,
impervious to ...
 D: undurchlässig für ...
 F: imperméable adj à, impénétrable adj pour,
impregnant n
 D: Tränkmittel n
 F: imprégnant m
impregnate v
 D: tränken v
 F: imprégner v
impregnated adj
 D: durchtränkt adj
 F: imprégné adj
impregnated, fully ~
 D: sattgetränkt adj
 F: imprégné adj jusqu'à saturation
impregnated gas-pressure cable
 D: Gasaußendruck-Kabel n
 F: câble m à compression externe de gaz
impregnated paper
 D: getränktes Papier
 F: papier m imprégné
impregnated paper insulated cable
 D: Kabel mit getränkter Papierisolierung
 F: câble m isolé au papier imprégné
impregnating compound
 D: Tränkmasse f, Imprägniermasse f
 F: matière f d'imprégnation

impregnating medium
 D: Tränkmittel n
 F: imprégnant m
impregnating resin
 D: Tränkharz n
 F: résine f imprégnatrice
impregnating tank
 D: Tränkgefäß n
 F: cuve f d'imprégnation
impregnating tray
 D: Tränkkorb m
 F: panier m d'imprégnation
impregnating varnish
 D: Tränklack m
 F: vernis m d'imprégnation
impregnation
 D: Imprägnierung f, Tränkung f
 F: imprégnation f
improvement n
 D: Verbesserung f
 F: amélioration f
impulse n (el.)
 D: Stoßwelle f, Spannungsstoß m
 F: onde f de choc
impulse breakdown strength
 D: Stoßdurchschlagfestigkeit f
 F: résistance f au claquage sous tension de choc
impulse current
 D: Stoßstrom m
 F: courant m de choc
impulse flashover voltage
 D: Überschlag-Stoßspannung f
 F: tension f de contournement au choc
impulse frequency
 D: Impulsfrequenz f
 F: fréquence f d'impulsion
impulse generator
 D: Stoßspannungsanlage f
 F: génératrice f de choc
impulse level
 D: Stoßpegel m
 F: seuil m de choc
impulse spark-over voltage
 D: Überschlag-Stoßspannung f
 F: tension f de contournement au choc
impulse test
 D: Stoßspannungs-Prüfung f, Stoßprüfung f (el.)
 F: essai m aux ondes de choc, essai m au choc

impulse voltage
D: Stoßspannung f
F: tension f de choc

impulse voltage behaviour
D: Stoßspannungsverhalten n
F: comportement m aux ondes de choc

impulse (voltage) strength
D: Stoßspannungsfestigkeit f
F: résistance f aux ondes de choc, tenue f aux ondes de choc

impulse voltage test
D: Stoßspannungs-Prüfung f, Stoßprüfung f (el.)
F: essai m aux ondes de choc, essai m au choc

impulse withstand voltage
D: Stehstoßspannung f
F: tension f de tenue au choc, tension f de tenue aux ondes de choc

impurity n
D: Verunreinigung f
F: contamination f, impureté f

inaccessible adj
D: unzugänglich adj
F: inaccessible adj

inaccuracy n
D: Ungenauigkeit f (Anzeige, Messung)
F: imprécision f, inexactitude f

inaccurate adj
D: ungenau adj
F: inexact adj, imprécis adj

inadmissible adj
D: unzulässig adj
F: inadmissible adj

incentive scheme
D: Akkordarbeit f
F: travail m à la pièce, travail m à forfait

incineration n
D: Veraschung f
F: incinération f

inclinable adj
D: kippbar adj
F: inclinable adj, basculant adj, renversable adj

inclination n
D: Neigung f
F: inclinaison f, basculement m

inclined adj
D: schräg adj
F: incliné adj, oblique adj

inclusions pl
D: Einschlüsse m pl
F: inclusions f pl, occlusions f pl

incombustibility n
D: Unbrennbarkeit f
F: non-inflammabilité f, incombustibilité f

incombustible adj
D: unbrennbar adj
F: non-inflammable adj, incombustible adj

incoming, testing of ~ materials
D: Wareneingangskontrolle f
F: contrôle m à la livraison, contrôle m à la réception du matériel

incoming inspection
D: Wareneingangskontrolle f
F: contrôle m à la livraison, contrôle m à la réception du matériel

incorporation n
D: Einlagerung f, Zwischenlagerung f
F: interposition f, entreposage m

increase v
D: vergrößern v
F: augmenter v, élargir v, grossir v, agrandir v

increase n
D: Erhöhung f, Steigerung f
F: augmentation f, élévation f

increment, in ~s of ...
D: in Stufen von ...
F: par paliers de ..., par échelons de ...

indelible adj
D: unauslöschlich adj (Farbe)
F: indélébile adj

indentation depth
D: Eindrucktiefe f
F: profondeur f de l'empreinte

indentation load
D: Eindrücklast f
F: charge f d'empreinte

indentation time
D: Eindrückzeit f
F: temps m d'empreinte

indicating dial
D: Meßuhr f
F: compteur m, indicateur m à cadran

indicating lamp
D: Signallampe f, Anzeigelampe f
F: voyant m lumineux, signal m lumineux, lampe-témoin f

indication n
D: Anzeige f

F: indication *f*, signalisation *f*, lecture *f*, affichage *m*

indicative, to be ~ of
D: Aufschluß geben über (z.B. Betriebsverhalten)
F: fournir *v* des renseignements sur

indicator
D: Anzeigevorrichtung *f*
F: indicateur *m*

indicator circuit
D: Anzeigestromkreis *m*
F: circuit *m* indicateur

indicator panel
D: Anzeigetafel *f*
F: panneau *m* indicateur de fonctionnement, tableau *m* indicateur

individually screened cable cores
D: einzeln abgeschirmte Kabeladern
F: conducteurs *m pl* de câble avec écran individuel

indoor installation
D: Innenraum-Verlegung *f*
F: pose *f* à l'intérieur

indoor plant
D: Innenraum-Anlage *f*
F: installation *f* intérieure

indoor termination
D: Innenraum-Endverschluß *m*
F: extrémité *f* intérieure

indoor wiring cable
D: Innenraumleitung *f*
F: câble *m* pour installation intérieure

induced current
D: Induktionsstrom *m*
F: courant *m* induit, courant *m* d'induction

induced voltage
D: induzierte Spannung, Induktionsspannung *f*
F: tension *f* induite

inductance *n*
D: Induktivität *f*
F: inductance *f*

induction current
D: Induktionsstrom *m*
F: courant *m* induit, courant *m* d'induction

induction furnace
D: Induktionsofen *m*
F: four *m* à induction

induction heating
D: Induktionsheizung *f*
F: chauffage *m* à induction

inductive conductor heating
D: induktive Leiterheizung
F: chauffage *m* de l'âme par induction

inductive coupling
D: induktive Kopplung
F: couplage *m* inductif

inductive current
D: Induktionsstrom *m*
F: courant *m* induit, courant *m* d'induction

inductive influence on neighbouring cables
D: induktive Beeinflussung benachbarter Kabel
F: effet *m* inductif sur des câbles voisins

inductive interference with neighbouring cables
D: induktive Beeinflussung benachbarter Kabel
F: effet *m* inductif sur des câbles voisins

inductive resistance
D: induktiver Widerstand
F: résistance *f* inductive

industrial, produced on an ~ scale
D: hergestellt im Fertigungsmaßstab
F: réalisé *adj* à l'échelle industrielle

industrial television
D: Industriefernsehen *n*
F: télévision *f* industrielle

ineffective *adj*
D: unwirksam *adj*
F: inefficace *adj*

inert *adj*
D: reaktionsträge *adj*
F: inerte *adj*

inert gas
D: Schutzgas *n*, reduzierendes Gas, Inertgas *n*
F: gaz *m* inerte, gaz *m* de protection, gaz *m* réducteur

inert gas arc welding
D: Schutzgasschweißen *n*
F: soudage *m* à arc en atmosphère protectrice

inexact *adj*
D: ungenau *adj*
F: inexact *adj*, imprécis *adj*

inexactitude *n*
D: Ungenauigkeit *f* (Anzeige, Messung)

inexactitude
   F: imprécision f, inexactitude f

infinitely variable
   D: stufenlos regelbar
   F: réglable sans à-coups, sans intervalles

infinitely variable gear
   D: stufenlos regelbares Getriebe
   F: engrenage m réglable sans à-coups

inflammability n
   D: Entzündbarkeit f
   F: inflammabilité f

inflammable adj (GB)
   D: brennbar adj, entflammbar adj
   F: combustible adj, inflammable adj

influence, inductive ~ on neighbouring cables
   D: induktive Beeinflussung benachbarter Kabel
   F: effet m inductif sur des câbles voisins

information material
   D: Unterlagen f pl (beschreibende oder zeichnerische Angaben)
   F: documents m pl, données f pl, documentation f

infra-red spectroscopy
   D: Infrarot-Spektroskopie f, IR-Spektroskopie f
   F: spectroscopie f infrarouge, spectroscopie f IR

infringement of a patent
   D: Patentverletzung f
   F: violation f d'un brevet, contrefaçon f d'un brevet

ingot n
   D: Drahtbarren m, Gußblock m
   F: lingot m

ingot mo(u)ld casting
   D: Kokillenguß m
   F: coulée f en coquille

ingots pl [met.]
   D: Formate n pl
   F: lingots m pl

ingredients of a compound
   D: Mischungsbestandteile m pl
   F: ingrédients m pl d'un mélange, composants m pl d'un mélange

ingress of moisture
   D: Eindringen von Feuchtigkeit
   F: pénétration f d'humidité

inherent quad coupling
   D: Imvierer-Kopplung f
   F: couplage m inhérent à la quarte, couplage m à l'intérieur de la quarte

inhibitor n
   D: Inhibitor m
   F: inhibiteur m

initial boiling point (I.B.P.)
   D: Siedebeginn (SB) m
   F: début m d'ébullition

initial pressure
   D: Anfangsdruck m
   F: pression f initiale

initial symmetric short-circuit current
   D: Anfangskurzschluß-Wechselstrom m
   F: courant m initial symétrique de court-circuit

initial temperature
   D: Eintrittstemperatur f
   F: température f d'entrée

initial value
   D: Ausgangswert m
   F: valeur f initiale

inject, to ~ a current
   D: einen Strom anlegen
   F: faire v passer un courant

injection mo(u)lding
   D: Spritzguß m
   F: moulage m par injection, fonte f injectée

ink-marking n
   D: Farbmarkierung f
   F: marquage m à l'encre, marquage m coloré

inlet n
   D: Einlauf m (in eine Maschine), Eintritt m, Einführung f (Kabel)
   F: entrée f

inlet insulator
   D: Einführungsisolator m
   F: isolateur m d'entrée

inlet temperature
   D: Eintrittstemperatur f
   F: température f d'entrée

inlet valve
   D: Einlaßventil n
   F: soupape f d'admission

inner conductor
   D: Innenleiter m
   F: conducteur m intérieur

inner diameter (ID)
   D: Innendurchmesser m, lichte Weite
   F: diamètre m intérieur

inner filling compound

inner filling sheath
 D: Zwickelmantelmischung f
 F: mélange m de bourrage
inner filling sheath
 D: gemeinsame gepreßte Aderumhüllung, Zwickelmantel m
 F: gaine f de bourrage, gaine f formant bourrage
inner semi-conducting layer
 D: Leiterdeckschicht f (schwachleitend), Leiterglättung f, Schirm (schwachleitend) über dem Leiter, innere Leitschicht
 F: écran m sur l'âme, écran m interne, couche f semi-conductrice interne
inoperative adj
 D: unwirksam adj
 F: inefficace adj
inorganic adj
 D: anorganisch adj
 F: inorganique adj
in-phase voltage
 D: Effektivspannung f, Wirkspannung f
 F: tension f efficace, tension f active
in-process testing
 D: Prüfung während der Fertigung
 F: essai m en cours de fabrication
input bobbin
 D: Einsatzspule f, Einsatztrommel f, Maschinenspule f, Maschinentrommel f, Werkstatttrommel f
 F: bobine f d'alimentation
input circuit
 D: Eingangskreis m
 F: circuit m d'entrée
input impedance
 D: Eingangsimpedanz f
 F: impédance f d'entrée
input reel
 D: Einsatzspule f, Einsatztrommel f, Maschinenspule f, Maschinentrommel f, Werkstatttrommel f
 F: bobine f d'alimentation
input resistance
 D: Eingangswiderstand m
 F: résistance f d'entrée
input voltage
 D: Primärspannung f
 F: tension f primaire
insensitive to ...
 D: unempfindlich gegen ...
 F: insensible adj à ...
insensitive, the measurements are ~ to small discharges
 D: die Messungen erfassen kleine Entladungen nicht mehr
 F: les mesures sont insensibles aux décharges de faible importance
insert v
 D: einsetzen v, einbauen v
 F: mettre v, placer v, insérer v
insertion n
 D: Einlagerung f, Zwischenlagerung f
 F: interposition f, entreposage m
inside diameter
 D: Innendurchmesser m, lichte Weite
 F: diamètre m intérieur
inside width
 D: lichte Weite
 F: diamètre m intérieur, largeur f intérieure, ouverture f
inside wiring
 D: innere Verdrahtung
 F: filerie f interne
inspect v
 D: besichtigen v
 F: examiner v, inspecter v
inspection n
 D: Untersuchung f, Prüfung f (Kontrolle)
 F: examen m, analyse f, contrôle m
inspection glass [mach.]
 D: Beobachtungsfenster n, Schauglas n, Schauloch n
 F: hublot m de regard, voyant m
inspection mark
 D: Prüfkennzeichen n
 F: marque f de contrôle
inspection officer
 D: Abnahmebeamter m
 F: réceptionnaire m
install v
 D: errichten v
 F: monter v, ériger v, installer v, assembler v
install v [cab.]
 D: auslegen v, verlegen v
 F: poser v
installation n
 D: Errichtung f, Montage f, Aufbau m
 F: implantation f, montage m, assemblage m
installation n [mach.]
 D: Anlage f

installation

F: installation f
installation, cable ~
 D: Verlegung von Kabeln
 F: pose f de câbles
installation below floor level
 D: Unterflur-Installation f
 F: installation f en sous-sol, installation f souterraine
installation conditions
 D: Legeverhältnisse n pl, Verlegebedingungen f pl
 F: conditions f pl de pose
installation depth [c. install.]
 D: Bettungstiefe f, Verlegetiefe f, Legungstiefe f
 F: profondeur f de pose
installation drawing
 D: Montagezeichnung f, Installationszeichnung f, Aufstellungszeichnung f
 F: plan m d'assemblage, plan m de montage
installation in free air
 D: Verlegung in Luft
 F: pose f à l'air libre
installation instructions pl
 D: Montageanleitung f
 F: instructions f pl de montage, notice f de montage
installation kit
 D: Montagesatz m
 F: ensemble m de montage
installation on the surface
 D: Aufputz-Installation f, Verlegung auf Putz
 F: pose f sur crépi, pose f apparente
installation rule
 D: Errichtungsvorschrift f
 F: prescription f d'installation, règle f d'installation
installation standard
 D: Errichtungsvorschrift f
 F: prescription f d'installation, règle f d'installation
installation under plaster
 D: Unterputz-Installation f, Verlegung unter Putz
 F: installation f sous crépi, pose f sous crépi, pose f encastrée
installation wires
 D: Installationsdrähte m pl (für Fernsprech- und Signalanlagen)
 F: fils m pl d'installation

installed capacity
 D: installierte Leistung, Ausbauleistung f
 F: puissance f installée
instantaneous breakdown strength
 D: Sofortdurchschlagfestigkeit f
 F: tenue f au claquage instantané
instructions pl **for use**
 D: Betriebsanleitung f, Bedienungsanleitung f
 F: mode m opératoire, mode m d'emploi, notice f d'utilisation, manuel m d'instruction
instrument n
 D: Gerät n
 F: appareil m, instrument m
insulant n
 D: Isolierstoff m, Isoliermaterial n
 F: isolant m
insulate v
 D: isolieren v
 F: isoler v
insulated conductor
 D: Ader f
 F: conducteur m isolé, fil m isolé
insulated neutral
 D: isolierter Sternpunkt
 F: neutre m isolé
insulated wire
 D: Ader f
 F: conducteur m isolé, fil m isolé
insulated wire
 D: Aderleitung f
 F: conducteur m (à âme rigide ou souple)
insulated wire
 D: Leitung f
 F: fil m isolé
insulating bell
 D: Glockenisolator m, Isolierglocke f
 F: isolateur m à cloche, cloche f isolante
insulating bush(ing)
 D: Isolierhülse f, Isolierbuchse f
 F: manchon m isolant, douille f isolante
insulating compound
 D: Adermischung f, Isoliermischung f
 F: mélange m isolant
insulating fluid
 D: Isolierflüssigkeit f
 F: liquide m isolant

insulating layer
D: Isolierschicht f
F: couche f isolante, paroi f isolante

insulating liquid
D: Isolierflüssigkeit f
F: liquide m isolant

insulating material
D: Isolierstoff m, Isoliermaterial n
F: isolant m

insulating oil
D: Isolieröl n
F: huile f isolante

insulating paper
D: Isolierpapier n
F: papier m isolant

insulating properties pl
D: Isoliervermögen n
F: pouvoir m isolant

insulating sleeve
D: Isolierhülse f, Isolierbuchse f
F: manchon m isolant, douille f isolante

insulating tape
D: Isolierband n
F: ruban m isolant

insulating varnish
D: Isolierlack m
F: vernis m isolant, vernis m d'émaillage

insulation
D: Isolierung f, Dielektrikum n
F: isolation f, isolant m, enveloppe f isolante, diélectrique m, isolement m

insulation, fully impregnated ~
D: vollimprägnierte Isolierung
F: isolation f à imprégnation totale

insulation against ground
D: Isolation gegen Erde
F: isolement m par rapport à la terre

insulation build-up
D: Isolierwickel m
F: reconstitution f d'isolant

insulation class
D: Wärmeklasse f
F: classe f d'isolement

insulation defect
D: Isolationsfehler m, Isolationsstörung f
F: défaut m d'isolement

insulation fault
D: Isolationsfehler m, Isolationsstörung f

F: défaut m d'isolement

insulation level
D: Isolationspegel m
F: niveau m d'isolement

insulation (class) rating
D: Reihenspannung f
F: tension f nominale d'isolement

insulation resistance
D: Isolationswiderstand m
F: résistance f d'isolement, résistance f diélectrique

insulation screen
D: Aderabschirmung f, Schirm über der Isolierung
F: écran m sur l'isolant

insulation shield (US)
D: Aderabschirmung f, Schirm über der Isolierung
F: écran m sur l'isolant

insulation test
D: Isolationsprüfung f
F: essai m d'isolement

insulation tester
D: Isolationsmesser m
F: appareil m de mesure d'isolement

insulation thickness
D: Isolierdicke f
F: épaisseur f d'isolant

insulator n
D: Isolator m
F: isolateur m

insulator, double groove ~
D: Glockenisolator mit doppelter Bundrille, Glockenisolator mit zwei Halsrillen
F: isolateur m à double rainure

insulator corrugation
D: Isolator-Rippen f pl
F: ondulation f d'isolateur

insulator string
D: Isolatorenkette f
F: chaîne f d'isolateurs

intact adj
D: unbeschädigt adj
F: intact adj

integral cooling of cables
D: direkte Kühlung von Kabeln
F: refroidissement m intégral des câbles, refroidissement m direct des câbles

integrated circuit (IC)
D: integrierter Schaltkreis
F: circuit m intégré

intelligible (linear) cross-talk
  D: verständliches (lineares) Nebensprechen
  F: diaphonie f intelligible (linéaire)
intensity n [el.]
  D: Stärke f
  F: intensité f, puissance f
interaction n
  D: Wechselwirkung f
  F: interaction f, action f réciproque
intercalated adj
  D: eingelagert adj, zwischengelagert adj
  F: interposé adj, entreposé adj
intercalated tapes
  D: dachziegelartig aufgebrachte Bänder
  F: rubans m pl imbriqués
intercalation n
  D: Einlagerung f, Zwischenlagerung f
  F: interposition f, entreposage m
interchangeable adj
  D: auswechselbar adj, austauschbar adj
  F: interchangeable adj
intercity cable
  D: Bezirkskabel n
  F: câble m régional, câble m suburbain
intercom cable
  D: Kabel für Gegensprechanlagen
  F: câble m d'intercommunication
intercommunication n
  D: Sprechverkehr m, Fernsprechverkehr m
  F: trafic m téléphonique
intercommunication cable
  D: Kabel für Gegensprechanlagen
  F: câble m d'intercommunication
interconnected system
  D: Verbundnetz n
  F: réseau m d'interconnexion, réseau m de liaison
interconnecting cable
  D: Verbindungskabel n, Schaltkabel n
  F: câble m de jonction, câble m de connexion
interconnection n
  D: Schaltung f, Verdrahtung f
  F: circuit m, montage m, schéma m de connexions, filerie f
interconnection system
  D: Verbundnetz n
  F: réseau m d'interconnexion, réseau m de liaison
intercrystalline brittleness [met.]
  D: interkristalline Brüchigkeit
  F: fragilité f intercristalline
intercrystalline crack [met.]
  D: interkristalliner Bruch
  F: cassure f intercristalline, cassure f intergranulaire
inter-exchange trunk cable [tel.]
  D: Amtsverbindungskabel n
  F: câble m de jonction entre centraux téléphoniques
interface n
  D: Grenzfläche f
  F: surface f de séparation, interface f
interface cable
  D: Schnittstellenkabel n
  F: câble m d'interface
interface pressure
  D: Grenzflächendruck m
  F: pression f à la surface de séparation
interfacial effect
  D: Grenzschicht-Effekt m
  F: effet m interfacial
interference n (effect)
  D: Störbeeinflussung f, Beeinflussung f
  F: effet m de perturbation, perturbation f, interférence f
interference, inductive ~ with neighbouring cables
  D: induktive Beeinflussung benachbarter Kabel
  F: effet m inductif sur des câbles voisins
interference elimination
  D: Entstörung f, Störbeseitigung f
  F: suppression f des parasites, déparasitage m
interference eliminator
  D: Störschutzeinrichtung f
  F: dispositif m antiparasites
interference field [com.]
  D: Störfeld n
  F: champ m perturbateur, champ m parasite
interference level [com. c.]
  D: Rauschpegel m, Geräuschpegel m, Störpegel m
  F: niveau m de bruit, niveau m des perturbations

interference of power cables with communication cables
 D: Beeinflussung von Nachrichtenleitungen durch Energieanlagen
 F: perturbation *f* des lignes de télécommunication par des lignes de transport d'énergie

interference protection
 D: Störschutz *m*
 F: antiparasitage *m*

interference source
 D: Störquelle *f*
 F: source *f* de perturbation

interference suppression
 D: Entstörung *f*, Störbeseitigung *f*
 F: suppression *f* des parasites, déparasitage *m*

interference suppression device
 D: Störschutzeinrichtung *f*
 F: dispositif *m* antiparasites

interference suppressor [com.]
 D: Störsperre *f*
 F: suppresseur *m* d'interférences

interference voltage
 D: Störspannung *f*, Beeinflussungsspannung *f*
 F: tension *f* perturbatrice, tension *f* parasite

interfering noise
 D: Störgeräusch *n*
 F: bruit *m* parasite, bruit *m* perturbateur

inter-layer coupling
 D: Lage-Lage Kopplung
 F: couplage *m* entre couches

interlinking of phases
 D: Phasenverkettung *f*
 F: interconnexion *f* des phases

interlock *v*
 D: blockieren *v*
 F: bloquer *v*

interlocked with
 D: gekoppelt mit
 F: lié *adj* à, couplé *adj* avec,

interlocked, carbon-loaded paper ~ with metallized paper
 D: dachziegelartig aufgebrachtes Rußpapier und metallisiertes Papier
 F: papier *m* carbone et papier métallisé imbriqués

interlocked tapes
 D: dachziegelartig aufgebrachte Bänder
 F: rubans *m pl* imbriqués

interlocking *n*
 D: Verriegelung *f*
 F: blocage *m*, verrouillage *m*

intermediate annealing [met.]
 D: Zwischenglühen *n*
 F: recuit *m* intermédiaire

intermediate piece
 D: Zwischenstück *n*, Verbindungsstück *n*, Anschlußstück *n*
 F: pièce *f* intermédiaire, pièce *f* de raccordement, raccord *m*, pièce *f* de jonction, adaptateur *m*

intermediate test
 D: Zwischenprüfung *f*
 F: essai *m* intermédiaire

intermediate wire [wire manuf.]
 D: Mitteldraht *m*
 F: fil *m* intermédiaire

intermediate wire gauge size
 D: Zwischendraht *m*
 F: fil *m* de diamètre intermédiaire

intermingle *v*
 D: vermischen *v*, mischen *v*
 F: mélanger *v*, mêler *v*

intermittent operation [el.]
 D: aussetzender Betrieb, Betrieb mit aussetzender Belastung
 F: service *m* intermittent, service *m* avec charge intermittente, régime *m* temporaire

intermittent operation
 D: periodischer Betrieb
 F: régime *m* périodique

intermittent process
 D: diskontinuierliches Verfahren, Chargenbetrieb *m*
 F: procédé *m* discontinu, service *m* en discontinu

intermittent service
 D: periodischer Betrieb
 F: régime *m* périodique

internal diameter
 D: Innendurchmesser *m*, lichte Weite
 F: diamètre *m* intérieur

internal gas pressure cable
 D: Gasinnendruck-Kabel *n*
 F: câble *m* à pression interne de gaz

internal mixer
 D: Innenmischer *m*, Kneter *m*

F: mélangeur m interne, malaxeur m

internal quad coupling
D: Imvierer-Kopplung f
F: couplage m inhérent à la quarte, couplage m à l'intérieur de la quarte

internal stress [mech.]
D: Eigenspannung f
F: contrainte f interne, tension f interne

internal wiring
D: innere Verdrahtung
F: filerie f interne

International Annealed Copper Standard (s. IACS)

interplay n
D: Wechselwirkung f
F: interaction f, action f réciproque

interpose v
D: zwischenschalten v
F: interposer v

interrupt v [el.]
D: abschalten v, ausschalten v
F: couper v, interrompre v, déconnecter v

interrupting capacity (US)
D: Ausschaltleistung f, Abschaltleistung f
F: puissance f de rupture, pouvoir m de coupure

intersection n
D: Knotenpunkt m
F: intersection f, point m nodal, nœud m, point m de jonction

interspace n
D: Zwischenraum m
F: espace m, intervalle m, jeu m

interstice n
D: Zwischenraum m
F: espace m, intervalle m, jeu m

interstices pl
D: Zwickelräume m pl (zwischen den Kabeladern)
F: interstices m pl

interval n
D: Zwischenraum m
F: espace m, intervalle m, jeu m

intimate bond
D: innige Verbindung
F: liaison f intime

intrinsically safe installation
D: eigensichere Anlage
F: installation f à sécurité intrinsèque

intrinsic viscosity
D: Eigenviskosität f, Grundviskosität f
F: viscosité f intrinsèque

introduce v
D: einführen v
F: insérer v, introduire v

inverse voltage
D: Sperrspannung f
F: tension f inverse, tension f d'arrêt

inverted type cable termination
D: umgekehrter Kabelendverschluß
F: extrémité f de câble du type inverti

investigation n
D: Untersuchung f, Prüfung f (Kontrolle)
F: examen m, analyse f, contrôle m

ion exchanger
D: Ionenaustauscher m
F: échangeur m d'ions

ionization n
D: Ionisation f
F: ionisation f

ionization by collision
D: Stoßionisation f
F: ionisation f par choc

ionization discharge
D: Glimmentladung f, Korona-Entladung f, Sprühentladung f
F: effluve f en couronne, décharge f par ionisation, décharge f en couronne

ionization extinction voltage
D: Ionisations-Aussetzspannung f
F: tension f d'extinction d'ionisation

ionization inception voltage
D: Ionisations-Einsetzspannung f
F: seuil m d'ionisation

ionization level
D: Ionisationspegel m
F: seuil m d'ionisation

ionizing discharge
D: Entladungsdurchschlag m
F: décharge f ionisante

irradiated PE
D: bestrahltes PE
F: polyéthylène m irradié

irradiation cross-linkable compound
D: strahlenvernetzbare Mischung
F: mélange m réticulable par irradiation

IR-spectroscopy n
D: Infrarot-Spektroskopie f, IR-Spektroskopie f

isolate v
 D: isolieren v
 F: isoler v
isolated neutral
 D: isolierter Sternpunkt
 F: neutre m isolé
isolating switch
 D: Trennschalter m
 F: sectionneur m, disjoncteur m
isolation n
 D: Isolation f, Isolierung f (Trennung)
 F: isolation f, isolement m

F: spectroscopie f infrarouge, spectroscopie f IR

J

jacket n
 D: Hülle f, Umhüllung f
 F: enveloppe f, revêtement m
jacket n [cab.]
 D: Mantel m
 F: gaine f
jacket removal tool [cab.]
 D: Rundschälwerkzeug n (zum schichtweisen Abtragen von extrudierten Kabel-Isolierungen und schwachleitenden Schichten), Schälwerkzeug n
 F: dispositif m de décortiquage (des couches isolantes et semiconductrices d'un câble), outil m de pelage, dispositif m de coupes minces
jacking up of a cable reel
 D: Aufbocken einer Kabeltrommel
 F: levage m d'un touret de câble
jaw n
 D: Einspannklaue f, Einspannklemme f, Klemmbacke f
 F: mâchoire f de serrage, mordache f
jaw n
 D: Greifer m (Raupenabzug)
 F: mâchoire f
jet n
 D: Düse f
 F: buse f, injecteur m, tuyère f
jet nozzle
 D: Sprühdüse f
 F: pulvérisateur m, atomiseur m

join v
 D: verbinden v
 F: raccorder v, lier v, joindre v, réunir v
joint v
 D: verbinden v
 F: raccorder v, lier v, joindre v, réunir v
joint n [cab.]
 D: Muffe f
 F: jonction f
joint n
 D: Verbindung f, Verbindungsstelle f
 F: jonction f
joint, to ~ cables
 D: Kabelverbindungen herstellen
 F: faire v des jonctions sur câble
joint box
 D: Muffengehäuse n
 F: boîte f de jonction
joint box
 D: Verbindungsmuffe f
 F: boîte f de jonction, jonction f
jointer n
 D: Monteur m
 F: monteur m
jointing n [cab.]
 D: Verbinden n
 F: raccordement m
joint protection box
 D: Schutzmuffe f
 F: manchon m protecteur
joint ring
 D: Dichtungsring m
 F: anneau m d'étanchéité, bague f d'étanchéité, joint m annulaire
joint sleeve
 D: Verbindungshülse f
 F: manchon m de jonction, manchon m de raccordement
jumper wire
 D: Schaltader f, Schaltdraht m
 F: fil m de connexion, jarretière f
junction n
 D: Abzweigung f
 F: dérivation f, raccordement m, branchement m
junction box [el.]
 D: Anschlußkasten m, Klemmenkasten m
 F: coffret m de distribution, boîte f de distribution, boîte f de dérivation, boîte f de connexion, coffret m de

junction
    raccordement, boîte f de jonction, boîte f à bornes
junction box
    D: Anschlußmuffe f
    F: manchon m de raccordement
junction cable
    D: Ringkabel n
    F: câble m de liaison circulaire
junction point
    D: Knotenpunkt m
    F: intersection f, point m nodal, nœud m, point m de jonction
jute bedding
    D: Jute-Polster n
    F: matelas m de jute
jute filler
    D: Jute-Beilauf m
    F: bourrage m jute
jute serving head
    D: Jute-Wickler m
    F: tête f à jute
jute spinner
    D: Jute-Wickler m
    F: tête f à jute
jute wrapping
    D: Jute-Umspinnung f
    F: revêtement m en jute
jute yarn
    D: Jute-Garn n
    F: filin m de jute

K

kaolin n
    D: Kaolin n
    F: caolin m, kaolin m
"killing" of rubber
    D: Totwalzen n (Kautschuk), Überwalzen n (Kautschuk)
    F: mastication f à mort, malaxage m à mort
kink n
    D: Knick m (in Leitung oder Kabel), Kinke f
    F: coque f
kinking n
    D: Kinkenbildung f
    F: formation f de coques
kinking, protection against ~ [cab.]
    D: Knickschutz m
    F: protection f contre la formation de coques
kit n
    D: Bausatz m, Werkzeugtasche f
    F: trousse f
kit, installation ~
    D: Montagesatz m
    F: ensemble m de montage
knead v
    D: kneten v, plastizieren v (mech.)
    F: malaxer v
kneader n
    D: Innenmischer m, Kneter m
    F: mélangeur m interne, malaxeur m
kneader mixer
    D: Mischkneter m
    F: malaxeur-mélangeur m
knee n
    D: Rohrbogen m, Rohrkrümmung f, Rohrknie n, Knierohr n, Krümmer m (Rohr)
    F: coude m, raccord m coudé
knock-down returnable shipping reel
    D: zerlegbare Kabeltrommel
    F: touret m de câble démontable non perdu
Kraft insulating paper
    D: Kraft-Isolierpapier n
    F: papier m isolant Kraft
Krarup cable
    D: Krarup-Kabel n
    F: câble m Krarup, câble m krarupisé, câble m à charge continue, câble m ferromagnétique

L

laboratory investigation
    D: Laboruntersuchung f
    F: essai m de laboratoire
laboratory roller mill
    D: Laborwalze f
    F: malaxeur m de laboratoire à cylindres
laboratory-scale trial
    D: Versuch im Labormaßstab
    F: essai m à l'échelle de laboratoire
laboratory stage
    D: Versuchsstadium n
    F: stade m expérimental

laboratory test
 D: Laboruntersuchung *f*
 F: essai *m* de laboratoire

lace *v* [cab.]
 D: abbinden *v*
 F: lier *v*

lacing board, cable ~
 D: Kabelformbrett *n*, Formbrett für Kabel
 F: gabarit *m* pour câbles, planche *f* de préparation pour câbles

lagging *n*
 D: Verschalung *f* (Kabeltrommeln)
 F: douvage *m*

lagging phase
 D: nacheilende Phase
 F: phase *f* en retard

laid in earth [c. install.]
 D: erdverlegt *adj*
 F: posé *adj* en terre, enterré *adj*

laid underground [c. install.]
 D: erdverlegt *adj*
 F: posé *adj* en terre, enterré *adj*

laminar insulation
 D: Mehrschicht-Isolierung *f*, Schichtisolierung *f*
 F: isolation *f* stratifiée, isolation *f* laminée

laminate *n*
 D: Schichtstoff *m*
 F: laminé *m*, stratifié *m*, plastique *m* laminé, produit *m* laminé

laminated fabric
 D: Hartgewebe *n*
 F: stratifié *m*, tissu *m* revêtu de résine synthétique

laminated insulation
 D: Mehrschicht-Isolierung *f*, Schichtisolierung *f*
 F: isolation *f* stratifiée, isolation *f* laminée

laminated material
 D: Schichtstoff *m*
 F: laminé *m*, stratifié *m*, plastique *m* laminé, produit *m* laminé

laminated paper
 D: Hartpapier *n*
 F: papier *m* dur, papier *m* imprégné de résine synthétique

laminated plastic
 D: Schichtstoff *m*
 F: laminé *m*, stratifié *m*, plastique *m* laminé, produit *m* laminé

laminated sheath
 D: Schichtenmantel *m*
 F: gaine *f* composite, gaine *f* complexe

laminated with ...
 D: kaschiert mit ...
 F: contrecouché *adj* de ..., contrecollé *adj* de ..., revêtu *adj* de ..., doublé *adj* de ...,

lamp cord
 D: Lampenschnur *f*
 F: cordon *m* de lampe

lamp indicator
 D: Schauzeichen *n*
 F: signalisation *f* visible

land of the screw [extr.]
 D: Schneckensteg *m*
 F: crête *f* de la vis

Lang's lay stranding
 D: Verseilung im Längsschlag
 F: câblage *m* long, câblage *m* Lang

lap *v*
 D: umwickeln *v* (mit Band), bewickeln *v* (mit Band), umspinnen *v* (mit Band), wickeln *v* (Band)
 F: enrubanner *v*, rubaner *v*

lapped covering
 D: gewickelte Umhüllung
 F: revêtement *m* rubané

lapped inner covering
 D: gemeinsame gewickelte Aderumhüllung
 F: revêtement *m* interne rubané

lapped insulation
 D: Bandisolierung *f*, gewickelte Isolierung
 F: isolation *f* rubanée

lapped joint
 D: gewickelte Muffe, Wickelmuffe *f*
 F: jonction *f* reconstituée

lapped paper insulation
 D: Isolierung aus Papierbandumspinnung, Papierbandisolierung *f*
 F: isolation *f* rubanée en papier, rubanage *m* en papier

lapped termination
 D: gewickelter Endverschluß
 F: extrémité *f* reconstituée

lapping *n*
 D: Umspinnung *f* (mit Band), Bandumspinnung *f*, Bewicklung *f* (mit Band), Schmalbandwicklung *f*

F: rubanage *m*
lapping angle [lapp.]
D: Spinnwinkel *m*
F: angle *m* de rubanage
lapping direction
D: Spinnrichtung *f*
F: sens *m* de rubanage, sens *m* d'enroulement
lapping head
D: Spinner *m* (Band), Spinnkopf *m* (Band), Bandwickler *m*
F: tête *f* de rubanage, tête *f* rubaneuse
lapping head speed
D: Spinnerdrehzahl *f*
F: vitesse *f* de tête rubaneuse
lapping machine
D: Bandwickelmaschine *f*, Spinnmaschine *f* (Band)
F: rubaneuse *f*
lapping of a joint
D: Auswickeln einer Verbindungsstelle
F: reconstitution *f* d'une jonction
lapping tension
D: Spinnspannung *f*, Spinnzug *m*
F: tension *f* de rubanage
large-capacity cable [tel.]
D: mehrpaariges Kabel, hochpaariges Kabel
F: câble *m* multipaire, câble *m* multitoron, câble *m* à grande capacité
large-diameter wire
D: dicker Draht
F: gros fil *m*, fil *m* de gros diamètre
large-scale trial
D: Großversuch *m*
F: essai *m* à grande échelle
large-size cables
D: Kabel mit großen Querschnitten
F: câbles *m pl* de grosses sections, gros câbles *m pl*
large-size wire
D: dicker Draht
F: gros fil *m*, fil *m* de gros diamètre
lashing machine
D: Anwendelmaschine *f* (Luftkabel)
F: machine *f* à poser l'hélice de support
lashing wire
D: Anwendeldraht *m* (Luftkabel)
F: fil *m* hélice de support
lateral, separate ~ water pipes
D: parallel zum Kabel verlegte Wasserrohre
F: tubes *m pl* à eau latéraux disposés séparément du câble
lateral cooling of cables
D: indirekte Kühlung von Kabeln
F: refroidissement *m* latéral des câbles, refroidissement *m* indirect des câbles
lattice network [el.]
D: Kettenleiter *m*
F: réseau *m* récurrent, système *m* itératif
launder *n* [c. c. r.]
D: Überführungsrinne *f*, Gießrinne *f*
F: rigole *f* de transfert, rigole *f* de coulée
lay *v* [cab.]
D: auslegen *v*, verlegen *v*
F: poser *v*
lay *n* [strand.]
D: Drall *m*, Schlag *m*
F: pas *m*, torsion *f*
lay changing gear
D: Drallwechselgetriebe *n*
F: variateur *m* de torsion
layer *n*
D: Lage *f*, Schicht *f*
F: couche *f*
layer, in consecutive ~s
D: lagenweise *adj*
F: en couches consécutives
layered cable
D: lagenverseiltes Kabel, Lagenkabel *n*
F: câble *m* à couches concentriques, câble *m* en couches
layer of wires
D: Drahtlage *f*
F: couche *f* de fils
layer-stranded cable
D: lagenverseiltes Kabel, Lagenkabel *n*
F: câble *m* à couches concentriques, câble *m* en couches
layer-stranding *n*
D: Lagenverseilung *f*
F: assemblage *m* par (en) couches, câblage *m* par (en) couches
layer thickness
D: Schichtdicke *f*
F: épaisseur *f* de couche
layer type cable

laying, cable ~
D: Verlegung von Kabeln
F: pose f de câbles

laying conditions
D: Legeverhältnisse n pl, Verlegebedingungen f pl
F: conditions f pl de pose

laying depth [c. install.]
D: Bettungstiefe f, Verlegetiefe f, Legungstiefe f
F: profondeur f de pose

laying in conduits
D: Verlegung in Röhren, Verlegung in Kanälen
F: pose f en caniveaux

laying in ducts
D: Verlegung in Röhren, Verlegung in Kanälen
F: pose f en caniveaux

laying in ducts [com. c.]
D: Verlegung in Formsteinen
F: pose f en blocs-tube

laying in earth
D: Verlegung in Erde, Erdverlegung f
F: pose f en pleine terre, pose f souterraine

laying in parallel
D: Verlegung nebeneinander, Parallelanordnung f
F: disposition f côte à côte, disposition f en nappe horizontale, disposition f en parallèle

laying on racks
D: Verlegung auf Pritschen
F: pose f sur tablettes

laying rollers [cab.]
D: Verlegerollen f pl
F: galets m pl de pose

laying side by side
D: Verlegung nebeneinander, Parallelanordnung f
F: disposition f côte à côte, disposition f en nappe horizontale, disposition f en parallèle

laying up n [cab.]
D: Seelenverseilung f, Aderverseilung f, Verseilung f (Seele)
F: assemblage m (des conducteurs)

laying-up allowance
D: Drallzuschlag m
F: supplément m de torsion

laying-up machine
D: Seelenverseilmaschine f, Aderverseilmaschine f
F: assembleuse f

lay out v
D: auslegen v (Werk, Anlage)
F: disposer v, arranger v

layout n
D: Auslegung f (Planung), Anordnung f, Anlage f (Auslegung)
F: disposition f, groupement m

layout drawing
D: Grundrißzeichnung f
F: plan m d'ensemble

lay plate [strand.]
D: Verseilscheibe f, Lochplatte f
F: plaque f de répartition, plaque f de guidage

lay ratio
D: Schlaglängen-Faktor m
F: taux m du pas

lay reversal point
D: Drallwechselstelle f
F: point m d'inversion de la torsion, point m de changement de la torsion

lay up v
D: verseilen v (Kabelseele)
F: assembler v

LD-PE (s. low-density PE)

L/D ratio [extr.]
D: Länge/Durchmesser-Verhältnis (L/D) (Extruder-Schnecke) n
F: rapport m L/D

lead n
D: Zuleitung f
F: conducteur m d'amenée, conducteur m d'alimentation

lead alloy
D: Bleilegierung f
F: alliage m de plomb

lead ball bath
D: Schrotkugelbad n, Bleikugelbad n
F: bain m de grenaille de plomb

lead cap
D: Bleikappe f
F: capot m de plomb

lead-covered cable
D: Bleimantelkabel n
F: câble m sous gaine de plomb

lead in v

lead

   D: einführen v
   F: insérer v, introduire v

lead-in n
   D: Zuleitung f
   F: conducteur m d'amenée, conducteur m d'alimentation

lead(ing)-in cable
   D: Einführungskabel n
   F: câble m d'entrée

leading phase
   D: voreilende Phase
   F: phase f en avance

lead-in insulator
   D: Einführungsisolator m
   F: isolateur m d'entrée

lead(ing)-in wire
   D: Teilnehmer-Anschlußleitung f, Hauszuführungsleitung f, Teilnehmereinführungsleitung f, Einführungsleitung f, Einführungsdraht m, Fernsprechteilnehmerleitung f
   F: ligne f d'abonné téléphonique (raccord à la ligne aérienne), ligne f de desserte d'abonné, fil m d'entrée d'abonné

lead-in wire
   D: Zuleitungsdraht m
   F: fil m d'amenée

lead melting kettle
   D: Bleischmelzwanne f
   F: creuset m à plomb

lead of a screw
   D: Ganghöhe einer Schnecke/Schraube
   F: pas m d'une vis

lead oxide
   D: Bleioxid n
   F: oxyde m de plomb

lead press
   D: Blei-(Mantel)-Presse f
   F: presse f de gainage à plomb, presse f à plomb

lead-sheath v
   D: Bleimantel aufpressen
   F: mettre v sous gaine de plomb

lead sheath
   D: Bleimantel m
   F: gaine f de plomb

lead sheath, to apply the ~
   D: Bleimantel aufpressen
   F: mettre v sous gaine de plomb

lead sheath, wire-reinforced ~
   D: Bleimantel mit Drahtarmierung
   F: gaine f de plomb avec armure en fils

lead-sheathed cable
   D: Bleimantelkabel n
   F: câble m sous gaine de plomb

lead-sheathed cable
   D: Bleimantelleitung f
   F: conducteur m sous gaine de plomb

lead-sheathing
   D: Ummanteln mit Blei
   F: mise f sous plomb

lead-sheathing press
   D: Blei-(Mantel)-Presse f
   F: presse f de gainage à plomb, presse f à plomb

lead-shot bath
   D: Schrotkugelbad n, Bleikugelbad n
   F: bain m de grenaille de plomb

lead sleeve
   D: Bleihülse f, Bleimuffe f
   F: manchon m de plomb

lead starvation
   D: Aussetzen des Bleiflusses
   F: raté m du flux de plomb

lead stearate
   D: Bleistearat n
   F: stéarate m de plomb

leak v
   D: durchsickern v
   F: suinter v, filtrer v (se)

leakage n
   D: Ableitung f
   F: dérivation f

leakage n
   D: Undichtigkeit f, Leckstelle f
   F: fuite f, non-étanchéité f

leakage attenuation [com. c.]
   D: Ableitungsdämpfung f
   F: affaiblissement m dû à la perditance

leakage current
   D: Ableit(ungs)strom m, Fehlerstrom m, Streustrom m, vagabundierender Strom, Verluststrom m
   F: courant m de fuite, courant m de défaut, courant m vagabond

leakage current loss [com. c.]
   D: Ableitungsdämpfung f
   F: affaiblissement m dû à la perditance

leakage current loss

leakage
D: Ableitungsverlust *m*
F: perte *f* par dérivation

leakage detection
D: Leckortung *f*
F: localisation *f* de fuites

leakage detection, automatic ~
D: automatische Leckstellenanzeige
F: détection *f* automatique de fuites

leakage field
D: Streufeld *n*
F: champ *m* de fuite

leakage formation
D: Leckbildung *f*
F: formation *f* de fuites

leakage loss [com. c.]
D: Ableitungsdämpfung *f*
F: affaiblissement *m* dû à la perditance

leakage loss
D: Ableitungsverlust *m*
F: perte *f* par dérivation

leakage path
D: Kriechweg *m*
F: ligne *f* de fuite

leakage test
D: Dichtigkeitsprüfung *f*
F: contrôle *m* d'étanchéité

leakance *n*
D: Ableitung *f*
F: dérivation *f*

leaky *adj*
D: undicht *adj*
F: non étanche *adj*

left-hand lay [strand.]
D: Linksdrall *m*, Linksschlag *m*
F: pas *m* à gauche

left-hand stranding
D: Linksschlag-Verseilung *f*
F: assemblage *m* à pas gauche, câblage *m* à pas gauche

left-hand(ed) thread
D: linksgängiges Gewinde
F: filet *m* à gauche

left-hand twist [strand.]
D: Linksdrall *m*, Linksschlag *m*
F: pas *m* à gauche

length, to cut to the required ~
D: auf die gewünschte Länge schneiden
F: couper *v* à la longueur voulue

length marking
D: Längenmarkierung *f*
F: marquage *m* métré

length of lay [strand.]
D: Schlaglänge *f*, Drallänge *f*
F: longueur *f* du pas

length of twist [strand.]
D: Schlaglänge *f*, Drallänge *f*
F: longueur *f* du pas

level control(ler)
D: Füllstandswächter *m*, Niveauwächter *m*
F: contrôleur *m* du niveau

level indicator
D: Füllstandsanzeiger *m*
F: indicateur *m* du niveau

liberation *n* [chem.]
D: Abspaltung *f*
F: libération *f*, dégagement *m*

life *n*
D: Lebensdauer *f*, Nutzungsdauer *f*
F: durée *f* de vie, vie *f*, durée *f* d'exploitation

life *n* [mach.]
D: Standzeit *f*
F: vie *f*

life test
D: Lebensdauerprüfung *f*
F: essai *m* de (durée de) vie

life test, accelerated ~
D: beschleunigte Lebensdauerprüfung
F: essai *m* accéléré de durée de vie

lift cable
D: Aufzugsleitung *f*, Fahrstuhlkabel *n*
F: câble *m* d'ascenseur

lifting carriage
D: Hubwagen *m*
F: chariot *m* élévateur

light-crack
D: Lichtriß *m*
F: craquelure *f* due à l'effet de la lumière

light-cracking *n*
D: Lichtrißbildung *f*
F: fissuration *f* sous l'effet de la lumière solaire

light-duty cable
D: Kabel für leichte Beanspruchungen
F: câble *m* pour contraintes faibles

light-fast *adj*
D: lichtbeständig *adj*, lichtecht *adj*
F: stable *adj* à la lumière, résistant *adj* à la lumière,

lighting cable
D: Beleuchtungskabel *n*
F: câble *m* pour éclairage luminescent

lightning

lightning, effects of ~
D: Blitzbeeinflussung f
F: effets m pl de foudre

lightning arrester
D: Blitzableiter m
F: parafoudre m

lightning conductor
D: Blitzableiter m
F: parafoudre m

lightning protection
D: Blitzschutz m
F: protection f contre la foudre

light plastic-sheathed flexible cord
D: leichte Kunststoffschlauchleitung
F: câble m souple sous gaine légère en plastique

light PVC-sheathed cable
D: Mantelleitung f, PVC-Mantelleitung f
F: câble m rigide sous gaine légère en PVC

light-sensitivity n
D: Lichtempfindlichkeit f
F: sensibilité f à la lumière, sensibilité f lumineuse

light (PVC-)sheathed flexible cord
D: leichte (PVC-)Schlauchleitung
F: câble m souple sous gaine légère (en PVC)

light-stability n
D: Lichtbeständigkeit f (Mischungen), Lichtfestigkeit f (Mischungen)
F: stabilité f à la lumière

light-stabilizer n
D: Lichtschutzmittel n
F: stabilisant m contre l'effet de la lumière

light-stable adj
D: lichtbeständig adj, lichtecht adj
F: stable adj à la lumière, résistant adj à la lumière,

lightweight aerial cable
D: Leichtbau-Luftkabel n
F: câble m aérien léger

lightweight coaxial cable
D: Leichtbau-Koaxialkabel n
F: câble m coaxial léger

lime box
D: Kreidekasten m (Kabelfertigung)
F: bac m à craie

lime milk
D: Kalkmilch f
F: lait m de chaux

limit n
D: Grenzwert m
F: valeur f limite, limite f

limitation of the electrical field
D: Feldbegrenzung f
F: limitation du champ électrique f

limiting value
D: Grenzwert m
F: valeur f limite, limite f

limit stop
D: Anschlag m (Arretierung)
F: butée f, arrêt m

limit switch
D: Endschalter m
F: interrupteur m de fin de course, interrupteur m terminal

limit temperature
D: Grenztemperatur f
F: température f limite

line n [mach.]
D: Anlage f
F: installation f

line n [com.]
D: Leitung f
F: ligne f

line, to be in ~ with
D: fluchten v
F: affleurer v, aligner v (s')

linear distortion
D: lineare Verzerrung
F: distorsion f linéaire

linear PE
D: geradkettiges PE
F: polyéthylène m à chaîne droite, polyéthylène m linéaire

linear resistance
D: linearer Widerstand
F: résistance f linéique

line attenuation [tel. c.]
D: Leitungsdämpfung f
F: affaiblissement m de la ligne

line cable
D: Netzanschlußkabel n
F: câble m d'alimentation réseau

line conductor
D: Phasenleiter m
F: conducteur m de phase

line connection
D: Netzanschluß m
F: branchement m au réseau, connexion f au réseau, alimentation f (sur) secteur

line constant

line
- D: Leitungskonstante f
- F: constante f de ligne

line current
- D: Netzstrom m
- F: courant m secteur, courant m de réseau

line density [com.]
- D: Durchdringung f
- F: densité f téléphonique, densité f de lignes principales

line inductance
- D: Leitungsinduktivität f
- F: inductance f de ligne

line loss [tel. c.]
- D: Leitungsdämpfung f
- F: affaiblissement m de la ligne

line noise
- D: Leitungsgeräusch n
- F: bruit m de circuit, bruit m de ligne

line of ducts
- D: Mehrlochkanal m, mehrzügiger Rohrstrang
- F: conduit m à plusieurs passages, caniveau m à passage multiple

line protection switch
- D: Schutzschalter m
- F: disjoncteur m de protection, interrupteur m de sécurité

liner n
- D: Innenbüchse f
- F: fourrure f

line resistance
- D: Leitungswiderstand m
- F: résistance f de ligne

line section [com. c.]
- D: Leitungsabschnitt m
- F: tronçon m de ligne

line speed [mach.]
- D: Fahrgeschwindigkeit f, Fertigungsgeschwindigkeit f, Arbeitsgeschwindigkeit f
- F: vitesse f de marche f, vitesse f de fabrication, vitesse f de production, vitesse f de travail

line telephony
- D: Sprechverkehr m, Fernsprechverkehr m
- F: trafic m téléphonique

line-to-earth voltage
- D: Leiter-Erdspannung f
- F: tension f étoilée

line to line fault
- D: Leitungsberührung f
- F: contact m entre fils

line-to-line voltage
- D: verkettete Spannung
- F: tension f composée, tension f entre phases

line under load
- D: belastete Leitung
- F: ligne f chargée, ligne f en charge

line voltage
- D: Netzspannung f
- F: tension f de réseau, tension f du secteur

line wire
- D: Leitungsdraht m
- F: fil m de ligne

lining n
- D: Futter n, Auskleidung f
- F: doublure f, revêtement m, fourrure f

link v
- D: verbinden v
- F: raccorder v, lier v, joindre v, réunir v

link box [cab.]
- D: Auskreuzungskasten m, Schaltkasten m
- F: boîte f de raccordement à la terre, boîte f de transposition

link cable
- D: Ringkabel n
- F: câble m de liaison circulaire

live adj
- D: stromführend adj, spannungführend adj
- F: sous tension, parcouru adj de courant,

live-washing n (of insulators)
- D: Abspritzen (von Isolatoren) im Betrieb
- F: rinçage m sous tension (des isolateurs)

load v
- D: laden v, belasten v
- F: charger v

load v [el., mech.]
- D: beanspruchen v, belasten v
- F: contraindre v, solliciter v, charger v

load v [mech., el.]
- D: speisen v, einspeisen v, beschicken v
- F: alimenter v, charger v

load n [el., mech.]

load

- D: Beanspruchung f, Belastung f, Last f
- F: contrainte f, sollicitation f, charge f

load, under ~ [el.]
- D: mit Last
- F: en charge

load centre [el.]
- D: Lastschwerpunkt m
- F: centre m de grande consommation

load current
- D: Belastungsstrom m
- F: courant m de charge

load curve, daily ~
- D: Tageslastdiagramm n
- F: courbe f journalière de charge

load cycles [el.]
- D: Lastzyklen m pl, Belastungszyklen m pl
- F: cycles m pl de charge

load density
- D: Lastdichte f
- F: densité f de charge

load distribution
- D: Lastverteilung f
- F: répartition f de la charge, dispatching m

loaded, heavily ~
- D: füllstoffreich adj
- F: fortement chargé, à haute teneur en charge

loaded audio cable
- D: Pupinkabel n
- F: câble m pupinisé

loaded cable
- D: bespultes Kabel
- F: câble m chargé

loaded cable, continuously ~
- D: Krarup-Kabel n
- F: câble m Krarup, câble m krarupisé, câble m à charge continue, câble m ferromagnétique

loaded line
- D: belastete Leitung
- F: ligne f chargée, ligne f en charge

loaded thin-wire cable
- D: bespultes dünndrähtiges Kabel
- F: câble m pupinisé avec âme en fils fins

loaded to capacity
- D: voll ausgelastet
- F: utilisé adj à pleine capacité, utilisé adj à plein

load factor
- D: Lastfaktor m
- F: facteur m de charge

load fluctuation
- D: Lastschwankung f
- F: fluctuation f de charge, variation f de charge

loading coil
- D: Pupin-Spule f, Belastungsspule f, Verstärkerspule f
- F: bobine f Pupin, bobine f de charge

loading coil case [com.]
- D: Spulenkasten m, Pupinspulenkasten m
- F: boîte f de charge, pot m de charge

loading coil unit
- D: Pupinspulensatz m, Spulensatz m
- F: jeu m de bobines de charge, unité f de charge (c. tél.)

loading cycle test
- D: Prüfung mit Belastungszyklen
- F: essai m aux cycles de charge

loading diagram
- D: Belastungsdiagramm n
- F: diagramme m de charge

loading material
- D: Füllstoff m
- F: matière f de charge, charge f

loading of reels
- D: Einsetzen von Spulen, Einsetzen von Trommeln
- F: montage m des bobines

loading (coil) pot [com.]
- D: Spulenkasten m, Pupinspulenkasten m
- F: boîte f de charge, pot m de charge

loading (coil) section
- D: Spulenfeldlänge f, Spulenfeld n
- F: section f de charge, section f de bobines Pupin

loading unit (tel. c.)
- D: Pupinspulensatz m, Spulensatz m
- F: jeu m de bobines de charge, unité f de charge (c. tél.)

load limit
- D: Grenzleistung f, Belastungsgrenze f
- F: charge f limite

load pause
- D: Belastungspause f
- F: intervalle m de charge

load peak [el.]
- D: Lastspitze f, Spitzenbelastung f
- F: pointe f de charge, charge f de

pointe
load variation
  D: Lastschwankung f
  F: fluctuation f de charge, variation f de charge

local cable
  D: Teilnehmer-Anschlußkabel n, Teilnehmer-Ortskabel n, Teilnehmer-Kabel n, Ortskabel n
  F: câble m urbain, câble m d'abonné

local call
  D: Ortsgespräch n
  F: conversation f urbaine

local cell
  D: Lokalelement n
  F: pile f locale, élément m galvanique localisé

local(ized) corrosion
  D: Lokalkorrosion f, Lochfraß m
  F: corrosion f localisée, corrosion f locale, corrosion f ponctuelle, pitting m

local distribution cable
  D: Aufteilungs-Ortskabel n
  F: câble m urbain de distribution

local exchange
  D: Ortsvermittlungsstelle f
  F: central m urbain

local exchange connection cable
  D: Ortsverbindungskabel n, Ortsanschlußkabel n
  F: câble m téléphonique de réseau local

local exchange network [tel.]
  D: Ortsnetz n
  F: réseau m urbain, réseau m local, réseau m municipal

local junction cable
  D: Ortsverbindungskabel n, Ortsanschlußkabel n
  F: câble m téléphonique de réseau local

locally confined
  D: örtlich begrenzt
  F: limité adj localement, localisé adj

locally limited
  D: örtlich begrenzt
  F: limité adj localement, localisé adj

local subscriber('s) connection cable
  D: Teilnehmer-Anschlußkabel n, Teilnehmer-Ortskabel n, Teilnehmer-Kabel n, Ortskabel n
  F: câble m urbain, câble m d'abonné

LoCap cable [com.]
  D: verlustarmes Kabel
  F: câble m à faible capacitance

locate, to ~ a fault
  D: eine Störung eingrenzen
  F: localiser v un défaut

locating the trouble (GB)
  D: Fehlersuche f, Fehlerortsbestimmung f, Fehlerortung f, Auffindung einer Störstelle
  F: localisation f d'un défaut

location of a factory
  D: Standort eines Werkes
  F: implantation f d'une usine

lock n
  D: Anschlag m (Arretierung)
  F: butée f, arrêt m

locking n
  D: Verriegelung f
  F: blocage m, verrouillage m

locking bolt
  D: Feststellschraube f
  F: vis f de blocage

locking ring
  D: Klemmring m
  F: bague f de serrage

locking screw
  D: Feststellschraube f
  F: vis f de blocage

lock washer
  D: Drehsicherungsscheibe f
  F: bague f de frein

long-chain polymers
  D: langkettige Polymere
  F: polymères m pl à longues chaînes

long distance call (US)
  D: Ferngespräch n
  F: conversation f interurbaine

long distance carrier frequency cable
  D: Trägerfrequenz-Fernkabel n
  F: câble m à courant porteur à grande distance

long distance coaxial cable
  D: koaxiales Fernkabel
  F: câble m coaxial à longue distance

long distance data transmission line
  D: Datenfernübertragungsleitung f
  F: ligne f de transmission d'informations à longue distance

long distance exchange
  D: Fernvermittlungsstelle f, Fernamt n

long

F: central *m* interurbain

long distance network
D: Weitverkehrsnetz *n*
F: réseau *m* de câbles à grande distance

long distance telephone cable
D: Weitverkehrskabel *n*, Weitverkehrs-Telefonkabel *n*, Telefon-Fernkabel *n*, Bezirkskabel *n*
F: câble *m* téléphonique à grande distance, câble *m* interurbain

long distance telephony
D: Weitverkehrs-Fernsprechtechnik *f*
F: téléphonie *f* à longue distance

long distance transmission
D: Fernübertragung *f*
F: transmission *f* à grande distance

long distance transmission line
D: Überlandleitung *f*
F: ligne *f* à grand transport d'énergie

longitudinal application
D: Längsaufbringung *f* (Bänder)
F: pose *f* longitudinale, disposition *f* longitudinale

longitudinal covering
D: Längsbedecken *n*
F: recouvrement *m* longitudinal

longitudinal covering machine
D: Längsbedeckungsmaschine *f*
F: machine *f* à revêtir en sens longitudinal

longitudinal direction
D: Längsrichtung *f*
F: sens *m* longitudinal, sens *m* de l'axe

longitudinal expansion coefficient
D: linearer Ausdehnungskoeffizient *m*
F: coefficient *m* de dilatation linéaire

longitudinally applied
D: längsaufgebracht *adj*
F: posé *adj* longitudinalement, disposé *adj* en long,

longitudinally water-proof
D: längswasserdicht *adj*
F: étanche *adj* à l'eau en sens longitudinal

longitudinal marking
D: Längsmarkierung *f*
F: marquage *m* longitudinal, repérage *m* longitudinal

longitudinal water tightness
D: Längswasserdichtigkeit *f*

F: étanchéité *f* longitudinale

long lay stranding
D: Verseilung im Längsschlag
F: câblage *m* long, câblage *m* Lang

long-time age(i)ng properties
D: Langzeit-Alterungs-Eigenschaften *f pl*
F: propriétés *f pl* de vieillissement de longue durée

long-time ag(e)ing test
D: Daueralterungsprüfung *f*
F: essai *m* de vieillissement de longue durée

long-time behaviour
D: Langzeitverhalten *n*
F: comportement *m* en (longue) durée

long-time dielectric strength of a cable
D: Zeit-Spannungsfestigkeit eines Kabels, Dauer-Spannungsfestigkeit eines Kabels
F: durée *f* de vie d'un câble, tenue *f* en longue durée d'un câble

long-time operation [el.]
D: Dauerbetrieb *m* (ununterbrochener Betrieb von mindestens 2,5 Std.)
F: service *m* de longue durée

long-time rupture strength [met.]
D: Dauerstandfestigkeit *f*
F: résistance *f* au fluage, résistance *f* à la rupture sous charge permanente

long-time strength [el.]
D: Dauerfestigkeit *f*, Langzeitfestigkeit *f*
F: tenue *f* en longue durée, longévité *f*

long-time test
D: Langzeitprüfung *f*, Langzeitversuch *m*, Dauerversuch *m*
F: essai *m* de (longue) durée, essai *m* continu

loop *n* [el.]
D: Schleife *f* (Leitungszusammenführung)
F: boucle *f*, circuit *m* fermé

loop *n*
D: Windung *f*
F: spire *f*

loop capacity
D: Schleifenkapazität *f*
F: capacité *f* de boucle

loop resistance

machine

- *D*: Schleifenwiderstand *m*
- *F*: résistance *f* de boucle

loop test
- *D*: Schleifenmessung *f*
- *F*: mesure *f* en boucle

loosening *n* [lapp.]
- *D*: Lockerung *f*, Lockerwerden *n*
- *F*: ramollissement *m*

loss *n*
- *D*: Verlust *m*
- *F*: perte *f*

loss angle (tan δ)
- *D*: Verlustwinkel *m* (tan δ)
- *F*: angle *m* de perte (tan δ)

losses, extra ~
- *D*: Zusatzverluste *m pl*
- *F*: pertes *f pl* supplémentaires

loss factor tg δ
- *D*: Verlustfaktor *m*
- *F*: facteur *m* de perte tg δ, facteur de puissance cos φ, tangente de l'angle de perte tg δ

lot *n* [cab.]
- *D*: Los *n*
- *F*: lot *m*

low capacitance cable [com.]
- *D*: verlustarmes Kabel
- *F*: câble *m* à faible capacitance

low-density PE (LD-PE)
- *D*: Hochdruck-PE *n*
- *F*: polyéthylène *m* basse densité, polyéthylène *m* haute pression

low frequency
- *D*: Tonfrequenz *f*, Niederfrequenz *f*
- *F*: audio-fréquence *f*, fréquence *f* vocale, basse fréquence *f*

low-loss... *adj*
- *D*: verlustarm *adj*
- *F*: à faibles pertes

low-ohmic *adj*
- *D*: niederohmig *adj*
- *F*: de faible valeur ohmique, de faible résistance

low pressure oil-filled cable
- *D*: Niederdruckölkabel *n*
- *F*: câble *m* sous basse pression d'huile

low pressure PE (LP-PE)
- *D*: Niederdruck-PE *n*
- *F*: polyéthylène *m* haute densité, polyéthylène *m* basse pression

low temperature brittleness
- *D*: Kältesprödigkeit *f*
- *F*: fragilité *f* à basse température

low temperature resistance
- *D*: Kältebeständigkeit *f*
- *F*: résistance *f* aux basses températures

low transmission voltage d.c. data transmission
- *D*: Gleichstrom-Datenübertragung mit niedriger Sendespannung
- *F*: transmission *f* d'informations en courant continu à basse tension d'émission

low-viscosity oil
- *D*: niedrigviskoses Öl
- *F*: huile *f* à faible viscosité

low voltage (LV)
- *D*: Niederspannung *f*
- *F*: basse tension *f* (BT)

low voltage cable
- *D*: Niederspannungskabel *n*
- *F*: câble *m* à basse tension

low voltage switchgear
- *D*: Niederspannungsschaltanlage *f*
- *F*: installation *f* de disjoncteurs basse tension

LP-PE (s. low pressure PE)

lubricant *n*
- *D*: Gleitmittel *n*, Schmiermittel *n*
- *F*: matière *f* lubrifiante, lubrifiant *m*

lubrication *n*
- *D*: Schmierung *f*
- *F*: lubrification *f*, graissage *m*

luminous control panel
- *D*: Leuchtbildwarte *f*
- *F*: tableau *m* de commande lumineux

luminous sensitivity
- *D*: Lichtempfindlichkeit *f*
- *F*: sensibilité *f* à la lumière, sensibilité *f* lumineuse

lump loaded circuit
- *D*: Leitung mit punktförmiger Ladung
- *F*: circuit *m* à charge concentrée

LV (s. low voltage)

M

machine, under running conditions of a ~
- *D*: bei laufender Maschine
- *F*: la machine étant en marche

machine cycle

machine

    D: Arbeitszyklus einer Maschine
    F: cycle *m* de marche d'une machine

machine downtime
    D: Brachzeit einer Maschine
    F: temps *m* d'attente d'une machine

machine drum
    D: Fertigungstrommel *f*
    F: touret *m* d'atelier

machine tool wire
    D: Werkzeugmaschinenleitung *f*
    F: conducteur *m* pour machines-outils

machining *n*
    D: spanabhebende Bearbeitung
    F: usinage *m* (à l'outil de coupe)

magnetic coupling
    D: magnetische Kopplung
    F: couplage *m* magnétique

magnetic shield
    D: magnetischer Schirm
    F: écran *m* magnétique

magnet wire
    D: Dynamodraht *m*
    F: fil *m* de bobinage, fil *m* de dynamo

magnification *n*
    D: Vergrößerung *f*
    F: agrandissement *m*, augmentation *f*, élargissement *m*

magnify *v*
    D: vergrößern *v*
    F: augmenter *v*, élargir *v*, grossir *v*, agrandir *v*

main cable
    D: Hauptkabel *n*, Hauptspeisekabel *n*
    F: câble *m* principal

main core unit [com. c.]
    D: Hauptbündel *n*
    F: faisceau *m* principal

main repeater station
    D: Hauptverstärkerstelle *f*
    F: station *f* principale de répéteurs

mains *n* [el.]
    D: Netz *n*
    F: réseau *m*, secteur *m*

mains
    D: Versorgungsnetz *n*
    F: réseau *m* d'alimentation

mains cable
    D: Netzkabel *n*
    F: câble *m* de réseau, câble *m* de distribution

mains current
    D: Netzstrom *m*
    F: courant *m* secteur, courant *m* de réseau

mains supply
    D: Versorgung aus dem Netz, Netzanschluß *m*
    F: alimentation *f* par le réseau, alimentation *f* (sur) secteur

mains supply lead
    D: Netzzuleitung *f*
    F: conduite *f* d'amenée de secteur

mains voltage
    D: Netzspannung *f*
    F: tension *f* de réseau, tension *f* du secteur

maintenance *n*
    D: Instandhaltung *f*
    F: entretien *m*, service *m*, maintenance *f*

maintenance instructions *pl*
    D: Wartungsvorschrift *f*
    F: instructions *f pl* d'entretien, manuel *m* d'entretien

main unit [com. c.]
    D: Hauptbündel *n*
    F: faisceau *m* principal

male die
    D: Patrize *f*
    F: poinçon *m*

malleableise *v* (GB) [met.]
    D: tempern *v*
    F: malléabiliser *v*

malleableize *v* (US) [met.]
    D: tempern *v*
    F: malléabiliser *v*

mandrel *n*
    D: Dorn *m*
    F: mandrin *m*, broche *f*, poinçon *m*

mandrel test
    D: Dornwickelprüfung *f*
    F: essai *m* d'enroulement

maneuver overvoltage
    D: Schaltüberspannung *f*
    F: surtension *f* de commutation, surtension *f* de manœuvre

manhandle, to ~ a cable
    D: ein Kabel von Hand einziehen
    F: tirer *v* un câble à la main

manhole *n* [c. install.]
    D: Einstiegöffnung *f*, Mannloch *n*
    F: entrée *f*, accès *m*, trou *m* d'homme, regard *m* de visite

manhole, cable jointing ~
    D: Muffenbunker *m*, Muffenbauwerk

manhole cover
- *n*, Kabelschacht *m*
- *F:* trou *m* d'homme, puits *m* de visite, puits *m* de jonction, chambre *f* de répartition, puits *m* à câbles

manhole cover
- *D:* Mannlochdeckel *m*, Schachtdeckel *m*
- *F:* couvercle *m* de trou d'homme

manometer *n*
- *D:* Druckmeßgerät *n*, Manometer *n*
- *F:* dispositif *m* de contrôle de la pression, manomètre *m*

man-sized tunnel
- *D:* begehbarer Tunnel
- *F:* tunnel *m* à dimension d'homme

manual control
- *D:* Handbetrieb *m*, Handsteuerung *f*
- *F:* opération *f* manuelle, commande *f* manuelle, opération *f* à main

manually operated
- *D:* handbetätigt *adj*
- *F:* commandé *adj* manuellement, à commande manuelle

manual operation
- *D:* Handbetrieb *m*, Handsteuerung *f*
- *F:* opération *f* manuelle, commande *f* manuelle, opération *f* à main

manufacturers' identification thread
- *D:* Firmenkennfaden *m*
- *F:* fil *m* distinctif du fournisseur

manufacturing control
- *D:* Fertigungskontrolle *f*
- *F:* contrôle *m* en cours de fabrication

manufacturing defect
- *D:* Fertigungsfehler *m*
- *F:* vice *m* de fabrication, défaut *m* de fabrication

manufacturing department
- *D:* Fertigungsabteilung *f*
- *F:* service *m* de production, atelier *m* de fabrication

manufacturing engineer
- *D:* Betriebsingenieur *m*
- *F:* ingénieur *m* de fabrication

manufacturing flaw
- *D:* Fertigungsfehler *m*
- *F:* vice *m* de fabrication, défaut *m* de fabrication

manufacturing length
- *D:* Fertigungslänge *f*
- *F:* longueur *f* de fabrication

manufacturing line
- *D:* Fertigungsstraße *f*
- *F:* chaîne *f* de fabrication

manufacturing planning
- *D:* Arbeitsvorbereitung *f*, Fertigungsvorbereitung *f*
- *F:* préparation *f* du travail

manufacturing programme
- *D:* Fertigungsprogramm *n*, Arbeitsprogramm *n* (Prod.)
- *F:* programme *m* de fabrication

manufacturing schedule
- *D:* Fertigungsprogramm *n*, Arbeitsprogramm *n* (Prod.)
- *F:* programme *m* de fabrication

manufacturing specification
- *D:* Fertigungsvorschrift *f*
- *F:* mode *m* opératoire

manufacturing stage
- *D:* Stadium der Fertigung
- *F:* étape *f* de fabrication, phase *f* de fabrication

manufacturing trial
- *D:* Versuchsfertigung *f*, Probefertigung *f*
- *F:* essai *m* de fabrication, production *f* à l'échelle expérimentale

mark *n* [cab.]
- *D:* Kennzeichen *n*
- *F:* marque *f*, code *m*

marked wire
- *D:* Zählader *f*
- *F:* fil *m* pilote, fil *m* compteur

marker *n* [com. c.]
- *D:* Markierungselement *n*
- *F:* élément *m* de marquage

marker *n* (com. c.)
- *D:* Markierung für fehlerhaftes Paar
- *F:* marqueur *m* de paires défectueuses

marker line
- *D:* Markierungsstrich *m*
- *F:* trait *m* de repère

marker thread
- *D:* Kennfaden *m*
- *F:* fil *m* d'identification, fil *m* distinctif, filin *m* de reconnaissance

marking *n* [cab.]
- *D:* Kennzeichnung *f*
- *F:* désignation *f*, identification *f*, marquage *m*, repérage *m*

marking by embossing
- *D:* Markierung durch Prägen
- *F:* marquage *m* en relief

marking element
- *D:* Zählelement *n*

marking

élément *m* de comptage
mass-impregnated *adj*
 D: massegetränkt *adj*
 F: imprégné *adj* de matière
mass-impregnated and drained insulation
 D: massearme Isolierung
 F: isolant *m* égoutté après imprégnation
master batch
 D: Farbkonzentrat *n*, Farbbatch *n*
 F: mélange *m* coloré maître
master batch
 D: Vormischung *f*, Grundmischung *f*
 F: mélange *m* mère, mélange *m* maître
masticate *v*
 D: kneten *v*, plastizieren *v* (mech.)
 F: malaxer *v*
masticator *n*
 D: Innenmischer *m*, Kneter *m*
 F: mélangeur *m* interne, malaxeur *m*
match *v* [contr.]
 D: abstimmen *v*
 F: accorder *v*, régler *v*
matching *n* [com.]
 D: Anpassung *f*
 F: adaptation *f*
matching attenuation
 D: Anpassungsdämpfung *f*
 F: affaiblissement *m* d'adaptation
matching loss
 D: Anpassungsdämpfung *f*
 F: affaiblissement *m* d'adaptation
matching relay repeater [com.]
 D: Anpassungsübertrager *m*
 F: transformateur *m* d'adaptation
matching transformer [com.]
 D: Anpassungsübertrager *m*
 F: transformateur *m* d'adaptation
material *n*
 D: Werkstoff *m*, Rohstoff *m*
 F: matière *f*, matière *f* première
material defect
 D: Materialfehler *m*
 F: défaut *m* du matériel
materials handling
 D: Materialfluß *m* (innerbetrieblich)
 F: transport *m* des matériaux
materials technology
 D: Werkstoff-Technologie *f*
 F: technologie *f* des matières
material testing
 D: Materialprüfung *f*
 F: essai *m* des matériaux
maximum admissible operating temperature
 D: maximal zulässige Betriebstemperatur
 F: température *f* de service maximale admissible
maximum asymmetric short-circuit current
 D: Stoßkurzschlußstrom *m*
 F: courant *m* maximum asymétrique de court circuit
maximum long-time strength
 D: Grenz-Dauerfestigkeit *f*
 F: tenue *f* maximale en longue durée
maximum voltage circuit-breaker
 D: Überspannungsschalter *m*
 F: interrupteur *m* à maximum de tension, disjoncteur *m* de surtension
meaningful *adj*
 D: aussagekräftig *adj* (Werte)
 F: significatif *adj*
mean value
 D: Mittelwert *m*
 F: valeur *f* moyenne
measured quantity
 D: Meßgröße *f*
 F: grandeur *f* mesurée
measured value
 D: Meßwert *m*
 F: valeur *f* mesurée
measuring arrangement
 D: Meßanordnung *f*, Meßschaltung *f*
 F: disposition *f* de mesure, montage *m* de mesure, couplage *m* de mesure
measuring bridge
 D: Meßbrücke *f*
 F: pont *m* de mesure
measuring cable
 D: Meßkabel *n*
 F: câble *m* de mesure
measuring circuit
 D: Meßkreis *m*
 F: circuit *m* de mesure
measuring device
 D: Meßgerät *n*
 F: appareil *m* de mesure
measuring electrode
 D: Meßelektrode *f*
 F: électrode *f* de mesure, sonde *f*
measuring equipment

measuring
  D: Meßgerät n
  F: appareil m de mesure
measuring error
  D: Fehlmessung f, Meßfehler m
  F: raté m de mesure, erreur f de mesure
measuring instrument
  D: Meßgerät n
  F: appareil m de mesure
measuring loop
  D: Meßschleife f
  F: boucle f de mesure
measuring point
  D: Meßpunkt m
  F: point m de mesure
measuring precision
  D: Meßgenauigkeit f
  F: précision f de mesure
measuring resistance
  D: Meßwiderstand m
  F: résistance f de mesure
measuring result
  D: Meßergebnis n
  F: résultat m de mesure
measuring room
  D: Meßraum m
  F: salle f de mesure
measuring set, portable cable ~
  D: Kabelmeßkoffer m
  F: valise f de mesure pour câbles
measuring setup
  D: Meßplatz m
  F: table f d'essai, poste m de mesure
measuring tape [cab.]
  D: Längenmeßband n, Meßband n
  F: bande f métreuse
measuring voltage
  D: Meßspannung f
  F: tension f de mesure
mechanical adj
  D: maschinell adj
  F: mécanique adj
mechanical characteristic
  D: mechanische Eigenschaft
  F: charactéristique f mécanique, propriété f mécanique
mechanically operated
  D: mechanisch betätigt
  F: à commande mécanique
mechanical property
  D: mechanische Eigenschaft
  F: charactéristique f mécanique, propriété f mécanique

mechanical strength
  D: mechanische Festigkeit
  F: résistance mécanique f
median value
  D: Medianwert m
  F: valeur f médiane
medium voltage cable
  D: Mittelspannungskabel n
  F: câble m à moyenne tension
meet v [test]
  D: einhalten v (Werte, Bedingungen)
  F: respecter v, observer v
meet, to ~ a requirement
  D: eine Forderung erfüllen, eine Bedingung erfüllen, einer Anforderung genügen
  F: satisfaire v à une demande, satisfaire v à une exigence
melt n
  D: Schmelze f
  F: matière f en fusion, fonte f (mét.)
melt (flow) index
  D: Schmelzindex m
  F: indice m de fluidité, indice m de fluage, indice m de fusion
melting
  D: Schmelzen n
  F: fonte f, fusion f
melting furnace
  D: Schmelzofen m
  F: four(neau) m de fusion
melting loss [smelt.]
  D: Abbrand m
  F: perte f au feu, déchet m
melting point
  D: Schmelzpunkt m
  F: point m de fusion
melting pot
  D: Schmelzkessel m (Bleipresse), Schmelztopf m (Bleipresse)
  F: pot m de presse
melting temperature
  D: Schmelztemperatur f
  F: température f de fusion
melt pressure [extr.]
  D: Masse-Druck m
  F: pression f de la matière en fusion
melt temperature [extr.]
  D: Masse-Temperatur f, Schmelzen-Temperatur f
  F: température f de la matière en fusion
membrane cells

membrane

D: Zellen f pl (im Öldruckausgleichsgefäß), Membranen f pl (im Öldruckausgleichsgefäß), pl
F: cellules f pl

mercury column
D: Quecksilbersäule f
F: colonne f de mercure

meshed network
D: vermaschtes Netz
F: réseau m maillé

messenger wire [tel. c.]
D: Tragseil n, Luftkabeltragseil n
F: câble m porteur, corde f de suspension

metal clad conductor
D: metallumhüllter Leiter
F: âme f plaquée de métal

metal-clad switch-gear
D: gekapselte Schaltanlagen
F: disjoncteurs m pl enfermés, disjoncteurs m pl blindés

metal-clad wiring cable
D: Rohrdraht m
F: câble m cuirassé

metal foil
D: Metallfolie f
F: feuille f métallique

metallized paper
D: metallisiertes Papier (Höchstädter Folie)
F: papier m métallisé

metallized paper screen [cab.]
D: Schirm aus metallisiertem Papier
F: écran m en papier métallisé

metallized paper screened cable
D: Höchstädter-Kabel (H-Kabel) n
F: câble m du type Hochstadter, câble m à écran en papier métallisé

metallographic examination
D: metallographische Prüfung
F: examen m métallographique, analyse f métallographique

metallographic test
D: metallographische Prüfung
F: examen m métallographique, analyse f métallographique

metal sheath
D: Metallmantel m
F: gaine f métallique

metal strip
D: Metallband n
F: feuillard m, bande f métallique

metal tape
D: Metallband n
F: feuillard m, bande f métallique

meter counter
D: Längenmeßvorrichtung f, Längenzählgerät n, Meterzähler m
F: compteur m métreur

metering n
D: Dosierung f
F: dosage m

metering device
D: Zuteilvorrichtung f
F: doseur m

metering section of a screw [extr.]
D: Homogenisierzone einer Schnecke
F: zone f d'homogénéisation d'une vis

meter marking
D: Längenmarkierung f
F: marquage m métré

method n
D: Verfahren n, Methode f
F: procédé m, méthode f, technique f

method of installation [cab.]
D: Verlegeart f
F: mode m de pose

method of laying [cab.]
D: Verlegeart f
F: mode m de pose

method of measurement
D: Meßmethode f
F: méthode f de mesure

method of operation
D: Betriebsart f
F: mode m d'exploitation, régime m de marche

mica tape
D: Glimmergewebeband n
F: ruban m mica

microcrystalline wax
D: mikrokristallines Wachs
F: cire f microcristalline

micrometer screw
D: Mikrometerschraube f
F: vis f micrométrique, palmer m

microphone cable
D: Mikrophonleitung f
F: câble m de microphone

microscopic inspection
D: mikroskopische Untersuchung
F: inspection f microscopique

microwave n
D: Mikrowelle f
F: micro-onde f

middle conductor
  D: Mittelleiter m
  F: conducteur m médian
migrate v
  D: abwandern v (Masse, Weichmacher)
  F: migrer v
migrating compound [cab.]
  D: abwandernde Masse
  F: matière f migrante
migration of compound [cab.]
  D: Masseverarmung f, Masseabwanderung f, Abwanderung von Masse
  F: migration f de matière, écoulement m de matière
migration of plasticizer
  D: Weichmacherwanderung f, Abwanderung des Weichmachers
  F: migration f du plastifiant
mill v [rub., plast.]
  D: walzen v
  F: malaxer v, mélanger v
milled crepe (rubber)
  D: Fell n
  F: nappe f de caoutchouc malaxé
Milliken conductor
  D: skineffektarmer Leiter (Milliken-Leiter)
  F: conducteur m Milliken
Milliken conductor cable
  D: Kabel mit skineffektarmen Leitern, Millikenleiter-Kabel n
  F: câble m à conducteurs Milliken
mine cable
  D: Bergwerkskabel n, Grubenkabel n
  F: câble m de mines
mine gallery cable
  D: Grubenstreckenkabel n
  F: câble m pour galeries de mines
mineral-insulated cable
  D: mineralisoliertes Kabel
  F: câble m à isolation minérale
mineral oil
  D: Mineralöl n
  F: huile f minérale
mine shaft cable
  D: Grubenschachtkabel n, Schachtkabel n
  F: câble m pour puits de mines
miniature cable
  D: Miniatur-Kabel n
  F: câble m miniature

mining cable
  D: Bergwerkskabel n, Grubenkabel n
  F: câble m de mines
misalignment n
  D: Fehlausrichtung f
  F: désalignement m
mismatching n
  D: Fehlanpassung f
  F: désadaptation f
mix v
  D: vermischen v, mischen v
  F: mélanger v, mêler v
mix v [rub., plast.]
  D: mischen v
  F: mélanger v
mixer n
  D: Mischer m, Rührwerk n
  F: mélangeur m
mixing mill
  D: Mischwalzwerk n
  F: mélangeur m à cylindres, mélangeur m à rouleaux, cylindre m malaxeur
mixing plant
  D: Mischanlage f
  F: installation f de préparation des mélanges
mixing rolls pl
  D: Mischwalzwerk n
  F: mélangeur m à cylindres, mélangeur m à rouleaux, cylindre m malaxeur
mixing screw [extr.]
  D: Mischschnecke f
  F: vis f de mélangeage
mixing shop
  D: Mischerei f
  F: atelier m de préparation des mélanges
mixture n
  D: Gemisch n
  F: mélange m, composition f
mobile equipment
  D: fahrbares Gerät
  F: équipement m mobile
mobile unit
  D: fahrbares Gerät
  F: équipement m mobile
mobility n
  D: Beweglichkeit f
  F: souplesse f, flexibilité f, mobilité f
model cable
  D: Modellkabel n

model

    F: maquette f de câble, modèle m de câble

mode of operation
    D: Arbeitsweise f
    F: fonctionnement m, mode m de fonctionnement, opération f

modify v
    D: abändern v, ändern v
    F: modifier v, changer v, réviser v

modulus of elasticity
    D: Elastizitätsmodul m
    F: module m d'élasticité

moisten v
    D: anfeuchten v, benetzen v, befeuchten v
    F: mouiller v, tremper v, humecter v

moisture n
    D: Feuchtigkeit f
    F: humidité f

moisture absorption
    D: Feuchtigkeitsaufnahme f
    F: reprise f d'humidité, absorption f d'humidité

moisture barrier
    D: Feuchtigkeitssperre f
    F: barrière f d'humidité

moisture content
    D: Feuchtegehalt m, Feuchtigkeitsgehalt m
    F: degré m d'humidité, teneur f en humidité

moisture permeation
    D: Eindringen von Feuchtigkeit
    F: pénétration f d'humidité

moisture-resistant adj
    D: feuchtigkeitsbeständig adj
    F: résistant adj à l'humidité

mold (s. mould)

molecular structure
    D: Molekulargefüge n
    F: structure f moléculaire

molecular weight, of high ~
    D: mit hohem Molekulargewicht, hochmolekular adj
    F: à haut poids moléculaire

molecular weight, of low ~
    D: niedermolekular adj
    F: à faible poids moléculaire

molten copper
    D: Kupferschmelze f
    F: cuivre m fondu

molten material
    D: Schmelze f
    F: matière f en fusion, fonte f (mét.)

monitoring n
    D: Überwachung f
    F: surveillance f

monobloc adj
    D: einteilig adj
    F: monobloc adj, indivisé adj, en une seule pièce

motor-driven adj
    D: motorangetrieben adj, motorisch adj
    F: commandé adj par moteur, motorisé adj, entraîné adj par moteur,

motor-driven roller for cable laying
    D: elektro-motorische Kabellegerolle
    F: rouleau m entraîné par moteur pour la pose du câble

motorized adj
    D: motorangetrieben adj, motorisch adj
    F: commandé adj par moteur, motorisé adj, entraîné adj par moteur,

mo(u)ld n
    D: Form f (Gießen, Pressen)
    F: moule m

mo(u)ld n [smelt.]
    D: Kokille f
    F: coquille f

mo(u)lded deflector
    D: aufgepreßter Deflektor
    F: déflecteur m surmoulé

mo(u)lded part
    D: Preßling m, Preßteil n, Formteil n
    F: pièce f moulée

mo(u)lding n
    D: Preßling m, Preßteil n, Formteil n
    F: pièce f moulée

mo(u)ld shrinkage
    D: Formenschwindmaß n
    F: retrait m au moulage

mount v
    D: errichten v
    F: monter v, ériger v, installer v, assembler v

mount v
    D: einsetzen v, einbauen v
    F: mettre v, placer v, insérer v

mounting base
    D: Grundplatte f
    F: plaque f de base, socle m

mounting bracket

mounting clip
D: Befestigungsklemme f
F: pince f d'ancrage, collier de fixation m

mounting clip
D: Befestigungsklemme f
F: pince f d'ancrage, collier de fixation m

movable adj
D: verschiebbar adj
F: déplaçable adj

movement n
D: Verschiebung f, Verlagerung f
F: déplacement m, décalage m

moving crosshead [met. extr. pr.]
D: Laufholm m
F: traverse f mobile

muller mixer
D: Kollergang m
F: mélangeur m à meules

multi-channel cable
D: Vielbandkabel n
F: câble m à bandes multiples

multiconductor cable
D: Mehrleiterkabel n, mehradriges Kabel
F: câble m multipolaire, câble m multiconducteur

multicontact plug
D: Mehrfachstecker m
F: fiche f multiple

multicore cable
D: Mehrleiterkabel n, mehradriges Kabel
F: câble m multipolaire, câble m multiconducteur

multilayer material
D: Verbundwerkstoff m
F: complexe m, matériau m composite

multimode optical fibre
D: Mehrmoden-Lichtleiter m
F: fibre f optique multimode

multipair cable [tel.]
D: mehrpaariges Kabel, hochpaariges Kabel
F: câble m multipaire, câble m multitoron, câble m à grande capacité

multipaired cable [tel.]
D: mehrpaariges Kabel, hochpaariges Kabel
F: câble m multipaire, câble m multitoron, câble m à grande capacité

multi-pass drum twisting machine
D: mehrgängige Trommelverseilmaschine
F: câbleuse f à tambour à plusieures passes

multiple core cable
D: Mehrleiterkabel n, mehradriges Kabel
F: câble m multipolaire, câble m multiconducteur

multiple duct conduit
D: Mehrlochkanal m, mehrzügiger Rohrstrang
F: conduit m à plusieurs passages, caniveau m à passage multiple

multiple extrusion
D: Mehrfachextrusion f
F: extrusion f multiple

multiple joint box
D: Aufteilungsmuffe f
F: boîte f de distribution, boîte f de division, boîte f de trifurcation

multiple pair cable [tel.]
D: mehrpaariges Kabel, hochpaariges Kabel
F: câble m multipaire, câble m multitoron, câble m à grande capacité

multiple pin plug
D: mehrpoliger Stecker
F: fiche f multipolaire

multiple plug
D: Mehrfachstecker m
F: fiche f multiple

multiple sheath
D: Schichtenmantel m
F: gaine f composite, gaine f complexe

multiple shift operation
D: Mehrschichtbetrieb m
F: travail m en plusieurs équipes

multiple stranding
D: Mehrfachverseilung f
F: câblage m multiple

multiple-twin quad
D: Dieselhorst-Martin-Vierer m, DM-Vierer m
F: quarte f Dieselhorst-Martin, quarte f DM

multiple-twin quad cable
D: Dieselhorst-Martin-Vierer- verseiltes Kabel, DM-Vierer-

multiple-twin
verseiltes Kabel, DM-Viererkabel *n*
F: câble *m* à quartes Dieselhorst-Martin, câble *m* à quartes DM

multiple-twin quad formation
D: Dieselhorst-Martin-Verseilung *f*, DM-Verseilung *f*
F: câblage *m* à quartes à paires

multiple way duct
D: Mehrlochkanal *m*, mehrzügiger Rohrstrang
F: conduit *m* à plusieurs passages, caniveau *m* à passage multiple

municipal network [tel.]
D: Ortsnetz *n*
F: réseau *m* urbain, réseau *m* local, réseau *m* municipal

mushroom insulator
D: Pilzisolator *m*
F: isolateur *m* en forme de champignon

mutual capacitance [tel.]
D: Betriebskapazität *f*
F: capacité *f* mutuelle

mutual heating
D: gegenseitige Erwärmung
F: échauffement *m* mutuel

mutual inductance
D: Gegeninduktivität *f*
F: induction *f* mutuelle

mutual interference
D: gegenseitige Störungen
F: interférence *f* mutuelle

N

naked eye, visible to the ~
D: mit bloßem Auge sichtbar
F: visible *adj* à l'œil nu

naphthene base crude oil
D: naphtenbasisches Rohöl
F: huile *f* brute naphténique

natural-coloured plastic
D: ungefärbter Kunststoff, farbloser Kunststoff
F: matière *f* plastique de couleur naturelle, matière *f* plastique non colorée, matière *f* plastique incolore

natural plastic (US)
D: ungefärbter Kunststoff, farbloser Kunststoff
F: matière *f* plastique de couleur naturelle, matière *f* plastique non colorée, matière *f* plastique incolore

natural rubber
D: Naturkautschuk *m*
F: caoutchouc *m* naturel

nd-cable
D: Kabel mit nicht abwandernder Tränkmasse, nd-Kabel *n*, Haftmassekabel *n*
F: câble *m* à matière non migrante, câble *m* nd

nd-compound *n*
D: Haftmasse *f*, nd-Masse *f*, nicht abwandernde Tränkmasse
F: matière *f* non migrante, matière *f* nd

near-end cross talk (NEX)
D: Nahnebensprechen *n*
F: paradiaphonie *f*

near-end crosstalk attenuation
D: Nahnebensprechdämpfung *f*
F: affaiblissement *m* paradiaphonique

nearest, to ~ ... mm
D: mit einer Genauigkeit von ... mm
F: à ... mm près, avec une précision de ... mm

negative conductor
D: Minusleiter *m*
F: conducteur *m* négatif

negative feed-back
D: Gegenkopplung *f*
F: contre-réaction *f*

negative lead
D: Minusleiter *m*
F: conducteur *m* négatif

negligible *adj*
D: vernachlässigbar *adj*
F: négligeable *adj*

Neoprene *n*
D: Neoprene *n* (Polychloropren-Kautschuk der Du Pont)
F: Neoprene *m*

net attenuation
D: Restdämpfung *f*
F: équivalent *m* net de transmission, affaiblissement *m* résiduel, affaiblissement *m* effectif

net loss
D: Restdämpfung *f*

network n [el.]
 D: Netz n
 F: réseau m, secteur m

network impedance
 D: Netzwiderstand m
 F: impédance f du réseau

neutral, earthed ~ (GB)
 D: geerdeter Sternpunkt (Nullpunkt)
 F: neutre m à la terre, neutre m mis à la terre

neutral, grounded ~ (US)
 D: geerdeter Sternpunkt (Nullpunkt)
 F: neutre m à la terre, neutre m mis à la terre

neutral, insulated ~
 D: isolierter Sternpunkt
 F: neutre m isolé

neutral, isolated ~
 D: isolierter Sternpunkt
 F: neutre m isolé

neutral, unearthed ~ (GB)
 D: nicht geerdeter Sternpunkt (Nullpunkt)
 F: neutre m non mis à la terre

neutral, ungrounded ~ (US)
 D: nicht geerdeter Sternpunkt (Nullpunkt)
 F: neutre m non mis à la terre

neutral conductor
 D: Nulleiter m, Mittelpunktsleiter m
 F: conducteur m neutre, fil m neutre, neutre m

neutral conductor, concentric ~
 D: konzentrischer Nulleiter
 F: neutre m concentrique, neutre m périphérique

neutralisation number
 D: Neutralisationszahl (NZ) f
 F: indice m de neutralisation

neutral point
 D: Nullpunkt m, Sternpunkt m
 F: neutre m, point m neutre, zéro m

neutral wire
 D: Nulleiter m, Mittelpunktsleiter m
 F: conducteur m neutre, fil m neutre, neutre m

NEX (s. near-end cross talk)

nick n
 D: Nut f, Aussparung f
 F: rainure f, encoche f, découpe f, évidement m, entaille f

nip between rolls
 D: Walzenspalt m (Mischungsherstellung), Walzenstellung f (Mischungsherstellung)
 F: écartement m entre cylindres, jeu m entre cylindres

nipple stand [strand.]
 D: Nippelbock m
 F: bâti m de filière

nitrile butadiene rubber
 D: Nitrilkautschuk m
 F: caoutchouc m nitrile

no-delay telephone system
 D: Fernsprechschnellverkehr m
 F: service m téléphonique instantané

noise field [com.]
 D: Störfeld n
 F: champ m perturbateur, champ m parasite

noise level [com. c.]
 D: Rauschpegel m, Geräuschpegel m, Störpegel m
 F: niveau m de bruit, niveau m des perturbations

noise suppression
 D: Entstörung f, Störbeseitigung f
 F: suppression f des parasites, déparasitage m

noise suppressor
 D: Geräuschfilter m
 F: filtre m de bruit

noise voltage
 D: Geräuschspannung f
 F: tension f de bruit, tension f psophométrique

no-load, at ~ [el.]
 D: ohne Last
 F: sans charge

no-load, cable at ~ [pow. c.]
 D: unbelastetes Kabel, Kabel in unbelastetem Zustand
 F: câble m non chargé, câble m en exploitation sans charge

no-load current
 D: Leerlaufstrom m
 F: courant m à vide

no-load voltage
 D: Leerlaufspannung f
 F: tension f à vide, tension f à circuit ouvert

nominal cross-section

nominal

nominal
D: Nennquerschnitt m
F: section f nominale

nominal load
D: Nennbelastung f
F: charge f nominale

nominal output [mach.]
D: Nennleistung f
F: debit m nominal

nominal power [el.]
D: Nennleistung f
F: puissance f nominale

nominal value
D: Nominalwert m, Nennwert m
F: valeur f nominale

nominal voltage
D: Nennspannung f
F: tension f nominale

non-bleeding cable
D: abgetropftes Kabel
F: câble m à matière écoulée

non-combustible adj
D: unbrennbar adj
F: non-inflammable adj,
incombustible adj

non-compacted conductor
D: nicht verdichteter Leiter
F: âme f non rétreinte

non-compensated length
D: nicht kompensierte Länge (beim Platzwechsel einer Blankdrahtleitung)
F: longueur f non compensée

non-cutting shaping
D: spanlose Bearbeitung
F: mise f en forme plastique

non-destructive test
D: zerstörungsfreie Prüfung
F: essai m non-destructif

non-draining cable
D: Kabel mit nicht abwandernder Tränkmasse, nd-Kabel n, Haftmassekabel n
F: câble m à matière non migrante, câble m nd

non-draining compound
D: Haftmasse f, nd-Masse f, nicht abwandernde Tränkmasse
F: matière f non migrante, matière f nd

non fire propagating
D: flammwidrig adj, einen Brand nicht weiterleitend
F: non propagateur de la flamme adj,
non propagateur de l'incendie adj,
non transmettant la flamme

non-inductive cable [com. c.]
D: induktionsfreies Kabel
F: câble m non-inductif

non-inflammable adj
D: unbrennbar adj
F: non-inflammable adj,
incombustible adj

non-intermittent adj
D: kontinuierlich adj
F: continu adj, en continu

non-loaded adj [tel. c.]
D: unbelastet adj, unbespult adj
F: non chargé adj, non pupinisé adj

non-loaded balanced line
D: unbespulte symmetrische Leitung
F: ligne f symétrique non pupinisée,
ligne f symétrique non chargée

non-magnetic armo(u)ring
D: unmagnetische Bewehrung
F: armure f amagnétique

non-metallic-sheathed cable
D: Kunststoffmantelkabel n
F: câble m sous gaine plastique, câble m sous gaine non-métallique

non-productive time [mach.]
D: Nebenzeit f
F: temps m auxiliaire, temps m mort

non-radial field cable
D: Kabel mit nicht radialem Feld
F: câble m à champ non radial

non-returnable reel [cab.]
D: Verkaufstrommel f, Einwegtrommel f
F: touret m perdu

non-return valve
D: Rückschlagventil n
F: soupape f de retenue

non-system-connected adj
D: netzunabhängig adj
F: indépendant adj du réseau

non-system-dependent adj
D: netzunabhängig adj
F: indépendant adj du réseau

non-vibrating adj
D: schwingungsfrei adj
F: anti-vibratoire adj

normalization n
D: Normung f, Vereinheitlichung f
F: standardisation f, normalisation f,
unification f

normalize v

notch n
 D: Nut f, Aussparung f
 F: rainure f, encoche f, découpe f, évidement m, entaille f

notched adj
 D: eingekerbt adj
 F: entaillé adj

notched bar impact test
 D: Kerbschlagprobe f
 F: essai m de choc sur éprouvette entaillée

notched type sleeve
 D: Kerbverbinder m
 F: manchon m à sertir

notch sensitivity
 D: Kerbempfindlichkeit f
 F: sensibilité f à l'entaille

notch toughness
 D: Kerbzähigkeit f
 F: résistance f au déchirement (à partir de l'entaille), dureté f à l'entaille

notch type cable lug
 D: Kerbkabelschuh m
 F: cosse f de câble à sertir

notch type joint
 D: Kerbverbindung f
 F: raccord m à sertir

nozzle n
 D: Düse f
 F: buse f, injecteur m, tuyère f

nuclear power station
 D: Kernkraftwerk n
 F: centrale f nucléaire, centrale f atomique

numbered cable core
 D: numerierte Kabelader
 F: conducteur m de câble numéroté

numbering n
 D: Numerierung f
 F: numérotage m

numbering of cable cores
 D: Aderzählfolge f
 F: ordre m de numération des conducteurs

number of cores
 D: Aderzahl f
 F: nombre m des conducteurs

number of double folds
 D: Falzzahl f
 F: nombre m de pliages répétés

D: spannungsfrei glühen
 F: normaliser v

number of revolutions per minute (r.p.m.)
 D: Drehzahl f (Umdrehungen pro Minute = U/Min), Geschwindigkeit f
 F: nombre m de tours par minute (t.p.m.), vitesse f de rotation, vitesse f

number-printing n
 D: Ziffernbedruckung f
 F: repérage m par chiffres imprimés

O

oblique adj
 D: schräg adj
 F: incliné adj, oblique adj

oblique head [extr.]
 D: Schrägkopf m
 F: tête f oblique

observation window [mach.]
 D: Beobachtungsfenster n, Schauglas n, Schauloch n
 F: hublot m de regard, voyant m

observe v [test]
 D: einhalten v (Werte, Bedingungen)
 F: respecter v, observer v

occupancy n
 D: Platzbedarf m, Raumbedarf m, Flächenbelegung f
 F: encombrement m

off-load period [el.]
 D: spannungslose Periode
 F: repos m

OFHC-copper n (oxygen free high conductivity copper)
 D: OFHC-Kupfer n (sauerstoffreies hochleitfähiges Kupfer)
 F: cuivre m OFHC (cuivre exempt d'oxygène, à haute conductivité)

ohmic coupling
 D: Ohmsche Kopplung
 F: couplage m ohmique

ohmic losses
 D: Kupferverluste m pl
 F: pertes f pl dans le cuivre

ohmic resistance
 D: ohmscher Widerstand
 F: résistance f ohmique

oil circulation

oil

    D: Ölkreislauf m
    F: circulation f d'huile

oil circulation cooling
    D: Ölumlaufkühlung f
    F: refroidissement m par circulation d'huile

oil duct [cab.]
    D: Ölkanal m
    F: canal m de circulation d'huile

oil expansion tank
    D: Ölausgleichsgefäß n, Öldruck-Ausgleichsgefäß n, Druck-Ausgleichsgefäß n, Ausgleichsgefäß n (Ölkabel)
    F: réservoir m à pression d'huile variable

oil feeding equipment
    D: Öleinspeisungsvorrichtung f
    F: dispositif m d'alimentation en huile

oil-filled cable
    D: Ölkabel n
    F: câble m à huile fluide

oil immersion ag(e)ing
    D: Alterung unter Öl
    F: vieillissement m dans l'huile

oil leakage
    D: Ölleckstelle f
    F: fuite f d'huile

oil level indicator
    D: Ölstandsanzeiger m
    F: indicateur m du niveau d'huile

oil oscillation
    D: Ölbewegung f (im Kabel)
    F: oscillation f d'huile

Oilostatic-cable n
    D: Hochdruck-Ölkabel im Stahlrohr, Oilostatic-Kabel n
    F: câble m en tube d'acier sous haute pression d'huile, câble m Oléostatique

oil/paper dielectric
    D: Öl/Papier-Dielektrikum n
    F: diélectrique m papier/huile

oil pressure
    D: Öldruck m
    F: pression f d'huile

oil pressure cable
    D: Öldruckkabel n
    F: câble m à pression d'huile

oil pressure pipe type cable
    D: Öldruck-Rohrkabel n
    F: câble m en tube à pression d'huile

oil pressure tank
    D: Ölausgleichsgefäß n, Öldruck-Ausgleichsgefäß n, Druck-Ausgleichsgefäß n, Ausgleichsgefäß n (Ölkabel)
    F: réservoir m à pression d'huile variable

oil reservoir
    D: Ölausgleichsgefäß n, Öldruck-Ausgleichsgefäß n, Druck-Ausgleichsgefäß n, Ausgleichsgefäß n (Ölkabel)
    F: réservoir m à pression d'huile variable

oil resistance
    D: Ölbeständigkeit f, Ölfestigkeit f
    F: résistance f à l'huile

oil-rosin compound
    D: Ölharzgemisch n
    F: mélange m oléo-résineux, mélange m huile-résine

oil soluble resin
    D: öllösliches Harz
    F: résine f oléosoluble

oleoresinous enamel
    D: Ölharzlack m
    F: vernis m oléo-résineux

one-man operation
    D: Einmannbedienung f
    F: commande f par une personne

one-piece... adj
    D: einteilig adj
    F: monobloc adj, indivisé adj, en une seule pièce

on-line remote data processing
    D: direkte Daten-Fernverarbeitung
    F: télétraitement m d'informations direct, télétraitement m d'informations on-line

on-line spark tester [cab.]
    D: Durchlaufprüfgerät n, Trockenprüfgerät n
    F: appareil m de contrôle d'ionisation par défilement continu, détecteur m de défauts à sec

ooze v
    D: durchsickern v
    F: suinter v, filtrer v (se)

open v
    D: aufkorben v (Armierungsdrähte), aufdrehen v (sich)
    F: détordre v (se)

open adj [c. install.]
    D: auf Putz

F: à la surface, apparent *adj,* sur crépi

open-circuit voltage
D: Leerlaufspannung *f*
F: tension *f* à vide, tension *f* à circuit ouvert

open helix
D: offene Wendel
F: hélice *f* de vide

opening *n*
D: Öffnung *f*
F: orifice *m,* ouverture *f*

open wire line [com. c.]
D: Freileitung *f*
F: fil *m* aérien

operate, to ~ a machine
D: eine Maschine fahren, eine Maschine bedienen
F: faire *v* marcher une machine, opérer *v* une machine

operating at full capacity
D: voll ausgelastet
F: utilisé *adj* à pleine capacité, utilisé *adj* à plein,

operating capacity
D: Betriebskapazität *f* (Anlage)
F: capacité *f* de service

operating condition
D: Betriebszustand *m*
F: état *m* de service

operating conditions
D: Betriebsbedingungen *f pl*
F: conditions *f pl* de travail, conditions *f pl* de fonctionnement, conditions *f pl* d'exploitation

operating cost
D: Betriebskosten *plt*
F: coût *m* d'exploitation

operating cycle
D: Arbeitsablauf *m,* Betriebsablauf *m*
F: phases *f pl* de travail, suite *f* des opérations, cycle *m* de travail, déroulement *m* des opérations

operating error
D: Bedienungsfehler *m,* Fehlbedienung *f*
F: fausse manœuvre *f,* erreur *f* de conduite, erreur *f* de manœuvre, erreur *f* de l'opérateur, erreur *f* de manipulation

operating expenses *pl*
D: Betriebskosten *plt*
F: coût *m* d'exploitation

operating field strength
D: Betriebsfeldstärke *f*
F: intensité *f* de service, gradient *m* de service

operating instruction
D: Betriebsanleitung *f,* Bedienungsanleitung *f*
F: mode *m* opératoire, mode *m* d'emploi, notice *f* d'utilisation, manuel *m* d'instruction

operating lever
D: Bedienungshebel *m*
F: levier *m* de commande

operating manual
D: Betriebsanleitung *f,* Bedienungsanleitung *f*
F: mode *m* opératoire, mode *m* d'emploi, notice *f* d'utilisation, manuel *m* d'instruction

operating performance
D: Betriebsverhalten *n*
F: performance *f* (en service), tenue *f* (en service)

operating platform
D: Arbeitsbühne *f*
F: plate-forme *f* de commande, plate-forme *f* de service

operating pressure
D: Betriebsdruck *m*
F: pression *f* de service

operating reliability
D: Betriebssicherheit *f,* Betriebszuverlässigkeit *f,* Zuverlässigkeit im Betrieb
F: sécurité *f* de fonctionnement, fiabilité *f* de service

operating safety
D: Betriebssicherheit *f,* Betriebszuverlässigkeit *f,* Zuverlässigkeit im Betrieb
F: sécurité *f* de fonctionnement, fiabilité *f* de service

operating sequence
D: Arbeitsablauf *m,* Betriebsablauf *m*
F: phases *f pl* de travail, suite *f* des opérations, cycle *m* de travail, déroulement *m* des opérations

operating side [mach.]
D: Bedienungsseite *f*
F: côté commande *m,* côté *m* manœuvre, côté *m* service

operating speed [mach.]
D: Fahrgeschwindigkeit *f,* Fertigungsgeschwindigkeit *f,*

operating

　　　Arbeitsgeschwindigkeit f
F: vitesse de marche f, vitesse f de fabrication, vitesse f de production, vitesse f de travail

operating stress
D: Betriebsbeanspruchung f
F: contrainte f de service

operating temperature
D: Betriebstemperatur f
F: température f de service, température f de fonctionnement

operating voltage
D: Betriebsspannung f
F: tension f de service, tension f de régime

operation n
D: Betätigung f, Bedienung f
F: commande f, manœuvre f, manipulation f

operation n [cab., mach.]
D: Betrieb m
F: fonctionnement m, service m, exploitation f, régime m

operation, in a single ~
D: in einem einzigen Arbeitsgang, in einem Durchgang
F: en une seule passe, en une même operation

operation, out of ~
D: außer Betrieb
F: hors service

operational adj
D: betriebsbereit adj
F: prêt adj à fonctionner, prêt adj à la mise en marche,, en ordre de marche

operational characteristics
D: Betriebseigenschaften f pl
F: caractéristiques f pl de service, caractéristiques f pl de fonctionnement

operational conditions
D: Betriebsbedingungen f pl
F: conditions f pl de travail, conditions f pl de fonctionnement, conditions f pl d'exploitation

operational leakage [com.]
D: Betriebsableitung f
F: perditance f de transmission

operationally reliable cables
D: betriebssichere Kabel
F: câbles m pl de bonne sécurité de fonctionnement, câbles m pl de fonctionnement sûr

operational range
D: Funktionsreichweite f
F: portée f de fonctionnement

operational reliability
D: Betriebssicherheit f, Betriebszuverlässigkeit f, Zuverlässigkeit im Betrieb
F: sécurité f de fonctionnement, fiabilité f de service

operation with cyclic loading
D: Betrieb mit zyklischer Belastung
F: régime m cyclique

operative attenuation [tel.]
D: Betriebsdämpfung f
F: affaiblissement m composite

operative attenuation unit [tel.]
D: Betriebsdämpfungsmaß n
F: unité f d'affaiblissement composite

operator n
D: Maschinenführer m, Bedienungsperson f
F: opérateur m, machiniste m

operator panel
D: Bedienungsfeld n
F: panneau m de commande

operator's control platform
D: Arbeitsbühne f
F: plate-forme f de commande, plate-forme f de service

operator's desk
D: Schaltpult n, Bedienungspult n, Steuerpult n
F: pupitre m de commande, poste m de commande

operator's error
D: Bedienungsfehler m, Fehlbedienung f
F: fausse manœuvre f, erreur f de conduite, erreur f de manœuvre, erreur f de l'opérateur, erreur f de manipulation

optical fibre
D: Lichtleiter m
F: fibre f optique

optical fibre cable
D: Lichtleiterkabel n
F: câble m à fibres optiques

optical fibre transmission
D: Lichtleiter-Nachrichtenübertragung f
F: transmission f par fibre optique

optical fibre transmission line

D: Lichtleiter-Nachrichten-Übertragungsanlage *f*
F: ligne *f* de transmission par fibre optique

optimization *n*
D: optimale Gestaltung, Optimierung *f*
F: optimisation *f*, optimalisation *f*

orbital laying head coiler [c. c. r.]
D: Überkopf-Aufwickelei *f*
F: enrouloir *m* au-dessus de la hauteur de la tête

order, out of ~
D: außer Betrieb
F: hors service

order-of-addition schedule (mixing)
D: Mischfolge *f*
F: ordre *m* d'addition des ingrédients

ordinary plastic-sheathed flexible cord
D: mittlere Kunststoffschlauchleitung
F: câble *m* souple sous gaine ordinaire en plastique

ordinary (PVC-)sheathed flexible cord
D: mittlere (PVC-)Schlauchleitung
F: câble *m* souple sous gaine ordinaire (en PVC)

ordinary tough-rubber sheathed flexible cord
D: leichte Gummischlauchleitung
F: câble *m* souple sous gaine ordinaire de caoutchouc

organization chart
D: Organisationsplan *m*
F: organigramme *m*

orifice *n*
D: Öffnung *f*
F: orifice *m*, ouverture *f*

original material
D: Ausgangsmaterial *n*
F: matière *f* de base, produit *m* de base, matière *f* première, matériel *m* rudimentaire

oscillate, to ~ cable units [strand.]
D: Bündel unregelmäßig zusammenschlagen
F: osciller *v* les faisceaux de câbles

oscillating face plate [strand]
D: oszillierende Verseilscheibe
F: plaque *f* de répartition oscillante

oscillation *n* [el.]
D: Schwingung *f*
F: oscillation *f*

outage *n*
D: Ausfall *m* (Anlage, Kabel), Betriebsstörung *f*
F: défaut *m*, panne *f*, défaillance *f*, incident *m* de fonctionnement

outage time [mach.]
D: Ausfallzeit *f*
F: temps *m* d'arrêt, temps *m* de panne, temps *m* d'immobilisation

outdoor communications cable
D: Nachrichten-Außenkabel *n*
F: câble *m* de communication extérieur

outdoor installation
D: Verlegung im Freien
F: pose *f* à l'extérieur

outdoor plant
D: Freiluft-Anlage *f*
F: installation *f* extérieure

outdoor termination
D: Freiluft-Endverschluß *m*
F: extrémité *f* extérieure

outer conductor
D: Außenleiter *m*
F: âme *f* extérieure, conducteur *m* extérieur

outer diameter (OD)
D: Außendurchmesser *m*
F: diamètre *m* extérieur

outer semi-conducting layer [cab.]
D: äußere Leitschicht
F: couche *f* semi-conductrice externe

outer sheath
D: Außenmantel *m*
F: gaine *f* extérieure, gaine d'étanchéité *f*

outlet *n*
D: Austritt *m*
F: sortie *f*

outlet temperature
D: Austrittstemperatur *f*
F: température *f* de sortie

outlet valve
D: Ablaßventil *n*, Auslaßventil *n*
F: soupape *f* de décharge, soupape *f* de vidange, soupape *f* d'émission, soupape *f* de sortie

output *n* [mach.]
D: Leistung *f*, Ausstoß *m*
F: performance *f*, débit *m*, efficacité *f*, rendement *m*, capacité *f*

output per shift
D: Schichtleistung *f*

output

F: production f par équipe

output voltage
D: Sekundärspannung f
F: tension f secondaire

oven n
D: Wärmeschrank m
F: étuve f

overall attenuation
D: Restdämpfung f
F: équivalent m net de transmission, affaiblissement m résiduel, affaiblissement m effectif

overall attenuation measurement
D: Restdämpfungsmessung zwischen den Leitungsenden
F: mesure f d'équivalents de transmission

overall diameter
D: Außendurchmesser m
F: diamètre m extérieur

overall dimensions
D: Außenabmessungen f pl
F: dimensions f pl extérieures

overall loss [tel.]
D: Betriebsdämpfung f
F: affaiblissement m composite

overall transmission loss
D: Restdämpfung f
F: équivalent m net de transmission, affaiblissement m résiduel, affaiblissement m effectif

overcurrent cut-out switch
D: Schutzschalter m
F: disjoncteur m de protection, interrupteur m de sécurité

overcurrent protection
D: Überstromschutz m
F: protection f contre les surintensités

overdimension n
D: Übermaß n, Überdicke f, Bearbeitungszugabe f
F: surépaisseur f

overflow pipe
D: Überlaufrohr n
F: tuyau m de trop-plein, trop-plein m

overflow valve
D: Überlaufventil n
F: soupape f de trop-plein

overhauling n
D: Instandsetzung f, Reparatur f
F: remise f en état, réparation f, dépannage m

overhead cable
D: Luftkabel n
F: câble m aérien, fil m aérien

overhead contact wire
D: Fahrdraht m, Schleifdraht m
F: fil m (de) trolley, fil m de contact

overhead crane
D: Laufkran m
F: pont m roulant

overhead line
D: Freileitung f
F: ligne f aérienne

overhead pay-off
D: Überkopfablauf m
F: dévidoir m au-dessus de la hauteur de la tête, dérouleur m au-dessus de la hauteur de la tête

overhead pull-off
D: Überkopfabzug m
F: cabestan m de tirage au-dessus de la hauteur de la tête

overhead travelling crane
D: Brückenkran m
F: pont-grue m

overheating n
D: übermäßige Erwärmung
F: surchauffe f, surchauffage m

overlap v
D: überlappen v
F: chevaucher v, recouvrir v (se)

overlap(ping) n
D: Überlappung f
F: recouvrement m, chevauchement m

overlap, with 50 % ~
D: mit 50% Überlappung
F: à 50 % de recouvrement

overlapping adj
D: überlappend adj
F: à recouvrement, chevauchant adj

overload n
D: Überlast f
F: surcharge f

overload, under ~ conditions
D: bei Überlastbetrieb
F: en surcharge

overload circuit breaker
D: Überlastschalter m
F: interrupteur m de surcharge

overload protection
D: Überstromschutz m
F: protection f contre les surintensités

overload temperature

over-mastication n
  D: Totwalzen n (Kautschuk), Überwalzen n (Kautschuk)
  F: mastication f à mort, malaxage m à mort

over-milling n
  D: Totwalzen n (Kautschuk), Überwalzen n (Kautschuk)
  F: mastication f à mort, malaxage m à mort

overpressure n
  D: Überdruck m
  F: surpression f

oversheath n [cab.]
  D: äußere Schutzhülle, Außenschutz m
  F: revêtement m extérieur

oversize n
  D: Übermaß n, Überdicke f, Bearbeitungszugabe f
  F: surépaisseur f

overvoltage n
  D: Überspannung f
  F: surtension f

overvoltage arrester
  D: Überspannungsableiter m
  F: parasurtension m

overvoltage circuit-breaker
  D: Überspannungsschalter m
  F: interrupteur m à maximum de tension, disjoncteur m de surtension

overvoltage protection
  D: Überspannungsschutz m
  F: protection f contre les surtensions

oxidation inhibitor
  D: Oxydationsinhibitor m, Oxydationsverzögerer m, Alterungsschutzmittel n, Antioxidans n
  F: inhibiteur m d'oxydation, antioxidant m, antioxygène m

oxidative decomposition
  D: oxydativer Abbau
  F: décomposition f par oxydation

oxidative degradation
  D: oxydativer Abbau
  F: décomposition f par oxydation

oxide film
  D: Oxidhaut f
  F: peau f oxydée, couche f d'oxyde

oxide inclusions
  D: Oxideinschlüsse m pl
  F: inclusions f pl d'oxyde

oxide skin
  D: Oxidhaut f
  F: peau f oxydée, couche f d'oxyde

oxidize v
  D: oxydieren v
  F: oxyder v

oxidized bitumen
  D: geblasenes Bitumen
  F: bitume m soufflé

oxygen bomb
  D: Sauerstoffbombe f
  F: bombe f à oxygène

oxygen content
  D: Sauerstoffanteil m
  F: degré m d'oxygène

ozone resistance
  D: Ozonbeständigkeit f
  F: résistance f à l'ozone

P

pack-former for wire
  D: Bündelungsvorrichtung für Draht
  F: dispositif m à empaqueter les fils métalliques

packing n
  D: Dichtung f
  F: joint m, joint m d'étanchéité

packing ring
  D: Dichtungsscheibe f
  F: rondelle f d'étanchéité

pad n (paper)
  D: Bandscheibe f
  F: galette f

paddle mixer
  D: Schaufelmischer m
  F: mélangeur m à palettes

pad holder [lapp.]
  D: Papierscheibenhalter m, Scheibenhalter m
  F: porte-galette f

pail-pack n
  D: Faßwickler m
  F: enrouleur m en forme de tonneau, fût m de bobinage pour fils métalliques

paint n

paint

- D: Anstrich *m*
- F: peinture *f*, enduit *m*

pair *n* [com. c.]
- D: Doppelader *f*, paarverseilte Leitung, Paar *n*
- F: paire *f*, fil *m* double, conducteur *m* jumelé

paired cable [com. c.]
- D: paarverseiltes Kabel, paarig verseiltes Kabel
- F: câble *m* à paires, câble *m* jumelé, câble *m* pairé

pairing *n*
- D: Paarverseilung *f*
- F: pairage *m*, assemblage *m* par paires

pair of cores
- D: Aderpaar *n*
- F: paire *f* de conducteurs

pair stranded in quad pair formation
- D: Doppelsternvierer *m*
- F: paire *f* câblée en étoile

pair stranding machine
- D: Paarverseilmaschine *f*
- F: paireuse *f*

pair twisting
- D: Paarverseilung *f*
- F: pairage *m*, assemblage *m* par paires

pair twisting machine
- D: Paarverseilmaschine *f*
- F: paireuse *f*

palletize *v*
- D: auf Paletten packen
- F: palettiser *v*

panel switching equipment
- D: Flachwähl-Anlage *f*
- F: installation *f* de sélecteurs à panneau

paper feed
- D: Papiervorschub *m*
- F: défilement *m* du papier

paper-insulated cable
- D: papierisoliertes Kabel, Papierkabel *n*
- F: câble *m* isolé au papier

paper-insulated core
- D: papierisolierte Ader
- F: conducteur *m* isolé au papier

paper-insulated lead-covered cable
- D: Papier-Bleikabel *n*, papierisoliertes Bleimantelkabel
- F: câble *m* isolé à papier sous gaine de plomb

paper-insulated lead-sheathed cable
- D: Papier-Bleikabel *n*, papierisoliertes Bleimantelkabel
- F: câble *m* isolé à papier sous gaine de plomb

paper-insulated mass-impregnated cable
- D: Papier-Masse-Kabel *n*, Massekabel *n*, massegetränktes Papierkabel
- F: câble *m* isolé à papier imprégné à matière visqueuse

paper-insulated wire
- D: papierisolierte Ader
- F: conducteur *m* isolé au papier

paper insulation
- D: Papierisolierung *f*
- F: isolant *m* papier

paper lapping
- D: Papierspinnen *n*
- F: rubanage *m* de papier

paper lapping head
- D: Papierspinnkopf *m*
- F: tête *f* de rubaneuse à papier, tête *f* à papier

paper lapping machine
- D: Papierspinnmaschine *f*, Plattiermaschine *f*
- F: rubaneuse *f* à papier

paper machine, continuous traveling wire cloth ~
- D: Langsieb-Papiermaschine *f*, Fourdrinier-Papiermaschine *f*
- F: machine *f* à papier à toile sans fin, machine *f* à papier Fourdrinier

paper-making, twin-wire ~ machine
- D: Doppellangsieb-Papiermaschine *f*
- F: machine *f* à papier à toile double sans fin

paper pad [lapp.]
- D: Papierscheibe *f*, Papierbandscheibe *f*
- F: galette *f* de papier

paper/plastic laminate insulation
- D: Papier/Kunststoff-Schichtenisolierung *f*
- F: isolant *m* stratifié en papier/matière plastique

paper pulp insulation
- D: Papierpulpisolierung *f*
- F: isolant *m* pâte à papier

paper ribbon insulation (US)

paper tape insulation
 D: Isolierung aus Papierbandumspinnung, Papierbandisolierung f
 F: isolation f rubanée en papier, rubanage m en papier

paper roll
 D: Papierrolle f
 F: rouleau m de papier

paper-slitting machine
 D: Papierschneidemaschine f, Papierbandschneidemaschine f
 F: machine f à couper les rubans de papier, machine f à découper le papier, découpeuse f à papier

paper string
 D: Papierkordel f
 F: ficelle f de papier

paper string, to apply the ~
 D: mit Papierkordel umspinnen
 F: guiper v

paper string wire (core)
 D: Papierkordelader f
 F: conducteur m à ficelle de papier

paper strip
 D: Papierstreifen m
 F: bande f de papier

paper tape break
 D: Papierbandriß m
 F: déchirure f du ruban de papier, rupture f du ruban de papier

paper tape cutting machine
 D: Papierschneidemaschine f, Papierbandschneidemaschine f
 F: machine f à couper les rubans de papier, machine f à découper le papier, découpeuse f à papier

paper tape insulation
 D: Isolierung aus Papierbandumspinnung, Papierbandisolierung f
 F: isolation f rubanée en papier, rubanage m en papier

paper tube [c. access.]
 D: Papierwickel m (vorgefertigt)
 F: fuseau m long de papier

paraffin base crude oil
 D: paraffinbasisches Rohöl
 F: huile f brute à la base de paraffine

parallel, cables laid in ~
 D: nebeneinander liegende Kabel, in einer Ebene liegende Kabel
 F: câbles m pl disposés en nappe

parallel, laying in ~
 D: Verlegung nebeneinander, Parallelanordnung f
 F: disposition f côte à côte, disposition f en nappe horizontale, disposition f en parallèle

parallel arrangement
 D: Verlegung nebeneinander, Parallelanordnung f
 F: disposition f côte à côte, disposition f en nappe horizontale, disposition f en parallèle

parallel circuit
 D: Parallelschaltung f
 F: montage m en parallèle, couplage m en parallèle

parallel connection
 D: Parallelschaltung f
 F: montage m en parallèle, couplage m en parallèle

parameter n
 D: Kennwert m, Parameter m
 F: paramètre m, valeur f caractéristique

parasitic current
 D: Fremdstrom m
 F: courant m parasitique

parasitic noise
 D: Störgeräusch n
 F: bruit m parasite, bruit m perturbateur

parasitic oscillation
 D: Störschwingung f
 F: onde f perturbatrice, oscillation f parasite

part by weight
 D: Gewichtsteil n
 F: partie f en poids

partial discharge [el.]
 D: Teilentladung f
 F: décharge f partielle

partial discharge-free
 D: teilentladungsfrei adj
 F: exempt adj de décharges partielles

partial discharge level test
 D: Teilentladungsprüfung f
 F: essai m de décharges partielles

partial discharge measurement
 D: Teilentladungsmessung f
 F: mesure f des décharges partielles

partial discharge resistance
 D: Teilentladungs-Beständigkeit f
 F: résistance f aux décharges partielles

particle size analysis
  D: Teilchengrößenanalyse f
  F: analyse f granulométrique
particle size distribution
  D: Korngrößenverteilung f, Teilchengrößenverteilung f
  F: répartition f granulométrique
particulars pl
  D: Daten pl, Angaben f pl
  F: données f pl, renseignements m pl
part subject to wear
  D: Verschleißteil n
  F: pièce f d'usure
party line
  D: Gemeinschaftsleitung f
  F: ligne f partagée
pass n [roll. m.]
  D: Durchgang m, Stich m
  F: passe f
pass, to ~ a test
  D: eine Prüfung bestehen
  F: passer v un essai, tenir v un essai, résister v à un essai
paste vt
  D: kleben vt
  F: coller vt, attacher vt
patent, to apply for a ~
  D: ein Patent anmelden
  F: déposer v une demande de brevet, demander v un brevet
patent, to grant a ~
  D: ein Patent erteilen
  F: accorder v un brevet, délivrer v un brevet
patent application
  D: Patentmeldung f
  F: demande f de brevet
patent application, examined ~
  D: Auslegeschrift f
  F: demande f de brevet examinée
patent application, published ~
  D: Auslegeschrift f
  F: demande f de brevet examinée
patent application, to file a ~
  D: ein Patent anmelden
  F: déposer v une demande de brevet, demander v un brevet
patent application, unexamined ~
  D: Offenlegungsschrift f
  F: demande f de brevet non examinée
patent claim
  D: Patentanspruch m
  F: revendication f d'un brevet, spécification f d'un brevet
patent infringement
  D: Patentverletzung f
  F: violation f d'un brevet, contrefaçon f d'un brevet
patent rights
  D: Schutzrechte n pl
  F: droits m pl de protection
pattern, taking ~ from
  D: in Anlehnung an
  F: suivant l'exemple de
pattern-making n
  D: Modellanfertigung f
  F: fabrication f de maquettes
pattern of types
  D: Typenspektrum n
  F: gamme f de types, éventail m de types
pay off v
  D: abwickeln v, abspulen v
  F: dérouler v, dévider v
pay-off n [wire manuf., cab.]
  D: Ablauf m
  F: déroulement m
pay-off-pak n
  D: Faßwickler m
  F: enrouleur m en forme de tonneau, fût m de bobinage pour fils métalliques
pay-off reel
  D: Ablaufspule f, Vorratstrommel f, Ablauftrommel f, Abwickeltrommel f
  F: bobine f débitrice, bobine f d'alimentation, bobine f de dévidage
pay-off stand [wire manuf., cab.]
  D: Ablaufbock m, Ablaufgestell n, Abwickelei f
  F: bâti m départ, dévidoir m, dérouleur m
PCM cable
  D: Pulscode-Modulationskabel n, PCM-Kabel n
  F: câble m de modulation par impulsion et codage, câble m MIC
PCP (s. polychloroprene)
PE (s. polyethylene)
peak n
  D: Spitze f (Spannung, Leistung)
  F: pointe f, crête f
peak hours pl
  D: Spitzenbelastungszeit f

peak load [el.]
D: Lastspitze f, Spitzenbelastung f
F: pointe f de charge, charge f de pointe

peak of corrugation
D: Wellenspitze f (beim Wellmantel)
F: crête f d'ondulation

peak value
D: Scheitelwert m, Spitzenwert m
F: valeur f de crête

peak voltage
D: Spitzenspannung f, Scheitelspannung f
F: tension f de crête, tension f de pointe

PE-compound n
D: PE-Mischung f
F: mélange m de PE

peel v
D: ablösen v (Folie, Schicht), abziehen v
F: peler v, séparer v, décoller v

peel v [c. access.]
D: schälen v (eine Schicht)
F: peler v

peel v (off)
D: abblättern v
F: écailler v (s'), décoller v (se)

peeling n
D: Ablösen n (Trennen)
F: pelage m, décollement m

peel strength
D: Haftvermögen n
F: adhérence f, adhésivité f

peephole n [mach.]
D: Beobachtungsfenster n, Schauglas n, Schauloch n
F: hublot m de regard, voyant m

pelletize v
D: granulieren v
F: granuler v

pelletizer n
D: Granulator m
F: granulateur m

pellets pl
D: Granulat n
F: granulés m pl

pencil v
D: anspitzen v (Isolierung)
F: appointer v

pencilled insulation
D: angespitzte Isolierung
F: isolation f appointée

pencilling tool
D: Konusschneider m, Radischneider m
F: dispositif m d'appointage

penetration n
D: Penetration f, Eindringung f
F: pénétration f

penetration of moisture
D: Eindringen von Feuchtigkeit
F: pénétration f d'humidité

penetration test
D: Eindringprüfung f
F: essai m de pénétration

percentage by weight
D: Gewichtsprozent n
F: pourcent(age) m en poids

percent in weight
D: Gewichtsprozent n
F: pourcent(age) m en poids

perform, to ~ a test
D: eine Prüfung durchführen
F: faire v un essai, effectuer v un essai

performance n [mach.]
D: Leistung f, Ausstoß m
F: performance f, débit m, efficacité f, rendement m, capacité f

performance n
D: Verhalten n
F: tenue f, allure f, comportement m, performance f

periodically changing lay
D: periodisch wechselnde Drallrichtung
F: pas m de câblage changeant périodiquement

periodic load duty [el.]
D: Dauerbetrieb mit periodisch veränderlicher Belastung
F: service m permanent à charge variant périodiquement, régime m permanent à charge variant périodiquement

periodic operation
D: periodischer Betrieb
F: régime m périodique

peripheral speed
D: Umfangsgeschwindigkeit f
F: vitesse f périphérique, vitesse f circonférentielle

permanent deformation
D: bleibende Verformung
F: déformation f permanente

permanent 324

permanent installation [cab.]
  D: feste Verlegung
  F: installation *f* fixe
permanent set
  D: bleibende Dehnung
  F: allongement *m* permanent, allongement *m* rémanent
permanent wiring
  D: feste Verdrahtung
  F: filerie *f* fixe
permeability *n*
  D: magnetische Leitfähigkeit
  F: perméabilité *f*
permeability to air
  D: Luftdurchlässigkeit *f*
  F: perméabilité *f* à l'air
permeability to gas
  D: Gasdurchlässigkeit *f*, Durchlässigkeit für Gas
  F: perméabilité *f* au gaz
permeable *adj*
  D: durchlässig *adj*
  F: perméable *adj*
permissible *adj*
  D: zulässig *adj*
  F: admissible *adj*
permissible variation
  D: Toleranz *f*
  F: tolérance *f*
permit, to ~ conclusions as to
  D: Aufschluß geben über (z.B. Betriebsverhalten)
  F: fournir *v* des renseignements sur
permittivity *n*
  D: Dielektrizitätskonstante (DK) *f*
  F: constante *f* diélectrique, permittivité *f*
permittivity, absolute ~
  D: absolute Dielektrizitätskonstante
  F: permittivité *f* absolue
permittivity, relative ~
  D: relative Dielektrizitätskonstante
  F: permittivité *f* relative
peroxide *n*
  D: Peroxid *n*
  F: peroxyde *m*
pervious *adj*
  D: durchlässig *adj*
  F: perméable *adj*
Peschel conduit (for house wiring)
  D: Peschelrohr *n*
  F: tube *m* en tôle plombée
PE-sheath *n*
  D: PE-Mantel *m*
  F: gaine *f* de PE
petroleum jelly
  D: Vaseline *f*, Petrol-jelly *n*
  F: vaseline *f*, gelée *f* de pétrole
petroleum jelly filling
  D: Abstopfen mit Petrol-jelly
  F: remplissage *m* en gelée de pétrole
petrol jelly
  D: Vaseline *f*, Petrol-jelly *n*
  F: vaseline *f*, gelée *f* de pétrole
petticoat insulator
  D: Glockenisolator *m*, Isolierglocke *f*
  F: isolateur *m* à cloche, cloche *f* isolante
phantom circuit
  D: Phantomkreis *m*, Phantomschaltung *f*, Viererkreis *m*, Kreisvierer *m*, Phantomleitung *f*
  F: circuit *m* fantôme, circuit *m* superposé, circuit *m* combiné
phantom circuit loading coil
  D: Phantompupinspule *f*
  F: bobine *f* de charge pour circuit fantôme
phantom phone connection
  D: Doppelsprechschaltung *f*
  F: montage *m* en phantôme
phantom telephony
  D: Doppelsprechen *n*
  F: téléphonie *f* fantôme, téléphonie *f* duplex
phantom-to-side unbalance
  D: Mitsprechkopplung *f*
  F: couplage *m* de diaphonie
phase, in ~
  D: phasengleich *adj*
  F: en phase
phase angle
  D: Phasenwinkel *m*
  F: angle *m* de phase
phase balance
  D: Phasengleichheit *f*
  F: équilibre *m* des phases, concordance *f* des phases
phase coincidence
  D: Phasengleichheit *f*
  F: équilibre *m* des phases, concordance *f* des phases
phase compensation
  D: Phasenausgleich *m*
  F: compensation *f* des phases
phase conductor

phase
  D: Phasenleiter m
  F: conducteur m de phase
phase constant
  D: Phasenmaß n
  F: constante f de phase
phase current
  D: Phasenstrom m
  F: courant m de phase
phase delay
  D: Phasenlaufzeit f
  F: temps m de propagation de phase
phase displacement
  D: Phasenverschiebung f
  F: déphasage m
phase distortion
  D: Phasenverzerrung f
  F: distorsion f de phase
phase lag
  D: Phasennacheilung f
  F: retard m de phase
phase lead
  D: Phasenvoreilung f
  F: avance f de phase
phase monitor
  D: Phasenausfall-Überwachungsgerät n
  F: dispositif m de contrôle des phases
phase shift
  D: Phasenverschiebung f
  F: déphasage m
phase to earth
  D: Phase gegen Erde
  F: phase f par rapport à la terre
phase-to-earth voltage
  D: Leiter-Erdspannung f
  F: tension f étoilée
phase to ground
  D: Phase gegen Erde
  F: phase f par rapport à la terre
phase to phase
  D: Phase gegen Phase
  F: phase f à phase
phase-to-phase fault
  D: zweipoliger Kurzschluß
  F: court-circuit m bipolaire
phase-to-phase voltage
  D: verkettete Spannung
  F: tension f composée, tension f entre phases
phase velocity
  D: Phasengeschwindigkeit f
  F: vitesse f de phase
phase voltage
  D: Phasenspannung f
  F: tension f de phase
physical circuit
  D: Stammkreis m, Stammleitung f
  F: circuit m combinant, circuit m réel
PIC (plastic insulated conductor) (US) [com. c.]
  D: kunststoffisolierte Ader
  F: conducteur m isolé au plastique
PIC-cable n (US)
  D: Kabel mit kunststoffisolierten Leitern
  F: câble m à conducteurs isolés au plastique
pickle v
  D: beizen v
  F: décaper v
pickling bath
  D: Beizbad n
  F: bain m de décapage
pickling plant
  D: Beizanlage f
  F: installation f de décapage
pickling solution
  D: Beizlösung f
  F: solution f de décapage
picture telegraphy transmission line
  D: Bildtelegraphie-Übertragungsleitung f
  F: ligne f de transmission phototélégraphique
piecework n
  D: Akkordarbeit f
  F: travail m à la pièce, travail m à forfait
pig n
  D: Massel f (Blei)
  F: saumon m
pig lead
  D: Blockblei n
  F: saumon m de plomb
pigment v
  D: färben v
  F: colorer v, teindre v
pigment n
  D: Farbstoff m
  F: pigment m, matière colorante f
PILC cable (US)
  D: Papier-Bleikabel n, papierisoliertes Bleimantelkabel
  F: câble m isolé à papier sous gaine de plomb
pilot conductor

pilot
  D: Prüfader f, Prüfdraht m, Prüfleiter m, Hilfsader f
  F: fil m d'essai, fil m pilote

pilot core
  D: Prüfader f, Prüfdraht m, Prüfleiter m, Hilfsader f
  F: fil m d'essai, fil m pilote

pilot installation
  D: Versuchsanlage f
  F: installation f d'essai, installation f expérimentale

pilot lamp
  D: Signallampe f, Anzeigelampe f
  F: voyant m lumineux, signal m lumineux, lampe-témoin f

pilot light
  D: Signallampe f, Anzeigelampe f
  F: voyant m lumineux, signal m lumineux, lampe-témoin f

pilot line [prod.]
  D: Versuchsstraße f
  F: ligne f expérimentale, ligne f d'essai

pilot on guider tip [extr.]
  D: Zentrierung am Führungsnippel
  F: dispositif m de centrage sur le poinçon guide

pilot wire
  D: Prüfader f, Prüfdraht m, Prüfleiter m, Hilfsader f
  F: fil m d'essai, fil m pilote

pinhole n
  D: Pore f
  F: pore m

pin insulator
  D: Stützisolator m
  F: isolateur m support, isolateur m rigide

pintle-mounted adj
  D: in Pinolen gelagert
  F: monté adj entre pointes

pintle-type spooler
  D: Pinolen-Wickler m
  F: bobinoir m à pointes, enrouleur m à pointes

pipe n
  D: Rohr n
  F: tube m, tuyau m

pipe bend
  D: Rohrbogen m, Rohrkrümmung f, Rohrknie n, Knierohr n, Krümmer m (Rohr)
  F: coude m, raccord m coudé

pipe clip
  D: Rohrschelle f
  F: bride f d'attache, collier m pour tubes

pipe connection
  D: Rohrverbindung f
  F: joint m de tuyaux

pipe hangers pl [vulc.]
  D: Rohraufhängung f
  F: berceau m

pipe joint
  D: Rohrverbindung f
  F: joint m de tuyaux

pipeline n
  D: Rohrleitung f
  F: tubulure f, conduite f

pipeline compression cable
  D: Gasaußendruck-Kabel im Stahlrohr
  F: câble m en tube sous compression externe de gaz

pipeline conduit
  D: Rohrstrang m
  F: conduit m, caniveau m

pipeline mixer
  D: Durchflußmischer m (Mischungsherstellung)
  F: mélangeur m en continu à courant

pipe suspension [vulc.]
  D: Rohraufhängung f
  F: berceau m

pipe system
  D: Rohrleitungssystem n
  F: tuyauterie f

pipe type cable
  D: Rohrkabel n
  F: câble m en tube

piping n
  D: Rohrleitungssystem n
  F: tuyauterie f

piston n [mach.]
  D: Stempel m, Kolben m, Plunger m
  F: piston m, fouloir m

piston stroke
  D: Kolbenhub m
  F: course f de piston

pit, cable ~
  D: Muffenbunker m, Muffenbauwerk n, Kabelschacht m
  F: trou m d'homme, puits m de visite, puits m de jonction, chambre f de répartition, puits m à câbles

pitch n [strand.]
  D: Schlaglänge f, Drallänge f

pitch n
 F: longueur f du pas
pitch n
 D: Steigung f (Gewinde, Schnecke, Bandspinnen)
 F: pas m
pitch n
 D: Teer m
 F: goudron m
pitch of corrugation
 D: Wellenlänge f (Wellmantel)
 F: pas m d'ondulation
pitting n
 D: Lokalkorrosion f, Lochfraß m
 F: corrosion f localisée, corrosion f locale, corrosion f ponctuelle, pitting m
pivoted adj
 D: ausschwenkbar adj, ausklappbar adj, schwenkbar adj, aufklappbar adj, drehbar gelagert
 F: pivotant adj, articulé adj
plain adj
 D: blank adj
 F: nu adj, brillant adj
plain conductor
 D: blanker Leiter
 F: âme f nue
plain lead-covered cable
 D: blankes Bleimantelkabel
 F: câble m sous gaine de plomb nu
plain sheath
 D: glatter Mantel
 F: gaine f lisse
plain surface
 D: glatte Oberfläche
 F: surface f lisse
planetary mixer
 D: Planetenrührwerk n
 F: agitateur m planétaire
planetary strander
 D: Korbverseilmaschine f
 F: câbleuse f à cage, assembleuse f à cage
planet-type stranding machine
 D: Korbverseilmaschine f
 F: câbleuse f à cage, assembleuse f à cage
plank n
 D: Daube f (Kabeltrommeln), Verschalbrett n
 F: douve f
planning n
 D: Projektierung f
 F: étude f, élaboration f d'un projet
planning of cable installations
 D: Planung von Kabelanlagen
 F: planification f d'installations de câbles
plant n [mach.]
 D: Anlage f
 F: installation f
plant n
 D: Betrieb m (Werk, Anlage), Werkstatt f
 F: usine f, atelier m
plant visitation (US)
 D: Werksbesichtigung f
 F: tour m de l'usine
plaster, under ~ [c. install.]
 D: unter Putz
 F: encastré adj, sous enduit, sous crépi
plastic deformation
 D: bleibende Verformung
 F: déformation f permanente
plastic flow
 D: plastisches Fließen
 F: écoulement m plastique
plastic-insulated cable
 D: Kunststoffkabel n, Kabel mit Kunststoff-Isolierung
 F: câble m (isolé) à matière plastique
plastic-insulated conductor cable
 D: Kabel mit kunststoffisolierten Leitern
 F: câble m à conducteurs isolés au plastique
plastic-insulated core
 D: kunststoffisolierte Ader
 F: conducteur m isolé au plastique
plastic-insulated power cable
 D: Kunststoff-Energiekabel n
 F: câble m d'énergie (isolé) à matière plastique
plastic insulation
 D: Kunststoff-Isolierung f
 F: isolant m plastique, isolant m synthétique
plasticity n
 D: Plastizität f
 F: plasticité f
plasticized PVC
 D: Weich-PVC n
 F: PVC m plastifié
plasticizer n
 D: Weichmacher m

plasticizer
   F: plastifiant m
plastic material
   D: Kunststoff m, Plast m
   F: matière f plastique, matière f synthétique, plastique m
plastics cable
   D: Kunststoffkabel n, Kabel mit Kunststoff-Isolierung
   F: câble m (isolé) à matière plastique
plastics-coated metal foil
   D: kunststoffkaschierte Metallfolie
   F: feuille f métallique doublée de matière plastique
plastics compound
   D: Kunststoff-Mischung f
   F: mélange m plastique
plastic sheath
   D: Kunststoffmantel m
   F: gaine f plastique
plastic-sheathed cable
   D: Kunststoffmantelkabel n
   F: câble m sous gaine plastique, câble m sous gaine non-métallique
plastic-sheathed flexible cord
   D: Kunststoffschlauchleitung f
   F: câble m souple sous gaine en plastique
plastic-sheathed flexible cord, light ~
   D: leichte Kunststoffschlauchleitung
   F: câble m souple sous gaine légère en plastique
plastic-sheathed flexible cord, ordinary ~
   D: mittlere Kunststoffschlauchleitung
   F: câble m souple sous gaine ordinaire en plastique
plastics mixing plant
   D: Kunststoff-Mischerei f
   F: installation f de préparation des mélanges plastiques
plastics power cable
   D: Kunststoff-Energiekabel n
   F: câble m d'énergie (isolé) à matière plastique
plastification n
   D: Plastifizierung f
   F: plastification f
plastificator n
   D: Plastifikator m
   F: plastificateur m
plastifier n
   D: Plastifikator m
   F: plastificateur m

plastometer n
   D: Plastometer n
   F: plastomètre m
plate n
   D: Platte f
   F: plaque f, plateau m
platform n
   D: Bühne f (Arbeitsplattform)
   F: plate-forme f
play of axis
   D: Achsenspiel n
   F: jeu m sur axe, jeu m à l'entraînement
plot, to ~ a graph
   D: graphisch darstellen
   F: représenter v graphiquement
plot, to ~ graphically
   D: graphisch darstellen
   F: représenter v graphiquement
plough, cable laying ~ (GB)
   D: Kabelpflug m
   F: charrue f de pose pour câbles
plow, cable laying ~ (US)
   D: Kabelpflug m
   F: charrue f de pose pour câbles
plug n
   D: Stecker m
   F: fiche f, prise f mâle
plug and socket connection
   D: Steckverbindung f, Steckanschluß m
   F: jonction f débrochable, prise f complète mâle et femelle, prise f débrochable
plug connector
   D: Stecker m
   F: fiche f, prise f mâle
plug-ended cord
   D: Stöpselschnur f
   F: cordon m avec fiche, cordon m de liaison
plug-in termination
   D: Aufsteck-Endverschluß m
   F: extrémité f embrochable
plug-on termination
   D: Aufsteck-Endverschluß m
   F: extrémité f embrochable
plug socket
   D: Steckbuchse f, Steckerbuchse f, Fassung f
   F: prise f femelle, fiche f femelle, douille f
plug vulcanized to the cable

plunger
- *D:* aufvulkanisierter Stecker
- *F:* fiche *f* vulcanisée sur le câble

plunger *n* [mach.]
- *D:* Stempel *m*, Kolben *m*, Plunger *m*
- *F:* piston *m*, fouloir *m*

plunger piston [met. extr. pr.]
- *D:* Tauchplunger *m*
- *F:* fouloir *m* plongeur

plunger press
- *D:* Stempelpresse *f*, Strangpresse *f*, Kolbenpresse *f*
- *F:* presse *f* à piston

p.m.e. (s. protective multiple earthing)

pneumatic conveying system
- *D:* pneumatische Förderanlage
- *F:* installation *f* de transport pneumatique

pneumatic operation
- *D:* Druckluftbetätigung *f*
- *F:* commande *f* à air comprimé, commande *f* pneumatique

pneu-wipe
- *D:* Gebläsetrockner *m*
- *F:* ventilateur *m* de séchage

point *v*
- *D:* anspitzen *v* (Draht)
- *F:* appointer *v*

pointwise measurement
- *D:* punktweises Messen
- *F:* mesure *f* par points

poise
- *D:* Poise *n* (Viskosität)
- *F:* poise *f*

polarity inversion test
- *D:* Prüfung mit wechselnder Polarität
- *F:* essai *m* à inversion de la polarité

pole changing
- *D:* Umpolung *f*, Polwechsel *m*, Umkehr der Polarität
- *F:* inversion *f* de polarité

pole-mounted insulator
- *D:* Stützisolator *m*
- *F:* isolateur *m* support, isolateur *m* rigide

pole-mounted termination
- *D:* Mast-Endverschluß *m*
- *F:* isolateur *m* de poteau

pole reversal
- *D:* Umpolung *f*, Polwechsel *m*, Umkehr der Polarität
- *F:* inversion *f* de polarité

poles, like ~
- *D:* gleichnamige Pole
- *F:* pôles *m pl* homologues, pôles *m pl* similaires

poles, similar ~
- *D:* gleichnamige Pole
- *F:* pôles *m pl* homologues, pôles *m pl* similaires

poling *n* [smelt.]
- *D:* Polen *n*
- *F:* travail *m* avec la perche

polyamide
- *D:* Polyamid (PA) *n*
- *F:* polyamide *m*

polychloroprene (PCP) *n*
- *D:* Polychloropren (PCP) *n*
- *F:* polychloroprène *m* (PCP)

polyester resin
- *D:* Polyesterharz *n*
- *F:* résine *f* polyester

polyethylene (PE) *n*
- *D:* Polyäthylen (PE) *n*
- *F:* polyéthylène *m* (PE)

polyisobutylene *n*
- *D:* Polyisobutylen *n*
- *F:* polyisobutylène *m*

polymer *n*
- *D:* Polymerisat *n*
- *F:* polymère *m*

polymerisation *n*
- *D:* Polymerisation *f*
- *F:* polymérisation *f*

polymer/paper laminated tape
- *D:* kunststoffbeschichtetes Papierband
- *F:* ruban *m* papier contrecouché d'un polymère

polyolefin, branched ~
- *D:* verzweigtes Polyolefin
- *F:* polyoléfine *m* ramifié

polypropylene *n*
- *D:* Polypropylen *n*
- *F:* polypropylène *m*

polystyrene *n*
- *D:* Polystyrol *n*
- *F:* polystyrène *m*

polytetrafluorethylene (PTFE) *n*
- *D:* Polytetrafluoräthylen (PTFE) *n*
- *F:* polytétrafluoréthylène *m* (PTFE)

polyvinyl chloride (PVC)
- *D:* Polyvinylchlorid (PVC) *n*
- *F:* chlorure *m* de polyvinyle (PVC), polychlorure *m* de vinyle (PCV)

population *n* [math.]
- *D:* Grundgesamtheit *f*

population

F: population f

porcelain insulator
D: Porzellanisolator m
F: isolateur m en porcelaine, porcelaine f

pore n
D: Pore f
F: pore m

pore-free adj
D: porenfrei adj
F: exempt adj de pores

porosimeter n
D: Porenprüfgerät n (Papier)
F: porosimètre m

porosity n
D: Luftdurchlässigkeit f (Papier)
F: porosité f

portable adj
D: tragbar adj
F: portatif adj

portable appliance
D: ortsveränderliches Gerät
F: appareil m portatif, appareil m mobile

portable cable measuring set
D: Kabelmeßkoffer m
F: valise f de mesure pour câbles

portable equipment
D: ortsveränderliches Gerät
F: appareil m portatif, appareil m mobile

portable telephone set
D: Streckenfernsprecher m
F: poste m téléphonique mobile

portal type pay-off
D: Portalwickler m (abwickelnd)
F: dérouleur m à portique

portal type take-up
D: Portalwickler m (aufwickelnd)
F: enrouleur m à portique

position control
D: Positionsregelung f
F: réglage m de position

positioning of reels
D: Einsetzen von Spulen, Einsetzen von Trommeln
F: montage m des bobines

position of a fault
D: Fehlerort m, Fehlerstelle f
F: position f d'un défaut

positively connected
D: kraftschlüssig verbunden
F: rendu adj solidaire, relié adj de façon positive

post insulator
D: Stützisolator m
F: isolateur m support, isolateur m rigide

potential difference
D: Spannungsunterschied m
F: différence f de potentiel

potential loss
D: Spannungsverlust m
F: perte f de tension, perte f de potentiel

potentiometer n
D: Spannungsteiler m, Potentiometer n
F: réducteur m de tension, potentiomètre m

pothead n
D: Endverschluß m, Endenabschluß m
F: extrémité f, accessoire m d'extrémité

pouring ladle [c. c. r.]
D: Gießpfanne f, Gießtopf m
F: poche f de coulée

pouring speed
D: Gießgeschwindigkeit f
F: vitesse f de coulée

pouring spout
D: Gießtülle f
F: bec m de coulée

pouring temperature
D: Gießtemperatur f
F: température f de coulée

pouring temperature
D: Einfülltemperatur f
F: température f de remplissage

pour point
D: Erstarrungspunkt m (Öle), Stockpunkt m (Öle)
F: point m de figeage

powdery adj
D: feinpulverig adj, pulverförmig adj
F: en poudre, pulvérulent adj

power n
D: Energie f
F: énergie f, puissance f

power n [el.]
D: Leistung f
F: puissance f

power n [mech.]
D: Stärke f
F: puissance f, force f

power, dielectric ~ factor cos φ

D: Verlustfaktor m
F: facteur m de perte tg δ, facteur de puissance cos φ, tangente de l'angle de perte tg δ f

power cable
D: Starkstromleitung f
F: câble m (souple) d'énergie

power cable
D: Energiekabel n, Starkstromkabel n
F: câble m d'énergie

power circuit
D: Starkstromleitung f (System)
F: ligne f à courant fort

power consumption
D: Stromverbrauch m, Energieverbrauch m
F: consommation f de courant, consommation f électrique, consommation f d'énergie

power current
D: Starkstrom m
F: courant m fort

power demand
D: Energiebedarf m, Leistungsbedarf m
F: demande f d'énergie, puissance f nécessaire

power dissipation
D: Verlustleistung f
F: puissance f de perte, dissipation f de puissance, puissance f dissipée

power distribution
D: Energieversorgung f, Energieverteilung f, Stromversorgung f
F: alimentation f en énergie électrique, distribution f d'énergie électrique, alimentation f en courant électrique

power distribution network
D: Starkstromnetz n
F: réseau m de distribution d'énergie, réseau m de transport d'énergie

powered by
D: angetrieben von
F: entraîné adj par

power engineering
D: Starkstromtechnik f
F: technique f des courants forts

power factor
D: Leistungsfaktor m
F: facteur m de puissance

power failure
D: Stromausfall m
F: panne f de courant, manque m de courant

power frequency
D: Starkstromfrequenz f
F: fréquence f industrielle

power frequency [el.]
D: Betriebsfrequenz f
F: fréquence f de régime

power induced noise [com. c.]
D: Starkstromgeräusch n, Stromversorgungsgeräusch n
F: bruit m induit

power input
D: Leistungsaufnahme f
F: puissance f absorbée

power level
D: Leistungspegel m
F: niveau m de puissance

power line
D: Starkstromleitung f (System)
F: ligne f à courant fort

power line carrier telephony
D: TFH-Telephonie f (Trägerfrequenzübertragung auf Hochspannungs-Leitungen)
F: téléphonie f à fréquence porteuse sur ligne à haute tension

power load
D: Strombelastung f
F: charge f électrique

power loss [el.]
D: Leistungsverlust m
F: perte f de puissance

power loss
D: Verlustleistung f
F: puissance f de perte, dissipation f de puissance, puissance f dissipée

power output
D: Leistungsabgabe f
F: puissance f disponible

power plug
D: Netzstecker m
F: fiche f de prise de courant

power rating
D: Belastbarkeit f, Strombelastbarkeit f
F: capacité f de charge, charge f limite, puissance f limite

power rating
D: Anschlußleistung f, Anschlußwert m
F: puissance f connectée, puissance f

power requirement
- D: Energiebedarf m, Leistungsbedarf m
- F: demande f d'énergie, puissance f nécessaire

power source
- D: Energiequelle f
- F: source f d'énergie

power station
- D: Kraftwerk n
- F: centrale f électrique

power supply
- D: Energieversorgung f, Energieverteilung f, Stromversorgung f
- F: alimentation f en énergie électrique, distribution f d'énergie électrique, alimentation f en courant électrique

power supply [el.]
- D: Einspeisung f
- F: alimentation f, arrivée f

power supply noise [com. c.]
- D: Starkstromgeräusch n, Stromversorgungsgeräusch n
- F: bruit m induit

power switch
- D: Netzschalter m
- F: interrupteur m de réseau

power system
- D: Starkstromnetz n
- F: réseau m de distribution d'énergie, réseau m de transport d'énergie

power transformer
- D: Netztransformator m
- F: transformateur m d'alimentation

power transmission
- D: Energieübertragung f
- F: transport m d'énergie

power transmission network
- D: Starkstromnetz n
- F: réseau m de distribution d'énergie, réseau m de transport d'énergie

practicable adj
- D: durchführbar adj
- F: réalisable adj, faisable adj, praticable adj

preadjustment n
- D: Voreinstellung f
- F: préréglage m

pre-assembled flexible cables and cords
- D: konfektionierte Leitungen
- F: cordons m pl et conducteurs façonnés, conducteurs m pl préassemblés

precipitate v [chem.]
- D: fällen v
- F: précipiter v

precipitate n [chem.]
- D: Niederschlag m, Ausscheidung f
- F: précipité m, dépôt m

precision adjustment
- D: Feineinstellung f
- F: réglage m minutieux, réglage m précis

precision of adjustment
- D: Einstellgenauigkeit f
- F: exactitude f de réglage, précision f de réglage

predischarge n
- D: Vorentladung f
- F: prédécharge f

pre-formed adj
- D: vorgeformt adj
- F: préformé adj

preheat v
- D: vorwärmen v
- F: préchauffer v

preheater n
- D: Vorwärmofen m
- F: four m de (pré-)chauffage

preheating furnace
- D: Vorwärmofen m
- F: four m de (pré-)chauffage

preheat zone
- D: Vorheizzone f
- F: zone f de préchauffage

pre-impregnated cable
- D: Kabel mit vorimprägnierter Papierisolierung, vorgetränktes Kabel
- F: câble m isolé au papier préimprégné, câble m préimprégné

pre-impregnated insulation
- D: vorimprägnierte Isolierung
- F: isolation f préimprégnée

preliminary treatment
- D: Vorbereitung f, Vorbehandlung f
- F: préparation f, traitement m préalable

pre-mix n
- D: Vormischung f, Grundmischung f
- F: mélange m mère, mélange m maître

pre-mo(u)lded termination
  D: vorgefertigter Endverschluß
  F: extrémité f prémoulée
preparation n
  D: Vorbereitung f, Vorbehandlung f
  F: préparation f, traitement m préalable
preparation of a compound
  D: Ansetzen einer Mischung, Mischungsaufbereitung f
  F: préparation f d'un mélange
preselection n
  D: Voreinstellung f
  F: préréglage m
presetting n
  D: Voreinstellung f
  F: préréglage m
prespiralled adj
  D: vordralliert adj
  F: préformé adj, prétordu adj
prespiralling n
  D: Vordrallierung f
  F: préformage m, prétorsion f
prespiralling head
  D: Vorverseilkopf m
  F: tête f de prétorsion
press block [met. extr. pr.]
  D: Preßkopf m
  F: bloc m de presse, tête f d'outillage
press roll
  D: Andruckrolle f
  F: rouleau m de pression, rouleau m de serrage
pressure, initial ~
  D: Anfangsdruck m
  F: pression f initiale
pressure-assisted oil-filled cable
  D: Öldruckkabel n
  F: câble m à pression d'huile
pressure cable
  D: Druckkabel n
  F: câble m sous pression
pressure contactor
  D: Druckwächter m
  F: dispositif m de contrôle de pression, avertisseur m de pression
pressure control device
  D: Druckmeßgerät n, Manometer n
  F: dispositif m de contrôle de la pression, manomètre m
pressure control(ler)
  D: Druckregler m
  F: régulateur m de pression

pressure drop
  D: Druckabfall m, Druckverlust m
  F: chute f de pression, dépression f, perte f de pression
pressure gas
  D: Druckgas n
  F: gaz m comprimé
pressure gauge
  D: Druckmeßgerät n, Manometer n
  F: dispositif m de contrôle de la pression, manomètre m
pressure loss
  D: Druckabfall m, Druckverlust m
  F: chute f de pression, dépression f, perte f de pression
pressure maintaining unit
  D: Druckhaltestation f
  F: poste m de tenue de la pression
pressure monitor
  D: Druckwächter m
  F: dispositif m de contrôle de pression, avertisseur m de pression
pressure pump
  D: Druckpumpe f
  F: pompe f foulante, pompe f refoulante, refouleur m
pressure ram
  D: Preßstempel m
  F: fouloir m de la presse
pressure reducing valve
  D: Druckminderungsventil n
  F: manodétendeur m
pressure regulator
  D: Druckregler m
  F: régulateur m de pression
pressure relief valve
  D: Überdruckventil n
  F: soupape f de sûreté, soupape f de surpression
pressure resistance
  D: Druckbeständigkeit f, Druckfestigkeit f
  F: résistance f à l'écrasement, résistance f à la pression
pressure-retaining sheath
  D: druckfester Mantel
  F: gaine f d'étanchéité à la pression
pressure-sensitive tape
  D: selbstklebendes Band
  F: ruban m auto-adhésif, ruban m auto-collant
pressure test
  D: Druckversuch m

pressure 334

    F: essai *m* de pression, essai *m* de compression
pressure-tight *adj*
    D: druckdicht *adj*
    F: étanche *adj* à la pression
pressure tightness
    D: Druckdichtigkeit *f*
    F: étanchéité *f* à la pression
pressure transducer [com.]
    D: Druckübertrager *m*, Druckgeber *m*
    F: transmetteur *m* de pression
pressure variations
    D: Druckschwankungen *f pl*
    F: alternance *f* des pressions et des dépressions
pressurization, telephone cable ~
    D: Druckgasschutz und -überwachung von Telefonkabeln
    F: contrôle *m* des câbles téléphoniques à gaz comprimé
pressurize *v*
    D: unter Druck setzen
    F: mettre *v* sous pression
pressurized water
    D: Druckwasser *n*
    F: eau *f* sous pression, eau *f* pressurisée
pressurizing plant
    D: Druckanlage *f*
    F: installation *f* de mise sous pression
pretreatment *n*
    D: Vorbereitung *f*, Vorbehandlung *f*
    F: préparation *f*, traitement *m* préalable
pretwisted *adj*
    D: vordralliert *adj*
    F: préformé *adj*, prétordu *adj*
pretwisting *n*
    D: Vordrallierung *f*
    F: préformage *m*, prétorsion *f*
pre-vulcanisation *n*
    D: Anvulkanisieren *n* (Vorvulkanisieren)
    F: prévulcanisation *f*
primary circuit
    D: Primärkreislauf *m*
    F: circuit *m* primaire
primary core unit [com. c.]
    D: Grundbündel *n*
    F: faisceau *m* élémentaire, faisceau *m* de base
primary unit [com. c.]
    D: Grundbündel *n*
    F: faisceau *m* élémentaire, faisceau *m* de base
primary voltage
    D: Primärspannung *f*
    F: tension *f* primaire
primary winding
    D: Primärwicklung *f*
    F: enroulement *m* primaire
prime conductor
    D: Primärleiter *m*
    F: conducteur *m* primaire
primer *n*
    D: Haftgrundierung *f*
    F: couche *f* de fond
print *v*
    D: bedrucken *v*
    F: imprimer *v*
printer *n*
    D: Bedruckungsvorrichtung *f*
    F: dispositif *m* d'impression
printing *n*
    D: Bedruckung *f*
    F: marquage *m* par impression
printing device
    D: Bedruckungsvorrichtung *f*
    F: dispositif *m* d'impression
probability calculus
    D: Wahrscheinlichkeitsrechnung *f*
    F: calcul *m* des probabilités
probability curve
    D: Wahrscheinlichkeitskurve *f*
    F: courbe *f* de probabilité
probability theory
    D: Wahrscheinlichkeitsrechnung *f*
    F: calcul *m* des probabilités
procedure *n*
    D: Verfahren *n*, Methode *f*
    F: procédé *m*, méthode *f*, technique *f*
process *v*
    D: verarbeiten *v*
    F: mettre *v* en œuvre, travailler *v*, convertir *v*
process *n*
    D: Verfahren *n*, Methode *f*
    F: procédé *m*, méthode *f*, technique *f*
process annealing [met.]
    D: Zwischenglühen *n*
    F: recuit *m* intermédiaire
process annealing
    D: Rekristallisationsglühung *f*
    F: recuit *m* de récristallisation
process (flow) chart

production

    D: Ablaufplan m, Ablaufdiagramm n, Arbeitsablaufdiagramm n, Flußdiagramm n, Fertigungsflußschema n
    F: organigramme m (prod.), ordinogramme m, graphique m de processus, diagramme m de déroulement

process control
    D: Fertigungskontrolle f
    F: contrôle m en cours de fabrication

process-control computer
    D: Prozeßrechner m
    F: calculateur m pour la conduite des processus industriels

process experience
    D: Erfahrung mit einer Fertigungsmethode
    F: expérience f faite avec une méthode de fabrication

processibility n
    D: Verarbeitbarkeit f
    F: aptitude f à la mise en œuvre

processing n
    D: Verarbeitung f
    F: mise f en œuvre

processing drum
    D: Einsatzspule f, Einsatztrommel f, Maschinenspule f, Maschinentrommel f, Werkstatttrommel f
    F: bobine f d'alimentation

processing reel
    D: Einsatzspule f, Einsatztrommel f, Maschinenspule f, Maschinentrommel f, Werkstatttrommel f
    F: bobine f d'alimentation

processing speed [mach.]
    D: Fahrgeschwindigkeit f, Fertigungsgeschwindigkeit f, Arbeitsgeschwindigkeit f
    F: vitesse de marche f, vitesse f de fabrication, vitesse f de production, vitesse f de travail

processing temperature
    D: Verarbeitungstemperatur f
    F: température f de mise en œuvre

produced on an industrial scale
    D: hergestellt im Fertigungsmaßstab
    F: réalisé adj à l'échelle industrielle

production control
    D: Fertigungskontrolle f
    F: contrôle m en cours de fabrication

production department
    D: Fertigungsabteilung f
    F: service m de production, atelier m de fabrication

production engineer
    D: Betriebsingenieur m
    F: ingénieur m de fabrication

production engineering
    D: Fertigungstechnik f
    F: technique f de fabrication, technique f de production

production engineering development
    D: fertigungstechnische Entwicklung
    F: étude f de la technique de fabrication

production flow time
    D: Durchlaufzeit f
    F: temps m de passage

production length
    D: Fertigungslänge f
    F: longueur f de fabrication

production line
    D: Fertigungsstraße f
    F: chaîne f de fabrication

production planning
    D: Arbeitsvorbereitung f, Fertigungsvorbereitung f
    F: préparation f du travail

production programme
    D: Fertigungsprogramm n, Arbeitsprogramm n (Prod.)
    F: programme m de fabrication

production rate [mach.]
    D: Fahrgeschwindigkeit f, Fertigungsgeschwindigkeit f, Arbeitsgeschwindigkeit f
    F: vitesse de marche f, vitesse f de fabrication, vitesse f de production, vitesse f de travail

production scheme
    D: Fertigungsprogramm n, Arbeitsprogramm n (Prod.)
    F: programme m de fabrication

production sequence
    D: Fertigungsablauf m, Produktionsablauf m
    F: cycle m de fabrication

production speed [mach.]
    D: Fahrgeschwindigkeit f, Fertigungsgeschwindigkeit f, Arbeitsgeschwindigkeit f
    F: vitesse de marche f, vitesse f de

production

fabrication, vitesse f de production, vitesse f de travail

production stage, developed to the ~
D: bis zur Fertigungsreife entwickelt
F: étudié jusqu'au stade de fabrication

production test
D: Prüfung während der Fertigung
F: essai m en cours de fabrication

production trial
D: Versuchsfertigung f, Probefertigung f
F: essai m de fabrication, production f à l'échelle expérimentale

profile wire
D: Profildraht m
F: brin m profilé, fil m profilé

program(me) control
D: Programmsteuerung f
F: commande f par programme

proofed cotton tape
D: gummibeschichtetes Baumwollband
F: ruban m de coton caoutchouté

proofed textile tape
D: gummiertes Textilband
F: ruban m textile caoutchouté

propagate v
D: ausbreiten v (sich)
F: étendre v (s'), propager v (se)

propagation
D: Ausbreitung f
F: propagation f, diffusion f

propagation coefficient
D: Übertragungskonstante f
F: exposant m linéique de propagation

propagation unit
D: Übertragungsmaß n
F: équivalent m de transmission, exposant m de transfert, unité f de propagation

proportioning n
D: Dosierung f
F: dosage m

protected against interference
D: induktionsgeschützt adj
F: protégé adj contre les interférences

protection against kinking [cab.]
D: Knickschutz m
F: protection f contre la formation de coques

protection by fuses
D: Absicherung f
F: protection f par fusibles

protection from contact [el.]
D: Berührungsschutz m
F: protection f contre des contacts accidentels

protective atmosphere
D: Schutzgasatmosphäre f
F: atmosphère f contrôlée, atmosphère f protectrice

protective coating
D: Schutzüberzug m, Schutzhülle f
F: revêtement m protecteur, revêtement m de protection, enveloppe f protectrice

protective conductor
D: Schutzleiter m
F: conducteur m de protection

protective contact
D: Schutzkontakt m
F: contact m de mise à la terre

protective cover(ing)
D: Schutzüberzug m, Schutzhülle f
F: revêtement m protecteur, revêtement m de protection, enveloppe f protectrice

protective covering [mach.]
D: Schutzabdeckung f, Sicherheitsabdeckung f
F: carter m de sécurité, carter m enveloppe, carter m de protection

protective device
D: Sicherheitsvorrichtung f, Schutzvorrichtung f
F: dispositif m de sécurité, dispositif m de protection

protective earth (GB)
D: Schutzerdung f
F: protection f par mise à la terre, mise f à la terre de protection

protective gas
D: Schutzgas n, reduzierendes Gas, Inertgas n
F: gaz m inerte, gaz m de protection, gaz m réducteur

protective ground (US)
D: Schutzerdung f
F: protection f par mise à la terre, mise f à la terre de protection

protective jacket
D: Schutzmantel m
F: gaine f de protection

protective multiple earthing (p.m.e.)
  D: Mehrfachschutzerdung f, Nullung f
  F: protection f par mise à la terre multiple, mise f à la terre de protection multiple, mise f au neutre

protective sheath
  D: Schutzmantel m
  F: gaine f de protection

protective spark gap
  D: Schutzfunkenstrecke f
  F: éclateur m de protection

protective switch
  D: Schutzschalter m
  F: disjoncteur m de protection, interrupteur m de sécurité

protective varnish coating
  D: Schutzanstrich m
  F: couche f de peinture protectrice, enduit m protecteur

Protodur-cable n
  D: Protodur-Kabel n
  F: câble m au Protodur

Protothen-cable n
  D: Protothen-Kabel n
  F: câble m au Protothen

proved adj
  D: bewährt adj
  F: éprouvé adj

proven adj
  D: bewährt adj
  F: éprouvé adj

proximity effect
  D: Näheeffekt m
  F: effet m de proximité

psophonetic curve [com. c.]
  D: Ohrkurve f
  F: courbe f psophonétique

PTFE (s. polytetrafluorethylene)

public distribution network
  D: EVU-Netz n
  F: réseau m de distribution public

public inquiry
  D: Einspruchsverfahren n
  F: enquête f publique

public utilities load
  D: EVU-Last f
  F: charge f des centrales électriques

published patent application
  D: Auslegeschrift f
  F: demande f de brevet examinée

pull v [c. install.]
  D: einziehen v (in Rohre)
  F: tirer v

pull n
  D: Zugkraft f
  F: effort m de traction, force f de traction

pull-back cylinder
  D: Rückzugzylinder m
  F: cylindre m de retour

pull-back ram
  D: Rückzugskolben m
  F: piston m de remontée, piston m de rappel

pullblock tyres
  D: Bandagen f pl (für Ziehscheiben an der Drahtziehmaschine)
  F: bandages m pl (pour les cônes de tréfilage)

pulley n
  D: Rolle f
  F: rouleau m, galet m

pull-in
  D: Einziehen n (von Kabeln in Rohre)
  F: tirage m

pulling eye [cab.]
  D: Ziehkopf m, Ziehöse f, Zugöse f
  F: œillet m de tirage, tête f de tirage, agrafe f de tirage, clou m de tirage

pulling grip [cab.]
  D: Ziehkopf m, Ziehöse f, Zugöse f
  F: œillet m de tirage, tête f de tirage, agrafe f de tirage, clou m de tirage

pulling head [cab.]
  D: Ziehkopf m, Ziehöse f, Zugöse f
  F: œillet m de tirage, tête f de tirage, agrafe f de tirage, clou m de tirage

pulling in
  D: Einziehen n (von Kabeln in Rohre)
  F: tirage m

pulling rope
  D: Zugseil n
  F: corde f de tirage

pull-off capstan
  D: Scheibenabzug m, Abzugscheibe f
  F: cabestan m de tirage, roue f de tirage, cabestan m tireur

pull-off device
  D: Abzugsvorrichtung f
  F: dispositif m de tirage

pull-off speed
  D: Abzugsgeschwindigkeit f
  F: vitesse f de tirage

pulped wire
  D: Pulp-Ader f, pulpisolierte Ader

pulped

F: conducteur *m* isolé à la pâte de papier

pulp-insulated wire
D: Pulp-Ader *f*, pulpisolierte Ader
F: conducteur *m* isolé à la pâte de papier

pulse-code modulation cable
D: Pulscode-Modulationskabel *n*, PCM-Kabel *n*
F: câble *m* de modulation par impulsion et codage, câble *m* MIC

pulse frequency
D: Impulsfrequenz *f*
F: fréquence *f* d'impulsion

pulverulent *adj*
D: feinpulverig *adj*, pulverförmig *adj*
F: en poudre, pulvérulent *adj*

pumped storage (hydroelectric) power station
D: Pumpspeicher(kraft)werk *n*
F: centrale *f* électrique à accumulation par pompage

pumping station
D: Pumpstation *f*
F: station *f* de pompage

pump output
D: Pumpenleistung *f*, Förderleistung einer Pumpe
F: capacité *f* de pompage, débit *m* d'une pompe

punching tool
D: Stanzwerkzeug *n*
F: outil *m* de découpage

punching with a die
D: Ausstanzen *n* (Prüfkörper)
F: découpage *m*, poinçonnage *m*

puncture *n* [el.]
D: Durchschlag *m*
F: claquage *m*, amorçage *m*, décharge *f* disruptive

puncture resistance
D: Durchschlagfestigkeit *f*, Spannungsfestigkeit *f*, elektrische Festigkeit, dielektrische Festigkeit
F: rigidité *f* diélectrique

Pupin coil
D: Pupin-Spule *f*, Belastungsspule *f*, Verstärkerspule *f*
F: bobine *f* Pupin, bobine *f* de charge

pupinization point
D: Spulenpunkt *m* (Pupinisierung)
F: point *m* de charge

Pupin loading
D: Bespulung *f*, Pupinisierung *f*
F: pupinisation *f*, charge *f* au moyen de bobines en série

puppet *n*
D: Puppe *f* (Rolle aus Walzfell)
F: billette *f*, poupée *f*

purchase specification
D: Liefervorschrift *f*
F: spécification *f* d'achat

purge *v* [extr.]
D: reinigen *v*
F: purger *v*

purging *n* [extr.]
D: Überlauf *m*
F: purges *f pl*

purging compound [extr.]
D: Reinigungsmischung *f*
F: mélange *m* de purification

purity, degree of ~
D: Reinheitsgrad *m*
F: degré *m* de pureté

push-button control
D: Druckknopfsteuerung *f*
F: commande *f* par bouton-poussoir

pushout, screw ~ device [extr.]
D: Schneckenausstoßvorrichtung *f*
F: extracteur *m* de vis

put through *v* [tel.]
D: durchschalten *v*
F: relier *v*, mettre *v* en communication

putting to service
D: Inbetriebnahme *f*
F: mise *f* en oeuvre, mise *f* en service

PVC (s. polyvinyl chloride)

PVC compound
D: PVC-Mischung *f*
F: mélange *m* de PVC

PVC insulation
D: PVC-Isolierung *f*
F: isolation *f* PVC

PVC sheath
D: PVC-Mantel *m*
F: gaine *f* de PVC

Q

quad *n*
D: Vierer *m*
F: quarte *f*

quadding n
 D: Viererverseilung f
 F: quartage m
quadding machine
 D: Viererverseilmaschine f
 F: quarteuse f
quad pair, pair stranded in ~ formation
 D: Doppelsternvierer m
 F: paire f câblée en étoile
quadrature-axis component of the voltage
 D: Querspannung f
 F: tension f transversale, composante f transversale d'une tension
quad twisting
 D: Viererverseilung f
 F: quartage m
quad twisting machine
 D: Viererverseilmaschine f
 F: quarteuse f
quality n
 D: Güteklasse f
 F: classe f de qualité, qualité f
quality control
 D: Güteprüfung f, Qualitätskontrolle f
 F: contrôle m de qualité, surveillance f de la qualité
quality control of raw material consignments
 D: Wareneingangskontrolle f
 F: contrôle m à la livraison, contrôle m à la réception du matériel
quality grade
 D: Güteklasse f
 F: classe f de qualité, qualité f
quality inspection
 D: Güteprüfung f, Qualitätskontrolle f
 F: contrôle m de qualité, surveillance f de la qualité
quality sample
 D: Ausfallmuster n
 F: échantillon m de qualité, échantillon m type
quality specification
 D: Gütevorschrift f
 F: spécification f de qualité
quality test
 D: Güteprüfung f, Qualitätskontrolle f
 F: contrôle m de qualité, surveillance f de la qualité
quantity to be measured
 D: Meßgröße f
 F: grandeur f mesurée

quench v
 D: abschrecken v
 F: tremper v
quick-acting lock with worm gear for impregnating tanks
 D: Bajonett-Schnellverschluß mit Schnecke und Schneckenrad für Tränkgefäße
 F: fermeture f rapide à baïonette avec roue hélicoïdale pour cuves d'imprégnation
quick-action locking device
 D: Schnellverschluß m
 F: fermeture f rapide
quick disconnect plug
 D: Schnelltrennstecker m
 F: fiche f de coupure rapide

R

rack n
 D: Gestell n, Rahmen m
 F: bâti m
rack, cable ~ [c. install.]
 D: Kabelpritsche f, Kabeltraggerüst n, Pritsche f
 F: tablette f à câbles, charpente pour câbles f
radial field cable
 D: Radialfeldkabel n
 F: câble m à champ radial
radiation n
 D: Strahlung f
 F: radiation f
radio frequency
 D: Hochfrequenz (HF) f
 F: haute fréquence f (HF), fréquence f radioélectrique
radio frequency cable
 D: Hochfrequenzkabel n
 F: câble m à haute fréquence, câble m à fréquence radioélectrique
radio frequency coaxial cable
 D: Hochfrequenz-Koaxialkabel n, koaxiales Hochfrequenzkabel
 F: câble m coaxial à haute fréquence, câble m coaxial à fréquence radioélectrique
railway cable
 D: Bahnkabel n

railway

F: câble *m* de chemin de fer
railway earth [com. c.]
D: Eisenbahnerde *f*
F: terre *f* de voie ferrée
railway station telecommunication cable
D: Bahnhofsfernmeldekabel *n*
F: câble *m* de télécommunication pour gares ferroviaires
railway telecommunication cable
D: Streckenfernmeldekabel *n*
F: câble *m* de télécommunication de parcours ferroviaire
raise *n*
D: Erhöhung *f*, Steigerung *f*
F: augmentation *f*, élévation *f*
ram *n* [mach.]
D: Stempel *m*, Kolben *m*, Plunger *m*
F: piston *m*, fouloir *m*
ramification of the molecular chains
D: Verzweigung der Molekülketten
F: ramification *f* des chaînes moléculaires
rammed refractory lining
D: Stampffutter bei Schmelzöfen
F: revêtement *m* de fourneau réfractaire damé
ramp *n*
D: Schnecke *f* (bei einer Kabeltrommel)
F: escargot *m*
ram press
D: Stempelpresse *f*, Strangpresse *f*, Kolbenpresse *f*
F: presse *f* à piston
ram truck
D: Dornstapler *m*
F: empileuse *f* à mandrins
random measurement
D: Stichprobenmessung *f*
F: mesure *f* sur prélèvement
random sample
D: Stichprobe *f*
F: échantillon *m* pris au hasard, éprouvette *f* prise au hasard
random test
D: Stichprobenprüfung *f*
F: essai *m* sur prélèvement
range *n*
D: Bereich *m*
F: gamme *f*, domaine *m*, plage *f*
range *n* [prod.]
D: Spektrum *n*

F: gamme *f*, éventail *m*
range, highly diversified ~ of products
D: breites Fabrikatespektrum, breites Fertigungsspektrum
F: gamme *f* de produits largement diversifiée
range of application
D: Anwendungsbereich *m*
F: sphère *f* d'application
range of dispersion
D: Streubereich *m*
F: plage *f* de dispersion
range of production
D: Fertigungsbereich *m*, Fertigungsspektrum *n*
F: gamme *f* de fabrication
range of scattering
D: Streubereich *m*
F: plage *f* de dispersion
range of types
D: Typenspektrum *n*
F: gamme *f* de types, éventail *m* de types
rapid-action locking device
D: Schnellverschluß *m*
F: fermeture *f* rapide
rapidity of response
D: Ansprechgeschwindigkeit *f*
F: rapidité *f* de réponse
rated load
D: Nennbelastung *f*
F: charge *f* nominale
rated output [mach.]
D: Nennleistung *f*
F: debit *m* nominal
rated power [el.]
D: Nennleistung *f*
F: puissance *f* nominale
rated power, total ~
D: installierte Leistung, Ausbauleistung *f*
F: puissance *f* installée
rated value
D: Nominalwert *m*, Nennwert *m*
F: valeur *f* nominale
rated voltage
D: Nennspannung *f*
F: tension *f* nominale
rate of cure
D: Vulkanisationsgeschwindigkeit *f*
F: vitesse *f* de vulcanisation
rate of flow
D: Strömungsgeschwindigkeit *f*,

raw material
D: Werkstoff m, Rohstoff m
F: matière f, matière f première

reactance n
D: Blindwiderstand m
F: réactance f

reaction coil
D: Rückkopplungsspule f
F: bobine f de réaction

reaction time
D: Ansprechzeit f
F: temps m de réponse

reactive current
D: Blindstrom m
F: courant m réactif

reactive impedance
D: Blindwiderstand m
F: réactance f

reactive power
D: Blindleistung f
F: puissance f réactive

reading n [el., vis.]
D: Anzeige f
F: indication f, signalisation f, lecture f, affichage m

reading, to take a ~
D: eine Ablesung vornehmen
F: faire v une lecture

ready for application, for service, for use
D: einsatzbereit adj
F: prêt adj à la mise en œuvre, à l'usage, au service

ready for operation
D: betriebsbereit adj
F: prêt adj à fonctionner, prêt adj à la mise en marche,, en ordre de marche

realizable adj
D: durchführbar adj
F: réalisable adj, faisable adj, praticable adj

real value
D: Istwert m
F: valeur f réelle

received, at the ~ stage
D: im Anlieferungszustand
F: à l'état vierge, à la livraison

receptacle n
D: Steckbuchse f, Steckerbuchse f, Fassung f
F: prise f femelle, fiche f femelle, douille f

recess n
D: Nut f, Aussparung f
F: rainure f, encoche f, découpe f, évidement m, entaille f

reciprocating motion
D: Hin- und Herbewegung f
F: mouvement m de va-et-vient, mouvement m alternatif

reciprocation n
D: Hin- und Herbewegung f
F: mouvement m de va-et-vient, mouvement m alternatif

recirculation n
D: Umpumpen n
F: circulation f par pompage, recyclage m

recirculation of cooling water
D: Kühlwasserrücklauf m
F: retour m d'eau de refroidissement

reclaim n
D: Regenerat n
F: régénéré m

reclaimed rubber
D: Kautschukregenerat n
F: caoutchouc m régénéré

re-cooling of cooling water
D: Rückkühlung von Kühlwasser
F: refroidissement m d'eau de retour

recorder n
D: Registriergerät n, Meßwertschreiber m
F: enregistreur m

recording instrument
D: Registriergerät n, Meßwertschreiber m
F: enregistreur m

recovery n
D: Rückgewinnung f
F: récupération f

recovery from stretching
D: elastische Erholung
F: reprise f élastique

recrystallization n
D: Rekristallisation f
F: récristallisation f

rectangular cross-section
D: rechteckiger Querschnitt
F: section f rectangulaire

rectangular section wire
D: Rechteckdraht m
F: fil m rectangulaire, fil m de section

rectangular
rectangulaire

rectangular waveguide
D: Rechteck-Hohlleiter m
F: guide m d'ondes rectangulaires

rectangular wire
D: Rechteckdraht m
F: fil m rectangulaire, fil m de section rectangulaire

recurrent network [el.]
D: Kettenleiter m
F: réseau m récurrent, système m itératif

recycling n
D: Umlauf m
F: circulation f

recycling n
D: Umpumpen n
F: circulation f par pompage, recyclage m

red lead
D: Bleimennige f
F: minium m de plomb

redraw rod [wire manuf.]
D: Grobdraht m, Drahtvormaterial n, Vorziehdraht m
F: fil m machine, fil m ébauche, fil m pour retréfilage

reduce v
D: vermindern v, verringern v
F: réduire v, diminuer v

reducing gas
D: Schutzgas n, reduzierendes Gas, Inertgas n
F: gaz m inerte, gaz m de protection, gaz m réducteur

reduction factor
D: Reduktionsfaktor m
F: facteur m réducteur, coefficient m de réduction

reduction gear
D: Reduktionsgetriebe n, Untersetzungsgetriebe n
F: réducteur m, engrenage m réducteur, démultiplicateur m

reduction steps [wire manuf.]
D: Ziehfolgen f pl, Ziehstufen f pl
F: étapes f pl de tréfilage

reel v
D: aufwickeln v, aufspulen v, spulen v, wickeln v, auftrommeln v
F: enrouler v, bobiner v

reel n
D: Spule f

F: bobine f

reel n [cab.]
D: Trommel f
F: touret m, bobine f

reel change
D: Spulenwechsel m
F: changement m de bobine

reel flange [cab.]
D: Trommelscheibe f, Trommelflansch m
F: joue f de touret

reeling drum
D: Aufwickeltrommel f
F: bobine f réceptrice

reference circuit
D: Bezugskreis m
F: circuit m de référence

reference equivalent
D: Bezugsdämpfung f
F: équivalent m de référence

reference quantity
D: Bezugsgröße f
F: grandeur f de référence

reference resistance
D: Vergleichswiderstand m
F: résistance f de comparaison

reference sample
D: Vergleichsmuster n
F: échantillon m témoin, échantillon m de comparaison, échantillon m de contrôle

reference value
D: Richtwert m
F: valeur f indicative, valeur f de référence, valeur f standard, valeur f approximée

reference voltage
D: Bezugsspannung f
F: tension f de référence

refill v
D: nachfüllen v, auffüllen v
F: remplir v, refaire v le plein

refining n
D: Raffination f
F: raffinage m

reflection, free of ~ [com. c.]
D: reflexionsfrei adj
F: non réfléchissant adj

reflection attenuation
D: Reflexionsdämpfung f, Fehlerdämpfung f
F: atténuation f de réflexion, affaiblissement m d'équilibrage,

reflection loss
 D: Reflexionsdämpfung f, Fehlerdämpfung f
 F: atténuation f de réflexion, affaiblissement m d'équilibrage, affaiblissement m des courants réfléchis

refraction index
 D: Brechungsindex m
 F: indice m de réfraction

refractory lining, rammed ~
 D: Stampffutter bei Schmelzöfen
 F: revêtement m de fourneau réfractaire damé

refrigeration unit
 D: Kühlaggregat n
 F: agrégat m réfrigérant, groupe m réfrigérant

regenerate v
 D: wiederaufbereiten v
 F: régénérer v

registration n [lapp.]
 D: Gangversatz m, Lagenversatz m
 F: chevauchement m

registration, with 50% ~
 D: mit 50% Überlappung
 F: à 50% de recouvrement

registration, with ... % ~ [lapp.]
 D: versetzt um ... %
 F: décalé adj de ... %

regulating range
 D: Regelbereich m
 F: plage f de régulation, gamme f de réglage

regulating transformer
 D: Regeltransformator m, Stelltransformator m
 F: transformateur m de réglage

regulation n [contr.]
 D: Regelung f, Einstellung f
 F: réglage m

regulations pl
 D: Bestimmungen f pl (Vorschriften)
 F: prescriptions f pl, règles f pl

regulator n
 D: Regler m
 F: régulateur m, appareil m de réglage

reinforced plastic
 D: verstärkter Kunststoff
 F: plastique m renforcé

reinforcement n [mech.]
 D: Verstärkung f
 F: renforcement m

reinforcement helix [cab.]
 D: Druckschutzwendel f
 F: frettage m

reinforcement tape spinner [cab.]
 D: Druckschutzspinner m
 F: enrouleur m du frettage

relative humidity
 D: relative Luftfeuchtigkeit
 F: degré m hygrométrique, humidité f relative

relative permittivity
 D: relative Dielektrizitätskonstante
 F: permittivité f relative

relay switch
 D: Schaltschütz n
 F: contacteur-disjoncteur m, contacteur-interrupteur m

release, to ~ for factory production
 D: für die Fertigung freigeben
 F: relâcher v pour la fabrication, passer v à la fabrication

release agent
 D: Trennmittel n
 F: agent m séparateur

release current
 D: Auslösestrom m
 F: courant m de déclenchement

reliability n
 D: Zuverlässigkeit f
 F: fiabilité f

reliability of operation
 D: Betriebssicherheit f, Betriebszuverlässigkeit f, Zuverlässigkeit im Betrieb
 F: sécurité f de fonctionnement, fiabilité f de service

remote control
 D: Fernsteuerung f, Fernbedienung f
 F: télécommande f, commande f à distance

remote monitoring
 D: Fernüberwachung f
 F: télésurveillance f, surveillance f à distance

remote supervision
 D: Fernüberwachung f
 F: télésurveillance f, surveillance f à distance

removable adj
 D: abnehmbar adj

removable
   F: amovible *adj*, démontable *adj*
removal of load [test]
   D: Entlasten *n*
   F: déchargement *m*
removal of oxygen
   D: Sauerstoffentzug *m*
   F: réduction *f* d'oxygène
remove *v* [cab.]
   D: absetzen *v* (Isolierung, Mantel)
   F: enlever *v*, découper *v*
remove *v*
   D: ausbauen *v*, abmontieren *v*
   F: démonter *v*, enlever *v*
remove, to ~ the insulation
   D: abisolieren *v*
   F: dénuder *v*, désisoler *v*
repair *n*
   D: Instandsetzung *f*, Reparatur *f*
   F: remise *f* en état, réparation *f*, dépannage *m*
repeatability *n*
   D: Wiederholbarkeit *f*
   F: reproductibilité *f*
repeated abrasion test
   D: Dauerabriebprüfung *f*
   F: essai *m* d'abrasion répétée
repeater *n*
   D: Verstärker *m*
   F: amplificateur *m*, répéteur *m*
repeater circuit
   D: Stromkreis mit Verstärkung
   F: circuit *m* à répéteur
repeater section
   D: Verstärkerfeld *n*
   F: section *f* (élémentaire) d'amplification
repeater station, main ~
   D: Hauptverstärkerstelle *f*
   F: station *f* principale de répéteurs
replace *v*
   D: ersetzen *v*
   F: remplacer *v*, substituer *v*
replaceable *adj*
   D: auswechselbar *adj*, austauschbar *adj*
   F: interchangeable *adj*
replenish *v*
   D: nachfüllen *v*, auffüllen *v*
   F: remplir *v*, refaire *v* le plein
representative sample
   D: Durchschnittsprobe *f*
   F: échantillon *m* de la qualité moyenne

reproducibility *n*
   D: Reproduzierbarkeit *f*
   F: réproductibilité *f*
requirement *n*
   D: Anforderung *f*
   F: exigence *f*, impératif *m*
requirement, to meet a ~
   D: eine Forderung erfüllen, eine Bedingung erfüllen, einer Anforderung genügen
   F: satisfaire *v* à une demande, satisfaire *v* à une exigence
reserve pair [com. c.]
   D: Reservepaar *n*, Ersatzaderpaar *n*
   F: paire *f* de réserve
reserve quad
   D: Reservevierer *m*
   F: quarte *f* de réserve
reservoir *n*
   D: Vorratsbehälter *m*
   F: réservoir *m*
reset *v*
   D: nachstellen *v*
   F: rajuster *v*, réajuster *v*
reset, automatic ~
   D: automatische Nulleinstellung
   F: remise *f* à zéro automatique
residence time [extr.]
   D: Verweilzeit *f*
   F: temps *m* de séjour, durée *f* de traitement
residual charge
   D: Restladung *f*
   F: charge *f* résiduelle
residual elongation
   D: Dehnungsrest *m*
   F: allongement *m* résiduel
residual set
   D: bleibende Dehnung
   F: allongement *m* permanent, allongement *m* rémanent
resin *n*
   D: Harz *n* (Kunstharz)
   F: résine *f*
resistance *n*
   D: Widerstand *m* (als el. Wert)
   F: résistance *f*
resistance *n*
   D: Beständigkeit *f*, Festigkeit *f*, Widerstandsfähigkeit *f*
   F: résistance *f*, stabilité *f*, tenue *f*
resistance, electrical ~ of conductor
   D: Leiterwiderstand *m*

F: résistance *f* électrique de l'âme

resistance, I.A.C.S. ~ (International Annealed Copper Standard/IEC)
D: Standard-Widerstand nach IEC (Kupfer)
F: résistance *f* I.A.C.S. (cuivre)

resistance, of high ~
D: hochohmig *adj*
F: de haute valeur ohmique, de grande résistance

resistance, of low ~
D: niederohmig *adj*
F: de faible valeur ohmique, de faible résistance

resistance annealer, continuous ~
D: kontinuierliche Widerstandsglühanlage
F: recuiseur *m* continu par résistance, installation *f* continue de recuit par résistance

resistance bridge
D: Widerstandsbrücke *f*
F: pont *m* de résistances

resistance heating
D: Widerstandsheizung *f*
F: chauffage *m* par résistance

resistance loss
D: Stromwärmeverlust *m*
F: perte *f* par effet Joule

resistance to bending fatigue
D: Dauerbiegefestigkeit *f*
F: résistance *f* de fatigue à la flexion, endurance *f* à la flexion

resistance to deformation
D: Formbeständigkeit *f*, Formänderungsbeständigkeit *f*
F: stabilité *f* de forme, résistance *f* à la déformation

resistance to low temperatures
D: Kältebeständigkeit *f*
F: résistance *f* aux basses températures

resistance to ozone
D: Ozonbeständigkeit *f*
F: résistance *f* à l'ozone

resistance to pressure at high temperatures
D: Wärmedruckbeständigkeit *f*
F: résistance *f* à la pression aux températures élevées

resistance to swelling
D: Quellbeständigkeit *f*
F: résistance *f* au gonflement

resistance to tearing
D: Einreißfestigkeit *f*, Weiterreißfestigkeit *f*
F: résistance *f* au déchirement

resistance to vibrations
D: Schwingungsfestigkeit *f*
F: résistance *f* aux vibrations

resistance welding
D: Widerstandsschweißen *n*
F: soudage *m* par résistance

resistant to ag(e)ing
D: alterungsbeständig *adj*
F: non-vieillissant *adj*

resistant to cold
D: kältebeständig *adj*
F: résistant *adj* au froid, résistant *adj* aux basses températures,

resistant to deformation
D: formbeständig *adj*
F: stable *adj* de forme

resistant to low temperatures
D: kältebeständig *adj*
F: résistant *adj* au froid, résistant *adj* aux basses températures,

resistant to tropical conditions
D: tropenfest *adj*
F: tropicalisé *adj*, résistant *adj* aux conditions tropicales,

resistivity *n*
D: spezifischer Widerstand
F: résistivité *f*

resistor *n*
D: Widerstand *m* (Gerät)
F: rhéostat *m*

resist *v* **to ...**
D: aushalten *v*
F: supporter *v*, résister *v* à ..., tenir *v*, soutenir *v*

responding speed
D: Ansprechgeschwindigkeit *f*
F: rapidité *f* de réponse

response time
D: Ansprechzeit *f*
F: temps *m* de réponse

restore, to ~ power
D: den Strom wieder einschalten
F: réenclencher *v* la puissance

resupply *v*
D: nachfüllen *v*, auffüllen *v*
F: remplir *v*, refaire *v* le plein

retained elongation
D: bleibende Dehnung
F: allongement *m* permanent,

retained

allongement *m* rémanent

retaining ring [extr.]
- D: Stauring *m*
- F: bague *f* de laminage

retarder *n*
- D: Verzögerer *m*
- F: retardateur *m*

retractile cord
- D: Handapparateschnur *f* (kleingewendelt, dehnbar), Geräteschnur *f* (für vielbewegte Verbindungen), hochbewegliche Verbindungsschnur
- F: cordon *m* souple rétractile

returnable reel [cab.]
- D: Leihtrommel *f*
- F: touret *m* non perdu

return conductor
- D: Rückleiter *m*
- F: conducteur *m* de retour, fil *m* de retour

return loss
- D: Anpassungsdämpfung *f*
- F: affaiblissement *m* d'adaptation

return loss between line and network (US)
- D: Reflexionsdämpfung *f*, Fehlerdämpfung *f*
- F: atténuation *f* de réflexion, affaiblissement *m* d'équilibrage, affaiblissement *m* des courants réfléchis

return loss unit [com. c.]
- D: Fehlerdämpfungsmaß *n*
- F: équivalent *m* d'affaiblissement d'équilibrage

return pipe
- D: Rücklaufrohr *n*
- F: tube *m* de retour

return stroke of the ram
- D: Rückzugbewegung des Preßstempels
- F: retour *m* du fouloir, recul *m* du fouloir

return valve
- D: Rückschlagventil *n*
- F: soupape *f* de retenue

return wire
- D: Rückleiter *m*
- F: conducteur *m* de retour, fil *m* de retour

reverberatory furnace
- D: Flammofen *m*
- F: four *m* à réverbère, fourneau *m* à réverbère

reversal of lay
- D: Drallwechsel *m*
- F: inversion *f* de la torsion, changement *m* de la torsion, changement *m* du pas de câblage

reversal of load
- D: Lastwechsel *m*
- F: alternance *f* de l'effort, cycle *m* de l'effort, cycle *m* de charge

reversed bending strength
- D: Wechselbiegefestigkeit *f*, Biegewechselfestigkeit *f*
- F: résistance *f* aux pliages alternés

reversed bending test
- D: Wechselbiegeprüfung *f*
- F: essai *m* de pliages alternés

reverse(d) lay stranding
- D: Kreuzschlagverseilung *f*, Verseilung im Gegenschlag, Gegenschlagverseilung *f*, Verseilung im Wechselschlag
- F: câblage *m* en couches croisées, câblage *m* en sens alterné

reverse voltage
- D: Sperrspannung *f*
- F: tension *f* inverse, tension *f* d'arrêt

reversing sheave
- D: Umlenkrolle *f*
- F: roue *f* de renvoi, galet *m* de renvoi, poulie *f* de renvoi

revise *v*
- D: abändern *v*, ändern *v*
- F: modifier *v*, changer *v*, réviser *v*

revolutions per minute (r.p.m.)
- D: Umdrehungen pro Minute (U/min, Upm)
- F: tours *m pl* par minute (t/min)

rewinding *n*
- D: Umwickeln *n* (Umspulen), Umtrommeln *n*
- F: rebobinage *m*, réenroulement *m*

rewinding stand
- D: Umwickelei *f*
- F: bobineuse *f*

ribbed *adj*
- D: geriffelt *adj*
- F: cannelé *adj*, strié *adj*, rainé *adj*

ribbed insulator
- D: Rippenisolator *m*
- F: isolateur *m* à nervures

right-angle connector

right-angle plug
D: Winkelstecker m
F: fiche f angulaire, fiche f rectangulaire

right-angle plug
D: Winkelstecker m
F: fiche f angulaire, fiche f rectangulaire

right-hand lay [strand.]
D: Rechtsdrall m, Rechtsschlag m
F: pas m à droite

right-hand stranding
D: Rechtsschlag-Verseilung f
F: assemblage m à pas droit, câblage m à pas droit

right-hand(ed) thread
D: rechtsgängiges Gewinde
F: filet m à droite

right-hand twist [strand.]
D: Rechtsdrall m, Rechtsschlag m
F: pas m à droite

right of way [c. install.]
D: Wegerecht n
F: droit m de passage

rigid adj
D: unempfindlich adj, kräftig adj, robust adj
F: robuste adj

rigid plastics
D: harte Kunststoffe
F: matières f pl plastiques rigides

rigid PVC
D: Hart-PVC n, weichmacherfreies PVC
F: PVC m rigide

rigid test
D: strenge Prüfung
F: essai m rigoureux, contrôle m serré, contrôle m rigoureux, contrôle m sévère

rigorous test
D: strenge Prüfung
F: essai m rigoureux, contrôle m serré, contrôle m rigoureux, contrôle m sévère

ring and ball method
D: Ring- und Kugelmethode (zur Bestimmung des Erweichungspunktes von Massen)
F: méthode f bille et anneau

ring code of cable cores
D: Ringmarkierung von Kabeladern
F: repérage m annulaire des conducteurs de câble

ring die
D: Matrize f
F: filière f

ringing test [tel. c.]
D: Abklingeln n, Durchklingeln n, Ausklingeln n, Klingelprüfung f
F: contrôle m de continuité, sonnage m

ring marking of cable cores
D: Ringmarkierung von Kabeladern
F: repérage m annulaire des conducteurs de câble

ring out v [tel. c.]
D: abklingeln v
F: sonner v

ring-out procedure [tel. c.]
D: Abklingeln n, Durchklingeln n, Ausklingeln n, Klingelprüfung f
F: contrôle m de continuité, sonnage m

rinse v
D: spülen v
F: rincer v

rise n
D: Erhöhung f, Steigerung f
F: augmentation f, élévation f

rising main
D: Steigleitung f
F: colonne f montante

river cable
D: Flußkabel n
F: câble m sous-fluvial

r.m.s.-voltage n
D: Effektivspannung f, Wirkspannung f
F: tension f efficace, tension f active

robust adj
D: unempfindlich adj, kräftig adj, robust adj
F: robuste adj

rod breakdown
D: Grobdrahtzug m
F: tréfilage m du fil machine

rod breakdown machine
D: Grobdrahtziehmaschine f
F: tréfileuse f pour fil machine

rod coil
D: Walzdrahtring m, Grobdrahtring m
F: couronne f de fil machine

rodent attack
D: Nagetier-Schäden m pl
F: détériorations f pl causées par des

rodent
rongeurs

rod rolling mill
D: Drahtwalzwerk n
F: laminoir m à fils métalliques

roll v [met.]
D: walzen v
F: laminer v

roll n
D: Walze f
F: rouleau m, cylindre m

rolled sheet
D: ausgezogene Platte
F: plaque f laminée

roller
D: Rolle f
F: rouleau m, galet m

roller (type) conveyor
D: Rollenförderer m
F: installation f de transport par rouleaux

roller-type accumulator [strand.]
D: Rollenspeicher m
F: accumulateur m du type rouleau

roll groove
D: Walzenkaliber n
F: calibre m des cylindres, cannelure f des cylindres

rolling cycle [met.]
D: Walzgang m
F: passe f de laminage, cycle m de laminage

rolling mill [met.]
D: Walzwerk n
F: laminoir m

rolling pass [met.]
D: Walzgang m
F: passe f de laminage, cycle m de laminage

rolling skin
D: Walzhaut f
F: pellicule f de laminage, croûte f de laminage

rolling train [met.]
D: Walzstraße f
F: train m de laminoirs

roll stand [met.]
D: Walzgerüst n
F: cage f de laminoir

room temperature
D: Raumtemperatur f
F: température f ambiante

root mean square (r.m.s.) value
D: Effektivwert m
F: valeur f efficace

rope n [cab.]
D: Seil n
F: câble m, corde f

rope lay strand
D: bündelverseilter Leiter
F: âme f câblée par faisceaux

ropiness
D: Dickflüssigkeit f, Zähflüssigkeit f
F: haute viscosité f

ropy adj
D: fadenziehend adj (Viskosität)
F: filant adj

rosin n
D: Harz n (Naturharz), Kolophonium n
F: colophane f

rotary die head
D: drehbarer Werkzeugkopf
F: tête f d'outils rotative

rotary furnace
D: Drehtrommelofen m
F: four m tubulaire tournant

rotating accumulator [strand.]
D: rotierender Speicher
F: moufle f rotative

rotation n
D: Umdrehung f (Achse)
F: rotation f

rotational speed
D: Drehzahl f (Umdrehungen pro Minute = U/Min), Geschwindigkeit f
F: nombre m de tours par minute (t.p.m.), vitesse f de rotation, vitesse f

rough v
D: vorwalzen v
F: cingler v, dégrossir v, ébaucher v

roughing mill
D: Vorwalzwerk n
F: laminoir m ébaucheur

roughing train
D: Vorwalzstraße f, Blockstraße f (Walzw.)
F: train m dégrossiseur, train m ébaucheur

round v
D: abrunden v (Kante)
F: arrondir v

round billet
D: Rundbolzen m, Rundknüppel m
F: billette f cylindrique

round conductor
D: Rundleiter m
F: âme f ronde, âme f circulaire

rounded edge
D: abgerundete Kante
F: côté m arrondi, tranche f arrondie

round off v
D: abrunden v (Kante)
F: arrondir v

round-robin test
D: Rundversuch m
F: essai m interlaboratoire

round wire
D: Runddraht m
F: fil m rond

round wire armo(u)ring
D: Runddraht-Bewehrung f, Runddraht-Armierung f
F: armure f en fils ronds

route n [cab.]
D: Trasse f
F: parcours m, tracé m

route section [c. install.]
D: Streckenabschnitt m, Abschnitt einer Strecke
F: tronçon m de ligne, tronçon m de liaison

routine test
D: Stückprüfung f
F: essai m de routine

royalty n
D: Lizenzgebühr f
F: taxe f et annuités sur brevet

r.p.m. (s. revolutions per minute)

rubber n
D: Gummi m (vulkanisierter Kautschuk)
F: caoutchouc m (vulcanisé)

rubber n
D: Kautschuk m (unvulkanisiert)
F: caoutchouc m

rubber-coated textile tape
D: gummiertes Textilband
F: ruban m textile caoutchouté

rubber compound
D: Gummimischung f
F: mélange m de caoutchouc

rubber-insulated wire with increased heat resistance
D: Gummiaderleitung mit erhöhter Wärmebeständigkeit
F: conducteur m isolé au caoutchouc avec résistance accrue aux températures élevées

rubber insulation
D: Gummiisolierung f
F: isolation f caoutchouc

rubber jacket core
D: Gummischlauchleitung f
F: câble m souple sous gaine de caoutchouc

rubber kneader
D: Gummikneter m, Banbury-Kneter m
F: mélangeur m à caoutchouc, mélangeur m Banbury, malaxeur m Banbury

rubber mixing plant
D: Gummimischerei f
F: installation f de préparation des mélanges de caoutchouc

rubber sheath
D: Gummi-Mantel m
F: gaine f de caoutchouc

rules pl
D: Bestimmungen f pl (Vorschriften)
F: prescriptions f pl, règles f pl

run n [cab.]
D: Trasse f
F: parcours m, tracé m

run, to ~ a machine
D: eine Maschine fahren, eine Maschine bedienen
F: faire v marcher une machine, opérer v une machine

run, to ~ into the machine
D: in die Maschine einlaufen
F: entrer v dans la machine

running cost
D: Betriebskosten pl t
F: coût m d'exploitation

running-in period [mach.]
D: Anlaufzeit f, Einlaufzeit f
F: temps m de démarrage, temps m d'accélération

running speed [mach.]
D: Fahrgeschwindigkeit f, Fertigungsgeschwindigkeit f, Arbeitsgeschwindigkeit f
F: vitesse f de marche f, vitesse f de fabrication, vitesse f de production, vitesse f de travail

running time of a machine
D: Laufzeit einer Maschine
F: durée f de fonctionnement d'une machine

rupture v
  D: zerreißen v
  F: déchirer v
rupture n
  D: Bruch m, Bruchstelle f
  F: rupture f, brisure f, cassure f
rural line [tel.]
  D: Landleitung f
  F: ligne f rurale
rust prevention
  D: Rostschutz m
  F: protection f contre la rouille
rust protection
  D: Rostschutz m
  F: protection f contre la rouille
rust-resisting adj
  D: nichtrostend adj, rostbeständig adj
  F: inoxydable adj

S

safety device
  D: Sicherheitsvorrichtung f, Schutzvorrichtung f
  F: dispositif m de sécurité, dispositif m de protection
safety guard [mach.]
  D: Schutzabdeckung f, Sicherheitsabdeckung f
  F: carter m de sécurité, carter m enveloppe, carter m de protection
sag n
  D: Durchhang m
  F: flèche f, mou m
sag clearance
  D: Durchhanghöhe f
  F: écart m de flèche, hauteur f de flèche
sag control [vulc.]
  D: Durchhangregelung f
  F: contrôle m de la flèche
sagging n
  D: Durchhängen n
  F: fléchissement m
sag sensing unit [vulc.]
  D: Durchhang-Abtastgerät n
  F: détecteur m de flèche
salt bath
  D: Salzbad n
  F: bain m de sel

same lay stranding
  D: Verseilung im Gleichschlag
  F: câblage m en même sens
sample n
  D: Probe f, Muster n, Prüfstück n
  F: éprouvette f, échantillon m
sample, taking of ~s
  D: Probenahme f
  F: prélèvement m d'échantillons, échantillonnage m
sample test
  D: Stückprüfung f
  F: essai m de routine
sampling n
  D: Probenahme f
  F: prélèvement m d'échantillons, échantillonnage m
sampling test
  D: Stichprobenprüfung f
  F: essai m sur prélèvement
sand v
  D: schmirgeln v
  F: émeriller v
sandwich covering
  D: schichtweise Bedeckung
  F: revêtement m en sandwich
sandwiched adj **between**
  D: eingelagert adj, zwischengelagert adj
  F: interposé adj, entreposé adj
saponification number
  D: Verseifungszahl f
  F: coefficient m de saponification, indice m de saponification
saponification value
  D: Verseifungszahl f
  F: coefficient m de saponification, indice m de saponification
SAT cable (s. Southatlantic telephone cable)
satin(ed) paper, satiny paper
  D: satiniertes Papier
  F: papier m satiné
saturation pressure
  D: Sättigungsdruck m
  F: pression f de saturation
SBR (s. styrene butadiene rubber)
scab n [met.]
  D: Zunder m
  F: calamine f
scalding compound
  D: Abbrühmasse f
  F: matière f d'échaudage

scale v (off)
 D: abblättern v
 F: écailler v(s'), décoller v(se)
scale n [met.]
 D: Zunder m
 F: calamine f
scale n
 D: Walzhaut f
 F: pellicule f de laminage, croûte f de laminage
scale division
 D: Skalenteilung f
 F: graduation f d'échelle
scale drawing
 D: maßstäbliche Zeichnung
 F: dessin m à l'échelle
scale loss [smelt.]
 D: Abbrand m
 F: perte f au feu, déchet m
scales pl
 D: Schuppen f pl
 F: écailles f pl, paillettes f pl
scaling n
 D: Schuppenbildung f
 F: écaillement m
scalp v
 D: fräsen v (Drahtbarren)
 F: scalper v
scalping n
 D: Befräsen n (Kupfer-Drahtbarren)
 F: scalpage m, décortiquage m
scan v
 D: abtasten v
 F: palper v, sonder v, balayer v
scanner n
 D: Abtastvorrichtung f, Fühler m
 F: palpeur m, scanner m, sonde f
scanning device
 D: Abtastvorrichtung f, Fühler m
 F: palpeur m, scanner m, sonde f
scanning test
 D: Durchlauf-Prüfung f, „Scanning"-Prüfung f, Ionisationsprüfung f
 F: essai m d'ionisation par défilement, essai m de «scanning»
scattering n [test]
 D: Streuung f
 F: dispersion f
schematic representation
 D: schematische Darstellung
 F: représentation f schématique, schéma m de principe
schematic wiring diagram
 D: Prinzipschaltbild n
 F: schéma m de principe
Schering bridge
 D: Schering-Brücke f
 F: pont m Schering
scope n
 D: Bereich m
 F: gamme f, domaine m, plage f
scope n (of application)
 D: Geltungsbereich m
 F: domaine m d'emploi
scorch v
 D: verbrennen vi
 F: brûler v, carboniser v
scorching n
 D: Anvulkanisation f (Elastomere)
 F: carbonisation f
scorching n (in extruder cylinder)
 D: Anbrennen n (im Extruder)
 F: grillage m (dans l'extrudeuse)
Scotland-Iceland telephone cable (SCOTICE cable)
 D: Schottland-Island-Kabel n
 F: câble m téléphonique de l'Ecosse à l'Islande
scrap n
 D: Schrott m, Abfälle m pl
 F: déchets m pl
scrap n [extr.]
 D: Überlauf m
 F: purges f pl
scrap copper
 D: Altkupfer n, Kupferabfälle m pl
 F: déchets m pl de cuivre
scrap cutter
 D: Abfallschere f
 F: cisailles f pl à déchets
scratch brushing
 D: Behandlung mit der Drahtbürste
 F: traitement m à la brosse métallique
scratchy noise [com.]
 D: Kratzgeräusch n
 F: bruit m de friture
screen v [el.]
 D: abschirmen v
 F: blinder v
screen n [el.]
 D: Abschirmung f, Schirm m
 F: écran m, blindage m
screen n
 D: Bildschirm m
 F: écran m, écran m de vision
screen analysis

screen

screen cross-section [cab.]
D: Schirmquerschnitt m
F: section f de l'écran

screened, individually ~ cable cores
D: einzeln abgeschirmte Kabeladern
F: conducteurs m pl de câble avec écran individuel

screened cable
D: abgeschirmtes Kabel, geschirmtes Kabel
F: câble m sous écran, câble m blindé

screened conductor cable
D: Kabel mit abgeschirmten Leitern
F: câble m à conducteurs sous écran

screened pair
D: geschirmtes Paar
F: paire f sous écran

screening n [el.]
D: Abschirmung f, Schirm m
F: écran m, blindage m

screening n
D: Auswahlprüfung f
F: essai m de prélèvement

screening n
D: Siebung f
F: criblage m, tamisage m

screening braid
D: Abschirmgeflecht n
F: écran m guipé

screening factor (GB)
D: Schirmfaktor m
F: facteur m d'écran

screening factor, electrical interference ~
D: Abschirmfaktor gegen elektrische Störungen
F: facteur m de blindage contre les perturbations électriques

screen pack [extr.]
D: Siebpackung f
F: paquet m de filtres

screen residue
D: Siebrückstand m
F: refus m de criblage, refus m du tamis

screw n [extr.]
D: Schnecke f
F: vis f

screw calipers pl
D: Schraublehre f
F: calibre m à vis

D: Siebanalyse f
F: analyse f au tamis

screw connection
D: Verschraubung f, Schraubverbindung f
F: vissage m, boulonnage m, raccord m à vis, raccord m fileté

screw(ed) joint
D: Verschraubung f, Schraubverbindung f
F: vissage m, boulonnage m, raccord m à vis, raccord m fileté

screw length nD (D = diameter) [extr.]
D: Schneckenlänge nD (D = Durchmesser)
F: longueur f de la vis nD (D = diamètre)

screw off v
D: abschrauben v
F: dévisser v

screw pushout device [extr.]
D: Schneckenausstoßvorrichtung f
F: extracteur m de vis

screw speed [extr.]
D: Schneckendrehzahl f
F: tours m pl de vis par minute, vitesse f de la vis

screw terminal [el.]
D: Klemmschraube f, Schraubklemme f
F: vis f de borne, borne f à vis

seal v
D: abdichten v
F: rendre v étanche, boucher v, étancher v

seal v [c. access.]
D: vergießen v
F: surmouler v, sceller v

seal n
D: Dichtung f
F: joint m, joint m d'étanchéité

sealed cable end
D: Kabelstumpf m
F: bout m de câble

sealing n
D: Abdichtung f, Dichtigkeit f
F: étanchéité f

sealing cap [cab.]
D: Verschlußkappe f
F: capot m d'étanchéité

sealing compound [c. acc.]
D: Vergußmasse f, Ausgußmasse f, Füllmasse f
F: matière f de remplissage

sealing compound

sealing
  D: Abdichtmasse *f*
  F: matière *f* d'étanchéité
sealing disc
  D: Dichtungsscheibe *f*
  F: rondelle *f* d'étanchéité
sealing end
  D: Endverschluß *m*, Endenabschluß *m*
  F: extrémité *f*, accessoire *m* d'extrémité
sealing end vulcanized to the cable
  D: aufvulkanisierter Endenabschluß
  F: extrémité *f* vulcanisée sur le câble
sealing ring
  D: Dichtungsring *m*
  F: anneau *m* d'étanchéité, bague *f* d'étanchéité, joint *m* annulaire
sealing washer
  D: Dichtungsscheibe *f*
  F: rondelle *f* d'étanchéité
sealing wrap [cab.]
  D: Dichtungswickel *m*
  F: rubanage *m* d'étanchéité
seamless extrusion of metal sheaths
  D: nahtloses Pressen von Metallmänteln
  F: filage *m* sans soudure des gaines métalliques
seamless tube
  D: nahtloses Rohr
  F: tube *m* sans soudure
seam welding
  D: Nahtschweißen *n*
  F: soudage *m* en ligne continue
secondary circuit
  D: Sekundärkreislauf *m*
  F: circuit *m* secondaire
secondary cooling
  D: Sekundärkühlung *f*
  F: refroidissement *m* secondaire
secondary voltage
  D: Sekundärspannung *f*
  F: tension *f* secondaire
second wire [com. c.]
  D: Meßader *f*
  F: fil *m* de test
section *n*
  D: Abschnitt *m*
  F: section *f*
section *n*
  D: Profil *n*
  F: profilé *m*
section, in ~s
  D: abschnittweise *adj*
  F: en sections
sectionalize *v*
  D: unterteilen *v*
  F: subdiviser *v*, sectionner *v*
section point for loading coil spacing [com. c.]
  D: Festpunkt für Spulenabstände
  F: point *m* de section pour l'écartement entre bobines de charge
section roll
  D: Profilwalze *f*
  F: cylindre *m* à profilés
sector angle
  D: Spitzenwinkel *m* (Sektorleiter)
  F: angle *m* au sommet
sector crest
  D: Sektorspitze *f*
  F: sommet *m* d'un secteur
sector edge
  D: Sektorkante *f*
  F: arête *f* de secteur
sector height
  D: Sektorhöhe *f* (des Leiters)
  F: hauteur *f* du secteur
sector peak
  D: Sektorspitze *f*
  F: sommet *m* d'un secteur
sector rollers
  D: Sektorverdichtungswalzen *f pl*
  F: rouleaux *m pl* (de rétreint) de secteur
sector-shaped conductor
  D: Sektorleiter *m*
  F: âme *f* sectorale
sector width
  D: Sektorbreite *f* (des Leiters)
  F: largeur *f* du secteur
sediment *n*
  D: Bodensatz *m*
  F: dépôt *m*, sédiment *m*
segmental conductor
  D: Segmentleiter *m*
  F: âme *f* segmentée
segregation *n*
  D: Ausscheidung *f*, Absonderung *f*
  F: ségrégation *f*, séparation *f*
segregation *n*
  D: Entmischung *f*
  F: ségrégation *f*, décomposition *f*, déshomogénéisation *f*
selector *n* (switch)
  D: Wählschalter *m*

selector

   F: commutateur-sélecteur *m*

self-adhering *adj*
   D: selbstklebend *adj*
   F: auto-collant *adj*, auto-adhésif *adj*

self-adhesive *adj*
   D: selbstklebend *adj*
   F: auto-collant *adj*, auto-adhésif *adj*

self-adhesive tape
   D: selbstklebendes Band
   F: ruban *m* auto-adhésif, ruban *m* auto-collant

self-ali(g)ning *adj*
   D: selbstzentrierend *adj*
   F: à centrage automatique

self-amalgamating tape
   D: selbstverschweißendes Band
   F: ruban *m* autosoudable, ruban *m* autosoudant, ruban *m* autoamalgamant

self-bonding *adj*
   D: selbstklebend *adj*
   F: auto-collant *adj*, auto-adhésif *adj*

self-centering *adj*
   D: selbstzentrierend *adj*
   F: à centrage automatique

self-contained oil-filled cable
   D: Niederdruckölkabel *n* (mit aufgepreßtem Metallmantel)
   F: câble *m* sous basse pression d'huile (sous gaine métallique)

self-contained system
   D: wartungsfreie Anlage
   F: installation *f* indépendante ne nécessitant pas d'entretien

self-curing *adj*
   D: selbstvulkanisierend *adj*
   F: auto-vulcanisant *adj*

self-disengaging *adj* [mach.]
   D: selbstausschaltend *adj*
   F: à débrayage automatique

self-extinguishing *adj*
   D: selbsterlöschend *adj*
   F: auto-extinguible *adj*

self-fusing tape
   D: selbstverschweißendes Band
   F: ruban *m* autosoudable, ruban *m* autosoudant, ruban *m* autoamalgamant

self-impedance *n*
   D: Eigenimpedanz *f*
   F: auto-impédance *f*

self-supporting aerial cable
   D: selbsttragendes Luftkabel
   F: câble *m* aérien autoporteur

self-supporting cable
   D: selbsttragendes Kabel
   F: câble *m* autoporteur

self-supporting overhead cable
   D: selbsttragendes Luftkabel
   F: câble *m* aérien autoporteur

self-vulcanizing *adj*
   D: selbstvulkanisierend *adj*
   F: auto-vulcanisant *adj*

selvage *n*
   D: Webkante *f*
   F: lisière *f*

selvedge *n*
   D: Webkante *f*
   F: lisière *f*

semi-conducting compound
   D: schwachleitende Mischung
   F: mélange *m* semi-conducteur

semi-conducting layer
   D: Leitschicht *f*, schwachleitende Schicht
   F: couche *f* semi-conductrice

semi-conducting rubber
   D: Leitgummi *m*
   F: caoutchouc *m* semi-conducteur

semi-conducting varnish
   D: Leitlack *m*
   F: vernis *m* semi-conducteur

semi-conductive compound
   D: schwachleitende Mischung
   F: mélange *m* semi-conducteur

semi-conductive layer
   D: Leitschicht *f*, schwachleitende Schicht
   F: couche *f* semi-conductrice

semi-finished product
   D: Halbfertigfabrikat *n*
   F: semi-produit *m*, demi-produit *m*, produit *m* semi-fini

sense *v*
   D: abtasten *v*
   F: palper *v*, sonder *v*, balayer *v*

sense of running [mach.]
   D: Laufrichtung *f*
   F: sens *m* de marche, sens *m* de défilement

sensibility *n*
   D: Empfindlichkeit *f*
   F: sensibilité *f*

sensibility to disturbances [com.]
   D: Störanfälligkeit *f*
   F: sensibilité *f* aux parasites,

sensibilité *f* aux perturbations
sensing device
  D: Abtastvorrichtung *f*, Fühler *m*
  F: palpeur *m*, scanner *m*, sonde *f*
sensing guide rollers [vulc.]
  D: Abtast-Führungsrollen *f pl*
  F: chandelles *f pl* de palpage
sensitivity *n*
  D: Empfindlichkeit *f*
  F: sensibilité *f*
sensor *n*
  D: Abtastvorrichtung *f*, Fühler *m*
  F: palpeur *m*, scanner *m*, sonde *f*
separate *v*
  D: ablösen *v* (Folie, Schicht), abziehen *v*
  F: peler *v*, séparer *v*, décoller *v*
separate lateral water pipes
  D: parallel zum Kabel verlegte Wasserrohre
  F: tubes *m pl* à eau latéraux disposés séparément du câble
separating element [com. c.]
  D: Trennelement *n*
  F: élément *m* de séparation
separation *n*
  D: Ausscheidung *f*, Absonderung *f*
  F: ségrégation *f*, séparation *f*
separation *n*
  D: Entmischung *f*
  F: ségrégation *f*, décomposition *f*, déshomogénéisation *f*
separator *n* (film)
  D: Trennfolie *f*, Trennschicht *f*
  F: séparateur *m*
series circuit
  D: Reihenschaltung *f*, Hintereinanderschaltung *f*
  F: montage *m* en série, connexion *f* en série, couplage *m* en série
series connection
  D: Reihenschaltung *f*, Hintereinanderschaltung *f*
  F: montage *m* en série, connexion *f* en série, couplage *m* en série
series interference voltage
  D: Serienstörspannung *f*
  F: tension *f* perturbatrice série
series resistance
  D: Längswiderstand *m*
  F: résistance *f* longitudinale, résistance *f* en série
served lead-covered cable
  D: Bleimantelkabel mit Außenschutz
  F: câble *m* sous gaine de plomb avec revêtement extérieur
service *n*
  D: Instandhaltung *f*
  F: entretien *m*, service *m*, maintenance *f*
service *n* [cab., mach.]
  D: Betrieb *m*
  F: fonctionnement *m*, service *m*, exploitation *f*, régime *m*
service, out of ~
  D: außer Betrieb
  F: hors service
service, to put to ~
  D: in Betrieb nehmen
  F: mettre *v* en service, mettre *v* en œuvre
service cable
  D: Anschlußkabel *n*
  F: câble *m* de raccordement
service cable [pow. c.]
  D: Stichkabel *n*, Hausanschlußkabel *n*
  F: câble *m* de raccordement domestique, câble *m* de branchement domestique
service conditions
  D: Betriebsbedingungen *f pl*
  F: conditions *f pl* de travail, conditions *f pl* de fonctionnement, conditions *f pl* d'exploitation
service drop cable [pow. c.]
  D: Stichkabel *n*, Hausanschlußkabel *n*
  F: câble *m* de raccordement domestique, câble *m* de branchement domestique
service life
  D: Lebensdauer *f*, Nutzungsdauer *f*
  F: durée *f* de vie, vie *f*, durée *f* d'exploitation
service life [mach.]
  D: Standzeit *f*
  F: vie *f*
service performance
  D: Betriebsverhalten *n*
  F: performance *f* (en service), tenue *f* (en service)
service reliability
  D: Betriebssicherheit *f*, Betriebszuverlässigkeit *f*, Zuverlässigkeit im Betrieb
  F: sécurité *f* de fonctionnement, fiabilité *f* de service

service side [mach.]
  D: Bedienungsseite f
  F: côté commande m, côté m manœuvre, côté m service

service voltage
  D: Betriebsspannung f
  F: tension f de service, tension f de régime

servicing n
  D: Instandhaltung f
  F: entretien m, service m, maintenance f

serving n [cab.]
  D: äußere Schutzhülle, Außenschutz m
  F: revêtement m extérieur

set v
  D: erstarren v, hartwerden v
  F: solidifier v (se), congéler v, durcir v

set v [adh.]
  D: abbinden v
  F: durcir v

set n
  D: Aggregat n
  F: agrégat m, groupe m

set, to ~ working
  D: in Betrieb nehmen
  F: mettre v en service, mettre v en œuvre

set free
  D: abspalten v
  F: fendre v, libérer v

set out v
  D: auslegen v (Werk, Anlage)
  F: disposer v, arranger v

set screw
  D: Verstellschraube f, Einstellschraube f, Stellschraube f
  F: vis f d'ajustage, vis f de réglage

setting n [contr.]
  D: Regelung f, Einstellung f
  F: réglage m

setting n
  D: Erstarrung f
  F: solidification f, congélation f

set up v [mach.]
  D: einrichten v
  F: régler v

set up v
  D: errichten v
  F: monter v, ériger v, installer v, assembler v

set-up n
  D: Errichtung f, Montage f, Aufbau m
  F: implantation f, montage m, assemblage m

set-up time [mach.]
  D: Rüstzeit f, Einrichtezeit f
  F: temps m de préparation, temps m de réglage

severe control
  D: strenge Prüfung
  F: essai m rigoureux, contrôle m serré, contrôle m rigoureux, contrôle m sévère

severe test
  D: strenge Prüfung
  F: essai m rigoureux, contrôle m serré, contrôle m rigoureux, contrôle m sévère

SF_6-insulated bus duct
  D: SF_6-isoliertes Leitersystem, SF_6-Rohrleiter m, SF_6-Rohrschiene f
  F: liaison f blindée isolée au SF_6, canalisation f blindée isolée au SF_6

SF_6-insulated metal clad tubular bus
  D: SF_6-isoliertes Leitersystem, SF_6-Rohrleiter m, SF_6-Rohrschiene f
  F: liaison f blindée isolée au SF_6, canalisation f blindée isolée au SF_6

shaft n [mach.]
  D: Welle f
  F: arbre m

shaft cable
  D: Grubenschachtkabel n, Schachtkabel n
  F: câble m pour puits de mines

shaft furnace
  D: Schachtofen m
  F: four m à cuve

shallow-water cable
  D: Küstenkabel n, armiertes Kabel für flache Küstengewässer
  F: câble m d'atterrissement, câble m côtier, câble m de bas fond

shaped conductor
  D: Profilleiter m
  F: âme f profilée

shaped plug
  D: Konturenstecker m
  F: fiche f profilée

shaped wire
  D: Profildraht m
  F: brin m profilé, fil m profilé

shaping degree
  D: Verdichtungsgrad m (Leiter),

Anwalzgrad m (Leiter)
F: coefficient m de rétreint

shave v
D: schälen v (Draht, Isolierung)
F: raser v

shaving n [wire manuf.]
D: Schaben n
F: rasage m

shear modulus
D: Gleitmodul m
F: module m d'élasticité au cisaillement

shear off v
D: abscheren v
F: cisailler v

shear strength
D: Scherfestigkeit f
F: résistance f au cisaillement

shear stress
D: Scherbeanspruchung f
F: effort m de cisaillement, contrainte f de cisaillement

sheath n
D: Hülle f, Umhüllung f
F: enveloppe f, revêtement m

sheath n [cab.]
D: Mantel m
F: gaine f

sheathed metal-clad wiring cable
D: umhüllter Rohrdraht
F: câble m cuirassé sous gaine

sheathing n
D: Ummantelung f
F: gainage m

sheathing compound
D: Mantelmischung f
F: mélange m gaine

sheath losses
D: Mantelverluste m pl
F: pertes f pl sur la gaine

sheath thickness [cab.]
D: Manteldicke f
F: épaisseur f de la gaine

sheave n
D: Scheibe f
F: roue f, galet m, poulie f, disque m

shed insulator
D: Glockenisolator m, Isolierglocke f
F: isolateur m à cloche, cloche f isolante

sheet n
D: Platte f
F: plaque f, plateau m

sheet n
D: Bahn f (Papier, Stoff)
F: bande f

sheet n (as taken from a mill)
D: Walzfell n (Mischungsherstellung)
F: nappe f

sheet of masticated rubber
D: Fell n
F: nappe f de caoutchouc malaxé

sheeting n
D: Bahn f (Papier, Stoff)
F: bande f

sheeting-out n [rub., plast.]
D: Plattenziehen n
F: tirage m en nappes

shelf ag(e)ing
D: Alterung durch Lagerung
F: vieillissement m au stockage

shelf cable
D: Küstenkabel n, armiertes Kabel für flache Küstengewässer
F: câble m d'atterrissement, câble m côtier, câble m de bas fond

shelf life
D: Lagerfähigkeit f (Werkstoffe), Haltbarkeit f (Werkstoffe), Lagerungsbeständigkeit f
F: limite f de stockage, stabilité f au stockage

shell n [met. extr. pr.]
D: Preßschale f
F: croûte f, chemise f

shield v [el.]
D: abschirmen v
F: blinder v

shield n [el.]
D: Abschirmung f, Schirm m
F: écran m, blindage m

shielded cable
D: abgeschirmtes Kabel, geschirmtes Kabel
F: câble m sous écran, câble m blindé

shielded conductor cable
D: Radialfeldkabel n
F: câble m à champ radial

shielded pair
D: geschirmtes Paar
F: paire f sous écran

shield factor (US)
D: Schirmfaktor m
F: facteur m d'écran

shielding n [el.]
D: Abschirmung f, Schirm m

shielding
F: écran m, blindage m

shielding braid
D: Abschirmgeflecht n
F: écran m guipé

shift, on a single ~ basis
D: im Einschichtbetrieb
F: en une seule équipe

shiftable adj
D: verschiebbar adj
F: déplaçable adj

shifting n
D: Verschiebung f, Verlagerung f
F: déplacement m, décalage m

shift operation
D: Schichtbetrieb m
F: travail m en équipes

shipping drum
D: Versandtrommel f
F: touret m d'expédition

shipping reel
D: Versandspule f, Versandtrommel f, Liefertrommel f
F: bobine f d'expédition

ship wiring cable
D: Schiffskabel n
F: câble m de navire, câble m de bord

shock protection [el.]
D: Berührungsschutz m
F: protection f contre des contacts accidentels

shop floor transport vehicle
D: Flurförderfahrzeug n
F: chariot m de manutention

shop lay-out
D: Anlage einer Werkstatt
F: disposition f dans un atelier

shore-end cable
D: Küstenkabel n, armiertes Kabel für flache Küstengewässer
F: câble m d'atterrissement, câble m côtier, câble m de bas fond

short-circuit v
D: kurzschließen v
F: mettre v en court-circuit, court-circuiter v

short-circuit behaviour
D: Kurzschlußverhalten n
F: tenue f en court-circuit

short-circuit conditions, under ~
D: im Kurzschlußfall
F: en cas de court-circuit

short-circuit current
D: Kurzschlußstrom m
F: courant m de court-circuit

short-circuit duration
D: Kurzschlußzeit f, Kurzschlußdauer f
F: temps m de court-circuit, durée f de court-circuit

short-circuited turn
D: Kurzschlußwindung f
F: spire f de court-circuit

short-circuit proof
D: kurzschlußsicher adj
F: résistant adj au court-circuit

short-circuit rating
D: Kurzschlußleistung f
F: puissance f de court-circuit

short-circuit strength
D: Kurzschlußfestigkeit f
F: résistance f aux courts-circuits

short-circuit time
D: Kurzschlußzeit f, Kurzschlußdauer f
F: temps m de court-circuit, durée f de court-circuit

short-circuit winding
D: Kurzschlußwindung f
F: spire f de court-circuit

short-time dielectric strength
D: Kurzzeit-Durchschlagfestigkeit f
F: tenue f au claquage de courte durée

short-time duty [el.]
D: Kurzzeitbetrieb m (mit gleichbleibender Last)
F: service m temporaire, régime m temporaire, service m de courte durée

short-time operation [el.]
D: Kurzzeitbetrieb m (mit gleichbleibender Last)
F: service m temporaire, régime m temporaire, service m de courte durée

short-time performance
D: Kurzzeitverhalten n
F: comportement m en courte durée

short-time service [el.]
D: Kurzzeitbetrieb m (mit gleichbleibender Last)
F: service m temporaire, régime m temporaire, service m de courte durée

short-time strength
D: Kurzzeitfestigkeit f

short-time test
 D: Kurzzeitprüfung f, Kurzzeitversuch m
 F: essai m de courte durée
shrink v
 D: schrumpfen v
 F: rétrécir v(se), contracter v(se)
shrinkage n
 D: Schrumpfung f
 F: retrait m, contraction f
shrinkage allowance
 D: Schrumpfmaß n
 F: grandeur f de retrait
shrinkhole n
 D: Lunker m
 F: retassure f
shrink on v
 D: aufschrumpfen v
 F: emmancher v à chaud
shrink-on cable accessories
 D: wärmeschrumpfende Kabelgarnituren
 F: accessoires m pl de câbles emmanchables à chaud
shrink-on sleeve
 D: Schrumpfmuffe f, Aufschrumpfmuffe f
 F: manchon m emmanché à chaud
shrink-on technique
 D: Wärmeschrumpftechnik f, Aufschrumpftechnik f
 F: technique f d'emmanchement à chaud
shrink-on termination
 D: wärmeschrumpfender Endverschluß, aufschrumpfbarer Endverschluß
 F: extrémité f emmanchable à chaud
shrink-on tube
 D: Schrumpfschlauch m
 F: tuyau m emmanchable à chaud, gaine f thermorétractable, manchon m thermorétractable
shrunk-on termination
 D: aufgeschrumpfter Endverschluß
 F: extrémité f emmanchée à chaud
shunt n
 D: Abzweigstromkreis m, Nebenschluß m
 F: circuit m dérivé, shunt m
shut down v [mach.]
 D: abschalten v, ausschalten v
 F: arrêter v
shut-off valve
 D: Absperrventil n
 F: soupape f d'arrêt
side, laying ~ by side
 D: Verlegung nebeneinander, Parallelanordnung f
 F: disposition f côte à côte, disposition f en nappe horizontale, disposition f en parallèle
side circuit
 D: Stammkreis m, Stammleitung f
 F: circuit m combinant, circuit m réel
side circuit loading coil
 D: Stammleitungsspule f, Stammkreisspule f, Stammpupinspule f
 F: bobine f de charge du circuit combinant
side of attendance [mach.]
 D: Bedienungsseite f
 F: côté commande m, côté m manœuvre, côté m service
side-to-phantom crosstalk
 D: Mitsprechen n
 F: diaphonie f entre réel et fantôme
side-to-phantom far-end crosstalk
 D: Gegenmitsprechen n
 F: télédiaphonie f entre réel et fantôme
side-to-side crosstalk
 D: Übersprechen n
 F: diaphonie f entre réel et réel
side-to-side crosstalk coupling
 D: Übersprechkopplung f, Nachbarvierer-Nebensprech-Kopplung f
 F: couplage m diaphonique entre réel et réel, couplage m diaphonique entre quartes voisines
side-to-side far-end crosstalk
 D: Gegenübersprechen n
 F: télédiaphonie f entre réel et réel
sieve analysis
 D: Siebanalyse f
 F: analyse f au tamis
sieving n
 D: Siebung f
 F: criblage m, tamisage m
sight glass [mach.]
 D: Beobachtungsfenster n, Schauglas n, Schauloch n
 F: hublot m de regard, voyant m

signal 360

signal board
 D: Anzeigetafel f
 F: panneau m indicateur de fonctionnement, tableau m indicateur

signal element [com.]
 D: Informationsschritt m
 F: élément m de signal

signal lamp
 D: Signallampe f, Anzeigelampe f
 F: voyant m lumineux, signal m lumineux, lampe-témoin f

signalling cable
 D: Signalkabel n
 F: câble m de signalisation

signalling core
 D: Signalader f
 F: fil m de signalisation

signal switchboard cable
 D: Signal-Schaltkabel n
 F: câble m de connexion pour installations de signalisation

significant adj
 D: aussagekräftig adj (Werte)
 F: significatif adj

sign marking
 D: Zeichenmarkierung f
 F: marquage m par symboles

silicone rubber
 D: Silikonkautschuk m
 F: caoutchouc m silicone

silk and cotton covered wire
 D: Seidenbaumwolldraht m
 F: fil m revêtu de soie et de coton

similar to
 D: in Anlehnung an
 F: suivant l'exemple de

simplex paper
 D: Simplex-Papier n (Einfachlagenpapier)
 F: papier m simplex, papier m en une couche

simulate v
 D: nachbilden v
 F: simuler v

singing frequency
 D: Pfeiffrequenz f
 F: fréquence f de sifflement

single conductor
 D: Einzelader f, Einzelleiter m
 F: brin m, élément m, monoconducteur m

single-conductor cable
 D: einadriges Kabel, Einleiterkabel n
 F: câble m monophasé, câble m unipolaire, câble m monoconducteur, câble m monopolaire

single-core cable
 D: einadriges Kabel, Einleiterkabel n
 F: câble m monophasé, câble m unipolaire, câble m monoconducteur, câble m monopolaire

single-core cable (with or without sheath)
 D: einadrige Leitung
 F: monoconducteur m (avec ou sans gaine)

single-core non-sheathed cable for internal wiring
 D: Verdrahtungsleitung f
 F: conducteur m pour filerie interne, fil m de câblage

single-core oil-filled cable
 D: Einleiterölkabel n
 F: câble m unipolaire à huile fluide

single-core sheathed conductor
 D: einadrige Leitung mit Mantel
 F: monoconducteur m sous gaine

single-core termination
 D: Einleiter-Endverschluß m
 F: boîte f d'extrémité unipolaire

single drive
 D: Einzelantrieb m
 F: commande f individuelle, commande f directe

single duct conduit
 D: einzügiger Rohrstrang
 F: caniveau m à passage simple

single-ended terminal wires
 D: einseitig herausgeführte Anschlußdrähte
 F: fils m pl de jonction unidirectionnels

single fault to earth (GB)
 D: Einfach-Erdschluß m
 F: défaut m à la terre simple

single fault to ground (US)
 D: Einfach-Erdschluß m
 F: défaut m à la terre simple

single-flighted screw [extr.]
 D: eingängige Schnecke
 F: vis f à un seul filet

single lead sheath, three-core ~ cable
 D: Dreibleimantelkabel n,

Dreimantelkabel *n*
F: câble *m* triplomb, câble *m* triplomb trigaine

single-line-to-earth fault
D: einpoliger Erdschluß
F: défaut *m* à la terre unipolaire

single-mode optical fibre [com.]
D: Einmoden-Lichtleiter *m*
F: fibre *f* optique monomode

single pair
D: Einzelpaar *n*
F: mono-paire *f*

single-phase current
D: Einphasenstrom *m*
F: courant *m* monophasé

single-piece... *adj*
D: einteilig *adj*
F: monobloc *adj*, indivisé *adj*, en une seule pièce

single-ply paper
D: Simplex-Papier *n* (Einfachlagenpapier)
F: papier *m* simplex, papier *m* en une couche

single-ram press
D: Einstempel-Presse *f*
F: presse *f* à un (seul) fouloir

single wire
D: Einzeldraht *m*
F: brin *m*

single-wire paper
D: Simplex-Papier *n* (Einfachlagenpapier)
F: papier *m* simplex, papier *m* en une couche

sink-pipe *n* [c. install.]
D: Rohrdüker *m*
F: tuyau *m* placé en lit de canal

site, at ~ [c. install.]
D: auf der Baustelle, am Montageort
F: sur chantier

site test on cables
D: Prüfung an verlegten Kabeln
F: essai *m* de câbles sur chantier

sizing roll
D: Profilwalze *f*
F: cylindre *m* à profilés

skid wire
D: Gleitdraht *m*
F: fil *m* de glissement

skilled worker
D: Facharbeiter *m*
F: ouvrier *m* qualifié

skim, to ~ off the dross
D: Schlacke abziehen
F: soutirer *v* la scorie, écrasser *v*

skin *n* [met. extr. pr.]
D: Preßschale *f*
F: croûte *f*, chemise *f*

skin *n* (casting)
D: Gußhaut *f*
F: croûte *f* de la fonte, peau *f* de la fonte, pellicule *f* de coulée

skin effect [el.]
D: Hauteffekt *m*, Skineffekt *m*, Stromverdrängung *f*
F: effet *m* de peau

slab *n*
D: Platte *f*
F: plaque *f*, plateau *m*

slab *n*
D: Walzplatte *f* (Mischungsherstellung)
F: mélange *m* en plaque

slackening *n*
D: Durchhängen *n*
F: fléchissement *m*

slack wire
D: zugspannungsloser Draht, durchhängender Draht
F: fil *m* lâche, fil *m* faisant flèche

slag *n*
D: Schlacke *f*
F: scorie *f*

SL-cable *n*
D: Dreibleimantelkabel *n*, Dreimantelkabel *n*
F: câble *m* triplomb, câble *m* triplomb trigaine

sleeve *n*
D: Buchse *f*
F: manchon *m*, douille *f*

sleeve *n* [c. access.]
D: Hülse *f*
F: manchon *m*

slide bar
D: Gleitschiene *f*
F: glissière *f*, chemin *m* de glissement, patin *m*

slide rail
D: Gleitschiene *f*
F: glissière *f*, chemin *m* de glissement, patin *m*

slide wire
D: Fahrdraht *m*, Schleifdraht *m*
F: fil *m* (de) trolley, fil *m* de contact

slip on v
  D: aufschieben v
  F: enfiler v

slip-on termination
  D: Aufschieb-Endverschluß m
  F: extrémité f emmanchable

slit, to ~ paper tapes
  D: Papierbänder schneiden
  F: découper v des rubans de papier

slitting cord
  D: Reißfaden m
  F: fil m de déchirement

sliver
  D: Flitter m (Draht)
  F: paillette f

sliver n [roll. m.]
  D: Walzsplitter m
  F: paille f de laminage

slope of a curve
  D: Abfall einer Kurve, Neigung einer Kurve
  F: inclinaison f d'une courbe, pente f d'une courbe

slope of a curve
  D: Anstieg einer Kurve
  F: pente f d'une courbe, montée f d'une courbe

slot n
  D: Nut f, Aussparung f
  F: rainure f, encoche f, découpe f, évidement m, entaille f

slot and tongue
  D: Nut und Feder
  F: rainure f et languette

slow-acting relay
  D: Verzögerungsrelais n
  F: relais m temporisé

slow down
  D: abbremsen v
  F: freiner v

slow-speed strander
  D: Korbverseilmaschine f
  F: câbleuse f à cage, assembleuse f à cage

small capacity cable [tel.]
  D: Kabel mit geringer Paarzahl, Kabel mit geringer Aderzahl, niedrigpaariges Kabel
  F: câble m à faible capacité, câble m à petit nombre de paires

small-diameter coaxial pair
  D: Kleinkoaxialpaar n
  F: paire f coaxiale de petit diamètre

small-diameter wire
  D: dünner Draht
  F: fil m de petit diamètre, fil m mince

small-gauge conductor
  D: Leiter mit kleinem Querschnitt
  F: âme f de petite section

small make-up cable [tel.]
  D: Kabel mit geringer Paarzahl, Kabel mit geringer Aderzahl, niedrigpaariges Kabel
  F: câble m à faible capacité, câble m à petit nombre de paires

small-size cables
  D: Kabel mit kleinen Querschnitten
  F: câbles m pl de petites sections

small-size conductor
  D: Leiter mit kleinem Querschnitt
  F: âme f de petite section

small-sized cable [tel.]
  D: Kabel mit geringer Paarzahl, Kabel mit geringer Aderzahl, niedrigpaariges Kabel
  F: câble m à faible capacité, câble m à petit nombre de paires

smooth-conductor cable
  D: Kabel mit metallener Leiterglättung
  F: câble m à écran métallique sur l'âme

smooth surface
  D: glatte Oberfläche
  F: surface f lisse

snaking of cables
  D: Schlangenverlegung von Kabeln, Verlegung von Kabeln in Schlangenlinien
  F: pose f des câbles en serpentins

sniffer, cable ~ [com. c.]
  D: Gasspürgerät n
  F: appareil m détecteur de gaz

snug fit
  D: Paßsitz m
  F: ajustement m

socket n
  D: Steckdose f
  F: prise f de courant

socket n
  D: Steckbuchse f, Steckerbuchse f, Fassung f
  F: prise f femelle, fiche f femelle, douille f

socket outlet
  D: Steckdose f

socket-outlet adapter
D: Abzweigstecker m
F: fiche f de dérivation

soft annealed wire
D: weichgeglühter Draht
F: fil m recuit

soft annealing
D: Weichglühen n
F: recuit m d'adoucissement

softener n
D: Erweicher m
F: émollient m

softening n
D: Erweichung f
F: ramollissement m

softening plant
D: Enthärtungsanlage f
F: installation f d'adoucissement, décarbonateur m

softening point
D: Erweichungspunkt m (Massen)
F: point m de ramollissement

soft-solder v
D: weichlöten v
F: souder v

soft soldering
D: Weichlöten n
F: soudage m tendre

soil n
D: Erdboden m
F: terre f

soil conductance
D: Bodenleitfähigkeit f
F: conductivité f du sol

solder n
D: Lot n
F: métal m d'apport, soudure f, brasure f

solderability n
D: Lötbarkeit f
F: soudabilité f

soldered joint
D: Lötverbindung f (weich), Lötstelle f
F: jonction f par soudure, soudure f, joint m soudé

soldered terminal lug
D: Lötkabelschuh m
F: cosse f de câble soudée

soldering n
D: Löten n
F: soudage m

soldering flux
D: Flußmittel n
F: flux m, fondant m

soldering joint
D: Lötverbindung f (weich), Lötstelle f
F: jonction f par soudure, soudure f, joint m soudé

soldering tin
D: Reibelot n, Lötzinn n
F: étain m à souder, étain m de soudage

soldering wire
D: Lötdraht m
F: fil m de soudure, soudure f en fil

solder stick
D: Lotstab m
F: barre f de soudure

solenoid valve
D: Magnetventil n
F: électrovanne f

solid adj
D: unempfindlich adj, kräftig adj, robust adj
F: robuste adj

solid conductor
D: eindrähtiger Leiter, Massivleiter m
F: âme f massive, âme f à un seul brin

solid dielectric
D: Isolierung aus extrudiertem homogenem Material
F: isolant m solide, isolant m sec

solid earthing of neutral (GB)
D: starre Sternpunkterdung
F: mise f à la terre rigide du neutre

solid grounding of neutral (US)
D: starre Sternpunkterdung
F: mise f à la terre rigide du neutre

solidification n
D: Erstarrung f
F: solidification f, congélation f

solidification point
D: Stockpunkt m, Einfrierpunkt m, Erstarrungspunkt m
F: point m de solidification, point m de congélation

solidification shrinkage
D: Erstarrungsschrumpfung f
F: retrait m par solidification

solidify v
D: erstarren v, hartwerden v
F: solidifier v (se), congéler v, durcir v

solid insulation
D: Isolierung aus extrudiertem homogenem Material

solid

F: isolant m solide, isolant m sec

solidly earthed neutral (GB)
D: starr geerdeter Sternpunkt
F: neutre m rigidement relié à la terre

solidly earthed system (GB)
D: Netz mit starr geerdetem Sternpunkt, starr geerdetes Netz
F: réseau m avec mise à la terre rigide du neutre, réseau m rigidement relié à la terre

solidly grounded neutral (US)
D: starr geerdeter Sternpunkt
F: neutre m rigidement relié à la terre

solidly grounded system (US)
D: Netz mit starr geerdetem Sternpunkt, starr geerdetes Netz
F: réseau m avec mise à la terre rigide du neutre, réseau m rigidement relié à la terre

solid PE
D: Voll-PE n
F: polyéthylène m

solid-state amplification
D: Halbleiter-Verstärkung f, Transistor-Verstärkung f
F: amplification f par semi-conducteurs, amplification f à transistors

solution
D: Lösung f
F: solution f

solvent resistance
D: Lösungsmittelbeständigkeit f
F: résistance f aux solvants

source of disturbance
D: Störquelle f
F: source f de perturbation

source of energy
D: Energiequelle f
F: source f d'énergie

source of power
D: Energiequelle f
F: source f d'énergie

Southatlantic telephone cable (SAT cable)
D: Südatlantisches Telefonkabel
F: câble m téléphonique de l'Atlantique du Sud

space n
D: Abstand m
F: distance f, écart m, intervalle m

space charge
D: Raumladung f
F: charge f d'espace, charge f spatiale

space factor
D: Füllfaktor m
F: coefficient m de remplissage, coefficient m de volume

spacer n
D: Abstandhalter m
F: séparateur m

space requirement
D: Platzbedarf m, Raumbedarf m, Flächenbelegung f
F: encombrement m

spacing n
D: Zwischenraum m
F: espace m, intervalle m, jeu m

span wire
D: Spanndraht m
F: fil m tendeur, fil m d'arrêt

spare n
D: Ersatzteil n
F: pièce f de rechange

spare pair [com. c.]
D: Reservepaar n, Ersatzaderpaar n
F: paire f de réserve

spare part
D: Ersatzteil n
F: pièce f de rechange

spare wire [com. c.]
D: Vorratsader f
F: fil m de réserve

spark n
D: Funken m
F: étincelle f

spark discharge
D: Funkenentladung f
F: décharge f par étincelles

sparker n [cab.]
D: Durchlaufprüfgerät n, Trockenprüfgerät n
F: appareil m de contrôle d'ionisation par défilement continu, détecteur m de défauts à sec

spark gap
D: Funkenstrecke f
F: éclateur m

spark-over n
D: Funkenüberschlag m, Überschlag m
F: contournement m, amorçage m

spark-over voltage
D: Überschlagspannung f
F: tension f de contournement, tension f d'éclatement, tension f

d'amorçage
spark test
 D: Spannungsprüfung *f*
 F: essai *m* diélectrique, essai *m* de tension
spark tester [cab.]
 D: Durchlaufprüfgerät *n*, Trockenprüfgerät *n*
 F: appareil *m* de contrôle d'ionisation par défilement continu, détecteur *m* de défauts à sec
speaking circuit
 D: Sprechkreis *m*
 F: circuit *m* téléphonique
speaking current
 D: Sprechstrom *m*
 F: courant *m* téléphonique
speaking wire
 D: Sprechader *f*
 F: fil *m* téléphonique
special rubber insulated cable
 D: Sonder-Gummiaderleitung *f*
 F: câble *m* spécial isolé au caoutchouc
specification *n*
 D: Pflichtenheft *n*
 F: cahier *m* des charges
specifications *pl*
 D: Bestimmungen *f pl* (Vorschriften)
 F: prescriptions *f pl*, règles *f pl*
specific gravity
 D: spezifisches Gewicht
 F: poids *m* spécifique, masse *f* volumique
specific insulation resistance
 D: spezifischer Isolationswiderstand
 F: résistance *f* spécifique d'isolement
specific resistance
 D: spezifischer Widerstand
 F: résistivité *f*
specified value
 D: Sollwert *m*
 F: valeur *f* spécifiée
specified voltage
 D: Bemessungsspannung *f*
 F: tension *f* spécifiée
specimen *n*
 D: Probe *f*, Muster *n*, Prüfstück *n*
 F: éprouvette *f*, échantillon *m*
spectral analysis
 D: Spektralanalyse *f*
 F: analyse *f* spectrale
spectrographic(al) analysis
 D: spektrographische Analyse
 F: analyse *f* spectrographique
spectrum *n* [prod.]
 D: Spektrum *n*
 F: gamme *f*, éventail *m*
spectrum, broad ~ of manufacturing activities
 D: breites Fabrikatespektrum, breites Fertigungsspektrum
 F: gamme *f* de produits largement diversifiée
speech channel
 D: Sprechkanal *m*, Fernsprechkanal *m*
 F: canal *m* téléphonique, voie *f* téléphonique
speech circuit
 D: Sprechkreis *m*
 F: circuit *m* téléphonique
speech frequency
 D: Sprechfrequenz *f*, Fernsprechfrequenz *f*
 F: fréquence *f* vocale, fréquence *f* téléphonique
speech power
 D: Sprechleistung *f*
 F: puissance *f* vocale
speech wire
 D: Sprechader *f*
 F: fil *m* téléphonique
speed *n*
 D: Drehzahl *f* (Umdrehungen pro Minute = U/Min), Geschwindigkeit *f*
 F: nombre *m* de tours par minute (t.p.m.), vitesse *f* de rotation, vitesse *f*
speed of rotation
 D: Drehgeschwindigkeit *f*, Umdrehungsgeschwindigkeit *f*
 F: vitesse *f* de rotation
speed range
 D: Drehzahlbereich *m*, Geschwindigkeitsbereich *m*
 F: gamme *f* de vitesses
speed variation
 D: Drehzahländerung *f*
 F: changement *m* de vitesse
sphere gap
 D: Kugelfunkenstrecke *f*
 F: éclateur *m* à sphères
spherical-shaped *adj*
 D: kugelförmig *adj*

spherical-shaped

F: sphérique *adj*

spider type die
D: Brückenmatrize *f*
F: filière *f* type croisillon

spill *n*
D: Flitter *m* (Draht)
F: paillette *f*

spill *n*
D: Überwalzung *f* (bei gewalztem Draht)
F: repliure *f* de laminage

spin, to ~ the paper string
D: mit Papierkordel umspinnen
F: guiper *v*

spindle hole
D: Achsbohrung *f* (Kabeltrommel)
F: trou *m* central

spinner *n*
D: Spinner *m* (Band), Spinnkopf *m* (Band), Bandwickler *m*
F: tête *f* de rubanage, tête *f* rubaneuse

spinning *n*
D: Bespinnung *f* (mit Kordel, Garn), Umspinnung *f* (mit Kordel, Garn)
F: guipage *m*

spinning head
D: Spinnkopf *m* (Garn, Kordel)
F: tête *f* guipeuse

spiral four quad (US)
D: Sternvierer *m*
F: quarte *f* étoile

spirally, to apply ~
D: wendelförmig aufbringen
F: poser *v* en hélice, enrouler *v* en hélice

spiral quad (US)
D: Sternvierer *m*
F: quarte *f* étoile

spiral strip paper insulation (US)
D: Isolierung aus Papierbandumspinnung, Papierbandisolierung *f*
F: isolation *f* rubanée en papier, rubanage *m* en papier

splice *v*
D: spleißen *v*
F: épisser *v*

splice *n*
D: Spleißstelle *f*, Spleiß *m*, Spleißverbindung *f*
F: épissure *f*, joint *m*, jonction épissée *f*

splice box [vulc.]
D: Teleskop-Rohr *n*
F: tube *m* télescopique

splice case [com. c.]
D: Spleißmuffengehäuse *n*
F: manchon *m* sur jonction épissée

splice closure [com. c.]
D: Spleißmuffengehäuse *n*
F: manchon *m* sur jonction épissée

spliced joint
D: Spleißstelle *f*, Spleiß *m*, Spleißverbindung *f*
F: épissure *f*, joint *m*, jonction épissée *f*

splicing *n* [cab.]
D: Verbinden *n*
F: raccordement *m*

splicing tool
D: Spleißgerät *n*
F: outil *m* à épisser

split *n*
D: Längsriß *m* (Draht)
F: crique *f*

split *adj*
D: zweigeteilt *adj*, zweiteilig *adj*, geteilt *adj*
F: en deux pièces, divisé *adj*

split conductor
D: Segmentleiter *m*
F: âme *f* segmentée

split off
D: abspalten *v*
F: fendre *v*, libérer *v*

spool *v*
D: aufwickeln *v*, aufspulen *v*, spulen *v*, wickeln *v*, auftrommeln *v*
F: enrouler *v*, bobiner *v*

spool *n*
D: Spule *f*
F: bobine *f*

spooler *n*
D: Wickler *m*, Umwickelei *f*
F: enrouleuse *f*, enrouleur *m*, bobineuse *f*

spooler, automatic ~
D: automatischer Spulapparat
F: bobinoir *m* automatique

spool flange
D: Spulenflansch *m*
F: joue *f* de bobine

spot check
D: Stichprobenprüfung *f*
F: essai *m* sur prélèvement

spray *n*

spray equipment
  D: Sprüheinrichtung f, Abspritzvorrichtung f
  F: dispositif m de pulvérisation, pulvérisateur m

spray nozzle
  D: Sprühdüse f
  F: pulvérisateur m, atomiseur m

spread v
  D: ausbreiten v (sich)
  F: étendre v (s'), propager v (se)

spreader box
  D: Aufteilungsmuffe f
  F: boîte f de distribution, boîte f de division, boîte f de trifurcation

spreader cap
  D: Aufteilungskappe f
  F: cornet m de division

spreader head
  D: Aufteilungskappe f
  F: cornet m de division

spreading n
  D: Ausbreitung f
  F: propagation f, diffusion f

spreading box
  D: Aufteilungsmuffe f
  F: boîte f de distribution, boîte f de division, boîte f de trifurcation

stability n
  D: Beständigkeit f, Festigkeit f, Widerstandsfähigkeit f
  F: résistance f, stabilité f, tenue f

stabilizer n
  D: stabilisierender Zusatz, Stabilisator m
  F: agent m stabilisant, stabilisant m

stabilizing agent
  D: stabilisierender Zusatz, Stabilisator m
  F: agent m stabilisant, stabilisant m

stack furnace
  D: Schachtofen m
  F: four m à cuve

stage of production
  D: Stadium der Fertigung
  F: étape f de fabrication, phase f de fabrication

staggered adj
  D: gestaffelt adj, abgestuft adj, versetzt adj (stufenweise),
  F: en quinconce, échelonné adj, décalé adj, gradué adj, étagé adj

staggering n [lapp.]
  D: Gangversatz m, Lagenversatz m
  F: chevauchement m

staining n
  D: Verfärbung f
  F: décoloration f, changement m de couleur

stainless adj
  D: nichtrostend adj, rostbeständig adj
  F: inoxydable adj

stainless steel
  D: rostfreier Stahl
  F: acier m inoxydable

staircase-type voltage
  D: Treppenspannung f
  F: tension f échelonnée

Stalpeth-sheath n
  D: Stalpeth-Mantel m (Stahl-Al-PE-Schichtenmantel)
  F: gaine f Stalpeth

standard n
  D: Eichmaß n
  F: jauge f, étalon f

standard coaxial pair
  D: Normalkoaxialpaar n
  F: paire f coaxiale standard

standard interface cable
  D: Standard-Schnittstellenkabel n
  F: câble m d'interface standard

standardisation n
  D: Normung f, Vereinheitlichung f
  F: standardisation f, normalisation f, unification f

standardization committee
  D: Normenausschuß m
  F: comité m de normalisation

standard part
  D: Normteil n
  F: pièce f standard, pièce f normalisée

standard resistance
  D: Eichwiderstand m
  F: résistance f étalon

standards pl
  D: Bestimmungen f pl (Vorschriften)
  F: prescriptions f pl, règles f pl

standard specification
  D: Norm f
  F: norme f, spécification f

standard stress
  D: Normalbeanspruchung f
  F: charge f normale

standard value

standard

- **standard**
  - D: Richtwert m
  - F: valeur f indicative, valeur f de référence, valeur f standard, valeur f approximée
- **stand-by aggregate**
  - D: Reserveaggregat n
  - F: agrégat m de réserve, agrégat m de secours, poste m de secours
- **stand-by power unit**
  - D: Notstrom-Aggregat n
  - F: groupe m électrogène de secours
- **stand-by unit**
  - D: Reserveaggregat n
  - F: agrégat m de réserve, agrégat m de secours, poste m de secours
- **standing wave** [el.]
  - D: stehende Welle
  - F: onde f stationnaire
- **star-quad** n
  - D: Sternvierer m
  - F: quarte f étoile
- **star quad cable**
  - D: sternviererverseiltes Kabel
  - F: câble m à quartes en étoile
- **star quadding**
  - D: Sternviererverseilung f
  - F: câblage m par quartes en étoile, fabrication f de quartes étoile
- **star quad formation**
  - D: Sternviererverseilung f
  - F: câblage m par quartes en étoile, fabrication f de quartes étoile
- **star quad twisting**
  - D: Sternviererverseilung f
  - F: câblage m par quartes en étoile, fabrication f de quartes étoile
- **start** v [mach.]
  - D: anfahren v, anschalten v, einschalten v
  - F: démarrer v, mettre v en marche
- **starting current**
  - D: Einschaltstrom m
  - F: courant m de démarrage
- **starting position** [mach.]
  - D: Anfahrstellung f
  - F: position f de mise en marche
- **starting time** [mach.]
  - D: Anlaufzeit f, Einlaufzeit f
  - F: temps m de démarrage, temps m d'accélération
- **start up** v [mach.]
  - D: anfahren v, anschalten v, einschalten v
  - F: démarrer v, mettre v en marche
- **starvation, lead ~**
  - D: Aussetzen des Bleiflusses
  - F: raté m du flux de plomb
- **state of cure**
  - D: Vulkanisationsgrad m
  - F: degré m de vulcanisation, stade m de vulcanisation
- **state of equilibrium**
  - D: Gleichgewichtszustand m
  - F: état m d'équilibre
- **state of the art, according to the latest ~**
  - D: nach dem neuesten Stand der Technik
  - F: selon les dernières règles de l'art
- **stationary**
  - D: stationär adj, feststehend adj
  - F: stationnaire adj, fixe adj
- **steady state condition**
  - D: Beharrungszustand m, Dauerzustand m
  - F: état m stationnaire, régime m établi, régime m permanent
- **steam** [vulc.]
  - D: Dampf m
  - F: vapeur f
- **steam** n
  - D: Wasserdampf m
  - F: vapeur f d'eau
- **steam atmosphere**
  - D: Dampfatmosphäre f
  - F: atmosphère f de vapeur
- **steam cure**
  - D: Dampfvulkanisation f
  - F: vulcanisation f à vapeur
- **steam pipe, continuous vulcanization high-pressure ~**
  - D: Dampfhochdruckrohr zur kontinuierlichen Vulkanisation
  - F: tube m de vulcanisation continue à vapeur à haute pression
- **steam pressure** [vulc.]
  - D: Dampfdruck m
  - F: pression f de vapeur
- **steam stop valve** [vulc.]
  - D: Dampfabsperrventil n
  - F: vanne f à vapeur
- **steam vulcanization**
  - D: Dampfvulkanisation f
  - F: vulcanisation f à vapeur
- **stearic acid**
  - D: Stearinsäure f

F: acide m stéarique
steel pipe
  D: Stahlrohr n
  F: tuyau m en acier, tube m d'acier
steel strip
  D: Bandeisen n, Stahlband n
  F: feuillard m d'acier
steel tape
  D: Bandeisen n, Stahlband n
  F: feuillard m d'acier
steel tape armo(u)r
  D: Bandeisen-Armierung f,
    Bandeisenbewehrung f,
    Stahlbandarmierung f,
    Stahlbandbewehrung f,
    Bandarmierung f, Bandbewehrung f
  F: armure f en feuillard d'acier
steel-tape-armo(u)red cable
  D: bandeisenbewehrtes Kabel,
    stahlbandarmiertes Kabel
  F: câble m armé en feuillard d'acier
steel tape armo(u)ring
  D: Bandeisen-Armierung f,
    Bandeisenbewehrung f,
    Stahlbandarmierung f,
    Stahlbandbewehrung f,
    Bandarmierung f, Bandbewehrung f
  F: armure f en feuillard d'acier
steel tape helix
  D: Stahlbandwendel f
  F: hélice f de feuillard d'acier
steel tape spinner
  D: Bandeisen-Spinner m, Eisenband-Wickler m
  F: enrouleur m à feuillard d'acier, tête f à feuillard
steel tape spooler
  D: Bandeisen-Wickler m
  F: bobinoir m à feuillard d'acier
steel taping head
  D: Bandeisen-Spinner m, Eisenband-Wickler m
  F: enrouleur m à feuillard d'acier, tête f à feuillard
steel wire
  D: Stahldraht m
  F: fil m d'acier
steel wire armouring
  D: Stahldrahtbewehrung f,
    Stahldrahtarmierung f
  F: armure f en fils d'acier

steep slopes, cable for installation on ~
  D: Steilhangkabel n
  F: câble m pour installation sur pentes raides
step, in ~s of ...
  D: in Stufen von ...
  F: par paliers de ..., par échelons de ...
step, to ~ down the voltage
  D: abspannen v
  F: abaisser v la tension
step, voltage increase in ~s
  D: stufenweise Spannungssteigerung
  F: élévation f de tension par paliers
stepless adj
  D: stufenlos adj
  F: continu adj, sans à-coups, sans intervalles
stepped sample [cab.]
  D: Stufenmuster n
  F: échantillon m étagé
"step-up" cure [vulc.]
  D: Stufenheizung f
  F: vulcanisation f échelonnée, vulcanisation f par paliers
stick v
  D: haften v, kleben vi
  F: adhérer v, coller v
stickiness n
  D: Klebrigkeit f
  F: glutinosité f, état m collant
sticking n
  D: Haftung f, Adhäsion f
  F: adhésion f, adhérance f, collage m
stiffness n
  D: Strammheit f (Gummimischungen)
  F: raideur f
stock length
  D: Lagerlänge f
  F: longueur f standard
stockscrew n [extr.]
  D: Förderschnecke f
  F: vis d'extrusion f
stokes n
  D: Stokes n (St) (Viskosität)
  F: stokes m
stop n
  D: Anschlag m (Arretierung)
  F: butée f, arrêt m
stop cock
  D: Absperrhahn m
  F: robinet m d'arrêt
stope cable
  D: Strossenleitung f

stope
  F: câble *m* de stross
stop joint
  D: Sperrmuffe *f*
  F: joint *m* d'arrêt
stop marks
  D: Bambusringe *m pl* (durch Rastzeiten beim Aufbringen von Kabelmänteln aus Blei oder Aluminium), Einschnürungen *f pl* (Met.-Strangpr.) Haltestellenmarkierungen *f pl* (Met.-Strangpr.)
  F: nœuds *m pl* de bambou
stoppage *n* [mach.]
  D: Anhalten *n*
  F: arrêt *m*
stoppage periods [met. extr. pr.]
  D: Haltezeiten *f pl*
  F: temps *m pl* d'arrêt
stopping device
  D: Anhaltevorrichtung *f*
  F: dispositif *m* d'arrêt
stop valve
  D: Absperrventil *n*
  F: soupape *f* d'arrêt
storage stability
  D: Lagerfähigkeit *f* (Werkstoffe), Haltbarkeit *f* (Werkstoffe), Lagerungsbeständigkeit *f*
  F: limite *f* de stockage, stabilité *f* au stockage
storage tank
  D: Vorratsbehälter *m*
  F: réservoir *m*
straight-chain PE
  D: geradkettiges PE
  F: polyéthylène *m* à chaîne droite, polyéthylène *m* linéaire
straighten *v*
  D: recken *v*, spannen *v*, strecken *v*
  F: allonger *v*, étendre *v*, tendre *v*
straighten *v*
  D: richten *v* (Draht)
  F: redresser *v*
straightened cable sample
  D: gestrecktes Kabelmuster
  F: échantillon *m* de câble étiré
straight joint
  D: Durchgangsmuffe *f*
  F: jonction *f* droite
straight plug
  D: Geradeausstecker *m*
  F: fiche *f* droite

straight-through joint
  D: Durchgangsmuffe *f*
  F: jonction *f* droite
strain *v* [el., mech.]
  D: beanspruchen *v*, belasten *v*
  F: contraindre *v*, solliciter *v*, charger *v*
strain *n* [el., mech.]
  D: Beanspruchung *f*, Belastung *f*, Last *f*
  F: contrainte *f*, sollicitation *f*, charge *f*
strain-bearing element [cab.]
  D: Zugentlastung *f*
  F: allégement *m* de contrainte, élément *m* compensateur de traction
strain-bearing member [cab.]
  D: Zugentlastung *f*
  F: allégement *m* de contrainte, élément *m* compensateur de traction
strainer *n* [extr.]
  D: Siebeinsatz *m*
  F: plaque-filtre *f*
strain hardening
  D: Kaltverfestigung *f*
  F: écrouissage *m*
strain in the material [mech.]
  D: Spannung im Material
  F: tension *f* dans le matériau
strain relief [cab.]
  D: Zugentlastung *f*
  F: allégement *m* de contrainte, élément *m* compensateur de traction
strand *v*
  D: verseilen *v* (Leiter)
  F: câbler *v*
strand *v*
  D: verseilen *v* (Kabelseele)
  F: assembler *v*
strand *n*
  D: Litze *f*
  F: toron *m*, cordon *m*
strand *n* [cab.]
  D: Seil *n*
  F: câble *m*, corde *f*
stranded conductor
  D: mehrdrähtiger Leiter
  F: âme *f* câblée
stranded element
  D: Verseilelement *n*
  F: élément *m* de câblage, élément *m*

stranded hook-up wire
D: Schaltlitze f
F: fil m à brins multiples

stranded wire
D: Litze f
F: toron m, cordon m

strander n
D: Verseilmaschine f
F: câbleuse f, assembleuse f

stranding n
D: Verseilung f
F: câblage m, assemblage m

stranding, same lay ~
D: Verseilung im Gleichschlag
F: câblage m en même sens

stranding allowance
D: Drallzuschlag m
F: supplément m de torsion

stranding angle
D: Verseilwinkel m
F: angle m de câblage

stranding axis
D: Verseilachse f
F: axe m de câblage

stranding cabler (US)
D: Verseilmaschine f
F: câbleuse f, assembleuse f

stranding cage
D: Verseilkorb m
F: cage f d'assemblage

stranding cage disc
D: Laufkranz m
F: couronne f d'assemblage

stranding closer
D: Verseilnippel m
F: filière f d'assemblage, filière f de câblage

stranding element
D: Verseilelement n
F: élément m de câblage, élément m câblé, élément m d'assemblage

stranding flyer
D: Verseilbügel m, Jochbügel m
F: archet m de câblage, flyer m de câblage

stranding head
D: Verseilkopf m
F: tête f de câblage, tête f d'assemblage

stranding in layers
D: Lagenverseilung f
F: assemblage m par (en) couches, câblage m par (en) couches

stranding machine
D: Verseilmaschine f
F: câbleuse f, assembleuse f

stranding nipple
D: Verseilnippel m
F: filière f d'assemblage, filière f de câblage

stranding point
D: Verseilpunkt m
F: point m de câblage

stranding support
D: Verseilkopf m
F: tête f de câblage, tête f d'assemblage

stranding with backtwist
D: Verseilung mit Rückdrehung (Rundleiter), spannungslose Verseilung (Rundleiter)
F: câblage m à détorsion

stranding without backtwist
D: Verseilung ohne Rückdrehung
F: câblage m sans détorsion

stranding without pretwist
D: gestreckte Verseilung
F: câblage m sans prétorsion

stranding with pretwist
D: Verseilung mit Vordrall (Sektorleiter), spannungslose Verseilung (Sektorleiter)
F: câblage m à préformage, câblage m à prétorsion

strand shield
D: Leiterdeckschicht f (schwachleitend), Leiterglättung f, Schirm (schwachleitend) über dem Leiter, innere Leitschicht
F: écran m sur l'âme, écran m interne, couche f semi-conductrice interne

straw-rope stranding
D: Strohverseilung f
F: câblage m en tortillon de paille

stray current
D: Ableit(ungs)strom m, Fehlerstrom m, Streustrom m, vagabundierender Strom, Verluststrom m
F: courant m de fuite, courant m de défaut, courant m vagabond

streamer n
D: Entladungskanal m
F: voie f de décharge

strength n

strength
  D: Beständigkeit f, Festigkeit f, Widerstandsfähigkeit f
  F: résistance f, stabilité f, tenue f
strength n [mech.]
  D: Stärke f
  F: puissance f, force f
strengthening n [mech.]
  D: Verstärkung f
  F: renforcement m
strength member [com. c.]
  D: Tragorgan n
  F: élément m de support
stress v [el., mech.]
  D: beanspruchen v, belasten v
  F: contraindre v, solliciter v, charger v
stress n [el., mech.]
  D: Beanspruchung f, Belastung f, Last f
  F: contrainte f, sollicitation f, charge f
stress concentration
  D: Beanspruchungshäufung f
  F: concentration f de contraintes
stress concentrations [el.]
  D: Feldkonzentrationen f pl
  F: concentrations f pl du champ électrique
stress cone [c. access.]
  D: feldsteuerndes Element, Steuerelement n, Wickelkeule f
  F: cône m de contrainte
stress control [el.]
  D: Feldsteuerung f, Feldregulierung f
  F: orientation f du champ électrique, régularisation f du champ électrique, régulation f du champ électrique
stress-controlling adj [el.]
  D: feldsteuernd adj
  F: orientant adj le champ électrique
stress cracking
  D: Ermüdungsbruch m
  F: cassure f de fatigue, rupture f de fatigue
stress cracking, environmental ~ [plast.]
  D: Spannungsrißbildung f pl
  F: fissuration f de contact, fissuration f sous contrainte
stress cracking resistance
  D: Spannungsrißbeständigkeit f
  F: résistance f à la fissuration sous contrainte, résistance f à la fissuration de contact

stress distribution [el.]
  D: Feldverteilung f
  F: répartition f du champ électrique, distribution f du champ électrique
stress grading [el.]
  D: Feldverteilung f
  F: répartition f du champ électrique, distribution f du champ électrique
stress relief [el.]
  D: Feldsteuerung f, Feldregulierung f
  F: orientation f du champ électrique, régularisation f du champ électrique, régulation f du champ électrique
stress relief ring [c. access.]
  D: Strahlungsring m
  F: anneau m de répartition du champ électrique
stress-relieving annealing
  D: Entspannungsglühen n
  F: recuit m de détente
stress-strain curve
  D: Dehnungs-Spannungs-Kurve f, Zug-Dehnungskurve f
  F: courbe f de tension-allongement
stretch
  D: recken v, spannen v, strecken v
  F: allonger v, étendre v, tendre v
stretch n
  D: elastische Dehnung
  F: allongement m élastique
stretching of the conductor
  D: Reckung des Leiters
  F: étirage m du conducteur
strict control
  D: strenge Prüfung
  F: essai m rigoureux, contrôle m serré, contrôle m rigoureux, contrôle m sévère
string n
  D: Kordel f
  F: ficelle f, cordelette f
stringent test
  D: strenge Prüfung
  F: essai m rigoureux, contrôle m serré, contrôle m rigoureux, contrôle m sévère
stringing-up n
  D: Einfädeln n (Drahtziehmaschine)
  F: enfilage m
string spinning
  D: Kordelbespinnung f
  F: guipage m

string spinning machine
D: Kordelspinnmaschine f
F: guipeuse f

strip n
D: Band n
F: ruban m, bande f

strip n
D: Profildraht m
F: brin m profilé, fil m profilé

strip, to ~ the cable sheath
D: abmanteln v
F: enlever v la gaine du câble, dépouiller v la gaine du câble

strip, to ~ the insulation
D: abisolieren v
F: dénuder v, désisoler v

strip chart recorder
D: Bandschreiber m
F: enregistreur m à papier déroulant

stripper, cable ~
D: Abisoliermaschine f
F: machine f à dénuder

stripping, cable ~ knife
D: Kabelmesser n
F: couteau m pour câbles

stripping, sheath ~ machine
D: Mantelabstreifmaschine f
F: dépouilleuse f de gaine

stripping device
D: Abstreifer m (an der Armiermaschine)
F: râcloir m

stripping of the conductor
D: Freilegen des Leiters
F: dénudage m du conducteur

stroke, piston ~
D: Kolbenhub m
F: course f de piston

structural return loss
D: Rückflußdämpfung f
F: affaiblissement m de régularité

structural steel
D: Konstruktionsstahl m
F: acier m de construction

stub cable
D: Abzweigkabel n
F: câble m de branchement, câble m de dérivation

stub cable
D: Kabelstumpf m
F: bout m de câble

stuffing box
D: Stopfbüchse f
F: presse-étoupe f

sturdy adj
D: unempfindlich adj, kräftig adj, robust adj
F: robuste adj

styrene butadiene rubber (SBR)
D: Styrol-Butadien-Kautschuk m
F: caoutchouc m styrène butadiène

Styroflex-helix n [cab.]
D: Styroflex-Wendel f
F: spirale f de Styroflex

Styroflex-insulated wire
D: Styroflex-isolierte Ader
F: conducteur m isolé au Styroflex

subcritical annealing
D: Rekristallisationsglühung f
F: recuit m de récristallisation

subdivide v
D: unterteilen v
F: subdiviser v, sectionner v

submarine cable
D: Seekabel n, Unterwasserkabel n
F: câble m sous-marin

submarine coaxial cable
D: Seekoaxialkabel n
F: câble m coaxial sousmarin

submarine laying
D: Unterwasserverlegung f
F: pose f sous-marine

submerged-pump cable
D: Tauchpumpenleitung f
F: câble m pour pompe immergée

submerged repeater
D: Unterseeverstärker m, Unterwasserverstärker m, Seekabelverstärker m
F: répéteur m immergé

submersible-pump cable
D: Tauchpumpenleitung f
F: câble m pour pompe immergée

subscriber n [tel.]
D: Teilnehmer m
F: abonné m

subscriber('s) cable
D: Teilnehmer-Anschlußkabel n, Teilnehmer-Ortskabel n, Teilnehmer-Kabel n, Ortskabel n
F: câble m urbain, câble m d'abonné

subscriber('s) drop wire
D: Teilnehmer-Anschlußleitung f, Hauszuführungsleitung f, Teilnehmereinführungsleitung f, Einführungsleitung f,

subscriber('s)
  Einführungsdraht m,
  Fernsprechteilnehmerleitung f
  F: ligne f d'abonné téléphonique
  (raccord à la ligne aérienne), ligne f
  de desserte d'abonné, fil m d'entrée
  d'abonné

subscriber's line [tel.]
  D: Anschlußleitung f,
  Hausanschlußleitung f
  F: ligne f d'abonné

subscriber's station
  D: Teilnehmeranschluß m
  F: poste m d'abonné

subsidence of ground
  D: Bodensenkung f, Senkung des Erdbodens
  F: tassement m de terre

subsoil water [c. install.]
  D: Grundwasser n
  F: eau f souterraine, nappe f d'eau souterraine

substance n (paper weight in g/m²)
  D: Flächengewicht n (Papier)
  F: grammage m

substation n
  D: Umspannwerk n
  F: sous-station f, poste m de transformation

substitute v
  D: ersetzen v
  F: remplacer v, substituer v

substitute n
  D: Ersatzmaterial n
  F: matériau m de remplacement

subsurface installation
  D: Unterflur-Installation f
  F: installation f en sous-sol, installation f souterraine

sub-unit n [com. c.]
  D: Grundbündel n
  F: faisceau m élémentaire, faisceau m de base

sub-zero properties
  D: Kälteeigenschaften unter 0 °C
  F: caractéristiques f pl aux températures en dessous de zéro

suck v
  D: ansaugen v, absaugen v
  F: aspirer v

suction n
  D: Absaugung f
  F: exhaustion f, aspiration f

suction hood
  D: Absaughaube f
  F: collecteur m de fumées

suction line
  D: Saugleitung f
  F: tubulure f d'aspiration, conduite f d'aspiration

suction pipe
  D: Absaugrohr n
  F: tube m d'aspiration

suction system
  D: Absauganlage f
  F: installation f d'aspiration

suitability n
  D: Eignung f
  F: aptitude f, qualification f

sulphur cross-linking
  D: Schwefelvernetzung f
  F: réticulation f au soufre

sulphur hexafluoride (SF₆)
  D: Schwefelhexafluorid (SF₆) n
  F: hexafluorure f de soufre (SF₆)

sump n
  D: Sammelbehälter m, Auffangbehälter m
  F: bâche f

sun-crack
  D: Lichtriß m
  F: craquelure f due à l'effet de la lumière

sun-cracking
  D: Lichtrißbildung f
  F: fissuration f sous l'effet de la lumière solaire

sun-cracking inhibitor
  D: Lichtschutzmittel n
  F: stabilisant m contre l'effet de la lumière

superconducting adj
  D: supraleitend adj
  F: supraconducteur adj (-trice)

superconducting cable
  D: Supraleiterkabel n
  F: câble m supraconducteur

superconductive adj
  D: supraleitend adj
  F: supraconducteur adj (-trice)

superconductivity n
  D: Supraleitung f
  F: supraconductibilité f

superconductor n
  D: Supraleiter m
  F: supraconducteur m

super-fine wire

surface

D: Feinstdraht m
F: fil m super-fin, fil m extra-fin

super-fine wire conductor
D: feinstdrähtiger Leiter
F: âme f en fils extra-fins, âme f en fils super-fins

superimpose v
D: überlagern v
F: superposer v

superimposition n
D: Überlagerung f
F: superposition f

superpose v
D: überlagern v
F: superposer v

superposed circuit
D: Phantomkreis m, Phantomschaltung f, Viererkreis m, Kreisvierer m, Phantomleitung f
F: circuit m fantôme, circuit m superposé, circuit m combiné

superposed circuit [pow. c.]
D: überlagerter Stromkreis
F: circuit m superposé

superposition n
D: Überlagerung f
F: superposition f

supertension n
D: Höchstspannung f
F: très haute tension f (THT)

supertension cable
D: Höchstspannungskabel n
F: câble m à très haute tension (THT)

supervision n
D: Überwachung f
F: surveillance f

supply v [mech., el.]
D: speisen v, einspeisen v, beschicken v
F: alimenter v, charger v

supply length
D: Lieferlänge f
F: longueur f de livraison, longueur f de bobine

supply line
D: Zuleitung f
F: conducteur m d'amenée, conducteur m d'alimentation

supply network
D: Versorgungsnetz n
F: réseau m d'alimentation

supply reel
D: Ablaufspule f, Vorratstrommel f, Ablauftrommel f, Abwickeltrommel f
F: bobine f débitrice, bobine f d'alimentation, bobine f de dévidage

supply stand [wire manuf., cab.]
D: Ablaufbock m, Ablaufgestell n, Abwickelei f
F: bâti m départ, dévidoir m, dérouleur m

supply system
D: Versorgungsnetz n
F: réseau m d'alimentation

supply tank
D: Vorratsbehälter m
F: réservoir m

supply voltage
D: Speisespannung f
F: tension f d'alimentation

support n
D: Halterung f
F: support m

support helix
D: Stützwendel f (im Hohlleiter)
F: hélice f de support

supporting rack, cable ~
D: Kabelendgestell n, Endgestell für Kabel
F: bâti m pour têtes de câbles, bâti m terminal

supporting roller
D: Stützrolle f
F: galet m support, rouleau m d'appui

supporting strand [tel. c.]
D: Tragseil n, Luftkabeltragseil n
F: câble m porteur, corde f de suspension

supporting wire
D: Tragdraht m
F: fil m porteur, câble m de support

surface, on the ~ [c. install.]
D: auf Putz
F: à la surface, apparent adj, sur crépi

surface cracks
D: Oberflächenrisse m pl
F: craquelures f pl en surface

surface defect
D: Oberflächenfehler m
F: défaut m superficiel, défaut m de surface, imperfection f superficielle

surface discharge
D: Gleitentladung f
F: décharge f superficielle

surface finish
 D: Oberflächenbeschaffenheit f,
   Oberflächengüte f
 F: qualité f de surface
surface imperfection
 D: Oberflächenfehler m
 F: défaut m superficiel, défaut m de
   surface, imperfection f superficielle
surface irregularity
 D: Oberflächenfehler m
 F: défaut m superficiel, défaut m de
   surface, imperfection f superficielle
surface layer welding
 D: Auftragsschweißung f
 F: soudure f à superposition
surface leakage current
 D: Kriechstrom m
 F: courant m de fuite superficiel
surface losses
 D: Oberflächenverluste m pl
 F: pertes f pl superficielles
surface-mounted switch
 D: Aufputz-Schalter m
 F: interrupteur m monté sur crépi
surface mounting
 D: Aufputz-Installation f, Verlegung
   auf Putz
 F: pose f sur crépi, pose f apparente
surface of granular structure
 D: körnige Oberfläche
 F: surface f de structure granulaire
surface protection
 D: Oberflächenschutz m
 F: protection f superficielle
surface quality
 D: Oberflächenbeschaffenheit f,
   Oberflächengüte f
 F: qualité f de surface
surface resistance
 D: Oberflächenwiderstand m
 F: résistance f superficielle
surface resistivity
 D: spezifischer
   Oberflächenwiderstand
 F: résistivité f de surface
surface roughness
 D: Oberflächenrauhigkeit f
 F: rugosité f de la surface
surface transfer impedance
 D: Kopplungswiderstand m
 F: résistance f de couplage
surface treatment
 D: Oberflächenbehandlung f
 F: traitement m de surface
surge current
 D: Stoßstrom m
 F: courant m de choc
surge diverter
 D: Überspannungsableiter m
 F: parasurtension m
surge protection
 D: Überspannungsschutz m
 F: protection f contre les surtensions
surge resistance
 D: Stoßspannungsfestigkeit f
 F: résistance f aux ondes de choc,
   tenue f aux ondes de choc
surge test
 D: Stoßspannungs-Prüfung f,
   Stoßprüfung f (el.)
 F: essai m aux ondes de choc, essai m
   au choc
surge voltage
 D: Stoßspannung f
 F: tension f de choc
surge voltage arrester
 D: Überspannungsableiter m
 F: parasurtension m
surge voltage strength
 D: Stoßspannungsfestigkeit f
 F: résistance f aux ondes de choc,
   tenue f aux ondes de choc
survey v
 D: besichtigen v
 F: examiner v, inspecter v
susceptance n
 D: Blindleitwert m
 F: susceptance f
suspender, cable ~
 D: Tragband n (Luftkabel)
 F: bride f de suspension
suspension n
 D: Aufhängung f
 F: suspension f
suspension insulator
 D: Kettenisolator m, Hängeisolator m
 F: isolateur m suspendu, isolateur m
   de suspension
suspension polymerisation
 D: Suspensionspolymerisation f
 F: polymérisation f en suspension
suspension PVC
 D: Suspension-PVC n
 F: PVC m de suspension
suspension strand [pow. c.]
 D: Tragorgan n

F: élément *m* porteur, porteur *m*

suspension strand [tel. c.]
 D: Tragseil *n*, Luftkabeltragseil *n*
 F: câble *m* porteur, corde *f* de suspension

suspension unit [pow. c.]
 D: Tragorgan *n*
 F: élément *m* porteur, porteur *m*

suspension wire
 D: Tragdraht *m* (für Fahrdraht)
 F: fil *m* de suspension (pour fil de contact)

sustained load
 D: Dauerbelastung *f*, Dauerlast *f*
 F: charge *f* continue, charge *f* permanente

sustained short-circuit current
 D: Dauerkurzschlußstrom *m*
 F: courant *m* de court-circuit permanent

swell *v*
 D: quellen *v*
 F: enfler *v* (s'), gonfler *v* (se)

swelling, resistance to ~
 D: Quellbeständigkeit *f*
 F: résistance *f* au gonflement

swinging-out *n*
 D: Ausschwenken *n*
 F: pivotement *m*

swing-out arm
 D: Schwenkarm *m*
 F: bras *m* pivotant, bras *m* amovible

switch *v* [el.]
 D: schalten *v*
 F: connecter *v*, brancher *v*, monter *v*, relier *v*

switch *n*
 D: Schalter *m*
 F: interrupteur *m*, disjoncteur *m*

switchboard *n*
 D: Schalttafel *f*
 F: tableau *m* de distribution, tableau *m* de commande

switchboard cable
 D: Schaltkabel *n*
 F: câble *m* de connexion

switch gear
 D: Schaltanlage *f*
 F: installation *f* de distribution, disjoncteur *m*, installation *f* de commutation

switching equipment [com.]
 D: Vermittlungseinrichtung *f*
 F: équipement *m* de commutation

switching station
 D: Schaltanlage *f*
 F: installation *f* de distribution, disjoncteur *m*, installation *f* de commutation

switching surge
 D: Schaltüberspannung *f*
 F: surtension *f* de commutation, surtension *f* de manœuvre

switch off *v* [el.]
 D: abschalten *v*, ausschalten *v*
 F: couper *v*, interrompre *v*, déconnecter *v*

switch on *v* [el.]
 D: einschalten *v*, anschalten *v*
 F: enclencher *v* (él.), mettre *v* sous tension, fermer *v* (circuit), mettre *v* en circuit

switch-on time
 D: Einschaltdauer *f*
 F: facteur *m* de marche, durée *f* de mise en circuit

switch-over *n*
 D: Umschaltung *f*
 F: commutation *f*

switch through *v* [tel.]
 D: durchschalten *v*
 F: relier *v*, mettre *v* en communication

swivel arm
 D: Schwenkarm *m*
 F: bras *m* pivotant, bras *m* amovible

swivelling *adj*
 D: ausschwenkbar *adj*, ausklappbar *adj*, schwenkbar *adj*, aufklappbar *adj*, drehbar gelagert
 F: pivotant *adj*, articulé *adj*

swivelling-out *n*
 D: Ausschwenken *n*
 F: pivotement *m*

symbol rate [com. c.]
 D: Zeichengeschwindigkeit *f*
 F: vitesse *f* des symboles

symmetric pair
 D: symmetrisches Paar *n*
 F: paire *f* symétrique

synchronous speed regulating device
 D: Gleichlaufregler *m*
 F: régulateur *m* de synchronisation de vitesses

synthetic insulation
 D: Kunststoff-Isolierung *f*

synthetic

    F: isolant *m* plastique, isolant *m* synthétique

synthetic material
    D: Kunststoff *m*, Plast *m*
    F: matière *f* plastique, matière *f* synthétique, plastique *m*

synthetic resin
    D: Kunstharz *n*
    F: résine *f* synthétique, résine *f* de synthèse, résine *f* artificielle

synthetic resin
    D: Kunststoff *m*, Plast *m*
    F: matière *f* plastique, matière *f* synthétique, plastique *m*

synthetic resin-bonded fabric
    D: Hartgewebe *n*
    F: stratifié *m*, tissu *m* revêtu de résine synthétique

synthetic resin-bonded paper
    D: Hartpapier *n*
    F: papier *m* dur, papier *m* imprégné de résine synthétique

synthetic resin cement
    D: Kunstharzkitt *m*
    F: ciment *m* de résine synthétique

synthetic resin compound
    D: Kunststoff-Mischung *f*
    F: mélange *m* plastique

system *n* [el.]
    D: Netz *n*
    F: réseau *m*, secteur *m*

system-connected, non-~ *adj*
    D: netzunabhängig *adj*
    F: indépendant *adj* du réseau

system-dependent, non-~ *adj*
    D: netzunabhängig *adj*
    F: indépendant *adj* du réseau

system earthed at one end only
    D: einseitig geerdetes System
    F: réseau *m* mis à la terre d'un côté seulement

system fault
    D: Netzstörung *f*
    F: dérangement *m* sur réseau

system planning and operation
    D: Planung und Betrieb von Stromnetzen
    F: conception *f* et exploitation de réseaux électriques

system voltage
    D: Netzspannung *f*
    F: tension *f* de réseau, tension *f* du secteur

system with insulated neutral
    D: Netz mit isoliertem Sternpunkt
    F: réseau *m* avec neutre isolé

system with the cable sheaths connected across the joints
    D: durchverbundenes Kabelsystem
    F: réseau *m* de câbles dont les gaines sont reliées entre elles à travers les jonctions

SZ-stranding *n*
    D: SZ-Verseilung *f*
    F: câblage *m* SZ

T

tackiness *n*
    D: Haftvermögen *n*
    F: adhérence *f*, adhésivité *f*

tackiness *n*
    D: Klebrigkeit *f*
    F: glutinosité *f*, état *m* collant

take-off stand [wire manuf., cab.]
    D: Ablaufbock *m*, Ablaufgestell *n*, Abwickelei *f*
    F: bâti *m* départ, dévidoir *m*, dérouleur *m*

take up *v*
    D: aufwickeln *v*, aufspulen *v*, spulen *v*, wickeln *v*, auftrommeln *v*
    F: enrouler *v*, bobiner *v*

take-up *n*
    D: Aufwickelei *f*, Wickler *m*
    F: enrouleur *m*, bobinoir *m*

take-up reel
    D: Aufwickelspule *f*, Aufwickeltrommel *f*
    F: bobine *f* réceptrice

take-up stand
    D: Aufwickelei *f*, Wickler *m*
    F: enrouleur *m*, bobinoir *m*

take-up unit
    D: Aufwickelei *f*, Wickler *m*
    F: enrouleur *m*, bobinoir *m*

taking into commission
    D: Inbetriebnahme *f*
    F: mise *f* en oeuvre, mise *f* en service

taking of samples
    D: Probenahme *f*
    F: prélèvement *m* d'échantillons, échantillonnage *m*

taking pattern from
  D: in Anlehnung an
  F: suivant l'exemple de
talc *n*
  D: Talkum *n*
  F: talc *m*
talc powder
  D: Talkum *n*
  F: talc *m*
tandem annealer
  D: Durchlaufglühanlage *f* (gekoppelt mit Feindraht-Ziehmaschine), kontinuierliche Drahtzieh- und Glühanlage
  F: installation *f* de recuit en tandem, tréfileuse *f* et recuiseur en continu
tandem arrangement [mech.]
  D: Hintereinander-Schaltung *f*, Tandemanordnung *f*
  F: disposition *f* en tandem
tandem connection [mech.]
  D: Hintereinander-Schaltung *f*, Tandemanordnung *f*
  F: disposition *f* en tandem
tandemized operation
  D: Tandembetrieb *m*
  F: fonctionnement *m* en tandem, opération *f* en tandem
tandem wire drawing, annealing and insulating line
  D: kontinuierliche Drahtzieh-, Glüh- und Isolier-Anlage
  F: installation *f* continue de tréfilage, recuit et isolement
tangential joint
  D: Tangentialmuffe *f*, spitzwinklige Abzweigmuffe
  F: boîte *f* tangentielle
tangential lapper
  D: Tangentialspinner *m*
  F: rubaneuse *f* tangentielle
tangential type lapping machine
  D: Tangentialspinner *m*
  F: rubaneuse *f* tangentielle
tap *v*
  D: abzweigen *v*
  F: brancher *v*, dériver *v*
tap *n*
  D: Anzapfung *f*
  F: prise *f*
tape *v*
  D: umwickeln *v* (mit Band), bewickeln *v* (mit Band), umspinnen *v* (mit Band), wickeln *v* (Band)
  F: enrubanner *v*, rubaner *v*
tape *n*
  D: Band *n*
  F: ruban *m*, bande *f*
tape break
  D: Bandriß *m* (Papier)
  F: déchirure *f* du ruban, rupture *f* du ruban
tape break monitor
  D: Bandrißwächter *m* (Papier)
  F: détecteur *f* de rupture du ruban
taped covering
  D: gewickelte Umhüllung
  F: revêtement *m* rubané
taped inner covering
  D: gemeinsame gewickelte Aderumhüllung
  F: revêtement *m* interne rubané
taped insulation
  D: Bandisolierung *f*, gewickelte Isolierung
  F: isolation *f* rubanée
tape(d) wrapping
  D: Umspinnung *f* (mit Band), Bandumspinnung *f*, Bewicklung *f* (mit Band), Schmalbandwicklung *f*
  F: rubanage *m*
tape insulation
  D: Bandisolierung *f*, gewickelte Isolierung
  F: isolation *f* rubanée
tape lapping head
  D: Spinner *m* (Band), Spinnkopf *m* (Band), Bandwickler *m*
  F: tête *f* de rubanage, tête *f* rubaneuse
taper *n*
  D: Verjüngung *f*
  F: conicité *f*, cône *m*
taper, to ~ down the original dielectric (for jointing or repairing)
  D: die Isolierung zurückschneiden (an der Verbindungs- oder Reparaturstelle)
  F: couper *v* l'isolant coniquement
tapered *adj*
  D: verjüngt *adj*, konisch *adj*
  F: effilé *adj*, à section décroissante, conique *adj*
tapering *n*
  D: Verjüngung *f*
  F: conicité *f*, cône *m*
tap hole [met.]

tap

    D: Abstichöffnung f
    F: trou m de percée, trou m de coulée

taping n
    D: Umspinnung f (mit Band), Bandumspinnung f, Bewicklung f (mit Band), Schmalbandwicklung f
    F: rubanage m

taping machine
    D: Bandwickelmaschine f, Spinnmaschine f (Band)
    F: rubaneuse f

tap line
    D: Abzweigleitung f
    F: ligne f de branchement, ligne f de dérivation, dérivation f

tapping n
    D: Anzapfung f
    F: prise f

tapping-off unit
    D: Abgangskasten m
    F: coffret m de branchement

tar n
    D: Teer m
    F: goudron m

TAT cable (s. Transatlantic telephone cable)

T-connector n
    D: Abzweigklemme f
    F: borne f en forme de T, borne f de dérivation, té m de dérivation

tear v
    D: zerreißen v
    F: déchirer v

tear n
    D: Reißen n
    F: rupture f, déchirure f, déchirement m

tearing n
    D: Reißen n
    F: rupture f, déchirure f, déchirement m

tearing strength
    D: Einreißfestigkeit f, Weiterreißfestigkeit f
    F: résistance f au déchirement

tear resistance
    D: Einreißfestigkeit f, Weiterreißfestigkeit f
    F: résistance f au déchirement

tear resistance (from a nick)
    D: Kerbzähigkeit f
    F: résistance f au déchirement (à partir de l'entaille), dureté f à l'entaille

technique n
    D: Verfahren n, Methode f
    F: procédé m, méthode f, technique f

tee connector
    D: Abzweigklemme f
    F: borne f en forme de T, borne f de dérivation, té m de dérivation

tee-joint n
    D: T-Abzweigmuffe f
    F: jonction f en forme de T

tee-off fitting
    D: T-Abzweigmuffe f
    F: jonction f en forme de T

telecommunication n
    D: Fernmeldeverkehr m, Nachrichtenübermittlung f
    F: télécommunication f

telecommunications cable
    D: Fernmeldekabel n, Nachrichtenkabel n
    F: câble m de télécommunication, câble m de communication

telecommunications engineering
    D: Fernmeldetechnik f
    F: technique f de télécommunication

telecommunications network
    D: Fernmeldenetz n
    F: réseau m de télécommunication

telecommunications system
    D: Fernmeldenetz n
    F: réseau m de télécommunication

telecontrol n
    D: Fernsteuerung f, Fernbedienung f
    F: télécommande f, commande f à distance

telegraphic noise
    D: Telegrafiegeräusch n
    F: bruit m télégraphique

telemetering cable
    D: Fernmeßkabel n
    F: câble m de télémesure

telephone cable
    D: Fernsprechkabel n, Telefonkabel n
    F: câble m téléphonique

telephone cable pressurization
    D: Druckgasschutz und -überwachung von Telefonkabeln
    F: contrôle m des câbles téléphoniques à gaz comprimé

telephone call
    D: Telefongespräch n
    F: conversation f téléphonique

telephone central office
 D: Fernsprechamt n, Telefonzentrale f
 F: bureau m téléphonique, central m téléphonique

telephone channel
 D: Sprechkanal m, Fernsprechkanal m
 F: canal m téléphonique, voie f téléphonique

telephone circuit
 D: Fernsprechleitung f, Sprechkreis m
 F: circuit m téléphonique

telephone connection
 D: Fernsprechanschluß m
 F: abonnement m téléphonique, abonné m téléphonique

telephone conversation
 D: Telefongespräch n
 F: conversation f téléphonique

telephone current
 D: Sprechstrom m
 F: courant m téléphonique

telephone density [com.]
 D: Durchdringung f
 F: densité f téléphonique, densité f de lignes principales

telephone distribution cable
 D: Ortsverbindungskabel n, Ortsanschlußkabel n
 F: câble m téléphonique de réseau local

telephone drop
 D: Teilnehmer-Anschlußleitung f, Hauszuführungsleitung f, Teilnehmereinführungsleitung f, Einführungsleitung f, Einführungsdraht m, Fernsprechteilnehmerleitung f
 F: ligne f d'abonné téléphonique (raccord à la ligne aérienne), ligne f de desserte d'abonné, fil m d'entrée d'abonné

telephone exchange
 D: Fernsprechamt n, Telefonzentrale f
 F: bureau m téléphonique, central m téléphonique

telephone frequency
 D: Sprechfrequenz f, Fernsprechfrequenz f
 F: fréquence f vocale, fréquence f téléphonique

telephone instrument (US)
 D: Telefonapparat m, Sprechstelle f
 F: appareil m téléphonique, poste m téléphonique

telephone line
 D: Telefonleitung f
 F: ligne f téléphonique

telephone loop
 D: Fernsprechdoppelleitung f
 F: circuit m téléphonique bifilaire

telephone network
 D: Fernsprechnetz n, Telefonnetz n
 F: réseau m téléphonique

telephone set
 D: Telefonapparat m, Sprechstelle f
 F: appareil m téléphonique, poste m téléphonique

telephone station
 D: Telefonapparat m, Sprechstelle f
 F: appareil m téléphonique, poste m téléphonique

telephone system
 D: Fernsprechnetz n, Telefonnetz n
 F: réseau m téléphonique

telephone traffic
 D: Sprechverkehr m, Fernsprechverkehr m
 F: trafic m téléphonique

telescoped sample [cab.]
 D: Stufenmuster n
 F: échantillon m étagé

telescopic adj
 D: ausziehbar adj
 F: extensible adj, télescopique adj

telescoping tube [vulc.]
 D: Teleskop-Rohr n
 F: tube m télescopique

teletransmission n
 D: Fernübertragung f
 F: transmission f à grande distance

television, combined ~ telephone service
 D: Fernsehgegensprechen n
 F: service m téléphonique et télévision combiné

television channel
 D: Fernsehkanal m
 F: voie de télévision f

television transmission
 D: Fernsehübertragung f
 F: transmission f de télévision

telex network

telex
  D: Fernschreibnetz n, Telex-Netz n
  F: réseau m télex
tellurium n
  D: Tellur n
  F: tellure m
temper n [met.]
  D: Härtegrad m
  F: degré m de dureté
temperature coefficient
  D: Temperaturbeiwert m, Temperaturkoeffizient m
  F: coefficient m de température
temperature control
  D: Temperaturregelung f
  F: réglage m de la température
temperature control by a liquid medium [extr.]
  D: Flüssigkeitstemperierung f
  F: réglage m de la température par un liquide thermique
temperature controller
  D: Temperaturregler m, Thermostat m
  F: thermostat m, régulateur m de température
temperature decrease
  D: Temperaturabfall m, Abfall der Temperatur, Absinken der Temperatur
  F: chute f de température, baisse f de la température
temperature dependence
  D: Temperaturabhängigkeit f
  F: dépendance f de la température
temperature-dependent adj
  D: temperaturabhängig adj
  F: dépendant adj de la température, influencé adj par la température,
temperature difference
  D: Grädigkeit f (Temp.Untersch.zw. Kühlmedien), Temperaturspiel n
  F: différence f de température
temperature drop
  D: Temperaturabfall m, Abfall der Temperatur, Absinken der Temperatur
  F: chute f de température, baisse f de la température
temperature gradient
  D: Temperaturgefälle n
  F: gradient m de température, gradient m thermique
temperature increase
  D: Temperaturerhöhung f, Anstieg der Temperatur, Erwärmung f
  F: élévation f de température, montée f de température
temperature–independent adj
  D: temperaturunabhängig adj
  F: indépendant adj de la température
temperature indicator
  D: Temperaturanzeiger m
  F: indicateur m de température
temperature limit
  D: Grenztemperatur f
  F: température f limite
temperature measurement
  D: Temperaturmessung f
  F: mesure f de température
temperature pick-up
  D: Temperaturfühler m
  F: palpeur m de température, sonde f pyrométrique
temperature profile
  D: Temperaturprofil n
  F: profil m de température
temperature recorder
  D: Temperaturschreiber m
  F: enregistreur m de température
temperature regulator
  D: Temperaturregler m, Thermostat m
  F: thermostat m, régulateur m de température
temperature rise
  D: Temperaturerhöhung f, Anstieg der Temperatur, Erwärmung f
  F: élévation f de température, montée f de température
temperature sensor
  D: Temperaturfühler m
  F: palpeur m de température, sonde f pyrométrique
temperature zones
  D: Temperaturzonen f pl
  F: zones f pl de température
temporary circuit
  D: Versuchsschaltung f, Prüfstromkreis m
  F: montage m expérimental (él.), couplage m expérimental, circuit m d'essai
tensile strength
  D: Zugfestigkeit f
  F: résistance f à la traction
tensile strength (at break)

tensile strength test
D: Reißfestigkeit f, Zerreißfestigkeit f
F: résistance f à la rupture
tensile strength test
D: Prüfung der Zerreißfestigkeit, Zerreißprüfung f, Zugfestigkeitsprüfung f
F: essai m de traction
tensile strength testing machine
D: Zugfestigkeitsprüfer m, Zerreißfestigkeits-Prüfmaschine f
F: machine f à essayer la résistance à la traction, machine f de traction
tensile stress
D: Zugbeanspruchung f, Dehnungsbeanspruchung f
F: contrainte f de traction, effort m de traction
tensile stress, cable for high ~es
D: zugfestes Kabel
F: câble m pour grands efforts de traction
tensile test
D: Prüfung der Zerreißfestigkeit, Zerreißprüfung f, Zugfestigkeitsprüfung f
F: essai m de traction
tension n
D: Spannung f
F: tension f
tension n [mech.]
D: Zugspannung f
F: tension f de traction
tension and compression test
D: Zugdruckversuch m
F: essai m de traction/compression
tension compensating device
D: Zugspannungs-Regelvorrichtung f
F: dispositif m de régulation de la traction, dispositif m de compensation de la tension
tension compensator
D: Zugspannungs-Regelvorrichtung f
F: dispositif m de régulation de la traction, dispositif m de compensation de la tension
tension control device
D: Zugspannungs-Regelvorrichtung f
F: dispositif m de régulation de la traction, dispositif m de compensation de la tension
tension meter
D: Zugspannungsmeßvorrichtung f
F: dispositif m de mesure de la tension de traction
tension wheel
D: Spannrad n (Properzi-Gießmaschine)
F: roue f de serrage
tentatively adv
D: versuchsweise adv
F: à titre d'essai
tentative standard
D: Vornorm f
F: norme f provisoire
terminal n [el.]
D: Klemme f, Anschlußklemme f, Verbindungsklemme f, Endenanschlußklemme f
F: borne f, connecteur m, borne f de raccordement
terminal n
D: Endverschluß m, Endenabschluß m
F: extrémité f, accessoire m d'extrémité
terminal bell [c. access.]
D: Einführungstrichter m
F: cornet m d'entrée
terminal block [el.]
D: Anschlußleiste f, Klemmleiste f
F: bloc m de connexion, réglette f de raccordement, réglette f à bornes, barrette f à bornes
terminal board [el.]
D: Anschlußleiste f, Klemmleiste f
F: bloc m de connexion, réglette f de raccordement, réglette f à bornes, barrette f à bornes
terminal box [el.]
D: Anschlußkasten m, Klemmenkasten m
F: coffret m de distribution, boîte f de distribution, boîte f de dérivation, boîte f de connexion, coffret m de raccordement, boîte f de jonction, boîte f à bornes
terminal lug
D: Kabelschuh m, Kabel-Abschlußhülse f, Anschlußöse f, Anschlußlasche f
F: cosse f de câble, attache f de conducteur, cosse f terminale
terminal plate
D: Klemmplatte f
F: plaque f à bornes
terminal rack
D: Kabelendgestell n, Endgestell für

terminal   384

Kabel
F: bâti *m* pour têtes de câbles, bâti *m* terminal

terminal screw [el.]
D: Klemmschraube *f*, Schraubklemme *f*
F: vis *f* de borne, borne *f* à vis

terminal strip [el.]
D: Anschlußleiste *f*, Klemmleiste *f*
F: bloc *m* de connexion, réglette *f* de raccordement, réglette *f* à bornes, barrette *f* à bornes

terminal wires, single-ended ~
D: einseitig herausgeführte Anschlußdrähte
F: fils *m pl* de jonction unidirectionnels

terminate, to ~ cables on to electrical plant
D: Kabel in elektrische Anlagen einführen
F: introduire *v* les câbles dans des installations électriques

terminating rack, cable ~
D: Kabelendgestell *n*, Endgestell für Kabel
F: bâti *m* pour têtes de câbles, bâti *m* terminal

termination *n*
D: Endverschluß *m*, Endenabschluß *m*
F: extrémité *f*, accessoire *m* d'extrémité

termite attack
D: Termitenschäden *m pl*
F: détériorations *f pl* causées par les termites

test *v*
D: prüfen *v*
F: essayer *v*, vérifier *v*, contrôler *v*

test *n*
D: Versuch *m*, Prüfung *f* (Erprobung), Test *m*
F: essai *m*, épreuve *f*, expérience *f*

test, to ~ the continuity of a coating
D: einen Überzug auf Porenfreiheit prüfen
F: essayer *v* la continuité d'un revêtement

test(ing) arrangement
D: Testanordnung *f*, Prüfanordnung *f*, Versuchsanordnung *f*
F: montage *m* d'essai, montage *m* expérimental, disposition *f* d'essai

test bench
D: Prüfstand *m*
F: plate-forme *f* d'essai, poste *m* d'essai

test cable
D: Versuchskabel *n*
F: câble *m* expérimental, câble *m* d'essai

test cell
D: Prüfzelle *f*
F: logette *f* d'essai

test certificate
D: Prüfbescheinigung *f*
F: certificat *m* d'essai

test circuit
D: Versuchsschaltung *f*, Prüfstromkreis *m*
F: montage *m* expérimental (él.), couplage *m* expérimental, circuit *m* d'essai

test conditions
D: Versuchsbedingungen *f pl*, Prüfbedingungen *f pl*
F: conditions *f pl* d'expérience, conditions *f pl* d'essai

test(ing) conductor
D: Prüfader *f*, Prüfdraht *m*, Prüfleiter *m*, Hilfsader *f*
F: fil *m* d'essai, fil *m* pilote

test current
D: Prüfstrom *m*
F: courant *m* d'essai

test duration
D: Versuchsdauer *f*, Prüfdauer *f*
F: durée *f* d'expérience, durée *f* d'essai

test field
D: Prüffeld *n*
F: champ *m* d'essai

test floor
D: Prüfstand *m*
F: plate-forme *f* d'essai, poste *m* d'essai

testing device
D: Prüfeinrichtung *f*, Prüfgerät *n*, Prüfvorrichtung *f*
F: équipement *m* d'essai, dispositif *m* d'essai

testing equipment
D: Prüfeinrichtung *f*, Prüfgerät *n*, Prüfvorrichtung *f*
F: équipement *m* d'essai, dispositif *m* d'essai

testing of incoming materials

testing period
D: Versuchsdauer f, Prüfdauer f
F: durée f d'expérience, durée f d'essai

testing station
D: Prüfstelle f
F: institut m de certification, station f d'essai, organisme m d'approbation

testing time
D: Versuchsdauer f, Prüfdauer f
F: durée f d'expérience, durée f d'essai

test(ing) installation
D: Versuchsanlage f
F: installation f d'essai, installation f expérimentale

test length
D: Prüflänge f
F: longueur f d'essai

test line
D: Prüfleitung f
F: ligne f d'essai

test mark
D: Prüfkennzeichen n
F: marque f de contrôle

test method
D: Prüfmethode f
F: méthode f d'essai

test piece
D: Prüfstück n, Prüfkörper m
F: échantillon m, éprouvette f

test procedure
D: Prüfverfahren n
F: mode m d'essai

test report
D: Prüfbericht m, Prüfprotokoll n
F: procès-verbal m d'essai

test requirements
D: Prüfanforderungen f pl
F: exigences f pl d'essai

test result
D: Prüfergebnis n, Prüfbefund m, Versuchsergebnis n
F: résultat m d'essai

test room
D: Meßraum m
F: salle f de mesure

test run
D: Probelauf m
F: marche f d'essai

test sample
D: Prüfstück n, Prüfkörper m
F: échantillon m, éprouvette f

test set
D: Prüfeinrichtung f, Prüfgerät n, Prüfvorrichtung f
F: équipement m d'essai, dispositif m d'essai

test setup
D: Testanordnung f, Prüfanordnung f, Versuchsanordnung f
F: montage m d'essai, montage m expérimental, disposition f d'essai

test-shield, concentric ~
D: konzentrischer Prüfschirm
F: écran m d'essai concentrique

test specification
D: Prüfvorschrift f
F: règle f d'essai

test specimen
D: Prüfstück n, Prüfkörper m
F: échantillon m, éprouvette f

test stand
D: Prüfstand m
F: plate-forme f d'essai, poste m d'essai

test voltage
D: Prüfspannung f
F: tension f d'essai

test(ing) wire
D: Prüfader f, Prüfdraht m, Prüfleiter m, Hilfsader f
F: fil m d'essai, fil m pilote

test wire [com. c.]
D: Meßader f
F: fil m de test

textile tape
D: Gewebeband n, Textilband n
F: ruban m textile

textile tape with interwoven metal wires
D: Textilband mit eingewebten Metalldrähten
F: toile f métallisée

theoretical value
D: rechnerischer Wert
F: valeur f théorique

thermal ag(e)ing
D: Wärmealterung f
F: vieillissement m thermique

thermal barrier
D: Wärmeschutz m (über Kabelisolierung)
F: isolation f thermique

thermal behaviour

thermal

    D: Wärmeverhalten n
    F: comportement m à la chaleur

thermal classification
    D: Wärmeklasse f
    F: classe f d'isolement

thermal conductivity
    D: Wärmeleitfähigkeit f, thermische Leitfähigkeit
    F: conductivité f calorifique, conductibilité f thermique

thermal-curing adj
    D: warmhärtend adj
    F: thermodurcissable adj

thermal degradation
    D: Abbau m (Kautschuk), thermischer Abbau (Kautschuk)
    F: dégradation f thermique

thermal expansion coefficient
    D: Wärmeausdehnungskoeffizient m
    F: coefficient m de dilatation thermique

thermal gradient
    D: Temperaturgefälle n
    F: gradient m de température, gradient m thermique

thermal liquid control [extr.]
    D: Flüssigkeitstemperierung f
    F: réglage m de la température par un liquide thermique

thermal-oxidative decomposition, time until ~
    D: Standzeit f (von Mischungen)
    F: temps m jusqu'à la décomposition thermo-oxydative

thermal power station
    D: Wärmekraftwerk n
    F: centrale f thermique

thermal resistance
    D: Wärmebeständigkeit f, Hitzebeständigkeit f, Wärmestandfestigkeit f
    F: résistance f à la chaleur, résistance f thermique, stabilité f thermique

thermal resistance
    D: Wärmewiderstand m, Wärmedurchgangswiderstand m
    F: résistance f thermique

thermal resistivity of the soil
    D: spezifischer Wärmewiderstand des Bodens
    F: résistivité f thermique du sol

thermal shock
    D: Wärmeschock m
    F: choc m thermique

thermal stability
    D: Wärmebeständigkeit f, Hitzebeständigkeit f, Wärmestandfestigkeit f
    F: résistance f à la chaleur, résistance f thermique, stabilité f thermique

thermo-accelerated ag(e)ing
    D: durch Wärme beschleunigte Alterung
    F: vieillissement m thermo-accéléré

thermocouple n
    D: Thermoelement n
    F: thermocouple m, thermoélément m

thermooxidative degradation
    D: thermooxidativer Abbau
    F: dégradation f thermo-oxydative

thermoplastic-insulated building wire
    D: Kunststoff-Aderleitung f
    F: conducteur m isolé à matière plastique

thermoplastic materials
    D: Thermoplaste m pl
    F: matières f pl thermoplastiques

thermoplastics pl
    D: Thermoplaste m pl
    F: matières f pl thermoplastiques

thermosetting adj
    D: warmhärtend adj
    F: thermodurcissable adj

thermosetting adhesive
    D: warmhärtender Klebstoff
    F: colle f thermodurcissable

thermosetting plastics
    D: wärmehärtbare Kunststoffe
    F: matières f pl plastiques thermodurcissables

thermosetting resins
    D: wärmehärtbare Kunststoffe
    F: matières f pl plastiques thermodurcissables

thermosetting synthetic materials
    D: wärmehärtbare Kunststoffe
    F: matières f pl plastiques thermodurcissables

thermostat n
    D: Temperaturregler m, Thermostat m
    F: thermostat m, régulateur m de température

thickness n
    D: Dicke f

F: épaisseur f
thickness compensation
 D: Dickenausgleich m
 F: compensation f de l'épaisseur
thickness measurement
 D: Dickenmessung f
 F: mesure f d'épaisseur
thin-film insulated magnet wire
 D: Dünnschicht-Lackdraht m
 F: fil m verni en couche mince
thinner n
 D: Verdünnungsmittel n
 F: agent m de dilution, diluant m
thinning n
 D: Durchmesserverringerung f
 F: réduction f du diamètre, rétreint m
thin-wall coating
 D: dünnwandiger Überzug
 F: revêtement m mince
thin-wire cable, loaded ~
 D: bespultes dünndrähtiges Kabel
 F: câble m pupinisé avec âme en fils fins
third-circuits coupling
 D: Dritte-Kreise-Kopplung f
 F: couplage m de tiers circuits
Thomson bridge
 D: Thomson-(Doppel)brücke f
 F: pont m (double) de Thomson
thorough examination
 D: eingehende Prüfung
 F: essai m détaillé, examen m détaillé, contrôle m minutieux
threading-up
 D: Einfädeln n (Drahtziehmaschine)
 F: enfilage m
thread of the screw [extr.]
 D: Schneckengang m, Gewindegang der Schnecke, Schneckengewinde n
 F: filet m de la vis, pas m de la vis, spire f de la vis
three-and-a-half core cable
 D: Dreieinhalbleiterkabel n
 F: câble m à trois conducteurs et demi
three-bowl calender
 D: Dreiwalzenkalander m
 F: calandre f à trois cylindres, calandre f à trois rouleaux
three-conductor cable
 D: dreiadriges Kabel, Dreifachkabel n, Dreileiterkabel n
 F: câble m triphasé, câble m à trois conducteurs
three-core cable
 D: dreiadriges Kabel, Dreifachkabel n, Dreileiterkabel n
 F: câble m triphasé, câble m à trois conducteurs
three-core cord
 D: Drillingsleitung f
 F: conducteur m trifil
three-core oil-filled cable
 D: Zwickelölkabel n
 F: câble m triphasé à huile fluide
three-core oil-filled cable
 D: Dreileiterölkabel n
 F: câble m tripolaire à huile fluide
three-core single lead sheath cable
 D: Dreibleimantelkabel n, Dreimantelkabel n
 F: câble m triplomb, câble m triplomb trigaine
three-core termination
 D: Dreileiter-Endverschluß m
 F: boîte f d'extrémité tripolaire
three-phase adj
 D: dreipolig adj
 F: tripolaire adj
three-phase (current) cable
 D: Drehstromkabel n
 F: câble m à courant triphasé
three-phase current
 D: Drehstrom m
 F: courant m triphasé
three-phase fault
 D: dreipoliger Kurzschluß
 F: court-circuit m tripolaire
three-phase rectifier
 D: Dreiphasengleichrichter m
 F: redresseur m triphasé
three-phase system with neutral
 D: Drehstromnetz mit Nulleiter
 F: secteur m triphasé avec conducteur neutre
three-pole adj
 D: dreipolig adj
 F: tripolaire adj
three-roll calender
 D: Dreiwalzenkalander m
 F: calandre f à trois cylindres, calandre f à trois rouleaux
throat, feed ~ [extr.]
 D: Trichtermündung f
 F: embouchure f de trémie
throat, hopper ~ [extr.]

throat
  D: Trichtermündung f
  F: embouchure f de trémie
through circuit [tel.]
  D: Durchgangsleitung f
  F: ligne f de transit
through-hardening n
  D: Durchhärtung f
  F: durcissement m à cœur
through line [tel.]
  D: Durchgangsleitung f
  F: ligne f de transit
throughput n
  D: Durchsatz m
  F: débit m
through-traffic n [com.]
  D: Durchgangsverkehr m
  F: trafic m de transit
tie v [cab.]
  D: abbinden v
  F: lier v
tied in with
  D: gekoppelt mit
  F: lié adj à, couplé adj avec,
tie line cable [tel.]
  D: Querverbindungskabel n
  F: câble m de jonction transversal
tight fit
  D: Paßsitz m
  F: ajustement m
tight fit, giving a ~
  D: fest anliegend, festsitzend adj
  F: étant bien serré
tight fit, making a ~
  D: fest anliegend, festsitzend adj
  F: étant bien serré
tight-fitting adj
  D: fest anliegend, festsitzend adj
  F: étant bien serré
tightness n
  D: Abdichtung f, Dichtigkeit f
  F: étanchéité f
tightness control
  D: Dichtigkeitsprüfung f
  F: contrôle m d'étanchéité
tilt n
  D: Neigung f
  F: inclinaison f, basculement m
tiltable adj
  D: kippbar adj
  F: inclinable adj, basculant adj, renversable adj
tiltable rotary furnace
  D: kippbarer Drehtrommelofen
  F: four m tubulaire tournant basculant
tilt angle
  D: Neigungswinkel m
  F: angle m d'inclinaison
tilting n
  D: Neigung f
  F: inclinaison f, basculement m
tilting mixer
  D: Kippmischer m
  F: mélangeur m basculant, mélangeur m renversable
time and motion study
  D: Arbeitsstudie f
  F: étude f du travail
time constant
  D: Zeitkonstante f
  F: constante f de temps
time factor
  D: Zeitkonstante f
  F: constante f de temps
time-lag relay
  D: Verzögerungsrelais n
  F: relais m temporisé
time of cure
  D: Vulkanisationsdauer f
  F: durée f de vulcanisation
time of efflux
  D: Auslaufzeit f (Viskositätsmessung)
  F: temps m d'écoulement
timer n
  D: Zeitschalter m
  F: automate m temporisé
time study
  D: Zeitstudie f
  F: mesure f du travail
time switch
  D: Zeitschalter m
  F: automate m temporisé
time-tested adj
  D: bewährt adj
  F: éprouvé adj
time until thermal-oxidative decomposition
  D: Standzeit f (von Mischungen)
  F: temps m jusqu'à la décomposition thermo-oxydative
tin n
  D: Zinn n
  F: étain n
tin-coating n
  D: Verzinnung f
  F: étamage m
tinned copper braid [cab.]

tinned copper mesh [cab.]
D: Kupfer-Gestrickband *n* (verzinnt)
F: tresse *f* en cuivre étamé

tinned wire
D: verzinnter Draht
F: fil *m* étamé

tinning *n*
D: Verzinnung *f*
F: étamage *m*

tinning solder
D: Reibelot *n*, Lötzinn *n*
F: étain *m* à souder, étain *m* de soudage

tinsel conductor
D: Lahnlitzenleiter *m*
F: fil *m* rosette

tinsel cord
D: Litzenleitung *f*
F: cordon *m*, toron *m*

tinsel wire
D: Litzendraht *m*
F: fil *m* torsadé

tip *n* [extr.]
D: Nippel *m*
F: poinçon *m*

tip of a screw [extr.]
D: Schneckenspitze *f*
F: pointe *f* de la vis

titanium white
D: Titanweiß *n*
F: blanc *m* de titane

titer *n* (yarn count; unit: denier)
D: Titer *m* (Feinheitsmaß für Fasern/Garn; Einheit: Denier (den))
F: titre *m* de fil (numéro de fil; unité: denier)

T-joint *n*
D: T-Abzweigmuffe *f*
F: jonction *f* en forme de T

to-and-fro movement
D: Hin- und Herbewegung *f*
F: mouvement *m* de va-et-vient, mouvement *m* alternatif

tolerance *n*
D: Toleranz *f*
F: tolérance *f*

tolerance bandwith
D: Toleranzbereich *m*
F: gamme *f* de tolérances

tolerance range
D: Toleranzbereich *m*

F: gamme *f* de tolérances

toll cable (US)
D: Weitverkehrskabel *n*, Weitverkehrs-Telefonkabel *n*, Telefon-Fernkabel *n*, Bezirkskabel *n*
F: câble *m* téléphonique à grande distance, câble *m* interurbain

toll call (US)
D: Ferngespräch *n*
F: conversation *f* interurbaine

toll exchange (US)
D: Fernvermittlungsstelle *f*, Fernamt *n*
F: central *m* interurbain

toll network (US)
D: Weitverkehrsnetz *n*
F: réseau *m* de câbles à grande distance

tooling *n*
D: Werkzeugbestückung *f*
F: outillage *m*

tools *pl* [extr., met.extr.pr., wire manuf.]
D: Werkzeuge *n pl*
F: outils *m pl*

top hat (annealing) furnace
D: Haubenglühofen *m*, Blankglühofen *m*
F: four *m* à tremper, four *m* pour recuit brillant

top-pouring *n*
D: fallender Guß
F: coulée *f* en chute, coulée *f* en plan incliné

torsion *n*
D: Verdrehung *f*
F: torsion *f*, giration *f*

torsional rigidity
D: Torsionssteifheit *f*
F: rigidité *f* de torsion

torsional stress
D: Torsionsbeanspruchung *f*
F: contrainte *f* de torsion

torsion test
D: Torsionsprüfung *f*
F: essai *m* de torsion

total attenuation
D: Dämpfungsmaß *n*
F: unité *f* d'affaiblissement, équivalent *m* d'affaiblissement

total attenuation
D: Gesamtdämpfung *f*
F: atténuation *f* totale

total cable equivalent
 D: Gesamtdämpfung *f*
 F: atténuation *f* totale

total coupling
 D: Gesamtkopplung *f*
 F: couplage *m* total

total loss
 D: Gesamtdämpfung *f*
 F: atténuation *f* totale

total rated power
 D: installierte Leistung, Ausbauleistung *f*
 F: puissance *f* installée

total transmission equivalent
 D: Dämpfungsmaß *n*
 F: unité *f* d'affaiblissement, équivalent *m* d'affaiblissement

touch potential
 D: Berührungsspannung *f*
 F: tension *f* de contact

touch voltage
 D: Berührungsspannung *f*
 F: tension *f* de contact

toughness *n*
 D: Zähigkeit *f*
 F: ténacité *f*

tough-pitch copper (t.p.c.)
 D: zähgepoltes Kupfer
 F: cuivre *m* raffiné, cuivre *m* tenace

tough-rubber sheathed cable
 D: Gummischlauchleitung *f*
 F: câble *m* souple sous gaine de caoutchouc

tough-rubber, heavy ~ sheathed flexible cable
 D: schwere Gummischlauchleitung
 F: câble *m* souple sous gaine épaisse de caoutchouc

tough-rubber, ordinary ~ sheathed flexible cord
 D: leichte Gummischlauchleitung
 F: câble *m* souple sous gaine ordinaire de caoutchouc

tough-rubber sheathing compound
 D: Gummimantelmischung für starke Beanspruchung
 F: mélange *m* gaine de caoutchouc pour contraintes fortes

tour through the factory (GB)
 D: Werksbesichtigung *f*
 F: tour *m* de l'usine

t.p.c. (s. tough-pitch copper)

trace, to ~ a fault
 D: eine Störung suchen
 F: détecter *v* un défaut

tracer *n* (US)
 D: Aderkennzeichnung *f*
 F: repérage *m* des conducteurs

tracer colo(u)r
 D: Markierungsfarbe *f* (Aderkennzeichnung)
 F: couleur *f* de repérage

tracer gas
 D: Spürgas *n*
 F: gaz *m* détecteur

tracer pair [com. c.]
 D: Zählpaar *n*
 F: paire *f* de comptage

tracer thread
 D: Kennfaden *m*
 F: fil *m* d'identification, fil *m* distinctif, filin *m* de reconnaissance

tracer wire
 D: Zähler *f*
 F: fil *m* pilote, fil *m* compteur

tracking *n*
 D: Kriechwegbildung *f*
 F: cheminement *m*

track(ing) resistance
 D: Kriechstromfestigkeit *f*
 F: résistance *f* au cheminement

tractive force
 D: Zugkraft *f*
 F: effort *m* de traction, force *f* de traction

trademark *n*
 D: Firmenkennzeichen *n*
 F: marque *f* de fabrique, marque *f* du fabricant

trademark rights
 D: Schutzrechte *n pl*
 F: droits *m pl* de protection

trailer, cable ~
 D: Kabelwagen *m*, Kabeltrommel-Anhänger *m*
 F: chariot *m* à câbles, chariot *m* à touret de câble

trailing cable
 D: Schleppleitung *f*, Leitungstrosse *f*, Kabel zum Auftrommeln, Trommelleitung *f*
 F: câble *m* de remorque, câble *m* d'enrouleur, câble *m* pour engin mobile

Transatlantic telephone cable (TAT cable)

D: Transatlantik-Telefonkabel (TAT-Kabel) n
F: câble m téléphonique transatlantique

transfer device
D: Umlenkvorrichtung f
F: dispositif m de renvoi

transfer head
D: Umlenkkopf m
F: tête f de renvoi

transfer launder [c. c. r.]
D: Überführungsrinne f, Gießrinne f
F: rigole f de transfert, rigole f de coulée

transfer of heat
D: Wärmeübergang m, Wärmeübertragung f
F: transmission f calorifique, transmission f de chaleur

transfer trough [c. c. r.]
D: Überführungsrinne f, Gießrinne f
F: rigole f de transfert, rigole f de coulée

transformer n [com.]
D: Übertrager m
F: transformateur m, translateur m

transformer connection
D: Transformator-Einführung f
F: prise f de transformateur, raccord m de transformateur, entrée f de transformateur

transformer entry
D: Transformator-Einführung f
F: prise f de transformateur, raccord m de transformateur, entrée f de transformateur

transformer station
D: Umspannwerk n
F: sous-station f, poste m de transformation

transformer tap
D: Transformator-Anzapfung f
F: prise f de transformateur

transformer termination
D: Transformator-Einführung f
F: prise f de transformateur, raccord m de transformateur, entrée f de transformateur

transformer type cable termination
D: Transformatoreinführungs-Endverschluß m
F: extrémité f de câble pour transformateur

transforming station
D: Umspannwerk n
F: sous-station f, poste m de transformation

transient caused by switching
D: Schaltüberspannung f
F: surtension f de commutation, surtension f de manœuvre

transient conditions pl
D: Übergangsbetrieb m
F: régime m transitoire

transient current
D: Ausgleichsstrom m, Übergangsstrom m
F: courant m compensateur, courant m transitoire

transient operation
D: Übergangsbetrieb m
F: régime m transitoire

transient wave
D: Wanderwelle f
F: onde f progressive, onde f mobile

transition joint
D: Übergangsmuffe f
F: joint m de transition

transition resistance
D: Übergangswiderstand m
F: résistance f de contact, résistance f de passage

transition sleeve
D: Übergangsmuffe f
F: joint m de transition

transition temperature [plast.]
D: Umwandlungstemperatur f
F: température f de transformation

translator n [com.]
D: Übertrager m
F: transformateur m, translateur m

transmission n
D: Übertragung f
F: transmission f

transmission band-width
D: Übertragungsbandbreite f
F: largeur f de bande de transmission

transmission capacity
D: Übertragungskapazität f
F: capacité f de transport, capacité f de transmission

transmission channel
D: Übertragungsweg m, Übertragungskanal m
F: voie f de transmission, voie f de transport

transmission

transmission characteristics
D: Übertragungs-Eigenschaften f pl
F: caractéristiques f pl de transmission

transmission equations [com.]
D: Übertragungs-Gleichungen f pl
F: équations f pl de transmission

transmission gain [tel. c.]
D: Entdämpfung f
F: compensation f de l'affaiblissement, compensation f de l'amortissement

transmission line, balanced ~ [tel.]
D: ausgeglichene Übertragungsleitung
F: ligne f de transmission équilibrée

transmission loss
D: Übertragungsverlust m
F: perte f de transmission, perte f de transport

transmission loss [tel. c.]
D: Leitungsdämpfung f
F: affaiblissement m de la ligne

transmission path
D: Übertragungsweg m, Übertragungskanal m
F: voie f de transmission, voie f de transport

transmission power
D: Übertragungsleistung f, übertragbare Leistung
F: puissance f à transporter

transmission quality
D: Übertragungsgüte f, Übertragungsqualität f
F: qualité f de transmission

transmission ratio [mech.]
D: Übersetzungsverhältnis n
F: rapport m d'engrenage, rapport m de transmission

transmission route, electrical ~
D: elektrischer Übertragungsweg
F: voie f de transmission électrique

transmission shaft
D: Antriebswelle f
F: arbre m de commande

transmission system
D: Übertragungssystem n, Übertragungsnetz n
F: système m de transmission, réseau m de transmission, réseau m de transport

transmission voltage
D: Übertragungsspannung f
F: tension f de transmission, tension f de transport

transmit v
D: übertragen v
F: transporter v, transmettre v

Transpacific telephone cable (TRANSPAC cable)
D: Transpazifik-Kabel n
F: câble m téléphonique transpacifique

transpose v
D: kreuzen v (Drähte zum Induktionsschutz)
F: transposer v

transposed conductors
D: gekreuzte Adern
F: conducteurs m pl transposés

transposed cores
D: gekreuzte Adern
F: conducteurs m pl transposés

transposed transmission line [com. c.]
D: Leitung mit Kreuzungsausgleich
F: ligne f de transmission avec transpositions

transposition n [com.c.]
D: Platzwechsel m (bei einer Fernsprechfreileitung)
F: transposition f

transverse motion
D: Querbewegung f
F: mouvement m transversal

transverse voltage
D: Querspannung f
F: tension f transversale, composante f transversale d'une tension

trap circuit
D: Sperrkreis m
F: circuit-bouchon m

travel, direction of cable ~
D: Laufrichtung des Kabels durch eine Maschine
F: sens m de passage du câble

travelling crane
D: Laufkran m
F: pont m roulant

travelling wave
D: Wanderwelle f
F: onde f progressive, onde f mobile

traverser n
D: Verlegearm m (Aufwickelei), Verlegevorrichtung f (Aufwickelei), Verteiler m (Aufwickelei)

traversing speed
 D: Verlegegeschwindigkeit f (beim Aufspulen)
 F: vitesse f de trancanage

traversing unit
 D: Verlegearm m (Aufwickelei), Verlegevorrichtung f (Aufwickelei), Verteiler m (Aufwickelei)
 F: dispositif de trancanage m, palpeur-guide m

tray n
 D: Schürze f (Mischwalzwerk)
 F: plateau m

tray, cable ~ [c. install.]
 D: Kabelpritsche f, Kabeltraggerüst n, Pritsche f
 F: tablette f à câbles, charpente pour câbles f

treatment n
 D: Behandlung f
 F: traitement m

treeing n
 D: Bäumchenbildung f (in Isolierstoffen unter el. Beanspruchung)
 F: treeing m, arborescence f

trefoil arrangement [c.install.]
 D: Dreiecksanordnung f
 F: disposition f en triangle, disposition f en trèfle

trench, cable ~
 D: Kabelgraben m
 F: tranchée f de câble

trial n
 D: Versuch m, Prüfung f (Erprobung), Test m
 F: essai m, épreuve f, expérience f

trial-and-error experiments
 D: empirische Versuche
 F: essais m pl empiriques

trial cable
 D: Versuchskabel n
 F: câble m expérimental, câble m d'essai

trial installation
 D: Versuchsanlage f
 F: installation f d'essai, installation f expérimentale

trial length
 D: Versuchslänge f, Probelänge f, Prüflänge f
 F: longueur f d'essai

trial production
 D: Versuchsfertigung f, Probefertigung f
 F: essai m de fabrication, production f à l'échelle expérimentale

trial run
 D: Probelauf m
 F: marche f d'essai

trial stage
 D: Versuchsstadium n
 F: stade m expérimental

triangular arrangement [c.install.]
 D: Dreiecksanordnung f
 F: disposition f en triangle, disposition f en trèfle

triangular-shape cable
 D: Dreieck-verseiltes Kabel
 F: câble m assemblé en forme triangulaire

trifurcating box
 D: Verzweigungsmuffe für drei Adern, Aufteilungsmuffe für drei Adern, Gabelmuffe für drei Adern
 F: boîte f tri-mono, boîte f de trifurcation

trifurcating joint
 D: Verzweigungsmuffe für drei Adern, Aufteilungsmuffe für drei Adern, Gabelmuffe für drei Adern
 F: boîte f tri-mono, boîte f de trifurcation

trim v
 D: abgleichen v
 F: ajuster v, compenser v, accorder v

trim v
 D: köpfen v (Drahtenden), beschneiden v, abschneiden v
 F: couper v, rogner v, cisailler v

trimming n
 D: Abgleichung f
 F: ajustement m, compensation f, équilibrage m, accord m

trimming n
 D: Entgraten n
 F: ébarbage m, ébavurage m

triple n [tel. c.]
 D: Dreier m
 F: câble m téléphonique à trois conducteurs

triple concentric cable
 D: konzentrisches Dreileiterkabel

F: câble *m* triphasé concentrique
triple-core cable
D: dreiadriges Kabel, Dreifachkabel *n*, Dreileiterkabel *n*
F: câble *m* triphasé, câble *m* à trois conducteurs
triple extruder head [extr.]
D: Dreifach-Spritzkopf *m*, Dreifach-Kopf *m*
F: tête *f* triple de boudineuse, tête *f* triple extrusion
triple extrusion
D: Dreifach-Extrusion *f*
F: extrusion *f* triple
tripping current
D: Auslösestrom *m*
F: courant *m* de déclenchement
trolley, cable ~
D: Kabelwagen *m*, Kabeltrommel-Anhänger *m*
F: chariot *m* à câbles, chariot *m* à touret de câble
trolley wire
D: Fahrdraht *m*, Schleifdraht *m*
F: fil *m* (de) trolley, fil *m* de contact
tropicalized *adj*
D: tropenfest *adj*
F: tropicalisé *adj*, résistant *adj* aux conditions tropicales,
tropic-proof *adj*
D: tropenfest *adj*
F: tropicalisé *adj*, résistant *adj* aux conditions tropicales,
trouble finding
D: Fehlersuche *f*, Fehlerortsbestimmung *f*, Fehlerortung *f*, Auffindung einer Störstelle
F: localisation *f* d'un défaut
trouble shooting (US)
D: Fehlersuche *f*, Fehlerortsbestimmung *f*, Fehlerortung *f*, Auffindung einer Störstelle
F: localisation *f* d'un défaut
trough
D: Trog *m*, Wanne *f*
F: bac *m*, cuve *f*, goulotte *f*
trough mixer
D: Trogmischer *m*
F: mélangeur *m* à cuve
true to size
D: maßhaltig *adj*, maßgerecht *adj*

F: à dimensions exactes, conforme *adj* à l'échelle,
trunk cable (GB)
D: Weitverkehrskabel *n*, Weitverkehrs-Telefonkabel *n*, Telefon-Fernkabel *n*, Bezirkskabel *n*
F: câble *m* téléphonique à grande distance, câble *m* interurbain
trunk call (GB)
D: Ferngespräch *n*
F: conversation *f* interurbaine
trunk exchange
D: Fernvermittlungsstelle *f*, Fernamt *n*
F: central *m* interurbain
trunk network
D: Weitverkehrsnetz *n*
F: réseau *m* de câbles à grande distance
tube *n*
D: Rohr *n*
F: tube *m*, tuyau *m*
tube *n* [com. c.]
D: Tube *f*
F: tube *m*
tube forming tool
D: Rohrformwerkzeug *n*
F: outil *m* pour le formage de tuyaux
tube-on method [extr.]
D: Schlauchreckverfahren *n*
F: extrusion *f* cône avec vide sur le poinçon, boudinage *m* sous vide
tube pole, tapered ~
D: nach oben verjüngter Rohrmast
F: poteau *m* tubulaire à section décroissante
tube strander
D: Rohrverseilmaschine *f*
F: toronneuse *f* tubulaire
tubing extrusion [extr.]
D: Schlauchreckverfahren *n*
F: extrusion *f* cône avec vide sur le poinçon, boudinage *m* sous vide
tubular mast, tapered ~
D: nach oben verjüngter Rohrmast
F: poteau *m* tubulaire à section décroissante
tubular stranding machine
D: Rohrverseilmaschine *f*
F: toronneuse *f* tubulaire
tubular test piece
D: schlauchförmiges Prüfstück

tundish *n*[c.c.r.]
  D: Gießpfanne *f,* Gießtopf *m*
  F: poche *f* de coulée
tune *v*
  D: abgleichen *v*
  F: ajuster *v,* compenser *v,* accorder *v*
tune *v*[contr.]
  D: abstimmen *v*
  F: accorder *v,* régler *v*
tungsten carbide (drawing) die
  D: Hartmetall-Ziehstein *m*
  F: filière *f* (de tréfilage) en métal dur, filière *f* (de tréfilage) en carbure de tungstène
tuning *n*
  D: Abgleichung *f*
  F: ajustement *m,* compensation *f,* équilibrage *m,* accord *m*
tuning *n*[contr.]
  D: Abstimmung *f*
  F: accord *m,* réglage *m*
turn *n*
  D: Windung *f*
  F: spire *f*
turnkey installation
  D: schlüsselfertige Anlage
  F: installation *f* (achevée) clé en main
turn off (US) *v*[el.]
  D: abschalten *v,* ausschalten *v*
  F: couper *v,* interrompre *v,* déconnecter *v*
turn on (US) *v*[el.]
  D: einschalten *v,* anschalten *v*
  F: enclencher *v* (él.), mettre *v* sous tension, fermer *v* (circuit), mettre *v* en circuit
twin *adj*
  D: doppeladrig *adj*
  F: bifilaire *adj*
twin cable [com. c.]
  D: paarverseiltes Kabel, paarig verseiltes Kabel
  F: câble *m* à paires, câble *m* jumelé, câble *m* pairé
twin cable
  D: doppeladriges Kabel
  F: câble *m* biphasé, câble *m* à deux conducteurs
twin (extruder) head
  D: Zweifach-Spritzkopf *m,* Doppelkopf *m*
  F: tête *f* double de boudineuse, tête *f* double extrusion
twin-head extrusion
  D: Doppelkopf-Extrusion *f,* Zweifach-Extrusion *f*
  F: extrusion *f* tête double
twin-layer *adj*
  D: doppellagig *adj*
  F: en double couche, en deux couches
twinning *n*
  D: Paarverseilung *f*
  F: pairage *m,* assemblage *m* par paires
twinning machine
  D: Paarverseilmaschine *f*
  F: paireuse *f*
twin-ram cable sheathing press
  D: Doppelstempel-Kabelmantelpresse *f*
  F: presse *f* de gainage à fouloir double
twin-ram press
  D: Doppelstempel-Presse *f*
  F: presse *f* à fouloir double
twin-wire *n*[com. c.]
  D: Doppelader *f,* paarverseilte Leitung, Paar *n*
  F: paire *f,* fil *m* double, conducteur *m* jumelé
twin-wire paper-making machine
  D: Doppellangsieb-Papiermaschine *f*
  F: machine *f* à papier à toile double sans fin
twist *v*
  D: verdrillen *v*
  F: torsader *v*
twist *n*
  D: Verdrehung *f*
  F: torsion *f,* giration *f*
twist *n*[strand.]
  D: Drall *m,* Schlag *m*
  F: pas *m,* torsion *f*
twist changing gear
  D: Drallwechselgetriebe *n*
  F: variateur *m* de torsion
twist changing point
  D: Drallwechselstelle *f*
  F: point *m* d'inversion de la torsion, point *m* de changement de la torsion
twist compensator
  D: Drall-Ausgleichsvorrichtung *f*
  F: compensateur *m* de torsion
twister *n*
  D: Verseilmaschine *f*

twister

F: câbleuse f, assembleuse f

twisting n
D: Verseilung f
F: câblage m, assemblage m

twisting closer
D: Verseilnippel m
F: filière f d'assemblage, filière f de câblage

twisting flyer
D: Verseilbügel m, Jochbügel m
F: archet m de câblage, flyer m de câblage

twisting section [strand.]
D: Tordierstrecke f
F: distance f de torsion

twisting test
D: Torsionsprüfung f
F: essai m de torsion

two-column type metal extrusion press
D: Strangpresse in Zweisäulenbauart
F: presse f à filer type à deux colonnes

two-conductor cable (US)
D: doppeladriges Kabel
F: câble m biphasé, câble m à deux conducteurs

two-phase fault
D: zweipoliger Kurzschluß
F: court-circuit m bipolaire

two-piece adj
D: zweigeteilt adj, zweiteilig adj, geteilt adj
F: en deux pièces, divisé adj

two-roller mill
D: Zweiwalzenmischwerk n
F: malaxeur m à deux cylindres

two-way telephone conversation
D: Doppelsprechen n
F: téléphonie f fantôme, téléphonie f duplex

two-wire telephone circuit
D: Fernsprechdoppelleitung f
F: circuit m téléphonique bifilaire

type n [cab.]
D: Bauart f, Typ m
F: construction f, type m

type designation
D: Typenbezeichnung f, Typenkurzzeichen n
F: code m de désignation

type of service
D: Betriebsart f
F: mode m d'exploitation, régime m de marche

type spectrum
D: Typenspektrum n
F: gamme f de types, éventail m de types

type test
D: Typprüfung f
F: essai m de type

U

UHV (s. ultra-high voltage)

ultimate elongation
D: Bruchdehnung f, Reißdehnung f
F: allongement m à la rupture

ultimate load
D: Grenzleistung f, Belastungsgrenze f
F: charge f limite

ultimate load
D: Bruchlast f
F: charge f de rupture

ultimate tensile strength
D: Reißfestigkeit f, Zerreißfestigkeit f
F: résistance f à la rupture

ultra-high voltage (UHV)
D: Ultra-Hochspannung f
F: ultra-haute tension f (UHT)

umbrella type insulator
D: Schirmisolator m
F: isolateur m type parapluie

unbalance n
D: Unsymmetrie f
F: déséquilibre m, asymétrie f, dissymétrie f

unbalance(d) current
D: Nebensprechstrom m
F: courant m diaphonique

unbalance level
D: Kopplungsniveau n
F: niveau m de couplage

unbalance to ground
D: Erdkopplung f
F: déséquilibre m par rapport à la terre

uncoil v
D: abwickeln v, abspulen v
F: dérouler v, dévider v

uncoloured plastic
D: ungefärbter Kunststoff, farbloser Kunststoff

uncouple v
D: entkoppeln v
F: neutraliser v, désaccoupler v

undamaged adj
D: unbeschädigt adj
F: intact adj

underground cable
D: Erdkabel n
F: câble m souterrain

underground cable system
D: unterirdisches Kabelnetz
F: réseau m de câbles souterrain

underground laying
D: Verlegung in Erde, Erdverlegung f
F: pose f en pleine terre, pose f souterraine

underground power station
D: Kavernenkraftwerk n
F: centrale f hydroélectrique souterraine

underwater amplifier
D: Unterseeverstärker m, Unterwasserverstärker m, Seekabelverstärker m
F: répéteur m immergé

underwater pipe [c. install.]
D: Rohrdüker m
F: tuyau m placé en lit de canal

unearthed neutral (GB)
D: nicht geerdeter Sternpunkt (Nullpunkt)
F: neutre m non mis à la terre

uneven adj
D: uneben adj
F: inégal adj, non plan adj

unexamined patent application
D: Offenlegungsschrift f
F: demande f de brevet non examinée

unfinished adj
D: unbearbeitet adj
F: non travaillé adj, non usiné adj

ungrounded neutral (US)
D: nicht geerdeter Sternpunkt (Nullpunkt)
F: neutre m non mis à la terre

unification n
D: Normung f, Vereinheitlichung f
F: standardisation f, normalisation f, unification f

F: matière f plastique de couleur naturelle, matière f plastique non colorée, matière f plastique incolore

uniform adj
D: einheitlich adj
F: homogène adj, uniforme adj

uniform distribution
D: gleichmäßige Verteilung
F: répartition f uniforme

unilateral drive
D: einseitiger Antrieb
F: commande f unilatérale

unintelligible (non linear) cross-talk
D: unverständliches (nicht lineares) Nebensprechen
F: diaphonie f inintelligible (non linéaire)

unit n
D: Aggregat n
F: agrégat m, groupe m

unit n [mach.]
D: Anlage f
F: installation f

unit n [com. c.]
D: Bündel n
F: faisceau m

unit binder
D: Bündel-Spinner m
F: tête f à lier les faisceaux

unit binder
D: Bündel-Haltewendel f
F: frettage m sur faisceaux

unit cable
D: Bündelkabel n, bündelverseiltes Kabel
F: câble m en faisceaux, câble m à conducteurs en faisceaux

unit capacity factor [mach.]
D: Ausnutzungsgrad m
F: coefficient m d'utilisation

unit lay-up
D: Bündelverseilung f
F: assemblage m par faisceaux, câblage m par faisceaux

unit-stranded cable
D: Bündelkabel n, bündelverseiltes Kabel
F: câble m en faisceaux, câble m à conducteurs en faisceaux

unit stranding
D: Bündelverseilung f
F: assemblage m par faisceaux, câblage m par faisceaux

unit stranding machine
D: Bündelverseilmaschine f
F: tordeuse f

unit-type stranded cable
  D: Bündelkabel n, bündelverseiltes Kabel
  F: câble m en faisceaux, câble m à conducteurs en faisceaux

unloaded adj[tel. c.]
  D: unbelastet adj, unbespult adj
  F: non chargé adj, non pupinisé adj

unloaded balanced line
  D: unbespulte symmetrische Leitung
  F: ligne f symétrique non pupinisée, ligne f symétrique non chargée

unloaded thin wire cable [tel. c.]
  D: unbelastetes dünndrähtiges Kabel
  F: câble m non chargé avec âme en fils fins

unloading n
  D: Entleeren n
  F: vidage m, vidange f, évacuation f

unmachined adj
  D: unbearbeitet adj
  F: non travaillé adj, non usiné adj

unpigmented plastic
  D: ungefärbter Kunststoff, farbloser Kunststoff
  F: matière f plastique de couleur naturelle, matière f plastique non colorée, matière f plastique incolore

unreeling n[cab.]
  D: Abtrommeln n
  F: déroulement m

unscreened cable
  D: ungeschirmtes Kabel
  F: câble m sans écran

unscrew v
  D: abschrauben v
  F: dévisser v

unserviceable adj
  D: betriebsuntauglich adj
  F: inutilisable adj

unskilled worker
  D: ungelernter Arbeiter
  F: ouvrier m non qualifié, manœuvre m

unsymmetry n
  D: Unsymmetrie f
  F: déséquilibre m, asymétrie f, dissymétrie f

unsystematic coupling
  D: unsystematische Kopplung
  F: couplage m non systématique

untight adj
  D: undicht adj
  F: non étanche adj

untreated adj
  D: unbearbeitet adj
  F: non travaillé adj, non usiné adj

untwist v
  D: aufkorben v (Armierungsdrähte), aufdrehen v (sich)
  F: détordre v (se)

unweighted noise voltage
  D: Fremdspannung f
  F: tension f non pondérée

unwind v
  D: abwickeln v, abspulen v
  F: dérouler v, dévider v

unwind v
  D: aufkorben v (Armierungsdrähte), aufdrehen v (sich)
  F: détordre v (se)

unwinding n[cab.]
  D: Abtrommeln n
  F: déroulement m

upstream adv
  D: entgegengesetzt der Fertigungsrichtung
  F: en amont

urban network [el.]
  D: Stadtnetz n
  F: réseau m urbain

urban supply system [el.]
  D: Stadtnetz n
  F: réseau m urbain

useful power [el.]
  D: Nutzleistung f
  F: puissance f utile

use of materials
  D: Einsatz von Materialien
  F: mise f au point de matériaux, utilisation f de matériaux

use of phantom circuits
  D: Phantomausnutzung f
  F: utilisation f de circuits fantôme

utilisation factor [mach.]
  D: Ausnutzungsgrad m
  F: coefficient m d'utilisation

utility n (US)
  D: Elektrizitäts-Versorgungsunternehmen (EVU) n
  F: société f de distribution d'électricité, entreprise f d'électricité, centrale f électrique

V

vacuum 1 to 10⁻³ torr
 D: Feinvakuum n
 F: vide m de 1 à 10^{-3} torr
vacuum 760 to 100 torr
 D: Grobvakuum n
 F: vide m de 760 à 100 torr
vacuum 100 to 1 torr
 D: Zwischenvakuum n
 F: vide m de 100 à 1 torr
vacuum, under ~
 D: unter Vakuum
 F: sous vide
vacuum annealing plant
 D: Vakuumglühanlage f
 F: installation f de recuit sous vide
vacuum drying
 D: Vakuumtrocknung f
 F: séchage m sous vide
vacuum pump
 D: Vakuumpumpe f
 F: pompe f à vide
vacuum-sealed adj
 D: vakuumdicht adj
 F: étanche adj au vide, hermétique adj
vacuum smearing [extr.]
 D: Schlauchreckverfahren n
 F: extrusion f cône avec vide sur le poinçon, boudinage m sous vide
vacuum-tight adj
 D: vakuumdicht adj
 F: étanche adj au vide, hermétique adj
vacuum tube amplifier
 D: Vakuumröhren-Verstärker m
 F: amplificateur m à tube à vide
valley of corrugation
 D: Wellental n (beim Wellmantel)
 F: fond m d'ondulation, gorge f d'ondulation
valley sealer [cab.]
 D: Beilauf m, Zwickelfüllung f, Lückenfüllung f
 F: bourrage m
value, approximate ~
 D: Annäherungswert m, Näherungswert m
 F: valeur f approchée, valeur f approximative
valve
 D: Ventil n
 F: valve f, soupape f
vapour n [vulc.]
 D: Dampf m
 F: vapeur f
vapour cure
 D: Dampfvulkanisation f
 F: vulcanisation f à vapeur
variable adj
 D: verstellbar adj, einstellbar adj, regelbar adj, regulierbar adj
 F: ajustable adj, réglable adj, orientable adj
variable load
 D: wechselnde Belastung
 F: charge f variable
variable oil pressure tank
 D: Ölausgleichsgefäß n, Öldruck-Ausgleichsgefäß n, Druck-Ausgleichsgefäß n, Ausgleichsgefäß n (Ölkabel)
 F: réservoir m à pression d'huile variable
variable ratio transformer
 D: Regeltransformator m, Stelltransformator m
 F: transformateur m de réglage
variable speed motor
 D: Motor mit regulierbarer Geschwindigkeit, Regelmotor m
 F: moteur m à vitesse réglable, moteur m à vitesse variable
variable temporary duty [el.]
 D: Kurzzeitbetrieb m (mit veränderlicher Last)
 F: service m temporaire variable, régime m temporaire variable
varnish n
 D: Lack m
 F: vernis m
varnish coating
 D: Lacküberzug m
 F: couche f de vernis, couche f de laque
varnished cambric (insulated) cable
 D: Lackbandkabel n
 F: câble m isolé à la toile vernie
varnished cambric insulation
 D: Lackgewebe-Isolierung f
 F: isolation f en toile vernie
varnished cambric tape
 D: Lackgewebe-Band n
 F: ruban m en toile vernie
varnished paper cable
 D: Lackpapierkabel n

varnished

   F: câble m isolé au papier verni
varnished tape
   D: Lackband n
   F: ruban m verni, ruban m laqué
varnish impregnation
   D: Lackimprägnierung f
   F: imprégnation f en vernis
vault, cable ~
   D: Muffenbunker m, Muffenbauwerk n, Kabelschacht m
   F: trou m d'homme, puits m de visite, puits m de jonction, chambre f de répartition, puits m à câbles
V-belt n
   D: Keilriemen m
   F: courroie f trapézoïdale
VDE approval mark
   D: VDE-Kennzeichen n
   F: marque f d'approbation VDE
VDE identification thread
   D: VDE-Kennfaden m
   F: fil m distinctif VDE, fil m d'identification VDE
VDE Regulations
   D: VDE-Bestimmungen f pl, VDE-Regeln f pl, VDE-Vorschriften f pl
   F: normes f pl VDE, règles f pl VDE, spécifications f pl VDE
VDE Rules
   D: VDE-Bestimmungen f pl, VDE-Regeln f pl, VDE-Vorschriften f pl
   F: normes f pl VDE, règles f pl VDE, spécifications f pl VDE
VDE Standards
   D: VDE-Bestimmungen f pl, VDE-Regeln f pl, VDE-Vorschriften f pl
   F: normes f pl VDE, règles f pl VDE, spécifications f pl VDE
VDE tracer thread
   D: VDE-Kennfaden m
   F: fil m distinctif VDE, fil m d'identification VDE
vehicle cable
   D: Kraftfahrzeugleitung f
   F: câble m pour automobile
vent n
   D: Entlüftungsloch n
   F: évent m
vent extruder
   D: Extruder mit Entgasungssystem
   F: boudineuse f à aération
vent hole
   D: Entlüftungsloch n
   F: évent m
ventilate v
   D: belüften v
   F: aérer v, ventiler v
ventilated air oven ag(e)ing
   D: Alterung im Umluftofen, Umluftalterung f
   F: vieillissement m en étuve à circulation d'air, vieillissement m par circulation d'air
ventilation n
   D: Belüftung f, Lüftung f
   F: ventilation f, aération f
ventilation hood
   D: Absaughaube f
   F: collecteur m de fumées
ventilation pipe
   D: Entlüftungsrohr n
   F: cheminée f d'aération, tube m d'évacuation, tube m de ventilation
ventilator n
   D: Gebläse n
   F: ventilateur m
verify v
   D: prüfen v
   F: essayer v, vérifier v, contrôler v
versus [math.]
   D: in Abhängigkeit von
   F: en fonction de
vertical arrangement
   D: senkrechte Anordnung
   F: disposition f verticale
vertical cage lapper
   D: vertikaler Korbspinner
   F: rubaneuse f verticale à cage
vertical cage type lapping machine
   D: vertikaler Korbspinner
   F: rubaneuse f verticale à cage
vertical cast
   D: stehender Guß
   F: coulée f verticale
vertical extrusion
   D: Vertikal-Extrusion f
   F: extrusion f verticale
vertical installation [cab.]
   D: Hochführung f
   F: installation f verticale
vertical lapping machine
   D: Vertikal-Spinnmaschine f
   F: rubaneuse f verticale
vertically adjustable
   D: in der Höhe verstellbar
   F: réglable adj en hauteur

vertical riser cable
  D: Steigleitung f
  F: colonne f montante

vertical twister, high speed ~ [com. c.]
  D: vertikale Schnellverseilmaschine
  F: câbleuse f verticale à grande vitesse

vertical wall duct [cab.]
  D: Hochführungsschacht m
  F: puits m de montée

vibration n [mech.]
  D: Schwingung f
  F: vibration f

vibration-free adj
  D: schwingungsfrei adj
  F: anti-vibratoire adj

vibration test machine
  D: Vibrations-Prüfmaschine f
  F: machine f à contrôler la tenue aux vibrations

vibratory feeder
  D: Schüttelrutsche f
  F: goulotte f oscillante, goulotte f à secousses

vibratory screen
  D: Rüttelsieb n
  F: tamis m à secousses

video frequency
  D: Fernsehfrequenz f
  F: vidéo-fréquence f

video pair
  D: Fernsehpaar n
  F: paire f de télévision

viewing screen
  D: Bildschirm m
  F: écran m, écran m de vision

virgin material [test]
  D: frisches Material, neues Material
  F: matière f neuve

viscosity n
  D: Viskosität f
  F: viscosité f

viscosity, high ~
  D: Dickflüssigkeit f, Zähflüssigkeit f
  F: haute viscosité f

viscosity, low ~
  D: Dünnflüssigkeit f
  F: faible viscosité f

viscous adj
  D: zähflüssig adj
  F: visqueux adj

visible to the naked eye
  D: mit bloßem Auge sichtbar
  F: visible adj à l'œil nu

visual control
  D: visuelle Prüfung
  F: examen m visuel, inspection f

visual examination
  D: visuelle Prüfung
  F: examen m visuel, inspection f

visual indication
  D: Leuchtanzeige f
  F: voyant m lumineux

visual signal
  D: Schauzeichen n
  F: signalisation f visible

voice channel
  D: Sprechkanal m, Fernsprechkanal m
  F: canal m téléphonique, voie f téléphonique

voice circuit
  D: Sprechkreis m
  F: circuit m téléphonique

voice frequency
  D: Sprechfrequenz f, Fernsprechfrequenz f
  F: fréquence f vocale, fréquence f téléphonique

voice frequency switchboard cable
  D: Niederfrequenz-Schaltkabel n
  F: câble m de connexion basse fréquence

voice frequency transmission
  D: Sprechfrequenzübertragung f
  F: transmission f de fréquences vocales

voice signal
  D: Sprechzeichen n
  F: signal m vocal

void n
  D: Hohlraum m
  F: vide m, cavité f

void formation
  D: Hohlraumbildung f
  F: formation f de vides

void-free adj
  D: frei von Luftblasen, frei von Hohlräumen, frei von Lufteinschlüssen
  F: exempt adj de bulles d'air, exempt adj de poches d'air,

voids pl
  D: Lufteinschlüsse m pl
  F: occlusions f pl d'air, poches f pl d'air, bulles f pl d'air

volatile

volatile components
D: flüchtige Bestandteile *m pl*
F: constituants *m pl* volatils, composants *m pl* volatils

volatilize *v*
D: verflüchtigen *v*
F: volatiliser *v*

voltage *n*
D: Spannung *f*
F: tension *f*

voltage, to cut off the ~
D: die Spannung abschalten
F: mettre *v* hors tension

voltage, to cut out the ~
D: die Spannung abschalten
F: mettre *v* hors tension

voltage between phases
D: verkettete Spannung
F: tension *f* composée, tension *f* entre phases

voltage control
D: Spannungsregelung *f*
F: réglage *m* de tension

voltage detector
D: Spannungsprüfgerät *n*
F: détecteur *m* de tension

voltage divider
D: Spannungsteiler *m*, Potentiometer *n*
F: réducteur *m* de tension, potentiomètre *m*

voltage drop
D: Spannungsabfall *m*
F: chute *f* de tension

voltage fluctuation
D: Spannungsschwankung *f*
F: fluctuation *f* de tension, variation *f* de tension

voltage gradient
D: Spannungsgradient *m*
F: gradient *m* de potentiel

voltage increase in steps
D: stufenweise Spannungssteigerung
F: élévation *f* de tension par paliers

voltage level
D: Spannungspegel *m*
F: niveau *m* de tension

voltage life characteristic curve [cab.]
D: Zeit-Spannungsfestigkeits-Kurve *f*
F: courbe *f* de vie

voltage life of a cable
D: Zeit-Spannungsfestigkeit eines Kabels, Dauer-Spannungsfestigkeit eines Kabels
F: durée *f* de vie d'un câble, tenue *f* en longue durée d'un câble

voltage life test
D: Dauerspannungsprüfung *f*
F: essai *m* de durée de vie

voltage loss
D: Spannungsverlust *m*
F: perte *f* de tension, perte *f* de potentiel

voltage rise
D: Spannungsanstieg *m*, Anstieg der Spannung
F: montée *f* de tension

voltage source
D: Spannungsquelle *f*
F: source *f* de tension

voltage stabilizer (additive in insulating compounds)
D: Spannungsstabilisator *m* (Zusatz in Isoliermischungen)
F: stabilisant *m* de tension

voltage-stabilizing *adj*
D: spannungsstabilisierend *adj* (Mischungsadditiv)
F: stabilisant *adj* électriquement

voltage step
D: Spannungsstufe *f*
F: gradin *m* de tension, palier *m* de tension

voltage stress
D: Spannungsbeanspruchung *f*
F: contrainte *f* de tension, contrainte *f* électrique

voltage surge
D: Stoßwelle *f*, Spannungsstoß *m*
F: onde *f* de choc

voltage tap
D: Spannungs-Abgriff *m*
F: prise *f* de tension

voltage test
D: Spannungsprüfung *f*
F: essai *m* diélectrique, essai *m* de tension

voltage to earth
D: Spannung gegen Erde
F: tension *f* par rapport à la terre, tension *f* simple

voltage variation
D: Spannungsschwankung *f*
F: fluctuation *f* de tension, variation *f* de tension

volume resistance (exclusive of surface resistance)
  D: Durchgangswiderstand m (ohne Oberflächenwiderstand)
  F: résistance f intérieure

volume resistivity
  D: spezifischer Durchgangswiderstand, spezifischer Widerstand
  F: résistivité f de volume

volumetric weight
  D: Raumgewicht n
  F: poids m par (unité de) volume, densité f

volume variation
  D: Volumenänderung f
  F: changement m du volume

volume weight
  D: spezifisches Gewicht
  F: poids m spécifique, masse f volumique

vulcanizate n
  D: Vulkanisat n
  F: produit m de vulcanisation

vulcanization n
  D: Vulkanisation f
  F: vulcanisation f

vulcanization in stages [vulc.]
  D: Stufenheizung f
  F: vulcanisation f échelonnée, vulcanisation f par paliers

vulcanization range
  D: Vulkanisationsbereich m
  F: intervalle m de vulcanisation

vulcanization rate
  D: Vulkanisationsgeschwindigkeit f
  F: vitesse f de vulcanisation

vulcanization time
  D: Vulkanisationsdauer f
  F: durée f de vulcanisation

vulcanize v
  D: vulkanisieren v
  F: vulcaniser v

vulcanized, plug ~ to the cable
  D: aufvulkanisierter Stecker
  F: fiche f vulcanisée sur le câble

vulcanized, sealing end ~ to the cable
  D: aufvulkanisierter Endenabschluß
  F: extrémité f vulcanisée sur le câble

vulcanized bitumen
  D: vulkanisiertes Bitumen
  F: bitume m vulcanisé

vulcanized material
  D: Vulkanisat n
  F: produit m de vulcanisation

vulcanizing agent
  D: Vulkanisationsmittel n
  F: agent m de vulcanisation

vulcanizing pan
  D: Heizkessel m, Vulkanisierkessel m
  F: autoclave m de vulcanisation

vulcanizing tube
  D: Vulkanisationsrohr n
  F: tube m de vulcanisation

W

wall clamp
  D: Rohrschelle f
  F: bride f d'attache, collier m pour tubes

wall duct
  D: Durchführungsrohr n
  F: douille f de traversée

wall thickness
  D: Wanddicke f
  F: épaisseur f de la paroi

wall tube
  D: Durchführungsrohr n
  F: douille f de traversée

warm-up time
  D: Aufheizzeit f
  F: temps m de chauffage

warning, audible ~
  D: akustisches Warnsignal
  F: signal m avertisseur acoustique

wash primer
  D: Haftgrundierung f
  F: couche f de fond

water absorption
  D: Wasseraufnahme f
  F: absorption f d'eau

water absorption capacity
  D: Wasseraufnahmefähigkeit f
  F: faculté f hygroscopique

water blocks, cable with ~ [tel. c.]
  D: diskontinuierlich abgestopftes Kabel
  F: câble m rempli de façon discontinue

water-cooled adj
  D: wassergekühlt adj
  F: refroidi adj à l'eau

water

water cooling
  D: Wasserkühlung f
  F: refroidissement m à l'eau
water cooling section
  D: Wasserkühlstrecke f
  F: section f de refroidissement par eau
water immersion
  D: Lagerung in Wasser, Wasserlagerung f, Eintauchen in Wasser
  F: immersion f dans l'eau
water level indicator
  D: Wasserstandsanzeiger m
  F: indicateur m de niveau d'eau
water penetration
  D: Eindringen von Wasser (in Kabel)
  F: infiltration f d'eau, pénétration f d'eau
water pressure
  D: Wasserdruck m
  F: pression f hydraulique, pression f d'eau
water-proof cable
  D: längswasserdichtes Kabel
  F: câble m étanche à l'eau, câble m imperméable à l'eau
water repellent
  D: wasserabstoßend adj
  F: hydrofuge adj, hydrophobe adj
water resistant
  D: wasserbeständig adj
  F: résistant adj à l'eau
water seal [vulc.]
  D: Wasserdichtung f
  F: joint m d'eau
water seepage
  D: Eindringen von Wasser (in Kabel)
  F: infiltration f d'eau, pénétration f d'eau
water seeping
  D: Eindringen von Wasser (in Kabel)
  F: infiltration f d'eau, pénétration f d'eau
water-tight cable
  D: längswasserdichtes Kabel
  F: câble m étanche à l'eau, câble m imperméable à l'eau
water tightness
  D: Wasserdichtigkeit f
  F: étanchéité f à l'eau
water vapour
  D: Wasserdampf m
  F: vapeur f d'eau
water vapour permeability
  D: Wasserdampfdurchlässigkeit f
  F: perméabilité f à la vapeur d'eau
wattful current
  D: Wirkstrom m
  F: courant m actif, courant m watté
wave n
  D: Welle f
  F: onde f
wave band
  D: Wellenbereich m (Schwingung)
  F: gamme f d'ondes
Waveconal-cable n (GB)
  D: Ceander-Kabel n
  F: câble m à neutre concentrique en fils métalliques disposés en méandres
wave formation, laying cables in a ~
  D: Schlangenverlegung von Kabeln, Verlegung von Kabeln in Schlangenlinien
  F: pose f des câbles en serpentins
wave-form concentric neutral conductor
  D: Ceander-Leiter m
  F: neutre m concentrique en fils métalliques disposés en méandres
waveguide n [com.]
  D: Hohlleiter m, Wellenleiter m
  F: guide m d'ondes
waveguide bundle
  D: Wellenleiterbündel n
  F: faisceau m de guide d'ondes
wavelength n
  D: Wellenlänge f
  F: longueur f d'onde
wave range
  D: Wellenbereich m (Schwingung)
  F: gamme f d'ondes
waviness n
  D: Welligkeit f
  F: ondulation f
wax, microcrystalline ~
  D: mikrokristallines Wachs
  F: cire f microcristalline
weak point [cab.]
  D: Schwachstelle f
  F: point m faible
wear n
  D: Verschleiß m, Abrieb m
  F: usure f
wearing part

wear part
D: Verschleißteil n
F: pièce f d'usure

weather v
D: bewittern v
F: exposer v aux intempéries

weatherability n
D: Wetterbeständigkeit f, Wetterfestigkeit f, Witterungsbeständigkeit f
F: résistance f aux intempéries

weathering test
D: Bewitterungsversuch m
F: essai m atmosphérique, essai m de résistance aux intempéries

weather resistance
D: Wetterbeständigkeit f, Wetterfestigkeit f, Witterungsbeständigkeit f
F: résistance f aux intempéries

web n
D: Bahn f (Papier, Stoff)
F: bande f

wedge ring
D: Keilring m
F: bague f conique

Weibull-curve n
D: Weibull-Kurve f
F: courbe f de Weibull

Weibull's (distribution) law
D: Weibull-Regel f (Weibull-Verteilung)
F: loi f de Weibull

weight loss
D: Gewichtsverlust m
F: perte f de masse, perte f de poids

weight per square meter
D: Flächengewicht n
F: poids m au mètre carré

weight per unit of volume
D: Raumgewicht n
F: poids m par (unité de) volume, densité f

weld v
D: verschweißen v
F: souder v

welded hard surfacing
D: Auftragsschweißung f
F: soudure f à superposition

welded joint
D: Schweißstelle f, Schweißverbindung f
F: soudure f, joint m soudé

welding n
D: Schweißen n
F: soudage m

welding, hot-air ~ with plastic welding rod
D: Heißluftschweißen mit Kunststoff-Drahtzufuhr
F: soudage m à air chaud avec fil de soudage plastique

welding bead
D: Schweißraupe f
F: cordon m de soudure

welding cable
D: Schweißleitung f
F: câble m de soudure

welding rod
D: Schweißstab m
F: baguette f de soudage

welding seam
D: Schweißnaht f
F: ligne f de soudure

welding wire
D: Schweißdraht m
F: fil m de soudage

wet v
D: anfeuchten v, benetzen v, befeuchten v
F: mouiller v, tremper v, humecter v

wet analysis
D: Naßanalyse f
F: analyse f humide

wet bulb temperature [air cond.]
D: Feuchtthermometer-Temperatur f, Feuchtkugel-Temperatur f
F: température f au thermomètre humide

wetting agent
D: Benetzungsmittel n, Netzmittel n
F: agent m mouillant, agent m humidificateur

Wheatstone bridge
D: Widerstandsbrücke f
F: pont m de résistances

wide-band cable
D: Breitbandkabel n
F: câble m à large bande

wide-band transmission
D: Breitband-Übertragung f
F: transmission f à large bande

widening n
D: Erweiterung f
F: extension f, élargissement m

width n
D: Breite f

width

F: largeur f
wind v
   D: aufwickeln v, aufspulen v, spulen v, wickeln v, auftrommeln v
   F: enrouler v, bobiner v
wind v [cab.]
   D: bewickeln v, umwickeln v, umspinnen v
   F: recouvrir v, enrouler v
winding n
   D: Wicklung f
   F: enroulement m, bobinage m
winding n
   D: Umwicklung f (mit Band)
   F: enrubannage m, recouvrement m
winding n (of coil, reel)
   D: Windung f
   F: spire f
winding direction
   D: Wickelrichtung f
   F: sens m d'enroulement
winding machine (for rewinding)
   D: Wickelmaschine f
   F: bobinoir m
winding speed
   D: Wickelgeschwindigkeit f
   F: vitesse f de bobinage
winding wire
   D: Wickeldraht m
   F: fil m de bobinage
wind up v
   D: aufwickeln v, aufspulen v, spulen v, wickeln v, auftrommeln v
   F: enrouler v, bobiner v
wiped solder joint
   D: Schmierplombe f
   F: soudure f à la louche
wiper n
   D: Abstreifer m (an der Armiermaschine)
   F: râcloir m
wiping gland
   D: Schmierplombe f
   F: soudure f à la louche
wiping nipple
   D: Schmierplombe f
   F: soudure f à la louche
wiping resin
   D: Streichharz n
   F: résine f à enduire
wiping solder
   D: Wischlot n, Weichlot n, Schmierlot n
   F: soudure f liquide
wiping solder seal
   D: Schmierplombe f
   F: soudure f à la louche
wire v
   D: verkabeln v
   F: câbler v
wire n
   D: Draht m
   F: fil m métallique
wire armo(u)r
   D: Drahtbewehrung f, Drahtarmierung f
   F: armure f en fils métalliques
wire-armo(u)red cable
   D: drahtbewehrtes Kabel, drahtarmiertes Kabel
   F: câble m armé en fils métalliques
wire armo(u)ring
   D: Drahtbewehrung f, Drahtarmierung f
   F: armure f en fils métalliques
wire bar
   D: Drahtbarren m, Gußblock m
   F: lingot m
wire binding, field-controlling ~ [c. access.]
   D: Strahlungsbund m, Drahtbund m
   F: frettage m en fil métallique pour l'orientation du champ électrique, frette f en fil métallique
wire binding sleeve
   D: Gummi-Einführungstülle f (gegen Ausfransen von Kabelenden), Gummitülle f (für Kabelenden)
   F: passe-fil m en caoutchouc
wire braid
   D: Drahtgeflecht n
   F: tresse f de fil métallique
wire braiding machine
   D: Drahtumflechtmaschine f
   F: machine f à tresser en fils métalliques
wire break
   D: Drahtbruch m, Drahtriß m
   F: casse-fil m, rupture f du fil
wire breakage
   D: Drahtbruch m, Drahtriß m
   F: casse-fil m, rupture f du fil
wire break monitor
   D: Drahtrißwächter m
   F: détecteur m de casses-fil, détecteur m de ruptures du fil

wire break switch
  D: Drahtbruchschalter m
  F: casse-fil m électrique
wire clamp
  D: Drahtklemme f
  F: serre-fil m
wire coil
  D: Drahtring m, Drahtbund m
  F: couronne f de fil métallique
wire covering
  D: Drahtumspinnung f
  F: recouvrement m du fil métallique
wire covering machine
  D: Drahtumspinnmaschine f
  F: machine f à recouvrir le fil métallique
wire diameter
  D: Drahtdurchmesser m
  F: diamètre m du fil métallique
wire drawing
  D: Drahtziehen n
  F: tréfilage m
wire drawing department
  D: Drahtzieherei f
  F: tréfilerie f
wire drawing machine
  D: Drahtziehmaschine f
  F: tréfileuse f, machine f à tréfiler
wire drawing speed
  D: Drahtziehgeschwindigkeit f
  F: vitesse f de tréfilage
wire enamel
  D: Drahtlack m
  F: vernis m pour fils
wire gauge
  D: Drahtdicke f, Drahtklasse f, Drahtlehre f
  F: grosseur f du fil métallique, jauge f des fils
wire grip
  D: Drahtklemme f
  F: serre-fil m
wire guide
  D: Drahtführung f
  F: guide-fil m
wire guide, automatic ~
  D: automatische Drahtführung (Wickler)
  F: trancanage m automatique du fil métallique
wire mesh guard
  D: Schutzgitter n
  F: grille f protectrice
wire packaging (barrel take-up)
  D: Aufwickeln von Draht (Faßwickler)
  F: enroulement m du fil (tonneau d'enroulement)
wire preheater
  D: Drahtvorwärmer m
  F: réchauffeur m de fil métallique
wire reclaiming system
  D: Rückgewinnungsanlage für Draht aus Kabelabfällen
  F: installation f de récupération du fil métallique à partir des déchets de câble
wire-reinforced lead sheath
  D: Bleimantel mit Drahtarmierung
  F: gaine f de plomb avec armure en fils
wire rewinding stand
  D: Drahtumwickelei f
  F: bobineuse f de fil métallique (pour rebobinage)
wire rod [wire manuf.]
  D: Grobdraht m, Drahtvormaterial n, Vorziehdraht m
  F: fil m machine, fil m ébauche, fil m pour retréfilage
wire rod
  D: Walzdraht m
  F: fil m machine laminé
wire rolling mill
  D: Drahtwalzwerk n
  F: laminoir m à fils métalliques
wire sharpening and threading machine
  D: Anspitzmaschine und Einziehmaschine (Draht)
  F: machine f à appointer et enfiler le fil métallique
wire size
  D: Drahtdicke f, Drahtklasse f, Drahtlehre f
  F: grosseur f du fil métallique, jauge f des fils
wire solder
  D: Lötdraht m
  F: fil m de soudure, soudure f en fil
wire spooler
  D: Drahtwickelmaschine f
  F: bobineuse de fil métallique f
wire straightening device
  D: Drahtrichtvorrichtung f

wire

F: redresseur *m* de fil

wire take-up, high-speed continuous ~
- **D:** Schnellaufwickelei für Draht
- **F:** enrouleur *m* de fil métallique à grande vitesse

wire-to-wire capacity
- **D:** Schleifenkapazität *f*
- **F:** capacité *f* de boucle

wire winding machine
- **D:** Drahtwickelmaschine *f*
- **F:** bobineuse de fil métallique *f*

wire-wrap connection
- **D:** lötfreie gewickelte Verbindung, Wickelverbindung *f* (lötfrei)
- **F:** connexion *f* enroulée, raccord *m* sans soudure

wire wrapping
- **D:** Drahtbewicklung *f*
- **F:** enroulement *m* de fil

wiring *n*
- **D:** Schaltung *f*, Verdrahtung *f*
- **F:** circuit *m*, montage *m*, schéma *m* de connexions, filerie *f*

wiring, inside ~
- **D:** innere Verdrahtung
- **F:** filerie *f* interne

wiring, internal ~
- **D:** innere Verdrahtung
- **F:** filerie *f* interne

wiring cable
- **D:** Verdrahtungsleitung *f*
- **F:** conducteur *m* pour filerie interne, fil *m* de câblage

wiring diagram
- **D:** Schaltplan *m*, Schaltschema *n*, Verdrahtungsplan *m*
- **F:** schéma *m* électrique, plan *m* de câblage, plan *m* des circuits, schéma *m* des connexions

wiring harness
- **D:** Kabelbaum *m*, Kabelsatz *m*
- **F:** harnais *m* de câbles, faisceau *m* de câbles, forme *f* de câbles

wiring scheme
- **D:** Schaltplan *m*, Schaltschema *n*, Verdrahtungsplan *m*
- **F:** schéma *m* électrique, plan *m* de câblage, plan *m* des circuits, schéma *m* des connexions

withstand *v*
- **D:** aushalten *v*
- **F:** supporter *v*, résister *v* à ..., tenir *v*, soutenir *v*

withstand, to ~ a test
- **D:** eine Prüfung bestehen
- **F:** passer *v* un essai, tenir *v* un essai, résister *v* à un essai

withstand voltage
- **D:** Stehspannung *f*
- **F:** tension *f* de tenue

wooden drum
- **D:** Holztrommel *f*
- **F:** touret *m* en bois

wooden reel
- **D:** Holztrommel *f*
- **F:** touret *m* en bois

workability *n*
- **D:** Formbarkeit *f*
- **F:** plasticité *f*, aptitude au façonnage *f*, aptitude *f* au moulage, malléabilité *f*

working ease
- **D:** leichte Bedienung, leichte Handhabung
- **F:** aisance *f* de manipulation, aisance *f* de manœuvre

working fluid
- **D:** Betriebsflüssigkeit *f*
- **F:** liquide *m* de service

working instructions *pl*
- **D:** Arbeitsanweisung *f*
- **F:** instructions *f pl* de travail

working order
- **D:** Betriebszustand *m*
- **F:** état *m* de service

working order, in ~
- **D:** betriebsbereit *adj*
- **F:** prêt *adj* à fonctionner, prêt *adj* à la mise en marche, , en ordre de marche

working pressure
- **D:** Betriebsdruck *m*
- **F:** pression *f* de service

work(ing) roll
- **D:** Arbeitswalze *f*
- **F:** cylindre *m* de travail

working side [mach.]
- **D:** Bedienungsseite *f*
- **F:** côté commande *m*, côté *m* manœuvre, côté *m* service

work measurement
- **D:** Zeitstudie *f*
- **F:** mesure *f* du travail

workplace layout
- **D:** Arbeitsplatzgestaltung *f*
- **F:** implantation *f* du poste de travail

work planning
  D: Arbeitsvorbereitung f, Fertigungsvorbereitung f
  F: préparation f du travail
workshop n
  D: Betrieb m (Werk, Anlage), Werkstatt f
  F: usine f, atelier m
woven shield
  D: Abschirmgeflecht n
  F: écran m guipé
wrap v [cab.]
  D: bewickeln v, umwickeln v, umspinnen v
  F: recouvrir v, enrouler v
wrap v
  D: umwickeln v (mit Band), bewickeln v (mit Band), umspinnen v (mit Band), wickeln v (Band)
  F: enrubanner v, rubaner v
wrapping n
  D: Wicklung f
  F: enroulement m, bobinage m
wrapping n
  D: Umwicklung f (mit Band)
  F: enrubannage m, recouvrement m
wrapping machine
  D: Umwicklungsmaschine f
  F: machine f à revêtir, machine f à enrouler
wrapping test
  D: Dornwickelprüfung f
  F: essai m d'enroulement
wrinkle n
  D: Falte f
  F: pli m
wrinkle-free adj
  D: faltenfrei adj
  F: exempt de plis, sans plis
wrinkling n
  D: Faltenbildung f
  F: plissement m, formation f de plis
wrought alloy
  D: Knetlegierung f
  F: alliage m de pétrissage

X

XLPE (s. cross-linked polyethylene)

Y

yarn spinning head
  D: Garnspinnkopf m
  F: tête f à filin
yield point
  D: Streckgrenze f, Dehn(ungs)grenze f, Elastizitätsgrenze f
  F: limite f d'élasticité, limite f d'allongement
yield strength
  D: Streckgrenze f, Dehn(ungs)grenze f, Elastizitätsgrenze f
  F: limite f d'élasticité, limite f d'allongement

Z

zero conductor
  D: Nulleiter m, Mittelpunktsleiter m
  F: conducteur m neutre, fil m neutre, neutre m
zero phase-sequence system
  D: Nullsystem n
  F: système m homopolaire
zero point
  D: Nullpunkt m, Sternpunkt m
  F: neutre m, point m neutre, zéro m
zinc-coated steel wire
  D: verzinkter Stahldraht
  F: fil m d'acier galvanisé
zinc oxide
  D: Zinkoxid n
  F: oxyde m de zinc

DICTIONNAIRE DE LA TECHNIQUE DES CÂBLES

PARTIE III

FRANÇAIS-ALLEMAND-ANGLAIS

A

abaisser *v* **la tension** [él.]
  D: abspannen *v*
  E: to step down the voltage
abonné *m* [tél.]
  D: Teilnehmer *m*
  E: subscriber *n*
abonnement *m* **téléphonique**
  D: Fernsprechanschluß *m*
  E: telephone connection
abonné *m* **téléphonique**
  D: Fernsprechanschluß *m*
  E: telephone connection
abrasion *f*
  D: Abrieb *m*
  E: abrasion *n*, wear *n*
absorption *f* **d'eau**
  D: Wasseraufnahme *f*
  E: water absorption
absorption *f* **de chaleur**
  D: Wärmeaufnahme *f*
  E: heat absorption
absorption *f* **de gaz**
  D: Gasaufnahme *f*
  E: gas absorption
absorption *f* **d'humidité**
  D: Feuchtigkeitsaufnahme *f*
  E: moisture absorption
accélérateur *m* [vulc.]
  D: Beschleuniger *m*
  E: accelerator *n*
accélération, temps d'~ [mach.]
  D: Anlaufzeit *f*, Einlaufzeit *f*
  E: starting time, acceleration time, running-in period
accès *m* [pose c.]
  D: Einstiegöffnung *f*, Mannloch *n*
  E: entrance *n*, manhole *n*
accessible, facilement ~
  D: leicht zugänglich
  E: easily accessible
accessoire *m* **d'extrémité**
  D: Endverschluß *m*, Endenabschluß *m*
  E: sealing end, termination *n*, terminal *n*, pothead *n*
accessoires *m pl*
  D: Garnituren *f pl*
  E: accessories *pl*
accessoires *m pl* **de câbles emmanchables à chaud**
  D: wärmeschrumpfende Kabelgarnituren
  E: shrink-on cable accessories, heat-shrinkable cable accessories
accord *m*
  D: Abgleichung *f*
  E: adjustment *n*, compensation *n*, trimming *n*, alignment *n*, tuning *n*
accord *m* [régl.]
  D: Abstimmung *f*
  E: tuning *n*, adjustment *n*
accorder *v*
  D: abgleichen *v*
  E: adjust *v*, compensate *v*, trim *v*, balance *v*, tune *v*
accorder *v* [régl.]
  D: abstimmen *v*
  E: tune *v*, adjust *v*, match *v*
accorder *v* **un brevet**
  D: ein Patent erteilen
  E: to grant a patent
accumulateur *m* [fabr.fils mét., câblage]
  D: Speicher *m*, Längenspeicher *m*
  E: accumulator *n*
accumulateur *m* **double** [câblage]
  D: Doppelspeicher *m*
  E: double accumulator
accumulateur *m* **du type rouleau** [câblage]
  D: Rollenspeicher *m*
  E: roller-type accumulator
accumulation, centrale électrique à ~ par pompage
  D: Pumpspeicher(kraft)werk *n*
  E: pumped storage (hydroelectric) power station
accumulation, zones à forte ~ [câb.]
  D: stark belegte Räume
  E: congested areas
accumulation *f* **de câbles** [pose c.]
  D: Häufung von Kabeln, Anhäufung von Kabeln, Ballung von Kabeln, Belegung mit Kabeln
  E: grouping of cables, accumulation of cables
acétate *m* **d'éthylène vinyle** (EVA)
  D: Äthylen-Vinyl-Azetat (EVA) *n*
  E: ethylene vinyl acetate (EVA)
acide *m* **stéarique**
  D: Stearinsäure *f*
  E: stearic acid
acier *m* **de construction**
  D: Konstruktionsstahl *m*
  E: structural steel

acier m inoxydable
 D: rostfreier Stahl
 E: stainless steel

à-coup, sans ~s
 D: stufenlos *adj*
 E: stepless *adj*, continuously adjustable, infinitely variable

acquisition f des données
 D: Datenerfassung f
 E: data collection, data acquisition

ACSR, âme ~ (fils d'aluminium câblés autour d'un fil central en acier)
 D: ACSR-Leiterseil n (Al-Leiter um einen Stahlkerndraht verseilt), Aluminiumleiter m (ACSR)
 E: aluminium conductor steel reinforced (ACSR)

action, piston à ~ double
 D: doppeltwirkender Plunger
 E: double-acting plunger

action f réciproque
 D: Wechselwirkung f
 E: interplay n, interaction n

adaptateur m
 D: Zwischenstück n, Verbindungsstück n, Anschlußstück n
 E: intermediate piece, connecting piece, adapter n, connector n, fitting n

adaptation f [com.]
 D: Anpassung f
 E: matching n

additif m
 D: Zusatzstoff m
 E: additive n

addition f
 D: Beimengung f
 E: addition n, admixture n

adhérance f
 D: Haftung f, Adhäsion f
 E: adhesion n, adherence n, bonding n, sticking n

adhérence f
 D: Haftvermögen n
 E: tackiness n, adhesive power, peel strength

adhérer v
 D: haften v, kleben vi
 E: adhere v, bond v, stick v

adhésif m
 D: Kleber m, Haftvermittler m, Klebstoff m
 E: adhesive n, bonding agent

adhésion f
 D: Haftung f, Adhäsion f
 E: adhesion n, adherence n, bonding n, sticking n

adhésion f
 D: Bindefestigkeit f
 E: bond strength, bonding strength, adhesiveness n

adhésivité f
 D: Haftvermögen n
 E: tackiness n, adhesive power, peel strength

adjonction f
 D: Beimengung f
 E: addition n, admixture n

adjuvant m
 D: Zusatzstoff m
 E: additive n

admissible *adj*
 D: zulässig *adj*
 E: admissible *adj*, permissible *adj*

aération f
 D: Belüftung f, Lüftung f
 E: ventilation n, aeration n

aérer v
 D: belüften v
 E: ventilate v, aerate v

affaiblissement m
 D: Dämpfung f
 E: damping n, attenuation n

affaiblissement m apparent
 D: Scheindämpfung f
 E: apparent attenuation

affaiblissement m composite [tél.]
 D: Betriebsdämpfung f
 E: effective attenuation, overall loss, operative attenuation

affaiblissement m d'adaptation
 D: Anpassungsdämpfung f
 E: matching attenuation, matching loss, return loss

affaiblissement m d'écho
 D: Echodämpfung f
 E: echo attenuation, active return loss

affaiblissement m de la ligne [c. tél.]
 D: Leitungsdämpfung f
 E: line attenuation, transmission loss, line loss

affaiblissement m d'équilibrage
 D: Reflexionsdämpfung f, Fehlerdämpfung f
 E: reflection attenuation, balance

affaiblissement *m* **de régularité**
D: Rückflußdämpfung *f*
E: structural return loss

affaiblissement *m* **des courants réfléchis**
D: Reflexionsdämpfung *f*, Fehlerdämpfung *f*
E: reflection attenuation, balance return loss, return loss between line and network (US), reflection loss, balance attenuation

affaiblissement *m* **diaphonique**
D: Nebensprechdämpfung *f*, Übersprechdämpfung *f*
E: crosstalk attenuation, crosstalk transmission equivalent

affaiblissement *m* **dû à la perditance** [c. com.]
D: Ableitungsdämpfung *f*
E: leakage attenuation, leakage loss, leakage current loss

affaiblissement *m* **effectif**
D: Restdämpfung *f*
E: net attenuation, net loss, overall attenuation, overall transmission loss

affaiblissement *m* **paradiaphonique**
D: Nahnebensprechdämpfung *f*
E: near-end crosstalk attenuation

affaiblissement *m* **résiduel**
D: Restdämpfung *f*
E: net attenuation, net loss, overall attenuation, overall transmission loss

affaiblissement *m* **sur images**
D: Vierpoldämpfung *f*, Wellendämpfung *f*
E: image attenuation constant

affaiblissement *m* **télédiaphonique**
D: Fernnebensprechdämpfung *f*, Gegennebensprechdämpfung *f*
E: far-end crosstalk attenuation

affichage *m*
D: Anzeige *f*
E: indication *n*, display *n*, reading *n*

affichage *m* **d'erreur**
D: Fehleranzeige *f*
E: error display, fault indication

affleurer *v*
D: fluchten *v*
E: to be flush, to be in alignment, to be in line with

agencement *m*
D: Zahnradgetriebe *n*, Getriebe *n*
E: gear(ing) *n*

agent *m* **anti-mousse**
D: Entschäumer *m*
E: anti-foaming agent

agent *m* **de dilution**
D: Verdünnungsmittel *n*
E: diluent *n*, thinner *n*

agent de durcissement *m*
D: Härter *m*
E: hardener *n*, curing agent

agent *m* **de gonflement**
D: Treibmittel *n* (Schaumstoffe), Blähmittel *n*
E: blowing agent

agent *m* **de réticulation**
D: Vernetzungsmittel *n*, Vernetzer *m*
E: cross-linking agent

agent *m* **de vulcanisation**
D: Vulkanisationsmittel *n*
E: vulcanizing agent

agent *m* **humidificateur**
D: Benetzungsmittel *n*, Netzmittel *n*
E: wetting agent

agent *m* **mouillant**
D: Benetzungsmittel *n*, Netzmittel *n*
E: wetting agent

agent *m* **séparateur**
D: Trennmittel *n*
E: release agent

agent *m* **soufflant**
D: Treibmittel *n* (Schaumstoffe), Blähmittel *n*
E: blowing agent

agent *m* **stabilisant**
D: stabilisierender Zusatz, Stabilisator *m*
E: stabilizing agent, stabilizer *n*

agglomération *f*
D: Zusammenballung *f*
E: agglomeration *n*, conglomeration *n*

agglomération, grande ~ urbaine [pose c.]
D: dicht besiedeltes Gebiet, Ballungszentrum *n*
E: heavily loaded locality, congested area

agglomération, zone de forte ~ [pose c.]
D: dicht besiedeltes Gebiet,

agglomération

Ballungszentrum n
E: heavily loaded locality, congested area

aggloméré m
D: Agglomerat n
E: agglomeration n, agglomerate n

agglomérer v
D: zusammenbacken v
E: agglomerate v, conglomerate v, cake v

agglutination f
D: Zusammenballung f
E: agglomeration n, conglomeration n

agglutiner v
D: zusammenbacken v
E: agglomerate v, conglomerate v, cake v

agitateur m
D: Rührwerk n
E: agitator n, mixer n

agitateur m planétaire
D: Planetenrührwerk n
E: planetary mixer

agrafe f de tirage [câb.]
D: Ziehkopf m, Ziehöse f, Zugöse f
E: pulling eye, pulling head, pulling grip

agrafer v
D: festklemmen v
E: cleat v, clamp v, cramp v

agrandir v
D: vergrößern v
E: increase v, extend v, enlarge v, magnify v

agrandissement m
D: Vergrößerung f
E: enlargement n, magnification n, increase n

agrégat m
D: Aggregat n
E: aggregate n, set n, unit n

agrégat m de réserve
D: Reserveaggregat n
E: stand-by unit, stand-by aggregate

agrégat m de secours
D: Reserveaggregat n
E: stand-by unit, stand-by aggregate

agrégat m réfrigérant
D: Kühlaggregat n
E: cooling set, refrigeration unit

aide m
D: Hilfsarbeiter m
E: helper n, unskilled worker

air m comprimé
D: Druckluft f
E: compressed air

air comprimé, commande à ~
D: Druckluftbetätigung f
E: pneumatic operation, compressed-air control

air m enfermé
D: eingeschlossene Luft
E: entrapped air

aisance f de manipulation
D: leichte Bedienung, leichte Handhabung
E: ease of manipulation, ease of operation, working ease

aisance f de manœuvre
D: leichte Bedienung, leichte Handhabung
E: ease of manipulation, ease of operation, working ease

ajustable adj
D: verstellbar adj, einstellbar adj, regelbar adj, regulierbar adj
E: adjustable adj, variable adj

ajustement m
D: Abgleichung f
E: adjustment n, compensation n, trimming n, alignment n, tuning n

ajustement m [méc.]
D: Paßsitz m
E: snug fit, tight fit

ajuster v
D: abgleichen v
E: adjust v, compensate v, trim v, balance v, tune v

alésage m
D: Bohrung f
E: bore n, hole n

aligner v
D: zum Fluchten bringen
E: align v

aligner v (s')
D: fluchten v
E: to be flush, to be in alignment, to be in line with

alimentation f
D: Zuführung f, Speisung f
E: feed n

alimentation f [él.]
D: Einspeisung f
E: power supply, feed-in n

alimentation f en billettes [pr. à filer]

alimentation f en courant électrique
  D: Energieversorgung f, Energieverteilung f, Stromversorgung f
  E: power supply, power distribution

alimentation f en énergie de secours
  D: Notstromversorgung f
  E: emergency power supply

alimentation f en énergie électrique
  D: Energieversorgung f, Energieverteilung f, Stromversorgung f
  E: power supply, power distribution

alimentation en huile, dispositif d'~
  D: Öleinspeisungsvorrichtung f
  E: oil feeding equipment

alimentation f par gravité
  D: Gefällezuführung f
  E: gravity feed

alimentation f par le réseau
  D: Versorgung aus dem Netz, Netzanschluß m
  E: mains supply, power supply

alimentation f (sur) secteur
  D: Versorgung aus dem Netz, Netzanschluß m
  E: mains supply, power supply

alimenté adj en courant
  D: stromgespeist adj
  E: current-fed adj

alimenter v [méc., él.]
  D: speisen v, einspeisen v, beschicken v
  E: feed v, charge v, load v, supply v

allégement m de contrainte [câb.]
  D: Zugentlastung f
  E: strain-bearing element, strain relief, strain-bearing member

alliage m
  D: Legierung f
  E: alloy n

alliage m d'aluminium
  D: Aluminiumlegierung f
  E: aluminium alloy

alliage m de pétrissage
  D: Knetlegierung f
  E: wrought alloy

alliage m de plomb
  D: Bleilegierung f
  E: lead alloy

allongement m
  D: Dehnung f
  E: elongation n, extension n, stretch n

allongement, essai d'~ à froid
  D: Kältedehnungsprüfung f
  E: elongation test at low temperature

allongement m à la rupture
  D: Bruchdehnung f, Reißdehnung f
  E: elongation at break, ultimate elongation, elongation at rupture

allongement m élastique
  D: elastische Dehnung
  E: stretch n

allongement m permanent
  D: bleibende Dehnung
  E: permanent set, residual set, retained elongation

allongement m rémanent
  D: bleibende Dehnung
  E: permanent set, residual set, retained elongation

allongement m résiduel
  D: Dehnungsrest m
  E: residual elongation

allonger v
  D: recken v, spannen v, strecken v
  E: straighten v, stretch v

allonger v
  D: dehnen v
  E: elongate v, extend v, expand vt

allure f
  D: Verhalten n
  E: behaviour n, performance n

allure f d'une courbe
  D: Kurvenverlauf m, Verlauf einer Kurve
  E: characteristic of a curve

alternance f
  D: Lastspiel n
  E: alternation of load

alternance f des pressions et des dépressions
  D: Druckschwankungen f pl
  E: pressure variations

alterné, en sens ~
  D: in wechselnder Richtung
  E: in alternating direction

aluminium m à haute conductibilité
  D: Leitaluminium (EC-Aluminium) n
  E: electrical conductor grade aluminium (EC-aluminium), high-conductivity aluminium

amagnétique, armure ~
  D: unmagnetische Bewehrung

amagnétique

    E: non-magnetic armo(u)ring

âme f **ACSR** (fils d'aluminium câblés autour d'un fil central en acier)
    D: ACSR-Leiterseil n (Al-Leiter um einen Stahlkerndraht verseilt), Aluminiumleiter m (ACSR)
    E: aluminium conductor steel reinforced (ACSR)

âme f **à section réduite**
    D: halber Leiter
    E: conductor with reduced cross-sectional area

âme f **à un seul brin**
    D: eindrähtiger Leiter, Massivleiter m
    E: solid conductor

âme f **câblée**
    D: mehrdrähtiger Leiter
    E: stranded conductor

âme f **câblée en couches concentriques**
    D: Leiter aus konzentrisch verseilten Drahtlagen
    E: concentric lay conductor, concentric strand

âme f **câblée par faisceaux**
    D: bündelverseilter Leiter
    E: rope lay strand

âme f **circulaire**
    D: Rundleiter m
    E: round conductor, circular conductor

âme f **compactée**
    D: verdichteter Leiter
    E: compact(ed) conductor, compacted strand, compressed strand

âme f **concentrique**
    D: konzentrischer Leiter
    E: concentric conductor

âme f **conductrice**
    D: Leiter m
    E: conductor n

âme f **creuse** [c. én.]
    D: Hohlleiter m
    E: hollow conductor

âme f **de petite section**
    D: Leiter mit kleinem Querschnitt
    E: small-size conductor, small-gauge conductor

âme f **en aluminium plaqué de cuivre**
    D: kupferplattierter Aluminiumleiter
    E: copper-clad aluminium conductor

âme f **en cuivre**
    D: Kupferleiter m
    E: copper conductor

âme f **en fils extra-fins**
    D: feinstdrähtiger Leiter
    E: extra-fine wire conductor, super-fine wire conductor, extra-flexible stranded conductor

âme f **en fils fins**
    D: feindrähtiger Leiter
    E: fine wire conductor, flexible stranded conductor

âme f **en fils super-fins**
    D: feinstdrähtiger Leiter
    E: extra-fine wire conductor, super-fine wire conductor, extra-flexible stranded conductor

âme f **extérieure**
    D: Außenleiter m
    E: outer conductor

amélioration f
    D: Verbesserung f
    E: improvement n

âme f **massive**
    D: eindrähtiger Leiter, Massivleiter m
    E: solid conductor

amenée, conduite d'~ de secteur
    D: Netzzuleitung f
    E: mains supply lead

âme f **non rétreinte**
    D: nicht verdichteter Leiter
    E: non-compacted conductor

âme f **nue**
    D: blanker Leiter
    E: bare conductor, plain conductor

âme f **plaquée de métal**
    D: metallumhüllter Leiter
    E: metal clad conductor

âme f **profilée**
    D: Profilleiter m
    E: shaped conductor

âme f **rétreinte**
    D: verdichteter Leiter
    E: compact(ed) conductor, compacted strand, compressed strand

âme f **ronde**
    D: Rundleiter m
    E: round conductor, circular conductor

âme f **sectorale**
    D: Sektorleiter m
    E: sector-shaped conductor

âme f **segmentée**

D: Segmentleiter *m*
E: segmental conductor, split conductor
amiante *m*
D: Asbest *m*
E: asbestos *n*
amiante-ciment, tube en ~
D: Asbestzementrohr *n*
E: asbestos cement pipe
amont, en ~
D: entgegengesetzt der Fertigungsrichtung
E: upstream *adv*
amorçage *m*
D: Funkenüberschlag *m*, Überschlag *m*
E: flash-over *n*, arc-over *n*, spark-over *n*
amorçage *m* [él.]
D: Durchschlag *m*
E: breakdown *n*, dielectric breakdown *n*, puncture *n*
amovible *adj*
D: abnehmbar *adj*
E: detachable *adj*, removable *adj*, dismountable *adj*
ampérage *m*
D: Stromstärke *f*
E: current intensity, amperage *n*
amplificateur *m*
D: Verstärker *m*
E: amplifier *n*, repeater *n*
amplificateur *m* **à tube à vide**
D: Vakuumröhren-Verstärker *m*
E: vacuum tube amplifier
amplification *f* [com.]
D: Verstärkung *f*
E: amplification *n*
amplification *f* **à transistors**
D: Halbleiter-Verstärkung *f*, Transistor-Verstärkung *f*
E: solid-state amplification
amplification *f* **par semi-conducteurs**
D: Halbleiter-Verstärkung *f*, Transistor-Verstärkung *f*
E: solid-state amplification
analyse *f*
D: Untersuchung *f*, Prüfung *f* (Kontrolle)
E: inspection *n*, check *n*, examination *n*, investigation *n*, analysis *n*
analyse *f* [ess.]
D: Bestimmung *f*

E: determination *n*, analysis *n*
analyse *f* **à décantation**
D: Schlämmanalyse *f*
E: analysis by elutriation, analysis by decantation
analyse *f* **au tamis**
D: Siebanalyse *f*
E: sieve analysis, screen analysis
analyse *f* **granulométrique**
D: Teilchengrößenanalyse *f*
E: particle size analysis
analyse *f* **humide**
D: Naßanalyse *f*
E: wet analysis
analyse *f* **métallographique**
D: metallographische Prüfung
E: metallographic examination, metallographic test
analyse *f* **par élutriation**
D: Schlämmanalyse *f*
E: analysis by elutriation, analysis by decantation
analyse *f* **spectrale**
D: Spektralanalyse *f*
E: spectral analysis
analyse *f* **spectrographique**
D: spektrographische Analyse
E: spectrographic(al) analysis
angle *m* **au sommet**
D: Spitzenwinkel *m* (Sektorleiter)
E: sector angle
angle *m* **de câblage**
D: Verseilwinkel *m*
E: stranding angle
angle *m* **de contact**
D: Umschlingungswinkel *m*
E: contact angle, angle of wrap
angle *m* **d'entrée à la filière** [fabr. fils mét.]
D: Ziehstein-Einlaufwinkel *m*
E: die approach angle
angle *m* **de pas**
D: Steigungswinkel *m*
E: angle of pitch
angle *m* **de perte** (tan δ)
D: Verlustwinkel *m* (tan δ)
E: loss angle (tan δ)
angle *m* **de phase**
D: Phasenwinkel *m*
E: phase angle
angle *m* **de rubanage** [rub.]
D: Spinnwinkel *m*
E: lapping angle
angle *m* **d'inclinaison**

angle

anneau *m* **de centrage**
 D: Zentrierring *m*
 E: eccentric ring

anneau *m* **de filière**
 D: Matrizenring *m*
 E: die ring

anneau *m* **de fond** [pr. à filer]
 D: Grundring *m*
 E: base ring

anneau *m* **de répartition du champ électrique** [access. c.]
 D: Strahlungsring *m*
 E: stress relief ring

anneau *m* **d'étanchéité**
 D: Dichtungsring *m*
 E: sealing ring, joint ring

antenne *f*
 D: Antenne *f*
 E: aerial *n*, antenna *n*

antenne *f* **collective**
 D: Gemeinschaftsantenne *f*
 E: community antenna

antimoine *m*
 D: Antimon *n*
 E: antimony *n*

antioxidant *m*
 D: Oxydationsinhibitor *m*,
   Oxydationsverzögerer *m*,
   Alterungsschutzmittel *n*,
   Antioxidans *n*
 E: antioxidant *n*, oxidation inhibitor

antioxygène *m*
 D: Oxydationsinhibitor *m*,
   Oxydationsverzögerer *m*,
   Alterungsschutzmittel *n*,
   Antioxidans *n*
 E: antioxidant *n*, oxidation inhibitor

antiparasitage *m*
 D: Störschutz *m*
 E: interference protection

anti-vibratoire *adj*
 D: schwingungsfrei *adj*
 E: vibration-free *adj*, non-vibrating *adj*, anti-vibration ...

appareil *m*
 D: Gerät *n*
 E: apparatus *n*, instrument *n*, device *n*, equipment *n*

appareil *m* **automatique d'essai de câbles**
 D: Kabelprüfautomat *m*
 E: automatic cable tester

appareil *m* **de contrôle de la dureté**
 D: Härteprüfer *m*, Durometer *n*
 E: hardness tester, durometer *n*

appareil *m* **de contrôle d'ionisation par défilement continu** [câb.]
 D: Durchlaufprüfgerät *n*,
   Trockenprüfgerät *n*
 E: on-line spark tester, continuous discharge detection apparatus, sparker *n*, spark tester

appareil *m* **de mesure**
 D: Meßgerät *n*
 E: measuring device, measuring instrument, measuring equipment

appareil *m* **de mesure de l'excentricité**
 D: Exzentrizitäts-Meßvorrichtung *f*
 E: eccentricity gauge

appareil *m* **de mesure d'isolement**
 D: Isolationsmesser *m*
 E: insulation tester

appareil *m* **de réglage**
 D: Regler *m*
 E: regulator *n*, control *n*, controller *n*

appareillage *m*
 D: Garnituren *f pl*
 E: accessories *pl*

appareillage *m* **accessoire**
 D: Zusatzeinrichtung *f*
 E: additional equipment, auxiliary equipment, ancillary equipment

appareillage *m* **complémentaire**
 D: Zusatzeinrichtung *f*
 E: additional equipment, auxiliary equipment, ancillary equipment

appareil *m* **mobile**
 D: ortsveränderliches Gerät
 E: portable appliance, mobile equipment, portable equipment

appareil *m* **portatif**
 D: ortsveränderliches Gerät
 E: portable appliance, mobile equipment, portable equipment

appareil *m* **téléphonique**
 D: Telefonapparat *m*, Sprechstelle *f*
 E: telephone set, telephone instrument (US), telephone station

apparent *adj* [pose c.]
 D: auf Putz
 E: on the surface, open *adj*

application *f* (**charge d'essai**)
 D: Aufsetzen *n* (Prüflast)
 E: application *n* (test load)

appliquer v
  D: aufbringen v
  E: apply v
appliquer v **une tension**
  D: eine Spannung anlegen
  E: to apply a voltage.
appointé, isolation ~e
  D: angespitzte Isolierung
  E: pencilled insulation
appointer v
  D: anspitzen v (Isolierung)
  E: pencil v
appointer v
  D: anspitzen v (Draht)
  E: point v
appointer, machine à ~ et enfiler le fil métallique
  D: Anspitzmaschine und Einziehmaschine (Draht)
  E: wire sharpening and threading machine
aptitude f
  D: Eignung f
  E: suitability n
aptitude f **à la mise en œuvre**
  D: Verarbeitbarkeit f
  E: processibility n
aptitude au durcissement f
  D: Härtbarkeit f
  E: hardenability n
aptitude au façonnage f
  D: Formbarkeit f
  E: plasticity n, workability n
aptitude f **au moulage**
  D: Formbarkeit f
  E: plasticity n, workability n
aptitude f **au pliage**
  D: Biegefähigkeit f
  E: bending capacity
arborescence f
  D: Bäumchenbildung f (in Isolierstoffen unter el. Beanspruchung)
  E: treeing n
arbre m [mach.]
  D: Welle f
  E: shaft n
arbre m **creux d'une cage de câblage**
  D: Hohlwelle eines Verseilkorbes
  E: cage barrel, barrel of a stranding cage
arbre m **de commande**
  D: Antriebswelle f
  E: transmission shaft, driving shaft
arc, résistance à l'~ électrique
  D: Lichtbogenbeständigkeit f
  E: arc resistance
arc m **d'enroulement**
  D: Umschlingungswinkel m
  E: contact angle, angle of wrap
archet m **de câblage**
  D: Verseilbügel m, Jochbügel m
  E: stranding flyer, twisting flyer
arête f
  D: Kante f
  E: edge n
arête f
  D: Grat m, Gußgrat m
  E: fin n, burr n, flash n
arête f **de secteur**
  D: Sektorkante f
  E: sector edge
armé adj
  D: bewehrt adj, armiert adj
  E: armo(u)red adj
armeuse f
  D: Armiermaschine f, Bewehrungsmaschine f
  E: armo(u)ring machine
armoire f **à câbles** [com.]
  D: Kabelschrank m
  E: cable cabinet
armoire f **d'appareillage**
  D: Schaltschrank m
  E: control cabinet
armoire f **de commande**
  D: Schaltschrank m
  E: control cabinet
armoire f **de distribution de câbles**
  D: Kabelverteilerschrank m
  E: cable distribution cabinet
armoire f **de régulation**
  D: Schaltschrank m
  E: control cabinet
armure f
  D: Bewehrung f, Armierung f
  E: armo(u)ring n, armo(u)r n
armure f **amagnétique**
  D: unmagnetische Bewehrung
  E: non-magnetic armo(u)ring
armure f **double**
  D: doppellagige Armierung
  E: double armo(u)ring
armure f **en feuillard d'acier**
  D: Bandeisen-Armierung f, Bandeisenbewehrung f,

armure

Stahlbandarmierung f,
Stahlbandbewehrung f,
Bandarmierung f, Bandbewehrung f
E: steel tape armo(u)ring, steel tape armo(u)r

armure f en fils d'acier
D: Stahldrahtbewehrung f,
Stahldrahtarmierung f
E: steel wire armouring

armure f en fils d'acier méplats
D: Stahlflachdraht-Bewehrung f,
Stahlflachdraht-Armierung f
E: flat steel wire armouring

armure f en fils méplats
D: Flachdrahtbewehrung f,
Flachdrahtarmierung f
E: flat wire armo(u)ring

armure f en fils métalliques
D: Drahtbewehrung f,
Drahtarmierung f
E: wire armo(u)ring, wire armo(u)r

armure f en fils ronds
D: Runddraht-Bewehrung f,
Runddraht-Armierung f
E: round wire armo(u)ring

arranger v
D: auslegen v (Werk, Anlage)
E: lay out v, set out v

arrêt m [mach.]
D: Anhalten n
E: stoppage n

arrêt m
D: Sperre f
E: barrier n

arrêt m d'urgence
D: Notabschaltung f
E: emergency shut-down

arrêter v [mach.]
D: abschalten v, ausschalten v
E: shut down v

arrivée f [él.]
D: Einspeisung f
E: power supply, feed-in n

arrondir v
D: abrunden v (Kante)
E: round v, round off v

articulé adj
D: ausschwenkbar adj, ausklappbar adj, schwenkbar adj, aufklappbar adj, drehbar gelagert
E: hinged adj, swivelling adj, pivoted adj

aspect m
D: Aussehen n (Oberfläche)
E: appearance n

aspiration f
D: Absaugung f
E: exhaust n, suction n

aspirer v
D: ansaugen v, absaugen v
E: suck v

assemblage m
D: Errichtung f, Montage f, Aufbau m
E: installation n, erection n, set-up n, assembly n

assemblage m (des conducteurs)
D: Seelenverseilung f, Aderverseilung f, Verseilung f (Seele)
E: core stranding, laying up n, cabling n

assemblage m à pas droit
D: Rechtsschlag-Verseilung f
E: right-hand stranding

assemblage m à pas gauche
D: Linksschlag-Verseilung f
E: left-hand stranding

assemblage m des conducteurs [câb.]
D: Seele f
E: core n (assembly)

assemblage m par (en) couches
D: Lagenverseilung f
E: layer-stranding n, stranding in layers

assemblage m par faisceaux
D: Bündelverseilung f
E: unit stranding, unit lay-up

assemblage m par paires
D: Paarverseilung f
E: pairing n, twinning n, pair twisting

assembler v
D: verseilen v (Kabelseele)
E: lay up v, strand v

assembler v
D: errichten v
E: set up v, install v, mount v, erect v, assemble v

assembleuse f
D: Seelenverseilmaschine f,
Aderverseilmaschine f
E: core-stranding machine, laying-up machine, core-strander n, cabler n

assembleuse f à cage
D: Korbverseilmaschine f
E: planetary strander, planet-type stranding machine, cage strander,

slow-speed strander
Association f des Electrotechniciens Allemands
 D: Verband Deutscher Elektrotechniker e.V. (VDE)
 E: Association of German Electrical Engineers
Association f des Ingénieurs Allemands
 D: Verein Deutscher Ingenieure (VDI)
 E: Association of German Engineers
asymétrie f
 D: Unsymmetrie f
 E: unbalance n, unsymmetry n, asymmetry n
atelier m
 D: Betrieb m (Werk, Anlage), Werkstatt f
 E: factory n, plant n, workshop n
atelier m **de fabrication**
 D: Fertigungsabteilung f
 E: production department, manufacturing department
atelier m **de préparation des mélanges**
 D: Mischerei f
 E: mixing shop
atmosphère f conditionnée
 D: klimatisierte Atmosphäre, konditionierte Luft
 E: conditioned atmosphere, conditioned air
atmosphère f contrôlée
 D: Schutzgasatmosphäre f
 E: controlled atmosphere, protective atmosphere
atmosphère f de vapeur
 D: Dampfatmosphäre f
 E: steam atmosphere
atmosphère f protectrice
 D: Schutzgasatmosphäre f
 E: controlled atmosphere, protective atmosphere
atomiseur m
 D: Sprühdüse f
 E: spray nozzle, jet nozzle
attache f
 D: Klemme f
 E: clamp n, clip n
attache f de câble
 D: Kabelschelle f, Kabelklemme f
 E: cable clamp, cable cleat, cable clip, cable grip

attache f de conducteur
 D: Kabelschuh m, Kabel-Abschlußhülse f, Anschlußöse f, Anschlußlasche f
 E: cable lug, terminal lug, cable eye
attacher v
 D: befestigen v
 E: fasten v, fix v, attach v
attacher vt
 D: kleben vt
 E: cement vt, glue vt, paste vt, bond vt
attaquer v [chim.]
 D: aufschließen v
 E: decompose v
attaquer v
 D: korrodieren v
 E: corrode v, attack v
atténuation f
 D: Dämpfung f
 E: damping n, attenuation n
atténuation f de réflexion
 D: Reflexionsdämpfung f, Fehlerdämpfung f
 E: reflection attenuation, balance return loss, return loss between line and network (US), reflection loss, balance attenuation
atténuation f totale
 D: Gesamtdämpfung f
 E: total cable equivalent, total loss, total attenuation
atterrir v un câble
 D: ein Kabel an Land ziehen
 E: to float a cable ashore
audio-fréquence f
 D: Tonfrequenz f, Niederfrequenz f
 E: audio frequency, voice frequency, low frequency
augmentation f
 D: Vergrößerung f
 E: enlargement n, magnification n, increase n
augmenter v
 D: vergrößern v
 E: increase v, extend v, enlarge v, magnify v
auto-adhésif adj
 D: selbstklebend adj
 E: self-bonding adj, self-adhering adj, self-adhesive adj
autoamalgamant, ruban ~
 D: selbstverschweißendes Band
 E: self-amalgamating tape, self-

autoamalgamant

    fusing tape
autoclave *m* de vulcanisation
    D: Heizkessel *m*, Vulkanisierkessel *m*
    E: vulcanizing pan, autoclave *n*
auto-collant *adj*
    D: selbstklebend *adj*
    E: self-bonding *adj*, self-adhering *adj*, self-adhesive *adj*
auto-extinguible *adj*
    D: selbsterlöschend *adj*
    E: self-extinguishing *adj*
auto-impédance *f*
    D: Eigenimpedanz *f*
    E: self-impedance *n*
automate *m* temporisé
    D: Zeitschalter *m*
    E: time switch, timer *n*
automatique, entièrement ~
    D: vollautomatisch *adj*, vollautomatisiert *adj*
    E: fully automatic, fully automated
automatisé, complètement ~
    D: vollautomatisch *adj*, vollautomatisiert *adj*
    E: fully automatic, fully automated
autoporteur, câble aérien ~
    D: selbsttragendes Luftkabel
    E: self-supporting aerial cable, self-supporting overhead cable
autosoudable, ruban ~
    D: selbstverschweißendes Band
    E: self-amalgamating tape, self-fusing tape
autosoudant, ruban ~
    D: selbstverschweißendes Band
    E: self-amalgamating tape, self-fusing tape
auto-vulcanisant *adj*
    D: selbstvulkanisierend *adj*
    E: self-curing *adj*, self-vulcanizing *adj*
auxiliaire *m*
    D: Hilfsarbeiter *m*
    E: helper *n*, unskilled worker
auxiliaire, dispositif ~
    D: Hilfsvorrichtung *f*
    E: auxiliary device
aval, en ~
    D: in Fertigungsrichtung
    E: downstream *adv*
avance *f*
    D: Vorschub *m*
    E: feed *n*, advance *n*
avance *f* de phase
    D: Phasenvoreilung *f*
    E: phase lead
avertisseur *m* de pression
    D: Druckwächter *m*
    E: pressure contactor, pressure monitor, pressure control device
axe *m* de câblage
    D: Verseilachse *f*
    E: stranding axis
axe *m* médian d'une machine
    D: Mittellinie einer Maschine
    E: centre line of a machine

B

bac *m*
    D: Trog *m*, Wanne *f*
    E: trough *n*
bac *m* à bitume
    D: Bitumenkasten *m*
    E: bitumen vat
bac *m* à craie
    D: Kreidekasten *m* (Kabelfertigung)
    E: lime box, chalk box
bac *m* de refroidissement
    D: Kühlrinne *f*, Kühlwanne *f*
    E: cooling trough
bâche *f*
    D: Sammelbehälter *m*, Auffangbehälter *m*
    E: sump *n*
bague *f* conique
    D: Keilring *m*
    E: wedge ring
bague *f* de centrage
    D: Zentrierring *m*
    E: eccentric ring
bague *f* de fond [pr. à filer]
    D: Grundring *m*
    E: base ring
bague *f* de frein
    D: Drehsicherungsscheibe *f*
    E: lock washer
bague *f* de laminage [extr.]
    D: Stauring *m*
    E: retaining ring
bague *f* de serrage
    D: Klemmring *m*
    E: clamp ring, clamping ring, locking

ring
bague f d'étanchéité
D: Dichtungsring m
E: sealing ring, joint ring
bague f d'une galette à papier [rub.]
D: Kern einer Papierscheibe
E: centre of a paper pad
baguette f de soudage
D: Schweißstab m
E: welding rod, filler rod
bain m de décapage
D: Beizbad n
E: pickling bath
bain m de grenaille de plomb
D: Schrotkugelbad n, Bleikugelbad n
E: lead ball bath, lead-shot bath
bain m de refroidissement
D: Kühlbad n
E: cooling bath
bain m de sel
D: Salzbad n
E: salt bath
bain m de tréfilage [fabr. fils mét.]
D: Ziehbad n
E: drawing bath
bain m de zinc
D: Zinkbad n
E: galvanizing bath
baisse f de la pression d'huile
D: Abfall des Öldrucks
E: drop of the oil pressure
baisse f de la température
D: Temperaturabfall m, Abfall der Temperatur, Absinken der Temperatur
E: temperature drop, temperature decrease
balance f
D: Ausgleich m
E: compensation n, balance n, balancing n, counterbalancing n, equalization n
balayer v
D: abtasten v
E: scan v, sense v
ballon, isolation ~
D: „Ballon"-Isolierung f
E: balloon insulation
banc m à deux cônes de tréfilage [fabr. fils mét.]
D: Einzelblock mit Doppelscheibe
E: double-deck drawing block
bandages m pl (pour les cônes de tréfilage)
D: Bandagen pl (für Ziehscheiben an der Drahtziehmaschine)
E: pullblock tyres
bande f
D: Bahn f (Papier, Stoff)
E: web n, sheeting n, sheet n
bande, enroulement papier à large ~
D: Breitbahnwicklung f (Papier)
E: broad-web paper wrapping
bande f de cuivre
D: Kupferband n, Bandkupfer n
E: copper tape, copper strip, copper strap
bande f de fréquences
D: Frequenzband n, Frequenzbereich m
E: frequency band, frequency range
bande f de fréquences transmise de façon effective
D: effektiv übertragenes Frequenzband
E: effectively transmitted frequency band
bande f de papier
D: Papierstreifen m
E: paper strip
bande f éliminée [com.]
D: Sperrbereich m
E: cut-off range suppression band
bande f métallique
D: Metallband n
E: metal strip, metal tape
bande f métreuse [câb.]
D: Längenmeßband n, Meßband n
E: measuring tape
barre f collectrice
D: Sammelschiene f
E: bus-bar n, bus-duct n
barre f coulée [coul. cont. lam.]
D: Gießstrang m
E: cast bar
barre f de soudure
D: Lotstab m
E: solder stick
barre f omnibus
D: Sammelschiene f
E: bus-bar n, bus-duct n
barrette f à bornes [él.]
D: Anschlußleiste f, Klemmleiste f
E: terminal block, terminal strip, terminal board, connecting block, connection strip

barrière f
  D: Sperre f
  E: barrier n

barrière f **d'humidité**
  D: Feuchtigkeitssperre f
  E: moisture barrier

basculant adj
  D: kippbar adj
  E: inclinable adj, tiltable adj

basculement m
  D: Neigung f
  E: inclination n, tilting n, tilt n

basse fréquence f
  D: Tonfrequenz f, Niederfrequenz f
  E: audio frequency, voice frequency, low frequency

basse tension (BT) f
  D: Niederspannung f
  E: low voltage (LV)

bâti m
  D: Gestell n, Rahmen m
  E: rack n, frame n

bâti m **de filière** [câblage]
  D: Nippelbock m
  E: nipple stand

bâti m **d'ensemble**
  D: Grundrahmen m, Fundamentrahmen m
  E: base frame

bâti m **départ** [fabr. fils mét., câb.]
  D: Ablaufbock m, Ablaufgestell n, Abwickelei f
  E: pay-off stand, supply stand, feed stand, take-off stand

bâti m **pour têtes de câbles**
  D: Kabelendgestell n, Endgestell für Kabel
  E: cable supporting rack, cable terminating rack, terminal rack

bâti m **terminal**
  D: Kabelendgestell n, Endgestell für Kabel
  E: cable supporting rack, cable terminating rack

bavure f
  D: Grat m, Gußgrat m
  E: fin n, burr n, flash n

bec m **de coulée**
  D: Gießtülle f
  E: pouring spout

berceau m [vulc.]
  D: Rohraufhängung f
  E: pipe suspension, pipe hangers pl

berceau m [câblage]
  D: Spulenhalter m, Spulenträger m, Joch n
  E: cradle n

berceau, disposé en ~ [pose c.]
  D: in Wiegenanordnung
  E: in cradled arrangement

biais, coupé en ~
  D: schräg geschnitten
  E: bias-cut adj

bifilaire adj
  D: doppeladrig adj
  E: bifilar adj, twin adj

bilatéral, commande ~e
  D: doppelseitiger Antrieb
  E: bilateral drive

billette f [pr. à filer]
  D: Bolzen m, Knüppel m
  E: billet n

billette f
  D: Puppe f (Rolle aus Walzfell)
  E: billet n, puppet n

billette, alimentation en ~s [pr. à filer]
  D: Bolzenbeschickung f
  E: billet loading

billette, dispositif de transport des ~s [pr. à filer]
  D: Blocktransportvorrichtung f
  E: billet handling device

billette f **cylindrique**
  D: Rundbolzen m, Rundknüppel m
  E: round billet

billette f **d'aluminium**
  D: Aluminiumbolzen m, Aluminiumpreßbolzen m, Aluminiumrundbarren m
  E: aluminium billet

biseauté, tranche ~e
  D: abgeschrägte Kante
  E: beveled edge

biseauter v
  D: abschrägen v
  E: bevel v, chamfer v

bitume m
  D: Bitumen n
  E: bitumen n

bitume m **soufflé**
  D: geblasenes Bitumen
  E: blown bitumen, oxidized bitumen

bitume m **vulcanisé**
  D: vulkanisiertes Bitumen
  E: vulcanized bitumen

bituminé adj

blanc m **de titane**
- D: Titanweiß n
- E: titanium white

blindage m [él.]
- D: Abschirmung f, Schirm m
- E: shield n, shielding n, screen n, screening n

blindé, disjoncteurs ~s
- D: gekapselte Schaltanlagen
- E: metal-clad switch-gear, cubicle type switch-gear

blinder v [él.]
- D: abschirmen v
- E: shield v, screen v

blocage m
- D: Verriegelung f
- E: blocking n, interlocking n, locking n

bloc m **de connexion** [él.]
- D: Anschlußleiste f, Klemmleiste f
- E: terminal block, terminal strip, terminal board, connecting block, connection strip

bloc m **de presse** [pr. à filer]
- D: Preßkopf m
- E: die block, press block

bloc-tube m
- D: Formstein m
- E: duct block

bloquer v
- D: blockieren v
- E: block v, interlock v

bobinage m
- D: Wicklung f
- E: winding n, wrapping n, coil n

bobinage m **de condensateur**
- D: Kondensatorwickel m
- E: capacitor roll, capacitor coil

bobine f
- D: Spule f
- E: coil n, reel n, bobbin n, spool n

bobine f [câb.]
- D: Trommel f
- E: reel n, drum n

bobine f **d'alimentation**
- D: Ablaufspule f, Vorratstrommel f, Ablauftrommel f, Abwickeltrommel f
- E: pay-off reel, supply reel

bobine f **d'alimentation**
- D: Einsatzspule f, Einsatztrommel f, Maschinenspule f, Maschinentrommel f, Werkstatttrommel f
- E: input bobbin, input reel, processing reel, processing drum

bobine f **débitrice**
- D: Ablaufspule f, Vorratstrommel f, Ablauftrommel f, Abwickeltrommel f
- E: pay-off reel, supply reel

bobine f **de câble**
- D: Kabeltrommel f
- E: cable drum, cable reel

bobine f **de charge**
- D: Pupin-Spule f, Belastungsspule f, Verstärkerspule f
- E: Pupin coil, loading coil

bobine f **de charge du circuit combinant**
- D: Stammleitungsspule f, Stammkreisspule f, Stammpupinspule f
- E: side circuit loading coil

bobine f **de charge pour circuit fantôme**
- D: Phantompupinspule f
- E: phantom circuit loading coil

bobine f **de dévidage**
- D: Ablaufspule f, Vorratstrommel f, Ablauftrommel f, Abwickeltrommel f
- E: pay-off reel, supply reel

bobine f **de réaction**
- D: Rückkopplungsspule f
- E: reaction coil, feedback coil

bobine f **d'expédition**
- D: Versandspule f, Versandtrommel f, Liefertrommel f
- E: despatch reel, shipping reel, delivery reel

bobine f **Pupin**
- D: Pupin-Spule f, Belastungsspule f, Verstärkerspule f
- E: Pupin coil, loading coil

bobiner v
- D: aufwickeln v, aufspulen v, spulen v, wickeln v, auftrommeln v
- E: wind v, wind up v, take up v, spool v, reel v, coil v

bobine f **réceptrice**
- D: Aufwickelspule f, Aufwickeltrommel f
- E: take-up reel

bobineuse

bobineuse *f*
  D: Wickler *m*, Umwickelei *f*
  E: coiler *n*, spooler *n*, take-up *n*, rewinding stand
bobineuse de fil métallique *f*
  D: Drahtwickelmaschine *f*
  E: wire winding machine, wire spooler
bobineuse *f* **de fil métallique** (pour rebobinage)
  D: Drahtumwickelei *f*
  E: wire rewinding stand
bobinoir *m*
  D: Aufwickelei *f*, Wickler *m*
  E: take-up unit, take-up *n*, take-up stand
bobinoir *m* **à feuillard d'acier**
  D: Bandeisen-Wickler *m*
  E: steel tape spooler
bobinoir *m* **à pointes**
  D: Pinolen-Wickler *m*
  E: pintle-type spooler
bobinoir *m* **automatique**
  D: automatischer Spulapparat
  E: automatic spooler
bobinoir *m* **double**
  D: Doppelspulapparat *m*, Doppelspuler *m*
  E: double-reel spooler, dual-reel take-up
boîte *f*
  D: Gehäuse *n*
  E: housing *n*, casing *n*, cabinet *n*
boîte *f* **à bornes** [él.]
  D: Anschlußkasten *m*, Klemmenkasten *m*
  E: distribution panel, terminal box, junction box, connection box
boîte *f* **de bifurcation**
  D: Gabelmuffe für zwei Adern, Verzweigungsmuffe für zwei Adern
  E: bifurcating joint
boîte *f* **de branchement**
  D: Abzweigkasten *m*, Abzweigdose *f*, Kabelverzweiger *m*, Abzweigmuffe *f*, Verteilerkasten *m*
  E: branch box, distributing box, branch joint, distributor box (US), distribution cabinet, connecting box
boîte *f* **de charge** [com.]
  D: Spulenkasten *m*, Pupinspulenkasten *m*
  E: loading (coil) pot, loading coil case
boîte *f* **de connexion** [él.]
  D: Anschlußkasten *m*, Klemmenkasten *m*
  E: distribution panel, terminal box, junction box, connection box
boîte *f* **de dérivation** [él.]
  D: Anschlußkasten *m*, Klemmenkasten *m*
  E: distribution panel, terminal box, junction box, connection box
boîte *f* **de dérivation**
  D: Abzweigkasten *m*, Abzweigdose *f*, Kabelverzweiger *m*, Abzweigmuffe *f*, Verteilerkasten *m*
  E: branch box, distributing box, branch joint, distributor box (US), distribution cabinet, connecting box
boîte *f* **de distribution**
  D: Aufteilungsmuffe *f*
  E: spreading box, spreader box, multiple joint box, distribution sleeve
boîte *f* **de distribution**
  D: Abzweigkasten *m*, Abzweigdose *f*, Kabelverzweiger *m*, Abzweigmuffe *f*, Verteilerkasten *m*
  E: branch box, distributing box, branch joint, distributor box (US), distribution cabinet, connecting box
boîte *f* **de division**
  D: Aufteilungsmuffe *f*
  E: spreading box, spreader box, multiple joint box, distribution sleeve
boîte *f* **de jonction** [él.]
  D: Anschlußkasten *m*, Klemmenkasten *m*
  E: distribution panel, terminal box, junction box, connection box
boîte *f* **de jonction**
  D: Verbindungsmuffe *f*
  E: connecting box, joint box, straight joint
boîte *f* **de jonction en fonte**
  D: gußeisernes Muffengehäuse
  E: cast iron joint box
boîte *f* **de raccordement**
  D: Anschlußdose *f*
  E: connection box, junction box

boîte *f* **de raccordement à la terre** [câb.]
 D: Auskreuzungskasten *m*,
  Schaltkasten *m*
 E: link box, cross-bonding box
boîte *f* **de raccordement domestique**
 D: Hausanschlußmuffe *f*
 E: house service box
boîte *f* **de transposition** [câb.]
 D: Auskreuzungskasten *m*,
  Schaltkasten *m*
 E: link box, cross-bonding box
boîte *f* **de trifurcation**
 D: Verzweigungsmuffe für drei Adern,
  Aufteilungsmuffe für drei Adern,
  Gabelmuffe für drei Adern
 E: trifurcating joint, trifurcating box
boîte *f* **d'extrémité de câble**
 D: Kabelendverschluß *m*
 E: cable termination
boîte *f* **d'extrémité tripolaire**
 D: Dreileiter-Endverschluß *m*
 E: three-core termination
boîte *f* **d'extrémité unipolaire**
 D: Einleiter-Endverschluß *m*
 E: single-core termination
boîte *f* **tangentielle**
 D: Tangentialmuffe *f*, spitzwinklige
  Abzweigmuffe
 E: tangential joint
boîte *f* **tri-mono**
 D: Verzweigungsmuffe für drei Adern,
  Aufteilungsmuffe für drei Adern,
  Gabelmuffe für drei Adern
 E: trifurcating joint, trifurcating box
bombe *f* **à air**
 D: Luftbombe *f*
 E: air bomb
bombe *f* **à oxygène**
 D: Sauerstoffbombe *f*
 E: oxygen bomb
bord *m*
 D: Kante *f*
 E: edge *n*
bordeler *v*
 D: umschlagen *v*, umbördeln *v*,
  bördeln *v*
 E: fold back *v*, flange *v*
border *v*
 D: umschlagen *v*, umbördeln *v*,
  bördeln *v*
 E: fold back *v*, flange *v*
bord *m* **rabattu**
 D: Umbördelung *f*

 E: flanging *n*
borne *f* [él.]
 D: Klemme *f*, Anschlußklemme *f*,
  Verbindungsklemme *f*,
  Endenanschlußklemme *f*
 E: terminal *n*, connector *n*,
  connecting terminal
borne *f* [c. com.]
 D: Anschlußklemme *f*
 E: binding post
borne *f* **à vis** [él.]
 D: Klemmschraube *f*,
  Schraubklemme *f*
 E: terminal screw, binding screw,
  screw terminal
borne *f* **de câble**
 D: Kabelklemme *f*
 E: cable terminal
borne *f* **de dérivation**
 D: Abzweigklemme *f*
 E: tee connector, T-connector *n*,
  branch connector, branch terminal
borne *f* **de raccordement** [él.]
 D: Klemme *f*, Anschlußklemme *f*,
  Verbindungsklemme *f*,
  Endenanschlußklemme *f*
 E: terminal *n*, connector *n*,
  connecting terminal
borne *f* **de terre**
 D: Erdungsklemme *f*, Erdklemme *f*
 E: ground clamp (US), ground
  terminal (US), earth terminal (GB),
  earth clamp (GB)
borne *f* **en forme de griffe**
 D: Tatzenklemme *f*
 E: claw-type clamp
borne *f* **en forme de T**
 D: Abzweigklemme *f*
 E: tee connector, T-connector *n*,
  branch connector, branch terminal
boucher *v*
 D: abdichten *v*
 E: seal *v*
boucle *f* [él.]
 D: Schleife *f*
  (Leitungszusammenführung)
 E: loop *n*, closed circuit
boucle *f* **de mesure**
 D: Meßschleife *f*
 E: measuring loop
boudinage *m*
 D: Extrudieren *n*, Extrusion *f*
 E: extrusion *n*

boudinage

boudinage m sous vide [extr.]
  D: Schlauchreckverfahren n
  E: tube-on method, tubing extrusion, vacuum smearing
boudiner v
  D: extrudieren v, umspritzen v
  E: extrude v
boudineuse f
  D: Schneckenpresse f, Extruder m
  E: extruder n
boudineuse f à aération
  D: Extruder mit Entgasungssystem
  E: vent extruder
boue f anodique
  D: Anodenschlamm m
  E: anode mud
boulon m de fondation
  D: Fundamentschraube f
  E: foundation bolt
boulonnage m
  D: Verschraubung f, Schraubverbindung f
  E: screw connection, bolted connection, bolted joint, screw(ed) joint
bourrage m [câb.]
  D: Beilauf m, Zwickelfüllung f, Lückenfüllung f
  E: filler n, valley sealer
bourrage m central
  D: Mittelblindader f
  E: centre blind core, centre filler
bourrage m jute
  D: Jute-Beilauf m
  E: jute filler
bourrelet m (sur mélangeur à caoutchouc)
  D: Wulst m (am Gummi-Mischwalzwerk)
  E: bank of rubber on a mill
bout m de câble
  D: Kabelstumpf m
  E: stub cable, sealed cable end
bout m de la billette [pr. à filer]
  D: Bolzenende n
  E: billet butt
bouton m de réglage
  D: Einstellknopf m
  E: control knob
bouton-poussoir, commande par ~
  D: Druckknopfsteuerung f
  E: push-button control
branchement m
  D: Abzweigung f
  E: branch n, tap n, junction n
branchement m au réseau
  D: Netzanschluß m
  E: line connection, mains supply, power supply
brancher v [él.]
  D: schalten v
  E: switch v, connect v
brancher v
  D: abzweigen v
  E: branch v, tap v
bras m (de malaxeur)
  D: Knetarm m
  E: blade n (of kneader)
bras m amovible
  D: Schwenkarm m
  E: swivel arm, swing-out arm
braser v
  D: hartlöten v
  E: braze v
bras m pivotant
  D: Schwenkarm m
  E: swivel arm, swing-out arm
brasure f
  D: Hartlot n
  E: brass solder, brazing solder, hard solder, brazing alloy
brasure f
  D: Lötverbindung f (hart)
  E: brazed joint, brazing joint
brevet, accorder un ~
  D: ein Patent erteilen
  E: to grant a patent
bride f
  D: Schelle f, Befestigungsschelle f
  E: clamp n, bracket n, clip n, cleat n
bride f d'attache
  D: Rohrschelle f
  E: collar band, wall clamp, pipe clip
bride f de suspension
  D: Tragband n (Luftkabel)
  E: cable suspender
brider v
  D: festklemmen v
  E: cleat v, clamp v, cramp v
brider v le câble
  D: Kabel mit Schellen befestigen
  E: to clamp a cable
brillant adj
  D: blank adj
  E: plain adj, bright adj, bare adj
brin m

brin m [câb.]
D: Einzeldraht m
E: single wire

brin m
D: Einzelader f, Einzelleiter m
E: single conductor

brin m **profilé**
D: Profildraht m
E: profile wire, shaped wire, strip n

briser v **la nappe de caoutchouc malaxé sur les cylindres** [caout.]
D: Fell von der Mischwalze abschneiden
E: to break the batch loose from the rolls

brisure f
D: Bruch m, Bruchstelle f
E: fracture n, break n, rupture n

broche f
D: Dorn m
E: mandrel n

brosse métallique, traitement à la ~
D: Behandlung mit der Drahtbürste
E: scratch brushing

broyage, installation de ~ des déchets de câbles
D: Zerkleinerungsanlage für Kabelabfälle
E: cable scrap granulators pl

bruit m **d'amplificateur**
D: Verstärkergeräusch n
E: amplifier noise

bruit m **de circuit**
D: Leitungsgeräusch n
E: line noise

bruit m **de friture** [com.]
D: Kratzgeräusch n
E: scratchy noise

bruit m **de ligne**
D: Leitungsgeräusch n
E: line noise

bruit m **induit** [c. com.]
D: Starkstromgeräusch n, Stromversorgungsgeräusch n
E: power induced noise, power supply noise

bruit m **parasite**
D: Störgeräusch n
E: interfering noise, parasitic noise

bruit m **perturbateur**
D: Störgeräusch n
E: interfering noise, parasitic noise

bruit m **télégraphique**
D: Telegrafiegeräusch n
E: telegraphic noise

brûler v
D: verbrennen vi
E: burn v, scorch v, combust v

BT (v. basse tension)

bull-block m [fabr. fils mét.]
D: Bull-Block m (Einscheiben-Vorsatzblock für große Profil-Abmessungen)
E: bull-block n

bulle f
D: Blase f
E: bubble n, blister n

bulle f **de gaz**
D: Gasblase f
E: gas bubble

bulle f **gazeuse**
D: Gasblase f
E: gas bubble

bulles f pl **d'air**
D: Lufteinschlüsse m pl
E: air inclusions, air pockets, voids pl

Buna m S (caoutchouc butadiène styrène)
D: Buna S m (Butadien-Styrol-Kautschuk)
E: Buna S (butadiene-styrene rubber), GRS (butadiene-styrene rubber) (US)

bureau m **de dessins**
D: Konstruktionsbüro n
E: drawing office, engineering department, designing office

bureau m **d'études**
D: Konstruktionsbüro n
E: drawing office, engineering department, designing office

bureau m **téléphonique**
D: Fernsprechamt n, Telefonzentrale f
E: telephone exchange, telephone central office

buse f
D: Düse f
E: nozzle n, jet n, orifice n

butée f
D: Anschlag m (Arretierung)
E: stop n, lock n, limit stop

C

cabestan *m* **de tirage**
 D: Scheibenabzug *m*, Abzugscheibe *f*
 E: pull-off capstan, haul-off capstan

cabestan *m* **de tirage au-dessus de la hauteur de la tête**
 D: Überkopfabzug *m*
 E: overhead pull-off

cabestan *m* **de tirage auxiliaire**
 D: Hilfsabzugsscheibe *f*
 E: auxiliary pull-off capstan

cabestan *m* **tireur**
 D: Scheibenabzug *m*, Abzugscheibe *f*
 E: pull-off capstan, haul-off capstan

câblage *m* **(âme)**
 D: Leiterverseilung *f*, Verseilung *f*
 E: conductor stranding, bunching *n*, stranding *n*, twisting *n*

câblage *m* **à détorsion**
 D: Verseilung mit Rückdrehung (Rundleiter), spannungslose Verseilung (Rundleiter)
 E: stranding with backtwist

câblage *m* **à pas droit**
 D: Rechtsschlag-Verseilung *f*
 E: right-hand stranding

câblage *m* **à pas gauche**
 D: Linksschlag-Verseilung *f*
 E: left-hand stranding

câblage *m* **à préformage**
 D: Verseilung mit Vordrall (Sektorleiter), spannungslose Verseilung (Sektorleiter)
 E: stranding with pretwist

câblage *m* **à prétorsion**
 D: Verseilung mit Vordrall (Sektorleiter), spannungslose Verseilung (Sektorleiter)
 E: stranding with pretwist

câblage *m* **à quartes à paires**
 D: Dieselhorst-Martin-Verseilung *f*, DM-Verseilung *f*
 E: multiple-twin quad formation

câblage *m* **en couches croisées**
 D: Kreuzschlagverseilung *f*, Verseilung im Gegenschlag, Gegenschlagverseilung *f*, Verseilung im Wechselschlag
 E: reverse(d) lay stranding

câblage *m* **en même sens**
 D: Verseilung im Gleichschlag
 E: same lay stranding

câblage *m* **en sens alterné**
 D: Kreuzschlagverseilung *f*, Verseilung im Gegenschlag, Gegenschlagverseilung *f*, Verseilung im Wechselschlag
 E: reverse(d) lay stranding

câblage *m* **en tortillon de paille**
 D: Strohverseilung *f*
 E: straw-rope stranding

câblage *m* **Lang**
 D: Verseilung im Längsschlag
 E: long lay stranding, Lang's lay stranding

câblage *m* **long**
 D: Verseilung im Längsschlag
 E: long lay stranding, Lang's lay stranding

câblage *m* **multiple**
 D: Mehrfachverseilung *f*
 E: multiple stranding

câblage *m* **par (en) couches**
 D: Lagenverseilung *f*
 E: layer-stranding *n*, stranding in layers

câblage *m* **par faisceaux**
 D: Bündelverseilung *f*
 E: unit stranding, unit lay-up

câblage *m* **par quartes en étoile**
 D: Sternviererverseilung *f*
 E: star quad formation, star quad twisting, star quadding

câblage *m* **sans détorsion**
 D: Verseilung ohne Rückdrehung
 E: stranding without backtwist

câblage *m* **sans prétorsion**
 D: gestreckte Verseilung
 E: stranding without pretwist

câblage *m* **SZ**
 D: SZ-Verseilung *f*
 E: SZ-stranding *n*

câble *m*
 D: Kabel *n*, Leitung *f*
 E: cable *n*

câble *m*
 D: Seil *n*
 E: rope *n*, strand *n*

câble *m* **à âme en aluminium**
 D: Aluminiumleiterkabel *n*
 E: aluminium conductor cable

câble *m* **à âme en cuivre**
 D: Kupferleiterkabel *n*

E: copper conductor cable
câble *m* **à bandes multiples**
  D: Vielbandkabel *n*
  E: multi-channel cable
câble *m* **à basse tension**
  D: Niederspannungskabel *n*
  E: low voltage cable
câble *m* **à ceinture**
  D: Gürtelkabel *n*
  E: belted cable
câble *m* **à champ non radial**
  D: Kabel mit nicht radialem Feld
  E: non-radial field cable
câble *m* **à champ radial**
  D: Radialfeldkabel *n*
  E: radial field cable, screened cable, shielded conductor cable
câble *m* **à charge continue**
  D: Krarup-Kabel *n*
  E: Krarup cable, continuously loaded cable
câble *m* **à compression**
  D: Außendruckkabel *n*
  E: compression cable
câble *m* **à compression externe de gaz**
  D: Gasaußendruck-Kabel *n*
  E: compression cable, impregnated gas-pressure cable, external gas pressure cable
câble *m* **à conducteur en aluminium**
  D: Aluminiumleiterkabel *n*
  E: aluminium conductor cable
câble *m* **à conducteur en cuivre**
  D: Kupferleiterkabel *n*
  E: copper conductor cable
câble *m* **à conducteurs en faisceaux**
  D: Bündelkabel *n*, bündelverseiltes Kabel
  E: unit cable, unit-stranded cable, bunched cable, unit-type stranded cable
câble *m* **à conducteurs isolés au plastique**
  D: Kabel mit kunststoffisolierten Leitern
  E: plastic-insulated conductor cable, PIC-cable *n* (US)
câble *m* **à conducteurs Milliken**
  D: Kabel mit skineffektarmen Leitern, Millikenleiter-Kabel *n*
  E: Milliken conductor cable
câble *m* **à conducteurs sous écran**
  D: Kabel mit abgeschirmten Leitern
  E: screened conductor cable
câble *m* **à couches concentriques**
  D: lagenverseiltes Kabel, Lagenkabel *n*
  E: layer-stranded cable, concentric layer cable, layered cable, layer type cable
câble *m* **à courant porteur**
  D: Trägerfrequenzkabel *n*
  E: carrier frequency cable, carrier cable
câble *m* **à courant porteur à grande distance**
  D: Trägerfrequenz-Fernkabel *n*
  E: long distance carrier frequency cable
câble *m* **à courant triphasé**
  D: Drehstromkabel *n*
  E: three-phase (current) cable
câble *m* **à deux conducteurs**
  D: doppeladriges Kabel
  E: double-core cable (GB), two-conductor cable (US), twin-cable
câble *m* **à diélectrique contrôlé**
  D: Kabel mit gesteuertem Dielektrikum (Ölkabel, Gasdruckkabel)
  E: cable with controlled dielectric, controlled dielectric cable
câble *m* **à écran en papier métallisé**
  D: Höchstädter-Kabel (H-Kabel) *n*
  E: Hochstadter cable, 'H'-type cable, metallized paper screened cable, shielded conductor cable
câble *m* **à écran métallique sur l'âme**
  D: Kabel mit metallener Leiterglättung
  E: smooth-conductor cable
câble *m* **aérien**
  D: Luftkabel *n*
  E: aerial cable, overhead cable
câble *m* **aérien autoporteur**
  D: selbsttragendes Luftkabel
  E: self-supporting aerial cable, self-supporting overhead cable
câble *m* **aérien léger**
  D: Leichtbau-Luftkabel *n*
  E: figure-eight cable, lightweight aerial cable
câble *m* **à faible capacitance** [com.]
  D: verlustarmes Kabel
  E: low capacitance cable, LoCap cable

câble

câble *m* à faible capacité [tél.]
  D: Kabel mit geringer Paarzahl, Kabel mit geringer Aderzahl, niedrigpaariges Kabel
  E: small capacity cable, small make-up cable, small-sized cable

câble *m* à fibres optiques
  D: Lichtleiterkabel *n*
  E: optical fibre cable

câble *m* à fréquence radioélectrique
  D: Hochfrequenzkabel *n*
  E: radio frequency cable, high-frequency cable

câble *m* à gaine ondulée
  D: Wellmantelkabel *n*
  E: cable with corrugated sheath

câble *m* à grande capacité [tél.]
  D: mehrpaariges Kabel, hochpaariges Kabel
  E: multiple pair cable, multipair cable, multipaired cable, large-capacity cable

câble *m* à grande puissance
  D: Hochleistungskabel *n*
  E: high power cable, heavy duty cable

câble *m* à haute fréquence
  D: Hochfrequenzkabel *n*
  E: radio frequency cable, high-frequency cable

câble *m* à haute tension
  D: Hochspannungskabel *n*
  E: high-voltage cable, H.V. cable, high-tension cable

câble *m* à huile fluide
  D: Ölkabel *n*
  E: oil-filled cable

câble *m* à huile fluide à haute pression
  D: Öl-Hochdruck-Kabel *n*
  E: high-pressure oil-filled cable

câble *m* à isolation minérale
  D: mineralisoliertes Kabel
  E: mineral-insulated cable

câble *m* à large bande
  D: Breitbandkabel *n*
  E: wide-band cable, broad-band cable

câble *m* à matière écoulée
  D: abgetropftes Kabel
  E: drained cable, non-bleeding cable

câble *m* à matière non migrante
  D: Kabel mit nicht abwandernder Tränkmasse, nd-Kabel *n*, Haftmassekabel *n*
  E: non-draining cable, nd-cable *n*

câble *m* (isolé) à matière plastique
  D: Kunststoffkabel *n*, Kabel mit Kunststoff-Isolierung
  E: plastics cable, plastic-insulated cable

câble *m* à moyenne tension
  D: Mittelspannungskabel *n*
  E: medium voltage cable

câble *m* à neutre concentrique en fils métalliques disposés en méandres
  D: Ceander-Kabel *n*
  E: Waveconal-cable *n* (GB)

câble *m* anti-giratoire
  D: verdrehungsfreies Kabel
  E: anti-twist cable

câble *m* à paires
  D: paarverseiltes Kabel, paarig verseiltes Kabel
  E: cable with pair formation, twin cable, paired cable

câble *m* à petit nombre de paires [tél.]
  D: Kabel mit geringer Paarzahl, Kabel mit geringer Aderzahl, niedrigpaariges Kabel
  E: small capacity cable, small make-up cable, small-sized cable

câble *m* à pression d'huile
  D: Öldruckkabel *n*
  E: oil pressure cable, pressure-assisted oil-filled cable

câble *m* à pression interne de gaz
  D: Gasinnendruck-Kabel *n*
  E: gas-filled internal pressure cable, internal gas pressure cable

câble *m* à quartes
  D: vierer-verseiltes Kabel
  E: cable with quad formation

câble *m* à quartes Dieselhorst-Martin
  D: Dieselhorst-Martin-Vierer-verseiltes Kabel, DM-Vierer-verseiltes Kabel, DM-Viererkabel *n*
  E: cable with multiple-twin quad formation, multiple-twin quad cable

câble *m* à quartes DM
  D: Dieselhorst-Martin-Vierer-verseiltes Kabel, DM-Vierer-verseiltes Kabel, DM-Viererkabel *n*
  E: cable with multiple-twin quad formation, multiple-twin quad

cable
câble *m* à quartes en étoile
  D: sternviererverseiltes Kabel
  E: cable with star quad combination, star quad cable
câble *m* à remplissage continu [c. tél.]
  D: über die ganze Länge abgestopftes Kabel, kontinuierlich gefülltes Kabel
  E: fully filled cable, continuously filled cable
câble *m* à remplissage total [c. tél.]
  D: über die ganze Länge abgestopftes Kabel, kontinuierlich gefülltes Kabel
  E: fully filled cable, continuously filled cable
câble *m* armé
  D: Panzerkabel *n*
  E: armo(u)red cable, shielded cable
câble *m* armé en feuillard d'acier
  D: bandeisenbewehrtes Kabel, stahlbandarmiertes Kabel
  E: steel-tape-armo(u)red cable
câble *m* armé en fils métalliques
  D: drahtbewehrtes Kabel, drahtarmiertes Kabel
  E: wire-armo(u)red cable
câble *m* à très haute tension (THT)
  D: Höchstspannungskabel *n*
  E: extra-high voltage cable, supertension cable, EHV-cable *n*
câble *m* à trois conducteurs
  D: dreiadriges Kabel, Dreifachkabel *n*, Dreileiterkabel *n*
  E: three-core cable, three-conductor cable, triple-core cable
câble *m* à trois conducteurs et demi
  D: Dreieinhalbleiterkabel *n*
  E: three-and-a-half core cable
câble *m* au Protodur
  D: Protodur-Kabel *n*
  E: Protodur-cable *n*
câble *m* au Protothen
  D: Protothen-Kabel *n*
  E: Protothen-cable *n*
câble *m* autoporteur
  D: selbsttragendes Kabel
  E: self-supporting cable
câble *m* biphasé
  D: doppeladriges Kabel
  E: double-core cable (GB), two-conductor cable (US), twin cable

câble *m* blindé
  D: abgeschirmtes Kabel, geschirmtes Kabel
  E: screened cable, shielded cable
câble *m* blindé
  D: Panzerkabel *n*
  E: armo(u)red cable
câble *m* CATV (câble de réception collective d'antenne de télévision)
  D: Kabel für (Orts-)Gemeinschafts-Fernsehantennen
  E: CATV cable (Community Antenna Television cable)
câble *m* chargé
  D: bespultes Kabel
  E: loaded cable
câble *m* chargé avec âme en fils fins [c. tél.]
  D: belastetes dünndrähtiges Kabel
  E: loaded thin-wire cable
câble *m* chauffant
  D: Heizkabel *n*
  E: heating cable
câble *m* coaxial
  D: Koaxialkabel *n*, konzentrisches Zweileiterkabel, konzentrisches Kabel
  E: coaxial cable, concentric cable
câble *m* coaxial à fréquence radioélectrique
  D: Hochfrequenz-Koaxialkabel *n*, koaxiales Hochfrequenzkabel
  E: high-frequency coaxial cable, radio frequency coaxial cable, coaxial cable for high-frequency transmission
câble *m* coaxial à haute fréquence
  D: Hochfrequenz-Koaxialkabel *n*, koaxiales Hochfrequenzkabel
  E: high-frequency coaxial cable, radio frequency coaxial cable, coaxial cable for high-frequency transmission
câble *m* coaxial à longue distance
  D: koaxiales Fernkabel
  E: long distance coaxial cable
câble *m* coaxial léger
  D: Leichtbau-Koaxialkabel *n*
  E: lightweight coaxial cable
câble *m* coaxial sousmarin
  D: Seekoaxialkabel *n*
  E: submarine coaxial cable
câble *m* composite

câble

D: kombiniertes Kabel
E: composite cable

câble *m* concentrique
D: Koaxialkabel *n*, konzentrisches Zweileiterkabel, konzentrisches Kabel
E: coaxial cable, concentric cable

câble *m* côtier
D: Küstenkabel *n*, armiertes Kabel für flache Küstengewässer
E: shore-end cable, shallow-water cable, shelf cable

câble *m* cryogénique
D: tiefgekühltes Kabel, Kryo-Kabel *n*
E: cryogenic cable

câble *m* cuirassé
D: Rohrdraht *m*
E: metal-clad wiring cable

câble *m* cuirassé sous gaine
D: umhüllter Rohrdraht
E: sheathed metal-clad wiring cable

câble *m* d'abonné
D: Teilnehmer-Anschlußkabel *n*, Teilnehmer-Ortskabel *n*, Teilnehmer-Kabel *n*, Ortskabel *n*
E: local subscriber('s) connection cable, telephone distribution cable, subscriber('s) cable, local cable

câble *m* d'alimentation
D: Einspeisungskabel *n*, Speisekabel *n*, Zuführungskabel *n*, Zuleitungskabel *n*
E: feeder *n*, feeder cable

câble *m* d'alimentation réseau
D: Netzanschlußkabel *n*
E: line cable

câble *m* d'allumage
D: Zündkabel *n*
E: ignition cable

câble *m* d'antenne
D: Antennenspeiseleitung *f*, Antennenzuleitung *f*, Antennenkabel *n*
E: antenna feeder, aerial feeder, antenna lead

câble *m* d'antenne à haute fréquence
D: Hochfrequenz-Antennenkabel *n*, HF-Antennenkabel *n*
E: high-frequency antenna cable

câble *m* d'ascenseur
D: Aufzugsleitung *f*, Fahrstuhlkabel *n*
E: lift cable

câble *m* d'atterrissement
D: Küstenkabel *n*, armiertes Kabel für flache Küstengewässer
E: shore-end cable, shallow-water cable, shelf cable

câble *m* d'avion
D: Flugzeug-Bordleitung *f*
E: aircraft wire

câble *m* de bas fond
D: Küstenkabel *n*, armiertes Kabel für flache Küstengewässer
E: shore-end cable, shallow-water cable, shelf cable

câble *m* de bord
D: Schiffskabel *n*
E: ship wiring cable

câble *m* de branchement
D: Abzweigkabel *n*
E: branch cable, stub cable

câble *m* de branchement domestique [c. én.]
D: Stichkabel *n*, Hausanschlußkabel *n*
E: service cable, branch cable, service drop cable

câble *m* de chauffage
D: Heizkabel *n*
E: heating cable

câble *m* de chemin de fer
D: Bahnkabel *n*
E: railway cable

câble *m* de commande
D: Steuerkabel *n*
E: control cable

câble *m* de communication
D: Fernmeldekabel *n*, Nachrichtenkabel *n*
E: telecommunications cable, communications cable

câble *m* de communication extérieur
D: Nachrichten-Außenkabel *n*
E: outdoor communications cable

câble *m* de connexion
D: Verbindungskabel *n*, Schaltkabel *n*
E: junction cable, connecting cable, interconnecting cable, switchboard cable

câble *m* de connexion basse fréquence
D: Niederfrequenz-Schaltkabel *n*
E: voice frequency switchboard cable

câble *m* de connexion pour installations de signalisation
D: Signal-Schaltkabel *n*
E: signal switchboard cable

câble *m* de dérivation

D: Abzweigkabel n
E: branch cable, stub cable

câble m de distribution [com.]
D: Aufteilungskabel n
E: distribution cable

câble m de distribution
D: Verteilerkabel n
E: distribution cable

câble m de drague
D: Baggerkabel n, Baggerleitung f
E: trailing cable, dredge cable

câble m de grand fond
D: Tiefseekabel n
E: deep sea submarine cable, deep sea cable

câble m de haute mer
D: Tiefseekabel n
E: deep sea submarine cable, deep sea cable

câble m de haveuse
D: Schrämleitung f
E: coal cutter cable

câble m de jonction
D: Verbindungskabel n, Schaltkabel n
E: junction cable, connecting cable, interconnecting cable, switchboard cable

câble m de jonction entre centraux téléphoniques [tél.]
D: Amtsverbindungskabel n
E: inter-exchange trunk cable

câble m de jonction transversal [tél.]
D: Querverbindungskabel n
E: tie line cable

câble m de liaison circulaire
D: Ringkabel n
E: link cable, junction cable

câble m de mesure
D: Meßkabel n
E: measuring cable

câble m de microphone
D: Mikrophonleitung f
E: microphone cable

câble m de mines
D: Bergwerkskabel n, Grubenkabel n
E: mining cable, mine cable

câble m de modulation par impulsion et codage
D: Pulscode-Modulationskabel n, PCM-Kabel n
E: pulse-code modulation cable, PCM cable

câble m de navire
D: Schiffskabel n
E: ship wiring cable

câble m (souple) d'énergie
D: Starkstromleitung f
E: power cable, flexible power cord

câble m d'énergie
D: Energiekabel n, Starkstromkabel n
E: power cable

câble m d'énergie (isolé) à matière plastique
D: Kunststoff-Energiekabel n
E: plastics power cable, plastic-insulated power cable

câble m d'enrouleur
D: Schleppleitung f, Leitungstrosse f, Kabel zum Auftrommeln, Trommelleitung f
E: trailing cable

câble m d'entrée
D: Einführungskabel n
E: lead(ing)-in cable, stub cable

câble m de raccordement
D: Anschlußkabel n
E: connection cable, service cable

câble m de raccordement domestique [c. én.]
D: Stichkabel n, Hausanschlußkabel n
E: service cable, branch cable, service drop cable

câble m de réception collective d'antenne de télévision
D: Ortsgemeinschaftsantennen-Fernsehkabel n
E: community antenna television (CATV) cable

câble m de remorque
D: Schleppleitung f, Leitungstrosse f, Kabel zum Auftrommeln, Trommelleitung f
E: trailing cable

câble m de réseau
D: Netzkabel n
E: mains cable, distribution cable

câble m de signalisation
D: Signalkabel n
E: signalling cable

câble m de soudure
D: Schweißleitung f
E: welding cable

câble m d'essai
D: Versuchskabel n
E: test cable, experimental cable, trial cable

câble

câble *m* **de stross**
  D: Strossenleitung *f*
  E: stope cable

câble *m* **de support**
  D: Tragdraht *m*
  E: supporting wire

câble *m* **de télécommunication**
  D: Fernmeldekabel *n*,
   Nachrichtenkabel *n*
  E: telecommunications cable,
   communications cable

câble *m* **de télécommunication de parcours ferroviaire**
  D: Streckenfernmeldekabel *n*
  E: railway telecommunication cable

câble *m* **de télécommunication pour gares ferroviaires**
  D: Bahnhofsfernmeldekabel *n*
  E: railway station telecommunication cable

câble *m* **de télémesure**
  D: Fernmeßkabel *n*
  E: telemetering cable

câble *m* **d'intercommunication**
  D: Kabel für Gegensprechanlagen
  E: intercom cable,
   intercommunication cable

câble *m* **d'interface**
  D: Schnittstellenkabel *n*
  E: interface cable

câble *m* **d'interface standard**
  D: Standard-Schnittstellenkabel *n*
  E: standard interface cable

câble *m* **domestique** [c. én.]
  D: Installationsleitung *f*,
   Hausinstallationsleitung *f*
  E: house wiring cable

câble *m* **du type Hochstadter**
  D: Höchstädter-Kabel (H-Kabel) *n*
  E: Hochstadter cable, 'H'-type cable,
   metallized paper screened cable,
   shielded conductor cable

câble *m* **en couches**
  D: lagenverseiltes Kabel, Lagenkabel *n*
  E: layer-stranded cable, concentric layer cable, layered cable, layer type cable

câble *m* **en exploitation sans charge** [c. én.]
  D: unbelastetes Kabel, Kabel in unbelastetem Zustand
  E: cable at no-load

câble *m* **en faisceaux**
  D: Bündelkabel *n*, bündelverseiltes Kabel
  E: unit cable, unit-stranded cable,
   bunched cable, unit-type stranded cable

câble *m* **en tube**
  D: Rohrkabel *n*
  E: pipe type cable

câble *m* **en tube à pression d'huile**
  D: Öldruck-Rohrkabel *n*
  E: oil pressure pipe type cable

câble *m* **en tube d'acier sous haute pression d'huile**
  D: Hochdruck-Ölkabel im Stahlrohr,
   Oilostatic-Kabel *n*
  E: high-pressure oil-filled pipe type cable, Oilostatic-cable *n*

câble *m* **en tube sous compression externe de gaz**
  D: Gasaußendruck-Kabel im Stahlrohr
  E: pipeline compression cable

câble *m* **en tube sous pression de gaz**
  D: Gasdruck-Rohrkabel *n*
  E: gas pressure pipe type cable

câble *m* **expérimental**
  D: Versuchskabel *n*
  E: test cable, experimental cable, trial cable

câble *m* **ferromagnétique**
  D: Krarup-Kabel *n*
  E: Krarup cable, continuously loaded cable

câble *m* **fini**
  D: fertiges Kabel
  E: finished cable

câble *m* **flottable**
  D: schwimmfähiges Kabel
  E: buoyant cable

câble *m* **HT**
  D: Hochspannungskabel *n*
  E: high-voltage cable, H.V. cable,
   high-tension cable

câble *m* **hydrofuge**
  D: Feuchtraumleitung *f*
  E: damp-proof wiring cable

câble *m* **interurbain**
  D: Weitverkehrskabel *n*,
   Weitverkehrs-Telefonkabel *n*,
   Telefon-Fernkabel *n*, Bezirkskabel *n*
  E: long distance telephone cable,

trunk cable (GB), toll cable (US)

câble *m* **isolé à la toile vernie**
- D: Lackbandkabel *n*
- E: varnished cambric (insulated) cable

câble *m* **isolé à papier imprégné à matière visqueuse**
- D: Papier-Masse-Kabel *n*, Massekabel *n*, massegetränktes Papierkabel
- E: paper-insulated mass-impregnated cable

câble *m* **isolé à papier sous gaine de plomb**
- D: Papier-Bleikabel *n*, papierisoliertes Bleimantelkabel
- E: paper-insulated lead-sheathed cable, paper-insulated lead-covered cable, PILC cable (US)

câble *m* **isolé au papier imprégné**
- D: Kabel mit getränkter Papierisolierung
- E: impregnated paper insulated cable

câble *m* **isolé au papier préimprégné**
- D: Kabel mit vorimprägnierter Papierisolierung, vorgetränktes Kabel
- E: pre-impregnated cable

câble *m* **jumelé**
- D: paarverseiltes Kabel, paarig verseiltes Kabel
- E: cable with pair formation, twin cable, paired cable

câble *m* **Krarup**
- D: Krarup-Kabel *n*
- E: Krarup cable, continuously loaded cable

câble *m* **krarupisé**
- D: Krarup-Kabel *n*
- E: Krarup cable, continuously loaded cable

câble *m* **méplat**
- D: Flachkabel *n*
- E: flat type cable

câble *m* **MIC**
- D: Pulscode-Modulationskabel *n*, PCM-Kabel *n*
- E: pulse-code modulation cable, PCM cable

câble *m* **miniature**
- D: Miniatur-Kabel *n*
- E: miniature cable

câble *m* **monoconducteur**
- D: einadriges Kabel, Einleiterkabel *n*
- E: single-core cable, single-conductor cable

câble *m* **monophasé**
- D: einadriges Kabel, Einleiterkabel *n*
- E: single-core cable, single-conductor cable

câble *m* **monopolaire**
- D: einadriges Kabel, Einleiterkabel *n*
- E: single-core cable, single-conductor cable

câble *m* **multiconducteur**
- D: Mehrleiterkabel *n*, mehradriges Kabel
- E: multicore cable, multiconductor cable, multiple core cable

câble *m* **multipaire** [tél.]
- D: mehrpaariges Kabel, hochpaariges Kabel
- E: multiple pair cable, multipair cable, multipaired cable, large-capacity cable

câble *m* **multipolaire**
- D: Mehrleiterkabel *n*, mehradriges Kabel
- E: multicore cable, multiconductor cable, multiple core cable

câble *m* **multitoron** [tél.]
- D: mehrpaariges Kabel, hochpaariges Kabel
- E: multiple pair cable, multipair cable, multipaired cable, large-capacity cable

câble *m* **nd**
- D: Kabel mit nicht abwandernder Tränkmasse, nd-Kabel *n*, Haftmassekabel *n*
- E: non-draining cable, nd-cable *n*

câble *m* **non chargé** [c. én.]
- D: unbelastetes Kabel, Kabel in unbelastetem Zustand
- E: cable at no-load

câble *m* **non chargé avec âme en fils fins** [c. tél.]
- D: unbelastetes dünndrähtiges Kabel
- E: unloaded thin wire cable

câble *m* **non-inductif**
- D: induktionsfreies Kabel
- E: screened conductor cable, non-inductive cable

câble *m* **Oléostatique**
- D: Hochdruck-Ölkabel im Stahlrohr, Oilostatic-Kabel *n*
- E: high-pressure oil-filled pipe type

câble

cable, Oilostatic-cable *n*

câble *m* pairé
D: paarverseiltes Kabel, paarig verseiltes Kabel
E: cable with pair formation, twin cable, paired cable

câble *m* porteur [c. tél.]
D: Tragseil *n*, Luftkabeltragseil *n*
E: supporting strand, suspension strand, aerial messenger, messenger wire

câble *m* posé en conduites
D: Röhrenkabel *n*
E: conduit cable

câble *m* pour appareils électrodomestiques
D: Hausgeräteleitung *f*
E: appliance wire

câble *m* pour appareils électroménagers
D: Hausgeräteleitung *f*
E: appliance wire

câble *m* pour automobile
D: Kraftfahrzeugleitung *f*
E: vehicle cable

câble *m* pour contraintes faibles
D: Kabel für leichte Beanspruchungen
E: light-duty cable

câble *m* pour contraintes sévères
D: Kabel für schwere Beanspruchungen
E: heavy-duty cable

câble *m* pour éclairage lumineux
D: Beleuchtungskabel *n*
E: lighting cable

câble *m* pour engin mobile
D: Schleppleitung *f*, Leitungstrosse *f*, Kabel zum Auftrommeln, Trommelleitung *f*
E: trailing cable

câble *m* pour galeries de mines
D: Grubenstreckenkabel *n*
E: gallery cable, mine gallery cable

câble *m* pour grands efforts de traction
D: zugfestes Kabel
E: cable for high tensile stresses

câble *m* pour installation fixe
D: Leitung für feste Verlegung
E: cable for fixed installation

câble *m* pour installation intérieure
D: Innenraumleitung *f*
E: indoor wiring cable

câble *m* pour installation sur pentes raides
D: Steilhangkabel *n*
E: cable for installation on steep slopes

câble *m* pour l'éclairage d'aéroports
D: Flugplatzbeleuchtungskabel *n*
E: airport lighting cable

câble *m* pour locaux humides
D: Feuchtraumleitung *f*
E: damp-proof wiring cable

câble *m* pour pompe immergée
D: Tauchpumpenleitung *f*
E: submersible-pump cable, submerged-pump cable

câble *m* pour puits de mines
D: Grubenschachtkabel *n*, Schachtkabel *n*
E: mine shaft cable, shaft cable

câble *m* pour trou de forage
D: Kabel für Tauchpumpen in Bohrlöchern, Leitung für Tauchpumpen in Bohrlöchern
E: borehole cable

câble *m* pour tubes fluorescentes
D: Leuchtröhrenleitung *f*
E: fluorescent tube cable

câble *m* préimprégné
D: Kabel mit vorimprägnierter Papierisolierung, vorgetränktes Kabel
E: pre-impregnated cable

câble *m* principal
D: Hauptkabel *n*, Hauptspeisekabel *n*
E: main cable, mains cable

câble *m* principal [tél.]
D: Amtskabel *n*
E: exchange cable

câble *m* pupinisé
D: Pupinkabel *n*
E: loaded audio cable, coil-loaded cable

câble *m* pupinisé avec âme en fils fins
D: bespultes dünndrähtiges Kabel
E: loaded thin-wire cable

câbler *v*
D: verseilen *v* (Leiter)
E: strand *v*

câbler *v*
D: verkabeln *v*
E: cable *v*, wire *v*

câble *m* régional
D: Bezirkskabel *n*
E: exchange cable, trunk cable,

intercity cable

câble *m* **rempli** [tél.]
D: abgestopftes Kabel
E: filled cable

câble *m* **rempli de façon continue** [c. tél.]
D: über die ganze Länge abgestopftes Kabel, kontinuierlich gefülltes Kabel
E: fully filled cable, continuously filled cable

câble *m* **rempli de façon discontinue** [c. tél.]
D: diskontinuierlich abgestopftes Kabel
E: cable with water blocks

câblerie *f*
D: Kabelwerk *n*
E: cable works, cable factory

câble *m* **rigide sous gaine légère en PVC**
D: Mantelleitung *f*, PVC-Mantelleitung *f*
E: light PVC-sheathed cable

câble *m* **sans écran**
D: ungeschirmtes Kabel
E: unscreened cable

câbles *m pl* **de fonctionnement sûr**
D: betriebssichere Kabel
E: operationally reliable cables, fail-safe cables

câbles *m pl* **de grosses sections**
D: Kabel mit großen Querschnitten
E: cables with big cross-sectional areas, large-size cables

câbles *m pl* **de petites sections**
D: Kabel mit kleinen Querschnitten
E: cables with small cross-sectional areas, small-size cables

câbles *m pl* **disposés en nappe**
D: nebeneinander liegende Kabel, in einer Ebene liegende Kabel
E: cables in flat formation, cables laid in parallel, cables laid side by side

câble *m* **souple**
D: Anschlußschnur *f*
E: flexible cord, flexible *n*, connecting cord

câble *m* **souple**
D: bewegliche Leitung, flexible Leitung
E: flexible cable, flexible cord, flexible *n*

câble *m* **souple de raccordement**
D: Geräte-Anschlußschnur *f*
E: appliance cord

câble *m* **souple méplat**
D: Flachleitung *f*
E: flat flexible cable, flat twin cable

câble *m* **souple méplat à fil rosette**
D: leichte Zwillingsleitung
E: flat twin tinsel cord

câble *m* **souple méplat sans gaine**
D: Zwillingsleitung *f*
E: flat twin flexible cord

câble *m* **souple mobile d'énergie**
D: bewegliche Starkstromleitung
E: flexible portable power cord

câble *m* **souple sous gaine de caoutchouc**
D: Gummischlauchleitung *f*
E: tough-rubber sheathed cable, rubber jacket core

câble *m* **souple sous gaine en plastique**
D: Kunststoffschlauchleitung *f*
E: plastic-sheathed flexible cord

câble *m* **souple sous gaine épaisse de caoutchouc**
D: schwere Gummischlauchleitung
E: heavy tough-rubber sheathed flexible cable

câble *m* **souple sous gaine légère (en PVC)**
D: leichte (PVC-)Schlauchleitung
E: light (PVC-)sheathed flexible cord

câble *m* **souple sous gaine légère en plastique**
D: leichte Kunststoffschlauchleitung
E: light plastic-sheathed flexible cord

câble *m* **souple sous gaine ordinaire en plastique**
D: mittlere Kunststoffschlauchleitung
E: ordinary plastic-sheathed flexible cord

câble *m* **souple sous gaine ordinaire de caoutchouc**
D: leichte Gummischlauchleitung
E: ordinary tough-rubber sheathed flexible cord

câble *m* **souple sous gaine ordinaire (en PVC)**
D: mittlere (PVC-)Schlauchleitung
E: ordinary (PVC-)sheathed flexible cord

câble *m* **souple sous gaine résistant aux températures élevées**

câble

  D: hitzebeständige Schlauchleitung
  E: heat-resistant sheathed flexible cable
câble *m* **sous basse pression d'huile**
  D: Niederdrucköllabel *n*
  E: low pressure oil-filled cable
câble *m* **sous basse pression d'huile** (sous gaine métallique)
  D: Niederdrucköllabel *n* (mit aufgepreßtem Metallmantel)
  E: self-contained oil-filled cable
câble *m* **sous écran**
  D: abgeschirmtes Kabel, geschirmtes Kabel
  E: screened cable, shielded cable
câble *m* **sous-fluvial**
  D: Flußkabel *n*
  E: river cable
câble *m* **sous gaine d'aluminium**
  D: Aluminiummantelkabel *n*
  E: aluminium-sheathed cable
câble *m* **sous gaine de plomb**
  D: Bleimantelkabel *n*
  E: lead-sheathed cable, lead-covered cable
câble *m* **sous gaine de plomb avec revêtement extérieur**
  D: Bleimantelkabel mit Außenschutz
  E: served lead-covered cable
câble *m* **sous gaine de plomb nu**
  D: blankes Bleimantelkabel
  E: cable with bare lead sheath, plain lead-covered cable
câble *m* **sous gaine double**
  D: doppelt-ummanteltes Kabel
  E: double-sheathed cable
câble *m* **sous gaine non-métallique**
  D: Kunststoffmantelkabel *n*
  E: plastic-sheathed cable, non-metallic-sheathed cable
câble *m* **sous gaine plastique**
  D: Kunststoffmantelkabel *n*
  E: plastic-sheathed cable, non-metallic-sheathed cable
câble *m* **sous haute pression d'huile**
  D: Öl-Hochdruck-Kabel *n*
  E: high-pressure oil-filled cable
câble *m* **sous-marin**
  D: Seekabel *n*, Unterwasserkabel *n*
  E: submarine cable
câble *m* **sous pression**
  D: Druckkabel *n*
  E: pressure cable

câble *m* **sous pression de gaz**
  D: Gasdruck-Kabel *n*
  E: gas pressure cable, gas-filled cable
câble *m* **souterrain**
  D: Erdkabel *n*
  E: buried cable, underground cable
câble *m* **spécial isolé au caoutchouc**
  D: Sonder-Gummiaderleitung *f*
  E: special rubber insulated cable
câble *m* **suburbain**
  D: Bezirkskabel *n*
  E: exchange cable, trunk cable, intercity cable
câble *m* **supraconducteur**
  D: Supraleiterkabel *n*
  E: superconducting cable
câble *m* **symétrique** [tél.]
  D: symmetrisches Kabel
  E: balanced pair cable
câble *m* **téléphonique**
  D: Fernsprechkabel *n*, Telefonkabel *n*
  E: telephone cable
câble *m* **téléphonique à grande distance**
  D: Weitverkehrskabel *n*, Weitverkehrs-Telefonkabel *n*, Telefon-Fernkabel *n*, Bezirkskabel *n*
  E: long distance telephone cable, trunk cable (GB), toll cable (US)
câble *m* **téléphonique à trois conducteurs** [c. tél.]
  D: Dreier *m*
  E: triple
câble *m* **téléphonique Commonwealth-Pacifique**
  D: Commonwealth-Pazifik-Kabel *n*
  E: Commonwealth-Pacific telephone cable (COMPAC cable)
câble *m* **téléphonique de l'Atlantique du Sud**
  D: Südatlantisches Telefonkabel
  E: Southatlantic telephone cable (SAT cable)
câble *m* **téléphonique de l'Ecosse à l'Islande**
  D: Schottland-Island-Kabel *n*
  E: Scotland-Iceland telephone cable (SCOTICE cable)
câble *m* **téléphonique de réseau local**
  D: Ortsverbindungskabel *n*, Ortsanschlußkabel *n*
  E: local exchange connection cable,

telephone distribution cable, local junction cable

câble *m* téléphonique d'Islande au Canada
D: Island-Kanada-Kabel *n*
E: Iceland-Canada telephone cable (ICECAN cable)

câble *m* téléphonique du Brésil aux Iles Canaries
D: Brasilien-Kanarische Inseln-Kabel *n*
E: Brazil-Canary Islands telephone cable (BRACAN cable)

câble *m* téléphonique du Canada à l'Ecosse
D: Kanada-Schottland-Kabel *n*
E: Canada-Scotland transatlantic telephone cable (CANTAT cable)

câble *m* téléphonique transatlantique
D: Transatlantik-Telefonkabel (TAT-Kabel) *n*
E: Transatlantic telephone cable (TAT cable)

câble *m* téléphonique transpacifique
D: Transpazifik-Kabel *n*
E: Transpacific telephone cable (TRANSPAC cable)

câble *m* terminé
D: fertiges Kabel
E: finished cable

câble *m* triphasé
D: dreiadriges Kabel, Dreifachkabel *n*, Dreileiterkabel *n*
E: three-core cable, three-conductor cable, triple-core cable

câble *m* triphasé à huile fluide
D: Zwickelölkabel *n*
E: three-core oil-filled cable

câble *m* triphasé concentrique
D: konzentrisches Dreileiterkabel
E: triple concentric cable

câble *m* triplomb
D: Dreibleimantelkabel *n*, Dreimantelkabel *n*
E: three-core single lead sheath cable, SL-cable *n*

câble *m* triplomb trigaine
D: Dreibleimantelkabel *n*, Dreimantelkabel *n*
E: three-core single lead sheath cable, SL-cable *n*

câble *m* tripolaire à huile fluide
D: Dreileiterölkabel *n*
E: three-core oil-filled cable

câble *m* unipolaire
D: einadriges Kabel, Einleiterkabel *n*
E: single-core cable, single-conductor cable

câble *m* unipolaire à huile fluide
D: Einleiterölkabel *n*
E: single-core oil-filled cable

câbleur *m*
D: Kabelhersteller *m*
E: cable maker, cable manufacturer

câble *m* urbain
D: Teilnehmer-Anschlußkabel *n*, Teilnehmer-Ortskabel *n*, Teilnehmer-Kabel *n*, Ortskabel *n*
E: local subscriber('s) connection cable, telephone distribution cable, subscriber('s) cable, local cable

câble *m* urbain de distribution
D: Aufteilungs-Ortskabel *n*
E: local distribution cable

câbleuse *f*
D: Verseilmaschine *f*
E: stranding machine, strander *n*, cabler *n*, twister *n*, stranding cabler (US)

câbleuse *f* à cage
D: Korbverseilmaschine *f*
E: planetary strander, planet-type stranding machine, cage strander, slow-speed strander

câbleuse *f* à grande vitesse
D: Schnellverseilmaschine *f*
E: high-speed strander

câbleuse *f* à tambour à plusieures passes
D: mehrgängige Trommelverseilmaschine *f*
E: multi-pass drum twisting machine

câbleuse *f* double torsion
D: Doppelschlag-Verseilmaschine *f*
E: double-twist strander

câbleuse *f* inversée (à flyer)
D: Bügelverseilmaschine *f*
E: flyer-type stranding machine

câbleuse *f* inversée (à flyer) double torsion à grande vitesse
D: Bügel-Doppelschlag-Schnellverseilmaschine *f*
E: double-twist flyer-type high-speed stranding machine

câbleuse *f* verticale à grande vitesse [c. com.]

câbleuse
    D: vertikale Schnellverseilmaschine
    E: high speed vertical twister

câblier *m* [pose c.]
    D: Kabellegeschiff *n*
    E: cable ship

cadre *m* **de base**
    D: Grundrahmen *m*, Fundamentrahmen *m*
    E: base frame

cage *f* [câblage]
    D: Korb *m*
    E: cage *n*

cage *f* **d'assemblage**
    D: Verseilkorb *m*
    E: stranding cage

cage *f* **de laminoir** [mét.]
    D: Walzgerüst *n*
    E: roll stand

cahier *m* **des charges**
    D: Pflichtenheft *n*
    E: specification *n*

caisse *f*
    D: Gehäuse *n*
    E: housing *n*, casing *n*, cabinet *n*

calamine *f*
    D: Zunder *m*
    E: scale *n*, scab *n*

calandre *f*
    D: Kalander *m*
    E: calender *n*

calandre *f* **à quatre cylindres**
    D: Vierwalzenkalander *m*
    E: four roll calender

calandre *f* **à quatre rouleaux**
    D: Vierwalzenkalander *m*
    E: four roll calender

calandre *f* **à trois cylindres**
    D: Dreiwalzenkalander *m*
    E: three-roll calender, three-bowl calender

calandre *f* **à trois rouleaux**
    D: Dreiwalzenkalander *m*
    E: three-roll calender, three-bowl calender

calculateur *m* **pour la conduite des processus industriels**
    D: Prozeßrechner *m*
    E: process-control computer

calcul *m* **des probabilités**
    D: Wahrscheinlichkeitsrechnung *f*
    E: probability theory, probability calculus

calibrage *m*
    D: Eichung *f*
    E: calibration *n*, adjusting *n*, gauging *n*

calibre *m* **à vis**
    D: Schraublehre *f*
    E: screw callipers *pl*

calibre *m* **des cylindres**
    D: Walzenkaliber *n*
    E: roll groove

canal *m* **de circulation d'huile** [câb.]
    D: Ölkanal *m*
    E: oil duct

canalisation *f* (câb.)
    D: Kabelanlage *f*
    E: cable installation

canalisation *f* **blindée isolée au SF$_6$**
    D: SF$_6$-isoliertes Leitersystem, SF$_6$-Rohrleiter *m*, SF$_6$-Rohrschiene *f*
    E: gas(SF$_6$)-insulated conductor system, compressed gas(SF$_6$)-insulated transmission line, SF$_6$-insulated metal clad tubular bus, SF$_6$-insulated bus duct

canal *m* **téléphonique**
    D: Sprechkanal *m*, Fernsprechkanal *m*
    E: telephone channel, voice channel, speech channel

caniveau *m* [pose c.]
    D: Kanalzug *m*, Rohrzug *m*
    E: duct *n*

caniveau *m*
    D: Rohrstrang *m*
    E: pipeline conduit

caniveau *m* **à passage multiple**
    D: Mehrlochkanal *m*, mehrzügiger Rohrstrang
    E: line of ducts, multiple duct conduit, multiple way duct

caniveau *m* **à passage simple**
    D: einzügiger Rohrstrang
    E: single duct conduit

caniveau *m* **de câble**
    D: Kabelkanal *m*
    E: cable duct

caniveau *m* **de câble à ventilation forcée**
    D: belüfteter Kabelkanal
    E: forced ventilated cable tunnel

cannelé *adj*
    D: geriffelt *adj*
    E: grooved *adj*, ribbed *adj*

cannelure *f* **des cylindres**

D: Walzenkaliber *n*
E: roll groove

caolin *m*
D: Kaolin *n*
E: china clay, kaolin *n*

caoutchouc *m*
D: Kautschuk *m* (unvulkanisiert)
E: rubber

caoutchouc *m* (vulcanisé)
D: Gummi *m* (vulkanisierter Kautschuk)
E: rubber

caoutchouc *m* (de) butyle
D: Butylkautschuk *m*
E: butyl rubber

caoutchouc *m* d'éthylène propylène (EPR)
D: EPR-Kautschuk *m*, Äthylen-Propylen-Kautschuk *m* (EPR)
E: ethylene-propylene rubber (EPR) *n*

caoutchouc *m* naturel
D: Naturkautschuk *m*
E: natural rubber

caoutchouc *m* nitrile
D: Nitrilkautschuk *m*
E: nitrile butadiene rubber

caoutchouc *m* régénéré
D: Kautschukregenerat *n*
E: reclaimed rubber

caoutchouc *m* sans protéine
D: enteiweißter Kautschuk
E: deproteinised rubber

caoutchouc *m* semi-conducteur
D: Leitgummi *m*
E: semi-conducting rubber

caoutchouc *m* silicone
D: Silikonkautschuk *m*
E: silicone rubber

caoutchouc *m* styrène butadiène
D: Styrol-Butadien-Kautschuk *m*
E: styrene butadiene rubber (SBR)

capacité *f* [él.]
D: Kapazität *f*
E: capacitance *n*

capacité *f* [mach.]
D: Leistung *f*, Ausstoß *m*
E: performance *n*, output *n*, efficiency *n*, capacity *n*

capacité, utilisé à pleine ~
D: voll ausgelastet
E: loaded to capacity, operating at full capacity

capacité *f* d'absorption
D: Saugfähigkeit *f*
E: absorption capacity

capacité *f* d'accumulateur [fabr. fils mét., câblage]
D: Speicherinhalt *m*
E: accumulator capacity

capacité *f* de boucle
D: Schleifenkapazität *f*
E: loop capacity, wire-to-wire capacity

capacité *f* de charge [él.]
D: Belastbarkeit *f*, Strombelastbarkeit *f*
E: current-carrying capacity, current rating, ampacity *n*, power rating

capacité *f* de moufle [fabr. fils mét., câblage]
D: Speicherinhalt *m*
E: accumulator capacity

capacité *f* de pompage
D: Pumpenleistung *f*, Förderleistung einer Pumpe
E: pump output, delivery of a pump

capacité *f* de service
D: Betriebskapazität *f* (Anlage)
E: operating capacity

capacité *f* de transmission
D: Übertragungskapazität *f*
E: transmission capacity

capacité *f* de transport
D: Übertragungskapazität *f*
E: transmission capacity

capacité *f* mutuelle [tél.]
D: Betriebskapazität *f*
E: mutual capacitance

capacité *f* par rapport à la terre
D: Kapazität gegen Erde
E: capacitance to earth

capot *m*
D: Abdeckhaube *f*
E: cover *n*, hood *n*

capot *m* [access. c.]
D: Kappe *f*
E: cap *n*

capot *m* de plomb
D: Bleikappe *f*
E: lead cap

capot *m* d'étanchéité [câb.]
D: Verschlußkappe *f*
E: sealing cap

captage *m* de fumées
D: Absaugung von Dämpfen

captage
E: drawing off of fumes

capteur m **de fumées**
D: Abzug m (Lüftung), Absaughaube f
E: exhaust n, exhaust hood, fume hood

capuchon m [access. c.]
D: Kappe f
E: cap n

caractéristique f
D: Kennlinie f
E: characteristic curve

caractéristique f **électrique**
D: elektrische Eigenschaft
E: electrical characteristic, electrical property

caractéristiques f pl **aux températures en dessous de zéro**
D: Kälteeigenschaften unter 0 °C
E: sub-zero properties

caractéristiques f pl **de fonctionnement**
D: Betriebseigenschaften f pl
E: operational characteristics

caractéristiques f pl **de service**
D: Betriebseigenschaften f pl
E: operational characteristics

caractéristiques f pl **de transmission**
D: Übertragungs-Eigenschaften f pl
E: transmission characteristics

caractéristiques f pl **dimensionelles**
D: Aufbau-Daten pl, Konstruktionsdaten pl
E: design data

carbonate m **de calcium**
D: Kreide f
E: calcium carbonate, chalk n

carbonisation f
D: Anvulkanisation f (Elastomere)
E: scorching n

carbonisation f **de l'isolant**
D: Anbrennen der Isolierung, Verkohlen der Isolierung
E: charring of the insulation

carbonisé adj
D: verkohlt adj
E: charred adj, carbonized adj

carboniser v
D: verbrennen vi
E: burn v, scorch v, combust v

carter m **de sécurité, de protection, carter enveloppe**
D: Sicherheitsabdeckung f, Schutzabdeckung f
E: guard n, protective covering, safety guard

cascade, installation de refroidissement en ~s
D: Kaskadenkühler m (Granulat)
E: cascades cooler

cascade, montage en ~
D: Kaskadenschaltung f
E: cascade connection

cas m **limite**
D: Grenzfall m
E: border-line case

cassant adj
D: spröde adj
E: brittle adj

cassant adj **à chaud**
D: warmbrüchig adj
E: hot-short adj

casse-fil m
D: Drahtbruch m, Drahtriß m
E: wire break, wire breakage

casse-fil m **électrique**
D: Drahtbruchschalter m
E: wire break switch

cassure f
D: Bruch m, Bruchstelle f
E: fracture n, break n, rupture n

cassure f **de fatigue**
D: Ermüdungsbruch m
E: fatigue crack, fatigue failure, fatigue fracture, stress cracking

cassure f **intercristalline** [mét.]
D: interkristalliner Bruch
E: intercrystalline crack

cassure f **intergranulaire** [mét.]
D: interkristalliner Bruch
E: intercrystalline crack

cave f **des câbles**
D: Kabelaufteilungskeller m (Fernsprechamt)
E: cable vault (tel. exchange)

cavité f
D: Hohlraum m
E: void n, cavity n

ceinture, câble à ~
D: Gürtelkabel n
E: belted cable

cellules f pl
D: Zellen f pl (im Öldruckausgleichsgefäß), Membranen f pl (im Öldruckausgleichsgefäß), pl
E: cells pl, membrane cells

cendre, teneur en ~s
D: Aschegehalt *m*
E: ash content

centrage *m*
D: Zentrierung *f*
E: centering *n*

centrage, à ~ automatique
D: selbstzentrierend *adj*
E: self-ali(g)ning *adj*, self-centering *adj*, autocentering *adj*

centrage, dispositif de ~ sur le poinçon guide [extr.]
D: Zentrierung am Führungsnippel
E: pilot on guider tip

centrage *m* **de l'écart entre la filière et le poinçon** [extr.]
D: Zentrierung von Mundstück und Nippel
E: adjustment of the gum space

central *m* [tél.]
D: Amt *n*
E: exchange *n* (GB), central *n* (US), central office

centrale *f* **atomique**
D: Kernkraftwerk *n*
E: nuclear power station

centrale *f* **électrique**
D: Kraftwerk *n*
E: power station, generating station

centrale *f* **électrique à accumulation par pompage**
D: Pumpspeicher(kraft)werk *n*
E: pumped storage (hydroelectric) power station

centrale *f* **hydroélectrique**
D: Wasserkraftwerk *n*
E: hydro-electric power station

centrale *f* **hydroélectrique souterraine**
D: Kavernenkraftwerk *n*
E: underground power station

centrale *f* **nucléaire**
D: Kernkraftwerk *n*
E: nuclear power station

centrale *f* **thermique**
D: Wärmekraftwerk *n*
E: thermal power station

central *m* **interurbain**
D: Fernvermittlungsstelle *f*, Fernamt *n*
E: trunk exchange (GB), toll exchange (US), long distance exchange

central *m* **téléphonique**
D: Fernsprechamt *n*, Telefonzentrale *f*
E: telephone exchange, telephone central office

central *m* **urbain**
D: Ortsvermittlungsstelle *f*
E: local exchange

centre *m* **de grande consommation** [él.]
D: Lastschwerpunkt *m*
E: load centre

centre *m* **d'une galette à papier** [rub.]
D: Kern einer Papierscheibe
E: centre of a paper pad

centricité *f*
D: Zentrizität *f*
E: centricity *n*

certificat *m* **de réception**
D: Abnahmeprotokoll *n*
E: acceptance certificate

certificat *m* **d'essai**
D: Prüfbescheinigung *f*
E: test certificate

chaîne *f* **CV**
D: CV-Anlage *f*, kontinuierliche Vulkanisationsanlage
E: CV-line *n*, continuous vulcanization line

chaîne *f* **de fabrication**
D: Fertigungsstraße *f*
E: manufacturing line, production line

chaîne *f* **de vulcanisation en continu**
D: CV-Anlage *f*, kontinuierliche Vulkanisationsanlage
E: CV-line *n*, continuous vulcanization line

chaîne *f* **d'isolateurs**
D: Isolatorenkette *f*
E: insulator string

chaînette *f*
D: Kettenlinie *f*
E: catenary *n*

chaînette, vulcanisation en ~
D: Kettenlinien-Vulkanisation *f*
E: catenary vulcanization

chaleur, dissiper la ~
D: die Wärme ableiten
E: to conduct away the heat, to carry away the heat, to dissipate the heat

chaleur *f* **due aux pertes**
D: Verlustwärme *f*
E: heat due to losses

chambre *f*
D: Kammer *f*
E: chamber *n*, cabinet *n*,

compartment n
chambre f de répartition
  D: Muffenbunker m, Muffenbauwerk n, Kabelschacht m
  E: cable pit, cable jointing chamber, cable jointing manhole, cable vault
champ m d'application
  D: Anwendungsgebiet n
  E: field of application
champ m de fuite
  D: Streufeld n
  E: leakage field
champ m d'essai
  D: Prüffeld n
  E: test field
champ électrique, concentrations du ~ [él.]
  D: Feldkonzentrationen f pl
  E: stress concentrations
champ électrique, limitation du ~
  D: Feldbegrenzung f
  E: limitation of the electrical field, field limitation
champ électrique, régulation du ~ [él.]
  D: Feldsteuerung f, Feldregulierung f
  E: stress control, stress relief, field control
champ m parasite [com.]
  D: Störfeld n
  E: noise field, interference field
champ m perturbateur [com.]
  D: Störfeld n
  E: noise field, interference field
chandelles f pl de palpage [vulc.]
  D: Abtast-Führungsrollen f pl
  E: sensing guide rollers
chanfreiner v
  D: abschrägen v
  E: bevel v, chamfer v
changement m de bobine
  D: Spulenwechsel m
  E: reel change
changement m de couleur
  D: Verfärbung f
  E: discoloration n, staining n
changement m de la torsion
  D: Drallwechsel m
  E: reversal of lay, change of lay
changement m de vitesse
  D: Drehzahländerung f
  E: speed variation
changement m du pas de câblage
  D: Drallwechsel m
  E: reversal of lay, change of lay
changement m du volume
  D: Volumenänderung f
  E: volume variation
changer v
  D: abändern v, ändern v
  E: modify v, alter v, change v, revise v
changer v de vitesse (engrenage) [méc.]
  D: schalten v
  E: change v (gear)
chantier, essai de câbles sur ~
  D: Prüfung an verlegten Kabeln
  E: site test on cables
chantier, essai sur ~
  D: Freigelände-Prüfung f
  E: field test
chantier, sur ~ [pose c.]
  D: auf der Baustelle, am Montageort
  E: at site
chapelle f
  D: Abzug m (Lüftung), Absaughaube f
  E: exhaust n, exhaust hood, fume hood
charactéristique f mécanique
  D: mechanische Eigenschaft
  E: mechanical characteristic, mechanical property
charge f
  D: Füllstoff m
  E: filler n, loading material
charge f [él.]
  D: Ladung f
  E: charge n
charge f [él., méc.]
  D: Beanspruchung f, Belastung f, Last f
  E: stress n, strain n, load n
charge, câble en exploitation sans ~ [c. én.]
  D: unbelastetes Kabel, Kabel in unbelastetem Zustand
  E: cable at no-load
charge, en ~ [él.]
  D: mit Last
  E: under load
charge, en ~s
  D: chargenweise adj
  E: in batch quantities
chargé, fortement ~
  D: füllstoffreich adj
  E: heavily loaded
chargé, fortement ~ [él., méc.]
  D: hochbeansprucht adj,

hochbelastet *adj*
 E: heavily loaded, heavily stressed, highly stressed

chargé, ligne ~e
 D: belastete Leitung
 E: loaded line, line under load

charge, sans ~ [él.]
 D: ohne Last
 E: at no-load

charge f au moyen de bobines en série
 D: Bespulung f, Pupinisierung f
 E: coil-loading n, Pupin loading

charge f constante
 D: gleichbleibende Belastung
 E: constant load

charge f continue
 D: Dauerbelastung f, Dauerlast f
 E: continuous load, sustained load

charge f continue [c. com.]
 D: Krarupisieren n
 E: continuous loading

charge f cyclique
 D: zyklische Belastung
 E: cyclic loading

charge f d'empreinte
 D: Eindrücklast f
 E: indentation load

charge f de pointe [él.]
 D: Lastspitze f, Spitzenbelastung f
 E: peak load, load peak

charge f de rupture
 D: Bruchlast f
 E: breaking load, ultimate load

charge f des centrales électriques
 D: EVU-Last f
 E: public utilities load

charge f d'espace
 D: Raumladung f
 E: space charge

charge f électrique
 D: Stromladung f
 E: current load, power load

chargé adj en noir
 D: rußgefüllt *adj*
 E: carbon black loaded

charge f limite
 D: Grenzleistung f, Belastungsgrenze f
 E: ultimate load, load limit

charge f limite [él.]
 D: Belastbarkeit f, Strombelastbarkeit f
 E: current-carrying capacity, current rating, ampacity n, power rating

charge f nominale
 D: Nennbelastung f
 E: rated load, nominal load

charge f normale
 D: Normalbeanspruchung f
 E: standard stress

charge f permanente
 D: Dauerbelastung f, Dauerlast f
 E: continuous load, sustained load

charger v
 D: laden v, belasten v
 E: charge v, load v

charger v [él., méc.]
 D: beanspruchen v, belasten v
 E: stress v, strain v, load v

charger v [méc., él.]
 D: speisen v, einspeisen v, beschicken v
 E: feed v, charge v, load v, supply v

charge f résiduelle
 D: Restladung f
 E: residual charge

charge f spatiale
 D: Raumladung f
 E: space charge

chargeur m de billettes [pr. à filer]
 D: Blocklader m
 E: billet loader

charge f variable
 D: wechselnde Belastung
 E: variable load, alternating load

chariot m à câbles
 D: Kabelwagen m, Kabeltrommel-Anhänger m
 E: cable trailer, cable trolley

chariot m à touret de câble
 D: Kabelwagen m, Kabeltrommel-Anhänger m
 E: cable trailer, cable trolley

chariot m de manutention
 D: Flurförderfahrzeug n
 E: shop floor transport vehicle

chariot m élévateur
 D: Hubwagen m
 E: lifting carriage

chariot m élévateur à fourche
 D: Gabelstapler m
 E: forklift truck

chariot m porte-outils
 D: Werkzeugschlitten m
 E: die slide

charpente pour câbles f [pose c.]

charpente

    D: Kabelpritsche *f*, Kabeltraggerüst *n*, Pritsche *f*
    E: cable tray, cable rack

charrue *f* de pose pour câbles
    D: Kabelpflug *m*
    E: cable laying plough (GB), cable laying plow (US)

chauffage *m*
    D: Beheizung *f*, Heizung *f*
    E: heating *n*

chauffage *m*
    D: Erwärmung *f*
    E: heating *n*, temperature rise

chauffage *m* à induction
    D: Induktionsheizung *f*
    E: induction heating

chauffage *m* de l'âme par induction
    D: induktive Leiterheizung
    E: inductive conductor heating

chauffage *m* du conteneur [pr. à filer]
    D: Aufnehmerheizung *f*
    E: container heating system

chauffage *m* par résistance
    D: Widerstandsheizung *f*
    E: resistance heating

chaux, couche de ~
    D: Kalkschicht *f*, Kalküberzug *m*
    E: chalk layer

chemin *m* de glissement
    D: Gleitschiene *f*
    E: slide bar, slide rail

chemin *m* de roulement de la grue
    D: Kranbahn *f*
    E: crane rail

cheminée *f* d'aération
    D: Entlüftungsrohr *n*
    E: exhaust pipe, exhaust flue, ventilation pipe

cheminement *m*
    D: Kriechwegbildung *f*
    E: tracking *n*

chemise *f* [pr. à filer]
    D: Preßschale *f*
    E: shell *n*, skin *n*

chenille *f* de tirage
    D: Raupenabzug *m*
    E: caterpillar pull-off, caterpuller *n*

chevauchant *adj*
    D: überlappend *adj*
    E: overlapping *adj*

chevauchement *m*
    D: Überlappung *f*
    E: overlap(ping) *n*

chevauchement *m* [rub.]
    D: Gangversatz *m*, Lagenversatz *m*
    E: registration *n*, staggering *n*

chevaucher *v*
    D: überlappen *v*
    E: overlap *v*

chiffre *m* distinctif [câb.]
    D: Kennziffer *f*
    E: code number

chlorure *m* de polyvinyle (PVC)
    D: Polyvinylchlorid (PVC) *n*
    E: polyvinyl chloride (PVC)

choc *m* thermique
    D: Wärmeschock *m*
    E: thermal shock, heat shock

chromatographie *f* en phase gazeuse
    D: Gaschromatographie *f*
    E: gas chromatographic analysis, gas chromatography

chute *f* de courant
    D: Stromabfall *m*
    E: current drop, current decrease

chute *f* de pression
    D: Druckabfall *m*, Druckverlust *m*
    E: pressure drop, pressure loss, head loss

chute *f* de température
    D: Temperaturabfall *m*, Abfall der Temperatur, Absinken der Temperatur
    E: temperature drop, temperature decrease

chute *f* de tension
    D: Spannungsabfall *m*
    E: voltage drop

ciment *m* de résine synthétique
    D: Kunstharzkitt *m*
    E: synthetic resin cement

cingler *v*
    D: vorwalzen *v*
    E: rough *v*, bloom *v*

circuit *m* [él.]
    D: Schaltung *f*, Verdrahtung *f*
    E: circuitry *n*, circuit arrangement, wiring *n*, cabling *n*, interconnection *n*

circuit *m* à charge concentrée
    D: Leitung mit punktförmiger Ladung
    E: lump loaded circuit

circuit *m* à répéteur
    D: Stromkreis mit Verstärkung
    E: repeater circuit

circuit *m* assimilé à un circuit à quatre

fils [com.]
  D: Stromkreis für Zweidraht-Getrenntlage-Verfahren
  E: four-wire type circuit

circuit-bouchon *m*
  D: Sperrkreis *m*
  E: block circuit, trap circuit

circuit *m* **combinant**
  D: Stammkreis *m*, Stammleitung *f*
  E: side circuit, physical circuit, combining circuit

circuit *m* **combiné**
  D: Phantomkreis *m*, Phantomschaltung *f*, Viererkreis *m*, Kreisvierer *m*, Phantomleitung *f*
  E: phantom circuit, superposed circuit

circuit *m* **d'alimentation**
  D: Versorgungsleitung *f*, Speiseleitung *f*
  E: feeding line, feeder *n*

circuit *m* **de base** [él.]
  D: Basisschaltung *f*
  E: grounded-base circuit

circuit *m* **de commande**
  D: Steuerkreis *m*, Regelkreis *m*
  E: control circuit

circuit *m* **de courant de rupture**
  D: Abschaltstromkreis *m*
  E: breaking circuit

circuit *m* **de mesure**
  D: Meßkreis *m*
  E: measuring circuit

circuit *m* **de mise à la terre**
  D: Erdungsleitung *f*
  E: earthing circuit (GB), grounding circuit (US)

circuit *m* **d'entrée**
  D: Eingangskreis *m*
  E: input circuit

circuit *m* **d'équilibrage**
  D: Ausgleichsleitung *f*
  E: equalizer *n*, equipotential connection, balancing circuit, equalizing circuit

circuit *m* **de référence**
  D: Bezugskreis *m*
  E: reference circuit

circuit *m* **de refroidissement**
  D: Kühlkreis *m*
  E: cooling circuit

circuit *m* **de réglage**
  D: Steuerkreis *m*, Regelkreis *m*
  E: control circuit

circuit *m* **de retour par la terre**
  D: Erdrückleitung *f*
  E: earth return circuit (GB), ground return circuit (US)

circuit *m* **dérivé**
  D: Abzweigstromkreis *m*, Nebenschluß *m*
  E: branch circuit, shunt *n*

circuit *m* **d'essai**
  D: Versuchsschaltung *f*, Prüfstromkreis *m*
  E: temporary circuit, test circuit, experimental circuit

circuit *m* **d'étalonnage**
  D: Eichkreis *m*
  E: calibration circuit

circuit *m* **électrique**
  D: Stromkreis *m*
  E: electric circuit *n*, electric circuit

circuit *m* **en pont**
  D: Brückenschaltung *f*
  E: bridge circuit

circuit *m* **fantôme**
  D: Phantomkreis *m*, Phantomschaltung *f*, Viererkreis *m*, Kreisvierer *m*, Phantomleitung *f*
  E: phantom circuit, superposed circuit

circuit *m* **fantôme avec retour par la terre**
  D: Phantomkreis mit Erdrückleitung
  E: ground phantom circuit

circuit *m* **fermé**
  D: geschlossener Kreis, geschlossener Kreislauf
  E: closed circuit

circuit *m* **fermé** [él.]
  D: Schleife *f* (Leitungszusammenführung)
  E: loop *n*, closed circuit

circuit *m* **indicateur**
  D: Anzeigestromkreis *m*
  E: indicator circuit

circuit *m* **intégré**
  D: integrierter Schaltkreis
  E: integrated circuit (IC)

circuit *m* **primaire**
  D: Primärkreislauf *m*
  E: primary circuit

circuit *m* **pupinisé**
  D: Pupinleitung *f*
  E: coil-loaded circuit

circuit *m* **réel**
  D: Stammkreis *m*, Stammleitung *f*
  E: side circuit, physical circuit, combining circuit

circuit *m* **secondaire**
  D: Sekundärkreislauf *m*
  E: secondary circuit

circuit *m* **superposé**
  D: Phantomkreis *m*, Phantomschaltung *f*, Viererkreis *m*, Kreisvierer *m*, Phantomleitung *f*
  E: phantom circuit, superposed circuit

circuit *m* **superposé** [c. én.]
  D: überlagerter Stromkreis *m*
  E: superposed circuit

circuit *m* **téléphonique**
  D: Fernsprechleitung *f*, Sprechkreis *m*
  E: telephone circuit, voice circuit, speech circuit

circuit *m* **téléphonique à fréquence porteuse à large bande**
  D: Breitband-Trägerfrequenz-Sprechkreis *m*
  E: broad-band carrier telephony speech circuit

circuit *m* **téléphonique bifilaire**
  D: Fernsprechdoppelleitung *f*
  E: two-wire telephone circuit, telephone loop

circulation *f*
  D: Umlauf *m*
  E: circulation *n*, recirculation *n*, recycling *n*

circulation *f* **d'eau de refroidissement**
  D: Kühlwasserumlauf *m*
  E: cooling water circulation

circulation *f* **d'huile**
  D: Ölkreislauf *m*
  E: oil circulation

circulation *f* **forcée**
  D: Zwangsumlauf *m* (Flüssigkeiten)
  E: forced circulation

circulation *f* **par pompage**
  D: Umpumpen *n*
  E: recycling *n*, recirculation *n*

cire *f* **microcristalline**
  D: mikrokristallines Wachs
  E: microcrystalline wax

cisaille *f* **à ébouter**
  D: Schopfschere *f*
  E: crop shear

cisailler *v*
  D: abscheren *v*
  E: shear off *v*

cisailler *v*
  D: köpfen *v* (Drahtenden), beschneiden *v*, abschneiden *v*
  E: crop *v*, trim *v*, cut *v*

cisailles *f pl* **à déchets**
  D: Abfallschere *f*
  E: cobble shears *pl*, scrap cutter

cisailles *f pl* **à porte-à-faux**
  D: fliegende Schere
  E: flying shear(s)

claquage *m* [él.]
  D: Durchschlag *m*
  E: breakdown *n*, dielectric breakdown, puncture *n*

claquer *v* [él.]
  D: durchschlagen *v*
  E: break down *v*

classe *f* **de qualité**
  D: Güteklasse *f*
  E: quality grade, quality *n*

classe *f* **d'isolement**
  D: Wärmeklasse *f*
  E: insulation class, thermal classification

climatisation *f*
  D: Klimatisierung *f*
  E: air-conditioning *n*

cloche *f* **d'égouttement**
  D: Tropfschirm *m* (Isolator)
  E: drop shield

cloche *f* **isolante**
  D: Glockenisolator *m*, Isolierglocke *f*
  E: shed insulator, cup insulator, bell-shaped insulator, dome-shaped insulator, petticoat insulator, insulating bell

clou *m* **de tirage** [câb.]
  D: Ziehkopf *m*, Ziehöse *f*, Zugöse *f*
  E: pulling eye, pulling head, pulling grip

code *m* [câb.]
  D: Kennzeichen *n*
  E: mark *n*, code *n*

code *m* **de couleur**
  D: farbige Kennzeichnung
  E: colo(u)r code, colo(u)r coding

code *m* **de désignation**
  D: Typenbezeichnung *f*, Typenkurzzeichen *n*
  E: code designation, type designation

coefficient m
  D: Beiwert m
  E: coefficient n, factor n
coefficient m **d'accumulation**
  D: Ballungsfaktor m
  E: grouping factor
coefficient m **d'affaiblissement**
  D: Dämpfungsfaktor m
  E: attenuation factor, damping coefficient
coefficient m **de couplage** [tél.]
  D: Kopplungsfaktor m
  E: coupling coefficient
coefficient m **de dilatation**
  D: Ausdehnungskoeffizient m
  E: coefficient of expansion, expansion coefficient
coefficient m **de dilatation linéaire**
  D: linearer Ausdehnungskoeffizient
  E: longitudinal expansion coefficient, coefficient of linear expansion
coefficient m **de dilatation thermique**
  D: Wärmeausdehnungskoeffizient m
  E: thermal expansion coefficient
coefficient m **de frottement**
  D: Reibungskoeffizient m
  E: friction coefficient
coefficient m **de réduction**
  D: Reduktionsfaktor m
  E: reduction factor
coefficient m **de remplissage**
  D: Füllfaktor m
  E: space factor, bulk factor
coefficient m **de rétreint**
  D: Verdichtungsgrad m (Leiter), Anwalzgrad m (Leiter)
  E: compression degree, shaping degree
coefficient m **de saponification**
  D: Verseifungszahl f
  E: saponification value, saponification number
coefficient m **de température**
  D: Temperaturbeiwert m, Temperaturkoeffizient m
  E: temperature coefficient
coefficient m **de transformation**
  D: Umrechnungsfaktor m
  E: conversion factor
coefficient m **de transmission calorifique**
  D: Wärmeübertragungskoeffizient m
  E: coefficient of heat transfer

coefficient m **de volume**
  D: Füllfaktor m
  E: space factor, bulk factor
coefficient m **d'utilisation** [mach.]
  D: Ausnutzungsgrad m
  E: utilisation factor, unit capacity factor
coffret m **de branchement**
  D: Abgangskasten m
  E: tapping-off unit
coffret m **de dérivation pour câbles** [com.]
  D: Verzweigergehäuse für Kabel
  E: cable distribution cabinet
coffret m **de raccordement** [él.]
  D: Anschlußkasten m, Klemmenkasten m
  E: distribution panel, terminal box, junction box, connection box
collage m
  D: Haftung f, Adhäsion f
  E: adhesion n, adherence n, bonding n, sticking n
colle f
  D: Kleber m, Haftvermittler m, Klebstoff m
  E: adhesive n, bonding agent
collecteur m **de fumées**
  D: Abzug m (Lüftung), Absaughaube f
  E: exhaust n, exhaust hood, fume hood
coller v
  D: haften v, kleben vi
  E: adhere v, bond v, stick v
coller v
  D: zusammenbacken v
  E: agglomerate v, conglomerate v, cake v
coller vt
  D: kleben vt
  E: cement vt, glue vt, paste vt, bond vt
colle f **thermodurcissable**
  D: warmhärtender Klebstoff
  E: thermosetting adhesive
collier m
  D: Schelle f, Befestigungsschelle f
  E: clamp n, bracket n, clip n, cleat n
collier chauffant m
  D: Heizband n
  E: heating collar
collier m **de câble**
  D: Kabelschelle f, Kabelklemme f
  E: cable clamp, cable cleat, cable clip,

collier

cable grip

collier de fixation m
- D: Befestigungsklemme f
- E: mounting clip, mounting bracket

collier m **de mise à la terre**
- D: Erdungsschelle f, Erdschelle f
- E: earth(ing) clip (GB), ground(ing) clip (US)

collier m **pour tubes**
- D: Rohrschelle f
- E: collar band, wall clamp, pipe clip

colonne f de mercure
- D: Quecksilbersäule f
- E: mercury column

colonne f montante
- D: Steigleitung f
- E: rising main, vertical riser cable

colophane f
- D: Harz n (Naturharz), Kolophonium n
- E: rosin n, gum rosin

coloration f
- D: Färbung f
- E: colo(u)ring n

coloré, mélange ~ dans la masse
- D: durchgefärbte Mischung
- E: colo(u)red compound

colorer v
- D: färben v
- E: colo(u)r v, dye v, stain v, pigment v

combustible adj
- D: brennbar adj, entflammbar adj
- E: flammable adj(US), inflammable adj(GB), , combustible adj

comité m **de normalisation**
- D: Normenausschuß m
- E: standardization committee

commande f
- D: Betätigung f, Bedienung f
- E: operation n, handling n, actuation n, control n

commande f [él., méc.]
- D: Steuerung f
- E: control n

commande, à ~ manuelle
- D: handbetätigt adj
- E: hand-operated adj, manually operated

commande, à ~ mécanique
- D: mechanisch betätigt
- E: mechanically operated

commande f à air comprimé
- D: Druckluftbetätigung f
- E: pneumatic operation, compressed-air control

commande f à courroie
- D: Riemenantrieb m
- E: belt drive

commande f à distance
- D: Fernsteuerung f, Fernbedienung f
- E: remote control, telecontrol n

commande f bilatérale
- D: doppelseitiger Antrieb
- E: bilateral drive

commande f directe
- D: Einzelantrieb m
- E: single drive, direct drive

commande f individuelle
- D: Einzelantrieb m
- E: single drive, direct drive

commande f manuelle
- D: Handbetrieb m, Handsteuerung f
- E: manual operation, hand operation, manual control

commandé adj manuellement
- D: handbetätigt adj
- E: hand-operated adj, manually operated

commande f par bouton-poussoir
- D: Druckknopfsteuerung f
- E: push-button control

commande f par chaîne
- D: Kettenantrieb m
- E: chain drive

commandé adj par moteur
- D: motorangetrieben adj, motorisch adj
- E: motor-driven adj, motorized adj

commandé adj par ordinateur
- D: rechnergesteuert adj
- E: computer-controlled adj

commande f par programme
- D: Programmsteuerung f
- E: program(me) control

commande f par une personne
- D: Einmannbedienung f
- E: one-man operation

commande f pneumatique
- D: Druckluftbetätigung f
- E: pneumatic operation, compressed-air control

commander v
- D: steuern v
- E: control v

commande f unilatérale
- D: einseitiger Antrieb

E: unilateral drive
commercial *adj*
  D: handelsüblich *adj*
  E: commercial *adj*
commercial, du type ~
  D: handelsüblich *adj*
  E: commercial *adj*
commutateur *m*
  D: Umschalter *m*
  E: change-over switch
commutateur-sélecteur *m*
  D: Wählschalter *m*
  E: selector *n* (switch)
commutation *f*
  D: Umschaltung *f*
  E: change-over *n*, switch-over *n*
compactage *m* **de l'âme**
  D: Verdichtung des Leiters
  E: compression of the conductor, compaction of the conductor
compacter *v*
  D: verdichten *v*
  E: compact *v*, compress *v*
compartiment *m*
  D: Kammer *f*
  E: chamber *n*, cabinet *n*, compartment *n*
compatibilité *f*
  D: Verträglichkeit *f*
  E: compatibility *n*
compensateur *m* **de torsion**
  D: Drall-Ausgleichsvorrichtung *f*
  E: twist compensator
compensation *f*
  D: Ausgleich *m*
  E: compensation *n*, balance *n*, balancing *n*, counterbalancing *n*, equalization *n*
compensation *f* **de l'affaiblissement** [c. tél.]
  D: Entdämpfung *f*
  E: damping reduction, transmission gain
compensation *f* **de l'amortissement** [c. tél.]
  D: Entdämpfung *f*
  E: damping reduction, transmission gain
compensation *f* **de la température**
  D: Temperaturausgleich *m*
  E: equalization of temperature, compensation of temperature
compensation de la tension, dispositif de ~
  D: Zugspannungs-Regelvorrichtung *f*
  E: tension control device, tension compensating device, tension compensator
compensation *f* **de l'épaisseur**
  D: Dickenausgleich *m*
  E: thickness compensation
compensation *f* **des défauts à la terre**
  D: Erdschlußkompensation *f*
  E: earth fault compensation (GB), ground fault compensation (US)
compensation *f* **des phases**
  D: Phasenausgleich *m*
  E: phase compensation
compensation *f* **par changement du pas de câblage** [c. com.]
  D: Ausgleichen durch Dralländerung
  E: compensation by alteration of twist
compensation *f* **par croisement** [c. com.]
  D: Ausgleichen durch Kreuzen
  E: compensation by crossing
compensation *f* **par groupement suivant les valeurs électriques** [c. com.]
  D: Ausgleichen durch Gruppieren nach elektrischen Werten
  E: compensation by grouping according to electrical values
complexe *m*
  D: Verbundwerkstoff *m*
  E: composite material, multilayer material, composite *n*
comportement *m*
  D: Verhalten *n*
  E: behaviour *n*, performance *n*
comportement *m* **à basse température**
  D: Kälteverhalten *n*
  E: behaviour at low temperatures
comportement *m* **à la chaleur**
  D: Wärmeverhalten *n*
  E: thermal behaviour
comportement *m* **aux ondes de choc**
  D: Stoßspannungsverhalten *n*
  E: impulse voltage behaviour
comportement *m* **en courte durée**
  D: Kurzzeitverhalten *n*
  E: short-time performance
comportement *m* **en (longue) durée**
  D: Langzeitverhalten *n*
  E: long-time behaviour
composante *f*
  D: Komponente *f*

composante
  E: component n, constituent n
composante f transversale d'une tension [él.]
  D: Querspannung f
  E: transverse voltage, quadrature-axis component of the voltage
composants m pl d'un mélange
  D: Mischungsbestandteile m pl
  E: ingredients of a compound
composants m pl volatils
  D: flüchtige Bestandteile m pl
  E: volatile components
composition f
  D: Gemisch n
  E: mixture n, blend n, compound n, composition n
compression f
  D: Zusammendrückung f
  E: compression n
compression f du sol [pose c.]
  D: Verdichtung des Erdbodens
  E: compression of the soil, compaction of the soil
comprimer v
  D: verdichten v
  E: compact v, compress v
compteur m
  D: Meßuhr f
  E: indicating dial
compteur m métreur
  D: Längenmeßvorrichtung f, Längenzählgerät n, Meterzähler m
  E: meter counter
concentration f de contraintes
  D: Beanspruchungshäufung f
  E: stress concentration
concentrations f pl du champ électrique [él.]
  D: Feldkonzentrationen f pl
  E: stress concentrations
conception f et exploitation de réseaux électriques
  D: Planung und Betrieb von Stromnetzen
  E: system planning and operation
concordance f des phases
  D: Phasengleichheit f
  E: phase balance, phase coincidence
condensateur m
  D: Kondensator m
  E: capacitor n
condensateur m antiparasites
  D: Störschutzkondensator m
  E: anti-interference capacitor, anti-noise capacitor
condensateur m de blocage
  D: Blockkondensator m
  E: blocking capacitor
condensateur m de couplage
  D: Koppelkondensator m
  E: coupling capacitor
conditionnement m d'air
  D: Klimatisierung f
  E: air-conditioning n
conditionneur m d'air
  D: Klimaanlage f
  E: air-conditioner n
conditions f pl aux limites
  D: Grenzbedingungen f pl, Randbedingungen f pl
  E: boundary conditions
conditions f pl de fonctionnement
  D: Betriebsbedingungen f pl
  E: operational conditions, operating conditions, service conditions
conditions f pl de pose
  D: Legeverhältnisse n pl, Verlegebedingungen f pl
  E: laying conditions, installation conditions
conditions f pl d'essai
  D: Versuchsbedingungen f pl, Prüfbedingungen f pl
  E: test conditions
conditions f pl de travail
  D: Betriebsbedingungen f pl
  E: operational conditions, operating conditions, service conditions
conditions f pl d'expérience
  D: Versuchsbedingungen f pl, Prüfbedingungen f pl
  E: test conditions
conditions f pl d'exploitation
  D: Betriebsbedingungen f pl
  E: operational conditions, operating conditions, service conditions
conditions f pl sur chantier [pose c.]
  D: Baustellen-Bedingungen f pl, Baustellen-Verhältnisse n pl, Bedingungen auf der Baustelle
  E: field conditions
conductance f
  D: Leitwert m
  E: conductance n
conducteur m
  D: Leiter m

E: conductor *n*

conducteur *m* (à âme rigide ou souple)
D: Aderleitung *f*
E: general purpose single-core non-sheathed cable, insulated wire

conducteur *adj* (-trice)
D: leitfähig *adj*, leitend *adj*
E: conductive *adj*

conducteur *m* à ficelle de papier
D: Papierkordelader *f*
E: paper string wire (core)

conducteur *m* à gaine séparable
D: Stegleitung *f*
E: flat webbed building wire

conducteur *m* à isolement air/papier (rubanage serré) [c. com.]
D: Festader *f*
E: air-space(d) paper-insulated core (tightly wrapped)

conducteur *m* à isolement air/papier (rubanage lâche) [c. com.]
D: Hohlader *f*
E: air-space(d) paper-insulated core (loosely wrapped)

conducteur *m* chauffant
D: Heizleitung *f*
E: heating wire

conducteur *m* d'alimentation
D: Zuleitung *f*
E: lead *n*, feeder *n*, lead-in *n*, supply line

conducteur *m* d'amenée
D: Zuleitung *f*
E: lead *n*, feeder *n*, lead-in *n*, supply line

conducteur *m* d'antenne
D: Antennenleitung *f*
E: antenna wire

conducteur *m* de commande
D: Steuerader *f*
E: control core

conducteur *m* de dérivation
D: Ableiter *m*
E: arrester *n*

conducteur *m* de direction
D: Richtungsader *f*
E: direction core

conducteur *m* de phase
D: Phasenleiter *m*
E: phase conductor, line conductor

conducteur *m* de protection
D: Schutzleiter *m*
E: protective conductor

conducteur *m* de retour
D: Rückleiter *m*
E: return conductor, return wire

conducteur *m* de terre
D: Erdleiter *m*, Erdleitung *f*, Erdseil *n*
E: earthing conductor (GB), grounding conductor (US), earth wire (GB), ground wire (US), guard wire

conducteur *adj* du courant électrique
D: elektrisch leitend
E: electrically conductive

conducteur *m* extérieur
D: Außenleiter *m*
E: outer conductor

conducteur *m* intérieur
D: Innenleiter *m*
E: inner conductor

conducteur *m* isolé
D: Ader *f*
E: core *n*, conductor *n*, insulated wire, insulated conductor

conducteur *m* isolé à la pâte de papier
D: Pulp-Ader *f*, pulpisolierte Ader
E: pulped wire, pulp-insulated wire

conducteur *m* isolé à matière plastique
D: Kunststoff-Aderleitung *f*
E: thermoplastic-insulated building wire

conducteur *m* isolé au caoutchouc avec résistance accrue aux températures élevées
D: Gummiaderleitung mit erhöhter Wärmebeständigkeit
E: rubber-insulated wire with increased heat resistance

conducteur *m* (à âme souple) isolé au caoutchouc résistant à la chaleur
D: wärmebeständige Gummiaderleitung
E: heat-resistant rubber-insulated cable

conducteur *m* isolé au papier
D: papierisolierte Ader
E: paper-insulated wire, paper-insulated core

conducteur *m* isolé au PE cellulaire
D: Zell-PE-isolierte Ader
E: cellular PE-insulated wire (core)

conducteur *m* isolé au plastique
D: kunststoffisolierte Ader
E: plastic-insulated core

conducteur *m* isolé au plastique [c. com.]

conducteur

    D: kunststoffisolierte Ader
    E: PIC (plastic insulated conductor) (US)

conducteur m isolé au Styroflex
    D: Styroflex-isolierte Ader
    E: Styroflex-insulated wire

conducteur m jumelé [c. com.]
    D: Doppelader f, paarverseilte Leitung, Paar n
    E: pair n, twin-wire n, dual wire

conducteur m médian
    D: Mittelleiter m
    E: middle conductor, centre conductor

conducteur m Milliken
    D: skineffektarmer Leiter (Milliken-Leiter)
    E: Milliken conductor

conducteur m négatif
    D: Minusleiter m
    E: negative lead, negative conductor

conducteur m neutre
    D: Nulleiter m, Mittelpunktsleiter m
    E: neutral conductor, neutral wire, zero conductor

conducteur m pour filerie interne
    D: Verdrahtungsleitung f
    E: single-core non-sheathed cable for internal wiring, wiring cable

conducteur m pour machines-outils
    D: Werkzeugmaschinenleitung f
    E: machine tool wire

conducteur m primaire
    D: Primärleiter m
    E: prime conductor

conducteur m résistant aux températures élevées
    D: hitzebeständige Aderleitung
    E: heat-resistant insulated wire

conducteurs m pl de câble avec écran individuel
    D: einzeln abgeschirmte Kabeladern
    E: individually screened cable cores

conducteur m sous gaine de plomb
    D: Bleimantelleitung f
    E: lead-sheathed cable

conducteurs m pl préassemblés
    D: konfektionierte Leitungen
    E: pre-assembled flexible cables and cords, cord sets

conducteurs m pl transposés
    D: gekreuzte Adern
    E: transposed conductors, transposed cores

conducteur m trifil
    D: Drillingsleitung f
    E: three-core cord

conducteur m vert-jaune
    D: grüngelbe Ader
    E: green-yellow core

conductibilité f
    D: Leitfähigkeit f, Leitvermögen n
    E: conductivity n

conductibilité, à haute ~
    D: hochleitfähig adj
    E: highly conductive, high-conductivity...

conductibilité f électrique
    D: elektrische Leitfähigkeit
    E: electrical conductivity

conductibilité f I.A.C.S. (cuivre)
    D: Standard-Leitfähigkeit nach IEC (Kupfer), I.A.C.S.-Leitfähigkeit f (Kupfer)
    E: I.A.C.S. conductivity (International Annealed Copper Standard/IEC)

conductibilité f thermique
    D: Wärmeleitfähigkeit f, thermische Leitfähigkeit
    E: thermal conductivity

conductible adj
    D: leitfähig adj, leitend adj
    E: conductive adj

conductivité f
    D: Leitfähigkeit f, Leitvermögen n
    E: conductivity n

conductivité f calorifique
    D: Wärmeleitfähigkeit f, thermische Leitfähigkeit
    E: thermal conductivity

conductivité f du sol
    D: Bodenleitfähigkeit f
    E: soil conductance

conductivité f I.A.C.S. (cuivre)
    D: Standard-Leitfähigkeit nach IEC (Kupfer), I.A.C.S.-Leitfähigkeit f (Kupfer)
    E: I.A.C.S. conductivity (International Annealed Copper Standard/IEC)

conduit m [pose c.]
    D: Kanalzug m, Rohrzug m
    E: duct n

conduit m
    D: Rohrstrang m
    E: pipeline conduit

conduit m à plusieurs passages

conduit *m* **de décharge**
  D: Abflußleitung *f*
  E: discharge line, drain pipe
conduite *f*
  D: Rohrleitung *f*
  E: pipeline *n*
conduite *f* **d'amenée de secteur**
  D: Netzzuleitung *f*
  E: mains supply lead
conduite *f* **d'aspiration**
  D: Saugleitung *f*
  E: suction line
conduite *f* **de câble**
  D: Kabelkanal *m*
  E: cable duct
conduite *f* **d'écoulement**
  D: Abflußleitung *f*
  E: discharge line, drain pipe
conduite *f* **pour l'introduction des câbles**
  D: Einführungskanal für Kabel
  E: conduit for leading in cables
cône *m*
  D: Verjüngung *f*
  E: tapering *n*, taper *n*
cône *m* **de condensateur**
  D: Kondensatorkeule *f*
  E: capacitor cone, condenser cone
cône *m* **de contrainte** [access. c.]
  D: feldsteuerndes Element, Steuerelement *n*, Wickelkeule *f*
  E: stress cone
cône *m* **de tréfilage** [fabr. fils mét.]
  D: Ziehkonus *m*, Ziehscheibe *f*
  E: drawing cone
cônes de tréfilage, banc à deux ~ [fabr. fils mét.]
  D: Einzelblock mit Doppelscheibe
  E: double-deck drawing block
conforme *adj* **à l'échelle**
  D: maßhaltig *adj*, maßgerecht *adj*
  E: true to size, accurate to size
congélation *f*
  D: Erstarrung *f*
  E: solidification *n*, setting *n*, hardening *n*, freezing *v*
congéler *v*
  D: erstarren *v*, hartwerden *v*
  E: solidify *v*, freeze *v*, set *v*, harden *v*

conicité *f*
  D: Verjüngung *f*
  E: tapering *n*, taper *n*
conique *adj*
  D: verjüngt *adj*, konisch *adj*
  E: tapered *adj*, conic(al) *adj*
connecter *v* [él.]
  D: schalten *v*
  E: switch *v*, connect *v*
connecteur *m* [él.]
  D: Klemme *f*, Anschlußklemme *f*, Verbindungsklemme *f*, Endenanschlußklemme *f*
  E: terminal *n*, connector *n*, connecting terminal
connecteur *m* (d'appareil)
  D: Gerätesteckdose *f*
  E: appliance connector
connecteur *m* **à vis**
  D: Schraubverbinder *m*
  E: bolt-on connector
connexion *f* **au réseau**
  D: Netzanschluß *m*
  E: line connection, mains supply, power supply
connexion *f* **de terre**
  D: Erdanschluß *m*, Erdungsanschluß *m*, Erdverbindung *f*
  E: earth connection (GB), ground connection (US)
connexion *f* **enroulée**
  D: lötfreie gewickelte Verbindung, Wickelverbindung *f* (lötfrei)
  E: wire-wrap connection
connexion *f* **en série**
  D: Reihenschaltung *f*, Hintereinanderschaltung *f*
  E: series circuit, series connection
consommation *f* **électrique, de courant, d'énergie**
  D: Energieverbrauch *m*, Stromverbrauch *m*
  E: current consumption, power consumption
constante *f* **d'affaiblissement**
  D: Dämpfungskonstante *f*
  E: attenuation constant
constante *f* **de ligne**
  D: Leitungskonstante *f*
  E: line constant
constante *f* **de phase**
  D: Phasenmaß *n*
  E: phase constant

constante *f* **de temps**
  D: Zeitkonstante *f*
  E: time constant, time factor

constante *f* **diélectrique**
  D: Dielektrizitätskonstante (DK) *f*
  E: dielectric constant, permittivity *n*

constante *f* **diélectrique effective**
  D: effektive Dielektrizitätskonstante
  E: effective dielectric constant

constituants *m pl* **volatils**
  D: flüchtige Bestandteile *m pl*
  E: volatile components

constitution *f* **de l'âme conductrice**
  D: Leiteraufbau *m*
  E: conductor design

constitution *f* **d'un câble**
  D: Kabelaufbau *m*, Aufbau eines Kabels, Kabelkonstruktion *f*
  E: cable design, cable make-up, construction of a cable, cable build-up, design of a cable

construction *f* [câb.]
  D: Bauart *f*, Typ *m*
  E: design *n*, type *n*, construction *n*

construction, ingénieur de ~ des câbles
  D: Kabelkonstrukteur *m*
  E: cable design engineer

construction *f* **d'un câble**
  D: Kabelaufbau *m*, Aufbau eines Kabels, Kabelkonstruktion *f*
  E: cable design, cable make-up, construction of a cable, cable build-up, design of a cable

contact *m* **à la terre**
  D: Erdschluß *m*
  E: earth fault (GB), ground fault (US)

contact *m* **de mise à la terre**
  D: Schutzkontakt *m*
  E: protective contact, earthing contact (GB)

contact *m* **entre fils**
  D: Leitungsberührung *f*
  E: line to line fault

contacteur-disjoncteur *m*
  D: Schaltschütz *n*
  E: contactor *n*, relay switch

contacteur-interrupteur *m*
  D: Schaltschütz *n*
  E: contactor *n*, relay switch

contamination *f*
  D: Verunreinigung *f*
  E: contamination *n*, impurity *n*

conteneur *m* **de billettes** [pr. à filer]
  D: Blockaufnehmer *m*, Bolzenaufnehmer *m*, Aufnehmer *m*, Preßtopf *m*, Rezipient *m*
  E: billet container

continu *adj*
  D: kontinuierlich *adj*
  E: continuous *adj*, non-intermittent *adj*

continu *adj*
  D: stufenlos *adj*
  E: stepless *adj*, continuously adjustable, infinitely variable

continu, en ~
  D: kontinuierlich *adj*
  E: continuous *adj*, non-intermittent *adj*

continu, en ~
  D: im Durchlaufverfahren
  E: in continuous operation

continuité, essayer la ~ d'un revêtement
  D: einen Überzug auf Porenfreiheit prüfen
  E: to test the continuity of a coating

continuité *f* **électrique**
  D: elektrischer Durchgang
  E: electrical continuity

contournement *m*
  D: Funkenüberschlag *m*, Überschlag *m*
  E: flash-over *n*, arc-over *n*, spark-over *n*

contracter *v* (se)
  D: schrumpfen *v*
  E: shrink *v*, contract *v*

contraction *f*
  D: Schrumpfung *f*
  E: shrinkage *n*, contraction *n*

contraindre *v* [él., méc.]
  D: beanspruchen *v*, belasten *v*
  E: stress *v*, strain *v*, load *v*

contrainte *f* [él., méc.]
  D: Beanspruchung *f*, Belastung *f*, Last *f*
  E: stress *n*, strain *n*, load *n*

contrainte *f* **continue**
  D: Dauerbeanspruchung *f*
  E: continuous stress

contrainte *f* **de cisaillement**
  D: Scherbeanspruchung *f*
  E: shear stress

contrainte *f* **de compression**
  D: Druckbeanspruchung *f*

E: compressive stress
contrainte *f* **de service**
 D: Betriebsbeanspruchung *f*
 E: operating stress
contrainte *f* **de tension**
 D: Spannungsbeanspruchung *f*
 E: voltage stress, electric stress
contrainte *f* **de torsion**
 D: Torsionsbeanspruchung *f*
 E: torsional stress
contrainte *f* **de traction**
 D: Zugbeanspruchung *f*, Dehnungsbeanspruchung *f*
 E: tensile stress
contrainte *f* **électrique**
 D: Spannungsbeanspruchung *f*
 E: voltage stress, electric stress
contrainte *f* **interne** [méc.]
 D: Eigenspannung *f*
 E: internal stress
contrecollé *adj* **de ...**
 D: kaschiert mit ...
 E: coated with ..., laminated with ..., backed with ...
contrecouché *adj* **de ...**
 D: kaschiert mit ...
 E: coated with ..., laminated with ..., backed with ...
contrefaçon *f* **d'un brevet**
 D: Patentverletzung *f*
 E: patent infringement, infringement of a patent
contre-pression *f* [extr.]
 D: Rückdruck *m*
 E: back pressure
contre-réaction *f*
 D: Gegenkopplung *f*
 E: negative feed-back
contre-traverse *f* [pr. à filer]
 D: Gegenholm *m*
 E: counterplaten *n*
contrôle *m*
 D: Untersuchung *f*, Prüfung *f* (Kontrolle)
 E: inspection *n*, check *n*, examination *n*, investigation *n*, analysis *n*
contrôle, dispositif de ~ des phases
 D: Phasenausfall-Überwachungsgerät *n*
 E: phase monitor
contrôle, système de ~ à gaz comprimé
 D: Druckgas-Überwachungssystem *n*
 E: gas pressure alarm system

contrôlé *adj* **à gaz comprimé**
 D: druckgasüberwacht *adj*
 E: gas pressure controlled
contrôle *m* **à la livraison**
 D: Wareneingangskontrolle *f*
 E: incoming inspection, testing of incoming materials, quality control of raw material consignments
contrôle *m* **à la réception du matériel**
 D: Wareneingangskontrolle *f*
 E: incoming inspection, testing of incoming materials, quality control of raw material consignments
contrôle *m* **de continuité** [c. tél.]
 D: Abklingeln *n*, Durchklingeln *n*, Ausklingeln *n*, Klingelprüfung *f*
 E: ringing test, ring-out procedure, buzz-out operation
contrôle *m* **de continuité** [él.]
 D: Durchgangsprüfung *f*, Prüfung auf Durchgang
 E: continuity check, continuity test
contrôle *m* **de la flèche** [vulc.]
 D: Durchhangregelung *f*
 E: catenary control, sag control
contrôle de la pression, dispositif de ~
 D: Druckmeßgerät *n*, Manometer *n*
 E: pressure gauge, pressure control device, manometer *n*
contrôle *m* **de qualité**
 D: Güteprüfung *f*, Qualitätskontrolle *f*
 E: quality inspection, quality test, quality control
contrôle *m* **des câbles téléphoniques à gaz comprimé**
 D: Druckgasschutz und -überwachung von Telefonkabeln
 E: telephone cable pressurization, gas pressure supervision of telephone cables, gas pressure control of telephone cables
contrôle *m* **d'étanchéité**
 D: Dichtigkeitsprüfung *f*
 E: tightness control, leakage test
contrôle *m* **d'impédance**
 D: Impedanz-Prüfung *f*
 E: impedance test
contrôle d'ionisation, appareil de ~ par défilement continu [câb.]
 D: Durchlaufprüfgerät *n*, Trockenprüfgerät *n*
 E: on-line spark tester, continuous discharge detection apparatus,

contrôle

sparker *n*, spark tester
contrôle du diamètre, dispositif de ~
  D: Durchmesser-Überwachungsgerät *n*
  E: diameter control device
contrôle *m* du séchage et de l'imprégnation
  D: Überwachung des Trocknungs- und Tränkvorgangs
  E: monitoring of the drying and impregnating process
contrôle *m* en cours de fabrication
  D: Fertigungskontrolle *f*
  E: process control, manufacturing control, production control
contrôle *m* minutieux
  D: eingehende Prüfung
  E: exhaustive test, close examination, thorough examination
contrôler *v*
  D: prüfen *v*
  E: check *v*, test *v*, verify *v*, control *v*
contrôle *m* rigoureux, serré, sévère
  D: strenge Prüfung
  E: severe test, rigorous test, rigid test, stringent test, severe control, strict control, exacting control
contrôleur *m* d'écoulement
  D: Strömungswächter *m*
  E: flow monitor
contrôleur *m* du niveau
  D: Füllstandswächter *m*, Niveauwächter *m*
  E: level control(ler)
contrôleur/enregistreur *m*
  D: Kontroll-/Schreibgerät *n*
  E: controller/recorder *n*
conversation *f* interurbaine
  D: Ferngespräch *n*
  E: trunk call (GB), toll call (US), long distance call (US)
conversation *f* téléphonique
  D: Telefongespräch *n*
  E: telephone call, telephone conversation
conversation *f* urbaine
  D: Ortsgespräch *n*
  E: local call
convertir *v*
  D: verarbeiten *v*
  E: process *v*, convert *v*
convoyeur *m*
  D: Förderanlage *f*
  E: conveying system, conveyor *n*, feed system
copolymère *m*
  D: Mischpolymerisat *n*, Copolymer *n*
  E: copolymer *n*
coque *f*
  D: Knick *m* (in Leitung oder Kabel), Kinke *f*
  E: kink *n*
coque, formation de ~s
  D: Kinkenbildung *f*
  E: kinking *n*
coque, protection contre la formation de ~s [câb.]
  D: Knickschutz *m*
  E: protection against kinking
coquille *f* [métallurg.]
  D: Kokille *f*
  E: mo(u)ld *n*
corbeille *f* d'enroulement
  D: Bundwickler *m*, Wickelkorb *m*
  E: coiling basket
corde *f*
  D: Seil *n*
  E: rope *n*, strand *n*
corde *f* d'allongement
  D: Verlängerungsschnur *f*
  E: extension cord
corde *f* de suspension [c. tél.]
  D: Tragseil *n*, Luftkabeltragseil *n*
  E: supporting strand, suspension strand, aerial messenger, messenger wire
corde *f* de tirage
  D: Zugseil *n*
  E: pulling rope
corde *f* de torsades
  D: Seil aus Würgelitzen
  E: compound bunch
cordelette *f*
  D: Kordel *f*
  E: string *n*
cordelettes *f pl*
  D: Beilaufschnüre *f pl*
  E: filler strings
cordon *m*
  D: Litze *f*
  E: strand *n*, bunch strand, stranded wire
cordon *m* [él.]
  D: Schnur *f*
  E: cord *n*
cordon *m*

cordon *m* ...
D: Litzenleitung *f*
E: tinsel cord

cordon *m* **avec fiche**
D: Stöpselschnur *f*
E: plug-ended cord

cordon *m* **d'alimentation d'appareil**
D: Geräte-Anschlußschnur *f*
E: appliance cord

cordon *m* **de lampe**
D: Lampenschnur *f*
E: lamp cord

cordon *m* **de liaison**
D: Stöpselschnur *f*
E: plug-ended cord

cordon *m* **de raccordement**
D: Anschlußschnur *f*
E: flexible cord, flexible *n*, connecting cord

cordon *m* **de raccordement d'appareil**
D: Geräte-Anschlußschnur *f*
E: appliance cord

cordon *m* **de soudure**
D: Schweißraupe *f*
E: welding bead

cordon *m* **prolongateur**
D: Verlängerungsschnur *f*
E: extension cord

cordons *m pl* **et conducteurs façonnés**
D: konfektionierte Leitungen
E: pre-assembled flexible cables and cords, cord sets

cordon *m* **souple**
D: Geräte-Anschlußschnur *f*
E: appliance cord

cordon *m* **souple**
D: bewegliche Leitung, flexible Leitung
E: flexible cable, flexible cord, flexible *n*

cordon *m* **souple rétractile**
D: Handapparateschnur *f* (kleingewendelt, dehnbar), Geräteschnur *f* (für vielbewegte Verbindungen), hochbewegliche Verbindungsschnur
E: retractile cord

cordon *m* **souple sous tresse**
D: Gummiaderschnur *f*
E: braided flexible cord

corne *f* **d'arc**
D: Funkenhorn *n*
E: arcing horn

corne *f* **de protection**
D: Funkenhorn *n*
E: arcing horn

cornet *m* **de division**
D: Aufteilungskappe *f*
E: spreader head, spreader cap

cornet *m* **d'entrée** [access. c.]
D: Einführungstrichter *m*
E: terminal bell, entrance bell

corps *m* **étranger**
D: Fremdkörper *m*, Fremdstoff *m*
E: impurity *n*, foreign matter

corroder *v*
D: korrodieren *v*
E: corrode *v*, attack *v*

corrosion, résistant à la ~
D: korrosionsfest *adj*
E: corrosion-resistant *adj*, corrosion-proof *adj*, anti-corrosive *adj*

corrosion *f* **électrolytique**
D: elektrolytische Korrosion
E: electrolytic corrosion

corrosion *f* **locale, localisée, ponctuelle**
D: Lokalkorrosion *f*, Lochfraß *m*
E: local(ized) corrosion, pitting *n*

corrosion *f* **par contact**
D: Kontaktkorrosion *f*
E: galvanic corrosion, bimetallic corrosion

cosse *f* **de câble**
D: Kabelschuh *m*, Kabel-Abschlußhülse *f*, Anschlußöse *f*, Anschlußlasche *f*
E: cable lug, terminal lug, cable eye

cosse *f* **de câble à poinçonner**
D: Preßkabelschuh *m*
E: crimped type cable termination, compression type cable lug

cosse *f* **de câble à sertir**
D: Kerbkabelschuh *m*
E: notch type cable lug

cosse *f* **de câble soudée**
D: Lötkabelschuh *m*
E: soldered terminal lug

cosse *f* **terminale**
D: Kabelschuh *m*, Kabel-Abschlußhülse *f*, Anschlußöse *f*, Anschlußlasche *f*
E: cable lug, terminal lug, cable eye

côte, disposition ~ à côte
D: Verlegung nebeneinander, Parallelanordnung *f*

côte

   E: laying side by side, laying in parallel, parallel arrangement

côté *m* arrondi
  D: abgerundete Kante
  E: rounded edge

côté commande *m* [mach.]
  D: Bedienungsseite *f*
  E: side of attendance, service side, operating side, working side

côté *m* manœuvre [mach.]
  D: Bedienungsseite *f*
  E: side of attendance, service side, operating side, working side

côté *m* service [mach.]
  D: Bedienungsseite *f*
  E: side of attendance, service side, operating side, working side

couche *f*
  D: Lage *f*, Schicht *f*
  E: layer *n*

couche, en ~s consécutives
  D: lagenweise *adj*
  E: in consecutive layers

couche, en deux ~s
  D: doppellagig *adj*
  E: double-layer *adj*, twin-layer *adj*, duplex *adj*

couche, en double ~
  D: doppellagig *adj*
  E: double-layer *adj*, twin-layer *adj*, duplex *adj*

couche de chaux *f*
  D: Kalkschicht *f*, Kalküberzug *m*
  E: chalk layer

couche *f* de fils
  D: Drahtlage *f*
  E: layer of wires

couche *f* de fond
  D: Haftgrundierung *f*
  E: primer *n*, wash primer

couche *f* de laque
  D: Lacküberzug *m*
  E: varnish coating

couche *f* de vernis
  D: Lacküberzug *m*
  E: varnish coating

couche *f* d'oxyde
  D: Oxidhaut *f*
  E: oxide film, oxide skin

couche *f* isolante
  D: Isolierschicht *f*
  E: insulating layer

couche *f* semi-conductrice
  D: Leitschicht *f*, schwachleitende Schicht
  E: semi-conducting layer, semi-conductive layer

couche *f* semi-conductrice externe [câb.]
  D: äußere Leitschicht
  E: outer semi-conducting layer

couche *f* semi-conductrice interne
  D: Leiterdeckschicht *f* (schwachleitend), Leiterglättung *f*, Schirm (schwachleitend) über dem Leiter, innere Leitschicht
  E: strand shield, inner semi-conducting layer

coude *m*
  D: Rohrbogen *m*, Rohrkrümmung *f*, Rohrknie *n*, Knierohr *n*, Krümmer *m* (Rohr)
  E: pipe bend, conduit bend, elbow *n*, knee *n*

coulage *m*
  D: Gießen *n* (in Formen)
  E: casting *n*

coulage *m* continu
  D: Strangguß *m*
  E: continuous casting

coulée *f*
  D: Gießen *n* (in Formen)
  E: casting *n*

coulée *f* continue
  D: Strangguß *m*
  E: continuous casting

coulée *f* continue laminage
  D: Gießwalzen *n*
  E: continuous casting and rolling (CCR)

coulée continue laminage, installation de ~
  D: Gießwalzanlage *f*
  E: continuous casting and rolling plant

coulée *f* en chute
  D: fallender Guß
  E: top-pouring *n*

coulée *f* en coquille
  D: Kokillenguß *m*
  E: ingot mo(u)ld casting, gravity die-casting

coulée *f* en plan incliné
  D: fallender Guß
  E: top-pouring *n*

coulée *f* verticale

couleur f
 D: Farbe f
 E: colo(u)r n
couleur, de ~ foncée
 D: dunkelgefärbt adj
 E: dark-coloured adj
couleur, de ~ résistante
 D: farbecht adj
 E: colo(u)r-fast adj
couleur f de repérage
 D: Markierungsfarbe f (Aderkennzeichnung)
 E: tracer colo(u)r
couleur naturelle, matière plastique de ~
 D: ungefärbter Kunststoff, farbloser Kunststoff
 E: uncoloured plastic, natural-coloured plastic, unpigmented plastic, natural plastic (US)
coupe, point d'éclair en ~ fermé
 D: Flammpunkt im geschlossenen Tiegel
 E: flash point in a closed cup
coupe, point d'éclair en ~ ouverte
 D: Flammpunkt im offenen Tiegel
 E: flash point in an open cup
coupé adj à longueur
 D: in abgepaßten Längen
 E: cut to length
coupe-circuit m [él.]
 D: Sicherung f
 E: fuse n
coupé adj **en biais**
 D: schräg geschnitten
 E: bias-cut adj
couper v [él.]
 D: abschalten v, ausschalten v
 E: switch off v, interrupt v, disconnect v, turn off (US) v, de-energize v, cut out v
couper v
 D: köpfen v (Drahtenden), beschneiden v, abschneiden v
 E: crop v, trim v, cut v
couper v **à la longueur voulue**
 D: auf die gewünschte Länge schneiden
 E: to cut to the required length
couper v **l'isolant coniquement**
 D: die Isolierung zurückschneiden (an der Verbindungs- oder Reparaturstelle)
 E: to taper down the original dielectric (for jointing or repairing)
coupes, dispositif de ~ minces [câb.]
 D: Rundschälwerkzeug n (zum schichtweisen Abtragen von extrudierten Kabel-Isolierungen und schwachleitenden Schichten), Schälwerkzeug n
 E: jacket removal tool
couplage m
 D: Kopplung f
 E: coupling n
couplage m **à l'intérieur de la quarte**
 D: Imvierer-Kopplung f
 E: inherent quad coupling, internal quad coupling
couplage m **de diaphonie**
 D: Mitsprechkopplung f
 E: phantom-to-side unbalance
couplage m **de mesure**
 D: Meßanordnung f, Meßschaltung f
 E: measuring arrangement, connections pl for measurement
couplage m **de tiers circuits**
 D: Dritte-Kreise-Kopplung f
 E: third-circuits coupling
couplage m **diaphonique**
 D: Nebensprechkopplung f
 E: crosstalk circuit, crosstalk coupling
couplage m **diaphonique entre quartes voisins**
 D: Übersprechkopplung f, Nachbarvierer-Nebensprech-Kopplung f
 E: side-to-side crosstalk coupling
couplage m **diaphonique entre réel et réel**
 D: Übersprechkopplung f, Nachbarvierer-Nebensprech-Kopplung f
 E: side-to-side crosstalk coupling
couplage m **en parallèle**
 D: Parallelschaltung f
 E: parallel circuit, parallel connection
couplage m **en série**
 D: Reihenschaltung f, Hintereinanderschaltung f
 E: series circuit, series connection
couplage m **entre couches**
 D: Lage-Lage Kopplung
 E: inter-layer coupling

couplage *m* entre éléments câblés non voisins
 D: Kopplung zwischen nicht-benachbarten Verseilelementen
 E: coupling between non-adjacent strands

couplage *m* expérimental
 D: Versuchsschaltung *f*, Prüfstromkreis *m*
 E: temporary circuit, test circuit, experimental circuit

couplage *m* galvanique
 D: galvanische Kopplung
 E: galvanic coupling

couplage *m* inductif
 D: induktive Kopplung
 E: inductive coupling

couplage *m* inhérent à la quarte
 D: Imvierer-Kopplung *f*
 E: inherent quad coupling, internal quad coupling

couplage *m* magnétique
 D: magnetische Kopplung
 E: magnetic coupling

couplage *m* non systématique
 D: unsystematische Kopplung
 E: unsystematic coupling

couplage *m* ohmique
 D: Ohmsche Kopplung
 E: ohmic coupling

couplage *m* par dérivation
 D: galvanische Kopplung
 E: galvanic coupling

couplage *m* total
 D: Gesamtkopplung *f*
 E: total coupling

couplé *adj* avec
 D: gekoppelt mit
 E: tied in with, interlocked with

courant *m*
 D: Strom *m*
 E: current *n*

courant, faire passer un ~
 D: einen Strom anlegen
 E: to inject a current, to apply a current

courant, sans ~
 D: stromlos *adj*
 E: currentless *adj*

courant *m* actif
 D: Wirkstrom *m*
 E: active current, wattful current

courant *m* à la terre
 D: Erdschlußstrom *m*
 E: earth leakage current (GB), earth fault current (GB), ground fault current (US)

courant *m* alternatif
 D: Wechselstrom *m*
 E: alternating current (a.c.)

courant *m* à vide
 D: Leerlaufstrom *m*
 E: no-load current

courant *m* compensateur
 D: Ausgleichsstrom *m*, Übergangsstrom *m*
 E: equalizing current, transient current, balancing current

courant *m* continu
 D: Gleichstrom *m*
 E: direct current (d.c.), continuous current

courant *m* d'alimentation
 D: Speisestrom *m*
 E: feed current

courant *m* de charge
 D: Ladestrom *m*
 E: capacitance current, charging current

courant *m* de charge
 D: Belastungsstrom *m*
 E: load current

courant *m* de choc
 D: Stoßstrom *m*
 E: surge current, impulse current

courant *m* de commande
 D: Steuerstrom *m*
 E: control current

courant *m* de coupure
 D: Abschaltstrom *m*
 E: breaking current

courant *m* de court-circuit
 D: Kurzschlußstrom *m*
 E: short-circuit current

courant *m* de court-circuit à la terre
 D: Erdschlußstrom *m*
 E: earth leakage current (GB), earth fault current (GB), ground fault current (US)

courant *m* de court-circuit permanent
 D: Dauerkurzschlußstrom *m*
 E: sustained short-circuit current

courant *m* de décharge
 D: Entladestrom *m*
 E: discharge current

courant *m* de déclenchement

D: Auslösestrom *m*
E: release current, tripping current

courant *m* **de défaut**
D: Ableit(ungs)strom *m*, Fehlerstrom *m*, Streustrom *m*, vagabundierender Strom, Verluststrom *m*
E: leakage current, fault current, stray current

courant *m* **de démarrage**
D: Einschaltstrom *m*
E: starting current

courant *m* **de Foucault** [él.]
D: Wirbelstrom *m*
E: eddy current

courant *m* **de fuite**
D: Ableit(ungs)strom *m*, Fehlerstrom *m*, Streustrom *m*, vagabundierender Strom, Verluststrom *m*
E: leakage current, fault current, stray current

courant *m* **de fuite superficiel**
D: Kriechstrom *m*
E: surface leakage current

courant *m* **de phase**
D: Phasenstrom *m*
E: phase current

courant *m* **de pleine charge**
D: Vollastrom *m*
E: full-load current

courant *m* **de réseau**
D: Netzstrom *m*
E: line current, mains current

courant *m* **d'essai**
D: Prüfstrom *m*
E: test current

courant *m* **diaphonique**
D: Nebensprechstrom *m*
E: crosstalk current, unbalance(d) current

courant *m* **d'induction**
D: Induktionsstrom *m*
E: induction current, induced current, inductive current

courant *m* **fort**
D: Starkstrom *m*
E: power current

courant *m* **induit**
D: Induktionsstrom *m*
E: induction current, induced current, inductive current

courant *m* **initial symétrique de court-circuit**
D: Anfangskurzschluß-Wechselstrom *m*
E: initial symmetric short-circuit current

courant *m* **maximum asymétrique de court circuit**
D: Stoßkurzschlußstrom *m*
E: maximum asymmetric short-circuit current

courant *m* **monophasé**
D: Einphasenstrom *m*
E: single-phase current

courant *m* **parasite** [él.]
D: Wirbelstrom *m*
E: eddy current

courant *m* **parasitique**
D: Fremdstrom *m*
E: parasitic current

courant permanent, essai de capacité de charge en ~
D: Dauerstrombelastungsprüfung *f*
E: continuous current carrying test

courant *m* **porteur**
D: Trägerstrom *m*
E: carrier current

courant *m* **réactif**
D: Blindstrom *m*
E: reactive current, idle current

courant *m* **secteur**
D: Netzstrom *m*
E: line current, mains current

courant *m* **téléphonique**
D: Sprechstrom *m*
E: telephone current, speaking current

courant *m* **transitoire**
D: Ausgleichsstrom *m*, Übergangsstrom *m*
E: equalizing current, transient current, balancing current

courant *m* **triphasé**
D: Drehstrom *m*
E: three-phase current

courant *m* **vagabond**
D: Ableit(ungs)strom *m*, Fehlerstrom *m*, Streustrom *m*, vagabundierender Strom, Verluststrom *m*
E: leakage current, fault current, stray current

courant *m* **watté**
D: Wirkstrom *m*

E: active current, wattful current
courbé, fil métallique ~
  D: vorgewölbter Draht
  E: curved wire
courbe, inclinaison d'une ~
  D: Abfall einer Kurve, Neigung einer Kurve
  E: decline of a curve, slope of a curve
courbe, montée d'une ~
  D: Anstieg einer Kurve
  E: slope of a curve
courbe, pente d'une ~
  D: Anstieg einer Kurve
  E: slope of a curve
courbe *f* caractéristique
  D: Kennlinie *f*
  E: characteristic curve
courbe *f* de probabilité
  D: Wahrscheinlichkeitskurve *f*
  E: probability curve
courbe *f* de refroidissement
  D: Abkühlkurve *f*
  E: cooling curve, heat dissipation diagram
courbe *f* des points d'ébullition
  D: Siedekurve *f*
  E: boiling curve
courbe *f* d'étalonnage
  D: Eichkurve *f*
  E: calibration curve
courbe *f* de tension-allongement
  D: Dehnungs-Spannungs-Kurve *f*, Zug-Dehnungskurve *f*
  E: stress-strain curve
courbe *f* de vie [câb.]
  D: Zeit-Spannungsfestigkeits-Kurve *f*
  E: voltage life characteristic curve
courbe *f* de Weibull
  D: Weibull-Kurve *f*
  E: Weibull-curve *n*
courbe *f* journalière de charge
  D: Tageslastdiagramm *n*
  E: daily load curve
courbe *f* psophonétique [c. com.]
  D: Ohrkurve *f*
  E: psophonetic curve
courbure *f*
  D: Krümmung *f*, Biegung *f*
  E: curvature *n*, bend *n*, deflection *n*
couronne *f* [él.]
  D: Korona *f*, Glimmen *n*
  E: corona *n*

couronne *f* (fil métallique/câble)
  D: Ring *m* (Draht/Kabel)
  E: coil *n*
couronne *f* d'assemblage
  D: Laufkranz *m*
  E: stranding cage disc, carriage *n* (carrying stranding cradles)
couronne *f* de fil machine
  D: Walzdrahtring *m*, Grobdrahtring *m*
  E: rod coil, coil of rod
couronne *f* de fil métallique
  D: Drahtring *m*, Drahtbund *m*
  E: coil of wire, wire coil
courroie *f* trapézoïdale
  D: Keilriemen *m*
  E: V-belt *n*
course *f* de piston
  D: Kolbenhub *m*
  E: piston stroke
court-circuit, en cas de ~
  D: im Kurzschlußfall
  E: under short-circuit conditions
court-circuit, mettre en ~
  D: kurzschließen *v*
  E: short-circuit *v*
court-circuit *m* bipolaire
  D: zweipoliger Kurzschluß
  E: two-phase fault, phase-to-phase fault
court-circuiter *v*
  D: kurzschließen *v*
  E: short-circuit *v*
court-circuit *m* tripolaire
  D: dreipoliger Kurzschluß
  E: three-phase fault
coût *m* d'exploitation
  D: Betriebskosten *plt*
  E: operating cost, operating expenses *pl*, running cost
couteau *m* pour câbles
  D: Kabelmesser *n*
  E: cable stripping knife
couvercle *m* de trou d'homme
  D: Mannlochdeckel *m*, Schachtdeckel *m*
  E: manhole cover
couverture *f*
  D: Abdeckung *f*
  E: cover *n*, covering *n*
couvre-joint, faisant ~ [rub.]
  D: die Stoßstellen überdeckend
  E: covering the butt joints

craie f
  D: Kreide f
  E: calcium carbonate, chalk n

craquelé adj
  D: rissig adj
  E: cracked adj, fissured adj

craquelure f
  D: Riß m
  E: crack n, fissure n

craquelure f **due à l'effet de la lumière**
  D: Lichtriß m
  E: sun-crack n, light-crack n

craquelures f pl **en surface**
  D: Oberflächenrisse m pl
  E: surface cracks

crasse f [mét.]
  D: Krätze f
  E: dross n

crépi, sous ~ [pose c.]
  D: unter Putz
  E: under plaster, concealed adj

crépi, sur ~ [pose c.]
  D: auf Putz
  E: on the surface, open adj

crête f
  D: Spitze f (Spannung, Leistung)
  E: peak n, crest n

crête f **de la vis** [extr.]
  D: Schneckensteg m
  E: land of the screw

crête f **d'ondulation**
  D: Wellenspitze f (beim Wellmantel)
  E: peak of corrugation

crête f **d'une onde** [câb.]
  D: Wellenkamm m
  E: crest of a wave

creuset m **à plomb**
  D: Bleischmelzwanne f
  E: lead melting kettle

criblage m
  D: Siebung f
  E: sieving n, screening n

cribleur m **à air**
  D: Windsichter m
  E: air classification plant, air-classifier n, air-sifter n

crique f
  D: Längsriß m (Draht)
  E: split n

cristal m
  D: Kristallit m (PE)
  E: crystal n, crystallite n

cristallinité f
  D: Kristallinität f
  E: crystallinity n

cristallite m
  D: Kristallit m (PE)
  E: crystal n, crystallite n

croisement m [c. com.]
  D: Kreuzen n
  E: crossing n, cross-connection n, cross-splicing n

croisement m **de routes** [pose c.]
  D: Kreuzen von Straßen
  E: crossing of roadways

croissance f **des grains**
  D: Kornwachstum n
  E: grain growth

croûte f [pr. à filer]
  D: Preßschale f
  E: shell n, skin n

croûte f **de la fonte**
  D: Gußhaut f
  E: skin n (casting)

croûte f **de laminage**
  D: Walzhaut f
  E: rolling skin, scale n

cryocâble m
  D: tiefgekühltes Kabel, Kryo-Kabel n
  E: cryogenic cable

CSPE (v. polyéthylène chlorosulfoné)

cuisson f [plast.]
  D: Aushärten n
  E: curing n

cuivre m **à haute conductibilité**
  D: Leitkupfer (EC-Kupfer) n
  E: electrical conductor grade copper (EC-copper), high-conductivity copper

cuivre m **blister**
  D: Blisterkupfer n
  E: blister copper

cuivre m **cathodique**
  D: Kathodenkupfer n
  E: cathode copper

cuivre m **cathodique électrolytique**
  D: KE-Kupfer n (Kathoden-Elektrolyt-Kupfer)
  E: CATH-copper n (electrolytic cathode copper)

cuivre m **électrolytique**
  D: Elektrolytkupfer n
  E: electrolytic copper

cuivre m **fondu**
  D: Kupferschmelze f
  E: molten copper

cuivre m OFHC (cuivre exempt d'oxygène, à haute conductivité)
D: OFHC-Kupfer n (sauerstoffreies hochleitfähiges Kupfer)
E: OFHC-copper n (oxygen free high conductivity copper)

cuivre m raffiné
D: zähgepoltes Kupfer
E: tough-pitch copper (t.p.c.)

cuivre m raffiné électrolytique
D: E-Kupfer n (Kupfer für die Elektrotechnik)
E: high-conductivity copper, electrical grade copper, ETP-Copper (electrolytic tough pitch copper) n

cuivre m tenace
D: zähgepoltes Kupfer
E: tough-pitch copper (t.p.c.)

culot m de filage [pr. à filer]
D: Preßrest m
E: discard n, butt-end n

culot de filage, expulsion du ~ [pr. à filer]
D: Ausstoßen des Preßrestes
E: ejection of the discard

cuve f
D: Trog m, Wanne f
E: trough n

cuve f de séchage
D: Trocknungsgefäß n
E: drying tank

cuve f d'imprégnation
D: Tränkgefäß n
E: impregnating tank

CV (v. vulcanisation continue)

cycle m de charge
D: Lastwechsel m
E: reversal of load, change of load

cycle m de fabrication
D: Fertigungsablauf m, Produktionsablauf m
E: production sequence

cycle m de laminage [mét.]
D: Walzgang m
E: rolling cycle, rolling pass

cycle m de l'effort
D: Lastwechsel m
E: reversal of load, change of load

cycle m de marche d'une machine
D: Arbeitszyklus einer Maschine
E: machine cycle

cycle m de travail
D: Arbeitsablauf m, Betriebsablauf m

E: flow of operation, operating sequence, flow process, operating cycle

cycles m pl de charge [él.]
D: Lastzyklen m pl, Belastungszyklen m pl
E: load cycles, current loading cycles

cycles m pl de chauffage
D: Wärmezyklen m pl
E: heat cycles

cycles m pl d'échauffement et de refroidissement
D: Erwärmungs- und Abkühlungszyklen
E: heating and cooling cycles

cycles m pl par seconde
D: Hertz (Hz)
E: cycles per second (cps), hertz

cycles m pl thermiques
D: Wärmezyklen m pl
E: heat cycles

cylindre f
D: Walze f
E: roll n, bowl n (calender)

cylindre m [extr.]
D: Zylinder m, Schneckengehäuse n
E: barrel n, cylinder n

cylindre m à profilés
D: Profilwalze f
E: sizing roll, section roll

cylindre m de pression [pr. à filer]
D: Arbeitszylinder m
E: main cylinder

cylindre m de retour
D: Rückzugzylinder m
E: pull-back cylinder

cylindre m de travail
D: Arbeitswalze f
E: work(ing) roll

cylindre m malaxeur
D: Mischwalzwerk n
E: mixing mill, mixing rolls pl

D

débit m [mach.]
D: Leistung f, Ausstoß m
E: performance n, output n, efficiency n, capacity n

débit m

débit *m*
D: Durchflußmenge *f*
E: flow rate, flow volume

débit *m*
D: Durchsatz *m*
E: throughput *n*

débit *m* **d'air**
D: Luftdurchsatz *m* (im Wärmeschrank)
E: air flow

débit *m* **d'une pompe**
D: Pumpenleistung *f*, Förderleistung einer Pumpe
E: pump output, delivery of a pump

debit *m* **nominal** [mach.]
D: Nennleistung *f*
E: rated output, nominal output

débrayage, à ~ automatique [mach.]
D: selbstausschaltend *adj*
E: self-disengaging *adj*

début *m* **d'ébullition**
D: Siedebeginn (SB) *m*
E: initial boiling point (I.B.P.)

décalage *m*
D: Verschiebung *f*, Verlagerung *f*
E: movement *n*, shifting *n*, displacement *n*

décalaminer *v*
D: entzundern *v*
E: descale *v*

décalé *adj*
D: gestaffelt *adj*, abgestuft *adj*, versetzt *adj* (stufenweise),
E: staggered *adj*, graded *adj*

décalé *adj* **de ... %** [rub.]
D: versetzt um ... %
E: with ... % registration

décapage, installation de ~
D: Beizanlage *f*
E: pickling plant

décapage *m* **discontinu** [fabr. fils mét.]
D: chargenweises Beizen
E: batch type pickling

décaper *v*
D: beizen *v*
E: pickle *v*

décarbonateur *m*
D: Enthärtungsanlage *f*
E: softening plant

décentrage *m*
D: Dezentrierung *f*
E: decentering *n*

décharge, intensité de ~
D: Entladungsintensität *f*
E: discharge intensity

décharge *f* **disruptive** [él.]
D: Durchschlag *m*
E: breakdown *n*, dielectric breakdown, puncture *n*

décharge *f* **en couronne**
D: Glimmentladung *f*, Korona-Entladung *f*, Sprühentladung *f*
E: corona discharge, ionization discharge

décharge *f* **ionisante**
D: Entladungsdurchschlag *m*
E: ionizing discharge

déchargement *m* [ess.]
D: Entlasten *n*
E: removal of load

décharge *f* **par étincelles**
D: Funkenentladung *f*
E: spark discharge

décharge *f* **par ionisation**
D: Glimmentladung *f*, Korona-Entladung *f*, Sprühentladung *f*
E: corona discharge, ionization discharge

décharge *f* **partielle** [él.]
D: Teilentladung *f*
E: partial discharge

décharge *f* **superficielle**
D: Gleitentladung *f*
E: surface discharge

déchargeur *m*
D: Ableiter *m*
E: arrester *n*

déchet *m* [métallurg.]
D: Abbrand *m*
E: scale loss, melting loss

déchets *m pl*
D: Schrott *m*, Abfälle *m pl*
E: scrap *n*

déchets *m pl* **de cuivre**
D: Altkupfer *n*, Kupferabfälle *m pl*
E: scrap copper, copper scrap

déchirement *m*
D: Reißen *n*
E: tearing *n*, breaking *n*, tear *n*, break *n*

déchirer *v*
D: zerreißen *v*
E: break *v*, tear *v*, rupture *v*

déchirure *f*
D: Reißen *n*
E: tearing *n*, breaking *n*, tear *n*, break *n*

déchirure f **du ruban de papier**
  D: Papierbandriß m
  E: paper tape break

décollement m
  D: Ablösen n (Trennen)
  E: peeling n, detachment n, detaching n

décoller v
  D: ablösen v (Folie, Schicht), abziehen v
  E: peel v, separate v, detach v

décoller v (se)
  D: abblättern v
  E: flake v (off), scale v (off), peel v (off)

décoloration f
  D: Verfärbung f
  E: discoloration n, staining n

décolorer v
  D: verblassen v
  E: fade v

décomposition f
  D: Entmischung f
  E: segregation n, decomposition n, separation n

décomposition f **par oxydation**
  D: oxydativer Abbau
  E: oxidative decomposition, oxidative degradation

décomposition thermo-oxydative, temps jusqu'à la ~
  D: Standzeit f (von Mischungen)
  E: time until thermal-oxidative decomposition

déconnecter v [él.]
  D: abschalten v, ausschalten v
  E: switch off v, interrupt v, disconnect v, turn off (US) v, de-energize v, cut out v

décortiquage m
  D: Befräsen n (Kupfer-Drahtbarren)
  E: scalping n, chipping n

décortiquage, dispositif de ~ (des couches isolantes et semiconductrices d'un câble) [câb.]
  D: Rundschälwerkzeug n (zum schichtweisen Abtragen von extrudierten Kabel-Isolierungen und schwachleitenden Schichten), Schälwerkzeug n
  E: jacket removal tool

découpage m
  D: Ausstanzen n (Prüfkörper)
  E: punching with a die, cutting with a die, die-cutting n

découpe f
  D: Aussparung f
  E: recess n, clearance n, slot n

découper v [câb.]
  D: absetzen v (Isolierung, Mantel)
  E: cut back v, remove v

découper v **des rubans de papier**
  D: Papierbänder schneiden
  E: to slit paper tapes

découpeuse f **à papier**
  D: Papierschneidemaschine f, Papierbandschneidemaschine f
  E: paper tape cutting machine, paper-slitting machine

découplage m **électrique**
  D: elektrische Entkopplung
  E: electrical decoupling

défaillance f
  D: Ausfall m (Anlage, Kabel), Betriebsstörung f
  E: failure n, breakdown n, outage n

défaillance f **du secteur**
  D: Netzausfall m
  E: power failure

défaut m
  D: Ausfall m (Anlage, Kabel), Betriebsstörung f
  E: failure n, breakdown n, outage n

défaut, sans ~s
  D: fehlerfrei adj
  E: correct adj, faultless adj, free from defects

défaut m **à la terre**
  D: Erdschluß m
  E: earth fault (GB), ground fault (US)

défaut m **à la terre double**
  D: Doppelerdschluß m
  E: double earth fault (GB), double ground fault (US)

défaut m **à la terre simple**
  D: Einfach-Erdschluß m
  E: single fault to earth (GB), single fault to ground (US)

défaut m **à la terre unipolaire**
  D: einpoliger Erdschluß
  E: single-line-to-earth fault

défaut m **de câble**
  D: Kabelfehler m
  E: cable defect, cable failure, cable fault

défaut m **de fabrication**
  D: Fertigungsfehler m

E: manufacturing defect, manufacturing flaw

défaut *m* de surface
D: Oberflächenfehler *m*
E: surface defect, surface imperfection, surface irregularity

défaut *m* d'isolement
D: Isolationsfehler *m*, Isolationsstörung *f*
E: insulation fault, insulation defect

défaut *m* du matériel
D: Materialfehler *m*
E: material defect

défaut *m* superficiel
D: Oberflächenfehler *m*
E: surface defect, surface imperfection, surface irregularity

défectueux *adj*
D: fehlerhaft *adj*
E: defective *adj*, faulty *adj*

défilement *m* du papier
D: Papiervorschub *m*
E: paper feed

déflecteur *m* [access. c.]
D: Deflektor *m*
E: deflector *n*

déflecteur *m* en une seule pièce
D: einteiliger Deflektor
E: one-piece deflector

déflecteur *m* surmoulé
D: aufgepreßter Deflektor
E: mo(u)lded deflector

déformation *f*
D: Formänderung *f*, Verformung *f*
E: deformation *n*, distortion *n*

déformation *f* à chaud
D: Deformation in der Wärme
E: heat deformation, heat distortion

déformation *f* élastique
D: elastische Verformung
E: elastic deformation

déformation *f* permanente
D: bleibende Verformung
E: permanent deformation, plastic deformation

dégagement *m* [chim.]
D: Abspaltung *f*
E: liberation *n*, cleavage *n*

dégazage *m*
D: Entgasung *f*
E: degassing *n*, degasification *n*

dégradation *f*
D: Abbau *m* (Werkstoffe), Zersetzung *f*
E: degradation *n*, decomposition *n*

dégradation *f* thermique
D: Abbau *m* (Kautschuk), thermischer Abbau (Kautschuk)
E: thermal degradation

dégradation *f* thermo-oxydative
D: thermooxidativer Abbau
E: thermooxidative degradation

degré *m* de dureté [mét.]
D: Härtegrad *m*
E: degree of hardness, temper *n*

degré *m* de pureté
D: Reinheitsgrad *m*
E: degree of purity

degré *m* de saturation
D: Sättigungsgrad *m*
E: degree of saturation

degré *m* de vulcanisation
D: Vulkanisationsgrad *m*
E: state of cure, degree of cure

degré *m* d'humidité
D: Feuchtegehalt *m*, Feuchtigkeitsgehalt *m*
E: moisture content

degré *m* d'oxygène
D: Sauerstoffanteil *m*
E: oxygen content

degré *m* Engler
D: Englergrad *m* (Öl-Viskosität)
E: Engler degree

degré *m* hygrométrique
D: relative Luftfeuchtigkeit
E: relative humidity

dégrossir *v*
D: vorwalzen *v*
E: rough *v*, bloom *v*

déjoint *m* [ruban. pap.]
D: Spinnfuge *f*, Fuge *f*, Stoßfuge *f*, Stoßkantenzwischenraum *m*
E: butt space, butt gap, gap *n*

délivrer *v* un brevet
D: ein Patent erteilen
E: to grant a patent

delta, monté en ~
D: in Dreieckschaltung
E: delta-connected *adj*

demande, satisfaire à une ~
D: eine Forderung erfüllen, eine Bedingung erfüllen, einer Anforderung genügen
E: to meet a requirement

demande *f* de brevet

demande

- D: Patentmeldung f
- E: patent application

demande de brevet, déposer une ~
- D: ein Patent anmelden
- E: to apply for a patent, to file a patent application

demande f de brevet examinée
- D: Auslegeschrift f
- E: published patent application, examined patent application

demande f de brevet non examinée
- D: Offenlegungsschrift f
- E: unexamined patent application

demande f d'énergie
- D: Energiebedarf m, Leistungsbedarf m
- E: power requirement, power demand

demander v un brevet
- D: ein Patent anmelden
- E: to apply for a patent, to file a patent application

démarrage, temps de ~ [mach.]
- D: Anlaufzeit f, Einlaufzeit f
- E: starting time, acceleration time, running-in period

démarrer v [mach.]
- D: anfahren v, anschalten v, einschalten v
- E: start v, start up v

demi-coquille
- D: Halbschale f
- E: half shell

déminéraliser v
- D: entsalzen v, demineralisieren v
- E: desalt v, desalinate v, demineralize v, deionize v

demi-produit m
- D: Halbfertigfabrikat n
- E: semi-finished product

démontable adj
- D: abnehmbar adj
- E: detachable adj, removable adj, dismountable adj

démonter v
- D: ausbauen v, abmontieren v
- E: remove v, dismount v

démultiplicateur m
- D: Reduktionsgetriebe n, Untersetzungsgetriebe n
- E: reduction gear

dénivellation m
- D: Höhenunterschied m
- E: difference of level

densité f
- D: Dichte f
- E: density n

densité f
- D: Raumgewicht n
- E: volumetric weight, density n, weight per unit of volume

densité f apparente
- D: Schüttgewicht n
- E: bulk density, apparent density

densité f apparente après vibration
- D: Stampfdichte f
- E: apparent density after vibration

densité f de charge
- D: Lastdichte f
- E: load density

densité f de courant
- D: Stromdichte f
- E: current density

densité f de lignes principales [com.]
- D: Durchdringung f
- E: telephone density, line density

densité f téléphonique [com.]
- D: Durchdringung f
- E: telephone density, line density

dénudage m du conducteur
- D: Freilegen des Leiters
- E: baring of the conductor, stripping of the conductor

dénuder v
- D: abisolieren v
- E: to remove the insulation, to strip the insulation

dénuder, machine à ~
- D: Abisoliermaschine f
- E: cable stripper

dépannage m
- D: Instandsetzung f, Reparatur f
- E: overhauling n, repair n

dépanner v
- D: eine Störung beseitigen
- E: to clear a fault

déparasitage m
- D: Entstörung f, Störbeseitigung f
- E: interference elimination, interference suppression, noise suppression

dépasser v
- D: überschreiten v
- E: exceed v

dépendance f de la température
- D: Temperaturabhängigkeit f
- E: temperature dependence

dépendant *adj* **de la fréquence**
  D: frequenzabhängig *adj*
  E: dependent on frequency, frequency-dependent *adj*
dépendant *adj* **de la température**
  D: temperaturabhängig *adj*
  E: temperature-dependent *adj*
déphasage *m*
  D: Phasenverschiebung *f*
  E: phase displacement, phase shift
déplaçable *adj*
  D: verschiebbar *adj*
  E: displaceable *adj*, shiftable *adj*, movable *adj*
déplacement *m*
  D: Verschiebung *f*, Verlagerung *f*
  E: movement *n*, shifting *n*, displacement *n*
dépolymérisation *f*
  D: Depolymerisation *f*
  E: depolymerisation *n*
déposer *v* **une demande de brevet**
  D: ein Patent anmelden
  E: to apply for a patent, to file a patent application
dépôt *m* [chim.]
  D: Niederschlag *m*, Ausscheidung *f*
  E: precipitate *n*
dépôt *m*
  D: Bodensatz *m*
  E: bottom settling, deposit *n*, sediment *n*
dépouiller *v* **la gaine du câble**
  D: abmanteln *v*
  E: to strip the cable sheath
dépouilleuse *f* **de gaine**
  D: Mantelabstreifmaschine *f*
  E: sheath stripping machine
dépression *f*
  D: Druckabfall *m*, Druckverlust *m*
  E: pressure drop, pressure loss, head loss
dépression, en ~
  D: ohne Druck
  E: depressurized *adj*
dérangement *m* **par les effets d'écho**
  D: Echostörungen *f pl*
  E: disturbances due to echo, echo troubles
dérangement *m* **sur réseau**
  D: Netzstörung *f*
  E: system fault
dérivation *f*
  D: Ableitung *f*
  E: leakage *n*, leakance *n*
dérivation *f*
  D: Abzweigung *f*
  E: branch *n*, tap *n*, junction *n*
dériver *v*
  D: abzweigen *v*
  E: branch *v*, tap *v*
déroulement *m* [fabr. fils mét., câb.]
  D: Ablauf *m*
  E: pay-off *n*
déroulement *m* [câb.]
  D: Abtrommeln *n*
  E: unreeling *n*, unwinding *n*
déroulement *m* **des opérations**
  D: Arbeitsablauf *m*, Betriebsablauf *m*
  E: flow of operation, operating sequence, flow process, operating cycle
dérouler *v*
  D: abwickeln *v*, abspulen *v*
  E: unwind *v*, pay off *v*, uncoil *v*
dérouleur *m* [fabr. fils mét., câb.]
  D: Ablaufbock *m*, Ablaufgestell *n*, Abwickelei *f*
  E: pay-off stand, supply stand, feed stand, take-off stand
dérouleur *m* **à portique**
  D: Portalwickler *m* (abwickelnd)
  E: portal type pay-off
dérouleur *m* **au-dessus de la hauteur de la tête**
  D: Überkopfablauf *m*
  E: overhead pay-off
désaccoupler *v*
  D: entkoppeln *v*
  E: balance out *v*, decouple *v*, uncouple *v*
désadaptation *f*
  D: Fehlanpassung *f*
  E: mismatching *n*
désaérateur *m*
  D: Entlüfter *m*
  E: exhaust fan
désaération *f*
  D: Entlüftung *f*
  E: exhaust *n*, deaeration *n*
désagréger *v* [chim.]
  D: aufschließen *v*
  E: decompose *v*
désalignement *m*
  D: Fehlausrichtung *f*
  E: misalignment *n*

désassembler

désassembler v
  D: abbauen v (Masch.), auseinandernehmen v, zerlegen v
  E: dismantle v, disassemble v

descente f d'antenne
  D: Antennenherabführung f, Antennenniederführung f
  E: antenna down-lead, aerial lead-in

descente f d'antenne
  D: Antennenspeiseleitung f, Antennenzuleitung f, Antennenkabel n
  E: antenna feeder, aerial feeder, antenna lead

déséquilibre m
  D: Unsymmetrie f
  E: unbalance n, unsymmetry n, asymmetry n

déséquilibre m de capacité
  D: kapazitive Kopplung, Kapazitätsunsymmetrie f
  E: capacitance unbalance, capacitance imbalance (US)

déséquilibre m par rapport à la terre
  D: Erdkopplung f
  E: unbalance to ground, earth coupling (GB)

déshomogénéisation f
  D: Entmischung f
  E: segregation n, decomposition n, separation n

déshumidifier v
  D: Feuchtigkeit entziehen
  E: dehumidify v, to extract humidity

déshydratant m
  D: Trocknungsmittel n
  E: desiccant n

déshydrater v
  D: Feuchtigkeit entziehen
  E: dehumidify v, to extract humidity

désignation f [câb.]
  D: Kennzeichnung f
  E: identification n, marking n, coding n

désisoler v
  D: abisolieren v
  E: to remove the insulation, to strip the insulation

dessaler v
  D: entsalzen v, demineralisieren v
  E: desalt v, desalinate v, demineralize v, deionize v

desséchant m
  D: Trocknungsmittel n
  E: desiccant n

dessèchement m du sol
  D: Austrocknung des Erdbodens, Bodenaustrocknung f
  E: drying (out) of the soil

dessécher v
  D: austrocknen v
  E: dry out v, desiccate vt, dehydrate vt

dessin m à l'échelle
  D: maßstäbliche Zeichnung
  E: scale drawing, dimensional drawing, drawing to scale

dessin m d'atelier
  D: Konstruktionszeichnung f
  E: construction drawing, design drawing

dessin m de fondation
  D: Fundamentzeichnung f
  E: foundation drawing

détaillé, examen ~
  D: eingehende Prüfung
  E: exhaustive test, close examination, thorough examination

détecter v un défaut
  D: eine Störung suchen
  E: to trace a fault

détecteur m de casses-fil
  D: Drahtrißwächter m
  E: wire break monitor

détecteur m de défauts
  D: Fehlerortungsgerät n, Fehlersuchgerät n
  E: fault detector, fault location unit

détecteur m de défauts à sec [câb.]
  D: Durchlaufprüfgerät n, Trockenprüfgerät n
  E: on-line spark tester, continuous discharge detection apparatus, sparker n, spark tester

détecteur m de flèche [vulc.]
  D: Durchhang-Abtastgerät n
  E: sag sensing unit, catenary sensing unit (on catenary vulcanization line)

détecteur de gaz, appareil ~ [c. com.]
  D: Gasspürgerät n
  E: cable sniffer

détecteur m de rupture du ruban
  D: Bandrißwächter m (Papier)
  E: tape break monitor

détecteur *m* de ruptures du fil métallique
 D: Drahtrißwächter *m*
 E: wire break monitor

détecteur *m* de tension
 D: Spannungsprüfgerät *n*
 E: voltage detector, spark tester

détection *f* automatique de fuites
 D: automatische Leckstellenanzeige
 E: automatic leakage detection

détérioration *f*
 D: Verschlechterung *f*
 E: deterioration *n*

détériorations *f pl* causées par des rongeurs
 D: Nagetier-Schäden *m pl*
 E: rodent attack

détériorations *f pl* causées par les termites
 D: Termitenschäden *m pl*
 E: termite attack

détermination *f*[ess.]
 D: Bestimmung *f*
 E: determination *n*, analysis *n*

détordre *v*(se)
 D: aufkorben *v* (Armierungsdrähte), aufdrehen *v* (sich)
 E: unwind *v*, open *v*, birdcage *v*, basket *v*, untwist *v*

détorsion *f* (formation de paniers/corbeilles des fils d'armure)
 D: Aufkorben *n* (Armierungsdrähte)
 E: birdcaging *n*, basketing *n*

détorsion, à ~ [câblage]
 D: mit Rückdrehung
 E: with backtwist

détorsion, sans ~ [câblage]
 D: ohne Rückdrehung
 E: without backtwist

dévider *v*
 D: abwickeln *v*, abspulen *v*
 E: unwind *v*, pay off *v*, uncoil *v*

dévidoir *m* [fabr. fils mét., câb.]
 D: Ablaufbock *m*, Ablaufgestell *n*, Abwickelei *f*
 E: pay-off stand, supply stand, feed stand, take-off stand

dévidoir *m* au-dessus de la hauteur de la tête
 D: Überkopfablauf *m*
 E: overhead pay-off

dévisser *v*
 D: abschrauben *v*
 E: unscrew *v*, screw off *v*

diagramme *m*
 D: Kurvenbild *n*, Diagramm *n*, graphische Darstellung
 E: diagram *n*, graph *n*, graphic representation, chart *n*

diagramme *m* de charge
 D: Belastungsdiagramm *n*
 E: loading diagram

diagramme *m* de déroulement
 D: Ablaufplan *m*, Ablaufdiagramm *n*, Arbeitsablaufdiagramm *n*, Flußdiagramm *n*, Fertigungsflußschema *n*
 E: flow chart, flow diagram, process (flow) chart

diamètre, gros, moyen, petit ~
 D: großer, mittlerer, kleiner Durchmesser
 E: large, medium, small diameter

diamètre *m* de la joue
 D: Flanschdurchmesser *m* (Kabeltrommel)
 E: flange diameter

diamètre *m* du fil métallique
 D: Drahtdurchmesser *m*
 E: wire diameter

diamètre *m* du tambour
 D: Kerndurchmesser *m* (Kabeltrommel)
 E: barrel diameter

diamètre *m* extérieur
 D: Außendurchmesser *m*
 E: overall diameter, outer diameter (OD)

diamètre *m* intérieur
 D: Innendurchmesser *m*, lichte Weite
 E: inner diameter (ID), inside diameter, internal diameter

diaphonie *f*
 D: Nebensprechen *n*
 E: crosstalk

diaphonie, exempt de ~
 D: nebensprechfrei *adj*
 E: crosstalk-proof *adj*

diaphonie *f* entre réel et fantôme
 D: Mitsprechen *n*
 E: side-to-phantom crosstalk

diaphonie *f* entre réel et réel
 D: Übersprechen *n*
 E: side-to-side crosstalk

diaphonie *f* inintelligible (non linéaire)
 D: unverständliches (nicht lineares)

diaphonie

Nebensprechen
E: unintelligible (non linear) crosstalk

diaphonie *f* intelligible (linéaire)
D: verständliches (lineares) Nebensprechen
E: intelligible (linear) cross-talk

diaphonomètre *m*
D: Nebensprechdämpfungsmesser *m*, Nebensprechmesser *m*
E: crosstalk meter

diélectrique *m*
D: Isolierung *f*, Dielektrikum *n*
E: insulation *n*, dielectric *n*

diélectrique, câble à ~ contrôlé
D: Kabel mit gesteuertem Dielektrikum (Ölkabel, Gasdruckkabel)
E: cable with controlled dielectric, controlled dielectric cable

diélectrique *m* papier/huile
D: Öl/Papier-Dielektrikum *n*
E: oil/paper dielectric

différence *f* de niveau
D: Höhenunterschied *m*
E: difference of level

différence *f* de potentiel
D: Spannungsunterschied *m*
E: potential difference

différence *f* de température
D: Grädigkeit *f* (Temp.Untersch.zw. Kühlmedien), Temperaturspiel *n*
E: temperature difference

diffusion *f*
D: Ausbreitung *f*
E: propagation *n*, spreading *n*

dilatation *f*
D: Ausdehnung *f*
E: expansion *n*, extension *n*, dilatation *n*

dilatation thermique, coefficient de ~
D: Wärmeausdehnungskoeffizient *m*
E: thermal expansion coefficient

dilater *v*(se)
D: ausdehnen *v*(sich)
E: expand *vi*, dilate *vi*

diluant *m*
D: Verdünnungsmittel *n*
E: diluent *n*, thinner *n*

dimension *f*
D: Abmessung *f*
E: dimension *n*

dimension, à ~s exactes
D: maßhaltig *adj*, maßgerecht *adj*
E: true to size, accurate to size

dimension *f* finale
D: Fertigmaß *n*
E: finishing dimension, finished size

dimensions *f pl* extérieures
D: Außenabmessungen *f pl*
E: overall dimensions

diminuer *v*
D: vermindern *v*, verringern *v*
E: reduce *v*, decrease *v*

dipforming *m* [fabr. fils mét.]
D: Tauchziehen *n*
E: dip forming (General Electric process for production of copper wire)

direction *f* de la torsion
D: Drallrichtung *f*, Schlagrichtung *f*
E: direction of lay, direction of twist

direction *f* du pas
D: Drallrichtung *f*, Schlagrichtung *f*
E: direction of lay, direction of twist

discontacteur *m*
D: Ausschalter *m*, Abschalter *m*
E: circuit breaker, cut-out switch, disconnecting switch

disjoncteur *m*
D: Ausschalter *m*, Abschalter *m*
E: circuit breaker, cut-out switch, disconnecting switch

disjoncteur *m*
D: Schalter *m*
E: switch *n*

disjoncteur *m* de protection
D: Schutzschalter *m*
E: line protection switch, overcurrent cut-out switch, protective switch

disjoncteur *m* de surtension
D: Überspannungsschalter *m*
E: overvoltage circuit-breaker, maximum voltage circuit-breaker

disjoncteurs, installation de ~ basse tension
D: Niederspannungsschaltanlage *f*
E: low voltage switchgear

disjoncteurs, installation de ~ haute tension
D: Hochspannungsschaltanlage *f*
E: high-voltage switchgear

disjoncteurs *m pl* blindés
D: gekapselte Schaltanlagen
E: metal-clad switch-gear, cubicle type switch-gear

disjoncteurs *m pl* **enfermés**
  D: gekapselte Schaltanlagen
  E: metal-clad switch-gear, cubicle type switch-gear

dispatching *m*
  D: Lastverteilung *f*
  E: load distribution, dispatching *n*

dispersion *n* [ess.]
  D: Streuung *f*
  E: scattering *n*, dispersion *f*

disposé *adj* **en berceau** [pose c.]
  D: in Wiegenanordnung
  E: in cradled arrangement

disposé *adj* **en long**
  D: längsaufgebracht *adj*
  E: longitudinally applied

disposer
  D: auslegen *v* (Werk, Anlage)
  E: lay out *v*, set out *v*

dispositif *m*
  D: Vorrichtung *f*
  E: device *n*, equipment *n*, facility *n*, appliance *n*

dispositif *m* **additionnel**
  D: Zusatzeinrichtung *f*
  E: additional equipment, auxiliary equipment, ancillary equipment

dispositif *m* **à empaqueter les fils métalliques**
  D: Bündelungsvorrichtung für Draht
  E: pack-former for wire

dispositif *m* **antiparasites**
  D: Störschutzeinrichtung *f*
  E: interference eliminator, interference suppression device

dispositif *m* **à onduler**
  D: Wellvorrichtung *f*
  E: corrugating device

dispositif *m* **auxiliaire**
  D: Hilfsvorrichtung *f*
  E: auxiliary device

dispositif *m* **d'alimentation en huile**
  D: Öleinspeisungsvorrichtung *f*
  E: oil feeding equipment

dispositif *m* **d'appointage**
  D: Konusschneider *m*, Radischneider *m*
  E: pencilling tool

dispositif *m* **d'arrêt**
  D: Anhaltevorrichtung *f*
  E: stopping device

dispositif *m* **d'audio-supression**
  D: Sprachsperre *f*
  E: audio-suppression device, guard circuit

dispositif *m* **de compensation de la tension**
  D: Zugspannungs-Regelvorrichtung *f*
  E: tension control device, tension compensating device, tension compensator

dispositif *m* **de contrôle du diamètre**
  D: Durchmesser-Überwachungsgerät *n*
  E: diameter control device

dispositif *m* **de coupe**
  D: Schneidvorrichtung *f*
  E: cutting device

dispositif *m* **de coupes minces** [câb.]
  D: Rundschälwerkzeug *n* (zum schichtweisen Abtragen von extrudierten Kabel-Isolierungen und schwachleitenden Schichten), Schälwerkzeug *n*
  E: jacket removal tool

dispositif *m* **de décortiquage** (des couches isolantes et semiconductrices d'un câble) [câb.]
  D: Rundschälwerkzeug *n* (zum schichtweisen Abtragen von extrudierten Kabel-Isolierungen und schwachleitenden Schichten), Schälwerkzeug *n*
  E: jacket removal tool

dispositif *m* **de déplacement du conteneur** [pr. à filer]
  D: Aufnehmer-Verschiebevorrichtung *f*
  E: container shifting device

dispositif *m* **de mesure de la tension de traction**
  D: Zugspannungsmeßvorrichtung *f*
  E: tension meter

dispositif *m* **de protection**
  D: Sicherheitsvorrichtung *f*, Schutzvorrichtung *f*
  E: safety device, protective device

dispositif *m* **de pulvérisation**
  D: Sprüheinrichtung *f*, Abspritzvorrichtung *f*
  E: spray equipment

dispositif *m* **de réglage de filière**
  D: Matrizenversteller *m*
  E: die adjuster

dispositif *m* **de régulation de la traction**
  D: Zugspannungs-Regelvorrichtung *f*

dispositif 478

    E: tension control device, tension compensating device, tension compensator

dispositif m de renvoi
    D: Umlenkvorrichtung f
    E: transfer device

dispositif m de sécurité
    D: Sicherheitsvorrichtung f, Schutzvorrichtung f
    E: safety device, protective device

dispositif m de serrage pour filière [fabr. fils mét.]
    D: Ziehsteinhalter m
    E: die holder

dispositif m d'essai
    D: Prüfeinrichtung f, Prüfgerät n, Prüfvorrichtung f
    E: testing equipment, test set, testing device

dispositif m d'essai de la continuité électrique [él.]
    D: Durchgangsprüfgerät n
    E: continuity tester

dispositif m de tirage
    D: Abzugsvorrichtung f
    E: pull-off device, haul-off device

dispositif m de tirage des câbles
    D: Kabel-Einziehvorrichtung f
    E: cable puller

dispositif de trancanage m
    D: Verlegearm m (Aufwickelei), Verlegevorrichtung f (Aufwickelei), Verteiler m (Aufwickelei)
    E: distributor n, traverser n, traversing unit

dispositif m d'impression
    D: Bedruckungsvorrichtung f
    E: printer n, printing device

disposition f
    D: Auslegung f (Planung), Anordnung f, Anlage f (Auslegung)
    E: layout n, arrangement n

disposition f côte à côte
    D: Verlegung nebeneinander, Parallelanordnung f
    E: laying side by side, laying in parallel, parallel arrangement

disposition f dans un atelier
    D: Anlage einer Werkstatt
    E: shop lay-out

disposition f de mesure
    D: Meßanordnung f, Meßschaltung f
    E: measuring arrangement, connections pl for measurement

disposition f des câbles
    D: Kabelanordnung f
    E: cable arrangement

disposition f d'essai
    D: Testanordnung f, Prüfanordnung f, Versuchsanordnung f
    E: experimental arrangement, test(ing) arrangement, test setup

disposition f en nappe horizontale
    D: Verlegung nebeneinander, Parallelanordnung f
    E: laying side by side, laying in parallel, parallel arrangement

disposition f en parallèle
    D: Verlegung nebeneinander, Parallelanordnung f
    E: laying side by side, laying in parallel, parallel arrangement

disposition f en tandem [méc.]
    D: Hintereinander-Schaltung f, Tandemanordnung f
    E: tandem arrangement, tandem connection

disposition f en trèfle [pose c.]
    D: Dreiecksanordnung f
    E: trefoil arrangement, triangular arrangement

disposition f en triangle [pose c.]
    D: Dreiecksanordnung f
    E: trefoil arrangement, triangular arrangement

disposition f longitudinale
    D: Längsaufbringung f (Bänder)
    E: longitudinal application

disposition f verticale
    D: senkrechte Anordnung
    E: vertical arrangement

disque m
    D: Scheibe f
    E: sheave n, disc n, pulley n

disque m d'écartement
    D: Abstandscheibe f
    E: disc spacer, disc insulator

disque m séparateur
    D: Abstandscheibe f
    E: disc spacer, disc insulator

dissipation f de la chaleur
    D: Wärmeableitung f
    E: heat dissipation, heat removal

dissipation f de puissance
    D: Verlustleistung f

E: power loss, power dissipation
dissiper *v* **la chaleur**
　D: die Wärme ableiten
　E: to conduct away the heat, to carry away the heat, to dissipate the heat
dissolution *f* (dans la bombe Wurzschmitt)
　D: Aufschluß *m* (in der Wurzschmitt-Bombe)
　E: decomposition *n* (in the Wurzschmitt-bomb)
dissoudre *v* [chim.]
　D: aufschließen *v*
　E: decompose *v*
dissymétrie *f*
　D: Unsymmetrie *f*
　E: unbalance *n*, unsymmetry *n*, asymmetry *n*
distance *f*
　D: Abstand *m*
　E: distance *n*, clearance *n*, interval *n*, space *n*
distance, à ~s égales
　D: in gleichen Abständen
　E: equispaced *adj*
distance *f* **d'axe en axe**
　D: Mittenabstand *m*, Achsabstand *m*
　E: centre-to-centre distance, centre spacing
distance *f* **de contournement** [él.]
　D: Schlagweite *f*
　E: flash-over distance
distance *f* **des centres**
　D: Mittenabstand *m*, Achsabstand *m*
　E: centre-to-centre distance, centre spacing
distance *f* **de torsion** [câblage]
　D: Tordierstrecke *f*
　E: twisting section
distance *f* **entre électrodes**
　D: Elektrodenabstand *m*
　E: electrode spacing, distance between electrodes, spark gap
distorsion *f*
　D: Verzerrung *f*
　E: distortion *n*
distorsion *f* **d'affaiblissement**
　D: Dämpfungsverzerrung *f*
　E: attenuation distortion, frequency distortion
distorsion *f* **de phase**
　D: Phasenverzerrung *f*
　E: phase distortion

distorsion *f* **linéaire**
　D: lineare Verzerrung
　E: linear distortion
distribuer *v*
　D: verteilen *v*
　E: distribute *v*, disperse *v*
distribution *f*
　D: Verteilung *f*
　E: dispersion *n*, distribution *n*
distribution *f* **d'énergie électrique**
　D: Energieversorgung *f*, Energieverteilung *f*, Stromversorgung *f*
　E: power supply, power distribution
distribution *f* **du champ électrique**
　D: Feldverteilung *f*
　E: stress grading, stress distribution
divisé *adj*
　D: zweigeteilt *adj*, zweiteilig *adj*, geteilt *adj*
　E: split *adj*, two-piece *adj*
documentation *f*
　D: Unterlagen *f pl* (beschreibende oder zeichnerische Angaben)
　E: information material, data *pl*, documents *pl*
documents *m pl*
　D: Unterlagen *f pl* (beschreibende oder zeichnerische Angaben)
　E: information material, data *pl*, documents *pl*
domaine *m*
　D: Bereich *m*
　E: range *n*, field *n*, scope *n*, area *n*
domaine *m* **d'application**
　D: Anwendungsgebiet *n*
　E: field of application
domaine *m* **d'ébullition**
　D: Siedebereich *m*
　E: boiling range
domaine *m* **d'emploi**
　D: Geltungsbereich *m*
　E: scope *n* (of application)
domaine *m* **d'utilisation**
　D: Anwendungsgebiet *n*
　E: field of application
données *f pl*
　D: Daten *pl*, Angaben *f pl*
　E: data *pl and sg*, details *pl*, particulars *pl*
données *f pl* **constructives**
　D: Aufbau-Daten *pl*, Konstruktionsdaten *pl*

données

E: design data

données *f pl* **de construction**
D: Aufbau-Daten *pl*, Konstruktionsdaten *pl*
E: design data

dosage *m*
D: Dosierung *f*
E: dosage *n*, proportioning *n*, metering *n*

doseur *m*
D: Zuteilvorrichtung *f*
E: metering device

double, en ~ couche
D: doppellagig *adj*
E: double-layer *adj*, twin-layer *adj*, duplex *adj*

double, piston à ~ effet
D: doppeltwirkender Plunger
E: double-acting plunger

doublé *adj* **de ...**
D: kaschiert mit ...
E: coated with ..., laminated with ..., backed with ...

double torsion *f*
D: Doppelschlag *m*
E: double twist

doublure *f*
D: Futter *n*, Auskleidung *f*
E: lining *n*

douille *f*
D: Buchse *f*
E: bushing *n*, bush *n*, sleeve *n*

douille *f* [access. c.]
D: Durchführung *f*
E: bushing *n*

douille *f*
D: Steckbuchse *f*, Steckerbuchse *f*, Fassung *f*
E: plug socket, connector socket, receptacle *n*, female contact, socket *n*

douille *f* **de traversée**
D: Durchführungsrohr *n*
E: wall tube, wall duct

douille *f* **isolante**
D: Isolierhülse *f*, Isolierbuchse *f*
E: insulating bush(ing), insulating sleeve

douvage *m*
D: Verschalung *f* (Kabeltrommeln)
E: lagging *n*

douve *f*
D: Daube *f* (Kabeltrommeln),
Verschalbrett *n*
E: plank *n*, batten *n*

drainage *m* **électrique**
D: elektrische Drainage
E: electrical drainage

droit *m* **de passage** [pose c.]
D: Wegerecht *n*
E: right of way

droits *m pl* **de protection**
D: Schutzrechte *n pl*
E: patent rights, trademark rights

ductilité *f*
D: Dehnbarkeit *f*
E: elasticity *n*, extensibility *n*, ductility *n*

durcir *v*
D: erstarren *v*, hartwerden *v*
E: solidify *v*, freeze *v*, set *v*, harden *v*

durcir *v* [plast.]
D: härten *v*
E: cure *v*

durcir *v* [col.]
D: abbinden *v*
E: harden *v*, set *v*

durcissable *adj*
D: härtbar *adj*
E: hardenable *adj*

durcissable, matière ~ à froid
D: kalthärtende Masse
E: cold-setting compound

durcissage *m* **à froid**
D: Kalthärten *n* (Gießharze)
E: cold-setting *n*

durcissement *m*
D: Härtung *f*
E: hardening *n*

durcissement *m* [plast.]
D: Aushärten *n*
E: curing *n*

durcissement, aptitude au ~
D: Härtbarkeit *f*
E: hardenability *n*

durcissement *m* **à cœur**
D: Durchhärtung *f*
E: through-hardening *n*

durcisseur *m*
D: Härter *m*
E: hardener *n*, curing agent

durée *f* **de court-circuit**
D: Kurzschlußzeit *f*, Kurzschlußdauer *f*
E: short-circuit time, short-circuit duration

durée f de fonctionnement d'une machine
  D: Laufzeit einer Maschine
  E: running time of a machine

durée f de mise en circuit
  D: Einschaltdauer f
  E: duty factor, switch-on time

durée f d'essai
  D: Versuchsdauer f, Prüfdauer f
  E: test duration, testing time, testing period

durée f de traitement [extr.]
  D: Verweilzeit f
  E: residence time

durée f de vie
  D: Lebensdauer f, Nutzungsdauer f
  E: life n, service life

durée de vie, essai accéléré de ~
  D: beschleunigte Lebensdauerprüfung
  E: accelerated life test

durée f de vie d'un câble
  D: Zeit-Spannungsfestigkeit eines Kabels, Dauer-Spannungsfestigkeit eines Kabels
  E: voltage life of a cable, long-time dielectric strength of a cable

durée f de vulcanisation
  D: Vulkanisationsdauer f
  E: time of cure, vulcanization time

durée f d'expérience
  D: Versuchsdauer f, Prüfdauer f
  E: test duration, testing time, testing period

durée f d'exploitation
  D: Lebensdauer f, Nutzungsdauer f
  E: life n, service life

durée f du séchage et de l'imprégnation
  D: Dauer der Trocknung und Tränkung
  E: duration of the drying and impregnating process

dureté f
  D: Härte f
  E: hardness n

dureté f à l'entaille
  D: Kerbzähigkeit f
  E: tear resistance (from a nick), notch toughness

duromètre m
  D: Härteprüfer m, Durometer n
  E: hardness tester, durometer n

E

eau f de refroidissement
  D: Kühlwasser n
  E: cooling water

eau f pressurisée
  D: Druckwasser n
  E: pressurized water

eau f réfrigérante
  D: Kühlwasser n
  E: cooling water

eau f sous pression
  D: Druckwasser n
  E: pressurized water

eau f souterraine [pose c.]
  D: Grundwasser n
  E: ground water, subsoil water

ébarbage m
  D: Entgraten n
  E: deburring n, trimming n

ébaucher v
  D: vorwalzen v
  E: rough v, bloom v

ébavurage m
  D: Entgraten n
  E: deburring n, trimming n

écaillement m
  D: Schuppenbildung f
  E: flaking n, scaling n

écailler v(s')
  D: abblättern v
  E: flake v(off), scale v(off), peel v(off)

écailles f pl
  D: Schuppen f pl
  E: flakes pl, scales pl

écart m
  D: Abstand m
  E: distance n, clearance n, interval n, space n

écart m de flèche
  D: Durchhanghöhe f
  E: sag clearance

écartement m [lam.]
  D: Spaltbreite f
  E: gap width

écartement m des électrodes
  D: Elektrodenabstand m
  E: electrode spacing, distance between electrodes, spark gap

écartement m entre cylindres [lam.]
  D: Walzenspalt m (Mischungsherstellung),

écartement

Walzenstellung *f* (Mischungsherstellung)
E: gap between rolls, nip between rolls

échange *m* de chaleur
D: Wärmeaustausch *m*
E: heat exchange

échange *m* thermique
D: Wärmeaustausch *m*
E: heat exchange

échangeur *m* de chaleur
D: Wärmeaustauscher *m*
E: heat exchanger

échangeur *m* d'ions
D: Ionenaustauscher *m*
E: ion exchanger

échangeur *m* thermique
D: Wärmeaustauscher *m*
E: heat exchanger

échantillon *m*
D: Probe *f*, Muster *n*, Prüfstück *n*
E: specimen *n*, sample *n*

échantillon *m* de câble étiré
D: gestrecktes Kabelmuster
E: straightened cable sample

échantillon *m* de comparaison
D: Vergleichsmuster *n*
E: reference sample, control sample

échantillon *m* de contrôle
D: Vergleichsmuster *n*
E: reference sample, control sample

échantillon *m* de la qualité moyenne
D: Durchschnittsprobe *f*
E: representative sample, average sample

échantillon *m* de qualité
D: Ausfallmuster *n*
E: reference sample, quality sample

échantillon *m* étagé [câb.]
D: Stufenmuster *n*
E: stepped sample, telescoped sample

échantillonnage *m*
D: Probenahme *f*
E: sampling *n*, taking of samples

échantillon *m* pris au hasard
D: Stichprobe *f*
E: random sample

échantillon *m* témoin
D: Vergleichsmuster *n*
E: reference sample, control sample

échantillon *m* type
D: Ausfallmuster *n*
E: reference sample, quality sample

échauffement *m*
D: Erwärmung *f*
E: heating *n*, temperature rise

échauffement *m* mutuel
D: gegenseitige Erwärmung
E: mutual heating

échelle, conforme à l'~
D: maßhaltig *adj*, maßgerecht *adj*
E: true to size, accurate to size

échelle, essai à l'~ naturelle
D: Versuch im praktischen Maßstab
E: full-scale trial

échelle, graduation d'~
D: Skalenteilung *f*
E: scale division

échelle de laboratoire, essai à l'~
D: Versuch im Labormaßstab
E: laboratory-scale trial

échelle industrielle, essai à l'~
D: Versuch im Betriebsmaßstab
E: commercial scale trial

échelle industrielle, réalisé à l'~
D: hergestellt im Fertigungsmaßstab
E: produced on an industrial scale, commercially produced

échelon, par ~s de ...
D: in Stufen von ...
E: in steps of ..., in increments of ...

échelonné *adj*
D: gestaffelt *adj*, abgestuft *adj*, versetzt *adj* (stufenweise),
E: staggered *adj*, graded *adj*

échelonné, isolant papier ~
D: geschichtete Papierisolierung
E: graded paper insulation

échelonnement *m* de l'isolant papier
D: Schichtung der Papier-Isolierung
E: gradation of the paper insulation

éclairage, câble pour l'~ d'aéroports
D: Flugplatzbeleuchtungskabel *n*
E: airport lighting cable

éclateur *m*
D: Funkenstrecke *f*
E: spark gap

éclateur *m* à sphères
D: Kugelfunkenstrecke *f*
E: sphere gap

éclateur *m* de protection
D: Schutzfunkenstrecke *f*
E: protective spark gap

écoulement *m* de matière [câb.]
D: Masseverarmung *f*, Masseabwanderung *f*,

Abwanderung von Masse
E: migration of compound, draining of compound
écoulement *m* d'un courant
D: Fließen eines Stroms
E: flow of a current
écoulement *m* par gravité
D: Fließen mit Gefälle
E: gravity flow
écoulement *m* plastique
D: plastisches Fließen
E: plastic flow
écouler *v*(s')
D: abfließen *v*
E: drain *v*
écouvillon *m*
D: Reinigungsmolch *m* (für Rohrleitungen), Molch *m* (Rohrreiniger)
E: go-devil *n*
écran *m* [él.]
D: Abschirmung *f*, Schirm *m*
E: shield *n*, shielding *n*, screen *n*, screening *n*
écran *m*
D: Bildschirm *m*
E: screen *n*, image screen, viewing screen
écran, conducteurs de câble avec ~ individuel
D: einzeln abgeschirmte Kabeladern
E: individually screened cable cores
écran *m* contre les effluves
D: Sprühschirm *m* (gegen el. Entladungen)
E: corona shield
écran *m* de mise à la terre
D: Erdungsschirm *m*
E: earth shield (GB), ground shield (US)
écran *m* d'essai concentrique
D: konzentrischer Prüfschirm
E: concentric test-shield
écran *m* de terre
D: Erdungsschirm *m*
E: earth shield (GB), ground shield (US)
écran *m* de vision
D: Bildschirm *m*
E: screen *n*, image screen, viewing screen
écran *m* électrostatique
D: statischer Schirm, elektrostatischer Schirm
E: electrostatic screen, electrostatic shield
écran *m* en cuivre
D: Kupferschirm *m*
E: copper screen
écran *m* en papier métallisé [câb.]
D: Schirm aus metallisiertem Papier
E: metallized paper screen
écran *m* en tresse de cuivre
D: Schirm aus Kupfer-Drahtgeflecht, Kupferschirmgeflecht *n*
E: copper-mesh shield, copper braid shielding, copper-mesh screen, braided copper screen
écran *m* guipé
D: Abschirmgeflecht *n*
E: screening braid, woven shield, shielding braid
écran *m* interne
D: Leiterdeckschicht *f* (schwachleitend), Leiterglättung *f*, Schirm (schwachleitend) über dem Leiter, innere Leitschicht
E: strand shield, inner semi-conducting layer
écran *m* magnétique
D: magnetischer Schirm
E: magnetic shield
écran *m* sur l'âme
D: Leiterdeckschicht *f* (schwachleitend), Leiterglättung *f*, Schirm (schwachleitend) über dem Leiter, innere Leitschicht
E: strand shield, inner semi-conducting layer
écran *m* sur l'isolant
D: Aderabschirmung *f*, Schirm über der Isolierung
E: insulation screen, core screen (GB), insulation shield (US)
écrasement, essai d'~
D: Druckversuch *m* (Rohre, Schaumkunststoffe)
E: crush(ing) test
écrasser *v*
D: Schlacke abziehen
E: to skim off the dross
écrouissage *m*
D: Kaltverfestigung *f*
E: strain hardening
écrouler *v*(s')
D: zusammenfallen *v*

écrouler
E: collapse v

effectuer v **un essai**
D: eine Prüfung durchführen
E: to perform a test, to carry out a test, to conduct a test

effet m **de couronne** [él.]
D: Korona f, Glimmen n
E: corona n

effet m **de peau** [él.]
D: Hauteffekt m, Skineffekt m, Stromverdrängung f
E: skin effect

effet m **de perturbation**
D: Störbeeinflussung f, Beeinflussung f
E: interference n (effect)

effet m **de proximité**
D: Näheeffekt m
E: proximity effect

effet m **inductif sur des câbles voisins**
D: induktive Beeinflussung benachbarter Kabel
E: inductive influence on neighbouring cables, inductive interference with neighbouring cables

effet m **interfacial**
D: Grenzschicht-Effekt m
E: interfacial effect

effets m pl **de foudre**
D: Blitzbeeinflussung f
E: effects pl of lightning

efficacité f [mach.]
D: Leistung f, Ausstoß m
E: performance n, output n, efficiency n, capacity n

efficacité f
D: Wirkungsgrad m
E: efficiency n

effilé adj
D: verjüngt adj, konisch adj
E: tapered adj, conic(al) adj

efflorescence f
D: Ausblühung f
E: bloom n, blooming n

effluve f **en couronne**
D: Glimmentladung f, Korona-Entladung f, Sprühentladung f
E: corona discharge, ionization discharge

effondrer v (s')
D: zusammenfallen v
E: collapse v

effort, câble pour grands ~s de traction
D: zugfestes Kabel
E: cable for high tensile stresses

effort m **de cisaillement**
D: Scherbeanspruchung f
E: shear stress

effort m **de compression**
D: Druckbeanspruchung f
E: compressive stress

effort m **de freinage**
D: Bremskraft f
E: braking effort

effort m **de traction**
D: Zugkraft f
E: pull n, tractive force

égalisation f
D: Ausgleich m
E: compensation n, balance n, balancing n, counterbalancing n, equalization n

égalisation f **de la température**
D: Temperaturausgleich m
E: equalization of temperature, compensation of temperature

égalisation f **des capacités mutuelles** [c. tél.]
D: Längsausgleich m
E: balancing of the mutual capacities

égoutté, isolant ~ après imprégnation
D: masseameme Isolierung
E: mass-impregnated and drained insulation

éjecteur m
D: Ausstoßvorrichtung f, Auswerfer m
E: ejector n

élaboration f **d'un projet**
D: Projektierung f
E: planning n

élaboré, méthode ~e
D: aufwendiges Verfahren
E: elaborate process

élargir v
D: aufweiten v
E: expand v, bulge v, bell out v, flare v

élargir v
D: vergrößern v
E: increase v, extend v, enlarge v, magnify v

élargissement m
D: Vergrößerung f
E: enlargement n, magnification n increase n

élasticité f
 D: Dehnbarkeit f
 E: elasticity n, extensibility n, ductility n

élastomère m
 D: Elastomer n
 E: elastomer n

électrode f **de mesure**
 D: Meßelektrode f
 E: measuring electrode

électrotechnique f
 D: Elektrotechnik f
 E: electrical engineering

électrovanne f
 D: Magnetventil n
 E: solenoid valve

élément m [câb.]
 D: Einzelader f, Einzelleiter m
 E: single conductor

élément m **câblé**
 D: Verseilelement n
 E: stranding element, stranded element

élément m **compensateur de traction** [câb.]
 D: Zugentlastung f
 E: strain-bearing element, strain relief, strain-bearing member

élément m **constitutif** [câb.]
 D: Bauelement n
 E: constructional element, component n

élément m **d'assemblage**
 D: Verseilelement n
 E: stranding element, stranded element

élément m **de câblage**
 D: Verseilelement n
 E: stranding element, stranded element

élément m **de comptage**
 D: Zählelement n
 E: marking element

élément m **de construction** [câb.]
 D: Bauelement n
 E: constructional element, component n

élément m **de direction**
 D: Richtungselement n
 E: direction element

élément m **de marquage** [c. com.]
 D: Markierungselement n
 E: marker n

élément m **de séparation** [c. com.]
 D: Trennelement n
 E: separating element

élément m **de signal** [com.]
 D: Informationsschritt m
 E: signal element

élément m **de support** [c. com.]
 D: Tragorgan n
 E: strength member

élément m **galvanique localisé**
 D: Lokalelement n
 E: local cell

élément m **porteur** [c. én.]
 D: Tragorgan n
 E: suspension strand, suspension unit

élévateur m (plateforme de travail)
 D: höhenverstellbare Arbeitsbühne
 E: elevator n (working platform)

élévation f
 D: Erhöhung f, Steigerung f
 E: increase n, raise n, rise n

élévation f **de température**
 D: Temperaturerhöhung f, Anstieg der Temperatur, Erwärmung f
 E: temperature rise, temperature increase

élévation f **de tension par paliers**
 D: stufenweise Spannungssteigerung
 E: voltage increase in steps

éliminer v **un défaut**
 D: eine Störung beseitigen
 E: to clear a fault

embouchure f **de trémie** [extr.]
 D: Trichtermündung f
 E: hopper throat, feed throat

embrochable, extrémité ~
 D: Aufsteck-Endverschluß m
 E: plug-in termination, plug-on termination

embrochable, extrémité facilement ~
 D: leicht aufsteckbarer Endverschluß
 E: easy-on termination

émeriller v
 D: schmirgeln v
 E: sand v, emery v

emmanchable, extrémité ~
 D: Aufschieb-Endverschluß m
 E: slip-on termination

emmanchable à chaud, extrémité ~
 D: wärmeschrumpfender Endverschluß, aufschrumpfbarer Endverschluß
 E: shrink-on termination, heat-

emmanchable
shrinkable termination
emmanché, extrémité ~e à chaud
D: aufgeschrumpfter Endverschluß
E: shrunk-on termination
emmanchement, technique d'~ à chaud
D: Wärmeschrumpftechnik f, Aufschrumpftechnik f
E: shrink-on technique, heat-shrinkage technique
emmancher v à chaud
D: aufschrumpfen v
E: heat-shrink v, shrink on v
émollient m
D: Erweicher m
E: softener n
empaqueter, dispositif à ~ les fils métalliques
D: Bündelungsvorrichtung für Draht
E: pack-former for wire
empileuse f à mandrins
D: Dornstapler m
E: ram truck
encastré adj [pose c.]
D: unter Putz
E: under plaster, concealed adj
encastrer v
D: einbetten v
E: embed v
enceinte f climatisée
D: klimatisierter Raum, konditionierter Raum
E: air-conditioned room
enclencher v (él.)
D: einschalten v, anschalten v
E: switch on v, turn on (US) v
encoche f
D: Nut f, Aussparung f
E: groove n, slot n, recess n, notch n, nick n
encombrement m
D: Platzbedarf m, Raumbedarf m, Flächenbelegung f
E: space requirement, occupancy n
endommagement m de la gaine de câble
D: Beschädigung des Kabelmantels
E: damage to the cable sheath
enduction f
D: Überziehen n (Masse, Kleber, Korrosionsschutz), Aufbringen n (Masse, Kleber, Korrosionsschutz)
E: flooding n, coating n
enduction f en craie
D: Kreideüberzug m
E: coating of whiting
enduire v
D: beschichten v
E: coat v
enduit m
D: Anstrich m
E: paint n, finish n
enduit, sous ~ [pose c.]
D: unter Putz
E: under plaster, concealed adj
enduit m anti-corrosif
D: Rostschutzanstrich m
E: anti-corrosion coating
enduit m protecteur
D: Schutzanstrich m
E: protective varnish coating
endurance f à la flexion
D: Dauerbiegefestigkeit f
E: resistance to bending fatigue, bending endurance, bending fatigue strength, flexural fatigue strength
énergie f
D: Energie f
E: power n, energy n
enfermé, air ~
D: eingeschlossene Luft
E: entrapped air
enfilage m
D: Einfädeln n (Drahtziehmaschine)
E: stringing-up n, threading-up n
enfiler v
D: aufschieben v
E: slip on v
enfler v (s')
D: quellen v
E: swell v
enfoncement, essai d'~
D: Durchdrückprüfung f
E: cut-through test
enfoncement, résistance à l'~
D: Durchdrückfestigkeit f
E: cut-through resistance
enfoncement, température d'~
D: Durchdrücktemperatur f
E: cut-through temperature
engrenage m
D: Zahnradgetriebe n, Getriebe n
E: gear(ing) n
engrenage m de changement de vitesse
D: Wechselgetriebe n

engrenage m réducteur
 D: Reduktionsgetriebe n, Untersetzungsgetriebe n
 E: reduction gear
engrenage m réglable sans à-coups
 D: stufenlos regelbares Getriebe
 E: infinitely variable gear
enlever v
 D: ausbauen v, abmontieren v
 E: remove v, dismount v
enlever v[câb.]
 D: absetzen v (Isolierung, Mantel)
 E: cut back v, remove v
enlever v la gaine du câble
 D: abmanteln v
 E: to strip the cable sheath
enlever v l'humidité
 D: Feuchtigkeit entziehen
 E: dehumidify v, to extract humidity
enquête f publique
 D: Einspruchsverfahren n
 E: public inquiry
enregistreur m
 D: Registriergerät n, Meßwertschreiber m
 E: recording instrument, recorder n
enregistreur m à diagramme circulaire
 D: Kreisdiagrammschreiber m
 E: circular chart recorder
enregistreur m à papier déroulant
 D: Bandschreiber m
 E: chart recorder, strip chart recorder
enregistreur m de température
 D: Temperaturschreiber m
 E: temperature recorder
enrobage m
 D: Überzug m, Beschichtung f
 E: coating n
enrober v
 D: einbetten v
 E: embed v
enroulement m
 D: Wicklung f
 E: winding n, wrapping n, coil n
enroulement m de fil
 D: Drahtbewicklung f
 E: wire wrapping
enroulement m du fil (tonneau d'enroulement)
 D: Aufwickeln von Draht (Faßwickler)
 E: wire packaging (barrel take-up)

enroulement m hélicoïdal
 D: wendelförmige Aufbringung
 E: helical application
enroulement m papier à large bande
 D: Breitbahnwicklung f (Papier)
 E: broad-web paper wrapping
enroulement m primaire
 D: Primärwicklung f
 E: primary winding
enrouler v
 D: aufwickeln v, aufspulen v, spulen v, wickeln v, auftrommeln v
 E: wind v, wind up v, take up v, spool v, reel v, coil v
enrouler v[câb.]
 D: bewickeln v, umwickeln v, umspinnen v
 E: wrap v, wind v, cover v
enrouler v en hélice
 D: wendelförmig aufbringen
 E: to apply helically, to apply spirally
enrouler v le câble dans la cale d'un navire
 D: Kabel in den Schiffsladeraum einschießen
 E: to coil the cable into the ship's hold
enrouleur m
 D: Aufwickelei f, Wickler m
 E: take-up unit, take-up n, take-up stand
enrouleur m à double bobine
 D: Doppelspulapparat m, Doppelspuler m
 E: double-reel spooler, dual-reel take-up
enrouleur m à feuillard d'acier
 D: Bandeisen-Spinner m, Eisenband-Wickler m
 E: steel tape spinner, steel taping head
enrouleur m à pointes
 D: Pinolen-Wickler m
 E: pintle-type spooler
enrouleur m à portique
 D: Portalwickler m (aufwickelnd)
 E: portal type take-up
enrouleur m automatique à double bobine
 D: automatische Doppelaufwickelei
 E: automatic double spooler
enrouleur m de fil métallique
 D: Drahtwickler m (stationär)
 E: dead block
enrouleur m de fil métallique à grande

enrouleur 488

vitesse
D: Schnellaufwickelei für Draht
E: high-speed continuous wire take-up

enrouleur *m* **du frettage** [câb.]
D: Druckschutzspinner *m*
E: reinforcement tape spinner

enrouleur *m* **en forme de tonneau**
D: Faßwickler *m*
E: pail-pack *n*, drum-pack *n*, pay-off-pak *n*, draw-pak *n*, D-pak *n*

enrouleuse *f*
D: Wickler *m*, Umwickelei *f*
E: coiler *n*, spooler *n*, take-up *n*, rewinding stand

enrouloir *m* **au-dessus de la hauteur de la tête** [coul. cont. lam.]
D: Überkopf-Aufwickelei *f*
E: orbital laying head coiler

enrubannage *m*
D: Umwicklung *f* (mit Band)
E: wrapping *n*, winding *n*

enrubanner *v*
D: umwickeln *v* (mit Band), bewickeln *v* (mit Band), umspinnen *v* (mit Band), wickeln *v* (Band)
E: lap *v*, tape *v*, wrap *v*

ensemble *m* **de montage**
D: Montagesatz *m*
E: installation kit

entaille *f*
D: Nut *f*, Aussparung *f*
E: groove *n*, slot *n*, recess *n*, notch *n*, nick *n*

entaillé *adj*
D: eingekerbt *adj*
E: notched *adj*

enterré *adj* [pose c.]
D: erdverlegt *adj*
E: laid in earth, buried *adj*, laid underground

entonnoir *m*
D: Trichter *m*
E: hopper *n*, funnel *n*

entonnoir *m* **de chargement** [extr.]
D: Fülltrichter *m*, Einfülltrichter *m*
E: feeding hopper

entraînement, unité d'~ hydraulique
D: hydraulisches Antriebsaggregat
E: hydraulic power pack

entraîné *adj* **par**
D: angetrieben von
E: powered by, driven by

entraîné *adj* **par moteur**
D: motorangetrieben *adj*, motorisch *adj*
E: motor-driven *adj*, motorized *adj*

entrée *f* [pose c.]
D: Einstiegöffnung *f*, Mannloch *n*
E: entrance *n*, manhole *n*

entrée *f*
D: Einlauf *m* (in eine Maschine), Eintritt *m*, Einführung *f* (Kabel)
E: inlet *n*, entrance *n*

entrée, cornet d'~ [access. c.]
D: Einführungstrichter *m*
E: terminal bell, entrance bell

entrée *f* **de câble**
D: Kabeleinführung *f*, Leitungseinführung *f*
E: cable entrance, cable inlet

entrée *f* **de conduit** [pose c.]
D: Kanalzugöffnung *f*
E: duct entrance

entrée *f* **de filière** [fabr. fils mét.]
D: Ziehsteineinlauf *m*
E: die approach

entrée *f* **de transformateur**
D: Transformator-Einführung *f*
E: transformer termination, transformer connection, transformer entry

entreposage *m*
D: Einlagerung *f*, Zwischenlagerung *f*
E: incorporation *n*, insertion *n*, intercalation *n*

entreposé *adj*
D: eingelagert *adj*, zwischengelagert *adj*
E: intercalated *adj*, sandwiched *adj* between,

entreprise *f* **d'électricité**
D: Elektrizitäts-Versorgungsunternehmen (EVU) *n*
E: electricity supply undertaking, electricity undertaking, utility (US) *n*

entrer *v* **dans la machine**
D: in die Maschine einlaufen
E: to enter the machine, to run into the machine

entretien *m*
D: Instandhaltung *f*
E: maintenance *n*, service *n*, servicing *n*

entretien, installation indépendante ne nécessitant pas d'~
  D: wartungsfreie Anlage
  E: self-contained system

enveloppante f
  D: Umhüllungslinie f (z.B. bei Leitern)
  E: contour line

enveloppe f
  D: Hülle f, Umhüllung f
  E: sheath n, covering n, jacket n

enveloppe f isolante
  D: Isolierung f, Dielektrikum n
  E: insulation n, dielectric n

enveloppe f protectrice
  D: Schutzüberzug m, Schutzhülle f
  E: protective coating, protective cover(ing)

épaisseur f
  D: Dicke f
  E: thickness n

épaisseur f de couche
  D: Schichtdicke f
  E: layer thickness

épaisseur f de la gaine [câb.]
  D: Manteldicke f
  E: sheath thickness

épaisseur f de la paroi
  D: Wanddicke f
  E: wall thickness

épaisseur f d'isolant
  D: Isolierdicke f
  E: insulation thickness

épanouissement m des conducteurs de câble
  D: Spreizen der Kabeladern, Auseinanderspreizen der Kabeladern, Ausbiegen von Kabeladern
  E: fanning out of the cable cores, bending out of the cable cores

épisser v
  D: spleißen v
  E: splice v

épissure f
  D: Spleißstelle f, Spleiß m, Spleißverbindung f
  E: splice n, spliced joint

époxy, résine ~ ou époxyde ou époxydique
  D: Epoxidharz n
  E: epoxy resin, epoxide resin

EPR (v. caoutchouc d'éthylène propylène)

épreuve f
  D: Versuch m, Prüfung f (Erprobung), Test m
  E: test n, trial n, experiment n

épreuve, qui a fait ses ~s en service
  D: im Betrieb bewährt
  E: field-proved adj

éprouvé adj
  D: bewährt adj
  E: proved adj, proven adj, time-tested adj

éprouvette f
  D: Probe f, Muster n, Prüfstück n
  E: specimen n, sample n

éprouvette f
  D: Prüfstück n, Prüfkörper m
  E: test sample, test piece, test specimen

éprouvette f de forme tubulaire
  D: schlauchförmiges Prüfstück
  E: tubular test piece

éprouvette f en forme d'haltère
  D: Prüfhantel f, hantelförmiges Prüfstück
  E: dumb-bell shaped test piece

éprouvette f prise au hasard
  D: Stichprobe f
  E: random sample

équations f pl de transmission [com.]
  D: Übertragungs-Gleichungen f pl
  E: transmission equations

équilibrage m
  D: Ausgleich m
  E: compensation n, balance n, balancing n, counterbalancing n, equalization n

équilibrage m d'affaiblissement
  D: Dämpfungsausgleich m, Dämpfungsentzerrung f
  E: attenuation equalization, attenuation compensation

équilibrage m de diaphonies
  D: Nebensprechausgleich m
  E: crosstalk balancing

équilibrage m de la tension
  D: Spannungsausgleich m
  E: compensation of voltage

équilibre m
  D: Ausgleich m
  E: compensation n, balance n, balancing n, counterbalancing n, equalization n

équilibre m de capacité

équilibre
  D: Kapazitätssymmetrie f
  E: capacitance balance
équilibre m des phases
  D: Phasengleichheit f
  E: phase balance, phase coincidence
équilibrer v [mach.]
  D: abgleichen v
  E: align v
équilibreur m
  D: Leitungsnachbildung f
  E: artificial balancing line, artificial line, balancing network
équipe, en une seule ~
  D: im Einschichtbetrieb
  E: on a single shift basis
équipe, travail en plusieurs ~s
  D: Mehrschichtbetrieb m
  E: multiple shift operation
équipement m
  D: Ausrüstung f
  E: equipment n, facilities pl
équipement m de commutation [com.]
  D: Vermittlungseinrichtung f
  E: switching equipment
équipement m d'essai
  D: Prüfeinrichtung f, Prüfgerät n, Prüfvorrichtung f
  E: testing equipment, test set, testing device
équipement m mobile
  D: fahrbares Gerät
  E: mobile unit, mobile equipment
équipement m supplémentaire
  D: Zusatzeinrichtung f
  E: additional equipment, auxiliary equipment, ancillary equipment
équivalent m d'affaiblissement
  D: Dämpfungsmaß n
  E: attenuation unit, attenuation equivalent, total transmission equivalent, total attenuation
équivalent m d'affaiblissement d'équilibrage [c. com.]
  D: Fehlerdämpfungsmaß n
  E: return loss unit
équivalent m d'affaiblissement diaphonique
  D: Nebensprechdämpfungsmaß n
  E: crosstalk attenuation unit
équivalent m de référence
  D: Bezugsdämpfung f
  E: reference equivalent
équivalent m de transmission
  D: Übertragungsmaß n
  E: propagation unit
équivalent m de transmission effective [c. tél.]
  D: Nutzdämpfung f
  E: effective transmission, effective transmission equivalent, overall transmission loss
équivalent m net de transmission
  D: Restdämpfung f
  E: net attenuation, net loss, overall attenuation, overall transmission loss
ériger v
  D: errichten v
  E: set up v, install v, mount v, erect v, assemble v
erreur f
  D: Fehler m
  E: defect n, error n, failure n, fault n
erreur f cumulée
  D: akkumulierter Fehler
  E: accumulated error
erreur f de conduite, de l'opérateur, de manipulation, de manœuvre
  D: Bedienungsfehler m, Fehlbedienung f
  E: faulty operation, operating error, operator's error
erreur f de mesure
  D: Fehlmessung f, Meßfehler m
  E: faulty measurement, measuring error
escargot m
  D: Schnecke f (bei einer Kabeltrommel)
  E: ramp n
espace m
  D: Zwischenraum m
  E: clearance n, gap n, interstice n, interspace n, interval n, spacing n
espace m annulaire
  D: Ringspalt m
  E: annular gap, annular passage
essai m
  D: Versuch m, Prüfung f (Erprobung), Test m
  E: test n, trial n, experiment n
essai, effectuer un ~
  D: eine Prüfung durchführen
  E: to perform a test, to carry out a test, to conduct a test
essai, faire un ~

D: eine Prüfung durchführen
E: to perform a test, to carry out a test, to conduct a test

essai *m* **à blanc**
D: Blindversuch *m*
E: blank trial, blank experiment, blank test

essai *m* **accéléré de durée de vie**
D: beschleunigte Lebensdauerprüfung *f*
E: accelerated life test

essai *m* **à grande échelle**
D: Großversuch *m*
E: large-scale trial

essai *m* **à l'échelle de laboratoire**
D: Versuch im Labormaßstab
E: laboratory-scale trial

essai *m* **à l'échelle industrielle**
D: Versuch im Betriebsmaßstab
E: commercial scale trial

essai *m* **à l'échelle naturelle**
D: Versuch im praktischen Maßstab
E: full-scale trial

essai *m* **à pleine charge**
D: Vollastprüfung *f*
E: full-load test

essai *m* **atmosphérique**
D: Bewitterungsversuch *m*
E: weathering test

essai *m* **au choc** [él.]
D: Stoßspannungs-Prüfung *f*, Stoßprüfung *f* (el.)
E: impulse voltage test, impulse test, surge test

essai *m* **au choc** [méc.]
D: Schlagprobe *f*
E: impact test

essai *m* **au rouge de Congo**
D: Kongo-Rot-Prüfung *f*
E: Congo Red test

essai *m* **aux cycles de charge**
D: Prüfung mit Belastungszyklen
E: loading cycle test, cyclic loading test

essai *m* **aux ondes de choc** [él.]
D: Stoßspannungs-Prüfung *f*, Stoßprüfung *f* (el.)
E: impulse voltage test, impulse test, surge test

essai *m* **comparatif**
D: Vergleichsprüfung *f*
E: comparative test

essai *m* **continu**
D: Langzeitprüfung *f*, Langzeitversuch *m*, Dauerversuch *m*
E: long-time test, continuous test

essai *m* **d'abrasion répétée**
D: Dauerabriebprüfung *f*
E: repeated abrasion test

essai *m* **d'allongement à froid**
D: Kältedehnungsprüfung *f*
E: elongation test at low temperature

essai *m* **d'allongement permanent**
D: Prüfung auf bleibende Dehnung
E: hot-set-test *n*

essai *m* **de câbles sur chantier**
D: Prüfung an verlegten Kabeln
E: site test on cables

essai *m* **de capacité de charge en courant permanent**
D: Dauerstrombelastungsprüfung *f*
E: continuous current carrying test

essai *m* **de choc à basse température**
D: Kälteschlagprüfung *f*
E: impact resistance test at low temperature

essai *m* **de choc sur éprouvette entaillée**
D: Kerbschlagprobe *f*
E: notched bar impact test

essai *m* **de choc thermique**
D: Wärmeschockprüfung *f*
E: heat shock test

essai *m* **d'éclatement**
D: Berstdruckprüfung *f*
E: bursting test

essai *m* **de compatibilité**
D: Verträglichkeitsprüfung *f*
E: compatibility test

essai *m* **de compression**
D: Druckversuch *m*
E: pressure test, compression test

essai *m* **de compression à chaud**
D: Wärmedruckprüfung *f*
E: hot pressure test

essai *m* **de continuité** [él.]
D: Durchgangsprüfung *f*, Prüfung auf Durchgang
E: continuity check, continuity test

essai *m* **d'écoulement** [câb.]
D: Abtropfprüfung *f*, Tropf- und Ablaufprüfung *f*
E: drainage test

essai *m* **de courte durée**
D: Kurzzeitprüfung *f*, Kurzzeitversuch *m*

E: short-time test

essai *m* d'écrasement
D: Druckversuch *m* (Rohre, Schaumkunststoffe)
E: crush(ing) test

essai *m* d'écrasement à chaud
D: Wärmedruckprüfung *f*
E: hot pressure test

essai *m* de décharges partielles
D: Teilentladungsprüfung *f*
E: partial discharge level test, corona level test

essai *m* de (durée) de vie
D: Lebensdauerprüfung *f*
E: life test

essai *m* de (longue) durée
D: Langzeitprüfung *f*, Langzeitversuch *m*, Dauerversuch *m*
E: long-time test, continuous test

essai *m* de durée de vie [él.]
D: Dauerspannungsprüfung *f*
E: voltage life test

essai *m* de fabrication
D: Versuchsfertigung *f*, Probefertigung *f*
E: trial production, production trial, manufacturing trial

essai *m* de fatigue [méc.]
D: Dauerversuch *m*, Ermüdungsversuch *m*
E: endurance test, fatigue test

essai *m* de fonctionnement
D: Funktionsprüfung *f*
E: functional test

essai *m* d'égouttement
D: Tropfprüfung *f* (an Tränkmassen)
E: dripping test

essai *m* de laboratoire
D: Laboruntersuchung *f*
E: laboratory test, laboratory investigation

essai *m* d'endurance [méc.]
D: Dauerversuch *m*, Ermüdungsversuch *m*
E: endurance test, fatigue test

essai *m* d'enfoncement
D: Durchdrückprüfung *f*
E: cut-through test

essai *m* de non-contamination
D: Verträglichkeitsprüfung *f*
E: compatibility test

essai *m* de non-propagation de la flamme
D: Flammwidrigkeitsprüfung *f*
E: flame resisting test, flame resistance test

essai *m* d'enroulement
D: Dornwickelprüfung *f*
E: mandrel test, wrapping test

essai *m* d'enroulement à basse température
D: Kältebiegeprüfung *f*, Kaltbiegeprüfung *f*, Kältewickelprüfung *f*
E: cold bending test, bending test at low temperature

essai *m* de pénétration
D: Eindringprüfung *f*
E: penetration test

essai *m* de pliage
D: Biegeprüfung *f*
E: bending test, flexural test

essai *m* de pliage à basse température
D: Kältebiegeprüfung *f*, Kaltbiegeprüfung *f*, Kältewickelprüfung *f*
E: cold bending test, bending test at low temperature

essai *m* de pliage à chaud
D: Warmbiegeprüfung *f*
E: hot bending test

essai *m* de pliage à froid
D: Kältebiegeprüfung *f*, Kaltbiegeprüfung *f*, Kältewickelprüfung *f*
E: cold bending test, bending test at low temperature

essai *m* de pliages alternés
D: Wechselbiegeprüfung *f*
E: reversed bending test

essai *m* de prélèvement
D: Auswahlprüfung *f*
E: sample test, screening *n*

essai *m* de pression
D: Druckversuch *m*
E: pressure test, compression test

essai *m* de pression à température élevée
D: Wärmedruckprüfung *f*
E: hot pressure test

essai *m* de réception
D: Abnahmeprüfung *f*
E: acceptance test, approval inspection

essai *m* de résistance à la propagation

de la flamme
  D: Flammwidrigkeitsprüfung f
  E: flame resisting test, flame resistance test
essai m **de résistance aux intempéries**
  D: Bewitterungsversuch m
  E: weathering test
essai m **de résistance aux secousses**
  D: Fallprüfung f
  E: drop test
essai m **de routine**
  D: Stückprüfung f
  E: routine test, sample test
essai m **de «scanning»**
  D: Durchlauf-Prüfung f, „Scanning"-Prüfung f, Ionisationsprüfung f
  E: scanning test
essai m **des matériaux**
  D: Materialprüfung f
  E: material testing
essai m **destructif**
  D: nicht zerstörungsfreie Prüfung
  E: destructive test
essai m **détaillé**
  D: eingehende Prüfung
  E: exhaustive test, close examination, thorough examination
essai m **de tension**
  D: Spannungsprüfung f
  E: dielectric test, voltage test, spark test
essai m **de tension alternative**
  D: Wechselspannungsprüfung f
  E: a.c. voltage test
essai m **de torsion**
  D: Torsionsprüfung f
  E: twisting test, torsion test
essai m **de traction**
  D: Prüfung der Zerreißfestigkeit, Zerreißprüfung f, Zugfestigkeitsprüfung f
  E: tensile test, tensile strength test
essai m **de traction/compression**
  D: Zugdruckversuch m
  E: tension and compression test
essai m **de type**
  D: Typprüfung f
  E: type test
essai m **de vieillissement**
  D: Alterungsprüfung f
  E: ag(e)ing test
essai m **de vieillissement de longue durée**
  D: Daueralterungsprüfung f
  E: long-time ag(e)ing test
essai m **d'homologation**
  D: Zulassungsprüfung f
  E: approval test
essai m **diélectrique**
  D: Spannungsprüfung f
  E: dielectric test, voltage test, spark test
essai m **d'ionisation par défilement**
  D: Durchlauf-Prüfung f, „Scanning"-Prüfung f, Ionisationsprüfung f
  E: scanning test
essai m **d'isolement**
  D: Isolationsprüfung f
  E: insulation test
essai m **en cours de fabrication**
  D: Prüfung während der Fertigung
  E: production test, in-process testing
essai m **en service**
  D: Betriebsversuch m
  E: field test, field trial, factory trial
essai m **en usine**
  D: Betriebsversuch m
  E: field test, field trial, factory trial
essai m **interlaboratoire**
  D: Rundversuch m
  E: round-robin test
essai m **intermédiaire**
  D: Zwischenprüfung f
  E: intermediate test
essai m **non-destructif**
  D: zerstörungsfreie Prüfung
  E: non-destructive test
essais m pl **empiriques**
  D: empirische Versuche
  E: trial-and-error experiments
essai m **sur chantier**
  D: Freigelände-Prüfung f
  E: field test
essai m **sur prélèvement**
  D: Stichprobenprüfung f
  E: sampling test, random test, spot check
essayer v
  D: prüfen v
  E: check v, test v, verify v, control v
estampage m
  D: Prägung f
  E: embossing n
estamper v
  D: prägen v
  E: emboss v

étagé *adj*
D: gestaffelt *adj*, abgestuft *adj*, versetzt *adj* (stufenweise),
E: staggered *adj*, graded *adj*

étagement *m* **de l'isolant papier**
D: Schichtung der Papier-Isolierung
E: gradation of the paper insulation

étain *m*
D: Zinn *n*
E: tin *n*

étain *m* **à souder**
D: Reibelot *n*, Lötzinn *n*
E: tinning solder, soldering tin

étain *m* **de soudage**
D: Reibelot *n*, Lötzinn *n*
E: tinning solder, soldering tin

étalon *m*
D: Eichmaß *n*
E: gauge *n*, standard *n*

étalonnage *m*
D: Eichung *f*
E: calibration *n*, adjusting *n*, gauging *n*

étamage *m*
D: Verzinnung *f*
E: tinning *n*, tin-coating *n*

étamage *m* **électrolytique**
D: galvanische Verzinnung
E: electro-tinning *n*

étamage *m* **galvanique**
D: galvanische Verzinnung
E: electro-tinning *n*

étamé, fil ~
D: verzinnter Draht
E: tinned wire

étanche, câble ~ à l'eau
D: längswasserdichtes Kabel
E: water-proof cable, water-tight cable

étanche, manchon de jonction ~ au gaz comprimé
D: druckgasdichte Muffe
E: gas pressure-tight joint

étanche, rendre ~
D: abdichten *v*
E: seal *v*

étanche *adj* **à l'air**
D: luftdicht *adj*
E: air-tight *adj*, hermetically sealed

étanche *adj* **à la pression**
D: druckdicht *adj*
E: pressure-tight *adj*

étanche *adj* **à l'eau en sens longitudinal**
D: längswasserdicht *adj*
E: longitudinally water-proof

étanche *adj* **au gaz**
D: gasundurchlässig *adj*
E: gas-tight *adj*, impermeable to gas

étanche *adj* **au vide**
D: vakuumdicht *adj*
E: vacuum-tight *adj*, vacuum-sealed *adj*

étanchéité *f*
D: Abdichtung *f*, Dichtigkeit *f*
E: sealing *n*, tightness *n*

étanchéité *f* **à l'air**
D: Luftabschluß *m*
E: exclusion of air, hermetic seal

étanchéité *f* **à la pression**
D: Druckdichtigkeit *f*
E: pressure tightness

étanchéité *f* **à l'eau**
D: Wasserdichtigkeit *f*
E: water tightness

étanchéité *f* **au gaz**
D: Gasdichtigkeit *f*, Gasundurchlässigkeit *f*
E: impermeability to gas, gas-tightness *n*, gas impermeability

étanchéité *f* **longitudinale**
D: Längswasserdichtigkeit *f*
E: longitudinal water tightness

étancher *v*
D: abdichten *v*
E: seal *v*

étape *f* **de fabrication**
D: Stadium der Fertigung
E: stage of production, manufacturing stage

étapes *f pl* **de tréfilage** [fabr. fils mét.]
D: Ziehfolgen *f pl*, Ziehstufen *f pl*
E: reduction steps

état *m* **collant**
D: Klebrigkeit *f*
E: stickiness *n*, tackiness *n*

état *m* **d'équilibre**
D: Gleichgewichtszustand *m*
E: state of equilibrium

état *m* **de service**
D: Betriebszustand *m*
E: working order, operating condition

état *m* **stationnaire**
D: Beharrungszustand *m*, Dauerzustand *m*
E: steady state condition

étendre *v*

étendre v
  D: recken v, spannen v, strecken v
  E: straighten v, stretch v

étendre v
  D: dehnen v
  E: elongate v, extend v, expand vt

étendre v(s')
  D: ausbreiten v(sich)
  E: spread v, propagate v

étincelle f
  D: Funken m
  E: spark n

étirage m
  D: Ziehen n (von Stangen, Profilen oder Draht)
  E: drawing n

étirage m
  D: Dehnung f
  E: elongation n, extension n, stretch n

étirage m **du conducteur**
  D: Reckung des Leiters
  E: stretching of the conductor

étiré, échantillon de câble ~
  D: gestrecktes Kabelmuster
  E: straightened cable sample

étirer v
  D: dehnen v
  E: elongate v, extend v, expand vt

étude f
  D: Projektierung f
  E: planning n

étude f **de la technique de fabrication**
  D: fertigungstechnische Entwicklung
  E: production engineering development

étude f **du travail**
  D: Arbeitsstudie f
  E: time and motion study

études f pl
  D: Entwicklungsarbeiten f pl
  E: development work

études f pl **continues**
  D: fortlaufende Untersuchungen
  E: continuing studies

étuve f
  D: Wärmeschrank m
  E: oven n, heating cabinet, heated cabinet

étuve f **à circulation d'air**
  D: Ofen mit Luftumwälzung, Umluftofen m
  E: forced-air oven, air oven

étuve f **de vieillissement Geer**
  D: Geer-Alterungsofen m
  E: Geer ag(e)ing oven

étuve f **ventilé**
  D: Ofen mit Luftumwälzung, Umluftofen m
  E: forced-air oven, air oven

EVA (v. acétate d'éthylène vinyle)

évacuation f **des calories**
  D: Wärmeableitung f
  E: heat dissipation, heat removal

évacuer v
  D: evakuieren v
  E: evacuate v

évaluation f
  D: Auswertung f
  E: evaluation n

évaporation f
  D: Verdampfung f
  E: evaporation n

évaser v
  D: aufweiten v
  E: expand v, bulge v, bell out v, flare v

évent m
  D: Entlüftungsloch n
  E: vent hole, vent n

éventail m [prod.]
  D: Spektrum n
  E: range n, spectrum n

éventail m **de types**
  D: Typenspektrum n
  E: pattern of types, range of types, type spectrum

évidement m
  D: Aussparung f
  E: recess n, clearance n, slot n

exacte, à dimensions ~s
  D: maßhaltig adj, maßgerecht adj
  E: true to size, accurate to size

exactitude f **de réglage**
  D: Einstellgenauigkeit f
  E: accuracy of adjustment, precision of adjustment

exactitude f **des dimensions prescrites**
  D: Maßhaltigkeit f
  E: accuracy to size, dimensional accuracy, dimensional stability, dimensional precision

examen m
  D: Untersuchung f, Prüfung f (Kontrolle)
  E: inspection n, check n, examination n, investigation n, analysis n

examen m **détaillé**
  D: eingehende Prüfung

examen

   E: exhaustive test, close examination, thorough examination

examen *m* métallographique
   D: metallographische Prüfung
   E: metallographic examination, metallographic test

examen *m* visuel
   D: visuelle Prüfung
   E: visual examination, visual control, inspection *n*

examiner *v*
   D: besichtigen *v*
   E: inspect *v*, survey *v*

excéder *v*
   D: überschreiten *v*
   E: exceed *v*

excentricité, appareil de mesure de l'~
   D: Exzentrizitäts-Meßvorrichtung *f*
   E: eccentricity gauge

exemple, suivant l'~ de
   D: in Anlehnung an
   E: similar to, taking pattern from

exempt *adj* de bulles d'air
   D: frei von Luftblasen, frei von Hohlräumen, frei von Lufteinschlüssen
   E: void-free *adj*

exempt *adj* de décharges partielles
   D: teilentladungsfrei *adj*
   E: free from partial discharges, partial discharge-free

exempt *adj* de défauts
   D: fehlerfrei *adj*
   E: correct *adj*, faultless *adj*, free from defects

exempt *adj* de diaphonie
   D: nebensprechfrei *adj*
   E: crosstalk-proof *adj*

exempt *adj* d'effet de couronne [él.]
   D: glimmfrei *adj*
   E: corona-free *adj*

exempt *adj* de poches d'air
   D: frei von Luftblasen, frei von Hohlräumen, frei von Lufteinschlüssen
   E: void-free *adj*

exempt *adj* de pores
   D: porenfrei *adj*
   E: pore-free *adj*, free of pinholes

exhaustion *f*
   D: Absaugung *f*
   E: exhaust *n*, suction *n*

exigence *f*
   D: Anforderung *f*
   E: requirement *n*, demand *n*

exigences *f pl* d'essai
   D: Prüfanforderungen *f pl*
   E: test requirements

expansion *f*
   D: Ausdehnung *f*
   E: expansion *n*, extension *n*, dilatation *n*

expérience *f*
   D: Versuch *m*, Prüfung *f* (Erprobung), Test *m*
   E: test *n*, trial *n*, experiment *n*

expérience *f* faite avec une méthode de fabrication
   D: Erfahrung mit einer Fertigungsmethode
   E: process experience

exploitation *f* [câb., mach.]
   D: Betrieb *m*
   E: operation *n*, service *n*, duty *n*

exploitation, câble en ~ sans charge [c. én.]
   D: unbelastetes Kabel, Kabel in unbelastetem Zustand
   E: cable at no-load

exploitation *f* (téléphonique) automatique
   D: Selbstwählbetrieb *m*, Selbstwählsystem *n*
   E: automatic telephone service, automatic dialling, automatic dial service

exposant *m* de transfert
   D: Übertragungsmaß *n*
   E: propagation unit

exposant *m* linéique de propagation
   D: Übertragungskonstante *f*
   E: propagation coefficient

exposer *v*
   D: aussetzen *v* (einwirken lassen)
   E: expose *v*

exposer *v* aux intempéries
   D: bewittern *v*
   E: weather *v*

exposition *f* (à la lumière; à la chaleur)
   D: Aussetzen *n* (dem Licht, der Wärme)
   E: exposure *n* (to)

expulsion *f* du culot de filage [pr. à filer]
   D: Ausstoßen des Preßrestes
   E: ejection of the discard

exsudation *f*

extrusion

    D: Ausschwitzen *n* (auf der Oberfläche von Kunststoffen)
    E: exudation *n*

exsuder *v*
    D: ausschwitzen *v*
    E: exude *v*

extendeur *m*
    D: Streckmittel *n* (Gummimischungen)
    E: extender *n*

extensibilité *f*
    D: Dehnbarkeit *f*
    E: elasticity *n*, extensibility *n*, ductility *n*

extensibilité, à ~ réduite
    D: dehnungsarm *adj*
    E: with limited extensibility

extensible *adj*
    D: ausziehbar *adj*
    E: extensible *adj*, telescopic *adj*

extension *f*
    D: Dehnung *f*
    E: elongation *n*, extension *n*, stretch *n*

extension *f*
    D: Erweiterung *f*
    E: extension *n*, enlargement *n*, widening *n*, expansion *n*

extracteur *m* **de vis** [extr.]
    D: Schneckenausstoßvorrichtung *f*
    E: screw pushout device

extrait *m* **aqueux**
    D: wäßriger Auszug
    E: aqueous extract

extrémité *f*
    D: Endverschluß *m*, Endenabschluß *m*
    E: sealing end, termination *n*, terminal *n*, pothead *n*

extrémité *f* **cylindrique**
    D: Zylinder-Endverschluß *m*
    E: cylinder pot-head

extrémité *f* **de câble du type inverti**
    D: umgekehrter Kabelendverschluß *m*
    E: inverted type cable termination

extrémité *f* **de câble pour les coffrets de disjoncteurs-interrupteurs**
    D: Schaltanlageneinführungs-Endverschluß *m*
    E: cable termination for metal-clad substations

extrémité *f* **de câble pour transformateur**
    D: Transformatoreinführungs-Endverschluß *m*
    E: transformer type cable termination

extrémité *f* **embrochable**
    D: Aufsteck-Endverschluß *m*
    E: plug-in termination, plug-on termination

extrémité *f* **emmanchable**
    D: Aufschieb-Endverschluß *m*
    E: slip-on termination

extrémité *f* **emmanchable à chaud**
    D: wärmeschrumpfender Endverschluß, aufschrumpfbarer Endverschluß
    E: shrink-on termination, heat-shrinkable termination

extrémité *f* **emmanchée à chaud**
    D: aufgeschrumpfter Endverschluß
    E: shrunk-on termination

extrémité *f* **extérieure**
    D: Freiluft-Endverschluß *m*
    E: outdoor termination

extrémité *f* **facilement embrochable**
    D: leicht aufsteckbarer Endverschluß
    E: easy-on termination

extrémité *f* **intérieure**
    D: Innenraum-Endverschluß *m*
    E: indoor termination

extrémité *f* **non étanche**
    D: blutender Endverschluß
    E: bleeding sealing end

extrémité *f* **prémoulée**
    D: vorgefertigter Endverschluß
    E: pre-mo(u)lded termination

extrémité *f* **reconstituée**
    D: gewickelter Endverschluß
    E: lapped termination

extrémité *f* **vulcanisée sur le câble**
    D: aufvulkanisierter Endenabschluß
    E: sealing end vulcanized to the cable

extrudabilité *f*
    D: Extrudierbarkeit *f*, Preßbarkeit *f*
    E: extrudability *n*

extruder *v*
    D: extrudieren *v*, umspritzen *v*
    E: extrude *v*

extrudeuse *f*
    D: Schneckenpresse *f*, Extruder *m*
    E: extruder *n*

extrusion *f*
    D: Extrudieren *n*, Extrusion *f*
    E: extrusion *n*

extrusion *f* **avec tolérances étroites**
    D: Extrusion mit engen Toleranzen
    E: close tolerance extrusion

extrusion f cône avec vide sur le poinçon [extr.]
  D: Schlauchreckverfahren n
  E: tube-on method, tubing extrusion, vacuum smearing

extrusion f de la gaine sur le câble
  D: Aufpressen des Mantels auf das Kabel
  E: extrusion of the sheath on to the cable

extrusion f en bourrage [extr.]
  D: Druckspritzverfahren n
  E: controlled pressure extrusion

extrusion f hydrostatique [mét.]
  D: hydrostatisches Extrudieren
  E: hydrostatic extrusion

extrusion f multiple
  D: Mehrfachextrusion f
  E: multiple extrusion

extrusion f «pression bourrage» [extr.]
  D: Druckspritzverfahren n
  E: controlled pressure extrusion

extrusion f tête double
  D: Doppelkopf-Extrusion f, Zweifach-Extrusion f
  E: twin-head extrusion

extrusion f triple
  D: Dreifach-Extrusion f
  E: triple extrusion

extrusion f verticale
  D: Vertikal-Extrusion f
  E: vertical extrusion

F

fabricant m de câbles
  D: Kabelhersteller m
  E: cable maker, cable manufacturer

fabrication f de maquettes
  D: Modellanfertigung f
  E: pattern-making n

fabrication f de quartes étoile
  D: Sternviererverseilung f
  E: star quad formation, star quad twisting, star quadding

fabrication f des câbles
  D: Kabelherstellung f
  E: cable making, cable manufacture

fabrication f discontinue
  D: chargenweise Fertigung
  E: batch type manufacturing process

fabrication f en continu
  D: kontinuierliche Fertigung
  E: continuous manufacture

facilement accessible
  D: leicht zugänglich
  E: easily accessible

facilement manœuvrable
  D: leicht bedienbar
  E: easy to operate

façonnage m à chaud
  D: Warmverformung f, Warmformung f, Warmverarbeitung f
  E: hot forming, hot-working n

façonnage m à froid
  D: Kaltformung f, Kaltumformung f
  E: cold-working n

façonnés, cordons et conducteurs ~
  D: konfektionierte Leitungen
  E: pre-assembled flexible cables and cords, cord sets

facteur m de blindage contre les perturbations électriques
  D: Abschirmfaktor gegen elektrische Störungen
  E: electrical interference screening factor

facteur m de charge
  D: Lastfaktor m
  E: load factor

facteur m d'écran
  D: Schirmfaktor m
  E: screening factor (GB), shield factor (US)

facteur m de distorsion
  D: Klirrfaktor m
  E: distortion factor

facteur m de marche
  D: Einschaltdauer f
  E: duty factor, switch-on time

facteur m de perte tg δ
  D: Verlustfaktor m
  E: loss factor tg δ, dissipation factor, dielectric power factor cos φ

facteur m de puissance
  D: Leistungsfaktor m
  E: power factor

facteur de puissance cos φ
  D: Verlustfaktor m
  E: loss factor tg δ, dissipation factor, dielectric power factor cos φ

facteur m réducteur

- D: Reduktionsfaktor *m*
- E: reduction factor

faculté *f* hygroscopique
- D: Wasseraufnahmefähigkeit *f*
- E: water absorption capacity

faible, à ~ poids moléculaire
- D: niedermolekular *adj*
- E: of low molecular weight

faire *v* des jonctions sur câble
- D: Kabelverbindungen herstellen
- E: to joint cables

faire *v* passer un câble par une machine
- D: Kabel durch eine Maschine laufen lassen
- E: to feed a cable through a machine

faire *v* passer un courant
- D: einen Strom anlegen
- E: to inject a current, to apply a current

faire *v* un essai
- D: eine Prüfung durchführen
- E: to perform a test, to carry out a test, to conduct a test

faisable *adj*
- D: durchführbar *adj*
- E: practicable *adj*, realizable *adj*

faisceau *m* [c. com.]
- D: Bündel *n*
- E: unit *n*, bunch *n*

faisceau *m* d'âmes
- D: Leiterbündel *n*
- E: conductor unit

faisceau *m* de base [c. com.]
- D: Grundbündel *n*
- E: primary unit, primary core unit, basic unit, sub-unit *n*

faisceau *m* de câbles
- D: Kabelbaum *m*, Kabelsatz *m*
- E: cable harness, wiring harness, cable assembly

faisceau *m* de guide d'ondes
- D: Wellenleiterbündel *n*
- E: waveguide bundle

faisceau *m* élémentaire [c. com.]
- D: Grundbündel *n*
- E: primary unit, primary core unit, basic unit, sub-unit *n*

faisceau *m* principal [c. com.]
- D: Hauptbündel *n*
- E: main unit, main core unit

famille *f* de câbles
- D: Kabelgruppe *f*
- E: cable group

fatigue *f*
- D: Ermüdung *f*
- E: fatigue *n*

fausse boîte de jonction
- D: Blindmuffe *f*
- E: dummy joint, dummy joint box

fausse manœuvre *f*
- D: Bedienungsfehler *m*, Fehlbedienung *f*
- E: faulty operation, operating error, operator's error

faux-élément *m* [c. tél.]
- D: Blindelement *n*
- E: dummy *n*

feeder *m*
- D: Einspeisungskabel *n*, Speisekabel *n*, Zuführungskabel *n*, Zuleitungskabel *n*
- E: feeder *n*, feeder cable

feeder *m* d'antenne
- D: Antennenspeiseleitung *f*, Antennenzuleitung *f*, Antennenkabel *n*
- E: antenna feeder, aerial feeder, antenna lead

fendre *v*
- D: abspalten *v*
- E: split off *v*, set free *v*

fermer *v* (circuit)
- D: einschalten *v*, anschalten *v*
- E: switch on *v*, turn on (US) *v*

fermer *v* par un capuchon
- D: verkappen *v*
- E: cap-seal *v*

fermeture *f* rapide
- D: Schnellverschluß *m*
- E: quick-action locking device, rapid-action locking device

fermeture *f* rapide à baïonette avec roue hélicoïdale pour cuves d'imprégnation
- D: Bajonett-Schnellverschluß mit Schnecke und Schneckenrad für Tränkgefäße
- E: quick-acting lock with worm gear for impregnating tanks

feuillard *m*
- D: Metallband *n*
- E: metal strip, metal tape

feuillard *m* d'acier
- D: Bandeisen *n*, Stahlband *n*
- E: steel tape, steel strip

feuille *f* [plast.]
  D: Folie *f*
  E: film *n*
feuille *f* [mét.]
  D: Folie *f*
  E: foil *n*
feuille *f* de construction
  D: Konstruktionsblatt *n*
  E: design sheet
feuille *f* métallique
  D: Metallfolie *f*
  E: metal foil
feuille *f* métallique doublée de matière plastique
  D: kunststoffkaschierte Metallfolie
  E: plastics-coated metal foil
fiabilité *f*
  D: Zuverlässigkeit *f*
  E: reliability *n*
fiabilité *f* de service
  D: Betriebssicherheit *f*, Betriebszuverlässigkeit *f*, Zuverlässigkeit im Betrieb
  E: operating reliability, operating safety, service reliability, functional reliability, reliability of operation, operational reliability
fibre *f* de verre
  D: Glasfaser *f*
  E: glass fibre (GB), glass fiber (US)
fibre *f* optique
  D: Lichtleiter *m*
  E: optical fibre
fibre *f* optique monomode [com.]
  D: Einmoden-Lichtleiter *m*
  E: single-mode optical fibre
fibre *f* optique multimode
  D: Mehrmoden-Lichtleiter *m*
  E: multimode optical fibre
ficelle *f*
  D: Kordel *f*
  E: string *n*
ficelle *f* de papier
  D: Papierkordel *f*
  E: paper string
fiche *f*
  D: Stecker *m*
  E: plug *n*, plug connector
fiche *f* angulaire
  D: Winkelstecker *m*
  E: angular plug, right-angle plug, right-angle connector
fiche *f* de coupure rapide
  D: Schnelltrennstecker *m*
  E: quick disconnect plug
fiche *f* de dérivation
  D: Abzweigstecker *m*
  E: socket-outlet adapter, distribution plug
fiche *f* de prise de courant
  D: Netzstecker *m*
  E: power plug
fiche *f* de raccordement
  D: Anschlußstecker *m*
  E: connector *n*, connecting plug
fiche *f* droite
  D: Geradeausstecker *m*
  E: straight plug
fiche *f* femelle
  D: Steckbuchse *f*, Steckerbuchse *f*, Fassung *f*
  E: plug socket, connector socket, receptacle *n*, female contact, socket *n*
fiche *f* méplate
  D: Flachstecker *m*
  E: flat plug
fiche *f* multiple
  D: Mehrfachstecker *m*
  E: multicontact plug, multiple plug
fiche *f* multipolaire
  D: mehrpoliger Stecker
  E: multiple pin plug
fiche *f* plate
  D: Flachstecker *m*
  E: flat plug
fiche *f* profilée
  D: Konturenstecker *m*
  E: shaped plug
fiche *f* rectangulaire
  D: Winkelstecker *m*
  E: angular plug, right-angle plug, right-angle connector
fiche *f* vulcanisée sur le câble
  D: aufvulkanisierter Stecker
  E: plug vulcanized to the cable
figure *f* de décharges
  D: Entladungsfigur *f*
  E: discharge pattern
fil *m* à brins multiples
  D: Schaltlitze *f*
  E: stranded hook-up wire
fil *m* aérien
  D: Luftkabel *n*
  E: aerial cable, overhead cable
fil *m* aérien [c. com.]

- D: Freileitung f
- E: open wire line

filage m **avec croûte** [pr. à filer]
- D: Pressen mit Schale
- E: extrusion with shell

filage m **de la gaine sur le câble**
- D: Aufpressen des Mantels auf das Kabel
- E: extrusion of the sheath on to the cable

filage m **sans croûte** [pr. à filer]
- D: Pressen ohne Schale
- E: extrusion without shell

filage m **sans soudure des gaines métalliques**
- D: nahtloses Pressen von Metallmänteln
- E: seamless extrusion of metal sheaths

filant adj
- D: fadenziehend adj (Viskosität)
- E: ropy adj

fil m **central**
- D: Mitteldraht m (Leiter)
- E: core wire

fil m **compteur**
- D: Zählader f
- E: pilot wire, marked wire, tracer wire

fil m **d'acier**
- D: Stahldraht m
- E: steel wire

fil m **d'acier galvanisé**
- D: verzinkter Stahldraht
- E: galvanized steel wire, zinc-coated steel wire

fil m **d'aluminium**
- D: Aluminiumdraht m
- E: aluminium wire

fil m **d'aluminium plaqué de cuivre**
- D: kupferplattierter Aluminiumdraht, kupferumhüllter Aluminiumdraht, Aluminiumdraht mit Kupfermantel
- E: copper-clad aluminium wire

fil m **d'amenée**
- D: Zuleitungsdraht m
- E: lead-in wire

fil m **d'ancrage**
- D: Abspanndraht m
- E: anchoring wire

fil m **d'armure**
- D: Bewehrungsdraht m, Armierungsdraht m
- E: armo(u)ring wire

fil m **d'arrêt**
- D: Spanndraht m
- E: guy wire, span wire

fil m **d'attache**
- D: Bindedraht m
- E: binding wire

fil m **de bobinage**
- D: Wickeldraht m
- E: winding wire

fil m **de câblage**
- D: Verdrahtungsleitung f
- E: single-core non-sheathed cable for internal wiring, wiring cable

fil m **de compensation**
- D: Ausgleichsleitung f
- E: equalizer n, equipotential connection, balancing circuit, equalizing circuit

fil m **de connexion**
- D: Schaltader f, Schaltdraht m
- E: jumper wire, cross-connecting wire, hook-up wire

fil m **de connexion**
- D: Verbindungsdraht m
- E: bond wire

fil m **de contact**
- D: Fahrdraht m, Schleifdraht m
- E: trolley wire, overhead contact wire, slide wire

fil m **de cuivre recuit**
- D: Kupferdraht, weichgeglüht
- E: copper wire, soft-annealed

fil m **de déchirement**
- D: Reißfaden m
- E: slitting cord

fil m **de diamètre final**
- D: Fertigdraht m
- E: final wire size

fil m **de diamètre intermédiaire**
- D: Zwischendraht m
- E: intermediate wire gauge size

fil m **de douille**
- D: Fassungsader f
- E: flexible wire for fittings (sockets)

fil m **de dynamo**
- D: Dynamodraht m
- E: magnet wire

fil m **de fusion**
- D: Schmelzdraht m, Schmelzleiter m
- E: fuse wire, fusing conductor

fil m **de garde**
- D: Erdleiter m, Erdleitung f, Erdseil n
- E: earthing conductor (GB), grounding conductor (US), earth

wire (GB), ground wire (US), guard wire

fil *m* de glissement
D: Gleitdraht *m*
E: skid wire

fil *m* de gros diamètre
D: dicker Draht
E: large-diameter wire, large-size wire

fil *m* de ligature
D: Bindedraht *m*
E: binding wire

fil *m* de ligne
D: Leitungsdraht *m*
E: line wire

fil *m* d'entrée d'abonné
D: Teilnehmer-Anschlußleitung *f*, Hauszuführungsleitung *f*, Teilnehmereinführungsleitung *f*, Einführungsleitung *f*, Einführungsdraht *m*, Fernsprechteilnehmerleitung *f*
E: drop wire (telephone cable to connect open wire lines on poles to subscribers' premises) (US), subscriber('s) drop wire, telephone drop, lead(ing)-in wire

fil *m* de petit diamètre
D: dünner Draht
E: small-diameter wire

fil *m* de réserve [c. com.]
D: Vorratsader *f*
E: spare wire

fil *m* de retour
D: Rückleiter *m*
E: return conductor, return wire

fil *m* de section rectangulaire
D: Rechteckdraht *m*
E: rectangular wire, rectangular section wire

fil *m* de signalisation
D: Signalader *f*
E: signalling core

fil *m* de sonnerie
D: Klingeldraht *m*
E: bell wire

fil *m* de soudage
D: Schweißdraht *m*
E: welding wire

fil *m* de soudure
D: Lötdraht *m*
E: cored solder, soldering wire, wire solder

fil *m* d'essai
D: Prüfader *f*, Prüfdraht *m*, Prüfleiter *m*, Hilfsader *f*
E: test(ing) wire, pilot wire, test(ing) conductor, pilot core, pilot conductor

fil *m* de suspension (pour fil de contact)
D: Tragdraht *m* (für Fahrdraht)
E: catenary wire, suspension wire

fil *m* de terre
D: Erddraht *m*
E: earth lead (GB), ground lead (US)

fil *m* de test [c. com.]
D: Meßader *f*
E: second wire, test wire

fil *m* d'identification
D: Kennfaden *m*
E: identification thread, marker thread, tracer thread

fil *m* d'identification VDE
D: VDE-Kennfaden *m*
E: VDE tracer thread, VDE identification thread

fil *m* distinctif
D: Kennfaden *m*
E: identification thread, marker thread, tracer thread

fil *m* distinctif du fournisseur
D: Firmenkennfaden *m*
E: manufacturers' identification thread

fil *m* distinctif VDE
D: VDE-Kennfaden *m*
E: VDE tracer thread, VDE identification thread

fil *m* double [c. com.]
D: Doppelader *f*, paarverseilte Leitung, Paar *n*
E: pair *n*, twin-wire *n*, dual wire

fil *m* dur
D: harter Draht, hartgezogener Draht
E: hard-drawn wire

fil *m* ébauche [fabr. fils mét.]
D: Grobdraht *m*, Drahtvormaterial *n*, Vorziehdraht *m*
E: wire rod, redraw rod

fil *m* écroui
D: harter Draht, hartgezogener Draht
E: hard-drawn wire

fil *m* émail-coton
D: Lackbaumwolldraht *m*
E: cotton-covered enamelled wire

fil *m* émaillé

D: Lackdraht m
E: enamel(l)ed wire, magnet wire
fil m émaillé guipé de coton
D: Lackbaumwolldraht m
E: cotton-covered enamelled wire
filerie f
D: Verdrahtung f
E: wiring n
filerie f fixe
D: feste Verdrahtung
E: permanent wiring, fixed wiring
filerie f interne
D: innere Verdrahtung
E: inside wiring, internal wiring
filerie f souple
D: flexible Verdrahtung
E: flexible wiring
filet m à droite
D: rechtsgängiges Gewinde
E: right-hand(ed) thread
filet m à gauche
D: linksgängiges Gewinde
E: left-hand(ed) thread
fil m étamé
D: verzinnter Draht
E: tinned wire
filet m de la vis [extr.]
D: Schneckengang m, Gewindegang der Schnecke, Schneckengewinde n
E: flight of the screw, thread of the screw
fil m extra-fin
D: Feinstdraht m
E: super-fine wire, extra-fine wire
fil m fabriqué en coulée continue laminage
D: Gießwalzdraht m
E: continuously cast and rolled rod
fil m faisant flèche
D: zugspannungsloser Draht, durchhängender Draht
E: slack wire
fil m fin
D: Feindraht m
E: fine wire, fine drawn wire
fil m fusible
D: Schmelzdraht m, Schmelzleiter m
E: fuse wire, fusing conductor
fil m hélice de support
D: Anwendeldraht m (Luftkabel)
E: lashing wire
filière f

D: Matrize f
E: ring die, female die
filière f [extr.]
D: Mundstück n, Düse f
E: die n
filière f d'assemblage
D: Verseilnippel m
E: stranding nipple, stranding closer, twisting closer, closing die
filière f de câblage
D: Verseilnippel m
E: stranding nipple, stranding closer, twisting closer, closing die
filière f de rétreint
D: Verdichtungswerkzeug n
E: compacting tool
filière f de tréfilage
D: Ziehstein m, Ziehwerkzeug n
E: drawing die
filière f (de tréfilage) en carbure de tungstène
D: Hartmetall-Ziehstein m
E: hard metal (drawing) die, tungsten carbide (drawing) die
filière f (de tréfilage) en métal dur
D: Hartmetall-Ziehstein m
E: hard metal (drawing) die, tungsten carbide (drawing) die
filières f pl en diamant [fabr. fils mét.]
D: Ziehdiamanten m pl, Diamantziehsteine m pl
E: diamond dies
filière f type croisillon
D: Brückenmatrize f
E: spider type die
filin m de jute
D: Jute-Garn n
E: jute yarn
filin m de reconnaissance
D: Kennfaden m
E: identification thread, marker thread, tracer thread
fil m intermédiaire [fabr. fils mét.]
D: Mitteldraht m
E: intermediate wire
fil m isolé
D: Ader f
E: core n, conductor n, insulated wire, insulated conductor
fil m isolé
D: Leitung f
E: insulated wire
fil m lâche

fil

- **fil** *m* **machine** [fabr. fils mét.]
  - *D:* zugspannungsloser Draht, durchhängender Draht
  - *E:* slack wire
- **fil** *m* **machine** [fabr. fils mét.]
  - *D:* Grobdraht *m*, Drahtvormaterial *n*, Vorziehdraht *m*
  - *E:* wire rod, redraw rod
- **fil** *m* **machine filé**
  - *D:* Preßdraht *m*
  - *E:* extruded rod
- **fil** *m* **machine laminé**
  - *D:* Walzdraht *m*
  - *E:* wire rod
- **fil** *m* **méplat**
  - *D:* Flachdraht *m*
  - *E:* flat wire
- **fil** *m* **métallique**
  - *D:* Draht *m*
  - *E:* wire *n*
- **fil** *m* **métallique courbé**
  - *D:* vorgewölbter Draht
  - *E:* curved wire
- **fil** *m* **métallique étamé électrolytiquement**
  - *D:* elektrolytisch verzinnter Draht
  - *E:* electro-tinned wire
- **fil** *m* **mince**
  - *D:* dünner Draht
  - *E:* small-diameter wire
- **fil** *m* **neutre**
  - *D:* Nulleiter *m*, Mittelpunktsleiter *m*
  - *E:* neutral conductor, neutral wire, zero conductor
- **fil** *m* **nu**
  - *D:* Blankdraht *m*
  - *E:* bare wire
- **fil** *m* **pilote**
  - *D:* Prüfader *f*, Prüfdraht *m*, Prüfleiter *m*, Hilfsader *f*
  - *E:* test(ing) wire, pilot wire, test(ing) conductor, pilot core, pilot conductor
- **fil** *m* **plat**
  - *D:* Flachdraht *m*
  - *E:* flat wire
- **fil** *m* **porte-câble**
  - *D:* Kabeltragdraht *m*
  - *E:* cable suspension wire
- **fil** *m* **porteur**
  - *D:* Tragdraht *m*
  - *E:* supporting wire
- **fil** *m* **pour retréfilage** [fabr. fils mét.]
  - *D:* Grobdraht *m*, Drahtvormaterial *n*, Vorziehdraht *m*
  - *E:* wire rod, redraw rod
- **fil** *m* **profilé**
  - *D:* Profildraht *m*
  - *E:* profile wire, shaped wire, strip *n*
- **fil** *m* **rectangulaire**
  - *D:* Rechteckdraht *m*
  - *E:* rectangular wire, rectangular section wire
- **fil** *m* **recuit**
  - *D:* weichgeglühter Draht
  - *E:* soft annealed wire
- **fil** *m* **revêtu de soie et de coton**
  - *D:* Seidenbaumwolldraht *m*
  - *E:* silk and cotton covered wire
- **fil** *m* **rond**
  - *D:* Runddraht *m*
  - *E:* round wire
- **fil** *m* **rosette**
  - *D:* Lahnlitzenleiter *m*
  - *E:* tinsel conductor
- **fils** *m pl* **de jonction unidirectionnels**
  - *D:* einseitig herausgeführte Anschlußdrähte
  - *E:* single-ended terminal wires
- **fils** *m pl* **d'installation**
  - *D:* Installationsdrähte *m pl* (für Fernsprech- und Signalanlagen)
  - *E:* installation wires
- **fil** *m* **super-fin**
  - *D:* Feinstdraht *m*
  - *E:* super-fine wire, extra-fine wire
- **fil** *m* **téléphonique**
  - *D:* Sprechader *f*
  - *E:* speaking wire, speech wire
- **fil** *m* **tendeur**
  - *D:* Spanndraht *m*
  - *E:* guy wire, span wire
- **fil** *m* **torsadé**
  - *D:* Litzendraht *m*
  - *E:* tinsel wire
- **filtre** *m* **de bruit**
  - *D:* Geräuschfilter *m*
  - *E:* noise suppressor
- **filtrer** *v* (se)
  - *D:* durchsickern *v*
  - *E:* ooze *v*, filter through *v*, leak *v*
- **fil** *m* **(de) trolley**
  - *D:* Fahrdraht *m*, Schleifdraht *m*
  - *E:* trolley wire, overhead contact wire, slide wire
- **fil** *m* **verni**
  - *D:* Lackdraht *m*

E: enamel(l)ed wire, magnet wire
fil m verni en couche mince
D: Dünnschicht-Lackdraht m
E: thin-film insulated magnet wire
fin f (fil métallique)
D: Auslauf-Ende n (Draht)
E: back-end n (wire)
finissage m
D: Endbearbeitung f, Endfertigung f
E: finishing n, completion n
finition f
D: Endbearbeitung f, Endfertigung f
E: finishing n, completion n
fissuration f de contact [plast.]
D: Spannungsrißbildung f
E: environmental stress cracking
fissuration f sous contrainte [plast.]
D: Spannungsrißbildung f
E: environmental stress cracking
fissuration f sous l'effet de la lumière solaire
D: Lichtrißbildung f
E: sun-cracking n, light-cracking n
fissure f
D: Riß m
E: crack n, fissure n
fissuré adj
D: rissig adj
E: cracked adj, fissured adj
fixation f du câble
D: Kabelfestlegung f, Festlegung von Kabeln
E: cable anchorage
fixe adj
D: stationär adj, feststehend adj
E: stationary adj, fixed adj
fixer v
D: befestigen v
E: fasten v, fix v, attach v
flamme, non transmettant la ~
D: flammwidrig adj, einen Brand nicht weiterleitend
E: flame-resistant adj, non fire propagating
flèche f
D: Durchhang m
E: sag n
flèche, écart de ~
D: Durchhanghöhe f
E: sag clearance
flèche, fil faisant ~
D: zugspannungsloser Draht, durchhängender Draht

E: slack wire
flèche, hauteur de ~
D: Durchhanghöhe f
E: sag clearance
fléchissement m
D: Durchhängen n
E: sagging n, slackening n
flexibilité f
D: Biegsamkeit f, Biegbarkeit f
E: flexibility n
flexible adj
D: biegsam adj
E: flexible adj
flexion f
D: Biegen n
E: bending n
flexions f pl répétées
D: Biegezyklen m pl
E: bending cycles
flottable, câble ~
D: schwimmfähiges Kabel
E: buoyant cable
fluage m
D: Kriechen n
E: creep n
fluage, résistance au ~ [mét.]
D: Dauerstandfestigkeit f
E: creep resistance, fatigue strength, creep strength, long-time rupture strength
fluage à froid, résistance au ~
D: Kaltfließbeständigkeit f
E: cold flow resistance
fluctuation f de charge
D: Lastschwankung f
E: load fluctuation, load variation
fluctuation f de courant
D: Stromschwankung f
E: current variation, fluctuation of current
fluctuation f de tension
D: Spannungsschwankung f
E: voltage fluctuation, voltage variation
fluidité f
D: Fließvermögen n
E: fluidity n, flow n
flux m
D: Flußmittel n
E: flux n, soldering flux
flyer m
D: Umlaufbügel m
E: flier n, flyer n

flyer

flyer *m* **de câblage**
  D: Verseilbügel *m*, Jochbügel *m*
  E: stranding flyer, twisting flyer

foncer *v*(se)
  D: nachdunkeln *v*
  E: darken *v*

fonction, en ~ de [math.]
  D: in Abhängigkeit von
  E: as a function of, versus

fonctionnement *m*
  D: Arbeitsweise *f*
  E: mode of operation, functioning *n*, operation *n*

fonctionnement *m* [câb., mach.]
  D: Betrieb *m*
  E: operation *n*, service *n*, duty *n*

fonctionnement, câbles de ~ sûr
  D: betriebssichere Kabel
  E: operationally reliable cables, fail-safe cables

fonctionnement *m* **en tandem**
  D: Tandembetrieb *m*
  E: tandemized operation

fondant *m*
  D: Flußmittel *n*
  E: flux *n*, soldering flux

fondation, boulon de ~
  D: Fundamentschraube *f*
  E: foundation bolt

fond *m* **d'ondulation**
  D: Wellental *n* (beim Wellmantel)
  E: valley of corrugation

fond *m* **du trou d'homme**
  D: Muffenbauwerks-Sohle *f*, Muffenbunker-Sohle *f*, Schachtsohle *f*
  E: floor of vault, floor of manhole

fondre *v* [él.]
  D: durchbrennen *v*
  E: blow *v*, fuse *v*

fonte *f*
  D: Schmelzen *n*
  E: melting *n*, fusion *n*

fonte *f* (mét.)
  D: Schmelze *f*
  E: melt *n*, molten material

fonte *f* **injectée**
  D: Spritzguß *m*
  E: injection mo(u)lding

force *f* [méc.]
  D: Stärke *f*
  E: strength *n*, power *n*, force *n*

force *f* **de traction**
  D: Zugkraft *f*
  E: pull *n*, tractive force

formage *m* **à froid**
  D: Kaltformung *f*, Kaltumformung *f*
  E: cold-working *n*

formage *m* **par immersion** [fabr. fils mét.]
  D: Tauchziehen *n*
  E: dip forming (General Electric process for production of copper wire)

formation *f* **de bulles**
  D: Blasenbildung *f*
  E: blistering *n*

formation *f* **de fuites**
  D: Leckbildung *f*
  E: leakage formation

formation *f* **de plis**
  D: Faltenbildung *f*
  E: creasing *n*, wrinkling *n*

formation *f* **de vides**
  D: Hohlraumbildung *f*
  E: void formation

forme *f* **de câbles**
  D: Kabelbaum *m*, Kabelsatz *m*
  E: cable harness, wiring harness, cable assembly

formulation *f* **d'un mélange**
  D: Ansatz einer Mischung, Mischungsansatz *m*
  E: compound formulation

formule *f* **d'un mélange**
  D: Rezept einer Mischung
  E: compound formula

fortement chargé [él., méc.]
  D: hochbeansprucht *adj*, hochbelastet *adj*
  E: heavily loaded, heavily stressed, highly stressed

foudre, effets de ~
  D: Blitzbeeinflussung *f*
  E: effects *pl* of lightning

fouloir *m* [mach.]
  D: Stempel *m*, Kolben *m*, Plunger *m*
  E: piston *n*, ram *n*, plunger *n*

fouloir *m* **creux** [pr. à filer]
  D: Hohlstempel *m*
  E: hollow ram

fouloir *m* **de la presse**
  D: Preßstempel *m*
  E: pressure ram

fouloir *m* **plongeur** [pr. à filer]
  D: Tauchplunger *m*
  E: plunger piston

four *m* **à cuve**
  D: Schachtofen *m*
  E: shaft furnace, stack furnace
four *m* **à induction**
  D: Induktionsofen *m*
  E: induction furnace
four *m* **à réverbère**
  D: Flammofen *m*
  E: reverberatory furnace
four *m* **à tremper**
  D: Haubenglühofen *m*, Blankglühofen *m*
  E: bell type (annealing) furnace, hood type (annealing) furnace, top hat (annealing) furnace
four *m* **d'attente** [coul. cont. lam.]
  D: Warmhalteofen *m*
  E: holding furnace
four *m* **de (pré-)chauffage**
  D: Vorwärmofen *m*
  E: preheater *n*, preheating furnace
four(neau) *m* **de fusion**
  D: Schmelzofen *m*
  E: melting furnace
four *m* **de maintien à température** [coul. cont. lam.]
  D: Warmhalteofen *m*
  E: holding furnace
four *m* **de réchauffage des billettes** [pr. à filer]
  D: Bolzenvorwärmofen *m*
  E: billet preheater
Fourdrinier, papier fabriqué sur machine ~
  D: Langsieb-Papier *n*
  E: Fourdrinier-machine paper
fourneau *m* **à réverbère**
  D: Flammofen *m*
  E: reverberatory furnace
fournir *v* **des renseignements sur**
  D: Aufschluß geben über (z.B. Betriebsverhalten)
  E: to be indicative of, to permit conclusions as to
four *m* **pour recuit brillant**
  D: Haubenglühofen *m*, Blankglühofen *m*
  E: bell type (annealing) furnace, hood type (annealing) furnace, top hat (annealing) furnace
fourreau *m*
  D: Matrizenhalter *m*
  E: die holder

fourreau *m* **porte-cables** [pose c.]
  D: Formsteinzug *m*
  E: duct-bank *n*
fourrure *f*
  D: Futter *n*, Auskleidung *f*
  E: lining *n*
fourrure *f*
  D: Innenbüchse *f*
  E: liner *n*
four *m* **tubulaire tournant**
  D: Drehtrommelofen *m*
  E: rotary furnace
four *m* **tubulaire tournant basculant**
  D: kippbarer Drehtrommelofen
  E: tiltable rotary furnace
fragile *adj*
  D: spröde *adj*
  E: brittle *adj*
fragilité *f*
  D: Brüchigkeit *f*, Sprödigkeit *f*
  E: brittleness *n*
fragilité *f* **à basse température**
  D: Kältesprödigkeit *f*
  E: low temperature brittleness
fragilité *f* **intercristalline** [mét.]
  D: interkristalline Brüchigkeit
  E: intercrystalline brittleness, cleavage brittleness
freiner *v*
  D: abbremsen *v*
  E: brake *v*, slow down *v*
fréquence *f* **cumulée** [math.]
  D: Summenhäufigkeit *f*
  E: cumulative frequency
fréquence *f* **de régime** [él.]
  D: Betriebsfrequenz *f*
  E: power frequency
fréquence *f* **d'erreurs**
  D: Fehlerhäufigkeit *f*
  E: error rate
fréquence *f* **de sifflement**
  D: Pfeiffrequenz *f*
  E: singing frequency
fréquence *f* **d'impulsion**
  D: Impulsfrequenz *f*
  E: pulse frequency, impulse frequency
fréquence *f* **industrielle**
  D: Starkstromfrequenz *f*
  E: power frequency
fréquence *f* **porteuse**
  D: Trägerfrequenz *f* (TF)
  E: carrier frequency
fréquence *f* **radioélectrique**

fréquence
- D: Hochfrequenz (HF) f
- E: high frequency (HF), radio frequency

fréquence f téléphonique
- D: Sprechfrequenz f, Fernsprechfrequenz f
- E: voice frequency, telephone frequency, speech frequency

fréquence f vocale
- D: Sprechfrequenz f, Fernsprechfrequenz f
- E: voice frequency, telephone frequency, speech frequency

frettage m [câb.]
- D: Druckschutzwendel f
- E: circumferential reinforcement tape, holding tape, reinforcement helix

frettage, enrouleur du ~ [câb.]
- D: Druckschutzspinner m
- E: reinforcement tape spinner

frettage m en fil métallique pour l'orientation du champ électrique [access. c.]
- D: Strahlungsbund m, Drahtbund m
- E: field-controlling wire binding

frettage m sur faisceaux
- D: Bündel-Haltewendel f
- E: unit binder

frettage m sur l'assemblage
- D: Seelen-Haltewendel f
- E: core binder

frette f de chauffage
- D: Heizbandage f
- E: heating tapes pl

frette f en fil métallique [access. c.]
- D: Strahlungsbund m, Drahtbund m
- E: field-controlling wire binding

fretting m
- D: Reibkorrosion f
- E: fretting corrosion

friction f
- D: Reibung f
- E: friction n

friction, à faible ~
- D: reibungsarm adj
- E: low friction ...

frigorifère m
- D: Kälteraum m
- E: cold-chamber n

frottement m
- D: Reibung f
- E: friction n

fuite f
- D: Undichtigkeit f, Leckstelle f
- E: leakage n

fuite f de matière
- D: Masseaustritt m
- E: bleeding of compound

fuite f d'huile
- D: Olleckstelle f
- E: oil leakage

fuseau m long de papier [access. c.]
- D: Papierwickel m (vorgefertigt)
- E: paper tube

fuser v [él.]
- D: durchbrennen v
- E: blow v, fuse v

fusible m [él.]
- D: Sicherung f
- E: fuse n

fusion f
- D: Schmelzen n
- E: melting n, fusion n

fût m de bobinage pour fils métalliques
- D: Faßwickler m
- E: pail-pack n, drum-pack n, pay-off-pak n, draw-pak n, D-pak n

fût m de touret [câb.]
- D: Trommelkern m
- E: barrel of a reel

G

gabarit m pour câbles
- D: Kabelformbrett n, Formbrett für Kabel
- E: cable forming board, cable lacing board

gainage m
- D: Ummantelung f
- E: sheathing n

gaine f [câb.]
- D: Mantel m
- E: sheath n, jacket n

gaine f complexe
- D: Schichtenmantel m
- E: composite layer sheath, laminated sheath, multiple sheath

gaine f composite
- D: Schichtenmantel m
- E: composite layer sheath, laminated sheath, multiple sheath

gaine f d'acier ondulée
D: Stahlwellmantel m
E: corrugated steel sheath

gaine f d'aluminium
D: Aluminiummantel m
E: aluminium sheath

gaine f d'aluminium filée sur câble
D: aufgepreßter Aluminiummantel
E: extruded aluminium sheath

gaine f d'aluminium polyéthylène contrecollé
D: Al-PE-Schichtenmantel m
E: Alpeth-sheath n (US)

gaine f de bourrage
D: gemeinsame gepreßte Aderumhüllung, Zwickelmantel m
E: extruded inner covering, inner filling sheath

gaine f de câble
D: Kabelmantel m
E: cable sheath, cable jacket

gaine f de caoutchouc
D: Gummi-Mantel m
E: rubber sheath

gaine f de PE
D: PE-Mantel m
E: PE-sheath n

gaine f de plomb
D: Bleimantel m
E: lead sheath

gaine f de plomb avec armure en fils
D: Bleimantel mit Drahtarmierung
E: wire-reinforced lead sheath

gaine f de protection
D: Schutzmantel m
E: protective jacket, protective sheath

gaine f de PVC
D: PVC-Mantel m
E: PVC sheath

gaine d'étanchéité f
D: Außenmantel m
E: outer sheath

gaine f d'étanchéité à la pression
D: druckfester Mantel
E: pressure-retaining sheath

gaine f extérieure
D: Außenmantel m
E: outer sheath

gaine f formant bourrage
D: gemeinsame gepreßte Aderumhüllung, Zwickelmantel m
E: extruded inner covering, inner filling sheath

gaine f lisse
D: glatter Mantel
E: plain sheath

gaine f métallique
D: Metallmantel m
E: metal sheath

gaine f ondulée
D: Wellmantel m, gewellter Mantel
E: corrugated sheath

gaine f ondulée en aluminium
D: Aluminium-Wellmantel m
E: corrugated aluminium sheath

gaine f ondulée en cuivre
D: Kupferwellmantel m
E: corrugated copper sheath

gaine f plastique
D: Kunststoffmantel m
E: plastic sheath

gaine f repliée en aluminium
D: gefalzter Aluminiummantel
E: folded aluminium sheath

gaine f Stalpeth
D: Stalpeth-Mantel m (Stahl-Al-PE-Schichtenmantel)
E: Stalpeth-sheath n

gaine f thermorétractable
D: Schrumpfschlauch m
E: heat-shrinkable tubing, shrink-on tube

galérie f des câbles
D: Kabeltunnel m
E: cable subway, cable tunnel, cable gallery

galet m
D: Rolle f
E: sheave n, roller n, pulley n

galet m de contact
D: Kontaktrolle f
E: contact sheave

galet m de renvoi
D: Umlenkrolle f
E: deflector roll, reversing sheave

galet m d'estampage
D: Prägerad n
E: embossing wheel

galets m pl de pose [câb.]
D: Verlegerollen f pl
E: laying rollers

galet m support
D: Stützrolle f
E: supporting roller

galette f

galette
  D: Bandscheibe *f*
  E: pad *n* (paper), coil *n* (metal tape)
galette *f* de papier [rub.]
  D: Papierscheibe *f*,
    Papierbandscheibe *f*
  E: paper pad
galvanisé, fil d'acier ~
  D: verzinkter Stahldraht
  E: galvanized steel wire, zinc-coated steel wire
gamme *f*
  D: Bereich *m*
  E: range *n*, field *n*, scope *n*, area *n*
gamme *f* [prod.]
  D: Spektrum *n*
  E: range *n*, spectrum *n*
gamme *f* de fabrication
  D: Fertigungsbereich *m*,
    Fertigungsspektrum *n*
  E: range of production
gamme *f* de fréquences
  D: Frequenzband *n*, Frequenzbereich *m*
  E: frequency band, frequency range
gamme *f* de produits largement diversifiée
  D: breites Fabrikatespektrum, breites Fertigungsspektrum
  E: highly diversified range of products, broad spectrum of manufacturing activities
gamme *f* de réglage
  D: Regelbereich *m*
  E: control range, regulating range
gamme *f* de tolérances
  D: Toleranzbereich *m*
  E: tolerance bandwith, tolerance range
gamme *f* de types
  D: Typenspektrum *n*
  E: pattern of types, range of types, type spectrum
gamme *f* de vitesses
  D: Drehzahlbereich *m*,
    Geschwindigkeitsbereich *m*
  E: speed range
gamme *f* d'ondes
  D: Wellenbereich *m* (Schwingung)
  E: wave range, wave band
gazage *m*
  D: Gasen *n*
  E: gassing *n*
gaz *m* comprimé
  D: Druckgas *n*
  E: compressed gas, pressure gas
gaz comprimé, contrôle des câbles téléphoniques à ~
  D: Druckgasschutz und -überwachung von Telefonkabeln
  E: telephone cable pressurization, gas pressure supervision of telephone cables, gas pressure control of telephone cables
gaz *m* de protection
  D: Schutzgas *n*, reduzierendes Gas, Inertgas *n*
  E: inert gas, protective gas, reducing gas
gaz *m* détecteur
  D: Spürgas *n*
  E: tracer gas
gaz *m* inerte
  D: Schutzgas *n*, reduzierendes Gas, Inertgas *n*
  E: inert gas, protective gas, reducing gas
gaz *m* réducteur
  D: Schutzgas *n*, reduzierendes Gas, Inertgas *n*
  E: inert gas, protective gas, reducing gas
gelée *f* de pétrole
  D: Vaseline *f*, Petrol-jelly *n*
  E: petroleum jelly, petrol jelly
génératrice *f* à courant alternatif
  D: Wechselstromgenerator *m*
  E: a.c. generator
génératrice *f* de choc
  D: Stoßspannungsanlage *f*
  E: impulse generator
giration *f*
  D: Verdrehung *f*
  E: torsion *n*, twist *n*
glissière *f*
  D: Gleitschiene *f*
  E: slide bar, slide rail
glutinosité *f*
  D: Klebrigkeit *f*
  E: stickiness *n*, tackiness *n*
gonflement, résistance au ~
  D: Quellbeständigkeit *f*
  E: resistance to swelling
gonfler (se)
  D: quellen *v*
  E: swell *v*
gorge *f* d'ondulation

goudron m
 D: Teer m
 E: tar n, pitch n
goudron m **de houille**
 D: Steinkohlenteer m
 E: coal tar
goudron m **minéral**
 D: Steinkohlenteer m
 E: coal tar
goulotte f
 D: Trog m, Wanne f
 E: trough n
goulotte f **à câbles** [pose c.]
 D: Kabelwanne f
 E: cable trough
goulotte f **à secousses**
 D: Schüttelrutsche f
 E: vibratory feeder
goulotte f **de refroidissement**
 D: Kühlrinne f, Kühlwanne f
 E: cooling trough
goulotte f **oscillante**
 D: Schüttelrutsche f
 E: vibratory feeder
gouttière f **de refroidissement**
 D: Kühlrinne f, Kühlwanne f
 E: cooling trough
gradient m
 D: Gradient m
 E: gradient n
gradient m **au conducteur**
 D: Leiterfeldstärke f
 E: conductor field strength, conductor gradient
gradient m **de potentiel**
 D: Spannungsgradient m
 E: voltage gradient
gradient m **de service**
 D: Betriebsfeldstärke f
 E: operating stress, operating field strength
gradient m **de température**
 D: Temperaturgefälle n
 E: temperature gradient, thermal gradient
gradient m **thermique**
 D: Temperaturgefälle n
 E: temperature gradient, thermal gradient
gradin m **de tension**
 D: Spannungsstufe f

 D: Wellental n (beim Wellmantel)
 E: valley of corrugation

graphique

 E: voltage step
graduation f **d'échelle**
 D: Skalenteilung f
 E: scale division
gradué adj
 D: gestaffelt adj, abgestuft adj, versetzt adj (stufenweise),
 E: staggered adj, graded adj
grain, structure à ~s fins
 D: feinkörnige Struktur
 E: fine-grain structure
grain, structure à gros ~s
 D: grobkörnige Struktur
 E: coarse-grain structure
grain m **de poussée** [pr. à filer]
 D: Preßscheibe f
 E: dummy block
graissage m
 D: Schmierung f
 E: lubrication n, greasing n
grammage m
 D: Flächengewicht n (Papier)
 E: substance n (paper weight in g/m²)
grandeur f **de référence**
 D: Bezugsgröße f
 E: reference quantity
grandeur f **de retrait**
 D: Schrumpfmaß n
 E: shrinkage allowance
grandeur f **mesurée**
 D: Meßgröße f
 E: quantity to be measured, measured quantity
granulaire adj
 D: körnig adj
 E: grained adj, granular adj
granulateur m
 D: Granulator m
 E: granulator n, granulating machine, dicer n, pelletizer n
granuler v
 D: granulieren v
 E: pelletize v, granulate v
granulés m pl
 D: Granulat n
 E: granules pl, pellets pl, granulate n
granuleux adj
 D: körnig adj
 E: grained adj, granular adj
graphique m
 D: Kurvenbild n, Diagramm n, graphische Darstellung
 E: diagram n, graph n, graphic

graphique
representation, chart n

graphique m de processus
D: Ablaufplan m, Ablaufdiagramm n, Arbeitsablaufdiagramm n, Flußdiagramm n, Fertigungsflußschema n
E: flow chart, flow diagram, process (flow) chart

grenaille de plomb, bain de ~
D: Schrotkugelbad n, Bleikugelbad n
E: lead ball bath, lead-shot bath

grenu adj
D: körnig adj
E: grained adj, granular adj

grillage m (dans l'extrudeuse)
D: Anbrennen n (im Extruder)
E: scorching n (in extruder cylinder)

grille f à câbles [pose c.]
D: Kabelrost m, Rost m
E: cable grate

grille f protectrice
D: Schutzgitter n
E: wire mesh guard

grip m de câble
D: Ziehstrumpf m (für Kabel)
E: cable stocking, cable grip

grip m de câble à double agrafe
D: Ziehstrumpf mit zwei Schlaufen
E: double-eye cable grip

gros câbles m pl
D: Kabel mit großen Querschnitten
E: cables with big cross-sectional areas, large-size cables

gros fil m
D: dicker Draht
E: large-diameter wire, large-size wire

grosseur f du fil métallique
D: Drahtdicke f, Drahtklasse f, Drahtlehre f
E: wire gauge, wire size

grosseur f du grain
D: Korngröße f
E: grain size

grossir v
D: vergrößern v
E: increase v, extend v, enlarge v, magnify v

grossissement m des grains
D: Kornwachstum n
E: grain growth

groupe m
D: Aggregat n
E: aggregate n, set n, unit n

groupe m électrogène de secours
D: Notstrom-Aggregat n
E: stand-by power unit, emergency generator set

groupement m
D: Auslegung f (Planung), Anordnung f, Anlage f (Auslegung)
E: layout n, arrangement n

groupement m de câbles [pose c.]
D: Häufung von Kabeln, Anhäufung von Kabeln, Ballung von Kabeln, Belegung mit Kabeln
E: grouping of cables, accumulation of cables

groupement m de longueurs de fabrication
D: Gruppieren von Fertigungslängen
E: grouping of factory lengths

groupe m réfrigérant
D: Kühlaggregat n
E: cooling set, refrigeration unit

grue, chemin de roulement de la ~
D: Kranbahn f
E: crane rail

grue f (à) portique
D: Portalkran m
E: gantry crane

guide m d'ondes [com.]
D: Hohlleiter m, Wellenleiter m
E: waveguide n

guide m d'ondes en fibres de verre
D: Glasfaser-Wellenleiter m
E: glass fibre waveguide

guide m d'ondes rectangulaire
D: Rechteck-Hohlleiter m
E: rectangular waveguide

guide-fil m
D: Drahtführung f
E: wire guide

guipage m
D: Bespinnung f (mit Kordel, Garn), Umspinnung f (mit Kordel, Garn)
E: spinning n

guiper v
D: mit Papierkordel umspinnen
E: to apply the paper string, to spin the paper string

guipeuse f
D: Kordelspinnmaschine f
E: string spinning machine

gutta-percha f
D: Guttapercha f

E: gutta percha

H

haltère, en forme d'~
D: hantelförmig *adj*
E: dumb-bell shaped

harnais *m* **de câbles**
D: Kabelbaum *m*, Kabelsatz *m*
E: cable harness, wiring harness, cable assembly

haute fréquence (HF) *f*
D: Hochfrequenz (HF) *f*
E: high frequency (HF), radio frequency

haute tension (HT) *f*
D: Hochspannung *f*
E: high voltage (HV), high tension

hauteur, réglable en ~
D: in der Höhe verstellbar
E: vertically adjustable

hauteur *f* **de flèche**
D: Durchhanghöhe *f*
E: sag clearance

hauteur de la tête, cabestan de tirage au-dessus de la ~
D: Überkopfabzug *m*
E: overhead pull-off

hauteur *f* **du secteur**
D: Sektorhöhe *f* (des Leiters)
E: sector height

haut polymère *m*
D: Hochpolymerisat *n*
E: high-polymer *n*

hélice, en ~ fermée [rub.]
D: auf Stoß
E: without butt gaps, in a closed helix

hélice, fil ~ de support
D: Anwendeldraht *m* (Luftkabel)
E: lashing wire

hélice, poser en ~
D: wendelförmig aufbringen
E: to apply helically, to apply spirally

hélice *f* **anti-torsion**
D: Gegenwendel *f*
E: anti-twist tape, counter helix

hélice *f* **colorée**
D: farbige Spirale, farbige Wendel
E: colo(u)red spiral, colo(u)red helix

hélice *f* **de feuillard d'acier**
D: Stahlbandwendel *f*
E: steel tape helix

hélice *f* **d'essai**
D: Wickellocke *f*
E: helical coil

hélice *f* **de support**
D: Stützwendel *f* (im Hohlleiter)
E: central spiral, support helix

hélice *f* **de vide**
D: offene Wendel
E: open helix

hélice *f* **fermée**
D: geschlossene Wendel
E: closed helix

hermétique *adj*
D: vakuumdicht *adj*
E: vacuum-tight *adj*, vacuum-sealed *adj*

hertz
D: Hertz (Hz)
E: cycles per second (cps), hertz

heures *f pl* **de pointe**
D: Spitzenbelastungszeit *f*
E: peak hours *pl*

hexafluorure *f* **de soufre**
D: Schwefelhexafluorid (SF6) *n*
E: sulphur hexafluoride (SF6)

HF (v. haute frequence)

homogène *adj*
D: einheitlich *adj*
E: uniform *adj*, consistent *adj*, homogeneous *adj*

homogénéisation, zone d'~ d'une vis [extr.]
D: Homogenisierzone einer Schnecke
E: metering section of a screw

homologation *f*
D: Zulassung *f*
E: approval *n*, certification *n*

hors service
D: außer Betrieb
E: out of operation, out of order, out of service

hotte *f*
D: Abzug *m* (Lüftung), Absaughaube *f*
E: exhaust *n*, exhaust hood, fume hood

hotte *f*
D: Kapelle *f* (Abzug)
E: hood *n*

HT (v. haute tension)

hublot *m* **de regard** [mach.]
D: Beobachtungsfenster *n*, Schauglas

hublot

    n, Schauloch *n*
    E: peephole *n,* sight glass, observation window, inspection glass

huile *f* à faible viscosité
    D: niedrigviskoses Öl
    E: low-viscosity oil

huile *f* à viscosité élevée
    D: hochviskoses Öl
    E: high-viscosity oil

huile *f* brute à la base de paraffine
    D: paraffinbasisches Rohöl
    E: paraffin base crude oil

huile *f* brute naphténique
    D: naphtenbasisches Rohöl
    E: naphthene base crude oil

huile *f* de condensateur
    D: Kondensatoröl *n*
    E: capacitor oil, condenser oil

huile *f* de tréfilage [fabr. fils mét.]
    D: Ziehöl *n*
    E: drawing oil

huile *f* isolante
    D: Isolieröl *n*
    E: insulating oil

huile *f* minérale
    D: Mineralöl *n*
    E: mineral oil

humecter *v*
    D: anfeuchten *v,* benetzen *v,* befeuchten *v*
    E: wet *v,* moisten *v*

humidité *f*
    D: Feuchtigkeit *f*
    E: humidity *n,* moisture *n*

humidité *f* de l'air
    D: Luftfeuchtigkeit *f*
    E: atmospheric humidity, humidity of the air

humidité *f* relative
    D: relative Luftfeuchtigkeit *f*
    E: relative humidity

hydrocarbure, polymères d'~
    D: Kohlenwasserstoffpolymere *n pl*
    E: hydrocarbon polymers

hydrofuge *adj*
    D: wasserabstoßend *adj*
    E: water repellent, hydrophobic *adj*

hydrophobe *adj*
    D: wasserabstoßend *adj*
    E: water repellent, hydrophobic *adj*

I

IACS (valeur standard de la résistivité du cuivre recuit) (selon la CEI)
    D: IACS (Standardwert des spezifischen Widerstandes von weichgeglühtem Kupfer) (nach IEC)
    E: IACS (International Annealed Copper Standard) (according to IEC)

identification *f* [câb.]
    D: Kennzeichnung *f*
    E: identification *n,* marking *n,* coding *n*

imbriqué, papier carbone et papier métallisé ~s
    D: dachziegelartig aufgebrachtes Rußpapier und metallisiertes Papier
    E: carbon-loaded paper interlocked with metallized paper

imbriqué, rubans ~s
    D: dachziegelartig aufgebrachte Bänder
    E: intercalated tapes, interlocked tapes

immerger *v*
    D: eintauchen *v*
    E: immerse *v,* dip *v*

immersion *f* dans l'eau
    D: Lagerung in Wasser, Wasserlagerung *f,* Eintauchen in Wasser
    E: immersion in water, water immersion

impédance *f*
    D: Scheinwiderstand *m*
    E: impedance *n*

impédance *f* caractéristique
    D: Wellenwiderstand *m*
    E: characteristic impedance

impédance *f* caractéristique de câble
    D: Kabelwiderstand *m*
    E: characteristic cable impedance

impédance *f* d'entrée
    D: Eingangsimpedanz *f*
    E: input impedance

impédance *f* du réseau
    D: Netzwiderstand *m*
    E: network impedance

impénétrable *adj* **pour**

impératif m
  D: Anforderung f
  E: requirement n, demand n

imperfection f **superficielle**
  D: Oberflächenfehler m
  E: surface defect, surface imperfection, surface irregularity

imperméabilité f
  D: Undurchlässigkeit f
  E: impermeability n

imperméabilité f **au gaz**
  D: Gasdichtigkeit f, Gasundurchlässigkeit f
  E: impermeability to gas, gas-tightness n, gas impermeability

imperméable, câble ~ à l'eau
  D: längswasserdichtes Kabel
  E: water-proof cable, water-tight cable

imperméable adj **à**
  D: undurchlässig für ...
  E: impermeable to ..., impervious to ..., impenetrable to ...

imperméable adj **au gaz**
  D: gasundurchlässig adj
  E: gas-tight adj, impermeable to gas

implantation f
  D: Errichtung f, Montage f, Aufbau m
  E: installation n, erection n, set-up n, assembly n

implantation f **d'une usine**
  D: Standort eines Werkes
  E: location of a factory

implantation f **du poste de travail**
  D: Arbeitsplatzgestaltung f
  E: workplace layout

imprécis adj
  D: ungenau adj
  E: inexact adj, inaccurate adj

imprécision f
  D: Ungenauigkeit f (Anzeige, Messung)
  E: inaccuracy n, inexactitude n

imprégnant m
  D: Tränkmittel n
  E: impregnating medium, impregnant n

imprégnation f
  D: Imprägnierung f, Tränkung f
  E: impregnation n

imprégnation, isolation à ~ totale
  D: vollimprägnierte Isolierung
  E: fully impregnated insulation

imprégnation f **en vernis**
  D: Lackimprägnierung f
  E: varnish impregnation

imprégné adj
  D: durchtränkt adj
  E: impregnated adj

imprégné adj **de matière**
  D: massegetränkt adj
  E: mass-impregnated adj, compound-impregnated adj

imprégné adj **jusqu'à saturation**
  D: sattgetränkt adj
  E: fully impregnated

imprégner v
  D: tränken v
  E: impregnate v

impression f
  D: Prägung f
  E: embossing n

impression, dispositif d'~
  D: Bedruckungsvorrichtung f
  E: printer n, printing device

imprimer v
  D: prägen v
  E: emboss v

imprimer v
  D: bedrucken v
  E: print v

impulsion f **de contrôle**
  D: Steuerimpuls m
  E: control signal pulse

impureté f
  D: Verunreinigung f
  E: contamination n, impurity n

inaccessible adj
  D: unzugänglich adj
  E: inaccessible adj

inadmissible adj
  D: unzulässig adj
  E: inadmissible adj

incendie, non propagateur de l'~
  D: flammwidrig adj, einen Brand nicht weiterleitend
  E: flame-resistant adj, non fire propagating

incident m **de fonctionnement**
  D: Ausfall m (Anlage, Kabel), Betriebsstörung f
  E: failure n, breakdown n, outage n

incinération f

incinération
  D: Veraschung f
  E: incineration n
inclinable adj
  D: kippbar adj
  E: inclinable adj, tiltable adj
inclinaison f
  D: Neigung f
  E: inclination n, tilting n, tilt n
inclinaison f d'une courbe
  D: Abfall einer Kurve, Neigung einer Kurve
  E: decline of a curve, slope of a curve
incliné adj
  D: schräg adj
  E: inclined adj, oblique adj
inclusions f pl
  D: Einschlüsse m pl
  E: inclusions pl
inclusions f pl d'oxyde
  D: Oxideinschlüsse m pl
  E: oxide inclusions
inclusions f pl granuleuses
  D: körnige Einschlüsse
  E: grained inclusions
incolore, matière plastique ~
  D: ungefärbter Kunststoff, farbloser Kunststoff
  E: uncoloured plastic, natural-coloured plastic, unpigmented plastic, natural plastic (US)
incombustibilité f
  D: Unbrennbarkeit f
  E: incombustibility n
incombustible adj
  D: unbrennbar adj
  E: non-inflammable adj, flame-proof adj, non-combustible adj, incombustible adj
incorporé adj
  D: eingebaut adj
  E: built-in adj, enclosed adj
incurvation f
  D: Krümmung f, Biegung f
  E: curvature n, bend n, deflection n
indélébile adj
  D: unauslöschlich adj (Farbe)
  E: indelible adj, fast adj
indépendant adj de la température
  D: temperaturunabhängig adj
  E: temperature-independent adj
indépendant adj du réseau
  D: netzunabhängig adj
  E: non-system-dependent adj, non-system-connected adj
indicateur m
  D: Anzeigevorrichtung f
  E: indicator n, display unit
indicateur m à cadran
  D: Meßuhr f
  E: indicating dial
indicateur m de courant
  D: Stromanzeiger m
  E: current indicator
indicateur m de défauts
  D: Fehleranzeiger m, Fehleranzeige-Einrichtung f
  E: error indicator, fault indicator
indicateur m de niveau d'eau
  D: Wasserstandsanzeiger m
  E: water level indicator
indicateur m d'erreur
  D: Fehleranzeiger m, Fehleranzeige-Einrichtung f
  E: error indicator, fault indicator
indicateur m de température
  D: Temperaturanzeiger m
  E: temperature indicator
indicateur m du niveau
  D: Füllstandsanzeiger m
  E: level indicator
indicateur m du niveau d'huile
  D: Ölstandsanzeiger m
  E: oil level indicator
indication f
  D: Anzeige f
  E: indication n, display n, reading n
indice m d'acide
  D: Säurezahl f
  E: acid number
indice m de fluage, de fluidité, de fusion
  D: Schmelzindex m
  E: melt flow index
indice m de neutralisation
  D: Neutralisationszahl (NZ) f
  E: neutralisation number
indice m de réfraction
  D: Brechungsindex m
  E: refraction index
indice m de saponification
  D: Verseifungszahl f
  E: saponification value, saponification number
indivisé adj
  D: einteilig adj
  E: single-piece... adj, one-piece... adj,

monobloc *adj*

inductance *f*
 D: Induktivität *f*
 E: inductance *n*

inductance *f* **de ligne**
 D: Leitungsinduktivität *f*
 E: line inductance

induction *f* **mutuelle**
 D: Gegeninduktivität *f*
 E: mutual inductance

inefficace *adj*
 D: unwirksam *adj*
 E: ineffective *adj*, inoperative *adj*

inégal *adj*
 D: uneben *adj*
 E: uneven *adj*

inerte *adj*
 D: reaktionsträge *adj*
 E: inert *adj*

inexact *adj*
 D: ungenau *adj*
 E: inexact *adj*, inaccurate *adj*

inexactitude *f*
 D: Ungenauigkeit *f* (Anzeige, Messung)
 E: inaccuracy *n*, inexactitude *n*

inférieur, être ~ à
 D: unterschreiten *v*
 E: to fall short of

infiltration *f* **d'eau**
 D: Eindringen von Wasser (in Kabel)
 E: water seeping, water seepage, water penetration

inflammabilité *f*
 D: Entzündbarkeit *f*
 E: inflammability *n*

inflammable *adj*
 D: brennbar *adj*, entflammbar *adj*
 E: flammable *adj* (US), inflammable *adj* (GB), , combustible *adj*

influence *f* **atmosphérique**
 D: Witterungseinfluß *m*
 E: atmospheric influence

influencé *adj* **par la température**
 D: temperaturabhängig *adj*
 E: temperature-dependent *adj*

ingénieur *m* **de construction des câbles**
 D: Kabelkonstrukteur *m*
 E: cable design engineer

ingénieur *m* **de fabrication**
 D: Betriebsingenieur *m*
 E: manufacturing engineer, production engineer

ingrédients *m pl* **d'un mélange**
 D: Mischungsbestandteile *m pl*
 E: ingredients of a compound

inhibiteur *m*
 D: Inhibitor *m*
 E: inhibitor *n*

inhibiteur *m* **d'oxydation**
 D: Oxydationsinhibitor *m*, Oxydationsverzögerer *m*, Alterungsschutzmittel *n*, Antioxidans *n*
 E: antioxidant *n*, oxidation inhibitor

inintelligible, diaphonie ~ (non linéaire)
 D: unverständliches (nicht lineares) Nebensprechen
 E: unintelligible (non linear) cross-talk

injecteur *m*
 D: Düse *f*
 E: nozzle *n*, jet *n*, orifice *n*

inorganique *adj*
 D: anorganisch *adj*
 E: inorganic *adj*

inoxydable *adj*
 D: nichtrostend *adj*, rostbeständig *adj*
 E: stainless *adj*, rust-resisting *adj*

insensible *adj* **à ...**
 D: unempfindlich gegen ...
 E: insensitive to ...

insensible, les mesures sont ~s aux décharges de faible importance
 D: die Messungen erfassen kleine Entladungen nicht mehr
 E: the measurements are insensitive to small discharges

insérer *v*
 D: einsetzen *v*, einbauen *v*
 E: insert *v*, mount *v*, fit *v*

inspecter *v*
 D: besichtigen *v*
 E: inspect *v*, survey *v*

inspection *f*
 D: visuelle Prüfung
 E: visual examination, visual control, inspection *n*

inspection *f* **microscopique**
 D: mikroskopische Untersuchung
 E: microscopic inspection

installation *f* [mach.]
 D: Anlage *f*
 E: plant *n*, unit *n*, installation *n*, equipment *n*, line *n*

installation

installation, câble pour ~ intérieure
  D: Innenraumleitung *f*
  E: indoor wiring cable
installation *f* à l'échelle industrielle
  D: Anlage im Betriebsmaßstab
  E: commercial size plant
installation *f* (achevée) clé en main
  D: schlüsselfertige Anlage
  E: turnkey installation
installation *f* continue de recuit par résistance
  D: kontinuierliche Widerstandsglühanlage
  E: continuous resistance annealer
installation *f* continue de tréfilage, recuit et isolement
  D: kontinuierliche Drahtzieh-, Glüh- und Isolier-Anlage
  E: tandem wire drawing, annealing and insulating line
installation *f* d'adoucissement
  D: Enthärtungsanlage *f*
  E: softening plant
installation *f* d'aspiration
  D: Absauganlage *f*
  E: suction system, exhaust system
installation *f* de commutation
  D: Schaltanlage *f*
  E: switching station, switch gear
installation *f* de décapage
  D: Beizanlage *f*
  E: pickling plant
installation *f* de disjoncteurs basse tension
  D: Niederspannungsschaltanlage *f*
  E: low voltage switchgear
installation *f* de disjoncteurs haute tension
  D: Hochspannungsschaltanlage *f*
  E: high-voltage switchgear
installation *f* de distribution
  D: Schaltanlage *f*
  E: switching station, switch gear
installation *f* de préparation des mélanges de caoutchouc
  D: Gummimischerei *f*
  E: rubber mixing plant
installation *f* de préparation des mélanges plastiques
  D: Kunststoff-Mischerei *f*
  E: plastics mixing plant
installation *f* de préparation des mélanges
  D: Mischanlage *f*
  E: mixing plant
installation *f* de réception collective d'antenne de télévision
  D: Großgemeinschaftsantennen-Anlage (GGA) *f*
  E: Community Antenna Television System (CATV)
installation *f* de recuit en tandem
  D: Durchlaufglühanlage *f* (gekoppelt mit Feindraht-Ziehmaschine), kontinuierliche Drahtzieh- und Glühanlage
  E: tandem annealer, continuous wire drawing and annealing machine
installation *f* de récupération d'acide
  D: Säurerückgewinnungsanlage *f*
  E: acid recovery plant
installation *f* de récupération du fil métallique à partir des déchets de câble
  D: Rückgewinnungsanlage für Draht aus Kabelabfällen
  E: wire reclaiming system
installation *f* de refroidissement en cascades
  D: Kaskadenkühler *m* (Granulat)
  E: cascades cooler
installation *f* de sélecteurs à panneau
  D: Flachwähl-Anlage *f*
  E: panel switching equipment
installation *f* d'essai
  D: Versuchsanlage *f*
  E: test(ing) installation, trial installation, pilot installation
installation *f* de télécommunication
  D: Fernmeldeanlage *f*
  E: telecommunications system
installation *f* de transport
  D: Förderanlage *f*
  E: conveying system, conveyor *n*, feed system
installation *f* de transport par rouleaux
  D: Rollenförderer *m*
  E: roller (type) conveyor
installation *f* en sous-sol
  D: Unterflur-Installation *f*
  E: subsurface installation, installation below floor level
installation *f* expérimentale
  D: Versuchsanlage *f*
  E: test(ing) installation, trial installation, pilot installation

installation f **extérieure**
  D: Freiluft-Anlage f
  E: outdoor plant
installation f **fixe** [câb.]
  D: feste Verlegung
  E: fixed installation, permanent installation
installation f **indépendante ne nécessitant pas d'entretien**
  D: wartungsfreie Anlage
  E: self-contained system
installation f **intérieure**
  D: Innenraum-Anlage f
  E: indoor plant
installation f **intérieure**
  D: Hausinstallation f
  E: house wiring
installation f **sous crépi**
  D: Unterputz-Installation f, Verlegung unter Putz
  E: buried wiring, concealed wiring, installation under plaster
installation f **souterraine**
  D: Unterflur-Installation f
  E: subsurface installation, installation below floor level
installation f **verticale** [câb.]
  D: Hochführung f
  E: vertical installation
installer v
  D: errichten v
  E: set up v, install v, mount v, erect v, assemble v
instantané, tenue au claquage ~e
  D: Sofortdurchschlagfestigkeit f
  E: instantaneous breakdown strength
institut m **de certification**
  D: Prüfstelle f
  E: approval organization, testing station
instructions f pl **de montage**
  D: Montageanleitung f
  E: fitting instructions pl, installation instructions pl
instructions f pl **d'entretien**
  D: Wartungsvorschrift f
  E: maintenance instructions pl
instructions f pl **de travail**
  D: Arbeitsanweisung f
  E: working instructions pl
instrument m
  D: Gerät n
  E: apparatus n, instrument n, device n, equipment n
intact adj
  D: unbeschädigt adj
  E: intact adj, undamaged adj
intelligible, diaphonie ~ (linéaire)
  D: verständliches (lineares) Nebensprechen
  E: intelligible (linear) cross-talk
intempéries f pl
  D: Witterungseinfluß m
  E: atmospheric influence
intempéries, exposer aux ~
  D: bewittern v
  E: weather v
intensité f [él.]
  D: Stärke f
  E: intensity n
intensité m **de champ au conducteur**
  D: Leiterfeldstärke f
  E: conductor field strength, conductor gradient
intensité f **de claquage**
  D: Durchschlagfeldstärke f
  E: breakdown stress, breakdown gradient, breakdown field strength
intensité f **de courant**
  D: Stromstärke f
  E: current intensity, amperage n
intensité f **de décharge**
  D: Entladungsintensität f
  E: discharge intensity
intensité f **de service**
  D: Betriebsfeldstärke f
  E: operating stress, operating field strength
intensité f **du champ** [él.]
  D: Feldstärke f
  E: field strength
interaction f
  D: Wechselwirkung f
  E: interplay n, interaction n
interchangeable adj
  D: auswechselbar adj, austauschbar adj
  E: interchangeable adj, replaceable adj
interconnexion f **des phases**
  D: Phasenverkettung f
  E: interlinking of phases
interface f
  D: Grenzfläche f
  E: interface n
interférence f

interférence

D: Störbeeinflussung *f,* Beeinflussung *f*
E: interference *n* (effect)

interférence *f* **mutuelle**
D: gegenseitige Störungen
E: mutual interference

interposé *adj*
D: eingelagert *adj,* zwischengelagert *adj*
E: intercalated *adj,* sandwiched *adj* between,

interposer *v*
D: zwischenschalten *v*
E: interpose *v,* insert *v*

interposition *f*
D: Einlagerung *f,* Zwischenlagerung *f*
E: incorporation *n,* insertion *n,* intercalation *n*

interrompre *v* [él.]
D: abschalten *v,* ausschalten *v*
E: switch off *v,* interrupt *v,* disconnect *v,* turn off (US) *v,* de-energize *v,* cut out *v*

interrupteur *m*
D: Ausschalter *m,* Abschalter *m*
E: circuit breaker, cut-out switch, disconnecting switch

interrupteur *m*
D: Schalter *m*
E: switch *n*

interrupteur *m* **à flotteur** [él.]
D: Schwimmerschalter *m*
E: float (type) switch

interrupteur *m* **à maximum de tension**
D: Überspannungsschalter *m*
E: overvoltage circuit-breaker, maximum voltage circuit-breaker

interrupteur *m* **automatique**
D: Selbstausschalter *m*
E: automatic cut-out

interrupteur *m* **de fin de course**
D: Endschalter *m*
E: limit switch

interrupteur *m* **de réseau**
D: Netzschalter *m*
E: power switch

interrupteur *m* **de sécurité**
D: Schutzschalter *m*
E: line protection switch, overcurrent cut-out switch, protective switch

interrupteur *m* **de surcharge**
D: Überlastschalter *m*
E: overload circuit breaker

interrupteur *m* **monté sur crépi**
D: Aufputz-Schalter *m*
E: surface-mounted switch

interrupteur *m* **terminal**
D: Endschalter *m*
E: limit switch

intersection *f*
D: Knotenpunkt *m*
E: intersection *n,* junction point

interstices *m pl*
D: Zwickelräume *m pl* (zwischen den Kabeladern)
E: interstices *pl*

intervalle *m*
D: Zwischenraum *m*
E: clearance *n,* gap *n,* interstice *n,* interspace *n,* interval *n,* spacing *n*

intervalle, sans ~s
D: stufenlos *adj*
E: stepless *adj,* continuously adjustable, infinitely variable

intervalle *m* **de charge**
D: Belastungspause *f*
E: load pause

intervalle *m* **de vulcanisation**
D: Vulkanisationsbereich *m*
E: curing range, vulcanization range

intervalle *m* **imperméable** [com.]
D: Sperrbereich *m*
E: cut-off range suppression band

introduction *f* **dans un conduit** [pose c.]
D: Einführen in einen Kanalzug
E: duct rodding

introduire *v*
D: einführen *v*
E: insert *v,* introduce *v,* lead in *v*

introduire *v* **les câbles dans des installations électriques**
D: Kabel in elektrische Anlagen einführen
E: to terminate cables on to electrical plant

inutilisable *adj*
D: betriebsuntauglich *adj*
E: unserviceable *adj*

inversion, essai à ~ de la polarité
D: Prüfung mit wechselnder Polarität
E: polarity inversion test

inversion *f* **de la torsion**
D: Drallwechsel *m*
E: reversal of lay, change of lay

inversion *f* **de polarité**
D: Umpolung *f,* Polwechsel *m,*

Umkehr der Polarität
E: change of polarity, pole reversal, pole changing

inverti, extrémité de câble du type ~
D: umgekehrter Kabelendverschluß
E: inverted type cable termination

ionisation f
D: Ionisation f
E: ionization n

ionisation f **par choc**
D: Stoßionisation f
E: ionization by collision, impact ionization

irradié, polyéthylène ~
D: bestrahltes PE
E: irradiated PE

isolant m
D: Isolierstoff m, Isoliermaterial n
E: insulating material, insulant n

isolant m
D: Isolierung f, Dielektrikum n
E: insulation n, dielectric n

isolant m **air/papier**
D: Papier-Luftraumisolierung f, Papier-Hohlraumisolierung f
E: air-space(d) paper insulation

isolant m **égoutté après imprégnation**
D: massearme Isolierung
E: mass-impregnated and drained insulation

isolant m **gazeux**
D: gasförmiger Isolierstoff
E: gaseous insulating material

isolant m **papier**
D: Papierisolierung f
E: paper insulation

isolant m **papier échelonné**
D: geschichtete Papierisolierung
E: graded paper insulation

isolant m **pâte à papier**
D: Papierpulpisolierung f
E: paper pulp insulation

isolant m **plastique**
D: Kunststoff-Isolierung f
E: plastic insulation, synthetic insulation

isolant m **sec**
D: Isolierung aus extrudiertem homogenem Material
E: solid insulation, solid dielectric

isolant m **solide**
D: Isolierung aus extrudiertem homogenem Material
E: solid insulation, solid dielectric

isolant m **stratifié en papier/matière plastique**
D: Papier/Kunststoff-Schichtenisolierung f
E: paper/plastic laminate insulation

isolant m **synthétique**
D: Kunststoff-Isolierung f
E: plastic insulation, synthetic insulation

isolateur m
D: Isolator m
E: insulator n

isolateur m **à cloche**
D: Glockenisolator m, Isolierglocke f
E: shed insulator, cup insulator, bell-shaped insulator, dome-shaped insulator, petticoat insulator, insulating bell

isolateur m **à double cloche**
D: Doppelglockenisolator m
E: double shed insulator

isolateur m **à double rainure**
D: Glockenisolator mit doppelter Bundrille, Glockenisolator mit zwei Halsrillen
E: double groove insulator

isolateur m **à nervures**
D: Rippenisolator m
E: ribbed insulator

isolateur m **d'entrée**
D: Einführungsisolator m
E: inlet insulator, lead-in insulator

isolateur m **de poteau**
D: Mast-Endverschluß m
E: pole-mounted termination

isolateur m **de suspension**
D: Kettenisolator m, Hängeisolator m
E: suspension insulator, chain insulator

isolateur m **de traversée**
D: Durchführungs-Isolator m
E: bushing insulator

isolateur m **en forme de champignon**
D: Pilzisolator m
E: mushroom insulator

isolateur m **en porcelaine**
D: Porzellanisolator m
E: porcelain insulator

isolateur m **en résine moulée**
D: Gießharz-Isolator m
E: casting resin insulator

isolateur m **en verre**

isolateur

- D: Glasisolator *m*
- E: glass insulator

isolateur *m* rigide
- D: Stützisolator *m*
- E: post insulator, pin insulator, pole-mounted insulator

isolateur *m* support
- D: Stützisolator *m*
- E: post insulator, pin insulator, pole-mounted insulator

isolateur *m* suspendu
- D: Kettenisolator *m*, Hängeisolator *m*
- E: suspension insulator, chain insulator

isolateur *m* type parapluie
- D: Schirmisolator *m*
- E: umbrella type insulator

isolation *f*
- D: Isolierung *f*, Dielektrikum *n*
- E: insulation *n*, dielectric *n*

isolation *f*
- D: Isolation *f*, Isolierung *f* (Trennung)
- E: isolation *n*

isolation *f* à imprégnation totale
- D: vollimprägnierte Isolierung
- E: fully impregnated insulation

isolation *f* ballon
- D: „Ballon"-Isolierung *f*
- E: balloon insulation

isolation *f* caoutchouc
- D: Gummiisolierung *f*
- E: rubber insulation

isolation *f* du conducteur
- D: Aderisolierung *f*
- E: core insulation

isolation *f* en toile vernie
- D: Lackgewebe-Isolierung *f*
- E: varnished cambric insulation

isolation *f* laminée
- D: Mehrschicht-Isolierung *f*, Schichtisolierung *f*
- E: laminated insulation, laminar insulation, composite bonded laminar insulation

isolation *f* par disques [c. com.]
- D: Scheibenisolierung *f*
- E: disc insulation

isolation *f* PVC
- D: PVC-Isolierung *f*
- E: PVC insulation

isolation *f* rubanée
- D: Bandisolierung *f*, gewickelte Isolierung
- E: tape insulation, taped insulation, lapped insulation

isolation *f* rubanée en papier
- D: Isolierung aus Papierbandumspinnung, Papierbandisolierung *f*
- E: paper tape insulation, lapped paper insulation, spiral strip paper insulation (US), paper ribbon insulation (US)

isolation *f* stratifiée
- D: Mehrschicht-Isolierung *f*, Schichtisolierung *f*
- E: laminated insulation, laminar insulation, composite bonded laminar insulation

isolation *f* thermique
- D: Wärmeschutz *m* (über Kabelisolierung)
- E: heat barrier, thermal barrier

isolé, câble ~ au papier
- D: papierisoliertes Kabel, Papierkabel *n*
- E: paper-insulated cable

isolé *adj* et blindé entièrement
- D: voll-isoliert und gekapselt (Schaltelemente)
- E: fully insulated and enclosed

isolement *m*
- D: Isolierung *f*, Dielektrikum *n*
- E: insulation *n*, dielectric *n*

isolement *m*
- D: Isolation *f*, Isolierung *f* (Trennung)
- E: isolation *n*

isolement *m* par rapport à la terre
- D: Isolation gegen Erde
- E: insulation against ground

isoler *v*
- D: isolieren *v*
- E: insulate *v*, isolate *v*

J

jarretière *f*
- D: Schaltader *f*, Schaltdraht *m*
- E: jumper wire, cross-connecting wire, hook-up wire

jauge *f*
- D: Eichmaß *n*
- E: gauge *n*, standard *n*

jaugeage m
  D: Eichung f
  E: calibration n, adjusting n, gauging n

jauge f **des fils**
  D: Drahtdicke f, Drahtklasse f, Drahtlehre f
  E: wire gauge, wire size

jauge f **d'excentricité**
  D: Exzentrizitäts-Meßvorrichtung f
  E: eccentricity gauge

jeu m
  D: Zwischenraum m
  E: clearance n, gap n, interstice n, interspace n, interval n, spacing n

jeu m **à l'entraînement**
  D: Achsenspiel n
  E: play of axis, backlash of axis

jeu m **de bobines de charge**
  D: Pupinspulensatz m, Spulensatz m
  E: loading coil unit, loading unit (tel. c.)

jeu m **entre cylindres** [lam.]
  D: Walzenspalt m (Mischungsherstellung), Walzenstellung f (Mischungsherstellung)
  E: gap between rolls, nip between rolls

jeu m **sur axe**
  D: Achsenspiel n
  E: play of axis, backlash of axis

joindre v
  D: verbinden v
  E: join v, joint v, connect v, link v

joint m
  D: Spleißstelle f, Spleiß m, Spleißverbindung f
  E: splice n, spliced joint

joint m
  D: Dichtung f
  E: seal n, packing n

joint m [ruban. pap.]
  D: Spinnfuge f, Fuge f, Stoßfuge f, Stoßkantenzwischenraum m
  E: butt space, butt gap, gap n

joint m **annulaire**
  D: Dichtungsring m
  E: sealing ring, joint ring

joint m **d'arrêt**
  D: Sperrmuffe f
  E: stop joint

joint m **d'eau** [vulc.]
  D: Wasserdichtung f
  E: water seal

joint m **d'étanchéité**
  D: Dichtung f
  E: seal n, packing n

joint m **de transition**
  D: Übergangsmuffe f
  E: transition joint, transition sleeve

joint m **de tuyaux**
  D: Rohrverbindung f
  E: pipe connection, pipe joint

jointif, rubanage ~
  D: anlappende Bandumspinnung
  E: butted taping

joints m pl **des grains**
  D: Korngrenzen f pl
  E: grain boundaries

joint m **soudé**
  D: Schweißstelle f, Schweißverbindung f
  E: welded joint

joint m **soudé**
  D: Lötverbindung f (weich), Lötstelle f
  E: soldered joint, soldering joint

jonction f [câb.]
  D: Muffe f
  E: joint n

jonction f
  D: Verbindung f, Verbindungsstelle f
  E: joint n, connection n

jonction, faire des ~s **sur câble**
  D: Kabelverbindungen herstellen
  E: to joint cables

jonction f **débrochable**
  D: Steckverbindung f, Steckanschluß m
  E: plug and socket connection

jonction f **droite**
  D: Durchgangsmuffe f
  E: straight joint, straight-through joint

jonction f **en forme de T**
  D: T-Abzweigmuffe f
  E: T-joint n, tee-joint n, tee-off fitting

jonction f **en résine moulée**
  D: Gießharz-Muffe f
  E: casting resin joint

jonction épissée f
  D: Spleißstelle f, Spleiß m, Spleißverbindung f
  E: splice n, spliced joint

jonction épissée, manchon sur ~ [c.

jonction
    com.]
    D: Spleißmuffengehäuse n
    E: splice case, splice closure
jonction f par soudure
    D: Lötverbindung f (weich), Lötstelle f
    E: soldered joint, soldering joint
jonction f reconstituée
    D: gewickelte Muffe, Wickelmuffe f
    E: lapped joint
joue f de bobine
    D: Spulenflansch m
    E: reel flange, spool flange
joue f de touret [câb.]
    D: Trommelscheibe f, Trommelflansch m
    E: reel flange, drum flange
jute, filin de ~
    D: Jute-Garn n
    E: jute yarn
jute, tête à ~
    D: Jute-Wickler m
    E: jute serving head, jute spinner
jute f compoundée
    D: compoundierte Jute
    E: compounded jute

K

kaolin m
    D: Kaolin n
    E: china clay, kaolin n
Krarup, câble ~
    D: Krarup-Kabel n
    E: Krarup cable, continuously loaded cable
krarupisation f [c. com.]
    D: Krarupisieren n
    E: continuous loading
krarupisé, câble ~
    D: Krarup-Kabel n
    E: Krarup cable, continuously loaded cable

L

lait m de chaux
    D: Kalkmilch f
    E: lime milk
lame f
    D: Klinge f
    E: blade n
laminé m
    D: Schichtstoff m
    E: laminate n, laminated plastic, laminated material
laminer v [mét.]
    D: walzen v
    E: roll v
laminer v à chaud
    D: warmwalzen v
    E: hot-roll v
laminer v à froid
    D: kaltwalzen v
    E: cold-roll v
laminoir m [mét.]
    D: Walzwerk n
    E: rolling mill
laminoir m à chaud
    D: Warmwalzwerk n
    E: hot-rolling mill
laminoir m à fils métalliques
    D: Drahtwalzen n
    E: wire rolling mill, rod rolling mill
laminoir m à froid
    D: Kaltwalzwerk n
    E: cold rolling mill
laminoir m ébaucheur
    D: Vorwalzwerk n
    E: blooming mill, roughing mill
lampe-témoin f
    D: Signallampe f, Anzeigelampe f
    E: pilot lamp, signal lamp, indicating lamp, pilot light
large bande, câble à ~
    D: Breitbandkabel n
    E: wide-band cable, broad-band cable
large bande, système à ~ à fréquence porteuse
    D: Breitband-Trägerfrequenzsystem n
    E: broad-band carrier system
largeur f
    D: Breite f
    E: width n, breadth n
largeur f de bande [com.]
    D: Bandbreite f
    E: band width
largeur f de bande de transmission
    D: Übertragungsbandbreite f

largeur f du secteur
  D: Sektorbreite f (des Leiters)
  E: sector width

largeur f intérieure
  D: lichte Weite
  E: inside diameter, inside width

L/D, rapport ~ [extr.]
  D: Länge/Durchmesser-Verhältnis (L/D) (Extruder-Schnecke) n
  E: L/D ratio

lecture f
  D: Anzeige f
  E: indication n, display n, reading n

lecture, faire une ~
  D: eine Ablesung vornehmen
  E: to take a reading

levage m d'un touret de câble
  D: Aufbocken einer Kabeltrommel
  E: jacking up of a cable reel

levier m de commande
  D: Bedienungshebel m
  E: hand lever, actuating lever, operating lever

liaison f [chim.]
  D: Bindung f
  E: bond n

liaison f blindée isolée au SF$_6$
  D: SF$_6$-isoliertes Leitersystem, SF$_6$-Rohrleiter m, SF$_6$-Rohrschiene f
  E: gas(SF$_6$)-insulated conductor system, compressed gas(SF$_6$)-insulated transmission line, SF$_6$-insulated metal clad tubular bus, SF$_6$-insulated bus duct

liaison f coaxiale
  D: Koaxialleitung f, konzentrische Leitung
  E: coaxial line, concentric-conductor line

liaison f de câble
  D: Kabelstrecke f
  E: cable route

liaison f de câbles
  D: Kabelanlage f
  E: cable installation

liaison f double [chim.]
  D: Doppelbindung f
  E: double bond

liaison f intime
  D: innige Verbindung
  E: intimate bond, close bond

liaisons f pl électriques
  D: elektrische Anschlüsse
  E: electrical connections

liant m
  D: Bindemittel n
  E: binder n, bonding agent

libération f [chim.]
  D: Abspaltung f
  E: liberation n, cleavage n

libérer v
  D: abspalten v
  E: split off v, set free v

lié adj à
  D: gekoppelt mit
  E: tied in with, interlocked with

lier v [câb.]
  D: abbinden v
  E: bind v, lace v, tie v

lier v
  D: verbinden v
  E: join v, joint v, connect v, link v

lier, tête à ~ les faisceaux
  D: Bündel-Spinner m
  E: unit binder

ligne f [com.]
  D: Leitung f
  E: line n

ligne f à conducteur concentrique
  D: Koaxialleitung f, konzentrische Leitung
  E: coaxial line, concentric-conductor line

ligne f à courant fort
  D: Starkstromleitung f (System)
  E: power line, power circuit

ligne f aérienne
  D: Freileitung f
  E: overhead line

ligne f à grand transport d'énergie
  D: Überlandleitung f
  E: long distance transmission line

ligne f artificielle
  D: Leitungsnachbildung f
  E: artificial balancing line, artificial line, balancing network

ligne f brisée
  D: gestrichelte Linie
  E: dashed line

ligne f brisée
  D: punktierte Linie
  E: dotted line

ligne f centrale d'une machine
  D: Mittellinie einer Maschine
  E: centre line of a machine

ligne

ligne *f* chargée
D: belastete Leitung
E: loaded line, line under load

ligne *f* coaxiale
D: Koaxialleitung *f*, konzentrische Leitung
E: coaxial line, concentric-conductor line

ligne *f* coaxiale pour trafic à longue distance
D: Koaxialleitung für den Fernverkehr
E: coaxial line for long distance traffic

ligne *f* d'abonné [tél.]
D: Anschlußleitung *f*, Hausanschlußleitung *f*
E: direct line, subscriber's line

ligne *f* d'abonné téléphonique (raccord à la ligne aérienne)
D: Teilnehmer-Anschlußleitung *f*, Hauszuführungsleitung *f*, Teilnehmereinführungsleitung *f*, Einführungsleitung *f*, Einführungsdraht *m*, Fernsprechteilnehmerleitung *f*
E: drop wire (telephone cable to connect open wire lines on poles to subscribers' premises) (US), subscriber('s) drop wire, telephone drop, lead(ing)-in wire

ligne *f* d'alimentation d'antenne
D: Antennenspeiseleitung *f*, Antennenzuleitung *f*, Antennenkabel *n*
E: antenna feeder, aerial feeder, antenna lead

ligne *f* de branchement
D: Abzweigleitung *f*
E: branch circuit, tap line

ligne *f* de dérivation
D: Abzweigleitung *f*
E: branch circuit, tap line

ligne *f* de desserte d'abonné
D: Teilnehmer-Anschlußleitung *f*, Hauszuführungsleitung *f*, Teilnehmereinführungsleitung *f*, Einführungsleitung *f*, Einführungsdraht *m*, Fernsprechteilnehmerleitung *f*
E: drop wire (telephone cable to connect open wire lines on poles to subscribers' premises) (US), subscriber('s) drop wire, telephone drop, lead(ing)-in wire

ligne *f* de fuite
D: Kriechweg *m*
E: leakage path

ligne *f* de soudure
D: Schweißnaht *f*
E: welding seam

ligne *f* d'essai [prod.]
D: Versuchsstraße *f*
E: pilot line

ligne *f* d'essai
D: Prüfleitung *f*
E: test line

ligne *f* de transit [tél.]
D: Durchgangsleitung *f*
E: through circuit, through line

ligne *f* de transmission avec transpositions [c. com.]
D: Leitung mit Kreuzungsausgleich
E: transposed transmission line

ligne *f* de transmission d'informations à longue distance
D: Datenfernübertragungsleitung *f*
E: long distance data transmission line

ligne *f* de transmission équilibrée [tél.]
D: ausgeglichene Übertragungsleitung
E: balanced transmission line

ligne *f* de transmission par fibre optique
D: Lichtleiter-Nachrichten-Übertragungsanlage *f*
E: optical fibre transmission line

ligne *f* de transmission phototélégraphique
D: Bildtelegraphie-Übertragungsleitung *f*
E: picture telegraphy transmission line

ligne *f* en charge
D: belastete Leitung
E: loaded line, line under load

ligne *f* expérimentale [prod.]
D: Versuchsstraße *f*
E: pilot line

ligne *f* partagée
D: Gemeinschaftsleitung *f*
E: party line

ligne *f* pupinisée
D: bespulte Leitung
E: coil-loaded line

ligne *f* rurale [tél.]

ligne f symétrique non chargée
  D: unbespulte symmetrische Leitung
  E: unloaded balanced line, non-loaded balanced line
ligne f symétrique non pupinisée
  D: unbespulte symmetrische Leitung
  E: unloaded balanced line, non-loaded balanced line
ligne f téléphonique
  D: Telefonleitung f
  E: telephone line
limitation du champ électrique f
  D: Feldbegrenzung f
  E: limitation of the electrical field, field limitation
limite f
  D: Grenzwert m
  E: limiting value, limit n
limite f absolue d'erreur
  D: absolute Fehlergrenze
  E: absolute limit of error
limite f d'allongement
  D: Streckgrenze f, Dehn(ungs)grenze f, Elastizitätsgrenze f
  E: yield point, yield strength, elastic limit
limite f d'écoulement
  D: Fließgrenze f
  E: flow limit
limite f de fluage
  D: Fließgrenze f
  E: flow limit
limite f d'élasticité
  D: Streckgrenze f, Dehn(ungs)grenze f, Elastizitätsgrenze f
  E: yield point, yield strength, elastic limit
limite f d'endurance
  D: Dauerfestigkeitsgrenze f
  E: fatigue limit, endurance limit
limite f de stockage
  D: Lagerfähigkeit f (Werkstoffe), Haltbarkeit f (Werkstoffe), Lagerungsbeständigkeit f
  E: shelf life, storage stability
limité adj localement
  D: örtlich begrenzt
  E: locally confined, locally limited
limites f pl des grains
  D: Korngrenzen f pl
  E: grain boundaries

D: Landleitung f
E: rural line

limiteur m de courant
  D: Strombegrenzer m
  E: current limiter
limure f de la gaine d'aluminium (pour la jonction)
  D: Befeilen des Aluminiummantels (zum Verbinden)
  E: filing of the aluminium sheath (for jointing)
lingot m
  D: Drahtbarren m, Gußblock m
  E: wire bar, ingot n
lingot m d'aluminium
  D: Aluminiumbarren m, Aluminiummassel f, Aluminiumkerbblock m
  E: aluminium ingot
lingots m pl [mét.]
  D: Formate n pl
  E: ingots pl
lingots m pl de cuivre
  D: Kupferdrahtbarren m pl
  E: copper wirebars
liquide m de refroidissement
  D: Kühlflüssigkeit f
  E: cooling liquid
liquide m de service
  D: Betriebsflüssigkeit f
  E: working fluid
liquide m de tréfilage
  D: Ziehflüssigkeit f
  E: drawing fluid
liquide m isolant
  D: Isolierflüssigkeit f
  E: insulating fluid, insulating liquid
lisière f
  D: Webkante f
  E: selvage n, selvedge n
livraison, à la ~
  D: im Anlieferungszustand
  E: in as-received condition, at the received stage, as delivered
localisateur m de défauts
  D: Fehlerortungsgerät n, Fehlersuchgerät n
  E: fault detector, fault location unit
localisation f de fuites
  D: Leckortung f
  E: leakage detection
localisation f d'un défaut
  D: Fehlersuche f, Fehlerortsbestimmung f, Fehlerortung f, Auffindung einer

localisation
    Störstelle
    E: fault location, fault finding, trouble finding, fault detection, trouble shooting (US), locating the trouble (GB)

localisé *adj*
    D: örtlich begrenzt
    E: locally confined, locally limited

localiser *v* **un défaut**
    D: eine Störung eingrenzen
    E: to locate a fault

logette *f* **d'essai**
    D: Prüfzelle *f*
    E: test cell

loi *f* **de Weibull**
    D: Weibull-Regel *f* (Weibull-Verteilung)
    E: Weibull's (distribution) law

loi *f* **gaussienne**
    D: Gaußsche Verteilung
    E: Gaussian (distribution) law

longévité *f* [él.]
    D: Dauerfestigkeit *f*, Langzeitfestigkeit *f*
    E: long-time strength

longitudinal, pose ~e
    D: Längsaufbringung *f* (Bänder)
    E: longitudinal application

longueur, couper à la ~ voulue
    D: auf die gewünschte Länge schneiden
    E: to cut to the required length

longueur *f* **de bobine**
    D: Lieferlänge *f*
    E: supply length, delivery length

longueur *f* **de fabrication**
    D: Fertigungslänge *f*
    E: manufacturing length, production length, factory length

longueur *f* **de la vis nD** (D = diamètre) [extr.]
    D: Schneckenlänge nD (D = Durchmesser)
    E: screw length nD (D = diameter)

longueur *f* **de livraison**
    D: Lieferlänge *f*
    E: supply length, delivery length

longueur *f* **de rupture**
    D: Reißlänge *f* (Papier)
    E: breaking length

longueur *f* **d'essai**
    D: Versuchslänge *f*, Probelänge *f*, Prüflänge *f*
    E: trial length, experimental length, test length

longueur *f* **d'onde**
    D: Wellenlänge *f*
    E: wavelength *n*

longueur *f* **du câble**
    D: Kabellänge *f*
    E: cable length

longueur *f* **du pas** [câblage]
    D: Schlaglänge *f*, Drallänge *f*
    E: length of lay, pitch *n*, length of twist

longueur *f* **immergée**
    D: Unterwasserlänge *f*
    E: immersed length

longueur *f* **libre entre mâchoires** [ess.]
    D: Einspannlänge *f*
    E: free length (of specimen) between clamps, clamping length

longueur *f* **non compensée**
    D: nicht kompensierte Länge (beim Platzwechsel einer Blankdrahtleitung)
    E: non-compensated length

longueur *f* **plongée**
    D: Unterwasserlänge *f*
    E: immersed length

longueur *f* **standard**
    D: Lagerlänge *f*
    E: stock length

lot *m* [câb.]
    D: Los *n*
    E: lot *n*

lover *v* **le câble dans la cale d'un navire**
    D: Kabel in den Schiffsladeraum einschießen
    E: to coil the cable into the ship's hold

lubrifiant *m*
    D: Gleitmittel *n*, Schmiermittel *n*
    E: grease *n*, lubricant *n*

lubrification *f*
    D: Schmierung *f*
    E: lubrication *n*, greasing *n*

M

machine *f* **à appointer et enfiler le fil métallique**
    D: Anspitzmaschine und Einziehmaschine (Draht)
    E: wire sharpening and threading

machine f **à contrôler la tenue aux vibrations**
  D: Vibrations-Prüfmaschine f
  E: vibration test machine
machine f **à couper les rubans de papier**
  D: Papierschneidemaschine f, Papierbandschneidemaschine f
  E: paper tape cutting machine, paper-slitting machine
machine f **à découper le papier**
  D: Papierschneidemaschine f, Papierbandschneidemaschine f
  E: paper tape cutting machine, paper-slitting machine
machine f **à enrouler**
  D: Umwicklungsmaschine f
  E: wrapping machine
machine f **à essayer la résistance à la traction**
  D: Zugfestigkeitsprüfer m, Zerreißfestigkeits-Prüfmaschine f
  E: tensile strength testing machine
machine f **à grand rendement, à grand débit, à grande puissance, à grande vitesse**
  D: Hochleistungsmaschine f
  E: high-capacity machine, high-speed machine, heavy-duty machine
machine f **à papier à tamis cylindrique**
  D: Rundsieb(papier-)maschine f
  E: cylinder paper machine
machine f **à papier à toile double sans fin**
  D: Doppellangsieb-Papiermaschine f
  E: twin-wire paper-making machine
machine f **à papier à toile sans fin**
  D: Langsieb-Papiermaschine f, Fourdrinier-Papiermaschine f
  E: continuous traveling wire cloth paper machine, Fourdrinier paper machine
machine f **à papier Fourdrinier**
  D: Langsieb-Papiermaschine f, Fourdrinier-Papiermaschine f
  E: continuous traveling wire cloth paper machine, Fourdrinier paper machine
machine f **à poser les câbles**
  D: Auslegemaschine für Kabel, Verlegemaschine für Kabel
  E: cable laying machine
machine f **à poser l'hélice de support**
  D: Anwendelmaschine f (Luftkabel)
  E: lashing machine
machine f **à recouvrir le fil métallique**
  D: Drahtumspinnmaschine f
  E: wire covering machine
machine f **à revêtir**
  D: Umwicklungsmaschine f
  E: wrapping machine
machine f **à revêtir en sens longitudinal**
  D: Längsbedeckungsmaschine f
  E: longitudinal covering machine
machine f **à tréfiler**
  D: Drahtziehmaschine f
  E: wire drawing machine
machine f **à tresser**
  D: Flechtmaschine f, Umflechtungsmaschine f, Klöppelmaschine f
  E: braiding machine, braider n
machine f **de traction**
  D: Zugfestigkeitsprüfer m, Zerreißfestigkeits-Prüfmaschine f
  E: tensile strength testing machine
machiniste m
  D: Maschinenführer m, Bedienungsperson f
  E: operator n, attendant n
mâchoire f
  D: Greifer m (Raupenabzug)
  E: jaw n
mâchoire f **de serrage**
  D: Einspannklaue f, Einspannklemme f, Klemmbacke f
  E: jaw n, fixing clamp, clamping jaw
main, posé à la ~
  D: von Hand aufgebracht
  E: hand-applied adj
maintenance f
  D: Instandhaltung f
  E: maintenance n, service n, servicing n
malaxage m **à mort**
  D: Totwalzen n (Kautschuk), Überwalzen n (Kautschuk)
  E: over-milling n, over-mastication n, "killing" of rubber
malaxer v
  D: kneten v, plastizieren v (mech.)
  E: masticate v, knead v
malaxer v [caout., plast.]

malaxer

- D: walzen v
- E: mill v

malaxeur m
- D: Innenmischer m, Kneter m
- E: internal mixer, kneader n, masticator n

malaxeur m **à deux cylindres**
- D: Zweiwalzenmischwerk n
- E: two-roller mill

malaxeur m **Banbury**
- D: Gummikneter m, Banbury-Kneter m
- E: rubber kneader, Banbury-mixer n, Banbury-kneader n

malaxeur m **de laboratoire à cylindres**
- D: Laborwalze f
- E: laboratory roller mill

malaxeur-mélangeur m
- D: Mischkneter m
- E: kneader mixer

malléabiliser v [mét.]
- D: tempern v
- E: malleableise v (GB), malleableize v (US)

malléabilité f
- D: Formbarkeit f
- E: plasticity n, workability n

malléabilité f **à chaud**
- D: Warmverformbarkeit f, Warmformbarkeit f
- E: hot-workability n

manchon m
- D: Buchse f
- E: bushing n, bush n, sleeve n

manchon m
- D: Stutzen m
- E: connecting piece, connection n

manchon m [access. c.]
- D: Hülse f
- E: sleeve n

manchon m **à poinçonner**
- D: Preßverbinder m
- E: compression type sleeve, crimped sleeve

manchon m **à sertir**
- D: Kerbverbinder m
- E: notched type sleeve

manchon m **de dilatation** [câb.]
- D: Dehnungsmuffe f
- E: expansion box

manchon m **de jonction**
- D: Verbindungshülse f
- E: joint sleeve, connecting sleeve

manchon m **de plomb**
- D: Bleihülse f, Bleimuffe f
- E: lead sleeve

manchon m **de raccordement**
- D: Verbindungshülse f
- E: joint sleeve, connecting sleeve

manchon m **de raccordement** [access. c.]
- D: Anschlußmuffe f
- E: junction box

manchon m **emmanché à chaud**
- D: Schrumpfmuffe f, Aufschrumpfmuffe f
- E: heat-shrinkage insulating sleeve, shrink-on sleeve, heat-shrinkable sleeve

manchon m **isolant**
- D: Isolierhülse f, Isolierbuchse f
- E: insulating bush(ing), insulating sleeve

manchon m **protecteur**
- D: Schutzmuffe f
- E: joint protection box

manchon m **sur jonction épissée** [c. com.]
- D: Spleißmuffengehäuse n
- E: splice case, splice closure

manchon m **thermorétractable**
- D: Schrumpfschlauch m
- E: heat-shrinkable tubing, shrink-on tube

mandrin m
- D: Dorn m
- E: mandrel n

mandrin m **creux** [pr. à filer]
- D: Hohldorn m
- E: hollow mandrel

mandrin m **de répartition de matière** [extr.]
- D: Strömungseinsatz m
- E: flow fixture

mandriner v
- D: aufweiten v
- E: expand v, bulge v, bell out v, flare v

manipulation f
- D: Betätigung f, Bedienung f
- E: operation n, handling n, actuation n, control n

manipulation, aisance de ~
- D: leichte Bedienung, leichte Handhabung
- E: ease of manipulation, ease of operation, working ease

manodétendeur m

manœuvrable, facilement ~
D: leicht bedienbar
E: easy to operate

manœuvre m
D: ungelernter Arbeiter
E: unskilled worker

manœuvre f
D: Betätigung f, Bedienung f
E: operation n, handling n, actuation n, control n

manomètre m
D: Druckmeßgerät n, Manometer n
E: pressure gauge, pressure control device, manometer n

manomètre m **à contact**
D: Kontaktmanometer n
E: contact manometer, contact-making pressure gauge

manostat m
D: Kontaktmanometer n
E: contact manometer, contact-making pressure gauge

manque m **de courant**
D: Stromausfall m
E: power failure, current breakdown

manque m **de tension secteur**
D: Netzausfall m
E: power failure

manuel, à commande ~le
D: handbetätigt adj
E: hand-operated adj, manually operated

manuel m **d'entretien**
D: Wartungsvorschrift f
E: maintenance instructions pl

manuel m **d'instruction**
D: Betriebsanleitung f, Bedienungsanleitung f
E: operating instruction, instructions pl for use, operating manual

manutention f
D: Flurförderwesen n
E: floor handling

manutention f
D: Transport m (innerbetrieblich)
E: handling n

maquette f **de câble**
D: Modellkabel n
E: model cable

marche, la machine étant en ~
D: bei laufender Maschine
D: Druckminderungsventil n
E: pressure reducing valve

E: under running conditions of a machine

marche, mettre en ~ [mach.]
D: anfahren v, anschalten v, einschalten v
E: start v, start up v

marche f **continue**
D: kontinuierlicher Betrieb
E: continuous operation

marche f **d'essai**
D: Probelauf m
E: trial run, test run

marche f **en avant**
D: Vorwärtsbewegung f
E: forward motion

marcher, faire ~ une machine
D: eine Maschine fahren, eine Maschine bedienen
E: to run a machine, to operate a machine

marquage m [câb.]
D: Kennzeichnung f
E: identification n, marking n, coding n

marquage m **à l'encre**
D: Farbmarkierung f
E: ink-marking n, colo(u)r marking

marquage m **coloré**
D: Farbmarkierung f
E: ink-marking n, colo(u)r marking

marquage m **en relief**
D: Markierung durch Prägen
E: marking by embossing

marquage m **hélicoïdal**
D: Wendelmarkierung f
E: helical marking

marquage m **longitudinal**
D: Längsmarkierung f
E: longitudinal marking

marquage m **métré**
D: Längenmarkierung f
E: meter marking, length marking

marquage m **par impression**
D: Bedruckung f
E: printing n

marquage m **par symboles**
D: Zeichenmarkierung f
E: sign marking

marque f [câb.]
D: Kennzeichen n
E: mark n, code n

marque f **d'approbation VDE**
D: VDE-Kennzeichen n

marque
    E: VDE approval mark
marque f de contrôle
    D: Prüfkennzeichen n
    E: test mark, inspection mark
marque f de fabrique
    D: Firmenkennzeichen n
    E: trademark n, brand mark
marque f d'homologation
    D: Zulassungszeichen n
    E: approbation mark, certification mark
marque f du fabricant
    D: Firmenkennzeichen n
    E: trademark n, brand mark
marqueur m de paires défectueuses
    D: Markierung für fehlerhaftes Paar
    E: marker n (com. c.), defective pair marker
masse f volumique
    D: spezifisches Gewicht
    E: specific gravity, volume weight
masse f volumique apparente
    D: Rohdichte f
    E: apparent density (paper)
mastication f à mort
    D: Totwalzen n (Kautschuk), Überwalzen n (Kautschuk)
    E: over-milling n, over-mastication n, "killing" of rubber
matelas m
    D: Polster n (unter der Bewehrung)
    E: bedding n
matériau m composite
    D: Verbundwerkstoff m
    E: composite material, multilayer material, composite n
matériau m de remplacement
    D: Ersatzmaterial n
    E: substitute n
matériel m
    D: Ausrüstung f
    E: equipment n, facilities pl
matériel m de remplissage [pose c.]
    D: Rückfüllung f, Auffüllmaterial n
    E: backfill n
matériel m rudimentaire
    D: Ausgangsmaterial n
    E: original material, basic material, raw material, feed stock
matière f
    D: Werkstoff m, Rohstoff m
    E: material n, raw material
matière colorante f
    D: Farbstoff m
    E: pigment n, colo(u)rant n
matière f d'alimentation
    D: Beschickungsmaterial n
    E: feed material
matière f de base
    D: Ausgangsmaterial n
    E: original material, basic material, raw material, feed stock
matière f de bitume
    D: Bitumenmasse f
    E: bitumen compound
matière f de charge
    D: Füllstoff m
    E: filler n, loading material
matière f d'échaudage
    D: Abbrühmasse f
    E: scalding compound
matière f de remplissage [c. tél.]
    D: Abstopfmasse f
    E: filling compound
matière f de remplissage [access. c.]
    D: Vergußmasse f, Ausgußmasse f, Füllmasse f
    E: filling compound, sealing compound, flooding compound
matière f de remplissage à chaud
    D: Warmvergußmasse f
    E: hot filling compound, hot pouring compound
matière f de remplissage à froid
    D: Kaltvergußmasse f, Kaltfüllmasse f
    E: cold filling compound, cold pouring compound
matière f d'étanchéité
    D: Abdichtmasse f
    E: sealing compound
matière f d'imprégnation
    D: Tränkmasse f, Imprägniermasse f
    E: impregnating compound
matière f durcissable à froid
    D: kalthärtende Masse
    E: cold-setting compound
matière f en fusion
    D: Schmelze f
    E: melt n, molten material
matière f lubrifiante
    D: Gleitmittel n, Schmiermittel n
    E: grease n, lubricant n
matière f migrante [câb.]
    D: abwandernde Masse
    E: migrating compound, draining compound

matière *f* nd
  D: Haftmasse *f*, nd-Masse *f*, nicht abwandernde Tränkmasse
  E: non-draining compound, nd-compound *n*

matière *f* neuve [ess.]
  D: frisches Material, neues Material
  E: virgin material

matière *f* non migrante
  D: Haftmasse *f*, nd-Masse *f*, nicht abwandernde Tränkmasse
  E: non-draining compound, nd-compound *n*

matière *f* plastique
  D: Kunststoff *m*, Plast *m*
  E: plastic material, synthetic material, synthetic resin

matière *f* plastique de couleur naturelle, incolore, non colorée
  D: ungefärbter Kunststoff, farbloser Kunststoff
  E: uncoloured plastic, natural-coloured plastic, unpigmented plastic, natural plastic (US)

matière *f* première
  D: Werkstoff *m*, Rohstoff *m*
  E: material *n*, raw material

matières *f pl* plastiques thermodurcissables
  D: wärmehärtbare Kunststoffe
  E: thermosetting synthetic materials, thermosetting plastics, thermosetting resins

matières *f pl* thermoplastiques
  D: Thermoplaste *m pl*
  E: thermoplastics *pl*, thermoplastic materials

matière *f* synthétique
  D: Kunststoff *m*, Plast *m*
  E: plastic material, synthetic material, synthetic resin

mécanique *adj*
  D: maschinell *adj*
  E: mechanical *adj*

mélange *m*
  D: Mischung *f*
  E: compound *n*

mélange *m* coloré dans la masse
  D: durchgefärbte Mischung
  E: colo(u)red compound

mélange *m* coloré maître
  D: Farbkonzentrat *n*, Farbbatch *n*
  E: master batch, colo(u)r batch, colo(u)r concentrate

mélange *m* de bourrage
  D: Zwickelmantelmischung *f*
  E: inner filling compound

mélange *m* de caoutchouc
  D: Gummimischung *f*
  E: rubber compound

mélange *m* de PE
  D: PE-Mischung *f*
  E: PE-compound *n*

mélange *m* de purification [extr.]
  D: Reinigungsmischung *f*
  E: purging compound

mélange *m* de PVC
  D: PVC-Mischung *f*
  E: PVC compound

mélange *m* en plaque
  D: Walzplatte *f* (Mischungsherstellung)
  E: slab *n*

mélange *m* gaine
  D: Mantelmischung *f*
  E: sheathing compound

mélange *m* gaine de caoutchouc pour contraintes fortes
  D: Gummimantelmischung für starke Beanspruchung
  E: tough-rubber sheathing compound

mélange *m* huile-résine
  D: Ölharzgemisch *n*
  E: oil-rosin compound

mélange *m* isolant
  D: Adermischung *f*, Isoliermischung *f*
  E: insulating compound

mélange *m* maître
  D: Vormischung *f*, Grundmischung *f*
  E: master batch, pre-mix *n*

mélange *m* mère
  D: Vormischung *f*, Grundmischung *f*
  E: master batch, pre-mix *n*

mélange *m* oléo-résineux
  D: Ölharzgemisch *n*
  E: oil-rosin compound

mélange *m* plastique
  D: Kunststoff-Mischung *f*
  E: plastics compound, synthetic resin compound

mélanger *v* [caout., plast.]
  D: mischen *v*
  E: mix *v*, blend *v*, compound *v*

mélanger *v*
  D: vermischen *v*, mischen *v*
  E: blend *v*, mix *v*, intermingle *v*

mélanger v[caout., plast.]
  D: walzen v
  E: mill v
mélange m réticulable par irradiation
  D: strahlenvernetzbare Mischung
  E: irradiation cross-linkable compound
mélange m semi-conducteur
  D: schwachleitende Mischung
  E: semi-conducting compound, semi-conductive compound
mélangeur m
  D: Mischer m, Rührwerk n
  E: mixer n
mélangeur m à caoutchouc
  D: Gummikneter m, Banbury-Kneter m
  E: rubber kneader, Banbury-mixer n, Banbury-kneader n
mélangeur m à charges
  D: Chargenmischer m
  E: batch mixer
mélangeur m à cuve
  D: Trogmischer m
  E: trough mixer
mélangeur m à cylindres
  D: Mischwalzwerk n
  E: mixing mill, mixing rolls pl
mélangeur m à meules
  D: Kollergang m
  E: muller mixer, edge runner mixer
mélangeur m à palettes
  D: Schaufelmischer m
  E: paddle mixer
mélangeur m à rouleaux
  D: Mischwalzwerk n
  E: mixing mill, mixing rolls pl
mélangeur m à tambour
  D: Trommelmischer m
  E: barrel mixer, drum mixer
mélangeur m à tonneau
  D: Trommelmischer m
  E: barrel mixer, drum mixer
mélangeur m Banbury
  D: Gummikneter m, Banbury-Kneter m
  E: rubber kneader, Banbury-mixer n, Banbury-kneader n
mélangeur m basculant
  D: Kippmischer m
  E: tilting mixer
mélangeur m discontinu
  D: Chargenmischer m
  E: batch mixer
mélangeur m du type à fluidification
  D: Fluidmischer m
  E: fluid mixer
mélangeur m en continu à courant
  D: Durchflußmischer m (Mischungsherstellung)
  E: flow mixer, pipeline mixer
mélangeur m interne
  D: Innenmischer m, Kneter m
  E: internal mixer, kneader n, masticator n
mélangeur m réfrigérant
  D: Kühlmischer m
  E: cooling mixer
mélangeur m renversable
  D: Kippmischer m
  E: tilting mixer
mêler v
  D: vermischen v, mischen v
  E: blend v, mix v, intermingle v
méplat adj
  D: abgeflacht adj
  E: flattened adj
mesure, appareil de ~ d'isolement
  D: Isolationsmesser m
  E: insulation tester
mesure, dispositif de ~ de la tension de traction
  D: Zugspannungsmeßvorrichtung f
  E: tension meter
mesure f comparative
  D: Vergleichsmessung f
  E: comparative measurement
mesure f de capacité
  D: Kapazitätsmessung f
  E: capacitance measurement
mesure f d'épaisseur
  D: Dickenmessung f
  E: thickness measurement
mesure f d'équivalents de transmission
  D: Restdämpfungsmessung zwischen den Leitungsenden
  E: overall attenuation measurement
mesure f des décharges partielles
  D: Teilentladungsmessung f
  E: partial discharge measurement
mesure f de température
  D: Temperaturmessung f
  E: temperature measurement
mesure du diamètre, appareil de ~
  D: Durchmessermeßgerät n
  E: diameter gauge, diameter

measuring device

mesure f du travail
D: Zeitstudie f
E: work measurement, time study

mesure f en boucle
D: Schleifenmessung f
E: loop test

mesure f par points
D: punktweises Messen
E: pointwise measurement

mesure f sur prélèvement
D: Stichprobenmessung f
E: random measurement

mesureur m du diamètre
D: Durchmessermeßgerät n
E: diameter gauge, diameter measuring device

métal m d'apport
D: Lot n
E: solder n

méthode f
D: Verfahren n, Methode f
E: process n, method n, technique n, procedure n

méthode f bille et anneau
D: Ring- und Kugelmethode (zur Bestimmung des Erweichungspunktes von Massen)
E: ring and ball method

méthode f de mesure
D: Meßmethode f
E: method of measurement

méthode f d'essai
D: Prüfmethode f
E: test method

méthode f d'extrusion
D: Spritzverfahren n, Extrusionsverfahren n
E: extrusion process

méthode f élaborée
D: aufwendiges Verfahren
E: elaborate process

méthode f éprouvée
D: bewährtes Verfahren
E: established practice

mettre v
D: einsetzen v, einbauen v
E: insert v, mount v, fit v

mettre v à la terre
D: erden v
E: earth v (GB), to connect to earth, ground (US) v

mettre v en circuit
D: einschalten v, anschalten v
E: switch on v, turn on (US) v

mettre v en communication [tél.]
D: durchschalten v
E: to connect through, put through v, switch through v

mettre v en marche [mach.]
D: anfahren v, anschalten v, einschalten v
E: start v, start up v

mettre v en œuvre
D: verarbeiten v
E: process v, convert v

mettre v en place
D: aufbringen v
E: apply v

mettre v hors tension
D: die Spannung abschalten
E: to cut off the voltage, to cut out the voltage

mettre v sous gaine de plomb
D: Bleimantel aufpressen
E: lead-sheath v, to apply the lead sheath

mettre v sous tension
D: eine Spannung anlegen
E: to apply a voltage

mettre v sous tension
D: einschalten v, anschalten v
E: switch on v, turn on (US) v

mettre v sous vide
D: evakuieren v
E: evacuate v

MIC, câble ~
D: Pulscode-Modulationskabel n, PCM-Kabel n
E: pulse-code modulation cable, PCM cable

micro-onde f
D: Mikrowelle f
E: microwave n

migration f
D: Ausbluten n (Farbe)
E: bleeding n

migration f de matière [câb.]
D: Masseverarmung f, Masseabwanderung f, Abwanderung von Masse
E: migration of compound, draining of compound

migration f du plastifiant
D: Weichmacherwanderung f, Abwanderung des Weichmachers

migration

    E: migration of plasticizer

migrer *v*
    D: abwandern *v* (Masse, Weichmacher)
    E: migrate *v*

mince, revêtement ~
    D: dünnwandiger Überzug
    E: thin-wall coating

minium *m* de plomb
    D: Bleimennige *f*
    E: red lead

minutieux, contrôle ~
    D: eingehende Prüfung
    E: exhaustive test, close examination, thorough examination

mis *adj* **à la terre**
    D: geerdet *adj*
    E: earthed *adj* (GB), grounded *adj* (US)

mise *f* **à la terre**
    D: Erdung *f*
    E: earthing *n* (GB), grounding *n* (US), connection to earth (GB), connection to ground (US)

mise *f* **à la terre de protection**
    D: Schutzerdung *f*
    E: protective earth (GB), protective ground (US)

mise *f* **à la terre de protection multiple**
    D: Mehrfachschutzerdung *f*, Nullung *f*
    E: protective multiple earthing (p.m.e.)

mise *f* **à la terre du neutre**
    D: Sternpunkterdung *f*
    E: earthing of neutral (GB), grounding of neutral (US)

mise *f* **à la terre rigide du neutre**
    D: starre Sternpunkterdung
    E: solid earthing of neutral (GB), solid grounding of neutral (US)

mise *f* **au neutre**
    D: Mehrfachschutzerdung *f*, Nullung *f*
    E: protective multiple earthing (p.m.e.)

mise *f* **au point de matériaux**
    D: Einsatz von Materialien
    E: use of materials, employment of materials, application of materials

mise *f* **en forme à chaud**
    D: Warmverformung *f*, Warmformung *f*, Warmverarbeitung *f*
    E: hot forming, hot-working *n*

mise *f* **en forme plastique**
    D: spanlose Bearbeitung
    E: non-cutting shaping

mise *f* **en oeuvre**
    D: Inbetriebnahme *f*
    E: commissioning *n*, putting to service, taking into commission

mise *f* **en œuvre**
    D: Verarbeitung *f*
    E: processing *n*

mise *f* **en place**
    D: Aufbringung *f*
    E: application *n*

mise *f* **en service**
    D: Inbetriebnahme *f*
    E: commissioning *n*, putting to service, taking into commission

mise *f* **sous plomb**
    D: Ummanteln mit Blei
    E: lead-sheathing *n*

mise sous pression, installation de ~
    D: Druckanlage *f*
    E: pressurizing plant

mobile *adj*
    D: beweglich (fliegend) angeordnet
    E: flying *adj*

mobilité *f*
    D: Beweglichkeit *f*
    E: flexibility *n*, mobility *n*

mode *m* **de fonctionnement**
    D: Arbeitsweise *f*
    E: mode of operation, functioning *n*, operation *n*

mode *m* **d'emploi**
    D: Betriebsanleitung *f*, Bedienungsanleitung *f*
    E: operating instruction, instructions *pl* for use, operating manual

mode *m* **de pose** [câb.]
    D: Verlegeart *f*
    E: method of laying, method of installation

mode *m* **d'essai**
    D: Prüfverfahren *n*
    E: test procedure

mode *m* **d'exploitation**
    D: Betriebsart *f*
    E: method of operation, mode of operation, type of service

modèle *m* **de câble**
    D: Modellkabel *n*
    E: model cable

mode *m* **opératoire**

mode m opératoire
  D: Betriebsanleitung f, Bedienungsanleitung f
  E: operating instruction, instructions pl for use, operating manual

mode m opératoire
  D: Fertigungsvorschrift f
  E: manufacturing specification

modifier v
  D: abändern v, ändern v
  E: modify v, alter v, change v, revise v

modulation, câble de ~ par impulsion et codage
  D: Pulscode-Modulationskabel n, PCM-Kabel n
  E: pulse-code modulation cable, PCM cable

modulation de groupe, équipement de ~ [com.]
  D: Gruppenumsetzer m
  E: group modulator

module m d'élasticité
  D: Elastizitätsmodul m
  E: modulus of elasticity

module m d'élasticité au cisaillement
  D: Gleitmodul m
  E: shear modulus

monobloc adj
  D: einteilig adj
  E: single-piece... adj, one-piece... adj, monobloc adj

monoconducteur m [câb.]
  D: Einzelader f, Einzelleiter m
  E: single conductor

monoconducteur m (avec ou sans gaine)
  D: einadrige Leitung
  E: single-core cable (with or without sheath)

monoconducteur m sous gaine
  D: einadrige Leitung mit Mantel
  E: single-core sheathed conductor

mono-paire f
  D: Einzelpaar n
  E: single pair

monophasé, courant ~
  D: Einphasenstrom m
  E: single-phase current

montage m [él.]
  D: Schaltung f, Verdrahtung f
  E: circuitry n, circuit arrangement, wiring n, cabling n, interconnection n

montage m
  D: Errichtung f, Montage f, Aufbau m
  E: installation n, erection n, set-up n, assembly n

montage m de base [él.]
  D: Basisschaltung f
  E: grounded-base circuit

montage m de mesure
  D: Meßanordnung f, Meßschaltung f
  E: measuring arrangement, connections pl for measurement

montage m des bobines
  D: Einsetzen von Spulen, Einsetzen von Trommeln
  E: positioning of reels, loading of reels

montage m d'essai
  D: Testanordnung f, Prüfanordnung f, Versuchsanordnung f
  E: experimental arrangement, test(ing) arrangement, test setup

montage m en cascade
  D: Kaskadenschaltung f
  E: cascade connection

montage m en parallèle
  D: Parallelschaltung f
  E: parallel circuit, parallel connection

montage m en fantôme
  D: Doppelsprechschaltung f
  E: phantom phone connection

montage m en série
  D: Reihenschaltung f, Hintereinanderschaltung f
  E: series circuit, series connection

montage m expérimental
  D: Testanordnung f, Prüfanordnung f, Versuchsanordnung f
  E: experimental arrangement, test(ing) arrangement, test setup

montage m expérimental (él.)
  D: Versuchsschaltung f, Prüfstromkreis m
  E: temporary circuit, test circuit, experimental circuit

montée f de température
  D: Temperaturerhöhung f, Anstieg der Temperatur, Erwärmung f
  E: temperature rise, temperature increase

montée f de tension
  D: Spannungsanstieg m, Anstieg der Spannung
  E: voltage rise

montée f d'une courbe
  D: Anstieg einer Kurve

montée
    E: slope of a curve
monter v
    D: errichten v
    E: set up v, install v, mount v, erect v, assemble v
monter v [él.]
    D: schalten v
    E: switch v, connect v
monteur m
    D: Monteur m
    E: jointer n, fitter n, erector n
montre, dans le sens des aiguilles d'une ~
    D: im Uhrzeigersinn
    E: clockwise adj
montre, dans le sens inverse des aiguilles d'une ~
    D: gegen den Uhrzeigersinn
    E: counterclockwise adj, anti-clockwise adj
mordache f
    D: Einspannklaue f, Einspannklemme f, Klemmbacke f
    E: jaw n, fixing clamp, clamping jaw
moteur m **à courant alternatif**
    D: Wechselstrommotor m
    E: a.c. motor
moteur m **à vitesse réglable**
    D: Motor mit regulierbarer Geschwindigkeit, Regelmotor m
    E: adjustable speed motor, variable speed motor
moteur m **à vitesse variable**
    D: Motor mit regulierbarer Geschwindigkeit, Regelmotor m
    E: adjustable speed motor, variable speed motor
moteur m **d'entraînement**
    D: Antriebsmotor m
    E: driving motor
motorisé adj
    D: motorangetrieben adj, motorisch adj
    E: motor-driven adj, motorized adj
mou m
    D: Durchhang m
    E: sag n
moufle f
    D: Tänzerrolle f
    E: float roll, floating roller, dancer n
moufle f **de régulation** [fabr.fils mét., câblage]
    D: Speicher m, Längenspeicher m
    E: accumulator n
moufle m **respirant** [câblage]
    D: atmender Speicher (SZ-Verseilung)
    E: breathing accumulator
moufle f **rotative** [câblage]
    D: rotierender Speicher
    E: rotating accumulator
mouiller v
    D: anfeuchten v, benetzen v, befeuchten v
    E: wet v, moisten v
moulage m **par injection**
    D: Spritzguß m
    E: injection mo(u)lding
moule m
    D: Form f (Gießen, Pressen)
    E: mo(u)ld n
mousse f (synthétique)
    D: Schaum-Kunststoff m
    E: foamed plastic, expanded plastic, cellular plastic
mouvement m **alternatif**
    D: Hin- und Herbewegung f
    E: reciprocation n, reciprocating motion, to-and-fro movement
mouvement m **de va-et-vient**
    D: Hin- und Herbewegung f
    E: reciprocation n, reciprocating motion, to-and-fro movement
mouvement m **transversal**
    D: Querbewegung f
    E: crosswise movement, transverse motion
multipaire, câble ~ [tél.]
    D: mehrpaariges Kabel, hochpaariges Kabel
    E: multiple pair cable, multipair cable, multipaired cable, large-capacity cable
multitoron, câble ~ [tél.]
    D: mehrpaariges Kabel, hochpaariges Kabel
    E: multiple pair cable, multipair cable, multipaired cable, large-capacity cable
murmure m **confus** [tél.]
    D: Babbeln n, unverständliches Nebensprechen
    E: babbling n

N

nappe *f*
 D: Walzfell *n* (Mischungsherstellung)
 E: band *n* (as taken from a mill), sheet *n* (as taken from a mill)

nappe, briser la ~ de caoutchouc malaxé sur les cylindres [caout.]
 D: Fell von der Mischwalze abschneiden
 E: to break the batch loose from the rolls

nappe, câbles disposés en ~
 D: nebeneinander liegende Kabel, in einer Ebene liegende Kabel
 E: cables in flat formation, cables laid in parallel, cables laid side by side

nappe, disposition en ~ horizontale
 D: Verlegung nebeneinander, Parallelanordnung *f*
 E: laying side by side, laying in parallel, parallel arrangement

nappe *f* **d'eau souterraine** [pose c.]
 D: Grundwasser *n*
 E: ground water, subsoil water

nappe *f* **de caoutchouc malaxé**
 D: Fell *n*
 E: sheet of masticated rubber, milled crepe (rubber)

navire *m* **câblier** [pose c.]
 D: Kabellegeschiff *n*
 E: cable ship

néfaste *adj*
 D: schädlich *adj*
 E: harmful *adj*, detrimental *adj*

négligeable *adj*
 D: vernachlässigbar *adj*
 E: negligible *adj*

Neoprene *m*
 D: Neoprene *n* (Polychloropren-Kautschuk der Du Pont)
 E: Neoprene *n*

neutraliser *v*
 D: entkoppeln *v*
 E: balance out *v*, decouple *v*, uncouple *v*

neutre *m*
 D: Nulleiter *m*, Mittelpunktsleiter *m*
 E: neutral conductor, neutral wire, zero conductor

neutre *m*
 D: Nullpunkt *m*, Sternpunkt *m*
 E: neutral point, zero point

neutre *m* **à la terre**
 D: geerdeter Sternpunkt (Nullpunkt)
 E: earthed neutral (GB), grounded neutral (US)

neutre *m* **concentrique**
 D: konzentrischer Nulleiter
 E: concentric neutral conductor

neutre *m* **concentrique en fils métalliques disposés en méandres**
 D: Ceander-Leiter *m*
 E: wave-form concentric neutral conductor

neutre *m* **isolé**
 D: isolierter Sternpunkt
 E: insulated neutral, isolated neutral

neutre *m* **mis à la terre**
 D: geerdeter Sternpunkt (Nullpunkt)
 E: earthed neutral (GB), grounded neutral (US)

neutre *m* **non mis à la terre**
 D: nicht geerdeter Sternpunkt (Nullpunkt)
 E: unearthed neutral (GB), ungrounded neutral (US)

neutre *m* **périphérique**
 D: konzentrischer Nulleiter
 E: concentric neutral conductor

neutre *m* **rigidement relié à la terre**
 D: starr geerdeter Sternpunkt
 E: solidly earthed neutral (GB), solidly grounded neutral (US)

niveau *m* **de bruit** [c. com.]
 D: Rauschpegel *m*, Geräuschpegel *m*, Störpegel *m*
 E: noise level, interference level

niveau *m* **de couplage**
 D: Kopplungsniveau *n*
 E: unbalance level, coupling level

niveau *m* **de puissance**
 D: Leistungspegel *m*
 E: power level

niveau *m* **des perturbations** [c. com.]
 D: Rauschpegel *m*, Geräuschpegel *m*, Störpegel *m*
 E: noise level, interference level

niveau *m* **de tension**
 D: Spannungspegel *m*
 E: voltage level

niveau *m* **d'isolement**
 D: Isolationspegel *m*
 E: insulation level

nocif *adj*

nocif
- D: schädlich *adj*
- E: harmful *adj*, detrimental *adj*

nœud *m*
- D: Knotenpunkt *m*
- E: intersection *n*, junction point

nœuds *m pl* **de bambou**
- D: Bambusringe *m pl* (durch Rastzeiten beim Aufbringen von Kabelmänteln aus Blei oder Aluminium), Einschnürungen *f pl* (Met.-Strangpr.) Haltestellenmarkierungen *f pl* (Met.-Strangpr.)
- E: bamboo rings, stop marks

noir *m* **au tunnel**
- D: Kanalruß *m*
- E: channel black

noir *m* **d'acétylène**
- D: Acetylenruß *m*
- E: acetylene black

noir *m* **de carbone**
- D: Ruß *m*
- E: carbon black

noir *m* **de fumée**
- D: Ruß *m*
- E: carbon black

noir *m* **de gaz**
- D: Gasruß *m*
- E: gas black

nombre *m* **de pliages alternés**
- D: Biegezahl *f*
- E: bending limit, bending value

nombre *m* **de pliages répétés**
- D: Falzzahl *f*
- E: number of double folds

nombre *m* **des conducteurs**
- D: Aderzahl *f*
- E: number of cores

nombre *m* **des fils**
- D: Fachung *f* (Garn)
- E: folding number

nombre *m* **de tours par minute** (t.p.m.)
- D: Drehzahl *f* (Umdrehungen pro Minute = U/Min), Geschwindigkeit *f*
- E: number of revolutions per minute (r.p.m.), rotational speed, speed *n*

non chargé *adj* [c. tél.]
- D: unbelastet *adj*, unbespult *adj*
- E: unloaded *adj*, non-loaded *adj*

non colorée, matière plastique ~
- D: ungefärbter Kunststoff, farbloser Kunststoff
- E: uncoloured plastic, natural-coloured plastic, unpigmented plastic, natural plastic (US)

non étanche *adj*
- D: undicht *adj*
- E: leaky *adj*, untight *adj*

non-étanchéité *f*
- D: Undichtigkeit *f*, Leckstelle *f*
- E: leakage *n*

non-inflammabilité *f*
- D: Unbrennbarkeit *f*
- E: incombustibility *n*

non-inflammable *adj*
- D: unbrennbar *adj*
- E: non-inflammable *adj*, flame-proof *adj*, non-combustible *adj*, incombustible *adj*

non plan *adj*
- D: uneben *adj*
- E: uneven *adj*

non propagateur de la flamme *adj*
- D: flammwidrig *adj*, einen Brand nicht weiterleitend
- E: flame-resistant *adj*, non fire propagating

non propagateur de l'incendie *adj*
- D: flammwidrig *adj*, einen Brand nicht weiterleitend
- E: flame-resistant *adj*, non fire propagating

non-propagation *f* **de la flamme**
- D: Flammwidrigkeit *f*
- E: flame resistance

non-propagation *f* **de l'incendie**
- D: Flammwidrigkeit *f*
- E: flame resistance

non pupinisé *adj* [c. tél.]
- D: unbelastet *adj*, unbespult *adj*
- E: unloaded *adj*, non-loaded *adj*

non réfléchissant *adj* [c. com.]
- D: reflexionsfrei *adj*
- E: flat *adj*, free of reflection

non soutenu *adj*
- D: freitragend *adj*
- E: cantilevered *adj*

non transmettant la flamme
- D: flammwidrig *adj*, einen Brand nicht weiterleitend
- E: flame-resistant *adj*, non fire propagating

non travaillé *adj*
- D: unbearbeitet *adj*
- E: untreated *adj*, unmachined *adj*,

non usiné *adj*
  D: unbearbeitet *adj*
  E: untreated *adj*, unmachined *adj*, unfinished *adj*

non-vieillissant *adj*
  D: alterungsbeständig *adj*
  E: resistant to ag(e)ing

normalisation *f*
  D: Normung *f*, Vereinheitlichung *f*
  E: standardisation *n*, normalization *n*, unification *n*

normaliser *v*
  D: spannungsfrei glühen
  E: normalize *v*

norme *f*
  D: Norm *f*
  E: standard specification

norme *f* **provisoire**
  D: Vornorm *f*
  E: tentative standard

normes *f pl* **VDE**
  D: VDE-Bestimmungen *f pl*, VDE-Regeln *f pl*, VDE-Vorschriften *f pl*
  E: VDE Regulations, VDE Rules, VDE Standards

notice *f* **de montage**
  D: Montageanleitung *f*
  E: fitting instructions *pl*, installation instructions *pl*

notice *f* **d'utilisation**
  D: Betriebsanleitung *f*, Bedienungsanleitung *f*
  E: operating instruction, instructions *pl* for use, operating manual

noyer *v*
  D: einbetten *v*
  E: embed *v*

nu *adj*
  D: blank *adj*
  E: plain *adj*, bright *adj*, bare *adj*

nuance *f* **de couleur**
  D: Farbtönung *f*
  E: colo(u)r shade

nuisible *adj*
  D: schädlich *adj*
  E: harmful *adj*, detrimental *adj*

numéro *m* **de fil**
  D: Garn-Nummer *f*
  E: count *n* (of yarn)

numéro-repère *m* [câb.]
  D: Kennziffer *f*
  E: code number

numérotage *m*
  D: Numerierung *f*
  E: numbering *n*

numéroté, conducteur de câble ~
  D: numerierte Kabelader
  E: numbered cable core

O

oblique *adj*
  D: schräg *adj*
  E: inclined *adj*, oblique *adj*

observer *v* [ess.]
  D: einhalten *v* (Werte, Bedingungen)
  E: meet *v*, observe *v*, comply with *v*

occlusions *f pl*
  D: Einschlüsse *m pl*
  E: inclusions *pl*

occlusions *f pl* **d'air**
  D: Lufteinschlüsse *m pl*
  E: air inclusions, air pockets, voids *pl*

occupation *f* [tél.]
  D: Belegung *f*
  E: engagement *n*, holding *n*

œillet *m* **de tirage** [câb.]
  D: Ziehkopf *m*, Ziehöse *f*, Zugöse *f*
  E: pulling eye, pulling head, pulling grip

œil nu, visible à l'~
  D: mit bloßem Auge sichtbar
  E: visible to the naked eye

œuvre, mettre en ~
  D: in Betrieb nehmen
  E: to put to service, to set working, to take into commission, to bring into commercial operation

OFHC, cuivre ~ (cuivre exempt d'oxygène, à haute conductivité)
  D: OFHC-Kupfer *n* (sauerstoffreies hochleitfähiges Kupfer)
  E: OFHC-copper *n* (oxygen free high conductivity copper)

ohmique, de faible valeur ~
  D: niederohmig *adj*
  E: low-ohmic *adj*, of low resistance

ohmique, de haute valeur ~
  D: hochohmig *adj*
  E: high-ohmic *adj*, of high resistance, highly resistive

onde *f*

onde
D: Welle f
E: wave n

onde f de choc [él.]
D: Stoßwelle f, Spannungsstoß m
E: impulse n (el.), voltage surge

onde f mobile
D: Wanderwelle f
E: travelling wave, transient wave

onde f perturbatrice
D: Störschwingung f
E: parasitic oscillation

onde f progressive
D: Wanderwelle f
E: travelling wave, transient wave

ondes f pl d'oscillation amortie
D: gedämpft schwingende Wellen
E: damped oscillation waves

onde f stationnaire [él.]
D: stehende Welle
E: standing wave

ondulation f
D: Welligkeit f
E: waviness n

ondulation f à anneaux fermés
D: geschlossene Ringwellung
E: closed corrugation

ondulation f d'isolateur
D: Isolator-Rippen f pl
E: insulator corrugation

opérateur m
D: Maschinenführer m, Bedienungsperson f
E: operator n, attendant n

opération f
D: Arbeitsweise f
E: mode of operation, functioning n, operation n

operation, en une même ~
D: in einem einzigen Arbeitsgang, in einem Durchgang
E: in a single operation

opération f à main
D: Handbetrieb m, Handsteuerung f
E: manual operation, hand operation, manual control

opération f continue
D: kontinuierlicher Betrieb
E: continuous operation

opération f en tandem
D: Tandembetrieb m
E: tandemized operation

opération f manuelle
D: Handbetrieb m, Handsteuerung f
E: manual operation, hand operation, manual control

opérer v une machine
D: eine Maschine fahren, eine Maschine bedienen
E: to run a machine, to operate a machine

optimalisation f
D: optimale Gestaltung, Optimierung f
E: optimization n

optimisation f
D: optimale Gestaltung, Optimierung f
E: optimization n

ordinogramme m
D: Ablaufplan m, Ablaufdiagramm n, Arbeitsablaufdiagramm n, Flußdiagramm n, Fertigungsflußschema n
E: flow chart, flow diagram, process (flow) chart

ordre, en ~ de marche
D: betriebsbereit adj
E: operational adj, ready for operation, in working order

ordre m d'addition des ingrédients
D: Mischfolge f
E: order-of-addition schedule (mixing)

ordre m de numération des conducteurs
D: Aderzählfolge f
E: numbering of cable cores

organigramme m
D: Organisationsplan m
E: organization chart

organigramme m (prod.)
D: Ablaufplan m, Ablaufdiagramm n, Arbeitsablaufdiagramm n, Flußdiagramm n, Fertigungsflußschema n
E: flow chart, flow diagram, process (flow) chart

organisme m d'approbation
D: Prüfstelle f
E: approval organization, testing station

orientable adj
D: verstellbar adj, einstellbar adj, regelbar adj, regulierbar adj
E: adjustable adj, variable adj

orientant adj le champ électrique [él.]

D: feldsteuernd *adj*
E: field-controlling *adj*, stress-controlling *adj*

orientation *f* **du champ électrique** [él.]
D: Feldsteuerung *f*, Feldregulierung *f*
E: stress control, stress relief, field control

orifice *m*
D: Öffnung *f*
E: opening *n*, orifice *n*, aperture *n*, bore *n*

oscillation *f* [él.]
D: Schwingung *f*
E: oscillation *n*

oscillation *f* **d'huile**
D: Ölbewegung *f* (im Kabel)
E: oil oscillation

oscillation *f* **parasite**
D: Störschwingung *f*
E: parasitic oscillation

osciller *v* **les faisceaux de câbles** [câblage]
D: Bündel unregelmäßig zusammenschlagen
E: to oscillate cable units

ôter *v*
D: entziehen *v*
E: extract *v*, remove *v*

outil *m* **à épisser**
D: Spleißgerät *n*
E: splicing tool

outil *m* **de découpage**
D: Stanzwerkzeug *n*
E: blanking die, punching tool

outil *m* **de pelage** [câb.]
D: Rundschälwerkzeug *n* (zum schichtweisen Abtragen von extrudierten Kabel-Isolierungen und schwachleitenden Schichten), Schälwerkzeug *n*
E: jacket removal tool

outil *m* **de poinçonnage** [access. c.]
D: Preßwerkzeug *n*
E: compression tool, crimping tool

outillage *m*
D: Werkzeugbestückung *f*
E: tooling *n*

outillage *m* **de boudineuse**
D: Extruderwerkzeuge *n pl*, Spritzwerkzeuge *n pl*
E: extruder dies *pl*, extrusion dies *pl*

outil *m* **pour le formage de tuyaux**
D: Rohrformwerkzeug *n*
E: tube forming tool

outils *m pl* [extr., pr.à filer, fabr. fils mét.]
D: Werkzeuge *n pl*
E: dies *pl*, tools *pl*

ouverture *f*
D: Öffnung *f*
E: opening *n*, orifice *n*, aperture *n*, bore *n*

ouverture *f*
D: lichte Weite
E: inside diameter, inside width

ouvrier *m* **non qualifié**
D: ungelernter Arbeiter
E: unskilled worker

ouvrier *m* **qualifié**
D: Facharbeiter *m*
E: skilled worker

oxyde *m* **de plomb**
D: Bleioxid *n*
E: lead oxide

oxyde *m* **de zinc**
D: Zinkoxid *n*
E: zinc oxide

oxyder *v*
D: oxydieren *v*
E: oxidize *v*

P

paille *f* **de laminage**
D: Walzsplitter *m*
E: sliver *n*

paillette *f*
D: Flitter *m* (Draht)
E: sliver *n*, spill *n*

paillettes *f pl*
D: Schuppen *f pl*
E: flakes *pl*, scales *pl*

pairage *m*
D: Paarverseilung *f*
E: pairing *n*, twinning *n*, pair twisting

paire *f* [c. com.]
D: Doppelader *f*, paarverseilte Leitung, Paar *n*
E: pair *n*, twin-wire *n*, dual wire

paire *f* **câblée en étoile**
D: Doppelsternvierer *m*
E: pair stranded in quad pair formation

paire *f* **coaxiale**

paire

paire f coaxiale de petit diamètre
D: Koaxialpaar n
E: coaxial pair

paire f coaxiale de petit diamètre
D: Kleinkoaxialpaar n
E: small-diameter coaxial pair

paire f coaxiale standard
D: Normalkoaxialpaar n
E: standard coaxial pair

paire f de comptage [c. com.]
D: Zählpaar n
E: tracer pair

paire f de conducteurs
D: Aderpaar n
E: pair of cores

paire f de direction
D: Richtungspaar n
E: direction pair

paire f de réserve [c. com.]
D: Reservepaar n, Ersatzaderpaar n
E: reserve pair, spare pair, extra pair

paire f de surveillance
D: Überwachungspaar n
E: alarm pair

paire f de télévision
D: Fernsehpaar n
E: video pair

paire f radio
D: Rundfunkpaar n
E: broadcast pair

paire f sous écran
D: geschirmtes Paar
E: screened pair, shielded pair

paire f symétrique
D: symmetrisches Paar
E: symmetric pair

paireuse f
D: Paarverseilmaschine f
E: twinning machine, pair stranding machine, pair twisting machine

pale f
D: Knetarm m
E: blade n (of kneader)

palette f
D: Knetarm m
E: blade n (of kneader)

palettiser v
D: auf Paletten packen
E: palletize v

palier, élévation de tension par ~s
D: stufenweise Spannungssteigerung
E: voltage increase in steps

palier, par ~s de ...
D: in Stufen von ...
E: in steps of ..., in increments of ...

palier m à billes
D: Kugellager n
E: ball-bearing

palier m de tension
D: Spannungsstufe f
E: voltage step

palmer m
D: Mikrometerschraube f
E: micrometer screw

palper v
D: abtasten v
E: scan v, sense v

palpeur m
D: Abtastvorrichtung f, Fühler m
E: scanning device, scanner n, sensing device, sensor n, detecting element

palpeur m de température
D: Temperaturfühler m
E: temperature pick-up, temperature sensor

palpeur-guide m
D: Verlegearm m (Aufwickelei), Verlegevorrichtung f (Aufwickelei), Verteiler m (Aufwickelei)
E: distributor n, traverser n, traversing unit

panier m d'enroulement
D: Bundwickler m, Wickelkorb m
E: coiling basket

panier m d'imprégnation
D: Tränkkorb m
E: impregnating tray

panne f
D: Ausfall m (Anlage, Kabel), Betriebsstörung f
E: failure n, breakdown n, outage n

panneau, installation de sélecteurs à ~
D: Flachwähl-Anlage f
E: panel switching equipment

panneau m de commande
D: Bedienungsfeld n
E: control panel, operator panel

panneau m indicateur de fonctionnement
D: Anzeigetafel f
E: indicator panel, signal board, display panel

panne f de courant
D: Stromausfall m
E: power failure, current breakdown

papier m abrasif

papier *m* **abrasif**
 D: Schmirgelpapier *n*
 E: abrasive paper
papier *m* **carbone**
 D: Rußpapier *n*
 E: carbon black paper
papier *m* **carbone et papier métallisé imbriqués**
 D: dachziegelartig aufgebrachtes Rußpapier und metallisiertes Papier
 E: carbon-loaded paper interlocked with metallized paper
papier *m* **crêpe**
 D: Krepp-Papier *n*
 E: crepe paper
papier *m* **crêpe bituminé**
 D: Bitumenkreppapier *n*
 E: bituminized crepe paper
papier *m* **duplex**
 D: Duplex-Papier *n* (Doppellagenpapier)
 E: duplex paper, double-ply paper
papier *m* **dur**
 D: Hartpapier *n*
 E: synthetic resin-bonded paper, laminated paper
papier *m* **émerisé**
 D: Schmirgelpapier *n*
 E: abrasive paper
papier *m* **en deux couches**
 D: Duplex-Papier *n* (Doppellagenpapier)
 E: duplex paper, double-ply paper
papier *m* **en une couche**
 D: Simplex-Papier *n* (Einfachlagenpapier)
 E: simplex paper, single-ply paper, single-wire paper
papier *m* **fabriqué sur machine Fourdrinier**
 D: Langsieb-Papier *n*
 E: Fourdrinier-machine paper
papier/huile, diélectrique ~
 D: Öl/Papier-Dielektrikum *n*
 E: oil/paper dielectric
papier *m* **imprégné**
 D: getränktes Papier
 E: impregnated paper
papier *m* **imprégné de résine synthétique**
 D: Hartpapier *n*
 E: synthetic resin-bonded paper, laminated paper

papier *m* **isolant**
 D: Isolierpapier *n*
 E: insulating paper
papier *m* **isolant Kraft**
 D: Kraft-Isolierpapier *n*
 E: Kraft insulating paper
papier *m* **(fabriqué sur) machine à tamis cylindrique**
 D: Rundsieb-Papier *n*
 E: cylinder machine paper
papier *m* **métallisé**
 D: metallisiertes Papier (Höchstädter Folie)
 E: metallized paper
papier *m* **plissé**
 D: Krepp-Papier *n*
 E: crepe paper
papier *m* **satiné**
 D: satiniertes Papier
 E: satin paper, satiny paper, satined paper
papier *m* **simplex**
 D: Simplex-Papier *n* (Einfachlagenpapier)
 E: simplex paper, single-ply paper, single-wire paper
papier verni, câble isolé au ~
 D: Lackpapierkabel *n*
 E: varnished paper cable
paquet *m* **de filtres** [extr.]
 D: Siebpackung *f*
 E: screen pack
paradiaphonie *f*
 D: Nahnebensprechen *n*
 E: near-end cross talk (NEX)
parafoudre *m*
 D: Blitzableiter *m*
 E: lightning conductor, lightning arrester
parallèle, disposition en ~
 D: Verlegung nebeneinander, Parallelanordnung *f*
 E: laying side by side, laying in parallel, parallel arrangement
paramètre *m*
 D: Kennwert *m*, Parameter *m*
 E: parameter *n*, characteristic value
parasurtension *m*
 D: Überspannungsableiter *m*
 E: surge diverter, surge voltage arrester, overvoltage arrester
parcours *m* [câb.]
 D: Trasse *f*

parcours
  E: route n, run n
parcouru adj **de courant**
  D: stromführend adj, spannungführend adj
  E: live adj, current-carrying adj
paroi f **isolante**
  D: Isolierschicht f
  E: insulating layer
partie f **en poids**
  D: Gewichtsteil n
  E: part by weight
pas m
  D: Steigung f (Gewinde, Schnecke, Bandspinnen)
  E: pitch n
pas m [câblage]
  D: Drall m, Schlag m
  E: lay n, twist n
pas m **à droite** [câblage]
  D: Rechtsdrall m, Rechtsschlag m
  E: right-hand lay, right-hand twist
pas m **à gauche** [câblage]
  D: Linksdrall m, Linksschlag m
  E: left-hand lay, left-hand twist
pas m **de câblage changeant périodiquement**
  D: periodisch wechselnde Drallrichtung
  E: periodically changing lay
pas m **de la vis** [extr.]
  D: Schneckengang m, Gewindegang der Schnecke, Schneckengewinde n
  E: flight of the screw, thread of the screw
pas m **d'ondulation**
  D: Wellenlänge f (Wellmantel)
  E: pitch of corrugation
pas m **d'une vis**
  D: Ganghöhe einer Schnecke/Schraube
  E: lead of a screw
passage, sens de ~ du câble
  D: Laufrichtung des Kabels durch eine Maschine
  E: direction of cable travel
passage m **d'antenne**
  D: Antennendurchführung f
  E: antenna duct, antenna lead-in (tube)
passage m **pour cable**
  D: Bohrung f (für den Kabeldurchlauf)
  E: cable passage, clear bore (for cable)
passe f [lam.]
  D: Durchgang m, Stich m
  E: pass n
passe, en une seule ~
  D: in einem einzigen Arbeitsgang, in einem Durchgang
  E: in a single operation
passe f **de laminage** [mét.]
  D: Walzgang m
  E: rolling cycle, rolling pass
passe-fil m **en caoutchouc**
  D: Gummi-Einführungstülle f (gegen Ausfransen von Kabelenden), Gummitülle f (für Kabelenden)
  E: wire binding sleeve
passer v **à la fabrication**
  D: für die Fertigung freigeben
  E: to release for factory production
passerelle f
  D: Laufboden m, Laufbühne f
  E: catwalk n
passer v **un essai**
  D: eine Prüfung bestehen
  E: to pass a test, to withstand a test
pâte de papier, conducteur isolé à la ~
  D: Pulp-Ader f, pulpisolierte Ader
  E: pulped wire, pulp-insulated wire
patin m
  D: Gleitschiene f
  E: slide bar, slide rail
patin m **de chenille**
  D: Raupenglied n
  E: caterpillar pad
PCP (v. polychloroprène)
PCV (v. chlorure de polyvinyle)
PE (v. polyéthylène)
peau f **de la fonte**
  D: Gußhaut f
  E: skin n (casting)
peau f **oxydée**
  D: Oxidhaut f
  E: oxide film, oxide skin
peinture f
  D: Anstrich m
  E: paint n, finish n
peinture protectrice, couche de ~
  D: Schutzanstrich m
  E: protective varnish coating
pelage m
  D: Ablösen n (Trennen)
  E: peeling n, detachment n, detaching n

pelage, outil de ~ [câb.]
  D: Rundschälwerkzeug n (zum schichtweisen Abtragen von extrudierten Kabel-Isolierungen und schwachleitenden Schichten), Schälwerkzeug n
  E: jacket removal tool

peler v
  D: ablösen v (Folie, Schicht), abziehen v
  E: peel v, separate v, detach v

peler v [access. c.]
  D: schälen v (eine Schicht)
  E: peel v

pellicule f de coulée
  D: Gußhaut f
  E: skin n (casting)

pellicule f de laminage
  D: Walzhaut f
  E: rolling skin, scale n

pénétration f
  D: Penetration f, Eindringung f
  E: penetration n

pénétration f d'eau
  D: Eindringen von Wasser (in Kabel)
  E: water seeping, water seepage, water penetration

pénétration f d'humidité
  D: Eindringen von Feuchtigkeit
  E: ingress of moisture, penetration of moisture, moisture permeation

pente f d'une courbe
  D: Abfall einer Kurve, Neigung einer Kurve
  E: decline of a curve, slope of a curve

pentes, câble pour installation sur ~ raides
  D: Steilhangkabel n
  E: cable for installation on steep slopes

perche, travail avec la ~ [métallurg.]
  D: Polen n
  E: poling n

perditance f [c. com.]
  D: Ableitung f, Ableitungsverlust m
  E: conductance n

perditance f de transmission [com.]
  D: Betriebsableitung f
  E: operational leakage

perdre v sa couleur
  D: verblassen v
  E: fade v

perdu, touret ~ [câb.]
  D: Verkaufstrommel f, Einwegtrommel f
  E: non-returnable reel

perdu, touret non ~ [câb.]
  D: Leihtrommel f
  E: returnable reel

performance f [mach.]
  D: Leistung f, Ausstoß m
  E: performance n, output n, efficiency n, capacity n

performance f
  D: Verhalten n
  E: behaviour n, performance n

performance f (en service)
  D: Betriebsverhalten n
  E: operating performance, service performance

périodes f pl par seconde
  D: Hertz (Hz)
  E: cycles per second (cps), hertz

permanence f de la teinte
  D: Farbbeständigkeit f
  E: colo(u)r-fastness, colo(u)r retention

perméabilité f
  D: magnetische Leitfähigkeit
  E: permeability n

perméabilité f à l'air
  D: Luftdurchlässigkeit f
  E: permeability to air

perméabilité f à la vapeur d'eau
  D: Wasserdampfdurchlässigkeit f
  E: water vapour permeability

perméabilité f au gaz
  D: Gasdurchlässigkeit f, Durchlässigkeit für Gas
  E: permeability to gas

perméable adj
  D: durchlässig adj
  E: permeable adj, pervious adj

permittivité f
  D: Dielektrizitätskonstante (DK) f
  E: dielectric constant, permittivity n

permittivité f absolue
  D: absolute Dielektrizitätskonstante
  E: absolute permittivity

permittivité f relative
  D: relative Dielektrizitätskonstante
  E: relative permittivity

peroxyde m
  D: Peroxid n
  E: peroxide n

perte f

perte
- D: Verlust m
- E: loss n

perte, à faibles ~s
- D: verlustarm adj
- E: low-loss... adj

perte f au feu [métallurg.]
- D: Abbrand m
- E: scale loss, melting loss

perte f au recuit
- D: Glühverlust m
- E: annealing loss

perte f d'écoulement
- D: Strömungsverlust m
- E: flow loss

perte f de masse
- D: Gewichtsverlust m
- E: weight loss

perte f de poids
- D: Gewichtsverlust m
- E: weight loss

perte f de potentiel
- D: Spannungsverlust m
- E: voltage loss, potential loss

perte f de pression
- D: Druckabfall m, Druckverlust m
- E: pressure drop, pressure loss, head loss

perte f de puissance [él.]
- D: Leistungsverlust m
- E: power loss

perte f de tension
- D: Spannungsverlust m
- E: voltage loss, potential loss

perte f de transmission
- D: Übertragungsverlust m
- E: transmission loss

perte f de transport
- D: Übertragungsverlust m
- E: transmission loss

perte f par dérivation
- D: Ableitungsverlust m
- E: leakage current loss, leakage loss

perte f par effet Joule
- D: Stromwärmeverlust m
- E: resistance loss

pertes f pl dans le cuivre [él.]
- D: Kupferverluste m pl
- E: ohmic losses

pertes f pl de Foucault [él.]
- D: Wirbelstromverluste m pl
- E: eddy current losses

pertes f pl dépendant du courant
- D: stromabhängige Verluste
- E: current-dependent losses, current-controlled losses

pertes f pl diélectriques
- D: dielektrische Verluste, Verluste im Dielektrikum
- E: dielectric losses

pertes f pl par courants parasites [él.]
- D: Wirbelstromverluste m pl
- E: eddy current losses

pertes f pl superficielles
- D: Oberflächenverluste m pl
- E: surface losses

pertes f pl supplémentaires
- D: Zusatzverluste m pl
- E: extra losses

pertes f pl sur la gaine
- D: Mantelverluste m pl
- E: sheath losses

pertes f pl sur l'âme
- D: Leiterverluste m pl
- E: conductor losses

perturbation f
- D: Störbeeinflussung f, Beeinflussung f
- E: interference n (effect)

perturbation f des lignes de télécommunication par des lignes de transport d'énergie
- D: Beeinflussung von Nachrichtenleitungen durch Energieanlagen
- E: interference of power cables with communication cables

phase, en ~
- D: phasengleich adj
- E: in phase

phase f à phase
- D: Phase gegen Phase
- E: phase to phase

phase f de fabrication
- D: Stadium der Fertigung
- E: stage of production, manufacturing stage

phase f en avance
- D: voreilende Phase
- E: leading phase

phase f en retard
- D: nacheilende Phase
- E: lagging phase

phase f par rapport à la terre
- D: Phase gegen Erde
- E: phase to earth, phase to ground

phases f pl de travail

plage

D: Arbeitsablauf m, Betriebsablauf m
E: flow of operation, operating sequence, flow process, operating cycle

pièce, en deux ~s
D: zweigeteilt adj, zweiteilig adj, geteilt adj
E: split adj, two-piece adj

pièce, en une seule ~
D: einteilig adj
E: single-piece... adj, one-piece... adj, monobloc adj

pièce f coulée
D: Gießling m
E: casting n

pièce f de jonction
D: Zwischenstück n, Verbindungsstück n, Anschlußstück n
E: intermediate piece, connecting piece, adapter n, connector n, fitting n

pièce f de raccordement
D: Zwischenstück n, Verbindungsstück n, Anschlußstück n
E: intermediate piece, connecting piece, adapter n, connector n, fitting n

pièce f de rechange
D: Ersatzteil n
E: spare part, spare n

pièce f d'usure
D: Verschleißteil n
E: wearing part, part subject to wear

pièce f intermédiaire
D: Zwischenstück n, Verbindungsstück n, Anschlußstück n
E: intermediate piece, connecting piece, adapter n, connector n, fitting n

pièce f moulée
D: Preßling m, Preßteil n, Formteil n
E: mo(u)lding n, mo(u)lded part

pièce f normalisée
D: Normteil n
E: standard part

pièce f standard
D: Normteil n
E: standard part

pigment m
D: Farbstoff m
E: pigment n, colo(u)rant n

pignon m de commande
D: Antriebsrad n
E: drive gear, driving gear

pile f locale
D: Lokalelement n
E: local cell

pince f
D: Klemme f
E: clamp n, clip n

pince f d'ancrage
D: Befestigungsklemme f
E: mounting clip, mounting bracket

pince f universelle
D: Kombizange f
E: combination pliers pl

piston m [mach.]
D: Stempel m, Kolben m, Plunger m
E: piston n, ram n, plunger n

piston m à action double
D: doppeltwirkender Plunger
E: double-acting plunger

piston m à double effet
D: doppeltwirkender Plunger
E: double-acting plunger

piston m de rappel
D: Rückzugskolben m
E: pull-back ram

piston m de remontée
D: Rückzugskolben m
E: pull-back ram

pitting m
D: Lokalkorrosion f, Lochfraß m
E: local(ized) corrosion, pitting n

pivotant adj
D: ausschwenkbar adj, ausklappbar adj, schwenkbar adj, aufklappbar adj, drehbar gelagert
E: hinged adj, swivelling adj, pivoted adj

pivotement m
D: Ausschwenken n
E: swinging-out n, swivelling-out n

placer v
D: einsetzen v, einbauen v
E: insert v, mount v, fit v

plage f
D: Bereich m
E: range n, field n, scope n, area n

plage f de dispersion
D: Streubereich m
E: range of scattering, range of dispersion

plage 550

plage *f* **de fréquences**
 D: Frequenzband *n*, Frequenzbereich *m*
 E: frequency band, frequency range

plage *f* **de régulation**
 D: Regelbereich *m*
 E: control range, regulating range

planche *f* **de préparation pour câbles**
 D: Kabelformbrett *n*, Formbrett für Kabel
 E: cable forming board, cable lacing board

plan *m* **d'assemblage**
 D: Montagezeichnung *f*, Installationszeichnung *f*, Aufstellungszeichnung *f*
 E: assembly drawing, erection drawing, installation drawing

plan *m* **de câblage**
 D: Schaltplan *m*, Schaltschema *n*, Verdrahtungsplan *m*
 E: wiring diagram, wiring scheme, circuit diagram

plan *m* **de construction**
 D: Konstruktionszeichnung *f*
 E: construction drawing, design drawing

plan *m* **de détail**
 D: Einzelzeichnung *f*, Teilzeichnung *f*
 E: detail drawing, component drawing

plan *m* **de fondation**
 D: Fundamentzeichnung *f*
 E: foundation drawing

plan *m* **de montage**
 D: Montagezeichnung *f*, Installationszeichnung *f*, Aufstellungszeichnung *f*
 E: assembly drawing, erection drawing, installation drawing

plan *m* **d'ensemble**
 D: Grundrißzeichnung *f*
 E: layout drawing

plan *m* **des circuits**
 D: Schaltplan *m*, Schaltschema *n*, Verdrahtungsplan *m*
 E: wiring diagram, wiring scheme, circuit diagram

planification *f* **d'installations de câbles**
 D: Planung von Kabelanlagen
 E: planning of cable installations

plaque *f*
 D: Platte *f*
 E: sheet *n*, plate *n*, slab *n*

plaqué, âme en aluminium ~ de cuivre
 D: kupferplattierter Aluminiumleiter
 E: copper-clad aluminium conductor

plaqué, fil d'aluminium ~ de cuivre
 D: kupferplattierter Aluminiumdraht, kupferumhüllter Aluminiumdraht, Aluminiumdraht mit Kupfermantel
 E: copper-clad aluminium wire

plaque *f* **à bornes**
 D: Klemmplatte *f*
 E: terminal plate

plaque *f* **de base**
 D: Grundplatte *f*
 E: base plate, mounting base

plaque *f* **de guidage** [câblage]
 D: Verseilscheibe *f*, Lochplatte *f*
 E: assembling plate, lay plate, face plate

plaque *f* **de recouvrement**
 D: Abdeckplatte *f*
 E: covering plate, guard plate

plaque *f* **de répartition** [câblage]
 D: Verseilscheibe *f*, Lochplatte *f*
 E: assembling plate, lay plate, face plate

plaque *f* **de répartition oscillante**
 D: oszillierende Verseilscheibe
 E: oscillating face plate

plaque-filtre *f* [extr.]
 D: Siebeinsatz *m*
 E: strainer *n*

plaque *f* **laminée**
 D: ausgezogene Platte
 E: rolled sheet

plaque *f* **protectrice**
 D: Abdeckplatte *f*
 E: covering plate, guard plate

plasticité *f*
 D: Plastizität *f*
 E: plasticity *n*

plastifiant *m*
 D: Weichmacher *m*
 E: plasticizer *n*

plastifiant *m* **derivé d'acide gras**
 D: Fettsäure-Weichmacher *m*
 E: fatty acid plasticizer

plastificateur *m*
 D: Plastifikator *m*
 E: plastifier *n*, plastificator *n*

plastification *f*
 D: Plastifizierung *f*
 E: plastification *n*

plastique *m*
 D: Kunststoff *m*, Plast *m*
 E: plastic material, synthetic material, synthetic resin

plastique *m* **cellulaire**
 D: Schaum-Kunststoff *m*
 E: foamed plastic, expanded plastic, cellular plastic

plastique *m* **laminé**
 D: Schichtstoff *m*
 E: laminate *n*, laminated plastic, laminated material

plastique *m* **renforcé**
 D: verstärkter Kunststoff
 E: reinforced plastic

plastomètre *m*
 D: Plastometer *n*
 E: plastometer *n*

plateau *m*
 D: Platte *f*
 E: sheet *n*, plate *n*, slab *n*

plateau *m*
 D: Schürze *f* (Mischwalzwerk)
 E: tray *n*

plate-forme *f*
 D: Bühne *f* (Arbeitsplattform)
 E: platform *n*

plate-forme *f* **de commande**
 D: Arbeitsbühne *f*
 E: operator's control platform, operating platform

plate-forme *f* **d'empilage**
 D: Stapelbühne *f*
 E: collection platform

plate-forme *f* **de service**
 D: Arbeitsbühne *f*
 E: operator's control platform, operating platform

plate-forme *f* **d'essai**
 D: Prüfstand *m*
 E: test stand, test floor, test bench

plein, utilisé à ~
 D: voll ausgelastet
 E: loaded to capacity, operating at full capacity

pleine charge *f*
 D: Vollast *f*
 E: full load

pli *m*
 D: Falte *f*
 E: crease *n*, wrinkle *n*

pli, exempt de ~s
 D: faltenfrei *adj*
 E: wrinkle-free *adj*, crease-free *adj*

pli, sans ~s
 D: faltenfrei *adj*
 E: wrinkle-free *adj*, crease-free *adj*

pliage *m*
 D: Biegen *n*
 E: bending *n*

pliage *m* [rub.]
 D: Knicken *n*
 E: creasing *n*

pliages, nombre de ~ alternés
 D: Biegezahl *f*
 E: bending limit, bending value

plier *v*
 D: falzen *v*
 E: fold *v*

plissement *m*
 D: Faltenbildung *f*
 E: creasing *n*, wrinkling *n*

plomb *m* **antimonié**
 D: Antimon-Blei *n*
 E: antimonial lead

plomb *m* **de câble**
 D: Kabelblei *n*
 E: cable lead

plonger *v*
 D: eintauchen *v*
 E: immerse *v*, dip *v*

poche *f* **de coulée** [coul. cont. lam.]
 D: Gießpfanne *f*, Gießtopf *m*
 E: tundish *n*, pouring ladle

poches *f pl* **d'air**
 D: Lufteinschlüsse *m pl*
 E: air inclusions, air pockets, voids *pl*

poids *m* **au mètre carré**
 D: Flächengewicht *n*
 E: weight per square meter

poids moléculaire, à haut ~
 D: mit hohem Molekulargewicht, hochmolekular *adj*
 E: of high molecular weight, high-molecular... *adj*

poids *m* **par (unité de) volume**
 D: Raumgewicht *n*
 E: volumetric weight, density *n*, weight per unit of volume

poids *m* **spécifique**
 D: spezifisches Gewicht
 E: specific gravity, volume weight

poinçon *m* [extr.]
 D: Nippel *m*
 E: tip *n*

poinçon *m*

poinçon

    D: Patrize *f*
    E: core die, male die
poinçon *m*
    D: Dorn *m*
    E: mandrel *n*
poinçon *m* **guide** [extr.]
    D: Führungsnippel *m*
    E: guider tip
poinçonnage *m*
    D: Ausstanzen *n* (Prüfkörper)
    E: punching with a die, cutting with a die, die-cutting *n*
point *m* **chaud**
    D: Heißstelle *f*
    E: hot spot
point *m* **d'alimentation**
    D: Speisepunkt *m*
    E: feeding point
point *m* **d'allumage**
    D: Zündpunkt *m*
    E: ignition point
point *m* **de branchement** [com.]
    D: Verzweiger *m*, Verzweigungspunkt *m*
    E: cross-connection point (C.C.P.), branching point
point *m* **d'ébullition**
    D: Siedepunkt *m*
    E: boiling point
point d'ébullition, à ~ élevé
    D: hochsiedend *adj*
    E: with a high boiling point
point d'ébullition, à bas ~
    D: niedrigsiedend *adj*
    E: with a low boiling point
point *m* **de câblage**
    D: Verseilpunkt *m*
    E: stranding point, die point
point *m* **de changement de la torsion**
    D: Drallwechselstelle *f*
    E: lay reversal point, twist changing point
point *m* **de charge**
    D: Spulenpunkt *m* (Pupinisierung)
    E: pupinization point
point *m* **d'éclair en coupe fermé**
    D: Flammpunkt im geschlossenen Tiegel
    E: flash point in a closed cup
point *m* **d'éclair en coupe ouverte**
    D: Flammpunkt im offenen Tiegel
    E: flash point in an open cup
point *m* **d'éclair en vase fermé**
    D: Flammpunkt im geschlossenen Tiegel
    E: flash point in a closed cup
point *m* **d'éclair en vase ouvert**
    D: Flammpunkt im offenen Tiegel
    E: flash point in an open cup
point *m* **de congélation**
    D: Stockpunkt *m*, Einfrierpunkt *m*, Erstarrungspunkt *m*
    E: solidification point, freezing point
point *m* **d'écoulement**
    D: Fließpunkt *m*
    E: flow point
point *m* **de figeage**
    D: Erstarrungspunkt *m* (Öle), Stockpunkt *m* (Öle)
    E: pour point, cloud point
point *m* **de fragilité**
    D: Brechpunkt *m*
    E: breaking point
point *m* **de fusion**
    D: Schmelzpunkt *m*
    E: melting point
point *m* **de goutte**
    D: Tropfpunkt *m*
    E: drop point
point *m* **de jonction**
    D: Knotenpunkt *m*
    E: intersection *n*, junction point
point *m* **de mesure**
    D: Meßpunkt *m*
    E: measuring point, check point
point *m* **de (mise à la) terre**
    D: Erdungspunkt *m*
    E: earth point
point *m* **de montée de cable**
    D: Kabelaufführungspunkt *m*
    E: cable distribution point, cable lifting point
point *m* **de ramollissement**
    D: Erweichungspunkt *m* (Massen)
    E: softening point
point *m* **de section pour l'écartement entre bobines de charge** [c. com.]
    D: Festpunkt für Spulenabstände
    E: section point for loading coil spacing
point *m* **de solidification**
    D: Stockpunkt *m*, Einfrierpunkt *m*, Erstarrungspunkt *m*
    E: solidification point, freezing point
point *m* **de sous-répartition** [com.]
    D: Verzweiger *m*,

Verzweigungspunkt m
E: cross-connection point (C.C.P.), branching point

point m d'inflammation
D: Entzündungspunkt m (Öle), Flammpunkt m, Brennpunkt m (chem.)
E: fire point, ignition point, flash point

point m d'inversion de la torsion
D: Drallwechselstelle f
E: lay reversal point, twist changing point

pointe f
D: Spitze f (Spannung, Leistung)
E: peak n, crest n

pointe, monté entre ~s
D: in Pinolen gelagert
E: pintle-mounted adj

pointe f de charge [él.]
D: Lastspitze f, Spitzenbelastung f
E: peak load, load peak

pointe f de la vis [extr.]
D: Schneckenspitze f
E: tip of a screw

pointe f locale de température
D: Heißstelle f
E: hot spot

point m faible [câb.]
D: Schwachstelle f
E: weak point

point m neutre
D: Nullpunkt m, Sternpunkt m
E: neutral point, zero point

point m nodal
D: Knotenpunkt m
E: intersection n, junction point

poise f
D: Poise n (Viskosität)
E: poise n

polarisation f
D: Vorspannung f
E: bias n

pôles m pl homologues
D: gleichnamige Pole
E: like poles, similar poles

pôles m pl similaires
D: gleichnamige Pole
E: like poles, similar poles

polyamide m
D: Polyamid (PA) n
E: polyamide n

polychloroprène m (PCP)
D: Polychloropren (PCP) n
E: polychloroprene (PCP) n

polychlorure m de vinyle (PCV)
D: Polyvinylchlorid (PVC) n
E: polyvinyl chloride (PVC)

polyéthylène m
D: Voll-PE n
E: solid PE

polyéthylène m (PE)
D: Polyäthylen (PE) n
E: polyethylene (PE) n

polyéthylène m à chaîne droite
D: geradkettiges PE
E: straight-chain PE, linear PE

polyéthylène m basse densité
D: Hochdruck-PE n
E: low-density PE (LD-PE), high-pressure PE (HP-PE)

polyéthylène m basse pression
D: Niederdruck-PE n
E: high-density PE (HD-PE), low pressure PE (LP-PE)

polyéthylène m cellulaire
D: Zell-PE n, verschäumtes PE, verzelltes PE
E: foamed PE, cellular PE, expanded PE

polyéthylène m chlorosulfoné (CSPE)
D: chlorsulfoniertes PE (CSPE)
E: chlorosulphonated PE (CSPE)

polyéthylène m haute densité
D: Niederdruck-PE n
E: high-density PE (HD-PE), low pressure PE (LP-PE)

polyéthylène m haute pression
D: Hochdruck-PE n
E: low-density PE (LD-PE), high-pressure PE (HP-PE)

polyéthylène m irradié
D: bestrahltes PE
E: irradiated PE

polyéthylène m linéaire
D: geradkettiges PE
E: straight-chain PE, linear PE

polyéthylène m mousse
D: Zell-PE n, verschäumtes PE, verzelltes PE
E: foamed PE, cellular PE, expanded PE

polyéthylène m réticulé
D: vernetztes Polyäthylen (VPE)
E: cross-linked polyethylene (XLPE)

polyéthylène m réticulé chimiquement (PRC)

polyéthylène

    D: chemisch vernetztes Polyäthylen (VPE)
    E: chemically cross-linked polyethylene (XLPE)

polyisobutylène
    D: Polyisobutylen n
    E: polyisobutylene n

polymère m
    D: Polymerisat n
    E: polymer n

polymère m greffé
    D: Pfropfpolymerisat n
    E: graft-polymer n

polymères m pl à longues chaînes
    D: langkettige Polymere
    E: long-chain polymers

polymères m pl d'hydrocarbure
    D: Kohlenwasserstoffpolymere n pl
    E: hydrocarbon polymers

polymérisation f en suspension
    D: Suspensionspolymerisation f
    E: suspension polymerisation

polyoléfine m ramifié
    D: verzweigtes Polyolefin
    E: branched polyolefin

polypropylène m
    D: Polypropylen n
    E: polypropylene n

polystyrène m
    D: Polystyrol n
    E: polystyrene n

polytétrafluoréthylène m (PTFE)
    D: Polytetrafluoräthylen (PTFE) n
    E: polytetrafluorethylene (PTFE) n

pompe f à vide
    D: Vakuumpumpe f
    E: vacuum pump

pompe f de (à) circulation
    D: Umwälzpumpe f
    E: circulating pump

pompe f foulante
    D: Druckpumpe f
    E: pressure pump, forcing pump

pompe immergée, câble pour ~
    D: Tauchpumpenleitung f
    E: submersible-pump cable, submerged-pump cable

pompe f refoulante
    D: Druckpumpe f
    E: pressure pump, forcing pump

ponctué adj et rayé
    D: strichpunktiert adj
    E: dash-dotted adj

pont m de localisation de défauts
    D: Fehlerort-Meßbrücke f
    E: fault location measuring bridge

pont m de mesure
    D: Meßbrücke f
    E: measuring bridge

pont m de résistances
    D: Widerstandsbrücke f
    E: resistance bridge, Wheatstone bridge

pont m (double) de Thomson
    D: Thomson-(Doppel)brücke f
    E: Thomson bridge, double bridge

pont-grue m
    D: Brückenkran m
    E: bridge crane, overhead travelling crane

pont m roulant
    D: Laufkran m
    E: overhead crane, travelling crane

pont m Schering
    D: Schering-Brücke f
    E: Schering bridge

population f [math.]
    D: Grundgesamtheit f
    E: population n

porcelaine f
    D: Porzellanisolator m
    E: porcelain insulator

pore m
    D: Pore f
    E: pore n, pinhole n

porosimètre m
    D: Porenprüfgerät n (Papier)
    E: porosimeter n

porosité f
    D: Luftdurchlässigkeit f (Papier)
    E: porosity n

portatif adj
    D: tragbar adj
    E: portable adj

porte-bobine m [câblage]
    D: Spulenhalter m, Spulenträger m, Joch n
    E: cradle n

porte-conteneur m [pr. à filer]
    D: Aufnehmerhalter m
    E: container holder

portée f d'appel [c. com.]
    D: Rufreichweite f
    E: calling range

portée f de fonctionnement
    D: Funktionsreichweite f

E: operational range
portée *f* **téléphonique** [c. com.]
D: Sprachreichweite *f*
E: audio range
porte-galette *m* [rub.]
D: Papierscheibenhalter *m*, Scheibenhalter *m*
E: pad holder
porte-outils *m* (machine à onduler)
D: Rillkopf *m* (Wellmaschine), Wellkopf *m*
E: corrugating head
porteur *m* [c. én.]
D: Tragorgan *n*
E: suspension strand, suspension unit
porteur *m* **de charge**
D: Ladungsträger *m*
E: charge carrier
pose *f*
D: Aufbringung *f*
E: application *n*
pose *f* **à l'air libre**
D: Verlegung in Luft
E: installation in free air
posé *adj* **à la main**
D: von Hand aufgebracht
E: hand-applied *adj*
pose *f* **à l'extérieur**
D: Verlegung im Freien
E: outdoor installation
pose *f* **à l'intérieur**
D: Innenraum-Verlegung *f*
E: indoor installation
pose *f* **apparente**
D: Aufputz-Installation *f*, Verlegung auf Putz
E: surface mounting, installation on the surface
pose *f* **de câbles**
D: Verlegung von Kabeln
E: cable installation, cable laying
pose *f* **en blocs-tube** [c. com.]
D: Verlegung in Formsteinen
E: laying in ducts
pose *f* **en caniveaux**
D: Verlegung in Röhren, Verlegung in Kanälen
E: laying in conduits, laying in ducts
pose *f* **encastrée**
D: Unterputz-Installation *f*, Verlegung unter Putz
E: buried wiring, concealed wiring, installation under plaster

pose *f* **en pleine terre**
D: Verlegung in Erde, Erdverlegung *f*
E: direct burial (in earth), burying *n* (in ground), underground laying, laying in earth
posé *adj* **en terre** [pose c.]
D: erdverlegt *adj*
E: laid in earth, buried *adj*, laid underground
posé *adj* **longitudinalement**
D: längsaufgebracht *adj*
E: longitudinally applied
poser *v* [câb.]
D: auslegen *v*, verlegen *v*
E: lay *v*, install *v*
poser *v* **en hélice**
D: wendelförmig aufbringen
E: to apply helically, to apply spirally
pose *f* **sous crépi**
D: Unterputz-Installation *f*, Verlegung unter Putz
E: buried wiring, concealed wiring, installation under plaster
pose *f* **sous-marine**
D: Unterwasserverlegung *f*
E: submarine laying
pose *f* **souterraine**
D: Verlegung in Erde, Erdverlegung *f*
E: direct burial (in earth), burying *n* (in ground), underground laying, laying in earth
pose *f* **sur crépi**
D: Aufputz-Installation *f*, Verlegung auf Putz
E: surface mounting, installation on the surface
pose *f* **sur tablettes**
D: Verlegung auf Pritschen
E: laying on racks
position *f* **de mise en marche**
D: Anfahrstellung *f*
E: starting position
position *f* **d'un défaut**
D: Fehlerort *m*, Fehlerstelle *f*
E: position of a fault
positive, relié de façon ~
D: kraftschlüssig verbunden
E: positively connected
poste *m* **d'abonné**
D: Teilnehmeranschluß *m*
E: subscriber's station
poste *m* **d'acquisition des données**
D: Datenerfassungsanlage *f*

E: data logging system

poste *m* de commande
D: Schaltpult *n*, Bedienungspult *n*, Steuerpult *n*
E: control desk, operator's desk, control console

poste *m* de commande
D: Schaltwarte *f*
E: control station

poste *m* de mesure
D: Meßplatz *m*
E: measuring setup, bench-mounted testing equipment

poste *m* de mesure des déséquilibres de capacité
D: Kopplungsmeßplatz *m*
E: capacity unbalance testing equipment

poste *m* de secours
D: Reserveaggregat *n*
E: stand-by unit, stand-by aggregate

poste *m* d'essai
D: Prüfstand *m*
E: test stand, test floor, test bench

poste *m* de transformation
D: Umspannwerk *n*
E: substation *n*, transforming station, transformer station

poste *m* téléphonique
D: Telefonapparat *m*, Sprechstelle *f*
E: telephone set, telephone instrument (US), telephone station

poste *m* téléphonique mobile
D: Streckenfernsprecher *m*
E: portable telephone set

pot *m* de charge [com.]
D: Spulenkasten *m*, Pupinspulenkasten *m*
E: loading (coil) pot, loading coil case

pot *m* de presse
D: Schmelzkessel *m* (Bleipresse), Schmelztopf *m* (Bleipresse)
E: melting pot

pot *m* de presse [pr. à filer]
D: Blockaufnehmer *m*, Bolzenaufnehmer *m*, Aufnehmer *m*, Preßtopf *m*, Rezipient *m*
E: billet container

poteau *m* tubulaire à section décroissante
D: nach oben verjüngter Rohrmast
E: tapered tube pole, tapered tubular mast

potentiel *m* de terre
D: Erdpotential *n*
E: earth potential (GB), ground potential (US)

potentiomètre *m*
D: Spannungsteiler *m*, Potentiometer *n*
E: voltage divider, potentiometer *n*

poudre, en ~
D: feinpulverig *adj*, pulverförmig *adj*
E: powdery *adj*, pulverulent *adj*

poulie *f*
D: Scheibe *f*
E: sheave *n*, disc *n*, pulley *n*

poulie *f* de guidage
D: Führungsrolle *f*, Leitrolle *f*
E: guide roller, guide pulley

poulie *f* de marche à vide
D: Leerlaufrolle *f*
E: idler pulley

poulie *f* de renvoi
D: Umlenkrolle *f*
E: deflector roll, reversing sheave

poulie *f* flottante
D: Tänzerrolle *f*
E: float roll, floating roller, dancer

poulie *f* mobile
D: Tänzerrolle *f*
E: float roll, floating roller, dancer *n*

poupée *f*
D: Puppe *f* (Rolle aus Walzfell)
E: billet *n*, puppet *n*

pourcent(age) *m* en poids
D: Gewichtsprozent *n*
E: percentage by weight, percent in weight

pouvoir *m* adhésif
D: Bindefestigkeit *f*
E: bond strength, bonding strength, adhesiveness *n*

pouvoir *m* de coupure
D: Ausschaltleistung *f*, Abschaltleistung *f*
E: breaking capacity (GB), interrupting capacity (US)

pouvoir *m* isolant
D: Isoliervermögen *n*
E: insulating properties *pl*

praticable *adj*
D: durchführbar *adj*
E: practicable *adj*, realizable *adj*

PRC (v. polyéthylène réticulé chimiquement)

préchauffage, zone de ~
  D: Vorheizzone f
  E: preheat zone
préchauffer v
  D: vorwärmen v
  E: preheat v
précipité m [chim.]
  D: Niederschlag m, Ausscheidung f
  E: precipitate n
précipiter v [chim.]
  D: fällen v
  E: precipitate v
précision, avec une ~ de ... mm
  D: mit einer Genauigkeit von ... mm
  E: to nearest ... mm, accurate within ... mm
précision f **de mesure**
  D: Meßgenauigkeit f
  E: accuracy of measurement, measuring precision
précision f **de réglage**
  D: Einstellgenauigkeit f
  E: accuracy of adjustment, precision of adjustment
prédécharge f
  D: Vorentladung f
  E: predischarge n
préformage m
  D: Vordrallierung f
  E: pretwisting n, prespiralling n
préformé adj [câblage]
  D: vordralliert adj
  E: pretwisted adj, prespiralled adj
préformé adj
  D: vorgeformt adj
  E: pre-formed adj
préimprégnée, isolation ~
  D: vorimprägnierte Isolierung
  E: pre-impregnated insulation
prélèvement m **d'échantillons**
  D: Probenahme f
  E: sampling n, taking of samples
préparation f
  D: Vorbereitung f, Vorbehandlung f
  E: preparation n, preliminary treatment, pretreatment n
préparation f **d'un mélange**
  D: Ansetzen einer Mischung, Mischungsaufbereitung f
  E: preparation of a compound, compound preparation
préparation f **du travail**
  D: Arbeitsvorbereitung f,
  Fertigungsvorbereitung f
  E: manufacturing planning, work planning, production planning
préréglage m
  D: Voreinstellung f
  E: presetting n, preselection n, preadjustment n
près, à ... mm ~
  D: mit einer Genauigkeit von ... mm
  E: to nearest ... mm, accurate within ... mm
prescription f **d'installation**
  D: Errichtungsvorschrift f
  E: installation rule, installation standard
prescriptions f pl
  D: Bestimmungen f pl (Vorschriften)
  E: specifications pl, rules pl, regulations pl, standards pl
presse f **à aluminium**
  D: Aluminium-(Mantel)-Presse f
  E: aluminium press, aluminium sheathing press
presse f **à filer pour gaines de câbles** [mét.]
  D: Strangpresse für Kabelmäntel
  E: cable sheathing press
presse f **à filer type à deux colonnes**
  D: Strangpresse in Zweisäulenbauart
  E: two-column type metal extrusion press
presse f **à filer type à quatre colonnes**
  D: Strangpresse in Viersäulenbauart
  E: four-column type metal extrusion press
presse f **à fouloir double**
  D: Doppelstempel-Presse f
  E: double-ram press, twin-ram press, double-acting press
presse f **à piston**
  D: Stempelpresse f, Strangpresse f, Kolbenpresse f
  E: ram press, plunger press
presse f **à plomb**
  D: Blei-(Mantel)-Presse f
  E: lead-sheathing press, lead press
presse f **à un (seul) fouloir**
  D: Einstempel-Presse f
  E: single-ram press
presse f **de gainage à fouloir double**
  D: Doppelstempel-Kabelmantelpresse f
  E: twin-ram cable sheathing press,

presse

       double-acting cable sheathing press, double-ram cable sheathing press
presse f **de gainage à plomb**
       D: Blei-(Mantel)-Presse f
       E: lead-sheathing press, lead press
presse f **de gainage en continu**
       D: kontinuierliche Kabelmantelpresse
       E: continuous cable sheathing press
presse-étoupe f
       D: Stopfbüchse f
       E: stuffing box, gland n
pression, installation de mise sous ~
       D: Druckanlage f
       E: pressurizing plant
pression, mettre sous ~
       D: unter Druck setzen
       E: pressurize v
pression f **à la surface de séparation**
       D: Grenzflächendruck m
       E: interface pressure
pression f **d'eau**
       D: Wasserdruck m
       E: hydraulic pressure, water pressure
pression f **d'éclatement**
       D: Berstdruck m
       E: bursting pressure
pression f **de filage**
       D: Preßdruck m
       E: extrusion pressure
pression f **de la matière en fusion** [extr.]
       D: Masse-Druck m
       E: melt pressure
pression f **de refoulement** [extr.]
       D: Rückdruck m
       E: back pressure
pression f **de saturation**
       D: Sättigungsdruck m
       E: saturation pressure
pression f **de serrage**
       D: Auflagedruck m
       E: contact pressure
pression f **de service**
       D: Betriebsdruck m
       E: operating pressure, working pressure
pression f **de vapeur** [vulc.]
       D: Dampfdruck m
       E: steam pressure
pression f **d'extrusion**
       D: Preßdruck m
       E: extrusion pressure
pression f **d'huile**
       D: Öldruck m
       E: oil pressure
pression f **hydraulique**
       D: Wasserdruck m
       E: hydraulic pressure, water pressure
pression f **initiale**
       D: Anfangsdruck m
       E: initial pressure
prêt adj **à fonctionner**
       D: betriebsbereit adj
       E: operational adj, ready for operation, in working order
prêt adj **à la mise en marche**
       D: betriebsbereit adj
       E: operational adj, ready for operation, in working order
prêt adj **à la mise en œuvre, à l'usage, au service**
       D: einsatzbereit adj
       E: ready for application, for service, for use
prétordu adj [câblage]
       D: vordralliert adj
       E: pretwisted adj, prespiralled adj
prétorsion f
       D: Vordrallierung f
       E: pretwisting n, prespiralling n
prévulcanisation f
       D: Anvulkanisieren n (Vorvulkanisieren)
       E: pre-vulcanisation n
prise f
       D: Anzapfung f
       E: tap n, tapping n
prise f [tél.]
       D: Belegung f
       E: engagement n, holding n
prise f **complète mâle et femelle**
       D: Steckverbindung f, Steckanschluß m
       E: plug and socket connection
prise f **débrochable**
       D: Steckverbindung f, Steckanschluß m
       E: plug and socket connection
prise f **de courant**
       D: Steckdose f
       E: socket n, socket outlet
prise f **de tension**
       D: Spannungs-Abgriff m
       E: voltage tap
prise f **de terre**
       D: Erdungsklemme f, Erdklemme f

prise f de terre
- D: ground clamp (US), ground terminal (US), earth terminal (GB), earth clamp (GB)

prise f de terre
- D: Erdanschluß m, Erdungsanschluß m, Erdverbindung f
- E: earth connection (GB), ground connection (US)

prise f de transformateur
- D: Transformator-Einführung f
- E: transformer termination, transformer connection, transformer entry

prise f de transformateur
- D: Transformator-Anzapfung f
- E: transformer tap

prise f femelle
- D: Steckbuchse f, Steckerbuchse f, Fassung f
- E: plug socket, connector socket, receptacle n, female contact, socket n

prise f mâle
- D: Stecker m
- E: plug n, plug connector

probabilité f cumulée [math.]
- D: Summenhäufigkeit f
- E: cumulative frequency

probabilité f de claquage [câb.]
- D: Ausfallwahrscheinlichkeit f, Fehlerwahrscheinlichkeit f
- E: failure probability

procédé m
- D: Verfahren n, Methode f
- E: process n, method n, technique n, procedure n

procédé m discontinu
- D: diskontinuierliches Verfahren, Chargenbetrieb m
- E: intermittent process, discontinuous operation, batch type process, batch operation

procès-verbal m de réception
- D: Abnahmeprotokoll n
- E: acceptance certificate

procès-verbal m d'essai
- D: Prüfbericht m, Prüfprotokoll n
- E: test report

production f à l'échelle expérimentale
- D: Versuchsfertigung f, Probefertigung f
- E: trial production, production trial, manufacturing trial

production f par équipe
- D: Schichtleistung f
- E: output per shift

produit m de base
- D: Ausgangsmaterial n
- E: original material, basic material, raw material, feed stock

produit m de vulcanisation
- D: Vulkanisat n
- E: vulcanized material, vulcanizate n

produit m d'extrusion
- D: Extrudat n
- E: extruded material, extrudate n

produit m laminé
- D: Schichtstoff m
- E: laminate n, laminated plastic, laminated material

produit m semi-fini
- D: Halbfertigfabrikat n
- E: semi-finished product

profil m d'écoulement plastique [extr.]
- D: Fließkanal m
- E: flow channel

profil m de température
- D: Temperaturprofil n
- E: temperature profile

profilé m
- D: Profil n
- E: section n

profondeur f de l'empreinte
- D: Eindrucktiefe f
- E: indentation depth

profondeur f de pénétration
- D: Eindringtiefe f
- E: depth of penetration

profondeur f de pose [pose c.]
- D: Bettungstiefe f, Verlegetiefe f, Legungstiefe f
- E: laying depth, depth of laying, depth below ground, depth under surface, installation depth

profondeur f d'ondulation
- D: Wellentiefe f (beim Wellmantel)
- E: depth of corrugation

programme m de fabrication
- D: Fertigungsprogramm n, Arbeitsprogramm n (Prod.)
- E: production programme, manufacturing programme, production scheme, manufacturing schedule

projet, élaboration d'un ~
- D: Projektierung f

projet

    E: planning n

propagation f
    D: Ausbreitung f
    E: propagation n, spreading n

propagation, essai de résistance à la ~ de la flamme
    D: Flammwidrigkeitsprüfung f
    E: flame resisting test, flame resistance test

propagation, résistance à la ~ de la flamme
    D: Flammwidrigkeit f
    E: flame resistance

propager v(se)
    D: ausbreiten v(sich)
    E: spread v, propagate v

propriété f adhésive
    D: Bindefestigkeit f
    E: bond strength, bonding strength, adhesiveness n

propriété f électrique
    D: elektrische Eigenschaft
    E: electrical characteristic, electrical property

propriété f mécanique
    D: mechanische Eigenschaft
    E: mechanical characteristic, mechanical property

protection, dispositif de ~
    D: Sicherheitsvorrichtung f, Schutzvorrichtung f
    E: safety device, protective device

protection f anticorrosion
    D: Korrosionsschutz m
    E: anti-corrosion protection

protection f anti-corrosive
    D: Korrosionsschutz m
    E: anti-corrosion protection

protection f cathodique
    D: kathodischer Korrosionsschutz
    E: cathodic protection

protection f contre des contacts accidentels [él.]
    D: Berührungsschutz m
    E: protection from contact, shock protection

protection f contre des contacts indirects [él.]
    D: Berührungsschutz m
    E: protection from contact, shock protection

protection f contre la formation de coques [câb.]
    D: Knickschutz m
    E: protection against kinking

protection f contre la foudre
    D: Blitzschutz m
    E: lightning protection

protection f contre la rouille
    D: Rostschutz m
    E: rust prevention, rust protection

protection f contre l'effet de couronne
    D: Glimmschutz m
    E: corona protection

protection f contre les défauts à la terre
    D: Erdschlußschutz m
    E: earth fault protection (GB), ground fault protection (US)

protection f contre les surintensités
    D: Überstromschutz m
    E: overcurrent protection, overload protection, excess current protection

protection f contre les surtensions
    D: Überspannungsschutz m
    E: overvoltage protection, surge protection

protection f par fusibles
    D: Absicherung f
    E: fusing n, protection by fuses

protection f par mise à la terre
    D: Schutzerdung f
    E: protective earth (GB), protective ground (US)

protection f par mise à la terre multiple
    D: Mehrfachschutzerdung f, Nullung f
    E: protective multiple earthing (p.m.e.)

protection f superficielle
    D: Oberflächenschutz m
    E: surface protection

protégé adj contre les interférences
    D: induktionsgeschützt adj
    E: protected against interference

proximité, effet de ~
    D: Näheeffekt m
    E: proximity effect

PTFE (v. polytetrafluoréthylène)

puissance f
    D: Energie f
    E: power n, energy n

puissance f [él.]
    D: Leistung f
    E: power n

puissance f [méc.]

puissance f
- D: Stärke f
- E: strength n, power n, force n

puissance f [él.]
- D: Stärke f
- E: intensity n

puissance f absorbée
- D: Leistungsaufnahme f
- E: power consumption, power input

puissance f absorbée
- D: Anschlußleistung f, Anschlußwert m
- E: power rating, connected load

puissance f apparente
- D: Scheinleistung f
- E: apparent power

puissance f à transporter
- D: Übertragungsleistung f, übertragbare Leistung
- E: transmission power

puissance f connectée
- D: Anschlußleistung f, Anschlußwert m
- E: power rating, connected load

puissance f de chauffage
- D: Heizleistung f
- E: heating power

puissance f de court-circuit
- D: Kurzschlußleistung f
- E: short-circuit rating

puissance f de perte
- D: Verlustleistung f
- E: power loss, power dissipation

puissance f de rupture
- D: Ausschaltleistung f, Abschaltleistung f
- E: breaking capacity (GB), interrupting capacity (US)

puissance f disponible
- D: Leistungsabgabe f
- E: power output

puissance f dissipée
- D: Verlustleistung f
- E: power loss, power dissipation

puissance f effective
- D: Wirkleistung f, Effektivleistung f
- E: active power

puissance f installée
- D: installierte Leistung, Ausbauleistung f
- E: installed capacity, total rated power

puissance f limite [él.]
- D: Belastbarkeit f, Strombelastbarkeit f
- E: current-carrying capacity, current rating, ampacity n, power rating

puissance f nécessaire
- D: Energiebedarf m, Leistungsbedarf m
- E: power requirement, power demand

puissance f nominale [él.]
- D: Nennleistung f
- E: rated power, nominal power

puissance f réactive
- D: Blindleistung f
- E: reactive power

puissance f utile [él.]
- D: Nutzleistung f
- E: useful power

puissance f vocale
- D: Sprechleistung f
- E: speech power

puits m à câbles
- D: Muffenbunker m, Muffenbauwerk n, Kabelschacht m
- E: cable pit, cable jointing chamber, cable jointing manhole, cable vault

puits m de jonction
- D: Muffenbunker m, Muffenbauwerk n, Kabelschacht m
- E: cable pit, cable jointing chamber, cable jointing manhole, cable vault

puits m de montée [câb.]
- D: Hochführungsschacht m
- E: cable shaft, vertical wall duct

puits m de visite
- D: Muffenbunker m, Muffenbauwerk n, Kabelschacht m
- E: cable pit, cable jointing chamber, cable jointing manhole, cable vault

pulvérisateur m
- D: Sprühdüse f
- E: spray nozzle, jet nozzle

pulvérisateur m
- D: Sprüheinrichtung f, Abspritzvorrichtung f
- E: spray equipment

pulvérulent adj
- D: feinpulverig adj, pulverförmig adj
- E: powdery adj, pulverulent adj

pupinisation f
- D: Bespulung f, Pupinisierung f
- E: coil-loading n, Pupin loading

pupinisé f
- D: pupinisiert adj
- E: coil-loaded adj

pupitre *m* **de commande**
 D: Schaltpult *n*, Bedienungspult *n*,
   Steuerpult *n*
 E: control desk, operator's desk,
   control console

pureté, degré de ~
 D: Reinheitsgrad *m*
 E: degree of purity

purger *v* [extr.]
 D: reinigen *v*
 E: purge *v*

purges *f pl* [extr.]
 D: Überlauf *m*
 E: scrap *n*, purging *n*

PVC (v. chlorure de polyvinyle)

PVC *m* **plastifié**
 D: Weich-PVC *n*
 E: plasticized PVC

PVC *m* **rigide**
 D: Hart-PVC *n*, weichmacherfreies PVC
 E: rigid PVC

Q

qualification *f*
 D: Eignung *f*
 E: suitability *n*

qualité *f*
 D: Güteklasse *f*
 E: quality grade, quality *n*

qualité *f* **de surface**
 D: Oberflächenbeschaffenheit *f*,
   Oberflächengüte *f*
 E: surface finish, surface quality

qualité *f* **de transmission**
 D: Übertragungsgüte *f*,
   Übertragungsqualität *f*
 E: transmission quality

quartage *m*
 D: Viererverseilung *f*
 E: quadding *n*, quad twisting

quarte *f*
 D: Vierer *m*
 E: quad *n*

quarte *f* **de réserve**
 D: Reservevierer *m*
 E: reserve quad

quarte *f* **Dieselhorst-Martin**
 D: Dieselhorst-Martin-Vierer *m*,
   DM-Vierer *m*
 E: multiple-twin quad, DM-quad *n*

quarte *f* **DM**
 D: Dieselhorst-Martin-Vierer *m*,
   DM-Vierer *m*
 E: multiple-twin quad, DM-quad *n*

quarte *f* **en étoile à courant porteur**
 D: Trägerfrequenz-Sternvierer *m*
 E: carrier frequency star quad

quarte *f* **étoile**
 D: Sternvierer *m*
 E: star-quad *n*, spiral quad (US),
   spiral four quad (US)

quarteuse *f*
 D: Viererverseilmaschine *f*
 E: quad twisting machine, quadding machine

quinconce, en ~
 D: gestaffelt *adj*, abgestuft *adj*,
   versetzt *adj* (stufenweise),
 E: staggered *adj*, graded *adj*

R

rabattre *v*
 D: umschlagen *v*, umbördeln *v*,
   bördeln *v*
 E: fold back *v*, flange *v*

raccord *m*
 D: Zwischenstück *n*,
   Verbindungsstück *n*,
   Anschlußstück *n*
 E: intermediate piece, connecting
   piece, adapter *n*, connector *n*,
   fitting *n*

raccord *m*
 D: Stutzen *m*
 E: connecting piece, connection *n*

raccord *m* **à sertir**
 D: Kerbverbindung *f*
 E: notch type joint

raccord *m* **à vis**
 D: Verschraubung *f*,
   Schraubverbindung *f*
 E: screw connection, bolted
   connection, bolted joint, screw(ed) joint

raccord *m* **boulonné**
 D: Klemmverbindung *f*
 E: clamped joint

raccord *m* **coudé**
D: Rohrbogen *m*, Rohrkrümmung *f*, Rohrknie *n*, Knierohr *n*, Krümmer *m* (Rohr)
E: pipe bend, conduit bend, elbow *n*, knee *n*

raccord *m* **de câble**
D: Kabelanschluß *m*
E: cable connection

raccord *m* **de transformateur**
D: Transformator-Einführung *f*
E: transformer termination, transformer connection, transformer entry

raccordement *m* [câb.]
D: Verbinden *n*
E: jointing *n*, splicing *n*, connecting *n*

raccordement *m*
D: Abzweigung *f*
E: branch *n*, tap *n*, junction *n*

raccorder *v*
D: verbinden *v*
E: join *v*, joint *v*, connect *v*, link *v*

raccord *m* **fileté**
D: Verschraubung *f*, Schraubverbindung *f*
E: screw connection, bolted connection, bolted joint, screw(ed) joint

raccord *m* **poinçonné**
D: Preßverbindung *f*
E: compressed joint, crimped joint

raccord *m* **sans soudure**
D: lötfreie gewickelte Verbindung, Wickelverbindung *f* (lötfrei)
E: wire-wrap connection

raccords *m pl* **électriques**
D: elektrische Anschlüsse
E: electrical connections

râcloir *m*
D: Abstreifer *m* (an der Armiermaschine)
E: stripping device, wiper *n*

râcloir *m*
D: Abstreifmesser *n*
E: doctor blade

râcloir *m* **en feutre**
D: Filzabstreifer *m*
E: felt stripper

radiation *f*
D: Strahlung *f*
E: radiation *n*

raffinage *m*
D: Raffination *f*
E: refining *n*

raffinage *m* **au feu**
D: Feuerraffination *f*
E: fire refining

raffinage *m* **du cuivre**
D: Kupferraffination *f*
E: copper refining

raffiné, cuivre ~ au feu
D: feuerraffiniertes Kupfer, Raffinade-Kupfer *n*
E: fire-refined copper

raideur *f*
D: Strammheit *f* (Gummimischungen)
E: stiffness *n*

rail *m* **de contact**
D: Stromschiene *f*
E: conductor rail, contact rail

rail *m* **de guidage**
D: Führungsschiene *f*, Laufschiene *f*
E: guide rail

rail *m* **de roulement**
D: Führungsschiene *f*, Laufschiene *f*
E: guide rail

rainé *adj*
D: geriffelt *adj*
E: grooved *adj*, ribbed *adj*

rainure *f*
D: Nut *f*, Aussparung *f*
E: groove *n*, slot *n*, recess *n*, notch *n*, nick *n*

rainure *f* **et languette**
D: Nut und Feder
E: slot and tongue

rajuster *v*
D: nachstellen *v*
E: reset *v*

ramification *f* **des chaînes moléculaires**
D: Verzweigung der Molekülketten
E: branching of the molecular chains, ramification of the molecular chains

ramollissement *m*
D: Erweichung *f*
E: softening *n*

ramollissement *m* [rub.]
D: Lockerung *f*, Lockerwerden *n*
E: loosening *n*

rapidité *f* **de réponse**
D: Ansprechgeschwindigkeit *f*
E: rapidity of response, responding speed

rapport

rapport *m* **d'engrenage** [méc.]
 D: Übersetzungsverhältnis *n*
 E: gear-ratio *n*, transmission ratio
rapport *m* **de transmission** [méc.]
 D: Übersetzungsverhältnis *n*
 E: gear-ratio *n*, transmission ratio
rapport *m* **L/D** [extr.]
 D: Länge/Durchmesser-Verhältnis (L/D) (Extruder-Schnecke) *n*
 E: L/D ratio
rasage *m* [fabr. fils mét.]
 D: Schaben *n*
 E: shaving *n*
raser *v*
 D: schälen *v* (Draht, Isolierung)
 E: shave *v*
raté *m* **de mesure**
 D: Fehlmessung *f*, Meßfehler *m*
 E: faulty measurement, measuring error
raté *m* **du flux de plomb**
 D: Aussetzen des Bleiflusses
 E: lead starvation
râtelier *m* **à câbles** [pose c.]
 D: Kabelrost *m*, Rost *m*
 E: cable grate
rayon *m* **de coude**
 D: Kantenradius *m* (Sektorleiter), Krümmungsradius *m* (Sektorleiter)
 E: corner radius, edge radius
rayon *m* **de courbure**
 D: Biegeradius *m*
 E: bending radius
réactance *f*
 D: Blindwiderstand *m*
 E: reactive impedance, reactance *n*
réaction *f*
 D: Rückkopplung *f*
 E: feedback *n*
réaction *f* **négative d'intensité**
 D: Stromgegenkopplung *f*
 E: current feedback
réajuster *v*
 D: nachstellen *v*
 E: reset *v*
réalisable *adj*
 D: durchführbar *adj*
 E: practicable *adj*, realizable *adj*
rebobinage *m*
 D: Umwickeln *n* (Umspulen), Umtrommeln *n*
 E: rewinding *n*
rebut *m*
 D: Kaltschweißstelle *f*
 E: cold shut, cold lap
réception, contrôle à la ~ du matériel
 D: Wareneingangskontrolle *f*
 E: incoming inspection, testing of incoming materials, quality control of raw material consignments
réception *f* **collective d'antenne de télévision**
 D: Gemeinschaftsantennenfernsehen *n*, Ortsantennen-Fernsehen *n*, Stadtgemeinschaftsantennen-Fernsehen *n*
 E: Community Antenna Television (CATV)
réception *f* **en usine**
 D: Abnahme im Werk
 E: factory acceptance
réceptionnaire *m*
 D: Abnahmebeamter *m*
 E: inspection officer
réchauffeur *m* **de fil métallique**
 D: Drahtvorwärmer *m*
 E: wire preheater
recherche *f* **fondamentale**
 D: Grundlagenforschung *f*
 E: fundamental research, basic research
reconstitué, extrémité ~e
 D: gewickelter Endverschluß
 E: lapped termination
reconstitué, jonction ~e
 D: gewickelte Muffe, Wickelmuffe *f*
 E: lapped joint
reconstituer *v*
 D: auswickeln *v* (Isolierung)
 E: build up *v*
reconstitution *f* **d'isolant**
 D: Isolierwickel *m*
 E: insulation build-up
reconstitution *f* **d'une jonction**
 D: Auswickeln einer Verbindungsstelle
 E: lapping of a joint, build-up of a joint
recouvrement *m*
 D: Abdeckung *f*
 E: cover *n*, covering *n*
recouvrement *m*
 D: Überlappung *f*
 E: overlap(ping) *n*
recouvrement *m*
 D: Umwicklung *f* (mit Band)

E: wrapping n, winding n
recouvrement, à ~
D: überlappend adj
E: overlapping adj
recouvrement, à 50 % de ~
D: mit 50 % Überlappung
E: half-lapped adj, with 50 % overlap, with 50 % registration
recouvrement m du fil métallique
D: Drahtumspinnung f
E: wire covering
recouvrement m longitudinal
D: Längsbedecken n
E: longitudinal covering
recouvrir v [câb.]
D: bewickeln v, umwickeln v, umspinnen v
E: wrap v, wind v, cover v
recouvrir v(se)
D: überlappen v
E: overlap v
récristallisation f
D: Rekristallisation f
E: recrystallization n
recuire v
D: glühen v
E: anneal v
recuire v [plast.]
D: tempern v
E: anneal v
recuiseur m
D: Glühanlage f
E: annealer n, annealing plant
recuiseur m continu par résistance
D: kontinuierliche Widerstandsglühanlage
E: continuous resistance annealer
recuiseur m en continu
D: Durchlaufglühanlage f
E: continuous annealing plant, continuous annealer
recuit m
D: Glühen n
E: annealing n
recuit, installation de ~ en continu
D: Durchlaufglühanlage f
E: continuous annealing plant, continuous annealer
recuit m brillant
D: Blankglühen n
E: bright annealing
recuit m d'adoucissement
D: Weichglühen n
E: soft annealing
recuit m de détente
D: Entspannungsglühen n
E: stress-relieving annealing
recuit m de récristallisation
D: Rekristallisationsglühung f
E: process annealing, subcritical annealing
recuit m intermédiaire [mét.]
D: Zwischenglühen n
E: intermediate annealing, process annealing
recuit par résistance, installation continue de ~
D: kontinuierliche Widerstandsglühanlage
E: continuous resistance annealer
recuit sous vide, installation de ~
D: Vakuumglühanlage f
E: vacuum annealing plant
recul m du fouloir
D: Rückzugbewegung des Preßstempels
E: return stroke of the ram
récupération f
D: Rückgewinnung f
E: recovery n
recyclage m
D: Umpumpen n
E: recycling n, recirculation n
redresser v
D: richten v (Draht)
E: straighten v
redresseur m de fil
D: Drahtrichtvorrichtung f
E: wire straightening device
redresseur m triphasé
D: Dreiphasengleichrichter m
E: three-phase rectifier
réducteur m
D: Reduktionsgetriebe n, Untersetzungsgetriebe n
E: reduction gear
réducteur m de tension
D: Spannungsteiler m, Potentiometer n
E: voltage divider, potentiometer n
réduction f de la section
D: Querschnittsverringerung f
E: area reduction
réduction f d'oxygène
D: Sauerstoffentzug m
E: removal of oxygen, deoxidation n

réduction f du diamètre
 D: Durchmesserverringerung f
 E: diameter reduction, thinning n

réduire v
 D: vermindern v, verringern v
 E: reduce v, decrease v

réduire v **le diamètre** (à) [fabr. fils mét.]
 D: herunterziehen v (auf)
 E: draw down v (to)

réenclencher v **la puissance**
 D: den Strom wieder einschalten
 E: to restore power

réenroulement m
 D: Umwickeln n (Umspulen), Umtrommeln n
 E: rewinding n

refaire v **le plein**
 D: nachfüllen v, auffüllen v
 E: replenish v, resupply v, refill v

refouleur m
 D: Druckpumpe f
 E: pressure pump, forcing pump

réfrigérant m
 D: Kühlmittel n
 E: coolant n, cooling medium, cooling agent

refroidi adj **à l'air**
 D: luftgekühlt adj
 E: air-cooled adj

refroidi adj **à l'eau**
 D: wassergekühlt adj
 E: water-cooled adj

refroidir v (se)
 D: abkühlen v
 E: cool v

refroidissement, section de ~
 D: Kühlstrecke f
 E: cooling section

refroidissement m **à air comprimé**
 D: Druckluftkühlung f
 E: cooling by compressed air

refroidissement m **à l'eau**
 D: Wasserkühlung f
 E: water cooling

refroidissement m **d'eau de retour**
 D: Rückkühlung von Kühlwasser
 E: re-cooling of cooling water

refroidissement m **de la filière**
 D: Matrizenkühlung f
 E: die cooling

refroidissement m **direct des câbles**
 D: direkte Kühlung von Kabeln
 E: integral cooling of cables, direct cooling of cables

refroidissement m **forcé** [câb.]
 D: Fremdkühlung f, Zwangskühlung f, künstliche Kühlung
 E: forced cooling, artificial cooling

refroidissement m **indirect des câbles**
 D: indirekte Kühlung von Kabeln
 E: lateral cooling of cables

refroidissement m **intégral des câbles**
 D: direkte Kühlung von Kabeln
 E: integral cooling of cables, direct cooling of cables

refroidissement m **latéral des câbles**
 D: indirekte Kühlung von Kabeln
 E: lateral cooling of cables

refroidissement m **par circulation d'huile**
 D: Ölumlaufkühlung f
 E: oil circulation cooling

refroidissement m **secondaire**
 D: Sekundärkühlung f
 E: secondary cooling

refus m **de criblage**
 D: Siebrückstand m
 E: screen residue

refus m **du tamis**
 D: Siebrückstand m
 E: screen residue

regard m **de visite** [pose c.]
 D: Einstiegöffnung f, Mannloch n
 E: entrance n, manhole n

régénéré m
 D: Regenerat n
 E: reclaim n

régénérer v
 D: wiederaufbereiten v
 E: regenerate v

régime m [câb., mach.]
 D: Betrieb m
 E: operation n, service n, duty n

régime m **cyclique**
 D: Betrieb mit zyklischer Belastung
 E: operation with cyclic loading

régime m **de marche**
 D: Betriebsart f
 E: method of operation, mode of operation, type of service

régime m **de secours**
 D: Notbetrieb m
 E: emergency operation, emergency service

régime m **établi**
 D: Beharrungszustand m,

règles

Dauerzustand *m*
  E: steady state condition
régime *m* périodique
  D: periodischer Betrieb
  E: periodic operation, intermittent operation, intermittent service
régime *m* permanent
  D: Beharrungszustand *m*, Dauerzustand *m*
  E: steady state condition
régime *m* permanent [él.]
  D: Dauerbetrieb mit gleichbleibender Belastung
  E: continuous duty, continuous operation
régime *m* permanent à charge temporaire [él.]
  D: Dauerbetrieb mit kurzzeitiger Belastung
  E: continuous duty with short-time loading
régime *m* permanent à charge variant périodiquement [él.]
  D: Dauerbetrieb mit periodisch veränderlicher Belastung
  E: periodic load duty
régime *m* temporaire [él.]
  D: aussetzender Betrieb, Betrieb mit aussetzender Belastung
  E: intermittent operation
régime *m* temporaire [él.]
  D: Kurzzeitbetrieb *m* (mit gleichbleibender Last)
  E: short-time service, short-time duty, short-time operation
régime *m* temporaire variable [él.]
  D: Kurzzeitbetrieb *m* (mit veränderlicher Last)
  E: variable temporary duty
régime *m* transitoire
  D: Übergangsbetrieb *m*
  E: transient operation, transient conditions *pl*
réglable *adj*
  D: verstellbar *adj*, einstellbar *adj*, regelbar *adj*, regulierbar *adj*
  E: adjustable *adj*, variable *adj*
réglable *adj* **en hauteur**
  D: in der Höhe verstellbar
  E: vertically adjustable
réglage *m*
  D: Regelung *f*, Einstellung *f*
  E: adjustment *n*, regulation *n*, setting *n*
réglage *m* [él., méc.]
  D: Steuerung *f*
  E: control *n*
réglage *m* **approximatif**
  D: Grobeinstellung *f*
  E: coarse adjustment
réglage *m* **de la température**
  D: Temperaturregelung *f*
  E: temperature control
réglage *m* **de la température par un liquide thermique** [extr.]
  D: Flüssigkeitstemperierung *f*
  E: thermal liquid control, temperature control by a liquid medium
réglage *m* **de position**
  D: Positionsregelung *f*
  E: position control
réglage *m* **de tension**
  D: Spannungsregelung *f*
  E: voltage control
réglage *m* **grossier**
  D: Grobeinstellung *f*
  E: coarse adjustment
réglage *m* **minutieux**
  D: Feineinstellung *f*
  E: fine adjustment, precision adjustment
réglage *m* **précis**
  D: Feineinstellung *f*
  E: fine adjustment, precision adjustment
règle *f* **d'essai**
  D: Prüfvorschrift *f*
  E: test specification
règle *f* **d'installation**
  D: Errichtungsvorschrift *f*
  E: installation rule, installation standard
régler *v*
  D: abstimmen *v*
  E: tune *v*, adjust *v*, match *v*
régler *v*
  D: steuern *v*
  E: control *v*
régler *v* [mach.]
  D: einrichten *v*
  E: set up *v*
règles *f pl*
  D: Bestimmungen *f pl* (Vorschriften)
  E: specifications *pl*, rules *pl*, regulations *pl*, standards *pl*
règles de l'art, selon les dernières ~

règles
- D: nach dem neuesten Stand der Technik
- E: according to the latest state of the art

règles *f pl* **VDE**
- D: VDE-Bestimmungen *f pl*, VDE-Regeln *f pl*, VDE-Vorschriften *f pl*
- E: VDE Regulations, VDE Rules, VDE Standards

réglette *f* **à bornes** [él.]
- D: Anschlußleiste *f*, Klemmleiste *f*
- E: terminal block, terminal strip, terminal board, connecting block, connection strip

réglette *f* **de raccordement** [él.]
- D: Anschlußleiste *f*, Klemmleiste *f*
- E: terminal block, terminal strip, terminal board, connecting block, connection strip

régularisation *f* **du champ électrique** [él.]
- D: Feldsteuerung *f*, Feldregulierung *f*
- E: stress control, stress relief, field control

régulateur *m*
- D: Regler *m*
- E: regulator *n*, control *n*, controller *n*

régulateur *m* **de pression**
- D: Druckregler *m*
- E: pressure regulator, pressure control(ler)

régulateur *m* **de synchronisation de vitesses**
- D: Gleichlaufregler *m*
- E: synchronous speed regulating device

régulateur *m* **de température**
- D: Temperaturregler *m*, Thermostat *m*
- E: temperature controller, thermostat *n*, temperature regulator

régulation de la traction, dispositif de ~
- D: Zugspannungs-Regelvorrichtung *f*
- E: tension control device, tension compensating device, tension compensator

régulation *f* **du champ électrique** [él.]
- D: Feldsteuerung *f*, Feldregulierung *f*
- E: stress control, stress relief, field control

relâcher *v* **pour la fabrication**
- D: für die Fertigung freigeben
- E: to release for factory production

relais *m* **temporisé**
- D: Verzögerungsrelais *n*
- E: time-lag relay, slow-acting relay

relié *adj* **de façon positive**
- D: kraftschlüssig verbunden
- E: positively connected

relier *v* [tél.]
- D: durchschalten *v*
- E: to connect through, put through *v*, switch through *v*

relier *v* [él.]
- D: schalten *v*
- E: switch *v*, connect *v*

relier *v* **à la terre**
- D: erden *v*
- E: earth *v* (GB), to connect to earth, ground (US) *v*

remblai *m* [pose c.]
- D: Bettungsmaterial *n*
- E: bedding material

remise *f* **à zéro automatique**
- D: automatische Nulleinstellung
- E: automatic reset

remise *f* **en état**
- D: Instandsetzung *f*, Reparatur *f*
- E: overhauling *n*, repair *n*

remplacement, matériau de ~
- D: Ersatzmaterial *n*
- E: substitute *n*

remplacer *v*
- D: ersetzen *v*
- E: replace *v*, substitute *v*

rempli, câble ~ de façon continue [c. tél.]
- D: über die ganze Länge abgestopftes Kabel, kontinuierlich gefülltes Kabel
- E: fully filled cable, continuously filled cable

remplir *v*
- D: nachfüllen *v*, auffüllen *v*
- E: replenish *v*, resupply *v*, refill *v*

remplissage *m* [c. tél.]
- D: Abstopfen *n*
- E: filling *n*, blocking *n*

remplissage *m*
- D: Füllen *n*, Füllung *f*
- E: filling *n*

remplissage *m* (caniveau de câble)
- D: Auffüllen *n* (Kabelgraben)
- E: backfilling *n*

remplissage, câble à ~ continu [c. tél.]
- D: über die ganze Länge abgestopftes

Kabel, kontinuierlich gefülltes Kabel
E: fully filled cable, continuously filled cable

remplissage, câble à ~ total [c. tél.]
D: über die ganze Länge abgestopftes Kabel, kontinuierlich gefülltes Kabel
E: fully filled cable, continuously filled cable

remplissage *m* **en gelée de pétrole** [c. tél.]
D: Abstopfen mit Petrol-jelly
E: petroleum jelly filling

rendement *m* [mach.]
D: Leistung *f*, Ausstoß *m*
E: performance *n*, output *n*, efficiency *n*, capacity *n*

rendement *m*
D: Wirkungsgrad *m*
E: efficiency *n*

renforcement *m* [méc.]
D: Verstärkung *f*
E: reinforcement *n*, strengthening *n*

renseignement, fournir des ~s sur
D: Aufschluß geben über (z.B. Betriebsverhalten)
E: to be indicative of, to permit conclusions as to

renseignements *m pl*
D: Daten *pl*, Angaben *f pl*
E: data *pl and sg*, details *pl*, particulars *pl*

renversable *adj*
D: kippbar *adj*
E: inclinable *adj*, tiltable *adj*

renvoi, dispositif de ~
D: Umlenkvorrichtung *f*
E: transfer device

réparation *f*
D: Instandsetzung *f*, Reparatur *f*
E: overhauling *n*, repair *n*

répartiteur *m* **de flux** [extr.]
D: Lochscheibe *f*
E: breaker plate

répartiteur *m* **d'installations de télécommunication**
D: Verteilergestell für Nachrichtenanlagen
E: distribution frame for telecommunications systems

répartition *f*
D: Verteilung *f*
E: dispersion *n*, distribution *n*

répartition *f* **de la charge**
D: Lastverteilung *f*
E: load distribution, dispatching *n*

répartition *f* **du champ électrique**
D: Feldverteilung *f*
E: stress grading, stress distribution

répartition *f* **gaussienne**
D: Gaußsche Verteilung
E: Gaussian (distribution) law

répartition *f* **granulométrique**
D: Korngrößenverteilung *f*, Teilchengrößenverteilung *f*
E: particle size distribution

répartition *f* **uniforme**
D: gleichmäßige Verteilung
E: even distribution, uniform distribution

repérage *m* [câb.]
D: Kennzeichnung *f*
E: identification *n*, marking *n*, coding *n*

repérage *m* **annulaire des conducteurs de câble**
D: Ringmarkierung von Kabeladern
E: ring marking of cable cores, ring code of cable cores

repérage *m* **coloré**
D: farbige Kennzeichnung
E: colo(u)r code, colo(u)r coding

repérage *m* **des conducteurs**
D: Aderkennzeichnung *f*
E: core identification, tracer *n* (US)

repérage *m* **hélicoïdal**
D: Wendelmarkierung *f*
E: helical marking

repérage *m* **longitudinal**
D: Längsmarkierung *f*
E: longitudinal marking

repérage *m* **par chiffres imprimés**
D: Ziffernbedruckung *f*
E: number-printing *n*

repère *m* **numérique** [câb.]
D: Kennziffer *f*
E: code number

répéteur *m*
D: Verstärker *m*
E: amplifier *n*, repeater *n*

répéteur *m* **à relais en courant continu** [com.]
D: Gleichstromübertrager *m*
E: d.c. relay repeater

répéteur *m* **immergé**

    D: Unterseeverstärker *m*,
       Unterwasserverstärker *m*,
       Seekabelverstärker *m*
    E: submerged repeater, underwater amplifier

replier *v*
    D: falzen *v*
    E: fold *v*

repliure *f* **de laminage**
    D: Überwalzung *f* (bei gewalztem Draht)
    E: spill *n*

réponse, temps de ~
    D: Ansprechzeit *f*
    E: response time, reaction time

repos *m* [él.]
    D: spannungslose Periode
    E: dead time interval, off-load period

représentation *f* **graphique**
    D: Kurvenbild *n*, Diagramm *n*, graphische Darstellung
    E: diagram *n*, graph *n*, graphic representation, chart *n*

représentation *f* **schématique**
    D: schematische Darstellung
    E: schematic representation, diagrammatic representation

représenter *v* **graphiquement**
    D: graphisch darstellen
    E: to plot a graph, to plot graphically

reprise *f* **d'humidité**
    D: Feuchtigkeitsaufnahme *f*
    E: moisture absorption

reprise *f* **élastique**
    D: elastische Erholung
    E: elastic recovery, recovery from stretching

réproductibilité *f*
    D: Reproduzierbarkeit *f*
    E: reproducibility *n*

reproductibilité *f*
    D: Wiederholbarkeit *f*
    E: repeatability *n*

réseau *m* [él.]
    D: Netz *n*
    E: network *n*, system *n*, mains *n*

réseau *m* **à courant alternatif**
    D: Wechselspannungssystem *n*, Wechselspannungsnetz *n*
    E: a.c. voltage system

réseau *m* **avec mise à la terre rigide du neutre**
    D: Netz mit starr geerdetem Sternpunkt, starr geerdetes Netz
    E: solidly earthed system (GB), solidly grounded system (US)

réseau *m* **avec neutre isolé**
    D: Netz mit isoliertem Sternpunkt
    E: system with insulated neutral

réseau *m* **d'alimentation**
    D: Versorgungsnetz *n*
    E: supply network, supply system, mains *n*

réseau *m* **datex**
    D: Datex-Netz *n*
    E: datex network

réseau *m* **de câbles à grande distance**
    D: Weitverkehrsnetz *n*
    E: long distance network, trunk network (GB), toll network (US)

réseau *m* **de câbles dont les gaines sont reliées entre elles à travers les jonctions**
    D: durchverbundenes Kabelsystem
    E: system with the cable sheaths connected across the joints

réseau *m* **de câbles souterrain**
    D: unterirdisches Kabelnetz
    E: underground cable system

réseau *m* **de communication à large bande**
    D: Breitbandkommunikationsnetz *n*, Breitbandsystem *n*
    E: broad-band communications network, broad-band system

réseau *m* **de communications**
    D: Nachrichtennetz *n*
    E: communications network

réseau *m* **de compensation**
    D: Ausgleichsnetzwerk *n*
    E: balancing network

réseau *m* **de distribution d'énergie**
    D: Starkstromnetz *n*
    E: mains *n*, power system, power transmission network, power distribution network

réseau *m* **de distribution public**
    D: EVU-Netz *n*
    E: public distribution network

réseau *m* **de liaison**
    D: Verbundnetz *n*
    E: interconnected system, interconnection system, grid (system) *n*

réseau *m* **de télécommunication**
    D: Fernmeldenetz *n*

réseau *m* **de transmission**
  D: Übertragungssystem *n*, Übertragungsnetz *n*
  E: transmission system
réseau *m* **de transport**
  D: Übertragungssystem *n*, Übertragungsnetz *n*
  E: transmission system
réseau *m* **de transport d'énergie**
  D: Starkstromnetz *n*
  E: mains *n*, power system, power transmission network, power distribution network
réseau *m* **d'interconnexion**
  D: Verbundnetz *n*
  E: interconnected system, interconnection system, grid (system) *n*
réseau *m* **local** [tél.]
  D: Ortsnetz *n*
  E: local exchange network, municipal network
réseau *m* **maillé**
  D: vermaschtes Netz
  E: meshed network
réseau *m* **mis à la terre d'un côté seulement**
  D: einseitig geerdetes System
  E: system earthed at one end only
réseau *m* **municipal** [tél.]
  D: Ortsnetz *n*
  E: local exchange network, municipal network
réseau *m* **récurrent** [él.]
  D: Kettenleiter *m*
  E: recurrent network, lattice network
réseau *m* **rigidement relié à la terre**
  D: Netz mit starr geerdetem Sternpunkt, starr geerdetes Netz
  E: solidly earthed system (GB), solidly grounded system (US)
réseau *m* **téléphonique**
  D: Fernsprechnetz *n*, Telefonnetz *n*
  E: telephone system, telephone network
réseau *m* **télex**
  D: Fernschreibnetz *n*, Telex-Netz *n*
  E: telex network
réseau *m* **urbain** [él.]
  D: Stadtnetz *n*
  E: urban network, urban supply system
réseau *m* **urbain** [tél.]
  D: Ortsnetz *n*
  E: local exchange network, municipal network
réservoir *m*
  D: Vorratsbehälter *m*
  E: storage tank, supply tank, reservoir *n*
réservoir *m* **à pression d'huile variable**
  D: Ölausgleichsgefäß *n*, Öldruck-Ausgleichsgefäß *n*, Druck-Ausgleichsgefäß *n*, Ausgleichsgefäß *n* (Ölkabel)
  E: oil expansion tank, variable oil pressure tank, oil pressure tank, oil reservoir
résidu *m* **de calcination**
  D: Glührückstand *m*
  E: ash *n*, ignition residue
résidu *m* **de distillation**
  D: Destillationsrückstand *m*
  E: distillation residue
résidu *m* **de recuit**
  D: Glührückstand *m*
  E: ash *n*, ignition residue
résilience *f*
  D: Schlagzähigkeit *f*, Schlagfestigkeit *f*
  E: impact strength, impact resistance
résine *f*
  D: Harz *n* (Kunstharz)
  E: resin *n*
résine *f* **à enduire**
  D: Streichharz *n*
  E: wiping resin
résine *f* **artificielle**
  D: Kunstharz *n*
  E: synthetic resin
résine *f* **de coumarone**
  D: Kumaronharz *n*
  E: Coumarone resin
résine *f* **de synthèse**
  D: Kunstharz *n*
  E: synthetic resin
résine *f* **époxy ou époxyde ou époxydique**
  D: Epoxidharz *n*
  E: epoxy resin, epoxide resin
résine *f* **imprégnatrice**
  D: Tränkharz *n*
  E: impregnating resin
résine *f* **moulée**

résine

D: Gießharz n
E: casting resin, cast resin
résine f oléosoluble
D: öllösliches Harz
E: oil soluble resin
résine f polyester
D: Polyesterharz n
E: polyester resin
résine f synthétique
D: Kunstharz n
E: synthetic resin
résistance f
D: Widerstand m (als el. Wert)
E: resistance n
résistance f
D: Beständigkeit f, Festigkeit f, Widerstandsfähigkeit f
E: stability n, durability n, resistance n, strength n
résistance, de faible ~
D: niederohmig adj
E: low-ohmic adj, of low resistance
résistance, de grande ~
D: hochohmig adj
E: high-ohmic adj, of high resistance, highly resistive
résistance f à l'abrasion
D: Abriebfestigkeit f, Abschleiffestigkeit f
E: abrasion resistance
résistance f à la chaleur
D: Wärmebeständigkeit f, Hitzebeständigkeit f, Wärmestandfestigkeit f
E: heat resistance, thermal resistance, thermal stability
résistance f à la déformation
D: Formbeständigkeit f, Formänderungsbeständigkeit f
E: form-stability n, dimensional stability, resistance to deformation, deformation resistance
résistance f à la fatigue [mét.]
D: Dauerfestigkeit f, Ermüdungsfestigkeit f
E: fatigue strength, fatigue resistance
résistance f à la fissuration de contact
D: Spannungsrißbeständigkeit f
E: stress cracking resistance
résistance f à la fissuration sous contrainte
D: Spannungsrißbeständigkeit f
E: stress cracking resistance

résistance f à la lumière
D: Lichtbeständigkeit f (Farben)
E: fastness to light
résistance f à la pression
D: Druckbeständigkeit f, Druckfestigkeit f
E: pressure resistance, compressive strength, crushing strength
résistance f à la pression aux températures élevées
D: Wärmedruckbeständigkeit f
E: resistance to pressure at high temperatures, hot deformation resistance, hot deformation strength
résistance f à la pression d'éclatement
D: Berstdruckfestigkeit f
E: bursting strength
résistance f à la propagation de la flamme
D: Flammwidrigkeit f
E: flame resistance
résistance f à l'arc électrique
D: Lichtbogenbeständigkeit f
E: arc resistance
résistance f à la rupture
D: Reißfestigkeit f, Zerreißfestigkeit f
E: tensile strength (at break), ultimate tensile strength
résistance f à la rupture en flexion
D: Umbruchfestigkeit f (Isolator)
E: cantilever strength
résistance f à la rupture sous charge permanente [mét.]
D: Dauerstandfestigkeit f
E: creep resistance, fatigue strength, creep strength, long-time rupture strength
résistance f à la traction
D: Zugfestigkeit f
E: tensile strength
résistance f à l'écrasement
D: Druckbeständigkeit f, Druckfestigkeit f
E: pressure resistance, compressive strength, crushing strength
résistance f à l'effet de corona
D: Koronabeständigkeit f, Glimmbeständigkeit f
E: corona resistance, glow stability
résistance f à l'effet de couronne
D: Koronabeständigkeit f, Glimmbeständigkeit f

E: corona resistance, glow stability
résistance f à l'enfoncement
  D: Durchdrückfestigkeit f
  E: cut-through resistance
résistance f à l'huile
  D: Ölbeständigkeit f, Ölfestigkeit f
  E: oil resistance
résistance f à l'ozone
  D: Ozonbeständigkeit f
  E: ozone resistance, resistance to ozone
résistance f au cheminement
  D: Kriechstromfestigkeit f
  E: track(ing) resistance
résistance f au choc mécanique
  D: Schlagzähigkeit f, Schlagfestigkeit f
  E: impact strength, impact resistance
résistance f au cisaillement
  D: Scherfestigkeit f
  E: shear strength
résistance f au claquage sous tension de choc
  D: Stoßdurchschlagfestigkeit f
  E: impulse breakdown strength
résistance f au déchirement
  D: Einreißfestigkeit f, Weiterreißfestigkeit f
  E: resistance to tearing, tear resistance, tearing strength
résistance f au déchirement (à partir de l'entaille)
  D: Kerbzähigkeit f
  E: tear resistance (from a nick), notch toughness
résistance f au feu
  D: Feuerbeständigkeit f, Feuerfestigkeit f
  E: fire-resistance n
résistance f au flambage
  D: Knickfestigkeit f
  E: buckling resistance, buckling strength
résistance f au fluage [mét.]
  D: Dauerstandfestigkeit f
  E: creep resistance, fatigue strength, creep strength, long-time rupture strength
résistance f au fluage [plast.]
  D: Fließbeständigkeit f
  E: flow resistance
résistance f au fluage à froid
  D: Kaltfließbeständigkeit f
  E: cold flow resistance
résistance f au gonflement
  D: Quellbeständigkeit f
  E: resistance to swelling
résistance f au pliage
  D: Biegefestigkeit f
  E: bending strength, flexural strength
résistance f au vieillissement
  D: Alterungsbeständigkeit f
  E: ag(e)ing resistance
résistance f aux acides
  D: Säurebeständigkeit f
  E: acid resistance
résistance f aux basses températures
  D: Kältebeständigkeit f
  E: low temperature resistance, resistance to low temperatures
résistance f aux courts-circuits
  D: Kurzschlußfestigkeit f
  E: short-circuit strength
résistance f aux craquelures
  D: Wärmeschockbeständigkeit f
  E: heat shock resistance
résistance f aux décharges partielles
  D: Teilentladungs-Beständigkeit f
  E: partial discharge resistance
résistance f aux efforts alternatifs
  D: Dauerwechselfestigkeit f
  E: endurance strength
résistance f aux efforts répétés
  D: Dauerwechselfestigkeit f
  E: endurance strength
résistance f aux intempéries
  D: Wetterbeständigkeit f, Wetterfestigkeit f, Witterungsbeständigkeit f
  E: weatherability n, weather resistance
résistance f aux ondes de choc
  D: Stoßspannungsfestigkeit f
  E: impulse (voltage) strength, surge voltage strength, surge resistance
résistance f aux pliages alternés
  D: Wechselbiegefestigkeit f, Biegewechselfestigkeit f
  E: reversed bending strength
résistance f aux pliages répétés
  D: Falzfestigkeit f
  E: folding endurance
résistance f aux solvants
  D: Lösungsmittelbeständigkeit f
  E: solvent resistance
résistance f aux vibrations

résistance

résistance f
- D: Schwingungsfestigkeit f
- E: resistance to vibrations

résistance f capacitive
- D: kapazitiver Widerstand
- E: capacitive resistance, capacitive reactance

résistance f d'adhésion
- D: Bindefestigkeit f
- E: bond strength, bonding strength, adhesiveness n

résistance f de boucle
- D: Schleifenwiderstand m
- E: loop resistance

résistance f de chauffage
- D: Heizwiderstand m
- E: heating resistor

résistance f de comparaison
- D: Vergleichswiderstand m
- E: reference resistance, comparative resistance

résistance f de contact
- D: Übergangswiderstand m
- E: contact resistance, transition resistance

résistance f de couplage
- D: Kopplungswiderstand m
- E: coupling resistance, surface transfer impedance

résistance f de fatigue à la flexion
- D: Dauerbiegefestigkeit f
- E: resistance to bending fatigue, bending endurance, bending fatigue strength, flexural fatigue strength

résistance f de ligne
- D: Leitungswiderstand m
- E: line resistance

résistance f de mesure
- D: Meßwiderstand m
- E: measuring resistance

résistance f d'entrée
- D: Eingangswiderstand m
- E: input resistance

résistance f de passage
- D: Übergangswiderstand m
- E: contact resistance, transition resistance

résistance f des bords au déchirement
- D: Kantenfestigkeit f
- E: edge tear resistance

résistance f de terre
- D: Erdungswiderstand m
- E: earth resistance (GB), ground resistance (US)

résistance f de transmission de chaleur
- D: Wärmeübergangswiderstand m
- E: heat transfer resistance, heat transmission resistance

résistance f diélectrique
- D: Isolationswiderstand m
- E: insulation resistance

résistance f d'isolement
- D: Isolationswiderstand m
- E: insulation resistance

résistance f effective
- D: Wirkwiderstand m
- E: active resistance, effective resistance

résistance f électrique de l'âme
- D: Leiterwiderstand m
- E: electrical resistance of conductor, conductor resistance

résistance f en série
- D: Längswiderstand m
- E: series resistance, ohmic resistance, positive-sequence resistance

résistance f étalon
- D: Eichwiderstand m
- E: standard resistance, calibrating resistance

résistance f hydraulique
- D: Strömungswiderstand m
- E: flow resistance, hydrodynamic resistance

résistance f I.A.C.S. (cuivre)
- D: Standard-Widerstand nach IEC (Kupfer)
- E: I.A.C.S. resistance (International Annealed Copper Standard/IEC)

résistance f inductive
- D: induktiver Widerstand
- E: inductive resistance

résistance f intérieure
- D: Durchgangswiderstand m (ohne Oberflächenwiderstand)
- E: volume resistance (exclusive of surface resistance)

résistance f limite de fatigue
- D: Dauerfestigkeitsgrenze f
- E: fatigue limit, endurance limit

résistance f linéique
- D: linearer Widerstand
- E: linear resistance

résistance f longitudinale
- D: Längswiderstand m
- E: series resistance, ohmic resistance,

positive-sequence resistance
résistance mécanique f
  D: mechanische Festigkeit
  E: mechanical strength
résistance f **ohmique**
  D: ohmscher Widerstand
  E: ohmic resistance
résistance f **spécifique d'isolement**
  D: spezifischer Isolationswiderstand
  E: specific insulation resistance
résistance f **superficielle**
  D: Oberflächenwiderstand m
  E: surface resistance
résistance f **thermique**
  D: Wärmebeständigkeit f,
    Hitzebeständigkeit f,
    Wärmestandfestigkeit f
  E: heat resistance, thermal resistance,
    thermal stability
résistance f **thermique**
  D: Wärmewiderstand m,
    Wärmedurchgangswiderstand m
  E: thermal resistance
résistant adj **à la chaleur**
  D: wärmebeständig adj
  E: heat-proof adj, heat-resistant adj
résistant adj **à la corrosion**
  D: korrosionsfest adj
  E: corrosion-resistant adj,
    corrosion-proof adj, anti-
    corrosive adj
résistant adj **à la flamme**
  D: feuerbeständig adj,
    flammenbeständig adj
  E: fire-resistant adj, fire-proof adj,
    flame-proof adj
résistant adj **à la lumière**
  D: lichtbeständig adj, lichtecht adj
  E: light-fast adj, light-stable adj
résistant adj **à l'eau**
  D: wasserbeständig adj
  E: water resistant
résistant adj **à l'humidité**
  D: feuchtigkeitsbeständig adj
  E: moisture-resistant adj
résistant adj **au court-circuit**
  D: kurzschlußsicher adj
  E: short-circuit proof
résistant adj **au feu**
  D: feuerbeständig adj,
    flammenbeständig adj
  E: fire-resistant adj, fire-proof adj,
    flame-proof adj

résistant adj **au froid**
  D: kältebeständig adj
  E: resistant to cold, cold-resistant adj,
    resistant to low temperatures
résistant adj **aux acides**
  D: säurebeständig adj
  E: acid-resistant adj, acid-proof adj
résistant adj **aux basses températures**
  D: kältebeständig adj
  E: resistant to cold, cold-resistant adj,
    resistant to low temperatures
résistant adj **aux conditions tropicales**
  D: tropenfest adj
  E: tropicalized adj, resistant to
    tropical conditions, tropic-proof
    adj
résister v **à ...**
  D: aushalten v
  E: withstand v, resist v to ...
résister v **à un essai**
  D: eine Prüfung bestehen
  E: to pass a test, to withstand a test
résistivité f
  D: spezifischer Widerstand
  E: volume resistivity, resistivity n,
    specific resistance
résistivité f **de surface**
  D: spezifischer
    Oberflächenwiderstand
  E: surface resistivity
résistivité f **de volume**
  D: spezifischer
    Durchgangswiderstand,
    spezifischer Widerstand
  E: volume resistivity
résistivité f **thermique du sol**
  D: spezifischer Wärmewiderstand des
    Bodens
  E: thermal resistivity of the soil
respecter v [ess.]
  D: einhalten v (Werte, Bedingungen)
  E: meet v, observe v, comply with v
respirer v [méc.]
  D: atmen v
  E: breathe v
résultat m **de mesure**
  D: Meßergebnis n
  E: measuring result
résultat m **d'essai**
  D: Prüfergebnis n, Prüfbefund m,
    Versuchsergebnis n
  E: test result
retardant adj **la flamme**

retardant

D: flammenhemmend *adj*,
flammenverzögernd *adj*
E: flame-retardant *adj*

retardateur *m*
D: Verzögerer *m*
E: retarder *m*

retard *m* **de phase**
D: Phasennacheilung *f*
E: phase lag

retassure *f*
D: Lunker *m*
E: shrinkhole *n*

réticulable *adj*
D: vernetzbar *adj*
E: cross-linkable *adj*

réticulation *f*
D: Vernetzung *f*
E: cross-linking *n*

réticulation *f* **au soufre**
D: Schwefelvernetzung *f*
E: sulphur cross-linking

réticulation *f* **chimique**
D: chemische Vernetzung
E: chemical cross-linking

réticulation *f* **par irradiation**
D: Strahlenvernetzung *f*
E: cross-linking by irradiation

réticulé, polyéthylène ~
D: vernetztes Polyäthylen (VPE)
E: cross-linked polyethylene (XLPE)

réticulé *adj* **par irradiation**
D: strahlenvernetzt *adj*
E: cross-linked by irradiation

retirer *v*
D: entziehen *v*
E: extract *v*, remove *v*

retour *m* **d'eau de refroidissement**
D: Kühlwasserrücklauf *m*
E: recirculation of cooling water

retour *m* **du fouloir**
D: Rückzugbewegung des
Preßstempels
E: return stroke of the ram

retour par la terre, circuit de ~
D: Erdrückleitung *f*
E: earth return circuit (GB), ground
return circuit (US)

retrait *m*
D: Schrumpfung *f*
E: shrinkage *n*, contraction *n*

retrait *m* **au chauffage**
D: Schrumpfung beim Erwärmen,
Wärmeschrumpfung *f*
E: heat-shrinkage *n*

retrait *m* **au moulage**
D: Formenschwindmaß *n*
E: mo(u)ld shrinkage

retrait *m* **par solidification**
D: Erstarrungsschrumpfung *f*
E: solidification shrinkage

rétrécir *v*
D: herunterziehen *v* (Metallmantel)
E: die down *v*

rétrécir *v* (se)
D: schrumpfen *v*
E: shrink *v*, contract *v*

rétreindre *v*
D: verdichten *v*
E: compact *v*, compress *v*

rétreindre *v*
D: herunterziehen *v* (Metallmantel)
E: die down *v*

rétreint *m*
D: Durchmesserverringerung *f*
E: diameter reduction, thinning *n*

rétreint, coefficient de ~
D: Verdichtungsgrad *m* (Leiter),
Anwalzgrad *m* (Leiter)
E: compression degree, shaping
degree

rétreint *m* **de l'âme**
D: Verdichtung des Leiters
E: compression of the conductor,
compaction of the conductor

réunir *v*
D: verbinden *v*
E: join *v*, joint *v*, connect *v*, link *v*

revendication *f* **d'un brevet**
D: Patentanspruch *m*
E: patent claim

revêtement *m*
D: Hülle *f*, Umhüllung *f*
E: sheath *n*, covering *n*, jacket *n*

revêtement *m*
D: Überzug *m*, Beschichtung *f*
E: coating *n*

revêtement *m* **de four**
D: Ofenauskleidung *f*
E: furnace lining

revêtement *m* **de fourneau réfractaire damé**
D: Stampffutter bei Schmelzöfen
E: rammed refractory lining

revêtement *m* **de protection**
D: Schutzüberzug *m*, Schutzhülle *f*
E: protective coating, protective

revêtement *m* **en jute**
 D: Jute-Umspinnung *f*
 E: jute wrapping
revêtement *m* **en sandwich**
 D: schichtweise Bedeckung
 E: sandwich covering
revêtement *m* **extérieur** [câb.]
 D: äußere Schutzhülle, Außenschutz *m*
 E: serving *n*, oversheath *n*
revêtement *m* **interne rubané**
 D: gemeinsame gewickelte Aderumhüllung
 E: taped inner covering, lapped inner covering
revêtement *m* **mince**
 D: dünnwandiger Überzug
 E: thin-wall coating
revêtement *m* **protecteur**
 D: Schutzüberzug *m*, Schutzhülle *f*
 E: protective coating, protective cover(ing)
revêtement *m* **rubané**
 D: gewickelte Umhüllung
 E: taped covering, lapped covering
revêtement *m* **sur l'assemblage**
 D: Seelenbedeckung *f*, Seelenbewicklung *f*
 E: core covering, core wrap(ping)
revêtir *v*
 D: beschichten *v*
 E: coat *v*
revêtu *adj* **de ...**
 D: kaschiert mit ...
 E: coated with ..., laminated with ..., backed with ...
réviser *v*
 D: abändern *v*, ändern *v*
 E: modify *v*, alter *v*, change *v*, revise *v*
rhéomètre *m*
 D: Strömungsmesser *m*
 E: flow meter
rhéostat *m*
 D: Widerstand *m* (Gerät)
 E: resistor *n*
rigide, matières plastiques ~s
 D: harte Kunststoffe
 E: rigid plastics
rigidité *f* **de torsion**
 D: Torsionssteifheit *f*
 E: torsional rigidity
rigidité *f* **diélectrique**
 D: Durchschlagfestigkeit *f*, Spannungsfestigkeit *f*, elektrische Festigkeit, dielektrische Festigkeit
 E: dielectric strength, breakdown strength, puncture resistance, electric strength
rigidité *f* **diélectrique instantanée**
 D: Sofortdurchschlagfestigkeit *f*
 E: instantaneous breakdown strength
rigole *f* **de coulée** [coul. cont. lam.]
 D: Überführungsrinne *f*, Gießrinne *f*
 E: launder *n*, transfer launder, transfer trough
rigole *f* **de transfert** [coul. cont. lam.]
 D: Überführungsrinne *f*, Gießrinne *f*
 E: launder *n*, transfer launder, transfer trough
rinçage *m* **sous tension** (des isolateurs)
 D: Abspritzen (von Isolatoren) im Betrieb
 E: live-washing *n* (of insulators)
rincer *v*
 D: spülen *v*
 E: rinse *v*, flush *v*
robinet *m* **d'arrêt**
 D: Absperrhahn *m*
 E: stop cock
robuste *adj*
 D: unempfindlich *adj*, kräftig *adj*, robust *adj*
 E: sturdy *adj*, robust *adj*, rigid *adj*, solid *adj*
rogner *v*
 D: köpfen *v* (Drahtenden), beschneiden *v*, abschneiden *v*
 E: crop *v*, trim *v*, cut *v*
rondelle *f* **d'étanchéité**
 D: Dichtungsscheibe *f*
 E: packing ring, sealing washer, gasket *n*, sealing disc
ronflement *m* **de modulation**
 D: Brumm-Modulation *f*
 E: hum-modulation *n*
rotation *f*
 D: Umdrehung *f* (Achse)
 E: rotation *n*
rotation *f* **en sens des aiguilles d'une montre** [mach.]
 D: Rechtsdrehung *f*
 E: clockwise rotation
rotation *f* **en sens inverse des aiguilles d'une montre** [mach.]
 D: Linksdrehung *f*

rotation

 E: counter-clockwise rotation
roue f
 D: Scheibe f
 E: sheave n, disc n, pulley n
roue f de coulée [coul. cont. lam.]
 D: Gießrad n
 E: casting wheel
roue f de renvoi
 D: Umlenkrolle f
 E: deflector roll, reversing sheave
roue f de serrage
 D: Spannrad n (Properzi-Gießmaschine)
 E: tension wheel
roue f de tirage
 D: Scheibenabzug m, Abzugscheibe f
 E: pull-off capstan, haul-off capstan
rouleau m
 D: Rolle f
 E: sheave n, roller n, pulley n
rouleau m
 D: Walze f
 E: roll n, bowl n (calender)
rouleau m d'appui
 D: Stützrolle f
 E: supporting roller
rouleau m de câble [pose c.]
 D: Kabelrolle f
 E: cable roller
rouleau m de papier
 D: Papierrolle f
 E: paper roll
rouleau m de pression
 D: Andruckrolle f
 E: press roll
rouleau m de serrage
 D: Andruckrolle f
 E: press roll
rouleau m dresseur
 D: Richtrolle f
 E: dressing roll
rouleau m entraîné par moteur pour la pose du câble
 D: elektro-motorische Kabellegerolle
 E: motor-driven roller for cable laying
rouleau-guide m
 D: Führungsrolle f, Leitrolle f
 E: guide roller, guide pulley
rouleaux m pl d'angle [pose c.]
 D: Eckrollen f pl
 E: corner rollers
rouleaux m pl (de rétreint) de secteur
 D: Sektorverdichtungswalzen f pl
 E: sector rollers
roulement m à billes
 D: Kugellager n
 E: ball-bearing n
ruban m
 D: Band n
 E: tape n, strip n, band n
ruban m adhésif
 D: Klebeband n
 E: adhesive tape
rubanage m
 D: Umspinnung f (mit Band), Bandumspinnung f, Bewicklung f (mit Band), Schmalbandwicklung f
 E: lapping n, taping n, tape(d) wrapping
rubanage m de papier
 D: Papierspinnen n
 E: paper lapping
rubanage m d'étanchéité [câb.]
 D: Dichtungswickel m
 E: sealing wrap
rubanage m en papier
 D: Isolierung aus Papierbandumspinnung, Papierbandisolierung f
 E: paper tape insulation, lapped paper insulation, spiral strip paper insulation (US), paper ribbon insulation (US)
rubanage m jointif
 D: anlappende Bandumspinnung
 E: butted taping
rubanage m stratifié (rubans papier/synthétiques)
 D: Papier/Kunststoff-Schichtenmaterial n (Bänder)
 E: bonded laminar material (paper/plastic tapes), bonded laminate (paper/plastic tapes)
ruban m auto-adhésif
 D: selbstklebendes Band
 E: self-adhesive tape, pressure-sensitive tape
ruban m autoamalgamant
 D: selbstverschweißendes Band
 E: self-amalgamating tape, self-fusing tape
ruban m auto-collant
 D: selbstklebendes Band
 E: self-adhesive tape, pressure-sensitive tape

ruban *m* **autosoudable**
D: selbstverschweißendes Band
E: self-amalgamating tape, self-fusing tape

ruban *m* **autosoudant**
D: selbstverschweißendes Band
E: self-amalgamating tape, self-fusing tape

ruban *m* **de chauffage**
D: Heizband *n*
E: heating collar

ruban *m* **de coton caoutchouté**
D: gummibeschichtetes Baumwollband
E: proofed cotton tape

ruban *m* **de coton de ligature**
D: Baumwollbindeband *n*
E: cotton binder tape

ruban *m* **de cuivre**
D: Kupferband *n*, Bandkupfer *n*
E: copper tape, copper strip, copper strap

ruban *m* **de feuille**
D: Folienband *n*
E: film tape

ruban *m* **en soie de verre**
D: Glasseidenband *n*
E: glass fibre tape

ruban *m* **en toile vernie**
D: Lackgewebe-Band *n*
E: varnished cambric tape

rubaner *v*
D: umwickeln *v* (mit Band), bewickeln *v* (mit Band), umspinnen *v* (mit Band), wickeln *v* (Band)
E: lap *v*, tape *v*, wrap *v*

rubaneuse *f*
D: Bandwickelmaschine *f*, Spinnmaschine *f* (Band)
E: taping machine, lapping machine

rubaneuse *f* **à papier**
D: Papierspinnmaschine *f*, Plattiermaschine *f*
E: paper lapping machine

rubaneuse *f* **centrale**
D: Zentralspinner *m*, Zentralwickler *m*
E: central spinner, concentric lapping machine, concentric lapper

rubaneuse *f* **horizontale à cage**
D: horizontaler Korbspinner
E: horizontal cage lapper, horizontal cage type lapping machine

rubaneuse *f* **tangentielle**
D: Tangentialspinner *m*
E: tangential lapper, tangential type lapping machine

rubaneuse *f* **verticale**
D: Vertikal-Spinnmaschine *f*
E: vertical lapping machine

rubaneuse *f* **verticale à cage**
D: vertikaler Korbspinner
E: vertical cage lapper, vertical cage type lapping machine

ruban *m* **Hessian**
D: Hessianband *n* (Jute)
E: hessian tape

ruban *m* **isolant**
D: Isolierband *n*
E: insulating tape, friction tape (US)

ruban *m* **laqué**
D: Lackband *n*
E: varnished tape

ruban *m* **mica**
D: Glimmergewebeband *n*
E: mica tape

ruban *m* **papier contrecouché d'un polymère**
D: kunststoffbeschichtetes Papierband
E: polymer/paper laminated tape

rubans *m pl* **imbriqués**
D: dachziegelartig aufgebrachte Bänder
E: intercalated tapes, interlocked tapes

ruban *m* **textile**
D: Gewebeband *n*, Textilband *n*
E: fabric tape, textile tape

ruban *m* **textile caoutchouté**
D: gummiertes Textilband
E: proofed textile tape, rubber-coated textile tape

ruban *m* **textile tissu de fils de cuivre**
D: Textilband mit eingewebten Kupferdrähten
E: fabric tape with interwoven copper wires, copper threaded textile tape

ruban *m* **thermosoudant**
D: warmverschweißendes Band
E: heat fusing tape

ruban *m* **verni**
D: Lackband *n*
E: varnished tape

rugosité *f* **de la surface**
D: Oberflächenrauhigkeit *f*

rugosité

  E: surface roughness
rupture f
  D: Reißen n
  E: tearing n, breaking n, tear n, break n
rupture f
  D: Bruch m, Bruchstelle f
  E: fracture n, break n, rupture n
rupture f **de fatigue**
  D: Ermüdungsbruch m
  E: fatigue crack, fatigue failure, fatigue fracture, stress cracking
rupture f **de l'âme**
  D: Leiterbruch m
  E: conductor break
rupture f **du fil**
  D: Drahtbruch m, Drahtriß m
  E: wire break, wire breakage
rupture f **du ruban de papier**
  D: Papierbandriß m
  E: paper tape break
rupture f **du ruban de papier ou du fil métallique**
  D: Abreißen von Papierband oder Draht
  E: break of paper tape or wire
rupture f **fragile**
  D: Sprödbruch m
  E: brittle fracture

S

sable m **compacté**
  D: verdichteter Sand
  E: compacted sand
salle f **de mesure**
  D: Meßraum m
  E: measuring room, test room
satisfaire v **à une demande**
  D: eine Forderung erfüllen, eine Bedingung erfüllen, einer Anforderung genügen
  E: to meet a requirement
satisfaire v **à une exigence**
  D: eine Forderung erfüllen, eine Bedingung erfüllen, einer Anforderung genügen
  E: to meet a requirement
saumon m
  D: Massel f (Blei)
  E: pig n, cake n
saumon m **de plomb**
  D: Blockblei n
  E: pig lead
scalpage m
  D: Befräsen n (Kupfer-Drahtbarren)
  E: scalping n, chipping n
scalper v
  D: fräsen v (Drahtbarren)
  E: scalp v
scanner m
  D: Abtastvorrichtung f, Fühler m
  E: scanning device, scanner n, sensing device, sensor n, detecting element
sceller v [access. c.]
  D: vergießen v
  E: encapsulate v, fill v, seal v
schéma m **de connexions** [él.]
  D: Schaltung f, Verdrahtung f
  E: circuitry n, circuit arrangement, wiring n, cabling n, interconnection n
schéma m **de principe**
  D: schematische Darstellung
  E: schematic representation, diagrammatic representation
schéma m **de principe** [él.]
  D: Prinzipschaltbild n
  E: schematic wiring diagram, elementary circuit diagram
schéma m **des connexions**
  D: Schaltplan m, Schaltschema n, Verdrahtungsplan m
  E: wiring diagram, wiring scheme, circuit diagram
schéma m **électrique**
  D: Schaltplan m, Schaltschema n, Verdrahtungsplan m
  E: wiring diagram, wiring scheme, circuit diagram
schéma m **fonctionnel**
  D: Funktionsschema n
  E: functional diagram, block diagram
scie f **volante**
  D: fliegende Säge
  E: flying saw
scorie f
  D: Schlacke f
  E: slag n, dross n
scorie, soutirer la ~
  D: Schlacke abziehen
  E: to skim off the dross
séchage m

séchage *m* **du sol**
D: Austrocknung des Erdbodens, Bodenaustrocknung *f*
E: drying (out) of the soil

séchage *m* **sous vide**
D: Vakuumtrocknung *f*
E: vacuum drying

sécher *v*
D: austrocknen *v*
E: dry out *v*, desiccate *vt*, dehydrate *vt*

secteur *m* [él.]
D: Netz *n*
E: network *n*, system *n*, mains *n*

secteur *m* **triphasé avec conducteur neutre**
D: Drehstromnetz mit Nulleiter
E: three-phase system with neutral

section *f*
D: Abschnitt *m*
E: section *n*

section *f* **(droite)**
D: Querschnitt *m*
E: cross-section *n*, cross-sectional area

section, à ~ décroissante
D: verjüngt *adj*, konisch *adj*
E: tapered *adj*, conic(al) *adj*

section, de ~ égale
D: querschnittsgleich *adj*
E: of equal cross-sectional area

section, en ~s
D: abschnittweise *adj*
E: in sections

section *f* **(élémentaire) d'amplification**
D: Verstärkerfeld *n*
E: repeater section

section *f* **de bobines Pupin**
D: Spulenfeldlänge *f*, Spulenfeld *n*
E: loading (coil) section

section *f* **de charge**
D: Spulenfeldlänge *f*, Spulenfeld *n*
E: loading (coil) section

section *f* **de l'écran** [câb.]
D: Schirmquerschnitt *m*
E: screen cross-section

section *f* **de refroidissement**
D: Kühlstrecke *f*
E: cooling section

section *f* **de refroidissement par air**
D: Luftkühlstrecke *f*
E: air cooling section

section *f* **de refroidissement par eau**
D: Wasserkühlstrecke *f*
E: water cooling section

section *f* **efficace calculée**
D: berechneter wirksamer Querschnitt
E: calculated effective area

section *f* **électriquement efficace**
D: elektrisch wirksamer Querschnitt
E: electrically effective cross-section

section *f* **géométrique**
D: geometrischer Querschnitt
E: geometrical cross-section

sectionner *v*
D: unterteilen *v*
E: sectionalize *v*, subdivide *v*

sectionneur *m*
D: Trennschalter *m*
E: isolating switch, disconnecting switch

section *f* **nominale**
D: Nennquerschnitt *m*
E: nominal cross-section

section *f* **rectangulaire**
D: rechteckiger Querschnitt
E: rectangular cross-section

sécurité, dispositif de ~
D: Sicherheitsvorrichtung *f*, Schutzvorrichtung *f*
E: safety device, protective device

sécurité *f* **de fonctionnement**
D: Betriebssicherheit *f*, Betriebszuverlässigkeit *f*, Zuverlässigkeit im Betrieb
E: operating reliability, operating safety, service reliability, functional reliability, reliability of operation, operational reliability

sécurité de fonctionnement, câbles de bonne ~
D: betriebssichere Kabel
E: operationally reliable cables, fail-safe cables

sécurité intrinsèque, installation à ~
D: eigensichere Anlage
E: intrinsically safe installation

sédiment *m*
D: Bodensatz *m*
E: bottom settling, deposit *n*, sediment *n*

segmenté, âme ~e

segmenté

segmenté
- D: Segmentleiter m
- E: segmental conductor, split conductor

ségrégation f
- D: Ausscheidung f, Absonderung f
- E: segregation n, exudation n

ségrégation f
- D: Entmischung f
- E: segregation n, decomposition n, separation n

sélection f **automatique**
- D: Selbstwählbetrieb m, Selbstwählsystem n
- E: automatic telephone service, automatic dialling, automatic dial service

sélection f **de la voie à fréquence porteuse**
- D: Trägerfrequenz-Kanalwahl f
- E: carrier frequency channel selection

semi-conducteur, mélange ~
- D: schwachleitende Mischung
- E: semi-conducting compound, semi-conductive compound

semi-produit m
- D: Halbfertigfabrikat n
- E: semi-finished product

sens, en ~ alterné
- D: in wechselnder Richtung
- E: in alternating direction

sens m **de câblage**
- D: Drallrichtung f, Schlagrichtung f
- E: direction of lay, direction of twist

sens m **de défilement** [mach.]
- D: Laufrichtung f
- E: direction of running, sense of running

sens m **de l'axe**
- D: Längsrichtung f
- E: longitudinal direction, axial direction

sens m **de marche** [mach.]
- D: Laufrichtung f
- E: direction of running, sense of running

sens m **d'enroulement**
- D: Spinnrichtung f
- E: lapping direction

sens m **d'enroulement**
- D: Wickelrichtung f
- E: winding direction

sens m **de passage du câble**
- D: Laufrichtung des Kabels durch eine Maschine
- E: direction of cable travel

sens m **de rotation** [mach.]
- D: Drehrichtung f
- E: direction of rotation

sens m **de rubanage**
- D: Spinnrichtung f
- E: lapping direction

sens m **de torsion**
- D: Drallrichtung f, Schlagrichtung f
- E: direction of lay, direction of twist

sens m **du pas de câblage**
- D: Drallrichtung f, Schlagrichtung f
- E: direction of lay, direction of twist

sens m **du pas de torsion**
- D: Drallrichtung f, Schlagrichtung f
- E: direction of lay, direction of twist

sensibilité f
- D: Empfindlichkeit f
- E: sensibility n, sensitivity n

sensibilité f **à la lumière**
- D: Lichtempfindlichkeit f
- E: light-sensitivity n, luminous sensitivity

sensibilité f **à l'entaille**
- D: Kerbempfindlichkeit f
- E: notch sensitivity

sensibilité f **aux parasites** [com.]
- D: Störanfälligkeit f
- E: sensibility to disturbances

sensibilité f **aux perturbations** [com.]
- D: Störanfälligkeit f
- E: sensibility to disturbances

sensibilité f **lumineuse**
- D: Lichtempfindlichkeit f
- E: light-sensitivity n, luminous sensitivity

sensible adj **à la chaleur**
- D: wärmeempfindlich adj
- E: heat-sensitive adj

sens m **longitudinal**
- D: Längsrichtung f
- E: longitudinal direction, axial direction

séparateur m
- D: Abstandhalter m
- E: spacer n

séparateur m
- D: Trennfolie f, Trennschicht f
- E: separator n (film)

séparateur m **du grain de poussée** [pr. à filer]

séparateur
D: Preßscheibentrenner *m*
E: dummy block separator

séparateur *m* pneumatique
D: Windsichter *m*
E: air classification plant, air-classifier *n*, air-sifter *n*

séparation *f*
D: Ausscheidung *f*, Absonderung *f*
E: segregation *n*, separation *n*, exudation *n*

séparer *v*
D: ablösen *v* (Folie, Schicht), abziehen *v*
E: peel *v*, separate *v*, detach *v*

serpentin *m*
D: Rohrschlange *f*
E: coiled pipe

serpentin, pose des câbles en ~s
D: Schlangenverlegung von Kabeln, Verlegung von Kabeln in Schlangenlinien
E: snaking of cables, laying cables in a wave formation

serpentin *m* de chauffage
D: Heizschlange *f*
E: heating coil

serrage, dispositif de ~ pour filière [fabr. fils mét.]
D: Ziehsteinhalter *m*
E: die holder

serré, étant bien ~
D: fest anliegend, festsitzend *adj*
E: giving a tight fit, close-fitting *adj*, tight-fitting *adj*, making a tight fit

serre-câble *m*
D: Kabelschelle *f*, Kabelklemme *f*
E: cable clamp, cable cleat, cable clip, cable grip

serre-câble *m* pneumatique [vulc.]
D: pneumatische Kabelklemme
E: air clamp

serre-fil *m*
D: Drahtklemme *f*
E: wire grip, wire clamp

serrer *v*
D: festklemmen *v*
E: cleat *v*, clamp *v*, cramp *v*

sertissage *m* hexagonal [access. c.]
D: Sechskantpressung *f*
E: hexagonal compression

service *m*
D: Instandhaltung *f*
E: maintenance *n*, service *n*, servicing *n*

service *m* [câb., mach.]
D: Betrieb *m*
E: operation *n*, service *n*, duty *n*

service, hors ~
D: außer Betrieb
E: out of operation, out of order, out of service

service, mettre en ~
D: in Betrieb nehmen
E: to put to service, to set working, to take into commission, to bring into commercial operation

service *m* avec charge intermittente [él.]
D: aussetzender Betrieb, Betrieb mit aussetzender Belastung
E: intermittent operation

service *m* continu
D: kontinuierlicher Betrieb
E: continuous operation

service *m* continu [él.]
D: Dauerbetrieb mit gleichbleibender Belastung
E: continuous duty, continuous operation

service *m* de courte durée [él.]
D: Kurzzeitbetrieb *m* (mit gleichbleibender Last)
E: short-time service, short-time duty, short-time operation

service *m* de longue durée [él.]
D: Dauerbetrieb *m* (ununterbrochener Betrieb von mindestens 2,5 Std.)
E: long-time operation

service *m* de production
D: Fertigungsabteilung *f*
E: production department, manufacturing department

service *m* en discontinu
D: diskontinuierliches Verfahren, Chargenbetrieb *m*
E: intermittent process, discontinuous operation, batch type process, batch operation

service *m* ininterrompu à charge intermittente [él.]
D: Dauerbetrieb mit aussetzender Belastung (DAB)
E: continuous duty with intermittent loading

service *m* ininterrompu à charge

service 584

variable [él.]
  D: Dauerbetrieb mit veränderlicher Belastung
  E: continuous duty with variable load
service m **intermittent** [él.]
  D: aussetzender Betrieb, Betrieb mit aussetzender Belastung
  E: intermittent operation
service m **permanent à charge variant périodiquement** [él.]
  D: Dauerbetrieb mit periodisch veränderlicher Belastung
  E: periodic load duty
service m **téléphonique automatique**
  D: Selbstwählbetrieb m, Selbstwählsystem n
  E: automatic telephone service, automatic dialling, automatic dial service
service m **téléphonique et télévision combiné**
  D: Fernsehgegensprechen n
  E: combined television telephone service
service m **téléphonique instantané**
  D: Fernsprechschnellverkehr m
  E: no-delay telephone system
service m **temporaire** [él.]
  D: Kurzzeitbetrieb m (mit gleichbleibender Last)
  E: short-time service, short-time duty, short-time operation
service m **temporaire variable** [él.]
  D: Kurzzeitbetrieb m (mit veränderlicher Last)
  E: variable temporary duty
seuil m **de choc**
  D: Stoßpegel m
  E: impulse level
seuil m **de fluage**
  D: Fließgrenze f
  E: flow limit
seuil m **d'ionisation**
  D: Ionisations-Einsetzspannung f
  E: ionization inception voltage
seuil m **d'ionisation**
  D: Ionisationspegel m
  E: ionization level
shunt m
  D: Abzweigstromkreis m, Nebenschluß m
  E: branch circuit, shunt n
signal m **avertisseur acoustique**
  D: akustisches Warnsignal
  E: audible warning
signalisation f
  D: Anzeige f
  E: indication n, display n, reading n
signalisation f **de défauts**
  D: Fehleranzeige f
  E: error display, fault indication
signalisation f **visible**
  D: Schauzeichen n
  E: lamp indicator, visual signal
signal m **lumineux**
  D: Signallampe f, Anzeigelampe f
  E: pilot lamp, signal lamp, indicating lamp, pilot light
signal m **vocal**
  D: Sprechzeichen n
  E: voice signal
significatif adj
  D: aussagekräftig adj (Werte)
  E: meaningful adj, significant adj
silo m **à granulés**
  D: Granulatsilo m
  E: granules storage bin
simuler v
  D: nachbilden v
  E: simulate v
société f **de distribution d'électricité**
  D: Elektrizitäts-Versorgungsunternehmen (EVU) n
  E: electricity supply undertaking, electricity undertaking, utility (US) n
socle m
  D: Grundplatte f
  E: base plate, mounting base
soie f **de verre**
  D: Glasseide f
  E: glass fibre yarn
solidaire, rendu ~
  D: kraftschlüssig verbunden
  E: positively connected
solidification f
  D: Erstarrung f
  E: solidification n, setting n, hardening n, freezing v
solidifier v (se)
  D: erstarren v, hartwerden v
  E: solidify v, freeze v, set v, harden v
sollicitation f [él., méc.]
  D: Beanspruchung f, Belastung f, Last f

E: stress n, strain n, load n

sollicitation f **permanente**
  D: Dauerbeanspruchung f
  E: continuous stress

solliciter v [él., méc.]
  D: beanspruchen v, belasten v
  E: stress v, strain v, load v

solution f
  D: Lösung f
  E: solution n

solution f **corrosive**
  D: aggressive Lösung
  E: corrosive solution

solution f **de décapage**
  D: Beizlösung f
  E: pickling solution

solution f **de tréfilage**
  D: Ziehlösung f
  E: drawing solution

solvant, résistance aux ~s
  D: Lösungsmittelbeständigkeit f
  E: solvent resistance

sommet m **d'un secteur**
  D: Sektorspitze f
  E: sector peak, sector crest

sonde f
  D: Abtastvorrichtung f, Fühler m
  E: scanning device, scanner n, sensing device, sensor n, detecting element

sonde f
  D: Meßelektrode f
  E: measuring electrode

sonde f **pyrométrique**
  D: Temperaturfühler m
  E: temperature pick-up, temperature sensor

sonder v
  D: abtasten v
  E: scan v, sense v

sonnage m [c. tél.]
  D: Abklingeln n, Durchklingeln n, Ausklingeln n, Klingelprüfung f
  E: ringing test, ring-out procedure, buzz-out operation

sonner v [c. tél.]
  D: abklingeln v
  E: buzz out v, ring out v

sortie f
  D: Austritt m
  E: outlet n, exit n, orifice n

sortie f **de filière** [fabr. fils mét.]
  D: Ziehsteinauslauf m
  E: die back relief

soudabilité f
  D: Lötbarkeit f
  E: solderability n

soudage m
  D: Löten n
  E: soldering n

soudage m
  D: Schweißen n
  E: welding n

soudage m **à air chaud avec fil de soudage plastique**
  D: Heißluftschweißen mit Kunststoff-Drahtzufuhr
  E: hot-air welding with plastic welding rod

soudage m **à arc en atmosphère protectrice**
  D: Schutzgasschweißen n
  E: inert gas arc welding

soudage m **à friction**
  D: Reibschweißen n
  E: friction welding

soudage m **à froid**
  D: Kaltschweißen n, Kaltpreßschweißen n
  E: cold welding, cold pressure welding

soudage m **à l'arc**
  D: Lichtbogenschweißen n
  E: arc welding

soudage m **en ligne continue**
  D: Nahtschweißen n
  E: seam welding

soudage m **par rapprochement**
  D: Stumpfschweißen n
  E: butt welding

soudage m **par résistance**
  D: Widerstandsschweißen n
  E: resistance welding

soudage m **tendre**
  D: Weichlöten n
  E: soft soldering

souder v
  D: verschweißen v
  E: weld v, fuse v

souder v
  D: weichlöten v
  E: soft-solder v

soudeuse f **par rapprochement**
  D: Stumpfschweißmaschine f
  E: butt welding machine

soudure f
  D: Lot n

soudure
  E: solder n
soudure f
  D: Schweißstelle f, Schweißverbindung f
  E: welded joint
soudure f
  D: Lötverbindung f (weich), Lötstelle f
  E: soldered joint, soldering joint
soudure, tube sans ~
  D: nahtloses Rohr
  E: seamless tube
soudure f **à la louche**
  D: Schmierplombe f
  E: wiped solder joint, wiping nipple, wiping gland, wiping solder seal
soudure f **à superposition**
  D: Auftragsschweißung f
  E: welded hard surfacing, build-up welding, surface layer welding
soudure f **bout à bout**
  D: Stumpfschweißen n
  E: butt welding
soudure f **en fil**
  D: Lötdraht m
  E: cored solder, soldering wire, wire solder
soudure f **froide**
  D: Kaltlötstelle f
  E: cold solder joint
soudure f **liquide**
  D: Wischlot n, Weichlot n, Schmierlot n
  E: wiping solder
soupape f
  D: Ventil n
  E: valve n
soupape f **d'admission**
  D: Einlaßventil n
  E: inlet valve
soupape f **d'arrêt**
  D: Absperrventil n
  E: stop valve, shut-off valve
soupape f **de décharge**
  D: Ablaßventil n, Auslaßventil n
  E: outlet valve, drain valve, discharge valve, exhaust valve
soupape f **d'émission**
  D: Ablaßventil n, Auslaßventil n
  E: outlet valve, drain valve, discharge valve, exhaust valve
soupape f **de retenue**
  D: Rückschlagventil n
  E: return valve, check valve, back-pressure valve, non-return valve
soupape f **de sortie**
  D: Ablaßventil n, Auslaßventil n
  E: outlet valve, drain valve, discharge valve, exhaust valve
soupape f **de sûreté**
  D: Überdruckventil n
  E: pressure relief valve
soupape f **de surpression**
  D: Überdruckventil n
  E: pressure relief valve
soupape f **de trop-plein**
  D: Überlaufventil n
  E: overflow valve, by-pass valve
soupape f **de vidange**
  D: Ablaßventil n, Auslaßventil n
  E: outlet valve, drain valve, discharge valve, exhaust valve
souple adj
  D: biegsam adj
  E: flexible adj
souplesse f
  D: Biegsamkeit f, Biegbarkeit f
  E: flexibility n
source f **de chaleur**
  D: Wärmequelle f
  E: heat source
source f **de courant**
  D: Stromquelle f
  E: current source
source f **d'énergie**
  D: Energiequelle f
  E: source of energy, source of power, power source
source f **de perturbation**
  D: Störquelle f
  E: interference source, source of disturbance
source f **de tension**
  D: Spannungsquelle f
  E: voltage source
sous-sol, installation en ~
  D: Unterflur-Installation f
  E: subsurface installation, installation below floor level
sous-sol m **de distribution des câbles**
  D: Kabelaufteilungskeller m (Fernsprechamt)
  E: cable vault (tel. exchange)
sous-station f
  D: Umspannwerk n
  E: substation n, transforming station, transformer station

soutenir v
  D: aushalten v
  E: withstand v, resist v to ...
soutenu, non ~
  D: freitragend adj
  E: cantilevered adj
souterrain, installation ~e
  D: Unterflur-Installation f
  E: subsurface installation, installation below floor level
soutirer v **la scorie**
  D: Schlacke abziehen
  E: to skim off the dross
spécification f
  D: Norm f
  E: standard specification
spécification f **d'achat**
  D: Liefervorschrift f
  E: purchase specification
spécification f **de qualité**
  D: Gütevorschrift f
  E: quality specification
spécification f **d'un brevet**
  D: Patentanspruch m
  E: patent claim
spécifications f pl **VDE**
  D: VDE-Bestimmungen f pl, VDE-Regeln f pl, VDE-Vorschriften f pl
  E: VDE Regulations, VDE Rules, VDE Standards
spectroscopie f **infrarouge**
  D: Infrarot-Spektroskopie f, IR-Spektroskopie f
  E: infra-red spectroscopy, IR-spectroscopy n
spectroscopie f **IR**
  D: Infrarot-Spektroskopie f, IR-Spektroskopie f
  E: infra-red spectroscopy, IR-spectroscopy n
sphère f **d'application**
  D: Anwendungsbereich m
  E: range of application
sphérique adj
  D: kugelförmig adj
  E: spherical-shaped adj
spirale f **colorée**
  D: farbige Spirale, farbige Wendel
  E: colo(u)red spiral, colo(u)red helix
spirale f **de fixation** [câb.]
  D: Haltewendel f
  E: binder n, holding tape, reinforcement helix
spirale f **de Styroflex** [câb.]
  D: Styroflex-Wendel f
  E: Styroflex-helix n
spire f
  D: Windung f
  E: winding n (of coil, reel), turn n, loop n
spire, en ~s jointives [rub.]
  D: auf Stoß
  E: without butt gaps, in a closed helix
spire f **de court-circuit**
  D: Kurzschlußwindung f
  E: short-circuited turn, short-circuit winding
spire f **de la vis** [extr.]
  D: Schneckengang m, Gewindegang der Schnecke, Schneckengewinde n
  E: flight of the screw, thread of the screw
spires f pl **d'un câble sur un touret**
  D: Windungen eines aufgetrommelten Kabels
  E: convolutions of a cable on a reel
stabilisant m
  D: stabilisierender Zusatz, Stabilisator m
  E: stabilizing agent, stabilizer n
stabilisant m **contre l'effet de la lumière**
  D: Lichtschutzmittel n
  E: light-stabilizer n, sun-cracking inhibitor
stabilisant m **de tension**
  D: Spannungsstabilisator m (Zusatz in Isoliermischungen)
  E: voltage stabilizer (additive in insulating compounds)
stabilisant adj **électriquement**
  D: spannungsstabilisierend adj (Mischungsadditiv)
  E: voltage-stabilizing adj
stabilité f
  D: Beständigkeit f, Festigkeit f, Widerstandsfähigkeit f
  E: stability n, durability n, resistance n, strength n
stabilité f **à la lumière**
  D: Lichtbeständigkeit f (Mischungen), Lichtfestigkeit f (Mischungen)
  E: light-stability n
stabilité f **au stockage**
  D: Lagerfähigkeit f (Werkstoffe),

stabilité

Haltbarkeit f (Werkstoffe), Lagerungsbeständigkeit f
E: shelf life, storage stability

stabilité f de forme
D: Formbeständigkeit f, Formänderungsbeständigkeit f
E: form-stability n, dimensional stability, resistance to deformation, deformation resistance

stabilité f de la couleur
D: Farbbeständigkeit f
E: colo(u)r-fastness, colo(u)r retention

stabilité f thermique
D: Wärmebeständigkeit f, Hitzebeständigkeit f, Wärmestandfestigkeit f
E: heat resistance, thermal resistance, thermal stability

stable adj à la lumière
D: lichtbeständig adj, lichtecht adj
E: light-fast adj, light-stable adj

stable adj de forme
D: formbeständig adj
E: form-stable adj, resistant to deformation

stade de fabrication, étudié jusqu'au ~
D: bis zur Fertigungsreife entwickelt
E: developed to the production stage

stade m de vulcanisation
D: Vulkanisationsgrad m
E: state of cure, degree of cure

stade m expérimental
D: Versuchsstadium n
E: trial stage, experimental stage, laboratory stage

standardisation f
D: Normung f, Vereinheitlichung f
E: standardisation n, normalization n, unification n

station f de commande
D: Schaltwarte f
E: control station

station f de pompage
D: Pumpstation f
E: pumping station

station f d'essai
D: Prüfstelle f
E: approval organization, testing station

stationnaire adj
D: stationär adj, feststehend adj
E: stationary adj, fixed adj

station f principale de répéteurs
D: Hauptverstärkerstelle f
E: main repeater station

stéarate m de plomb
D: Bleistearat n
E: lead stearate

stocker v le cable dans la cale d'un navire
D: Kabel in den Schiffsladeraum einschießen
E: to coil the cable into the ship's hold

stokes m
D: Stokes n (St) (Viskosität)
E: stokes n

stratifié m
D: Schichtstoff m
E: laminate n, laminated plastic, laminated material

stratifié m
D: Hartgewebe n
E: synthetic resin-bonded fabric, laminated fabric

strié adj
D: geriffelt adj
E: grooved adj, ribbed adj

structure f à grains fins
D: feinkörnige Struktur
E: fine-grain structure

structure f à gros grains
D: grobkörnige Struktur
E: coarse-grain structure

structure f cristalline
D: kristallines Gefüge
E: crystalline structure

structure f moléculaire
D: Molekulargefüge n
E: molecular structure

subdiviser v
D: unterteilen v
E: sectionalize v, subdivide v

substituer v
D: ersetzen v
E: replace v, substitute v

suie f
D: Ofenruß m
E: furnace black

suinter v
D: durchsickern v
E: ooze v, filter through v, leak v

suite f des opérations
D: Arbeitsablauf m, Betriebsablauf m
E: flow of operation, operating sequence, flow process, operating

cycle
suivant l'exemple de
 D: in Anlehnung an
 E: similar to, taking pattern from
superposer v
 D: überlagern v
 E: superpose v, superimpose v
superposition f
 D: Überlagerung f
 E: superposition n, superimposition n
supplément m **de torsion** [câblage]
 D: Drallzuschlag m
 E: stranding allowance, laying-up allowance
support m
 D: Halterung f
 E: holder n, support n
support m **de déflecteur**
 D: Deflektorhalter m
 E: deflector support
support m **du conteneur** [pr. à filer]
 D: Aufnehmerhalter m
 E: container holder
supporter v
 D: aushalten v
 E: withstand v, resist v to ...
suppresseur m **d'écho**
 D: Echosperre f
 E: echo suppressor
suppresseur m **d'interférences** [com.]
 D: Störsperre f
 E: interference suppressor
suppression f **des parasites**
 D: Entstörung f, Störbeseitigung f
 E: interference elimination, interference suppression, noise suppression
supprimer v **un défaut**
 D: eine Störung beseitigen
 E: to clear a fault
supraconducteur m
 D: Supraleiter m
 E: superconductor n
supraconducteur adj (-trice)
 D: supraleitend adj
 E: superconducting adj, superconductive adj
supraconductibilité f
 D: Supraleitung f
 E: superconductivity n
surcharge f
 D: Überlast f
 E: overload n

surcharge, en ~
 D: bei Überlastbetrieb
 E: under overload conditions
surchauffage m
 D: übermäßige Erwärmung
 E: overheating n
surchauffe f
 D: übermäßige Erwärmung
 E: overheating n
surépaisseur f
 D: Übermaß n, Überdicke f, Bearbeitungszugabe f
 E: oversize n, overdimension n
surface f [mach.]
 D: Stellfläche f
 E: floor space, floor area
surface, à la ~ [pose c.]
 D: auf Putz
 E: on the surface, open adj
surface f **de séparation**
 D: Grenzfläche f
 E: interface n
surface f **de structure granulaire**
 D: körnige Oberfläche
 E: surface of granular structure
surface f **lisse**
 D: glatte Oberfläche
 E: smooth surface, plain surface
surintensités, protection contre les ~
 D: Überstromschutz m
 E: overcurrent protection, overload protection, excess current protection
surmoulé, déflecteur ~
 D: aufgepreßter Deflektor
 E: mo(u)lded deflector
surmouler v [access. c.]
 D: vergießen v
 E: encapsulate v, fill v, seal v
surpression f
 D: Überdruck m
 E: overpressure n, excess pressure
surtension f
 D: Überspannung f
 E: overvoltage n, surge voltage
surtension f **de commutation**
 D: Schaltüberspannung f
 E: switching surge, maneuver overvoltage, transient caused by switching
surtension f **de manœuvre**
 D: Schaltüberspannung f
 E: switching surge, maneuver

surtension
  overvoltage, transient caused by switching
surveillance f
  D: Überwachung f
  E: monitoring n, supervision n
surveillance f **à distance**
  D: Fernüberwachung f
  E: remote supervision, remote monitoring
surveillance f **de la qualité**
  D: Güteprüfung f, Qualitätskontrolle f
  E: quality inspection, quality test, quality control
susceptance f
  D: Blindleitwert m
  E: susceptance n
suspension f
  D: Aufhängung f
  E: suspension n
suspension, PVC de ~
  D: Suspension-PVC n
  E: suspension PVC
système m **à courant porteur**
  D: TF-System n (Trägerfrequenzsystem)
  E: carrier system
système m **à large bande**
  D: Breitbandkommunikationsnetz n, Breitbandsystem n
  E: broad-band communications network, broad-band system
système m **de mise à la terre**
  D: Erdungsanlage f
  E: earth(ing) system (GB), ground(ing) system (US)
système m **de transmission**
  D: Übertragungssystem n, Übertragungsnetz n
  E: transmission system
système m **de transmission à courants porteurs**
  D: Trägerfrequenz-Übertragungssystem n
  E: carrier frequency transmission system
système m **de transmission basse fréquence**
  D: Niederfrequenz-Übertragungssystem n
  E: audio frequency transmission system
système m **homopolaire**
  D: Nullsystem n
  E: zero phase-sequence system
système m **itératif** [él.]
  D: Kettenleiter m
  E: recurrent network, lattice network
SZ, câblage ~
  D: SZ-Verseilung f
  E: SZ-stranding n

T

tableau m **de commande**
  D: Schalttafel f
  E: control panel, switchboard n
tableau m **de commande lumineux**
  D: Leuchtbildwarte f
  E: luminous control panel
tableau m **de distribution**
  D: Schalttafel f
  E: control panel, switchboard n
tableau m **indicateur**
  D: Anzeigetafel f
  E: indicator panel, signal board, display panel
table f **d'essai**
  D: Meßplatz m
  E: measuring setup, bench-mounted testing equipment
tablette f **à câbles** [pose c.]
  D: Kabelpritsche f, Kabelträggerüst n, Pritsche f
  E: cable tray, cable rack
talc m
  D: Talkum n
  E: talc n, talc powder
tambour m **de touret** [câb.]
  D: Trommelkern m
  E: barrel of a reel
tamisage m
  D: Siebung f
  E: sieving n, screening n
tamis m **à secousses**
  D: Rüttelsieb n
  E: vibratory screen
tandem, disposition en ~ [méc.]
  D: Hintereinander-Schaltung f, Tandemanordnung f
  E: tandem arrangement, tandem connection
tandem, fonctionnement en ~
  D: Tandembetrieb m

téléphonie

E: tandemized operation
tandem, opération en ~
  D: Tandembetrieb *m*
  E: tandemized operation
tangente *f* de l'angle de perte tg δ
  D: Verlustfaktor *m*
  E: loss factor tg δ, dissipation factor, dielectric power factor cos φ
tassement *m* de terre
  D: Bodensenkung *f*, Senkung des Erdbodens
  E: subsidence of ground
taux *m* de cendre
  D: Aschegehalt *m*
  E: ash content
taux *m* de défaillances
  D: Ausfallrate *f*
  E: failure rate
taux *m* d'erreur
  D: Fehlerhäufigkeit *f*
  E: error rate
taux *m* du pas
  D: Schlaglängen-Faktor *m*
  E: lay ratio
taxe *f* et annuités sur brevet
  D: Lizenzgebühr *f*
  E: royalty *n*
technique *f*
  D: Verfahren *n*, Methode *f*
  E: process *n*, method *n*, technique *n*, procedure *n*
technique *f* de communication
  D: Nachrichtentechnik *f*
  E: communications engineering
technique *f* de fabrication
  D: Fertigungstechnik *f*
  E: production engineering
technique *f* d'emmanchement à chaud
  D: Wärmeschrumpftechnik *f*, Aufschrumpftechnik *f*
  E: shrink-on technique, heat-shrinkage technique
technique *f* de production
  D: Fertigungstechnik *f*
  E: production engineering
technique *f* des câbles
  D: Kabeltechnik *f*
  E: cable engineering
technique *f* des courants forts
  D: Starkstromtechnik *f*
  E: power engineering
technique *f* de télécommunication
  D: Fernmeldetechnik *f*
  E: telecommunications engineering
technique *f* recherchée
  D: aufwendiges Verfahren
  E: elaborate process
technologie *f* des matières
  D: Werkstoff-Technologie *f*
  E: materials technology
té *m* de dérivation
  D: Abzweigklemme *f*
  E: tee connector, T-connector *n*, branch connector, branch terminal
teindre *v*
  D: färben *v*
  E: colo(u)r *v*, dye *v*, stain *v*, pigment *v*
teinte *f*
  D: Farbtönung *f*
  E: colo(u)r shade
télécommande *f*
  D: Fernsteuerung *f*, Fernbedienung *f*
  E: remote control, telecontrol *n*
télécommunication *f*
  D: Fernmeldeverkehr *m*, Nachrichtenübermittlung *f*
  E: telecommunication *n*
télédiaphonie *f*
  D: Fernnebensprechen *n*, Gegennebensprechen *n*
  E: far-end cross talk (FEX)
télédiaphonie *f* entre réel et fantôme
  D: Gegenmitsprechen *n*
  E: side-to-phantom far-end crosstalk
télédiaphonie *f* entre réel et réel
  D: Gegenübersprechen *n*
  E: side-to-side far-end crosstalk
téléphone *m* automatique
  D: Fernsprech-Selbstanschluß *m*
  E: automatic telephone
téléphonie *f* à audio-fréquence
  D: Niederfrequenzfernsprechen *n*
  E: audio frequency telephony
téléphonie *f* à courants porteurs
  D: Trägerstromfernsprechen *n*
  E: carrier current telephony
téléphonie *f* à fréquence porteuse sur ligne à haute tension
  D: TFH-Telephonie *f* (Trägerfrequenzübertragung auf Hochspannungs-Leitungen)
  E: power line carrier telephony
téléphonie *f* à longue distance
  D: Weitverkehrs-Fernsprechtechnik *f*
  E: long distance telephony

téléphonie *f* **duplex**
 D: Doppelsprechen *n*
 E: two-way telephone conversation, phantom telephony

téléphonie *f* **fantôme**
 D: Doppelsprechen *n*
 E: two-way telephone conversation, phantom telephony

télescopique *adj*
 D: ausziehbar *adj*
 E: extensible *adj*, telescopic *adj*

télésurveillance *f*
 D: Fernüberwachung *f*
 E: remote supervision, remote monitoring

télétraitement *m* **d'informations direct**
 D: direkte Daten-Fernverarbeitung
 E: on-line remote data processing, direct remote data processing

télétraitement *m* **d'informations on-line**
 D: direkte Daten-Fernverarbeitung
 E: on-line remote data processing, direct remote data processing

télévision *f* **industrielle**
 D: Industriefernsehen *n*
 E: closed-circuit television (factory), industrial television

télévision *f* **par câble**
 D: Kabelfernsehen *n*
 E: closed-circuit television

Télévision Scolaire
 D: Schulfernsehen *n*
 E: Educational Television (ETV)

tellure *m*
 D: Tellur *n*
 E: tellurium *n*

température *f* **à l'âme**
 D: Leitertemperatur *f*
 E: conductor temperature

température *f* **ambiante**
 D: Raumtemperatur *f*
 E: room temperature, ambient temperature

température *f* **ambiante**
 D: Umgebungstemperatur *f*
 E: ambient temperature

température *f* **au thermomètre humide**
 [cond. d'air]
 D: Feuchtthermometer-Temperatur *f*, Feuchtkugel-Temperatur *f*
 E: wet bulb temperature

température *f* **au thermomètre sec**
 [cond. d'air]
 D: Trockenkugel-Temperatur *f*, Trockenthermometer-Temperatur *f*
 E: dry bulb temperature

température *f* **de coulée**
 D: Gießtemperatur *f*
 E: pouring temperature, casting temperature

température *f* **de déformation à chaud**
 D: Erweichungstemperatur *f*
 E: heat distortion temperature

température *f* **de filage**
 D: Preßtemperatur *f*
 E: extrusion temperature

température *f* **de fonctionnement**
 D: Betriebstemperatur *f*
 E: operating temperature

température *f* **de fragilité**
 D: Sprödigkeitstemperatur *f*
 E: brittleness temperature

température *f* **de fusion**
 D: Schmelztemperatur *f*
 E: melting temperature

température *f* **de la matière en fusion**
 [extr.]
 D: Masse-Temperatur *f*, Schmelzen-Temperatur *f*
 E: melt temperature

température *f* **de mise en œuvre**
 D: Verarbeitungstemperatur *f*
 E: processing temperature

température *f* **d'enfoncement**
 D: Durchdrücktemperatur *f*
 E: cut-through temperature

température *f* **d'entrée**
 D: Eintritts-, Anfangstemperatur *f*
 E: inlet temperature, initial temperature

température *f* **d'équilibre**
 D: Gleichgewichtstemperatur *f*
 E: equilibrium temperature

température *f* **de ramollissement**
 D: Erweichungstemperatur *f*
 E: heat distortion temperature

température *f* **de remplissage**
 D: Einfülltemperatur *f*
 E: pouring temperature, filling temperature

température *f* **de service**
 D: Betriebstemperatur *f*
 E: operating temperature

température *f* **de service maximale**

admissible
 D: maximal zulässige Betriebstemperatur
 E: maximum admissible operating temperature

température f de sortie
 D: Austrittstemperatur f
 E: outlet temperature

température f de transformation [plast.]
 D: Umwandlungstemperatur f
 E: transition temperature

température f d'extrusion
 D: Preßtemperatur f
 E: extrusion temperature

température f en surcharge
 D: Überlasttemperatur f
 E: emergency temperature, overload temperature

température f limite
 D: Grenztemperatur f
 E: limit temperature, temperature limit

temps m alloué
 D: Vorgabezeit f
 E: allowed time

temps m auxiliaire [mach.]
 D: Nebenzeit f
 E: ancillary time, non-productive time, handling time, down time

temps m d'accélération [mach.]
 D: Anlaufzeit f, Einlaufzeit f
 E: starting time, acceleration time, running-in period

temps m d'arrêt [mach.]
 D: Stillstandszeit f, Totzeit f
 E: down-time n, idle time, dead time

temps m pl d'arrêt [pr. à filer]
 D: Haltezeiten f pl
 E: stoppage periods

temps m d'attente d'une machine
 D: Brachzeit einer Maschine
 E: machine downtime

temps m de chauffage
 D: Aufheizzeit f
 E: warm-up time, heating-up time

temps m d'écoulement
 D: Auslaufzeit f (Viskositätsmessung)
 E: time of efflux, flow time

temps m de coupure [él.]
 D: Abschaltzeit f
 E: cut-out time

temps m de court-circuit
 D: Kurzschlußzeit f, Kurzschlußdauer f
 E: short-circuit time, short-circuit duration

temps m de démarrage [mach.]
 D: Anlaufzeit f, Einlaufzeit f
 E: starting time, acceleration time, running-in period

temps m d'empreinte
 D: Eindrückzeit f
 E: indentation time

temps m de panne [mach.]
 D: Ausfallzeit f
 E: down-time n, outage time

temps m de passage [prod.]
 D: Durchlaufzeit f
 E: production flow time

temps m de préparation [mach.]
 D: Rüstzeit f, Einrichtezeit f
 E: set-up time

temps m de propagation de groupe [com.]
 D: Gruppenlaufzeit f
 E: group propagation time, group delay time

temps m de propagation de phase
 D: Phasenlaufzeit f
 E: phase delay

temps m de réglage [mach.]
 D: Rüstzeit f, Einrichtezeit f
 E: set-up time

temps m de réponse
 D: Ansprechzeit f
 E: response time, reaction time

temps m de séjour [extr.]
 D: Verweilzeit f
 E: residence time

temps m d'immobilisation [mach.]
 D: Ausfallzeit f
 E: down-time n, outage time

temps m jusqu'à la décomposition thermo-oxydative
 D: Standzeit f (von Mischungen)
 E: time until thermal-oxidative decomposition

temps m mort [mach.]
 D: Stillstandszeit f, Totzeit f
 E: down-time n, idle time, dead time

ténacité f
 D: Zähigkeit f
 E: toughness n

tendre v
 D: recken v, spannen v, strecken v
 E: straighten v, stretch v

teneur, à haute ~ en charge
  D: füllstoffreich *adj*
  E: heavily loaded
teneur f en cendres
  D: Aschegehalt *m*
  E: ash content
teneur f en humidité
  D: Feuchtegehalt *m*, Feuchtigkeitsgehalt *m*
  E: moisture content
tenir v
  D: aushalten *v*
  E: withstand *v*, resist *v* to ...
tenir v un essai
  D: eine Prüfung bestehen
  E: to pass a test, to withstand a test
tension f
  D: Spannung *f*
  E: voltage *n*, tension *n*
tension, mettre hors ~
  D: die Spannung abschalten
  E: to cut off the voltage, to cut out the voltage
tension, mettre sous ~
  D: eine Spannung anlegen
  E: to apply a voltage
tension, sous ~
  D: stromführend *adj*, spannungführend *adj*
  E: live *adj*, current-carrying *adj*
tension f à circuit ouvert
  D: Leerlaufspannung *f*
  E: open-circuit voltage, no-load voltage
tension f active
  D: Effektivspannung *f*, Wirkspannung *f*
  E: active voltage, in-phase voltage, effective voltage, r.m.s.-voltage *n*
tension f alternative
  D: Wechselspannung *f*
  E: a.c. voltage, alternating voltage
tension f auxiliaire
  D: Hilfsspannung *f*
  E: auxiliary voltage
tension f à vide
  D: Leerlaufspannung *f*
  E: open-circuit voltage, no-load voltage
tension f composée
  D: verkettete Spannung
  E: phase-to-phase voltage, line-to-line voltage, voltage between phases
tension f continue
  D: Gleichspannung *f*
  E: direct voltage, d.c. voltage, continuous voltage
tension f continue vibrée
  D: zerhackte Gleichspannung
  E: chopped d.c. voltage
tension f d'alimentation
  D: Speisespannung *f*
  E: supply voltage
tension f d'amorçage
  D: Überschlagspannung *f*
  E: flash-over voltage, spark-over voltage, arc-over voltage
tension f dans le matériau [méc.]
  D: Spannung im Material
  E: strain in the material
tension f d'arrêt
  D: Sperrspannung *f*
  E: inverse voltage, reverse voltage
tension f de bruit
  D: Geräuschspannung *f*
  E: noise voltage
tension f de choc
  D: Stoßspannung *f*
  E: impulse voltage, surge voltage
tension f de claquage
  D: Durchschlagspannung *f*
  E: breakdown voltage, disruptive voltage
tension f d'éclatement
  D: Überschlagspannung *f*
  E: flash-over voltage, spark-over voltage, arc-over voltage
tension f de commande
  D: Steuerspannung *f*, Regelspannung *f*
  E: control voltage, control tension
tension f de contact
  D: Berührungsspannung *f*
  E: contact voltage, touch voltage, touch potential
tension f de contournement
  D: Überschlagspannung *f*
  E: flash-over voltage, spark-over voltage, arc-over voltage
tension f de contournement au choc
  D: Überschlag-Stoßspannung *f*
  E: impulse flashover voltage, impulse spark-over voltage
tension f de crête
  D: Spitzenspannung *f*,

Scheitelspannung *f*
 E: peak voltage, crest voltage
tension *f* de décharge
 D: Entladungsspannung *f*
 E: discharge voltage
tension *f* de distribution
 D: Versorgungsspannung *f*
 E: distribution voltage
tension *f* de mesure
 D: Meßspannung *f*
 E: measuring voltage
tension *f* de perforation
 D: Durchschlagspannung *f*
 E: breakdown voltage, disruptive voltage
tension *f* de phase
 D: Phasenspannung *f*
 E: phase voltage
tension *f* de pointe
 D: Spitzenspannung *f*, Scheitelspannung *f*
 E: peak voltage, crest voltage
tension *f* de polarisation
 D: Vorspannung *f*
 E: bias *n*
tension *f* de référence
 D: Bezugsspannung *f*
 E: reference voltage
tension *f* de régime
 D: Betriebsspannung *f*
 E: operating voltage, service voltage
tension *f* de réglage
 D: Steuerspannung *f*, Regelspannung *f*
 E: control voltage, control tension
tension *f* de réseau
 D: Netzspannung *f*
 E: mains voltage, line voltage, system voltage
tension *f* de rubanage
 D: Spinnspannung *f*, Spinnzug *m*
 E: lapping tension
tension *f* de service
 D: Betriebsspannung *f*
 E: operating voltage, service voltage
tension *f* d'essai
 D: Prüfspannung *f*
 E: test voltage
tension *f* de tenue
 D: Stehspannung *f*
 E: withstand voltage
tension *f* de tenue au choc
 D: Stehstoßspannung *f*
 E: impulse withstand voltage
tension *f* de tenue au courant alternatif
 D: Stehwechselspannung *f*
 E: a.c. withstand voltage
tension *f* de tenue aux ondes de choc
 D: Stehstoßspannung *f*
 E: impulse withstand voltage
tension *f* de traction
 D: Zugspannung *f*
 E: tension *n*
tension *f* de transmission
 D: Übertragungsspannung *f*
 E: transmission voltage
tension *f* de transport
 D: Übertragungsspannung *f*
 E: transmission voltage
tension *f* d'extinction d'ionisation
 D: Ionisations-Aussetzspannung *f*
 E: ionization extinction voltage
tension *f* disruptive
 D: Durchschlagspannung *f*
 E: breakdown voltage, disruptive voltage
tension *f* du secteur
 D: Netzspannung *f*
 E: mains voltage, line voltage, system voltage
tension *f* échelonnée
 D: Treppenspannung *f*
 E: staircase-type voltage
tension *f* efficace
 D: Effektivspannung *f*, Wirkspannung *f*
 E: active voltage, in-phase voltage, effective voltage, r.m.s.-voltage *n*
tension *f* entre phases
 D: verkettete Spannung
 E: phase-to-phase voltage, line-to-line voltage, voltage between phases
tension *f* étoilée
 D: Leiter-Erdspannung *f*
 E: phase-to-earth voltage, line-to-earth voltage
tension *f* induite
 D: induzierte Spannung, Induktionsspannung *f*
 E: induced voltage
tension *f* interne [méc.]
 D: Eigenspannung *f*
 E: internal stress
tension *f* inverse
 D: Sperrspannung *f*

tension

E: inverse voltage, reverse voltage
tension f nominale
D: Nennspannung f
E: nominal voltage, rated voltage
tension f nominale d'isolement
D: Reihenspannung f
E: insulation (class) rating
tension f non pondérée
D: Fremdspannung f
E: external voltage, unweighted noise voltage
tension f parasite
D: Störspannung f, Beeinflussungsspannung f
E: interference voltage, disturbing voltage
tension f par rapport à la terre
D: Spannung gegen Erde
E: voltage to earth
tension f perturbatrice
D: Störspannung f, Beeinflussungsspannung f
E: interference voltage, disturbing voltage
tension f perturbatrice série
D: Serienstörspannung f
E: series interference voltage
tension f primaire
D: Primärspannung f
E: primary voltage, input voltage
tension f psophométrique
D: Geräuschspannung f
E: noise voltage
tension f secondaire
D: Sekundärspannung f
E: secondary voltage, output voltage
tension f simple
D: Spannung gegen Erde
E: voltage to earth
tension f spécifiée
D: Bemessungsspannung f
E: specified voltage
tension f transversale [él.]
D: Querspannung f
E: transverse voltage, quadrature-axis component of the voltage
tenue f
D: Verhalten n
E: behaviour n, performance n
tenue f
D: Beständigkeit f, Festigkeit f, Widerstandsfähigkeit f
E: stability n, durability n, resistance

n, strength n
tenue f (en service)
D: Betriebsverhalten n
E: operating performance, service performance
tenue f au claquage de courte durée
D: Kurzzeit-Durchschlagfestigkeit f
E: short-time dielectric strength
tenue f au claquage instantané
D: Sofortdurchschlagfestigkeit f
E: instantaneous breakdown strength
tenue f au fluage
D: Fließhalten n
E: flow behaviour
tenue f aux craquelures
D: Rißbeständigkeit f
E: cracking resistance
tenue f aux ondes de choc
D: Stoßspannungsfestigkeit f
E: impulse (voltage) strength, surge voltage strength, surge resistance
tenue de la pression, poste de ~
D: Druckhaltestation f
E: pressure maintaining unit
tenue f en court-circuit
D: Kurzschlußverhalten n
E: short-circuit behaviour
tenue f en courte durée
D: Kurzzeitfestigkeit f
E: short-time strength
tenue f en longue durée [él.]
D: Dauerfestigkeit f, Langzeitfestigkeit f
E: long-time strength
tenue f en longue durée d'un câble
D: Zeit-Spannungsfestigkeit eines Kabels, Dauer-Spannungsfestigkeit eines Kabels
E: voltage life of a cable, long-time dielectric strength of a cable
tenue f maximale en longue durée
D: Grenz-Dauerfestigkeit f
E: maximum long-time strength
tenue f sous tension alternative
D: Wechselspannungsfestigkeit f
E: a.c. voltage strength
tenue f sous tension continue
D: Gleichspannungsfestigkeit f
E: d.c. voltage strength
terminaison f à 4 fils [com.]
D: Vierdraht-Abschluß m
E: four-wire termination
terminer v par un capuchon

D: verkappen v
E: cap-seal v

terrassement, travaux de ~ [pose c.]
D: Erdarbeiten f pl
E: earth work, excavation work

terre f
D: Erdboden m
E: soil n, ground n, earth n

terre f [él.]
D: Erde f
E: earth n (GB), ground n (US)

terre, par rapport à la ~
D: gegen Erde
E: to ground, to earth

terre de voie ferrée f [c. com.]
D: Eisenbahnerde f
E: railway earth

tête f à deux feuillards
D: zweifacher Eisenband-Wickler
E: dual steel taping head

tête f à feuillard
D: Bandeisen-Spinner m, Eisenband-Wickler m
E: steel tape spinner, steel taping head

tête f à filin
D: Garnspinnkopf m
E: yarn spinning head

tête f à jute
D: Jute-Wickler m
E: jute serving head, jute spinner

tête f à lier les faisceaux
D: Bündel-Spinner m
E: unit binder

tête f à onduler
D: Rillkopf m (Wellmaschine), Wellkopf m
E: corrugating head

tête f à papier
D: Papierspinnkopf m
E: paper lapping head

tête f d'assemblage
D: Verseilkopf m
E: stranding head, stranding support

tête f de boudineuse
D: Spritzkopf m (Extruder), Extruderkopf m
E: extrusion head, extruder head

tête f de câblage
D: Verseilkopf m
E: stranding head, stranding support

tête f de compression [câblage]
D: Verdichter m
E: compacting head

tête f de frettage
D: Wendelspinner m (für Haltewendel)
E: binder head

tête f de la billette [pr. à filer]
D: Bolzenspitze f
E: billet nose

tête f de prétorsion
D: Vorverseilkopf m
E: prespiralling head

tête f de renvoi
D: Umlenkkopf m
E: transfer head

tête f de revêtement d'assemblage [câb.]
D: Seelenspinnkopf m
E: core binder head

tête f de rubanage
D: Spinner m (Band), Spinnkopf m (Band), Bandwickler m
E: spinner n, lapping head, tape lapping head

tête f de rubanage centrale
D: Zentralspinnkopf m
E: concentric lapping head

tête f de rubaneuse à papier
D: Papierspinnkopf m
E: paper lapping head

tête f de tirage [câb.]
D: Ziehkopf m, Ziehöse f, Zugöse f
E: pulling eye, pulling head, pulling grip

tête f d'extrusion
D: Spritzkopf m (Extruder), Extruderkopf m
E: extrusion head, extruder head

tête f double de boudineuse
D: Zweifach-Spritzkopf m, Doppelkopf m
E: twin (extruder) head, double (extruder) head, dual (extruder) head

tête f double de rubanage
D: Doppelspinnkopf m
E: duplicate lapping head, dual lapping head

tête f double extrusion
D: Zweifach-Spritzkopf m, Doppelkopf m
E: twin (extruder) head, double (extruder) head, dual (extruder) head

tête f d'outillage [pr. à filer]
D: Preßkopf m

tête

E: die block, press block

tête f d'outils rotative
D: drehbarer Werkzeugkopf
E: rotary die head

tête f équerre [extr.]
D: Querkopf m
E: cross-head n

tête f guipeuse
D: Spinnkopf m (Garn, Kordel)
E: spinning head

tête f oblique [extr.]
D: Schrägkopf m
E: oblique head

tête f rubaneuse
D: Spinner m (Band), Spinnkopf m (Band), Bandwickler m
E: spinner n, lapping head, tape lapping head

tête f rubaneuse centrale
D: Zentralspinnkopf m
E: concentric lapping head

tête f transversale [extr.]
D: Querkopf m
E: cross-head n

tête f triple de boudineuse [extr.]
D: Dreifach-Spritzkopf m, Dreifach-Kopf m
E: triple extruder head

tête f triple extrusion [extr.]
D: Dreifach-Spritzkopf m, Dreifach-Kopf m
E: triple extruder head

thermocouple m
D: Thermoelement n
E: thermocouple n

thermodurcissable adj
D: warmhärtend adj
E: thermosetting adj, heat-curing adj, thermal-curing adj

thermodurcissable, matières plastiques ~s
D: wärmehärtbare Kunststoffe
E: thermosetting synthetic materials, thermosetting plastics, thermosetting resins

thermoélément m
D: Thermoelement n
E: thermocouple n

thermoplastique, matières ~s
D: Thermoplaste m pl
E: thermoplastics pl, thermoplastic materials

thermorétractable, manchon ~
D: Schrumpfschlauch m
E: heat-shrinkable tubing, shrink-on tube

thermosouder v
D: warmverschweißen v
E: heat-seal v

thermostat m
D: Temperaturregler m, Thermostat m
E: temperature controller, thermostat n, temperature regulator

THT (v. très haute tension)

tirage m
D: Einziehen n (von Kabeln in Rohre)
E: pulling in, pull-in n, drawing in

tirage, dispositif de ~ des câbles
D: Kabel-Einziehvorrichtung f
E: cable puller

tirage m en nappes [caout., plast.]
D: Plattenziehen n
E: sheeting-out n

tirer v [pose c.]
D: einziehen v (in Rohre)
E: pull v

tirer v un câble à la main
D: ein Kabel von Hand einziehen
E: to manhandle a cable

tireté m
D: gestrichelte Linie
E: dashed line

tissu m
D: Gewebe n
E: fabric n

tissu m de verre
D: Glasfasergewebe n
E: glass fibre fabric

tissu m revêtu de résine synthétique
D: Hartgewebe n
E: synthetic resin-bonded fabric, laminated fabric

titre, à ~ d'essai
D: versuchsweise adv
E: tentatively adv

titre m de fil (numéro de fil; unité: denier)
D: Titer m (Feinheitsmaß für Fasern/Garn; Einheit: Denier (den))
E: titer n (yarn count; unit: denier)

t/min (v. tours par minute)

toile f
D: Gewebe n
E: fabric n

toile f (d')émeri

toile f métallisée
D: Textilband mit eingewebten Metalldrähten
E: textile tape with interwoven metal wires

toile vernie, câble isolé à la ~
D: Lackbandkabel
E: varnished cambric (insulated) cable

toile vernie, ruban en ~
D: Lackgewebe-Band n
E: varnished cambric tape

tôle f de protection
D: Abdeckblech n
E: covering sheet, cover plate

tôle f de recouvrement
D: Abdeckblech n
E: covering sheet, cover plate

tolérance f
D: Toleranz f
E: tolerance n, permissible variation, allowance n

tolérance f étroite
D: enge Toleranz
E: close tolerance

tordeuse f
D: Bündelverseilmaschine f
E: bunching machine, unit stranding machine

tordeuse f double-torsion à grande vitesse
D: Hochleistungs-Doppelschlag-Bündelverseilmaschine f, Doppelschlag-Bündel-Schnellverseilmaschine f
E: double-twist high-speed bunching machine

toron m
D: Leiterseil n
E: conductor strand

toron m
D: Litze f
E: strand n, bunch strand, stranded wire

toron m de câble
D: Kabellitze f
E: cable strand

toronner v
D: verwürgen v, verlitzen v
E: bunch-strand v, bunch v

toronneuse f tubulaire
D: Rohrverseilmaschine f
E: tubular stranding machine, tube strander

torsade f
D: Würgelitze f, Litzenleiter m
E: bunched conductor

torsader v
D: verdrillen v
E: twist v

torsader v
D: verwürgen v, verlitzen v
E: bunch-strand v, bunch v

torsion f
D: Verdrehung f
E: torsion n, twist n

torsion f [câblage]
D: Drall m, Schlag m
E: lay n, twist n

torsion, à ~ [câblage]
D: ohne Rückdrehung
E: without backtwist

tour m de l'usine
D: Werksbesichtigung f
E: tour through the factory (GB), plant visitation (US)

tour f de réfrigération
D: Kühlturm m
E: cooling tower

tour f de vernissage
D: Lackierturm m
E: enamelling tower

touret m [câb.]
D: Trommel f
E: reel n, drum n

touret m d'atelier
D: Fertigungstrommel f
E: machine drum

touret m de câble
D: Kabeltrommel f
E: cable drum, cable reel

touret m de câble démontable non perdu
D: zerlegbare Kabeltrommel
E: knock-down returnable shipping reel

touret m d'expédition
D: Versandtrommel f
E: shipping drum, shipping reel

touret m en bois
D: Holztrommel f
E: wooden reel, wooden drum

touret m non perdu [câb.]
D: Leihtrommel f
E: returnable reel

touret *m* **perdu** [câb.]
  D: Verkaufstrommel *f*, Einwegtrommel *f*
  E: non-returnable reel

tours *m pl* **de vis par minute** [extr.]
  D: Schneckendrehzahl *f*
  E: screw speed

tours *m pl* **par minute** (t/min)
  D: Umdrehungen pro Minute (U/min, Upm)
  E: revolutions per minute (r.p.m.)

tracé *m* [câb.]
  D: Trasse *f*
  E: route *n*, run *n*

traction *f* **de retenue**
  D: Bremszug *m*
  E: back pull, back tension

trafic *m* **de transit** [com.]
  D: Durchgangsverkehr *m*
  E: through-traffic *n*

trafic *m* **téléphonique**
  D: Sprechverkehr *m*, Fernsprechverkehr *m*
  E: telephone traffic, line telephony, intercommunication *n*

train *m* **dégrossisseur**
  D: Vorwalzstraße *f*, Blockstraße *f* (Walzw.)
  E: roughing train, blooming train

train *m* **de laminoirs** [mét.]
  D: Walzstraße *f*
  E: rolling train

train *m* **ébaucheur**
  D: Vorwalzstraße *f*, Blockstraße *f* (Walzw.)
  E: roughing train, blooming train

train *m* **finisseur**
  D: Fertigwalzstraße *f*
  E: finishing train

trait *m* **de repère**
  D: Markierungsstrich *m*
  E: marker line

traitement *m*
  D: Behandlung *f*
  E: treatment *n*

traitement *m* **de surface**
  D: Oberflächenbehandlung *f*
  E: surface treatment

traitement *m* **préalable**
  D: Vorbereitung *f*, Vorbehandlung *f*
  E: preparation *n*, preliminary treatment, pretreatment *n*

traitement *m* **thermique**
  D: Wärmebehandlung *f*
  E: heat treatment

traitement *m* **thermique** [mét.]
  D: Vergüten *n*
  E: hardening and tempering operation, heat treatment

trait *m* **plein**
  D: durchgehende Linie
  E: full line

trancanage, dispositif de ~
  D: Verlegearm *m* (Aufwickelei), Verlegevorrichtung *f* (Aufwickelei), Verteiler *m* (Aufwickelei)
  E: distributor *n*, traverser *n*, traversing unit

trancanage *m* **automatique du fil métallique**
  D: automatische Drahtführung (Wickler)
  E: automatic wire guide

tranche *f*
  D: Kante *f*
  E: edge *n*

tranche *f* **arrondie**
  D: abgerundete Kante
  E: rounded edge

tranche *f* **biseautée**
  D: abgeschrägte Kante
  E: beveled edge

tranchée *f* **de câble**
  D: Kabelgraben *m*
  E: cable trench

transformateur *m* [com.]
  D: Übertrager *m*
  E: transformer *n*, translator *n*

transformateur *m* **d'adaptation** [com.]
  D: Anpassungsübertrager *m*
  E: matching relay repeater, matching transformer

transformateur *m* **d'alimentation**
  D: Netztransformator *m*
  E: power transformer

transformateur *m* **de réglage**
  D: Regeltransformator *m*, Stelltransformator *m*
  E: regulating transformer, variable ratio transformer

transformateur *m* **du courant**
  D: Stromwandler *m*
  E: current transformer

transformateur *m* **(de) haute tension**
  D: Hochspannungstransformator *m*

translateur *m* [com.]
  D: Übertrager *m*
  E: transformer *n*, translator *n*
transmetteur *m* **de pression** [com.]
  D: Druckübertrager *m*, Druckgeber *m*
  E: pressure transducer
transmettre *v*
  D: übertragen *v*
  E: carry *v*, transmit *v*
transmission *f*
  D: Übertragung *f*
  E: transmission *n*
transmission *f* **à grande distance**
  D: Fernübertragung *f*
  E: long distance transmission, teletransmission *n*
transmission *f* **à large bande**
  D: Breitband-Übertragung *f*
  E: wide-band transmission, broad-band transmission
transmission *f* **calorifique**
  D: Wärmeübergang *m*, Wärmeübertragung *f*
  E: heat transfer, heat transmission, transfer of heat
transmission *f* **de chaleur**
  D: Wärmeübergang *m*, Wärmeübertragung *f*
  E: heat transfer, heat transmission, transfer of heat
transmission *f* **de données**
  D: Datenübertragung *f*
  E: data transmission
transmission *f* **de fréquences vocales**
  D: Sprechfrequenzübertragung *f*
  E: voice frequency transmission
transmission *f* **de télévision**
  D: Fernsehübertragung *f*
  E: television transmission
transmission *f* **d'informations**
  D: Datenübertragung *f*
  E: data transmission
transmission *f* **d'informations en courant continu à basse tension d'émission**
  D: Gleichstrom-Datenübertragung mit niedriger Sendespannung
  E: low transmission voltage d.c. data transmission
transmission *f* **par chaîne**
  D: Kettenantrieb *m*
  E: chain drive
transmission *f* **par fibre optique**
  D: Lichtleiter-Nachrichtenübertragung *f*
  E: optical fibre transmission
transmissions numériques, câble pour ~
  D: Kabel für Datenübertragung
  E: data transmission cable
transport *m* **de courant continu à haute tension**
  D: Hochspannungs-Gleichstrom-Übertragung (HGÜ) *f*
  E: high-voltage d.c. transmission
transport *m* **de grandes (fortes) puissances**
  D: Hochleistungsübertragung *f*
  E: bulk power transmission
transport *m* **d'énergie**
  D: Energieübertragung *f*
  E: power transmission
transport *m* **des matériaux**
  D: Materialfluß *m* (innerbetrieblich)
  E: materials handling
transporter *v*
  D: übertragen *v*
  E: carry *v*, transmit *v*
transport pneumatique, installation de ~
  D: pneumatische Förderanlage
  E: pneumatic conveying system
transposer *v*
  D: kreuzen *v* (Leitungen)
  E: cross-connect *v*, cross-splice *v*
transposer *v*
  D: kreuzen *v* (Drähte zum Induktionsschutz)
  E: transpose *v*
transposition *f* [c. com.]
  D: Kreuzen *n*
  E: crossing *n*, cross-connection *n*, cross-splicing *n*
transposition *f*
  D: Platzwechsel *m* (bei einer Fernsprechfreileitung)
  E: transposition *n*
transposition *f* **des gaines de câbles**
  D: Auskreuzen von Kabelmänteln
  E: cross-bonding of cable sheaths
travail *m* **à forfait**
  D: Akkordarbeit *f*
  E: piecework *n*, incentive scheme

travail

travail *m* **à la pièce**
 D: Akkordarbeit *f*
 E: piecework *n*, incentive scheme

travail *m* **avec la perche** [métallurg.]
 D: Polen *n*
 E: poling *n*

travail *m* **en équipes**
 D: Schichtbetrieb *m*
 E: shift operation

travailler *v*
 D: verarbeiten *v*
 E: process *v*, convert *v*

travaux *m pl* **de terrassement** [pose c.]
 D: Erdarbeiten *f pl*
 E: earth work, excavation work

traverse *f* **de touret** [câb.]
 D: Trommelkern *m*
 E: barrel of a reel

traversée *f* [access. c.]
 D: Durchführung *f*
 E: bushing *n*

traversée *f* **d'antenne**
 D: Antennendurchführung *f*
 E: antenna duct, antenna lead-in (tube)

traverse *f* **mobile** [pr. à filer]
 D: Laufholm *m*
 E: moving crosshead

treeing *m*
 D: Bäumchenbildung *f* (in Isolierstoffen unter el. Beanspruchung)
 E: treeing *n*

tréfilage *m*
 D: Drahtziehen *n*
 E: wire drawing

tréfilage *m* **à dimensions fines** [fabr. fils mét.]
 D: Feinzug *m*, Fertigzug *m*
 E: finishing pass

tréfilage *m* **du fil machine**
 D: Grobdrahtzug *m*
 E: rod breakdown

tréfiler *v* **des fils de gros, moyens, petits diamètres**
 D: Drähte ziehen auf dicke, mittlere, kleine Durchmesser
 E: to draw wires down to large, medium, small diameters

tréfilerie *f*
 D: Drahtzieherei *f*
 E: wire drawing department

tréfileuse *f*
 D: Drahtziehmaschine *f*
 E: wire drawing machine

tréfileuse *f* **et recuiseur en continu**
 D: Durchlaufglühanlage *f* (gekoppelt mit Feindraht-Ziehmaschine), kontinuierliche Drahtzieh- und Glühanlage
 E: tandem annealer, continuous wire drawing and annealing machine

tréfileuse *f* **pour fil machine**
 D: Grobdrahtziehmaschine *f*
 E: rod breakdown machine

trémie *f*
 D: Trichter *m*
 E: hopper *n*, funnel *n*

trémie *f* **d'alimentation** [extr.]
 D: Fülltrichter *m*, Einfülltrichter *m*
 E: feeding hopper

trempe *f* [mét.]
 D: Vergüten *n*
 E: hardening and tempering operation, heat treatment

tremper *v* [métallurg.]
 D: abschrecken *v*
 E: chill *v*, quench *v*

tremper *v*
 D: anfeuchten *v*, benetzen *v*, befeuchten *v*
 E: wet *v*, moisten *v*

tremper *v*
 D: eintauchen *v*
 E: immerse *v*, dip *v*

très haute tension (THT) *f*
 D: Höchstspannung *f*
 E: extra-high voltage (EHV), supertension *n*

tresse *f*
 D: Beflechtung *f*, Geflecht *n*, Umflechtung *f*
 E: braid *n*, braiding *n*

tresse *f* **de coton**
 D: Baumwollumklöppelung *f*, Baumwollgeflecht *n*
 E: cotton braiding, braided cotton covering

tresse *f* **de fil métallique**
 D: Drahtgeflecht *n*
 E: wire braid

tresse *f* **en cuivre étamé** [câb.]
 D: Kupfer-Gestrickband *n* (verzinnt)
 E: tinned copper braid, tinned copper mesh

tresse *f* **en fils de cuivre**

tresser, machine à ~ en fils métalliques
  D: Kupferdrahtgeflecht n
  E: copper wire braiding, copper braiding
tresser, machine à ~ en fils métalliques
  D: Drahtumflechtmaschine f
  E: wire braiding machine
treuil m de câble
  D: Kabelwinde f
  E: cable winch
triage m pneumatique
  D: Windsichten n
  E: air classification
triangle, monté en ~
  D: in Dreieckschaltung
  E: delta-connected adj
triangulaire, câble assemblé en forme ~
  D: Dreieck-verseiltes Kabel
  E: triangular-shape cable
triplomb, câble ~
  D: Dreibleimantelkabel n, Dreimantelkabel n
  E: three-core single lead sheath cable, SL-cable n
tripolaire adj
  D: dreipolig adj
  E: three-pole adj, three-phase adj
tronçon m de câble
  D: Kabelabschnitt m
  E: cable section
tronçon m de liaison [pose c.]
  D: Streckenabschnitt m, Abschnitt einer Strecke
  E: route section
tronçon m de ligne [c. com.]
  D: Leitungsabschnitt m
  E: line section
tronçon m de ligne [pose c.]
  D: Streckenabschnitt m, Abschnitt einer Strecke
  E: route section
troncs m pl de bouleaux
  D: Birkenstämme m pl (zum Polen beim Kupferschmelzen)
  E: birch trunks, birch poles
tropicalisé adj
  D: tropenfest adj
  E: tropicalized adj, resistant to tropical conditions, tropic-proof adj
trop-plein m
  D: Überlaufrohr n
  E: overflow pipe

trou m
  D: Bohrung f
  E: bore n, hole n
trou m central
  D: Achsbohrung f (Kabeltrommel)
  E: spindle hole
trou m de coulée [mét.]
  D: Abstichöffnung f
  E: tap hole
trou m de percée [mét.]
  D: Abstichöffnung f
  E: tap hole
trou m de poing [com.]
  D: Handloch n
  E: handhole n
trou m de remplissage
  D: Einfüllöffnung f
  E: filling hole
trou m d'homme [pose c.]
  D: Einstiegöffnung f, Mannloch n
  E: entrance n, manhole n
trou m d'homme
  D: Muffenbunker m, Muffenbauwerk n, Kabelschacht m
  E: cable pit, cable jointing chamber, cable jointing manhole, cable vault
trousse f
  D: Bausatz m, Werkzeugtasche f
  E: kit n
tube m
  D: Rohr n
  E: tube n, pipe n
tube m [c. com.]
  D: Tube f
  E: tube f
tube m à eau de refroidissement
  D: Kühlwasserrohr n
  E: cooling water pipe
tube m coaxial
  D: Koax-Tube f
  E: coaxial tube
tube m d'acier
  D: Stahlrohr n
  E: steel pipe
tube m d'aspiration
  D: Absaugrohr n
  E: suction pipe
tube m de refroidissement
  D: Kühlrohr n
  E: cooling tube
tube m de retour
  D: Rücklaufrohr n
  E: return pipe

tube 604

tube *m* **d'évacuation**
 D: Entlüftungsrohr *n*
 E: exhaust pipe, exhaust flue, ventilation pipe

tube *m* **de ventilation**
 D: Entlüftungsrohr *n*
 E: exhaust pipe, exhaust flue, ventilation pipe

tube *m* **de vulcanisation**
 D: Vulkanisationsrohr *n*
 E: vulcanizing tube

tube *m* **de vulcanisation continue à vapeur à haute pression**
 D: Dampfhochdruckrohr zur kontinuierlichen Vulkanisation
 E: continuous vulcanization high-pressure steam pipe

tube *m* **en amiante-ciment**
 D: Asbestzementrohr *n*
 E: asbestos cement pipe

tube *m* **en tôle plombée**
 D: Peschelrohr *n*
 E: Peschel conduit (for house wiring)

tube *m* **ondulée en cuivre**
 D: Kupferwellrohr *n*
 E: corrugated copper tube

tubes *m pl* **à eau latéraux disposés séparément du câble**
 D: parallel zum Kabel verlegte Wasserrohre
 E: separate lateral water pipes

tube *m* **sans soudure**
 D: nahtloses Rohr
 E: seamless tube

tube *m* **télescopique** [vulc.]
 D: Teleskop-Rohr *n*
 E: telescoping tube, splice box

tubulure *f*
 D: Rohrleitung *f*
 E: pipeline *n*

tubulure *f*
 D: Stutzen *m*
 E: connecting piece, connection *n*

tubulure *f* **d'aspiration**
 D: Saugleitung *f*
 E: suction line

tunnel *m* **à dimension d'homme**
 D: begehbarer Tunnel
 E: man-sized tunnel

tunnel *m* **des câbles**
 D: Kabeltunnel *m*
 E: cable subway, cable tunnel, cable gallery

tuyau *m*
 D: Rohr *n*
 E: tube *n*, pipe *n*

tuyau *m* **à ailettes**
 D: Rippenrohr *n*
 E: fin tube

tuyau *m* **de trop-plein**
 D: Überlaufrohr *n*
 E: overflow pipe

tuyau *m* **emmanchable à chaud**
 D: Schrumpfschlauch *m*
 E: heat-shrinkable tubing, shrink-on tube

tuyau *m* **en acier**
 D: Stahlrohr *n*
 E: steel pipe

tuyau *m* **placé en lit de canal** [pose c.]
 D: Rohrdüker *m*
 E: sink-pipe *n*, underwater pipe

tuyau *m* **serpentin**
 D: Rohrschlange *f*
 E: coiled pipe

tuyauterie *f*
 D: Rohrleitungssystem *n*
 E: pipe system, piping *n*

tuyeau *m*
 D: Schlauch *m*
 E: tube *n*, hose *n*

tuyère *f*
 D: Düse *f*
 E: nozzle *n*, jet *n*, orifice *n*

type *m* [câb.]
 D: Bauart *f*, Typ *m*
 E: design *n*, type *n*, construction *n*

U

UHT (v. ultra-haute tension)

ultra-haute tension *f*
 D: Ultra-Hochspannung *f*
 E: ultra-high voltage (UHV)

unidirectionnel, fils de jonction ~s
 D: einseitig herausgeführte Anschlußdrähte
 E: single-ended terminal wires

unification *f*
 D: Normung *f*, Vereinheitlichung *f*
 E: standardisation *n*, normalization *n*, unification *n*

uniforme *adj*

D: einheitlich adj
E: uniform adj, consistent adj, homogeneous adj

unilatérale, commande ~
D: einseitiger Antrieb
E: unilateral drive

unité f d'affaiblissement
D: Dämpfungsmaß n
E: attenuation unit, attenuation equivalent, total transmission equivalent, total attenuation

unité f d'affaiblissement composite [tél.]
D: Betriebsdämpfungsmaß n
E: operative attenuation unit

unité f d'affaiblissement diaphonique
D: Nebensprechdämpfungsmaß n
E: crosstalk attenuation unit

unité f de charge (c. tél.)
D: Pupinspulensatz m, Spulensatz m
E: loading coil unit, loading unit (tel. c.)

unité f d'entraînement hydraulique
D: hydraulisches Antriebsaggregat
E: hydraulic power pack

unité f de propagation
D: Übertragungsmaß n
E: propagation unit

usinage m (à l'outil de coupe)
D: spanabhebende Bearbeitung
E: cutting n, machining n

usine f
D: Betrieb m (Werk, Anlage), Werkstatt f
E: factory n, plant n, workshop n

usine f de câbles
D: Kabelwerk n
E: cable works, cable factory

usure f
D: Verschleiß m, Abrieb m
E: wear n

utilisation f de circuits fantôme
D: Phantomausnutzung f
E: use of phantom circuits

utilisation f de matériaux
D: Einsatz von Materialien
E: use of materials, employment of materials, application of materials

utilisé adj **à plein**
D: voll ausgelastet
E: loaded to capacity, operating at full capacity

utilisé adj **à pleine capacité**
D: voll ausgelastet
E: loaded to capacity, operating at full capacity

V

valeur f approchée
D: Annäherungswert m, Näherungswert m
E: approximate value

valeur f approximative
D: Annäherungswert m, Näherungswert m
E: approximate value

valeur f approximée
D: Richtwert m
E: reference value, standard value, approximate value

valeur f caractéristique
D: Kennwert m, Parameter m
E: parameter n, characteristic value

valeur f comparative
D: Vergleichswert m
E: reference value, comparative value

valeur f de crête
D: Scheitelwert m, Spitzenwert m
E: peak value, crest value, amplitude n

valeur f de référence
D: Richtwert m
E: reference value, standard value, approximate value

valeur f efficace
D: Effektivwert m
E: effective value, root mean square (r.m.s.) value

valeur f indicative
D: Richtwert m
E: reference value, standard value, approximate value

valeur f initiale
D: Ausgangswert m
E: initial value

valeur f limite
D: Grenzwert m
E: limiting value, limit n

valeur f médiane
D: Medianwert m
E: median value

valeur f mesurée
D: Meßwert m

valeur

E: measured value

valeur *f* moyenne
D: Mittelwert *m*
E: mean value, average value

valeur *f* nominale
D: Nominalwert *m*, Nennwert *m*
E: nominal value, rated value

valeur *f* réelle
D: Istwert *m*
E: actual value, real value

valeur *f* spécifiée
D: Sollwert *m*
E: specified value, desired value

valeur *f* standard
D: Richtwert *m*
E: reference value, standard value, approximate value

valeur standard de la résistivité du cuivre recuit (selon la CEI) (v. IACS)

valeur *f* théorique
D: rechnerischer Wert
E: calculated value, theoretical value

valise *f* de mesure pour câbles
D: Kabelmeßkoffer *m*
E: portable cable measuring set

valve *f*
D: Ventil *n*
E: valve *n*

vanne *f* à vapeur [vulc.]
D: Dampfabsperrventil *n*
E: steam stop valve

vapeur *f* [vulc.]
D: Dampf *m*
E: steam *n*, vapour *n*

vapeur *f* d'eau
D: Wasserdampf *m*
E: water vapour, steam *n*

variateur *m* de torsion
D: Drallwechselgetriebe *n*
E: lay changing gear, twist changing gear

variateur *m* de vitesse
D: Wechselgetriebe *n*
E: change gear

variation *f* de charge
D: Lastschwankung *f*
E: load fluctuation, load variation

variation *f* de courant
D: Stromschwankung *f*
E: current variation, fluctuation of current

variation *f* de fréquence
D: Frequenzschwankung *f*
E: frequency variation, frequency fluctuation

variation *f* de tension
D: Spannungsschwankung *f*
E: voltage fluctuation, voltage variation

vase, point d'éclair en ~ fermé
D: Flammpunkt im geschlossenen Tiegel
E: flash point in a closed cup

vase, point d'éclair en ~ ouvert
D: Flammpunkt im offenen Tiegel
E: flash point in an open cup

vaseline *f*
D: Vaseline *f*, Petrol-jelly *n*
E: petroleum jelly, petrol jelly

ventilateur *m*
D: Gebläse *n*
E: fan *n*, blower *n*, ventilator *n*, air wiper, blast *n*, pneu-wipe *n*

ventilation *f*
D: Belüftung *f*, Lüftung *f*
E: ventilation *n*, aeration *n*

ventilation *f* forcée
D: künstliche Belüftung
E: forced ventilation

ventiler *v*
D: belüften *v*
E: ventilate *v*, aerate *v*

vérifier *v*
D: prüfen *v*
E: check *v*, test *v*, verify *v*, control *v*

vernis *m*
D: Lack *m*
E: varnish *n*, enamel *n*

vernis *m* d'émaillage
D: Isolierlack *m*
E: insulating varnish

vernis *m* d'imprégnation
D: Tränklack *m*
E: impregnating varnish

vernis-émail *m*
D: Einbrennlack *m*
E: baking enamel, baking varnish

vernis *m* isolant
D: Isolierlack *m*
E: insulating varnish

vernis *m* oléo-résineux
D: Ölharzlack *m*
E: oleoresinous enamel

vernis *m* pour fils
D: Drahtlack *m*
E: wire enamel

vernis *m* **semi-conducteur**
 D: Leitlack *m*
 E: semi-conducting varnish, conducting varnish

verrouillage *m*
 D: Verriegelung *f*
 E: blocking *n*, interlocking *n*, locking *n*

verrouillage *m* **à baïonnette**
 D: Bajonettverschluß *m*
 E: bayonet joint

vert-jaune, conducteur ~
 D: grüngelbe Ader
 E: green-yellow core

vessie *f*
 D: Blase *f*
 E: bubble *n*, blister *n*

vibration *f* [méc.]
 D: Schwingung *f*
 E: vibration *n*

vice *m* **de fabrication**
 D: Fertigungsfehler *m*
 E: manufacturing defect, manufacturing flaw

vidage *m*
 D: Entleeren *n*
 E: unloading *n*, emptying *n*

vidange *f*
 D: Entleeren *n*
 E: unloading *n*, emptying *n*

vide *m*
 D: Hohlraum *m*
 E: void *n*, cavity *n*

vide, mettre sous ~
 D: evakuieren *v*
 E: evacuate *v*

vide, sous ~
 D: unter Vakuum
 E: under vacuum

vide *m* **de 1 à 10^{-3} torr**
 D: Feinvakuum *n*
 E: vacuum 1 to 10^{-3} torr

vide *m* **de 760 à 100 torr**
 D: Grobvakuum *n*
 E: vacuum 760 to 100 torr

vide *m* **de 100 à 1 torr**
 D: Zwischenvakuum *n*
 E: vacuum 100 to 1 torr

vidéo-fréquence *f*
 D: Fernsehfrequenz *f*
 E: video frequency

vide *m* **poussé** (10^{-3} à 10^{-6} torr)
 D: Hochvakuum *n*
 E: high vacuum (10^{-3} to 10^{-6} torr)

vie *f*
 D: Lebensdauer *f*, Nutzungsdauer *f*
 E: life *n*, service life

vie *f* [mach.]
 D: Standzeit *f*
 E: life *n*, service life

vieillir *v*
 D: altern *v*
 E: age *v*

vieillissement *m*
 D: Alterung *f*
 E: ag(e)ing *n*

vieillissement *m* **accéléré**
 D: beschleunigte Alterung
 E: accelerated ag(e)ing

vieillissement *m* **au stockage**
 D: Alterung durch Lagerung
 E: shelf ag(e)ing

vieillissement *m* **dans l'huile**
 D: Alterung unter Öl
 E: oil immersion ag(e)ing

vieillissement de longue durée, propriétés de ~
 D: Langzeit-Alterungs-Eigenschaften *f pl*
 E: long-time age(i)ng properties

vieillissement *m* **en étuve à circulation d'air**
 D: Alterung im Umluftofen, Umluftalterung *f*
 E: ventilated air oven ag(e)ing, circulating air ag(e)ing

vieillissement *m* **par circulation d'air**
 D: Alterung im Umluftofen, Umluftalterung *f*
 E: ventilated air oven ag(e)ing, circulating air ag(e)ing

vieillissement *m* **thermique**
 D: Wärmealterung *f*
 E: thermal ag(e)ing

vieillissement *m* **thermo-accéléré**
 D: durch Wärme beschleunigte Alterung
 E: thermo-accelerated ag(e)ing

vierge, à l'état ~
 D: im Anlieferungszustand
 E: in as-received condition, at the received stage, as delivered

violation *f* **d'un brevet**
 D: Patentverletzung *f*
 E: patent infringement, infringement of a patent

vis f [extr.]
  D: Schnecke f
  E: screw n
vis f à un seul filet [extr.]
  D: eingängige Schnecke
  E: single-flighted screw
viscosité f
  D: Viskosität f
  E: viscosity n
viscosité, faible ~
  D: Dünnflüssigkeit f
  E: low viscosity
viscosité, haute ~
  D: Dickflüssigkeit f, Zähflüssigkeit f
  E: ropiness n, high viscosity
viscosité f intrinsèque
  D: Eigenviskosität f, Grundviskosität f
  E: intrinsic viscosity
vis f d'ajustage
  D: Verstellschraube f, Einstellschraube f, Stellschraube f
  E: set screw, adjusting screw
vis f de blocage
  D: Feststellschraube f
  E: locking screw, locking bolt
vis f de borne [él.]
  D: Klemmschraube f, Schraubklemme f
  E: terminal screw, binding screw, screw terminal
vis f de boudineuse
  D: Extruderschnecke f
  E: extrusion screw
vis f de mélangeage [extr.]
  D: Mischschnecke f
  E: mixing screw
vis f de réglage
  D: Verstellschraube f, Einstellschraube f, Stellschraube f
  E: set screw, adjusting screw
vis d'extrusion f [extr.]
  D: Förderschnecke f
  E: stockscrew n
visible adj **à l'œil nu**
  D: mit bloßem Auge sichtbar
  E: visible to the naked eye
vis f micrométrique
  D: Mikrometerschraube f
  E: micrometer screw
visqueux adj
  D: zähflüssig adj
  E: viscous adj

vissage m
  D: Verschraubung f, Schraubverbindung f
  E: screw connection, bolted connection, bolted joint, screw(ed) joint
vitesse f
  D: Drehzahl f (Umdrehungen pro Minute = U/Min), Geschwindigkeit f
  E: number of revolutions per minute (r.p.m.), rotational speed, speed n
vitesse f circonférentielle
  D: Umfangsgeschwindigkeit f
  E: peripheral speed, circumferential speed
vitesse f de bobinage
  D: Wickelgeschwindigkeit f
  E: winding speed
vitesse f de coulée
  D: Gießgeschwindigkeit f
  E: casting speed, pouring speed, casting rate
vitesse f d'écoulement
  D: Strömungsgeschwindigkeit f, Fließgeschwindigkeit f
  E: flow rate, flow velocity, rate of flow
vitesse f de fabrication [mach.]
  D: Fahrgeschwindigkeit f, Fertigungsgeschwindigkeit f, Arbeitsgeschwindigkeit f
  E: line speed, production speed, running speed, production rate, operating speed, processing speed
vitesse f de la bobine
  D: Spulendrehzahl f
  E: bobbin speed
vitesse f de la vis [extr.]
  D: Schneckendrehzahl f
  E: screw speed
vitesse de marche f [mach.]
  D: Fahrgeschwindigkeit f, Fertigungsgeschwindigkeit f, Arbeitsgeschwindigkeit f
  E: line speed, production speed, running speed, production rate, operating speed, processing speed
vitesse f de passage [prod.]
  D: Durchlaufgeschwindigkeit f
  E: feed rate, line speed, running speed
vitesse f de phase
  D: Phasengeschwindigkeit f
  E: phase velocity

vitesse f de production [mach.]
  D: Fahrgeschwindigkeit f,
    Fertigungsgeschwindigkeit f,
    Arbeitsgeschwindigkeit f
  E: line speed, production speed,
    running speed, production rate,
    operating speed, processing speed

vitesse f de rotation
  D: Drehzahl f (Umdrehungen pro
    Minute = U/Min),
    Geschwindigkeit f
  E: number of revolutions per minute
    (r.p.m.), rotational speed, speed n

vitesse f des symboles [c. com.]
  D: Zeichengeschwindigkeit f
  E: symbol rate

vitesse f de tête rubaneuse
  D: Spinnerdrehzahl f
  E: lapping head speed

vitesse f de tirage
  D: Abzugsgeschwindigkeit f
  E: pull-off speed

vitesse f de trancanage
  D: Verlegegeschwindigkeit f (beim
    Aufspulen)
  E: distribution speed, traversing
    speed

vitesse f de travail [mach.]
  D: Fahrgeschwindigkeit f,
    Fertigungsgeschwindigkeit f,
    Arbeitsgeschwindigkeit f
  E: line speed, production speed,
    running speed, production rate,
    operating speed, processing speed

vitesse f de tréfilage
  D: Drahtziehgeschwindigkeit f
  E: wire drawing speed

vitesse f de vulcanisation
  D: Vulkanisationsgeschwindigkeit f
  E: rate of cure, vulcanization rate

vitesse f d'extrusion
  D: Preßgeschwindigkeit f
  E: extrusion rate

vitesse f périphérique
  D: Umfangsgeschwindigkeit f
  E: peripheral speed, circumferential
    speed

voie f de décharge
  D: Entladungskanal m
  E: streamer n, discharge channel

voie de télévision f
  D: Fernsehkanal m
  E: television channel

voie f de transmission
  D: Übertragungsweg m,
    Übertragungskanal m
  E: transmission path, transmission
    channel, channel n

voie f de transmission électrique
  D: elektrischer Übertragungsweg
  E: electrical transmission route

voie f de transport
  D: Übertragungsweg m,
    Übertragungskanal m
  E: transmission path, transmission
    channel, channel n

voie f téléphonique
  D: Sprechkanal m, Fernsprechkanal
    m
  E: telephone channel, voice channel,
    speech channel

voiture-laboratoire f pour l'essai des câbles
  D: Kabelmeßwagen m, Meßwagen
    für Kabel
  E: cable testing truck

volant adj
  D: beweglich (fliegend) angeordnet
  E: flying adj

volatil, composants ~s
  D: flüchtige Bestandteile m pl
  E: volatile components

volatil, constituants ~s
  D: flüchtige Bestandteile m pl
  E: volatile components

volatiliser v
  D: verflüchtigen v
  E: volatilize v

voyant m [mach.]
  D: Beobachtungsfenster n, Schauglas
    n, Schauloch n
  E: peephole n, sight glass,
    observation window, inspection
    glass

voyant m lumineux
  D: Leuchtanzeige f
  E: visual indication

voyant m lumineux
  D: Signallampe f, Anzeigelampe f
  E: pilot lamp, signal lamp, indicating
    lamp, pilot light

vulcanisation f
  D: Vulkanisation f
  E: vulcanization n, curing n

vulcanisation, chaîne de ~ en continu
  D: CV-Anlage f, kontinuierliche

vulcanisation

    Vulkanisationsanlage
    E: CV-line *n*, continuous vulcanization line
vulcanisation *f* à froid
    D: Kaltvulkanisation *f*
    E: cold cure, cold vulcanization
vulcanisation *f* à vapeur
    D: Dampfvulkanisation *f*
    E: steam vulcanization, steam cure, vapour cure
vulcanisation *f* continue (CV)
    D: kontinuierliche Vulkanisation (CV), Durchlaufvulkanisation *f*
    E: continuous vulcanization (CV)
vulcanisation *f* échelonnée [vulc.]
    D: Stufenheizung *f*
    E: vulcanization in stages, "step-up" cure
vulcanisation *f* en chaînette
    D: Kettenlinien-Vulkanisation *f*
    E: catenary vulcanization
vulcanisation *f* par paliers [vulc.]
    D: Stufenheizung *f*
    E: vulcanization in stages, "step-up" cure
vulcanisé, extrémité ~e sur le câble
    D: aufvulkanisierter Endenabschluß
    E: sealing end vulcanized to the cable
vulcanisé, fiche ~e sur le câble
    D: aufvulkanisierter Stecker
    E: plug vulcanized to the cable
vulcaniser *v*
    D: vulkanisieren *v*
    E: vulcanize *v*, cure *v*

Z

zéro *m*
    D: Nullpunkt *m*, Sternpunkt *m*
    E: neutral point, zero point
zinc, oxyde de ~
    D: Zinkoxid *n*
    E: zinc oxide
zone *f* d'alimentation [extr.]
    D: Einzugszone *f*
    E: feeding zone
zone *f* d'ébullition
    D: Siedebereich *m*
    E: boiling range
zone *f* de chauffage [extr.]
    D: Heizzone *f*
    E: heating zone
zones *f pl* de température
    D: Temperaturzonen *f pl*
    E: temperature zones